FEDERAL TAXATION OF ESTATES, TRUSTS AND GIFTS

Revised Third Edition

Ira Mark Bloom

*Justice David Josiah Brewer Distinguished
Professor of Law
Albany Law School of Union University*

F. Ladson Boyle

*Charles E. Simon, Jr. Professor of Federal Law
University of South Carolina School of Law*

John T. Gaubatz

*Professor of Law
University of Miami School of Law*

Lewis D. Solomon

*Theodore Rinehart Professor of Business Law
George Washington University National Law Center*

LexisNexis™

Library of Congress Catalog Card Number: 2002109637
Reprinted in 2003

ISBN 0-8205-6111-8

Editorial Offices
744 Broad Street, Newark, NJ 07102 (973) 820-2000
201 Mission Street, San Francisco, CA 94105-1831 (415) 908-3200
701 East Water Street, Charlottesville, VA 22902-7587 (804) 972-7600
www.lexis.com

ACKNOWLEDGMENTS

The following copyright holders have graciously consented to the reprint of excerpts from their published works:

Anne L. Alstott, *The Uneasy Liberal Case Against Income and Wealth Transfer Taxation: Response to Professor McCaffery*, 51 TAX L. REV. 363, 363-367 (1996);

William D. Andrews, *The Accessions Tax Proposal*, 22 TAX L. REV. 589, 591-595 (1967);

F. Ladson Boyle, *Evaluating Split-Interest Valuation*, 24 GA. L. REV. 1 (1989);

F. Ladson Boyle, *Fiduciary Accounting Basics*, 1 PROB. PRAC. REP. No. 8 (August 1989);

F. Ladson Boyle, *Present Interest Gifts in Trust: Donor and Donee Problems*, 29 GONZAGA L. REV. 453 (1993-94);

F. Ladson Boyle, *Tax Consequences of Equitable Adjustments*, 37 S.C. L. REV. 583 (1986);

George Cooper, *A Voluntary Tax? New Perspectives on Sophisticated Estate Tax Avoidance* 107-110 (Brookings Inst. 1979);

George Cooper, *Taking Wealth Taxation Seriously*, 34 THE RECORD 24, 34-43, 46-49 (1979), published with permission from The Record of the Association of the Bar of the City of New York;

Laura E. Cunningham, *Remember the Alamo: The IRS Needs Ammunition in Fight Against FLP*, 86 TAX NOTES 1461 (Special Supplement, Mar. 13, 2000), published with permission of Tax Analysts;

Joseph M. Dodge, *Beyond Estate and Gift Tax Reform: Including Gifts and Bequests in Income*, 91 HARV. L. REV. 1177, 1178-1179, 1185-1186, 1188-1192, 1208-1210 (1978);

Joseph M. Dodge, *Taxing Gratuitous Transfers Under a Consumption Tax*, 51 TAX L. REV. 529, 593-595 (1996);

William G. Gale and Joel Slemrod, *The Estate Tax: Not Dead Yet*, 93 TAX NOTES 807 (2001), published with permission of Tax Analysts;

Barry L. Isaacs, *Do We Want a Wealth Tax in America?*, 32 U. MIAMI L. REV. 23, 35-37, 46-49 (1977), reprinted from the University of Miami Law Review which holds the copyright;

Gerald R. Jantscher, *The Aims of Death Taxation*, reprinted from DEATH, TAXES, AND FAMILY PROPERTY 46-49, 54-55 (E. Halbach, ed. 1977) with permission of The West Publishing Company;

Edward J. McCaffery, *The Uneasy Case for Wealth Transfer Taxation*, 104 YALE L.J. 283-365 (1994), reprinted by permission of The Yale Law Journal Company and Fred B. Rothman & Company from The Yale Law Journal;

DEDICATIONS

Ira Mark Bloom
To Josh and Becky.

F. Ladson Boyle
To my loving wife Susan, to Elizabeth and Travis,
and to Captain Quirk who gave me a curiosity for tax.

John T. Gaubatz
To my beloved wife Kathy, to the memory of our beloved son Daniel, and
to the memory of Wally Blum, who taught me everything I needed to know
about tax law.

Lewis D. Solomon
To Janet and Michael

PREFACE

We believe that the most effective pedagogical approach to the federal taxation of estates, trusts, and gifts is one that combines the analytical and problem-method approaches. Materials concentrating on one approach are inherently weaker than those utilizing both. Traditionally, *problem method* materials tend to be theoretically weak, and virtually unusable by teachers who wish to emphasize the structural development of the law. Conversely, materials which focus on the analytical structure of the field tend to leave to the student the task of developing an understanding of the basic operation of the rules.

By combining both approaches, this coursebook bridges the gap between the analytical and problem-method approaches to teaching and learning this difficult field. Thus, the materials include the judicious use of structured problems to facilitate an understanding of the doctrinal framework, analytical processes, and policy issues.

This third edition presents a comprehensive study of the tax aspects involved in the wealth transfer process.[1] Early chapters outline the basic structure of, and develop the underlying policy questions inherent in, the underlying gift, estate, and generation-skipping tax systems. The material then explores how these tax systems, plus the relevant income tax rules—especially the grantor trust provisions of subchapter J—apply to various transactions, most of which are in the nature of testamentary substitutes. In a departure from the first edition, the income taxation of estates and non-grantor trusts, in significantly expanded form, is covered in Chapter 14. There exists sufficient materials in that chapter to teach a separate course on subchapter J taxation. The book ends with a chapter on options for reforming the tax systems.

Ease and enjoyment of student learning can be seen in various characteristics of the materials. The first is an intentional redundancy. Themes are developed early, and then reiterated and expanded upon as later materials explore more complex areas. The effect is that the student will see important concepts two or three times. This is enough, according to educational psychologists, to cement the concepts in the student's mind.

The second characteristic of the book is its attempt to be on the *cutting edge*. Thus, the book contains not only changes made by the Economic Growth and Tax Relief Act of 2001, but developments that have occurred in early 2002. Further, although the book relies on well-recognized leading cases, it also includes recent and significant cases, rulings, and regulations which either break new ground or expand on existing law.

---

[1] We treat community property in an integrated way in this book by raising community property intersections in the context of specific transfer and income tax provisions. We have also attempted to identify the specific community property issues so that they may be focused upon or avoided - as the course dictates.

The book also features the liberal use of text and textual materials describing the area being studied. In many cases, the book explains the rationale for rules and explores whether they should continue. In this sense, the book does not seek to *hide the ball.*

In writing the book, we have adopted editorial conventions. With respect to reproduced cases and materials, we have excised many citations and footnotes, and have renumbered any remaining footnotes. Further, for ease of reading we have reformatted the cases and materials to follow a consistent pattern. With respect to original text, we have used *he, she,* and *he or she* interchangeably, except as the context suggests otherwise.

As anyone who has produced a book knows, the task cannot be accomplished without the assistance of many people. Each of us received support from our respective Deans. For the third edition, Elizabeth Fritz Bailey and Andrea Painter Easler, students at the University of South Carolina School of Law, and Harrison Aldrich, Kristie Haslinger and Meghan Mahaney, students at Albany Law School, provided significant editorial assistance. Recent estate and gift tax students at Albany and the University of South Carolina also provided helpful input. The secretarial support at University of South Carolina, particularly Nancy Shealy, made working with the manuscript easier. Professor David Pratt, Albany Law School, provided helpful comments on retirement benefits in Chapter 11. Cristina Gegenschatz at Matthew Bender eased the pain of production. Finally, thanks to the many who assisted, but are unnamed.

February 2002

Ira Mark Bloom
F. Ladson Boyle
John T. Gaubatz
Lewis D. Solomon

TABLE OF CONTENTS

TABLES

INDEX

Part I

INTRODUCTION

This book is designed as a basic teaching text for studying the federal taxation of estates, trusts, and gifts. As such, it explores the federal transfer tax system, composed of the federal estate tax, the federal gift tax, and the federal generation-skipping transfer tax, as well as the federal income taxation of estates, trusts, and gifts. The book approaches this study by first describing the basic structure of each of the four taxes. Thereafter, emphasis changes to the study of how each tax responds to a series of types of transactions that trigger taxation. Being transactionally based, the book contains many Problems, which can provide the basis of study and discussion.

Chapter 1 provides a brief look at the history of and policies underlying the tax systems studied in this book. A summary description of the four taxes contained in Chapter 2 provides the background for succeeding Parts.

Chapter 1

BACKGROUND

The structure and application of virtually any mature tax system can be understood only in the context of its history and policies. Portions of that history and those policies that are relevant to the details of the taxation of estates, trusts, and gifts are included throughout this book. This chapter discusses the general history and policies of those taxes. It also identifies the sources of applicable federal tax law studied in this book.

§ 1.01 History of Federal Taxation of Estates, Trusts, and Gifts

Estates, trusts, and gifts have long been the subject of taxation in this country. Transfer taxes have taken the form of stamp taxes on legacies, inheritance taxes on the receipt of property by reason of death, and estate taxes on the transfer of property by reason of death. Taxation of the income of trusts and estates has existed since the earliest days of the federal income tax system.

[A] Estate and Gift Taxation

The development of the federal taxation of gratuitous transfers can be divided into three parts. The first can be described as the era of temporary transfer taxation, in which death taxes were imposed for limited periods to provide short-term financing of federal expenses. The second covers the transition of death taxes to a more generalized transfer tax. The third represents modern developments, including major changes made by Congress in 2001.

Early history. Federal taxation of transfers began with various types of death taxes passed as expedient measures designed to meet an economic emergency. Such death taxes were usually repealed after the emergency passed. The first such tax was a 1797 documentary stamp tax, at a maximum rate of 2%. It was levied on the documentary receipts given for legacies and shares in intestate estates.[1] The tax thus indirectly taxed the receipt of the legacies and inheritances until its repeal in 1802.[2]

In 1862, Congress shifted to directly taxing the receipt of legacies and inheritances by enacting an inheritance tax to help finance the Civil War. The tax was initially limited to personal property but was subsequently extended to devises and inheritance of real property, and had a maximum rate of 6%.[3] To illustrate the operation of that tax, assume that a decedent died owning

---

[1] *See* 1 Stat. 527, 536 (1797).

[2] *See* 2 Stat. 148 (1802).

[3] *See* 12 Stat. 432, 485 (1862); 13 Stat. 223, 285–289 (1864); 14 Stat. 98, 140 (1866).

3

$10 million in real property, which he devised equally to four children. The 1862 federal inheritance tax was levied against each child's $2.5 million legacy. Congress repealed the tax in 1870.[4]

In 1898, Congress again enacted a graduated inheritance tax, this time with a maximum rate of 15%. This tax introduced the concept of the graduated tax—determining the rate of the tax by the size of the devise to the beneficiary and by reference to the beneficiary's relationship to the decedent.[5] It was repealed in 1902.[6]

Finally, Congress enacted the beginnings of the current federal estate tax in 1916 to finance World War I.[7] This tax differed from earlier federal death taxes in that it was not an inheritance tax. Rather than taxing the beneficiary's receipt of a legacy or bequest, Congress imposed the 1916 tax on the transfer of property by a decedent to a beneficiary. The tax was on the giver, rather than on the taker. To illustrate its operation, again assume that a decedent died owning $10 million in real property, which he devised equally to four children. Rather than tax the receipt of $2.5 million by each child, the estate tax applied to the decedent's $10 million testamentary transfer. However, the value of the property passing continued to determine the tax. Congress imposed the tax not on the property in the estate, but on the decedent's net estate, that is, the estate reduced by deductions for such items as administration expenses and claims. Like its immediate predecessor, the estate tax was a graduated tax, and it provided for a maximum rate of 10% on amounts in excess of $5 million. The tax rates were subsequently increased to a maximum of 25% on amounts in excess of $10 million.

Death taxation has repeatedly been challenged as a violation of the Constitutional prohibition on direct taxes; it has been routinely upheld on the ground that the tax is an excise tax and not a direct tax because it does not apply to the property given or received, but to the privilege of giving or receiving it.[8]

The shift to a transfer tax. The 1916 estate tax applied only to assets that passed in estate-like transactions. Included assets were those that the decedent owned at death and which were "subject to administration," as well as assets which the decedent had transferred (1) "in contemplation of death," or (2) in a manner "intended to take effect" on the decedent's death. Because the estate tax did not apply to outright gifts, an individual generally could avoid the tax by making outright transfers during life. Thus, the estate tax was uneven in its application. Taxation depended on the nature of the gratuitous transfer.

This unevenness was first addressed in 1924, when Congress enacted a federal gift tax as a backstop to the estate tax.[9] However, the 1924 gift tax

---

[4] *See* 16 Stat. 256–257 (1870).

[5] *See* 30 Stat. 448, 464–66 (1898), *as amended* 31 Stat. 938, 948 (1901).

[6] *See* 32 Stat. 96, 97 (1902).

[7] *See* Rev. Act of 1916, ch. 463, §§ 200-212, 39 Stat. 756, 777-780.

[8] *See* Scholey v. Rew, 91 U.S. (23 Wall.) 331 (1874) (upholding the 1862 inheritance tax); Knowlton v. Moore, 178 U.S. 41 (1900) (holding the 1898 inheritance tax constitutional); New York Trust Co. v. Eisner, 256 U.S. 345 (1921) (validating the 1916 estate tax).

[9] *See* Rev. Act of 1924, ch. 234, § 301(b), 43 Stat. 253, 304.

was repealed in 1926[10] in favor of an amendment to the estate tax which contained an irrebuttable presumption that lifetime transfers within two years of the donor's death were made in contemplation of death, thus making them subject to the estate tax.[11] In 1932, however, the Supreme Court held this presumption to be unconstitutional on procedural due process grounds.[12] Thereupon, Congress in 1932 reenacted a gift tax in response to the need for revenue caused by the Great Depression.[13]

The basic structures of the 1916 estate tax and the 1932 gift tax are contained in Chapters 11 and 12: the present estate and gift tax provisions of the Internal Revenue Code of 1986. Although significant changes have occurred over the years in a number of details, the basic framework has remained constant: the gift tax applies to the lifetime transfer of interests in property for less than adequate consideration, and the estate tax applies to property owned at death or passing as a result of statutorily-defined, testamentary-like transactions.

The modern changes. As originally enacted, the estate and gift tax systems were generally separate and distinct. The gift tax applied to taxable gifts, which were defined as gross gifts (gifts less an annual per donee exclusion, initially $5,000 in 1932, but subsequently reduced to $3,000) minus three types of deductions, including a $30,000 cumulative lifetime exemption. Thus, in any year, a donor could make gifts of $3,000 to any number of donees tax-free because of the annual per donee exclusion, and a donor could give an additional $30,000 tax-free during his lifetime. The tax was calculated on cumulative taxable gifts during the donor's life, at progressive rates set at 75% of the estate tax rates on the same amounts transferred.

The estate tax was based on gross assets in the estate minus deductions, including a $60,000 exemption. The tax was calculated at the higher rate, without regard to prior gifts. As a result, an individual paid a lower tax if he transferred some or all of his property during lifetime, rather than holding the property until his death. A lower tax was possible for a variety of reasons: (1) some gifts could be excluded from taxation using the annual exclusion; (2) others were freed from tax using the gift tax lifetime exemption; (3) because gift tax rates were lower than estate tax rates, any dollar of taxable gift was taxed at a rate lower than the corresponding estate tax rate; and (4) because the gift tax was separate from the estate tax, any gift was removed from an estate tax at the donor's top marginal estate tax rate, and taxed (at least initially) at the lowest gift tax marginal rate.

The separate gift and estate taxes were merged in 1976. In recognition of the fact that wealthy families were able to undermine the progressive gift and estate tax structure by using the tax advantages inherent in making lifetime gifts, Congress acted to remove most of those advantages by requiring that lifetime gifts be taken into account in calculating the estate tax. The Tax Reform Act of 1976 enacted a "unified" estate and gift tax system.[14] Among

---

[10] *See* Rev. Act of 1926, ch. 27, § 1200, 44 Stat. 9, 125.

[11] *See* Rev. Act of 1926, ch. 27, § 302(c), 44 Stat. 9, 70.

[12] *See* Heiner v. Donnan, 285 U.S. 312 (1932).

[13] *See* Rev. Act of 1932, ch. 29, §§ 501-532, 44 Stat. 169, 245-59.

[14] *See* Pub. L. No. 94-455, § 2001, 90 Stat. 1520, 1846-53.

other items, that Act (1) replaced the separate gift and estate tax rate schedules with a unified rate schedule applicable to both lifetime and at death taxable transfers, and (2) replaced the $30,000 gift tax exemption and $60,000 estate tax exemption with a single unified credit against federal wealth transfer taxes. In short, post-1976 gratuitous transfers, whenever made, would generally be taxed in the same manner. As explained in the legislative history:

> As a matter of equity, the Congress believed that the tax burden imposed on transfers of the same amount of wealth should be substantially the same whether the transfers are made both during life and at death or made only upon death. As a practical matter, the preferences for lifetime transfers are available only for wealthier individuals who are able to afford lifetime transfers. The preferences for lifetime transfers are not generally available for those of small and moderate wealth since they generally want to retain their property until death to assure security during lifetime. Therefore, the Congress believes that the preferences for lifetime transfers principally benefit the wealthy and resulted in eroding the transfer tax base.[15]

The other major change in the gift and estate taxes began in 1948, with the adoption of a deduction for transfers to the donor's or decedent's spouse.[16] As originally enacted, the deduction was limited to one-half of the net estate (estate after expenses and losses) and was designed to equalize the tax treatment of couples residing in common law and community property jurisdictions. The thrust of the deduction was changed in the Economic Recovery Tax Act of 1981, which enacted an unlimited marital deduction for the value of property given or devised to a spouse in specified ways.[17]

Less revolutionary changes were also made by the 1981 Act, which was generally aimed at reducing the overall impact of transfer taxes, and restricting their application to the wealthy. First, the Act increased the annual gift tax exclusion from $3,000 to $10,000, thereby allowing larger gifts to pass tax free. Second, the Act reduced the maximum transfer tax rate from the then 70% to a planned 1988 rate of 50% (although ultimately the reduction from 55% to 50% was repealed). Third, and most strikingly, the Act increased the unified credit from $42,500 to $192,800 in six annual steps ending in 1987. This meant that after 1986, an estate of up to $600,000 was exempt from federal wealth transfer taxation. The purpose of these changes was to initiate a policy that only "large" wealth transfers be subject to gift and estate taxes, as was clear from the legislative history:

> [Previously], with a unified credit of $47,000, cumulative transfers of $175,625 [could] be made without the imposition of any transfer taxes. The amount of the credit was intended to exempt small-and-moderate-sized estates from the estate and gift taxes. However, inflation has been increasing the estate and gift tax burden by eroding

---

[15] Staff of the Joint Committee on Taxation, General Explanation of the Tax Reform Act of 1976, 526 (1976).

[16] See Rev. Act of 1948, ch. 168, § 361, 62 Stat. 110, 117-121.

[17] See Pub. L. No. 97-34, § 403, 95 Stat. 172, 301-305.

the value of the credit and pushing estates and gifts into higher brackets. In addition, the committee believes that the amount of the credit, established in 1976 and fully effective in 1981, is inadequate to provide relief for estates containing farms, ranches, and small businesses which often are forced to dispose of family business to pay the estate or gift tax.

　　The committee believes that the existing unified credit should be increased to offset the effects of inflation and to provide estate and gift tax relief to small estates, especially those which primarily consist of family businesses.[18]

The Revenue Act of 1987[19] delayed the reduction of the maximum transfer tax rate to 50%: the maximum estate and gift tax rates were frozen at 55% until 1993; thereafter, the maximum rate was scheduled to decline to 50%. In addition, the 1987 Act included provisions that required a phase out of the benefit of rates lower than the maximum by imposing a 5% surcharge on taxable estates exceeding $10 million.[20] The Revenue Reconciliation Act of 1993 amendment to that provision,[21] however, permanently maintained the maximum rate of 55%. Consequently, the maximum rate did not decline to 50% as provided for in the Revenue Act of 1987.

In 1990, Congressional action added Chapter 14 to the Internal Revenue Code.[22] These complex Code sections were aimed at various transactions that the Treasury Department and Congress perceived as abusive.

The Taxpayer Relief Act of 1997[23] made a few changes in the wealth transfer tax area. Most significantly, the unified credit was scheduled to increase over nine years so that the exemption equivalent would increase from $600,000 in 1997 to $1 million in 2006. The phase in of the increased exemption amount was much lower in the earlier years, as indicated below:

Year	Applicable Credit Amount	Unified Credit Equivalent
1997	$192,800	$600,000
1998	$202,050	$625,000
1999	$211,300	$650,000
2000	$220,550	$675,000
2001	$220,550	$675,000
2002	$229,800	$700,000
2003	$229,800	$700,000
2004	$287,300	$850,000
2005	$326,300	$950,000
2006	$345,800	$1,000,000

The 1997 Act also indexes various benchmarks for inflation, *e.g.*, the $10,000 gift tax annual exclusion and the $1 million GST exemption. However, the

---

[18] House Ways and Means Committee, H.R. Rep. No. 97–201, 97th Cong., 1st Sess. 154 (1981).

[19] *See* Pub. L. No. 100-203, tit. x, 101 Stat. 1330-382.

[20] *See* Revenue Act of 1987, § 2001(c)(2).

[21] *See* Pub. L. No. 103–66, 103rd Cong., 2d Sess., § 13208(a).

[22] *See* Omnibus Budget Reconciliation Act of 1990, § 11602.

[23] *See* Pub. L. No. 105-34, 111 Stat. 788.

unified credit is not indexed after the increase is fully phased in. The Act also added a new estate tax section that excludes from estate taxation all or part of the value of decedents' interests in qualifying closely held family businesses.

Continuing the theme of the 1997 Act, the Economic Growth and Tax Relief Reconciliation Act of 2001 (Tax Act of 2001)[24] heads the transfer tax towards extinction. For the immediate future, the Tax Act of 2001 does three things. First, the Act introduces a schedule of reductions in the top marginal rate applicable to gifts, estates and GST taxes. Second, the Act accelerates and magnifies the 1997 increases in the exemption amount for estate and GST (but not gift) taxes. Third, the Act ties the GST exemption to the exemption equivalent of the estate tax unified credit, beginning in 2004. The rate and exemption schedule for estate and GST taxes under the new law is as follows:

Taxable Event in:	Top Rate	Exemption Equivalent
2002	50% (5% surtax repealed)	$1 million (indexing for $1 million GST exemption continues)
2003	49%	$1 million (indexing for $1 million GST exemption continues)
2004	48%	$1.5 million (indexing for GST exemption eliminated)
2005	47%	$1.5 million
2006	46%	$2 million
2007	45%	$2 million
2008	45%	$2 million
2009	45%	$3.5 million

While doing this, the Act de-unifies the gift and estate taxes, beginning in 2004. At that time, the gift tax exemption amount freezes at $1 million, even though the estate and GST tax exemption amounts continue to climb.

In the same time frame, the Tax Act of 2001 phases out the § 2011 state death tax credit, by reducing it to 75% in 2002, 50% in 2003, 25% in 2004 and nothing in 2005. See § 2011(b). After 2004, an estate will be allowed an unlimited state death tax deduction. See §§ 2011(g) and 2058.

For the more distant future, the Tax Act of 2001 calls for the repeal of the estate and GST taxes for decedents who die after December 31, 2009, or GST transfers that occur after 2009, and the reduction of the gift tax rate to the top marginal income tax rate (set by other provisions in the Act at 35%). This repeal is coupled, however, with a provision returning the estate and GST tax to year 2001 rates in 2011. See § 2011(a).[25] Supposedly, the latter provision was required by budget negotiations, but it is widely perceived to be a game of political "chicken" challenging a future Congress to continue the repeal of estate and generation-skipping taxes.

---

[24] See Pub. L. No. 107-16, 115 Stat. 38.

[25] All provisions of the Tax Act of 2001 are scheduled to expire on December 31, 2010. This sunset provision was necessary to comply with the Congressional Budget Act of 1974, and it means that, unless a later Congress re-enacts these changes, the estate, gift, and GST laws will be restored on January 1, 2011. See Tax Act of 2001 § 901.

Assuming nothing changes before 2010, the Tax Act of 2001 reintroduces carryover basis for property received from a decedent who dies in 2010. As currently designed, this provision will give the transferee a basis equal to the lesser of their fair market value on the date of death or their adjusted basis in the hands of the decedent. Thus, the basis in loss assets still step-down, although the step-up in basis for appreciated assets is limited or denied. *See* §§ 1014(f) and 1022(a). Further, the decedent's executor will be permitted to allocate to specific noncash assets an aggregate $1.3 million basis increase, although the basis of any asset may not be increased above its fair market value. *See* § 1022(b)(2)(B). Additionally, the basis of property transferred to a surviving spouse can be increased by $3 million, for assets passing outright or in certain marital trusts. *See* § 1022(b), (c). The $1.3 million adjustment is increased by any unused capital losses, net losses and certain "built-in" losses of the decedent, and both the $1.3 million and $3 million figures are indexed for inflation. *See* § 1022(b)(2)(C). The basis increase allowed the estates of nonresidents who are not U.S. citizens will be limited to $60,000, to be indexed for inflation after December 31, 2009. *See* § 1022(b)(3).

Other changes include liberalizing the deduction under § 2031(c) for certain conservation easements by eliminating certain restrictions, and repealing the § 2057 Qualified Family Owned Business Interest rules for estates of decedents dying after 2003. *See* § 2057(j). The GST exemption allocation rules were modified. *See* Chapter 5.

[B] Generation-Skipping Transfer Tax

The third transfer tax is the generation-skipping transfer (GST) tax, first enacted by the Tax Reform Act of 1976, and completely restructured by the Tax Reform Act of 1986. Its purpose is to ensure (subject to certain exceptions) that a transfer tax is collected each time property passes between generations. It was needed because gift and estate taxes could effectively be eliminated on some inter-generational transfers by creating interests that spanned succeeding generations. For example, although the gift or estate tax applies to the creation of a trust paying income to the grantor's child for his life with the corpus passing to the grantor's grandchildren, no transfer tax applies when the child dies and the grandchildren become entitled to the property. The GST tax was designed to fill this void.

The 1976 GST tax system was designed to apply only to trusts (or equivalent transactions) that had beneficiaries in at least two separate generations below the generation of the grantor. A GST tax was imposed only upon the distribution of assets to the beneficiary in the younger of the two generations (or the termination of the interests of the beneficiary in the older of the two generations). The tax did not apply to direct gifts to a single generation, no matter how remote.

Because the 1976 GST tax did not apply to direct gifts to remote generations, the tax was easy to avoid by those who had sufficient resources. They could make gifts to grandchildren and great-grandchildren without fear of the impact of such transfers on the lives of the children. Because the GST tax was meant to apply to these recipients, it was deemed sufficiently flawed to require replacement. Therefore, the 1976 GST tax system was retroactively repealed by the Tax Reform Act of 1986, and replaced with a new system.[26]

The current GST tax system applies to generation-skipping transfers made by lifetime transfers after September 25, 1985, and under most wills (or revocable trusts), whenever executed, if the decedent died after 1986. Unlike the prior law, it taxes both outright transfers to, and transfers in trust for the benefit of, any beneficiary who is in a generation younger than the generation of the grantor's children. In effect, direct skips without intervening enjoyment by a person in an intermediate generation are taxed, as are remainder interests in generation-skipping trusts. Thus, for example, a bequest by *D* to her grandchild, *GC,* is subject to the tax. Similarly, if *D* creates a trust, income payable to child for life, remainder to *GC,* the GST tax applies when the child dies and *GC* obtains possession. To restrict its application to gifts by the wealthy, the GST tax includes a $1 million exemption, which will be adjusted for inflation beginning in 1999.[27]

[C] Income Taxation of Gifts, Estates, and Trusts

The federal income tax in general purports to tax income of an individual from any source. However, since 1913, the Code has excluded property acquired by gift, devise, bequest, or inheritance from the definition of gross income.[28] The current Code provision represents a slightly modified version of the original language.[29]

Although property acquired gratuitously is not subject to income taxation, income earned on property held by a trust or estate may be income to the beneficiary of the trust or estate. Between 1913 and 1954, Congress devised and refined a statutory system for taxing trust and estate income to either the fiduciary estate or the beneficiary, depending on whether the income was accumulated or distributed.

Trusts over which the grantor retained beneficial powers were recognized early on as a separate category for income tax purposes. Beginning in 1924, separate rules were adopted under the predecessor of § 676 to tax the grantor on income of trusts when the grantor retained a variety of economic controls.[30] Those rules did not, however, expressly apply to reversionary interests or retained nonbeneficial powers, such as the right to add new beneficiaries to the trust. Use of such interests and powers blossomed in the 1930s. Extensive litigation tested the effectiveness of those trusts as devices to shift the income tax burden from the grantor, culminating in *Helvering v. Clifford*, 309 U.S. 331 (1940) (reproduced at § 2.06[C][3], *infra*). This case was followed in 1946 by the *Clifford* Regulations which delineated the Treasury's position on the impact of *Helvering v. Clifford* on the taxation of grantor trusts. These

---

[26] *See* §§ 2601–2663.

[27] Indexing continues through 2003. Beginning in 2004, the GST exemption will be the same as the estate tax exemption. For example, the GST exemption in 2004 will be $1.5 million. *See* § 2631.

[28] *See* Rev. Act of 1913, ch. 16, § 2(B), 38 Stat. 114.

[29] *See* § 102(a).

[30] *See* Rev. Act of 1924, ch. 234, § 219(g), 43 Stat. 253, 277.

regulations were, in turn, adopted by Congress in 1954, as §§ 671–678, and continue as the law today, although modified somewhat over the years.

§ 1.02 Policies Underlying Federal Taxation of Estates, Trusts, and Gifts

The imposition of federal wealth transfer taxes has been and continues to be a controversial political problem.[31] In justifying any particular form of federal wealth transfer taxation, you should be aware that wealth transfer taxes have greatly declined in importance as sources of revenue for the federal government.[32] Before World War II, federal gift and estate taxes generated about 7% of total federal tax revenues. In 2000, federal wealth transfer taxes contributed $29 billion, which was only about 1.4% of the $2 trillion total federal tax revenues for 2000.[33]

Apart from revenue raising, federal wealth transfer taxation has another, more questionable goal: the leveling of wealth.[34] This goal, which has a long history in the United States, was openly stated in the legislative history to the Tax Reform Act of 1976, which noted that federal wealth transfer taxes are imposed to "increase the progressivity of our tax system and help prevent excessive concentrations of inherited wealth."[35]

As early as the end of the nineteenth century, public opinion in the United States turned in favor of the taxation of wealth at death, and more specifically, application of a progressive death tax structure. Individuals of great wealth, perhaps responding to the notoriety of the "robber baron" era, professed support of death taxes on the rich. Andrew Carnegie wrote of graduated death taxes as follows:

> Of all forms of taxation this seems the wisest. Men who continue hoarding great sums all their lives, the use of which for public ends would work good to the community from which it chiefly came, should be made to feel that the community, in the form of the State, cannot thus be deprived of its proper share. By taxing estates heavily at death the State marks its condemnation of the selfish millionaire's unworthy life.

> It is desirable that nations should go much further in this direction. Indeed it is difficult to set bounds to the share of a rich man's estate which should go at his death to the public through the agency of the State, and by all means such taxes should be graduated, beginning at nothing upon moderate sums to dependents, and increasing rapidly as the amount swells, until the millionaire's hoard, as of Shylock's, at least "The other half comes to the privy coffer of the State." This

---

[31] *See, e.g.,* Edward J. McCaffrey, *The Uneasy Case for Wealth Transfer Taxation,* 104 YALE L. J. 283 (1994).

[32] *See generally* Louis Eisenstein, *The Rise and Decline of the Estate Tax,* 11 TAX L. REV. 223 (1956).

[33] *See* Analytical Perspectives, Budget of U.S. Gov't at 35 (2001).

[34] *See* Mark L. Ascher, *Curtailing Inheritance,* 89 MICH. L. REV. 69, 150 (1990).

[35] H.R. Rep. No. 94–1380, 94th Cong., 2d Sess. 5 (1976). *See generally* Michael J. Graetz, *To Praise the Estate Tax, Not to Bury It,* 93 YALE L. J. 259 (1983).

policy works powerfully to induce the rich man to attend to the administration of wealth during his life, which is the end that Society should always have in view, as being by far the most fruitful for the people. Nor need it be feared that this policy would sap the root of enterprise and render men less anxious to accumulate, for, to the class whose ambition it is to leave great fortunes and be talked about after their death, it will attract even more attention, and, indeed, be a somewhat nobler ambition to have enormous sums paid over to the State from their fortunes.[36]

Although an economic class among those most likely to be affected by a wealth transfer tax, even professionals of the early twentieth century, recognized a basic fairness of the concept. One attorney wrote:

There can hardly be a more fit subject for taxation than unearned fortunes, nor a more appropriate season for imposing the tax upon them than during the transmission of the property to the persons appointed by the law or the will of the former owner to receive it upon his death. At a time when property is, by reason of death without ownership, the state steps in and takes, as revenue, its share for the privilege it extends to the heir or devisee of receiving a portion; and if the diffusion of wealth is to be preferred to its concentration in the hands of those who have not produced it—and this seems to be the prevailing trend of public opinion—the inheritance tax offers a simple expedient for bringing about that result.[37]

As noted in the *Final Report of the American Assembly on Death, Taxes and Family Property*:

At the same time, transfers of substantial wealth tend to conflict with other basic social values, including . . . dispersal of economic power, reward according to merit, and avoidance of rigid class distinctions.

Excessive unearned wealth . . . may arouse deep-seated resentment, and possibly alienation from society, over someone's "getting something for nothing."

There also may be adverse economic implications in permitting significant wealth transfers, including loss of potential tax revenues, tolerance of continuing concentrations of economic power, inefficiency in investment resource allocation and reduced incentives to productivity among heirs.[38]

Opponents of wealth transfer taxes have traditionally raised the objection that such a tax reduces individual incentives and destroys investment capital by transferring wealth from the private sector to public hands. For example, arguing in 1924, that federal estate tax rates should be reduced, then Secretary of the Treasury Andrew Mellon stated:

---

[36] ANDREW CARNEGIE, THE GOSPEL OF WEALTH 14, 21–22 (Harvard Press, 1962) (quoting NORTH AMERICAN REVIEW (June 1889)).

[37] Peter V. Ross, *Inheritance Taxation,* 19 CASE & COMMENT 452, 453 (1913).

[38] DEATH, TAXES AND FAMILY PROPERTY, 183–84 (E. Halbach, Jr., ed. 1977).

Death taxes are taxes upon capital. It is obvious that, if the government to maintain itself, were to take 50 percent of every estate, small or large, and if on the average in the course of a generation a man could not double his inheritance, there would be an actual depletion of capital within the country and ultimately nothing would be left to tax. [39]

More recently, the *Final Report of the American Assembly on Death, Taxes and Family Property* stated:

Examined from an economic perspective, the right to transfer wealth has the positive values of fostering incentives in the form of rewarding industry, ingenuity and creativity, encouraging capital formation through saving and investment, permitting continuity of ongoing enterprise, and supporting diversity in priorities. In addition, such transfers are, indeed, often justified by significant, if not always evident, economic contributions by those who receive them. [40]

The opposition to wealth transfer taxes is very much alive, as evidenced by the Tax Act of 2001 which came close to a total, permanent repeal of the estate, gift, and generation-skipping transfer tax systems. [41] Chapter 15 sets forth a comprehensive discussion of the policy issues surrounding repeal.

Whether permanent repeal of wealth transfer taxation is imminent is uncertain. In their seminal article on progressive taxation, *The Uneasy Case for Progressive Taxation*, [42] Blum and Kalven may have identified best the political realities:

But in the end it is the implications about economic inequality which impart significance and permanence to the issue and institution of progression. Ultimately a serious interest in progression stems from the fact that a progressive tax is perhaps the cardinal instance of the democratic community struggling with its hardest problem.

§ 1.03   Sources of Federal Tax Law [43]

The primary source of federal income tax law is the Internal Revenue Code of 1986. Sometimes the Code constitutes the basic, and often the only relevant, statutory source of tax law. The constitutionality of the federal transfer tax systems enacted under the Code is not in doubt. Early on, the Supreme Court held that both the estate and gift taxes were validly imposed excise taxes, rather than constitutionally infirm unapportioned direct taxes. [44]

---

[39] Andrew Mellon, *Economic Aspects of Estate and Inheritance Taxation,* 39 Trust; Companies 708–09 (1924).

[40] *Supra* note 37.

[41] *See, e.g.*, Family Heritage Preservation Act of 1997, H.R. 902 and S. 75, 105th Cong., 1st Sess. (1997). *See also* Charles O. Galvin, *To Bury the Estate Tax, Not to Praise It,* 52 TAX NOTES 1413 (1991); Joel C. Dobris, *A Brief for the Abolition of All Transfer Taxes,* 35 SYRACUSE L. REV. 1215 (1984).

[42] 19 U. CHI. L. REV. 417, 520 (1952).

[43] Adapted in part from LAURIE L. MALMAN ET AL., PROBLEMS, CASES AND MATERIALS ON FEDERAL INCOME TAXATION 5–10 (1994).

[44] *See* New York Trust Co. v. Eisner, 256 U.S. 345 (1921) (upholding the estate tax); Bromley v. McCaughn, 280 U.S. 124 (1929) (upholding the gift tax).

In contrast, the Supreme Court has also held that taxation of income from real or personal property is an unconstitutional direct tax because it is not apportioned.[45] The Sixteenth Amendment's adoption in 1913, ensured that the income tax would be characterized as an indirect tax and, thus, constitutional.[46] More recently, the Supreme Court in *United States v. Carlton*[47] upheld the constitutionality of a limited retroactive tax on the grounds that due process was not violated because the enactment had a rational legislative purpose. Based on *Carlton*, courts have upheld the constitutionality of the 1993 retroactive freeze of the estate and gift tax rates above 50%.[48]

[A] Legislative Materials

Legislative history may provide assistance in interpreting certain provisions of the Code. Such history includes drafts of prior bills, hearings held before House and Senate committees, and the reports of the House Ways and Means and Senate Finance Committees. Conference committee reports and Congressional floor debates may also illuminate the tax law as enacted. Courts and taxpayers often use comments made in the reports of House and Senate committees or by the members in charge of the bill on its way through Congress to justify that a conclusion is in accordance with Congressional intent. Quotations from relevant committee and conference reports will be frequent throughout this book.

In recent years, the staff of the Joint Committee on Taxation has published. explanations (sometimes referred to as the blue book) after the enactment of major tax acts. The weight accorded these explanations is unclear because they are published after the passage of the bill.

[B] Administrative Materials

The administrative materials are essentially divided into Treasury Regulations, Revenue Rulings and Revenue Procedures. The Regulations, promulgated by the Treasury Department, constitute the most formal and authoritative administrative interpretation of the Internal Revenue Code. Under I.R.C. § 7805(a) the Secretary of the Treasury is authorized to "prescribe all needful rules and regulations for the enforcement" of the internal revenue laws. The Secretary of the Treasury has delegated authority to issue regulations to the Commissioner of Internal Revenue, subject to the approval of the Assistant Secretary of the Treasury for Tax Policy. The Regulations interpret the Code for the guidance of taxpayers as well as the staff of the Internal Revenue Service.

Regulations take two forms: interpretive and legislative. Interpretative regulations are designed to explain and illustrate the rules of the statute and enjoy a presumption of correctness. The extent to which an interpretative

---

[45] *See* Pollock v. Farmers' Loan & Trust Co., 157 U.S. 429, *reh'g granted,* 158 U.S. 601 (1895).

[46] *See* Brushaber v. Union Pacific R.R., 240 U.S. 1 (1916)(upholding constitutionality of income tax). *See also* New York Trust Co. v. Eisner, 256 U.S. 345 (1921) (upholding the estate tax); Bromley v. McCaughn, 280 U.S. 124 (1929) (upholding the gift tax).

[47] 512 U.S. 26 (1994).

[48] *See, e.g.,* Quarty v. United States, 170 F.3d 961 (9th Cir. 1999).

regulation is binding on the courts usually depends on the length of time a regulation has been in force and the consistency with which a regulation has been maintained. A court may declare an interpretive regulation invalid if the regulation is not supported by or is inconsistent with the statute.

Legislative regulations are regulations issued pursuant to a statutory provision that carves out for the Treasury explicit rule making authority. Certain provisions of the Code are particularly general and through regulation specifically delegate to the Treasury the task of providing the specific rules and guidance omitted from the Code.[49] A court may declare a rule making regulation invalid only if it is beyond the scope of Congressional intent.

The Internal Revenue Service (the Service) also issues revenue rulings, revenue procedures, private letter rulings, technical advice memoranda, and field service advice. Revenue rulings address substantive tax issues and reflect the Commissioner's official interpretation of the tax law. While generally binding on Service officials, revenue rulings are usually given less weight by the courts than are regulations because rulings are often viewed as merely reflecting the Commissioner's opinion. The Service states that taxpayers in substantially similar situations may rely on published rulings, although the Service has authority to amend or revoke a ruling.

A revenue procedure is a statement of procedure affecting the rights or duties of taxpayers and usually provides guidance to taxpayers for dealings with the Service. For example, there are revenue procedures which provide guidance to taxpayers as to how to file requests for private letter rulings.

Both revenue rulings and revenue procedures are published weekly in the Internal Revenue Bulletin. Published rulings and procedures are then accumulated semi-annually in a bound volume called the Cumulative Bulletin.

As stated above, the Service also issues private letter rulings, technical advice memoranda, and field service advice. A private letter ruling is a written statement issued to a taxpayer or her authorized representative by the National Office of the Internal Revenue Service interpreting and applying the tax laws to the taxpayer's specific set of facts. Taxpayers usually request a letter ruling to be sure of the tax consequences of planned transactions. A taxpayer requesting a private letter ruling is charged a user fee. Despite the implementation of user fees, there has been no significant decline in the number of ruling requests.

A technical advice memorandum (TAM) is an interpretation of the proper application of the tax laws and regulations furnished by the National Office of the Internal Revenue Service on the request of a District Office of the Internal Revenue Service in connection with an examination of a taxpayer's claim for refund or credit. Unlike revenue rulings and revenue procedures, private letter rulings and technical advice memoranda have no precedential effect and may only be relied upon by the taxpayer who requested the ruling (or advice). In addition, a taxpayer may rely on a private letter ruling only to the extent that the taxpayer accurately states all material facts in the ruling request and to the extent that the law remains unchanged after the Service issues the ruling.

---

[49] *See, e.g.,* § 2663.

Field service advice (FSA) is provided by the national office to a Field Office at the request of the Field Office. When field service advice is sought, the taxpayer is typically not involved in the process, but is not mandatory. The conclusion of the National Office in the field service advice is not a final determination. The Field Office may exercise independent judgment using the field service advice as one factor in resolving a taxpayer dispute.

The increased exposure of tax advisors and tax return preparers to penalties suggests that taxpayers will probably seek (and tax advisors and tax return preparers will insist on) a private letter ruling before undertaking a speculative transaction or before filing a return on a completed transaction. However, the Service will not always respond to a request for a private letter ruling. There are certain specific issues on which the Service will not issue a ruling or will not ordinarily issue a ruling. In addition, the Service refuses to give rulings on "inherently factual" matters prior to a taxpayer filing a return, issues in litigation, and matters to be addressed in future rule-making regulations. Information on areas or issues on which the Service will not rule is published in revenue procedures.

[C] Treatment of Tax Returns

Before moving on to the judicial sources of the tax law, consider the administrative treatment given tax returns. Taxpayers required to file an income tax or a gift tax return must do so annually.[50] The estate tax return is due nine months after the decedent's death.[51] Returns submitted by the taxpayer to a District Office of the Internal Revenue Service may not be audited. If a return is audited, the examining officer may find a deficiency (too little tax paid) or an overassessment (too much tax paid). The general statute of limitations on the Service is three years, so that the Service must assess a deficiency within three years after the return is filed. The statute of limitations is extended in cases where the taxpayer omitted from gross income more than 25% of the amount reported on a return (six years), failed to file a return (no limit), or filed a false or fraudulent return (no limit).[52] If a deficiency is asserted and the taxpayer and examining agent cannot reach an agreement on the alleged deficiency, the taxpayer may appeal to the Regional Appeals Office of the Internal Revenue Service. If the one-level administrative appeal procedure does not produce an agreement, the Service may issue a Notice of Deficiency (a 90-day letter) and the controversy may go into litigation. If the taxpayer wants to contest the deficiency notice before paying it, the taxpayer then has 90 days to petition the Tax Court and litigate.

The 90-day letter is often referred to as the taxpayer's ticket to the Tax Court. The failure to exhaust administrative remedies provides a basis for the Tax Court imposing a discretionary penalty.[53] Alternatively, the taxpayer may pay the asserted deficiency, file a claim for a refund, and, if the claim is denied, sue for a refund in either the United States Court of Federal Claims or district court.

---

[50] *See* §§ 6012, 6019.

[51] *See* § 6018.

[52] *See* §§ 6501(a), (c), (e)(1).

[53] *See* § 6673(a)(1)(c).

[D]　Judicial Function and Judicial Materials

If a taxpayer refuses to pay a deficiency, she may file a petition in the United States Tax Court seeking a redetermination of the proposed deficiency within a prescribed time period.[54] The case will be tried, without a jury, before one of the judges of the Tax Court. Although there is only one Tax Court, the judges serving on the Tax Court sit in a number of cities throughout the United States. For taxpayers with small proposed tax deficiencies (*i.e.*, the amount of the tax deficiency is $50,000 or less for any one taxable year), the Tax Court offers informal procedures designed to expedite the resolution and reduce the expense of tax litigation. If a taxpayer elects this informal, small case procedure, the outcome of the case cannot be appealed by either the taxpayer or the Service.[55] Although a taxpayer cannot generally be required to pay a proposed deficiency while her case is pending before the Tax Court,[56] if the Tax Court upholds the deficiency, interest accrues on the unpaid deficiency from the due date of the return.[57]

Should a taxpayer fail to file a petition with the Tax Court within the time permitted or lose in the Tax Court, various collection procedures are available to the Internal Revenue Service.[58] These include distraint (seizure and sale of a taxpayer's personal and real property) and the imposition of liens. If the Service believes that the collection of a deficiency may be jeopardized by delay, it may demand immediate payment of a tax without reference to the time limitations and restrictions generally in effect.

Instead of litigating in the Tax Court, the taxpayer may pay the full amount of the tax or additional tax proposed by the Service, and thereafter, file an administrative claim for a refund for the overpayment of taxes. If there is administrative inaction for a specified time period or if the claim is disallowed, the taxpayer may then file a suit for a refund in a federal district court in the district in which the taxpayer resides or in the United States Court of Federal Claims. In federal district court either the taxpayer or the government may demand a jury trial. A court of federal claims case is tried without a jury.

In litigation, the decision of the Internal Revenue Service is generally presumed correct for purposes of determining who has the burden of proof, except in cases where the government alleges fraud. Also, § 7491 places the burden of proof on the Service if the taxpayer submits credible evidence on a factual issue and has complied with the substantiation and cooperation requirements of that section.

Decisions by the Tax Court (except small claims procedures) or a federal district court are appealable by right by either party to a United States Court of Appeals for the appropriate circuit, as are decisions in the Court of Federal Claims. The United States Supreme Court rarely ventures into the tax field to review decisions of an appellate court.

---

[54] *See* §§ 6211(a), 6212(a), 6213(a).

[55] *See* § 7463(a), (b).

[56] *See* § 6213(a).

[57] *See* § 6601(a).

[58] *See* § 6213(c).

Interest at an adjustable rate is payable by taxpayers with respect to deficiencies and by the government on overpayments.[59] This interest rate is keyed to market rates. The interest rate taxpayers pay to the government on deficiencies equals the rate on short term Treasury bonds (*i.e.*, the average market yield on outstanding marketable obligations of the United States with a maturity of three years or less) plus 3 percentage points. The interest rate the government pays taxpayers on overpayments is the same: it equals the rate on short term Treasury bonds plus 3 percentage points.[60] Additional penalties are assessed for late filing,[61] failure to file a return,[62] failure to pay a tax shown,[63] and for fraud.[64] Accuracy related penalties are imposed for, among other items, negligence, substantial understatement of income tax, and any substantial valuation misstatement.[65] Criminal prosecution may also be instituted for, among other offenses, fraud, or a willful failure to file a return.

[E] Nonacquiescence in Decisions

It may startle some students to learn that when the taxpayer wins a case in the Tax Court which the Internal Revenue Service believes to be based on an erroneous legal concept, the Service may announce, whether or not it appeals the decision, that it does not acquiesce in the decision. Nonacquiescence puts other taxpayers on notice of a disputed issue and indicates that the Service may litigate the same issue when it arises again. The decision, unless reversed on appeal, is binding as to the Service in the case itself. On the other hand, by acquiescing in a determination adverse to the government, the Service indicates that it will not continue to contest the issue when it arises in other cases. In its published revenue rulings, the Internal Revenue Service may also announce whether or not it will follow a decision of the United States Court of Federal Claims, a district court, or a court of appeals.

Acquiescence and nonacquiescence indicate the Service's views. They are not given great weight, and may be repudiated by a court. Sometimes the Service will announce that it has changed its mind, *i.e.*, substituted an acquiescence for a nonacquiescence, or vice versa.

[F] State Law as a Source of Federal Tax Results

Commissioner v. Estate of Bosch

387 U.S. 456 (1967)

Mr. Justice Clark delivered the opinion of the Court.

---

[59] *See* §§ 6621, 6601, 6611(a).

[60] *See* § 6621(a).

[61] *See* § 6651(a)(1).

[62] *See* § 6651(a)(1).

[63] *See* § 6651(a)(2).

[64] *See* § 6663.

[65] *See* § 6662.

These two federal estate tax cases present a common issue for our determination: Whether a federal court or agency in a federal estate tax controversy is conclusively bound by a state trial court adjudication of property rights or characterization of property interests when the United States is not made a party to such proceeding.

Issue

In *Commissioner of Internal Revenue v. Estate of Bosch*, 363 F.2d 1009, the Court of Appeals for the Second Circuit held that since the state trial court had "authoritatively determined" the rights of the parties, it was not required to delve into the correctness of that state court decree. In *Second National Bank of New Haven, Executor v. United States*, 351 F.2d 489, another panel of the same Circuit held that the "decrees of the Connecticut Probate Court . . . under no circumstances can be construed as binding" on a federal court in subsequent litigation involving federal revenue laws. Whether these cases conflict in principle or not, which is disputed here, there does exist a widespread conflict among the circuits over the question and we granted certiorari to resolve it. We hold that where the federal estate tax liability turns upon the character of a property interest held and transferred by the decedent under state law, federal authorities are not bound by the determination made of such property interest by a state trial court.

[Although both cases involved aspects of the Federal estate tax marital deduction, which are addressed in Chapter 3, resolution of both cases depended on the effect of applicable state law. In *Bosch,* the issue was whether a general power of appointment had been validly released under New York property law.[66] A lower New York State court held that the release was ineffective under New York law. In *Second National Bank*, the issue was whether, under Connecticut probate law, decedent's will required that taxes be paid from the surviving spouse's bequest so as to reduce the marital deduction. A lower Connecticut court held that the taxes were not payable from the bequest.]

Commissioner of Internal Revenue v. Estate of Bosch

[In 1930, the decedent created a revocable trust that benefited his wife for her lifetime, and upon her death she was granted a general power of appointment over the trust assets. In 1951, the decedent's wife released the general power of appointment and converted it into a special power. When the decedent died, his estate claimed an estate tax marital deduction for the value of the trust. On audit, the Service disallowed the deduction because of the spouse's release of the power of appointment. To qualify for the estate tax marital deduction in effect at the time of the decedent's death, the power needed to be general, not special. Eventually the estate filed a petition in the Tax Court.]

. . .

The ultimate outcome of the controversy hinged on whether the release executed by Mrs. Bosch in 1951 was invalid—as she claimed it to be—in which

---

[66] For both tax and non-tax purposes, a general power of appointment is a power in the donee of the power (decedent's wife in *Bosch*) to name as the principal beneficiary any one of the following: the donee, her creditors, the donee's estate or the creditor's of the donee's estate. *See* I.R.C. § 2041(b); RESTATEMENT OF PROPERTY (SECOND), DONATIVE TRANSFERS, § 11.4. Eds.

case she would have enjoyed a general power of appointment at her husband's death and the trust would therefore qualify for the marital deduction. While the Tax Court proceeding was pending, the respondent filed a petition in the Supreme Court of New York for settlement of the trustee's account; it also sought a determination as to the validity of the release under state law. The Tax Court, with the Commissioner's consent, abstained from making its decision pending the outcome of the state court action. The state court found the release to be a nullity; the Tax Court then accepted the state court judgment as being an 'authoritative exposition of New York law and adjudication of the property rights involved,' 43 T.C. 120, 124, and permitted the deduction. On appeal, a divided Court of Appeals affirmed. It held that '(t)he issue is . . . not whether the federal court is "bound by" the decision of the state tribunal, but whether or not a state tribunal has authoritatively determined the rights under state law of a party to the federal action.' 363 F.2d, at 1013. The court concluded that the 'New York judgment, rendered by a court which had jurisdiction over parties and subject matter, authoritatively settled the rights of the parties, not only for New York, but also for purposes of the application to those rights of the relevant provisions of federal tax law.' *Id.*, at 1014. It declared that since the state court had held the wife to have a general power of appointment under its law, the corpus of the trust qualified for the marital deduction. We do not agree and reverse.

[The detailed facts and lower court rulings in *Second National Bank* are omitted.]

. . .

The problem of what effect must be given a state trial court decree where the matter decided there is determinative of federal estate tax consequences has long burdened the Bar and the courts. This Court has not addressed itself to the problem for nearly a third of a century. In *Freuler v. Helvering*, 291 U.S. 35 (1934), this Court, declining to find collusion between the parties on the record as presented there, held that a prior in personam judgment in the state court to which the United States was not made a party, "[o]bviously . . . had not the effect of res judicata, and could not furnish the basis for invocation of the full faith and credit clause . . . ." At 43. In *Freuler*'s wake, at least three positions have emerged among the circuits. The first of these holds that ". . . if the question at issue is fairly presented to the state court for its independent decision and is so decided by the court the resulting judgment if binding upon the parties under the state law is conclusive as to their property rights in the federal tax case . . . ." *Gallagher v. Smith*, 223 F.2d 218, at 225.

The opposite view is expressed in *Faulkerson's Estate v. United States*, 301 F.2d 231. This view seems to approach that of *Erie R. Co. v. Tompkins*, 304 U.S. 64 (1938), in that the federal court will consider itself bound by the state court decree only after independent examination of the state law as determined by the highest court of the State. The Government urges that an intermediate position be adopted; it suggests that a state trial court adjudication is binding in such cases only when the judgment is the result of an adversary proceeding in the state court. *Pierpont v. C.I.R.*, 336 F.2d 277. Also see the dissent of Friendly, J., in *Bosch*.

We look at the problem differently. First, the Commissioner was not made a party to either of the state proceedings here and neither had the effect of res judicata, *Freuler v. Helvering, supra*; nor did the principle of collateral estoppel apply. It can hardly be denied that both state proceedings were brought for the purpose of directly affecting federal estate tax liability. Next, it must be remembered that it was a federal taxing statute that the Congress enacted and upon which we are here passing. Therefore, in construing it, we must look to the legislative history surrounding it. We find that the report of the Senate Finance Committee recommending enactment of the marital deduction used very guarded language in referring to the very question involved here. It said that "proper regard," not finality, "should be given to interpretations of the will" by state courts and then only when entered by a court "in a bona fide adversary proceeding." S. Rep. No. 1013, Pt. 2, 80th Cong., 2d Sess., 4. We cannot say that the authors of this directive intended that the decrees of state trial courts were to be conclusive and binding on the computation of the federal estate tax as levied by the Congress. If the Congress had intended state trial court determinations to have that effect on the federal actions, it certainly would have said so—which it did not do. On the contrary, we believe it intended the marital deduction to be strictly construed and applied. Not only did it indicate that only "proper regard" was to be accorded state decrees but it placed specific limitations on the allowance of the deduction as set out in §§ 2056(b), (c), and (d). These restrictive limitations clearly indicate the great care that Congress exercised in the drawing of the Act and indicate also a definite concern with the elimination of loopholes and escape hatches that might jeopardize the federal revenue. This also is in keeping with the long-established policy of the Congress, as expressed in the Rules of Decision Act, 28 U.S.C.§ 1652. There it is provided that in the absence of federal requirements such as the Constitution or Acts of Congress, the "laws of the several states . . . shall be regarded as rules of decision in civil actions in the courts of the United States, in cases where they apply." This Court has held that judicial decisions are "laws of the . . . state" within the section. *Erie R. Co. v. Tompkins, supra; Cohen v. Beneficial Loan Corp.,* 337 U.S. 541 (1949); *King v. Order of United Commercial Travelers,* 333 U.S. 153 (1948). Moreover, even in diversity cases this Court has further held that while the decrees of "lower state courts" should be "attributed some weight . . . the decision [is] not controlling . . ." where the highest court of the State has not spoken on the point. *King v. Order of United Commercial Travelers, supra,* at 160–161. And in *West v. American Tel. & Tel. Co.,* 311 U.S. 223 (1940), this Court further held that "an intermediate appellate state court . . . is a datum for ascertaining state law which is not to be disregarded by a federal court unless it is convinced by other persuasive data that the highest court of the state would decide otherwise." At 237. . . . Thus, under some conditions, federal authority may not be bound even by an intermediate state appellate court ruling. It follows here then, that when the application of a federal statute is involved, the decision of a state trial court as to an underlying issue of state law should a fortiori not be controlling. This is but an application of the rule of *Erie R. Co. v. Tompkins, supra,* where state law as announced by the highest court of the State is to be followed. This is not a diversity case but the same principle may be applied for the same reasons, viz., the underlying substantive rule involved is based on state law and the State's highest court is the best authority on its own law. If there be no decision by that court then federal authorities must apply what they find to be the state law after giving "proper regard" to relevant rulings of other courts of the State. In this respect, it may be said to be, in effect, sitting as a state court. *Bernhardt v. Polygraphic Co.*, 350 U.S. 198 (1956).

We believe that this would avoid much of the uncertainty that would result from the "non-adversary" approach and at the same time would be fair to the taxpayer and protect the federal revenue as well.

The judgment in *Second National Bank* is therefore affirmed while that in *Bosch* is reversed and remanded for further proceedings not inconsistent with this opinion. It is so ordered.

[Dissenting opinions of Justices Douglas, Harlan and Fortas are omitted.]

Revenue Ruling 73–142

1973–1 C.B. 405

[During his lifetime the decedent petitioned a lower state court to construe a trust document. Contrary to the decisions of the highest court of the state, the lower court in a non-adversary proceeding construed the trust document in a way that limited the decedent's powers in the trust. If the Internal Revenue Service considered itself bound by the state court's erroneous construction, the trust assets would not be subject to estate taxation when the decedent died.]

In light of the holding in *Commissioner v. Estate of Herman J. Bosch*, 387 U.S. 456 (1967), the specific question asked is the effect to be given the above-mentioned court decree in determining the estate tax consequences of the trust. In *Bosch* the Supreme Court of the United States held that where the Federal estate tax liability turns upon the character of a property interest held and transferred under state law, federal authorities are not bound by a determination made of such property interest by a state trial court. Recognizing that state law as announced by the highest court of the state is to be followed, the Court held that, where there is no decision by the highest court, the federal court must apply what it finds state law to be, after giving proper regard to decisions of other courts of the state.

A close reading of the *Bosch* decision discloses that it does not in any way indicate that a lower court decree that is inconsistent with the ruling by the state's highest court on the particular issue is void as between the parties to the action. The problem involved in *Bosch* concerns the effect to be given such lower court decree where the same issue is critical in the determination of a federal tax question. The Court concluded that 'federal authorities are not bound' by a determination of a property interest by a state trial court. This does not mean that the parties to the state court action are not bound by the decree.

In this case the lower court had jurisdiction over the parties and over the subject matter of the proceeding. Thus, the time for appeal having elapsed, its judgment is final and conclusive as to those parties, regardless of how erroneous the court's application of the state law may have been. Consequently, after the time for appeal had expired, the grantor-decedent did not have the power [that would require inclusion of the trust in the decedent's gross estate.] The rights and powers which would otherwise have brought the value of the trust corpus within the estate tax provisions were thus effectively cut off before his death.

Unlike the situation in *Bosch,* the decree in this case was handed down before the time of the event giving rise to the tax (that is, the date of the grantor's death). Thus, while the decree would not be binding on the Government as to questions relating to the grantor's power under the trust prior to the date of the decree, it is controlling after such date since the decree, in and of itself, effectively extinguished the power. In other words, while there may have been a question whether the grantor had such power prior to the decree, there is no question that he did not have the power thereafter.

Accordingly, it is held that the value of the property transferred to the inter vivos trust is not includible in the grantor-decedent's gross estate.

———

Because the federal wealth transfer and income taxes purport to tax the ownership of rights, powers, and interests, their application is inherently dependent on the state property law that defines those rights, powers, and interests. "State law creates legal interests and rights. The federal revenue acts designate what interests or rights, so created, shall be taxed."[67] On the other hand, the tax laws need not, and do not, organize those interests and rights along lines identical to those of the various states. Once the right exists, it is for Congress to determine what the tax effect will be.

The significant impact that variations in state law can have on federal tax results leads to a variety of problems. The first is the necessity of defining what exactly is the applicable state law. Initially, this may include a conflicts of law issue, to determine which state's law controls.[68] As *Bosch* indicates, the difficulties do not cease there, however. The Supreme Court has long held that statutes and decisions of the highest state court constitute applicable state law.[69] Thus, in the many cases in which the local state court of last resort has not decided the point, a Federal court confronting the tax issue must determine what the state's highest court's decision would be if it were presented with identical facts.

This necessity for relying on state law to define tax results suggests the *Bosch* problem: what is the effect of a state court decision on the rights of

---

[67] Morgan v. Commissioner, 309 U.S. 78, 80 (1940).

[68] *See, e.g.,* Connecticut Bank & Trust Co. v. United States, 330 F. Supp. 997 (D. Conn. 1971), *rev'd on other grounds,* 465 F.2d 760 (2d Cir. 1972).

[69] *See* King v. Order of United Commercial Travelers of America, 333 U.S. 153 (1948); Erie R.R. v. Tompkins, 304 U.S. 64 (1938).

the parties to the transaction which is alleged to be subject to taxation? In other terms, what is the effect upon the Service of lower state court decisions? In *Bosch,* the Court decided that if the Service was not a party to the state court proceeding (as it rarely is) the Federal courts are not bound by that court's determination of the rights of the parties. Rather, the Federal court must make an independent evaluation of the parties' rights under state law. Thus, it is possible to have one result binding for state property law purposes, and another equally binding for federal tax purposes.

A major consequence of variations in state law is forum shopping. Because a person's domicile may determine the jurisdiction whose law will determine the validity of a transaction, individuals may move to obtain a more favorable succession law climate or other tax benefits. Estate planning documents may expressly state that the law of a particular jurisdiction is to be applied to the interpretation of the document in an attempt to obtain a favorable property law climate within which to have the validity of particular provisions determined.

The *Bosch* doctrine arises in numerous contexts throughout the course.[70] For a systematic analysis of how federal courts and the Service have applied *Bosch* in the past, see Gilbert Paul Verbit, *State Court Decisions in Federal Transfer Tax Litigation, Bosch Revisited,* 23 REAL PROP. PROB. & TR. J. 407 (1988); Paul L. Caron, *The Role of State Court Decisions in Federal Tax Litigation: Bosch, Erie, and Beyond,* 71 ORE. L. REV. 781 (1992); Paul L. Caron, *The Federal Courts of Appeals' Use of State Court Decisions in Tax Cases: "Proper Regard" Means "No Regard,"* 46 OKLA. L. REV. 443 (1993); and F. Ladson Boyle, *When It's Broke Fix It: Reforming Irrevocable Trusts to Change the Tax Consequences,* 53 TAX LAW 821 (2000).

Professor Gans suggests that the *Bosch* doctrine should be overruled in the marital deduction context. *See* Mitchell M. Gans, *Federal Transfer Taxation and the Role of State Law: Does the Marital Deduction Strike the Proper Balance?,* EMORY L. J. 871, 931-933. *See generally* Ira Mark Bloom, *How Federal Wealth Transfer Taxes Affect the Development of Property Law,* 48 CLEVE. ST. L. REV. 661 (2000).

Problems

1. During his life, *D* conveyed land to *B* by means of an invalid conveyance. After *D*'s death, his executor sued to recover the land. A lower state court ruled against the executor, and the case was not appealed. Property owned by a decedent at his death is subject to estate taxation. Do you think that the land will be taxable to *D*'s estate? Would your answer be different if during his life, *D* had unsuccessfully sued *B* to recover the land?

2. What if *D* received $100,000 for the land although the land's fair market value was $250,000? Consider § 2043.

---

[70] *See, e.g.,* Estate of Vissering v. Commissioner, discussed in Chapter 3.

§ 1.04   Resources

Throughout these materials, reference is made to particular sections of the Internal Revenue Code of 1986, and the Treasury Regulations adopted pursuant to it. You should obtain a copy of that Code and its Regulations. Further, there are several excellent treatises and compendiums which discuss in depth specific subject matter pertaining to the federal taxation of estates, trusts, and gifts. The following are recommended secondary sources:

Wealth Transfer Taxation

> BORIS I. BITTKER, FEDERAL TAXATION OF INCOME, ESTATES AND GIFTS (Warren, Gorham & Lamont, 3rd ed. 1999).

> PAUL L. CARON, GRAYSON M. P. McCOUCH & KAREN C. BURKE, FEDERAL WEALTH TRANSFER TAX ANTHOLOGY (Anderson 1998).

> RICHARD B. STEPHENS, STEPHEN A. LIND, GUY B. MAXFIELD AND DENNIS A. CALFEE, FEDERAL ESTATE AND GIFT TAXATION (Warren, Gorham & Lamont 7th ed. 1997).

Income Taxation of Estates, Gifts and Trusts

> BORIS I. BITTKER AND LAWRENCE LOKKEN, FEDERAL TAXATION OF INCOME, ESTATES AND GIFTS (Warren, Gorham & Lamont 3rd ed. 1999).

> JONATHAN G. BLATTMACHR AND ARTHUR M. MICHAELSON, INCOME TAXATION OF ESTATES AND TRUSTS (PLI 14th ed. 1996).

> M. CARR FERGUSON, JAMES J. FREELAND & RICHARD B. STEVENS ASCHER, FEDERAL INCOME TAXATION OF ESTATES AND BENEFICIARIES (Aspen Law & Business 3rd ed. 1998).

> HOWARD M. ZARITSKY AND NORMAN H. LANE, FEDERAL INCOME TAXATION OF ESTATES AND TRUSTS (Warren, Gorham & Lamont 3rd ed. 2001).

Valuation

> JOHN A. BOGDANSKI, FEDERAL TAX VALUATION (Warren Gorham & Lamont 1996).

Estate Planning

> A. JAMES CASNER AND JEFFREY N. PENNELL, ESTATE PLANNING (Aspen Law & Business 6th ed. 1995).

> JOHN L. PESCHEL & EDWARD D. SPURGEON, FEDERAL TAXATION OF TRUSTS, GRANTORS, AND BENEFICIARIES (Warren Gorham and Lamont 3rd ed. 1997).

> JOHN R. PRICE, CONTEMPORARY ESTATE PLANNING (Aspen Law & Business 2nd ed. 2000).

> JEFFREY A. SCHOENBLUM, MULTISTATE AND MULTINATIONAL ESTATE PLANNING (Aspen Law & Business 2nd ed. 1999).

> HAROLD WEINSTOCK, PLANNING AN ESTATE (Clark Boardman Callaghan 4th ed. 1995).

Apart from treatises and other books, the major source of guidance comes from law review articles, technical journals, and institute proceedings. Significant journals include:

> ESTATE PLANNING (Warren, Gorham & Lamont).
>
> PROBATE PRACTICE REPORTER (Probate Practice Reporter, LLC).
>
> REAL PROPERTY, PROBATE AND TRUST JOURNAL (American Bar Association).
>
> TRUSTS AND ESTATES (Intertec Publishing Corporation).

Institute Proceedings

> UNIVERSITY OF MIAMI PHILIP E. HECKERLING INSTITUTE ON ESTATE PLANNING (Lexis Publishing).
>
> NEW YORK UNIVERSITY INSTITUTE ON FEDERAL TAXATION (Lexis Publishing).
>
> MAJOR TAX PLANNING (UNIVERSITY OF SOUTHERN CALIFORNIA INSTITUTE ON TAXATION) (Lexis Publishing).

In addition, conference materials such as those published by the *Practicing Law Institute* may be helpful.

Chapter 2

OVERVIEW OF FEDERAL TAXATION OF ESTATES, TRUSTS AND GIFTS

This Chapter explores the structural foundations of the various tax systems studied in this course and the interrelationships among the systems. You will use this knowledge as the basis for later detailed discussions of each system's operation and then for transactional analysis. Specifically, this Chapter first provides a general overview of the structure of the federal gift tax and the federal estate tax. Then, the unification of the federal gift and estate tax systems is addressed as well as the de-unification scheduled for 2004. Thereafter, the structure of federal generation-skipping transfer tax is highlighted. Finally, we address those aspects of the federal income tax system that apply when property is gratuitously transferred.

Before providing a general overview of gift taxes and estate taxes, it is necessary to have an understanding of how the threshold for taxation is determined. Smaller estates are not subject to estate taxation and lifetime transfers are not subject to gift taxation until a cumulative total is reached.

Until 1977, donors were permitted a $30,000 lifetime exclusion from gift taxes. Estates were similarly permitted a $60,000 deduction from the value of the taxable estate before computing estate taxes. In 1976, Congress abandoned the deduction regime and adopted the concept of a single credit to offset either gift taxes or estate taxes. With a unified system, a taxpayer can make lifetime gifts that exhaust the unified credit, or only use a part or none of it. The portion not used during lifetime is available to reduce or eliminate estate taxes.

With the change from a deduction to a unified credit system, it was more difficult for practitioners and clients to perceive the value of the credit. Quickly, however, a short-hand developed: the exemption equivalent. Moreover, the Code needed to convert the credit to an exclusion amount for various purposes, such as the size of an estate for filing purposes.

In 1977, the credit was $29,800, which translated into an exemption equivalent of $120,000. From 1977 to 1987, the unified credit and the exemption equivalent rose each year until the credit reached $192,800 and the exemption equivalent reached $600,000. In 1997, Congress again adjusted the unified credit to increase year by year until 2006, when it was scheduled to reach $345,800, which is an exemption equivalent of $1 million. When drafting the 1997 changes, Congress chose to state the change in the credit as the "Applicable Credit Amount" by references to the "applicable exclusion amount," which is the same as an exemption equivalent. In 2001, Congress made dramatic changes to the threshold of taxation, effective for years after 2001. Thus, from 1997 until 2010, the applicable credit amount and the exemption equivalent are as follows:

Year	Applicable Credit Amount	Exemption Equivalent
1997	$192,800	$600,000
1998	$202,050	$625,000
1999	$211,300	$650,000
2000	$220,550	$675,000
2001	$220,550	$675,000
2002	$345,800	$1,000,000
2003	$345,800	$1,000,000
2004	$555,800	$1,500,000
2005	$555,800	$1,500,000
2006	$780,800	$2,000,000
2007	$780,800	$2,000,000
2008	$780,800	$2,000,000
2009	$1,455,800	$3,500,000
2010	credit repealed	unlimited

Because the estate tax credit is in transition until 2011,[1] the text will refer to the unified credit using the statutory term "applicable credit amount." Students need to pay particular attention to the calendar year involved in all examples and discussions to determine the appropriate applicable credit amount and the exemption equivalent. Moreover, the amount of tax due will depend on the type of transfer because the gift tax exemption amount remains a constant $1 million and is not indexed for inflation.

Before the Tax Act of 2001 rate changes, the maximum estate tax rate was 55%. The Act reduces the top rate as follows:

Taxable Event In	Top Rate
2002	50%
2003	49%
2004	48%
2005	47%
2006	46%
2007	45%
2008	45%
2009	45%

The Tax Act of 2001 repealed the 5% estate and gift tax surcharge on taxable estates or taxable gifts that exceed $10 million for taxable transfers occurring after 2001.

§ 2.01   Federal Gift Tax Structure

Code: §§ 2001, and 2501 through 2512.

Regulations: Treas. Reg. § 25.2502–1.

The federal gift tax liability is calculated in four steps. First, the Code defines what transactions are subject to the tax, *i.e.*, what transfers are

---

[1] There is no estate tax credit in 2010 because there is no estate tax. In 2011, the exemption equivalent amount reverts to $1 million.

treated as gifts. Second, the Code allows some transfers to be removed (deducted) from those subject to the tax. Third, a tax is calculated by applying a rate table to the remaining transfers. Fourth, the taxpayer is allowed to reduce the tax by a credit. The gift tax is imposed on the donor of the gift, with secondary donee liability if the donor does not pay the tax.

A "gift" for gift tax purposes is a transfer: (1) of a beneficial interest in property, (2) beyond the control of the transferor, (3) for less than full and adequate consideration in money or money's worth. As will be developed in Chapter 4, the definition of what constitutes a gift for tax purposes is expansive, and it includes both direct and indirect transfers.

Once the transfers subject to the gift tax have been identified, it is necessary to determine which of those transfers are taxable, i.e., which "taxable gifts" were made during the taxable period. Three concepts—split gifts, exclusions, and deductions—are applied to reduce coverage of the tax. First, § 2513 permits married taxpayers to treat certain transfers as made one-half by each. Second, some transactions are "excludable," i.e., the transaction is statutorily excluded from the definition of taxable gifts. The most common exclusion is authorized by § 2503(b), which excludes gifts of present interests up to $10,000 (as adjusted for inflation starting in 1999) per donee per taxable year.[2] Less common are exclusions under § 2503(e) for certain medical and educational expenses and the § 2503(f) waiver for certain pension transactions. Third, the Code allows certain transfers to be "deducted" from taxable gifts, thereby reducing the amount of gifts subject to tax. Section 2523 permits a deduction for gifts of certain transfers to the donor's spouse, and § 2522 allows a deduction for gifts to charity.

Once the amount of taxable gifts is determined, the donor's tax liability for the year can be calculated. This is done by aggregating the donor's taxable gifts for the current year with the aggregate of taxable gifts made by the taxpayer in prior years. In other words, the donor adds together all taxable gifts made at anytime. A *first tentative tax* is calculated under §§ 2501(a)(1), 2502(a), and 2001(c) on this sum using the rate tables contained in federal estate tax § 2001. Second, the current rate tables under § 2001(c) are again applied only to those taxable gifts made in prior years, to determine a *second tentative tax*. Third, § 2502(a) provides that this *second tentative tax* is subtracted from the *first tentative tax* to determine the taxpayer's gift tax liability on the current calendar year's taxable gifts.

The effect of cumulating present gifts with prior gifts for the purposes of calculating the current tax is to maintain the progressive nature of the gift tax in the face of multiple transfers made in different tax years. This cumulation has been a part of gift taxes since its beginnings in 1932. Pursuant to Treasury Regulations § 25.2502–1, the gift tax is determined by a six-step process calculated as follows:

Example: During calendar year 2002, *X* made a taxable gift (after exclusions and deductions) of $750,000. He had made a taxable gift of $100,000 in 1998.

(1) Amount of taxable gifts for current year $750,000

---

[2] In 2002, the gift tax annual exclusion is $11,000. *See* Rev. Proc. 2001-59, I.R.B. 2001-52 (Dec. 24, 2001).

(2) Plus total amount of taxable gifts for
preceding calendar periods 100,000
(3) Total for calculating tentative tax year $850,000
(4) Tax computed on item 3 in accordance
with § 2001(c) rate schedule
(first tentative gift tax) year $287,300
(5) Minus tax computed on item 2 computed in
same way (second tentative gift tax) . . . . -23,800
(6) Tax for current year before credit $263,500

Finally, § 2505 allows the taxpayer to reduce the amount of the tax by subtracting any unused part of a "unified credit" from the amount of tax owed. Its use is mandatory.[3] The credit reduces the tax, dollar for dollar. To the extent the credit is not used in one year, it may be used in succeeding years. The applicable credit amount for 2002 is $345,800, which exceeds the tentative gift tax and allows this transfer to pass tax free.

In the above example, the available credit would be $345,800 less the $23,800 credit allowable on last year's taxable gift of $100,000. Because the credit cannot exceed the tax imposed, the credit allowed against the tentative gift tax liability will equal $263,500. Thus, there will be no gift tax liability. Understand that by making total taxable gifts of $850,000, X has used up much of the credit. He has an available credit of $58,500 remaining, that is, $345,800 minus the sum of: (1) $23,800 (credit used against the 1998 taxable gift) and (2) $263,500 (credit used against the 2002 taxable gift).

The credit was added to the gift tax calculation in 1976, applicable to taxable years beginning in or after 1977. Thus, if X had made the $100,000 taxable gift in 1970 rather than in 1998, there would have been no credit used in a prior year to reduce the $345,800 credit available in 2002. As a result, $82,300 of credit would remain after taking the $263,500 credit applied against the tax generated by the $750,000 current taxable gift, rather than the $58,500 remaining if the $100,000 gift were made in 1998.

Problems

1. Assume D, a widower, made no prior taxable gifts. Consider I.R.C. §§ 2501, 2502, 2505 and 6019.

a. In 2000, D makes taxable gifts aggregating $200,000 (net of the $10,000 annual exclusion) to A. What are the gift tax ramifications of the transfer? What is the amount of the gift tax payable? Must D file a gift tax return?

b. In 2001, D makes a taxable gift of $250,000 (net of the annual exclusion) to B. What are the gift tax consequences of the transfer? Must D file a gift tax return?

c. In 2002, D makes a taxable gift of $650,000 (net of the annual exclusion) to C. What are the gift tax consequences of the transfer? Must D file a gift tax return?

d. What is the amount of gift tax due if D makes all three gifts in 2002?

---

[3] See Rev. Rul. 79–398, 1979–2 C.B. 338.

§ 2.02　Federal Estate Tax Structure

Code: I.R.C. §§ 2001, 2002, 2010, 2011, 2033 through 2044, 2051, and 2053.

Regulations: None.

The basic structure of the federal estate tax is as follows: the transactions to which the tax applies are accumulated to determine the *gross estate,* which is then reduced by applicable *deductions,* resulting in the *taxable estate.* The *estate tax imposed* is then determined on the sum of the *taxable estate* and *adjusted taxable gifts* (most taxable gifts since 1976), reduced by the gift tax payable on the taxable gifts. Finally, the *estate tax imposed* is reduced by allowable *credits* to determine the *estate tax payable.*

Briefly stated, the basic operation of the estate tax is as follows:

The gross estate. Section 2001(a) imposes the estate tax on the taxable estate of a citizen or resident of the United States.[4] In turn, the taxable estate depends upon the amount of the gross estate, a broadly defined term that encompasses four major categories. Under § 2033, the gross estate first includes all property that the decedent owned at death. Second, because the power to obtain property is treated as the equivalent of owning the property, § 2041 includes in the gross estate property over which the decedent possessed a general power of appointment exercisable during life or at death. Third, §§ 2036 through 2040 and 2042 include in the gross estate property previously transferred by the decedent in transactions that the Code treats as the substantial equivalent of testamentary transfers. Further, § 2044 includes in the gross estate property obtained by the decedent from the decedent's spouse, even if the decedent does not own it or have a general power of appointment over it, if that property passed to the decedent free of transfer taxation as part of the marital deduction. Investigating the reasons for inclusion of property in the gross estate is one of the central themes of this book.

The first of these reasons for including property in the gross estate—ownership of the property—is addressed in § 2033, which includes all property, real or personal, tangible or intangible, wherever situated, that the decedent owned at death.

The second reason for inclusion—the right to exercise a power to obtain someone else's property—is addressed in § 2041. Under that section, property that the decedent could have obtained through exercise of a general power of appointment (defined to include any power exercisable in favor of the holder, including powers to invade corpus), or could have transmitted by will (a testamentary general power), is includable in the gross estate.

The third reason—inclusion because the decedent dealt with the property during lifetime in a testamentary manner—is addressed in a number of sections of the Code. Specifically, the gross estate includes:

(1)　the value of property transferred by the decedent during life with certain retained "strings," specifically:

(a)　where the decedent retained a life income interest in the transferred property or in the enterprise underlying the

---

[4] Section 2101(a) imposes an estate tax on the taxable estate of a nonresident who is not a citizen of the United States.

transferred property or the power to control the beneficial enjoyment of the transferred property (§ 2036);

    (b)   where the decedent retained a proscribed reversionary interest and others only could obtain possession and enjoyment of the property by surviving the decedent (§ 2037); or

    (c)   where the decedent retained the power to alter, amend, revoke, or terminate the transfer (§ 2038);

(2)   the value of contractual payments to beneficiaries by reason of surviving the decedent under any agreement by which the decedent had the right to a payment during his life (§ 2039);

(3)   the value of all property held in joint tenancy except:

    (a)   to the extent it can be shown that the surviving co-tenant contributed to the acquisition or improvement of the property (§ 2040(a)); and

    (b)   one-half of certain joint property interests between husband and wife (§ 2040(b));

(4)   the value of proceeds of insurance on the decedent's life:

    (a)   receivable by the decedent's personal representative (§ 2042(a)); or

    (b)   receivable by any other beneficiary if the decedent possessed, at the time of her death, any "incident of ownership" over the policy (§ 2042(b)); and

(5)   the value of some types of property because of transfers by the decedent within three years of the decedent's death, specifically, property that would have been includable in the decedent's gross estate under §§ 2036, 2037, 2038 or 2042, if the decedent had not made the transfer (§§ 2035(a)).

In addition, § 2044 includes property in the gross estate if it previously passed tax-free to the decedent as "qualified terminable interest property," thus qualifying for the gift or estate tax marital deduction. This result parallels inclusion under § 2033 for property previously devised to the decedent spouse outright, and under § 2041 for property transferred in a trust that qualified for the marital deduction because the decedent spouse was given a general power of appointment.[5]

An important aspect of determining the gross estate is the valuation of assets subject to the tax. Section 2031 states that "[t]he value of the gross estate . . . shall be determined by including to the extent provided . . . the value at the time of his death of all property, real or personal, tangible or intangible, wherever situated." Relief from the mischance of dying at the height of the stock market is provided by § 2032, which allows the estate to be valued as of six months after the date of death. Additional relief is provided in the case of estates composed mostly of farm or business real estate. Section 2032A allows such estate property to be valued based on its actual use, rather

---

[5] Under the special valuation rules of Chapter 14, gross estate inclusion is also required in very particularized transactions. *See* §§ 2701(d), 2704(a).

than its (assumably) higher market value, as long as the property continues to be used in the same way by family members after the decedent's death.

Deductions. After determining the value of the gross estate, it is necessary to determine the deductions allowed by the Code. Deductions from the decedent's gross estate allowed in determining the amount of the decedent's taxable estate include amounts for:

(1) certain expenses and indebtedness, *i.e.*, funeral expenses, administration expenses, claims against the estate, mortgages and other indebtedness with respect to property included in the decedent's gross estate, and certain marital property settlements (§ 2053);

(2) casualty losses with respect to estate assets (§ 2054);

(3) certain transfers to charity of assets included in the decedent's gross estate (§ 2055);

(4) certain transfers to the decedent's surviving spouse of assets included in the decedent's gross estate (§§ 2056 and 2056A). This deduction is known as the estate tax marital deduction.

(5) certain transfers of Qualified Family Owned Business Interests to Qualified Heirs (§ 2057);[6] and

(6) state inheritance, estate and other death taxes paid for decedents dying after 2004 (§ 2058).

Subtracting these deductions from the gross estate mathematically leaves what is called the taxable estate. *See* § 2051. The estate tax imposed by § 2001(a) is based on the rate schedule provided by that section.

Calculation of the tax. For decedents who did not make any taxable gifts after 1976, the estate tax imposed is simply the tax on the taxable estate amount under § 2001(c). For example, the calculation of the estate tax imposed in 2002, on a taxable estate of $1.1 million, if no post-1976 taxable gifts were made, would be as follows:

Item	*Amount*
Taxable estate	$1,100,000
Adjusted taxable gifts	0
Total	$1,100,000
Tax on $1.1 million	$386,800
Estate tax imposed (before the allowance of any applicable credits)	$386,800

Credits. Finally, the estate tax liability is determined by subtracting a variety of credits from the estate tax imposed under § 2001. These credits include: (1) the applicable credit amount (a unified credit) which excludes from taxation a taxable estate of $1 million to $3.5 million depending on the year of the decedent's death, or no tax in 2010 (§ 2010(a)); (2) a credit for state

---

[6] I.R.C. § 2057, enacted in 1997 as § 2033A but subsequently renumbered 2057, provides a deduction for some property owned by a decedent at death if the requirements of the section are satisfied. The Tax Act of 2001 repeals § 2057 for estates of decedents dying after 2003.

death taxes until 2005 (§ 2011); (3) a credit for federal gift taxes paid on pre-1977 transactions included in the gross estate (§ 2012); (4) a credit for part or all of the estate taxes paid on assets recently included in another decedent's estate (§ 2013); and (5) a credit for foreign death taxes paid on estate assets (§ 2014).

The § 2010 applicable credit amount will always be allowable and, absent the unusual situation described in § 2010(b), the applicable credit amount will equal the amount set out at the beginning of this Chapter. The credit is equivalent to the applicable credit amount; *i.e.,* if the applicable credit amount had been allowed as a deduction, rather than as a credit, gross estates valued at the applicable credit amount or less would have resulted in a zero taxable estate and no estate tax would be imposed.

The other credits may, but will not necessarily, be allowable in the particular case. This depends on the date of the decedent's death and the actual payment of state death taxes, taxable gifts made before 1977, foreign death taxes, and whether included property was recently taxed in another estate. In the overwhelming majority of estates only the §§ 2010 and 2011 credits will need to be available.

The effect of the §§ 2010 and 2011 credits may be illustrated by determining the federal estate tax payable on a 2002 decedent's taxable estate of $1.1 million (where the decedent made no taxable gifts). Based on the computational scheme of § 2001(b), the estate tax imposed is $386,800. Sections 2010 and 2011 provide that the estate tax imposed shall be reduced by the allowable credits under these sections. Thus, we first reduce the estate tax imposed of $386,800 by $345,800, the credit allowed under § 2010 in 2002; and then by the § 2011 credit of $29,100 which is determined by application of the § 2011(b) rate schedule, as modified by the Tax Act of 2001.[7] The federal estate tax payable is $11,900 and the state estate tax is at least $29,100 for a combined estate tax due of $41,000. If the decedent died in 2003 or 2004, the combined federal estate tax and state estate tax total of $41,000 would remain the same although the Treasury would receive more and the state, potentially less ($21,600 and $19,400 in 2003; $31,300 and $9,700 in 2004) because § 2011 phases out.

Problems

1. *A*, a widow, died in 2002 with the following assets: savings account ($15,000), checking account ($1,500), certificates of deposit ($43,000), stocks and bonds ($378,000), auto ($6,000), real estate ($254,000), which is subject to a recourse mortgage of $30,000, joint and survivor checking account with her son *J* in which she contributed all the funds ($2,500), and personal and household goods ($15,000). *A* also was the beneficiary of a testamentary trust created under the will of her late husband *H*, pursuant to which she was

---

[7] In this example, the § 2011 credit amount is based on an adjusted taxable estate of $1,040,000; *i.e.,* the taxable estate of $1.1 million less $60,000. *See* § 2011(b) (last sentence defines adjusted taxable estate as the taxable estate less $60,000). By application of § 2011(b), the credit amount in the example is $38,800, but the Tax Act of 2001 allows only 75% of that amount in 2002. In 2003, only 50% is allowed and in 2004, only 25%. After 2004, no credit is allowed, but § 2058 permits state estate tax to be deducted. The state death tax credit is discussed in Chapter 3.

entitled to the income from the trust payable at least annually and over which she had a power to appoint the entire trust assets in favor of herself during her life or to the estate on her death. The value of the trust corpus equals $500,000. The amount of funeral and administration expenses equals $25,000. Her will provides that all of her estate is to pass to *J*.

a. What is the amount of *A*'s gross estate for federal estate tax purposes? Consider §§ 2033, 2040, and 2041.

b. What is her estate tax, assuming that *A* made no taxable gifts during her life and that her state of domicile imposes a death tax equal to the maximum state death tax credit? Consider §§ 2051, 2053, 2001, 2010, and 2011.

c. Who is liable for the payment of the tax? Consider § 2002.

§ 2.03   The Unified Gift and Estate Tax System

Before the Tax Reform Act of 1976, gift taxes were imposed on the transfer of taxable gifts, which were defined as gross gifts (gifts less a $3,000 per donee annual exclusion) less three types of deductions (including a $30,000 cumulative lifetime deduction). The tax was calculated by applying a progressive rate (which was set at 75% of the estate tax rate structure) to the sum of taxable gifts for the year plus taxable gifts in prior years. Thus, the tax was progressive over the lifetime of the donor.

Because the pre-1976 estate and gift tax systems were generally separate and distinct, an individual could pay a lower transfer tax if he transferred some or all of his property during his lifetime, rather than retaining ownership of the property until death. This tax reduction resulted from several aspects of the gift tax: (1) an additional $30,000 could be given tax-free because of the lifetime exemption deduction; (2) even if lifetime gifts exceeded both the exclusion and the exemption, the tax rate was only three-fourths that of the estate tax rate (although the exemption deduction for the estate tax was $60,000); and (3) each dollar transferred during life was removed from the top marginal estate tax rate, to be taxed (at least initially) at the lowest gift tax marginal rate.[8] An additional reason why lifetime transfers were (and still are) advantageous, was the ability to make annual exclusion gifts ($3,000 before 1977 and $10,000 (indexed for inflation) thereafter) that were entirely free from both gift and estate taxes.

By unifying the gift tax with the estate tax, the 1976 amendments to the Code, effective January 1, 1977, removed most of the tax advantages of gifts enjoyed prior to 1977. The three structural changes were: (1) an individual and his estate had one overall exemption equivalent amount; (2) both gift and estate taxes were imposed by applying one unified rate schedule; and (3) the estate tax was imposed by taking into account adjusted taxable gifts so that each dollar transferred during life used up the marginal tax bracket that would have applied had the taxable gift not been made.

---

[8] Another advantage to gifts was that no gift tax was imposed on the money used to pay the tax. Because the applicable credit amount for gifts made after 2003 will be limited to $1 million, whereas the applicable credit amount for estates of decedents dying after 2003 will be higher, making gifts to pay gift taxes may no longer be perceived as an advantage for many individuals.

The technical implementation of unification is complex. Section 2001(b)(1)(B) requires that "adjusted taxable gifts," defined by § 2001(b) (flush sentence), be added to the amount of the taxable estate for the purposes of calculating the tentative estate tax. Once this tentative tax is calculated, the estate may subtract gift taxes payable with respect to gifts made by the decedent after December 31, 1976, from the tentative tax,[9] with the remainder constituting the estate tax imposed. The effect of this process is to push the taxable estate into a bracket higher than that in which it would have been had adjusted taxable gifts not been included in the calculation. It is this cumulation which forms the heart of unification of the estate tax and the gift tax. Finally, the estate tax imposed is reduced by the § 2010 applicable credit amount (ignoring all other credits).

Consider the effect of unification by comparing two relatively simple examples:

Example 1: In 2001, *D* made a taxable gift of $100,000. In 2003, he died with a taxable estate of $1 million. Assume no other gifts.

By applying the unified rate schedule of § 2001(c), as prescribed by § 2502(a), the gift tax imposed on the taxable gift of $100,000 is $23,800. However, the gift produces no gift tax payable because the applicable credit amount of $23,800 is allowed under § 2505. When *D* dies in 2003, the taxable estate of $1 million is cumulated with $100,000 in adjusted taxable gifts under § 2001(b)(1), producing a tentative tax rate base of $1.1 million. The tax on this amount is $386,800 and no gift tax is subtracted because none was payable on the $100,000 gift. From the $386,800, estate tax applicable credit amount of $345,800 is subtracted, leaving an estate tax payable of $41,000 (ignoring the state death tax credit).

Example 2: *D* made no taxable gifts. He died in 2003, with a taxable estate of $1.1 million.

D's taxable estate and tentative tax rate base are both $1,100,000 because *D* made no taxable gifts. The tax on this amount is $386,800. Of course, no gift tax is subtracted because there were no gifts that could have generated gift tax liability. From the $386,800, the estate tax applicable credit amount of $345,800 is subtracted, leaving an estate tax payable of $41,000 (ignoring the state death tax credit).

By unifying gift and estate taxes, the same amount of tax is payable in both examples. It does not matter whether all property is held until death as in Example 2 or some property is gifted as in Example 1.

Although Congress unified the gift and estate tax systems in 1976, the combined transfer tax liability will not always be the same if gifts are made, rather than holding all wealth until death. There are two main structural reasons. First, virtually all gifts that fall within the applicable gift tax exclusion exceptions escape transfer taxation altogether. The gift tax annual exclusion of $11,000 (reflecting an inflation adjustment in 2002) per donee is the major exclusion provision in this area.

---

[9] This second tentative tax is calculated using current rate tables to avoid the possibility of the taxpayer who made gifts before 1982 or after 2001 from benefiting from lower rates in subsequent years. *See* § 2001(b)(2).

Second, when gifts generate gift tax liability, the overall transfer tax may be less than if the gifts had not been made. Before considering the reasons for decreased overall transfer tax liability, it is necessary to understand how the gift and estate tax liability is calculated if prior gifts generated gift taxes. The same initial steps must be taken: (1) the taxable estate is added to the adjusted taxable gifts to obtain the tentative tax rate base, and the tentative tax. Now, however, it is necessary to (2) calculate the gift tax on the prior gifts (including any gifts included in the gross estate), which is (3) subtracted from the tentative tax. Again, if only the § 2010 credit is taken into account, the applicable credit amount will be subtracted from the resulting figure to determine the tax due.

The calculation in the case of taxable gifts not included in the gross estate is illustrated by the following example:

Example 3: The decedent made a gift of $760,000 in 1997. The gift tax payable was $55,500 (a gift tax of $248,300 imposed on a taxable gift of $750,000 ($760,000 minus the $10,000 exclusion) less the then allowable credit of $192,800). The decedent died in 2003, with a taxable estate of $750,000.

The estate tax imposed under § 2001 on the taxable estate of $750,000 is computed as follows: the adjusted taxable gifts were $750,000 which, when added to the taxable estate, produced a tentative tax rate base of $1.5 million and a tentative tax of $555,800. This amount is reduced by $55,500, the gift tax payable on the 1997 gift.[10] The tax due will be $154,500 ($555,800 tentative tax, less the $345,800 applicable credit amount and less the $55,500 gift tax paid credit (before consideration of the § 2011 credit)).

If the gift upon which a gift tax was paid is included in the decedent's gross estate, for example as a result of a retained power or interest (see Chapters 7-9), the gift tax paid still reduce the estate tax due.

Example 4: In 1997, the decedent furnished the entire consideration of $1,520,000 for property taken in the joint names of the decedent and her daughter. The result was a taxable gift of $750,000 (the value of her daughter's one-half interest, minus the $10,000 annual exclusion amount allowed in 1997), with a $55,500 gift tax payable. Assume the decedent died in 2003, when the jointly held property was worth $1.5 million and the decedent had a taxable estate, including all of the jointly held property, of $2 million.

The estate tax imposed under § 2001 on the $2 million taxable estate would be $725,300, computed as follows: the tentative tax rate base was $2 million, comprised of the taxable estate of $2 million and no adjusted taxable gifts. The taxable gift of $750,000 did not constitute an adjusted taxable gift because the gift was included in the gross estate under § 2040. The tentative tax on $2 million is $780,800, which is then reduced by the gift tax payable of $55,500 on the post-1976 taxable gift. The $725,300 balance is the estate tax imposed by § 2001, which is reduced further by the applicable credit amount of $345,800,

---

[10] Technically, the gift tax payable is the gift tax which would have been imposed based on the rate schedule in force when the decedent died, not when the gift was made. *See* § 2001(b)(2).

leaving an estate tax due of $379,500 (before consideration of the § 2011 credit).

On further analysis, the overall estate and gift taxes may be less if the decedent incurred gift tax liability. This is because the gift tax is a tax exclusive basis. The estate tax is applied to the total assets of the decedent, including those assets used to pay the tax, the gift tax applies only to those assets transferred to the donee. It does not apply to the assets used to pay the tax. The tax-exclusive/tax-inclusive distinction is sometimes referred to as the failure either to gross-up the gift tax or net-down the estate tax. This distinction permits a greater amount of property to be conveyed during life-time, rather than if the wealth holder transferred an equivalent amount of property at death.[11]

The distinction between the gift tax-exclusive system and the estate tax-inclusive system may be illustrated as follows:

> **Example 5:** *X,* who is in the 50% wealth transfer tax bracket, wishes to make a gratuitous transfer of $1 million during her lifetime or at death. She could transfer $667,000 by a taxable gift and pay a gift tax of $333,000 (50% of $667,000).

If *X* transferred $1 million at death, an estate tax of $500,000 would be imposed, leaving only $500,000 for the devisee. In other words, if the applicable rate equals 50%, two-thirds of the owner's property may pass to a beneficiary by gift whereas only one-half of the property may pass to the beneficiary if transferred at death.

Finally, there is another reason why unification may not produce the same transfer tax liability without regard to whether gifts are made or all property is held until death. Absent a few exceptions, the unified system does not account for changes in value over time. For example, the value of stock in year one for gift tax purposes may be more (or less) than its date of death value.

The failure to equate the two taxes may be justified, in the sense that the gift tax is collected earlier than is the estate tax. Thus the government gets the advantage of the use of the money for a longer period of time. The differential also may compensate somewhat for the capital gains tax advantage of assets included in the gross estate, which are allowed a stepped-up basis,[12] rather than the donor's carryover basis for the gifted property. See the discussion of basis in § 2.05, *infra.*

Problems

(Take into account only the § 2010 credit and ignore state death taxes.)

1. In 2003, *D* made taxable gifts of $1 million exclusive of the annual exclusion. He died later in the same year with a taxable estate of $11,000. What

---

[11] *See* John T. Gaubatz, *The Unfinished Task of Estate and Gift Tax Reform,* 63 Iowa L. Rev. 85, 85–89 (1977).

[12] When the estate tax is repealed in 2010, §§ 1014(f) and 1022 provide for carryover basis, subject to a complicated set of adjustments. When the estate tax repeal sunsets in 2011 and as a result the 2001 version of the estate tax is restored, carryover basis is repealed. *See* Tax Act of 2001 § 901.

is the estate tax liability? What is the estate tax liability if *D* had not made any adjusted taxable gifts, but died with a taxable estate of $1,011,000?

2. *B* owned $1.5 million in unproductive assets. In 2002, she transferred $111,000 by gift, which qualified for one gift tax annual exclusion. If *B* died later that year, what is the estate tax liability if *B*'s taxable estate was $1,389,000? Explain why this amount is less than *B*'s liability had she made no lifetime transfers.

3. *A* owned $1.5 million in unproductive assets. In 1997, *A* made a taxable gift of $700,000 in a manner which did not qualify for the gift tax annual exclusion. Assume *A* died in 2003. Further assume that *A*'s taxable estate is $1.5 million, less the amount transferred in 1997 and the gift taxes she paid on the 1997 transfer. What is the combined gift and estate tax liability (taking into account only the § 2010 credit)? Why is it less than if *A* died in 2003 with a taxable estate of $1.5 million?

§ 2.04 De-Unification of Estate and Gift Taxes

Code: §§ 2001, 2010, 2502, and 2505.

Regulations: None.

Under the Tax Act of 2001, the applicable credit amount for gift taxes does not increase in 2004 and later years when the applicable exclusion amount for estate tax purposes rises to $1.5 million and eventually to $3.5 million by 2009. The consequence of this is to "de-unify" the gift tax from the estate tax during a taxpayer's lifetime. No longer is the amount that may be given away free of tax the same as the amount that may pass free of estate taxes when a taxpayer dies.

Example 6: In 2005, *A* transfers $1.5 million to a trust for the benefit of her daughter. The transfer does not qualify for the gift tax annual exclusion. *A* will owe $210,000 in gift taxes ($555,800 tentative tax less the applicable credit amount of $345,000). If, instead of making the gift, *A* died in 2005 with a taxable estate of $1.5 million, the tentative tax would be $555,800, the applicable tax credit amount would be $555,800 and her estate would owe no tax.

The system "re-unifies" at the time of a taxpayer's death because lifetime gifts potentially are still adjusted taxable gifts, and gift taxes paid during life are still a credit against the estate tax.

Example 7: In 2005, *A* transfers $1 million to a trust for the benefit of her daughter. The transfer does not qualify for the gift tax annual exclusion. *A* will owe no gift taxes ($345,800 tentative tax less the applicable credit amount of $345,800). If *A* dies later that year with a taxable estate of $1 million, her combined taxable estate and adjusted taxable gifts total $2 million. The tentative tax is $780,800, the applicable credit amount is $555,800, and her estate owes $225,000 in estate tax.

Also, any gift taxes paid on adjusted taxable gifts will be credited against the estate tax. *See* § 2001(b)(2).

For taxpayers who do not make taxable gifts, the system remains unified until the estate tax is repealed in 2010. If a taxpayer makes gifts that result in the payment of gift taxes, the system still operates as before.

Example 8: In 2010, A transfers $5 million to a trust for the benefit of her daughter. The transfer does not qualify for the gift tax annual exclusion. A will owe $2,045,000 in gift taxes ($2,390,800 tentative tax less the applicable credit amount of $345,800). If, instead of making the gift, A died in 2010 with a taxable estate of $5 million (or a greater amount), there would be no estate tax.

The net effect of the 2004-2010 de-unification is likely a decrease in taxable gifts. For many taxpayers who would consider making taxable gifts, retaining ownership of assets until death likely or at least possibly means the avoidance of any transfer tax and the potential for an income tax step-up in basis.

Example 9: In 2010, A transfers $1.5 million to a trust for the benefit of her daughter. The transfer does not qualify for the tax annual exclusion. A will owe $210,000 in gift taxes ($555,800 tentative tax less the applicable credit amount of $345,800). If the income tax basis of the transferred assets is -0-, § 1015 permits the donee to increase the basis by the amount of the gift tax $210,000.[13] If, instead of making the gift, A died in 2010 with a taxable estate of $1.5 million, there would be no estate tax and the daughter will have an income tax basis of $1.3 million in the inherited assets.

The consequence of discouraging gifts is likely higher values for estates of decedents and more income taxes paid by the wealthy because of the disincentive to make gifts of income producing property. It also means a slow down in the transmission of wealth from older generations to younger generations—a result not intended by those that argue that the purpose of wealth transfer taxes is to de-centralize large concentrations of wealth!

§ 2.05 Generation-Skipping Transfer Tax

Code: §§ 2601, 2611, 2612, 2613, 2631, 2641, 2642, 2651, and 2652.

Regulations: None.

The unified gift and estate system is based on the premise that property should be taxed at each generation. When, however, beneficiaries do not have the equivalent of ownership, for example, when they hold only life or term interests, gift and estate taxation at each generation level can be avoided. Subject to important exceptions, the generation-skipping transfer (GST) tax system fills the gaps in the estate and gift tax systems and ensures that property will be taxed once each generation.

The structure of the GST tax system parallels the gift and estate tax systems. First, the tax requires a taxable event, *i.e.*, a generation-skipping transfer. In that event, the transfer is valued using the general gift and estate tax valuation rules. Next, the taxable amount (the value of the generation-skipping transfer less applicable reductions) is ascertained. Third, the tax

---

[13] In this example, all of the gift tax paid increases basis because all of the gift tax is attributable to appreciation. If the donor had a basis of $750,000 in the transferred assets, only half of the gift tax paid would be an addition to basis. *See* § 1015(d)(6).

imposed on the taxable amount is calculated. Finally, the tax imposed may be reduced by a credit for state GST taxes on transfers before 2005.

[A] The Taxable Event

Under the GST tax system, there are three types of generation-skipping transfers: (1) a direct skip, (2) a taxable termination, and (3) a taxable distribution. *See* § 2611.

A direct skip includes a transfer to an individual who is more than one generation younger than the transferor, *i.e.*, a transfer that "skips" a generation, in the sense that no estate or gift tax will be imposed at the level of the intervening generation. A direct skip is illustrated as follows:

> **Example 1:** Grandfather, *GF*, bequeaths $2 million to his granddaughter, *GD*, child of *C*.

Although the estate tax will tax the bequest at *GF*'s death, the bequest to *GD* will not be subject to estate and gift taxation at *C*'s generation level; no one in *C*'s generation has any interest or power over the property which would trigger estate or gift taxation. Hence, transfer taxation at *C*'s generation would otherwise be avoided without a GST tax system. The GST tax system treats the transfer as a taxable event—a direct skip.

Taxable terminations arise under trusts or trust equivalents.[14] A taxable termination occurs on the termination of an interest when the result of the termination is that the property in the transaction avoids estate and gift taxation at the intervening generation. A taxable termination is illustrated by the following testamentary trust disposition under a grandparent's will:

> **Example 2:** Grandmother, *GM*, creates a trust, income to son, *S*, for life, remainder to grandchild, *GC*. *S* dies after *GM* created the trust.

When *S* dies, the trust is not subject to estate taxation because *S* had no interest in the trust property. Hence, when *GC* becomes entitled to possession of the property, taxation at *S*'s generation level could be avoided but for a GST tax system. The GST tax system treats *S*'s death as a taxable event—a taxable termination.

A taxable distribution also occurs in the context of trusts. The concept involves the distribution of property from a trust to beneficiaries more than one generation younger than the person who created the trust. A taxable distribution is illustrated by the following bequest:

> **Example 3:** Grandparent, *GP*, creates a trust, income to daughter, *D*, for life, remainder to grandchild, *GC*, with power in the trustee to invade the corpus for *GC*. Pursuant to that power, the trustee invades corpus for *GC*. When *GC* receives corpus, estate and gift taxation on that property is bypassed at the intervening generation level of the daughter. However, the GST tax system treats the distribution of the corpus as a taxable event—a taxable distribution.

---

[14] As will be seen in Chapter 5, a direct skip may occur on the creation of certain trusts.

[B] Taxable Amount

The taxable amount varies depending on the type of generation-skipping transfer. *See* §§ 2621–2623. As a general rule, however, the taxable amount will be the value of the property involved in the particular generation-skipping transfer, reduced by a limited number of items, as described in Chapter 5.

[C] Calculation of the GST Tax

Section 2602 imposes the GST tax by multiplying the taxable amount under the generation-skipping transfer by the *applicable rate.* The applicable rate is the product of the maximum estate tax rate (50% in 2002 and decreasing as shown in the chart on page 28) and the *inclusion ratio* (§ 2641). The inclusion ratio is a mechanism designed to allocate the benefit of a $1 million (as adjusted for inflation) for 2002 and 2003 and equal to the applicable exclusion amount in 2004-2009 ($1.5 million to $3.5 million) per transferor GST tax exemption. *See* §§ 2631, 2632, 2642.

Determining the inclusion ratio (or fraction) first requires the calculation of the exclusion ratio (or applicable fraction). The exclusion ratio has as its numerator the portion of the GST exemption amount (not to exceed $1 to $3.5 million, depending on the tax year) allocated to the transfer; the denominator is the value of the property subject to the generation-skipping transfer. This *applicable fraction* is then subtracted from 1 to determine the inclusion ratio.

> **Example 1:** Grandfather dies in 2004, having made no generation-skipping transfers during his lifetime. His will devises $1.5 million to a grandchild and the residue of his estate to a child from which all taxes are payable. The bequest is a generation-skipping transfer (a direct skip) and the personal representative allocates the entire $1.5 million GST exemption to the direct skip.

The amount of the GST tax that will be imposed on the $1.5 million depends on the applicable rate, the product of the maximum estate tax rate of 48% in 2004, and the inclusion ratio. The inclusion ratio, in turn, depends on the exclusion ratio. In this example, the exclusion ratio will be 1 because both the numerator and denominator are $1.5 million. The numerator is the allocated GST exemption amount of $1.5 million, and the denominator is the value of the property which passes pursuant to the generation-skipping transfer—also $1.5 million. The inclusion ratio, determined by subtracting the exclusion ratio of 1 from 1, will be zero.

Whenever a zero inclusion ratio applies, there can be no generation-skipping transfer tax imposed. Quite simply, any taxable amount multiplied by zero must always be zero.

If the inclusion ratio is greater than zero, a GST tax will be imposed, as shown in the following example:

> **Example 2:** A grandparent's will bequeaths $1 million to a grandchild, with all taxes payable from the residue. Assume the grandparent's GST exemption was fully allocated during the grandparent's lifetime and the grandparent died in 2002. The inclusion ratio in this example is 1 (1 − 0/$1 million),

and the GST tax imposed will be $500,000, which is the product of the $1 million taxable amount times 50% times the inclusion ratio of 1.

[D] Section 2604 Credit

The GST tax system allows only one credit: a credit for state GST tax imposed on taxable terminations and distributions occurring before 2005. *See* § 2604. This credit is analogous to the § 2011 credit under the estate tax system. In response to the credit, many states have enacted a GST tax which taxes GST transfers to the extent of the credit allowed by § 2604. The Tax Act of 2001 repeals the credit for GST transfers occurring after December 31, 2004.

§ 2.06   The Federal Income Tax System[15]

[A] Income Tax Consequences of Gifts and Bequests

Code: I.R.C. §§ 1(h), 102(a), 1014(a), 1015(a), and 1041.

Regulations: None.

Although the receipt of a gift or bequest enriches the recipient, the receipt does not have any direct income tax ramifications.[16] Section 102(a) excludes the receipt of a gift or bequest from the gross income of the donee or recipient. Similarly, the donor generally will not realize a gain (or a loss) when making a gift because making a gift is not deemed a taxable event.[17] However, any income subsequently generated by the property received will be included in the donee's or recipient's gross income. Thus, under § 102(b), gifts and bequests have significant secondary income tax effects.

Another secondary income tax effect of gifts is that any gain or loss on the transferred asset is generally realized upon its disposition by the donee. For the purpose of determining gain on the sale of property acquired by gift, generally § 1015(a) provides that the donee's basis equals the donor's basis subject to adjustments which may occur during the time the donee holds the property.[18] Under this carryover basis approach, the pre-gift appreciation is deferred and is taxed to the donee on the donee's sale or other disposition of the property. For gifts made after 1976, the allowable increase in basis for gift taxes paid (not to exceed fair market value) under § 1015(d)(6) is restricted to that portion (fraction) of the tax which is attributable to "net appreciation in value" of the gift.

---

[15] This discussion assumes that you have a basic understanding of the federal income taxation of individuals.

[16] The special rules for income and deductions in respect of a decedent are considered in Chapter 14.

[17] *See* Taft v. Bowers, 278 U.S. 470 (1929).

[18] To prevent the gifting of losses, the donee's basis for loss purposes will be the property's fair market value at the time of the gift if the value is less than the donor's adjusted basis in the property. *See* § 1015(a). *But see* § 1041 (no limitation on interspousal gifts).

Until 2010 and after 2010, § 1014(a) provides that the basis for determining gain or loss from the sale of property passing or acquired from a decedent[19] generally equals its fair market value on the date of the decedent's death or the alternative valuation date if the personal representative elects to use this date in valuing the estate for federal estate tax purposes. The decedent's basis becomes irrelevant for the purposes of thereafter calculating gain or loss on the disposition by the beneficiary. Thus, if property owned by a decedent appreciates in value after he acquired it, there will be no income tax on the pre-death appreciation. Similarly, any pre-death decline in the value is nondeductible for income tax purposes.

Because of the loss of the tax payable on pre-death appreciation, a stepped-up basis to inherited property has often come under attack. Indeed, the Tax Reform Act of 1976 sought to modify the Code so that the basis of property passing or acquired from a decedent dying after December 31, 1976, was to be carried over from the decedent, with specified adjustments, to the recipient of the property. However, this change was subsequently repealed by the Crude Oil Windfall Profit Tax Act of 1980. The reasons in favor of the carryover basis approach were summarized in the following excerpt:

> Prior law [step-up basis] resulted in an unwarranted discrimination against those persons who sell their property prior to death as compared with those whose property was not sold until after death. Where a person sells appreciated property before death, the resulting gain is subject to the income tax. However, if the sale of the property could be postponed until after the owner's death, all of the appreciation occurring before death would not be subject to the income tax.
>
> This discrimination against sale occurring before death created a substantial "lock-in" effect. Persons in their later years who might otherwise sell property were effectively prevented from doing so because they realized that the appreciation in that asset would be taxed as income if they sold before death, but would not be subject to income tax if they held the asset until their death. The effect of this "lock-in" was often to distort the allocation of capital between competing sources.
>
> In order to eliminate these problems, Congress believed that the basis of property acquired from or passing from a decedent should have the same basis in the hands of the recipient as it has in the hands of the decedent, i.e., a "carryover basis." This will have the effect of eliminating the unwarranted difference in treatment between lifetime and testamentary transfers.[20]

Compare this with the following excerpt setting forth the reasons for the repeal of the carryover basis provisions:

---

[19] Under § 1014(b) property is deemed acquired from a decedent if the property is includable in the decedent's gross estate for estate tax purposes. When a spouse dies owning an interest in community property, however, both halves of the community property receive a step-up (or step-down) basis under § 1014(b)(6). See § 3.01[B][2].

[20] Staff of the Joint Committee on Taxation, General Explanation of the Tax Reform Act of 1976, 94th Cong., 2d Sess. 552 (1976).

A number of administration problems concerning the carryover basis provisions have been brought to the attention of the committee. Administrators of estates have testified that compliance with the carryover basis provisions has caused a significant increase in the time required to administer an estate and has resulted in raising the overall cost of administration. The committee believes that the carryover basis provisions are unduly complicated.[21]

The Tax Act of 2001 resurrects carryover basis for the one year the estate tax is repealed: 2010.[22] Assets included in a decedent's estate will have a basis equal to the lesser of (1) fair market value on the date of death or (2) the adjusted basis in the hands of the decedent. Basis step-down in loss assets in retained. *See* §§ 1014(f), 1022 (a).

The decedent's personal representative will be permitted to allocate to specific noncash assets an aggregate basis increase of $1.3 million. No asset basis may be increased above fair market value. *See* § 1022(b)(2)(B). In addition, the basis of property transferred to a surviving spouse may be increased by $3 million, with respect to assets passing outright or in certain marital trusts. *See* § 1022(b)(c).

The $1.3 million basis adjustment can be further increased by any unused capital losses, net operating losses, and certain "built-in" losses of the decedent, and both the $1.3 million and $3 million figures are indexed for inflation. *See* § 1022(b)(2)(C).

No basis adjustment will be permitted for certain types of assets, such as items of income in respect of a decedent and property acquired by the decedent by gift (other than from his or her spouse) during the three-year period ending on the date of the death. *See* § 1022(d)(1). The estates of nonresidents who are not U.S. citizens will be allowed a basis increase only up to $60,000, but this is also indexed for inflation after December 31, 2009. *See* § 1022(b)(3).

Congress adopted several special rules to prevent the carryover basis rules from creating special problems:

(a) Gain or loss on the transfer of property in satisfaction of a pecuniary bequest after 2009 will be recognized only to the extent that the fair market value of the property at the time of the transfer exceeds its fair market value on the date of the decedent's death, rather than its carryover. *See* § 1040.

(b) The $250,000 exclusion for the gain on the sale of a principal residence is extended to estates and heirs, if the decedent used the property as a principal residence for two or more years during the five-year period prior to the sale. The decedent's period of occupancy is added to any actual occupancy by the heir, with respect to the heir's sale. *See* § 121(d).

(c) Section 684, which currently taxes a donor on the appreciation in property contributed to a foreign trust or estate, will be extended to include testamentary transfers to foreign individuals. *See* § 684.

---

[21] Report of the Committee on Finance, United States Senate, Crude Oil Windfall Profit Tax Act of 1979, 96th Cong., 1st Sess. 122 (1979).

[22] In many respects, the carryover basis regime in 2010 is more complex than the system that Congress repealed in 1980 because it was "unduly complicated." *See* Joseph M. Dodge, *A Deemed Realization Approach Is Superior to Carryover Basis (And Avoids Most of the Problems of Estate and Gift Tax),* 54 Tax L. Rev. 421 (2001).

Problems

1. *D* makes a gift of stock to *X*. *D*'s basis for the stock equals $1,000. The stock, a capital asset, has a fair market value of $10,000 at the date of the gift. Assume *D* pays no federal gift tax on the transfer. *X* sells the shares one year later for:

 (i) $15,000;

 (ii) $5,000;

 (iii) $500.

 a. In each of the above, does the donee or the donor realize the gain (or loss)? When? Consider § 1001(a).

 b. What is the amount of the gain (or loss)?

 c. How would your answer change if the donor was the spouse of the donee? *See* § 1041.

 d. What income tax considerations should enter into a property owner's decision whether to transfer property which has appreciated in value? Depreciated in value?

2. What result upon the sale in each of the three situations in (1) above if *D* died when the stock was worth $10,000, and the stock was left as a bequest to *X* in the decedent's will?

3. *D*'s basis for stock is $10,000. The shares are worth $1,000 at the date of the gift. Assume *D* pays no federal gift tax with respect to the transfer.

 a. Does *X* realize gain (or loss) and in what amount, if *X* sells the shares for:

 (i) $15,000 (is the basis for determining loss useful?);

 (ii) $500;

 (iii) $5,000?

 b. Can the donee take advantage of the pre-gift depreciation in the value of the property?

 c. Would you recommend that an individual owning property with a basis in excess of the fair market value transfer the property by gift? What should the prospective donor do instead of making a gift of property which has declined in value?

 d. Would any of your answers to (a)-(c) change if the donee were the donor's spouse? *See* § 1041.

[B] Federal Income Tax Consequences of Attempted Income Splitting

Gifts have often been used to reduce income taxes payable on the income earned by the transferred assets. Three points explain this reason for making gifts. First, each member of the family is a separate individual for federal income tax purposes, and every individual is entitled to file his or her own separate income tax return. *See* § 6012(a). Second, each individual filing a tax return generally has a personal exemption (§ 151) and a standard deduction (§ 63(c)), which can be used to shelter income from taxation. Third, because the income tax rate structure is progressive, shifting income to a lower bracket taxpayer can reduce the tax payable on the income. For these reasons, a high income family member might want to shift income to a lower income family member, purely to save on the family tax bill.[23] Income shifting, however, will be thwarted if the donor is unwilling to relinquish sufficient control of the asset. Under the "assignment of income doctrine," the donor may still be taxed on income which is received by the donee.[24]

It has been particularly common to shift income to the children of the donor. Although parents and their children are members of the same household, income generated from property owned by a child is taxable to that child, not to the parents, even though the income producing property may have been received as a gift from the parents. At the same time, the parents may feel secure in their ability to control the child's property after the "gift," leaving the family control of the assets in approximately the same condition as it was before the transfer.

Because intra-family transfers, especially when the recipient is very young, are perceived dominantly to have been used to reduce the income tax burden on the family, attempts have been made from time to time to limit the practice. A broad scale attack on the practice was launched in the Tax Reform Act of 1986. That Act diminished the reasons for income splitting in four significant ways. The Act first reduced the top marginal rates and dramatically reduced the number of marginal rates. This created a situation in which the recipient's marginal rate would rapidly equal the donor's marginal rate, thus removing the primary incentive for tax motivated giving. Second, the personal exemption was disallowed for an individual who is eligible to be claimed as a dependent on another taxpayer's return (for example, a child eligible to be claimed on the parents' return). See § 151(d)(2). Third, the standard deduction for dependent children was generally limited to $500 as increased by indexing for inflation ($750 in 2002). See § 63(c)(5). Finally, the Act directly attacked the tax benefits of gifts to minor children by requiring the children to pay tax on the income generated on assets gratuitously transferred to them at the parent's rate. As stated in the legislative history of § 1(g):

> The committee believes that the present law rules governing the taxation of minor children provide inappropriate tax incentives to shift income-producing assets among family members. In particular, the committee is aware that the treatment of a child as a separate taxpayer encourages parents whose income would otherwise be taxed at a high marginal rate bracket to transfer income-producing property to a child to ensure that the income is taxed at the child's lower marginal rates. In order to reduce the opportunities for tax avoidance through intra-family transfers of income-producing property, the committee concluded that it is generally appropriate to tax

---

[23] Non-tax considerations, such as a concern for the financial stability of the prospective donee, may discourage the transfer in spite of the tax benefits.

[24] The assignment of income doctrine has been codified for trust transfers under the grantor trust rules. *See also* Helvering v. Horst, 311 U.S. 112 (1940).

the income on property transferred . . . to a minor child at the parent's marginal rates. [25]

This so-called "kiddie" tax provision does not prohibit the shifting of income to minor children, nor does it change the child's rate structure on earned income. The earned income continues to be taxed to the child at her marginal tax rate. The provision did remove the tax incentive for shifting income producing assets to the minor by requiring that the tax on net unearned income of a child under age 14 [26] be calculated at the parents' marginal tax rate.

Problems

1. On January 1 of the current year, Nicole's parents, who are in the 35% income tax bracket, transfer a substantial sum of money into a custodial savings account for her. During the year, the savings account earns $10,000 of interest. Assume that Nicole is 13 at the end of the tax year and that she has no other unearned income and no itemized deductions directly connected with the production of income. What are the income tax consequences to Nicole for the $10,000 of income she must report? Consider §§ 1(g), 63(c)(5) and 151(d)(2). What amount in taxes was saved by this assignment of income from the parents to their child? (Assume the standard deduction is $750.)

2. What would Nicole's income tax liability have been if, in Problem 1, she already was 14?

[C]　Federal Income Taxation of Trusts and Estates

Code: §§ 641 through 663, 671 through 678, 1014, and 1015.

Regulations: None.

[1]　The Tax Structure

A trust is a common receptacle for gifts or bequests of property. The trust may exist for a considerable amount of time. For example, it may be used to preserve assets for one beneficiary while another beneficiary enjoys the income from the assets or to manage the property for the primary beneficiary. Furthermore, whenever an individual dies, the decedent's assets are held by the personal representative for some period of time, while the creditors are paid and estate taxes are determined. The probability that income will be produced while property is held by a trust or a decedent's estate necessitated a tax law response to the existence of these entities. This response is contained in Subchapter J of the Code, §§ 641 through 682, the details of which are considered in Chapter 14.

In some respects, Subchapter J treats trusts and estates as separate taxable entities. The income tax imposed is determined the same way that the Code

---

[25] Senate Finance Committee Report on H.R. 3838, Tax Reform Act of 1986, 99th Cong., 2d Sess. 862 (1986).

[26] Apparently, age 14 was selected because this is the age at which children may work in certain employment under the Fair Labor Standards Act.

taxes individuals. Thus, an entity's taxable income must be calculated by subtracting deductions from gross income. Generally, an estate or trust will have the same items of gross income and deductions as individuals, except that an estate or trust is entitled to a special deduction for the distributions it makes to beneficiaries.[27]

Because trusts and estates are entitled to the special deduction for distributions, these entities are treated, in part, as income conduits similar to a partnership. The income and deductions pass through the trust or estate to the beneficiary to the extent of distributions. By adopting the conduit approach, Congress created a need to identify the income which would be taxable to beneficiaries and for which an estate or trust would receive a distribution deduction. The 1954 Congress adopted the concept of "distributable net income." The following legislative history explains this concept:

> Your committee's bill contains the basic principles of existing law under which estates and trusts are treated as separate taxable entities, but are generally regarded as conduits through which income passes to the beneficiary. The estate or trust is taxed in general in the same manner as an individual, but is allowed an additional deduction for income distributions to its beneficiaries.
>
> . . .
>
> The bill adopts the general principle that to the extent of the trust's current income all distributions are deductible by the estate or trust and taxable to the beneficiaries. This approach represents a basic departure from the general rule of the existing law that taxable distributions must be traced to the income of the estate or trust for the current year.
>
> However, this approach requires the use of a measure to impose an outside limit on the total distributions deductible by the estate or trust and taxable to the beneficiary. In general, the measure adopted by the bill for this purpose is taxable income, [with several modifications].
>
> The bill adheres to the conduit theory of the existing law. This means that an estate or trust is in general treated as a conduit through which income passes to the beneficiary. In order to implement this theory in a satisfactory manner, it is necessary to include in the measure items of income and deductions which are not reflected in taxable income. The bill adopts the concept of "distributable net income" as the measure and adjusts the amount of the distributions deductible by the estate or trust and taxable to the beneficiaries by eliminating not only capital gains and losses but items of income and expenses which do not enter into the computation of taxable income. Thus, the distributable net income of an estate or trust is defined as its taxable income for the current year, excluding capital gains and losses not distributed by the estate or trust, the portion of extraordinary cash dividends and taxable stock

---

[27] Also, estates and trusts will apply §§ 1014 and 1015 in determining the basis for property acquired from a decedent or settlor.

dividends allocated to principal (in the case of simple trusts described below), and the dividends received exclusion, but including tax-exempt interest and foreign income of foreign trusts.

The approach adopted by the bill eliminates the necessity, in determining the taxability of distributions, of tracing such distributions to the income of the estate or trust for the current taxable year.[28]

The statutory term of art "distributable net income" (DNI) is the cornerstone for determining the income tax liability of estates and trusts, as well as the beneficiaries of estates and trusts. Through the mechanics of § 643, taxable income is allocated among the entity and its beneficiaries. DNI limits the amount of the §§ 651(a) and 661(a) deductions that estates and trusts are allowed for distributions to beneficiaries and the amount §§ 652(a) and 662(a) require beneficiaries to report as income.

To determine DNI and taxable income, a fiduciary must allocate receipts and disbursements between principal and income under the terms of the governing instrument or applicable state law. Thus, fiduciary accounting income (FAI) plays an important role in determining the tax liability of beneficiaries.

A relatively simple example illustrates how FAI and DNI are computed:

Example: A trust is required to distribute all of its income to its sole beneficiary and make no other distributions. It has the following items of income and expense:

Gross income from real estate rentals	$15,000
Interest on corporate bonds	$25,000
Short term capital gains	$25,000
Real estate rental expenses	-$5,000

The FAI of the trust that is distributable to the beneficiary is computed as follows:

Rental income	$15,000
Corporate bond interest	$25,000
Less rental expenses	-$5,000
FAI	$35,000[29]

DNI is calculated by computing the entity's taxable income (without the distribution deduction) with certain adjustments as follows:

Gross income from real estate rentals	$15,000
Interest on corporate bonds	$25,000
Short term capital gain	$25,000
Gross income	$65,000

Normal deductions are allowed:

Real estate rental expenses	-$5,000

---

[28] S. Rep. No. 1622, H.R. 8300, 83rd Cong., 2d Sess. 82–83 (1954).

[29] The capital gains are not in FAI because capital gains are allocated to principal under state fiduciary accounting rules. Thus, the amount the trust must distribute to the beneficiary is $35,000.

Personal exemption (§ 642(b))	-$300
Taxable income before the distribution deduction	$59,700

Under § 643, the capital gain income must be subtracted in the computation of DNI and the personal exemption deduction must be added back:

Plus personal exemption (§ 643(a)(2))	$300
Less capital gains (§ 643(a)(3))	-$25,000
DNI	$35,000

Computation of the trust's taxable income continues by permitting the trust a distribution deduction equal to the lesser of DNI ($35,000) or the amount distributed ($35,000):

Less distribution deduction	$35,000
Taxable Income	$24,700

Once the taxable income of a trust or estate is determined, the tax is imposed by applying the rate table for trusts and estates. *See* § 1(e). Under this table (as amended by the Tax Act of 2001) there are five tax brackets. For 2004 and 2005, these rates are scheduled to be 15%, 26%, 29%, 34% and 37.6%, and through 2010, these rates are scheduled to be 15%, 25%, 28%, 33% and 35%. In 2001, trust income in excess of $8,900 is taxed at the top rate of 39.1%. The tax liability may be reduced by various credits.

Under Subchapter J, estate and trust beneficiaries may be required to include the amount of the distributions in gross income. *See* §§ 652, 662. [30] The beneficiary of the trust in the example must report as gross income the amount that is required to be distributed, *i.e.,* $35,000. *See* § 652(a).

[2] Tax Minimization Opportunities

The creation of trusts can have federal income tax ramifications for both the donor and the beneficiaries. Because a trust is a separate taxable entity under the Code, a settlor can shift income from the settlor's return (at the marginal rate) to a trust (at the trust's marginal rate) by transferring income producing property to the trust. This can produce very limited income tax savings, provided the trust is kept sufficiently small, so that it does not generate too much income. For example, in 2002, the maximum amount that could have been saved by having taxable income of $9,200 taxed at brackets below 38.6% was $1,022.

Further, the trust or estate has the flexibility of transferring some of the income to beneficiaries, allowing for the shifting of income for tax purposes. Although the trust or estate is allowed a deduction for distributions to beneficiaries, the beneficiaries report the receipts as income on their returns. [31] Thus, with some limitations, the Code allows the trustee to determine

---

[30] Generally, the basis of property in the hands of the trust or estate will carry over to the beneficiary whether or not the beneficiary has to include the receipt in gross income. If, however, the fiduciary elects to recognize a gain or loss on the distribution, the beneficiary's basis may be adjusted accordingly. *See* § 643(e) discussed in Chapter 14.

[31] The trust income received by the beneficiary retains the same character in the hands of the beneficiary as it had when received by the trust. *See* §§ 652(b), 662(b).

the effective taxable rate on the income by choosing whether to have it taxed to the trust (at its marginal rate) or the beneficiary (at the beneficiary's marginal rate). In the family trust context, this power allows for the minimization of income taxes, especially where the beneficiary is a minor who has attained age 14, with little other income.

Problems

1. A decedent's estate has taxable income of $24,700 during its current taxable year. What is the tax imposed under § 1(e)?

[3] Grantor Trusts

Special rules also apply to trusts in which the grantor retains various powers or interests. These rules parallel the "string provisions" of the estate tax provisions. The problem is illustrated by the famous case *Helvering v. Clifford*.

Helvering v. Clifford

309 U.S. 331 (1940)

Mr. Justice Douglas delivered the opinion of the Court.

In 1934 respondent declared himself trustee of certain securities which he owned. All net income from the trust was to be held for the "exclusive benefit" of respondent's wife. The trust was for a term of five years, except that it would terminate earlier on the death of either respondent or his wife. On termination of the trust the entire corpus was to go to respondent, while all "accrued or undistributed net income" and "any proceeds from the investment of such net income" was to be treated as property owned absolutely by the wife. During the continuance of the trust respondent was to pay over to his wife the whole or such part of the net income as he in his "absolute discretion" might determine.

[The trust instrument also gave Clifford, the trustee, administrative powers broader than normal, and provided that he was to be held to a lower than normal standard of fiduciary responsibility.]

It was stipulated that while the "tax effects" of this trust were considered by respondent they were not the "sole consideration" involved in his decision to set it up, as by this and other gifts he intended to give "security and economic independence" to his wife and children. It was also stipulated that respondent's wife had substantial income of her own from other sources; that there was no restriction on her use of the trust income, all of which income was placed in her personal checking account, intermingled with her other funds, and expended by her on herself, her children and relatives; that the trust was not designed to relieve respondent from liability for family or household expenses and that after execution of the trust he paid large sums from his personal funds for such purposes.

Respondent paid a federal gift tax on this transfer. During the year 1934 all income from the trust was distributed to the wife who included it in her individual return for that year. The Commissioner, however, determined a deficiency in respondent's return for that year on the theory that income from the trust was taxable to him. The Board of Tax Appeals sustained that redetermination (38 B.T.A. 1532). The Circuit Court of Appeals reversed (105 F.2d 586). We granted certiorari because of the importance to the revenue of the use of such short term trusts in the reduction of surtaxes.

. . .

The broad sweep of [§ 61(a)] indicates the purpose of Congress to use the full measure of its taxing power within those definable categories (*Cf. Helvering v. Midland Mutual Life Insurance Co.*, 300 U.S. 216). Hence our construction of the statute should be consonant with that purpose. Technical considerations, niceties of the law of trusts or conveyances, or the legal paraphernalia which inventive genius may construct as a refuge from surtaxes should not obscure the basic issue. That issue is whether the grantor after the trust has been established may still be treated, under this statutory scheme, as the owner of the corpus. *See Blair v. Commissioner*, 300 U.S. 5, 12. In the absence of more precise standards or guides supplied by statute or appropriate regulations, the answer to that question must depend on an analysis of the terms of the trust and all the circumstances attendant on its creation and operation. And where the grantor is the trustee and the beneficiaries are members of his family group, special scrutiny of the arrangement is necessary lest what is in reality but one economic unit be multiplied into two or more by devices which, though valid under state law, are not conclusive so far as [§ 61(a)] is concerned.

In this case we cannot conclude as a matter of law that respondent ceased to be the owner of the corpus after the trust was created. Rather, the short duration of the trust, the fact that the wife was the beneficiary, and the retention of control over the corpus by respondent all lead irresistibly to the conclusion that respondent continued to be the owner for purposes of [§ 61(a)].

So far as his dominion and control were concerned it seems clear that the trust did not effect any substantial change. In substance his control over the corpus was in all essential respects the same after the trust was created, as before. The wide powers which he retained included for all practical purposes most of the control which he as an individual would have. There were, we may assume, exceptions, such as his disability to make a gift of the corpus to others during the term of the trust and to make loans to himself. But this dilution in his control would seem to be insignificant and immaterial, since control over investment remained. If it be said that such control is the type of dominion exercised by any trustee, the answer is simple. We have at best a temporary reallocation of income within an intimate family group. Since the income remains in the family and since the husband retains control over the investment, he has rather complete assurance that the trust will not effect any substantial change in his economic position. It is hard to imagine that respondent felt himself the poorer after this trust had been executed or, if he did, that it had any rational foundation in fact. For as a result of the terms of the trust and the intimacy of the familial relationship respondent retained the substance of full enjoyment of all the rights which previously he had in the property. That might not be true if only strictly legal rights were considered. But when the benefits flowing to him indirectly through the wife are added to the legal rights he retained, the aggregate may be said to be a fair equivalent of what he previously had. To exclude from the aggregate those indirect benefits would be to deprive [§ 61(a)] of considerable vitality and to treat as immaterial what may be highly relevant considerations in the creation of such family trusts. For where the head of the household has income in excess of normal needs, it may well make but little difference to him (except income-taxwise) where portions of that income are routed-so long as it stays in the family group. In those circumstances the all-important factor might be retention by him of control over the principal. With that control in his hands he would keep direct command over all that he needed to remain in substantially the same financial situation as before. Our point here is that no one fact is normally decisive but that all considerations and circumstances of the kind we have mentioned are relevant to the question of ownership and are appropriate foundations for findings on that issue. Thus, where, as in this case, the benefits directly or indirectly retained blend so imperceptibly with the normal concepts of full ownership, we cannot say that the triers of fact committed reversible error when they found that the husband was the owner of the corpus for the purposes of [§ 61(a)]. To hold otherwise would be to treat the wife as a complete stranger; to let mere formalism obscure the normal consequences of family solidarity; and to force concepts of ownership to be fashioned out of legal niceties which may have little or no significance in such household arrangements.

We should add that liability under [§ 61(a)] is not foreclosed by reason of the fact that Congress made specific provision in [§ 676] for revocable trusts, but failed to adopt the Treasury recommendation in 1934, *Helvering v. Wood*, [308 U.S. 344], that similar specific treatment should be accorded income from short term trusts. Such choice, while relevant to the scope of [§ 676], *Helvering v. Wood*, [supra], cannot be said to have subtracted from [§ 61(a)] what was already there. Rather, on this evidence it must be assumed that the choice was between a generalized treatment under [§ 61(a)] or specific treatment under a separate provision (such as was accorded revocable trusts under [§ 676]); not between taxing or not taxing grantors of short term trusts. In view of the broad and sweeping language of [§ 61(a)], a specific provision covering short term trusts might well do no more than to carve out of [§ 61(a)] a defined group of cases to which a rule of thumb would be applied. The failure of Congress to adopt any such rule of thumb for that type of trust must be taken to do no more than to leave to the triers of fact the initial determination of whether or not on the facts of each case the grantor remains the owner for purposes of [§ 61(a)].

In view of this result we need not examine the contention that the trust device falls within the rule of *Lucas v. Earl*, 281 U.S. 111 and *Burnet v. Leininger*, 285 U.S. 136, relating to the assignment of future income; or that respondent is liable under [§ 676], taxing grantors on the income of revocable trusts.

The judgment of the Circuit Court of Appeals is reversed and that of the Board of Tax Appeals is affirmed.

Reversed.

————

In response to *Clifford*, the Treasury Department issued detailed regulations governing the taxation of trusts over which the grantor retained powers and interests. These "Clifford Regulations" controlled until Congress specifically addressed the problem in the 1954 Code. That legislative response is now found in the "grantor trust" rules of §§ 671 through 678 (Subpart E of Subchapter J).

Section 671 provides that a grantor trust is taxed on the income generated by a trust if the grantor retained any interest or power specified in §§ 673 through 677. To the extent the grantor trust rules apply and the grantor is treated as the owner of the trust, the other provisions of Subchapter J are supplanted. *See* § 671(a).

Section 672 sets forth a number of key definitions for application of Subpart E. Most notably, adverse and non-adverse parties are defined to distinguish persons who have an economic interest in a trust and those who are not affected by a retained power or interest of the grantor. In addition, § 672(e) provides that a grantor is deemed to have the same interest in, or power over, a trust held by the grantor's spouse. The marital unit is one for income tax purposes.

Section 673 causes a grantor to be taxed on the income generated by a trust if the grantor has a reversionary interest in either the income or principal of the trust that has a value in excess of 5% of the trust principal at the inception of the trust. For example, if a grantor transfers property to a trust to benefit *A* for a ten year term certain, but the grantor retains a sufficiently large reversionary interest in the trust assets at the end of the trust term, the income—both ordinary and capital gains—generated by the trust's assets will be taxed to the grantor because the value of the reversionary interest exceeds 5%. This is true even though the income is actually distributed to *A*, not the grantor. *A* gets the cash flow from the trust, but the grantor must report the income of the trust on the grantor's personal income tax return.

Sections 674 and 675 cause a grantor to be taxed on income generated by a trust if the grantor retains, or a non-adverse person has, certain controls over the trust. For example, a grantor who serves as trustee of a trust is taxed on the trust income if the grantor, as trustee, has the discretion to sprinkle income among several trust beneficiaries or to accumulate the income. *See* § 674(a). It is not necessary for the grantor to have any beneficial interest in the trust assets for these sections to apply.

Section 676 causes a grantor to be taxed if the grantor has the power to revoke a trust and take back the property transferred to the trust. Section 676(b) makes this rule applicable even if the power is not currently exercisable. If the power to revoke can be exercised in the future and the 5% rule of § 673 is not satisfied, the grantor is taxed.[32] For example, if a grantor transfers property to a trust to benefit *A* for life, but the grantor retains the right to revoke the trust after ten years, both ordinary and capital gains are taxed to the grantor. This example is functionally the equivalent of the § 673 example above.

Section 677 addresses retention of interests in the trust income or corpus. The grantor is taxed if the trust income (1) may be distributed to the grantor or the grantor's spouse; (2) may be accumulated for future distribution to the grantor or the grantor's spouse; or (3) may be used to pay life insurance premiums on the life of the grantor. Also, to the extent trust income is used by the trustee to pay for items of support or maintenance for a person the grantor is obligated to support or maintain, § 677(b) causes the trust income to be taxed to the grantor. For example, a grantor transfers a life insurance policy insuring the grantor's life and cash to a trust. Any income generated by the trust will be taxed to the grantor under § 677(a)(3) if the trust income could be used to pay the life insurance premiums.

Section 678 applies the grantor trust rules to individuals other than the grantor. In certain circumstances, a beneficiary of a trust is treated as a grantor of a trust and subject to the grantor trust rules when the beneficiary has substantial control over the income or principal of the trust. For example, a beneficiary of a trust has a right to demand a distribution of all the income earned by the trust each year. Under § 678, the beneficiary will be taxed on the trust's income, even if the income is not demanded in a particular year. Section 678 is not applicable, however, if any one of the grantor trust provisions under §§ 671 through 677 causes the grantor to be taxed on the income. *See* § 678(b).

The grantor trust rules are discussed in much greater detail in Chapters 7 through 13.

---

[32] For purposes of this subsection, you may assume that when the power to revoke can be exercised, it will be exercised to revert the trust assets to the grantor and then the 5% rule applies.

Part II

BASICS OF WEALTH TRANSFER TAXATION

This Part includes chapters which develop the basic rules underlying the federal gift tax, federal estate tax, and federal generation-skipping transfer tax. Chapter 3 develops the basics of federal estate taxation and approaches such subjects as the concept of ownership of property at death, the basis for taxing general powers of appointment, and the valuation of assets for transfer tax purposes. Chapter 4 investigates basic federal gift taxation, including the definition of taxable gift and the standards governing the exclusion of assets from taxable gifts. Chapter 5 is a limited excursion into the federal generation-skipping transfer tax.

Chapter 3

ESTATE TAXATION BASICS

As outlined in Chapter 2, calculating the estate tax entails a four step process: (1) determining the value of the gross estate; (2) subtracting the value of deductions to ascertain the taxable estate; (3) applying the estate tax rate table; and (4) subtracting allowable credits. These steps are developed in more detail in this and subsequent chapters.

§ 3.01 Determining the Gross Estate

Section 2031 defines the gross estate as including those interests in property that are described by §§ 2033 through 2044. This Chapter explores the concept of actual and virtual ownership at death. Section 2033 prescribes gross estate inclusion for interests owned at death, and § 2041 requires inclusion for interests subject to the power of disposition at death.

The valuation of includable as well as deductible interests is sufficiently important to warrant separate discussion in this Chapter. Later chapters consider sections that pertain to gross estate inclusion of interests subject to testamentary-like powers and interests.

[A] The Concept of Property

Underlying all gross estate inclusion provisions is the existence of property. Consider the following case. It arose under § 2033, which taxes interests in "property" the decedent owned at death.

First Victoria National Bank v. United States

620 F.2d 1096 (5th Cir. 1980)

[Decedent, through prior use of land for the planting of rice, was entitled under a government crop control program to continue production. The production right passed to his heirs and devisees on his death. The Commissioner asserted that the "rice history acreage" constituted "property" for purposes of § 2033. The court, analogizing the allotment to business good will, held it to be an asset of the estate.]

Goldberg, Circuit Judge:

. . .

As we attempt to resolve this question, we necessarily must wrestle with the meaning of the label "property." Documentation of the history and derivation of many interests which are today denominated "property" would require philosophers, professors of jurisprudence, and scholars of economics to call upon their full erudition and exegetic talents. The shelves of our jurisprudence are tomed with obituaries of species of property long ago tolled. Announcements of the nascence of other species which were unheard of and unspeculated upon centuries ago populate further volumes.

Although the varieties of property may not be infinite, any attempt to enumerate every species of property would beggar the mind and intellect of even the wisest of persons. Avoiding this Sisyphian endeavor, we embark on a Delphian one. As we begin, we must remind ourselves that "property" is an expansionist term. Its mooring is contemporary rather than historical.

The attempt to define "property" is an elusive task. There is no cosmic synoptic definiens that can encompass its range. The word is at times more cognizable than recognizable. It is not capable of anatomical or lexicographical definition or proof. It devolves upon the Court to fill in the definitional vacuum with the substance of the economics of our time.

The Restatement of Property uses the word "property" to denote legal relations between persons with respect to a thing, *see* 1 Restatement of Property 3 (1936), but does not attempt to define which "things" constitute "property." The Supreme Court has said that "[t]he accurate delimitation of the concept of 'property' would afford a theme especially apposite for amplificative philosophic disquisition." *Gleason v. Thaw*, 236 U.S. 558, 660 (1915). Legal encyclopedias can provide us an interminable string of definitions suggested by various courts. *See, e.g.,* 73 C.J.S. *Property* § 1 (1951).

. . .

"Property" evolves over time. It can be described as the bundle of rights attached to things conferred by law or custom, or as everything of value which a person owns that is or may be the subject of sale or exchange . . . . Both of these definitions contemplate the possibility that law or custom may create property rights where none were earlier thought to exist.

. . .

The precise question before us is whether "rice acreage history" is "property" for purposes of the estate tax laws. In deciding this question, we start with the basic principle that "unless there is some special reason intrinsic to the particular provision (under consideration) . . ., the general word 'property' has a broad reach in tax law." *DuPont de Nemours & Co. v. United States*, 471 F.2d 1211, 1218, 200 Ct.Cl. 391 (1973).

. . .

"Rice acreage history" is not only devisable and descendible, but also transferable inter vivos. Those heirs who inherited [the] rice farming operations, by filing the requisite document with the county commission, were able to retain possession of the "rice history acreage" possessed by [the decedent] the moment before his death. They could have converted the value of the rice acreage history into cash by selling it to others. . . . [Footnote omitted.] When an interest possesses these attributes, there can be no doubt that its value must be included in the owner's estate, for the focus of the estate tax is on the passage of an interest at death.

[B] Assets Owned at Death: Section 2033

Code: § 2033.

Regulations: Treas. Reg. § 20.2033–1.

[1] In General

By requiring gross estate inclusion of property "to the extent of the interest therein of the decedent at the time of his death," § 2033 carries out the basic principle of estate taxation: taxation of property owned at death. The tests normally used to determine if § 2033 applies are (1) whether the decedent owned an interest in property immediately before death, and (2) whether the decedent had the right to transfer (or transmit) that interest at death.

Connecticut Bank & Trust Co. v. United States

465 F.2d 760 (2d Cir. 1972)

[Decedents were killed in Virginia when the car in which they were riding exploded after being struck by a tractor-trailer truck. The executors of the decedents' Connecticut estates commenced wrongful death actions in New York against the New Jersey corporation that owned the truck. The suits were settled before going to trial. The recovery, which was made on the assumption of instantaneous deaths, included nothing for post-mortem pain and suffering.

The executors held the proceeds for distribution in accordance with the terms of the decedents' wills under the Connecticut wrongful death statute (Connecticut General Statutes § 45-280) which provided, *inter alia*:

> All damages recovered for injuries resulting in death . . . shall be distributed as personal estate in accordance with the last will and testament of the deceased if there is one or, if not, in accordance with the law concerning the distribution of intestate personal estate, provided such damages shall not be subject to taxation under the provisions of Chapter 216.

The executors did not include the proceeds in the decedents' gross estates for the federal estate tax. The Commissioner assessed deficiencies based upon the recovery against each of the estates. The deficiencies were paid, and these suits were filed for refunds.]

Robert P. Anderson, Circuit Judge:

. . .

The crucial issue to be decided under section 2033 is whether or not the value of an action for wrongful death is "property . . . of the decedent at the time of his death." Much of the Government's argument and the opinion of

Issue

the court below rest on the differences between the Connecticut statutory scheme for wrongful death recovery and the more common pattern of recovery in the majority of the states based upon "Lord Campbell's Act," which provides for a direct right of action on behalf of designated beneficiaries of the decedent to recover for his wrongful death, with damages to be measured by the loss to the survivors . . . . The Connecticut statutes, on the other hand, provide for a right of action in the executor or administrator, with damages to be measured on the basis of the loss of the decedent's ability to carry on life's activities, *Floyd v. Fruit Industries, Inc.*, 144 Conn. 659, 669–677, 136 A.2d 918, 923–927 (1957). In addition, by recent amendments, the wrongful death proceeds in Connecticut are distributed according to the terms of the decedent's will, if there is one, and are subject to the general claims of the estate. The differences in results under the two types of statutes may be more theoretical than real, *cf. Foran v. Carangelo*, 153 Conn. 356, 362, 216 A.2d 638, 641 (1966), but in any event, these differences have little relevance concerning the question of whether or not the right of action for wrongful death was property owned at death.

Simple logic mandates the conclusion that an action for wrongful death cannot exist until a decedent has died, at which point, he is no longer a person capable of owning any property interests. The Government's reply to this is that at the very instant of death the right of action arose which the decedent was then capable of owning at death. The only authorities cited for this position, however, are cases where preexisting property interests were valued as of the instant of death, but valuation at time of death of prior existing interests is a far different concern from that in this case where the property interest itself has sprung from the fact that the death has taken place.

While it is true that Congress may constitutionally place an excise tax on property created by death, as well as upon property transferred by death [citations omitted], section 2033 does not read so broadly. In a discussion of the estate tax the Supreme Court described the scope of § 2033: "What this law taxes is not the interest to which the legatees and devisees succeeded on death, but the interest which ceased by reason of the death," *Y.M.C.A. of Columbus, Ohio v. Davis*, 264 U.S. 47, 50 (1924). Where, as here, there was no property interest in the decedent which passed by virtue of his death, but rather one which arose after his death, such an interest is not property owned at death and not part of the gross estate under section 2033.

This construction of the relevant statutes is supported both by Connecticut law and Treasury Department Revenue Rulings. The Connecticut Supreme Court has stated that under Connecticut statutes "no person, during his lifetime, can possess an action or right of action embracing, as elements of damage, his own death or any of its direct consequences," *Foran, supra,* 153 Conn. n. 2 at 360, 216 A.2d at 641. Connecticut General Statute section 45-280 specifically states that wrongful death proceeds are not part of the gross estate for state succession tax purposes, and the Probate Court Administrator, a Connecticut Superior Court Judge, has ruled that wrongful death proceeds are not part of the gross estate for purposes of determining the probate court fee.

The Treasury Department has issued three Revenue Rulings concerning the inclusion of wrongful death proceeds under section 2033, all of which hold that the proceeds are not part of the gross estate. In this case, the Government tries to distinguish them because they concerned rights of action arising under New Jersey and Virginia state law and the federal Death on the High Seas Act, 46 U.S.C. § 761; however, the rationale of those rulings is fully applicable here. In *Rev. Rul. 54–19,* 1954–1 C.B. 179, 180, the Department stated: "Inasmuch as the decedent had no right of action or interest in the proceeds at the time of his death, nothing 'passed' from the decedent to the beneficiaries. Accordingly, the amounts recovered by the beneficiaries would not be includible in the decedent's gross estate for federal estate tax purposes." It held that such proceeds were not part of the gross estate in *Rev. Rul. 68–88,* 1968–1 C.B. 397, 398, because "[t]he right of action for wrongful death does not accrue until death occurs," and in *Rev. Rul. 69–8,* 1969–1 C.B. 219, because "[t]he decedent in his lifetime never had an interest in either the right of action or the proceeds." *See also Rev. Rul. 55–581,* 1955–2 C.B. 381, holding that an allotment paid by the armed services to designated beneficiaries of servicemen who die in active duty is not part of the gross estate; and *Rev. Rul. 55–87,* 1955–1 C.B. 112, holding that a lump sum payment for funeral expenses to social security recipients is not taxable under section 2033.

. . .

The judgments of the district court are reversed and the cases remanded for the determination of the amounts of the refunds due to the respective appellants and for their costs.

———

The Service no longer contests the question raised in *Connecticut Bank, i.e.,* whether wrongful death proceeds are includable in the gross estate under § 2033, except in cases where recovery is for pre-mortem suffering. *See* Rev. Rul. 75–127, 1975–1 C.B. 297.

The second test of § 2033, the ability to transmit property, means that interests which terminate on the decedent's death are not includable under § 2033. As explained by the Service in Private Letter Ruling 7949021:

> [I]f the only interest which a decedent owns, and has ever owned, in property is an estate for his own life, nothing will be included in his gross estate under section 2033 because he owns no interest which he can transmit at his death. *Frazer v. Commissioner,* 6 T.C. 1255 (1946), *aff'd,* 162 F.2d 167 (3rd Cir. 1947); *Rev. Rul. 66–86,* 1966–1 C.B. 219. Likewise, a remainder limited to the life of the remainderman, or a remainder that divests if the remainderman predeceases the life tenant is not taxable to the remainderman's estate because his interest in the property terminates at his death. *Nelson v. Commissioner,* 47 T.C. 279 (1966), *rev'd on other grounds,* 396 F.2d 519 (2d Cir. 1968); *Rev. Rul. 67–370,* 1967–2 C.B. 325. Similarly, a future interest which is contingent upon a decedent's survival is not taxable to his estate under section 2033 if he fails to survive. *Nelson v. Commissioner, supra*; Rev. Rul. 67–370, *supra.*

The question of what interest a decedent owned in property at the time of death is governed by local law. Once this determination is made, however, the way in which the particular interest is taxed is a question for the Federal law. *See Morgan v. Commissioner*, 309 U.S. 78 (1940).

It is important to recognize that an "interest in property" is distinct, and may only be a part of the underlying "property," and that § 2033 does not require that the decedent have owned all of the property itself. Thus, if under her parent's will the decedent had inherited a vested remainder interest in a trust, that remainder would be included in the decedent's estate, even if she died before the termination of the prior interest. *See, e.g., Estate of Patterson v. Commissioner*, 736 F.2d 32 (2d Cir. 1984). However, as will be seen in § 3.03 *infra*, the delay in possession inherent to future interests will affect the valuation of the interest.

In scope, § 2033 is the most commonly applicable gross estate inclusion provision. Assuming the decedent owned a transmissible interest, the property subject to tax can be real or personal, tangible or intangible. Thus, § 2033 applies to such common assets as cash, tangible personal property, and real property not disposed of before death. *See Estate of Whitt v. Commissioner*, 751 F.2d 1548 (11th Cir. 1985) (property ineffectively deeded to decedent's son). It applies to uncommon assets, such as the right to publicity if descendible under applicable state law. *See Estate of Andrews v. United States*, 850 F.Supp. 1279 (E.D.Va. 1994) (Virginia law). *See generally* Ray D. Madoff, *Taxing Personhood: Estate Taxes and The Compelled Commodification of Identity*, 17 Va. Tax Rev. 759 (1998). It does not matter where the property is located. *See, e.g., Norstar Bank v. United States*, 644 F. Supp. 1112 (N.D.N.Y. 1986) (realty located in France included in the gross estate of a United States citizen). Notwithstanding the court's opinion in *First Victoria National Bank*, students should note that courts generally have not given § 2033 the extremely broad application that § 61 (the definition of gross income) has for income tax purposes.

Problems

1. *D* owned "tax exempt" municipal bonds. Are the bonds includable in her gross estate? *See* Treas. Reg. § 20.2033–1(a).

2. *D* owned a term life insurance policy on the life of her brother. If *D* predeceases her brother, is the policy includable in *D*'s gross estate?

3. *D* died as a result of an automobile accident in which driver, *A*, was at fault. *D* survived a week after the accident before dying. Immediately after *D*'s death, the personal representative of *D*'s estate instituted a negligence action against *A* claiming $400,000 in damages for pain and suffering by *D* during the week, and $500,000 in damages for causing *D*'s death. *A*'s insurance company settled for $500,000, of which $300,000 was designated for the wrongful death and $200,000 for the pain and suffering. What amount would be included in *D*'s gross estate? *See* Rev. Rul. 75-127, 1975-1 C.B. 297.

4. Decedent purchased a $200,000 bond on January 1, paying 8% annual interest; $8,000 on June 30 and $8,000 on December 31. On June 29 of the same year, decedent died. What would be included in decedent's gross estate?

5. Assume *A* owned 1000 shares of General Motors Corporation common stock. Under which of the following sets of facts would dividends declared and paid on the stock be includable in her gross estate? Assume that *A* died on November 1, and that the dividend was received on November 15.

a. Dividend declared and payable to owners of record on November 4.

b. Dividend declared and payable to owners of record on October 28.

c. Dividend declared on October 28, but payable to owners of record on November 4.

d. Dividend declared on November 4, but payable to owners of record on October 28.

Compare Estate of Corbett v. Commissioner, 12 T.C. 163 (1949), *with Estate of Lockie v. Commissioner,* 21 T.C. 64 (1953); Rev. Rul. 54–399, 1954–2 C.B. 279.

6. In *Connecticut Bank,* the wrongful death proceeds were distributed in accordance with the decedents' wills. If one of the beneficiaries of the estates died before the wrongful death proceeds had been disbursed, what, if anything, would have been includable in the beneficiary's estate under § 2033? *See Estate of Houston v. Commissioner,* T.C. Memo 1982–362.

[2] Interests of the Surviving Spouse

Code: § 2034.

Regulations: Treas. Reg. § 20.2034–1.

[a] Common Law Interests

Section 2034 requires gross estate inclusion of property "to the extent of any interest therein of the surviving spouse, existing at the time of the decedent's death as a result of dower or curtesy, or by virtue of a statute creating an estate in lieu of dower or curtesy." This section is designed to ensure estate taxation of property passing to the surviving spouse from the decedent. This is the case even though the surviving spouse's interest may be created by state law, and even if the decedent could not have avoided the surviving spouse's interest. Section 2034 has been interpreted to require inclusion of homestead rights as well. *See Estate of Johnson v. Commissioner,* 718 F.2d 1303 (5th Cir. 1983) (Texas law).

[b] Community Property Interests

Under § 2033, the decedent's gross estate includes only property that is owned at death. It taxes only the decedent's one-half of community property. The survivor's corresponding community property interest is vested. Thus, this property is not included in the gross estate of the deceased spouse for estate tax purposes. In contrast, all separate property of the deceased spouse in a community property regime is included in the gross estate.

Ultimately, the classification of property has a major impact on the estate tax burden. In turn, the classification will depend on the applicable state community property laws. *Estate of Kenly v. Commissioner,* T.C. Memo 1996–516, illustrates the complexities involved in the classification process. In

Kenly, the decedent died intestate, domiciled in Arizona, owning California realty that was traceable to a previously owned New Mexico parcel. California law required the Tax Court to use Arizona law and New Mexico law to determine whether the property had been transmuted into community property. In *Wilmington Trust Co. v. United States*, 85–2 U.S.T.C. ¶ 13,625 (Fed. Cir. 1985), the court held that income from trusts received by the decedent's spouse before the decedent's death was not community property under Texas law, and, therefore, no part of it was includable in the decedent's gross estate under § 2033. In *Estate of Young v. Commissioner*, 110 T.C. 297 (1998), real property titled as joint tenants in the name of husband and wife was not community property taxable under 2033.

The classification of property as community or separate also significantly impacts the property's basis for income tax purposes. Pursuant to § 1014(b)(6), the surviving spouse is deemed to have acquired her one-half interest in community property from the deceased spouse. As a result, the basis in her one-half interest in what was previously community property will be the estate tax value of the decedent's interest, whether or not the surviving spouse succeeds to the deceased spouse's interest.

The application of § 1014(b)(6) to community property may be illustrated as follows:

Example: Assume that publicly traded stock was acquired as community property with an adjusted basis of $60 per share. At the first spouse's death, the stock had an estate tax value of $90 per share.

The deceased spouse's one-half interest in the stock would be included in his gross estate under § 2033, at an estate tax value of $45 per share. Pursuant to the general rule of § 1014, the surviving spouse, or whoever received the decedent's one-half interest, would have a basis of $45 per share. By application of § 1014(b)(6), the surviving spouse's basis in her preexisting one-half would automatically become $45, resulting in a total adjusted basis of $90 per share.

In effect, community property receives an enormous income tax advantage over separate property if the value of community property has appreciated from its pre-death basis. Thus, in the above example, if a husband and wife in a non-community property state acquired the stock as tenants in common or jointly, the surviving spouse's basis would remain at $30 per share while only the recipient of the husband's one-half share would be eligible for a step-up in basis under § 1014. Of course, if the community property had declined in value by the time of the first spouse's death, § 1014(b)(6) would disadvantage the surviving spouse, because the basis in the stock would be reduced by all of the decline in value and not just one-half.

Although § 2034 applies to property owned by a decedent that passes by operation of law to the surviving spouse, or which may be elected by the surviving spouse, it does not apply to the surviving spouse's interest in community property. Unlike dower (and the dower substitutes), community property interests are vested upon creation; they are not inchoate as are dower and curtesy rights, nor do they depend upon the continuation of the marital status.

A few community property states have quasi-community property. This is property that was acquired during marriage in a separate property regime, and would have been classified as community property if the property had been acquired in a community property regime. The only case on point holds that quasi-community property should be treated as an expectancy so that the entire value of the property is included in the decedent's gross estate, rather than only half of the value. *See Estate of Sbicca v. Commissioner*, 35 T.C. 96 (1960).

Problems

1. Decedent died owning a parcel of realty, but its classification of separate or community property was uncertain. A lower state court determined that the property was held by the decedent and his surviving spouse as community property. Is the Service precluded from contending that the property was the separate property of the decedent? *See Estate of Kenly v. Commissioner*, T.C. Memo 1996–516.

2. While *H* and *W* were domiciliaries of a community property state, *H* purchased publicly traded stock at $80 per share. The stock is now worth $150 per share, and the couple now lives in a non-community property state. What action might be suggested? What advice would be suggested if the stock was now worth $30 per share, but the couple still resided in a community property state? Suppose the couple resided in a non-community property state?

3. *H* and *W,* as tenants in common, purchased publicly traded stock at $80 per share while they were domiciliaries of a non-community property state. The stock is now worth $150, and the couple now lives in a community property state. What action might be suggested? What advice would be suggested if the stock was now worth $30 per share, but the couple still resided in a non-community property state? Suppose the couple resided in a community property state?

§ 3.02 Powers Equivalent to Ownership: Section 2041

Code: § 2041.

Regulations: Treas. Reg. § 20.2041–1(a) through (c).

[A] In General

Estate of Alperstein v. Commissioner

613 F.2d 1213 (2d Cir. 1979),
cert. denied sub. nom.,
Greenberg v. Commissioner,
446 U.S. 918 (1980)

[Decedent's husband, Harry Alperstein, died in July 1967. His valid will created a trust, the income of which was payable to decedent during her life, with the remainder to pass as she appointed by will. In January 1967, the decedent entered a nursing home, in which she remained until shortly before her death. In December 1967, she was declared incompetent, and her daughter was appointed her guardian.

Decedent's estate tax return excluded the trust created by her husband's will. The Commissioner entered a deficiency for the tax which would have been generated by its inclusion, citing decedent's ownership of the general power of appointment. His position was upheld by the Tax Court, and the estate appealed.]

Friendly, Circuit Judge:

. . .

Appellant does not question that, so far as language is concerned, the power of appointment conferred by Article Fourth of Harry Alperstein's will [was a general power under section 2041]. The claim is that, despite this section 2041(a)(2) is inapplicable because, under the stipulated facts, Fannie Alperstein was never able after her husband's death to exercise the power vested in her by his will—a situation allegedly not present in any of the cases that have sustained the taxability of powers against attacks of the same general sort as that mounted here.[1]

I.

We start, as always, with the words of the statute [citation omitted]. The operative verb in section 2041(a)(2) is "has." Beyond cavil Mrs. Alperstein "had" a general power of appointment at the time of her death. This had been granted by her husband's will and nothing done by the New York courts purported to take it away. Even if we assume that the judgment of Fannie Alperstein's incompetence conclusively established her inability to exercise this power, that judgment was subject to being vacated if her mental condition changed for the better. The argument is rather that although Mrs. Alperstein "had" such a power, it was not "exercisable" at the time of her death since she had long since been declared incompetent and in fact had been so ever since her husband had died. However, the word "exercisable" is found not in the operative portion of the statute but in a section addressed to how broad a power must be in order to be "general." The natural meaning of the words is that "exercisable" is shorthand for "which by its terms may be exercised," and not that section 2041(a)(2) is limited to cases where the decedent could in fact exercise the power at the moment of death—something which, in the absence of a previous will or similar instrument, could rarely occur.

---

[1] In fact, Mrs. Alperstein's inability ever to have exercised the power is not so clear as appellant's counsel asserts. Harry Alperstein's will was executed on September 23, 1953. This stipulation that Mrs. Alperstein was incompetent to execute a valid will after her husband's death on July 6, 1967, does not negate her capacity to have exercised the power prior to his death. Absent contrary specification by the donor, New York law does not require the donee of a testamentary power to provide for its exercise in a will executed subsequent to the donor's death. *See* N.Y. Est., Powers & Trusts Law § 10–6.1. Indeed, Mrs. Alperstein could have exercised the power by a will made even before Harry's will was executed. *See, e.g., In re* Tucker's Trust, 41 Misc. 2d 405, 244 N.Y.S.2d 356 (Sup. Ct. 1963). However, we do not find it necessary to rest decision on this ground.

II.

The meaning which thus emerges from the words of the statute is strongly reinforced by the legislative history. Section 2041 reflects, in all respects here relevant, the Powers of Appointment Act of 1951. The latter was a substantial amendment of the amendments to section 811 of the Internal Revenue Code of 1939 that were included in the Revenue Act of 1942.

[The court noted that only the exercise of general powers was taxed before 1942, and that the Revenue Act of 1942 provided that post-1942 powers held at death would be taxed, whether exercised or not.]

The 1942 amendments extended the policy of taxing powers, regardless of exercise, to general powers created before the enactment of the amendments [section 403(d)(1)]. However, the amendments sought to mitigate the retroactive impact of this by allowing a grace period in which all holders of general powers might release their power without estate tax consequences, *id.* section 403(d)(3), and by extending this grace period in the case of holders who were "under a legal disability to release such power" until six months after termination of their disability, *id.* section 403(d)(2) . . . . Senate Report No. 1631, [77th Cong., 2d Sess. 232 (1942)], suggested that legal incompetents such as insane people, minors, and unborn children might be expected to benefit from this exemption. *Id.* at 234. Beyond demonstrating that when Congress wished to make a dispensation for incompetents, it has known how to say so, the fact that the 1942 Congress felt it necessary to include this provision strongly suggests its belief that the existence of a legal disability by the holder of a general power would not prevent inclusion of property subject to that power in the estate . . . .

In the case of pre-1942 powers, the 1951 Act returned to the criterion of pre-1942 law by taxing only those general powers that had been exercised . . . .

We find no force in the . . . argument that Congress' concern in 1951 for those holders of pre-1942 powers who are "unwary" or "powerless to help themselves," S. Rep. No. 382, [82d Cong., 1st Sess. 2, 1951] U.S. Code Cong. & Admin. News at 1531, which led to a change from the policy of the 1942 Act with respect to such powers, may allow the courts to manifest a similar concern for holders of post-1942 powers . . . . This position ignores the strict division between pre- and post-1942 powers which is at the heart of the 1951 Act.

Further support for the construction that the 1951 Act embraced all general powers regardless of the donee's capacity to exercise them is furnished by a provision in the marital deduction, originally enacted by section 361(a) of the Revenue Act of 1948 and now codified as amended in I.R.C. section 2056(b)(5). This provides that property passing in trust to a surviving spouse will qualify for exclusion from the decedent's estate, *inter alia,* if the surviving spouse is entitled to all income from the property for life; if the surviving spouse has the power to appoint such property in favor of herself or the estate; and if the power to appoint such property, "whether exercisable by will or during life, is exercisable by such spouse alone and in all events." The Internal Revenue Service has long held that competency under local law is irrelevant for determining whether a power is "exercisable" within the meaning of the marital deduction. *Rev. Rul. 55–518,* 1955–2 C.B. 384; *Rev. Rul. 75–350,* 1975–2 C.B. 367. This conclusion is virtually dictated by the consideration that "[o]therwise, in view of the possibility that any given person may become legally incompetent during his or her lifetime, no trust could ever qualify under section 2056(b)(5)." *Rev. Rul. 75–350, supra,* 1975–2 C.B. at 368 . . . .

III.

We find no basis for a contrary view in the Service's rulings and regulations.
. . .

IV.

Although appellant may be right in contending that no decision upholding the estate taxation of property subject to a general power of appointment has presented facts quite so humanly appealing in favor of the donee as this, the general thrust of the case law in appellate courts is decidedly unfavorable to her.

While the Supreme Court has not had occasion to rule on the effect of incompetency of the holder of a general power on taxability under section 2041, *Commissioner v. Estate of Noel,* 380 U.S. 678 (1965), strongly indicated the Court's probable approach. *Noel* required a construction of I.R.C. section 2042, which provides *inter alia* that a decedent's estate is taxable for the proceeds of insurance policies on the life of the decedent "with respect to which the decedent possessed at his death any of the incidents of ownership, exercisable alone or in conjunction with any other person." Immediately before boarding a plane doomed to a fatal crash, the decedent in *Noel* purchased several flight insurance policies which he left with his wife on the ground. The decedent's estate contended that on these facts there had been no exercisable incidents of ownership within the meaning of the statute. While acknowledging that "there was no practical opportunity" to exercise ownership power, the Court concluded:

> It would stretch the imagination to think that Congress intended to measure estate tax liability by an individual's fluctuating, day-to-day, hour-by-hour capacity to dispose of property which he owns. We hold that estate tax liability for policies "with respect to which the decedent possessed at his death any of the incidents of owner-ship" depends on a general, legal power to exercise ownership, without regard to the owner's ability to exercise it at a particular moment.

Id. at 684.

[The court then discusses *Pennsylvania Bank & Trust Co. v. United States,* 597 F.2d 382 (3d Cir. 1979), *aff'g* 451 F. Supp. 1296 (W.D. Pa. 1978); *Bagley v. United States,* 433 F.2d 1266 (5th Cir. 1971); and *Fish v. United States,* 432 F.2d 1278 (9th Cir. 1970), each holding various general powers includable in the donee's estate notwithstanding his incompetence.]

Against this array of unfavorable decisions by the Supreme Court and courts of appeals, all of which emphasize the creation of rights and pay scant regard to the possibility of their exercise, taxpayer relies on four recent decisions of courts of first instance that are now under appeal to the Court of Appeals for the Fifth Circuit: *Finley v. United States*, 404 F. Supp. 200 (S.D. Fla. 1975); *Estate of Gilchrist v. Commissioner*, 65 T.C. 5 (1977); *Williams v. United States*, 78–2 U.S.T.C. ¶ 13,264 (W.D. Texas 1978); and *Estate of Reid v. Commissioner*, 71 T.C. 816 (1979). Whether correctly decided or not, *Gilchrist* is readily distinguishable; it dealt not with a testamentary power of appointment but with a clause conferring on the widow "full rights to transfer all the remainder of my property, both real and personal, so long as she may live." The court held that under Texas law the appointment of guardians transformed, for the period of incompetency, Mrs. Gilchrist's general power over corpus to one limited by an ascertainable standard within section 2401(b)(1). *Estate of Reid*, which relies heavily on *Gilchrist*, is even more remote from the instant case, as it deals with the effect of legal incompetence on taxation under I.R.C. section 2036(a)(2). In our view, *Finley* and, if the decedent in *Williams* possessed a testamentary power of appointment, that case also, were wrongly decided.

In sum we hold, on the basis of statutory language, legislative history (particularly the interaction of section 2041(a)(1) with the marital deduction, section 2056(b)(5)), administrative interpretation and case law, that when an instrument has conferred a testamentary power which by its terms can be exercised in favor of the donee's estate, the property subject to the power is part of the donee's gross estate even though the donee, by virtue of incompetency, was unable to make a valid will at any time after the power was granted.

Affirmed.

———

Early in the history of the federal estate tax, no special provision was made for taxing property when the decedent possessed a power to obtain the property, but did not possess a property interest. Early cases attempted to tax decedents, as owners, who had the right to trust income for life and the power to obtain the principal, or to appoint it to others. The attempts failed in *United States v. Field*, 255 U.S. 257 (1921), in which the power was exercised by the decedent in favor of others, and later in *Helvering v. Safe Deposit & Trust Co.*, 316 U.S. 56 (1942), in which it was not exercised. The *Field* result was anticipated by Congress, which added a provision to the Code taxing exercises of such powers by the decedent. Congress responded to *Safe Deposit & Trust Co.* by adding what is now § 2041(a)(2), which taxes to the decedent-holder all general powers created after October 21, 1942, whether or not exercised by the decedent.

The application of § 2041 does not require that the decedent's power be labeled a power of appointment or termed a power of appointment under local law. It requires only that the decedent, in fact, have a legally recognized power to obtain property for himself, his creditors, his estate or the creditors of his estate. Such a power may be classified as a power of appointment, a power of invasion, a power to withdraw, or any other designation for state property law purposes; for the purposes of § 2041, it is a general power of appointment. *See* Treas. Reg. § 20.2041–1(b)(1) (second, third, fifth, and sixth sentences). Because a person who holds such a power could be the owner of the property merely by exercising the power for his own benefit, he is treated as the owner of the property for estate tax purposes. Even a trustee who has uncontrolled discretion to invade trust for the trustee's personal benefit has a taxable power of appointment.

The power does not need to be exercisable directly in favor of the decedent, as long as it may be exercised for his economic benefit. The statute expressly defines as a general power a power exercisable in favor of the decedent's creditors or the creditor's of the decedent's estate. *See* § 2041(b)(1). Further, Treasury Regulation § 20.2041–1(c)(1) defines the term "general powers" to include powers:

> (1) "[t]o meet the estate tax, or any other taxes, debts, or charges which are enforceable against the estate," and

> (2) "[f]or the purpose of discharging a legal obligation of the decedent or for his pecuniary benefit. . . ."

This same regulation provides that a power of appointment is not a general power if, by its terms, it is either:

> (1) exercisable only in favor of one or more designated persons or classes other than the decedent or his creditors, or the decedent's estate or the creditors of his estate, or

> (2) expressly not exercisable in favor of the decedent or his creditors, or the decedent's estate or the creditors of his estate.

[B] Limitations on the Taxation of Powers

Estate of Vissering v. Commissioner

990 F.2d 578 (10th Cir. 1993)

Logan, Circuit Judge.

The estate of decedent Norman H. Vissering appeals from a judgment of the Tax Court determining that he held at his death a general power of appointment as defined by I.R.C. § 2041, and requiring that the assets of a trust of which he was cotrustee be included in his gross estate for federal estate tax purposes. The appeal turns on whether decedent held powers permitting him to invade the principal of the trust for his own benefit unrestrained by an ascertainable standard relating to health, education, support, or maintenance. The trust was created by decedent's mother in Florida and specifies that Florida law controls in the interpretation and administration of its provisions.

The estate argues that decedent was not a trustee at the time of his death because a New Mexico court's adjudication that he was incapacitated two months before his death divested him of those powers. Decedent was not formally removed as trustee; if he ceased to serve it was by operation of Florida law. However, we assume for purposes of this opinion that decedent continued as trustee until his death and that his powers are to be adjudged as if he were fully competent to exercise them at the time of his death.

The trust at issue was created by decedent's mother, and became irrevocable on her death in 1965. Decedent and a bank served as cotrustees. Under the dispositive provisions decedent received all the income from the trust after his mother's death. On decedent's death (his wife, a contingent beneficiary, predeceased him), remaining trust assets were to be divided into equal parts and passed to decedent's two children or were held for their benefit. Decedent developed Alzheimer's disease and entered into a nursing home in 1984, but he tendered no resignation as trustee, nor did his guardian or conservator do so on his behalf after he was found to be incapacitated.

. . .

Under I.R.C. § 2041 a decedent has a general power of appointment includable in his estate if he possesses at the time of his death a power over assets that permits him to benefit himself, his estate, his creditors, or creditors of his estate. A power vested in a trustee, even with a cotrustee who has no interest adverse to the exercise of the power, to invade principal of the trust for his own benefit is sufficient to find the decedent trustee to have a general power of appointment, unless the power to invade is limited by an ascertainable standard relating to health, education, support, or maintenance. Treas. Reg. § 20.2041–1(c), –3(c)(2). *See, e.g., Estate of Sowell v. Commissioner*, 708 F.2d 1564, 1568 (10th Cir. 1983) (invasion of trust corpus in case of emergency or illness is an ascertainable standard under § 2041(b)(1)(A)); *Gaskill v. United States*, 561 F. Supp. 73, 78 (D. Kan. 1983) (life estate with power of disposition but not to consume the proceeds did not create general power of appointment under § 2041(b)(1)(A)), *aff'd mem.*, 787 F.2d 1446 (10th Cir. 1986); *see also Merchants Nat'l Bank v. Commissioner*, 320 U.S. 256, 261 (1943) (invasion of trust corpus for "the comfort, support, maintenance and/or happiness of my wife" is not a fixed standard for purposes of charitable deductions); *Ithaca Trust Co. v. United States*, 279 U.S. 151, 154 (1929) (invasion of trust corpus for any amount "that may be necessary to suitably maintain [decedent's wife] in as much comfort as she now enjoys" is a fixed standard for purposes of charitable deduction).

The relevant provisions of the instant trust agreement are as follows:

> During the term of [this trust], the Trustees shall further be authorized to pay over or to use or expend for the direct or indirect benefit of any of the aforesaid beneficiaries, whatever amount or amounts of the principal of this Trust as may, in the discretion of the Trustees, be required for the continued comfort, support, maintenance, or education of said beneficiary.

Tax Ct. ex. 3-C at 5–6. The Internal Revenue Service (IRS) and the Tax Court focused on portions of the invasion provision providing that the trust principal could be expended for the "comfort" of decedent, declaring that this statement rendered the power of invasion incapable of limitation by the courts.

[1] We look to state law (here Florida's) to determine the legal interests and rights created by a trust instrument, but federal law determines the tax consequences of those interests and rights. *Morgan v. Commissioner*, 309 U.S. 78, 80 (1940); *Maytag v. United States*, 493 F.2d 995, 998 (10th Cir. 1974). The absence of clear and controlling state precedent regarding the use of the term "comfort" in trust documents for purposes of determining a general power of appointment under federal estate tax law has prompted the estate and amici to request that we certify this question to the Supreme Court of Florida. Because recent changes in Florida trust law significantly curtail the number of trusts that might be affected by such a certification,[2] and because the language of each trust document in any event requires individualized attention, we deny the motion to certify to the Florida Supreme Court.

[2] Despite the decision in *Barritt v. Tomlinson*, 129 F. Supp. 642 (S.D. Fla. 1955), which involved a power of invasion broader than the one before us, we believe the Florida Supreme Court would hold that a trust document permitting invasion of principal for "comfort," without further qualifying language, creates a general power of appointment. Treas. Reg. § 20.2041–1(c). *See First Virginia Bank v. United States*, 490 F.2d 532, 533 (4th Cir. 1974) (under Virginia law, right of invasion for beneficiary's "comfort and care as she may see fit" not limited by an ascertainable standard); *Lehman v. United States*, 448 F.2d 1318, 1320 (5th Cir. 1971) (under Texas law, power to invade corpus for "support, maintenance, comfort, and welfare" not limited by ascertainable standard); *Miller v. United States*, 387 F.2d 866, 869 (3d Cir. 1968) (under Pennsylvania law, power to make disbursements from principal in amounts "necessary or expedient for [beneficiary's] proper maintenance, support, medical care, hospitalization, or other expenses incidental to her comfort and well-being" not limited by ascertainable standard); *Estate of Schlotterer v. United States*, 421 F. Supp. 85, 91 (W.D. Pa. 1976) (power of consumption "to the extent deemed by [beneficiary] to be desirable not only for her support and maintenance but also for her comfort and pleasure" not limited by ascertainable standard); *Doyle v. United States*, 358 F. Supp. 300, 309–10 (E.D. Pa. 1973) (under Pennsylvania law, trustees' "uncontrolled discretion" to pay beneficiary "such part or parts of the principal of said trust fund as may be necessary for her comfort, maintenance and support" not limited by ascertainable standard); *Stafford v. United States*, 236 F. Supp. 132, 134 (E.D. Wisc. 1964) (under Wisconsin law, trust permitting husband "for his use, benefit and enjoyment during his lifetime," unlimited power of disposition thereof "without permission of any court, and with the right to use and enjoy the principal, as well as the income, if he shall have need thereof for his care, comfort or enjoyment" not limited by ascertainable standard).

---

[2] In 1990 the Florida legislature amended its law governing trusts such as the one before us to limit a trustee beneficiary's power to make distributions of principal or income to himself sufficiently to eliminate its inclusion in the trustee's estate as a general power of appointment under § 2041(b)(1)(A). Fla. Stat. Ann. § 737.402(4)(a). The statute applies to all instruments executed after June 30, 1991, and to preexisting trusts unless the settlor amends the instrument to negate the effect of the statute before the later of July 1, 1994, or three years after the date on which the trust becomes irrevocable. *Id.* § 737.402(4)(b). The statute does not apply to the situation before us, of course, because this decedent died in 1988. In light of the amendments, however, there cannot be a large number of Florida trusts in which the parties in interest have no power to accept or negate the statutory change.

[3] However, there is modifying language in the trust before us that we believe would lead the Florida courts to hold that "comfort," in context, does not permit an unlimited power of invasion. The instant language states that invasion of principal is permitted to the extent "required for the continued comfort" of the decedent, and is part of a clause referencing the support, maintenance and education of the beneficiary. Invasion of the corpus is not permitted to the extent "determined" or "desired" for the beneficiary's comfort but only to the extent that it is "required." Furthermore, the invasion must be for the beneficiary's "continued" comfort, implying, we believe, more than the minimum necessary for survival, but nevertheless reasonably necessary to maintain the beneficiary in his accustomed manner of living. These words in context state a standard essentially no different from the examples in the Treasury Regulation, in which phrases such as "support in reasonable comfort," "maintenance in health and reasonable comfort," and "support in his accustomed manner of living" are deemed to be limited by an ascertainable standard. Treas. Reg. § 20.2041–1(c)(2). *See, e.g., United States v. Powell*, 307 F.2d 821, 828 (10th Cir. 1962) (under Kansas law, invasion of the corpus if "it is necessary or advisable . . . for the maintenance, welfare, comfort or happiness" of beneficiaries, and only if the need justifies the reduction in principal, is subject to ascertainable standard); *Hunter v. United States*, 597 F. Supp. 1293, 1295 (W.D. Pa. 1984) (power to invade for "comfortable support and maintenance" of beneficiaries is subject to ascertainable standard).

We believe that had decedent, during his life, sought to use the assets of the trust to increase significantly his standard of living beyond that which he had previously enjoyed, his cotrustee would have been obligated to refuse to consent, and the remainder beneficiaries of the trust could have successfully petitioned the court to disallow such expenditures as inconsistent with the intent of the trust instrument. The Tax Court erred in ruling that this power was a general power of appointment includable in decedent's estate.

Reversed and Remanded.

––––––

The concept of an ascertainable standard is discussed in detail in Treasury Regulation § 20.2041–1(c). Whether trustees' powers are limited by an ascertainable standard has been the source of much controversy. For example, compare *Estate of Vissering v. Commissioner* with Technical Advice Memorandum 9125002 (a trust was included in the decedent's gross estate because the decedent-trustee had the power to invade the trust for his own "health, support and reasonable comfort, best interest and welfare"), and Private Letter Ruling 9203047 (invasion for "comfort" to defray expenses arising out of sickness, accidents and disability was subject to ascertainable standard).

Estate of Little v. Commissioner, 87 T.C. 599 (1986), suggests that two questions must be answered: (1) is the standard "ascertainable" and (2) does the ascertainable standard relate to the decedent's health, support, or education? If, under applicable law, the standard does not relate to the decedent's health, support, or education, determining whether the standard is ascertainable is unnecessary. Applying California law, the Tax Court in *Little* determined that a power to invade for general happiness was not limited by a standard relating to the decedent's health, education, or support, and thus, was a general power for estate tax purposes.

Problems

1. Under applicable state law, assume that the power to appoint to one's estate is a special power. If the decedent held such a power, would the property subject to the power be included in decedent's gross estate under § 2041? *See Morgan v. Commissioner*, 309 U.S. 78 (1940).

2. In *Connecticut Bank & Trust Co. v. United States*, *supra*, the Internal Revenue Service contended that the decedent had a general power of appointment because the wrongful death proceeds would pass under decedent's will. Why was the Service unsuccessful with the argument?

3. *W* transfers property to a lifetime trust under which her husband, *H*, will receive the income for life, with the remainder distributable at *H*'s death as he may appoint by will. If *H* fails to appoint the property, the trust provides that the remainder will be distributed among their issue. When *H* dies, is the trust property includable in his gross estate?

4. You represent *H*. He wants to create a testamentary trust for his wife *W*, if she survives him. He also wants to give *W* some power to obtain the property in the trust.

    a. How would you draft the power so that it would not trigger adverse estate tax consequences on *W*'s death?

    b. Would you advise giving *W* the lifetime power to invade the corpus for her maintenance, comfort, and happiness?

    c. To what extent does (should) state law play in your planning considerations?

§ 3.03   Valuation Issues

Code: §§ 2031, 2032, 2032A, 2703, and 2704(a).

Regulations: Treas. Reg. §§ 20.2031–1(b), –2(a) and (b), –7(a), (d)(1) and (2); and 25.2703–1(a) and (b).

The value of the property must be determined whatever the reason for inclusion in the gross estate. Similarly, valuation is required of items that are deductible from the gross estate, as well as some interests giving rise to credits. The rules regarding valuation are contained in §§ 2031 through 2032A.[3]

Section 2031 controls valuation in the vast majority of estates. Its overriding valuation rule requires inclusion in the gross estate of an amount equal to the fair market value of the interest on the date of the decedent's death. Section 2032 allows a personal representative to elect to value the estate as of six months after the decedent's death. A § 2032 election may be appropriate

---

[3] *See generally* JOHN A. BOGDANSKI, FEDERAL TAX VALUATION (Warren Gorham & Lamont 1996).

when there has been a decline in the overall value of the interests in property that will be included in the gross estate. Section 2032A provides yet another valuation method if the estate contains substantial amounts of real estate used for farming or in a closely held business. This elective statute permits a personal representative to value that property based on its special use, rather than at its market value. The latter valuation would probably be higher as it would reflect the property's highest and best use.

[A]   Valuation "At the Time of Death"

Goodman v. Granger

243 F.2d 264 (3d Cir. 1957),
cert. denied, 355 U.S. 835 (1957)

Kalodner, Circuit Judge.

On October 19, 1944, June 1, 1945 and May 26, 1946, decedent entered into identical contracts of employment with Gimbel Brothers covering the years ending January 31, 1945, January 31, 1946 and January 31, 1947, respectively. Each contract provided for a basic salary of $50,000 per year, and for additional "contingent benefits" of $2,000 per year for fifteen years "after the employee ceases to be employed by the employer" by reason of death or otherwise. The post-employment "contingent payments" were to be made only if the employee duly performed the services agreed upon and did not engage in a competing business within a specified period after termination of his employment; and they were to be reduced if his post-employment earnings from a non-competing business plus the contingent payments exceeded seventy-five percent of his yearly average compensation under the contracts. Any of the fifteen annual contingent payments which fell due after the employee's death were to be paid to his estate, or to a nominee designated in his will.

. . .

After the decedent's death Gimbels paid the $6,000 annual installments provided by the three separate contracts ($2,000 each) to the taxpayer in her capacity as administratrix as they became due. She filed with the Collector a timely federal estate tax return and included the three contracts at a value of $15,000. Upon audit of the return, the Internal Revenue Agent in Charge, Pittsburgh, increased the value of the three contracts from $15,000 to $66,710.34, the present worth of $90,000, payable in equal annual installments of $6,000 a year over a period of fifteen years. The increase in the value of the contracts resulted in a deficiency of $15,958.18, including interest, which was assessed against and paid by the taxpayer, and for the recovery of which she brought the suit here involved.

. . .

The sum of the taxpayer's position is (1) what is taxed is "the value" of the decedent's interest in his contract that "ceased by reason of death," not the value of what is received by the recipient (the administratrix); otherwise stated, "the value" of the decedent's interest in his contract was to be determined as "of the moment before death."

The government's position may be summarized as follows: (1) the estate tax is measured by the value of property transferred by death and here an absolute right to the fifteen deferred compensation payments passed by decedent's death to the taxpayer inasmuch as the possibility of forfeiture was extinguished by decedent's death; (2) the government properly valued the right to the deferred compensation payments in the same manner as an annuity for a term certain, *i.e.,* at the commuted value in accordance with the applicable Treasury Regulations.

As earlier noted, the District Court agreed with the taxpayer's view. In doing so it stated:

> It seems clear under the authorities and the statute and the regulations that the value of the contract rights *is limited to the interest of the decedent during his lifetime.* That interest, under the testimony and by a fair preponderance of the evidence, is valueless. There was no fair market value on which to base a deficiency assessment. (emphasis supplied)

It may be noted parenthetically that the taxpayer's testimony as to lack of value, adverted to by the District Court, was premised on the circumstance that the employment contracts specified four contingencies which, if any of them had occurred, would have forfeited the decedent's right to the deferred compensation payments.

. . .

It is clear that the decedent's interest in the employment contracts was "property" includible in his gross estate [§ 2033]. Determination of the time when that interest is to be valued is the crux of the dispute.

We have had the benefit of thorough discussions by both the government and the taxpayer of the nature of the federal estate tax. Both parties cited *Knowlton v. Moore,* 1900, 178 U.S. 41; *Young Men's Christian Association of Columbus, Ohio v. Davis,* 1924, 264 U.S. 47; and *Edwards v. Slocum,* 1924, 264 U.S. 61. The government cited them for the proposition that the subject of the tax is neither the property of the decedent, nor the property of the legatee, but rather the transfer of assets affected by death. The taxpayer emphasizes the language in these cases which supports the theory that what is taxed is the value of the interest that ceased by reason of death, not the value of what is received by the recipient. We are in accord with both of these general axioms which aid in clarifying the nature of the federal estate tax. However, the cases cited and the principles drawn therefrom are not decisive of the question posed by this case. While the nature of the tax has been discussed in numerous Supreme Court cases, the question of the proper time to determine the nature of the decedent's interest and the value thereof requires a more particularized analysis.

The taxpayer has ignored the very nature of the tax which it is urged is dispositive of this case. True, the tax reaches the " '. . . interest which ceased by reason of the death.' " *Knowlton v. Moore,* 178 U.S. at page 49, but the reference there was to the distinction between an estate tax and an inheritance tax. The inheritance tax is levied upon the individual shares of the decedent's estate after distribution to the legatees; the estate tax is imposed upon the total estate of the decedent which is transferred to the legatees [§ 2031]. The estate tax has been characterized as "an excise imposed upon the transfer of or shifting in relationships to property at death." *United States Trust Co. of New York v. Helvering*, 1939, 307 U.S. 57, 60. The estate and inheritance taxes have the common element of being based upon the transmission of property from the dead to the living. *New York Trust Co. v. Eisner*, 1921, 256 U.S. 345. In *Knowlton v. Moore, supra*, the Supreme Court recognized this basic principle when it said, 178 U.S. at page 56:

> . . . tax laws of this nature in all countries rest in their essence upon the principle that death is the generating source from which the particular taxing power takes its being, and that it is the power to transmit, or the transmission from the dead to the living, on which such taxes are more immediately rested.

Since death is the propelling force for the imposition of the tax, it is death which determines the interests to be includible in the gross estate. Interests which terminate on or before death are not a proper subject of the tax. Assets may be acquired or disposed of before death, [and] possibilities of the loss of an asset may become actualities or may disappear. Upon the same principle underlying the inclusion of interests in a decedent's gross estate, valuation of an interest is neither logically made nor feasibly administered until death has occurred. The taxpayer's theory of valuing property before death disregards the fact that generally the estate tax is neither concerned with changes in property interests nor values prior to death.[4] The tax is measured by the value of assets transferred by reason of death, the critical value being that which is determined as of the time of death.

. . .

Here the employment contracts provided for additional "contingent" compensation of $6,000 per year for fifteen years to be paid to Blum or his estate after the termination of his employment by reason of death or otherwise. True, the right to these payments was forfeitable upon the occurrence of any of the specified contingencies. However, forfeiture as a result of the contingencies never occurred during Blum's lifetime, and any possibility of their occurrence was extinguished by his death. Gimbels has been making and the estate has been collecting the payments provided by the contracts. Valuation of the right to these payments must be determined as of the time of Blum's death when the limiting factor of the contingencies would no longer be considered. Death ripened the interest in the deferred payments into an absolute one, and death permitted the imposition of the tax measured by the value of that absolute interest in property.

---

[4] *Cf.* Newell v. Commissioner of Internal Revenue, 66 F.2d 102 (7th Cir. 1993), for the effect of the death of a key officer and shareholder in a corporation upon the valuation of stock in the corporation included in his gross estate. Also, in valuing a partnership interest of a decedent, goodwill attributable to the decedent's personal efforts is not valued due to the decedent's loss to the partnership. Estate of Gannon, 21 T.C. 1073 (1954); Estate of Maddock, 16 T.C. 324 (1951).

In *Mearkle's Estate v. Commissioner of Internal Revenue*, 3 Cir., 1942, 129 F.2d 386, we considered the proper method of valuing an annuity upon the death of the decedent which by its terms was payable to the decedent during his life and to his wife for her life. The criterion adopted was the purchase price of an annuity contract upon the life of the wife measured by her life expectancy on the date of her husband's death. There is no reference in this test to the husband's life expectancy upon the date of his death or to the joint expectancies of the decedent and his wife. The value of decedent's interest in the annuity up to the time of his death is not considered, and, as in the situation here involved, death cuts off prior limiting factors.

For the reasons stated the judgment of the District Court will be reversed with directions to proceed in accordance with this opinion.

———

In *Estate of McClatchy v. Commissioner*, 147 F.3d 1089 (9th Cir. 1998), *rev'g*, 106 T.C. 206 (1996), the decedent owned stock of a publicly traded corporation. As explained (147 F.3d at 1091): "Because of his position with the corporation and his ownership interest, McClatchy was subject to federal securities law restrictions on the sale or disposition of his Class B shares as an affiliate of the corporation." The limitations apply based on the identity of the owner. Thus, "[u]pon McClatchy's death, however, the shares passed to the estate, which was not an affiliate of the corporation. The estate therefore was not subject to the securities law restrictions applicable to decedent."

The Tax Court followed *Goodman* and held that restrictions which terminated at a decedent's death were to be disregarded in valuing property at the "moment of death." The Ninth Circuit reversed the Tax Court and made a factual finding that restrictions did not lapse at death. It concluded (147 F.3d at 1093-1095):

> The affiliate or non-affiliate status of an estate depends on the status of the executor or other person who serves "in any similar capacity." 17 C.F.R. 230.144(a)(2)(ii). The personal representatives for the estate were not issued letters testamentary until 25 days after McClatchy's death. The restrictions therefore did not evaporate at the moment of death.

> Making the amount of estate tax dependent on the affiliate or non-affiliate status of the executor contradicts the principle that valuation should not depend on the status of the recipient. . . .

The Commissioner's position would lead to the following anomaly described by the estate in its brief: Taxpayer A, an affiliate, and Taxpayer B, a non-affiliate, each own $1,000,000 worth of stock, but because of the securities laws restrictions, Taxpayer A's shares are worth only $800,000. Taxpayer A's estate plan uses non-affiliate executors, while Taxpayer B's uses affiliate executors. Thus, when Taxpayer A dies, his $800,000 interest is worth $1,000,000 to his estate, whereas Taxpayer B's $1,000,000 interest is worth $800,000 to his. The result is that, by using affiliate executors, a non-affiliate decedent, who transfers a more valuable asset than an affiliate decedent, pays less estate tax than the affiliate decedent.

. . .

The increase in the stock's value was occasioned, not by death, but by transfer to a non-affiliate estate; death alone did not alter the value. Moreover, the value of the estate is determined by the interest of the decedent at the time of death. Therefore, the stock should be valued in the hands of the decedent.

———

The "moment of death" valuation rule offers estate planning opportunities. Taxpayers may structure voting rights or other control powers in family businesses (as distinct from restrictions imposed by outsiders) to terminate on death.

Consider the facts in *Harrison v. Commissioner*, T.C. Memo 1987–8. Shortly before his death, the decedent and his two children formed a limited partnership. The decedent contributed property worth approximately $60 million and received a general and limited partnership interest. The children were also general and limited partners. Under the agreement, any general partner could dissolve the partnership, but the right to dissolve ended on that general partner's death. Immediately before the decedent's death, his limited partnership interest, because of the right to dissolve, was worth about $60 million. Because the dissolution right ended on death, the Tax Court held that the value of the interest at the moment of death—only $33 million—controlled.

In response to the *Harrison* gambit, Congress enacted § 2704(a), which treats the lapse of a decedent's right to liquidate as a taxable transfer. Thus, if the decedent in *Harrison* died today, his gross estate would include $60 million. First, based on *Goodman*, § 2033 would require gross estate inclusion of $33 million. In addition, § 2704(a) would require inclusion of $27 million. That is, the difference between $60 million—the value of decedent's interest in the partnership immediately before decedent's death (taking into account the right to liquidate)—and the value after the lapse of the liquidation right, $33 million.

[1] General Valuation Aspects

The gross estate is defined by § 2031 as the sum of the interests in property that are includable in the gross estate, based on valuation as of the date decedent dies. The general valuation guidelines, based on a facts and circumstances test, are contained in Treasury Regulation § 20.2031–1(b): "[F]air market value is the price at which the property would change hands between a willing buyer and a willing seller, neither being under any compulsion to buy or sell and both having reasonable knowledge of relevant facts."

Determining the fair market value of an item of property is often a relatively simple matter. Cash obviously needs no valuation. Banks and savings and loans will readily provide account balances as of the date of death. Insurance companies certify life insurance policy values on standard Internal Revenue Service forms.[5] Publicly traded stocks and bonds have regularly quoted values that can be obtained from most major newspapers and brokerage houses. Technically, the price per share is defined in Treasury Regulation § 20.2031–2(b)(1) as the mean between the highest and lowest quoted selling price on the date of death. This regulation also provides guidance relating to valuation when a decedent dies on a weekend, a day stock is not traded, or other situations.

Valuation can be difficult, even in the case of assets having readily available market quotations. For example, market quotations may overvalue a decedent's shares in a publicly traded corporation if the decedent owns such a large percentage of stock that a sale would depress the market. In such a case, a discount for "blockage" may be allowed. *See Rifkind v. United States*, 5 Cl. Ct. 362 (1984); Treas. Reg. § 20.2031–2(e). In *Estate of McClatchy v. Commissioner*, 147 F.3d 1089 (9th Cir. 1998), which was discussed above, the IRS conceded that a "blockage discount" of 15% should be used in valuing the stock. *But see Estate of Van Horne v. Commissioner*, 720 F.2d 1114 (9th Cir. 1983) (blockage discount denied in absence of proof that a sale of stock would depress market).

When the asset is unique or does not have regular market quotations, valuation becomes difficult. In these cases, expert appraisal is typically required. For example, the Regulations specifically mention an appraiser's evaluation of household and personal effects. *See* Treas. Reg. § 20.2031–6(b). Even with appraisers, however, valuation disputes arise. Valuation is not an exact science. As the Tax Court noted, "[w]e are again asked to resolve a dispute over the fair market value of property, a process which has been described as 'weighing evidence of expert guesswork.'" *Estate of Carr v. Commissioner*, T.C. Memo 1985–19 (*quoting Andrews v. Commissioner*, T.C. Memo 1976–106).

The imprecise nature of the valuation process is illustrated by *Estate of Curry v. Commissioner*, 74 T.C. 540 (1980), *acq.* 1981-2 C.B. 1. The decedent was a lawyer who had contracted with another attorney to carry on litigation for which the decedent had contingent fee contracts. After holding that the contractual right to share in the fees was "property" for purposes of § 2033, the Tax Court valued the contingent fees in several cases that were pending before the Indian Claims Court at the decedent's death. The court stated:

> We have carefully evaluated the nature and the type of cases involved in the light of the expert testimony received, the stage of the litigation at the date of death, [the successor attorney's] experience and past successes in this relatively esoteric area, the impact of delay so characteristic of Indian Claims litigation, and the possibility of competing claims for some of the fees. We recognize

---

[5] Valuation of life insurance and annuity contracts issued by life insurance companies is addressed in Treasury Regulation § 20.2031–8, which directs valuation at replacement cost. Replacement cost is what the insurance company would charge to issue the policy or contract, if available. Otherwise, the valuation is the insurance company's "interpolated terminal reserve" value, or its internal accounting charge in the policy. Such information would be furnished on request by the life insurance company. Taxation of life insurance is discussed in Chapter 10, *infra*.

> that, while there were ultimately substantial awards in some instances, in estimating the date-of-death value of these claims, we must be satisfied with some imprecision. But inexactitude is often a byproduct in estimating claims or assets without an established market and provides no excuse for failing to value the claims before us in the light of the vicissitudes attending their recovery.

74 T.C. at 551.

Valuation being uncertain naturally leads to disputes between the estate and the Service; both rely on experts.[6] This has led in turn to some pressure being exerted by the courts to force settlement of valuation disputes. Consider *Estate of Carr v. Commissioner*, T.C. Memo 1985–19:

> Prior to and during trial we admonished counsel that a factual issue of this nature is clearly more properly suited to the give and take of the settlement process than adjudication. As stated in *Buffalo Tool & Die Mfg. Co. v. Commissioner*, 74 T.C. 441, 452 (1980):
>
> > We are convinced that the valuation issue is capable of resolution by the parties themselves through an agreement which will reflect a compromise Solomon-like adjustment, thereby saving the expenditure of time, effort, and money by the parties and the Court—a process not likely to produce a better result. Indeed, each of the parties should keep in mind that, in the final analysis, the Court may find the evidence of valuation by one of the parties sufficiently more convincing than that of the other party, so that the final result will produce a significant financial defeat for one or the other, rather than a middle-of-the-road compromise which we suspect each of the parties expects the Court to reach.
>
> The parties, therefore, are well aware of the fact that we may, in an appropriate case, refuse to reach a compromise where one or more of the valuations submitted to us are the result of overzealous advocacy that ignores common sense. We cannot, however, abdicate our responsibility to determine a factual dispute, including fair market value, where as in this case the parties have failed or refused to do so by agreement.

In valuing real estate, the most persuasive evidence will be the sales price for comparable properties, including sales made after the decedent's death. *See, e.g., First Nat'l Bank v. United States*, 763 F.2d 891 (7th Cir. 1985). Other factors, including assessments, may be considered. *See Estate of Frieders v. Commissioner*, 687 F.2d 224 (7th Cir. 1982), *cert. denied*, 460 U.S. 1011 (1983).

Problems

1. Assume *A* died on Tuesday evening. She owned 10,000 shares of XYZ stock, a security listed on the New York Stock Exchange. On the date of her death, 630,000 shares of XYZ stock were traded. The high (and opening) trading price for that date was $75 per share; the low (and closing) price was $50 per share. What is the value of the XYZ stock in her estate?

---

[6] *See generally*, Wendy C. Gerzog, *Contingencies and the Estate Tax*, 5 Fla. Tax Rev. 49 (2001).

2. To the extent that appraisers are necessary to determine the value of a decedent's assets, what characteristics will you want in the appraisers you hire? Consider §§ 6662(a), (b), (g), and 6701.

3. After the estate tax return is filed, the Commissioner alleges that real property included on the return is worth $50,000 more than its appraised value. What steps could be taken to convince the agent that the valuation is accurate? Consider § 7517.

[2] Restricted Markets

Code: §§ 2703 and 2704.

Regulations: None.

United States v. Cartwright

411 U.S. 546 (1973)

Mr. Justice White delivered the opinion of the Court.

At the time of her death in 1964, Ethel B. Bennett owned approximately 8,700 shares of three mutual funds that are regulated by the Investment Company Act of 1940, 15 U.S.C. § 80a-1 *et seq.* The 1940 Act seeks generally to regulate publicly held companies that are engaged in investing in securities. Open-end investment companies, or mutual funds, "dominate" this industry. Unquestionably, the unique characteristic of mutual funds is that they are permitted, under the Act, to market their shares continuously to the public, but are required to be prepared to redeem outstanding shares at any time. The redemption "bid" price that a shareholder may receive is set by the Act at approximately the fractional value per share of the fund's net assets at the time of redemption. In contrast, the "asked" price, or the price at which the fund initially offers its shares to the public, includes not only the net asset value per share at the time of sale, but also a fixed sales charge or "sales load" assessed by the fund's principal underwriter who acts as an agent in marketing the fund's shares. Sales loads vary within fixed limits from mutual fund to mutual fund, but all are paid to the fund's underwriters; the charges do not become part of the assets of the fund. The sales loads of the funds held by the decedent ranged from seven and eight percent to one percent of the fractional net asset value of the funds' shares.

Private trading in mutual fund shares is virtually nonexistent. . . . Respondent is the executor of the decedent's estate. On the federal estate tax return, he reported the value of the mutual fund shares held by the decedent at their redemption price, which amounted to about $124,400. The Commissioner assessed a deficiency based upon his valuation of the shares at their public offering or asked price, pursuant to Treas. Reg. § 20.2031–8(b). Valued on that basis, the shares were worth approximately $133,300. Respondent paid the deficiency of about $3,100, including interest, filed a timely claim for a refund, and, when that claim was denied, commenced a refund action in Federal District Court on the ground that the valuation based on § 20.2031–8(b) was unreasonable. The District Court agreed with respondent and held the

Regulation invalid. 323 F. Supp. 769. The Court of Appeals affirmed. 457 F.2d 567. We granted the Government's petition for certiorari, 409 U.S. 840, because of the conflict among the circuits. . . .

[T]he United States maintains that the redemption price does not reflect the price that a willing buyer would pay, inasmuch as the mutual fund is under a statutory obligation to redeem outstanding shares whenever they are offered. According to the Government, the only market for mutual fund shares that has both willing buyers and willing sellers is the public offering market. Therefore, the price in that market, the asked price, is an appropriate basis for valuation. The central difficulty with this argument is that it unrealistically bifurcates the statutory scheme for the trading in mutual fund shares. To be sure, the fund is under an obligation to redeem its shares at the stated price. But, at the time of the original purchases, both the fund and the purchasers are aware of that duty and both willingly enter into the sale transactions nonetheless. As Judge Winner correctly observed in *Hicks v. United States*, 335 F. Supp. 474, 481 (Colo. 1971):

> Viewing the contract in this light meets every test of the "willing buyer-willing seller" definition usually applied in the determination of market value. The "willing buyer" is the fully informed person who agrees to buy the shares, agreeing at that time to sell them to the fund—the only available repurchaser—at the redemption price. The "willing seller" is the fund which sells the shares at market value plus a load charge, and which agrees to buy the shares back at market less the load charge. That is the market, and it is the only market. It is a market made up of informed buyers and an informed seller, all dealing at arm's length.

In the context of the Investment Company Act, the redemption price may thus be properly viewed only as the final step in a voluntary transaction between a willing buyer and a willing seller. As a matter of statutory law, holders of mutual fund shares cannot obtain the "asked" price from the fund. That price is never paid by the fund; it is used by the fund when selling its shares to the public—and even then the fund receives merely the net asset value per share from the sale, with the sales load being paid directly to the underwriter. In short, the only price that a shareholder may realize and that the fund—the only buyer—will pay is the redemption price. In the teeth of this fact, Regulation section 20.2031–8(b) purports to assign a value to mutual fund shares that the estate could not hope to obtain and that the fund could not offer.

In support of the Regulation, the Government stresses that many types of property are taxed at values above those which could be realized during an actual sale. For example, ordinary corporate stock is valued at its fair market price without taking into account the brokerage commission that a seller must generally pay in order to sell the stock. Respondent does not contend that the approach is inappropriate or that, for example, the value of ordinary stock in an estate should be the market price at the time less anticipated brokerage fees. But section 20.2031–8(b) operates in an entirely different fashion. The regulation includes as an element of value the commission cost incurred in the hypothetical purchase of the mutual fund shares already held in the decedent's estate. If that principle were carried over to the ordinary stock situation, then a share traded at $100 on the date of death would be valued, not at $100, as it now is, but at, say, $102, representing the "value" plus the fee that a person buying the stock on that day would have to pay. It hardly need be said that such a valuation method is at least inconsistent with long-established Treasury practice and would appear at odds with the basic notions of valuation embodied in the Internal Revenue Code. *See Estate of Wells v. Commissioner*, 50 T. C. 871, 880 (1968) (Tannenwald, J., dissenting).

Even if it were assumed that the public offering price were somehow relevant to the value of mutual fund shares privately held, there would still be the difficulty that shares so held are, in important respects, similar to ordinary corporate stock held subject to a restrictive agreement (such as a first-refusal right at a specified price). With respect to the value of such stock, the Treasury Regulations have provided that the price that may be obtained in the marketplace does not control. Rather, so long as the restriction is a bona fide one, the value of the shares in the hands of the restricted stockholder is determined in accordance with the terms of the restriction (Treas. Reg. § 20.2031–2(h)). Outstanding mutual fund shares are likewise held subject to a restriction, as the Court of Appeals noted. 457 F.2d, at 571. Those shares may not be "sold" at the public offering price. By statute, they may be "sold" back to the mutual fund only at the redemption price. We see no valid justification for disregarding this reality connected with the ownership of mutual fund shares.

. . .

We recognize that normally "Treasury regulations must be sustained unless unreasonable and plainly inconsistent with the revenue statutes." *Commissioner v. South Texas Lumber Co.*, [333 U.S. 496 (1948)] at 501. But even if the Regulation contested here is not, on its face, technically inconsistent with section 2031 of the Internal Revenue Code, it is manifestly inconsistent with the most elementary provisions of the Investment Company Act of 1940 and operates without regard for the market in mutual fund shares that the Act created and regulates. Congress surely could not have intended section 2031 to be interpreted in such a manner. The Regulation also imposes an unreasonable and unrealistic measure of value. We agree with Judge Tannenwald, who stated at the very outset of the dispute over Regulation section 20.2031–8(b), that "it does not follow that, because [the Commissioner] has a choice of alternatives, his choice should be sustained where the alternative chosen is unrealistic. In such a situation the regulations embodying that choice should be held to be unreasonable." *Estate of Wells v. Commissioner*, 50 T. C., at 878 (dissenting opinion).

The judgment of the Court of Appeals is affirmed.

It is so ordered.

Mr. Justice Stewart, with whom The Chief Justice and Mr. Justice Rehnquist join, dissenting.

———

The court in *Cartwright* noted that buy-sell agreements are often entered into for business interests, and that such agreements may impact on the value of the underlying business interest to the estate. For example, the agreement may obligate the estate to sell the estate's interest, and the buyer to buy it. It may, on the other hand, constitute only an option, in that it obligates the estate to sell, but does not obligate the buyer to purchase the shares unless she so desires. Even less definite would be a right of first refusal; for example, an agreement obligating the estate only if it decided to sell, at which point the estate would have to offer the asset to the buyer for the agreed price. Such agreements are commonly used to control ownership of closely-held corporations and to provide a means for termination of partnerships on the death of a partner. *See Bischoff v. Commissioner,* 69 T.C. 32 (1977).

Section 2703(a) provides that the value of property for estate (and gift) tax purposes is determined without regard to any option, agreement, right to acquire or use the property at less than fair market value, or any restriction on the right to sell or use such property, unless (2703(b)):

(1) the option, agreement, right, or restriction is a bona fide business arrangement;

(2) the option, agreement, right, or restriction is not a device to transfer such property to members of the decedent's family for less than full and adequate consideration; and

(3) the terms of the option, agreement, right, or restriction are comparable to those obtained in a similar arrangement entered into by persons in an arm's length transaction.[7]

The legislative history explains the reasons for enacting § 2703:

> The committee believes that buy-sell agreements are common business planning arrangements and that buy-sell agreements generally are entered into for legitimate business reasons that are not related to transfer tax consequences. Buy-sell agreements are commonly used to control the transfer of ownership in a closely held business, to avoid expensive appraisals in determining purchase price, to prevent the transfer to an unrelated party, to provide a market for the equity interest, and to allow owners to plan for future liquidity needs in advance. However, the committee is aware of the potential of buy-sell agreements for distorting transfer tax value. Therefore, the committee establishes rules that attempt to distinguish between agreements designed to avoid estate taxes and those with legitimate business agreements. These rules generally

---

[7] *See* Estate of True v. Commissioner, T.C. Memo 2001-167 (§ 2703(a) barred valuation based on a buy-sell agreement).

disregard a buy-sell agreement that would not have been entered into by unrelated parties acting at arm's length.[8]

Section 2704(b) also relates to restrictions on property for valuation purposes. As explained in *Kerr v. Commissioner*, 113 T.C. 449, 462 (2000):

> Section 2704(b) generally provides that, where a transferor and his family control a corporation or partnership, a[n applicable] restriction on the right to liquidate the corporation or partnership shall be disregarded in determining the value of an interest that has been transferred from the transferor to a family member if, after the transfer, the restriction on liquidation either lapses or can be removed by the family.[9]

Section 2704(b) is more easily understood in the context of gift taxation which has generated litigation involving the application of 2704(b) to liquidation restrictions in partnership and LLC agreements. *See* Chapter 4, § 4.02[B].

Sections 2703 and 2704, together with §§ 2701 and 2702, were adopted in response to various valuation "tricks" that taxpayers were employing to reduce value. While these sections ended specific targeted techniques, such as the use of lapsing rights in *Harrison*, discussed in § 3.03[A] *supra*, we will see in later chapters that the effectiveness of these sections to stop overall valuing planning is in considerable doubt.

Problems

1. At the time of her death, *A* owned 1,000 shares of a mutual fund that had a "bid" (sale) price of $20 and an "ask" (purchase) price of $22. If this is an "open end" fund (a fund that continually takes in capital to make investments, and redeems shares of those who wish to sell them), what is the value of the shares for estate tax purposes? Does it make any difference whether the fund expressly applies a "load" (commission) when shares are purchased?

2. *A* died owning 100 shares of XYZ, a publicly traded stock, the average sale price of which was $50 on the day of her death. On the average, full-service retail brokers charge a commission of $100 to consummate the sale of this number of shares. Could the personal representative reduce the $5,000 value of the stock by the $100 selling commission that would be paid if the stock were sold through a broker?

3. *A* owned a two-year old automobile with a "Blue Book" wholesale value (the amount a used car dealer would pay for the vehicle) of $14,000 and a retail value (the amount it would cost to buy a comparable vehicle) of $16,000. The personal representative sold the automobile a few weeks after *A*'s death to a dealer for $13,600, to liquidate the estate. What impact would this event have on the valuation of the vehicle? *See* Treas. Reg. § 20.2053–3(d)(2).

---

[8] Senate Finance Committee Report on S. 3209, Revenue Reconciliation Act of 1990, 101st Cong., 2d Sess. 60 (1990).

[9] Under § 2704(b)(3)(B), an applicable restriction does not include "any restriction on liquidation imposed, or required to be imposed, by any Federal or State law."

[3] Valuation of Family Business Interests[10]

Code: § 2031.

Regulations: Treas. Reg. §§ 20.2031–2 and –3.

[a] In General

Particularly difficult to value are stocks in closely held corporations, interests in partnerships, and other business interests. These types of assets present the most frequently litigated valuation questions. Minimal guidance is provided by § 2031(b), which states:

> (b) Valuation of unlisted stock and securities. In the case of stock and securities of a corporation the value of which, by reason of their not being listed on an exchange and by reason of the absence of sales thereof, cannot be determined with reference to bid and asked prices or with reference to sales prices, the value thereof shall be determined by taking into consideration, in addition to all other factors, the value of stock or securities of corporations engaged in the same or a similar line of business which are listed on an exchange.

This is expanded slightly by Treasury Regulation § 20.2031–2(f). More guidance is provided in the following Revenue Ruling and *Estate of Bright, infra.*

Revenue Ruling 59–60

1959–1 C.B. 237

SECTION 1. PURPOSE.

The purpose of this Revenue Ruling is to outline and review in general the approach, methods and factors to be considered in valuing shares of the capital stock of closely held corporations for estate tax and gift tax purposes. The methods discussed herein will apply likewise to the valuation of corporate stocks on which market quotations are either unavailable or are of such scarcity that they do not reflect the fair market value.

SEC. 2. BACKGROUND AND DEFINITIONS.

. . .

.03 Closely held corporations are those corporations the shares of which are owned by a relatively limited number of stockholders. Often the entire stock issue is held by one family. The result of this situation is that little, if any, trading in the shares takes place. There is, therefore, no established market for the stock and such sales as occur at irregular intervals seldom reflect all of the elements of a representative transaction as defined by the term "fair market value."

---

[10] Sections 2703 and 2704, discussed in § 3.03[A][2], *supra*, also apply to the valuation of family business interests.

SEC. 3. APPROACH TO VALUATION.

.01 A determination of fair market value, being a question of fact, will depend upon the circumstances in each case. No formula can be devised that will be generally applicable to the multitude of different valuation issues arising in estate and gift tax cases. Often, an appraiser will find wide differences of opinion as to the fair market value of a particular stock. In resolving such differences, he should maintain a reasonable attitude in recognition of the fact that valuation is not an exact science. A sound valuation will be based upon all the relevant facts, but the elements of common sense, informed judgment and reasonableness must enter into the process of weighing those facts and determining their aggregate significance.

.02 The fair market value of specific shares of stock will vary as general economic conditions change from "normal" to "boom" or "depression," that is, according to the degree of optimism or pessimism with which the investing public regards the future at the required date of appraisal. Uncertainty as to the stability or continuity of the future income from a property decreases its value by increasing the risk of loss of earnings and value in the future. The value of shares of stock of a company with very uncertain future prospects is highly speculative. The appraiser must exercise his judgment as to the degree of risk attaching to the business of the corporation which issued the stock, but that judgment must be related to all of the other factors affecting value.

.03 Valuation of securities is, in essence, a prophesy as to the future and must be based on facts available at the required date of appraisal. As a generalization, the prices of stocks which are traded in volume in a free and active market by informed persons best reflect the consensus of the investing public as to what the future holds for the corporations and industries represented. When a stock is closely held, is traded infrequently, or is traded in an erratic market, some other measure of value must be used. In many instances, the next best measure may be found in the prices at which the stocks of companies engaged in the same or a similar line of business are selling in a free and open market.

SEC. 4. FACTORS TO CONSIDER.

.01 It is advisable to emphasize that in the valuation of the stock of closely held corporations or the stock of corporations where market quotations are either lacking or too scarce to be recognized, all available financial data, as well as all relevant factors affecting the fair market value, should be considered. The following factors, although not all-inclusive are fundamental and require careful analysis in each case:

(a) The nature of the business and the history of the enterprise from its inception.

(b) The economic outlook in general and the condition and outlook of the specific industry in particular.

(c) The book value of the stock and the financial condition of the business.

(d) The earning capacity of the company.

(e) The dividend-paying capacity.

(f) Whether or not the enterprise has goodwill or other intangible value.

(g) Sales of the stock and the size of the block of stock to be valued.

(h) The market price of stocks of corporations engaged in the same or a similar line of business having their stocks actively traded in a free and open market, either on an exchange or over-the-counter.

––––––––

[b] Valuation Discounts

In recent years, taxpayers, their advisors, and the Service have focused on the valuation of minority interests in businesses and undivided interests in property. The economic basis for the taxpayers' view is that a willing buyer would not pay a willing seller a pro rata value for a minority interest in a business.[11]

Estate of Bright v. United States

658 F.2d 999 (5th Cir. 1981)

Anderson, III, Circuit Judge:

[Mary Frances Smith Bright and her husband owned 55% of the stock of several companies. They held the stock as their community property under Texas law. Thirty of the remaining forty-five percent was owned by one unrelated person, and the remaining fifteen percent was owned by two or three other individuals. Mrs. Bright's will named her husband executor, and devised her interest in the stock to him as trustee of a trust for the primary benefit of her four children.

Before trial, the district judge ruled that "no element of control can be attributed to the decedent in determining the value of the decedent's interest in the stock. . . ."]

The only issue facing the en banc court is whether the district court erred in entering the above-quoted pretrial order. . . .

. . .

First, the government argues that the property to be valued for estate tax purposes is an undivided one-half interest in the control block of 55 percent of the stock, and that the proper method of valuation would be to value the 55 percent control block, including a control premium, and then take one-half thereof . . . . Both parties agree that, under Texas law, the stock at issue was the community property of Mr. and Mrs. Bright during her life, that Mrs. Bright's death dissolved the community, that upon death the community is divided equally, that each spouse can exercise testamentary disposition over only his or her own half of the community, and that "only the decedent's half is includable in his gross estate for federal tax purposes." *Commissioner v. Chase Manhattan Bank,* 259 F.2d [231 (5th Cir. 1958)] at 239. . . .

––––––––

[11] The willing buyer-willing seller is the fundamental standard of valuation. *See* Treas. Reg. § 20.2031–1(b).

The estate points out that the government's argument overlooks the fact that the block of stock is subject to the right of partition under Texas law at the instance of either the surviving spouse or the estate of the deceased's spouse. Tex. Prob. Code Ann. § 385 (Vernon 1980). [citation omitted] Thus, the estate has no means to prevent the conversion of its interest into shares representing a 27.5 percent block, and we conclude that the estate's interest is the equivalent of a 27.5 percent block of the stock. . . .

Having determined that the property which is to be valued for estate tax purposes is the 27.5 percent block of stock owned by the estate, we turn to the government's second argument, which is based on the doctrine of family attribution between the successive holders of interest to be taxed, the decedent, the executor, and the legatee, on the one hand, and the related party, Mr. Bright, on the other. The government argues that the following facts are relevant and should have been considered by the district court in valuing the 27.5 percent block: the fact that Mr. and Mrs. Bright were husband and wife and held their stock during her lifetime as a control block of 55 percent; the fact that Mr. Bright held the estate's 27.5 percent block after her death as executor and subsequently as trustee of the testamentary trust for their children, while he simultaneously held another 27.5 percent block in his individual capacity, thus continuing the control block after death; and the fact that the government might be able to adduce evidence that Mr. Bright, as executor or trustee, would not be willing to sell the estate's 27.5 percent block as a minority interest, but would be willing to sell it only as part of the block of 55 percent including his individually-owned stock so that a substantial control premium could be realized. . . . For several reasons, we reject the government's attempt to import into this area of the estate tax law this kind of family attribution. . . .

. . .

In *United States v. Land*, [303 F.2d 170 (5th Cir. 1962)], this court held that a restrictive agreement, which depressed the value of a partnership interest but which by its terms expired at decedent's death, did not affect value for estate tax purposes because the estate tax is an excise tax on the transfer of property at death and accordingly valuation is to be made at the time of the transfer, *i.e.*, at death, and the valuation is to be measured by the interest that actually passes. 303 F.2d at 172. It follows necessarily from our *Land* holding that the fact that Mr. and Mrs. Bright held their stock during her lifetime as a control block of 55 percent is an irrelevant fact. It is a fact which antedates her death, and no longer exists at the time of her death. . . .

Beginning at least as early as 1940, the Tax Court has uniformly valued a decedent's stock for estate tax purposes as a minority interest when the decedent himself owned less than 50 percent, and despite the fact that control of the corporation was within the decedent's family. [Citations omitted.] Similarly, many district courts have either expressly or impliedly rejected the application of family attribution to an estate's stock in the valuation process for estate tax purposes [citations omitted]. Our research has uncovered no cases, and the government has cited none, which have attributed family owned stock to the estate's stock in determining the value thereof for estate tax purposes.

. . .

We conclude that the case law reflects long established precedent that family attribution should not apply to lump a decedent's stock with that of related parties for estate tax valuation purposes. . . .

Our second reason for rejecting this kind of family attribution is our conclusion that the doctrine is logically inconsistent with the willing buyer-seller rule set out in [Treasury] Regulation section 20.2031–1(b). . . .

It is apparent from the language of the regulation that the "willing seller" is not the estate itself, but a hypothetical seller. . . .

The notion of the "willing seller" as being hypothetical is . . . supported by the theory that the estate tax is an excise tax on the transfer of property at death and accordingly that the valuation is to be made as of the moment of death and is to be measured by the interest that passes, as contrasted with the interest held by the decedent before or the interest held by the legatee after death. Earlier in this opinion, we noticed that our *United States v. Land, supra,* decision logically requires a holding that the relationship between Mr. and Mrs. Bright and their stock is an irrelevant, before death fact. Thus, it is clear that the "willing seller" cannot be identified with Mrs. Bright, and therefore there can be no family attribution with respect to those related to Mrs. Bright. Similarly, the dictum in *Land*—that valuation is not determined by the value of the interest in the hands of the legatee—means that the "willing seller" cannot be identified with Mr. Bright as executor or as trustee of the testamentary trust. Therefore, there can be no family attribution based on identity of the executor and trustee, Mr. Bright. . . . The *Land* dictum also comports with common sense. It would be strange indeed if the estate tax value of a block of stock would vary depending upon the legatee to whom it was devised.

. . .

For the foregoing reasons, we Affirm.

Alvin B. Rubin, Circuit Judge, with whom Vance, Frank M. Johnson, Jr., Politz and Hatchett, Circuit Judges, join, dissenting:

. . .

While my colleagues discuss at length why the value of the 27.5 percent interest should not be enhanced because it is part of a majority block and thus controls the corporation, they do not discuss why it should be discounted to one-half its public value because it is a minority interest. An appraisal based on "public value" of $4.4 million might be increased if control-value is considered. It does not necessarily follow that, because the control-value premium cannot be added, a subtraction because the stock represents a minority interest is correct.

. . .

[Dissenting opinion of Judge Tate omitted.]

––––––

In Rev. Rul. 93–12, 1993–1 C.B. 202, the Service revoked Rev. Rul. 81–253, 1981–2 C.B. 187, which held that the market value of stock a parent gave to his children could not be discounted because the shares were minority interests. Now, following cases such as *Estate of Bright*, the Service concedes that the interests should be valued without regard to the family relationship. In Rev. Rul. 93–12, the Service further conceded that in valuing stock transferred in equal amounts from a father to his children, the shares transferred do not have to be aggregated and valued as if they represent a controlling interest. The fact that corporate control may rest in the family does not mean that each individual shareholder has such control. The concession makes it advantageous for a business owner to give minority interests to children and other relatives while still living, instead of through a will.

––––––

Besides minority interest discounts, taxpayers also assert discounts for lack of marketability. This discount is based on the precept that the market for a closely held business stock is limited when compared to publicly traded business stock.

The following excerpt from *Estate of Berg v. Commissioner*, T.C. Memo 1991–279, *aff'd in part, rev'd in part*, 976 F.2d 1163 (8th. Cir. 1992), considers the minority discount and the discount for lack of marketability in valuing stock in a closely-held real estate holding company for estate tax purposes:

> The valuation of stock in a closely held corporation, including the appropriate discounts to apply, must take into account all relevant facts and circumstances of the particular corporation at issue. The courts have long recognized that the shares of stock of a corporation which represent a minority interest are usually worth less than a proportionate share of the value of the assets of the corporation. *Estate of Bright v. United States*, 658 F.2d 999 (5th Cir. 1981) (en banc); *Ward v. Commissioner*, 87 T.C. 78, 106 (1986); *Harwood v. Commissioner*, 82 T.C. 239 (1984), *aff'd. without published opinion* 786 F.2d 1174 (9th Cir. 1986); *Estate of Andrews v. Commissioner*, 79 T.C. 938 (1982); *Estate of Zaiger v. Commissioner*, 64 T.C. 927 (1975); *Estate of de Guebriant v. Commissioner*, 14 T.C. 611 (1950), *rev'd on other grounds sub nom. Claflin v. Commissioner*, 186 F.2d 307 (2d Cir. 1951). The minority discount is recognized because the holder of a minority interest lacks control over corporate policy, cannot direct the payment of dividends, and cannot compel a liquidation of corporate assets.
>
> A lack of marketability discount, on the other hand, reflects the fact that there is no ready market for shares in a closely held corporation. *Ward v. Commissioner*, *supra*; *Estate of Andrews v.*

Commissioner, supra at 953. The burden is on petitioner to establish
the appropriate discounts in the instant case.

Courts have used the lack of market discounts to conclude that a willing buyer
would not pay a willing seller a pro rata amount for an undivided interest
in a piece of property. *See generally*, James R. Repetti, *Minority Discounts:
The Alchemy in Estate and Gift Taxation*, 50 Tax L. Rev. 415 (1995). For
example, in *Estate of Williams v. Commissioner*, T. C. Memo. 1998-59, the
decedent made lifetime transfers of half interests in two large tracts of
timberland. After determining the fair market value of each tract, the court
considered whether the value of a half interest should be discounted.

> The applicability and extent of a discount for a fractional interest is
> a question of fact to be decided based on the entire record. Estate of
> Fawcett v. Commissioner, 64 T.C. 889, 898, 1975 WL 3029 (1975);
> Estate of Campanari v. Commissioner, 5 T.C. 488, 492, 1945 WL 37
> (1945). Courts have held that the sum of all fractional interests can
> be less than the whole and have used fractional interest discounts to
> value undivided interests. Estate of Bonner v. United States, 84 F.3d
> 196, 197 (5th Cir.1996); Estate of Bright v. United States, 658 F.2d
> 999 (5th Cir.1981); see, e.g., Estate of Wildman v. Commissioner, T.C.
> Memo.1989-667 (40-percent discount); Estate of van Loben Sels v.
> Commissioner, T.C. Memo.1986-501 (60-percent discount).

The court rejected the Service's contention that the only appropriate discount
should be for the cost of partition. It accepted the testimony of the taxpayer's
expert.

> [He] testified that the fractional interests at issue here should be
> discounted by 20 percent due to lack of marketability and by 30
> percent for lack of control and the necessity of resorting to partition
> and related costs to liquidate one's interest, for a total discount of 44
> percent. He concluded that a marketability discount is appropriate
> because of the 9-month marketing time and 10-percent real estate
> commission cost involved in selling real property in that particular
> market. He said that the holder of a fractional interest in real estate
> lacks control because he or she cannot unilaterally decide how to man-
> age it. Wiggins noted that a partition action can take a considerable
> amount of time and expense. He estimated that partition costs would
> be $164,400 for the 1980 transfer, $172,500 for the 1983 transfer, and
> $76,500 for the estate property because the properties are irregularly
> shaped parcels and contain pineland, swampland, and riverfront
> acreage.

A further discount may be allowed for so-called "built in capital gains"
because of the 1986 repeal of corporate tax doctrine known as "General
Utilities." That income tax rule provided that corporations did not realize gain
on its appreciated assets when distributed to its shareholders in liquidation
of the entity. As a result of the 1986 legislation, gain is recognized. In response
to this change, estates should be able to discount the value of a decedent's
interest in a closely held corporation based on the built in capital gains

liability inside the entity. *See Estate of Welch v. Commissioner*, 85 AFTR2d 2000-534 (6th Cir. 2000).[12]

Problems

1. Assume *D* owned a majority interest in closely held corporation *A* and a minority interest in closely held corporation *B*. How should the stock interests be valued for estate tax purposes?

2. Assume *D* died owning 40 million shares of General Motors stock. Would you use the same method of valuing that stock in his estate as you would use for valuing 100 shares? Would the problem differ if *D* were a recognized sculptor, and who died owning as many of his sculptures as those owned by others? *See Estate of Smith v. Commissioner*, 57 T.C. 650 (1972), *aff'd* 510 F.2d 479 (2d. Cir. 1975).

[4] Valuation of Partial Interests

Code: §§ 2031 and 7520.

Regulations: Treas. Reg. §§ 20.2031–7, 20.7520–1(a)(1), (b), (c), and 20.7520–3(b)(1), (b)(3), (b)(4).

A further valuation problem arises when a decedent owns only a partial interest in property, such as an unexpired term of years, a remainder, or a reversion.[13] Valuation depends on the expected time of possession of that interest and requires valuation in accordance with actuarial principles.

Before the enactment of § 7520, valuation of partial interests had been addressed by using a fixed interest rate.[14] Congress enacted § 7520 to prevent revenue losses when actual interest rates varied from the prescribed rate. Effective for transfers after April 30, 1989, § 7520 generally provides that the value of a partial interest is determined under tables (or formulae) prescribed by the Treasury, using an interest rate equal to 120% of the federal mid-term rate, for the month in which the valuation date falls. The federal mid-term rate is the average market yield on outstanding U.S. government obligations with a term of over three years, but less than nine years.

In 1999, the Treasury published actuarial valuation rules and tables for estate and gift tax purposes.[15] Although the regulations address only the most

---

[12] The Service now agrees that a discount for built in capital gains is appropriate. *See* Eisenberg v. Commissioner, 155 F.3d 50 (2d Cir. 1998), *acq.* 1999-4 I.R.B. 4. *Eisenberg*, a gift tax case, is discussed in Chapter 4, 4.02[B] *infra*.

[13] Undivided concurrent interests such as tenancies in common will involve discounts to reflect the lack of marketability, control problems, and possibly partition costs. *See, e.g.,* Mooneyhan v. Commissioner, T.C. Memo 1991–178; Estate of Williams v. Commissioner, T.C. Memo 1998-59.

[14] The fixed rate was changed infrequently. From 1971, until November 30, 1983, the rate was 6%. From December 1, 1983, until April 30, 1989, the rate was 10%.

[15] *See* Treas. Reg. § 20.2031–7 (estate tax regulation); Treas. Reg. § 25.2512–5 (gift tax regulation adopting estate tax regulation).

basic actuarial valuation problems,[16] even these may at first seem daunting. Consider the following example, which is adapted from the regulations.

> **Example: Remainder payable at an individual's death.** The decedent, or the decedent's estate, was entitled to receive certain property worth $50,000 upon the death of the decedent's elder sister, to whom the income was bequeathed for life. The decedent died in February 2002. At the time of the decedent's death, the elder sister was 47 years 5 months old. In February 2002, the § 7520 rate was 5.6%. Under Table S in paragraph (d)(7) of this section [of the regulations], the remainder factor at 5.6% for determining the present value of the remainder interest due at the death of a person aged 47, the number of years nearest the elder sister's actual age at the decedent's death, is 0.22468. The present value of the remainder interest at the date of the decedent's death is, therefore, $11,234 ($50,000 × 0.22468).[17]

Furthermore, the valuation tables for annuities, life estates, and remainders under § 2031 cannot be used in all circumstances. Treasury Regulations under § 7520 take the position that a value which is based on an individual's age is valued under the standard tables, unless the individual is suffering from a deteriorating physical condition of advanced stages such that death is imminent. For this purpose, death is imminent if it is likely to occur within one year. *See* Treas. Reg. § 20.7520–3(b)(2). To this extent, the Regulations merely restate the Service's long standing position in Rev. Rul. 80–80, 1980–1 C.B. 194 (clarifying Rev. Rul. 66–307, 1966–2 C.B. 429). *See Estate of Fabric v. Commissioner*, 83 T.C. 932 (1984) (Service compelled to use the tables when the measuring life lived more than one year). The Regulations go on to provide that the standard tables apply unless "there is at least a 50 percent probability that the individual will not survive for more than 1 year from the valuation date." This is significantly different from the old rule of Rev. Rul. 80–80, which applied the standard tables unless there was no "reasonable possibility of survival for more than a very brief period," and that death is not "clearly imminent" if the chance that the individual will survive for a year or more "is not so remote as to be negligible."

Problems

1. Decedent was the vested remainderman of a trust established by his mother, in which the mother had retained the income for her life. When his mother was 69 years old, decedent died. At the decedent's death at age 40, the trust consisted of publicly traded stock having a fair market value of $100,000. What is the value of the trust interest includable in decedent's gross estate, assuming an 8% 7520 interest rate? What if the 7520 rate is 5%?

---

[16] More complex calculations, requiring, for example, valuation depending on the possibility of surviving two or more people, require reference to other tables which may be obtained in IRS Publication 1457. Further, the regulations state that the Service can provide a special valuation factor for unusual cases. *See* Treas. Reg. § 20.2031–7(d)(4). In such situations, however, prudence might dictate engaging the services of an actuary.

[17] Treas. Reg. § 20.2031–7(d)(5).

2. S transferred $100,000 to T in trust, providing that D, or D's estate, is entitled to receive all of the income generated by the trust property for a ten year period. At the end of this ten year term, T is directed to distribute all of the trust corpus to E. Assume that at all times the trust corpus was worth $100,000 and the 7520 interest rate is 8%. Is anything included in D's gross estate if he dies at the end of the fifth year? If so, how is it valued?

3. Assume the same facts as in Problem 2, except that D is to receive only the first $6,000 of income each year, with the balance to be added to the trust corpus. Again, D dies at the end of the fifth year. What result?

4. Consider the valuation of the "contingent payments" in *Goodman v. Granger* (§ 3.03[A], *supra*). What is the present value of employer provided post-employment "contingent payments" payable at the rate of $6,000 per year for 15 years, assuming an 8% applicable interest rate under § 7520?

5. S transferred $100,000 to T in trust. The income was payable to A for A's life and the remainder to B if living at A's death and, if B is not then living, to C or C's estate. Assume the applicable 7520 interest rate is 8%.

    a. If A is 69 when B dies, what would be included in B's gross estate?

    b. If A is 69 when C dies after B died, what would be included in C's gross estate, and how would you value it?

    c. If C dies before both A, age 69, and B, age 69, what amount would be included in C's gross estate?

[B] Alternate Valuation: Section 2032

Code: § 2032.

Regulations: Treas. Reg. § 20.2032–1(a), (d), and (f).

Section 2032 allows the personal representative to elect to value the gross estate based on a valuation date six months after the decedent's death. It was enacted as a relief against the estate declining in value after death and before the due date for the estate tax return. The § 2032 election must be made, however, for all or none of the estate assets. The personal representative cannot selectively use §§ 2031 and 2032 to obtain the lowest (or highest) value for each asset. Thus, a decline in the value of only a few assets may not justify an alternate valuation date election.

On its face, § 2032 would appear to present no significant valuation difficulties beyond those arising under § 2031. The appearance, however, is deceiving. For example, some assets, such as zero-coupon bonds, will increase in value over time because of their own terms, giving rise to the question whether that increase should be reflected in the alternate valuation.[18] Second,

---

[18] A "zero coupon bond" is a bond that is issued at a substantial discount and does not make periodic payments of interest to the bondholder, but matures at par. For example, a corporation might sell a bond for $500 that will mature in nine years. At maturity the bond is redeemed for $1,000. Although the bond has no interest payments, the bond is increasing at an average of 8% annually from the date of issue to the date of maturity. If the bond is sold by its owner before maturity, its value will reflect both the amount of time until maturity and current interest rates. If it is assumed that interest rates are stable over the entire eight year term of the bond, the bond will steadily increase in value from the date of issue to the date of maturity as a result of the passage of time.

valuation after death inherently presents the problem of dealing with assets disposed of between death and the alternate valuation date: how can you value an asset no longer in the estate at the time set for valuing it?

The Code responds directly to both questions. Section 2032(a)(3) requires that assets whose value are affected by the mere lapse of time must be included at their date of death value, adjusted by changes in value not related to the mere passage of time. This, of course, has produced questions about what constitutes a change in value affected by the mere lapse of time. *Compare* Rev. Rul. 55–379, 1955–1 C.B. 449 (interest on insurance), *with* Rev. Rul. 63–52, 1963–1 C.B. 173 (death of non-decedent insured). On the second issue, § 2032(a)(1) requires valuation as of the date on which the estate disposes of the asset, if the alternate valuation date is used. Again, however, this leaves open the question of what constitutes a "disposition" of the asset in the statutory sense, which again has produced significant litigation. *See, e.g., Hertsche v. United States*, 244 F. Supp. 347 (D. Or. 1965), *aff'd* 366 F.2d 93 (9th Cir. 1966) (date of probate order controls over date of delivery to legatee).

When an asset is subject to a contingency other than a mere lapse of time, the alternate value may be significantly different six months after the decedent's death. For example, in *Estate of Aldrich v. Commissioner*, T.C. Memo. 1983–543, a contingent legal fee was collected and the alternate valuation date elected. The amount received was fully includable in the gross estate. However, if by the alternate value date it was apparent that no fee would be collected, the estate tax value of the contingent fee would be zero.

Finally, although the reason for the § 2032 election is to prevent taxation of estate assets at unrealistically high values, the election can also have an impact on the income tax status of the assets in the estate by determining the stepped-up basis of the assets. Thus, in estates that pass tax-free, there would be a temptation to use alternate valuation if the estate value was higher on the later date. Perceiving such elections as abusive, in 1984, Congress enacted § 2032(c), which permits the use of alternate valuation only when an estate has decreased in value and the election will reduce estate taxes payable. This provision was further amended by the Tax Reform Act of 1986, to limit, but not bar, the election under the newly enacted generation-skipping transfer tax system. For an analysis of the requirements of alternative valuation and the factors to consider before making the election, see Ted D. Englebrecht and James M. Turner, *Alternate Valuation Has Side Effects*, 21 Est. Plan. 154 (May/June 1994).

Problems

1. *D*'s gross estate consists of the following assets, with different values as of the indicated dates:

Asset	Date of Death	Six months after Date of Death
Real Estate	$300,000	$200,000
Stocks	550,000	600,000
Inventory	500,000	510,000
Patent with 5 yrs. to run at death	150,000	135,000

Asset	Date of Death	Six months after Date of Death
Receivables	100,000	80,000
Total	$~~1,600,000~~ 2,600,000	$1,525,000 ~~3,520,000~~

The stocks were distributed to D's sole beneficiary three months after D's death when they were worth $560,000. Dividends of $2,000 on the stock were received by the estate after D's death, but before the stock was distributed. Royalties on the patent of $20,000 were received by the estate in the first six months after D's death. In addition, $20,000 of receivables had been collected in the first six months.

a. Can the personal representative elect to value the estate under § 2032?

b. What would be the impact under § 2032 if (1) D died before the record date for the dividend, and (2) the estate collected an additional $20,000 of receivables during the first six months after D's death?

c. How would the results differ if D died after the record date for the dividend?

[C]   Special Use Valuation: Section 2032A

Code: § 2032A.

Regulations: Treas. Reg. § 20.2032A–3, –4, and –8.

Section 2032A permits the personal representative to elect to value certain "qualified real property" on the basis of its actual use value, rather than its fair market value as determined by its highest and best use. As explained, the section was enacted in 1976, to relieve the burden of estate taxation on cash-poor farmers and other owners of real property.

> The Congress believed that, when land is actually used for farming purposes or in other closely held businesses (both before and after the decedent's death), it is inappropriate to value the land on the basis of its potential "highest and best use" especially since it is desirable to encourage the continued use of property for farming and other small business purposes. Valuation on the basis of highest and best use, rather than actual use, may result in the imposition of substantially higher estate taxes. In some cases, the greater estate tax burden makes continuation of farming, or the closely held business activities, not feasible because the income potential from these activities is insufficient to service extended tax payments or loans obtained to pay the tax. Thus, the heirs may be forced to sell the land for development purposes. Also, where the valuation of land reflects speculation to such a degree that the price of the land does not bear a reasonable relationship to its earning capacity, the Congress believed it unreasonable to require that this "speculative value" be included in an estate with respect to land devoted to farming or closely held businesses.

Joint Committee on Taxation, 94th Cong., 2d Sess., General Explanation of Tax Reform Act of 1976, 537 (1976).

As enacted and amended over the years, § 2032A specifically targets and limits the benefit of special use valuation to relatively small farmers and businessmen.[19] First, the real property qualifying for the election is limited to that used in farming or in closely held businesses where the decedent or a member of her family materially participated in its operation for a substantial period of time. Second, the real property must constitute a significant portion of the decedent's estate. Third, the maximum amount by which the gross estate may be reduced by the personal representative electing special use valuation § 2032A is $750,000, as adjusted for inflation since 1998. The amount in 2002 is $820,000. Fourth, the recipients must be qualified heirs who must continue the use of the property for a significant period, generally, ten years after the decedent's death. A premature disposition or cessation of use can result in recapturing the estate tax which was lost by invoking the special use valuation.

Comprehensive treatment of § 2032A, the longest statute under Subtitle B of the Code, is beyond the purview of this book. Instead, the discussion focuses on the most important conceptual questions under § 2032A.[20]

The key question is which real property qualifies for the election. Section 2032A(b)(1) requires that at the time of the decedent's death the real property is being used by the decedent or a member of his family for a "qualified use." Section 2032A(b)(2) defines "qualified use" as the devotion of property to "(1) use as a farm for farming purposes as those terms are defined in § 2032A(e)(4), or (2) use in a trade or business other than the trade or business of farming."

Treasury Regulation § 20.2032A–3(b)(1) provides the following guidance on what constitutes a "trade or business" other than farming:

> Under section 2032A, the term trade or business applies only to an active business such as a manufacturing, mercantile, or service enterprise, or to the raising of agricultural or horticultural commodities, as distinguished from passive investment activities. The mere passive rental of property to a party other than a member of the decedent's family will not qualify. The decedent or a member of the decedent's family must own an equity interest in the farm operation. A trade or business is not necessarily present even though an office and regular hours are maintained for management of income producing assets, as the term "business" is not as broad under section 2032A as under section 162 [which applies for income tax purposes].

Also, the decedent or a member of his family must have owned the real property and materially participated in the operation of the farm or other business during five of the eight years before the decedent's death. *See* § 2032A(b)(1)(C). Whether there has been "material participation" is determined by § 1402(a)(1) and Treasury Regulation § 20.2032A–3. The purpose

---

[19] The decedent must also be a United States citizen or resident, and the real property must be located in the United States.

[20] Should you wish to delve further into the area, you should consult more extensive works. *See, e.g.*, Stephen E. Martin, *2032A Special Valuation—Often Overlooked Opportunities,* 29 U. Miami Inst. on Est. Plan., Ch. 19 (1995); Richard B. Stephens et al., Federal Estate and Gift Taxation, ¶ 4.04 (Warren, Gorham & Lamont 7th ed. 1997) (providing over 50 pages of treatment).

of the requirement is, of course, to prevent tax avoidance where the property is not truly an asset of family heritage.

If a qualified use exists, the next question is whether the property represents a significant enough portion of the decedent's estate to qualify for relief. This requires consideration of two statutory tests under § 2032A(b)(1):

(1) Did the adjusted value of real and personal property used in the trade or business constitute 50% of the adjusted value of decedent's gross estate?

(2) If so, did the adjusted value of the qualifying real property constitute 25% of the adjusted value of the decedent's gross estate?

For both tests, the actual fair market value—not the special use value—of the property is determined and then adjusted for unpaid mortgages or other encumbrances. *See* § 2032A(b)(3).

In addition, pursuant to the first sentence of § 2032A(b)(1), the property must pass to the "qualified heirs" of the decedent. A "qualified heir" includes the decedent's spouse, ancestors, lineal descendants (or their spouses), or parents. *See* § 2032A(e)(1), (2). Furthermore, those takers must agree to pay a recapture tax if they fail to continue to use the property for qualifying purposes for the statutorily required time. *See* § 2032A(b)(1)(D).

Section 2032A(c) provides for the recapture of the tax benefits of special use valuation if, within the first ten years after the decedent's death, the qualifying heir makes a lifetime disposition of qualifying real property outside the family, or ceases to use the property for a qualified use. The reason for the recapture rule was explained as follows:

> [T]he Congress recognized that it would be a windfall to the beneficiaries of an estate to allow real property used for farming or closely held business purposes to be valued for estate tax purposes at its farm or business value unless the beneficiaries continue to use the property for farm or business purposes, at least for a reasonable period of time after the decedent's death. Also, the Congress believed that it would be inequitable to discount speculative values if the heirs of the decedent realize these speculative values by selling the property within a short time after the decedent's death.

Joint Committee on Taxation, 94th Cong., 2d Sess., General Explanation of Tax Reform Act of 1976, 537 (1976).

The Taxpayer Relief Act of 1997 extended retroactive relief to the decedent's lineal descendants, so that the rental to an applicable family member on a net cash basis does not constitute the cessation of qualified use. *See* § 2032A(c)(7)(E).

Compliance with the substantive provisions alone is not sufficient to obtain relief. In addition, § 2032A(d) requires the personal representative to make a timely election on the estate tax return,[21] which has been described as a "fairly laborious process."[22] In 1984, and again under the Taxpayer Relief Act

---

[21] A special use valuation election under § 2032A may be made in conjunction with an alternate valuation date election. *See* Rev. Rul. 83–31, 1983–1 C.B. 225.

[22] Estate of McAlpine, Jr. v. Commissioner, 968 F.2d 459, 460 (5th Cir. 1992).

of 1997, Congress liberalized the election requirements. Substantial compliance with the election rule regulations may not be preclusive of special use valuation if the personal representative subsequently furnishes the deficient information or signatures of the qualifying heirs agreeing to pay any recapture tax. *See* § 2032A(d)(3).

Problem

D died with a gross estate of $2 million which included real property that was used by the decedent at his death in a truck farming business. What additional information do you need to determine whether the personal representative can make a special use valuation election under § 2032A? Would it matter if *D* devised the farm to his surviving spouse, a nephew, or to an unrelated person? Would it matter if *D* had rented the farm to a nephew before *D*'s death? What would happen if a valid § 2032A election was made, but seven years after *D*'s death, the nephew, who was the devisee of the property, leased it to *D*'s brother? Would it matter if the nephew sold it to *D*'s brother?

§ 3.04 Deduction Provisions

The taxable estate is determined by reducing the value of the gross estate by various deductions. There are six types of deductions recognized in the Code: (1) § 2053 allows the deduction of valid claims, and the expenses of administration; (2) § 2054 relieves the estate tax burden if property is destroyed by casualty during estate administration; (3) § 2055 allows the deduction of some interests passing to charities; (4) § 2056 permits a deduction for most interests in property passing to the surviving spouse; (5) § 2057 allows a deduction, until 2004, for some or all of a decedent's interest in a family owned business; and (6) § 2058 allows to estates of decedents dying after 2004 a deduction for state death taxes. These sections are addressed below.

[A] Section 2053: Expenses and Debts

Code: §§ 2043 and 2053.

Regulations: Treas. Reg. § 20.2053–1(a), (b), (c); –3(a), (b), (c); –4, –7, and –8.

[1] In General

Because the estate tax is imposed on the privilege of passing property at death, its application should logically be limited to that property that gratuitously passes from the decedent to someone else at the decedent's death. A number of factors, however, can make this amount less than the sum of the assets owned (or otherwise includable in the gross estate) by the decedent. Administration of the estate must occur. The personal representative (administrator or executor), the attorneys, and accountants for the estate must be paid for their services. Also, the decedent must be buried (or the body otherwise disposed of), requiring the expenditure of funds. Further, most decedents have creditors at the time of death. These items reduce the assets available for distribution. Their deduction is allowed by § 2053. This section provides a deduction for administration expenses, funeral expenses, claims against the estate, and unpaid mortgages. The deductions under §§ 2053 and 2054 reflect that it is appropriate to tax only the decedent's net wealth, not the decedent's gross assets.

[2] Administration Expenses

Administration expenses include all of the expenses commonly associated with the administration of an estate, such as personal representative's commissions, attorneys' fees, surrogate's fees, appraiser's fees, and expenses for selling property.[23]

Estate of Smith v. Commissioner

510 F.2d 479 (2d Cir. 1975)
cert. denied sub. nom. Lowe v. Commissioner
423 U.S. 827 (1975)

Robert P. Anderson, Circuit Judge:

David Smith, a sculptor, died on May 23, 1965 possessed of 425 pieces of sculpture, which he had created, along with cash and other liquid assets totalling $210,647.08 . . . .

Had the large number of artistic works which he left at his death been generally known and had all of these works been immediately placed on the market they would have brought substantially less than could be received by feeding them slowly into the market over a period of time. Shortly after Smith's death, therefore, the executors began an orderly process of gradual liquidation of the Estate's holdings of sculpture through Marlborough-Gerson Galleries, which was entitled to a commission on each piece of sculpture sold in accordance with a 1963 contract that was subsequently renewed by the executors in 1968 and 1970.

. . .

From the time of Smith's death to August 21, 1973, the executors paid to the Galleries, with the approval of the Surrogate's Court, the total sum of $1,583,544.67 in commissions for sales of Smith's works, but the Tax Court allowed the Estate only $750,447.74 as deductions for sales commissions under section 2053(a) of the Internal Revenue Code . . . (26 U.S.C. § 2053(a)) and Treas. Reg. section 20.2053–3. This allowance was the exact amount necessary to pay the decedent's debts, the expenses of administration, and taxes as finally adjudicated.

---

[23] The personal representative may elect to deduct administration expenses, but not funeral expenses, against the estate's income tax, rather than against the estate tax. *See* § 642(g). This would normally be done if the estate were estate-tax-free, or if the income tax marginal rate were higher. *See* Treas. Reg. § 20.2053–3. Also included is interest on federal and state death taxes if that interest is allowable as an administration expense under applicable state law. *See* Rev. Rul. 81–256, 1981–2 C.B. 183; Rev. Rul. 79–252, 1979–2 C.B. 333.

. . .

Both section 222 of the New York Surrogate's Court Act [now 11-1.1 of the Estates, Powers and Trusts Law] and Treas. Reg. section 20.2053-3, like most state laws concerning executors and administrators, require an administrative expense to be "necessary" in order to be allowable. *See* 31 Am. Jur. 2d *Executors and Administrators* §§ 524, 527 (1967); *In re Rosenberg's Estate*, 169 Misc. 92, 6 N.Y.S.2d 1009, 1012–1013 (Sur. Ct. 1938). Normally, therefore, a Surrogate's court decree approving expenditures by an executor as proper administrative expenses under New York law will be controlling and will not raise questions concerning possible discrepancies between section 2053 of the Internal Revenue Code . . . and Treas. Reg. section 20.2053-3(d)(2). *See* Treas. Reg. section 20.2053-1(b)(2) ("The decision of a local court as to the amount and allowability under local law of a claim or administration expense will ordinarily be accepted if the court passes upon the facts upon which deductibility depends"); *Dulles v. Johnson*, 273 F.2d 362 (2d Cir. 1959), *cert. den.*, 364 U.S. 834 (1960); *Sussman v. United States*, 236 F. Supp. 507 (E.D.N.Y. 1962).

As noted in *Pitner v. United States*, 388 F.2d 651, 659 (5th Cir. 1967), however, the interest of the federal government in taxing the passage of property from a decedent's estate to individual beneficiaries or to a trustee will not always completely or accurately be reflected in a state's interests in supervising the fiduciary responsibilities of executors. In the present case, appellants' claims for administration expenses were not contested in the Surrogate's Court and there is some question as to whether some of these expenses were in fact incurred for the benefit of the estate in accordance with the general purpose of section 2053 rather than for the benefit of individual beneficiaries. *See Commercial Nat. Bank of Charlotte v. United States*, 196 F.2d 182, 183–184 (4th Cir. 1952); *cf. United States v. Stapf*, 375 U.S. 118, 130–131 (1963), *reh'g denied*, 375 U.S. 981 (1964). In such circumstances, the federal courts cannot be precluded from reexamining a lower state court's allowance of administration expenses[24] to determine whether they were in fact necessary to carry out the administration of the estate or merely prudent or advisable in preserving the interests of the beneficiaries. *Cf. Commissioner v. Estate of Bosch*, 387 U.S. 456 (1967); *Commercial Nat. Bank of Charlotte*

---

[24] Such administrative expenses must be the "type intended to be deductible" (United States v. Stapf, 375 U.S. 118, 130 (1964)), ultimately a question of Federal law. *See* Pitner v. United States, 388 F.2d 651 (5th Cir. 1967). The holding in *Pitner* differs from the interpretation placed upon it by Judge Mulligan in his dissent. The court in that case assumed that the expense deduction was allowable by the laws of the jurisdiction under which the estate was being administered, and yet held that:

[i]n the determination of deductibility under section 2053(a)(2), it is not enough that the deduction be allowable under state law. It is necessary as well that the deduction be for an "administration expense" within the meaning of that term as it is used in the statute, and that the amount sought to be deducted be reasonable under the circumstances. These are both questions of Federal law and establish the outside limits for what may be considered allowable deductions under section 2053(a)(2).

388 F.2d at 659.

Thus, the Fifth Circuit, as well as the Tax Court, have rejected the proposition that the only requirement for deductibility under § 2053(a) is the allowability of the expense under state law.

v. United States, 196 F.2d 182, 185 (4th Cir. 1952); Treas. Reg. § 20.2053–1(b)(2). Viewed from this standpoint, the Tax Court's determination that the additional sales of sculpture were not necessary to preserve the estate or to effect its distribution did not involve a refusal to follow New York law, but rather was the result of a de novo inquiry into the factual necessity for these expenditures.

It is, therefore, unnecessary to pass on whether Treasury Regulation section 20.2053–3(d)(2) is invalid if read to deny a deduction properly allowed by state law. As the determination of the Tax Court is not clearly erroneous, it is affirmed.

Mulligan, Circuit Judge (dissenting):

I dissent with respect but without reluctance. Section 2053(a) of the Internal Revenue Code provides that in determining a decedent's taxable estate there shall be a deduction from the gross estate of

> such amounts . . . for administration expenses . . . as are allowable by the laws of the jurisdiction, whether within or without the United States, under which the estate is being administered.

The estate here was administered in the State of New York and the selling commissions at issue here were held to be allowable as proper expenses by the Surrogate of Warren County in several separate accountings. The Code unambiguously provides for their deduction if allowed by the jurisdiction administering the estate and neither the Commissioner of Internal Revenue nor the Tax Court, in my view, can properly reverse the State Court determination. Congress has explicitly left the matter in the hands of the state.

In a case squarely in point, the Sixth Circuit reversed the Tax Court's denial of deductibility, stating:

> By the literal language of section 2053(a), Congress has left the deductibility of administrative expenses to be governed by their chargeability against the assets of the estate under state law. As otherwise stated, Congress has committed to the considered judgment of the states whether a particular expense is allowable as a proper or necessary charge against estate assets. In the situation before us, the expenses were admittedly allowable under Michigan law. They were paid out of probate assets and they were approved in two different accountings filed with the probate court. Hence, they are deductible under section 2053(a).

. . .

Since I believe there was a failure to recognize the command of the Code, I would characterize the error here as one of law and not of fact, which would make the "clearly erroneous" test set by the majority inapplicable. . . .

———

On the question raised in the principal case, whether "allowable" expenses are to be defined purely by local law or by the federal courts, there is a diversity of opinion. The Seventh Circuit has held that it is sufficient that local law allows the expense. *See Ballance v. Commissioner*, 347 F.2d 419 (7th Cir. 1965). Until 1997, the Sixth Circuit was aligned with the Seventh Circuit. *See Estate of Millikin v. Commissioner*, 125 F.3d 339 (6th Cir. 1997) (overruling *Park v. Commissioner*, 475 F.2d 673 (6th Cir. 1973)).

In *United States v. White*, 650 F. Supp. 904 (W.D.N.Y. 1987), the district court held the probate court's determination that a particular expense is necessary is subject to Service review if the Service shows that the probate court failed to pass on the factors on which deductibility depends. In reversing the district court, the appellate court (853 F.2d 107 (2d Cir. 1988)) stated that there is nothing in the wording of § 2053, its Regulations, or its legislative history that would preclude the Service from independently evaluating the factors governing deductibility using state law. The issue, as viewed by the Second Circuit, was not a matter of federal versus state law, but one of interpretation of state law. After granting certiorari, 489 U.S. 1051 (1989), the Supreme Court, in a *per curiam* decision, 110 S. Ct. 273 (1989), dismissed a writ of certiorari as "improvidently granted," thereby allowing to stand the Second Circuit decision supporting the Service's authority to investigate an estate's legal fees and personal representative's commissions for federal estate tax purposes, despite a state probate court's approval of these expenses.

According to the Second Circuit, Congress did not intend for § 2053 to make state trial court decrees determinative of federal deductibility without federal inquiry. Thus, the Service may make its own assessment of the validity of administration expenses under applicable state law as determined by the state's highest court. *See also Estate of Love v. Commissioner*, 923 F.2d 335 (4th Cir. 1991) (federal law controlled whether a payment made by the decedent's estate, pursuant to a foal-sharing agreement the decedent had executed as part of her horse breeding business, was deductible as an administration expense for estate tax purposes). *See, e.g., Marcus v. DeWitt*, 704 F.2d 1227 (11th Cir. 1983). *Smith* was distinguished by the Tax Court in *Estate of Vatter v. Commissioner*, 65 T.C. 633 (1975), on the ground that the will in *Vatter* gave the executor the power to sell the real estate which he sold, while in *Smith* the proceeds from the statues were to be placed in a testamentary trust. *See generally*, Paul L. Caron, *Must an Administration Expense Allowed by State Law Also Meet a Federal Necessity Test?* 70 J. Tax'n 352 (June 1989).

The necessity of the asserted expenses or payment continues to trouble the Service and the courts. Often, bequests and other distributions attempt to masquerade as expenses. For example, in *Estate of Suzuki v. Commissioner*, T.C. Memo 1991–624, the court rejected an expense deduction for payments made to the decedent's husband pursuant to an agreement between the decedent's husband and son. The husband agreed not to contest inter vivos trusts established by the mother, in return for the payments for which the deduction was claimed.

In addition to permitting a deduction for expenses related to the administration of a decedent's estate, an estate may deduct administration expenses in connection with property includable in the gross estate, but not subject to probate. *See* § 2053(b); Treas. Reg. § 20.2053–8. Such expenses might include, for example, attorneys' fees and trustees' commissions for distributing the corpus of a revocable living trust which was includable in the decedent's gross estate under § 2038. Treasury Regulation § 20.2053–1(a)(2) provides that the expenses in this second category are deductible if they would have been deductible had the property been subject to creditors' claims. The expense must be paid within the time period for assessing taxes in the estate under § 6501. This period is typically three years and nine months, unless an extension to file is granted. *See* § 2053(b).

Problems

1. In *Estate of Smith, supra*, could the expenses disallowed by the court as estate tax deductions be taken by the estate or its beneficiaries as deductions for income tax purposes against the income generated by the sale of the paintings? Consider §§ 162 and 212.

2. Local law allows the family of the decedent to pay creditors and distribute the decedent's property without formal administration. In doing this, the family incurred attorneys' fees and other costs. Are those fees and costs deductible? *See Pitner v. United States*, 388 F.2d 651 (5th Cir. 1967) (applying Texas law).

[3] Funeral Expenses

The estate may deduct reasonable funeral expenses if local law allows. *See* Treas. Reg. § 20.2053–2. A bequest for the perpetual care of the decedent's burial lot may be eligible for the funeral expense deduction, provided the bequest is permitted by local law, and the decedent is buried there. *See* Rev. Rul. 57–530, 1957–2 C.B. 621.

[4] Claims and Mortgages

An estate may deduct enforceable claims against the estate that represent personal obligations of the decedent at his death (§ 2053(a)(3)) and mortgages on property included in the gross estate (§ 2053(a)(4)), subject to a number of limitations. First, of course, the claim or mortgage must be allowed under local law. Otherwise, its payment would be in the nature of a gift.

In addition, if the claim, mortgage, or indebtedness is founded on a promise or agreement, deductibility generally requires that the liability be a bona fide contract for full and adequate consideration in money or money's worth.[25] This prevents the deduction for claims from substituting for bequests as discussed in greater detail below.

Common types of claims are contract debts, expenses of the last illness,[26] unpaid taxes and assessments, and tort liability claims.

---

[25] An exception to this requirement is that a charitable pledge may be deducted if it would have been deductible under § 2055 and the decedent had bequeathed, rather than pledged, the donation.

[26] The personal representative has the option to deduct certain medical bills on either the decedent's final income tax return or on the estate tax return. *See* § 213(c). The Service has ruled that the disallowed portion of medical care expenses (the portion that does not exceed 7½% of

Example 1: The decent obtained an unsecured bank loan which had an unpaid balance of $10,000 at death. In addition, the decedent, a single person, owed a total of $5,000 for federal and state income taxes.

The claim of $10,000 is deductible because the decedent contracted the liability for full consideration and the claim is enforceable against the estate. Similarly, the amount of unpaid income taxes is a valid claim and deductible. Thus, the combined amount of $15,000 is deductible in computing the decedent's taxable estate.

———

Estate of O'Neal v. United States

258 F.3d 1265 (11th Cir. 2001)

HILL, Circuit Judge:

I. FACTUAL BACKGROUND

[Mrs. O'Neal and her husband were minority shareholders in O'Neal Steel, Inc., a closely-held family corporation. In 1987, the O'Neals gave all their stock to their children and grandchildren. Mr. O'Neal died approximately nine months after the gifts were made. Mrs. O'Neal paid $810,000 in gift taxes with a timely filed return. The statute of limitations expired to assess additional gift taxes against Mr. and Mrs. O'Neal. Relying on tranferee liability nevertheless, the government asserted a liability against the donees for an additional $9,407,226 in gift taxes allegedly due by Mrs. O'Neal. (Under transferee liability, the government has an extra year to assess a tax.) A similar assertion was made on account of Mr. O'Neal's gifts. Mrs. O'Neal died in July 1994. Her timely filed estate tax return reflected no estate taxes due on a negative taxable estate. The negative value resulted from a $9,407,226 deduction taken for "claims for reimbursement of transfer gift tax liability by donees of 1987 gifts." The estate claimed the deduction using the government's per share stock values and proposed transferee tax liability. More than nine months after Mrs. O'Neal's death, the donees and the government settled the gift tax controversy. The parties agreed that the donees had a transferee liability of $487,814 for gift taxes, plus interest. Thereafter, the probate court ruled that the donees' claims were valid and enforceable and they were reimbursed $563,314 from the estate.]

. . .

---

adjusted gross income for income tax purposes) cannot be deducted for estate tax purposes. *See* Rev. Rul. 77–357, 1977–2 C.B. 328. The personal representative's decision should be based on the relative tax savings under the two taxes. Because of a lower top marginal bracket for income tax purposes (nominally 38.6% in 2002) as compared to a top rate percent for estate tax purposes (50% in 2002), the personal representative may decide to deduct medical care expenses for estate tax purposes.

IV. DISCUSSION

A. Section 2053(a)(3)—Claims Against the Estate

1. In General

. . . For purposes of this appeal, the relevant deductions are found in subsection (a)(3) of Section 2053 for "claims against the estate." 26 U.S.C. 2053(a)(3). The statute is silent regarding the date for valuing claims against the estate. [Footnote omitted.] In general, the amounts that may be deducted as claims against a decedent's estate are such only as represent personal obligations of the decedent existing at the time of his or her death, whether or not then matured. Treas. Reg. § 20.2053-4. [Footnote omitted.] However, the regulations go on to state that a deduction will be allowed for a claim against the estate even "though its exact amount is not then known, provided it is ascertainable with reasonable certainty, and will be paid." Treas. Reg. § 20.2053-1(b)(3).

2. Contentions of the Parties

Here there is no dispute that the estate is entitled to a deduction with respect to claims against the estate by the nine heirs for reimbursement of their transferee gift tax liability on the 1987 gifts of stock by Mrs. O'Neal. [Footnote omitted.] As to the amount of the deduction, the estate argues that we must ignore the tax court settlement made by the grandchildren donees nine months after Mrs. O'Neal's death and instead use the $9,407,226 demand amount asserted by the government in its own statutory notices of deficiency. The government contends that the tax court settlement figure of $563,314, as found by the district court and approved by the probate court, is the proper amount of the deduction as it represents the actual amount of taxes ultimately paid.

3. The Split Among the Circuits

How do we value this deduction for a claim against the estate? Do we take a valuation snapshot on the day Mrs. O'Neal died? Or, do we consider events occurring after her death, such as the tax court settlement between the grandchildren donees and the government? These questions reflect the dilemma where a valid, enforceable claim may exist at the time of the decedent's death, but subsequent events may relieve the estate of all or a portion of its liability for the claim. [Footnote omitted.] In this context, two distinct and irreconcilable lines of cases have been spawned.

There are those circuits that strictly follow the 1929 Supreme Court decision in *Ithaca Trust Co. v. United States*, 279 U.S. 151, 49 S.Ct. 291, 73 L.Ed. 647 (1929), and its general rule that post-death events must not be considered in valuing the amount of the deduction, as "[t]he estate so far as may be is settled as of the date of the testator's death." [Footnote omitted.] And, there are those that follow the 1929 Eighth Circuit decision in *Jacobs v. Commissioner*, 34 F.2d 233 (8th Cir.1929), *cert. denied*, 280 U.S. 603, 50 S.Ct. 85, 74 L.Ed. 647 (1929), and its approach that post-death events must be considered, as "[t]he claims which Congress intended to be deducted were actual claims, not theoretical ones." [Footnote omitted.]

We prefer to follow the analysis used by the Supreme Court in *Ithaca Trust*, 49 S.Ct. at 291. [Footnote omitted.] In *Ithaca Trust*, the decedent bequeathed property to charity and reserved a life estate in his spouse. The widow died six months after her husband died, but before his estate tax return was filed.

The question presented was whether the charitable deduction should be calculated using the actuarial value of the widow's life expectancy at the date of her husband's death (a decrease in value), or calculated by using the actual and known date of her death (an increase in value). The Supreme Court concluded that the charitable deduction had to be valued based on the wife's probable life expectancy as of her husband's date of death rather than the known fact that she died only six months after her husband.

Cited many times, Justice Holmes, writing for a unanimous court, reasoned:

> The first impression is that it is absurd to resort to statistical probabilities when you know the fact. But this is due to inaccurate thinking. The estate so far as may be is settled as of the date of the testator's death. . . . The tax is on the act of the testator not on the receipt of property by the legatees. . . . Therefore, the value of the thing to be taxed must be estimated as of the time when the act is done. But the value of property at a given time depends upon the relative intensity of the social desire for it at that time, expressed in the money that it would bring in the market. . . . Like all values, as the word is used by the law, it depends largely on more or less certain prophecies of the future, and the value is no less real at that time if later the prophecy turns out false than when it comes out true. . . . Tempting as it is to correct uncertain probabilities by the now certain fact, we are of opinion that it cannot be done, but that the value of the wife's life interest must be estimated by the mortality tables.

49 S.Ct. at 291-292. [Footnote omitted.]

We therefore align ourselves with the more persuasive and better-reasoned opinions of those circuits that follow *Ithaca Trust*. [Footnote omitted.] Our case is very similar to *Estate of Smith v. Commissioner*, 198 F.3d 515 (5th Cir.1999) and *Estate of McMorris v. Commissioner*, 243 F.3d 1254 (10th Cir.2001).

In the *Estate of Smith* case, Exxon Corporation sued Ms. Smith to recoup an alleged overpayment of oil and gas lease royalties. In November 1990, Ms. Smith died, while Exxon's motion for summary judgment was pending. Three months later the district court granted summary judgment for Exxon and referred the calculation of damages to a special master. Exxon claimed it was owed $2,482,719 by the estate. *Estate of Smith*, 198 F.3d at 519.

Ms. Smith's estate tax return was filed in July 1991, eight months after her death, five months after the summary judgment in Exxon's favor, yet before the final calculation of damages by the special master. Her estate tax return included a Section 2053(a)(3) deduction of $2,482,719 for Exxon's demand claim against the estate. In March 1992, fifteen months after Ms. Smith's death and nine months after her estate tax return had been filed, the estate settled with Exxon for $681,840, an amount equal to only 27.5% of the Section 2053(a)(3) deduction claimed originally. *Id.*

The government assessed a deficiency against the estate, arguing that the Section 2053(a)(3) deduction should be limited to the amount actually paid. Relying on *Ithaca Trust*, the Fifth Circuit held that the post-death settlement event could not be considered in determining the amount of the deduction:

> [W]e hold that the claim generating the estate tax deduction under [Section] 2053(a)(3) . . . must be valued as of the date of the death of the decedent and thus must appraised [sic] on information known or available up to (but not after) that date. We therefore vacate and remand with instructions to the Tax Court that it admit and consider evidence of pre-death facts and occurrences that are relevant to the date-of-death value of Exxon's claim, without admitting or considering post-death facts and occurrences such as the Estate's settlement with Exxon, which occurred some fifteen months after Decedent's death.

Id. at 517-18.

Similarly, in *Estate of McMorris*, Mr. McMorris died in 1990 owning 13.4 shares of stock in NW Transport Service, Inc. The stock was listed on Mr. McMorris' estate tax return at an appraised value of $1,726,562 per share at the date of his death. The shares passed to Mrs. McMorris, and this price per share value became her basis in the stock. Mrs. McMorris then entered into an agreement with NW Transport to redeem the stock for $2,200,000 per share, payable over 120 months at ten percent interest. *Estate of McMorris*, 243 F.3d at 1256.

Mrs. McMorris died in 1991. On her federal estate tax return, her estate claimed Section 2053(a)(3) deductions of $3,960,525 for her 1991 federal individual income taxes, and $641,222 for her 1991 state individual income taxes. Both tax liabilities resulted largely from the gain generated by the NW Transport stock redemption. Id. In 1994, the government issued a notice of deficiency to Mr. McMorris' estate, claiming that the value of the NW Transport stock was $3,618,040 per share, not the $1,726,562 per share claimed on his estate tax return. Mr. McMorris' estate contested the determination and, in 1996, after lengthy negotiations, the parties settled, meeting almost halfway at $2,500,00 per share. This value then became the new basis for the stock redeemed by Mrs. McMorris. Due to her increased basis, the taxable gain generated by the redemption was eliminated and she realized a loss. *Id.*

In January 1996, Mrs. McMorris' estate filed an amended 1991 individual federal income tax return seeking a refund of $3,332,443. [Footnote omitted.] It did not, however, file an amended estate tax return decreasing the amount of the Section 2053(a)(3) deduction originally claimed for federal and state income taxes.

By this time, Mrs. McMorris' estate was already embroiled in tax court litigation with the government on unrelated issues. The estate's filing of an amended income tax return, but not an amended estate tax return, caused the government to react. It filed an amended answer in tax court, claiming that the estate was no longer entitled to such a large Section 2053(a)(3) deduction as the tax liabilities upon which it was based were now subject to a refund. The government argued that the deductions should reflect the per share stock value reached in the 1996 settlement between Mr. McMorris' estate and the government, not the 1991 per share appraised value at Mr. McMorris' date of date. The tax court agreed. *Id.* at 1257.

Relying upon *Ithaca Trust*, the Tenth Circuit reversed the tax court and held that the 1996 post-death settlement event could not be considered in determining the amount of the deduction. It remanded with directions to "*vacate* the determination of the estate tax deficiency at issue [based on the settlement value] and to recalculate any remaining *unrelated* deficiencies owing." *Id.* at 1263 (emphasis added). As the *Estate of McMorris* date of death value was already established, the Section 2053(a)(3) deduction stood as originally filed; it was unnecessary for the Tenth Circuit to request a recalculation upon remand. *Id.*

By contrast, in *Estate of Smith*, the date of death value was not established when the Fifth Circuit chose to follow *Ithaca Trust* and disregard post-death events. *Estate of Smith*, 198 F.3d at 526. The date of death value was unknown. The amount claimed by Ms. Smith's estate to be the date of death value was only the litigation demand amount being made by Exxon at her date of death. It was therefore necessary for the Fifth Circuit to request a recalculation upon remand. *Id.*

We face a similar situation here. We conclude that the Section 2053(a)(3) deduction should be the value at Mrs. O'Neal's date of death. We still, however, do not know what that value is. As in *Estate of Smith*, it is not necessarily the amount of the demand being made by the government at Mrs. O'Neal's death. Like the Fifth Circuit, we must remand this case to the district court for a recalculation of the deduction. *Id; see also Estate of Van Horne v. Commissioner*, 720 F.2d 1114 (9th Cir.1983) (date of death valuation for spousal support obligation); *Propstra v. United States*, 680 F.2d 1248 (9th Cir.1982) (date of death valuation for encumbered real estate where "as a matter of law, when claims are for sums certain and are legally enforceable as of the date of death, post-death events are not relevant in computing the permissible deduction").

4. The Proper Valuation in this Case

Based upon the foregoing discussion, we find that the district court erred when it considered the post-death tax court settlement amount of $563,314 determined some nine months after Mrs. O'Neal's death in calculating the value of the estate's Section 2053(a)(3) deduction. Yet, conversely, we find that no case holds that the value at the date of death is the demand amount, $9,407,226, being made here by the government at the date of death. *See, e.g., Estate of Smith*, 198 F.3d at 519. We therefore vacate the opinion of the district court on this issue and remand for evidentiary hearing on valuation.

On remand, the district court is instructed neither to admit nor consider evidence of post-death occurrences when determining the date of death value of the Section 2053(a)(3) deduction. *Id.* at 526. It will be incumbent on each party to supply the district court with relevant evidence of pre-death facts and occurrences supporting the date of death value of the deduction as advocated by that party. *Id.* The district court will then, by using informed judgment, reasonableness and common sense, weighing all relevant facts and evaluating their aggregate significance, determine a sound valuation. [Footnote omitted] *See* Revenue Ruling, 1959-1 C.B. 237, Rev. Rul. 59-60 (1959). . . .

V. CONCLUSION

As to the central issue on appeal, we conclude that the value of the deduction claimed by the estate for claims against the estate under Section 2053(a)(3) must be valued as of the date of the decedent's death. All events occurring after the decedent's death that alter the value must be disregarded. That part of the district court order considering post-death events in limiting the amount of the deduction is vacated. This issue is remanded to the district court for an evidentiary hearing with instructions to value the deduction at the date of death.

AFFIRMED in PART; VACATED in PART; and REMANDED with INSTRUCTIONS.

The deduction for unpaid mortgages and other indebtedness turns on whether the estate is liable for the debt. *See* Treas. Reg. § 20.2053–7. If the estate is liable, the mortgage or debt is deductible, but the entire value of the property subject to the encumbrance is included in the gross estate. If the estate is not liable, perhaps as a result of nonrecourse borrowing, the mortgage is not deductible. Only the net value of the property is includable in the gross estate.

Example 2: The decedent owned a residence with an unpaid mortgage of $40,000 upon which the decedent was personally liable. The residence had a value of $100,000 at the decedent's death. He also owned a piece of investment property worth $500,000, upon which he had borrowed $200,000 without personal liability.

Because of decedent's personal liability on the residence debt, his gross estate includes the $100,000 value, but is entitled to a $40,000 deduction under § 2053. Conversely, the estate only includes $300,000 in the gross estate as a result of the investment property, but is not entitled to a deduction for the mortgage debt.[27]

The deduction for taxes is the subject of express regulation. *See* Treas. Reg. § 20.2053–6. Deductible taxes may include property taxes that have accrued before the decedent's death, plus unpaid income and gift taxes. Consistent with § 2053(c)(1)(B), deductions are not allowed for income taxes on income received after the decedent's death or for death taxes.[28]

---

[27] For income tax purposes, a beneficiary's income tax basis in property subject to a mortgage includes the amount of the indebtedness. *See* Crane v. Commissioner, 331 U.S. 1 (1947). Therefore, the basis of the investment property would be $500,000, and the basis for the residence would be $100,000.

[28] Note, however, that in unusual cases a deduction for state and foreign death taxes may be allowed if the benefit of the tax reduction inures to the benefit of a charity. This allowance, prescribed by § 2053(d), *as amplified by* Treasury Regulation § 20.2053–9, is beyond the scope of this book.

When the claims against a decedent's estate and the expenses of administration exceed the value of the property subject to claims, Treasury Regulation § 20.2053–1(c) limits the § 2053 deduction to the value of the property subject to claims, plus the amount actually paid from property not subject to claims within the nine months of the decedent's death. However, in *Estate of Snyder v. United States*, 84 A.F.TR.2d 99-5963 (1999), the Court of Federal Claims refused to limit a deduction for environmental clean-up costs when those costs exceeded the value of the decedent's probate estate. Before his death, the decedent transferred most of his assets to a revocable trust that became irrevocable upon his death.

Problems

1. Local law requires that claims against the estate be filed with the probate court within three months after publication to creditors, but allows the personal representative to pay untimely claims in the personal representative's discretion. A claim was filed beyond the time set by statute, but the personal representative did not contest it. Can it be deducted under § 2053? *Compare Estate of McDowell*, T.C. Memo 1986–27, *following Estate of Van Horne v. Commissioner*, 78 T.C. 728 (1982), *aff'd* 720 F.2d 1114 (9th Cir. 1983), *and Propstra v. United States*, 680 F.2d 1248 (9th Cir. 1982), *with Estate of Hagmann v. Commissioner*, 60 T.C. 465 (1973), *aff'd* 492 F.2d 796 (5th Cir. 1974).

2. Decedent agreed to pay his ex-spouse $1,000 per month for her life. How would the ex-spouse's death six months after the decedent affect the deduction? *Compare Estate of Van Horne v. Commissioner*, 78 T.C. 728 (1982), *aff'd* 720 F.2d 1114 (9th Cir. 1983), *cert. denied*, 466 U.S. 980 (1984), *with Estate of Chesterton v. United States*, 551 F.2d 278 (Ct. Cl.), *cert. denied*, 434 U.S. 96 (1977).

3. Decedent and his unmarried cohabitant had a written agreement to share expenses and assets. At his death, decedent left property, otherwise includable in the gross estate, to the cohabitant. Are the amounts deductible under § 2053? *See United States v. Carlson*, U.S.T.C. ¶ 13,570 (D. Minn. 1983); Andrew R. Lee, *Estate and Disposition Planning Issues for Same-Sex or Unmarried Couples*, 141 Tr. & Est. 51 (2002).

4. Before she died, the decedent borrowed $100,000 from XYZ, Inc. She owned 50% of the corporation. The decedent's son was the sole beneficiary of the decedent's will and owned the remaining 50% of XYZ. Because he was the sole beneficiary of the estate, the decedent's son did not file on behalf of the corporation against the decedent's estate within the four months claim statute of limitations. Can the estate deduct the $100,000 as a debt owed by the decedent?

5. Shortly before his death, *D* purchased 100 shares of stock on margin for $10,000. The stock was selling for $100 per share. *D* paid his broker $8,000 cash and received a $2,000 loan from the broker. His broker retained the stock as security for the loan. A few days later, when the stock was selling for $85 per share, *D* died without having paid the loan. Will *D*'s estate have to include this stock in the gross estate, and if so, at what value? *Consider* Treas. Reg. § 20.2031–2(g).

[5] Consideration Requirement

When a claim, an unpaid mortgage, or any other debt of the estate is based on a promise or agreement, the estate must show that the liability was incurred for full and adequate consideration in money or money's worth. *See* § 2053(c)(1)(A). If this were not required, property owners could easily avoid the estate tax by contracting for love and affection or other sufficient, but non-monetary, consideration to leave property to their loved ones.

Under § 2043, a relinquishment of marital rights arising at death does not constitute consideration in money or money's worth. Thus, a claim against the estate, based on the decedent's antenuptial promise to leave his spouse money, would not be deductible if the claim is based on the spouse's relinquishment of elective share rights. *See Estate of Hermann v. Commissioner*, 85 F.3d 1032 (2d Cir. 1996). On the other hand, if the spouse relinquished other rights, for example her share in community income, valid consideration may be found. *See Estate of Carli v. Commissioner*, 84 T.C. 649 (1985). Similarly, the effective release of the right to support constitutes consideration in money or money's worth for purposes of § 2053. *See, e.g, Estate of Kosow*, 45 F.3d 1524 (11th Cir. 1995); Rev. Rul. 77–314, 1977–2 C.B. 349. If, however, support rights cannot be released under local law, the result would be different. *See Natchez v. United States*, 705 F.2d 671 (2d Cir. 1983) (applying New York law to a provision in a separation agreement that released support rights).

Marital dissolution arrangements can have significant estate tax consequences. If any part of the obligations of the property settlement remain unpaid at the death of the obligor spouse, the surviving ex-spouse usually will file a claim against, and collect from, the estate of the obligor. The question thus arises whether the claim will qualify for a deduction from the gross estate under § 2053. Assuming the claim is valid, the answer depends, in part, on when the decedent died and, in part, on the nature of the agreement. If the decedent died before July 19, 1984, the agreement had to have been incorporated in the divorce decree for the claim to be deductible. Before that date, § 2043 did not treat any release of marital rights pursuant to agreement to be for consideration.[29] The express language of § 2053(c)(1)(A) generally limits application of the section to claims based upon a "promise or agreement," and requires that they be supported by consideration in money or money's worth. Section 2043(b) provides that, for the purposes of the estate tax, the release of marital rights generally does not constitute consideration in money or money's worth. Thus, a claim based solely upon a property settlement agreement releasing marital rights would not qualify for deduction.

Since July 18, 1984, § 2043(b)(2) has treated a claim based on an agreement as deductible if the agreement was excused from gift taxation by § 2516, discussed at § 4.01[B][2], *infra*. Since that date, agreements which do not satisfy the gift tax test presumably must still be incorporated into the divorce decree if claims under them are to be deductible for estate tax purposes.

---

[29] The "divorce decree" exception was created by the Supreme Court in Harris v. Commissioner, 340 U.S. 106 (1950) (reproduced in Chapter 4 at § 4.01[B][2], *infra*), which held that, for gift tax purposes, a claim based on a decree was not based on a "promise or agreement," and therefore, not subject to the gift tax. This exception applies as well to the claims under § 2053(c). *See* Rev. Rul. 60–160, 1960–1 C.B. 374.

[6] Settlement of Claims

If a claim or mortgage is deductible, payments in settlement of the item are deductible. *See* Treas. Reg. § 20.2053–1(b)(2). Conversely, payments in settlement of claims not supported by consideration are not deductible. *See, e.g., Bank of New York v. United States*, 526 F.2d 1012 (3d Cir. 1975).

A decedent's estate is not entitled to deduct a payment made in settlement of a contest involving the decedent's will because the payment does not fall into any of the various categories of deductible expenses under § 2053. In *Estate of Moore v. Commissioner*, T.C. Memo 1987–587, for example, a $40,000 payment to decedent's brother who contested decedent's will was held to constitute a nondeductible claim. In effect, the $40,000 was treated as a bequest to a beneficiary.

Problems

1. The decedent promised to leave his heirs property under his will, but he failed to do so. Had he in fact left the heirs the promised property, it would have been subject to estate taxation. If the heirs litigate and settle the claim with the personal representative, are the amounts paid in settlement deductible? *See* §§ 2043(a), 2053(a), (c)(1)(A); *Estate of Morse v. Commissioner*, T.C.Memo. 1987-587; *Estate of Luce v. United States*, 444 F. Supp. 347 (W.D. Mo. 1977).

[7] Community Property

State specific community property rules may affect whether administration expenses and claims will be deductible under § 2053. For example, because the survivor's one-half share is not chargeable with funeral expenses in California, New Mexico, and Texas, deduction of the entire funeral expense should be allowable under § 2053. *See* Rev. Rul. 71–168, 1971–1 C.B. 271. Deductions for administration expenses depend on whether the survivor's share is subject to administration. If the share is subject to administration, only one-half of the administration expenses would likely be deductible. *See Lang's Estate v. Commissioner*, 97 F.2d 867 (9th Cir. 1938) (Washington law). *But see Stapf*, § 3.04[C][5] *infra* (under applicable Texas law, the surviving spouse was charged with 35% of the expenses). On the other hand, if the surviving spouse's share is not subject to administration, as in Nevada, all of the administration expenses should be deductible. Where separate property of the deceased spouse is also being administered, apportionment may be appropriate. *See* Rev. Rul. 66–21, 1966–1 C.B. 219.

The deductibility of claims will depend on the composition of the assets owned by the decedent, as well as the character of the claims. For example, if the decedent only owned community property at death, community debts would be deductible up to one-half of their value. *See Stapf*, § 3.04[C][5] *infra*. On the other hand, if the community property is insufficient to pay a debt incurred by the deceased spouse, the separate property of the deceased spouse subject to the claim is allowed as a deduction. *See Lang's Estate v. Commissioner*, 97 F.2d 867 (9th Cir. 1938).

[B] Section 2054: Casualties

Code: § 2054.

Regulations: None.

Section 2054 allows an estate to deduct fire, storm, theft, shipwreck and casualty losses that occur during the settlement of an estate. This section has not produced significant litigation. Presumably, losses through malfeasance that do not rise (descend) to the level of criminal will not qualify for deduction. *See, e.g., Estate of Shlensky v. Commissioner*, T.C. Memo 1977–148 (defaults of co-executor).

Because theft and casualty losses are deductible from income, the estate may choose to claim the loss for fiduciary income tax purposes in those cases in which it would produce a greater deduction. *See* §§ 642(g), 165(c)(3). However, this election should be unusual because only losses in excess of 10% of adjusted gross income are deductible under § 165(h).

[C] The Estate Tax Marital Deduction

Code: §§ 2056, 2056A, 2044, and 2207A.

Regulations: Treas. Reg. §§ 20.2056(a)–1(a), –1(b), –2(a), –2(b); 20.2056(b)–1, –3, –4(a), –5(a), –5(e), –5(f), –5(g), –7(a), –7(b)(1) and (2), –7(d); 20.2056(c)–1(a); 20.2056A–1, –2; 20.2044–1; and 20.2207A–1.

[1] In General

Under § 2056, most property interests that pass to the surviving spouse may be deducted from the gross estate when calculating the taxable estate. The estate tax marital deduction was originally designed to equalize the favorable treatment available to spouses who owned property as community property. Under community property regimes, the decedent owned only one-half of the community assets, and the surviving spouse the other half. As a result, only one-half of community property was included in the gross estate of the decedent. In contrast, if the propertied spouse died first, all separate property owned at death was included in the decedent's estate.[30]

Initially enacted in 1948, the marital deduction limited a deduction for property passing to the surviving spouse to one-half of the "adjusted gross estate." The latter term was defined as the gross estate minus deductions under §§ 2053 and 2054, with adjustments for community property.[31] In 1976, the maximum deduction was expanded to allow a minimum deduction of $250,000, *i.e.*, a deduction equaling the greater of $250,000 or one-half of the

---

[30] If, however, the non-propertied spouse died first, estate taxation would not occur at the decedent's death because the predeceasing spouse would not have a transmissible ownership interest in the surviving spouse's separate property. In such cases, an estate tax advantage for non-community property existed because one-half of a couple's community property would be subject to estate taxation regardless of which spouse died first.

[31] *See* § 2056(c)(2)(B) (repealed by Pub. L. No. 97–34 § 403(a)(1)(A), 95 Stat. 301); *see generally* Charles L. B. Lowndes et al., Federal Estate and Gift Taxes § 17.3 (3rd ed. 1974).

adjusted gross estate. Finally, the Economic Recovery Tax Act of 1981 (ERTA), removed all quantitative limitations on the marital deduction. [32]

Since 1982, the marital deduction has been unlimited in the sense that any qualified property passing to the surviving spouse can be deducted up to, and including, the entire estate of the decedent. The shift to an unlimited estate tax marital deduction signaled a shift in the rationale for the deduction. According to the legislative history, Congress "believed that a husband and a wife should be treated as one economic unit for purposes of estate and gift taxes, as they generally are for income tax purposes. Accordingly, no tax should be imposed on transfers between a husband and wife." [33] The unlimited marital deduction permits a decedent to pass the entire estate to the surviving spouse free of estate taxes. As to this tax-free portion, the marital deduction defers the payment of the Federal estate tax on the portion of the estate that remains until the death of the survivor.

Understand that adoption of an unlimited marital deduction did not affect the equality of tax treatment given to estates in community and non-community property states. Taxation of all property passing or which passed to the surviving spouse may be deferred in both types of jurisdictions. In non-community states, this is because of the marital deduction alone; in community states, because one-half qualifies for the deduction and one-half is not taxed because it is deemed not to be owned by the decedent under community property laws. [34]

[2]　Marital Deduction Rules

The technical requirements for the estate tax marital deduction under § 2056 are: (1) the decedent must be a U.S. citizen or resident; (2) a surviving spouse must exist; (3) the spouse must be a U.S. citizen; (4) property, or an interest in property, must pass to the surviving spouse from the decedent; (5) the property, or interest in property, transferred to the spouse must be included in the decedent's gross estate; and (6) the surviving spouse must receive a "deductible" interest.

[a]　Surviving Spouse Requirement

Although the term "surviving spouse" is not specifically defined by statute or regulation, the Service defines the term as "a legal status that arises from the termination of a lawful marital union by the death of the other mate." Rev. Rul. 76–155, 1976–1 C.B. 286. In turn, surviving spouse status depends on the applicable state law of the decedent's domicile. *See Estate of Steffke v. Commissioner,* 538 F.2d 730 (7th Cir.), *cert. denied,* 429 U.S. 1022 (1976); Rev. Rul. 67–442, 1967–2 C.B. 65.

When both spouses die simultaneously, local law determines the order of death in the absence of an express provision in the governing document. The

---

[32] Under a transitional rule, an unlimited marital deduction may not be allowed for certain wills and revocable trusts that were executed before September 12, 1981. *See* § 403(e)(2) of ERTA.

[33] Senate Finance Committee, S. Rep. No. 97–144, Economic Recovery Tax Act of 1981, 97th Cong., 1st Sess. 127 (1981).

[34] Separate property of a spouse in a community property state is treated the same way as separate property in a non-community property regime.

statutory presumption normally provided is either that of the original 1940 version or the revised version of the Uniform Simultaneous Death Act (USDA).[35] When death occurs simultaneously, each individual is presumed to have died last with respect to his or her own property; each is presumed to have died last with respect to one-half of all jointly held property; and the insured is presumed to have survived the beneficiary with respect to life insurance. The decedent's will may provide that in the event that the decedent and the spouse die in a common disaster under circumstances in which the order of death cannot be determined, the spouse is deemed to survive. When this happens, the Treasury Regulations permit a marital deduction. *See* Treas. Reg. § 20.2056(e)–2(e).

[b]   Citizenship Requirement

Section 2056(d) denies the estate tax marital deduction for property passing to a surviving spouse who is not a United States citizen. Notwithstanding the disallowance rule of § 2056(d), a marital deduction is permitted for property passing to a non-citizen surviving spouse if the assets are devised to a "qualified domestic trust," often referred to as a Q-DOT. The Q-DOT marital deduction is not a true marital deduction in the same manner provided by § 2056. The value of the Q-DOT property is not included in the surviving spouse's estate. Instead, Q-DOT treatment postpones the estate taxes payable by the estate that claimed a deduction for the Q-DOT.

The Q-DOT rules of § 2056A are complex, but may be summarized. A Q-DOT: (1) must have at least one trustee who is a United States citizen or a domestic corporation; (2) the trust must provide that no corpus distributions be made without the trustee having the right to withhold applicable taxes from the distribution; and (3) the personal representative must file an election to claim a marital deduction for the trust property. Understand that the Q-DOT requirements are in addition to all the other marital deduction requirements when the surviving spouse is a United States citizen. Special rules permit a reformation of a non-qualifying devise to a non-citizen spouse. *See* § 2056(D)(5)(A). Alternatively, the Q-DOT rules do not apply if the surviving spouse becomes a United States citizen by the time the decedent's estate tax return is filed. *See* Treas. Reg. § 20.2056A–1(b). The Taxpayer Relief Act of 1997 added subsection (c)(3) to § 2056A to permit an arrangement that is not a trust, but that has "substantially the same effect as a trust," to qualify as a Q-DOT.

[c]   Passing and Gross Estate Inclusion Requirements

Marital deduction allowance depends on an interest in property passing from the decedent to the surviving spouse. *See* § 2056(a). This passing requirement—effectively the transfer of a property interest to the surviving spouse from the decedent—may be satisfied under several statutory situations enumerated by § 2056(c). Passing includes an interest in property that: (1) is bequeathed or devised; (2) is inherited from the decedent spouse; (3) the

---

[35] Under the revised USDA version, the person dying first is deemed to have survived the second person to die if the second dies within 120 hours of the first decedent.

surviving spouse succeeds to under some spousal protection statute, such as dower or elective share; (4) was transferred by the decedent during lifetime to the eventual surviving spouse; (5) the surviving spouse succeeds to ownership of by operation of law under joint ownership systems; (6) the decedent possessed a general power of appointment, and the surviving spouse was the appointee or taker in default of the exercise of the power; and (7) the surviving spouse receives as the beneficiary of life insurance proceeds on the decedent's life.

Although § 2056(c) purports to enumerate the sanctioned means for passing property, the regulations recognize other qualifying means, *e.g.,* certain annuity arrangements. Further, the passing requirement may be satisfied by various postmortem means that are sanctioned under the regulations. These include the receipt of property by: (1) certain settlements (*see* Treas. Reg. § 20.2056(c)–2(d));[36] (2) elections under or against the will (*see* Treas. Reg. § 20.2056(c)–2(c)); and (3) disclaimers. In addition, the Internal Revenue Service has recognized passing by antenuptial agreements. *See* Rev. Rul. 68–271, 1968–1 C.B. 409.

Section 2056(a) (last clause) provides a parallel requirement for the marital deduction allowance: the interest in property that passes to the surviving spouse from the decedent must be an interest that is includable in the decedent's gross estate. This requirement ensures against a tax shelter effect—avoiding estate taxation on items not in the gross estate that pass to the surviving spouse. For example, assume that *H* and *W* own jointly held property worth $100,000. Although $100,000 is deemed to pass to *W* as survivor under § 2056(c), a marital deduction would be allowed for only $50,000 because that is the amount includable in *H*'s gross estate as a result of § 2040(b).

[d] Deductible Interest Requirement

The mere passing of an interest in property from the decedent to the surviving spouse is not sufficient to obtain a marital deduction. The interest must be such that it is "deductible" rather than "nondeductible." Although the Regulations provide four categories that render an interest nondeductible, only the fourth category—marital disallowance for terminable interests—has major significance. *See* Treas. Reg. § 20.2056(a)–2(b). This "terminable interest rule" represents a major part of modern estate planning, and is separately considered in the next section.

Problems

1. *W* obtained a Mexican divorce. She then married *H2*, who died domiciled in Wisconsin. Is *W H2*'s surviving spouse for marital deduction purposes? Should it matter whether the divorce would or would not be recognized in

---

[36] In Estate of Mergott v. United States, 86 A.F.T.R. 2000-6634 (D. N.J. 2000), the decedent's widow and his estate settled several claims she made against the estate for a lump sum payment $135,000 and a transfer of a parcel of land. The court determined that the widow had no right under the decedent's will to land or the payment and as a result denied a marital deduction. The opinion does not imply the settlement did not resolve a bona fide controversy.

Wisconsin? *See Estate of Steffke v. Commissioner*, 538 F.2d 730 (7th Cir. 1976), *cert. denied*, 429 U.S. 1026 (1976); *Estate of Goldwater v. Commissioner*, 539 F.2d 878 (2d Cir. 1976); Rev. Rul. 67–442, 1967–2 C.B. 65; *cf. Estate of Spalding v. Commissioner*, 537 F.2d 666 (2d Cir. 1976).

2. The passing requirement may be satisfied if the surviving spouse receives property "as a bona fide recognition of enforceable rights of the surviving spouse in the decedent's estate." *See* Treas. Reg. § 20.2056(c)–2(d)(2). If the surviving spouse receives a property settlement based on good faith, arm's length negotiation as to enforceable rights, is the passing requirement satisfied without regard to whether the rights were actually enforceable? *See Estate of Brandon v. United States*, 828 F.2d 493 (8th Cir. 1987), *on remand*, 91 T.C. 829 (1988).

3. What will the marital deduction consequences be if the surviving spouse surrenders property to avoid a lawsuit? *See Schroder v. United States*, 924 F.2d 1547 (10th Cir. 1991).

4. Do the following situations give rise to a marital deduction?

a. The surviving spouse serves as executrix of the decedent's estate and is paid $10,000 for administering the estate.

b. The surviving spouse holds a mortgage on a building owned by the decedent, and the estate satisfies the mortgage obligation in full.

c. *H* established an irrevocable trust in which his son was income beneficiary for *H*'s life and *H*'s wife, *W*, was entitled to the remainder. *H* died ten years later, and the trust corpus was distributed to *W*.

[3]   The Terminable Interest Rule

Jackson v. United States

376 U.S. 503 (1964)

Mr. Justice White delivered the opinion of the Court.

. . .

Petitioners are the widow-executrix and testamentary trustee under the will of George Richards who died a resident of California on May 27, 1951. Acting under the Probate Code of California, the state court, on June 30, 1952, allowed Mrs. Richards the sum of $3,000 per month from the corpus of the estate for her support and maintenance, beginning as of May 27, 1951, and continuing for a period of 24 months from that date. Under the terms of the order, an allowance of $42,000 had accrued during the 14 months since her husband's death. This amount, plus an additional $3,000 per month for the remainder of the two-year period, making a total of $72,000, was in fact paid to Mrs. Richards as widow's allowance.

On the federal estate tax return filed on behalf of the estate, the full $72,000 was claimed as a marital deduction. . . .

The issue . . . is whether the interest in property passing to Mrs. Richards as widow's allowance would "terminate or fail" upon the "lapse of time, upon the occurrence of an event or contingency, or upon the failure of an event or contingency to occur."

We accept the Court of Appeals' description of the nature and characteristics of the widow's allowance under California law.[37] In that State, the right to a widow's allowance is not a vested right and nothing accrues before the order granting it. The right to an allowance is lost when the one for whom it is asked has lost the status upon which the right depends. If a widow dies or remarries prior to securing an order for a widow's allowance, the right does not survive such death or remarriage. The amount of the widow's allowance that has accrued and is unpaid at the date of death of the widow is payable to her estate but the right to future payments abates upon her death. The remarriage of a widow subsequent to an order for an allowance likewise abates her right to future payments. 317 F.2d 821, 825.

In light of these characteristics of the California widow's allowance, Mrs. Richards did not have an indefeasible interest in property at the moment of her husband's death since either her death or remarriage would defeat it. If the order for support allowance had been entered on the day of her husband's death, her death or remarriage at any time within two years thereafter would terminate that portion of the interest allocable to the remainder of the two-year period. As of the date of Mr. Richards' death, therefore, the allowance was subject to failure or termination "upon the occurrence of an event or contingency." That the support order was entered in this case 14 months later does not, in our opinion, change the defeasible nature of the interest.

Petitioners ask us to judge the terminability of the widow's interest in property represented by her allowance as of the date of the Probate Court's order rather than as of the date of her husband's death. The court's order, they argue, unconditionally entitled the widow to $42,000 in accrued allowance of which she could not be deprived by either her death or remarriage. It is true that some courts have followed this path, but it is difficult to accept an approach that would allow a deduction of $42,000 on the facts of this case, a deduction of $72,000 if the order had been entered at the end of two years from Mr. Richards' death and none at all if the order had been entered immediately upon his death. . . . [J]udging deductibility as of the date of the Probate Court's order ignores the Senate Committee's admonition that in considering terminability of an interest for purposes of a marital deduction "the situation is viewed as at the date of the decedent's death." S. Rep. No. 1013, Part 2, 80th Cong., 2d Sess., p. 10. We prefer the course followed by both the Court of Appeals for the Ninth Circuit . . . and by the Court of Appeals for the Eighth Circuit. . . . Both courts have held the date of death of the testator to be the correct point of time from which to judge the nature of a widow's allowance for the purpose of deciding terminability and deductibility. . . . This is in accord with the rule uniformly followed with regard to interests other than the widow's allowance—that qualification for the marital deduction must be determined as of the time of death.

Our conclusion is confirmed by [§ 2056(b)(3)], which saves from the operation of the terminable-interest rule interests that by their terms may (but do

---

[37] [Presently, Cal. Prob. Code §§ 6540–6545. Eds.]

not in fact) terminate only upon failure of the widow to survive her husband for a period not in excess of six months. The premise of this provision is that an interest passing to a widow is normally to be judged as of the time of the testator's death rather than at a later time when the condition imposed may be satisfied; hence, the necessity to provide an exception to the rule in the case of a six months' survivorship contingency in a will. A gift conditioned upon eight months' survivorship, rather than six, is a nondeductible terminable interest for reasons that also disqualify the statutory widow's allowance in California, where the widow must survive and remain unmarried at least to the date of an allowance to become indefeasibly entitled to any widow's allowance at all.

Petitioners contend, however, that the sole purpose of the terminable-interest provisions of the Code is to assure that interests deducted from the estate of the deceased spouse will not also escape taxation in the estate of the survivor. This argument leads to the conclusion that since it is now clear that unless consumed or given away during Mrs. Richards' life, the entire $72,000 will be taxed to her estate, it should not be included in her husband's. But as we have already seen, there is no provision in the Code for deducting all terminable interests that become nonterminable at a later date and therefore taxable in the estate of the surviving spouse if not consumed or transferred. . . .

We are mindful that the general goal of the marital deduction provisions was to achieve uniformity of federal estate tax impact between those States with community property laws and those without them. But the device of the marital deduction that Congress chose to achieve uniformity was knowingly hedged with limitations, including the terminable-interest rule. These provisions may be imperfect devices to achieve the desired end, but they are the means that Congress chose. To the extent it was thought desirable to modify the rigors of the terminable-interest rule, exceptions to the rule were written into the Code. Courts should hesitate to provide still another exception by straying so far from the statutory language as to allow a marital deduction for the widow's allowance provided by the California statute. The achievement of the purposes of the marital deduction is dependent to a great degree upon the careful drafting of wills; we have no fear that our decision today will prevent either the full utilization of the marital deduction or the proper support of widows during the pendency of an estate proceeding.

Affirmed.

Mr. Justice Douglas dissents.

––––––––

Under § 2056(b)(1), and subject to carefully crafted exceptions discussed below, no marital deduction is allowed for an interest in property passing to a surviving spouse if the interest meets each of the following three conditions.[38]

---

[38] Only the first condition needs to be met if the personal representative or a trustee is directed to acquire the interest for the surviving spouse. See § 2056(b)(1)(C).

(1) The interest passing to the surviving spouse may, when viewed at the time of the decedent's death, terminate or fail "on the lapse of time, on the occurrence of an event or contingency, or on the failure of an event or contingency to occur. . . ." *See* § 2056(b)(1). For example, if the interest of a surviving spouse will terminate on his remarriage, it constitutes a terminable interest, even though the surviving spouse may never remarry. Similarly, a life estate constitutes a terminable interest because it terminates at the death of the life tenant.

(2) The interest in property passes or has passed for less than adequate and full consideration from the decedent to someone other than the surviving spouse or the estate of the surviving spouse. *See* § 2056(b)(1)(A). This provision is satisfied, for example, if the decedent's children are given the remainder after the surviving spouse's life estate.

(3) Because of the passing of the interest to another person, such person, or her heirs or assigns, may possess or enjoy any part of such property on the termination or failure of the surviving spouse's interest. *See* § 2056(b)(1)(B). Again, this provision is satisfied by a remainder in the children after a life estate in the surviving spouse because on the termination of the life estate, the remainder beneficiaries will be capable of enjoyment.

Furthermore, the personal representative cannot bypass these rules by using terminable interest assets to satisfy a bequest to the surviving spouse. If a devise may be funded by assets that do not qualify for the marital deduction, under the *tainted asset rule* the amount of the marital deduction is reduced by the amount of those assets, whether or not nonqualifying assets are, in fact, used. *See* § 2056(b)(2). The devise is deemed satisfied by assets that do not qualify.

The rationale for the terminable interest rule lies in the attempt to equalize the treatment of married couples in common law and community property jurisdictions by § 2056. Under community property regimes, the surviving spouse is entitled to a one-half vested interest in the community assets. Ordinarily, most, if not all, assets are held in fee simple. Accordingly, the survivor receives a one-half interest in fee simple in the community assets. The terminable interest rule attempts generally to mimic this result, and bars a marital deduction for less than outright dispositions in common law states (as well as for separate property in community property regimes).

Problems

1. Two years ago, *X* created a trust, the income of which was payable to *H* for twenty years, reversion to *X*. This year *H* died, survived by *X* and *H*'s wife, *W*. *H*'s will left his income interest in the trust to *W*. Does the bequest violate the terminable interest rule?

2. *H*'s will left *H*'s farm, Blackacre, to *A* for *A*'s life, remainder to *H*'s wife, *W*. Does the devise to *W* violate the terminable interest rule?

3. The decedent owns a patent outright that she devises to her husband (or her husband's estate). Does the value of the patent qualify for the marital deduction?

4. The decedent's will directs the personal representative to purchase an annuity for decedent's spouse paying $10,000 per year for the spouse's life. Is a marital deduction available for the annuity?

[4] Exceptions to the Terminable Interest Rule

Alleviating the harshness of the terminable interest rule are a number of exceptions that allow desirable estate planning techniques. The most common exceptions are discussed below.[39]

[a] Limited Survivorship Clauses

As noted in *Jackson, supra*, one exception to the terminable interest rule permits a decedent to condition receipt of property by the surviving spouse on the spouse's surviving the deceased for up to six months. *See* § 2056(b)(3). Were it not for § 2056(b)(3), the beneficiary-spouse's interest would constitute a nondeductible terminable interest because of the gift over, if the spouse did not survive.[40] Because of this provision, a testamentary disposition to a surviving spouse that requires her survival for up to six months after the testator's death does not violate the terminable interest rule.

In addition to this six month rule, § 2056(b)(3) allows a decedent to condition the surviving spouse's taking on not dying as a result of a common disaster. Both kinds of conditional bequests are designed to avoid requiring families to undergo the expense and delay of administering the same assets in both estates.

Consistent with the general operation of the terminable interest rule, § 2056(b)(3) requires that the spouse, in fact, take the interest, notwithstanding the survivorship clause. If the beneficiary-spouse dies within the six months (without regard to the cause of death) or as a result of a common disaster with the decedent, no marital deduction would be available because no interest would pass from the decedent to the surviving spouse.

Problems

1. In his will, *H* named his spouse, *W,* as the beneficiary of the residue on the condition that she survive until his personal representative distributes the assets in the probate estate. Does this bequest qualify for the marital deduction if *W* does survive? *See* Rev. Rul. 88–90, 1988–2 C.B. 335. What if it is possible that under state law *W*'s interest would not terminate even if

---

[39] See § 2056(b)(6) related to a deduction for life insurance, and § 2056(b)(8) relating to a deduction under a charitable remainder trust, discussed later in this Chapter. Under the § 2056(b)(8) exception, the value of the surviving spouse's income interest in a charitable remainder trust may be deductible.

[40] In response to the problem, California law mandates that survival terms beyond six months must be reduced to six months. *See* Cal. Prob. Code § 21525. However, the decedent must have intended that the disposition qualify for the estate tax marital deduction before this reduction statute comes into play. *See* Estate of Heim v. Commissioner, 914 F.2d 1322 (9th Cir. 1990).

she failed to survive until distribution? *See Estate of Tilyou v. Commissioner,* 470 F.2d 693 (2d Cir. 1973), *rev'g* 56 T.C. 1362 (1971).

2. The decedent's will provided that the residue would pass to her husband if he survived until the will was admitted to probate. Under state law, the decedent's will could have been admitted to probate more than six months after death. Does the residuary devise qualify for the marital deduction? *See Estate of Robertson v. United States,* 903 F.2d 1034 (5th Cir. 1990).

[b] Life Estate Power of Appointment Arrangement

Before 1982, the major exception to the terminal interest rule was provided by § 2056(b)(5). This provision permits a trust to qualify for the estate tax marital deduction if:

(1) all trust income is payable to the surviving spouse, at least, annually for life;

(2) during the surviving spouse's lifetime, no other person can be a beneficiary of the trust;

(3) the surviving spouse is given an "all events" general power of appointment under which the surviving spouse can appoint the trust property to himself or to his estate.

Examples of income interests that do not qualify include: (1) an income interest that terminates on remarriage; (2) a term of years; or (3) a provision in favor of a third party that may or may not apply during the surviving spouse's lifetime, such as a requirement to distribute trust income to a child until the child reaches a specified age.

A trust's administrative provisions may give the trustee power to restrict the spouse's right to income and negate the estate tax marital deduction. To avoid this problem, Treasury Regulation § 20.2056(b)–5(f)(5) provides that the marital deduction is not lost if the trustee may not invest in unproductive assets without the consent of the surviving spouse.

A personal residence and other personal property may be held in trust, even if the property does not produce income, if the spouse is permitted to use the property. In addition, property interests not in trust may satisfy the requirements of § 2056(b)(5). For example, if the surviving spouse was given a life interest and a general power to appoint the property at death, the deduction is allowed for the full value of property.

While no one other than the surviving spouse may have the authority to make distributions to anyone other than herself, the trustee can be given a power to distribute trust property to the surviving spouse. Moreover, the surviving spouse may have a power to distribute the trust property to third parties.

Not all general powers of appointment will satisfy the § 2056(b)(5) requirement. The power must be exercisable in favor of either the surviving spouse or the spouse's estate. A power to appoint to the creditors of the spouse's estate, or a power exercisable with the consent of another person, is a general power of appointment under § 2041, but does not satisfy § 2056(b)(5). There can be no substantive restriction on the grant of the power or on the power's exercise for the requirements of § 2056(B)(5) to be met.

Section 2056(b)(5) permits a marital deduction for less than the entire value of the property passing to the trust. It is possible that only a specific portion qualifies. *See* § 2056(b)(5) (final sentence). For many years, the exact meaning of "specific portion" was unknown. In *Estate of Alexander v. Commissioner*, 82 T.C. 34 (1984), *aff'd*, No. 8401600 (4th Cir. Apr. 3, 1985), the Tax Court invalidated a Regulation, holding that the term "specific portion" includes a fixed dollar amount. *See also Northeastern Pennsylvania Nat'l Bank & Trust Co. v. United States*, 387 U.S. 213 (1967). Under the court's holding, appreciation in certain marital deduction property could be excluded from the surviving spouse's taxable estate.

In 1992, in response to *Alexander*, Congress enacted § 2056(b)(10), which effectively codifies the Regulation that was declared invalid by the *Alexander* court.[41] The legislative history explains that § 2056(b)(10) was enacted to ensure that appreciation did not escape taxation in the surviving spouse's estate: "[a] Treasury regulation defines 'a specific portion' to be a fractional or percentage share of a property interest."

Before 1982, a testamentary power of appointment marital trust, or a (b)(5) trust as it is sometimes called, was used extensively by decedents to provide surviving spouses with an interest in property that satisfied the marital deduction rules of § 2056, but was something less than an outright devise. The element of control was the overwhelming factor that resulted in the use of a trust by the decedent. Sometimes the desire to control was to provide the surviving spouse with asset management or to have someone other than the spouse control the assets in the trust. This was particularly significant when the marital trust was funded with a controlling interest in a family business. The decedent may have hoped that the trust assets would ultimately be distributed as the decedent desired when the surviving spouse died. A (b)(5) trust gave the surviving spouse a general power of appointment to direct the disposition of the trust assets at death in any manner he chose. As a practical matter, however, the power of appointment required the spouse to affirmatively exercise the power. Many powers go unexercised. When they do, the trust property passes by the default provisions of the power of appointment.

The right to exercise powers led some taxpayers to make "deals" with their spouses concerning the exercise of the power. In *Chapman v. Citizens and Southern Nat'l Bank*, 395 S.E.2d 446 (S.C. App. 1990), the surviving spouse-decedent was granted a general power of appointment to comply with the estate tax laws in effect when the husband signed his will. Nevertheless, there were numerous letters in the record that established that the decedent had promised her husband that she would not exercise the power. Finding that a confidential relationship existed between the decedent and her husband, the court imposed a constructive trust on the property that the decedent appointed, because the decedent broke her promise not to exercise the power of appointment. The court rejected the argument made by the decedent's children that not permitting the decedent to exercise the power of appointment

---

41 *See* § 2056(b)(10) (imposing the same requirements under §§ 2056(b)(6) and (b)(7)).

was "tax fraud." The court rejected this argument because the decedent did not change her mind about following her husband's wishes until after he died. For a different state court result, see *In re Estate of O'Rourke*, 610 N.Y.S.2d 704 (Sur. 1994), in which the court sustained the exercise of the power of appointment.

Problems

1. Decedent creates a trust with income payable annually to his surviving spouse for life, remainder as she appoints to her estate, or in default of the exercise of the power of appointment, to his children.

a. Would this trust qualify under § 2056(b)(5)?

b. Would your answer change if the trustee could invade corpus for the couple's children? *See Estate of Weisberger v. Commissioner*, 29 T.C. 217 (1957).

c. Would your answer change if the trustee could invade corpus for the surviving spouse's child to the extent necessary for the child's support? *See* Treas. Reg. § 20.2056(b)–5(j); Rev. Rul. 85–35, 1985–1 C.B. 328.

2. Decedent and her husband executed mutual wills, each of which provided that the testator's property would pass to the other spouse if he or she survived. Upon the second decedent's death, one-half would pass to the children of each spouse. At the same time, they executed a contract in which they agreed not to revoke the wills. Under local law, that contract is binding on the survivor, if carried out by the decedent. Decedent died with her mutual will in force. Would the assets passing to her husband qualify for the marital deduction under 2056(b)(5)? *See Estate of Opal*, 450 F.2d 1085 (2d Cir. 1971); *Batterton v. United States*, 406 F.2d 247 (5th Cir. 1968), *cert. denied*, 395 U.S. 934 (1969).

[c] Qualified Terminable Interest Property (QTIP) Exception

In 1981, Congress added § 2056(b)(7), permitting a marital deduction for another type of disposition that otherwise would violate the nondeductible terminal interest rule under § 2056(b)(1). This additional exception sanctions a marital deduction for qualified terminable interest property (QTIP) dispositions. The exception entitles the decedent's estate to a marital deduction for property if (1) the surviving spouse has the absolute right to annual income from the property for life; (2) no one has an exercisable right during the surviving spouse's life to appoint any interest to anyone other than the surviving spouse; and (3) the personal representative elects to treat the interest as QTIP property. No power of appointment is necessary for the surviving spouse. Thus, the first spouse to die can control the ultimate disposition of the QTIP property.

Estate of Spencer v. Commissioner

43 F.3d 226 (6th Cir. 1995)

Merritt, Chief Judge

In this estate tax case, Mrs. Ernestine W. Spencer, a surviving spouse who is also the executrix of her husband's estate, disagrees with the Internal Revenue service and the Tax Court because they have disallowed $1.2 million in assets as a marital deduction from her husband's taxable estate. Internal Revenue Code § 2056(b)(7) provides for the deductibility of "qualified terminable interest property," or so-called "QTIP." The QTIP provision, § 2056(b)(7)(B), Title 26, allows a life estate in property to qualify for deductibility if (1) the surviving spouse receives all income from the property, (2) no one can appoint the property away from the surviving spouse during her lifetime, and (3) the proper statutory election is made by the personal representative of decedent's estate on decedent's estate tax form.

. . .

I. Facts of the Case

On September 24, 1984, the decedent, Mr. John D. Spencer of Licking County, Ohio, executed the John D. Spencer Trust Agreement. It provided that upon decedent's death two trusts would be established; Trust A, the QTIP Trust, for his surviving spouse, and Trust B for his children. Trust A is the subject of the current dispute.

Trust A was to be funded by the amount elected under § 2056(b)(7) by the executor after decedent's death.[42] The Trust Agreement further provided that all income from trust principal would be distributed to the surviving spouse on at least a quarterly basis and that no one could grant income or principal to anyone other than the spouse during her lifetime. The Trust Agreement named decedent's spouse, Mrs. Ernestine W. Spencer, as the trustee.

On the same day, the decedent executed his Will naming Mrs. Spencer executor of his estate. The will gave her almost complete discretion to determine the amount of the QTIP election. The will had a non-binding provision elsewhere in its text indicating that the decedent anticipated "that my Executor will elect to minimize the estate tax payable [by] my estate."

Mr. Spencer died in March 1987. Mrs. Spencer survived him, and began her multiple roles of trustee, executrix and surviving spouse. As executrix, she determined the gross estate to have a value of approximately $1.9 million. On December 3, 1987, she appointed approximately $1.2 million of the estate to Trust A, the QTIP Trust, and used the unified tax credit of $600,000 plus certain administrative costs to reduce the taxable estate to zero. She filed Form 706, the estate tax form, with the IRS on December 5, 1987, claiming the entire value of Trust A to be exempt from taxation under § 2056(b)(7). On this form, she made the QTIP election required by law. On November 8,

---

42 [The effect of the provision was that the QTIP trust was to be funded with assets only to the extent that the decedent's executor made the QTIP election. Thus, to the extent that a QTIP election was not made, property passed to Trust B for the benefit of the decedent's children. Eds.]

1990, the IRS disallowed this deduction from decedent's estate and sent Mrs. Spencer a tax bill for $416,477.62. On behalf of decedent's estate, she appealed this finding to the Tax Court. *See* T. C. M. 1992–579. It ruled in favor of the IRS, and Mrs. Spencer appealed once more.

II. § 2056(b)(7)

Code § 2001 imposes a tax on all transfers of estates by deceased United States citizens. Section 2056(a) then provides for a "marital deduction," which generally excludes from present taxation all property passing from a decedent to a surviving spouse that will later be taxed in the estate of the surviving spouse. Currently there is no limit to the amount that may be claimed as a marital deduction. But § 2056(b)(1) makes an exception to this deduction for transfers of "terminable interests," defined as any interest that will terminate or fail upon the lapse of time or occurrence of a stated condition. An example of a terminable interest would be a life estate in the surviving spouse with the remainder in the decedent's children. Thus, the general rule is that terminable interests are included in the taxable estate. Confusion arises because this exception is itself subject to a number of counter-exceptions that permit certain kinds of terminable interests to be excluded from the taxable estate. The subject of this litigation is the counter-exception created by § 2056(b)(7), which deals with "qualified terminable interest property."

The Economic Recovery Tax Act of 1981 made a number of revisions to the estate tax code. Among others it raised the total amount of the unified credit, abolished the fifty-percent (50%) cap on the marital deduction, and added § 2056(b)(7) to the tax code. By abolishing the cap on the marital deduction, Congress intended to address the problem of taxing a single estate "one and one-half times, *i.e.*, one-half on the death of the first spouse and again fully upon the death of the second spouse." H. R. Rep. 201 at 159.

Congress added § 2056(b)(7) primarily to allow a decedent to provide for a surviving spouse while controlling the ultimate disposition of the property after the surviving spouse's death. *See* H. R. Rep. 201 at 159–60. Before the addition of § 2056(b)(7), a person planning an estate was forced to choose between either leaving property outright to the surviving spouse or leaving it to the surviving children because under prior law simply granting a life estate to the surviving spouse with remainder in the decedent's children resulted in the property's inclusion in the taxable estate. Section 2056(b)(5) had already provided an exception to the terminal interest exception to the marital deduction by allowing deductions of a life estate with a general power of appointment in the surviving spouse. But this one exception was not considered sufficient because there are situations when a decedent would want to remove discretion from the surviving spouse so as to ensure the ultimate disposition of the estate after the death of the spouse. This concern led Congress to revise the estate tax code, including the addition of § 2056(b)(7).

In this case, the facts have been stipulated by the parties, and we must make only a legal determination. Accordingly, our review of the Tax Court's decision in this case is *de novo. Smith v. Commissioner*, 926 F.2d 1470 (6th Cir. 1991).

The IRS argues that the QTIP deduction should be disallowed because the executrix's power to determine the amount of the election constitutes an impermissible power to appoint property away from the surviving spouse under § 2056(b)(7)(B)(ii)(II) during the period between the testator's death and the date of the election. On the other hand, Mrs. Spencer points out that under the terms of trust, none of the property in Trust A can be appointed away from her until after her death. Once in the trust, the property meets the requirements of § 2056(b)(7)(B), and, she argues, should qualify for the QTIP counter-exception and not be included in the taxable estate.

To resolve this issue, we must answer one decisive question: does the surviving spouse's interest in qualified terminable interest property have to be determinable on the date of decedent's death, or may the estate adopt a wait and see attitude and determine the QTIP property later on the date of the QTIP election? The IRS argues that decedent's date of death is the correct determination date.

We do not think this meaning is what Congress intended when it passed the election provision for QTIP property. Congress deliberately crafted the broad language of § 2056(b)(7)(B)(v): "An election under [§ 2056(b)(7)] with respect to *any property* shall be made by the executor on the return of tax imposed by § 2001." (Emphasis added.) Congress did not use the words "any existing qualified terminable interest property" or "any property meeting the above definition as of the date of decedent's death" or any similar limiting language, and we are not prepared to read such a limitation into this statute. The language "any property" should be given its ordinary meaning. Nowhere in the legislative history of § 2056(b)(7) do we find an indication that Congress intended a different reading of the statute. Our reading is reinforced by the history of the rule against appointments away from the surviving spouse. History suggests that the main reason Congress included the language against appointments away from the surviving spouse was to ensure that the property subject to the QTIP deduction would be taxed in the spouse's estate:

> There must be no power in any person (including the spouse) to appoint any part of the property subject to the qualifying income interest to any person other than the spouse during the spouse's life. This rule . . . will insure that the value of the property not consumed by the spouse is subject to tax upon the spouse's death (or earlier disposition).

H.R. Rep. 201 at 161.

Since Trust A property in the instant case qualifies as QTIP, it will be included in the surviving spouse's estate upon her death under § 2044. Were we to adopt the Commissioner's interpretation, we would be adding an unnecessary restriction. The words of the statute are plain: no property meets the definition of QTIP until the proper election is made, and no QTIP election can be made until the estate tax form is filed. § 2056(b)(7)(B)(v). Since no property can be QTIP until the election is made, the proper date to determine if property satisfies the requirement of § 2056(b)(7) is on the date of the election.

In support of the position that QTIP property must be ascertained as of the date of death rather than the date of election, the Commissioner cites a thirty year-old Supreme Court case, *Jackson v. United States*, 376 U.S. 503, 507–09

(1964), the central holding of which is that interests are to be examined for terminability as of the date of decedent's death. At the date of decedent's death, Mrs. Spencer had the discretion to decide what property went to Trust A and what did not. The Commissioner argues that this was an impermissible power to appoint property away from the surviving spouse, and the $1.2 million election does not meet the definition of "qualified terminable interest" under § 2056(b)(7)(B)(ii)(II). Therefore, it must be included in decedent's taxable estate.

Jackson is readily distinguishable from this case and not in point. In *Jackson*, after her husband's death, a widow received a court-ordered temporary allowance for her support and maintenance payable from his estate. The Supreme Court held that because the widow's allowance arose from a right under state law that had not vested in her as of her husband's date of death, it could not be included as part of the marital deduction because it did not meet the definition of any counter-exception to the rule that terminable interests are to be included in the taxable estate. *Jackson* at 507. In the instant case, the decedent used an estate planning device unknown when *Jackson* was decided—the QTIP counter-exception to the terminable interest rule. Because the *Jackson* court ruled on the proper determination date for an interest that is not an exception to the terminal interest rule, and not subject to a later election, we do not think it is dispositive of this issue.

Section 2056(b)(7) creates a new and different legislative scheme. Under the election provision, no property anywhere can be considered QTIP until an election is made by the executor on Form 706, which can only be done after the date of death. When the Commissioner's interpretation is carried to its logical extent, no property could ever satisfy the statutory definition of QTIP because the election for the surviving spouse cannot be made until after the date of decedent's death. This simple fact highlights the major problem with the Commissioner's interpretation of § 2056(b)(7).

An old judicially created rule used to interpret taxing statutes, like the date-of-death rule in the *Jackson* case, may not be used to displace the language of the statute itself. When interpreting statutes, generally the plain language of the statute is given effect, and "in determining the meaning of the statute, we look not only to the particular statutory language, but to the design of the statute as a whole and to its object and policy." *Crandon v. United States*, 494 U.S. 152, 158 (1990).

The IRS would have us adopt an interpretation that would force property to satisfy every requirement for the QTIP counter-exception on the date of decedent's death except the requirement of election. This would effectively reduce the election requirement to a mere formality, defeat its apparent purpose and its most reasonable interpretation. We hold that the date of the QTIP election is the proper date to determine if property satisfies the requirements of § 2056(b)(7).

. . .

IV. Additional Reasons

Our decision is reinforced by the decisions of the Fifth Circuit in *Clayton*[43] and the Eighth Circuit in *Robertson,*[44] which reached the same conclusion as ours. After exhaustively detailing the legislative history of § 2056(b)(7) and taking the IRS to task for overzealous revenue collection, the *Clayton* court, however, unnecessarily created a legal fiction that the QTIP election is somehow considered "retroactive" to the date of decedent's death. 976 F.2d at 1495. The Eighth Circuit followed suit. This *nunc pro tunc* treatment of the QTIP election is unnecessary for the reasons previously stated. The election provision is plain on its face and need not be read retroactively.

The IRS has failed to present a valid policy argument supporting their interpretation other than maximizing estate taxation. The IRS currently permits effectively identical dispositions of property provided the decedent has a savvy estate planner. For example, the decedent could have effectuated his goal of minimizing his estate taxes by simply leaving all of his property to Trust A. Acting under § 2518, Mrs. Spencer would then only have had to disclaim whatever property she wished to designate for the trust benefitting decedent's children. She would have had as much discretion as she enjoyed under decedent's will, and the decedent would have enjoyed the same tax benefits and results as under his actual estate plan.

Finally, it is significant that in a 1986 private letter ruling the IRS held that if the surviving spouse was also the executor, even though her interest was contingent upon her making an election identical to Mrs. Spencer's, this interest qualified for the QTIP counter-exception. Priv. Ltr. Rul. 8631005 (April 23, 1986). Although this ruling cannot be cited as precedent under 26 U.S.C. § 6110(J)(3), it highlights the confusion this section has engendered at the IRS. More importantly, the fact that the IRS has done an about face since 1986 makes us even more reluctant to adopt their interpretation of this statute without an understandable articulation of a tax policy supporting it. *See I.N.S. v. Cardoza-Fonseca*, 480 U.S. 421 (1987) (agency's interpretation that conflicts with agency's prior interpretation entitled to considerably less deference than a consistently held agency view.)

Therefore, the judgment of the Tax Court is Reversed and the case remanded for further proceedings consistent with this opinion.

The Service has conceded the contingent income issue involved in *Spencer*. Treasury Regulation § 20.2056(b)–7(d)(3) provides that "a qualifying income interest for life that is contingent upon the executor's election under § 2056(b)(7)(B)(v)" will not be precluded, on that basis, from qualification as a "qualifying income interest for life" within the meaning of § 2056(b)(7)(B)(ii).[45]

---

[43] [Estate of Clayton v. Commissioner, 976 F.2d 1486 (5th Cir. 1992). Eds.]

[44] [Estate of Robertson v. Commissioner, 15 F.3d 779 (8th Cir. 1994). Eds.]

[45] This problem does not exist under § 2056(b)(5) arrangements because the surviving spouse, or her estate, must have a general power of appointment over any income not payable to the spouse or her estate.

Analytically, the QTIP requirements parallel the requirements in § 2056(b)(5) insofar as the surviving spouse must have the absolute right to annual income for life, and no person during the spouse's lifetime can have the power to appoint the property to anyone other than the surviving spouse.[46] In fact, the applicable regulations under § 2056(b)(5) apply to QTIPs. *See* Treas. Reg. § 20.2056(b)–7(d)(2). Furthermore, a QTIP election may be allowed over a specific portion of property provided the specific portion is expressed as a percentage or fraction pursuant to the mandate of § 2056(b)(10), which is discussed at § 3.04[C][4][b].

Proposed Treasury Regulations § 1.643(b)-1, which relates to the definition of trust income, also impacts on the gift and estate tax marital deductions. The Treasury Department explains:

> Certain transfers of property in trust for the benefit of the spouse qualify for the marital deduction for gift and estate tax purposes. These transfers include a life estate with a general power of appointment described in sections 2523(e) and 2056(b)(5) and qualified terminal interest property described in sections 2523(f) and 2056(b)(7). One of the requirements of these provisions is that the spouse must be entitled for life to all the income from the trust property. The rules for determining whether the spouse is entitled to all the income from either a life estate with a general power of appointment trust or a qualified terminable interest trust are set forth in section 20.2056(b)– 5(f) of the Estate Tax Regulations and section 25.2523(e)–1(f) of the Gift Tax Regulations. These rules provide that if an interest is transferred in trust, the spouse is entitled for life to all the income from the entire interest or a specific portion of the entire interest if the effect of the trust is to give the spouse substantially that degree of beneficial enjoyment of the trust property during the spouse's life which the principles of the law of trusts accord a person who is unqualifiedly designated as the life beneficiary of a trust.
>
> The proposed regulations will provide that a spouse's interest satisfies the income standard set forth in sections 20.2056(b)–5(f) and 25.2523(e)–1(f) if the spouse is entitled to income as defined under a state statute that provides for a reasonable apportionment between the income and remainder beneficiaries of the total return of the trust and that meets the requirements of section 1.643(b)–1(a). As the examples under section 1.643(b)–1(a) make clear, reasonable apportionment can be accomplished through a unitrust definition of income or by giving the trustee the power to make equitable adjustments between income and principal. In addition, a conforming amendment is made to section 20.2056A–5(c)(2) providing rules regarding distributions of income from a qualified domestic trust.[47]

---

[46] The QTIP requirement is more stringent than the (b)(5) exception because even the surviving spouse may not have a lifetime power to appoint property to someone other than herself, which is permissible under (b)(5).

[47] Supplementary Information for Proposed Treasury Regulations Redefining Income, 66 Fed. Reg. 10396, 10398 (February 15, 2001).

What constitutes a right to income has proved troubling. For example, in *Estate of Novotny v. Commissioner*, 93 T.C. 12 (1989), the decedent left her surviving spouse a life estate in real property. The will imposed on the surviving spouse the duty to pay real estate taxes, to make mortgage payments, and to provide for repairs and maintenance for the property. The court found, however, that the duties were no more restrictive than the limits imposed: (1) on the decedent and the surviving spouse as signers of a deed of trust secured by the property, and (2) on the surviving spouse under local law as a life tenant. The court, therefore, held that where the limits imposed on a life estate received by a surviving spouse do not exceed the limits independently applicable to that spouse, those limits did not result in the failure of the property to qualify as terminable interest property.

The QTIP exception differs from the § 2056(b)(5) exception in that it is not necessary for the surviving spouse to have a power over the corpus (and in fact may have no lifetime power to appoint to anyone other than the surviving spouse). In fact, Congress enacted the QTIP exception to avoid forcing a decedent "to choose between surrendering control of the entire estate [to the surviving spouse] to avoid imposition of estate tax at death or reducing tax benefits to insure inheritance by the children."[48]

The Service has challenged the QTIP deduction in a number of cases alleging that someone had the power to appoint the QTIP trust property to someone other than the surviving spouse. For example, QTIP treatment was denied in *Estate of Manscill v. Commissioner*, 98 T.C. 413 (1992), because the trustee had the power to appoint corpus to the surviving spouse's daughter with the consent of the surviving spouse. The power violated the limitation that no person (including the surviving spouse) could have the power to appoint property to anyone other than the surviving spouse.

The QTIP exception also differs from the § 2056(b)(5) arrangement, and indeed from other qualifying arrangements, because the personal representative must make a QTIP election for the estate to obtain a marital deduction for the QTIP disposition. A timely QTIP election is made on the federal estate tax return.[49] In contrast, no election is required to obtain a marital deduction under other qualifying arrangements; however, a marital deduction is mandatory under other arrangements.[50] *See Estate of La Sala v. Commissioner*, 71 T.C. 752 (1979).

QTIP trusts have become a popular estate planning device since their adoption in 1981. Although they allow the testator to limit the surviving spouse's control over disposition of the trust property, the popularity of QTIPs is not solely based on this characteristic. This is considered later in § 3.04[C][5][b].

---

[48] House Ways and Means Committee, H.R. Rep. No. 97–201, Economic Recovery Tax Act of 1981, 97th Cong., 1st Sess. 160 (1981).

[49] Because of problems with personal representatives inadvertently failing to make the election, the Service modified IRS Form 706 to provide an automatic QTIP election, unless an affirmative election is made not to qualify to permissible devises for the deduction.

[50] If the surviving spouse's property interest is in the form of a joint and survivor annuity with the decedent, no election is required. *See* § 2056(b)(7)(C)(ii). In that case, the personal representative must elect against qualification. *Id.* In other cases, a marital deduction may be avoided, in part or in whole, by a qualified disclaimer.

Problems

1. Will a devise of a residence to the surviving spouse for as long as he wants to live there qualify for the marital deduction? *See Peacock v. United States,* 914 F.2d 230 (11th Cir. 1990). *But see* Priv. Ltr. Rul. 8736004 (Texas homestead does not qualify because of loss on abandoning).

2. Assume the trustee is authorized to make payments of trust principal for a surviving spouse's benefit if the spouse becomes disabled. Will this power bar compliance with § 2056(b)(7)? *See* Priv. Ltr. Rul. 8706008 (relying on Rev. Rul. 85–35, 1985–1 C.B. 328); Priv. Ltr. Rul. 8503009.

3. Will dower rights qualify for the marital deduction under § 2056(b)(7) in those jurisdictions in which the surviving spouse is not entitled to take a fee interest?

4. Would a QTIP election be valid if the trust property consisted of non-income producing property, such as works of art? *See* Tech. Adv. Mem. 9237009.

[d] Estate Trusts

Another exception to the terminal interest rule is the *estate trust.* This type of marital trust is the only type of trust that qualifies for the federal estate tax marital deduction under § 2056 and does not require that trust income be paid to the surviving spouse for life. The estate trust may permit the discretionary payment of income to the surviving spouse or require the accumulation of income if the remainder passes to the spouse's estate at death. For the trust to qualify, no one other than the surviving spouse may have any beneficial interest in the trust. The reason that the trust qualifies for the marital deduction is that this type of trust is not a terminal interest. Nothing passes to anyone else upon the surviving spouse's death. Instead, the trust assets must pass to the spouse's estate. *See* Rev. Rul. 68–554, 1968–2 C.B. 412; *see also* Treas. Reg. § 20.2056(c)–2(b).

Estate trusts are useful when the decedent is likely to devise non-income producing assets to a marital trust. With the estate trust, it is not necessary for the trust assets to be income producing during the spouse's lifetime or to give the spouse the right to make non-productive assets productive, as is required with (b)(5) and (b)(7) trusts. During the spouse's lifetime, the trustee controls the trust assets. Of course, the spouse will necessarily control the ultimate disposition of the trust assets because the remainder interest in trust must pass to the spouse's estate for distribution under the spouse's will, or to the spouse's intestate heirs.

[e] Other Forms of the Marital Deduction

Besides the various types of trusts discussed above that qualify for the estate tax marital deduction, it is possible to obtain a marital deduction for life insurance proceeds or annuities held by an insurance company. *See* § 2056(b)(6). It is necessary for the surviving spouse to receive annually the interest earned by the funds and for the surviving spouse the have an "all events" general power of appointment. In addition, it is possible to qualify for the marital deduction a combined devise to a surviving spouse and charity. See § 2056(b)(8) and the discussion at § 3.04[D][6] *infra.*

[f] Section 2044: Estate Tax Inclusion Following a QTIP Election

Section 2044 can only be understood in the context of the marital deduction under the QTIP exception. Section 2056(b)(7) only requires the surviving spouse have the absolute right to trust income (or the nontrust equivalent), for life. Because the marital deduction is allowed for the value of the trust, or trust equivalent, without requiring the surviving spouse to have a general power of appointment, property qualifying for the marital deduction under § 2056(b)(7) is not included in the survivor's estate under either § 2033 or § 2041. The life estate would terminate at death, thus negating taxation under § 2033. No power being required, § 2041 would not apply.

Congress enacted § 2044 as a counterpart to the QTIP provision. Under § 2044, the survivor's gross estate includes any property in which the decedent had a "qualifying income interest for life," as defined by § 2056(b)(7), if a gift or estate tax marital deduction had been claimed at the time the interest was created. Section 2044 ensures that property for which the decedent's estate was allowed a marital deduction will be taxed in the estate of the surviving spouse, absent any lifetime transfer of the income interest by the surviving spouse.

Section 2044 requires gross estate inclusion of the value of the property in which the beneficiary spouse, now the decedent, enjoyed the income. The decedent is treated as if he owned the property at death even though the decedent had only a terminable interest in it.[51] Further, the Regulations presume that, if the spouse had a qualifying income interest for life in the property, a QTIP election was made when the interest was created, and, therefore, § 2044 applies. The decedent's personal representative has the burden to overcome this presumption. *See* Treas. Reg. § 20.2044–1(c). The Regulations provide the following example:

> Under *D*'s will, assets valued at $800,000 in *D*'s gross estate (net of debts, expenses and other charges, including death taxes, payable from the property) passed in trust with income payable to *S* for life. Upon *S*'s death, the trust principal is to be distributed to *D*'s children. *D*'s personal representative elected under section 2056(b)(7) to treat the entire trust property as qualified terminable interest property and claimed a marital deduction of $800,000. *S* made no disposition of the income interest during *S*'s lifetime under section 2519. On the date of *S*'s death, the fair market value of the trust property was $740,000. *S*'s personal representative did not elect the alternate valuation date.

---

[51] Absent a specific provision to the contrary in the decedent's will (or revocable trust), the decedent's estate is entitled to recover the estate tax paid by the estate on the transfer of qualified terminable interest property at the spouse's death from the recipients of the property. *See* § 2207A(c). This result reflects Congress's assumption that property subject to a terminable interest qualifying for the marital deduction may ultimately pass to persons other than the natural objects of the surviving spouse's (or the donee-spouse's) bounty. The recovery provision prevents the spouse's estate from being liable for estate taxes on a transfer directed by the decedent-spouse (or the donor-spouse), such as to children of a prior marriage. The taxes are recoverable from the trustee if the property is in trust, or from the person who has received the trust property "if the property does not remain in trust." Treas. Reg. § 20.2207A–1(e).

The amount included in *S*'s gross estate pursuant to section 2044 is $740,000.

Treas. Reg. § 20.2044–1(e), Example (1).

The amount includable under § 2044 is dependent on the extent to which the QTIP election was made. If the election was a fraction or percentage, only part of the property will be included in the surviving spouse's gross estate (assuming that the spouse's personal representative proves that something less than a full marital deduction was allowed in the first estate). *See* Treas. Reg. § 20.2044–1(d).

There is one exception to gross estate inclusion under § 2044 where a QTIP marital deduction has been allowed.[52] Section 2044 will not apply if, during lifetime, the beneficiary spouse disposed of the income interest in a manner that triggered § 2519, the gift tax equivalent to § 2044. In that case the trust would have already been taxed under § 2519, and estate taxation would be redundant. Section 2519 is discussed in Chapter 4, § 4.03[B][2], *infra*.

[handwritten margin note: Exception]

Problems

1. If the decedent's will created a qualified terminable interest trust, but no QTIP election was made, would the trust property be included in the surviving spouse's gross estate at her death?

2. Should § 2044 mandatorily apply if the decedent spouse's estate made no QTIP election but claimed a marital deduction based on the duty of consistency? *See Estate of Letts v. Commissioner*, 109 T.C. 290 (1997)? Would it matter if, due the trustee's mismanagement, the surviving spouse did not actually receive all of the QTIP trust income? *See Estate of Soberdash v. Commissioner*, T.C. Memo 1997–362.

[g] Valuation Rules

Estate of Bonner v. United States

84 F.3d 196 (5th Cir. 1996)

PER CURIAM: The estate of Louis F. Bonner, Sr., Appellant ("the estate") filed suit to recover a refund of approximately $425,000 in estate taxes assessed by and paid to the Internal Revenue Service ("IRS" or "the government"). The estate and the government filed cross motions for summary judgment based on a joint stipulation of facts, but differing interpretations of the applicable law. The district court granted summary judgment for the government, ordering that the estate was not entitled to a refund of any estate taxes paid. We reverse.

---

[52] If a QTIP election was made, but there would be no federal estate tax payable even if a QTIP election was not made, § 2044 will not apply because the QTIP will be deemed null and void. *See* Rev. Proc. 2001-38, 2001-24 I.R.B. 335.

FACTS

The estate's decedent ("Bonner") died on January 11, 1989. At the time of his death, Bonner owned the following properties:

1) A fee simple 62.5 percent undivided interest in real property consisting of 2,107.33 acres in Angelina County, Texas ("the ranch");

2) A fee simple 50 percent undivided interest in real property located in New Mexico ("New Mexico property");

3) A fee simple 50 percent undivided interest in a 56 foot pleasure boat ("the boat").

The remaining 37.5 percent interest in the ranch, 50 percent interest in the New Mexico Property and 50 percent interest in the boat were owned by a trust established by the will of Bonner's wife ("Mrs. Bonner") who died on December 7, 1986. The parties also stipulated that the fair market values of 100 percent fee ownership of the properties on the date of Bonner's death were $1,800,000 for the ranch, $175,000 for the New Mexico property and $30,000 for the boat.

Mrs. Bonner's estate elected to claim a marital deduction for the bequest to the trust under the Internal Revenue Code ("I.R.C."), 26 U.S.C. § 2056(b)(7). The trust satisfied the test for qualified terminable interest property (QTIP) under that provision. Accordingly, a marital deduction was allowed to Mrs. Bonner's estate for the value of these property interests passing to the trust. As required by I.R.C. section 2044, the value of these undivided interests held by the trust were included in the taxable estate of Bonner upon his subsequent death. The undivided interests owned by Bonner at his death were included in his taxable estate pursuant to I.R.C. section 2033.

Per the appraisal submitted by the estate as part of its summary judgment evidence, the fair market value of Bonner's interest in the ranch claimed on the estate's tax return included a 45 percent discount (below 62.5 percent of $1,800,000) based on the fact that is was a fractional undivided interest. The New Mexico property and the boat were likewise discounted on the estate's tax return. The government did not stipulate to the appropriate amount of discount, if any, based on the undivided nature of the interests in question in the event that the Court finds that a discount is allowable as a matter of law.

On cross motions for summary judgment, the district court, adopting the reasoning of the government, held that the estate is not entitled to a refund of estate tax, granted the government's motion for summary judgment and denied the estate's motion for summary judgment.

STANDARD OF REVIEW

This appeal is taken from a final summary judgment predicated upon stipulated facts and the district court's interpretation of a federal statute, which we review de novo. . . .

AVAILABILITY OF FRACTIONAL INTEREST DISCOUNT

The sole question before us is whether the estate is precluded from applying a fractional interest discount against the value of these three properties for federal estate tax purposes.

We begin by recognizing that valuation of interests in property for federal tax purposes is a question of fact. *Propstra v. United States*, 680 F.2d 1248, 1251 (9th Cir. 1982). Further, courts have consistently recognized that the sum of all fractional interests in a property is less than the whole and have upheld the use of fractional interest discounts in valuing undivided interests. *See, e.g. Estate of Bright v. United States*, 658 F.2d 999 (5th Cir. 1981) (*en banc*). The discount is an acknowledgment of the restrictions on sale or transfer of property when more than one individual or entity hold undivided fractional interests. *Estate of Wildman v. C.I.R.*, 58 T.C. Memo 1006, 1989 WL 153505 (1989). Potential costs and fees associated with partition or other legal controversies among owners, along with a limited market for fractional interests and lack of control, are all considerations rationally related to the value of an asset. *See id.*

The government takes the position that the interest held by the QTIP trust and the interest held by Bonner merged at the time of Bonner's death, pursuant to the plain language of section 2044 [footnote omitted], extinguishing the fractional undivided interests and resulting in 100 percent fee ownership of the assets by the estate.

Section 2031(a) provides that the value of a decedent's gross estate includes the value of property included in his gross estate pursuant to sections 2033 and 2044. Under section 2033, a decedent's gross estate includes the value of all property that decedent owned at the time of his death. Under section 2044(a) and (b)(1)(A), it also includes the value of any property for which a deduction was allowed for the decedent's spouse's taxable estate under section 2056 by reason of the QTIP provisions of section 2056(b)(7). Property thus includable in the gross estate of the decedent "shall be treated as property passing from the decedent." 26 U.S.C. § 2044(c). The government contends, and the district court found, that the "plain language of section 2044 resulted in 100 percent fee ownership by the estate at the moment of Bonner's death, and precluded any potential problems with fractional ownership." Such a reading is not supported by precedent or logic. In *Estate of Bright v. United States*, 658 F.2d 999 (5th Cir. 1981), this Court, sitting en banc, rejected a similar argument, there termed the "doctrine of family attribution." In that case, Bright held a 27½ percent interest in an asset as executor of his deceased wife's estate, while simultaneously holding an additional 27½ percent interest in the same asset in his individual capacity. This Court rejected the government's contention that Bright's interests for estate tax purposes should be treated as one 55 percent interest in the asset.

In *Bright,* we considered Reg. 20.2031–1(b), which provides:

> The fair market value is the price at which the property would change hands between a willing buyer and a willing seller, neither being under any compulsion to buy or to sell and both having reasonable knowledge of relevant facts.

The "willing seller" is not the estate itself, but is a hypothetical seller. Therefore, family attribution, which depends on the identity of seller as the legatee and the executor, cannot control the value of the asset.

The question before us is controlled by the holding in *Bright*. Although section 2044 contemplates that the QTIP property will be treated as having passed from Bonner for estate tax purposes, the statute does not require, nor logically contemplate that in so passing, the QTIP assets would merge with other assets. The assets in the QTIP trust could have been left to any recipient of Mrs. Bonner's choosing, and neither Bonner nor the estate had any control over their ultimate disposition. We are precluded from considering evidence submitted by the government regarding who actually received the assets. An estate tax is an excise tax on the transfer of property at death and accordingly the valuation is made as of the moment of death and must be measured by the interest that passes, as contrasted with the interest held by the decedent before death or the interest held by the legatee after death. *Bright*, 658 F.2d at 1006.

In addition to arguing that section 2044 mandates merging of the Bonners' fractional interests in the assets, the government also argues that public policy dictates that the Bonners not use the QTIP device to avoid paying taxes on the unified value of the property. In fact, public policy mitigates in favor of the estate's position in this litigation. The estate of each decedent should be required to pay taxes on those assets whose disposition that decedent directs and controls, in spite of the labyrinth of federal tax fictions. In this case, Mrs. Bonner controlled the disposition of her assets, first into a trust with a life interest for Bonner and later to the objects of her largesse. The assets, although taxed as if they passed through Bonner's estate, in fact were controlled at every step by Mrs. Bonner, which a tax valuation with a fractional interest discount would reflect. At the time of Bonner's death, his estate did not have control over Mrs. Bonner's interests in the assets such that it could act as a hypothetical seller negotiating with willing buyers free of the handicaps associated with fractional undivided interests. The valuation of the assets should reflect that reality.

CONCLUSION

Based on the foregoing, we reverse the summary judgment for the government. Because the record discloses a genuine issue of material fact concerning the appropriate value of the fractional interest discounts, we remand to the district court for further proceedings consistent with this opinion.

Reversed and Remanded.

————

The Tax Court in *Estate of Mellinger v. Commissioner*, 112 T. C. 26 (1999), followed *Bonner*. Subsequently, the Internal Revenue Service acquiesced in result only. *See* 1999-2 C.B. XVI.

Revenue Ruling 84–105

1984–2 C.B. 197

ISSUE

What are the estate and gift tax consequences when a pecuniary bequest for the benefit of the surviving spouse is inadequately satisfied by the executor under the circumstances described below?

FACTS

The decedent *D* died on July 1, 1977. *D*'s will provided for a bequest of 200x dollars to be used to establish a testamentary trust for the benefit of *D*'s surviving spouse *S*. The will provided that trust income is payable to *S* for *S*'s life and that a general power of appointment over the trust assets may be exercised by *S* at any time. The terms of the trust meet the general requirements of section 2056(b)(5) of the Internal Revenue Code for allowance of a marital deduction for *D*'s estate. The residue of the estate was bequeathed to *C*, the child of *D* and *S*. *D*'s executor filed a timely estate tax return for the estate on March 20, 1978, claiming a marital deduction of 200x dollars for the bequest to establish the trust. At that time the executor believed that the trust for the benefit of *S* would eventually be fully funded. The trust was established by the executor and initially funded with 100x dollars on April 1, 1979. However, final funding of *S*'s trust was delayed until the administration of *D*'s estate could be completed.

On July 15, 1983, the executor distributed an additional 60x dollars worth of tangible and intangible assets to *S*'s trust. Income was paid to *S* with respect to the 160x dollars worth of corpus for the period between *D*'s death and the time the amounts were placed in trust. The remaining 40x dollars worth of the bequest was never distributed to the trust. In order for the remaining 40x dollars portion of the bequest to be satisfied, the executor would have had to sell some of *D*'s farm land that would otherwise become a part of the residue for the benefit of *C*. The executor's final account showing only 160x dollars worth of assets had been distributed to the trust was approved by an order of the local probate court on July 22, 1983. *S* did not object or attempt to appeal the order of the court, which became final on August 22, 1983.

LAW AND ANALYSIS

Section 2056(a) of the Code provides that, in computing the decedent's taxable estate, a marital deduction is allowable for the value of property passing from the decedent to the surviving spouse.

Section 20.2056(e)–2(d)(1) provides that if, as a result of a controversy involving the decedent's will, or involving any bequest or devise thereunder, the surviving spouse assigns or surrenders a property interest in settlement of the controversy, the interest so assigned or surrendered is not considered as having passed from the decedent to the surviving spouse. Section 2511 of the Code provides that the gift tax applies to a transfer of property by gift, whether the transfer is in trust or otherwise, whether the gift is direct or indirect, and whether the transferred property is real or personal, tangible, or intangible.

Section 2518 of the Code provides that if a person makes a qualified disclaimer with respect to any interest in property, the estate, gift, and generation-skipping transfer tax provisions of the Code shall apply to such interest as if the interest had never been transferred to such person.[53] A qualified disclaimer must be made within 9 months of the date on which the transfer creating the interest in such person is made. In the absence of a qualified disclaimer, a property interest bequeathed to a person is treated as passing by will to that person from the decedent, for purposes of the estate, gift, and generation-skipping transfer tax provisions of the Code. In the present case, S could have recovered the 40x dollar amount by routinely asserting in the local probate court the right as beneficiary under D's will to have the bequest adequately satisfied. The fact that some of the land would have had to be either sold or severed to satisfy fully the bequest to S would not have impaired S's claim for full satisfaction. The failure of S to raise an objection to the underfunding of the testamentary trust at some time before the expiration of S's right to appeal the final order of the local probate court in effect constituted an irrevocable transfer to C by S of the 40x dollar amount.

S's acquiescence in the underfunding of the trust is not an assignment or surrender of a property interest in settlement of a controversy described in section 20.2056(e)–2(d)(1) of the regulations. Further, S's acquiescence is not a qualified disclaimer because S made no disclaimer of the 40x dollar amount within 9 months of D's death.

For purposes of the estate and gift tax provisions of the Code, the amount of property that passed from D to S under D's will was 200x dollars, notwithstanding the underfunding of S's trust. The 40x dollar amount that was diverted by D's executor from S to C is a gift by S to C on August 22, 1983.

HOLDING

The estate tax marital deduction allowable to D's estate for the bequest in trust to S is 200x dollars. The distribution of 40x dollars to C is a taxable gift by S.

Bonner illustrates how a carefully planned estate and estate administration may produce estate tax savings. By dividing the ownership of assets between

---

[53] [Section 2518 is considered in detail in Chapter 4. Eds.]

a husband and wife during their joint lives, it is possible to affect valuation of those assets, if the estate planning documents maintain that separate ownership and selection of assets for distribution during the first spouse's estate do not undo the division.

With every opportunity there is the potential for disaster, or so it seems. While *Bonner* offers opportunities, pitfalls exist. For example, where a decedent dies owning a controlling interest in a corporation, but devises it partially to a surviving spouse and partially to others, the value of the controlling interest in the decedent's estate will exceed the value of the two smaller blocks when distributed. This becomes critical for purposes of valuing the block left to the spouse for marital deduction purposes.

Rev. Rul. 84–105 presents a different but related issue. When a surviving spouse does not insist on receiving the full value of the marital deduction, a taxable transfer results, and a gift tax can arise.

Valuation of the interest qualifying for the marital deduction depends, in part, on how the underlying property interest was treated for gross estate inclusion purposes. Because the personal representative will usually use date of death values, those values will control for marital deduction purposes. If the alternate valuation date or special use valuation rules were elected, however, these methods would apply in valuing the interests qualifying for the marital deduction. *See* Treas. Reg. § 20.2032–1(g); Priv. Ltr. Rul. 8433011.

Valuation problems arise because the value, for marital deduction purposes, of property passing to the surviving spouse is the net value of any deductible interest. Thus, several factors must be taken into account in calculating the amount of the marital deduction, including: (1) the effect of encumbrances; (2) the effect of obligations on the surviving spouse; and (3) the effect of death taxes. *See, e.g., United States v. Stapf*, 375 U.S. 118 (1963) (reduction in widow's election situation); *Estate of Chiles v. United States*, 843 F.2d 367 (9th Cir. 1988) (reduction for taxes); *Estate of Preisser v. Commissioner*, 90 T.C. 767 (1988) (reduction for mortgage debt).

In *Commissioner v. Estate of Hubert*, 520 U.S. 93, (1997), the Supreme Court ruled on a difficult issue under § 2056(b)(4). Should the value of the marital deduction be reduced if the expenses of administration were payable from income that otherwise would be payable to the surviving spouse?[54] Based on Treasury Regulation § 20.2056(b)(4), the Service took the position that the payment of *any* expenses from such income *ipso facto* constituted a "material limitation" on the right to receive income so that the marital deduction should be reduced dollar for dollar by expenses payable from such income. The Court rejected this position, and because the Service failed to make any other arguments, the Court ultimately allowed a marital deduction without reduction for expenses that were paid from trust income.

Dissenting and concurring opinions invited the Service to change the *Hubert* result by regulation; in 1999, the Treasury issued final Regulations that detail the tax treatment of estate administration expenses that are charged against

---

[54] The same issue also implicated the amount of the charitable deduction under § 2055. *See* § 2055(c).

marital or charitable shares. The final regulations jettison the material limitation standard that was applicable in *Hubert* and with it, the dependence of whether estate administration expenses were payable from estate principal or income. *See* Jonathan G. Blattmachr, Mitchell M. Gans and Carlyn S. McCaffrey, *The Anti-Hubert Regulations*, 87 TAX NOTES 969 (May 15, 2000).

The Regulations make a distinction between "estate transmission expenses" and "estate management expenses." Estate management expenses are those expenses that could have been incurred by the decedent during life or by the beneficiaries, had they received the property on the date of death without any intervening period of administration. Estate management expenses include, for example, costs of maintaining and preserving estate assets during the estate administration, investment advisory fees, stock brokerage commissions, custodial fees, and interest. Treas. Reg. §§ 20.2055–3(b)(1)(i), 20.2056(b)–4(d)(1)(i). Estate transmission expenses are expenses that would not have been incurred but for the decedent's death and the resultant need to collect the decedent's assets, pay debts and wealth transfer taxes, and distribute the decedent's property to the beneficiaries. Estate transmission expenses include, for example, personal representative commissions and attorney fees (except to the extent they are specifically related to investment, preservation, and maintenance of the assets), probate fees, expenses incurred in construction proceedings and defending against will contests, and appraisal fees. Any expense that is not an estate management expense is an estate transmission expense. Treas. Reg. §§ 20.2055–3(b)(1)(ii), 20.2055–3(b)(2), 20.2056(b)–4(d)(1)(ii), 20.2056(b)–4(d)(2).

Three rules may be derived from Treasury Regulations §§ 20.2056–4(d)(2) thru (4): (1) estate transmission expenses that are payable from the surviving spouse's marital share will reduce the marital deduction whether payable from estate principal or estate income; (2) estate management expenses that are payable from the surviving spouse's marital share will not reduce the marital deduction whether payable from estate principal or estate income; and (3) the marital deduction will be reduced if management expenses are payable from the marital share but are not for the benefit of the surviving spouse.[55]

Problems

1. If *D* is the sole owner of a corporation, and bequeathed a 51% interest in the corporation to his spouse, *W,* will the marital deduction amount reflect a premium for control? *See Estate of Chenoweth v. Commissioner*, 88 T.C. 1577 (1987); *Pillsbury v. Commissioner*, T.C. Memo 1992–425. How would the marital deduction amount be affected if instead, *D* bequeathed only 49% of the stock in the corporation to *W*?

2. At her death the surviving spouse owned outright 40% of stock in a closely held corporation. Another 40% of the stock was held in a trust for which a marital deduction under § 2056(b)(7) had been allowed to the estate of her predeceased spouse. Should minority discounts apply in valuing the stock interests?

---

[55] The *Hubert* regulations are discussed in further detail in Chapter 14.

3. Assume that local law provides that any estate taxes payable by the estate are allocated proportionately among the beneficial interests in the estate, without regard to whether the particular interest generated any tax. Assuming that the surviving spouse takes part of the estate, and that the spouse's interest otherwise would qualify for the marital deduction, what would be the impact of the local rule on the calculation of the estate tax? *Consider Estate of Murphy v. United States*, 524 F. Supp. 862 (W.D. Wis. 1981).

4. The decedent's will leaves her entire $20 million estate to the surviving spouse. The state death tax law of the decedent's domicile does not provide for an unlimited marital deduction, and as a result, the decedent's estate pays $2 million in state death taxes. What is the amount of the estate tax marital deduction permitted the decedent's estate? *See Estate of Chiles v. United States*, 843 F.2d 367 (9th Cir. 1988).

[5]   Estate Planning Considerations

[a]   In General

Estate tax marital deduction planning usually involves planning within the context of a family. Whatever the family situation, the assumed goal is to keep as much wealth within the family and pay as few transfer taxes as possible.

A primary planning consideration is whether it is even necessary to be concerned with the federal estate tax marital deduction. If the combined estates of a married couple do not exceed the applicable exclusion amount (the amount that would generate a tax exactly equal to the applicable credit—for example, $1 million in 2002), the testator may freely transfer all of his property to his spouse at death without tax concerns, unless he devises property to others based on non-tax considerations.

Although the marital property will be taxed in the surviving spouse's estate, the applicable credit will offset the estate consequences on the value of the marital property, provided consumption equals or exceeds any income and appreciation produced by the property during the life of the surviving spouse.[56] This conclusion, it must be noted, assumes that the value of the combined marital property remains below the applicable exclusion amount on the surviving spouse's death. However, determining that the surviving spouse's estate will be less than the applicable exclusion amount is not always readily ascertainable when the couple sign their estate planning documents. The length of time before the second death and the growth in value of the assets is usually totally unknown.

Assuming spousal wealth exceeds, or may exceed, the applicable exclusion amount, marital deduction planning will be appropriate to achieve the goal of maximizing wealth within the family by minimizing federal estate taxes. The planning approach of a zero taxable estate by passing all of the property to the surviving spouse—the maximum unlimited marital deduction—is tempting. The document is very simple.

---

[56] Although there may be no federal estate tax for modest size estates, state death taxes may be imposed under certain state death tax systems.

Unfortunately, using the unlimited marital deduction may produce adverse tax and non-tax consequences. The major tax problem is that this approach may produce a larger-than-necessary tax on the death of the surviving spouse. With an unlimited martial deduction, the first-spouse-to-die's taxable estate could be reduced to zero, but in the process, the applicable exclusion amount of the first-spouse-to-die is wasted. In turn, the surviving spouse's exemption may not be sufficient to avoid the imposition of estate tax when she dies.

Consider a worst case scenario based on both spouses dying in 2002, when the applicable exclusion amount is $1 million.

Example: *H* died in 2002, with a gross estate of $2 million, which he devised to *W*. *H*'s taxable estate would be zero, as would the federal estate tax payable. *W* died ten days later in 2002, with a gross estate that consisted of only the marital property devised to her with an estate tax value of $2 million. For simplicity, assume that neither spouses' estate incurred expenses, or had claims under § 2053.

W's taxable estate would be $2 million, but only the first $1 million would be sheltered from federal estate tax by the 2010 credit. Thus, a federal estate tax would be payable on the second $ 1 million; $250,000 would be taxed at the 41% bracket, $250,000 at the 43% bracket, and $500,000 at the 45% bracket. The estate tax of $435,000 would then be allocated between the federal Treasury ($360,300) and the applicable state ($74,700, based on 75% of the § 2011(b) state death tax credit available in 2002).

Beyond the additional tax cost imposed on *W*'s estate from using the unlimited estate tax marital deduction in this example, consider the human dimension. Assume the couple has two children. Leaving the estate outright to *W* afforded her the opportunity to divert assets from the children. This may not be what the first-spouse-to-die wanted, particularly if the widow is the children's stepmother, and was (or might become) antagonistic to the children. Similarly, even in the case of a nuclear family, a predeceasing spouse may be concerned about the widow remarrying, and ultimately diverting the assets from the children to the new spouse.

Estate planners have devised a number of solutions to the problem of minimizing the overall tax burden on the family while ensuring benefits for family members other than the surviving spouse. In the above example, the solution is to plan the estate so that the decedent's applicable exclusion amount is fully used, while passing the remaining assets to, or for the use of, the surviving spouse.

The plan is implemented by appropriate will drafting. The will is drafted to pass the marital devise to, or for the use of, the surviving spouse in a form that qualifies for the marital deduction and in an amount sufficient to eliminate federal estate taxes, taking into account the applicable credit amount.[57] The balance of the estate can then be left to family members in a so-called "credit shelter disposition" (sometimes referred to as the "bypass trust" when the balance is left in trust), which will not generate federal estate taxes because of the applicable credit.

---

[57] It is also possible to fine tune the approach by relying on other credits.

In short, the plan is to pass sufficient assets to the surviving spouse that qualifies for the marital deduction, so that the taxable estate will equal the applicable exclusion amount.[58] The tax imposed on the taxable estate amount will equal the amount of the applicable credit amount so that no federal estate tax is payable. This plan is referred to as the *reduce to zero* approach.

Planners have also responded to the problem caused by the nature of will drafting. How can the necessary marital deduction amount, that depends on the death of that testator at a future, uncertain time, be determined? The solution lies in the use of martial deduction formula clauses that can be drafted to obtain the optimal marital deduction amount under the *reduce to zero* approach.

The following is a sample of a marital deduction formula clause in a will that entitles the surviving spouse to the dollar amount (often referred to as the pecuniary amount) necessary to zero-out the federal estate taxes on the death of the first-spouse-to-die:

> I give to my surviving spouse that pecuniary amount equal to the smallest amount necessary to eliminate the federal estate tax liability for my estate, taking into account all other deductions that are allowed to my estate, and the applicable credit under § 2010 of the Internal Revenue Code, as amended.[59]

As applied to the example above, where *H* and *W* both died in 2002, the formula amount would be $1 million. With a marital deduction of $1 million,

---

[58] If taxable gifts were made, the size of the taxable estate may be less than the exemption equivalent amount needed to zero-out the estate tax.

[59] An alternative to a pecuniary marital deduction clause is a pecuniary credit shelter amount formula with the residue passing to the surviving spouse in a qualifying form. Yet another formula approach involves drafting both the credit shelter and marital deduction provisions as fractions of the residuary estate.

The funding of pecuniary dispositions can cause unwanted capital gains to an estate if the pecuniary amount is satisfied with assets that have appreciated during estate administration. In our example, when *H* died in 2002, the pecuniary bequest produced by a pecuniary marital bequest was $1 million. If the personal representative satisfied this bequest with stock at an estate tax value of $800,000, the estate would have a $200,000 capital gain on funding. See Kenan v. Commissioner, 114 F.2d 217 (2d Cir. 1940) and Rev. Rul. 60-87, 1960-1 C.B. 286, both of which are set forth in section § 14.05[E][1].

In response to the gain on funding problem, estate planners mandated that pecuniary bequests be satisfied by using assets based on estate tax values. In the above situation, the pecuniary bequest of $1 million would not be satisfied by distributing the stock that had an estate tax value of $800,000. An additional $200,000 in cash or other assets with an estate tax value of $200,000 would be necessary. On the other hand, if the estate had an asset with an estate tax value of $1 million, but a date of distribution value of only $800,000 (or even a value of nothing!), the pecuniary bequest would be satisfied by using this asset. This raises potential Rev. Rul. 84-105 problems if not funded with other assets. *See* § 3.04[C][4][g].

The potential for minimizing the value of the surviving spouse's estate was of great concern to the Government. In response, the Service issued the famous (infamous) Rev. Proc. 64-19, 1964-1 C.B. 682. With Rev. Proc. 64-19, the Service announced that a pecuniary marital bequest would be disallowed as violative of the terminable interest rule if the personal representative had discretionary funding powers that could result in minimizing the value of property received by the surviving spouse. At the same time, Rev. Proc. 64-19 sanctioned funding based on estate tax values if the personal representative did not have the discretion to distort the value of property passing to the surviving spouse.

the taxable estate will also be $1 million, and the resulting tax imposed under § 2001 will be zeroed-out by the applicable credit of $345,800 permitted under § 2010 for the year 2002.

If, however, H and W die in 2004, when the applicable exclusion amount under § 2010 is $1.5 million, the smallest amount necessary to zero-out H's estate would be $500,000. H's taxable estate would be $1.5 million with a marital deduction of $500,000, and the tax would be zeroed out by the credit of $555,800, under § 2010. In effect, the formula clause is self-adjusting for future events, such as the increasing applicable credit amount or changes in asset values and asset profiles between the date the will is executed and death of the testator.

The "reduce to zero" approach is most effective where: (1) one spouse owns most of the family property and is likely to die first; and (2) the family wealth is between one and two exemption equivalents (for example, $1 million and $2 million in 2002). If the combined estates exceed twice the value of the exemption equivalent, other techniques must be used to further reduce taxes. In larger estates, it may make sense to subject some property to tax when the first spouse dies, to avoid taxing the property at a higher marginal rate when the surviving spouse dies.[60]

> **Example:** If both spouses are likely to die relatively close together, the estate should be planned so that approximately equal amounts are taxed in each estate. This prevents property in either estate from being taxed at a rate higher than the highest marginal rate applicable to the other estate. This can be accomplished by providing in the will of the first-spouse-to-die that sufficient property pass to the surviving spouse to equalize the size of the two spouses' estates.[61]

The non-tax difficulties with leaving the entire estate to the surviving spouse may also be alleviated (but not eliminated) in the midst of tax planning. For example, the reduce to zero approach described above necessarily passes some interests to persons other than the surviving spouse, thereby protecting children and other beneficiaries favored by the decedent. The protection could be increased by passing the property that is not in the credit shelter devise to a QTIP trust, which would qualify for the marital deduction, but deny the surviving spouse any power to dispose of the corpus.

The example, however, also suggests a potential problem with the reduce to zero approach. The credit shelter disposition may unduly favor other family members at the expense of the surviving spouse, and leave the surviving spouse with insufficient assets to maintain an acceptable lifestyle. Indeed, in modest estates, the reduce to zero approach may entitle the surviving spouse to an amount that is less than the spouse's elective statutory share amount under applicable state law. This encourages the spouse to exercise the right of election under the applicable state protection statute. This problem may be alleviated in some jurisdictions by making the surviving spouse a beneficiary under the credit shelter disposition. By leaving the surviving spouse an

---

[60] With the increased exemption level and decreasing top marginal rate in the next few years, this technique will be unnecessary. By 2006, there will a flat tax of 46% and for 2007-2009 a flat tax of 45%.

[61] See Rev. Rul. 82–63, 1982–1 C.B. 139 (recognizing equalization clauses).

income interest in the credit shelter disposition, an election against the will may be effectively barred or at least reduced. This solution is not possible in all jurisdictions, however.[62] The only limitation from the tax point of view on the credit shelter disposition is that the surviving spouse's interest must not be such that the trust will be includable in the surviving spouse's gross estate on her death. The purpose of the trust, after all, is to bypass estate taxation when the surviving spouse dies.

In the final analysis, planning for the estate tax marital deduction depends on the first spouse to die having a surviving spouse. Because orders of death are uncertain, it will take lifetime actions to ensure optimal tax results. The gift tax marital deduction is taken up in Chapter 4, 4.03[B], infra.

[b] The Flexible QTIP Device

QTIP trusts have many advantages in planning for the estate tax marital deduction. The major advantage of the QTIP disposition is that it allows the testator to control the identity of the remainder beneficiaries. The surviving spouse does not need to control the remainder for QTIP qualification.[63] Thus, the testator can use a QTIP trust to provide income for a spouse, but preserve the property for ultimate distribution to the decedent's children, and still qualify the devise for the marital deduction. The QTIP marital trust is particularly attractive when either of the spouses have children from an earlier marriage. Alternatively, the testator could provide the surviving spouse with some control by giving him, for example, a testamentary special power of appointment over the remainder.

The tax advantage offered by QTIPs is that the decedent's personal representative can determine what part of the trust will qualify for the marital deduction. That determination is made when the estate tax return is filed, allowing for very flexible tax planning. The personal representative can choose to qualify only part of the QTIP trust for the marital deduction and, assuming the automatic six month extension of time to file has been requested, the election can be made up to fifteen months after the decedent's death. Thus, the personal representative has the flexibility to elect an amount that would, for example, equalize the estates of the spouse and the decedent. If the surviving spouse has a larger potential estate than the decedent, the personal representative can forgo the QTIP election and have the assets taxed at the decedent's lower marginal tax rate. Similarly, if the surviving spouse is in poor health with a short life expectancy, failing to elect QTIP treatment would allow the surviving spouse's estate to benefit from the § 2013 credit for previously taxed property.[64] At the same time, the spouse can be given as many powers for her protection (such as invasion powers limited by a support standard) and as restricted dispositive powers (such as a special power to appoint) as the testator deems advisable.

---

[62] In those jurisdictions, a spousal election could be avoided by leaving the surviving spouse the elective share amount outright.

[63] Because women statistically outlive men, the QTIP regime has been criticized as a sexist device. See Joseph M. Dodge, *A Feminist Perspective on the QTIP Trust and the Unlimited Marital Deduction*, 76 N.C. L. Rev. 1729 (1998); Wendy C. Gerzog, *The Illogical and Sexist QTIP Provisions: I Just Can't Say It Ain't So*, 76 N.C. L. Rev. 1597 (1998).

[64] *See* discussion at § 3.07[D], *infra*.

[c] Credit-Shelter Dispositions

The non-marital portion of the will, often referred to as credit-shelter or by-pass disposition, is the property that can be sheltered by the applicable credit amount of the first-spouse-to-die. Absent lifetime gifts, the credit-shelter disposition will be the amount of the exemption equivalent in the year of the decedent's death. For example, if the decedent dies in 2002 or 2003, the credit-shelter disposition amount may equal $1 million.

Absent spousal protection rules under applicable state law, the predeceasing spouse can completely bypass the surviving spouse in the credit-shelter disposition. Thus, the first-spouse-to-die can make a credit-shelter disposition, outright or in trust, in favor of anyone other than the surviving spouse. Common beneficiaries are children and other family members, although non-relatives could be beneficiaries to the exclusion of family members.

If the testator wants the surviving spouse to be a beneficiary of the credit-shelter disposition, a trust must be structured so that it will not be taxable to the spouse's estate. Such a trust is commonly known as either the "credit-shelter trust" or the "family trust." The former name has been appended because of the tax purpose of the trust. The latter name comes from the dispositive purpose of the trust, which typically provides for the income to the spouse during her life, with the distribution of the principal to other family members, usually children, at her death. At the spouse's death, the trust will not be included in the spouse's gross estate because the spouse has only a life income interest that terminates at death. The survivor has no interest in the trust property being included in the gross estate under § 2033 at the time of his death.

The independent trustee of a family trust may be given the power to invade the trust principal for, or distribute the income to, the surviving spouse or the remaindermen, or both. In these situations, the trustee holds only a special power of appointment, unless the trustee has a power to appoint to himself, his estate, his creditors, or the creditors of his estate. *See* § 2041(b)(1).

A family trust cast in the form of a life income interest to the surviving spouse, with a remainder to the children in equal shares, is maybe too rigid.[65] The surviving spouse or the children may need part of the trust principal to meet their medical or other expenses. In an inflationary spiral, the income from the trust principal may be inadequate for the needs of the surviving spouse. It is possible to give the surviving spouse expanded control and enjoyment of the trust assets by naming that spouse as the trustee or a co-trustee of the family without subjecting the trust to estate taxation at her death.

One technique for adding to the surviving spouse's beneficial interest is to give her an invasion power subject to an ascertainable standard under § 2041(b)(1). That section negates the application of § 2041 when a person has the power to invade the trust principal for her own benefit limited by "an ascertainable standard relating to . . . [her] health, education, support, or

---

[65] A mandatory life estate for the spouse may be undesirable since it can result in greater income taxes than if an independent trustee had the discretion to distribute the income to the spouse, as well as to other beneficiaries who are in lower income tax brackets.

maintenance. . . ." Thus, such a power can be freely given. Care must be taken, however, in drafting the power. Giving the surviving spouse the right to invade the trust principal for her "comfort, welfare, or happiness" is not considered to be conforming to the standard, and would result in taxation of the property to her estate. *See* Treas. Reg. § 20.2041–1(c)(2).

Another option that expands the spouse's control is to grant the surviving spouse a special power to appoint the remainder at death. The permissible appointees often include the decedent's issue, as well as named or unnamed charities. Because the power is not exercisable in the spouse's favor, § 2041 does not require that the property be included in the spouse's gross estate at her death. Giving a surviving spouse a special power of appointment over the family trust allows the surviving spouse a "second look" at the share of the takers in default of exercise, which is commonly the couple's children. This provides flexibility in the family wealth transmission process during the surviving spouse's lifetime. Changes may occur in the health and financial needs of the remaindermen. Some children will likely do better financially than others, while one or more may have little capacity for money management. Others may suffer from physical or mental disabilities. Moreover, the ability of the surviving spouse to designate the share of the takers of the trust property affords the surviving spouse a power of "disappointment," and thus, considerable economic clout over the children.

Not all cases call, however, for a special power. This would be particularly true where the surviving spouse is not the parent of the children, or where there is rancor between the children and the surviving spouse that the decedent does not share. Each case must be decided on its own facts.

Problem

Assume you are drafting the estate planning documents for a married couple. What professional responsibility problems do you see? For example, what problems do you see in recommending the use of a QTIP trust by the wealth holder spouse? In answering, consider American Bar Association, Model Rules of Professional Conduct (1983), Rule 1.7 Conflict of Interest:

General Rule:

(a) A lawyer shall not represent a client if the representation of that client will be directly adverse to another client, unless:

(1) the lawyer reasonably believes the representation will not adversely affect the relationship with the other client; and

(2) each client consents after consultation.

(b) A lawyer shall not represent a client if the representation of that client may be materially limited by the lawyer's responsibilities to another client or to a third person, or by the lawyer's own interests, unless

(1) the lawyer reasonably believes the representation will not be adversely affected; and

(2) the client consents after consultation. When representation of multiple clients in a single matter is undertaken, the

consultation shall include explanation of the implications of the common representation and the advantages and risks involved.

COMMENT:

Other Conflict Situations

Conflicts of interest in a context other than litigation sometimes may be difficult to assess. Relevant factors in determining whether there is potential for adverse effects include the duration and intimacy of the lawyer's relationship with the client or clients involved, the functions being performed by the lawyer, the likelihood that actual conflict will arise and the likely prejudice to the client from the conflict if it does arise. The question is often one of proximity and degree.

[d] Community Property

As in common law states, the wealthier spouse may make lifetime transfers of property to the less wealthy spouse in a manner that qualifies for the unlimited gift tax marital deduction. This provides the latter spouse with assets sufficient to fund the devise sheltered by the applicable exclusion amount should he or she die first. Because of the unlimited gift tax marital deduction under § 2523, no gift tax consequences result on a couple converting (also known as transmuting): (1) community property into separate property; (2) community property into a joint tenancy arrangement; or (3) separate property into community property. If both spouses join in giving community property to a third person, each spouse is treated as making a transfer of one-half interest in the property. The transfer of each is subject to gift tax liability.

United States v. Stapf

375 U.S. 118 (1963)

Mr. Justice Goldberg delivered the opinion of the Court.

. . .

Lowell H. Stapf died testate on July 29, 1953, a resident and domiciliary of Texas, a community property jurisdiction. At the time of his death he owned, in addition to his separate estate, a substantial amount of property in community with his wife. His will required that his widow elect either to retain her one-half interest in the community or to take under the will and allow its terms to govern the disposition of her community interest. If Mrs. Stapf were to elect to take under the will, she would be given, after specific bequests to others, one-third of the community property and one-third of her husband's separate estate. By accepting this bequest she would allow her one-half interest in the community to pass, in accordance with the will, into a trust for the benefit of the children. It was further provided that if she chose to take under the will the executors were to pay "all and not merely one-half" of the community debts and administration expenses.

The relevant facts and computations are not in dispute. The decedent's separate property was valued at $65,100 and the community property at

$258,105. The only debts were community debts totalling $32,368. The administration expenses, including attorneys' fees, were $4,073. If Mrs. Stapf had not elected to take under the will, she would have retained her fully vested one-half interest in the community property ($129,052) that would have been charged with one-half of the community debts ($16,184) and 35 percent of the administration expenses ($1,426). Thus, as the parties agree, she would have received a net of $111,443.

In fact Mrs. Stapf elected to take under the will. She received, after specific bequests to others, one-third of the combined separate and community property, a devise valued at $106,268, which was $5,175 less than she would have received had she retained her community property and refused to take under the will.

In computing the net taxable estate, the executors claimed a marital deduction under [§ 2056(a)] for the full value of the one-third of decedent's separate estate ($22,367) that passed to his wife under the will. The executors also claimed a deduction for the entire $32,368 of community debts as "claims against the estate" under [§ 2053(a)(3)] and for the entire $4,073 of expenses as "administration expenses" under [§ 2053(a)(2)]. The Commissioner of Internal Revenue disallowed the marital deduction and the deductions for claims and administration insofar as these represented debts (50 percent) and expenses (35 percent) chargeable to the wife's one-half of the community. . . . [T]he Court of Appeals, with one judge dissenting on all issues, held that each of the claimed deductions was allowable in full. . . . For reasons stated below, we hold that the Commissioner was correct and that none of the disputed deductions is allowable.

I. The Marital Deduction

By electing to take under the will, Mrs. Stapf, in effect, agreed to accept the property devised to her and, in turn, to surrender property of greater value to the trust for the benefit of the children. This raises the question of whether a decedent's estate is allowed a marital deduction under [§ 2056(b)(4)(B)] where the bequest to the surviving spouse is on the condition that she convey property of equivalent or greater value to her children. The Government contends that, for purposes of a marital deduction, "the value of the interest passing to the wife is the value of the property given her less the value of the property she is required to give another as a condition to receiving it." On this view, since the widow had no net benefit from the exercise of her election, the estate would be entitled to no marital deduction. Respondents reject this net benefit approach and argue that the plain meaning of the statute makes detriment to the surviving spouse immaterial.

. . .

The disputed deduction turns upon the interpretation of (1) the introductory phrase "any obligation imposed by the decedent with respect to the passing of such interest," and (2) the concluding provision that "such . . . obligation shall be taken into account in the same manner as if the amount of a gift to such spouse of such interest were being determined."

The Court of Appeals, in allowing the claimed marital deduction, reasoned that since the valuation is to be "as if" a gift were being taxed, the legal analysis should be the same as if a husband had made an inter vivos gift to his wife on the condition that she give something to the children. In such a case, it was stated, the husband is taxable in the full amount for his gift. The detriment incurred by the wife would not ordinarily reduce the amount of the gift taxable to the husband, the original donor. The court concluded:

> "Within gift tax confines the community property of the widow passing under the will of the husband to others may not be 'netted' against the devise to the widow, and thus testator, were the transfer inter vivos, would be liable for gift taxes on the full value of the devise."

309 F. 2d 592, 598.

This conclusion, based on the alleged plain meaning of the final gift-amount clause of [§ 2056(b)(4)(B)] is not supported by a reading of the entire statutory provision. First, [§ 2056(a)] allows a marital deduction only for the decedent's gifts or bequests that pass "to his surviving spouse." In the present case the effect of the devise was not to distribute wealth to the surviving spouse, but instead to transmit, through the widow, a gift to the couple's children. The gift-to-the-surviving-spouse terminology reflects concern with the status of the actual recipient or donee of the gift. What the statute provides is a "marital deduction"—a deduction for gifts to the surviving spouse—not a deduction for gifts to the children or a deduction for gifts to privately selected beneficiaries. The appropriate reference, therefore, is not to the value of the gift moving from the deceased spouse but to the net value of the gift received by the surviving spouse.

Second, the introductory phrases of [§ 2056(b)(4)(B)] provide that the gift-amount determination is to be made "where such interest or property is incumbered in any manner, or where the surviving spouse incurs any obligation imposed by the decedent with respect to the passing of such interest. . . ." The Government, drawing upon the broad import of this language, argues: "An undertaking by the wife to convey property to a third person, upon which her receipt of property under the decedent's will is conditioned, is plainly an 'obligation imposed by the decedent with respect to the passing of such interest.'" Respondents contend that "incumbrance or obligation" refers only to "a payment to be made out of property passing to the surviving spouse." Respondents' narrow construction certainly is not compelled by a literal interpretation of the statutory language. Their construction would embrace only, for example, an obligation on the property passing whereas the statute speaks of an obligation "with respect to the passing" gift. Finally, to arrive at the real value of the gift "such . . . obligation shall be taken into account. . . ." In context we think this relates the gift-amount determination to the net economic interest received by the surviving spouse.

This interpretation is supported by authoritative declarations of congressional intent. The Senate Committee on Finance, in explaining the operation of the marital deduction, stated its understanding as follows:

"If the decedent bequeaths certain property to his surviving spouse *subject*, however, to her agreement, or a charge on the property, for payment of $1,000 to X, the value of the bequest (and, accordingly, the value of the interest passing to the surviving spouse) is the value, reduced by $1,000, of such property." S. Rep. No. 1013, 80th Cong., 2d Sess., Pt. 2, p. 6. (Emphasis added.)

The relevant Treasury Regulation is directly based upon, if not literally taken from, such expressions of legislative intent. [Treas. Reg. § 20.2056(b)–4(b).] The Regulation specifically includes an example of the kind of testamentary disposition involved in this case:

"A decedent bequeathed certain securities to his wife in lieu of her interest in property held by them as community property under the law of the State of their residence. The wife elected to relinquish her community property interest and to take the bequest. For the purpose of the marital deduction, the value of the bequest is to be reduced by the value of the community property interest relinquished by the wife."[66]

We conclude, therefore, that the governing principle, approved by Congress and embodied in the Treasury Regulation,[67] must be that a marital deduction is allowable only to the extent that the property bequeathed to the surviving spouse exceeds in value the property such spouse is required to relinquish.

The purpose [for the marital deduction] is only to permit a married couple's property to be taxed in two stages and not to allow a tax-exempt transfer of wealth into succeeding generations. Thus the marital deduction is generally restricted to the transfer of property interests that will be includable in the surviving spouse's gross estate.[68] Respondents' construction of [§ 2056(a)] would, nevertheless, permit one-half of a spouse's wealth to pass from one generation to another without being subject either to gift or estate taxes.[69]

---

[66] [10] Treas. Reg. 105, § 81.47c (b)(3) (1949), now Treas. Reg. § 20.2056(b)–4(b)(3) (1958). . . .
See Charles Lowndes and Robert Kramer, Federal Estate and Gift Taxes (1962), § 17.4:
What the Regulations are driving at seems to be this. If a decedent bequeaths property to his wife in lieu of her interest in community property, which is not part of his estate and which does not pass to her from him, it seems clear that the only thing that the surviving spouse actually receives from the decedent is the excess of the interest bequeathed to her over and above the value of her interest in the community property. Therefore, this should be the only amount that qualifies for the marital deduction. . . .

[67] [11] This Court has frequently "given considerable and in some cases decisive weight to . . . interpretative Regulations of the Treasury and of other bodies that were not of adversary origin." *Skidmore v. Swift & Co.*, 323 U.S. 134, 140. Although the weight to be given to an interpretative rule varies with its statutory and legislative context, a Treasury Regulation is particularly persuasive when, as in this case, it is supported by declarations of congressional intent.

[68] [13] The congressional concern with the eventual taxability of marital-deduction property is indicated by the terminable interest rule of § [2056(b)(1)]. . . .

[69] The Court of Appeals recognized the effect of its decision: "Here estate taxes are due now on the property of the husband with the devise to the widow excluded. It is a part of the marital deduction or exclusion on which taxes are deferred to the estate of the widow to be assessed on so much of it as survives on another day. The net of the transfer by the widow became subject to gift taxes at the time of the transfer. The property transferred by the widow will, to the extent of an amount equal to the devise to her, escape both gift and estate taxes." 309 F. 2d 592, 598. For an illustration of the tax effects of the decision, see the dissent of Judge Wisdom. 309 F. 2d, at 608–609.

We do not believe that this result, squarely contrary to the concept of the marital deduction, can be justified. . . . Furthermore, since in a community property jurisdiction one-half of the community normally vests in the wife, approval of the claimed deduction would create an opportunity for tax reduction that, as a practical matter, would be more readily available to couples in community property jurisdictions than to couples in common-law jurisdictions. Such a result, again, would be unnecessarily inconsistent with a basic purpose of the statute.

Since in our opinion the plain meaning of [§ 2056(a)] does not require the interpretation advanced by respondents, the statute must be construed to accord with the clearly expressed congressional purposes and the relevant Treasury Regulation. We conclude that, for estate tax purposes, the value of a conditional bequest to a widow should be the value of the property given to her less the value of the property she is required to give to another. In this case the value of the property transferred to Mrs. Stapf ($106,268) must be reduced by the value of the community property she was required to relinquish ($111,443). Since she received no net benefit, the estate is entitled to no marital deduction.

. . .

The judgment of the Court of Appeals for the Fifth Circuit is reversed and the case remanded for proceedings in accordance with this opinion.

It is so ordered.

———

Estate planning for couples residing or holding property in community property states will differ from planning for those in common law jurisdictions. A typical plan would include a non-marital deduction trust in an amount sufficient to take advantage of the unified credit. A marital deduction trust would be funded with separate property of the deceased and the decedent's share of the community property. The advantage of funding the marital deduction portion with community property is the avoidance of conflict that may result if the community property is controlled equally by the surviving spouse and the decedent's other beneficiaries. Depending on the nature of the property, such conflict could result in liquidation of the asset, with its attendant disadvantages.

Where the decedent spouse's share of the community property passes to the survivor, all of the former community property then held by the surviving spouse will be subject to federal estate taxation. As an alternative, the planner may use the *widow's or widower's election,* which may be created in two ways: voluntary or forced.

The *voluntary widow's* (or *widower's) election* allows the surviving spouse to retain her one-half share of the community property, as well as receive the benefits provided in the decedent spouse's will. A typical will designed to trigger the election would provide that the entire community property is placed in trust for the benefit of the surviving spouse for the spouse's life. In addition, the surviving spouse may be given a power to appoint her one-half share of the community property by will. The survivor may also be given the power to withdraw trust principal in excess of her one-half share. Any power over the deceased spouse's one-half share should be limited by an ascertainable standard. Other beneficiaries, such as the children, would be the remaindermen. Under such a plan, one-half of the community property will be included in the decedent spouse's estate. The survivor's share of the community property is not viewed as passing under the decedent's will and is not taxed as part of the decedent's gross estate.

The *forced widow's* (or *widower's*) *election* requires the survivor to choose between accepting the devise specified in the decedent's will or demanding his right to one-half of the community property. Even if the survivor elects to take under the will, only the decedent's half of the total community property will be taxable to the decedent's estate. The survivor's share of the community property is not viewed as passing under the decedent's will and is not taxed as part of the decedent's gross estate. *See Pacific Nat'l Bank of Seattle v. Commissioner*, 40 B.T.A. 128 (1939). However, as illustrated by *Stapf, supra*, if the surviving spouse elects to take under the will, the marital deduction amount will be reduced by the value that spouse relinquished.

The typical forced widow's election scheme involves a conditional bequest in trust for the widow for life, with remainder to children or other preferred beneficiaries. The bequest is conditioned on the widow agreeing to allow her share of community property to pass under the trust. By this arrangement, the widow is forced to take under the will—effectively receiving a life interest in the husband's community property share—in return for which, she must relinquish a remainder interest in her community property share. Simply put, the widow transfers a remainder interest in return for a life interest. Assuming the widow elects against taking under the will, she typically is deprived of any interest in the decedent's community property share.

Under the typical forced widow's election, the widow is deemed to purchase the life interest in her husband's share of community property.[70] Whether the survivor made a gift and if so, the amount of the gift, depends upon the actuarial value at the time of the decedent's death of: (1) the remainder interest in the survivor's half of the community property and (2) the survivor's life estate in the decedent's half of the community property. The value on the date of the decedent's death of the remainder interest in the community property, surrendered by the surviving spouse in excess of the life estate, received by the surviving spouse (reduced by taxes and other charges), constitutes a taxable gift under § 2501. *See Estate of Bressani v. Commissioner*, 45 T.C. 373 (1966), *acq.* 1966–2 C.B. 4.

Problem

1. Under her husband's marital election will, *D* received a life estate and general testamentary power over the remainder of the trust of the community

---

[70] The cost of the life interest, valued at time of election, may be recovered by amortization deductions. *See* Gist v. United States, 423 F.2d 1118 (9th Cir. 1970). *But see* § 167(e) (denying depreciation deduction for term interests if a related party owns the remainder interest) and § 273 (denying amortization deduction term interests gratuitously acquired.)

property. When *D* dies, can her estate deduct the value of her half of the community property from the value of the trust? *See Steinman v. Commissioner*, 69 T.C. 804 (1978).

[D] The Estate Tax Charitable Deduction: Section 2055

Code: § 2055.

Regulations: Treas. Reg. § 20.2055–2(a)(2), –2(b).

Section 2055 allows an estate to take a charitable deduction equal to the value of most, but not all, interests in property that the decedent transfers at death to a qualifying charitable organization. Unlike the rules of § 170 which limit the income tax charitable deduction, there are neither limitations on the total amount of the estate tax charitable deduction, nor are there distinctions on the type of qualified charitable organizations or the uses to which the organizations will put the bequests. *See* § 2055(a) (but note the limitations of § 2055(e) on private foundations). Outright devises to charitable organizations reduce the decedent's gross estate and lessen the estate tax. In addition, an estate tax deduction may also be available with respect to certain lifetime charitable transfers if the property is included in the decedent's gross estate.

As discussed below, a decedent can make a charitable devise for a partial interest in property. These *split-interest* devises may take the form of a remainder interest or a current income interest in a trust.[71] The portion of the property not left to charity is devised to non-charitable beneficiaries. When a split-interest devise is made, only a portion of the value of the devise qualifies for the estate tax charitable deduction, and only if made in a manner that meets a number of complex rules. *See* §§ 2055, 664; Treas. Reg. § 20.2055–2(e); Treas. Reg. § 20.2055–2(e)(2)(v) (adopting the rules of § 664).

To qualify for the various charitable deductions, the decedent must make the devise to a qualified charitable organization. The rules for qualification of charitable organizations are complex. *See* § 2055(a); Treas. Reg. § 20.2055–1. Students should not confuse the terms *charitable organization* and *exempt organization*. A charitable organization describes an organization to which gifts and bequests are deductible, while an exempt organization is one that does not pay income tax.

Estate of Starkey v. United States

223 F.3d 694 (7th Cir. 2000)

MANION, Circuit Judge.

I. Background

Kenneth Starkey's will created an educational trust for his grandchildren and a charitable trust. Section 5.02 of the will, the provision at issue,

---

[71] Trusts that provide a charity with an income interest for a period of time typically are called *charitable lead trusts*, discussed at § 3.04[D][10] *infra*.

instructed the trustees of the charitable trust to distribute the income as follows:

> Half of the income from the trust is to go to Lawndale Community Church in Chicago, Illinois provided that Wayne Gordon is still the pastor of it at the time of my death and that church will receive this until the time that he is no longer pastor. The Trustees are to manage the property of the Trust *for the benefit of this beneficiary, missionaries preaching the Gospel of Christ, and Milligan College.*

(Emphasis added.) Section 5.03 authorized the trustees to distribute the net income or corpus of the trust to or for the benefit of a beneficiary "at any time and from time to time as the Trustees deem advisable." One week later, Mr. Starkey executed the following codicil to his will:

> My Last Will and Testament in Items IV and V, created two trusts, the former an educational trust and the latter a charitable trust. My Last Will and Testament further provided that the trusts would eventually end even though they were educational and charitable in nature and therefore not subject to the Rule against Perpetuities twenty-one years after the death of my last descendant alive at the time of my own demise. My last Will and Testament did not dispose of the residue of the trusts upon the occurrence of the terminating events. I specifically leave the residues of both trusts to Milligan College.

Mr. Starkey died about three weeks later. The Estate claimed a charitable deduction of about $1.3 million on its federal estate tax return for the amount Mr. Starkey had left to the charitable trust and asked the IRS to determine that the trust was exempt from taxation. The IRS declined to do so. It noted various defects in the trust instrument and issued a directive on how the Estate might remedy them. *See Estate of Starkey v. United States*, 58 F.Supp.2d 939, 944 (S.D.Ind.1999).

In response, the Estate petitioned the state probate court to amend Section 5.02 of the will to allow the trustees, in their discretion, to distribute trust income to eight specific beneficiary groups (in effect replacing the "missionaries" phrase in Section 5.02 with the eight specific groups). The motion stated that the groups "all fit the description of those intended by the testator to benefit from this trust, [Lawndale Community Church], missionaries preaching the Gospel of Christ, and Milligan College." The Estate then filed an amended petition stating that the part of Section 5.02 referring to "missionaries preaching the Gospel of Christ" had "created confusion as to whether the phrase . . . defines the beneficiary Lawndale Community Church or whether missionaries preaching the Gospel of Christ creates a [separate] class of beneficiaries." The amended petition no longer sought to substitute specifically named groups for the "missionaries" phrase; it retained the phrase and argued that it was meant simply to describe the Lawndale Community Church. The Estate requested the state court to construe the phrase accordingly.

In the verified petition, Mr. Starkey's son stated that the Lawndale Community Church was well known for its missionary program and that, in fact, its missionary program was the only such program his father supported. The

Estate also offered the testimony of Dr. Lynn Franken, a former associate dean of the College of Arts and Sciences at Butler University, who received her doctorate in English language and literature. Dr. Franken is trained as a grammarian, someone who studies the relationship between words and meaning. She opined that the "missionaries" phrase did not create a separate class of beneficiaries, but merely described the Lawndale Community Church. The probate court agreed and construed the phrase "missionaries preaching the Gospel of Christ" in Section 5.02 "as merely descriptive of Lawndale Community Church" and "as not creating a separate class of beneficiaries to which the trustees could distribute income or corpus."

The next day the IRS issued the Estate an estate tax deficiency in the amount of $520,178 (plus penalties). Despite the probate court's construction of the will, the IRS maintained that the will created three trust beneficiaries: the Lawndale Community Church, a group of missionaries, and Milligan College. The IRS thus disallowed the Estate a charitable deduction because the trust assets were split between charitable and noncharitable beneficiaries (concluding that while the Lawndale Community Church and Milligan College were both qualified charities, a group of unknown missionaries was not) and the amount of the charitable bequest was unascertainable.

Shortly thereafter, the Estate petitioned the probate court to appoint a *guardian ad litem* to represent the interests of the unknown "missionaries preaching the Gospel of Christ" so they could appeal the probate court's ruling that they—whoever they might be—are not beneficiaries. The Indiana Court of Appeals, in an unpublished opinion, affirmed the ruling of the probate court. It held that the "missionaries" phrase "is most logically interpreted in the context of the will as standing in apposition to, and describing, the Lawndale Community Church." The guardian sought transfer to the Indiana Supreme Court, but it declined to hear the case.

After the state court proceedings concluded, the Estate paid the assessment and filed a refund claim with the IRS. The Estate claimed that the trust qualified for a charitable deduction because in his will, as interpreted by the state courts, Mr. Starkey had intended to create only two beneficiaries (the Lawndale Community Church and Milligan College), both of which are charities. The IRS disallowed the refund claim, and the Estate filed this action against the United States under 28 U.S.C. § 1346(a)(1) (allowing taxpayers to sue for relief from erroneously assessed taxes).

Both sides moved for summary judgment. The district court framed the issue as whether Mr. Starkey had "intended that the portion of his estate transferred to the [charitable] trust would be used by the trustees exclusively for charitable purposes, and whether the language he used in the grant to the trust restricted the trustees to such use. . . ." *Estate of Starkey*, 58 F.Supp.2d at 955. The district court held that the probate and appellate courts' decisions did not bind it, and it was only required to give them "proper" weight. The court determined that "proper" was not much because the probate court proceedings were not adversarial due to the absence of the IRS. *Id.* at 951. Yet, although the United States received notice of both the probate and appellate proceedings, it did not contest them or even appear. The district court disagreed with the state courts' interpretation of the "missionary" phrase and concluded that Mr. Starkey more likely intended to benefit a group of missionaries in addition to the church and the college. *Id.* at 956-57. Because the trustees had the discretion to distribute an undesignated amount of trust corpus or income to a group of "missionaries" potentially for personal purposes, the court held that Mr. Starkey had failed to create a charitable trust. *Id.* at 957-58. The district court ruled that the Estate was not entitled to a charitable deduction and entered judgment for the Government. The Estate appeals this ruling.

II. Discussion

. . .

A. Relevant Tax Principles

. . . A decedent's taxable estate is determined by deducting from the gross estate transfers for public, charitable or religious uses (among other things). *Id.* at 2055(a). The entire amount transferred to a trust for the benefit of a qualified charity is deductible. *Id.* at 2055(a)(3). [Footnote omitted.]

To qualify for the charitable deduction, the charitable bequest must be ascertainable at the time of the transfer. *Estate of Marine v. Commissioner of Internal Revenue*, 990 F.2d 136, 138 (4th Cir.1993) ("Ascertainability at the date of death of the amount going to charity is the test."). If a will provides a trustee with discretion to distribute trust assets to charities and to individuals for their personal use, the amount bequeathed to the charities might not be ascertainable at the time of the transfer. *See Merchants Nat. Bank of Boston v. Commissioner of Internal Revenue*, 320 U.S. 256, 257-58, 263, 64 S.Ct. 108, 88 L.Ed. 35 (1943); *see also Estate of Marine*, 990 F.2d at 138-39. Such a trust, where the assets are "split" between charitable and noncharitable beneficiaries, is known as a "split-interest" trust. *See* 26 U.S.C. § 2055(e)(2). With such a trust, the estate can only take a charitable deduction if the charitable interest of the trust is presently ascertainable. *See id.* at §§ 2055(e)(2)(A) & (B), 2055(e)(3); *see also* Treas. Reg. § 20.2055-2(a) ("If a trust is created or property is transferred for both a charitable and a private purpose, deduction may be taken of the value of the charitable beneficial interest only insofar as that interest is presently ascertainable, and hence severable from the noncharitable interest.").

The will's codicil clearly states that Mr. Starkey intended to set up a charitable trust, and the IRS acknowledges that this was indeed his intent. Its dispute with the Estate is over the type of charitable trust he intended to create and, more specifically, whom he intended to benefit. The IRS acknowledges that if Mr. Starkey intended the "missionaries" phrase to create two beneficiaries (Lawndale Community Church and Milligan College, both of which are qualified charities), then the value of the charitable interest would be ascertainable and hence deductible. In that case, the trust would not be a split-interest trust because both the trust beneficiaries would be qualified charities and the trust assets could only be used for their benefit. As a result, the charitable portion of the trust would be ascertainable (it would be the entire value of the trust). [Footnote omitted.] If, however, Mr. Starkey intended to benefit a group of missionaries in addition to the church and the college, the IRS argues that then Mr. Starkey will have created a split-interest trust with both charitable and noncharitable beneficiaries. In that case the trust assets would not have been specifically divided among the charitable and noncharitable beneficiaries. Because the charitable portion of the trust would thus not be ascertainable, the Estate would not qualify for a charitable deduction. *See* Treas. Reg. § 20.2055-2(a). We agree with the IRS that this is the "ultimate issue" and thus must now determine whom Mr. Starkey intended to assist financially in preaching the Gospel of Christ, and if the will sufficiently expresses his intent.

B. Kenneth Starkey's Probable Intent

Both parties agree that Indiana law governs our analysis of Mr. Starkey's will. *Estate of Bowgren v. Commissioner of Internal Revenue*, 105 F.3d 1156, 1161 (7th Cir.1997). In Indiana, the primary goal in interpreting a will is to determine and give effect to the testator's intent as expressed in the will, and determining this intent is a question of law. *Gladden v. Jolly*, 655 N.E.2d 590, 592 (Ind.Ct.App.1995); *Hershberger v. Luzader*, 654 N.E.2d 841, 842 (Ind.Ct.App.1995). The Estate notes that the probate court determined that Mr. Starkey intended the charitable trust to have only two beneficiaries, and it argues that the district court should have adopted this determination of Mr. Starkey's intent because it was affirmed by the Indiana Court of Appeals, "the highest Indiana Court which has addressed the issue."

The Supreme Court has made clear that we are not bound by the probate court's decision: "where the federal estate tax liability turns upon the character of a property interest held and transferred by the decedent under state law, federal authorities are not bound by the determination made of such property interests by a state trial court." *Commissioner of Internal Revenue v. Estate of Bosch*, 387 U.S. 456, 457, 87 S.Ct. 1776, 18 L.Ed.2d 886 (1967). Intermediate state appellate decisions, however, are presumed to be a correct indicator (or "datum") of state law which we may not disregard unless other decisions convince us "that the highest court of the state would decide otherwise." *Id.* at 465, 87 S.Ct. 1776 (emphasis omitted). But Bosch also tells us that if a state's supreme court has not resolved an issue, we have to apply what we "find to be the state law after giving 'proper regard' to relevant rulings of other courts of the State." *Id.*

While the Supreme Court did not expand upon what it meant by "proper regard," we note that the Indiana Court of Appeals did not publish its decision. As a result, it is questionable whether we may simply presume that it correctly indicates Indiana law—whether we may "properly regard" it as precedent— even though it is, of course, directly on point. *See* Ind. R. App. P. 15(A)(3) (unpublished decisions shall not "be regarded as precedent nor cited before any court except for the purpose of establishing the defense of res judicata, collateral estoppel or the law of the case."). . . . But while an unpublished opinion is normally not presumed to be an indicator or "datum" of state law as a published (precedential) decision would be, *Bosch*, 387 U.S. at 465, 87 S.Ct. 1776, we note that arguably (although no one seems to have made the argument) it is the law of the case, which is one of the exceptions under Ind.

R. App. P. 15(A)(3) for when unpublished decisions "may be regarded as precedent." *Supra*. Anyway, regardless of the extent to which it may be viewed as a "datum" of state law, we are persuaded by the Indiana Court of Appeals' analysis in this matter.

The Court of Appeals concluded that the "missionaries" phrase was ambiguous and then construed this ambiguity. [Based on the testimony of a grammarian and taking into account extrinsic evidence, the court held that missionary phrase did not constitute a separate class of beneficiaries but modified the bequest to the Lawndale Community Church]. . . .

Lastly, the IRS argues that the state courts' construction of the "missionaries" phrase should be rejected because "the state court proceedings . . . were instituted for the sole purpose of decreasing the estate's tax liability." We have no doubt that they were; it is not unusual not to want assets, which have already been taxed, to be taxed again. This desire is not impermissible. The only inquiry here is whether Mr. Starkey intended to draft his will so as to *permissibly* reduce, or even avoid, his estate's tax liability. In this regard, the IRS candidly acknowledged at oral argument that Mr. Starkey did not have an illegal intent. The charitable trust was not a "tax dodge." Mr. Starkey was not, for example, trying to shuffle money between family members to "shelter it" from tax while really keeping it within the family. [Footnote omitted.] His charitable intent, and his estate's attempt to implement it, were both perfectly permissible. [Footnote omitted.]

III. Conclusion

. . . Because our objective in construing Mr. Starkey's will is to determine and give effect to his true intent, "rather than have that intent frustrated," *Gladden*, 655 N.E.2d at 592, we hold that "missionaries preaching the Gospel of Christ" in Section 5.02 of Kenneth Starkey's will modifies "this beneficiary" ("the Lawndale Community Church"). As so construed, the bequest to the trust qualifies for a charitable deduction under 26 U.S.C. § 2055(a)(3).

The judgment of the district court in favor of the defendant is REVERSED and the case is remanded for judgment to be entered in favor of the plaintiff.

The deduction for outright devises of property, other than cash, is the property's fair market value, which is determined by the price that a willing buyer would pay a willing seller. The regular rules determine the value of property devised to charity. *See* §§ 2031 and 2032. When the devise to charity is only for a partial interest in property, additional rules apply to determine valuation. *See* Treas. Reg. § 20.2055–2(f).

Comparable to § 2056(b)(4), the amount of the charitable deduction must take into account any taxes that may be payable from the charitable bequest. *See* § 2055(c). Regulations outlining the effect of administration expenses on the charitable deduction were promulgated in response to the Supreme Court's decision in *Hubert*, discussed at § 3.04[C][4], *supra* and § 14.04[B][4][b] *infra*. *See* § 20.2055–3(b).

[1] Deferred Charitable Devises

As an alternative to a devise of the decedent's entire interest in property, a testator may choose testamentary deferred giving. With this option, the enjoyment of the devise to charity is deferred, rather than the devise itself. The charitable beneficiary receives an immediate interest in property with possession or enjoyment delayed until a future date. The advantage of a deferred charitable gift is that a decedent's estate receives some estate tax benefit, while a non-charitable beneficiary enjoys the property before it ultimately passes to charity.

Section 2055 does not allow an estate deduction for all transfers of a partial interest in property. *See* § 2055(e)(2); Treas. Reg. § 20.2055–2(e). An estate tax charitable deduction is allowed only for the value of the charitable remainder if the interest is in the form of a qualified charitable remainder trust, a pooled income fund or a remainder interest in a personal residence or farm. *See* § 2055(e); Treas. Reg. § 20.2055–2(e)(2)(ii), (e)(2)(iii). The qualification rules are complex and strictly enforced by the Service.

Devises of remainder interests in trust must be distinguished from devises of undivided interests in property. If the donor transfers an undivided portion of her entire interest in property, consisting of a fraction or percentage of every substantial interest or right owned by the donor over the entire term of the donor's interest, a charitable deduction will be allowed for the value of the fractional interest without complying with the split-interest transfer rules. *See* Treas. Reg. § 20.2055–2(e)(2)(i).

[2] Reasons for Restrictions on Charitable Remainder Trusts

Through the Tax Reform Act of 1969, Congress imposed strict rules for obtaining estate, gift, and income tax deductions for the value of charitable remainder interests. Senate Finance Committee Report 91–552 explains the general reasons for the change:

> The rules of present law for determining the amount of a charitable contribution deduction in the case of gifts of remainder interests in trust do not necessarily have any relation to the value of the benefit which the charity receives. This is because the trust assets may be invested in a manner so as to maximize the income interest with the result that there is little relation between the interest assumptions used in calculating present values and the amount received by the charity. For example, the trust corpus can be invested in high-income, high-risk assets. This enhances the value of the income interest but decreases the value of the charity's remainder interest.

> The committee agrees . . . that a taxpayer should not be allowed to obtain a charitable contribution deduction for a gift of a remainder interest in trust to a charity which is substantially in excess of the amount the charity may ultimately receive. To provide a closer correlation between the charitable contributions deduction and the ultimate benefit to charity, [and subject to exceptions for non-trust

gifts of residential, and farm property and pooled income fund arrangements] a deduction [will] not be allowed for a gift of a remainder interest [unless] in trust to charity [and] unless the gift takes a specified form: namely, an annuity trust (under which the income beneficiary is to receive a stated dollar amount annually) or a unitrust (under which the income beneficiary is to receive an annual payment based on a fixed percentage of the trust's assets).

[3]　General Rules for Charitable Remainder Trusts

A charitable remainder trust provides for a specified distribution (1) at least annually, (2) to at least one non-charitable beneficiary, (3) for a term of years, or for the life of the noncharitable beneficiary, or the lives of several beneficiaries, and (4) with an irrevocable remainder to be paid over to a charity. There are two types of charitable remainder trusts: charitable remainder annuity trusts and charitable remainder unitrusts. *See* § 2055(e)(2).[72]

The qualified charitable organization must fit the description of organizations defined in § 170(c) and 2055(a). The trust must also name, or allow the trustee to select, an alternative qualified charitable remainderman in case the named charitable beneficiary does not qualify under § 170(c) at the time of any distribution. *See* Treas. Reg. § 1.664–2(a)(6)(iv).

Although a charitable trust is created upon the decedent's death, a testamentary charitable remainder trust is allowed a reasonable period for administration of the decedent's estate before the trust must be funded and payments begin. Nevertheless, the obligation to pay the annuity or the unitrust amount must arise as of the decedent's death, with a catch-up payment when the trust is finally funded.

The payment period must be for the life of the individual beneficiary or lives of the beneficiaries, or for a term not exceeding 20 years. The payment can be terminated upon a qualified contingency, as long as the termination will not occur later than the beneficiary's death, or the end of the stated term of years. The fact that a beneficiary's payout may terminate sooner because of the qualified contingency does not result in an increased charitable deduction. *See* § 664(d)(1)(A), (2)(A).

The trust does not qualify if any person has the power to alter the amount paid to any noncharitable beneficiary. Nevertheless, an independent trustee may be given the authority to sprinkle the required payment among several beneficiaries. For example, a corporate trustee may be permitted to distribute the required payout among the decedent's children, in the trustee's discretion.

Because the trust can make no payment to, or for the use of, any person other than the named noncharitable beneficiaries and the charity, the trust

---

[72] Because of the complexity of the rules and the frequency that taxpayers were requesting private letter rulings concerning the qualifications of a split interest charitable trust, the Service issued several Revenue Procedures setting forth forms for many of the common alternative annuity trusts and unitrusts. *See* Rev. Proc. 89–20, 1989–1 C.B. 841; Rev. Proc. 90–30, 1990–1 C.B. 534; Rev. Proc. 90–31, 1990–1 C.B. 539; and Rev. Proc. 90–32, 1990–1 C.B. 546. Unfortunately, developments since 1990 make the forms outdated on certain issues.

cannot be subject to a power to invade, amend, or revoke for the benefit of any person other than a qualified charity.[73]

The trust is not qualified unless it provides that the noncharitable payment is prorated during the first tax year and the final tax year. As an alternative to proration in the final year, the trust may provide that the payments are to terminate with the last payment preceding the beneficiary's death.

The payment amount must be made at least once annually, although it may be made a reasonable time after the close of the tax year. Also, a charitable remainder trust cannot contain any provision that would restrict the trustee from: (1) investing the trust property so as to obtain a reasonable return or (2) disposing of the trust assets. *See* Treas. Reg. § 1.664–1(a)(3).

Certain rules that apply to private foundations also apply to charitable remainder trusts, such as the private foundation rules imposing excise taxes or penalties on self-dealing and on taxable expenditures. Thus, a charitable remainder trust must include provisions that would prohibit engaging in activities that would subject it to private foundation excise taxes.[74]

The valuation of the charitable remainder is complex. Treasury Regulation § 20.2055–2(f) defers to Treasury Regulation § 1.664–4 to calculate the value. The income tax regulation provides very complex rules for determining the value of the charitable deduction. The varying interest rate rule of § 7520 is incorporated with a special rule that permits (1) the use of the interest rate in the month of the decedent's death, or (2) the interest rate applicable for the two months preceding the month of the decedent's death, if either of those will provide a larger charitable deduction.

The Taxpayer Relief Act of 1997 added subsections (d)(1)(D) and (d)(2)(D), which require both charitable remainder annuity trusts and charitable remainder unitrusts to have a charitable remainder equal to at least 10% of the value of the property contributed to the trust. Failing the 10% charitable remainder rule, results in the trust not qualifying under § 664, *i.e.,* the trust is not exempt from income taxes and the donor or the donor's estate will receive no charitable deduction.

[4] The Charitable Remainder Annuity Trust

In a charitable remainder annuity trust (often referred to as a CRAT), the decedent devises property to a trust that provides an annuity for the benefit of at least one noncharitable beneficiary, with the remainder interest passing to a qualified charity. If the charitable remainderman qualifies, the devise of the remainder interest qualifies for estate tax charitable deductions. The charitable remainder annuity trust must satisfy the following conditions.

---

[73] The grantor of an inter-vivos split-interest trust, however, may retain the right to revoke, by will, the interest of any noncharitable beneficiary. The donor may also retain the right to change the charitable remainderman as long as another qualified charitable beneficiary is named instead. *See* Treas. Reg. § 1.664–2(a)(4).

[74] While it is only necessary to include limitations against self-dealing and taxable expenditures, it may be prudent to also expressly prohibit a failure to distribute income, excess business holdings, and "jeopardy" investments. *See* § 4947. In fact, many state statutes mandate such prohibitions.

The trust must pay a sum certain to at least one noncharitable beneficiary, who must be living at the time the trust is created. The amount paid must be between 5% and 50% of the initial fair market value of the trust. *See* § 664(d)(1)(A). The amount must be paid at least annually either for the life or lives of the noncharitable beneficiary or beneficiaries, or for a term not to exceed 20 years. *See* § 664(d)(1)(A). The trust may not pay any other amount to any person. When the time for paying the amount to the noncharitable beneficiary terminates, the remainder must be paid to the charitable organization or remain in trust for the organization's use.

When the annuity payment is expressed as a dollar amount, rather than as a percent of the initial fair market value, there is a danger that the amount expressed may prove to be less than 5% or greater than 50% of the fair market value of the trust as finally determined for federal tax purposes. Fractional or percentage annuities cannot violate the 5% minimum or 50% payout, unless the trust property is later revalued, causing the earlier payments to be more or less than the proper amount based upon the subsequent revaluation. Such an overpayment or underpayment would violate the requirement that the payments under the annuity be a sum certain. This problem must be avoided by providing a method in the trust for correcting payments in the event of subsequent revaluation. Failure to include such an adjustment provision in the trust will disqualify the trust. *See* Treas. Reg. § 1.664–2(a)(1)(iii).

The trust cannot provide for a fixed percentage payout to be increased upon the occurrence of some condition. For example, the payout percentage cannot be increased for the life of a successor beneficiary after the death of a previous beneficiary.

No additional contributions can be made to a charitable remainder annuity trust after it is initially funded. *See* Treas. Reg. § 1.664–2(b).

[5]   Charitable Remainder Unitrust

In a charitable remainder unitrust (often referred to as a CRUT), the decedent devises a present interest in a qualified unitrust to at least one noncharitable beneficiary, with the remainder to a charitable organization. Unlike the annuity trust, in which the annuity is a sum certain, the unitrust involves a variable annual payment. The yearly distribution is calculated according to the value of the trust property determined from year to year.

The payment term must be for the life or lives of an individual beneficiary or beneficiaries living at the time the trust is created, or for a term not to exceed 20 years. The trust may not make any payment to any other person. When the noncharitable interest terminates, the remainder interest must be paid to, or held for the use of, a qualified charitable organization. *See* § 664(d)(2)(A).

The fixed percentage of the annual payment must be between 5% and 50% of the annual value of the trust property. *See* § 664(d)(2)(A). The annual payment must be expressed as a percentage or a fraction, not as a dollar amount. This standard type of charitable remainder unitrust is sometimes referred to as CRUT. As a variation, a trust (NI-CRUT) may limit any annual payment to the actual amount of income received, if the income is less than the fixed percentage amount. *See* § 664(d)(3). When the payments are limited, the trust may also provide that the difference between the fixed percentage amount and the actual income earned may be paid in subsequent years, when the annual payment is less than the income, but a "make-up" provision is not mandatory. *See* § 664(d)(3). This type of trust is referred to as a net income make-up only charitable remainder unitrust, abbreviated as NIM-CRUT.

The unitrust must be valued at least once a year on the same valuation date. The same valuation method must be used each time. The trust will be disqualified unless the instrument provides that subsequent adjustments may be made in payments based on incorrect valuations.

Unlike the charitable remainder annuity trust, additional contributions may be made to the charitable remainder unitrust. The trust must include a specific provision for the valuation of additional contributions for purposes of determining the payout to the beneficiary in the year of contribution, unless the trust prohibits additional contributions. If the additional contribution is made after the date of valuation, it is valued at the time of its contribution. Income earned on the additional contribution is not considered in the valuation for that year. When an additional contribution is made before the valuation date, the additional property is valued at the valuation date, including any income earned since its contribution. The trust must also provide for subsequent adjustments for undervaluation or overvaluation.

[6] Comparison Between CRATs and CRUTs

The essential difference between a CRAT and a CRUT is that in a CRAT there is an annual fixed dollar obligation during the term of the trust. In contrast, the annual obligation under a CRUT must be redetermined each year based on the value of the trust principal on the applicable annual date of valuation.

Because CRATs must make fixed annual payments, the noncharitable beneficiaries will not share in any appreciation in the trust principal. Conversely, they will not suffer if the trust principal depreciates in value. The noncharitable beneficiaries in CRUTs share in the vicissitudes of the trust over the trust term. CRATs are easier to administer than CRUTs, which will require revaluation of the trust principal annually.

Because of the complexity of the rules and the frequency that taxpayers were requesting private letter rulings concerning the qualifications of a split interest charitable trust, the Service issued several Revenue Procedures setting forth forms for many of the common alternative annuity trusts and unitrusts.[75]

[7] Marital Deduction; Charitable Remainder Trusts

When Congress adopted the QTIP provisions of § 2056(b)(7) in 1981, it also adopted § 2056(b)(8). This provision permits a decedent to leave a surviving spouse a lifetime interest or a term interest not to exceed 20 years in either

---

[75] *See* Rev. Proc. 89–20, 1989–1 C.B. 841; Rev. Proc. 90–30, 1990–1 C.B. 534; Rev. Proc. 90–31, 1990–1 C.B. 539; and Rev. Proc. 90–32, 1990–1 C.B. 546.

a unitrust or an annuity trust, with a remainder interest passing to charity. The marital deduction is based on the actuarial value of the spouse's interest. The charitable deduction is similarly computed based on the value of the remainder interest. The value of the two interests equal the value of the property devised to the (b)(8) trust. When the spouse dies, the trust is not included in the spouse's estate.

Alternatively, a decedent may devise property to a QTIP trust with the remainder interest in the trust passing to charity at the spouse's death. Under this arrangement, the decedent's estate receives a marital deduction for the full value of the assets devised to the trust. When the spouse dies, the QTIP is included in the spouse's estate, but a charitable deduction is allowed for the full value of the trust. This negates any adverse effect of including the trust in the spouse's estate.

[8] The Pooled Income Fund

With a pooled income fund charitable contribution, the decedent devises property to the fund, providing a life income interest in the property for at least one noncharitable beneficiary, and contributing the remainder to a 50% (public) charitable organization.[76] Properly made, transfers to a pooled income fund made at death qualify for the estate tax charitable deduction as a split-interest transfer. The contributed property must be commingled with other property contributed to the fund by other donors. The fund cannot invest in tax exempt securities. The pooled income fund must be maintained by the remainder organization and cannot have a donor or a noncharitable beneficiary as trustee. The income received each year by the income beneficiary is determined by the rate of return earned by the fund annually. The pooled income fund, however, does not have to provide for an alternative remainderman.

[9] Partial Interest Contributions (Not in Trust)

To qualify for the estate tax charitable deduction, devises of a remainder interest in a personal residence or farm to a charity cannot be in trust. A devise of a remainder interest in a personal residence or farm, when use of the property is given to a noncharitable beneficiary, cannot meet the requirements of a charitable remainder trust or a pooled income fund because the trustee of a charitable remainder trust or a pooled income fund must have unrestricted power to invest and dispose of trust or fund assets. The devise of the remainder interest must be of the property itself, not the proceeds of the sale of the property.

Estates are permitted a charitable deduction for an irrevocable transfer of easement in real property that satisfies the rules of income tax § 170(h). *See* § 2055(f); Treas. Reg. § 20.2055–2(e)(2)(iv). In addition, the Taxpayer Relief Act of 1997 added a provision to permit the personal representative of a decedent's estate to elect to exclude from the gross estate up to 40% of the value of the land subject to a qualified conservation easement. *See* § 2031(c).

---

[76] This organization is described in § 170(b)(1)(A).

The section is complex, but the legislative history gives some insight into the parameters of the exclusion:

> The Senate amendment allows a personal representative to elect to exclude from the taxable estate 40% of the value of any land subject to a qualified conservation easement that meets the following requirements:
>
> > (1) the land is located within 25 miles of a metropolitan area (as defined by the Office of Management and Budget) or a national park or wilderness area, or within 10 miles of an Urban National Forest (as designated by the Forest Service of the U.S. Department of Agriculture);
> >
> > (2) the land has been owned by the decedent or a member of the decedent's family at all times during the three-year period ending on the date of the decedent's death; and
> >
> > (3) a qualified conservation contribution (within the meaning of sec. 170(h)) of a qualified real property interest (as generally defined in sec. 170(h)(2)(C)) was granted by the decedent or a member of his or her family.
>
> . . .
>
> The . . . maximum exclusion for land subject to a qualified conservation easement is limited to $100,000 in 1998, $200,000 in 1999, $300,000 in 2000, $400,000 in 2001, and $500,000 in 2002 and thereafter. The exclusion for land subject to a qualified conservation easement may be taken in addition to the maximum exclusion for qualified family owned business interests (*i.e.,* there is no coordination between the two provisions). The conference agreement provides that *de minimis* commercial recreational activity that is consistent with the conservation purpose, such as the granting of hunting and fishing licenses, will not cause the property to fail to qualify under this provision.

Effective for decedents dying after the year 2000, the 2001 Tax Act repeals the distance requirement for conservation easements. As a result, the exclusion is available for any property located in the United States or in a United States territory. *See* § 2031(c)(8)(A).

[10] Charitable Lead Trusts

A charitable lead trust is a trust that pays annually to a qualifying charity organization or qualifying charitable organizations either (1) a guaranteed annuity (charitable lead annuity trust), or (2) a fixed percentage of the fair market value determined annually of the trust principal (charitable lead unitrust). No estate tax deduction is available for a lead trust unless it is in one of these two forms. *See* § 2055(e)(2)(B) and Treas. Reg. § 20.2055-2(e)(vi) and (vii). A charitable lead annuity trust is often abbreviated as CLAT; a charitable lead unitrust is often abbreviated as CLUT.

An estate tax deduction is available for the actuarial value of the charity's present interest in the charitable lead trust.[77] The trust term may either be

---

[77] CLATs are most popular when the § 7520 rate is low.

for the life of an individual or a term of years. In April 2000, the Internal Revenue Service issued Proposed Treasury Regulation §§ 20.2055 (e)(2)(vi)(a) and (vii)(a) which limit the individuals whose lives may be used to measure the duration of the charitable lead interest.

Although charitable lead trusts are not private foundations, certain rules that apply to private foundations also apply to charitable lead trusts, such as the private foundation rules that impose excise taxes or penalties on self-dealing pursuant to § 4941. *See* I.R.C. §§ 4947(a)(2) and 4947(b)(3)(A). Charitable lead trusts are not exempt from federal income tax. However, distribution to the charitable annuitants or unitrust holders should qualify for an income tax charitable deduction under § 642(c), discussed in Chapter 14, § 14.07, *infra*.

[E]   Family-Owned Business Deduction (FOBD): Section 2057

Code: § 2057.

Regulations: None.

Effective until 2004, § 2057 permits a decedent's estate to deduct from the gross estate the adjusted value of the decedent's interest in all, or some, of the decedent's qualified family owned business interests (Q-FOBIs).[78]

Section 2057 specifically targets and limits the benefit of the family owned business interest deduction exclusion (FOBI) to relatively small farmers and businessmen, in part by relying heavily on the complex rules of § 2032A, discussed in § 3.03[C], *supra*. First, the decedent must be a United States citizen or resident, and the principal place of the family-owned business (FOB) must be in the United States for eligibility under § 2057. Second, the decedent's family-owned business interest (FOBI) qualifies for the § 2057 deduction only if the decedent or a member of her family materially participated in the operation of the business for a substantial period of time. Third, the FOBI must represent a significant portion of the decedent's estate. Fourth, the recipients of the decedent's interest in the FOB must be qualified heirs who are required to materially participate in the FOB for a significant period after the decedent's death. A premature disposition or cessation of participation can result in recapturing some or all of the estate tax (with interest) that was lost by use of the FOBD from the qualified heirs who must sign a written recapture agreement. Also, the Q-FOBI deduction is not automatic, but must be elected by the executor. *See* § 2057(b)(1)(B). *See generally* Stephen E. Martin, *Practical Aspects of Qualified Family Owned Business Interests*, 35 Univ. of Miami Est. Plng Inst. ch. 14 (2001).

The FOBD is also quantitatively limited: the deductible amount cannot exceed the lesser of the adjusted value of the decedent's interest in the FOB, or $675,000. *See* § 2057(a)(2). Furthermore, the overall benefit of the applicable exclusion amount and the § 2057 deduction cannot exceed $1.3 million.

---

[78] Originally enacted by the Taxpayer Relief Act of 1997 as 2033A as an election to exclude property from the gross estate, the 1998 Technical Corrections Act renumbered 2033A as 2057 and converted the exclusion to a deduction.

See § 2057(a)(3). Thus, if an estate is allowed the maximum § 2057 deduction of $675,000 for 2002 or 2003, the allowable credit under § 2011 will equal $202,050, which is the equivalent of an exclusion amount of $625,000. *See* § 2057(a)(3). Because the applicable exclusion amount is $1.5 million beginning in 2004, the 2001 Tax Act repealed § 2057 for decedents dying after 2003.

[F] The State Death Tax Deduction: Section 2058

Code: § 2058.

The 2001 Tax Act repeals the state death tax credit, § 2011, effective for estates of decedents who die after 2004. *See* § 3.07[B], *infra* (discussing § 2011 and its phaseout). Because the amount paid in state death taxes is a deduction instead of a credit, the total tax bill for decedent's estate will rise, unless the decedent's state of domicile repeals its death tax. For example, if a decedent dies in 2005 with a $2 million taxable estate, the federal estate tax would be $225,000, before taking into account state death taxes. Under § 2011, before amendment by the 2001 Tax Act, a state death tax credit of $99,600 was available. Under the pre-2001 law, the net federal tax would have been $125,400 and the state would have been received $99,600. The total of both taxes is $225,000. If it is assumed that the state will still tax the decedent's estate $99,600, the federal taxable estate is reduced to $1,900,600 and the federal estate tax is $180,270. The total of both taxes is now $279,870—a $54,870 increase. This result occurs because the $99,600 deduction reduced federal estate taxes by only $44,730; whereas, the old § 2011 credit reduced federal estate taxes dollar for dollar.

§ 3.05 Determining the Tax

As outlined in Chapter 2, once the taxable estate is determined (by subtracting the deductions from the gross estate), the tax is calculated by first determining a tentative tax on the sum of the taxable estate and adjusted taxable gifts, and then subtracting a tax calculated on post-1976 gifts. From this, the estate is entitled to subtract any available credits, including the applicable credit amount, the credit for pre-1977 gifts, the credit for state death taxes, and the credit for foreign death taxes.

§ 3.06 Credits Against the Estate Tax Imposed

The tax imposed by § 2001 may be reduced by various credits. The most significant credit is the unified credit against estate tax under § 2010, which will be available to all estates. The § 2011 state death tax credit depends on applicable state death tax systems, although it is repealed for estates of decedents who die after 2004. The § 2012 gift tax credit is applicable only if the decedent made taxable gifts before 1977 that are included in the gross estate. The § 2013 credit for prior transfers serves to prevent the double taxation of property when a decedent and legatee die within a short time of each other, so that the same property is included in the gross estate of each. Section 2014 depends on the decedent owning property that is subject to death taxation by a foreign country.

[A] Unified Credit: Section 2010

Code: § 2010.

Regulations: None.

Section 2010 is the most important credit in the estate tax system. Every estate is entitled to the credit. Unless the decedent made gifts in the latter part of 1976 or the executor elected a deduction under § 2057, discussed in § 3.04[E], *supra*, the section allows the estate a credit amount that corresponds to the applicable exclusion amount to offset the estate tax imposed by § 2001. *See* Chapter 2 for a discussion of the unified credit and applicable exclusion amount.

The § 2010 credit effectively exempts "modest" estates from federal estate taxation. Unless the decedent has adjusted taxable gifts under § 2001(b), there can be no federal estate tax liability if the taxable (not gross) estate does not exceed the applicable exclusion amount. *See* § 2001(b). The applicable exclusion amount of $1 million in 2002, for the § 2010 credit can be illustrated as follows:

Example 1: Assume the decedent died in 2002, with a taxable estate of $1 million. Further assume the decedent made no adjusted taxable gifts. The tax imposed on a taxable estate of $1 million is $345,800. The § 2010 credit in 2002, of $345,800 eliminates the federal estate tax liability.

The only major limitation on the § 2010 credit is that the credit cannot exceed the estate tax imposed under § 2001. *See* § 2010(d). In effect, the credit can only reduce the liability of an estate. The credit is not refundable.

Example 2: The decedent died in 2002, with a taxable estate of $500,000, having made no gifts. The estate tax imposed under § 2001 is $155,800. Although the otherwise allowable credit in 2002 is $345,800, the credit allowed will be limited to $155,800.

Unlike the gift tax unified credit, the § 2010 credit is not reduced by any credit used to reduce the tax on prior taxable gifts made by the decedent. For example, if the decedent made no prior taxable gifts and made a $100,000 gift in 1985, it would have been tax-free in 1985 because of the § 2505 credit. Assume that he dies in 2002, with a taxable estate of $900,000. Because the $100,000 gift is cumulated with the $900,000 taxable estate for the purposes of calculating the tentative tax, the tentative tax imposed under § 2001 would be $345,800. The estate is entitled to subtract only the gift tax payable on the $100,000 gift from the $345,800 to determine the estate tax imposed under § 2001. The gift tax paid, however, was zero. Therefore, unless the full $345,800 estate tax credit is allowed, the estate would produce a tax, even though the total assets equal the $1 million designed to pass tax-free under the unified credit. Section 2010 recognizes this necessity, and does not require adjustment for the prior use of the gift tax unified credit.

[B] Credit for State Death Taxes: Section 2011

Code: § 2011.

Regulations: None.

Section 2011 allows a credit against the federal estate tax imposed under § 2001 for state death taxes paid on property included in the gross estate for decedents who die before 2005.

The overwhelming majority of states have death tax systems that impose a tax that equals the maximum credit allowable under § 2011(b). The system is sometimes referred to as a SOP, sponge tax or pick-up tax, since it sops up the allowable federal credit. In those SOP tax states, the effect of the Tax Act of 2001 may be significant reductions in revenue. *See Repeal of Federal Estate Tax Would Have Effect on States* (Federation of Tax Administrators), 2001 Tax Notes Today 2001 TNT 48-102 (Mar. 8, 2001).

Curiously, in some SOP tax states, revenues will not decline because the state has incorporated the § 2011 table amount as in effect before 2001. For example, New York's SOP tax is pegged to the § 2011 table amount that was in effect in 1998. *See* N.Y. Tax Law 951(a) and 952(a). Consider the above example and assume the decedent dies in 2002 in New York. Although the allowable federal credit will only $25,350 (75% of the table amount), New York will impose a tax of $33, 800 since that was the credit allowable in 1998.

It remains to be seen how states will respond to the Tax Act of 2001. Consider Florida, which is constitutionally prohibited from imposing a death tax other than a SOP tax. Unless Florida amends its constitution, it will collect no tax in 2005 since the Tax Act of 2001 repeals the § 2011 credit beginning that year.

The state death tax credit dates to 1926, and was the result of two movements by the states and others following World War I. *See generally* E.M. Perkins, *State Action Under the Federal Estate Tax Credit Clause,* 13 N.C. L. REV. 271 (1935). The first movement was a cry to repeal the federal estate tax. The estate tax was adopted to finance World War I. At its conclusion, the states urged repeal so that the ability to obtain death tax revenues would be returned to the states. Rather than repeal the tax, however, Congress compromised, and allowed a credit for state death taxes to the extent the state tax did not exceed 25% of the federal tax liability.

Secondly, a movement started in some states to repeal their death taxes in an attempt to attract wealthy citizens. For example, in its 1924 general election, Florida adopted a constitutional provision prohibiting the imposition of state death taxes. This led others to suggest that the federal credit be retained and expanded, so as to negate any advantage to the non-taxing states. The tension between those seeking repeal of the federal estate tax and those seeking protection of state death taxes from invidious competition resulted in the estate tax credit under the Revenue Act of 1926. Pursuant to the Act, the credit for state death taxes was set at an amount equal to 80% of the federal tax imposed on a decedent's estate, based on the rate schedule enacted under the same Revenue Act of 1926. At the same time, that Act imposed the federal estate tax on the net estate, defined as gross estate less deductions, including a $100,000 exemption deduction.

This history can be seen in the current structure of the table. The 1926 exemption is reflected in the sum of (1) the $60,000 figure used to calculate the "adjusted taxable estate," and (2) the $40,000 minimum amount for which a credit will be given. It can also be seen by comparing the rates in the table with the 1926 estate tax rates.

The significance of the credit depends on the manner in which the decedent's state imposes death taxes. Over the years, many states have followed Florida by adopting a SOP, sponge tax or pick-up tax designed to impose a tax at exactly the level of the credit, on the assumption that such a tax will not impose any burden on estates beyond that imposed by the federal tax. For example, the Colorado statute reads: "[a] tax in the amount of the federal credit is imposed on the transfer of the taxable estate of every domiciliary." Colo. Rev. Stat. § 39–23.5–103(1). In short, the state sponge tax system adopts the federal estate tax system (including federal exemption levels), but applies the table in § 2011(b) as a rate schedule.

A few states utilize an independent death tax system. Often they use data from the federal estate tax return, adjusted for out-of-state property. State exemption levels, however, may vary from the federal exemption amount, and the state tax rate may differ markedly from that in § 2011. Thus, state death taxes may be imposed when none are imposed at the federal level. If the exemption is lower, or the rates imposed are higher, the federal credit may only partially cover the death tax imposed by the state. Still other states rely on an inheritance system. Under an inheritance tax system, a tax is determined by reference to who receives particular property. Differing rates apply based on the relationship of the recipient to the decedent. For example, the New Jersey inheritance tax system exempts property received by a surviving spouse and children (and their spouses) from taxes. Brothers and sisters are taxed. Other relatives and persons who have no blood relationship to the decedent are taxed at higher rates. In these jurisdictions, the effect of the credit will depend on the rates actually applied to the situation.

Both inheritance tax and estate tax states have an additional "pick-up" tax. Under this provision, the state imposes an additional tax which, when added to the basic state death tax, equals the maximum credit allowable under § 2011. This guarantees the state's benefit from the credit in the unusual event that the state death tax is insufficient to allow the estate to fully utilize the credit. The pick-up tax applies, for example, if the regular death tax is only $10,000, but the federal death tax credit is $15,000. On those facts, the pick-up (or sponge) tax is $5,000.

The credit under § 2011 is subject to several limitations. First, the credit cannot exceed the federal estate tax imposed under § 2001, reduced by the unified credit amount under § 2010. *See* § 2011(f). In effect, the § 2011 credit is not refundable; it can only reduce federal estate tax liability. There will be no credit allowable on a taxable estate that is less than the applicable exclusion where the decedent made no adjusted taxable gifts because the unified credit would prevent any tax from being imposed on that amount.

Second, the § 2011 credit cannot exceed the amount of state death taxes actually paid, and for which credit is claimed, within four years after the federal estate tax return is due to be filed. *See* § 2011(c).[79]

Third, the credit is limited to the amounts set forth in the table contained in § 2011(b), as applied to the amount of the "adjusted taxable estate," defined as the taxable estate, less $60,000. *See* § 2011(b) (last sentence). Operation of the table is illustrated in the following example:

Example: The decedent died unmarried in 2001. She was a domiciliary of a state that taxes estates in an amount that exceeds the 2011 credit, and made no gifts to charity. The state imposed an estate tax of $45,500. The decedent's federal taxable estate was $1.1 million.

In the example, the decedent's taxable estate ($1.1 million) less $60,000 equals $1,040,000. Applying the table, the maximum credit allowable under § 2011 is $33,800. The first limitation—a credit that does not exceed the federal estate tax liability after the unified credit—does not apply here because the federal estate tax liability before application of the state death tax credit would be $41,000. Section 2001 imposes a tax of $386,800 on a $1.1 million taxable estate, from which the applicable § 2010 unified credit of $220,550 can be subtracted, producing a federal estate tax liability of $166,250. Assuming that the estate actually paid the state death tax, the full $33,800 credit would be allowed.

The 2001 Tax Act repeals the § 2011 credit for estates of decedents who die after 2004. Moreover, the Act reduces the § 2011 credit 25% each year from 2002 until 2004. Thus, in 2002, the maximum amount of the credit allowed is 75% of the amount computed under § 2011; in 2003, the maximum amount is 50% of the amount computed under § 2011; and in 2004, the maximum amount is 25% of the amount computed under § 2011. For 2005 and thereafter, § 2058 permits an unlimited deduction for state death taxes paid. *See* § 3.04[F], *supra*, for a discussion of § 2058.

The impact of the Tax Act of 2001 change to § 2011 may be illustrated by reference to the above example. If the decedent died in 2002, the allowable credit would only be 75% of the § 2011 table amount of $38,800, that is, a credit of $25,350. If death occurred in 2004, then the 2011 would only be $8,450 (25% of $33,800).

Problem

1. Would you advise a client to move from New York to Florida to avoid higher New York taxes? Can you think of a way to minimize New York death tax without requiring a change in domicile?

[C]   Gift Taxes Paid Credit: Section 2012

Code: §§ 2012 and 2001(b)(2).

Regulations: None.

---

[79] There are a few exceptions to this time rule, including measuring the four-year period by the extension period granted for filing the estate tax return. *See* §§ 2011(c) and 2015.

In very limited circumstances, § 2012 allows an estate to obtain a credit for certain gift taxes that a decedent has paid.

The first requirement for application of § 2012 is that property upon which the federal gift tax was imposed be included in the decedent's gross estate. *See* § 2012(a). Thus, it requires that the gift be of a nature that it triggers §§ 2035 through 2040 or § 2042. For example, if the decedent had created an irrevocable trust during 1975, in which he retained the income for life and gave the remainder to his child, a gift tax would have been due on the value of the remainder. Assuming he died in 2002, the then corpus (the remainder in possession) would be includable in the gross estate under § 2036(a)(1), and the estate would be allowed to take the gift tax paid as a credit against the estate tax generated by the trust. The second requirement for application of the credit is that the gift have been made before 1977. *See* § 2012(e).

Assuming a credit is allowable, the credit will equal the lesser of: (1) the gift tax paid on the gift; or (2) the estate tax attributable to the gift. *See* § 2012(a).

Gift taxes payable on post-1976 gifts that are included in the gross estate may be subtracted from the tentative tax due. *See* § 2001(b)(2). This provides the equivalent of a credit for the gift taxes on those transactions that effectively parallel the operation of § 2012.

[D] Credit for Tax on Prior Transfers: Section 2013

Code: § 2013.

Regulations: None.

A tax on prior transfers (TPT) credit may be available under § 2013 if the decedent has received property from a person whose estate paid an estate tax on the transfer of the property to the decedent. Specifically, a credit will be allowed if the decedent died within ten years after the prior transferor's death, or if the prior transferor dies within two years after the decedent's death.

The § 2013 credit for the estate tax paid on prior transfers is designed to diminish the impact of taxation on separate transfers of the same property within a short period of time.

Example: *A*, the transferor, died in 2002 bequeathed $75,000 to *B*, which was charged with the payment of $25,000 of estate taxes. In the following year *B* died. Without regard to the credit, the remaining $50,000, after payment of estate taxes in *A*'s estate, would generate another estate tax of $24,500 (assuming *B*'s estate was in the 49% marginal bracket).

In the example, the initial $75,000 would have been subject to two transfers (one from *A* to *B* and the second from *B* to his legatee). Therefore, the money would be subject to two federal transfer taxes, totaling $49,500, within a year's time. To avoid this double taxation, Congress enacted the TPT credit. *B*'s estate would be allowed a credit under § 2013, which would cancel or reduce the $24,500 second tax.

The credit is the lesser of two amounts. The first limitation is defined as the estate tax attributable to the property transferred to the second decedent and paid by the transferor's estate. *See* § 2013(b); Treas. Reg. § 20.2013–2(a). The value of the property transferred by the transferor must take into account the extent to which the bequest is diminished by applicable death taxes. Thus, in the above example, the value of the transferred property would be $50,000 (the $75,000 bequest less the $25,000 federal estate tax paid on the bequeathed property).[80]

The estate tax attributable to the transferred property is determined by creating a fraction. The numerator of the fraction is the value of the property transferred to the decedent less any applicable death taxes paid therefrom as a result of the transfer. The denominator is the value of the transferor's taxable estate less the amount of any death taxes paid by the estate. This fraction is then applied against the estate tax paid by the transferor's estate. Thus, in the above example, if *A* died in 2002, with a taxable estate of $3 million, the estate tax paid after subtracting the unified credit would equal $930,000. The amount of the net estate (after estate taxes is $2,070,000). The first limitation, the estate tax attributable to the transferred property, is determined by multiplying the fraction $50,000 / $2,070,000 by the estate tax of $930,000. Thus the first limitation equals $22,464.[81]

The second limitation on the § 2013 credit is defined as "[t]he amount of the federal estate tax attributable to the transferred property in the present decedent's estate." *See* Treas. Reg. § 20.2013–3(a) (explaining § 2013(c)). First, the estate tax on the decedent's entire taxable estate is computed. Then, the estate tax without inclusion of the transferred amount is computed. The difference equals the second limitation. Assume that *B* died in 2003, with a taxable estate of $2 million. The estate tax on *B*'s estate would be $435,000, taking into account the transferred amount of $50,000. If the $50,000 were excluded, the estate tax would be $24,500 less. Accordingly, the first limitation of $22,464, being less than the second limitation of $24,500 would control.[82] *B*'s estate would, therefore, be entitled to a credit of no more than $22,464.

The amount determined by comparing the two limitations is not necessarily the allowable credit. This amount will be creditable only if the decedent and the transferor die within two years of each other. If the decedent dies between two and ten years after the transferor's death, the credit will be a percentage of the determined amount. *See* § 2013(a). After ten years, no credit is available.

As this brief discussion illustrates, § 2013 is a complex statute. Other adjustments may be necessary. For example, if the decedent was the surviving spouse of the transferor and the transferor's estate claimed a marital deduction for the transferred property, then a § 2013 credit is not allowed. *See* § 2013(d)(3). This result is correct because the marital deduction shielded the

---

[80] Note that this example disregards possible state death taxes.

[81] The difference between the amount of tax charged against the devise and the amount of tax attributable to the devise under the first limitation can occur when the decedent's will provides for other than a proportionate tax apportionment.

[82] In Estate of Meyer v. Commissioner, 83 T.C. 350 (1984), *aff'd* 778 F.2d 125 (2d Cir. 1985), the decedent received property from several persons who predeceased him. The estate wanted to aggregate the estate taxes paid by the multiple transferors to calculate the two limitations. The court held that the maximum credit for each transfer must be computed separately.

property from tax in the transferor's estate. There will be no double taxation of the property.[83] State death taxes, charitable deductions, and encumbrances against the property are examples of situations that call for adjustments. *See* Treas. Reg. § 20.2013–4(b).

Difficulties in applying § 2013 also arise if the inherited interest is an income interest. Although the income generated by the trust will be includable in the decedent's gross estate, the income interest itself will not be includable because it terminates on the decedent's death. *See* § 2033. Nonetheless, a credit may be allowed under § 2013 for the actuarial value of the income interest. Treasury Regulation § 20.2013–1(a) provides:

> There is no requirement that the transferred property be identified in the estate of the present decedent or that the property be in existence at the time of the decedent's death. It is sufficient that the transfer of the property was subjected to federal estate tax in the estate of the transferor and that the transferor died within the prescribed period of time.

Consistent with this Regulation, the Service ruled that § 2013 applies to the value of a life estate. *See* Rev. Rul. 59–9, 1959–1 C.B. 232. *See also* Treas. Reg. § 20.2013–4 (Example 2).[84] The § 2013 credit will be denied where deaths occur simultaneously or otherwise as a result of a common accident. *See Estate of Harrison v. Commissioner*, 115 T.C. 116 (2000) (applying § 7520); *Estate of Carter v. United States*, 921 F.2d 63 (5th Cir. 1991); *Estate of Marks v. Commissioner*, 94 T.C. 720 (1990); Treas. Reg. 20.7520–3(b)(3)(iii).

Because the § 2013 credit is available for the value of an income interest, planning opportunities exist when a surviving spouse is the beneficiary of the credit-shelter (by-pass) trust and estate taxes are payable in the estate of the first-spouse-to-die. The potential credit may increase when the spouse is the beneficiary of a QTIP trust and, either no QTIP election was made for the trust, or only a partial election was made. The mathematics of computing the credit are quite complex in the life income interest situations, but the potential tax savings may be significant.

---

[83] On the other hand, if a marital deduction was disallowed under § 2056(d) because the surviving spouse was not United States citizen, the estate of the surviving spouse is entitled to a credit under § 2013. The credit would be for the full amount of the estate tax paid with respect to property received from the decedent spouse's estate, regardless of when the decedent spouse died. *See* § 2056(d)(3). This effectively substitutes for the marital deduction in the earlier estate, but guarantees that the property is taxed once.

[84] The credit will, of course, depend on the possibility of valuing the interest actuarially. *See* Treas. Reg. § 20.2013–4(a). Following normal valuation principles, actual life expectancy may be taken into account if the income beneficiary's death was imminent when the interest was created. *See* Priv. Ltr. Rul. 8512004 (*citing* Rev. Rul. 80–80, 1980–1 C.B. 194). Surprisingly, the Service has also ruled that an income interest which will terminate on remarriage can be valued for credit purposes. *See* Rev. Rul. 85–111, 1985–2 C.B. 196. Valuation may not be possible if the trustee has broad discretion to invade corpus for another, or if the trustee can invest in unproductive property, thereby depriving the income beneficiary of income. *See* Holbrook v. United States, 575 F.2d 1288 (9th Cir. 1978). On the other hand, if a power to invade corpus is subject to an ascertainable standard, the credit may be available. *Cf.* Estate of Weinstein v. United States, 820 F.2d 201 (6th Cir. 1987). Various situations involving the right to a § 2013 credit for income interests are summarized in Priv. Ltr. Rul. 8608002.

[E] Credit for Foreign Death Taxes: Section 2014

Code: § 2014.

Regulations: None.

Section 2014 allows an estate to obtain a credit for death taxes paid to a foreign country for property situated in the foreign country. The credit is designed to mitigate the effect of double taxation. Because the location of property is irrelevant for purposes of imposing the United States estate tax, double taxation could occur. For example, real property located in France that was owned by a United States citizen would be subject to both United States and French death taxes. *See Norstar Bank v. United States*, 644 F. Supp. 1112 (N.D. N.Y. 1986).

Assuming death taxes were paid to a foreign country for property owned by the decedent, and assuming that the property was also includable in the decedent's gross estate, § 2014(b) provides that the credit cannot exceed the lesser of two amounts. The first limitation is the amount of foreign death taxes attributable to the subject property. As was the case with the estate tax credit under § 2013, this amount can be determined by creating a fraction. In this case, the numerator of the fraction is the value the foreign country places on property that is includable in the gross estate. The denominator is the value of all property subject to death taxation in the foreign country. The fraction is then multiplied by the death tax imposed by the foreign country. The regulations provide elaborate examples of how to compute the first limitation. *See* Treas. Reg. § 20.2014–2.

The second limitation is the amount of the federal estate tax that is attributable to the property situated in the foreign country. Again, the amount is determined by creating a fraction. The numerator of the fraction is the value of the property for federal estate tax purposes. The denominator is the value of all property included in the gross estate. These values may have to be adjusted by marital and charitable deductions. The fraction is then multiplied by the federal estate tax liability, taking into account the credits under §§ 2010 through 2012. *See* Treas. Reg. § 20.2014–3.

As was true with the state death credit under § 2011, § 2014 provides that the foreign death taxes be paid and a credit claimed within four years after the estate tax return is required to be filed. *See* § 2014(e).

The following example illustrates the impact of § 2014:

Example: The decedent, a United States citizen, died in 2002, owning real property located in Country A. This property was the only property owned by the decedent in Country A. Its value was $200,000, and the death tax imposed thereon by Country A was $20,000. Assume a federal gross and taxable estate of $2 million.

Because this was the only real property owned by the decedent in Country A, the fraction equals 1/1 ($200,000/$200,000) and the first limitation equals $20,000. The second limitation is determined by comparing the value of the realty situated in Country A with the decedent's gross estate. Thus, the applicable fraction would be one-tenth ($200,000/$2 million). Because the federal estate tax liability in 2002, after subtracting the unified credit, is

$435,000, the second limitation would be $43,500. Thus, a § 2014 credit of $20,000 is allowable.

Note, if the decedent's gross estate were $1.2 million instead of $2 million, the second limitation would be less than the first limitation amount of $20,000. Although the applicable fraction would be one-sixth ($200,000/$1.2 million), it would be applied against a tax liability of $82,000 to produce a second limitation amount of $13,667.

Whether property was actually situated in the foreign country for the purposes of § 2014 is determined by using the rules for determining the situs of property owned by nonresidents who are not citizens of the United States. *See* §§ 2014(a), 2104, and 2105. By applying § 2105, the court in *Estate of Borne v. Commissioner*, 577 F. Supp. 115 (N.D. Ind. 1983), concluded that bank deposits held in a Canadian bank were not situated in Canada despite the fact that the decedent was a resident of Canada. In another case, *Estate of Schwartz v. Commissioner*, 83 T.C. 943 (1984), *acq.* 1986–1 C.B. 1, the Tax Court cast doubt on the *Borne* conclusion. In both *Schwartz* and *Borne*, the United States citizen was a resident of the foreign country. Unlike *Borne*, however, the *Schwartz* case took into account the foreign residence.

§ 3.07 Tax Payment

Under § 2002, the estate tax is imposed on the executor. The executor is defined in § 2203 to include the administrator or other person in possession of the property of the decedent. The executor is given a right of reimbursement against (1) the beneficiaries of life insurance (§ 2206), (2) the trustee of property generating taxes because of a general power of appointment (§ 2207) or qualified income interest taxable under § 2044 (§ 2207A), and (3) property included because of a grantor's retained income interest (§ 2207(B)).

For taxpayers who do not have the ability to pay the estate tax in full on the due date, several code sections provide possible avenues to pay the estate tax liability in installments. Section 6161 permits an estate to request an extension to pay the tax to the extent the estate is illiquid. The request is made annually. Interest accrues on the unpaid tax at the prevailing rate provided by § 6601. The maximum extension permitted under § 6161 is ten years. Section 6163 permits the executor to elect to defer estate taxes that are attributable to reversions and remainders.

Section 6166 provides elective relief to estates that include a significant amount of interest in a qualifying, closely held business.[85] Specifically, § 6166 applies if the value of the decedent's qualifying, closely held business interests exceed 35% of the value of the adjusted gross estate, defined as the gross estate less deductions allowed under §§ 2053 and 2054. The relief permits the personal representative to pay only interest on the estate tax attributable to

---

[85] The decedent's interest may be as a sole proprietor. It may also be a partnership interest if the decedent's gross estate included at least 20% of the value of the total capital interest in the partnership, or there were fewer than 16 partners. Similarly, the qualifying interest may be as a shareholder if at least 20% of the voting stock's value is included in the decedent's gross estate, or the corporation had less than 46 shareholders. *See* § 6166(b)(1), as amended by the Tax Act of 2001.

gross estate inclusion of the closely held business interest for the first four years, following the ninth month after the original due date of the estate tax return. Thereafter, the tax attributable to the includable interest, plus interest, is payable in up to ten equal annual installments.

Lower interest rates on the tax attributable to closely held business interests are also available under § 6601(j). Pursuant to the Taxpayer Relief Act of 1997, the interest rate on the first $1 million as adjusted for inflation that exceeds the applicable exemption amount was reduced from 4% to 2%. Interest on amount over the 2% portion is 45% of the interest rate that would otherwise be payable on a tax deficiency.

If the personal representative elects to defer payment of the estate tax under various extension provisions, the Service will not allow interest on the estate tax to be deducted until the interest accrues. *See* Rev. Rul. 80–250, 1980–2 C.B. 278. The interest accruing on a § 6166 deferral is not allowed as a § 2053 administration expense, however. *See* § 2053(c)(1)(D).

Chapter 4

GIFT TAXATION BASICS

As described in Chapter 2, chapter 12 of the Code provides the basic structure for gift taxation. *Gross gifts* made each year are reduced by *deductions* to determine *taxable gifts*. A tentative gift tax is imposed on the taxable gifts made each year at the marginal tax rate by taking into account taxable gifts in previous periods. The tentative gift tax is then reduced by any unused unified credit amount. The remaining balance, if any, is the donor's gift tax liability.

Generally, chapter 12 does not apply to a gift of intangible property by a nonresident, non-United States citizen. *See* § 2501(a)(2). However, § 2501(a)(3) may subject gifts of intangibles to gift taxation if made by certain expatriates. *See also* § 2511(b).

When reading this Chapter, you should bear in mind the various planning considerations raised in the following questions:

1. What are the tax advantages or disadvantages of making a transfer by gift instead of at death?

2. Although there appear to be transfer tax advantages in making gifts, can all taxpayers take advantage of these tax savings?

3. If a husband and wife collectively own assets valued at $2.3 million with an aggregate basis of $400,000, what planning considerations should be taken into account to maximize overall tax savings under the federal gift, estate, and income tax systems?

§ 4.01 Gross Gifts

The Code does not use the term *gross gift*. Nonetheless, the term reflects that the gift tax system does not take into account all gratuitous transfers. It is used to mean what otherwise would constitute gifts for gift tax purposes, less applicable exclusions. The term *gross gift* is analogous to the term *gross estate* under the estate tax.

[A] Definition of "Gift"

Code: §§ 2501(a), 2511, and 2512.

Regulations: Treas. Reg. §§ 25.2511–1(g) and 25.2512–8.

To determine gross gifts, it is necessary to ascertain what constitutes a gift for gift tax purposes. The Code provides that a tax is imposed on "the transfer of property by gift during [each] calendar year by any, resident or nonresident, individual." § 2501(a)(1). The concept of a "gift" for federal gift tax purposes is not defined by the Code, however.

Commissioner v. Wemyss

324 U.S. 303 (1945)

Mr. Justice Frankfurter delivered the opinion of the Court.

In 1939 taxpayer proposed marriage to Mrs. More, a widow with one child. Her deceased husband had set up two trusts, one half the income of which was for the benefit of Mrs. More and the other half for that of the child with provision that, in the event of Mrs. More's remarriage, her part of the income ceased and went to the child. The corpus of the two trusts consisted of stock which brought to Mrs. More from the death of her first husband to her remarriage, about five years later, an average income of $5,484 a year. On Mrs. More's unwillingness to suffer loss of her trust income through remarriage the parties on May 24, 1939, entered upon an agreement whereby taxpayer transferred to Mrs. More a block of shares of stock. Within a month they married. The Commissioner ruled that the transfer of this stock, the value of which, $149,456.13, taxpayer does not controvert, was subject to the Federal Gift Tax. . . . Accordingly, he assessed a deficiency which the Tax Court upheld, 2 T.C. 876, but the Circuit Court of Appeals reversed the Tax Court, 144 F.2d 78. We granted certiorari to settle uncertainties in tax administration engendered by seemingly conflicting decisions. 323 U.S. 703.

The answer to our problem turns on the proper application of [§§ 2501(a) and 2512(b)] to the immediate facts. . . .

In view of the major role which the Tax Court plays in Federal tax litigation, it becomes important to consider how that court dealt with this problem. Fusing, as it were, [§§ 2501(a) and 2512(b)], the Tax Court read them as not being limited by any common law technical notions about "consideration." And so, while recognizing that marriage was of course a valuable consideration to support a contract, the Tax Court did not deem marriage to satisfy the requirement of [§ 2512(b)] in that it was not a consideration reducible to money value. Accordingly, the Court found the whole value of the stock transferred to Mrs. More taxable under the statute and the relevant Treas. Reg. [§ 25.2512–8]: "A consideration not reducible to a money value, as love and affection, promise of marriage, etc., is to be wholly disregarded, and the entire value of the property transferred constitutes the amount of the gift." In the alternative, the Tax Court was of the view that if Mrs. More's loss of her trust income rather than the marriage was consideration for the taxpayer's transfer of his stock to her, he is not relieved from the tax because he did not receive any money's worth from Mrs. More's relinquishment of her trust income, and, in any event, the actual value of her interest in the trust, subject to fluctuations of its stock earnings, was not proved. One member of the Tax Court dissented, deeming that the gift tax legislation invoked ordinary contract conceptions of "consideration."

The Circuit Court of Appeals rejected this line of reasoning. It found in the marriage agreement an arm's length bargain and an absence of "donative intent" which it deemed essential: "A donative intent followed by a donative act is essential to constitute a gift; and no strained and artificial construction of a supplementary statute should be indulged to tax as a gift a transfer actually lacking donative intent." 144 F.2d 78, 82.

Sections [2501(a) and 2512(b)] are not disparate provisions. Congress directed them to the same purpose, and they should not be separated in application. Had Congress taxed "gifts" simpliciter, it would be appropriate to assume that the term was used in its colloquial sense, and a search for "donative intent" would be indicated. But Congress intended to use the term "gifts" in its broadest and most comprehensive sense. H. Rep. No. 708, 72d Cong., 1st Sess., p. 27; S. Rep. No. 665, 72d Cong., 1st Sess., p. 39; *cf. Smith v. Shaughnessy*, 318 U.S. 176; *Robinette v. Helvering*, 318 U.S. 184. Congress chose not to require an ascertainment of what too often is an elusive state of mind. For purposes of the gift tax it not only dispensed with the test of "donative intent." It formulated a much more workable external test, that where "property is transferred for less than an adequate and full consideration in money or money's worth," the excess in such money value "shall, for the purposes of the tax imposed by this title, be deemed a gift. . . ." And Treasury Regulations have emphasized that common law considerations were not embodied in the gift tax.

To reinforce the evident desire of Congress to hit all the protean arrangements which the wit of man can devise that are not business transactions within the meaning of ordinary speech, the Treasury Regulations make clear that no genuine business transaction comes within the purport of the gift tax by excluding "a sale, exchange, or other transfer of property made in the ordinary course of business (a transaction which is bona fide, at arm's length, and free from any donative intent)." Treas. Reg. [§ 25.2512–8]. Thus on finding that a transfer in the circumstances of a particular case is not made in the ordinary course of business, the transfer becomes subject to the gift tax to the extent that it is not made "for an adequate and full consideration in money or money's worth." *See* 2 Paul, Federal Estate and Gift Taxation (1942) p. 1113.

The Tax Court in effect found the transfer of the stock to Mrs. More was not made at arm's length in the ordinary course of business. It noted that the inducement was marriage, took account of the discrepancy between what she got and what she gave up, and also of the benefit that her marriage settlement brought to her son. These were considerations the Tax Court could justifiably heed, and heeding, decide as it did. Its conclusion on the issue before it was no less to be respected than were the issues which we deemed it was entitled to decide as it did in *Dobson v. Commissioner*, 320 U.S. 489; *Commissioner v. Heininger*, 320 U.S. 467; *Commissioner v. Scottish American Co.*, 323 U.S. 119.

If we are to isolate as an independently reviewable question of law the view of the Tax Court that money consideration must benefit the donor to relieve a transfer by him from being a gift, we think the Tax Court was correct. To be sure, the Revenue Act of 1932 does not spell out a requirement of benefit to the transferor to afford relief from the gift tax. Its forerunner, section 320 of the 1924 Act, was more explicit in that it provided that the excess of the transfer over "the consideration received shall . . . be deemed a gift." It will hardly be suggested, however, that in re-imposing the gift tax in 1932 Congress meant to exclude transfers that would have been taxed under the 1924 Act. The section taxing as gifts transfers that are not made for "adequate and full [money] consideration" aims to reach those transfers which are withdrawn from the donor's estate. To allow detriment to the donee to satisfy the requirement of "adequate and full consideration" would violate the purpose of the statute and open wide the door for evasion of the gift tax. *See* 2 Paul, *supra*, at 1114.

Reversed.

Mr. Justice Roberts dissents, and would affirm the judgment for the reasons given in the opinion of the Circuit Court of Appeals.

Merrill v. Fahs

324 U.S. 308 (1945)

Mr. Justice Frankfurter delivered the opinion of the Court. This is a companion case to *Commissioner v. Wemyss* [citations omitted].

On March 7, 1939, taxpayer, the petitioner, made an antenuptial agreement with Kinta Desmare. Taxpayer, a resident of Florida, had been twice married and had three children and two grandchildren. He was a man of large resources, with cash and securities worth more than $5,000,000, and Florida real estate valued at $135,000. Miss Desmare's assets were negligible. By the arrangement entered into the day before their marriage, taxpayer agreed to set up within ninety days after marriage an irrevocable trust for $300,000, the provisions of which were to conform to Miss Desmare's wishes. The taxpayer was also to provide in his will for two additional trusts, one, likewise in the amount of $300,000, to contain the same limitations as the inter vivos trust, and the other, also in the amount of $300,000, for the benefit of their surviving children. In return Miss Desmare released all rights that she might acquire as wife or widow in taxpayer's property, both real and personal, excepting the right to maintenance and support. The inducements for this agreement were stated to be the contemplated marriage, desire to make fair requital for the release of marital rights, freedom for the taxpayer to make appropriate provisions for his children and other dependents, the uncertainty surrounding his financial future and marital tranquility. That such an antenuptial agreement is enforceable in Florida is not disputed . . . . The parties married, and the agreement was fully carried out.

. . .

Like the *Wemyss* case, this case turns on the proper application of [§ 2512(b)] . . . . Taxpayer claims that Miss Desmare's relinquishment of her marital rights constituted "adequate and full consideration in money or money's worth." The Collector, relying on the construction of a like phrase in the estate tax, contends that release of marital rights does not furnish such "adequate and full consideration."

. . .

The guiding light is what was said in *Estate of Sanford v. Commissioner*, 308 U.S. 39, 44: "The gift tax was supplementary to the estate tax. The two are in pari materia and must be construed together." The phrase on the meaning of which decision must largely turn—that is, transfer for other than "an adequate and full consideration in money or money's worth"—came into the gift tax by way of estate tax provisions. It first appeared in the Revenue Act of 1926. [The predecessor of § 2053(c)(1)(A)] allowed deductions from the value of the gross estate of claims against the estate to the extent that they were bona fide and incurred "for an adequate and full consideration in money or money's worth." It is important to note that the language of previous Acts which made the test "fair consideration" was thus changed after courts had given "fair consideration" an expansive construction.

The first modern estate tax law had included in the gross estate transfers in contemplation of, or intended to take effect in possession or enjoyment at, death, except "a bona fide sale for a fair consideration in money or money's worth." § 202(b), Revenue Act of 1916. Dower rights and other marital property rights were intended to be included in the gross estate, since they were considered merely an expectation, and in 1918 Congress specifically included them. § 40 Stat. 1057, 1097. This provision was for the purpose of clarifying the existing law. H. Rep. No. 767, 65th Cong., 2d Sess., p. 21. In 1924 Congress limited deductible claims against an estate to those supported by "a fair consideration in money or money's worth," § 303(a)(1), 43 Stat. 253, 305, employing the same standard applied to transfers in contemplation of death, H. Rep. No. 179, 68th Cong., 1st Sess., pp. 28, 66. Similar language was used in the gift tax, first imposed by the 1924 Act, by providing "Where property is sold or exchanged for less than a fair consideration in money or money's worth" the excess shall be deemed a gift. § 43 Stat. 253, 314 . . . .

When the gift tax was re-enacted in the 1932 Revenue Act, the restrictive phrase "adequate and full consideration" as found in the estate tax was taken over by the draftsman.

To be sure, in the 1932 Act Congress specifically provided that relinquishment of marital rights for purposes of the estate tax shall not constitute "consideration in money or money's worth." The Committees of Congress reported that if the value of relinquished marital interests "may, in whole or in part, constitute a consideration for an otherwise taxable transfer (as has been held to be so), or an otherwise unallowable deduction from the gross estate, the effect produced amounts to a subversion of the legislative intent . . . ." H.Rep. No. 708, 72d Cong., 1st Sess., p. 47; S. Rep. No. 665, 72d Cong., 1st Sess., p. 50. Plainly, the explicitness was one of cautious redundancy to prevent "subversion of the legislative intent." Without this specific provision, Congress undoubtedly intended the requirement of "adequate and full consideration" to exclude relinquishment of dower and other marital rights with respect to the estate tax.

We believe that there is every reason for giving the same words in the gift tax the same reading. Correlation of the gift tax and the estate tax still requires legislative intervention. *Commissioner v. Prouty*, 115 F.2d 331, 337. But to interpret the same phrases in the two taxes concerning the same subject matter in different ways where obvious reasons do not compel divergent treatment is to introduce another and needless complexity into this already irksome situation. Here strong reasons urge identical construction. To hold otherwise would encourage tax avoidance. *Commissioner v. Bristol, supra,* at 136; . . . And it would not fulfill the purpose of the gift tax in discouraging family settlements so as to avoid high income surtaxes. H. Rep. No. 708, 72d Cong., 1st Sess., p. 28; S. Rep. No. 665, 72d Cong., 1st Sess., p. 40. There is thus every reason in this case to construe the provisions of both taxes harmoniously. *Estate of Sanford v. Commissioner, supra.*[1]

Affirmed.

Mr. Justice Roberts dissents.

Mr. Justice Reed, dissenting.

Petitioner was obligated to create the trust upon consideration of the relinquishment of marital rights and did so, and hence this is not a case involving marriage alone as consideration. Through the tables of mortality, the value of a survivor's right in a fixed sum receivable at the death of a second party may be adequately calculated . . . .

It seems to us clear that with the judicial history of the difficulties in estate and gift taxes as to the transfer of marital rights when Congress expressly provided that relinquishment of dower, curtesy or other statutory estate was not "consideration" for estate tax purposes and left the gift tax provision without such a limitation, it intended that these rights be accorded a different treatment under these sections. This has been the determination of the Tax Court.

In our view this judgment should be reversed.

The Chief Justice and Mr. Justice Douglas join in this dissent.

———

Commissioner v. Wemyss and *Merrill v. Fahs* illustrate one of the most significant aspects between the intersection of contract law and gift taxation. Because gift taxation seeks to avoid untaxed depletion of the donor's estate, transfers for inadequate consideration constitute gifts for gift tax purposes. *See, e.g.,* Estate of Costanza v. Commissioner, T.C. Memo. 2001-128 (gift on transfer by parent to son in return for installment note because transaction was not bona fide). As *Wemyss* indicates, the consideration must pass to the transferor—a transferee's assumption of an obligation (or passing of property) to another is not enough. In short, a gift in the tax sense occurs to the extent that the value of a transferred interest in property exceeds the value of property interests received in return. In effect, a gift occurs if the value of the potential estate has been depleted by a lifetime transfer. After all, it was to prevent the tax-free depletion of the estate (and thus the avoidance of the estate tax) which led to the passage of the gift tax.

The concentration on consideration in § 2512 means that a transfer need not be a *gift* for property law purposes. As *Wemyss* and *Merrill* illustrate, gifts for tax purposes may arise in a contractual setting. For example, the assignment of a contract right is a transfer of intangible property and is expressly

---

[1] Treasury Regulation [§ 25.2512–8] is inapplicable. To find that the transaction was "made in the ordinary course of business" is to attribute to the Treasury a strange use of English.

taxed by § 2511. Similarly, the creation of third-party contract rights is an indirect transfer that is also expressly addressed in § 2511. Rather than concentrate on the property law categorization of the transaction, the Code focuses on the consideration for the transfer. The gift tax applies to transactions for inadequate consideration as well as to those purely gratuitous transactions which have no consideration other than love and affection. According to the regulations, "[d]onative intent on the part of the transferor is not an essential element in the application of the gift tax to the transfer." *See* Treas. Reg. § 25.2511–1(g)(1). Rather than ascertaining the donor's "elusive state of mind," the Code shifts the issue to whether the transfer is made for less than an equivalent consideration in money or money's worth. This effectively avoids the possibility of the donor structuring a gratuitous transfer as a sale (commonly referred to as a bargain sale) to avoid the gift tax.

Unfortunately, the shift of concern to consideration does not negate the importance of the donor's "elusive state of mind." Indeed, Treasury Regulation § 25.2511–1(g)(1) expressly excludes "ordinary business transactions" from the definition of a gift. "A transaction which is bona fide, at arm's length, and free from any donative intent" is not a gift. Treas. Reg. § 25.2512–8. This, of course, reintroduces the necessity for an inquiry into donative intent.[2] On the other hand, the donor need not be engaged in business to qualify for the bad business deal exception. *See* Anderson v. Commissioner, 8 T.C. 706 (1947), *acq.* 1947–2 C.B. 1. The outer limits of the exception are, therefore, unclear. The bad business-deal analysis has been applied to a political contribution. *See* Stern v. United States, 436 F.2d 1327 (5th Cir. 1971) (before amendment of § 2501(a) to add subsection (a)(5)). Further, the Supreme Court suggested in Harris v. Commissioner (reproduced at § 4.01[B][2], *infra*) that the concept could apply to marital transfers.

In all events it is clear that for a taxable gift to occur, there first must be a transfer under local law. Thus, for example, if an attempted gift lacks delivery and is therefore invalid, no gift for federal gift tax purposes can occur. *See* Estate of Kincade v. Commissioner, 69 T.C. 247 (1977) (attempted gift of bearer bonds by depositing them in a safety deposit box). There are two corollaries to this requirement. First, the putative donor must have owned an interest in property. Second, the interest must have been transferable. For example, an employee does not make a taxable gift of employee death benefits if (1) he has no power to alter the benefit or its timing and (2) the recipient is designated by the employer, even though the benefit would cease if the decedent quit employment. *See* Estate of DiMarco v. Commissioner, 87 T.C. 653 (1986) (reproduced at § 4.01[A][2], *infra*).

Consideration passing to the transferor must be economic, but can represent the reduction of a legal obligation on the transferor's part. Most significantly, transfers in satisfaction of a parent's or spouse's support obligation are not gifts in the tax sense. *See, e.g.,* Rev. Rul. 68–379, 1968–2 C.B. 414. *See generally* RICHARD B. STEPHENS ET AL., FEDERAL ESTATE AND GIFT TAXATION ¶ 10.02[5] (7th ed. 1997).

---

[2] Donative intent is relevant for income tax purposes. "Detached and disinterested generosity" is the test used to determine whether a transaction is a *gift* which may be excluded from income under § 102. *See* Duberstein v. United States, 363 U.S. 278 (1960).

Consideration will also be recognized when the donee agrees to pay the donor's gift tax. *See* Rev. Rul. 71–232, 1971–1 C.B. 275. Specifically, if the donee agrees to pay the gift tax on the transfer, the value of the donor's gift is only the difference between the value of the property and the amount of the gift tax, or the "net gift."

Example: A donor in the 50% bracket for gift tax purposes transfers $100,000 to a donee, provided the donee agrees to pay the gift tax, the donor's net gift will be $ 66,667 ($100,000 minus the gift tax of $33,333 which constitutes consideration received by the donor).[3] *Net gifts* are discussed in *Estate of Sachs v. Commissioner* (reproduced at § 6.02[B], *infra*).

Problems

1. *D* paid $21,000 for a new car. *D*, who has made no prior taxable gifts during the current year, transferred title and keys to her 16 year old son, saying, "This is for you. Now, I won't have to drive you everywhere." *D* asks you whether she should file a federal gift tax return reporting the transaction. (Assume that *D* is not married.)

     a. What would you advise her?

     b. What would be the result if *D* sold the car to her son for $12,000?

     c. What would be the result if *D* sold the car to her son in return for her son's agreement to pay $12,000 to his sister (*D*'s daughter), a 21 year old college student whose tuition *D* otherwise was paying?

2. *D* purchased a used car for $4,000 from Junior's Used Cars. The fair market value of the car was only $2,500.

     a. Has *D* made a gift of $1,500 to Junior?

     b. Would the result be different if *D* and Junior were relatives?

3. In 2002, Donor transfers real property to Donee worth $1.1 million in return for Donee's promise to pay the gift tax. Assume Donor made no prior taxable gifts, but earlier in the year made a cash gift to Donee that fully used the Donor's gift tax annual exclusion. What is the amount of the taxable gift?

4. *G* promised to give *X* 1,000 shares of stock in corporation *Q* (valued at $25,000) if *X* refrained from smoking for one year. One year later, the shares have a value of $30,000 and a basis in *G*'s hands of $18,000. *X*, having refrained from smoking for the year, receives the shares from *G* on the promised date. Has *G* made a taxable gift? If so, when? Assuming no gift tax because of the unified credit, what basis would *X* take in the stock? *See* Farid-Es-Sultaneh v. Commissioner, 160 F.2d 812 (2d Cir. 1947). Would G have any capital gains or ordinary income?

5. Son owes $500 to a merchant.

---

[3] The example assumes that the gift tax annual exclusion has already been exhausted for the calendar year. The net gift amount is determined by simple algebra: The net gift (n) plus the tax on the net gift ($0.50n$) equals the total amount transferred. In the example, $n + 0.50n = $100,000; 1.50n = $100,000$ and $n = $66,667$. IRS Publication 904 explains the solution to net gift calculations and to other situations that involve interrelated computations.

a. Father pays the store $500 in complete satisfaction of son's debt. Has father made a transfer of property by gift?

b. Father satisfies son's debt to the merchant by performing services for the merchant. Has either the father or the merchant made a transfer of property by gift?

6. Taxpayer and her husband agreed that he would create a testamentary trust for her and she would transfer her one-half share of community property into the trust after his estate had been administered. Assume that, at her husband's death, taxpayer's community property interest exceeded the value of the trust interest created for her. Will a gift occur at her husband's death or when she transfers the property into the trust? *See* Rev. Rul. 69–346, 1969–1 C.B. 227.

[1] Release of Dominion and Control

Code: §§ 2501, 2511, and 2512(b).

Regulations: Treas. Reg. §§ 25.2511–1(c), (h)(4) & (5); 25.2511–2(b), (c), (f); and 25.2512–8.

Burnet v. Guggenheim

288 U.S. 280 (1933)

Mr. Justice Cardozo delivered the opinion of the Court.

The question to be decided is whether deeds of trust made in 1917, with a reservation to the grantor of a power of revocation, became taxable as gifts under the Revenue Act of 1924 when in 1925 there was a change of the deeds by the cancellation of the power.

On June 28, 1917, the respondent, a resident of New York, executed in New Jersey two deeds of trust, one for the benefit of his son, and one for the benefit of his daughter. The trusts were to continue for ten years, during which period part of the income was to be paid to the beneficiary and part accumulated. At the end of the ten year period the principal and the accumulated income were to go to the beneficiary, if living; if not living, then to his or her children; and if no children survived, then to the settlor in the case of the son's trust, and in the case of the daughter's trust to the trustees of the son's trust as an increment to the fund. The settlor reserved to himself . . . an unrestricted power to modify, alter or revoke the trusts except as to income, received or accrued . . . . The power to modify, alter or revoke was eliminated from the deeds, and thereby canceled and surrendered, in July, 1925.

In the meantime Congress had passed the Revenue Act of 1924 which included among its provisions a tax upon gifts. "For the calendar year 1924 and each calendar year thereafter . . . a tax . . . is hereby imposed upon the transfer by a resident by gift during such calendar year of any property wherever situated, whether made directly or indirectly . . . ."

On November 8, 1924, more than eight months before the cancellation of the power of revocation, the Commissioner of Internal Revenue, with the approval of the Secretary of the Treasury, adopted and promulgated the following regulation: "The creation of a trust, where the grantor retains the power to revest in himself title to the corpus of the trust, does not constitute a gift subject to tax, but the annual income of the trust which is paid over to the beneficiaries shall be treated as a taxable gift for the year in which so paid. Where the power retained by the grantor to revest in himself title to the corpus is not exercised, a taxable transfer will be treated as taking place in the year in which such power is terminated." Regulations 67, Article I.

The substance of this regulation has now been carried forward into the Revenue Act of 1932, which will give the rule for later transfers (section 2511 and Treas. Reg. § 25.2511–2(c) and (f)).

. . .

"Taxation is not so much concerned with the refinements of title as it is with the actual command over the property taxed—the actual benefit for which the tax is paid." *Corliss v. Bowers*, 281 U.S. 376, 378 [other citations omitted]. While the powers of revocation stood uncancelled in the deeds, the gifts, from the point of view of substance, were inchoate and imperfect. By concession there would have been no gift in any aspect if the donor had attempted to attain the same result by the mere delivery of the securities into the hands of the donees. A power of revocation accompanying delivery would have made the gift a nullity. *Basket v. Hassell*, 107 U.S. 602. By the execution of deeds and the creation of trusts, the settlor did indeed succeed in divesting himself of title and transferring it to others [citations omitted], but the substance of his dominion was the same as if these forms had been omitted. *Corliss v. Bowers, supra*. He was free at any moment, with reason or without, to revest title in himself, except as to any income then collected or accrued. As to the principal of the trusts and as to income to accrue thereafter, the gifts were formal and unreal. They acquired substance and reality for the first time in July, 1925, when the deeds became absolute through the cancellation of the power.

The argument for the respondent is that Congress in laying a tax upon transfers by gift made in 1924 or in any year thereafter had in mind the passing of title, not the extinguishment of dominion. In that view the transfer had been made in 1917 when the deeds of trust were executed. The argument for the Government is that what was done in 1917 was preliminary and tentative, and that not till 1925 was there a transfer in the sense that must have been present in the mind of Congress when laying a burden upon gifts. Petitioner and respondent are at one in the view that from the extinguishment of the power there came about a change of legal rights and a shifting of economic benefits which Congress was at liberty, under the Constitution, to tax as a transfer effected at that time [citations omitted]. The question is not one of legislative power. It is one of legislative intention.

With the controversy thus narrowed, doubt is narrowed too. Congress did not mean that the tax should be paid twice, or partly at one time and partly at another. If a revocable deed of trust is a present transfer by gift, there is not another transfer when the power is extinguished. If there is not a present transfer upon the delivery of the revocable deed, then there is such a transfer upon the extinguishment of the power. There must be a choice, and a consistent choice, between the one date and the other. To arrive at a decision, we have therefore to put to ourselves the question, which choice is it the more likely that Congress would have made . . . ?

The respondent invokes the rule that in the construction of a taxing act doubt is to be resolved in favor of the taxpayer. *United States v. Merriam*, 263 U.S. 179; *Gould v. Gould*, 245 U.S. 151 . . . . It happens that the taxpayer before us made his deeds in 1917, before a transfer by gift was subject to a tax. We shall alleviate his burden if we say that the gift was then complete. On the other hand, we shall be heightening the burdens of taxpayers who made deeds of gift after the Act of 1924. In making them, they had the assurance of a treasury regulation that the tax would not be laid . . . .

The tax upon gifts is closely related both in structure and in purpose to the tax upon those transfers that take effect at death . . . . The two statutes are plainly in pari materia . . . . The tax upon estates, as it stood in 1924, was the outcome of a long process of evolution; it had been refined and perfected by decisions and amendments almost without number. The tax on gifts was something new. Even so, the concept of a transfer, so painfully developed in respect of taxes on estates, was not flung aside and scouted in laying this new burden upon transfers during life. Congress was aware that what was of the essence of a transfer had come to be identified more nearly with a change of economic benefits than with technicalities of title.

. . .

The argument for the respondent, if pressed to the limit of its logic, would carry him even farther than he has claimed the right to go. If his position is sound that a power to revoke does not postpone for the purpose of taxation the consummation of the gift, then the income of these trusts is exempt from the tax as fully as the principal. What passed to the beneficiaries was the same in either case, an interest inchoate and contingent till rendered absolute and consummate through receipt or accrual before the act of revocation. Congress did not mean that recurring installments of the income, payable under a revocable conveyance which had been made by a settlor before the passage of this statute, should be exempt, when collected, from the burden of the tax.

The judgment is reversed.

Estate of Sanford v. Commissioner

308 U.S. 39 (1939)

Mr. Justice Stone delivered the opinion of the Court.

This and its companion case, *Rasquin v. Humphreys*, [308 U.S. 54] . . . present the single question of statutory construction whether in the case of an inter vivos transfer of property in trust, by a donor reserving to himself the power to designate new beneficiaries other than himself, the gift becomes complete and subject to the gift tax imposed by the federal revenue laws at the time of the relinquishment of the power. Correlative questions, important only if a negative answer is given to the first one, are whether the gift becomes complete and taxable when the trust is created . . . .

In 1913, before the enactment of the first gift tax statute of 1924, decedent created a trust of personal property for the benefit of named beneficiaries, reserving to himself the power to terminate the trust in whole or in part, or to modify it. In 1919 he surrendered the power to revoke the trust by an appropriate writing in which he reserved "the right to modify any or all of the trusts" but provided that this right "shall in no way be deemed or construed to include any right or privilege" in the donor "to withdraw principal or income from any trust." In August, 1924, after the effective date of the gift tax statute, decedent renounced his remaining power to modify the trust. After his death in 1928, the Commissioner following the decision in *Hesslein v. Hoey*, 91 F.2d 954, in 1937, ruled that the gift became complete and taxable only upon decedent's final renunciation of his power to modify the trusts.

. . .

In ascertaining the correct construction of the statutes taxing gifts, it is necessary to read them in the light of the closely related provisions of the revenue laws taxing transfers at death, as they have been interpreted by our decisions . . . . When the gift tax was enacted Congress was aware that the essence of a transfer is the passage of control over the economic benefits of property rather than any technical changes in its title. *See* Burnet v. Guggenheim, 288 U.S. 280, 287. Following the enactment of the gift tax statute this Court in *Reinecke v. Northern Trust Co.*, 278 U.S. 339 (1929) held that the relinquishment at death of a power of revocation of a trust for the benefit of its donor was a taxable transfer [citations omitted]; and similarly in *Porter v. Commissioner*, 288 U.S. 436 (1933), that the relinquishment by a donor at death of a reserved power to modify the trust except in his own favor is likewise a transfer of the property which could constitutionally be taxed under the provisions of § 302(d) of the 1926 Revenue Act . . . although enacted after the creation of the trust [citations omitted]. Since it was the relinquishment of the power which was taxed as a transfer and not the transfer in trust, the statute was not retroactively applied [citations omitted].

. . .

There is nothing in the language of the statute, and our attention has not been directed to anything in its legislative history to suggest that Congress had any purpose to tax gifts before the donor had fully parted with his interest in the property given, or that the test of the completeness of the taxed gift was to be any different from that to be applied in determining whether the donor has retained an interest such that it becomes subject to the estate tax upon its extinguishment at death. The gift tax was supplementary to the estate tax. The two are *in pari materia* and must be construed together. *Burnet v. Guggenheim* . . . . An important, if not the main, purpose of the gift tax was to prevent or compensate for avoidance of death taxes by taxing the gifts of property *inter vivos* which, but for the gifts, would be subject in its original or converted form to the tax laid upon transfers at death.

. . .

It is plain that the contention of the taxpayer in this case that the gift becomes complete and taxable upon the relinquishment of the donor's power to revoke the trust cannot be sustained unless we are to hold, contrary to the policy of the statute and the reasoning in the *Guggenheim* case, that a second tax will be incurred upon the donor's relinquishment at death of his power to select new beneficiaries, or unless as an alternative we are to abandon our ruling in the *Porter* case. The Government does not suggest . . . that we should depart from our earlier rulings, and we think it clear that we should not do so both because we are satisfied with the reasoning upon which they rest and because departure from either would produce inconsistencies in the law . . . .

There are other persuasive reasons why the taxpayer's contention cannot be sustained. By [§ 6324(b)], the donee of any gift is made personally liable for the tax to the extent of the value of the gift if the tax is not paid by the donor. It can hardly be supposed that Congress intended to impose personal liability upon the donee of a gift of property, so incomplete that he might be deprived of it by the donor the day after he had paid the tax. Further, [§ 2522] exempts from the tax, gifts to religious, charitable, and educational corporations and the like. A gift would seem not to be complete, for purposes of the tax, where the donor has reserved the power to determine whether the donees ultimately entitled to receive and enjoy the property are of such a class as to exempt the gift from taxation. Apart from other considerations we should hesitate to accept as correct a construction under which it could plausibly be maintained that a gift in trust for the benefit of charitable corporations is then complete so that the taxing statute becomes operative and the gift escapes the tax even though the donor should later change the beneficiaries to the non-exempt class through exercise of a power to modify the trust in any way not beneficial to himself.

. . .

Affirmed.

———

For a gift to be complete for gift tax purposes, the donor must relinquish sufficient dominion and control over the property so that it is no longer subject to her will. *See* Treas. Reg. § 25.2511–2(b). Examples of retained control that will cause a gift to be deemed incomplete include the power to "revoke a transfer," "name new beneficiaries," and "change the interests of the beneficiaries as between themselves unless the power is a fiduciary power limited by a fixed or ascertainable standard." *See* Treas. Reg. § 25.2511–2(c). If the donor retains only the power to "change the manner or time of enjoyment," however, a gift is complete. *See* Treas. Reg. § 25.2511–2(b). These, and other issues, are discussed in Chapters 8 and 9, *infra*.

Some common third-party beneficiary contracts produce no gift tax effects until fulfilled by the promisor. Often, the gift is deemed incomplete because a part of the contract permits the promisee (donor) to revoke or to otherwise modify the terms of the contract. An insurance policy in which the policy owner has the right to change beneficiaries and cash in the policy is an example. A United States savings bond registered in the name of the donor, but payable at his death to a named donee, and which gives the registered owner the right to exchange the bond for cash, is another example.

Problems

1. Mother establishes a joint bank account for herself and Arlene, her daughter. Under the account, either may withdraw funds. Mother deposits $15,000 to the account. Is there a gift for tax purposes when the money is deposited? If not, when would there be a completed gift? *Consider* Treas. Reg.§ 25.2511-2(f).

2. On August 1, 2000, *D* gratuitously issued his $25,000 note, with interest, payable to *A*. The note is enforceable under state law. *D* pays on the note on January 2, 2002. When has *D* made a gift—in 2000, 2002, or some other year? *See* Rev. Rul. 84–25, 1984–1 C.B. 191.

3. Four years ago, *D*, who then had a net worth of $100,000, guaranteed a bank loan for a friend, *A*, in the amount of $100,000. This year *A* defaulted on the loan, the bank obtained a judgment against *D*, and the bank levied on *D*'s assets. The levy yielded only $40,000. When, if at all, did *D* make a gift, and in what amount? *Consider* Bradford v. Commissioner, 34 T.C. 1059 (1960), and Treasury Regulations §§ 25.2511–1(c) and 25.2512–8. *Cf.* Abrams v. United States, 1988–1 U.S.T.C. (CCH) ¶ 13,769 (S.D.N.Y. 1988) (discharge of lien).

[2]　Transfer of Property

Code: §§ 2511 and 7872.

Regulations: Treas. Reg. §§ 25.2511–1; 1.7872–1(a), –4(a), and (b).

The gift tax only applies if there has been a "transfer of property" that constitutes a gift. This section explores the "transfer of property" requirement.

Dickman v. Commissioner

465 U.S. 330 (1984)

Chief Justice Burger delivered the opinion of the Court:

[Mr. and Mrs. Dickman made substantial no-interest demand loans over several years to their son and a family corporation. After Mr. Dickman died, the Commissioner asserted a gift tax deficiency against his estate and Mrs. Dickman for the value of the use of the loaned amounts.]

We granted certiorari to resolve a conflict among the Circuits as to whether intrafamily, interest-free demand loans result in taxable gifts of the value of the use of the money lent.

.　.　.

II

A

The statutory language of the federal gift tax provisions purports to reach any gratuitous transfer of any interest in property. Section 2501(a)(1) of the Code imposes a tax upon "the transfer of property by gift." Section 2511(a) highlights the broad sweep of the tax imposed by § 2501 . . . .

B

In asserting that interest-free demand loans give rise to taxable gifts, the Commissioner does not seek to impose the gift tax upon the principal amount of the loan, but only upon the reasonable value of the use of the money lent. The taxable gift that assertedly results from an interest-free demand loan is the value of receiving and using the money without incurring a corresponding obligation to pay interest along with the loan's repayment.[4] Is such a gratuitous transfer of the right to use money a "transfer of property" within the intendment of § 2501(a)(1)?

We have little difficulty accepting the theory that the use of valuable property—in this case money—is itself a legally protectible property interest. Of the aggregate rights associated with any property interest, the right of use of property is perhaps of the highest order. One court put it succinctly:

> "Property" is more than just the physical thing—the land, the bricks, the mortar—it is also the sum of all the rights and powers incident to ownership of the physical thing. It is the tangible and the intangible. Property is composed of constituent elements and of these elements the right to use the physical thing to the exclusion of others is the most essential and beneficial.

Without this right all other elements would be of little value . . . . *Passailaigue v. United States*, 224 F. Supp. 682, 686 (M.D. Ga. 1963) (footnote omitted).

What was transferred here was the use of a substantial amount of cash for an indefinite period of time. An analogous interest in real property, the use under a tenancy at will, has long been recognized as a property right. *E.g.*, Restatement (Second) of Property § 1.6 (1977). For example, a parent who grants to a child the rent-free, indefinite use of commercial property having a reasonable rental value of $8000 a month has clearly transferred a valuable property right. The transfer of $100,000 in cash, interest-free and repayable on demand, is similarly a grant of the use of valuable property. Its uncertain tenure may reduce its value, but it does not undermine its status as property. In either instance, when the property owner transfers to another the right to use the object, an identifiable property interest has clearly changed hands.

---

[4] [5] The Commissioner's tax treatment of interest-free demand loans may perhaps be best understood as a two-step approach to such transactions. Under this theory, such a loan has two basic economic components: an arm's-length loan from the lender to the borrower, on which the borrower pays the lender a fair rate of interest, followed by a gift from the lender to the borrower in the amount of that interest. *See Crown v. Commissioner*, 585 F.2d 234, 240 (7th Cir. 1978).

The right to the use of $100,000 without charge is a valuable interest in the money lent, as much so as the rent-free use of property consisting of land and buildings. In either case, there is a measurable economic value associated with the use of the property transferred. The value of the use of money is found in what it can produce; the measure of that value is interest—"rent" for the use of the funds. We can assume that an interest-free loan for a fixed period, especially for a prolonged period, may have greater value than such a loan made payable on demand, but it would defy common human experience to say that an intra-family loan payable on demand is not subject to accommodation; its value may be reduced by virtue of its demand status, but that value is surely not eliminated.

This Court has noted in another context that the making of an interest-free loan results in the transfer of a valuable economic right: "It is virtually self-evident that extending interest-free credit for a period of time is equivalent to giving a discount equal to the value of the use of the purchase price for that period of time." *Catalano, Inc. v. Target Sales, Inc.*, 446 U.S. 643, 648 (1980) (*per curiam*).

Against this background, the gift tax statutes clearly encompass within their broad sweep the gratuitous transfer of the use of money. Just as a tenancy at will in real property is an estate or interest in land, so also is the right to use money a cognizable interest in personal property. The right to use money is plainly a valuable right, readily measurable by reference to current interest rates; the vast banking industry is positive evidence of this reality. Accordingly, we conclude that the interest-free loan of funds is a "transfer of property by gift" within the contemplation of the federal gift tax statutes.[5]

Our holding that an interest-free demand loan results in a taxable gift of the use of the transferred funds is fully consistent with one of the major purposes of the federal gift tax statute: protection of the estate tax and the income tax. The legislative history of the gift tax provisions reflects that Congress enacted a tax on gifts to supplement existing estate and income tax laws . . . .

A substantial no-interest loan from parent to child creates significant tax benefits for the lender quite apart from the economic advantages to the

---

[5] Petitioners argue that no gift tax consequences should attach to interest-free demand loans because no "transfer" of property occurs at the time the loan is made. Petitioners urge that the term "transfer" "connotes a discrete, affirmative act whereby a person conveys something to another person, not a continuous series of minute failures to require return of something loaned." Brief for Petitioners 22. We decline to adopt that construction of the statute.

In order to make a taxable gift, a transferor must relinquish dominion and control over the transferred property. *See* Treas. Reg. § 25.2511–2(b). At the moment an interest-free demand loan is made, the transferor has not given up all dominion and control; he could terminate the transferee's use of the funds by calling the loan. As time passes without a demand for repayment, however, the transferor allows the use of the principal to pass to the transferee, and the gift becomes complete. *See ibid*; Rev. Rul. 69–347, 1969–1 Cum. Bull. 227; Rev. Rul. 69–346, 1969–1 Cum. Bull. 227. As the Court of Appeals realized, 690 F.2d, at 819, the fact that the transferor's dominion and control over the use of the principal is relinquished over time will become especially relevant in connection with the valuation of the gifts that result from such loans; it does not, however, alter the fact that the lender has made a gratuitous transfer of property subject to the federal gift tax.

borrower. This is especially so when an individual in a high income tax bracket transfers income-producing property to an individual in a lower income tax bracket, thereby reducing the taxable income of the high-bracket taxpayer at the expense, ultimately, of all other taxpayers and the government. Subjecting interest-free loans to gift taxation minimizes the potential loss to the federal fisc generated by the use of such loans as an income tax avoidance mechanism for the transferor. Gift taxation of interest-free loans also effectuates Congress' desire to supplement the estate tax provisions. A gratuitous transfer of income-producing property may enable the transferor to avoid the future estate tax liability that would result if the earnings generated by the property—rent, interest, or dividends—became a part of the transferor's estate. Imposing the gift tax upon interest-free loans bolsters the estate tax by preventing the diminution of the transferor's estate in this fashion.

III

Petitioners contend that administrative and equitable considerations require a holding that no gift tax consequences result from the making of interest-free demand loans. In support of this position, petitioners advance several policy arguments; none withstands studied analysis.

A

Petitioners first advance an argument accepted by the Tax Court in *Crown v. Commissioner, supra*:

> [O]ur income tax system does not recognize unrealized earnings or accumulations of wealth and no taxpayer is under any obligation to continuously invest his money for a profit. The opportunity cost of either letting one's money remain idle or suffering a loss from an unwise investment is not taxable merely because a profit could have been made from a wise investment. 67 T.C., at 1063–1064.

Thus, petitioners argue, an interest-free loan should not be made subject to the gift tax simply because of the possibility that the money lent might have enhanced the transferor's taxable income or gross estate had the loan never been made.

This contention misses the mark. It is certainly true that no law requires an individual to invest his property in an income-producing fashion, just as no law demands that a transferor charge interest or rent for the use of money or other property. An individual may, without incurring the gift tax, squander money, conceal it under a mattress, or otherwise waste its use value by failing to invest it. Such acts of consumption have nothing to do with lending money at no interest. The gift tax is an excise tax on transfers of property; allowing dollars to be idle involves no transfer. If the taxpayer chooses not to waste the use value of money, however, but instead transfers the use to someone else, a taxable event has occurred. That the transferor himself could have consumed or wasted the use value of the money without incurring the gift tax does not change this result. Contrary to petitioners' assertion, a holding in favor of the taxability of interest-free loans does not impose upon the transferor a duty profitably to invest; rather, it merely recognizes that certain tax consequences inevitably flow from a decision to make a "transfer of property by gift." 26 U.S.C. § 2501(a)(1).

B

Petitioners next attack the breadth of the Commissioner's view that interest-free demand loans give rise to taxable gifts. Carried to its logical extreme, petitioners argue, the Commissioner's rationale would elevate to the status of taxable gifts such commonplace transactions as a loan of the proverbial cup of sugar to a neighbor or a loan of lunch money to a colleague. Petitioners urge that such a result is an untenable intrusion by the government into cherished zones of privacy, particularly where intrafamily transactions are involved.

Our laws require parents to provide their minor offspring with the necessities and conveniences of life; questions under the tax law often arise, however, when parents provide more than the necessities, and in quantities significant enough to attract the attention of the taxing authorities. Generally, the legal obligation of support terminates when the offspring reach majority. Nonetheless, it is not uncommon for parents to provide their adult children with such things as the use of cars or vacation cottages, simply on the basis of the family relationship. We assume that the focus of the Internal Revenue Service is not on such traditional familial matters. When the government levies a gift tax on routine neighborly or familial gifts, there will be time enough to deal with such a case.

Moreover, the tax law provides liberally for gifts to both family members and others; within the limits of the prescribed statutory exemptions, even substantial gifts may be entirely tax free. First, under § 2503(e) of the Code, amounts paid on behalf of an individual for tuition at a qualified educational institution or for medical care are not considered "transfer[s] of property by gift" for purposes of the gift tax statutes. More significantly, section 2503(b) of the Code provides an annual exclusion from the computation of taxable gifts of $10,000 per year, per donee; this provision allows a taxpayer to give up to $10,000 annually to each of any number of persons, without incurring any gift tax liability. The "split gift" provisions of Code § 2513(a), which effectively enables a husband and wife to give each object of their bounty $20,000 per year without liability for gift tax, further enhances the ability to transfer significant amounts of money and property free of gift tax consequences. Finally, should a taxpayer make gifts during one year that exceed the § 2503(b) annual gift tax exclusion, no gift tax liability will result until the unified credit of Code § 2505 has been exhausted. These generous exclusions, exceptions, and credits clearly absorb the sorts of de minimis gifts petitioners envision and render illusory the administrative problems that petitioners perceive in their "parade of horribles."

. . .

IV

As we have noted, Congress has provided generous exclusions and credits designed to reduce the gift tax liability of the great majority of taxpayers.

Congress clearly has the power to provide a similar exclusion for the gifts that result from interest-free demand loans. Any change in the gift tax consequences of such loans, however, is a legislative responsibility, not a judicial one. Until such a change occurs, we are bound to effectuate Congress' intent to protect the estate and income tax systems with a broad and comprehensive tax upon all "transfer[s] of property by gift." *Cf. Diedrich v. Commissioner,* 457 U.S. 191, 199 (1982).

We hold, therefore, that the interest-free demand loans shown by this record resulted in taxable gifts of the reasonable value of the use of the money lent. Accordingly, the judgment of the United States Court of Appeals for the Eleventh Circuit is Affirmed.

Justice Powell, with whom Justice Rehnquist joins, dissenting. [Opinion omitted.]

———

In response to the *Dickman* Court's invitation to legislate, Congress enacted § 7872. This section recharacterizes below-market interest rate loans by imputing payment of interest to the borrower at the applicable federal interest rate. Section 7872 also treats the lender as constructively *giving* the borrower the funds for the payment of the constructive interest and thereby making a gift for gift tax purposes. For example, if a father loans his son $100,000 interest-free, § 7872 treats the son as transferring an imputed interest amount to the father, and then the father retransferring the interest back to the son as a gift. *See generally* Brien D. Ward, *The Taxation of Interest-Free Loans,* 61 Tul. L. Rev. 849 (1987). As described in the legislative history to § 7872:

> Loans that are subject to [§ 7872] and that do not require payment of interest, or require payment at a rate below the statutory rate (referred to as the "Applicable Federal Rate"), are recharacterized as an arm's-length transaction in which the lender made a loan to the borrower in exchange for a note requiring the payment of interest at the Applicable Federal Rate. This rule results in the parties being treated as if:
>
> (1) The borrower paid interest to the lender that may be deductible to the borrower and is included in income by the lender; and
>
> (2) The lender (a) made a gift subject to the gift tax (in the case of a gratuitous transaction) . . . .

Joint Committee on Taxation, General Explanation of the Revenue Provisions of the Deficit Reduction Act of 1984, 528–529 (1984).

The mere fact that a gift is a transfer of a future interest does not prevent its current taxation as a gift. A transfer by a remainderman or by the creator of the future interest is the transfer of "an interest" in property under § 2511. *See* Lazarus v. Commissioner, 513 F.2d 824 (9th Cir. 1975); Treas. Reg. §§ 25.2511–1(e), –1(h)(6); Rev. Rul. 79–238, 1979–2 C.B. 339. That the interest may not carry with it any right to immediate possession or enjoyment of the property is irrelevant.

On the other hand, a gift of services is not subject to gift taxation. For example, in *Hogle v. Commissioner*, 165 F.2d 352 (10th Cir. 1947), the issue was

> whether or not annual earnings of two trusts, from trading in securities and commodities carried on by the trusts under Hogle's direction, amounted to gifts by Hogle to the trusts.
>
> The trust was irrevocable and Hogle retained no right to alter or amend the trust instrument, or to change the beneficial interests. None of the principal or income could revest in Hogle. [The trusts] provided that any losses resulting from trading in excess of the "profits and various income returns thereof" should be made good by Hogle, and that any such losses should not become an indebtedness of the trustee or the beneficiaries, but that any such losses made good by Hogle should be returned to him out of the first profits that accrued from further transactions.

The court found for the taxpayer. It determined that the taxpayer provided services, not property, to the trusts and their beneficiaries. "What, in fact and in reality, Hogle gave to the trusts in the taxable years was his expert services in carrying on the trading, personal services in the management of the trusts. Hogle could give or withhold his personal services in carrying on trading on margin for the trusts."

The Service concedes that the gift of services is not subject to gift taxation because the gift is not property. *See* Rev. Rul. 66–167, 1966–1 C.B. 20.

Problems

1. On January 1, Father lends his son $1 million. In return, the son executes a promissory note agreeing to pay the entire $1 million on demand. The note does not require the payment of interest. Assume that the applicable interest rate for the purposes of § 7872 equals 8% and that the loan remains outstanding on December 31. What is the amount of the gift under § 7872?

2. D, age 60, loaned $500,000 to X, age 35, in return for X's promise to pay $500,000 to Y at D's death. What are the gift tax consequences of the loan?

3. Parent gives the rent-free use of the family beach house to adult child. What are the gift tax consequences if:

   a. Child personally uses the beach house?

   b. Child rents the beach house to a tenant?

Would your answers depend on whether parent regularly rented the property or used it for personal use?

———

Besides the requirement that the donor transfer property, gift taxation requires a donor to make a voluntary transfer. While this requirement may easily be satisfied, sometimes it is not.

Estate of DiMarco v. Commissioner

87 T.C. 653 (1986), acq. Rev. Rul. 92–68, 1992–2 C.B. 257.

Sterrett, Chief Judge: By notice of deficiency dated May 4, 1983, respondent determined a deficiency in petitioner's Federal estate tax of $17,830.88. As a result of concessions by both parties, the only issue presented in this case is whether the present value of a survivor's income benefit payable with respect to the decedent by decedent's employer is an adjusted taxable gift within the meaning of section 2001.

. . .

Petitioner is the Estate of Anthony F. DiMarco . . . .

Anthony F. DiMarco . . . died on November 16, 1979, survived by his wife, Joan M. DiMarco, and five children. He had been employed continuously by the International Business Machines Corp. (IBM) as an active, regular, full-time, permanent employee from January 9, 1950, until his death. On May 2, 1953, decedent and Joan M. DiMarco were married; he had not been previously married. Decedent's parents were not dependent upon him for their support at any time between the date when his employment with IBM began and the date of his marriage to Joan M. DiMarco. At the time of his death, decedent was employed as an electrical engineer at a salary of $5,250 per month. He was not an officer of the corporation and did not have a written employment contract.

On November 16, 1979, and at all other times relevant to this proceeding, IBM maintained a noncontributory Group Life Insurance and Survivors Income Benefit Plan (hereinafter referred to as the plan) for the benefit of its regular employees . . . .

The plan provided group term life insurance pursuant to a group contract between IBM and the Prudential Life Insurance Co. of America. The amount of insurance payable under the plan was dependent on the length of the employee's service with the company.

The plan also provided a survivor's income benefit on an uninsured and unfunded basis; that is, all survivors income benefits were paid out of IBM's general assets. With the exception of fewer than 30 top executives, all regular IBM employees, including decedent, were covered automatically by the survivors income benefit portion of the plan. At the time of decedent's death, the amount of the survivors income benefit was equal to three times the employee's regular annual compensation. Under the terms of the plan, the benefit was payable only to an employee's surviving spouse, certain minor and dependent children, and dependent parents. Payment was made semimonthly, at the monthly rate of one-quarter of the employee's regular monthly compensation, and continued until the total benefit was paid. However, payments continued only so long as there remained at least one eligible survivor, and if the employee left no eligible survivor at death, no benefit was payable.

Decedent never had any power to alter, amend, revoke, or terminate the plan in whole or in part. He had no power to select or change the beneficiaries of the survivors income benefit; no power to change the amount, form, or timing of the survivors income benefit payments; no power to substitute other benefits for the survivors income benefit; and, other than by resigning his employment with IBM, no power to terminate his coverage under the plan. However, IBM expressly reserved the right, in its discretion, to modify the plan if it determined that it was advisable to do so.

Joan M. DiMarco, as decedent's surviving spouse, was entitled under the plan to receive a survivors income benefit, payable semimonthly, in the amount of $656.25.[6] Decedent did not report the survivors income benefit as a gift on a gift tax return, and petitioner did not report it either as part of the gross estate or as an adjusted taxable gift on decedent's Federal estate tax return. However, the existence of the survivors income benefit was reported by petitioner on Schedule I of decedent's Federal estate tax return.

In his notice of deficiency, respondent "determined that an adjusted taxable gift of the present value of the IBM Survivor Annuity was made by the decedent on the date of death as it was not susceptible of valuation until the date of death." Respondent then determined that the present value of the survivors income benefit was $135,885,[7] and he added this amount, as an adjusted taxable gift, to the taxable estate of decedent in computing the amount of the deficiency. . . .

[T]he survivors income benefit that is payable by IBM to Joan M. DiMarco is an adjusted taxable gift within the meaning of section 2001 only if it is also a taxable gift within the meaning of section 2503 that was made by decedent after December 31, 1976.

. . .

First, it appears that respondent argues that decedent made a completed transfer of a property interest in the survivors income benefit for gift tax purposes on January 9, 1950, but that because the interest could not be valued at that time, it was necessary to treat the transfer as an open transaction and to value the transferred property and impose the gift tax on the date of decedent's death, when the property interest finally became subject to valuation. In the alternative, respondent appears to argue that decedent made an

---

[6] Under the terms of the plan, decedent's surviving spouse was entitled to receive these semimonthly payments until her death, remarriage, or the exhaustion of the total amount of the survivors income benefit. If she died or remarried prior to the exhaustion of the fund, the semimonthly payments would be continued to decedent's other eligible survivors.

[7] Petitioner does not dispute that this value represents the present value of the survivor's income benefit.

incomplete transfer of a property interest in the survivors income benefit for gift tax purposes on January 9, 1950, because the property interest could not be valued at that time, but that the transfer became complete on November 16, 1979, when decedent died, because the transferred property could then and for the first time be valued.

. . .

In view of the fact that a transfer of property that becomes complete because the donor's death terminates a power to change the beneficiaries of the transferred property is not subject to gift tax, we decline to hold that a transfer of property that becomes complete because the donor's death makes it possible for the first time to value the transferred property is subject to the gift tax.

. . .

We reject any suggestion by respondent either that transfers of property are incomplete for gift tax purposes simply because "no realistic value can be placed" on the property at the time the transfer occurs, or that transfers of property become complete for gift tax purposes only when the value of the transferred property can be easily ascertained.

Respondent also argues that completed transfers of property for gift tax purposes can and should be treated as open transactions in those cases where the transferred property is difficult to value, and that valuation of the transferred property and the imposition of the gift tax should be postponed until the value of the property can be readily determined. We reject this contention. The clear language of the statute and the regulations requires that transferred property be valued for gift tax purposes at the time the transfer becomes complete . . . . As a result, property must be valued and the gift tax imposed at the time a completed transfer of the property occurs.

We also agree with petitioner that decedent never made a taxable gift of any property interest in the survivors income benefit because we find no act by decedent that qualifies as an act of "transfer" of an interest in property.

. . .

Moreover, we question whether decedent ever owned a property interest in the survivor's income benefit that he was capable of transferring during his lifetime.

. . .

---

[3] Specific Inclusionary Sections

Code: §§ 2514, 2515, and 2519.

Regulations: None.

In contrast with the estate tax, in which many sections require inclusion of particular types of assets in the gross estate, the gift tax contains only three sections that separately prescribe gift taxation for particular types of transactions.[8] First, § 2514 treats an exercise or release (and some lapses) of a general power of appointment as a transfer of property. This section is discussed in Chapter 12, § 12.01[A][1], *infra*. Second, § 2515 requires that any generation-skipping transfer tax paid on *direct skip* transfers be added to the value of the transferred property for gift tax purposes. Section 2515 is discussed in Chapter 5. Lastly, § 2519 provides that if, during a lifetime, a spouse either partially or fully disposes of an income interest in property for which a marital deduction was allowed by the making of a (QTIP) election, the spouse will be deemed to have transferred the underlying remainder interest in the property. Section 2519 is discussed in conjunction with the gift tax marital deduction later in this Chapter. *See* § 4.03[B][2], *infra*.

[4] Gift-Splitting

Code: §§ 2503(b) and 2513.

Regulations: Treas. Reg. § 25.2513–1, –2(a)(1), and –2(c).

The last major way in which the Code defines gifts for transfer tax purposes is in the concept of the *split gift*. Section 2513 allows married taxpayers to treat gifts to third parties as having been made one-half by each.

Section 2513 is another provision enacted to equalize the tax treatment of donors in non-community property jurisdictions with donors in community property states. In a community property jurisdiction, a gift of community property to a third party is treated as a gift by each spouse of one half of the property, because each spouse owns one-half of the gifted property before the gift. For example, if $22,000 in community cash is transferred to a couple's son in 2002, each spouse is deemed to have made a gift of $11,000. Each, therefore, is entitled to a $11,000 per-donee annual exclusion under § 2503(b) (discussed at § 4.01[B][1], *infra*), and the transfer would pass tax free. In a non-community property state, on the other hand, a gift of $22,000 of *family assets* titled in one spouse's name is treated as a gift by that spouse. The donor is entitled only to a single $11,000 annual exclusion in the absence of § 2513, resulting in a taxable gift of $11,000.

The election to treat a gift as a split gift can produce significant tax savings, given the progressive and cumulative nature of the federal gift tax. Under a split gift, in 2002 each spouse is entitled to exclude $11,000, as indexed for inflation, per donee of the gift under the annual exclusion contained in § 2503(b).[9] The split gift annual exclusion thereby doubles the available exclusions for married couples. Further, in the case of multiple donees, the effect can multiply.

---

[8] In addition to the provisions of the gift tax, chapter 14 of the Code (§§ 2701 through 2704) can result in an individual being deemed to have made a gift for gift tax purposes. This can occur when, for example, the holder of corporate distribution rights fails to exercise those rights. *See* § 2701(d). Gifts can also arise because chapter 14 requires that special valuation rules be applied to transactions that would be for full and adequate consideration if normal valuation principles were used. *See* §§ 2701 and 2702. The specific application of provisions under chapter 14 are considered throughout this chapter.

[9] Section 2503(b) provides for an annual exclusion of $10,000 per donee, but inflation indexing has increased this to $11,000 in 2002. *See* Rev. Proc. 2001-59, I.R.B. 2001-52 (December 24, 2001) §4.19(1).

Example: In 2002, husband and wife with four adult children can give, free of federal gift tax, annual outright gifts of $22,000 per child, or an annual total of $88,000.

Second, gift-splitting also doubles the available unified credit. Each spouse may give gift-tax free his unified credit equivalent, based on the applicable credit amount in effect for the year of the gift. By using the split-gift election, twice the unified credit equivalent can pass because two applicable credit amounts are available.

Example: In 2002, by using gift splitting one spouse can effectively make a gift of $2,022,000 to a single donee and incur no gift tax liability. Under § 2513, both spouses would be deemed to have transferred $1,011,000 to the donee. Each would be entitled to a $11,000 annual exclusion. Thus, each would be treated as having made a gross gift of $1 million. Assuming no deductions are available, each would be treated as having made a taxable gift of $1 million. Thus, the tax on each (assuming no prior taxable gifts) would be $345,800. Each, however, would be entitled to a unified credit of $345,800. As a result, neither spouse would incur gift tax liability. This compares with a net gift tax liability of $445,780 on a gift of $2,022,000 if made by a single individual.

To elect the provisions of § 2513, four technical requirements must be met: (1) both spouses must be citizens or residents of the United States at the time of the gift (Treas. Reg. § 25.2513–1(a)); (2) the donor-spouse cannot create a general power of appointment in the non-donor spouse (Treas. Reg. § 25.2513–1(b)(3)); (3) the parties must be married at the time of the gift (although they need not remain married at the time the return is filed) (Treas. Reg. § 25.2513–1(a)) and neither may remarry during the calendar year in which the gift was made, although death of one before the filing of the gift tax return does not prevent gift-splitting (Treas. Reg. § 25.2513–2(c)); and (4) the spouses must consent to the split-gift treatment by filing a gift tax return signifying their consent to a gift of more than $11,000 (in 2002), as indexed for inflation (Treas. Reg. § 25.2513–2(a)(1)).

Because split-gift treatment results in taxable gifts being attributed to both spouses, the election can have an impact beyond its effect on the gift in question. First, the non-donor spouse is jointly and severally liable for the gift tax on the gift. *See* § 2513(d). Second, if one of the spouses dies with the gift tax unpaid, the split-gift liability can produce a § 2053 deduction. Finally, after the gift, the non-donor spouse is treated as having made prior taxable gifts, thereby increasing the marginal rate applicable to any subsequent gifts that spouse makes. When that spouse dies, he is treated as having made adjusted taxable gifts which inflate his rate base for calculating the tentative estate tax. On the other hand, if the gifted property is later included in the gross estate of one or the other, the split gift is recognized expressly in calculating the tax liability. Under § 2001(d), any gift tax payable by the decedent's spouse is deemed payable by the decedent if the gift is included in the decedent's gross estate. This will determine how much the tentative tax will be reduced by gift taxes payable on prior transfers under § 2001(b)(2).

[B] Excludable Transfers

The Code excludes a number of transfers from gift taxation. The most significant exclusion allows a donor to exclude up to $11,000 (in 2002), as adjusted for inflation, in annual gifts to each donee. *See* § 2503(b). Certain transfers for educational purposes may also be excludable from the gift tax base.

There are two other significant exclusions. Section 2516 exempts certain transfers pursuant to a property settlement in divorce, by defining them as having been made for full and adequate consideration. Section 2518 deems *qualified disclaimers* not to be transfers for the purposes of gift taxation. Less significant exclusions allow a donor to exclude gifts of medical expenses paid to the provider of medical services (§ 2503(e)), transfers to political organizations (§ 2501(a)(5)), and certain waivers of pension rights by a spouse (§ 2503(f)).

[1] Annual Exclusion: Sections 2503(b) and 2503(c)

Code: § 2503(b) and (c).

Regulations: Treas. Reg. § 25.2503–3 and –4.

[a] In General: Section 2503(b)

Section 2503(b) allows a donor to exclude from gross gifts up to $11,000 (in 2002), as indexed for inflation, in gifts of present interests made to each donee in each tax year. The reason for the exclusion, "on the one hand, is to obviate the necessity of keeping an account of and reporting numerous small gifts, and, on the other, to fix the amount sufficiently large to cover in most cases wedding and Christmas gifts and occasional gifts of relatively small amounts."[10]

By ensuring that the gift tax will not apply to relatively small gifts, the exclusion eases the administrative burden on both taxpayers and tax authorities. Excluded transfers never enter into the gift tax computational process. Indeed, if all gifts for the tax year are less than the maximum allowable exclusion, a gift tax return does not have to be filed. *See* § 6019(1).

Congress has occasionally modified the amount of the exclusion. For many years before 1982, the exclusion was set at $3,000. Effective for transfers in 1982, Congress increased the exclusion to $10,000 because "inflation has substantially reduced [its] real value." Senate Finance Committee, S. Rep. No. 97–144, Economic Recovery Tax Act of 1981, 97th Cong., 1st Sess. 129 (1981). In 1997, Congress amended § 2503(b) to provide that the $10,000 annual exclusion will be indexed for inflation, starting in 1999. The indexing is in $1,000 increments, with rounding down to the next lowest $1,000 multiple. *See* § 2503(b)(2). The amount of the annual exclusion in 2002 is $11,000. For purposes of discussion, this text uses $11,000 as the amount of the exclusion, although in years after 2002, the amount may be larger, depending on the amount of inflation. Students should determine if the actual amount has increased to a higher amount in the applicable year.

---

[10] S. Rep. No. 775, 72d Cong., 1st Sess. (1932), *reprinted in* 1939–1 C.B. (Part 2) 496, 525–26.

For transfers in trust, each beneficiary, not the trustee, is the donee to whom the exclusion applies. *See Helvering v. Hutchings*, 312 U.S. 393 (1941). For transfers to corporations, the stockholders are deemed the recipients of the gift. *See* Treas. Reg. § 25.2511–1(h)(1); *Heringer v. Commissioner*, 235 F.2d 149 (9th Cir. 1956). Nonetheless, multiple exclusions will not be allowed because the requirement that a majority of the shareholders must act before any property can be distributed to the shareholders prevents the given interests from qualifying for the annual exclusion. *See* Rev. Rul. 71–443, 1971–2 C.B. 337. *See also Estate of Stinson v. United States*, 85 AFTR2d Par. 2000-690 (7th Cir. 2000); *Chanin v. United States*, 393 F.2d 972 (Ct. Cl. 1968); *Estate of Hollingsworth v. Commissioner*, 86 T.C. 91 (1986).

Even though a transfer of a future interest is a gift for tax purposes, it will not qualify for the annual exclusion. Section 2503(b) by its own terms applies only to transfers "other than gifts of future interests in property." The following excerpt from a Senate Finance Committee Report (S. Rep. No. 665, 72d Cong., 1st Sess. 41 (1932) *reprinted in* 1939–1 C.B. Part 2 496, 526) provides the rationale for the present interest requirement:

> The term "future interest in property" refers to any interest or estate, whether vested or contingent, limited to commence in possession or enjoyment at a future date. The [exclusion] being available only in so far as the donees are ascertainable, the denial of the [exclusion] in the case of gifts of future interests is dictated by the apprehended difficulty, in many instances, of determining the number of eventual donees and the values of their respective gifts.

In effect, the present interest requirement prevents a donor from cumulating exclusions by dividing the interests of donees on temporal lines to reduce gift taxes.

Maryland National Bank v. United States

Heavily criticized case

609 F.2d 1078 (4th Cir. 1979)

Butzner, Circuit Judge:

Maryland National Bank, executor of the estate of Katherine L. N. Willis, deceased, appeals the district court's denial of claims for refund of gift taxes based on the disallowance of seventeen $3,000 exclusions in both 1971 and 1972. Before her death, Mrs. Willis contended that her transfers into an inter vivos trust were in part gifts to the beneficiaries of income qualifying for the annual $3,000 per donee exclusion from taxation under I.R.C. § 2503(b), and she sought to value the worth of the income interests by reference to the actuarial tables [under the forerunner of Treasury Regulation § 25.2512–5]. The district court ruled that the gifts did not qualify for exclusion, and it held that use of the actuarial tables was impermissible. We affirm.

The relevant, historical facts are not in dispute. By successive assignments in 1971 and 1972, Mrs. Willis transferred her one-half interest in a partnership owning real estate into an inter vivos trust for the benefit of seventeen members of her family. The other one half of the partnership was held in trust under the will of E. Paul Norris. The partnership property had been owned by members of these two families, Norris and Willis (descendants of a common ancestor), for over 70 years. One tract was a farm; the other was waterfront property which contained recreational facilities, including a tennis court and swimming pool. Both tracts contained rental housing. Mrs. Willis had rented one of the houses on the waterfront property for a number of years before and after placing her interest in trust. The Norris family owned and occupied rent free another dwelling on this piece of land. Despite gross receipts from rents and farming, between 1968 and 1976 the partnership produced a net income of only $774.91 in 1971. That income was not distributed to the partners. All other years showed net losses, which aggregated $42,000 for the years 1963 through 1972 and $13,000 during the period 1973–76.

Under the partnership agreement the partners held options on portions of the land. They also held rights of first refusal on any resale to third parties of land purchased under the options. A large portion of the waterfront property, approximately 45 acres including the recreational facilities, could not be partitioned for sale.

The Willis trust named as trustees three of the seventeen beneficiaries and directed them to disburse "the entire net income of the trust estate" at least annually among the beneficiaries in set proportions. The trustees were given broad powers, without incurring liability, to invest in or retain non-productive assets. They were required to disburse within three years rather than reinvest the net proceeds received from any sale of the partnership's land unless the proceeds were "used to purchase an additional or increased interest in [the original holdings], whether the purchase is of the real estate directly or indirectly by purchase of an interest in a partnership or other entity holding said real estate." Thus, the trustees could not convert the unproductive real estate into other holdings. The trustees had no explicit duty to make the property generate income.

. . .

Only gifts of "present interest" are eligible for exclusion under § 2503(b) of the Internal Revenue Code. The parties agree that the corpus of the trust was a gift of a future interest that cannot be excluded. Therefore, the unqualified right to receive profits from the operation of the partnership's business presents the only arguable circumstance for holding that the beneficiaries received an excludable present income interest.

Mrs. Willis' executor contends that the provisions of the trust agreement are controlling. The executor insists that Mrs. Willis was entitled to the $3,000 exclusions under the statute and regulations because the trustees absolutely must disburse annually to the beneficiaries all the income from the partnership interest. In response, the government says one must probe deeper: that before the executor can rely on the disbursal clause of the trust, the executor must prove that income will be available for distribution. Lacking such proof, the government continues, the beneficiaries have only a future interest, not a present interest qualifying for exclusion within the meaning of the statute and regulations.

The Internal Revenue Code does not define either future or present interest. The Service, however, has stated that " '[f]uture interest' is a legal term, and includes reversions, remainders, and other interests or estates, whether vested or contingent, and whether or not supported by a particular interest or estate, which are limited to commence in use, possession, or enjoyment at some future date or time" (Treas. Reg. § 25.2503–3(a) (1958)). In contrast, a present interest is "[a]n unrestricted right to the immediate use, possession, or enjoyment of property or the income from property . . . ." (Treas. Reg. § 2503–3(b) (1958)). The Supreme Court in *Fondren v. Commissioner*, 324 U.S. 18, 20–21 (1945), construing these definitions, held that the distinction turns on whether the donor conferred a real and immediate benefit upon the donee:

> [I]t is not enough to bring the exclusion into force that the donee has vested rights. In addition he must have the right presently to use, possess or enjoy the property. These terms are not words of art, like "fee" in the law of seizing, . . . but connote the right to substantial present economic benefit. The question is of time, not when title vests, but when enjoyment begins. Whatever puts the barrier of a substantial period between the will of the beneficiary or donee now to enjoy what has been given him and that enjoyment makes the gift one of a future interest within the meaning of the regulation.

The Internal Revenue Code's "present interest" differs from the technical concept of a present estate for life or a term of years, because even a vested interest may be considered a "future interest" for gift tax purposes if the donee gets no immediate use, possession, or enjoyment of the property. The donor is entitled to the exclusion only if he has conferred on the donee "the right to substantial present economic benefit." 324 U.S. at 20.

These principles are exemplified by *Commissioner v. Disston*, 325 U.S. 442 (1945). There the trust had income, but it placed such limitations on disbursement that the Court concluded that only a future interest was created. It was in that context that the Court explained:

> In the absence of some indication from the face of the trust or surrounding circumstances that a steady flow of some ascertainable portion of income to the [beneficiary] would be required, there is no basis for a conclusion that there is a gift of anything other than for the future. The taxpayer claiming the exclusion must assume the burden of showing that the value of what he claims is other than a future interest. 325 U.S. at 449.

The absence of a steady flow of ascertainable income to the beneficiary can result just as surely from a lack of any prospect of income as it can from restrictions on the trustees' power to disburse income. In either event the result is the same, and the exclusion should be denied because no present interest was conveyed. *Disston* places a dual burden on the taxpayer—the first is implicit, the second explicit. The taxpayer must show that the trust will receive income, and, second, that some ascertainable portion of the income will flow steadily to the beneficiary.

Application of these principles to the facts of this case presents little difficulty. The executor has failed to prove that the partnership has produced any income for distribution to the beneficiaries, that steps have been taken to eliminate the losses it has sustained annually, or that there will be any income in the foreseeable future. Moreover, the trust authorizes the trustees to hold this unproductive property, and it bars them from reinvesting for more than three years the proceeds from the sale of partnership real estate, which is the trust's only significant asset, into stocks, bonds, or other real estate to generate income. In sum, neither the circumstances of the case nor the provisions of the trust realistically establish that the beneficiaries actually will receive a steady flow of income.

The executor, however, urges that this hiatus in the proof can be filled by use of the actuarial tables, which calculate the present value of an estate for a term of years by assuming a prescribed rate of return on the corpus. *See* Treas. Reg. § 25.2512–9(f) (1970). It is undisputed that if use of the tables is permissible, the present worth of each beneficiary's interest would exceed $3,000.

The tables are appropriate only when there is proof that some income will be received by the trust beneficiaries. "Where the property may yield no income at all . . . the tables are not applicable." *Elise McK. Morgan v. Commissioner*, 42 T.C. 1080, 1088 (1964), *aff'd*, 353 F.2d 209 (4th Cir. 1965). The tables are designed to calculate the value of a present interest, not create it. Indeed, even if it is assumed that the disbursal clause of the trust standing alone is facially sufficient to create a present interest, the uncertainty that the beneficiaries will receive income precludes exclusion, whether or not resort is had to the tables. *See Berzon v. Commissioner*, 534 F.2d 528 (2d Cir. 1976); *Stark v. United States*, 477 F.2d 131 (8th Cir. 1973); *Fischer v. Commissioner*, 288 F.2d 574 (3d Cir. 1961). Although the Willis trust gave the beneficiaries an unconditional right to receive income, bestowing this right did not of itself create a present interest. Without any prospect of income, the bare right to receive income was illusory, and all that characterized the gift was the future enjoyment of the corpus.

Rosen v. Commissioner, 397 F.2d 245 (4th Cir. 1968), upon which the executor primarily relies, is readily distinguishable. In that case, the evidence disclosed, and the government acknowledged, that a gift in trust of publicly traded corporate stock conferred a present interest, even though the stock had never paid dividends. The corporation was a profitable enterprise, and it had retained its earnings for growth. The trustees intended to hold the stock, although they had authority to sell, because they anticipated that dividends would be paid in the future and the stock would enhance in value. The income component of the gift was currently reflected by the stock's growth. Pointing out that the present income interest had value, we concluded that use of the tables would not "result in an 'unrealistic and unreasonable' valuation." 397 F.2d at 247.

Unlike the corporation in *Rosen*, the Willis partnership was not a profitable enterprise. It consistently operated at a loss. The executor's use of the tables, if allowed, would create an income value from assets that have never shown any capacity to produce income for the trust. Use of the tables under these circumstances would convert a portion of the future interest into a present interest by a simple computation. This legerdemain would surely transgress the statutory ban on the exclusion of future interests.

. . .

Affirmed.

K. K. Hall, Circuit Judge, dissenting. [Opinion omitted.]

———

The taxpayer in *Maryland National Bank* made transfers to a trust and claimed a present interest annual exclusion based on the actuarial value of the income the trust should generate. The court disallowed the present interest because the asset transferred to the trust had no history of producing income and there was little prospect that it would in the future. Students should note, however, that if the taxpayer had made an outright gift of the partnership interest to the donees, it is likely that the partnership interests would have qualified for present interest gifts. The taxpayer is no longer attempting to qualify an assumed income stream from a non-income producing asset as a present interest gift. Moreover, if the property transferred to the trust had been income producing, the valuation tables could have been used to value a projected income stream from the property and that projected value would have qualified for a present interest under § 2503(b).

The importance of gifting present interests, that is, the right to the present economic enjoyment of the property, is reflected in Treasury Regulation § 25.2503–3(b). The issue arises in a number of common estate planning situations. For example, if the trustee of a trust has unlimited discretion to accumulate income for future distribution to *A*, *A*'s life interest in the trust does not constitute a present interest. *See* Treas. Reg. § 25.2503–3(c), Example 1. Thus, in *Ritland v. Commissioner*, T.C. Memo 1986–298, the exclusion was denied because the beneficiaries were only entitled to income at the trustee's discretion. Therefore, the beneficiaries lacked any immediate right to income, even though the income beneficiaries were also the trustees. The fact that their unanimous consent was required negated any individual's right to income.

The future interest problem arises in a number of contexts. For example, in *Calder v. Commissioner*, 85 T.C. 713 (1985), the taxpayer created trusts funded with paintings which her deceased husband, the famous artist, had left her. The trust provided that the beneficiaries were entitled to the annual income from the corpus, and the trustees were authorized to convert the non-income producing art works into income producing property. Interpreting the seminal case of *Commissioner v. Disston*, 325 U.S. 442 (1945), the court held that a taxpayer must prove: (1) that the trust will receive income, (2) that some portion of that income will flow steadily to the beneficiary, and (3) that the portion of income flowing out to the beneficiary can be ascertained. 85 T.C. at 727–28. Applying these three principles, the court found that the taxpayer had not made a gift of a present interest because there was no showing that the trusts, consisting of non-income producing property, would generate any income for the beneficiaries. The court rejected the argument that, because the trustees had a fiduciary obligation to make the trust property productive, a present interest had passed to the beneficiaries. The court thus aligned itself with *Maryland National Bank* and several other courts which have disallowed the gift tax annual exclusion when the gift in trust consists of non-income producing property. *See, e.g., Estate of Berzon v. Commissioner*, 63 T.C. 601 (1975), *aff'd*, 534 F.2d 528 (2d Cir. 1976).

Similarly, in *Estate of Babbitt v. Commissioner*, 87 T.C. 1270 (1986), the decedent apparently made completed gifts of realty to various children and grandchildren under which the donees would not receive anything until after the property was sold. The Tax Court held that the gifts were of future interests because the donees did not receive immediate enjoyment of the realty.

Note that the critical factor in determining whether the right of the income beneficiary will qualify for the annual exclusion is the power of the beneficiary to demand its present distribution. Thus, Rev. Rul. 75–415, 1975–2 C.B. 374, 375, states:

> The fact that the payment of income or principal is not required to commence immediately but is subject to the demand of the income beneficiary does not constitute the barrier to present enjoyment of the transferred interest contemplated by the Supreme Court [in *Fondren v. United States*, 324 U.S. 18 (1945)]. Thus, the mere fact that the beneficiary must first make that demand, which must be complied with, does not preclude the classification of the interest as a present interest.

In short, interests that are present interests but for a contingency, will qualify for present interest treatment if the contingency is within the control of the donee. *Cf.* Rev. Rul. 75–415, 1975–2 C.B. 374 (gift of income after three years or earlier termination of enrollment in institution of higher education does not qualify).

Further, the fact that the beneficiary's right is limited by a spendthrift provision does not sufficiently restrict a right to demand distribution so as to negate the exclusion. Under Rev. Rul. 54–344, 1954–2 C.B. 319, the transfer of a present right to enjoy the income of a trust for life or a period of years "will not be held to be one of a future interest in property solely because of the inclusion of a provision or clause which prohibits the income beneficiary from alienating, assigning or otherwise anticipating such income."

Some taxpayers, unhappy with the maximum amount of the annual exclusion, concoct various plans to circumvent the limitation. *Bies v. Commissioner*, below is an example of one that did not work.

Estate of Bies v. Commissioner

T.C. Memo. 2000-338

PARR, J.

The sole issue for decision [Footnote omitted] is whether annual transfers of closely held corporation stock made by Marie A. Bies (decedent) to two daughters-in-law during the years 1985 through 1995, and to a granddaughter-in-law during the years 1991 through 1995, were, in substance, indirect transfers of stock to decedent's sons and grandson. We hold they were.

FINDINGS OF FACT

. . . .

Mueller-Bies Funeral Home was founded in 1906 by decedent's father, Charles Mueller. Decedent's father was succeeded in the business by decedent's husband, Albert Sr. In 1962, Albert Sr. incorporated the business as Mueller-Bies Funeral Home, Inc. (MBI). Decedent was a member of the MBI board of directors and treasurer of the corporation from 1985 until the year of her death.

. . . .

Beginning in 1985, and each year until her death, decedent transferred shares of MBI stock to [her son] Albert, [his wife] Gayle, [her son] Gregory, and [his wife] Loretta. Beginning in 1991, and each year until her death, decedent transferred shares of MBI stock to [her grandson] James and his wife Cheryl. Each transfer was to an individual, and each transfer was the number of shares or fraction of a share calculated by Mr. Grayson to be equal in value to $10,000.

The procedure was the same for each of the 27 transfers at issue: Mr Grayson [the decedent's attorney] would prepare the certificates to transfer MBI shares to Albert, Gayle, Gregory, and Loretta, and at the same time, he would prepare the certificates for the shares transferred from Gayle to Albert, and from Loretta to Gregory. After Mr. Grayson had prepared all transfer documents, he would deliver them to the funeral home for endorsement. Albert, as president of MBI, endorsed all the certificates before delivery to the donees, including the shares that would be issued to Albert and Gregory once Gayle and Loretta endorsed the certificates for transfer. Gayle and Loretta transferred the shares received from decedent to their husbands upon receipt. [Footnote omitted] Mr. Grayson would retrieve the documents after they were signed, and the transfers were then recorded in the corporate stock ledger. After their marriage, the transfers of shares from decedent to James and Cheryl, and from Cheryl to James, were made according to this same procedure.

Decedent did not file a Form 709, United States Gift Tax Return, with respect to any of these transfers, nor were any taxable gifts reported on Form 706, United States Estate (and Generation-Skipping Transfer) Tax Return.

OPINION

Respondent determined that decedent's transfers of MBI stock to Gayle, Loretta, and Cheryl were, in substance, indirect transfers of additional shares to Albert, Gregory, and James, respectively. Respondent contends that decedent transferred the MBI stock through Gayle, Loretta, and Cheryl to Albert, Gregory, and James, respectively, for the purpose of obtaining additional annual gift tax exclusions.

Petitioner asserts that decedent's transfers of MBI stock to Gayle, Loretta, and Cheryl were, both in form and substance, transfers only to Gayle, Loretta, and Cheryl.

Respondent's determinations of fact are presumptively correct, and petitioner bears the burden of proving by a preponderance of the evidence that those determinations are erroneous. *See* Rule 142(a); [Footnote omitted] Welch v. Helvering, 290 U.S. 111, 115, 54 S.Ct. 8, 78 L.Ed. 212 (1933).

Section 2001(a) provides that a tax is imposed on the transfer of the taxable estate of every decedent who is a citizen or resident of the United States. The tax imposed is equal to the excess of a tentative tax computed on the sum of the taxable estate and the adjusted taxable gifts over the aggregate amount of tax that would have been payable with respect to gifts made by the decedent after December 31, 1976, using the unified rate schedule in effect at the date of death. *See* sec. 2001(b). The term "adjusted taxable gifts" means the total amount of the taxable gifts (within the meaning of section 2503) made by the decedent after December 31, 1976, other than gifts which are includable in the gross estate. *See id.*

In general, a tax is imposed for each calendar year on the transfer of property by gift by any individual, whether the gift is made directly or indirectly. *See* secs. 2501(a), 2511(a). The term "taxable gifts" means the total amount of gifts made during the calendar year, less certain deductions. *See* sec. 2503(a). However, the first $10,000 of gifts of a present interest in property made by a donor to any person in a calendar year is excluded from taxable gifts. *See* sec. 2503(b).

As a general rule, we will respect the form of a transaction. We will not apply the substance over form principles unless the circumstances so warrant. *See* Gregory v. Helvering, 293 U.S. 465, 55 S.Ct. 266, 79 L.Ed. 596 (1935); Estate of Jalkut v. Commissioner, 96 T.C. 675, 686, 1991 WL 64935 (1991). Courts have applied the substance over form principles in gift tax cases to determine the real donee and value of the property transferred. *See, e.g.,* Heyen v. United States, 945 F.2d 359, 363 (10th Cir.1991); Estate of Cidulka v. Commissioner, T.C. Memo.1996-149. In these cases, the indirect transfers of the property to the intended donees were the result of a prearranged plan. *See, e.g.,* Heyen v. United States, *supra* at 361 (donor transferred stock to 29 straws who either did not know they were receiving stock or believed that they were participating in stock transfers or had agreed before receiving the stock to its retransfer, 27 of whom then retransferred the stock to the donor's intended donees); Estate of Cidulka v. Commissioner, *supra* (father's 14 transfers of stock to daughter-in-law, who, on the same day, transferred the stock to her husband, provided "inference" of an "understanding" between father and daughter-in-law that her shares would be merely a pass-through of shares to her husband).

Section 2511(a) requires consideration of whether decedent made indirect transfers. Accordingly, we must decide whether Gayle, Loretta, and Cheryl were merely intermediate recipients of decedent's indirect transfers of stock to Albert, Gregory, and James, respectively, or were the intended beneficiaries of decedent's bounty. *See* Heyen v. United States, *supra* at 362; Estate of Cidulka v. Commissioner, *supra.*

We consider the objective facts of the transfers and the circumstances under which they were made evidence of decedent's actual intent in making the stock transfers. *See* United States v. Estate of Grace, 395 U.S. 316, 323, 89 S.Ct. 1730, 23 L.Ed.2d 332 (1969); Heyen v. United States, *supra* at 362–363; sec. 25.2511-1(g)(1), Gift Tax Regs. The evidence shows that the simultaneous transfers were all part of a prearranged single transaction.

It is clear that decedent arranged to give annually to each recipient the number of MBI shares that would avoid imposition of the gift tax. This fact, by itself, is not evidence of an ulterior purpose in making the stock transfers to Gayle, Loretta, and Cheryl. *See* Gregory v. Helvering, *supra* at 469 ("The legal right of a taxpayer to decrease the amount of what otherwise would be his taxes, or altogether avoid them, by means which the law permits, cannot be doubted."). However, it is also clear from the record that Gayle, Loretta, and Cheryl had preexisting agreements to transfer the shares to their husbands. Mr. Grayson testified that he knew before decedent made the gifts that the wives had agreed to transfer the shares to their husbands. Moreover, decedent was treasurer of MBI and a member of its board of directors; therefore, it cannot be denied that she knew Gayle, Loretta, and Cheryl made immediate transfers of the shares to Albert, Gregory, and James, respectively.

Decedent executed her will in 1989. The will provided for the bequest of the MBI stock that decedent held at death to her sons, or to the survivor of them. Thus, in the event either of her sons had predeceased decedent, decedent did not intend for the surviving spouse of the deceased son to take any shares. This provision is evidence of decedent's intentions regarding ownership of MBI stock by her daughters-in-law.

Furthermore, decedent made no inter vivos or testamentary transfers of MBI stock to either [of her daughters] Joanne or Barbara, because neither daughter was committed to the funeral home business. However, decedent made transfers of stock to Gayle even though she knew that Gayle did not want to be in the funeral home business. This is strong evidence that the stock transfers to the daughters-in-law actually were indirect transfers to her sons.

The 1986 and 1991 [buy-sell] agreements show that Albert, Gregory, and James anticipated owning collectively all the MBI shares. Mr. Grayson, Albert, Loretta, Gayle, James, and Cheryl testified that the shares in the closely held corporation were transferred to the husbands so that in the event Albert, Gregory, or James predeceased his wife, MBI would purchase the shares and provide the surviving spouse liquidity. This testimony is not supported by the facts.

Upon the death of Gregory, MBI did not redeem all his shares. Rather, Loretta inherited the shares, and none of those shares was sold to MBI until after Loretta reached a conditional agreement with Albert for the purchase of enough of his shares to equalize their ownership interests. Although Loretta testified that the MBI shares "had absolutely no value" to her, it is evident from Loretta's retention of almost twice the amount of shares initially transferred through her by decedent, and by Loretta's agreement with Albert for the purchase of more shares, that, contrary to her testimony, Loretta preferred owning MBI stock to cash. The objective evidence does not support the purported reason for the stock transfers between the spouses.

Viewed as a whole, the evidence shows the daughters-in-law were merely intermediate recipients, and that decedent intended to transfer the stock to her lineal descendants who were committed to continuing the operation of the funeral home business. We conclude that the inter vivos transfers of the MBI shares to Gayle, Loretta, and Cheryl were, in fact, indirect transfers of additional shares to decedent's sons and grandson.

————

Problems

1. What are the federal gift tax consequences of the following?

a. A widow, who has made no prior taxable gifts, wishes to give her adult son $500 outright. *See* § 2503(b).

b. Starting in 1992, a wealthy widower, who has made no prior taxable gifts, gave $10,000 each year, for ten years, (*i.e.* 1992 to 2001), to each of six adult family members. *See* § 2503(b). Must he file a gift tax return? *See* § 6019. Having made $600,000 in gifts, how much of the donor's applicable credit amount has been consumed?

c. A widow, who has made no prior taxable gifts, gives her adult daughter $23,000 outright in each of two successive years.

d. A widower, who had made no prior taxable gifts, gave his married daughter and her husband a $28,000 gift to use as a down payment on a house.

2. *S* transfers $100,000 to an irrevocable trust, the income of which is to be shared equally by *A* and *B* for 10 years, remainder to *C*. How many annual exclusions are available for *S*, and in what amount if the § 7520 rate is 8%? *See* Treas. Reg. § 25.2503–3(a).

3. *S* transfers $100,000 to an irrevocable trust, the income of which is payable to *M*, his 65 year old mother, for her life, and the corpus of which is to be distributed to *D*, *S*'s daughter, who is age twenty on the day the trust is created. What portion of the $100,000 is included in *S*'s taxable gifts for the year, assuming that the applicable interest rate for the purposes of § 7520 equals 8%? What would be the result if the § 7520 was 7%? *See* Treas. Reg. §§ 25.2512–5(c), –5(d), –5(f).

4. *S* transfers $100,000 to an irrevocable trust, the income of which is payable to *A* for *A*'s life, with the corpus payable to *B* at *A*'s death. The trustee is given the power to invade the corpus for the benefit of either *A* or *B*. Does the trust qualify for the annual exclusion? Would the result be any different if the trustee only had the power to invade the corpus for *A* alone? *See* § 2503(b), second sentence; Treas. Reg. § 25.2503–3(c), Example 4.

5. Assume *S* created an irrevocable inter vivos trust, under which the trustee was to pay income to *A* or accumulate it and add it to corpus in the trustee's discretion. The corpus was payable to *B* after 15 years.

a. Does the trust qualify for an annual exclusion? *See* Treas. Reg. § 25.2503–3(c), Example 1.

b. Would the result be different if the corpus were payable to *A* at the end of the 15 years?

[b] Gifts in Trust: *Crummey* Trusts and Gifts to Minors

An outright gift of property to a donee is a simple example of a present interest gift. On the other hand, a gift to a trust for someone's benefit is generally a future interest.[11] Nevertheless, donors who give property to minors, and to some adults, often wish to withhold the property from the donee until he is capable of dealing with it, but still want the transfer to qualify for the present interest annual exclusion.

From the desire to make annual exclusion gifts in trust, two avenues have evolved. From a line of cases and administrative rules, a properly drafted demand trust, commonly called a *Crummey trust,* can qualify as a present interest. The crux of a *Crummey* trust is the power or right of the beneficiary or beneficiaries to withdraw, for a limited period of time, each new transfer made to the trust by the donor. In addition, for minor donees, the donor may also use § 2503(c) to qualify gifts in trust as present interest transfers and, thus, meet the statutory requirements for the annual exclusion.

Estate of Cristofani v. Commissioner

97 T.C. 74 (1991)
acq. in result, 1992–1 C.B. 1
acq. in result, 1992–2 C.B. 1
acq. in result, 1996–2 C.B. 1

FINDINGS OF FACT

Petitioner is the Estate of Maria Cristofani, deceased, Frank Cristofani, executor. Maria Cristofani (decedent) died testate on December 16, 1985. At the time of her death, decedent resided in the State of California. Petitioner's Federal estate tax return (Form 706) was timely filed with the Internal Revenue Service Center in Fresno, California.

Decedent has two children, Frank Cristofani and Lillian Dawson. Decedent's children were both born on July 9, 1948. They were in good health during the years 1984 and 1985.

Decedent has five minor grandchildren. During 1984 and 1985, the parents of decedent's grandchildren were the legal guardians of the person of their respective minor children. There were no independently appointed guardians of decedent's grandchildren's property.

On June 11, 1984, decedent executed a durable power of attorney which named her two children, Frank Cristofani and Lillian Dawson, as her Attorneys in Fact. On that same day, decedent executed her will.

---

[11] *See* Treas. Reg. § 25.2503–3(c), Example 2; Rev. Rul. 79–47, 1979–1 C.B. 312; Phillips v. Commissioner, 12 T.C. 216 (1949).

On June 12, 1984, decedent executed an irrevocable trust entitled the Maria Cristofani Children's Trust I (Children's Trust). Frank Cristofani and Lillian Dawson were named the trustees of the Children's Trust.

In general, Frank Cristofani and Lillian Dawson possessed the following rights and interests in the Children's Trust corpus and income. Under Article Twelfth, following a contribution to the Children's Trust, Frank Cristofani and Lillian Dawson could each withdraw an amount not to exceed the amount specified for the gift tax exclusion under section 2503(b). Such withdrawal period would begin on the date of the contribution and end on the 15th day following such contribution. Under Article Third, Frank Cristofani and Lillian Dawson were to receive equally the entire net income of the trust quarter-annually, or at more frequent intervals. After decedent's death, under Article Third, the Trust Estate was to be divided into as many equal shares as there were children of decedent then living or children of decedent then deceased but leaving issue. Both Frank Cristofani and Lillian Dawson survived decedent, and thus the Children's Trust was divided into two equal trusts. Under Article Third, if a child of decedent survived decedent by 120 days, that child's trust would be distributed to the child. Both Frank Cristofani and Lillian Dawson survived decedent by 120 days, and their respective trusts were distributed upon the expiration of the 120-day waiting period. During the waiting period, Frank Cristofani and Lillian Dawson received the entire net income of the separate trusts as provided for in Article Third.

In general, decedent's five grandchildren possessed the following rights and interests in the Children's Trust. Under Article Twelfth, during a 15-day period following a contribution to the Children's Trust, each of the grandchildren possessed the same right of withdrawal as described above regarding the withdrawal rights of Frank Cristofani and Lillian Dawson. Under Article Twelfth, the trustee of the Children's Trust was required to notify the beneficiaries of the trust each time a contribution was received. Under Article Third, had either Frank Cristofani or Lillian Dawson predeceased decedent or failed to survive decedent by 120 days, his or her equal portion of decedent's Children's Trust would have passed in trust to his or her children (decedent's grandchildren).

Under Article Third, the trustees, in their discretion, could apply as much of the principal of the Children's Trust as necessary for the proper support, health, maintenance and education of decedent's children. In exercising their discretion, the trustees were to take into account several factors, including "The Settlor's desire to consider the Settlor's children as primary beneficiaries and the other beneficiaries of secondary importance."

Decedent intended to fund the corpus of the Children's Trust with 100 percent ownership of improved real property, on which a warehouse was located, identified as the 2851 Spring Street, Redwood City, California, property (Spring Street property). Decedent intended that a one-third undivided interest in the Spring Street property be transferred to the Children's Trust during each of the 3 taxable years 1984, 1985, and 1986. The Spring Street property was unencumbered property at all times pertinent to this case.

Consistent with her intent, decedent transferred, on December 17, 1984, an undivided 33-percent interest in the Spring Street property to the

Children's Trust by a quitclaim deed. Similarly, in 1985, decedent transferred a second undivided 33-percent interest in the Spring Street property to the Children's Trust by a quitclaim deed which was recorded on November 27, 1985. Decedent intended to transfer her remaining undivided interest in the Spring Street property to the Children's Trust in 1986. However, decedent died prior to making the transfer, and her remaining interest in the Spring Street property remained in her estate.

The value of the 33-percent undivided interest in the Spring Street property that decedent transferred in 1984 was $70,000. The value of the 33-percent undivided interest in the Spring Street property that decedent transferred in 1985 also was $70,000.

Decedent did not report the two $70,000 transfers on Federal gift tax returns. Rather, decedent claimed seven annual exclusions of $10,000 each under section 2503(b) for each year 1984 and 1985. These annual exclusions were claimed with respect to decedent's two children and decedent's five grandchildren.

There was no agreement or understanding between decedent, the trustees, and the beneficiaries that decedent's grandchildren would not exercise their withdrawal rights following a contribution to the Children's Trust. None of decedent's five grandchildren exercised their rights to withdraw under Article Twelfth of the Children's Trust during either 1984 or 1985. None of decedent's five grandchildren received a distribution from the Children's Trust during either 1984 or 1985.

Respondent allowed petitioner to claim the annual exclusions with respect to decedent's two children. However, respondent disallowed the $10,000 annual exclusions claimed with respect to each of decedent's grandchildren claimed for the years 1984 and 1985. Respondent determined that the annual exclusions that decedent claimed with respect to her five grandchildren for the 1984 and 1985 transfers, of the Spring Street property, were not transfers of present interests in property. Accordingly, respondent increased petitioner's adjusted taxable gifts in the amount of $100,000.

OPINION

Section 2001(a) imposes a tax on the transfer of the taxable estate of every decedent who is a citizen or resident of the United States. The tax imposed is equal to the excess of the tentative tax on the sum of the amount of the taxable estate and the amount of adjusted taxable gifts, over the amount of tax which would have been payable as a gift tax with respect to gifts made by a decedent after December 31, 1976 (section 2001(b)). The term "adjusted taxable gifts" means the total amount of taxable gifts (within the meaning of section 2503) made by a decedent after December 31, 1976, other than gifts which are includable in the gross estate of the decedent (section 2001(b)). Section 2503(a) defines "taxable gifts" as the total amount of gifts made during the calendar year, less certain statutory deductions.

Section 2503(b) provides that the first $10,000 of gifts to any person during a calendar year shall not be included in the total amount of gifts made during such year. A trust beneficiary is considered the donee of a gift in trust for purposes of the annual exclusion under section 2503(b). Sec. 25.2503–2(a), Gift Tax Regs.; Helvering v. Hutchings, 312 U.S. 393 (1941). The section 2503(b) exclusion applies to gifts of present interests in property and does not apply to gifts of future interests in property. Sec. 2503(b) and Treas. Reg. § 25.2503–3(a). The regulations define a future interest to include "reversions, remainders, and other interests or estates, whether vested or contingent, and whether or not supported by a particular interest or estate, which are limited to commence in use, possession or enjoyment at some future date or time." Sec. 25.2503–3(a), Gift Tax Regs.; see Commissioner v. Disston, 325 U.S. 442 (1945); Fondren v. Commissioner, 324 U.S. 18 (1945). The regulations further provide that "An unrestricted right to the immediate use, possession, or enjoyment of property or the income from property (such as a life estate or term certain) is a present interest in property. An exclusion is allowable with respect to a gift of such an interest (but not in excess of the value of the interest)." Treas. Reg. § 25.2503–3(b).

In the instant case, petitioner argues that the right of decedent's grandchildren to withdraw an amount equal to the annual exclusion within 15 days after decedent's contribution of property to the Children's Trust constitutes a gift of a present interest in property, thus qualifying for a $10,000 annual exclusion for each grandchild for the years 1984 and 1985. Petitioner relies upon Crummey v. Commissioner, 397 F.2d 82 (9th Cir. 1968), rev'g on this issue T.C. Memo. 1966–144.

In Crummey v. Commissioner, T.C. Memo. 1966–144, aff'd in part and rev'd in part, 397 F.2d 82 (9th Cir. 1968), the settlors created an irrevocable living trust for the benefit of their four children, some of whom were minors. The trustee was required to hold the property in equal shares for the beneficiaries. Under the terms of the trust, the trustee, in his discretion, could distribute trust income to each beneficiary until that beneficiary obtained the age of 21. When the beneficiary was age 21 and up until age 35, the trustee was required to distribute trust income to each beneficiary. When the beneficiary was age 35 and over, the trustee was authorized, in his discretion, to distribute trust income to the beneficiary or his or her issue. Upon the death of a beneficiary, his or her trust share was to be distributed to that beneficiary's surviving issue subject to certain age requirements. If a beneficiary died without issue, then his or her trust share was to be distributed equally to the trust shares of the surviving children of the grantors. In addition, each child was given an absolute power to withdraw up to $4,000 in cash of any additions to corpus in the calendar year of the addition, by making a written demand upon the trustee prior to the end of the calendar year.

Relying on these powers, the settlors claimed the section 2503(b) exclusion on transfers of property to the trust for each trust beneficiary. Respondent permitted the settlors to claim the exclusions with respect to the gifts in trust to the beneficiaries who were adults during the years of the additions. However, respondent disallowed exclusions with respect to the gifts in trust to the beneficiaries who were minors during such years. Respondent disallowed the exclusions for the minor beneficiaries on the ground that the minors' powers were not gifts of present interests in property.

In deciding whether the minor beneficiaries received a present interest, the Ninth Circuit specifically rejected any test based upon the likelihood that the minor beneficiaries would actually receive present enjoyment of the property. Instead, the court focused on the legal right of the minor beneficiaries to demand payment from the trustee. The Ninth Circuit, relying on *Perkins v. Commissioner*, 27 T.C. 601 (1956), and *Gilmore v. Commissioner*, 213 F.2d 520 (6th Cir. 1954), *rev'g* 20 T.C. 579 (1953), stated:

> All exclusions should be allowed under the *Perkins* test or the "right to enjoy" test in *Gilmore*. Under *Perkins*, all that is necessary is to find that the demand could not be resisted. We interpret that to mean legally resisted and, going on that basis, we do not think the trustee would have any choice but to have a guardian appointed to take the property demanded. [*Crummey v. Commissioner*, 397 F.2d at 88.]

The court found that the minor beneficiaries had a legal right to make a demand upon the trustee, and allowed the settlors to claim annual exclusions, under section 2503(b), with respect to the minor trust beneficiaries.

The Ninth Circuit recognized that there was language in a prior case, *Stifel v. Commissioner*, 197 F.2d 107 (2d Cir. 1952), *aff'g* 17 T.C. 647 (1951), that seemed to support a different test.

> As we read the *Stifel* case, it says that the court should look at the trust instrument, the law as to minors, and the financial and other circumstances of the parties. From this examination it is up to the court to determine whether it is likely that the minor beneficiary is to receive any present enjoyment of the property. If it is not likely, then the gift is a "future interest." [*Crummey v. Commissioner*, 397 F.2d at 85.]

As previously stated, the Ninth Circuit rejected a test based on the likelihood that an actual demand would be made. Respondent does not rely on or cite *Stifel* in his brief. We believe that the test set forth in *Crummey v. Commissioner*, *supra*, is the correct test.

Subsequent to the opinion in *Crummey*, respondent's revenue rulings have recognized that when a trust instrument gives a beneficiary the legal power to demand immediate possession of corpus, that power qualifies as a present interest in property. *See Rev. Rul. 85–24*, 1985–1 C.B. 329, 330 ("When a trust instrument gives a beneficiary the power to demand immediate possession of corpus, the beneficiary has received a present interest. *Crummey v. Commissioner*, 397 F.2d 82 (9th Cir. 1968)"); *Rev. Rul. 81–7*, 1981–1 C.B. 474 ("The courts have recognized that if a trust instrument gives a beneficiary the power to demand immediate possession and enjoyment of corpus or income, the beneficiary has a present interest. *Crummey v. Commissioner*, 397 F.2d 82 (9th Cir. . . . [1968])"). While we recognize that revenue rulings do not constitute authority for deciding a case in this Court, we mention them to show respondent's recognition that a trust beneficiary's legal right to demand immediate possession and enjoyment of trust corpus or income constitutes a present interest in property for purposes of the annual exclusion under section 2503(b). We also note that respondent allowed the annual exclusions with respect to decedent's two children who possessed the same right of withdrawal as decedent's grandchildren.

In the instant case, respondent has not argued that decedent's grandchildren did not possess a legal right to withdraw corpus from the Children's Trust within 15 days following any contribution, or that such demand could have been legally resisted by the trustees. In fact, the parties have stipulated that "following a contribution to the Children's Trust, each of the grandchildren possessed the *same right of withdrawal as* . . . the withdrawal rights of Frank Cristofani and Lillian Dawson." (Emphasis added.) The legal right of decedent's grandchildren to withdraw specified amounts from the trust corpus within 15 days following any contribution of property constitutes a gift of a present interest. *Crummey v. Commissioner, supra.*

On brief, respondent attempts to distinguish *Crummey* from the instant case. Respondent argues that in *Crummey* the trust beneficiaries not only possessed an immediate right of withdrawal, but also possessed "substantial, future economic benefits" in the trust corpus and income. Respondent emphasizes that the Children's Trust identified decedent's children as "primary beneficiaries," and that decedent's grandchildren were to be considered as "beneficiaries of secondary importance."

Generally, the beneficiaries of the trust in *Crummey* were entitled to distributions of income. Trust corpus was to be distributed to the issue of each beneficiary sometime following the beneficiary's death. *See Crummey v. Commissioner,* T.C. Memo. 1966–144. Aside from the discretionary actions of the trustee, the only way any beneficiary in *Crummey* could receive trust corpus was through the demand provision which allowed each beneficiary to demand up to $4,000 in the year in which a transfer to the trust was made. The Ninth Circuit observed:

> In our case . . . if no demand is made in any particular year, the additions are forever removed from the uncontrolled reach of the beneficiary since, with exception of the yearly demand provision, the only way the corpus can ever be tapped by a beneficiary, is through a distribution at the discretion of the trustee." [*Crummey v. Commissioner,* 397 F.2d at 88.]

In the instant case, the primary beneficiaries of the Children's Trust were decedent's children. Decedent's grandchildren held contingent remainder interests in the Children's Trust. Decedent's grandchildren's interests vested only in the event that their respective parent (decedent's child) predeceased decedent or failed to survive decedent by more than 120 days. We do not believe, however, that *Crummey* requires that the beneficiaries of a trust must have a vested present interest or vested remainder interest in the trust corpus or income, in order to qualify for the section 2503(b) exclusion.

As discussed in *Crummey,* the likelihood that the beneficiary will actually receive present enjoyment of the property is not the test for determining whether a present interest was received. Rather, we must examine the ability of the beneficiaries, in a legal sense, to exercise their right to withdraw trust corpus, and the trustee's right to legally resist a beneficiary's demand for payment. *Crummey v. Commissioner,* 397 F.2d at 88. Based upon the language of the trust instrument and stipulations of the parties, we believe that each grandchild possessed the legal right to withdraw trust corpus and that the trustees would be unable to legally resist a grandchild's withdrawal demand. We note that there was no agreement or understanding between decedent, the trustees, and the beneficiaries that the grandchildren would not exercise their withdrawal rights following a contribution to the Children's Trust.

Respondent also argues that since the grandchildren possessed only a contingent remainder interest in the Children's Trust, decedent never intended to benefit her grandchildren. Respondent contends that the only reason decedent gave her grandchildren the right to withdraw trust corpus was to obtain the benefit of the annual exclusion.

We disagree. Based upon the provisions of the Children's Trust, we believe that decedent intended to benefit her grandchildren. Their benefits, as remaindermen, were contingent upon a child of decedent's dying before decedent or failing to survive decedent by more than 120 days. We recognize that at the time decedent executed the Children's Trust, decedent's children were in good health, but this does not remove the possibility that decedent's children could have predeceased decedent.

In addition, decedent's grandchildren possessed the power to withdraw up to an amount equal to the amount allowable for the 2503(b) exclusion. Although decedent's grandchildren never exercised their respective withdrawal rights, this does not vitiate the fact that they had the legal right to do so, within 15 days following a contribution to the Children's Trust. Events might have occurred to prompt decedent's children and grandchildren (through their guardians) to exercise their withdrawal rights. For example, either or both of decedent's children and their respective families might have suddenly and unexpectedly been faced with economic hardship; or, in the event of the insolvency of one of decedent's children, the rights of the grandchildren might have been exercised to safeguard their interest in the trust assets from their parents' creditors. In light of the provisions in decedent's trust, we fail to see how respondent can argue that decedent did not intend to benefit her grandchildren.

Finally, the fact that the trust provisions were intended to obtain the benefit of the annual gift tax exclusion does not change the result. As we stated in *Perkins v. Commissioner, supra,*

> regardless of the petitioners' motives, or why they did what they in fact did, the legal rights in question were created by the trust instruments and could at any time thereafter be exercised. Petitioners having done what they purported to do, their tax-saving motive is irrelevant. [*Perkins v. Commissioner*, 27 T.C. at 606.]

Based upon the foregoing, we find that the grandchildren's right to withdraw an amount not to exceed the section 2503(b) exclusion, represents a present interest for purposes of section 2503(b). Accordingly, petitioner is entitled to claim annual exclusions with respect to decedent's grandchildren as a result of decedent's transfers of property to the Children's Trust in 1984 and 1985.

Decision will be entered for the petitioner.

Reviewed by the Court.

————

In Rev. Rul. 73–405, 1973–2 C.B. 321, the Service sanctions the use of a *Crummey* demand power to obtain the gift tax annual exclusion. The Service requires, however, that the power holder be given sufficient notice and a reasonable time to exercise the withdrawal power. *See* Rev. Rul. 81–7, 1981–1 C.B. 474. In Rev. Rul. 81–7, the Service held that a trust instrument created and funded on December 29, which gave a legally competent adult beneficiary the power to demand the principal through December 31 of the same year, did not qualify as a present interest eligible for the annual exclusion under § 2503(b) where neither the grantor nor the trustee informed the beneficiary of the demand right with respect to the initial contribution to the trust before the demand right lapsed. The grantor's conduct made the demand right illusory and effectively deprived the donee-beneficiary of the power.

Rev. Rul. 81–7 was distinguished in Rev. Rul. 83–108, 1983–2 C.B. 167, in which the grantor set up an irrevocable trust on December 29th for his adult daughter, the beneficiary, who was given the right to withdraw the lesser of the amount to the trust or $3,000. The trustee was required to give the beneficiary written notice of the withdrawal right within ten days of the initial transfer or any subsequent transfer. The withdrawal right had to be exercised within 45 days after written notice. On January 6, the beneficiary received written notice of her withdrawal right. Although the beneficiary was not notified until the following year, the power had not lapsed. The beneficiary was notified of the existence of the power, and she had 45 days from the notification date to exercise the power of withdrawal. The *Crummey* power created a present gift interest, and the exclusion was available in the year of trust creation. It did not matter for purposes of the exclusion that the time period in which the beneficiary could exercise the right was in a different calendar year than the one in which the trust was created and the property transferred. The length of time between the creation of the trust and the end of the calendar year was important in Rev. Rul. 81–7 because the withdrawal power lapsed at the end of the calendar year.

In *Action on Decision 1996–010*, the Service revised its previous acquiescence (*Action on Decision 1992–09*) in *Cristofani*. The Service stated that it would consider whether the donor actually intended that the power holders possess a bona fide withdrawal right, rather than focusing on the interests held by the beneficiaries after the expiration of the power.

The Service indicated that it will not contest the gift tax annual exclusion where the trust instrument gives the power holders a bona fide unrestricted legal right to demand immediate possession and enjoyment of trust income or corpus. The annual exclusion for a withdrawal power held by a current income beneficiary or vested remainder beneficiary will not be challenged because these persons "have a continuing economic interest in the trust and must weigh the benefit of a present withdrawal against their long term interests." The gift tax annual exclusion will be challenged, however, where "the withdrawal rights are not in substance what they purport to be in form." *See generally* Bradley E.S. Fogel, *The Emperor Does Not Need Clothes — the Expanding Use of "Naked" Crummey Withdrawal Powers to Obtain Federal Gift Tax Annual Exclusions*, 73 Tul. L. Rev. 555 (1998).

All relevant facts and circumstances of each case will be considered, and the annual exclusion will be denied whenever there is a prearranged understanding that the *Crummey* power will not be exercised, or when the exercise of the *Crummey* power would result in "adverse consequences" to the donee, such as losing other rights or gifts under the trust or other arrangements. The Service used this reasoning to deny annual exclusions in Technical Advice Memorandum 9628004. Following *Cristofani*, the Tax Court in *Kohlsaat v. Commissioner*, T.C. Memo 1997–212, rejected the Service's attempt to impute a prearranged agreement by contingent beneficiaries not to exercise their demand powers.

A properly drafted *Crummey* trust will provide a donor with a present interest transfer that can qualify for the § 2503(b) gift tax exclusion. Assuming the non-donor spouse consents under § 2513 for split-gift treatment, the exclusion amounts may be doubled. *See* Private Letter Rul.LTR 200130030. For the donee of a *Crummey* power, the tax issues are more complex. For a discussion of the issues, see Chapter 12, § 12.01[C][1], *infra*.

[c] Trusts for Minors: Section 2503(c)

Besides making gifts to *Crummey* trusts, under § 2503(c) a donor can make a present interest exclusion gift to a trust that benefits a minor. Section 2503(c) permits the grantor to obtain the annual exclusion, yet have the beneficiary's interest in the trust subject to some restrictions. Three basic provisions are required by § 2503(c). The trust instrument must provide that: (1) the donated interest and the income therefrom *may* be expended by, or for the benefit of, the donee before he attains age 21; (2) any unexpended balance will pass to the donee when he or she attains age 21; and (3) if the donee dies before age 21, any unexpended balance will be payable to the estate of the donee or as the donee may appoint under a general power of appointment. Thus, a trust created under § 2503(c) can restrict the minor's right to receive income currently, provided the income or corpus *may* be distributed currently to the minor and unexpended amounts will be distributed to the minor on reaching age 21, or to the minor's estate or appointees on the minor's earlier death.

The requirement that the trust assets be payable to the minor or the minor's estate is strictly enforced. For example, in *Ross v. Commissioner*, 652 F.2d 1365 (9th Cir. 1981), the trust provided that if the beneficiary died before age 21 and failed to appoint his interest, then it "should be distributed to such deceased child's heirs at law." The court held, under local law, that "heirs at law" did not constitute the minor's "estate," and denied the exclusion. In short, because § 2503(c)(2)(B) uses the term "estate," the trust must also use this term.

It is important to note, however, that only the "interest" given to the minor must satisfy the rules of § 2503(c). An income interest can qualify as easily as an interest in the principal. Thus, a § 2503(c) trust may be set up with an income interest, without an accompanying interest in the principal, provided: (1) the trustee is given unlimited discretion to distribute all of the income during the beneficiary's minority; (2) the accumulated income is distributed to the beneficiary on reaching age 21 or is subject to the beneficiary's demand right; and (3) if the beneficiary should die before reaching 21, the accumulated income is payable to the beneficiary's estate or as the beneficiary may appoint by will. *See Commissioner v. Herr*, 303 F.2d 780 (3d Cir. 1962).

In Rev. Rul. 68–670, 1968–2 C.B. 413, the Service concluded that "the right to receive trust income until [the beneficiary] reaches majority or his earlier death meets the requirements of section 2503(c) of the Code and is not treated as a future interest for purposes of section 2503(b), even though the beneficiary has no interest in the trust corpus." The trust principal may be distributable in the trustee's discretion before age 21. This is not mandatory because the present value of the principal does not qualify for the § 2503(c) annual exclusion and the principal is not distributable at age 21.

Section 2503(c) contemplates that the trustee will have discretion to use the interest for the minor's benefit from the time of the transfer to the trust until the minor reaches majority. The following Revenue Rulings analyze the restrictions a grantor may impose on a trustee's discretion.

Revenue Ruling 69–345

1969–1 C.B. 226

Advice has been requested whether a transfer in trust meets the requirements of section 2503(c) of the Internal Revenue Code of 1954, in the circumstances described below.

The trustee's discretionary power to use the property during the beneficiary's minority is subject to the following provision:

> The trustee shall distribute to or for the benefit of the beneficiary, until he attains the age of twenty-one years, so much of the income and principal of the trust estate as may be necessary in the sole discretion of the trustee for the care, support, education, and welfare of the beneficiary. In determining whether such need exists, the trustee shall take into consideration other resources available to the beneficiary and other payments made to him or for his benefit.

The restrictions placed on the trustee's power to expend trust property for the benefit of the minor beneficiary are greater than those restrictions placed on a guardian under state law.

The beneficiary's parents owned considerable property and had other sources of income more than sufficient to meet their legal obligation for his support. In addition the beneficiary held substantial property in his own name (previously acquired by gift and inheritance).

. . .

Section 25.2503–4(b) of the regulations provides that a transfer does not fail to satisfy the conditions of section 2503(c) of the Code by reason of the mere fact that there is left to the discretion of a trustee the determination of the amounts, if any, of the income or property to be expended for the benefit of the minor and the purpose for which the expenditure is to be made, provided there are no substantial restrictions under the terms of the trust instrument on the exercise of such discretion.

Under the terms of the subject trust, the trust property may be used for the minor's benefit only in the event that his needs are not adequately provided for by his parents and only after his separate property has been expended. It is evident from the trust instrument and the surrounding circumstances that, at the time of the transfer, the trustee was not authorized to expend any portion of the trust for the care, support, or education of the minor beneficiary.

In view of the foregoing, it is concluded that the above trust provision imposes an effective condition precedent that is not satisfied and, hence, imposes a substantial restriction on the trustee's power to use the property for the minor's benefit that a court of equity would apply to compel compliance by the trustees . . . . Accordingly, it is held that the trustee's powers do not meet the requirements of section 2503(c) of the Code. For this reason the annual exclusion provided by section 2503(b) is not allowable with respect to transfers to the trust.

Although the trustee of a § 2503(c) trust must have broad discretion to distribute the income and principal for the minor's benefit, one district court approved a provision in a § 2503(c) trust specifically prohibiting trust assets from being used to pay an obligation of support that the beneficiary's parents are required to provide. *See Upjohn v. United States*, 30 A.F.T.R.2d (P-H) 72–5918, 72–2 U.S.T.C. (CCH) ¶ 12,858 (W.D. Mich. 1972). While this type of restriction is favorably cited by many commentators, the Service has not acquiesced in the decision and one district court decision is not substantial authority on which to unequivocally rely. Moreover, donors may want the flexibility and security of having trust funds available for support. In addition, the Service may take the position that how the trust is used (and not whether the use violated the trust's terms) determines the tax consequences.

Revenue Ruling 74–43

1974–1 C.B. 285

The Internal Revenue Service has given further consideration to *Rev. Rul. 60–218*, 1960–1 C.B. 378. That Revenue Ruling holds that a gift to a minor by means of a trust, which provides that the beneficiary, upon reaching age 21, may compel immediate distribution of the trust or may elect to extend the term of the trust and receive distribution of the corpus according to the provisions set forth in the trust instrument, is not considered to be a gift of a present interest so as to qualify under the provisions of section 2503(c) of the Internal Revenue Code of 1954 for the exclusion provided for in section 2503(b). Stated otherwise, if a beneficiary is required to perform a positive act to terminate a trust, upon reaching the age of 21, the gift does not qualify for the annual exclusion.

. . .

Contrary to the Service's argument, *Rev. Rul. 60–218* was not followed in *Griffith v. United States*, 63–1 U.S.T.C. [Paragraph 12,124] (S.D. Tex. 1962), where the donor conveyed various properties in trust to three minor children and gave them (or their guardians) the right to terminate the trusts at any time, if legally capable of acting for themselves. If the trusts were not sooner terminated, they were to automatically terminate when the beneficiary reached age 30.

In *Martha J. Heidrich*, 55 T.C. 746 (1971), *Rev. Rul. 60–218* was distinguished on the basis that in *Heidrich* the beneficiary, upon reaching age 21, had a *continuing* right to terminate the trust by giving written notice to the trustee. If the trust was not sooner terminated, it was to automatically terminate when the beneficiary reached age 25. In allowing the annual exclusion, the court held that:

> . . . [W]here the only impediment to the donee's use and possession of the unexpended trust funds will be the submission of a written demand to the trustee and where the written demand will be purely within the donee's power to make, we must conclude that the trust funds will pass to the donee at the time the right to make written demand accrues.

By reason of the trend of the foregoing decisions, the Service will no longer take the position that anything other than an "automatic termination" at age 21 will disqualify a trust for the benefit of a minor that otherwise meets the requirements of section 2503(c) as a present interest.

Accordingly, a gift to a minor in trust, with the provision that the beneficiary has, upon reaching age 21, either (1) a continuing right to compel immediate distribution of the trust corpus by giving written notice to the trustee, or to permit the trust to continue by its own terms, or (2) a right during a limited period to compel immediate distribution of the trust corpus by [giving] written notice to the trustee which if not exercised will permit the trust to continue by its own terms, will not be considered to be the gift of a future interest as the gift satisfies the requirements of section 2503(c) of the Code, and the exclusion provided for in section 2503(b) is allowable.

Rev. Rul. 60–218 is hereby revoked.

———

In *Levine's Estate v. Commissioner*, 526 F.2d 717, 718 (2d Cir. 1975),

> a Connecticut resident, established identical irrevocable trusts for five grandchildren whose ages then ranged from two to fifteen years.

The corpus of each trust consisted of common stock of New Haven Moving Equipment Corporation. The shares were valued at $3,750. Unless a designated "Independent Trustee" saw fit in his discretion to direct otherwise, the trustees were to retain all income generated until the grandchild-beneficiary reached age twenty-one. At that time, the accumulated income would be distributed in toto. Thereafter, the beneficiary would receive payments at least annually of all income earned by the trust. If the grandchild died before his twenty-first birthday, all accumulated income would go to the estate of the grandchild.

Based on *Commissioner v. Herr*, 303 F.2d 780 (3d Cir. 1962), the Service conceded that the pre-21 income interest qualified for the present interest exclusion. The taxpayer sought to exclude as a present interest gift both the pre-21 income interest and post-21 income stream. The Second Circuit in *Levine* disagreed, holding (526 F.2d at 721):

> The taxpayers urge that we are required to treat the post-21 income interests as one with the pre-21 income interests, but that the remainder interests should be considered a separate gift. The taxpayers recognize that the combined pre- and post-21 income interests do not qualify as a present interest when viewed solely in the light of section 2503(b). This is so because the accumulation of income before age 21 works as a postponement of immediate enjoyment. In addition, the combined income interests fail to meet the criteria of section 2503(c)(2).
>
> The Levines seek to overcome these obstacles by means of an ingenious argument. The combination of pre-21 and post-21 income interests resembles a unitary life estate, they argue. The only reason it cannot qualify as a section 2503(b) present interest, they urge, is the accumulation provision that permits enjoyment to be delayed until age 21. But, they say, section 2503(c) as interpreted by *Herr* permits the future interest characteristic of the pre-21 income interests to be disregarded for the purpose of receiving the section 2503(b) exclusion. In other words, they assert that *Herr* and section 2503(c) in effect transform the pre-21 income interests into present interests. Then, by a giant leap, the taxpayers conclude that a single, lifetime present interest is produced by linking the pre-21 *constructive* present interests with the post-21 income interests.
>
> A study of the statutory language, however, convinces us that Congress did not contemplate such an "off-again, on-again" elusive treatment of the pre-21 segment of the transfers in trust. Moreover, we cannot be unmindful of the rule of construction that Congress permits exclusions only as a matter of grace, and the exclusions sections are to be strictly construed against the taxpayer . . . . Nor does the legislative history prove more helpful to the taxpayers.

[d]   Other Methods to Make Gifts to Minors: Custodial Accounts

Outright gifts to minors and trusts for minors can save estate taxes by qualifying for the annual exclusion and avoiding taxation of later appreciation of the transferred property. An outright transfer constitutes a completed gift and qualifies for the gift tax annual exclusion. *See* Rev. Rul. 55–400, 1955–2 C.B. 319. Nevertheless, an outright transfer to a minor is probably the least attractive alternative from a non-tax perspective. First, the disability of the minority requires a court appointed guardian, with attending expenses and restrictions, to deal with the property. Second, the donor may not want the property to be subject to the donee's absolute control on attaining majority, typically 18 years of age. Third, many donors are wary of giving property directly to a minor, for fear that the minor will lack the maturity necessary to avoid waste.

The Uniform Gifts to Minors Act, the Revised Uniform Gifts to Minors Act, and the Uniform Transfers to Minors Act respond to the need for a method of effectively conveying property to minors without requiring the appointment of a guardian to manage it. These statutes solve the management and control problems by creating the mechanism under which the property can be vested in the minor, and yet be managed without the formality of a guardianship or the inherent expense of a trust.

All states have some form of a gifts to minors act. The most common models are the Uniform Transfers to Minors Act (UTMA) and the Revised Uniform Gifts to Minors Act (UGMA). Neither of these Acts provide a universal solution to the problems facing prospective donors. First, because both Acts allow only a single minor to be the subject of a single custodianship, it is impossible to use the statutory form to provide for discretionary distributions to several minors based on need. If that type of arrangement is desirable, a trust is a more appropriate device. Second, the custodianship established under either act must terminate with the majority of the minor (as defined for the purposes of the Act—typically, ages 18 or 21). If the donor wishes to delay the donee's control of the assets beyond that age, a trust is required.

Rev. Rul. 59–357 holds that custodial gifts are complete and qualify for the gift tax annual exclusion. If the age when the property will pass to the donee is reduced from 21 to 18 years, to accord with a state's statutes defining adulthood, gifts pursuant to the amended statute continue to qualify for the exclusion. *See* Rev. Rul. 73–287, 1973–2 C.B. 321.

Besides the gift tax issue, custodian accounts raise significant estate tax and income tax issues if either the donor of the account or the parent of the minor beneficiary serves as the custodian. For a discussion, see Chapter 9.

The annual exclusion and, particularly, gifts in trust that qualify for the annual exclusion have been analyzed and criticized by commentators. For a sample of the issues and suggestions for change see Robert B. Smith, *Should We Give Away the Annual Exclusion?*, 1 FLA. TAX. REV. 361, 407–41 (1993); F. Ladson Boyle, *Present Interest Gifts in Trust: Donor and Donee Problems*, 29 GONZ. L. REV. 454–97 (1994).

Problems

1. *W* wants to place property in an irrevocable trust for her minor grandson, age 15. The trust instrument is subject to the following terms and conditions:

a. The third party trustee may use the income and principal for the beneficiary before he reaches 30 "as she deems necessary" for the maintenance, support, and education of the beneficiary;

b. If the beneficiary dies before reaching age 21, the trust property and accumulated income will be paid to his estate;

c. The beneficiary, on attaining age 21 may, within 30 days thereafter, request that the trust terminate by giving written notice to the trustee. If the beneficiary fails to exercise this right, the trust continues automatically until the beneficiary reaches age 30, at which time the trust will terminate. The principal and accumulated income will then be paid over to the beneficiary.

Is the annual per-donee exclusion available under § 2503(c)? *See* Heidrich v. Commissioner, 55 T.C. 746 (1971); Williams v. U. S., 378 F.2d 693 (Ct. Cl. 1967); and Illinois Nat'l Bank v. U.S., 756 F. Supp. 1117 (C.D. Ill. 1991).

2. *H* and *W* want to transfer property to their grandchildren who are minors. Should *H* and *W* transfer property to the beneficiaries: (1) outright, (2) under the Uniform Transfers to Minors Act, (3) to a § 2503(c) trust, or (4) to a *Crummey* trust?

[2]   Transfers for Certain Educational Purposes

[a]   Direct Transfers to Educational Institutions: Section 2503 (e)

In addition to the annual per-donee exclusion, a donor may exclude amounts paid for certain educational expenses. *See* § 2503(e).[12] The exclusion for educational expenses is limited to tuition. Thus, it excludes books, supplies, and room and board. The tuition expenses must be paid directly to an educational organization described in § 170(b)(1)(A)(ii): "an educational organization which normally maintains a regular faculty and curriculum and normally has a regularly enrolled body of pupils or students in attendance at the place where its educational activities are regularly carried on." Thus, the definition of an educational organization does not limit the availability of the exclusion to college or university expenses. *See* Tech. Advice Memo. 199941013 (exclusion applied for prepaid tuition at private school for preschool through 12th grade). Additionally, the donee of the educational expenses need not be a minor or a dependent of the donor for the payments to qualify for the exclusion. *See* Tech. Advice Memo. 199941013 (transfer on behalf of grandchildren qualified for exclusion). On the other hand, a donor will not receive an exclusion under § 2503(e) for transfers to a trust that will make direct payments of tuition expenses. *See* Treas. Reg. § 25.2503–6(c), Example 3.

---

[12] Section 2503(e) also provides an exclusion for certain medical payments. *See* § 4.01[B][5][e], *infra*.

Problem

F, a widower, had an adult son in law school. In 2002, *F* paid $12,000 directly to the university for the son's annual tuition. In the same year, *F* gave his son $16,000 for living expenses while in school. What is the amount of *F*'s taxable gifts for the year?

[b] College Tuition Programs: Section 529

Enacted in 1996, § 529 was substantially revised and liberalized by the Tax Acts of 1997 and 2001. Although § 529 involves both college savings plans and prepaid college tuition plans, this discussion focuses only on college savings plans because prepaid tuition plans are very restricted. Basically college savings plans are plans established by a state (or instrumentality thereof) which permit a taxpayer to open and contribute cash to an account for a designated beneficiary. The plan is exempt from income tax; as a result, a tax-free buildup can occur in the account. Although cash distributions are taxable to the distributee to the extent of earnings, distributions for qualified higher education expenses (QHEE), including tuition, books, and room and board, are not taxable to the distributee. Liberal income tax exclusion rules apply for rollovers and change of beneficiaries.

Cash contributions to a qualified tuition plan are treated as completed gifts of a present interest which are not excludible under § 2503(e). *See* § 529(c)(2)(A). Since the account owner can change the beneficiary at will, the treatment of § 529 savings accounts as completed gifts is an exception to the general gift tax rule that a gift is not complete if the donor retains dominion and control over the property. *See* § 4.01[A], *supra*.

As a general rule, distributions from a college savings account are not treated as gifts. *See* § 529(c)(5)(A). However, a gift will occur when there is a change in the designated beneficiary but only if the new beneficiary is in a generation younger than that of the designated beneficiary. *See* § 529(c)(5)(B). If the change in beneficiary is treated as a gift, the designated beneficiary, not the account owner, is deemed to make the gift. *See* Prop. Treas. Reg § 1.529-5(b)(3)(ii) and (iii).

Section 529 provides a special gift tax election whereby the account owner in one year may elect to treat up to five times the gift tax annual exclusion amount as qualifying for the gift tax annual exclusion. *See* § 529(c)(2)(B).

Example: In 2002, an individual opens a college savings plan and contributes $55,000 thereto. She could elect to exclude $11,000 in the year of the gift and treat the balance ($44,000) as a gift in the next four years. Thus, $11,000 would be available for the § 2503(b) exclusion in each of the next four years.[13]

Because split-gift treatment is allowed, the gift tax annual exclusion amount may be used by both spouses when one spouse contributes to a section 529 plans. *See* Prop. Treas. Reg § 1.529-5(b)(2)(ii) and (iii).

---

[13] If the exclusion increased to $12,000 in 2005, then $1,000 added to the account owner in 2005 would qualify for the gift tax annual exclusion. *See* Prop. Treas. Reg. § 1.529-5(b)(2)(iv).

Example: In 2002, W opens up a college savings account in the amount of $110,000. If H consents to split-gift treatment, and the 5 year spread-out election is made, the $110,000 could be entirely excluded from gift taxation. Each spouse would be treated as making a present interest gift of $11,000 for each of the five years, 2002-2006.

Absent one situation, there will be no estate consequences to the donor-account owner. In such a case, the owner's estate will include the portion of the contributions that were allocable to years after the year in which the owner died. For example, if the owner contributed $55,000 in 2002 and made the spread-out election but died in 2003, $33,000 (the total amount allocable to 2004-2006) would be includible in the account owner's gross estate. *See* § 529(c)(4)(C). On the other hand, if the designated beneficiary dies while the account is still open, the designated beneficiary's gross estate will include the value of the interest in the qualified tuition plan. *See* § 529(c)(4)(B).

Due in large part to very favorable tax rules, college savings programs are becoming popular. As financial columnist Andrew Tobias wrote even before the 2001 Act amendments that made § 529 plans even more attractive: "Almost anybody saving for college would be crazy not at least to consider them [529 plans]." (http://www.andrewtobias.com/newcolumns/991215.html). *See generally* Michael Schlesinger, *Qualified State Tuition Programs: More Favorable After 2001 Act*, 28 Est. Plng. 412 (2001); A.L. Spitzer and Christopher E. Houston, *Section 529 College Savings Plans Better than Ever*, 33 Exempt Org. Tax Rev. 23 (July 2001); Joseph F. Hurley, The Best Way to Save for College — a Complete Guide to 529 Plans (2002-2003 Edition). Joseph Hurley also maintains an incredibly useful website, "The Internet Guide to 529 Plans" at http://www.savingforcollege.com/.

Problem

In August of 2002, *M* contributed $20,000 to a college savings account for his daughter, *B*, under a section 529 plan. One month earlier, *M* had made a $8,000 outright gift to *B*. What would be the amount of the gross gift with respect to the college saving account? What would be the taxable gift if *M*'s spouse agreed to split gift treatment but only for the college savings account?

[c] Coverdell IRAs: Section 530

Section 530 provides for educational IRAs which Congress renamed Coverdell IRAs in honor of the late senator who was a moving force in the area. As significantly liberalized by the 2001 Act, § 530 permits an individual to open a Coverdell IRA for an individual and contribute up to $2,000 per year. Although the contribution is not deductible, the account is exempt from income taxes; thus, like § 529 plans, there will be a tax-free build up in the account.

The gift and estate tax consequences are similar to those for § 529 accounts. *See* § 530(d)(3). Thus, the contribution will be the gift of a present interest but not excludible under § 2503(e). A gift will occur only if the current beneficiary is replaced by a younger generation beneficiary; in such case, the existing beneficiary will be the donor. Because the contribution amount cannot exceed $2,000, the elective spread-out rule of § 529 does not apply. As a result, the death of the account owner or beneficiary should not result in estate taxation.

Unlike § 529 plans, Coverdell IRAs can be used at any educational level and may include public, private and religious schools; further, qualified elementary and educational expenses include a wide array of items, such as daycare, uniforms and certain computer technology. *See* § 530(b)(2) and (4). Distributions for qualified expenses, including any income earned on the account, are generally not subject to income tax. *See* § 530(d). On the other hand, contributions cannot be made to a Coverdell IRA once a potential contributor's income level (modified adjusted gross income) exceeds $110,000 in the case of individuals and $220,000 for joint filers. Nor can contributions be made once an individual has reached age 18. *See* § 530(b)(1)(A)(ii). Generally, the designated beneficiary must receive the account balance on attaining age 30. *See* § 530(b)(1)(E).

[3] Transfers in Marital Dissolution Context: Section 2516

Code: §§ 2516 and 2043(b).

Regulations: None.

Harris v. Commissioner

340 U.S. 106 (1950)

Mr. Justice Douglas delivered the opinion of the Court.

The federal estate tax and the federal gift tax, as held in a line of cases ending with *Commissioner v. Wemyss*, 324 U.S. 303 [reproduced at § 4.01[A]], and *Merrill v. Fahs*, 324 U.S. 308, [reproduced at § 4.01[A]] are construed in pari materia, since the purpose of the gift tax is to complement the estate tax by preventing tax-free depletion of the transferor's estate during his lifetime. Both the gift tax and the estate tax exclude transfers made for "an adequate and full consideration in money or money's worth." In the estate tax this requirement is limited to deductions for claims based upon "a promise or agreement";[14] but the consideration for the "promise or agreement" may not be the release of marital rights in the decedent's property.[15] In the *Wemyss* and *Merrill* cases the question was whether the gift tax was applicable to premarital property settlements. If the standards of the estate tax were to be applied ex proprio vigore in gift tax cases, those transfers would be taxable because there was a "promise or agreement" touching marital rights in property. We sustained the tax, thus giving "adequate and full consideration in money or money's worth" the same meaning under both statutes insofar as premarital property settlements or agreements are concerned.

The present case raises the question whether *Wemyss* and *Merrill* require the imposition of the gift tax in the type of post-nuptial settlement of property rights involved here.

---

[14] [*See* § 2053(c). Eds.]

[15] [*See* § 2043(b). Eds.]

Petitioner divorced her husband, Reginald Wright, in Nevada in 1943. Both she and her husband had substantial property interests. They reached an understanding as respects the unscrambling of those interests, the settlement of all litigated claims to the separate properties, the assumption of obligations, and the transfer of properties.

Wright received from petitioner the creation of a trust for his lifetime of the income from her remainder interest in a then-existing trust; an assumption by her of an indebtedness of his of $47,650; and her promise to pay him $416.66 a month for ten years.

Petitioner received from Wright 21/90 of certain real property in controversy; a discontinuance of a partition suit then pending; an indemnification from and assumption by him of all liability on a bond and mortgage [sic] on certain real property in London, England; and an indemnification against liability in connection with certain real property in the agreement. It was found that the value of the property transferred to Wright exceeded that received by petitioner by $107,150. The Commissioner assessed a gift tax on the theory that any rights which Wright might have given up by entering into the agreement could not be adequate and full consideration.

If the parties had without more gone ahead and voluntarily unraveled their business interests on the basis of this compromise, there would be no question that the gift tax would be payable. For there would have been a "promise or agreement" that effected a relinquishment of marital rights in property. It therefore would fall under the ban of the provision of the estate tax which by judicial construction has been incorporated into the gift tax statute.

But the parties did not simply undertake a voluntary contractual division of their property interests. They were faced with the fact that Nevada law not only authorized but instructed the divorce court to decree a just and equitable disposition of both the community and the separate property of the parties.[16] The agreement recited that it was executed in order to effect a settlement of the respective property rights of the parties "in the event a divorce should be decreed"; and it provided that the agreement should be submitted to the divorce court "for its approval." It went on to say, "It is of the essence of this agreement that the settlement herein provided for shall not become operative in any manner nor shall any of the Recitals or covenants herein become binding upon either party unless a decree of absolute divorce between the parties shall be entered in the pending Nevada action."

If the agreement had stopped there and were in fact submitted to the court, it is clear that the gift tax would not be applicable. That arrangement would not be a "promise or agreement" in the statutory sense. It would be wholly conditional upon the entry of the decree; the divorce court might or might not accept the provisions of the arrangement as the measure of the respective obligations; it might indeed add to or subtract from them. The decree, not the

---

[16] At the time of the divorce Nevada Compiled Laws (Supp. 1931–1941) § 9463 provided: "In granting a divorce, the court may award such alimony to the wife and shall make such disposition of the community and separate property of the parties as shall appear just and equitable, having regard to the respective merits of the parties and to the condition in which they will be left by such divorce, and to the party through whom the property was acquired, and to the burdens, if any, imposed upon it for the benefit of the children . . . ."

arrangement submitted to the court, would fix the rights and obligations of the parties. That was the theory of *Commissioner v. Maresi*, 156 F.2d 929, and we think it sound.

Even the Commissioner concedes that the result would be correct in case the property settlement was litigated in the divorce action. That was what happened in *Commissioner v. Converse*, 163 F.2d 131, where the divorce court decreed a lump-sum award in lieu of monthly payments provided by the separation agreement. Yet without the decree there would be no enforceable, existing agreement whether the settlement was litigated or unlitigated. Both require the approval of the court before an obligation arises. The happenstance that the divorce court might approve the entire settlement, or modify it in unsubstantial details, or work out material changes seems to us unimportant. In each case it is the decree that creates the rights and the duties; and a decree is not a "promise or agreement" in any sense—popular or statutory.

But the present case is distinguished by reason of a further provision in the undertaking and in the decree. The former provided that "the covenants in this agreement shall survive any decree of divorce which may be entered." And the decree stated "It is ordered that said agreement and said trust agreements forming a part thereof shall survive this decree." The Court of Appeals turned the case on these provisions. It concluded that since there were two sanctions for the payments and transfers—contempt under the divorce decree and execution under the contract—they were founded not only on the decree but upon both the decree and a "promise or agreement." It therefore held the excess of the value of the property which petitioner gave her husband over what he gave her to be taxable as a gift.

We, however, think that the gift tax statute is concerned with the source of rights, not with the manner in which rights at some distant time may be enforced. Remedies for enforcement will vary from state to state. It is "the transfer" of the property with which [§ 2511] is concerned, not the sanctions which the law supplies to enforce transfers. If "the transfer" of marital rights in property is effected by the parties, it is pursuant to a "promise or agreement" in the meaning of the statute. If "the transfer" is effected by court decree, no "promise or agreement" of the parties is the operative fact. In no realistic sense is a court decree a "promise or agreement" between the parties to a litigation. If finer, more legalistic lines are to be drawn, Congress must do it.

If, as we hold, the case is free from any "promise or agreement" concerning marital rights in property, it presents no remaining problems of difficulty. The Treasury Regulations [§ 25.2512–8] recognize as tax free "a sale, exchange, or other transfer of property made in the ordinary course of business (a transaction which is bona fide, at arm's length, and free from any donative intent)." This transaction is not "in the ordinary course of business" in any conventional sense. Few transactions between husband and wife ever would be; and those under the aegis of a divorce court are not. But if two partners on dissolution of the firm entered into a transaction of this character or if chancery did it for them, there would seem to be no doubt that the unscrambling of the business interests would satisfy the spirit of the Regulations. No reason is apparent why husband and wife should be under a heavier handicap absent a statute which brings all marital property settlements under the gift tax.

. . .

Reversed.

Mr. Justice Frankfurter, joined by Mr. Justice Black, Mr. Justice Burton, and Mr. Justice Minton, dissenting. [The dissenting opinion is omitted.]

———

The *Harris* doctrine did not end the uncertainty of gift tax application to marital dissolutions. Nor did the doctrine end the problems in the estate tax area. For example, a § 2053 estate tax deduction for a claim against the estate, founded on a promise or agreement, must be based on adequate consideration in money or money's worth. *See* Chapter 3, § 3.04[A][5], *supra*.

Based on *Harris*, the Service agrees that if a divorce decree incorporates the terms of a separation agreement, a subsequent transfer will be deemed to arise out of a judicial obligation, so long as the court had the independent power to modify the provisions of the agreement. *See* Rev. Rul. 60–160, 1960–1 C.B. 374. As a result, the transfer is deemed to be for full consideration in money or money's worth. On the other hand, the Service has asserted that if the divorce court is bound by the terms of the settlement agreement and must, under state law, incorporate the agreement into the divorce decree, then the subsequent claim or transfer will be deemed to arise out of the settlement agreement, resulting in the application of the full consideration rules. *See* Rev. Rul. 75–395, 1975–2 C.B. 370. The Second Circuit rejected this argument in *Natchez v. United States*, 705 F.2d 671 (2d Cir. 1983). The mere power of a court to approve a settlement and incorporate it into a divorce decree removes the payments from being founded on a promise or agreement, at least in a case where the agreement would have been void in the absence of the decree.

Section 2516 extends the gift tax exclusion to many, but not all, marital dissolution transfers which are not embraced under the *Harris* doctrine. It applies equally to property settlement agreements and agreements setting support obligations. Thus, transfers made in exchange for the release of a child's support rights (to the extent that those rights can be released) will not be subject to gift taxation if the requirements of § 2516 are met. Unlike property settlements, however, support agreements are limited to "a reasonable allowance for the support of issue of the marriage during minority." *See* § 2516.

The § 2516 requirement for a divorce means that the section is inapplicable to property settlements in permanent separation situations. In this circumstance, as well as in the case of a transfer occurring before a divorce, the transfer may be deductible under the gift tax marital deduction provisions of § 2523, discussed later in this Chapter, if the requirements of that section are fulfilled. Otherwise, the parties are left to establish the value of the support rights given up in the agreement: "[T]he transfer of property pursuant to the property settlement agreement of the parties incident to a legal separation results in a taxable gift to the extent that the value of the transferred property may exceed the value of any support rights transferred." *See* Rev. Rul. 68–379, 1968–2 C.B. 414; *see also* Treas. Reg. § 25.2512–8.

Note also that § 2516 may *not* be necessary to establish the consideration for a particular marital transfer. As discussed earlier, transfers made to support minor children, for example, have been held to satisfy the adequate and full consideration requirement of § 2512(b). *See Helvering v. United States Trust Company*, 111 F.2d 576 (2d Cir. 1940), *cert. denied*, 311 U.S. 678 (1940); *see also* Rev. Rul. 77–314, 1977–2 C.B. 349; Rev. Rul. 71–67, 1971–1 C.B. 271.

Problems

1. *H* and *W* cannot agree on a property settlement before they are divorced. *H* does not want to give *W* anything. The court, in granting their divorce, orders *H* to pay $100,000 to *W*.

    a. Has *H* made a gift for gift tax purposes when he pays this judgment?

    b. Assume that *H* dies before the transfer, but after the divorce, and that *W* files a claim for the payment in *H*'s estate. Would *H*'s estate receive a deduction under § 2053?

2. *H* and *W* enter into a separation agreement whereby *H* agrees to pay *W* $1,000 per month for her support until she dies or remarries, and a lump-sum payment of $250,000 for the release of her property rights in *H*'s estate. The agreement is effective even if no divorce occurs. They are divorced six months later, but the divorce court merely issues a decree of divorce. No reference is made to any payments or the separation agreement. When *H* later makes the payments called for by the agreement, are the transfers subject to the gift tax?

[4] Disclaimers: Section 2518

Code: § 2518.

Regulations: Treas. Reg. §§ 25.2818–2; 1.7520–1(a), (b); 25.7520–3(b)(1), (b)(3), and (b)(4).

Estate of Monroe v. Commissioner

124 F.3d 699 (5th Cir. 1997), rev'g 104 T.C. 352 (1995)

Edith H. Jones, Circuit Judge:

I. BACKGROUND

. . .

On April 28, 1989, Louise S. Monroe died at the age of 91, leaving a multimillion dollar estate. J. Edgar Monroe (Monroe), her husband, became executor of the estate. Monroe, who was then 92 years old, sought help from Robert Monroe, his nephew, in administering the estate. An estate tax return was timely filed in March 1990. Edgar Monroe died in May 1990.

The Monroes had no children, but Louise Monroe's will made 31 specific cash bequests to extended family members, long-time employees, and friends, as well as 4 bequests to corporate entities. Louise Monroe also made bequests in trust to two grandnieces and a grandnephew, giving each a treasury bond with a $500,000 face value. Monroe was the residual beneficiary of his wife's estate.

The will called for each bequest to bear its portion of the death taxes. Touche Ross, the accounting firm retained by the estate, also determined that generation-skipping transfer taxes would have to be borne by some of the individual legatees. The tax impact on the legatees under these circumstances would be substantial, amounting in some cases to 75%–80% of the individual bequests. However, projections showed that tax liability was significantly reduced if legatees disclaimed their legacies. Deeply concerned about the high tax burden on the individual bequests, Monroe and Robert Monroe decided to pursue disclaimers as a means of reducing the overall federal tax liability . . . .

With assistance from the accountants, Monroe and Robert Monroe identified 29 legatees to approach about renouncing. Robert Monroe rehearsed with one of the accountants his presentation to the legatees. In substance, Robert Monroe made the following points: his uncle was upset about the amount of taxes that would have to be paid by the estate and the legatees; each bequest would be significantly reduced by taxes; his uncle would like each legatee to disclaim his or her bequest; each legatee who disclaimed would be giving up a right; and any disclaimer had to be voluntary and without consideration.

Monroe personally asked Kathleen Gooden Hayward, Monroe's grandniece and one of the legatees of a $500,000 treasury bond, as well as four household employees to give up their bequests. Robert Monroe made some version of his presentation to the remaining 24 legatees on the list.

In December 1989, each of the 29 legatees signed a disclaimer, conceded by the Commissioner to be valid and effective under Louisiana law. The total amount disclaimed was $892,781, and this amount was included in the marital deduction on the estate tax return as money which passed to Monroe.

In late December 1989 and January 1990, Monroe wrote each of the disclaimants a personal check in an amount approximately equal to the gross amount of the bequest renounced. Each check bore the notation "gift." Inadvertently, Monroe failed to file a 1989 gift tax return for the December 1989 gifts. However, in 1991, a timely gift tax return was filed covering all the gifts made in January 1990, and an amended gift tax return was filed for the 1989 taxable year.

. . .

Some of the disclaimants were told by the nephew that Monroe had always taken care of them and had never cheated them or that Monroe was a generous man. Many of the disclaimants anticipated that Monroe would continue to care for them financially or was likely to make a bequest to them in his will. Some disclaimants believed that executing the disclaimer would be in their best long-term interest, because they did not wish to upset Monroe by refusing to renounce.

The Tax Court agreed with the Commissioner on 28 of 29 disclaimers . . . .

II. THE TAX COURT DECISION

. . .

Section 2518(b) provides that "the term 'qualified disclaimer' means an irrevocable and unqualified refusal by a person to accept an interest in property but only if . . . (3) such person has not accepted the interest or any of its benefits . . . ." [footnote omitted].

In concluding that all but one of the disclaimers were not qualified within the meaning of § 2518, the Tax Court reasoned that the disclaimants expected, for one reason or another, that they would receive their renounced bequests in the form of a gift or legacy from Monroe. Furthermore, the testimony of many of the disclaimants suggests that they feared what would happen if they refused to renounce their bequests.

. . .

[The Tax Court determined that the] disclaimants may not have explicitly negotiated with or bargained with Monroe or the nephew for consideration in return for executing their disclaimers. Each of the disclaimants other than Helene Tebo, however, was induced or, in some instances, coerced, into executing a disclaimer. Under these circumstances, the consideration for their disclaimers was the implied promise that they would be better off if they did what Monroe wanted them to do than if they refused to do so. Their disclaimers thus were not "unqualified" as required by section 2518.

. . .

III. THE PARTIES' CONTENTIONS

On appeal, the estate contends that the Tax Court confused the two tests for acceptance of a disclaimed interest within the meaning of § 2518(b)(3). The estate relies on the Treasury Regulations interpreting § 2518(b)(3): A qualified disclaimer cannot be made with respect to an interest in property if the disclaimant has accepted the interest or any of its benefits, expressly or impliedly, prior to the disclaimer. Acceptance is manifested by an affirmative act which is consistent with ownership of the interest in property . . . . In addition, the acceptance of any consideration in return for making the disclaimer is an acceptance of the benefits of the entire interest disclaimed. Gift Tax Regs. § 25.2518–2(d)(1).

The estate argues that this regulation sets up two distinct ways that the disclaimer can be "unqualified": by a legatee's explicitly or implicitly accepting the interest or its benefits before making the disclaimer, or by his receiving consideration in return for making the disclaimer. Accordingly, since the Commissioner has not argued that the disclaimants accepted the benefits of their legacies prior to executing the disclaimers, the only issue is whether the disclaimants received consideration for making the disclaimers.

The Estate further argues that the Tax Court invalidated the disclaimers based on evidence of the disclaimants' motive or expectation and not based upon evidence that the disclaimants received valid consideration for executing the disclaimers. Belief that one will be the beneficiary of future gifts by Monroe or be remembered in Monroe's will is insufficient to establish consideration in the absence of some actual promise or agreement to provide such future benefits. In support, the estate cites *Philpot v. Gruninger*, 81 U.S. (14 Wall.) 570, 577 (1872), where the Supreme Court observed:

> There is a clear distinction sometimes between the motive that may induce to enter into a contract and the consideration of a contract. Nothing is consideration that is not regarded as such by both parties . . . an expectation of results often leads to the formation of a contract, but neither the expectation nor the result is the [consideration].

In addition, the estate points to several private letter rulings that have approved disclaimers under § 2518 where the disclaimants clearly expected that executing disclaimers would benefit them in the long run . . . .

IV. DISCUSSION

. . .

If the disclaimers in this case fail to meet the requirements of § 2518, it is either because they were not "irrevocable and unqualified," or because the disclaimants had "accepted the interest or any of its benefits." The Treasury regulations further explain that acceptance of the interest within the meaning of § 2518(b)(3) includes not only explicit or implied acceptance of the interest or any of its benefits, but also the receipt of consideration in return for executing the disclaimer. *See* Treas. Reg. § 25.2518–1(d)(1).

Unqualified means "not modified by reservations or restrictions." *Id.* Under the plain meaning of the statute, an "irrevocable and unqualified" disclaimer is a relinquishment of a legal right that is incapable of being retracted or revoked by the disclaimant and is not modified by reservations or restrictions that limit its enforceability. None of the written disclaimers challenged by the Commissioner can be attacked as being subject to revocation or subject to some condition: the documents executed by the disclaimants are irrevocable and unqualified on their face.

Monroe's gifts, given after the disclaimants renounced their bequests, do not change the irrevocability of the disclaimers: once executed, the disclaimers were effective to give up the legatees' rights to their respective bequests from Louise Monroe's estate. The Commissioner, unlike the Tax Court, seems to be implying that the legatees actually revoked their disclaimers by accepting the gifts from Monroe. But even if the disclaimants subsequently received and accepted a payment from Monroe, the Commissioner has not demonstrated how such acceptance affects the enforceability of the previously executed disclaimer. The disclaimants still had no right to such a payment from the estate or from Monroe. Thus, the disclaimers were not revoked.

But irrevocability is a side issue. The real bone of contention is whether the disclaimers were "unqualified," and whether unqualified has some meaning beyond the possibilities carefully delineated in the applicable Treasury

Regulations. None of the written disclaimers articulates any kind of disabling qualification, of course. Nevertheless, the Tax Court and the Commissioner assert that because all but one of the disclaimants "expected," because they were "induced" or "coerced" by Monroe, that they would eventually receive their bequests in the form of a gift or legacy, their renunciations were "qualified" to the extent of the expectation. As the Tax Court later put it, a disclaimer is not "unqualified" if it rests on an "implied promise" that the disclaimant will be better off executing the disclaimer than not doing so. Further, according to the Tax Court, the "implied promise" may exist even though the disclaimants did not negotiate or bargain with Monroe for later recompense.

We disagree with this interpretation of "unqualified." It is inconsistent with a holistic reading of section 2518(b), contrary to the governing Treasury Regulations and the Service's letter rulings, and intolerably, unnecessarily vague.

Section 2518(b) describes a covered disclaimer as one which is "unqualified . . . but only if [the disclaimant] . . . has not accepted the interest or any of its benefits." A "qualification," therefore, would seem to depend on the tangible receipt of property, *i.e.*, the "interest or any of its benefits." That is also the most sensible understanding of an unqualified disclaimer. One who disclaims an interest in property must do so without getting something in exchange; and since property has been given up, it follows that a "qualified disclaimer" would be one in which the renunciation is not complete because property has been kept or received in return.

The Commissioner and Tax Court would eliminate this statutory symmetry by holding that a disclaimer of property is "qualified" even though something less than property, *e.g.* an "expectation" or "implied promise," is received in return. While their reading would enhance the government's ability to disqualify disclaimers, it also rests on an incomprehensible subjective standard. How likely is it, in tax terms, that people would disclaim "a bird in the hand" purely altruistically? Yet the clear inference to be drawn from the Tax Court's approach to this case is that a "qualified disclaimer" demands no less than disinterest in the "property or its benefits." The court voided all of the disclaimers here except that of Ms. Tebo, who acted solely for personal reasons in executing a disclaimer. On the contrary, as the Service's letter rulings indicate, a primary purpose of the law authorizing qualified disclaimers is to facilitate post-mortem estate tax planning and to increase family wealth on the "expectation" that there will thus remain more wealth to pass on to disclaimants in the future. Consequently, if the Tax Court's subjective interpretation of "unqualified" disclaimer is accepted, it undermines the very purpose for which the provision was enacted. It also ensures litigation in virtually every disclaimer situation, because it can be assumed that heirs and legatees rarely execute disclaimers for tax purposes without having had some "expectations" or "inducements" based on conversations with advisers on the prospective benefits of such a course of action.

Not only does the statutory language conflict with the Tax Court's interpretation of an "unqualified disclaimer," but the Treasury Regulations are also incompatible with the "expectation" or "implied promise" theory. This is not to say that we are required to enforce Treasury Regulations instead of the statute, but rather, that the regulations mirror the correct understanding of the statute better than the Commissioner's and Tax Court's present positions. The regulations set forth two situations in which a disclaimer expresses a mere qualified refusal to accept an interest in property: when the disclaimant accepts, expressly or impliedly, the interest or any of its benefits; and when the disclaimant receives "consideration" in return for executing the disclaimer. *See* Treas. Reg. § 25.2518–2(d)(1). Consistent with our interpretation, a disclaimant cannot purport to disclaim, while taking actual advantage of the property "or any of its benefits." Further, the disclaimant cannot accept "benefits" from the property by receiving consideration in exchange for the disclaimer. The juxtaposition in the regulation between the "implied" acceptance of the interest or any of its benefits and the "consideration" that must be received in exchange for a disclaimer is not accidental. One may impliedly accept the benefits of property, for instance by pledging it as security for a loan, and therefore act inconsistently when making an alleged disclaimer. On the other hand, only by receiving "consideration" in the classic sense does one receive "property" or any of its benefits in exchange for executing the disclaimer. We thus agree with the estate that to have accepted the benefits of a disclaimed interest, the disclaimant must have received actual consideration in return for renouncing his legacy.

A disclaimant's mere expectation of a future benefit in return for executing a disclaimer will not render it "unqualified." "Consideration," used deliberately in the regulations, is a term of art. *See Philpot v. Gruninger*, 81 U.S. (14 Wall.) 570, 577 (1872); *Fire Ins. Ass'n v. Wickham*, 141 U.S. 564, 579 (1891) (to constitute consideration, promise "must have been offered by one party, and accepted by the other, as one element of the contract"). This is the way the regulations are written, and it is consistent with the Commissioner's letter rulings, which are properly cited as evidence of how the Commissioner has interpreted the law in the past. *See Transco Exploration Co.*, 949 F.2d at 840. In each of the three rulings cited above [LTR 8701001, LTR 9427030, and LTR 9509003], the obvious expectation that the disclaimant would be better off in the long-run by renouncing his interest in favor of the decedent's spouse did not violate the bar against acceptance of the disclaimed interest or its benefits. . . . In one letter ruling, the surviving spouse proposed to set up an inter vivos trust calling for the same distributions at her death as were provided in the trust established by the decedent. *See* LTR 9427030. In each case, the Commissioner cited the lack of an agreement between the parties as to what the disclaimants were to receive in the future. The Commissioner implicitly recognized the distinction between the expectation that renouncing is in the disclaimant's best interest and an expectation that rises to the level of consideration. The charitable contribution cases also recognize this distinction. *See, e.g., Wardwell*, 301 F.2d at 638 ("Motivation and personal expectation do not destroy the reality and genuineness of a given transaction, even in tax cases"). Thus, the question for each disclaimer is whether the decision to disclaim was part of mutually-bargained-for consideration or a mere unenforceable hope of future benefit, whether that unenforceable hope springs from family ties, long-term friendship or employment, or a generalized fear that benefits will be withheld in the future absent execution of the disclaimer.

. . .

The rehearsed presentation by Robert Monroe does not in itself support a finding that there was consideration. He explained the estate tax problems created by the decedent's will and how executing the disclaimers would affect the distribution of property. He informed the legatees that they were giving up a right and that he could not promise them anything in return for that. The only potentially questionable part of the presentation was the reference to his uncle's generosity. The Tax Court found that the intent of this statement was to inform the disclaimants that the probability that they would receive something from Monroe in the future was good. Conversely, if the legatees refused to disclaim, they were unlikely to receive anything from Monroe subsequently, because their refusal would be against Monroe's wishes. Even assuming that the Tax Court correctly ascertained Robert Monroe's intention, his statements merely reminding the disclaimants of Monroe's history of generosity, without demonstrating that the individual legatee did or could reasonably be expected to interpret such a reminder as a promise, do not invalidate the disclaimers. It is only where the evidence indicates that Robert or Edgar Monroe went further than this rehearsed presentation, or that a particular legatee interpreted this as a promise, [footnote omitted] that the Tax Court's findings might be supported. Furthermore, even if the record shows that Robert or Edgar Monroe went too far in their representations to a specific legatee, that does not support a generalization applicable to other disclaimants.

Turning to an evaluation of the record relevant to each disclaimer, we conclude that for the majority of the disclaimants, the evidence as a matter of law does not support a finding of any agreement that would amount to consideration for the execution of the disclaimers. The duty to defer to the Tax Court's findings of fact applies only insofar as the Tax Court correctly applied the law, which it did not do here. And in any event, with regard to most of the disclaimers, there is no specific evidence other than that which only supports a finding that the disclaimers were made without consideration. In addition to testimony indicating that they were made no promises and that they understood that they were giving up any right to claim something from Louise Monroe's estate, many legatees testified to some personal reason inconsistent with improper inducement or coercion by Monroe . . . .

Step-transaction / Substance-over-form

Finally, we disagree with the Commissioner's contention that the Tax Court's decision should be affirmed on substance-over-form or step-transaction grounds. While the disclaimants, to varying degrees, may have thought they would eventually receive something from Monroe, even the actual amount of their legacy, the evidence shows that most really believed they were, in fact, giving up their legacy under Louise Monroe's will. Several legatees sought outside counsel before making their decision. As long as there was no implicit agreement that they would receive something from Monroe in return for their disclaimers, the fact that the legatees understood they were giving up their rights and actually did, in a manner effective under Louisiana law, give up their rights is sufficient. There is no evidence that any of the legatees who executed disclaimers that we have held to be "qualified disclaimers" under § 2518(b) believed they were receiving their inheritance under Louise Monroe's will when they received Edgar Monroe's gifts. Accordingly, Monroe's subsequent gifts do not change the legitimacy or legal effect of the legatee's renunciations.

. . .

VI.

For the foregoing reasons, we REVERSE in part and REMAND . . . .

King, Circuit Judge, dissenting: [dissenting opinion omitted].

———

In *Drye v. United States*, 528 U.S. 49 (1999), the Supreme Court ruled that a disclaimer did not usurp a federal tax lien. The taxpayer disclaimed an interest in his mother's estate pursuant to local law (Arkansas). The Court determined, however, the tax lien attached and could not be defeated by the disclaimer.

———

For many years there were numerous problems with the validity of disclaimers for federal transfer tax purposes. The effect of state law was uncertain, and specific parameters did not exist. *See United States v. Irving*, 511 U.S. 224 (1992); *Jewett v. Commissioner*, 455 U.S. 305 (1982); *see generally* Grayson M.P. McCouch, *Timely Disclaimers and Taxable Transfers,* 47 U. Miami L. Rev. 1043 (1993). In 1976, Congress responded to the problems that had arisen by adding §§ 2518 and 2046 to the Code. Section 2518 contains detailed rules governing disclaimers for gift tax purposes. Section 2046 adopts the § 2518 rules for estate tax purposes.[17]

The basic approach of § 2518 is to limit the tax benefit to written disclaimers made either within nine months of the creation of the disclaimed interest or power or the majority of the disclaimant. *See* § 2518(b). This avoids both the uncertainty of the "reasonable time" standard applied by state law and the possibility of delaying a disclaimer until the interest becomes possessory, which is possible in some jurisdictions. Partial disclaimers are possible, as are disclaimers of discrete interests. *See* § 2518(c)(1).

Subsequent to the adoption of §§ 2518 and 2045, it became clear that those sections had failed to achieve uniformity in the treatment of disclaimers in one important respect. Because disclaimers were required to be effective under local law to be effective for tax purposes, variations in local law could still defeat favorable tax treatment in some jurisdictions, while allowing it in others. This problem was cured in 1981, by the adoption of § 2518(c)(3), which treats a timely transfer of an interest to the person who would have taken

———

[17] Section 2518 also applies for generation-skipping transfer tax purposes. *See* § 2654(c).

under an effective disclaimer as though it were a disclaimer valid under state law.

By refusing to accept the bequeathed interests, and thereby allowing others to benefit instead, a devise can be changed for both property and tax purposes. A variety of tax situations can suggest the use of a disclaimer. As *Monroe* illustrates, disclaimers can reduce the size of the taxable estate by increasing deductible interests, such as the marital deduction. This can occur if children disclaim interests in a decedent's estate which then pass to the surviving spouse and, as a result, increase the amount of the marital deduction. *See* Treas. Reg. § 20.2056(d)–1(b). *See also* Estate of Lassiter v. Commissioner, T. C. Memo 2000-324.

> **Example:** H devises property in trust for Wife for life, remainder to child. The trustee has the power to invade corpus for the child. As a result, the trust does not qualify for the QTIP election. If, however, the child makes a qualified disclaimer under § 2518, then a QTIP election could be made for the trust.

The possibility of income tax savings can also be the basis for a disclaimer. A devisee having a higher marginal income tax rate might choose to avoid additional income being taxed at those rates by disclaiming income-producing property in favor of its passing to a family member with lower rates. Similarly, a personal representative who is also a legatee may disclaim the personal representative's fee, and thereby receive the funds as an untaxed legacy, rather than as taxed income. *See* Rev. Rul. 66–167, 1966–1 C.B. 20. Of course, to the extent that the received interest is taxed either way it is received, the effectiveness of this planning technique depends on the progressivity of the respective tax rate schedules.

Because of the effect that disclaimers can have on the ultimate tax liability of the estate and its beneficiaries, creative use of disclaimers has come to be called "post-mortem estate planning" and has generated comment in the estate planning literature. *See, e.g.,* Virginia F. Coleman, *Disclaimers–New Developments, Opportunities and Unsettled Areas,* 33 Inst. on Est. Plan. ch.16. (1999).

Problems

1. Under *X*'s will, *A* receives a specific bequest of *X*'s boat. *B* is designated as the residuary legatee. *A* neither wanted the leaky old boat nor any tax liability from disposing of it. What should *A* do?

2. *C* is the residuary legatee under *Y*'s will. *C* is also named as the executor of *Y*'s estate. As executor, *C* is entitled to a fee for the administrative services he renders. Under what circumstances should *C* disclaim the right to payment for these fees?

3. The decedent, age 55, died intestate in 2002 survived by a spouse, two adult children, and one minor child. The gross estate was valued at $5 million. Under applicable state law, the intestate estate is divided one-half to the surviving spouse, age 45, and one-half to the decedent's three children (ages 21, 19, and 17). What are the decedent's estate taxes? If the children are willing to disclaim all or a portion of their inheritance, how much should they

disclaim? What will the decedent's estate taxes and the estate taxes of the surviving spouse be, assuming that the surviving spouse dies one year after the decedent?

[5] Miscellaneous Exclusions

Code: §§ 2501(a)(5); 2503(e) and (f).

Regulations: Treas. Reg. § 25.2503–6.

Several particular types of transfers are also specifically excludable from the taxable estate, including transfers to educational institutions for tuition, transfers for medical care, political donations, and the waiver of federally-protected pension rights by an employee's spouse.

[a] Unlimited Exclusion for Certain Transfers for Educational or Medical Expenses: Section 2503(e)

In addition to the annual per-donee exclusion, a donor may exclude amounts paid for certain medical care expenses. *See* § 2503(e).[18] Medical expenses, such as diagnosis, treatment, and insurance, paid by the donor to the service provider are also excludable. *See* § 2503(e)(2)(B). The amounts must, however, be paid directly to the provider of the medical services. No exclusion is available when the donor reimburses the donee for medical expenses paid by the donee, whether the donor makes the payments before or after the donee pays the expenses. *See* Rev. Rul. 82–98, 1982–1 C.B. 141.

[b] Transfers to Political Organizations: Section 2501(a)(5)

Under § 2501(a)(5), transfers to political organizations for the use of the organization are excluded from the definition of a taxable transfer for gift tax purposes. To qualify, the organization must qualify as a political organization under § 527(e)(1).

[c] Waiver of Pension Rights: Section 2503(f)

Under § 2503(f), if before an employee's death the employee's spouse waives his right to the joint and survivor pension otherwise mandated by the Retirement Equity Act of 1984, that waiver does not constitute a gift for tax purposes.

§ 4.02 Valuation of Lifetime Gratuitous Transfers

Code: §§ 2512 and 7520.

Regulations: Treas. Reg. § 25.2512–1, –5.

---

[18] Section 2503(e) also excludes transfers for certain educational expenses, discussed earlier in § 4.01[B][2][a], *supra*.

[A]　In General

Once a taxable transfer of property has been made and applicable exclusions are taken into account, the gift must be valued to determine the amount subject to tax, or to value any present interest in the transferred property to determine whether the full annual exclusion applies. Consistent with the general valuation principle for estate tax purposes, the gift tax employs the fair market value standard. *See* Treas. Reg § 25.2512–1. Unlike the estate tax, neither special use valuation nor alternate valuation date elections are allowed. In short, the value of a gift for gift tax purposes is its fair market value on the date of the gift. *See* § 2512.[19]

The gift tax regulations closely parallel the estate rules for valuing various types of property.[20] In fact, the regulations provide identical actuarial valuation tables for remainders, life estates, and annuities.[21] Further, the buy-sell valuation rules of § 2703, and the treatment of lapsing rights under § 2704 (a) and (b), apply for both estate and gift tax purposes. Section 2704(b) is considered in *Estate of Jones v. Commissioner, infra*.

Many assets, like cash or marketable securities, are simple to value. Many other assets are hard to value and generate controversy.[22] Many times the valuation disputes lead to litigation and the testimony of competing valuation experts. Consider the following excerpt from *Lefrak v. Commissioner*, T.C. Memo 1993–526, which involved the valuation of buildings:

> Section 2501 provides for a tax on gifts by individuals. Section 2512(a) provides that, in the case of a gift of property, its value at the date of the gift shall be considered the amount of such gift. Accordingly, the principal issue we must decide in the instant case is the value of the buildings conveyed on December 30, 1976, by petitioner to his children, or the trusts of which they were beneficiaries.
>
> The law with respect to the value of property for gift tax purposes is well developed. The issue is one of fact, and all factors bearing on such issue must be considered . . . . Although we must consider the entire record, we have broad discretion in selecting a method of valuation, *Estate of O'Connell v. Commissioner* . . . and the weight to be given the facts in reaching our conclusion because "finding market value is, after all, something for judgment, experience, and reason." *Colonial Fabrics, Inc. v. Commissioner* . . . . Because valuation is necessarily an approximation, the figure at which the Court arrives need not be one as to which there is specific testimony, if it is within the range of figures that may properly be deduced from the evidence. *Silverman v. Commissioner* . . . ; *Alvary v. United States* . . . .

---

[19] *See generally* JOHN A. BOGDANSKI, FEDERAL TAX VALUATION (Warren Gorham & Lamont).

[20] For example, the estate and gift tax regulations are virtually identical for valuing publicly traded stocks and bonds. *Compare* Treas. Reg. § 20.2031–2 *with* Treas. Reg. § 25.2512–2.

[21] See Treas. Reg. § 25.2512–5 (gift tax regulation), adopting Treas. Reg. § 20.2031–7 (estate tax actuarial valuation regulation).

[22] The valuation issues for family business interests is considered in the next subdivision *See* § 4.02[B], *infra*.

The regulations promulgated under § 2512 provide the standard to be used in fixing the value of the donated property:

> The value of the property is the price at which such property would change hands between a willing buyer and a willing seller, neither being under any compulsion to buy or sell, and both having reasonable knowledge of relevant facts. The value of a particular kind of property is not the price that a forced sale of the property would produce. Nor is the fair market value of an item of property the sale price in a market other than that in which such item is most commonly sold to the public, taking into account, the location of the item wherever appropriate . . . . [§ 25.2512–1, Gift Tax Regs.]

The willing buyer-willing seller standard generally is used in valuing gratuitously transferred property. *United States v. Cartwright* . . . . The standard is an objective test using hypothetical buyers and sellers in the marketplace, and is not a personalized one which envisions a particular buyer and seller. *Estate of Andrews v. Commissioner* . . . ; *Kolom v. Commissioner* . . . . Furthermore, the value of a gift is measured by the value of the property passing from the donor, not according to what the donee received. *Estate of Bright v. United States* . . . ; *Connecticut Bank & Trust Co. v. United States* . . . ; *Goodman v. Commissioner* . . . ; *Ward v. Commissioner* . . . ; *Cullman v. Commissioner* . . . ; sec. 25.2511–2(a), Gift Tax Regs. Where the donated property is encumbered by a mortgage, the value of the gift is measured by the equity in the property remaining after deduction of the mortgage indebtedness. *Laughinghouse v. Commissioner* . . . .

As is customary in valuation cases, the parties have relied extensively on expert opinion evidence to support their respective values of the interests in the buildings under the willing buyer-willing seller standard. We evaluate opinion evidence in the light of the qualifications of the expert and all other evidence of value. *Parker v. Commissioner* . . . . We are not, however, bound by the formulas or opinions proffered by expert witnesses, especially when they are contrary to our judgment, but we may reach a decision on value based on our own analysis of all the evidence in the record. *Silverman v. Commissioner* . . . ; *IT & S of Iowa, Inc. v. Commissioner* . . . . While we may adopt the opinion of an expert in its entirety, *Buffalo Tool & Die Manufacturing Co. v. Commissioner* . . . , we may be selective in the use of any portion of such an opinion. *Parker v. Commissioner* . . . .

Valuation in the gift tax setting also presents some unique problems. One of the more interesting is the attempt to include as a part of the gift an agreement that the gift will revert to the donor if it is determined to be taxable. Such a provision was held in *Commissioner v. Procter*, 142 F.2d 824 (4th Cir. 1944), *cert. denied*, 323 U.S. 765 (1944), to be against public policy because it discouraged legitimate government efforts to enforce the gift tax. Since then, courts have also ruled ineffective clauses calling for price adjustments if a court determines that the price is inadequate for gift tax purposes. *See Harwood v. Commissioner*, 82 T.C. 239 (1984), *aff'd* 786 F.2d 1174 (9th Cir. 1986), *cert. denied* 479 U.S. 1007 (1986). *Harwood* distinguished *King v. United States*, 545 F.2d 700 (10th Cir. 1976), which recognized as valid a price adjustment clause made in the ordinary course of business. Since *Harwood*, the Service has relied on *Procter* to disregard a price adjustment clause that did not require a prior court determination. *See* Rev. Rul. 86–41, 1986–1 C.B. 300. The Tax Court then followed Rev. Rul. 86–41 in *Ward v. Commissioner*, 87 T.C. 78 (1986), and held that the *Procter* result controls to avoid a price adjustment clause, even if court determination was not a prerequisite.

[B]   Valuation of Family Business Interests

Over the past 25 years, estate planners for family businesses have been able to exploit the concept of fair market value. *See* Laura Cunningham, *Remember the Alamo: the IRS Needs Ammunition in Fight Against the FLP*, 86 Tax Notes 1461 (Special Supplement, Mar. 13, 2000) (Citing articles from the 1970s that identified problems). Consider Professor Cunningham's description of *Estate of Frank v. Commissioner*, T.C. Memo. 1995-132:

> In 1988 Anthony Frank owned roughly 50.2 percent of the outstanding common stock of Magton, Inc. His wife Margaret owned approximately 13.5 percent, and the remaining shares were held by the couple's adult children. The corporation, which operated a number of beach motels, had a net asset value of close to $9,900 per share. On October 24, 1988, Anthony's son, acting under a power of attorney executed by his father some months earlier, transferred a portion of Anthony's stock representing 18 percent of the total Magton stock to Margaret, thereby reducing Anthony's stock ownership to slightly more that 32 percent, and increasing Margaret's to 31.5 percent. Two days later Anthony died, and 15 days later, on November 10, 1988, Margaret died. Both estates claimed discounts from the net asset value of the stock due to the lack of a ready market for the shares, and due to the lack of control exercisable by each decedent with respect to the corporation. The Tax Court found appropriate discounts of 30 percent for lack of marketability (bringing the per share value down to $6,910) and an additional 20 percent to reflect that fact that neither decedent held a controlling interest in the corporation, resulting in a final per share value of $5,558.
>
> Focusing solely on the minority discount, the Tax Court's ruling essentially holds that Anthony's wealth was reduced by $851,312 two days before his death.[23] The sole cause of this decline was the transfer of shares valued by the court at $503,048 to Margaret. Where did the remaining $348,246 in wealth go? As far as the federal transfer tax system was concerned, it disappeared.

The disappearing wealth phenomena occurs in large part because the fair market value for a minority interest in a family business is discounted for

---

[23] Before the gift, Anthony held 252 shares worth $ 6,910 per share, or $ 1,741,320. After the gift, he held 161 shares (a minority interest) worth $ 5,528 per share, or $ 890,008.

lack of control. Coupled with discounts for lack of marketability, it is now common-place for property values to be discounted by 35–40%. In recent years, family limited partnerships and limited liability companies (LLCs) have become the favored vehicles to set in motion the disappearing wealth phenomena. The *Jones* case, which follows, illustrates how a FLP property is formed over individually-owned property and how wealth can disappear when limited partnership interests in the FLP are then gifted.

Estate of Jones v. Commissioner

116 T.C. 121 (2001)

COHEN, J.:

Respondent determined a deficiency of $ 4,412,527 in the 1995 Federal gift tax of W.W. Jones II. The issues for decision . . . [include] Whether the transfers of assets on formation of Jones Borregos Limited Partnership (JBLP) and Alta Vista Limited Partnership (AVLP) (collectively, "the partnerships") were taxable gifts pursuant to section 2512(b) . . . and the fair market value of interests in the partnerships transferred by gift after formation. . . .

FINDINGS OF FACT

. . .

For most of his life, [W.W. Jones II] decedent worked as a cattle rancher in southwest Texas. Decedent had one son, A.C. Jones, and four daughters, Elizabeth Jones, Susan Jones Miller, Kathleen Jones Avery, and Lorine Jones Booth.

During his lifetime, decedent acquired, by gift or bequest, the surface rights to several large ranches, including the Jones Borregos Ranch, consisting of 25,669.49 acres, and the Jones Alta Vista Ranch, consisting of 44,586.35 acres. These ranches were originally acquired by decedent's grandfather and have been held by decedent's family for several generations. The land on these ranches is arid natural brushland, and commercial uses include raising cattle and hunting.

Motivated by his desire to keep the ranches in the family, decedent became involved in estate planning matters beginning in 1987. In 1994, decedent's certified public accountant suggested that decedent use partnerships as estate and business planning tools. Following up on this suggestion, A.C. Jones prepared various projections for decedent concerning a hypothetical transfer of the ranches to partnerships and the discounted values that would attach to the partnership interests for gift tax purposes.

A.C. Jones, Elizabeth Jones, Susan Jones Miller, Kathleen Jones Avery, and Lorine Jones Booth each owned a one-fifth interest in the surface rights of the Jones El Norte Ranch. They acquired this ranch by bequest from decedent's aunt in 1979. The Jones El Norte Ranch was also originally owned by decedent's grandfather and has also been owned by decedent's extended family for several generations.

Effective January 1, 1995, decedent and A.C Jones formed JBLP under Texas law. Decedent contributed the surface estate of the Jones Borregos Ranch, livestock, and certain personal property in exchange for a 95.5389-percent limited partnership interest. The entire contribution was reflected in the capital account of decedent. A.C. Jones contributed his one-fifth interest in the Jones El Norte Ranch in exchange for a 1-percent general partnership interest and a 3.4611-percent limited partnership interest.

On January 1, 1995, the same day that the partnership was effectively formed, decedent gave to A.C. Jones an 83.08-percent interest in JBLP, leaving decedent with a 12.4589-percent limited partnership interest. Decedent used a document entitled "Gift Assignment of Limited Partnership Interest" to carry out the transfer. The document stated that decedent intends that A.C. Jones receive the gift as a limited partnership interest.

Also effective January 1, 1995, decedent and his four daughters formed AVLP under Texas law. Decedent contributed the surface estate of the Jones Alta Vista Ranch in exchange for an 88.178-percent limited partnership interest. The contribution was reflected in decedent's capital account. Susan Jones Miller and Elizabeth Jones each contributed their one-fifth interests in the Jones El Norte Ranch in exchange for 1-percent general partnership interests and 1.9555-percent limited partnership interests, and Kathleen Jones Avery and Lorine Jones Booth each contributed their one-fifth interest in the Jones El Norte Ranch in exchange for 2.9555-percent limited partnership interests. The following chart summarizes the ownership structure of AVLP immediately after formation:

Partner	Percentages	Interest
Elizabeth Jones	1.0	General
	1.9555	Limited
Susan Jones Miller	1.0	General
	1.9555	Limited
Kathleen Jones Avery	2.9555	Limited
Lorine Jones Booth	2.9555	Limited
Decedent	88.178	Limited

On January 1, 1995, the same day that the partnership was effectively formed, decedent gave to each of his four daughters a 16.915-percent interest in AVLP, leaving decedent with a 20.518-percent limited partnership interest. Decedent used four separate documents, one for each daughter, entitled "Gift Assignment of Limited Partnership Interest" to carry out the transfers. Each document stated that decedent intended for his daughters to receive the gifts as limited partnership interests.

Section 5.4 of the AVLP agreement originally provided that the general partners could not sell any real property interest that was owned by the partnership without first obtaining the consent of partners owning a majority interest in the partnership. This section was later amended so that partners owning 85 percent of the partnership must consent to a sale of real property.

On January 1, 1995, the Jones Alta Vista Ranch had a fair market value of $ 10,254,860, and the Jones Borregos Ranch, livestock, and personal property that were contributed by decedent to JBLP had a fair market value of $ 7,360,997. . . . At the time that decedent transferred interests in the partnerships by gift to his children, the net asset values (NAV) of the underlying partnership assets that were held by AVLP and JBLP were $ 11,629,728 and $ 7,704,714, respectively. JBLP and AVLP had bases in their assets of $ 562,840 and $ 1,818,708, respectively.

Attached to his 1995 Federal gift tax return, decedent included a valuation report prepared by Charles L. Elliott, Jr. (Elliott), who also testified as the estate's expert at trial. The partnerships were valued on the return and by Elliott at trial using the NAV method on a "minority interest, nonmarketable" basis. Nowhere in his report did Elliott purport to be valuing assignee interests in the partnership. The valuation report arrived at an NAV for the partnerships and then applied secondary market, lack-of-marketability, and built-in capital gains discounts. The expert report concluded that a 66-percent discount from NAV is applicable to the interest in JBLP and that a 58-percent discount is applicable to the interest in AVLP. On the return, decedent reported gifts of "an 83.08 percent limited partnership interest" in JBLP valued at $ 2,176,864 and a "16.915 percent limited partnership interest" in AVLP to each of his four daughters, valued at $ 821,413 per interest.

In an affidavit executed on January 12, 1999, A.C. Jones stated that the gifts that he and his sisters received from decedent were "limited partnership interests". The sole activity of AVLP is the rental of its real property. AVLP produces an average annual yield of 3.3 percent of NAV.

OPINION

Gift at the Inception of the Partnerships

In an amendment to the answer, respondent contends that decedent made taxable gifts upon contributing his property to the partnerships. Using the value reported by decedent on his gift tax return, respondent argues that, if decedent gave up property worth $ 17,615,857 and received back limited partnership interests worth only $ 6,675,156, decedent made taxable gifts upon the formation of the partnerships equal to the difference in value.

In *Estate of Strangi v. Commissioner*, 115 T.C. 478, 489–490 (2000), a decedent formed a family limited partnership with his children and transferred assets to the partnership in return for a 99-percent limited partnership interest. After his death, his estate claimed that, due to lack-of-control and lack-of-marketability discounts, the value of the limited partnership interest was substantially lower than the value of the property that was contributed by the decedent. The Commissioner argued that the decedent had made a gift when he transferred property to the partnership and received in return a limited partnership interest of lesser value. The Court held that, because the taxpayer received a continuing interest in the family limited partnership and his contribution was allocated to his own capital account, the taxpayer had not made a gift at the time of contribution.

In *Shepherd v. Commissioner*, 115 T.C. 376, 379–381 (2000), the taxpayer transferred real property and stock to a newly formed family partnership in which he was a 50-percent owner and his two sons were each 25-percent owners. Rather than allocating contributions to the capital account of the contributing partner, the partnership agreement provided that any contributions would be allocated pro rata to the capital accounts of each partner according to ownership. Because the contributions were reflected partially in the capital accounts of the noncontributing partners, the value of the noncontributing partners' interests was enhanced by the contributions of the taxpayer. Therefore, the Court held that the transfers to the partnership were indirect gifts by the taxpayer to his sons of undivided 25-percent interests in the real property and stock. *See id.* at 389.

The contributions of property in the case at hand are similar to the contributions in Estate of Strangi and are distinguishable from the gifts in Shepherd. Decedent contributed property to the partnerships and received continuing limited partnership interests in return. All of the contributions of property were properly reflected in the capital accounts of decedent, and the value of the other partners' interests was not enhanced by the contributions of decedent. Therefore, the contributions do not reflect taxable gifts. . . .

Valuation of Decedent's Gifts of Limited Partnership Interests

A gift of property is valued as of the date of the transfer. *See* sec. 2512(a). The gift is measured by the value of the property passing from the donor, rather than by the property received by the donee or upon the measure of enrichment to the donee. *See* sec. 25.2511-2(a), Gift Tax Regs. The fair market value of the transferred property is the price at which the property would change hands between a willing buyer and willing seller, neither being under any compulsion to buy or to sell and both having reasonable knowledge of relevant facts. *See* United States v. Cartwright, 411 U.S. 546, 551 (1973); sec. 25.2512-1, Gift Tax Regs. The hypothetical willing buyer and the hypothetical willing seller are presumed to be dedicated to achieving the maximum economic advantage. *See* Estate of Davis v. Commissioner, 110 T.C. 530, 535 (1998). Transactions that are unlikely and plainly contrary to the economic interests of a hypothetical willing buyer or a hypothetical willing seller are not reflective of fair market value. *See* Estate of Strangi v. Commissioner, 115 T.C. 478, 491 (2000); Estate of Newhouse v. Commissioner, 94 T.C. 193, 232 (1990); Estate of Hall v. Commissioner, 92 T.C. 312, 337 (1989).

As is customary for valuation issues, the parties rely extensively on the opinions of their respective experts to support their differing views about the fair market value of the gifts of partnership interests. The estate relies on Elliott, a senior member of the American Society of Appraisers and a principal in the business valuation firm of Howard Frazier Barker Elliott, Inc. Respondent relies on Francis X. Burns (Burns), a candidate member of the American Society of Appraisers and a principal in the business valuation firm of IPC Group, Inc. Each expert prepared a report.

We evaluate the opinions of the experts in light of the demonstrated qualifications of each expert and all other evidence in the record. *See* Estate of Davis v. Commissioner, *supra* at 536. We are not bound by the formulae and opinions proffered by expert witnesses, especially when they are contrary to our judgment. Instead, we may reach a determination of value based on our own examination of the evidence in the record. Where experts offer contradicting estimates of fair market value, we decide what weight to give those estimates by examining the factors used by the experts in arriving at their conclusions. *See id.* Moreover, because valuation is necessarily an approximation, it is not required that the value that we determine be one as to which there is specific testimony, provided that it is within the range of figures that properly may be deduced from the evidence. *See* Silverman v. Commissioner, 538 F.2d 927, 933 (2d Cir. 1976), *affg.* T.C. Memo. 1974-285. The experts in this case agree that, in ascertaining the fair market value of each gift of interest in the partnerships, one starts with the fair market value of the underlying assets of each partnership and then applies discounts for factors that limit the value of the partnership interests.

[Valuation issues for the transferred interest in JBLP omitted]

Value of Interests in AVLP

The estate relies on the conclusions of Elliott, who opined that the value of each transferred interest in AVLP is subject to a secondary market discount of 45 percent, a discount for lack of marketability equal to 20 percent, and an additional discount for built-in capital gains. Burns opined that the transferred interests are entitled to a secondary market discount of 38 percent, a discount for lack of marketability equal to 7.5 percent, and no discount for built-in capital gains.

An owner of a 16.915-percent limited partnership interest in AVLP does not have the ability to remove a general partner. As such, a hypothetical buyer would have minimal control over the management and business operations. Also, a 16.915-percent limited partnership interest in AVLP is not readily marketable, and any hypothetical purchaser would demand a significant discount. In calculating the overall discount for the AVLP interests, both experts use data from different issues of the same publication regarding sales of limited partnership interests on the secondary market. The publication was the primary tool used by both experts.

Burns, using the May/June 1995 issue, opined that interests in real estate-oriented partnerships with characteristics similar to AVLP traded at discounts due to lack of control equal to 38 percent on January 1, 1995. The May/June 1995 issue contained data regarding the sale of limited partnership interests during the 60-day period ended May 31, 1995. Burns classified AVLP as a low-debt partnership making current distributions.

Elliott, using the May/June 1994 issue, opined that similar partnerships traded at a secondary market discount of 45 percent. The secondary market discount is an overall discount encompassing discounts for both lack of control and lack of marketability for minority interests in syndicated limited partnerships. The May/June 1994 issue contained data regarding the sale of limited partnership interests during the 60-day period ended May 31, 1994.

The estate argues that Burns' conclusion, which is based on data found in the May/June 1995 issue, is flawed because such information was not available on January 1, 1995, the date the gift was made. The estate contends that, since a gift of property is valued, pursuant to section 2512(a), as of the date of the transfer, posttransfer data cannot affect our decision. However, Burns does not use the posttransfer data to prove directly the value of the transferred interests. Instead, he uses the May/June 1995 issue to show what value would have been calculated if, on January 1, 1995, decedent had looked at transactions involving the sale of interests in similarly situated partnerships occurring at that point in time. Data regarding such transactions involving similarly situated partnerships were available on the valuation date. Therefore, the data available in the May/June 1995 issue are relevant as they provide insight into what information would have been found if, on January 1, 1995, decedent had looked at transactions occurring on or near the valuation date.

The data on which Burns relied show that interests in similarly situated partnerships were trading at a 38-percent discount from April 2 to May 31, 1995. The data on which Elliott relied show that interests in similarly situated partnerships were trading at a 45-percent discount from April 2 to May 31, 1994. Therefore, transfers of interests on or around January 1, 1995, would have been trading at a discount somewhere between 38 and 45 percent. Because the data on which Burns relied are closer in time to the transfer date of the 16.915-percent AVLP interests, we give greater weight to his determination. Recognizing that the valuation process is always imprecise, a 40-percent discount is reasonable. This discount is a reduction in value for an interest trading on the secondary market and encompasses discounts for lack of control and lack of marketability.

Elliott opines that an additional 20-percent discount for lack of marketability is applicable because the partnerships that are the subject of the data in the publication are syndicated limited partnerships. He believes that, although there is a viable market for syndicated limited partnership interests, a market for nonsyndicated, family limited partnership interests does not exist. The additional 20-percent discount opined by Elliot is also attributable to sections 8.4 and 8.5 of the AVLP agreement, which attempt to limit the transferability of interests in AVLP. In calculating the additional discount, Elliott relied on data found in various restricted stock and initial public offering studies.

Elliott acknowledges that the secondary market for syndicated partnerships is not a strong market and that a large discount for lack of marketability is already built into the secondary market discount. Although Elliott adjusts his analysis of the data found in the restricted stock and initial public offering studies to take into consideration the lack-of-marketability discount already allowed, his adjustment is inadequate. His cumulation of discounts does not survive a sanity check.

Sections 8.4 and 8.5 of the AVLP agreement do not justify an additional 20-percent discount. An option of the partnership or the other partners to purchase an interest for fair market value before it is transferred to a third party, standing alone, would not significantly reduce the value of the partnership interest. Nevertheless, the right of the partnership to elect to pay the purchase price in 10 annual installments with interest set at the minimum rate allowed by the rules and regulations of the Internal Revenue Service would increase the discount for lack of marketability. Texas courts have been willing to disregard option clauses that unreasonably restrain alienation. *See* Procter v. Foxmeyer Drug Co., 884 S.W.2d 853, 859 (Tex. App. 1994). We express no opinion whether this election is enforceable under Texas law. Because this clause would cause uncertainty as to the rights of an owner to receive fair market value for an interest in AVLP, a hypothetical buyer would pay less for the partnership interest. *See* Estate of Newhouse v. Commissioner, 94 T.C. 193, 232–233 (1990); Estate of Moore v. Commissioner, T.C. Memo. 1991-546. We believe that an additional discount equal to 8 percent for lack of marketability, to the NAV previously discounted by 40 percent, is justified.

[The Court then rejects an additional discount for built-in capital gains]

CONCLUSION

The schedules below summarize our conclusions as to fair market value for the transferred . . . AVLP limited partnership interests:

16.915-Percent Interest in AVLP

NAV of limited partnership	$ 11,629,728
	16.915%
Pro rata NAV	$1,967,168
Secondary market (40%)	(786,867)
	$ 1,180,301
Lack of marketability discount (8%)	(94,424)
Fair Market Value	$ 1,085,877

Estate of Dailey v. Commissioner, T.C. Memo. 2001-263, is the logical extension of cases such as Jones: the formation of a LLP or LLC to hold non-business assets. In *Estate of Dailey*, the taxpayer formed a LLP to hold stock in Exxon and AT&T. She then gifted minority interests in the LLP for which a 40% discount was sustained by the Tax Court.

The Service has failed in its argument that discounts based on applicable restrictions on the right to liquidate a partnership should not be taken into account based on § 2704(b). *See, e.g., Kerr v. Commissioner*, 113 T.C. 449 (1999). Although that section bars discounts due to applicable restrictions on liquidation rights in partnerships or corporations, § 2704(b)(3)(B) excepts from the definition of applicable restrictions, restrictions that are no more restrictive than under applicable state law. Quite naturally, estate planners have formed partnerships and corporations in states whose laws are very restrictive.

The Service has been unsuccessful in denying discounts in the most egregious of cases: the formation of entities by taxpayers whose death is imminent. *See, e.g., Estate of Strangi v. Commissioner*, 115 T.C. 478 (200); *Church v. United States*, 2000-1 U.S.T.C. ¶ 60,369 (W.D. Tex. 2000). *See generally* Jay A. Soled, *Use of Judicial Doctrines in Resolving Transfer Tax Controversies*, 42 Boston Coll. L. Rev. 587(2001) (includes discussion of *Estate of Murphy v. Commissioner*, T.C. Memo 1990-4721 where the Service prevailed); Walter D. Schwidetzky, *Last-gasp Estate Planning: The Formation of Family Limited Liability Entities Shortly Before Death*, 21 Va. Tax Rev. 1 (2001).

In 1986, Congress repealed the corporate income tax doctrine known as "General Utilities." That corporate tax rule provided that a corporation did not realize gain when it distributed appreciated assets to its shareholders in liquidation of the entity. As a result of the 1986 legislation, gain is recognized when the fair market value of the distributed corporate assets exceed the adjusted basis. In response to this change, taxpayers began to argue that the "built in gain" inside the entity and the corresponding corporate tax liability was a basis to discount the value of a transferred interest in a closely held corporation.

The Service's denial of a discount was overruled in *Eisenberg v. Commissioner*, 155 F.3d 50 (2nd Cir. 1998) and the Commissioner has acquiesced. 1999-4 I. R. B. 4 (January 25, 1999). A.O.D. 1999-001 summarized the Eisenberg fact pattern and the government's concession.

> The taxpayer made several transfers to her son and grandchildren of shares in her closely-held C corporation. She timely filed gift tax returns for these transfers. On these returns, the taxpayer discounted the value of the gifts by an amount she attributed to the potential capital gains tax liability of the corporation upon liquidation, or upon the sale or distribution of its assets. The Commissioner disputed this discount and issued notices of deficiency. On cross motions for summary judgment, the Tax Court found for the Commissioner. It held that:

>> no reduction in the value of closely held stock to reflect potential capital gains is warranted where the evidence fails to establish that a liquidation of the corporation or sale of the corporation's assets is likely to occur. [citations omitted.]

> *Eisenberg v. Commissioner*, T.C. Memo. 1997-483.

> The Second Circuit reversed the Tax Court and held that, in valuing closely-held stock, a discount for the built in capital gains tax liabilities could apply depending on the facts presented. The court noted that the Tax Court itself had recently reached a similar conclusion in *Estate of Davis v. Commissioner*, 110 T.C. 530 (1998).

> We acquiesce in this opinion to the extent that it holds that there is no legal prohibition against such a discount.[24] The applicability of such a discount, as well as its amount, will hereafter be treated as factual matters to be determined by competent expert testimony based upon the circumstances of each case and generally applicable valuation principles.

---

[24] Because capital gains may be avoided under partnership income tax law, the Tax Court in *Jones v. Commissioner*, *supra*, agreed with the service that a discount was not allowable in that context.

Problem

Should Congress do something to curb valuation reduction techniques? If so, what should it do? *See* Laura Cunningham, *Remember the Alamo: the IRS Needs Ammunition in Fight Against the FLP*, 86 TAX NOTES 1461 (Special Supplement, Mar. 13, 2000); William S. Blatt, *Minority Discounts, Fair Market Value, and the Culture of Estate Taxation*, 52 TAX L. REV. 225 (1997); James O. Repetti, *Minority Discounts: The Alchemy in Estate and Gift Taxation*, 50 TAX L. REV. 415 (1995).

———

[C] Donor's Retention of an Interest in Property

[1] The Rule of *Robinette*

Robinette v. Helvering

318 U.S. 184 (1943)

Mr. Justice Black delivered the opinion of the Court.

. . .

In 1936, the petitioner, Elise Paumgarten (nee Robinson), was thirty years of age and was contemplating marriage; her mother, Meta Biddle Robinette, was 55 years of age and was married to the stepfather of Miss Robinson. The three, daughter, mother and stepfather, had a conference with the family attorney, with a view to keeping the daughter's fortune within the family. An agreement was made that the daughter should place her property in trust, receiving a life estate in the income for herself, and creating a second life estate in the income for her mother and stepfather if she should predecease them. The remainder was to go to her issue upon their reaching the age of 21, with the further arrangement for the distribution of the property by the will of the last surviving life tenant if no issue existed. Her mother created a similar trust, reserving a life estate to herself and her husband and a second or contingent life estate to her daughter. She also assigned the remainder to the daughter's issue. The stepfather made a similar arrangement by will. The mother placed $193,000 worth of property in the trust she created, and the daughter did likewise with $680,000 worth of property.

The parties agree that the secondary life estates in the income are taxable gifts, and this tax has been paid. The issue is whether there has also been a taxable gift of the remainders of the two trusts . . . . [The Court then determined that there had been.] The last argument is that "in any event, in computing the value of the remainders herein, allowance should be made for the value of the grantor's reversionary interest." Here, unlike the Smith case [*Smith v. Shaughnessy*, 318 U.S. 176 (1942)], the government does not concede that the reversionary interest of the petitioner should be deducted from the total value. In the Smith case, the grantor had a reversionary interest which depended only upon his surviving his wife, and the government conceded that the value was therefore capable of ascertainment by recognized actuarial methods. In this case, however, the reversionary interest of the grantor depends not alone upon the possibility of survivorship but also upon the death of the daughter without issue who should reach the age of 21 years. The petitioner does not refer us to any recognized method by which it would be possible to determine the value of such a contingent reversionary remainder.

It may be true, as the petitioners argue, that trust instruments such as these before us frequently create "a complex aggregate of rights, privileges, powers and immunities and that in certain instances all these rights, privileges, powers and immunities are not transferred or released simultaneously." But before one who gives his property away by this method is entitled to deduction from his gift tax on the basis that he had retained some of these complex strands it is necessary that he at least establish the possibility of approximating what value he holds. Factors to be considered in fixing the value of this contingent reservation as of the date of the gift would have included consideration of whether or not the daughter would marry; whether she would have children; whether they would reach the age of 21; etc. Actuarial science may have made great strides in appraising the value of that which seems to be unappraisable, but we have no reason to believe from this record that even the actuarial art could do more than guess at the value here in question. Humes v. United States, 276 U.S. 487, 494.

The judgment of the Circuit Court of Appeals is Affirmed.

———

The *Robinette* rule is contained in Treasury Regulation § 25.2511–1(e).

[2] Actuarial Valuation

The actuarial principles that apply to estates also apply to gifts. *See* Chapter 3, § 3.03, *supra* (discussing actuarial valuation for estate tax purposes). Treasury Regulation § 25.2512-5 sets forth the valuation rules for income and remainder interests, annuities and unitrusts.

Problem

R was the beneficiary under a trust that provided income to *A* for 10 years, reversion to *R*. Two years after trust creation, *R* assigns her interest to *X*. The trust was worth $100,000 on date of assignment. Has *R* made a gift and if so, how would you value the gift?

[3] Section 2702

Enacted as part of the Revenue Reconciliation Act of 1990, § 2702 provides valuation rules for certain grantor retained interests.[25] As a general rule,

---

[25] Section 2702 also applies if the interest is retained by the grantor's spouse, ancestors of the grantor, or ancestor's of the grantor's spouse and even spouses of qualifying ancestors. *See*

trust interests retained by a grantor are valued, for gift tax purposes, at zero unless the interest retained by the grantor is a qualified interest, as explained below. The zero valuation rule for the retained interest applies if the gift taxable portion of the transfer is to a member of the grantor's family. Section 2704(c)(2) defines *family* to include the grantor's spouse or siblings, the ancestors or descendants of the grantor or the grantor's spouse, and the spouses of such siblings, ancestors, and descendants. For example, if a grantor transfers to her child a remainder interest in a trust over nonresidential property and retains the income for life, the value of the child's remainder is deemed to be equal to the value of the entire property placed in trust.

The Senate Finance Committee Report on S. 3209, the Revenue Reconciliation Act of 1990, 101st Cong., 2d Sess. 60–61 (1990), provides the rationale for § 2702:

> [T]he committee is concerned about the undervaluation of gifts valued [pursuant] to Treasury tables. Based on average rates of return and life expectancy, those tables are seldom accurate in a particular case, and therefore, may be subject to adverse selection. Because the taxpayer decided what property to give, when to give it, and often controls the return on the property, use of Treasury tables undervalues the transferred interests, in the aggregate, more often than not. Therefore, the committee determines that the valuation problems inherent in trusts and term interests in property are best addressed by valuing retained interests at zero unless they take an easily valued form—as an annuity or unitrust interest. By doing so, the bill draws upon present law rules valuing split interests in property for purposes of the charitable deduction.

To avoid the impact of § 2702, the grantor's retained interest must be a "qualified interest" which, under § 2702(b) means:

(1) an interest consisting of the right to receive fixed amounts payable, not less frequently than annually, like an annuity called a GRAT;.[26]

(2) an interest consisting of the right to receive amounts that are payable not less frequently than annually, and annually constitute a fixed percentage of the fair market value of the property in the trust, like an unitrust called a GRUT;[27] or

(3) a noncontingent remainder (reversion) after an annuity or unitrust interest.

These qualified interests are valued using § 7520, so that the gift is the difference between the value of the transferred property and the value of the retained interest. *See* § 2702(a)(2)(B). Another exception to this "zero valuation" rule is for a trust that consists solely of a residence to be used as a personal residence by the persons holding the term interests in the trust. *See*

---

§ 2702(a)(1). This rule is not applicable, however, if the spouse, ancestor, or spouse of the ancestor is the transferee, rather than being someone who retained an interest in the property transferred by the donor. *See* Treas. Reg. § 25.2702–2(d)(1), Example 3.

[26] The analogous charitable remainder annuity trust is discussed in Chapter 3.

[27] The analogous charitable remainder unitrust is discussed in Chapter 3.

§ 2702(a)(3)(A)(ii). Section 2702 will be considered in more detail in Chapter 7.

Section 2702 is comprehensively treated in Grayson M.P. McCouch, *Rethinking Section 2702*, 2 FLA. TAX REV. 99 (1994). For a detailed analysis of § 2702 and the other provisions of chapter 14, see Louis A. Mezzullo, *Valuation Rules Under Chapter 14*, Real Property, Probate and Trust Law Section, American Bar Association (1995). For a further discussion of the problems that led to the enactment of § 2702, see F. Ladson Boyle, *Evaluating Split-Interest Valuation*, 24 GA. L. REV. 1 (1989). *See also Walton v. Commissioner*, 115 T.C. 589 (2000).

Problem

It is possible to create a short-term GRAT, for example, for 2 years, where the value of the annuity is so high that there is no value to the remainder gift. These are referred to as zeroed-out GRATs. The hope is that the property will appreciate and that all of the appreciation will pass transfer tax free to the remainder beneficiary after the brief term. Can you imagine the benefits of transferring a minority interest in a FLP to a zeroed-out GRAT? *See* Leo L. Schmolka, *FLPs and GRATs: What to Do?*, 86 TAX NOTES 1473 (Special Supplement, Mar. 13, 2000).

[4]   Section 2701

For many years, taxpayers used various techniques to *freeze* the value of interests in property. One popular vehicle was the preferred stock recapitalization. Typically, the older generation of a family would transfer ownership of the common or junior interest in the entity to younger generations while retaining the preferred interest. Because much of the value of the entity was allocated to the preferred interest, the transfer of the common or junior interest generated very little if any gift tax consequences. A similar technique involved partnerships that provided some partners with a preferred, but limited right to income.

Many times the preferred interest controlled the entity, and thus, the older generation could control the payment of dividends, liquidation, conversion, puts, or call rights. By the exercise or nonexercise of these powers, the older generation was able to effect a tax free transfer of value to the younger generation.

The Revenue Reconciliation Act of 1990 included § 2701 to prevent the tax-free transfer of value using various preferred and common interests. The complex rules provide for valuation of the retained interests by assuming that all distribution (*i.e.*, dividends), liquidation, conversion, put or call rights will be exercised in a manner that will provide the lowest value for the retained interest. Like § 2702, the general rule is that a retained payment right will be valued at zero unless the right is a qualified payment right, which is defined under § 2701(c)(3). *See* §§ 2701(a)(3). The following example is adapted from Treasury Regulations § 25.2701(e), Examples 1 and 2.

Example: P, an individual, holds all the outstanding stock of X Corporation. Assume the fair market value of P's interest in X immediately prior to the transfer is $ 1.5 million. X is recapitalized so that P holds 1,000 shares of $ 1,000 par value preferred stock bearing a noncumulative dividend of $ 100 per share and 1,000 shares of voting common stock. P transfers the common stock to P's child.

Section 2701 applies to the transfer because P has transferred an equity interest (the common stock) to a member of P's family and immediately thereafter holds an applicable retained interest (the preferred stock). P's preferred dividend right is valued at zero because it is a distribution right in a controlled entity, but is not a qualified payment right. The amount of P's gift is $ 1.5 million ($ 1.5 million minus $ 0). P may elect, however, to treat the dividend right as a qualified payment right as provided in § 25.2701-2(c)(2).

The lengthy statute is the basis for even longer regulations. Detailed coverage of the § 2701 rules are beyond the scope of this text.

Problems

1. What is the amount of the gross gift on creation of the following trusts, assuming that the value of the corpus is $100,000, G is the grantor, A is unrelated to G and is 55 years old, C is unrelated to G and is 35 years old, and the applicable rate under § 7520 is 8%?

    a. Income payable to A for life.

    b. Income payable to A for life, remainder to C or C's estate.

    c. Income payable to A for life, remainder to C if C survives A.

    d. Income payable to A for life, remainder to C if C then has children surviving. At the time of the transfer C has three living children and is beyond child bearing age.

    e. Income payable to A for life, remainder to C if C then has children surviving. At the time of the transfer C is unmarried and childless.

2. What would be your answers if the facts are the same as in Problem 1 except that A was G's child? A was G's nephew?

§ 4.03   Gift Tax Deductions

Once gross gifts are determined, the amount of taxable gifts can be calculated by subtracting from gross gifts the available deductions. Only two deductions are allowed for gift tax purposes: (1) a charitable contribution deduction under § 2522, and (2) a gift tax marital deduction under § 2523. Both closely parallel the equivalent deductions in the estate tax area.

[A]   Charitable Deduction: Section 2522

Code: § 2522.

Regulations: None.

[1] Generally

As does its estate tax counterpart, § 2522(a) allows a deduction for most gifts to qualified charities.[28] Like § 2055, § 2522 places no limit on the size of qualifying gifts or on the percentage of the donor's assets which qualify for the deduction. Comparable to § 2055(d)(2), § 2522(c)(2) imposes restrictions on deductions for interests in charitable trusts and severely limits the deduction for partial dispositions outside trusts.

A donor may make inter vivos transfers to charity that qualify for both an income tax and a gift tax deduction. Complex rules under § 170 govern the income tax deduction, and penalties exist for overvaluing charitable gifts. *See* § 6662. In addition, donors are required to obtain appraisals and substantiate valuation of gifts. *See* Treas. Reg. § 1.170A–13. Before 1997, taxpayers were required to file gift tax returns for gifts to charity. *See* § 6019. In 1997, Congress amended the filing requirements to relieve taxpayers from filing gift tax returns if the donor transferred her entire interest in gifted property to the qualified charity. *See* § 6019(3). For split interest transfers, the donor is still required to file a gift tax return.

[2] Deferred Inter Vivos Charitable Giving

Corresponding to the testamentary split-interest charitable trust, an inter vivos transfer may be made to a trust similar to those described at § 3.04[D][1]. A donor may create a charitable remainder trust, a charitable lead trust, or make a gift to a pooled income fund.

Lifetime deferred giving can have gift tax consequences.[29] If a donor transfers an interest to a beneficiary other than a charitable organization, the transfer may involve a taxable gift. Whether a gift tax applies depends on the amount and circumstances of the gift.

For the donor who retains the only nonqualified interest in a qualified charitable remainder trust, there are no gift tax consequences. If the donor's spouse is the only income beneficiary, the donor has made two gifts: one to a charity and one to a noncharitable income beneficiary—the donor's spouse. Although the gift to the spouse is a terminable interest, which ordinarily would not qualify for the marital deduction, the terminable interest qualifies for the gift tax marital deduction. *See* § 2523(g). Thus, the transaction is not subject to gift tax. If on the other hand, the donor transfers an income interest to someone other than the donor's spouse, the donor has again made two gifts: one to a charity and one to a noncharitable individual. The gift to the noncharitable individual is taxable and must be valued and reported.

The above discussion assumes that the gifts were irrevocable and thus complete for gift tax purposes. However, if the donor reserves the right to revoke the interest of a noncharitable beneficiary that does not come into possession until after the donor dies, the donor has not made a complete gift to the noncharitable beneficiary. The right to revoke must be limited to a

---

[28] Surprisingly, however, the qualifying charities are not identical under both tax systems. *Compare* § 2055(a) *with* § 2522(a).

[29] Lifetime deferred giving transfers can also have estate tax consequences; these are discussed in Chapter 7, § 7.01[B][1], *infra*.

testamentary revocation. A right to revoke, exercisable during the donor's lifetime, disqualifies the charitable deduction for the transfer to the charitable remainder trust or the pooled income fund. Thus, there would be no gift tax deduction—there would be a taxable gift of the remainder interest.

Lifetime deferred giving transfers can also have estate tax consequences. For a donor who transfers property to a charitable remainder trust, but retains a life interest, most or all of the value of the trust assets are included in the donor's gross estate. [30] The estate in turn will receive an estate tax charitable deduction for the value of the remainder interest that passes to the charitable beneficiary. If no other noncharitable beneficiaries have an interest in the trust property, the charitable deduction should offset the inclusion. For a discussion of how to compute the inclusion, see Rev. Rul. 82–105, 1982–1 C.B. 133, in Chapter 7.

[B]　Marital Deduction: Section 2523

Code: § 2523.

Regulations: None.

[1]　In General

Under § 2523, a donor may deduct the value of all gifts of property to the donee spouse, subject to the same type of limitations that apply to the estate tax marital deduction. As explained by the Senate Finance Committee (S. Rep. No. 97–144, Economic Recovery Tax Act of 1981, 97th Cong., 1st Sess. 127 (1981)):

> [A] husband and wife should be treated as one economic unit for purposes of estate and gift taxes, as they generally are for income tax purposes. Accordingly, no tax should be imposed on transfers between husband and wife.

The deduction applies for transfers of property of any type, whether separate property or community property, subject only to two limitations. Gifts to spouses who are not United States citizens are not deductible. *See* § 2523(i). Instead, annual exclusion gifts to noncitizen spouses are permitted and the maximum amount of the annual exclusion is $100,000 rather than $10,000 ($11,000 in 2002). *See* § 2523(i)(2). The $100,000 is indexed for inflation since 1998 and is $110,000 in 2002. *See* Rev. Proc. 2001-59, I.R.B. 2001-52 §4.19(2).

The second limitation generally parallels the estate nondeductible terminable interest rule, with similar exceptions. [31] There are five categories of exceptions to the nondeductible terminable interest rule of § 2523(b). First, if no one receives an interest in property as a result of the termination, or if the donor did not create the terminable interest, the spouse's terminable interest qualifies for the gift tax marital deduction. Second, gifts to spouses qualify for the marital deduction if the spouse is given both a life estate and

---

[30] *See* Rev. Rul. 82–105.

[31] *See* Chapter 3, § 3.04[C][4], *supra*. The legislative history provides that the gift tax marital deduction rules are to be construed by applying the estate tax marital deduction rules. S. Rep. No. 1013, Part 2, 80th Cong., 2d Sess. 29.

a general power to appoint the remainder or the remainder is to pass to the donee-spouse's estate. *See* § 2523(e). Third, the deduction is allowed if the transferred interest qualifies as "qualified terminable interest property" (QTIP), using the estate tax definitions and rules, and the donor makes a QTIP election. *See* § 2523(f). Fourth, a marital deduction is allowed for a spouse's interest in a qualified charitable remainder. *See* § 4.03[A][2], *supra*. Finally, a gift tax marital deduction is allowed on the creation of joint tenancies between spouses. *See* § 2523(d).

Because most inter-spousal transfers produce no tax, § 6019(a) exempts inter-spousal transfers qualifying under § 2523 from gift tax filing requirements. The only exception is if the deduction is claimed as a result of a QTIP election. The election must be made on or before the due date for the return, taking into account applicable extensions of time. *See* § 2523(f)(4).

The inter vivos QTIP trust represents an important estate planning tool for clients. As was discussed in chapter 3, § 3.04[C][4], *supra*, significant estate tax savings are achieved when the value of each spouse's estate is approximately equal, or both spouses have an estate equal to the exemption equivalent. Notwithstanding the tax advantages, the monied spouse may be reluctant to transfer substantial assets to the other spouse just to save estate taxes. This is most acute when it is a second marriage and both spouses have children by prior marriages. The inter vivos QTIP trust solves the dilemma. The monied spouse can transfer assets to a QTIP trust for the other spouse and retain control of the QTIPed assets when the spouse dies. The monied spouse's estate is reduced by the amount transferred to the QTIP trust and the other spouse's estate is increased, thus, providing estate equalization in the event the nonmonied spouse dies first.

Some donors will hesitate to lose economic benefit of the property transferred to the QTIP in the event that the donee-spouse dies first. The donor does not want the remaindermen to receive the trust assets until both spouses die. The gift tax marital deduction regulations permit the donor to retain an income interest in the QTIP trust following the donee's life interest without the assets of the QTIP trust being included in the donor's estate. *See* Treas. Reg. § 25.2523(f)–1(f), Examples 10 and 11. Thus, the donor may transfer assets to a trust for the benefit of the donee-spouse for life and retain a secondary life interest in the QTIP trust assets. The transfer will qualify for the gift tax marital deduction, if a QTIP election is made, and the trust assets will be taxed in the donee-spouse's estate under § 2044. However, the trust assets will not be included in the donor's estate unless the personal representative of the donee-spouse's estate makes an estate tax QTIP election for the trust.

[2] Section 2519

Code: §§ 2207A(b) and 2519.

Regulations: None.

Section 2519 parallels the operation of estate tax § 2044 by imputing a transfer by the donee-spouse or surviving spouse when a QTIP election was previously made. Specifically, if the donee or surviving spouse transfers any part of her income interest in a QTIP trust, § 2519 deems a transfer of all other interests in the trust. *See* Treas. Reg. § 25.2519–1(g), Examples 1 and 2. The Service also takes the position that the donee-spouse's or surviving spouse's purchase of the remainder interest triggers application of § 2519. *See* Priv. Ltr. Rul. 199936036.

When the spouse gratuitously transfers her entire income interest, § 2511 in conjunction with § 2519 appears to result in a gift tax on the entire value of the trust. However, § 2207A(b), as interpreted by Treasury Regulation § 20.2207A–1(e), entitles the spouse to recover the gift taxes on the remainder interests from the trustee of the QTIP trust. Because the spouse is liable for the gift tax, this scheme effectively results in a net gift and the Service has agreed. *See* Priv. Ltr. Rul. 200044034 (on assignment of interest). Priv. Ltr. Rul. 200122036 (on renunciation of interest). *See generally Revisiting Purchases of Remainder Interests in QTIP Trusts*, 27 Est. Plng. 99 (2000).

In conjunction with § 2044, § 2519 ensures that if property is allowed to pass tax free between spouses based on a QTIP election, the property will be taxed to the donee spouse or the donee spouse's estate. The property is ultimately taxed on the earlier of the date on which the donee spouse disposes of all or part of the qualifying terminable interest, by gift, sale, or otherwise, during the spouse's lifetime, or on the donee spouse's death. For a general discussion of § 2519, *see* Michael J. Jones and Deeann L. Thompson, *Inter Vivos Transfer of a QTIP Interest*, 57 Inst. on Fed. Tax'n 19-1 (1999).

Problems

1. In year 1, *H* creates an irrevocable trust of $100,000 with income to *W* for life, remainder to his Son. *H* makes a QTIP election. In year 3, when the trust corpus is still worth $100,000, *W*, age 65, gifts her entire income interest to Daughter. *W* is in the 50% gift tax bracket and has used up her Applicable Exclusion Amount. What is the value of the gift imputed to *W* assuming the §7520 interest rate is 8%?

2. In year 1, *H* creates an irrevocable trust of $100,000 with income to his wife, *W*, for life, reversion to *H*. *H* makes a QTIP election so that none of the $100,000 is subject to gift tax or to a reduction in the Applicable Exclusion Amount. In year 2, *H* dies when the trust is worth $100,000 and *W* is 71. One year later, *W* transfers her income interest in the trust to *D*. What are the tax consequences in each year?

3. In year 1, *W* creates an irrevocable trust of $100,000 with income to *H* for life, then income to W for life, if she survives *H*, remainder to his Daughter. *W* makes a QTIP election. In year 3, when the trust corpus is still worth $100,000, *W* dies.

a. Are there any estate tax issues for *W*'s estate?

b. Would your answer in (a) be different if *H* died in year 2?

[C] Limitation on Deductions: Section 2524

As a general rule, there are no quantitative limitations on either the marital or charitable deductions. Because the Code provides for deductions in addition to the § 2503(b) exclusion, however, it is occasionally necessary to interrelate the operation of the exclusion with the marital deduction under § 2523 and the charitable deduction under § 2522. Both sections provide for deductions equal to the full value of the property transferred, without taking into account the existence of the annual exclusion. Thus, at first blush, it would appear possible to deduct and exclude more than the value of the transfer (up to but not in excess of the § 2503(b) present interest annual exclusion). Under § 2524, however, deductions are limited to the "extent that the gifts . . . are included in the amount of gifts against which such deductions are applied." Because § 2503(b) operates to exclude value from gifts, it reduces the amount of gifts against which deductions are applied (*i.e.,* gross gifts). Therefore, it prevents any excess deductions.

> **Example:** In 2002, S transfers $50,000 to a qualifying charity and $20,000 to S's daughter. Because the gift to the charity qualifies for the gift tax annual exclusion, only a charitable deduction of $39,000 is allowed as a result of § 2524. After the annual exclusion for the gift to the daughter, a taxable gift of $9,000 results for the year. If instead a $50,000 charitable contribution deduction were allowed on top of the annual exclusion for the charitable gift, there would be no taxable gift in 2002—an unacceptable result because there would have been a $9,000 taxable gift if S only made a gift to the daughter in 2002.

§ 4.04 Unification Revisited

Code: §§ 2001(b), (f); 2504(c); and 6501(c)(9).

Regulations: Teas. Reg. §§ 20.2001-1; 25.2504-2; 301.6501(c)-1(f).

Taxable gifts are taken into account when calculating subsequent gift and estate taxes. The finality of valuation results was open to question, however. In Rev. Rul. 84–11, 1984–1 C.B. 201, the Service ruled that, in certain cases, improperly valued gifts could be revalued in determining the gift tax consequences for later gifts, even though the statute of limitations had run for assessing any additional gift tax. Specifically, Rev. Rul. 84–11 holds that although § 2504(c) requires that the value used for prior gifts be respected when a gift tax "has been assessed or paid" on the gift, revaluation is not barred if the earlier gift produced no gift tax liability because of the applicable credit amount.

Even more significantly, the Service took the position that for purposes of determining § 2001 "adjusted taxable gifts" at the time of a decedent's death, valuation of lifetime gifts could be re-examined. Most courts agreed with the Service. *See Evanson v. United States,* 30 F.3d 960 (9th Cir. 1994); *Stalcup v. United States,* 946 F.2d 1125 (5th Cir. 1991); *Estate of Smith v. Commissioner,* 94 T.C. 872 (1990). *But see Boatman's First Nat'l Bank v. United States,* 705 F. Supp. 1407 (W.D. Mo. 1988).

In 1997, Congress settled the matter with the adoption of § 2001(f) and the modification of § 6501(c)(9). Moreover, Congress also added a provision that permits a taxpayer to seek a declaratory judgment in the Tax Court whenever the Service issues a final notice of redetermination of value. *See* § 7477. This makes a judicial review of the Service's action available even if the change in value does not cause the payment of taxes (because of the applicable credit amount).

In response to these legislative changes, the Treasury Department issued regulations that treat the valuation of gifts made after August 5, 1997 differently from gifts made before August 6, 1997. *See generally* Edward Kessel and Joan Agran, *Final Regs. On Disclosure of Gifts Liberalized, But Problems Remain*, 27 EST. PLNG. 147 (2000). [32] When a taxpayer makes a gift after August 5, 1997, valuation of the gift is final when the statute of limitations expires if the taxpayer complies with the "adequate disclosure" reporting requirements of Treasury Regulation § 301.6501(c)-1(f). The general premise of the regulation is that the Internal Revenue Service must be reasonably apprised "of the nature of the gift and the basis for the value so reported." *See* Treas. Reg. § 301.6501(c)-1(f)(2). The regulation enumerates the information that must be disclosed: the return must describe the property, identify the donee and relationship between the donor and the donee, explain in detail the methodology used to value the property, and disclose any position taken on the return that is contrary to Treasury Department regulations or revenue rulings. Alternatively, the donor may submit an appraisal report prepared by a qualified appraiser. *See* Treas. Reg. § 301.6501(c)-1(f)(3) (defining qualified appraiser and setting forth necessary contents of the appraisal report.)

Taxpayers who make transfers that are not intended to be taxable gifts may wish to report such transfers and make adequate disclosures to start the running of the statute of limitations. *See generally* Michael D. Mulligan, *Adequate Disclosure: Its Impact on Gift Tax Return Strategies*, 28 EST. PLAN. 3 (2001).

Example: In 2002, taxpayer makes a gift of present interest in a family limited partnership. Based on aggressive discounts, the taxpayer believes that the interest is worth just under the annual exclusion amount.

Although the taxpayer is not required to file a gift tax return, she may be well-advised to do so to start the running of the statute of limitations.

For decedents' estates, adjusted taxable gifts may not be revalued for transfers made after August 5, 1997 if the decedent filed a gift tax return and satisfied the adequate disclosure rules of Treasury Regulation § 301.6501(c)-1(f). *See* Treas. Reg. § 20.2001-1(b).

---

[32] Treasury Regulation § 25.2504-2(a) provides valuation finality for gifts made before August 6, 1997 only if a gift tax was assessed or paid and the time for assessment of tax has expired. For gifts that did not result in the assessment or payment of a tax or for issues other than valuation, the regulation does not provide finality. Treasury Regulation § 20.2001-1(a) provides that when gifts were made prior to August 6, 1997, the value of the gift may be redetermined for purposes of "adjusted taxable gifts."

Chapter 5

GENERATION-SKIPPING TRANSFER TAX BASICS[1]

This Chapter deals with the taxation of transfers that skip, or may skip, generations, such as transfers from grandparents to grandchildren. As used in this Chapter, the term "generation-skipping transfers" refers to the spectrum of transactions in which the transferor conveys property to, or for the benefit of, an individual more than one generation removed from himself. Thus, generation-skipping transfers include the simple hypothetical above, as well as more complex arrangements in which, for example, a trust spans three or four generations, with successive or concurrent interests in each.

The Chapter first provides an historical background for generation-skipping transfer (GST) taxation. Thereafter, the structure of the GST tax system, as enacted by the Tax Reform Act of 1986, and as later amended, is explored. This foundation will enable you to understand the impact of GST taxes on issues considered later in this book.

§ 5.01 Historical Background

The ability to avoid estate or gift taxation by making transfers that skip at least one generation level has long been recognized.[2] Generation-skipping has been possible under the estate and gift tax system because the taxable event only occurs when an individual both owns and transfers property.[3]

The prototypical generation-skipping arrangement involves a trust for a child for life, with remainder to a grandchild. When the child dies, the property is not subject to estate tax because the child's interest in the property terminates at death. If, instead, the child had received the property outright, the property would be subject to estate tax at the child's death when she died and transmitted the property to her children. Thus, the prototypical arrangement avoids an estate tax at the child's generation level.

Congress perceived generation-skipping transfers as a problem because these transfers enabled wealthy families to undermine the progressive tax

---

[1] Portions of this Chapter are adapted from Ira Mark Bloom, *Federal Generation-Skipping Transfer Taxation: How Should the States Respond?* 51 ALB. L. REV. 817 (1987).

[2] *See, e.g.,* Erwin N. Griswold, *Powers of Appointment and the Federal Estate Tax,* 52 HARV. L. REV. 929, 959–60 (1939); Harold Weinstock, *The A-B-C's of Generation Skipping Trusts,* 52 TAXES 68 (1974). A proposal for taxation of generation-skipping transfers was made as early as 1941. *See* Willard C. Mills, III *Transfers from Life Tenant to Remaindermen in Relation to the Federal Estate Tax,* 19 TAXES 195 (1941). Major generation-skipping proposals can be traced to that date. *See* Gilbert Paul Verbit, *Annals of Tax Reform: The Generation-Skipping Transfer,* 25 U.C.L.A. L. REV. 700, 702–16 (1978).

[3] Technically, estate and gift taxation may also apply when an individual does not own property, but exercises or possesses a general power of appointment over property. *See* §§ 2041, 2514.

system by avoiding the imposition of estate tax at various generations.[4] Congress responded to this problem by enacting a GST tax system in the Tax Reform Act of 1976. The 1976 GST tax system was a separate succession tax, imposed at the termination of the intervening estate, payable from the property in the trust, and calculated to approximate the transfer tax effect the property would have if it passed to the recipient from the recipient's parent.[5]

The 1976 GST tax system did not, however, effectively prevent avoidance of transfer taxes at every generation level. The weakness of the system was that it subjected property to GST tax only if a person in a skipped generation received some enjoyment of the property.[6] For example, the *life estate to child, remainder to grandchild* sequence was subject to GST tax at the death of the child because she had enjoyed the property. Thus, under the 1976 system, it was easy to avoid the GST tax by completely bypassing a skipped generation. For example, an outright devise to a grandchild, or a devise in trust for a grandchild, was not subject to GST tax because no person in the child's generation level enjoyed the property.[7]

In addition to being avoidable, the 1976 GST tax system suffered from being both fantastically complex and overly broad in that it contained no general exemption level. Thus, generation-skipping transfers, however small, could be subject to tax, contrary to the purpose of the GST tax system. In effect, the system was a trap for the unwary. These weaknesses in the tax forced Congress to rethink the 1976 GST tax,[8] and restructure it in 1986.

With the Tax Reform Act of 1986, Congress repealed the GST tax system it had enacted ten years earlier, and replaced it with a new generation-skipping tax system.[9] The 1986 system substantially broadened the reach of the tax,

---

[4] Although generation-skipping arrangements are theoretically available to everyone, the vast majority of families find it feasible only to make outright transfers of property. This undoubtedly stems, in part, from the uncertainty of less wealthy individuals about whether medical and other emergency expenses would be met if their principal were tied up in trust. *See Federal Estate and Gift Taxes: Public Hearings and Panel Discussions Before the House Comm. on Ways and Means*, 94th Cong., 2d Sess. 476 n. 1 (1976) (Statement of Thomas J. Reese).

[5] Other generation-skipping proposals had been studied and reported by the American Law Institute. *See* AMERICAN LAW INSTITUTE, FEDERAL ESTATE AND GIFT TAXATION (1969).

[6] *See generally* Ira Mark Bloom, *The Generation-Skipping Loophole: Narrowed, But Not Closed, By the Tax Reform Act of 1976*, 53 WASH. L. REV. 31 (1977); RICHARD B. COVEY, GENERATION-SKIPPING TRANSFERS IN TRUST (3rd ed. 1978); Joseph M. Dodge, *Generation-Skipping Transfers after the Tax Reform Act of 1976*, 125 U. PA. L. REV. 1265 (1977); Richard B. Stephens & Dennis Calfee, *Skip to M'Loo*, 32 TAX L. REV. 443 (1977).

[7] Estate planners understood that generation-skipping transfer taxation could be avoided by the device of *layering*, whereby separate trusts or bequests were created for each generation.

[8] Considerable time was expended on unsuccessful efforts to repeal, but not replace, the old generation-skipping system. *See, e.g.*, Additional Estate and Gift Tax Issues, 1981: *Hearings on S. 1695 Before the Subcomm. on Estate and Gift Taxation of the Senate Comm. on Finance*, 98th Cong., 1st Sess. (1981); *Estate Tax Issues, 1983: Hearings on S. 1252 Before the Subcomm. on Estate and Gift Taxation of the Senate Comm. on Finance*, 98th Cong., 1st Sess. (1983) (considering generation-skipping repeal). *But see* Ira Mark Bloom, *Needed: An Effective Generation-Skipping Tax*, 13 TAX NOTES 1142 (1981).

[9] The Tax Reform Act of 1986 repealed the 1976 generation-skipping tax system. Tax Reform Act of 1986, 99 Pub. L. No. 514, § 1433(c) 100 Stat. 2731 (1986) [Act]. The Act replaced it with a new generation-skipping system. Act, at §§ 1431–1433.

and added an increased exemption. Moreover, the new system is comparatively easier to understand. Simplification resulted from taxing generation-skipping transfers at a flat rate (the maximum federal estate tax rate), rather than attempting to determine and mimic an additional federal gift or estate tax that would have been paid if the property were taxed at each generation. By using the highest marginal rate, Congress assumed that taxable generation-skipping transfers are made predominantly by the wealthiest people.

Between 2002 and 2009, the maximum GST tax rate deceases in conformity with the reduction in maximum estate tax rates discussed in Chapters 1 and 2. Between 2004 and 2009, the amount of transfers that are exempt from the GST increase in lockstep with increases in the estate tax Applicable Exclusion Amount discussed in Chapters 1 and 2. Although the 2001 Tax Act repeals the GST tax for transfers occurring in 2010, the GST tax will be back in full force on January 1, 2011 unless Congress decides otherwise. *See* Footnote 25 on page 8.

§ 5.02　Structure of the Generation-Skipping Transfer Tax System[10]

Code: §§ 2601, 2602, 2611, 2612, 2613, 2651, and 2652.

Regulations: Treas. Reg. §§ 26.2611–1, 26.2612–1(d), 26.2652–1(a)(1)–(a)(2), and –6, Example 1.

Section 2601 imposes a tax on generation-skipping transfers that occur after October 22, 1986.[11] There are three types of generation-skipping transfers: a direct skip, a taxable termination, and a taxable distribution. *See* § 2611(a). Section 2602 provides the method for imposing the GST tax: multiply the taxable amount of the generation-skipping transfer by the applicable rate.

The GST tax is designed to supplement the estate tax system. It is not surprising, therefore, that the technical operation of the GST tax system depends on an understanding of the gift and estate tax systems. For example, as explained in the next section, a transfer constitutes a direct skip only if the transfer is also subject to either gift or estate taxation. Conversely, neither a taxable termination nor a taxable distribution occur simultaneously with the imposition of either an estate tax or a gift tax.

Application of the tax starts with a determination of the "transferor." Under § 2652(a) and Treasury Regulation § 26.2652–1(a)(1), the transferor is the person who was most recently subject to estate or gift taxes with respect to the property. Generally, the transferor is the decedent in the case of a testamentary transfer, and the donor in the case of a transfer subject to gift taxes. There are exceptions, however. For example, a person with a general power of appointment is a transferor after the exercise or lapse of the power (even

---

[10] For a more detailed discussion of the GST tax, see CAROL HARRINGTON ET AL., GENERATION-SKIPPING TRANSFER TAX (Warren, Gorham & Lamont 1995).

[11] Generally, generation-skipping transfers made before October 23, 1986 are grandfathered under the effective date rules. However, some transfers before October 23, 1986 are taxable; particularly irrevocable, inter vivos trusts created after September 25, 1985. *See* § 5.02[A][2], *infra.*

by death). Also, as discussed below, once the GST tax applies, the generation of the transferor changes.

The key to the application of the GST tax is the determination of *skip persons*. If no skip persons are involved in the transfer, the trust is not subject to the GST tax. A skip person is defined by § 2613(a) as anyone who is two or more generations below the generation of the grantor.[12] For example, a decedent's grandchildren are skip persons.

For purposes of the GST tax, whether someone is related to the transferor is determined by looking up to the grandparent of the transferor and then counting down generations. *See* § 2651(b)(1), (b)(2). The following rules help resolve the application of the rule when an individual may be assigned to more than one generation or is not directly related to the transferor.

1. Half-bloods are treated as whole bloods, and persons legally adopted count as related (but a relative cannot be moved up a generation by adoption). *See* § 2651(b)(3).

2. A spouse (or former spouse) of a related individual is treated as being in the same generation as the related person. *See* § 2651(c).

3. Individuals who may be assigned to more than one generation are assigned to the youngest generation. *See* § 2651(f)(1).[13] For example, someone who marries a cousin will not move the cousin up the GST assignment hierarchy, but may move him down.

4. Beneficiaries who are not related to the grantor are assigned to the child's generation if the beneficiary is more than 12½ years younger than the Grantor, but not more than 37½ years younger. Beneficiaries who are more than 37½ years younger are assigned to lower generations in 25-year groups (*i.e.,* 37½ to 62½, 62½ to 87½, etc.).

5. If an estate, trust, partnership, or corporation is a beneficiary, the generation assignment is based on who owns the beneficial interests in the entity. *See* § 2651(f)(2).[14]

[A]   Direct Skips

Code: §§ 2612, 2613, 2623, 2651, and 2652.

Regulations: Treas. Reg. §§ 26.2612–1(a),–1(e)(2) through–1(e)(3), and–1(f), Examples 1, 2, 6, 7.

Direct skips can be of several types. The easiest to understand is an outright transfer that skips generations. Other types of direct skips are possible, as described below.

---

[12] Conversely, § 2613(b) defines a nonskip person as any person who is not a skip person.

[13] Section 511 of the Taxpayer Relief Act of 1997 amended § 2651 by renumbering existing subsection (e) as (f) and adding a new subsection (e), effective on GST taxable events occurring after December 31, 1997.

[14] *Id.*

[1] Outright Transfers

Section 2612(c)(1) generally defines a direct skip as a transfer to a skip person of an interest in property that is subject to gift or estate tax. The simplest examples involve outright transfers.

Example 1: Lifetime Direct Skip. Grandparent makes a taxable gift of $100,000 to Grandchild in 2002, having previously exhausted the gift tax annual exclusion and the unified credit amount. The Grandparent is in the 50% gift tax bracket.

This transfer constitutes a direct skip. The first element of a direct skip is satisfied: the transfer is clearly subject to gift tax. *See* Chapter 4. Grandparent, as donor, will incur a gift tax liability of $50,000. Second, the transfer of $100,000, Grandparent's entire interest in the property, is also a transfer of an interest in property for GST purposes. Finally, the transfer is to a skip person because Grandchild is two generations below the transferor, Grandparent, who is the donor for gift tax purposes. *See* § 2652(a)(1)(B).[15] Grandchild is a skip person, as defined by § 2613(a)(1), because Grandchild is assigned to the second generation below Grandparent. *See* § 2651(b)(1).

Once a transfer is determined to be a direct skip, the tax is calculated by applying the applicable rate to the taxable amount. Section 2623 prescribes that the value of the property received by the transferee is used to determine the taxable amount. Although "transferee" is an undefined term, Grandchild, as the recipient of the gift, is clearly the transferee in Example 1. In turn, § 2624 provides that the value of the property will be its gift tax value, $100,000 in Example 1. Thus, assuming an applicable rate of 50%,[16] the GST tax imposed will be $50,000 because no tax credit is allowed for direct skips. *See* § 2604. Grandparent, as transferor, will be required to pay a GST tax of $50,000. *See* §§ 2603(a)(3), 2662.[17]

At this point it appears that Grandparent, having made a taxable gift of $100,000, will be required to pay a gift tax of $50,000 and a GST tax of $50,000. The gift tax, however, is more than $50,000 because § 2515 provides that any taxable gift must be increased by the amount of any GST tax on the transferor of the direct skip gift. Under § 2515, the taxable gift is $150,000 (the original $100,000 taxable gift plus the $50,000 GST tax), and the gift tax imposed is $75,000 (the original $50,000 plus a $25,000 gift tax on the amount of the $50,000 GST tax). In sum, the total tax on the transfer is $125,000 (the sum of a $50,000 GST tax and a $75,000 gift tax). Thus, the gift requires that Grandparent expend $225,000 for Grandchild to receive $100,000 when the transfer is fully taxable for gift tax and GST tax purposes.

---

[15] If split gift treatment were elected, Grandparent's spouse would be the transferor of one-half of the gift. *See* § 2652(a)(2).

[16] For purposes of illustrating the general taxation of generation-skipping transfers in this and the following examples, the applicable rate is assumed at 50%. The actual rate may vary from zero to 50% in 2002. In years after 2002, the maximum rate will be lower than 50% because the maximum GST tax rate is the maximum estate tax rate. Determination of the rate is discussed at § 5.02[D][2], *infra*.

[17] The GST tax must be reported on Form 709, U.S. Gift (and Generation-Skipping Transfer) Tax return.

The purpose of § 2515 is to equate the tax effects of direct skips by gift with those that would result for lifetime transfers that did not direct skip, but passed through two successive generations at the top tax bracket. To illustrate the point, consider the following example which assumes that the donor has exhausted the unified credit against the gift tax, that the gift tax annual exclusion is not available, and that the gifts will be taxed at a 50% rate:

Example 2: In 2002, Grandparent transfers $150,000 to Child. Grandparent pays a gift tax of $75,000 on the $150,000. With the $150,000, Child transfers $100,000 to Grandchild and pays gift tax of $50,000. This assumes that the gift by Child to Grandchild is taxable at the maximum gift tax rate of 50% and the annual exclusion is not available.

In Example 2, the combined gift tax is $125,000. Grandchild receives $100,000. This is, as illustrated in Example 1, the result that § 2515 produces for direct skips by gift.

Direct skips can also occur as a result of a devise or bequest:

Example 3: Grandparent devises $100,000 to her Grandchild. Grandparent's will provides that all death taxes, but not GST taxes, are payable from the residuary estate, rather than from pecuniary devises. Grandparent dies in 2002.

In Example 3, a direct skip occurs because:

1. There is a transfer to a skip person of an interest in property that is subject to estate tax. *See* § 2612(c)(1).

2. The property required to fund the devise will be property owned at death and, therefore, includable in Grandparent's gross estate under § 2033. Grandparent is the transferor for GST tax purposes because the property is subject to estate tax.[18] *See* § 2652(a). Further, Grandparent has clearly transferred her entire interest in the $100,000.

3. Grandchild is a skip person because, as a relative of Grandparent, the transferor, she is assigned to the second generation below the generation assignment of Grandparent. *See* §§ 2613(a)(1), 2651(b)(1).

The taxable amount in Example 3 initially appears to be $100,000 because the taxable amount is the estate tax value of the property received by the transferee.[19] *See* §§ 2623, 2624(a). This conclusion, however, ignores the statutory requirement that Grandparent's personal representative first pay the GST tax imposed from the property constituting the direct skip. *See* § 2603(b). Note that the GST tax imposed will be charged to the devise because Grandparent's will did not specifically refer to the GST tax when directing that all death taxes be paid out of the residue. *See* § 2603(b).

The legislative history under the Tax Reform Act of 1986 explains that direct skips are taxed on a tax exclusive basis by stating that "the amount subject to tax is the value [net of tax] of the property received by the transferee," or

---

[18] Absent an election, however, the decedent's spouse will be the transferor over QTIP property. *See* § 2652(a)(3); § 5.03[A][2], *infra.*

[19] The alternate and special use valuation provisions might control in some situations. *See* § 2624(b).

the tax is imposed on a *tax-exclusive* basis. General Explanation of the Tax Reform Act of 1986, at 1266 (Joint Committee on Taxation 1987).

In effect, the GST tax imposed (the product of the taxable amount and the applicable rate, which is assumed to be 50%) cannot be determined without knowing the taxable amount. In turn, the taxable amount cannot be determined without first knowing the amount of generation-skipping transfer tax imposed. The analogy is similar to that of a net gift as discussed in Chapter 4. There is an algebraic solution to this interdependent variable problem. Assuming a 50% rate, the value of the generation-skipping transfer in a direct skip will be 66.667% of the value of the devise.[20] Thus, the taxable amount in the example will be $66,667, which, based on the 50% rate, produces a GST tax of $33,333.

Ultimately, Grandchild inherits $66,667 because no credit for state GST taxes is allowed for direct skips. *See* § 2604(a). Note also that there is no estate tax provision comparable to § 2515, so no adjustment is necessary for the amount of the GST tax.

[2] Direct Skips in Trust

So far, only outright transfers that constitute direct skips have been considered. Transfers in trust may also constitute direct skips. The following example illustrates how a testamentary trust may constitute a direct skip:

Example 4: Direct Skip in Trust. Grandparent creates a trust under his will in the amount of $100,000 with income payable to Grandchild until age 25, remainder to Grandparent's Child. The will specifically provides that all taxes, including GST taxes, are payable from the residue.

Recall that a direct skip occurs when a transfer is subject to estate tax if the interest in property is transferred to a skip person. *See* § 2612(c)(1). By definition, a trust is a skip person if all interests in the trust are held by skip persons. *See* § 2613(a)(2)(A). Further, this trust is a skip person even though Child is a beneficiary assigned to only the first generation below Grandparent, and, therefore, appears to give the trust a beneficiary who is not a skip person. *See* § 2613(b). Section 2652(c)(1)(A) alters that tentative result by providing that a person does not have an interest in trust for GST tax purposes if that person only has the future right to receive trust income or corpus. *See also* Treas. Reg. §26.2612-1(e)(1). A person does have an interest in property held in trust if that person has the present right to trust income or corpus, or is a current, permissible recipient of trust income or corpus. In Example 4 (Direct Skip in Trust), Grandchild has the only interest in property held in trust;

---

[20] The actual generation-skipping transfer equals the difference between the amount of the pre-tax devise and the amount of the GST tax. Based on a 50% GST tax rate in 2002, the amount of the tax is .50 times the amount of the generation-skipping transfer. Thus, in formula terms:

Devise before tax = devise after tax + .50 (devise after tax)

Algebra changes the formula to:

Devise after tax = devise before GST tax/1.50, or the devise times 66.667%.

Child's interest is a future right to receive the corpus. Therefore, Child's interest is ignored, and the trust is a skip person.[21]

A transfer not in trust may be deemed to be a transfer in trust for GST tax purposes if the arrangement has substantially the same effect as a trust. *See* § 2652(b)(1). An example would be a devise of a life estate in Blackacre by Grandparent to Grandchild 1, remainder to Grandchild 2. Because the transaction has the same effect as a transfer in trust, it is treated as a transfer to a trust that, because no nonskip person owns an interest, is a skip person. *See* §§ 2612(c)(1), 2613(a)(2)(A), 2651(b), 2652(b), (c).

Because the trust in the Example 4 is a skip person, the requirements for a direct skip are met. The interest in property that the trust (actually the trustee) receives is the legal interest, or the full $100,000. Accordingly, the taxable amount of the direct skip will be $100,000 because no taxes were chargeable to the devise. *See* §§ 2603, 2623, 2624. A trust may also be a skip person if no person has an "interest" in the trust, so long as no nonskip person can ever receive any of the trust property. *See* § 2613(a)(2)(B). The classic application of this rule is to accumulation trusts. For example, the trust would be a skip person if income were to be accumulated for ten years, with trust property then payable to Grandchild.

Problems

1. Would a direct skip occur if a testator devised property to:

a. A second cousin who was 50 years younger than the testator?

b. A child of the testator's spouse who was 50 years younger than the testator?

c. An unrelated person who was 50 years younger than the testator?

2. In Example 1 (Outright Lifetime Direct Skip) above, Grandparent needed $225,000 to pay all of the taxes and for the Grandchild to receive $100,000. Assume Grandparent did not make the gift, but owned the $225,000 at death. Based on a 50% GST tax and estate tax rate and assuming the unified credit and GST exemption have been exhausted, how much after taxes could Grandchild receive from Grandparent if taxes were payable out of the $225,000?

3. What is the result in Problem 2 if the estate taxes and GST taxes are not paid out of the Grandchild's devise?

4. Grandparent creates a trust with income to be accumulated or distributed to Grandchild as the trustee decides; after ten years the trust property is to be paid to Grandchild.

---

[21] The result in Example 4 (Direct Skip in Trust) is confirmed in Technical Advice Memorandum 9105006, in which the Service held that the entire value of real property was subject to the GST tax where a decedent devised a life estate in the property to a skip person and a remainder interest to a nonskip person. For purposes of the GST tax, the devise constituted a transfer to a deemed trust, and the trust was considered to be both a skip person under § 2613(a)(2) and the transferee of a direct skip under the present interest rule of § 2652(c)(1)(A). Because the taxable amount under § 2623 in a direct skip situation is the value of the property received by the transferee, the Service concluded that the entire value of the real property (not just the actuarial value of the life estate) is subject to GST tax.

a. Is the trust a skip person?

b. Assume the income could also be distributed to a child of Grandchild. Would the trust be a skip person?

5. In 2002, Grandparent creates a trust with income to Grandchild for life, remainder to Great-Grandchild. The trustee has the power to invade corpus for the President of the United States. Is the trust a nonskip person because the President, as permissible recipient of trust property, is a nonskip person?

6. Can a direct skip be avoided by interposing an entity? For example, would a devise by Grandparent to a corporation wholly owned by Grandchild constitute a direct skip?

[B]　Taxable Terminations

Code: §§ 2612, 2621, and 2622.

Regulations: Treas. Reg. § 26.2612–1(b) and –1(f). Examples 4, 8, 9, 10, and 11.

The second manner in which a generation-skipping transfer occurs is by a taxable termination.

[1]　In General

Section 2612(a)(1) generally provides that a taxable termination occurs on the termination of a person's interest in trust. When applying taxable termination rules, recall that a trust may include any arrangement that has substantially the same effect as a trust. *See* § 2652(b)(1).

A taxable termination is defined in such a way that it has both positive and negative requirements. On the positive side, § 2612(a)(1) requires the termination of an interest in property held in trust. On the negative side, the same section excludes from the definition, terminations in which: (1) a nonskip person has an interest in the trust property immediately after the termination, or (2) distributions can only be made to nonskip persons after the termination. Complex? Yes!

Example 1: Grandparent creates a trust with income payable to Child for life, remainder to Grandchild.

First, recall that creation of the trust in the example was not a GST taxable event because the trust is not a skip person, having a nonskip person, Child, as a beneficiary. However, a taxable termination occurs when Child dies. In terms of the positive requirements of § 2612(a)(1), Child had an interest in property held in trust, as defined by § 2652(c), which generally states that the beneficiary must have a present right to trust property or be a permissible current recipient of trust property. Child has an interest in trust property because he has the present right to receive trust income. In addition, the second positive requirement for a taxable termination is also met because Child's interest terminates by death.

In Example 1, the first negative requirement does not prevent the transaction from being defined as a taxable termination. That requirement, or exception to the concept of a taxable termination, is triggered if a nonskip person has an interest in trust property immediately after the termination. Grandchild, who has the right to receive trust corpus, is the only beneficiary of the trust who has an interest in the trust property as that concept is defined by § 2652(c). Grandchild, however, being assigned to the second generation below the generation assignment of the transferor, is a skip person. Because the application of the exception requires that a nonskip person have an interest, this exception does not apply in the example.

Example 1 further illustrates the application of the second negative require- ment, that a termination is taxable if, after the termination, a distribution to a skip person is possible. This provision is phrased in § 2612(a)(1) as a double negative, *i.e.*, that a termination is taxable "unless . . . at no time" there is a possibility of a distribution to a skip person. The effect, however, is positive; if a distribution to a skip person is possible after the termination, the termination is taxable. Note that this exception requires that all trust beneficiaries be identified, assigned to generations, and classified as skip or nonskip persons. In Example 1, Grandchild is the only remaining possible recipient of trust distributions. Because she is assigned to the second genera- tion below that of Child, she is classified as a skip person. Thus, after the termination a distribution can only be made to a skip person, so the second exception does not apply. Because neither exception exists in Example 1, a taxable termination occurs on Child's death.

The impact of the exceptions can be seen in the following example:

Example 2: Grandparent creates a trust with income payable to children, *A* and *B*, with all income to the survivor, and on the survivor's death trust property to Grandchild. *A* dies. Thereafter, *B* dies.

There is no taxable termination when *A* dies, but there is a taxable termina- tion when *B* dies. Although *A* had an interest in the trust property, immedi- ately upon the termination of that interest a nonskip person, *B*, had an interest in the property. Accordingly, the first disqualifying situation arises and no taxable termination occurs. However, when *B* dies, neither of the disqualifying situations arise, and a taxable termination occurs.

[2]   Taxable Amount in Case of Taxable Termination

Section 2622 provides that the taxable amount in the case of taxable termination will be the value of the property involved in the taxable termina- tion less expenses that are similar to those that would be allowable under § 2053.

Example 3: Grandparent creates a trust with $80,000 in corporate stock, with income to Child for life, remainder to Grandchild. Thereafter, Child dies when the trust property has a value of $102,000. The trustee's commis- sions on terminating the trust are $2,000.

In Example 3, the amount of the taxable generation-skipping transfer is $100,000, or $102,000 reduced by the $2,000 commissions.

Note also that § 2624(c) allows the trust to value the trust property six months after death in accordance with § 2032, if the termination takes place because of the death of an individual.

[3]　Tax Computation for a Taxable Termination

The GST tax on a taxable termination is determined somewhat differently than is the tax on a direct skip, in that taxable terminations are taxed on a tax-inclusive basis—the tax is on an amount that includes the eventual tax. On the surface, the process appears to be the same, in that the GST tax in the case of a taxable termination is the product of the taxable amount and the applicable rate. *See* § 2602. In reality, however, the amount of the tax differs. To illustrate the difference, assume the facts in Example 3 above. The amount of the taxable termination is $100,000 ($102,000 minus $2,000 commissions). Based on an applicable rate of 50%, the GST tax imposed is $50,000, so that Grandchild receives $50,000. In a direct skip by devise, the tax would be imposed on the amount received by Child, and, unlike the tax on taxable terminations, would not apply to the amount used to pay the tax. For example, a donor who sets aside $100,000 for a gift to a skip person and to pay the GST tax on the gift could make a $66,667 gift to a skip person resulting in a $33,333 GST tax liability.

Following the analogy of the estate tax, if the taxable termination occurs at the same time as, and as a result of, the death of an individual before 2005, a credit of up to 5% of the federal GST tax is allowed for state GST taxes paid. *See* § 2604. Thus, if in Example 3 a state imposed a GST tax equal to the allowable federal credit, the state would impose a tax of $1,500 in 2002. This amount would be creditable against the federal GST tax. Not surprisingly, many states have enacted a GST tax system that is designed to pick up the amount of tax that will be creditable under § 2604. *See generally*, Ira Mark Bloom, *Federal Generation-Skipping Taxation: How Should The States Respond?* 51 ALB. L. REV. 817 (1987). The Tax Act of 2001 repeals § 2604 for generation-skipping transfers that occur after December 31, 2004. The number of states that will continue to tax GST transfers after 2004 is unknown.

Problems

1. Grandparent creates a trust with income to Child for life. On Child's death the income is to be accumulated for ten years with trust property, then paid to Grandchild. Will a taxable termination occur when Child dies?

2. Grandparent creates a trust with income payable to Child, or Grandchild, for ten years, with trust property then payable to Grandchild. The trustee exercises its discretion by paying annual income to Child. When will a taxable termination occur?

3. In Problem 2, what are the GST tax consequences of Child dying at the end of the fifth year?

4. Grandparent creates a trust with income to Child for life, then income to Grandchild 1 for life, remainder to Grandchild 2. The trustee has the power to invade corpus as may be necessary for the support of Child's independently wealthy Sister. Will a taxable termination occur when Child dies (assuming Sister is still living)?

[C]   Taxable Distributions

Code: §§ 2612 and 2621.

Regulations: Treas. Reg. §§ 26.2612–1(c), –1(f). Examples 12 and 13.

The third type of taxable event under the GST tax is a taxable distribution. When applying taxable distribution rules, recall that a trust may include any arrangement that has substantially the same effect as a trust. *See* § 2652(b)(1).

[1]   In General

Section 2612(b) defines a taxable distribution as any distribution from a trust to a skip person, unless a direct skip or taxable termination also occurs on the distribution. In addition, the trust's payment of GST taxes on the taxable distribution from the trust constitutes an additional taxable distribution. *See* § 2621(b).

> **Example 1:** Grandparent creates a trust with income payable to Child for ten years, corpus to Grandchild, with power in the trustee to invade corpus for the benefit of Grandchild. The trustee exercises this power and distributes some trust corpus to Grandchild.

The distribution of corpus constitutes a taxable distribution. Grandchild is a skip person and the distribution does not otherwise constitute a taxable termination or direct skip.

> **Example 2:** Grandparent creates a trust with income payable to Child or Grandchild in the amounts the trustee determines in its discretion. The trustee exercises this power and distributes some trust income to Grandchild.

The distribution of trust income to Grandchild constitutes a taxable distribution. Grandchild is a skip person and the distribution does not otherwise constitute a taxable termination or direct skip.

[2]   Other Considerations Involving Taxable Distributions

Note that both taxable terminations and direct skips take precedence over taxable distributions, in the sense that any transaction that constitutes either a taxable termination or a direct skip by definition is not a taxable distribution. *See* § 2612(b). Consider the following example involving a taxable termination and a taxable distribution:

> **Example 3:** Grandparent creates a trust with income to Child for life, remainder to Grandchild. When Child dies, the trust is distributed to Grandchild.

A taxable termination occurs at Child's death. Thus, although the distribution of corpus to Grandchild, a skip person, otherwise would constitute a taxable distribution, the transaction is treated only as a taxable termination; the distribution does not itself constitute a taxable event.

Section 2612(b) also states that a taxable distribution is a distribution from a trust, thus distinguishing other types of distributions. In many ways, of course, this result is guaranteed by excluding direct skips from the definition of taxable distributions, because many direct skips occur by outright distribution from the transferor or the transferor's estate. The limitation of taxable distributions to trusts also means that the precedence rule for direct skips has meaning only when a direct skip is made from a trust. Consider the following:

> **Example 4:** Grandparent creates a trust with income to Spouse for ten years, remainder to Child, with an immediately exercisable power in Spouse to appoint the property to anyone. Spouse exercises her power by appointing some of the trust property to Grandchild.

The distribution of trust corpus to Grandchild is a direct skip because Grandchild is a skip person and the transfer of the property by exercise of the general power of appointment is subject to gift tax. Although the distribution would also constitute a taxable distribution, the direct skip takes precedence.

[3]　Taxable Amount in Case of Taxable Distribution

Section 2621 provides that the taxable amount in the case of a taxable distribution is the value of the property received, less tax-related expenses for determining the GST tax consequences.

> **Example 5:** Grandparent creates a trust with income to Child for life, remainder to Grandchild with power in the trustee to invade principal for Grandchild. Assume the trustee in 2002 partially invades corpus, giving Grandchild $21,000. Grandchild pays $1,000 for tax advice to determine the GST tax consequences of the distribution.

A taxable distribution occurs when the distribution is made. Grandchild is a skip person, and the distribution is not a direct skip or a taxable termination. The taxable amount is $20,000, which is the difference between the distributed amount, and the expenses associated with the distribution.

[4]　Tax Computation for a Taxable Distribution

The GST tax on the taxable amount in the case of a taxable distribution is the product of the taxable amount and the applicable rate. *See* § 2602. Assuming an applicable rate of 50% in 2002, the GST tax imposed in the above example is $10,000. As discussed above, with respect to taxable terminations, taxable distributions are taxed on a tax inclusive basis. *Tax inclusive* means that the funds used to pay taxes are also subject to tax, unlike the tax on direct skips, which is imposed on the amount received by the beneficiary. For taxable terminations, the beneficiary must pay a tax on the gross amount received. Thus, the taxes come out of the transferred property.

The § 2604 credit for state GST taxes paid may also apply in the case of taxable distributions, if the distribution occurs at the time and as a result of the death of an individual. In most cases, however, a taxable termination also will occur at the same time, and the credit will be allowed because of the taxable termination, not the taxable distribution.

Problems

1. Grandparent creates a trust with income payable to Child or Grandchild as the trustee decides in its discretion, remainder to Grandparent's contemporary, *X*. The trustee distributes income to Grandchild. Does a taxable distribution occur on the income distribution?

2. Grandparent creates a testamentary trust to pay income to a Child for life, remainder to a Grandchild with power in the trustee to invade corpus for the Grandchild. The trust provides that any GST taxes on a taxable distribution shall be paid from trust property. The trustee invades corpus for the Grandchild in the amount of $100,000. If the applicable rate is 50%, the GST tax payable by the trust on that amount will be $50,000. What will be the ultimate taxable distribution amount? *See* § 2621(b).

[D] The GST Tax Computation

[1] The GST Exemption

Code: §§ 2631, 2632, 2641(f), and 2642.

Regulations: Treas. Reg. §§ 26.2632–1(a) and –1(b)(1)(i).

Under § 2631 as enacted in 1986, every person had a $1 million exemption that may be allocated to potential GST transfers. The Tax Reform Act of 1997 indexed the $1 million exemption for inflation in $10,000 increments. In 2002, the indexed amount is $1.1 million. The 2001 Tax Act increases the exemption to equal the Applicable Exclusion Amount beginning in 2004 and eliminates indexing. Thus, the GST exemption will equal $1.5 million in 2004 and 2005, $2 million in 2006-2008, and $3.5 million in 2009. This provision is intended to exclude many estates and trusts from the GST tax. The statute effectively provides a "default" allocation of the exemption in the absence of an affirmative allocation:

> First, the exemption is allocated to lifetime direct skips. Next the 2001 Tax Act mandates that any remaining GST exemption be allocated to lifetime indirect skips, defined by § 2632(c) to include most trusts created after Decmber 31, 2000 that have a reasonable prospect of being subject to the GST tax in the future. Then, the exemption is allocated to testamentary direct skips. Finally, the exemption is allocated to nonindirect lifetime skips and testamentary transfers that may have GST implications. *See* § 2632(b), (c) and (e).

The allocation is deemed to be made to direct skips and to lifetime transfers that are indirect skips, unless the transferor elects out. *See* §2632(b), (c). Transfers that are indirect skips and thus subject to the deemed allocation rule are defined by § 2632(c) to include most trusts that have a reasonable prospect of being subject to the GST tax in the future.

Both the deemed allocation and the election out are irrevocable after the due date of the return. *See* Treas. Reg. § 26.2632–1(b)(1)(ii), –1(b)(2)(i). Filing a return and paying a direct skip tax is sufficient to elect out of a deemed allocation. *See* Treas. Reg. § 26.2632–1(b)(i).

For transfers by gift, the value for allocation is the gift tax return value, if the gift return is filed in a timely manner. For a transferor who dies before the gift tax return is due, the decedent's personal representative may make the allocation on a gift return. This return is due the earlier of the normal due date of the gift tax return or the due date of Form 706. For transfers subject to estate taxes, the estate tax value (or alternate valuation value) is used. A timely allocation of exemption relates back to the time of transfer. *See* § 2642(b)(1). As will be seen in later chapters, the transferor may not be permitted to allocate the GST exemption and no deemed allocations will be made during the period that the transferor retains too much control over the lifetime transfer.

If the allocation is not timely made, the allocation is effective as of the date of allocation and the GST value is the value at the time the allocation is made. If the donor dies before a late allocation is made, the allocation is effective as of the date of death. *See* Treas. Reg. § 26.2632–1(d)(1). For late lifetime allocations, the transferor may elect to value transferred assets (except for life insurance) as of the first day of the month in which allocation is made. Treasury Regulation § 26.2632–1(b)(2)(i) and –1(d)(1) permit formula allocations of exemption, *e.g.*, "the allocation may be expressed in terms of the amount necessary to produce an inclusion ratio of zero."

The 2001 Tax Act added a provision for "substantial compliance" with the GST allocation rules. *See* § 2642(g). Congress wanted to provide some relief from the highly technical rules for allocating GST exemption when the transferor attempted to allocate GST exemption to provide the lowest inclusion ratio. Also, the 2001 Tax Act added a provision permitting retroactive allocations of GST exemption when there is an unnatural order of deaths. *See* § 2632(d). For example, if a parent creates a trust for a child and the child dies unexpectedly before the parent, the trust may pass to grandchildren and be subject to the GST tax. Section 2632(d) permits the parent to make a retroactive allocation of any unused GST exemption to a trust to avoid the GST tax.

[2]   The Applicable Rate

Code: § 2641.

Regulations: Treas. Reg. § 26.2641–1.

The examples considered so far in this Chapter have assumed that the applicable rate for calculating the GST tax is 50% and that as a result the GST tax is 50% of the taxable amount. In some cases, however, the applicable rate may be less than 50%, or even zero.

Variation in the rate used to calculate the GST tax is caused by the § 2641 definition of the applicable rate. That section defines the applicable rate as the product of:

(1)   the maximum federal estate tax rate (50% in 2002 and lower in later years), and

(2)   the inclusion ratio with respect to the transfer.

Thus for example, if the inclusion ratio is 1, the applicable rate will be 50% in 2002. If the inclusion ratio is less than 1, the applicable rate will be less than 50% in 2002. If the inclusion ratio is zero, the applicable rate will be zero. For years after 2002, the maximum GST tax rate will be lower than 50%.

[3] Inclusion Ratio

Code: § 2642.

Regulations: Treas. Reg. § 26.2642–1.

The inclusion ratio is defined by § 2642(a). The purpose of the ratio is to take into account the generation-skipping exemption amount (GST exemption). For 2002, this amount is $1.1 million. *See* §§ 2631, 2632. The ratio accomplishes this objective by freeing from taxation any portion of the transfer that comes from assets sheltered by the exemption.

Section 2642(a) defines the inclusion ratio as 1 minus an applicable fraction. The denominator of the applicable fraction is usually the value of the property in the direct skip or the value of the trust property in which a generation-skipping transfer might later occur. *See* § 2642(a)(2)(B), (b). The numerator of the applicable fraction is the amount of the available GST exemption that is allocated to the direct skip or to the trust transfer.

> **Example 1:** In 2002, Grandparent transfers $1 million to Grandchild and pays the applicable gift tax, if any. Having made no prior allocations, Grandparent allocates a portion of her GST exemption to the property.

The inclusion ratio is zero. The value of the transferred property involved in this direct skip is $1 million. Because she allocated $1 million of GST exemption to the transferred property that has a value of $1 million, the applicable fraction (exclusion ratio) is 1 ($1 million/$1 million). Thus, the inclusion ratio is zero (1 minus 1).

> **Example 2:** In 2002, Grandparent creates a trust of $200,000 with income payable to Child or accumulated as trustee decides. The trust is to terminate after ten years and the corpus distributed to Grandchild and Great-Grandchild. Grandparent allocates $200,000 of GST exemption to the trust. At the time of termination, the value of the trust is $2 million.

Although no generation-skipping transfer occurs on the trust's creation (because the transaction is not a direct skip), a generation-skipping transfer (a taxable termination) will occur after ten years. Because Grandparent allocated part of his exemption to the trust, however, the inclusion ratio for the trust is zero. The termination will not produce a tax even though the termination value of the trust exceeds the $200,000 of GST exemption allocated to it at the time of creation.

> **Example 3:** In 2002, Grandparent dies establishing a testamentary trust with income payable to Child for life, remainder to Grandchild. The trust corpus has an estate tax value of $2 million. Federal and state death taxes on the trust property are payable from the residue, *i.e.*, not from the GST trust. Within the time prescribed for filing Grandparent's estate tax return, the personal representative allocates $1 million of the Grandparent's GST exemption to the testamentary trust.

In Example 3, the inclusion ratio is one-half. The applicable fraction is one-half, determined by dividing that portion of the GST exemption allocated to the trust ($1 million) by the value of the property transferred to the trust ($2 million). The inclusion ratio, one minus the applicable fraction, is therefore one-half. Thus, the applicable rate for any distribution from the trust will be one-half of the maximum estate tax rate in effect at the time of the taxable event.

A complicating factor in determining the inclusion ratio is that the GST exemption must be allocated by the time the transferor's estate tax return is due. This is true even though the generation-skipping transfer (taxable termination or taxable distribution) might not occur until decades later.

The 2001 Tax Act added a relief provision that permits a trust which has an inclusion ratio greater than zero but less than one to be divided into separate trusts with inclusion ratios of zero and one. *See* § 2642(a)(3). The division may be made at any time so long as the trust is divided on a fractional basis and the succession of interests is the same.

[4] Sample Calculations

As described above, the GST tax is the product of the taxable amount and the applicable rate (maximum estate rate times inclusion ratio). In this section, calculation of this tax for the various types of transfers is illustrated.

[a] GST Tax Imposed on a Direct Skip

The easiest calculation is on direct skips:

Example 4: Grandparent died in 2002. Her will left a Grandchild $2 million, with GST taxes payable from the residue and not out of the Grandchild's $2 million devise. Grandparent's personal representative allocated $1 million of GST exemption to this property. (The balance of Grandparent's GST exemption was either used previously or allocated to other devises.)

The transfer is a direct skip. The amount of the generation-skipping transfer is $2 million. The applicable fraction is one-half. Accordingly, the inclusion ratio is one-half. The GST tax imposed is $500,000, computed as follows:

GST amount	$2,000,000
Applicable rate	
Estate tax rate of 50% times inclusion ratio of .50 (1 - ½)	× 25%
GST tax imposed on D's residuary estate	$ 500,000

[b] GST Tax Imposed on a Taxable Termination

The calculation of the tax on a taxable termination is tax-inclusive:

Example 5: In 1995, Grandparent created a testamentary trust with income to Child for life, remainder to Grandchild in the amount of $1 million. Grandparent previously allocated her entire GST exemption to other transfers. At Child's death in 2002, the property was worth $2.1 million, with termination expenses of $100,000.

The GST tax imposed will be $1 million. The amount of the generation-skipping transfer is $2 million ($2.1 million less termination expenses). The applicable fraction is zero because no exemption was allocated to the trust. The inclusion ratio is, therefore, one (one minus zero). Thus, the applicable rate is 50% (estate tax rate of 50% times the inclusion ratio of 1). The amount of the transfer times the applicable rate equals $1 million.

[c] GST Tax Imposed on a Taxable Distribution

The calculation of the GST tax on taxable distributions is similar to the tax on taxable terminations:

> **Example 6:** In 1995, Grandparent created a trust containing stock worth $1 million with income payable to Child for ten years, corpus to Grandchild with power in the trustee to invade principal for the benefit of Grandchild. Grandparent allocated $400,000 of his GST exemption to the trust. In 2002, the trustee distributed stock worth $100,000 to Grandchild.

The distribution of corpus constituted a taxable distribution. The GST tax imposed was $30,000, computed as follows: the amount of the generation-skipping transfer is $100,000; the applicable fraction is $\frac{2}{5}$ ($400,000 / $1,000,000); the inclusion ratio ratio is $\frac{3}{5}$ (1 minus $\frac{2}{5}$); the applicable rate is 30% (50% maximum estate tax rate times $\frac{3}{5}$); and the tax is $30,000 ($100,000 times 30%).

[5] The Section 2604 Credit

Code: § 2604.

Regulations: None.

As noted above, § 2604 allows a credit for state GST taxes paid on transfers that occur before 2005. The credit is, however, both qualitatively and quantitatively limited, as well as time limited. First, the credit only applies to generation-skipping transfers that generate federal GST tax and that are triggered by the death of an individual. Second, the credit is not available for direct skips. Third, the creditable amount cannot exceed 5% of the federal tax imposed. Finally, there is no credit for state taxes paid on GST transfers that occur after 2004 because the 2001 Tax Act repeals § 2604 for transfers beginning in 2005.

The most common event triggering the credit is the death of the income beneficiary of a trust who was entitled to all of the trust income.

> **Example 7:** In 1992, Grandparent created a trust for Child for life, remainder to Grandchild. No part of Grandparent's GST exemption was allocated to the trust. Child dies in 2002. At Child's death, the trust property has a value of $550,000, and termination expenses are $50,000. The alternate valuation date is not elected, and, therefore, the taxable amount of the generation-skipping transfer is $500,000. The GST tax imposed is $250,000, based on a 50% applicable rate.

A credit against the $250,000 tax imposed is allowable if a state GST tax is actually paid. The credit cannot exceed $12,500 (5% of the federal GST tax imposed).

The trust need not have a sole income beneficiary. The credit is also available when other taxable terminations occur, as long as the taxable event is caused by the death of an individual. For example, a taxable termination caused by the death of a beneficiary who was a permissible recipient of trust income or corpus would qualify for the state GST tax credit.

A significant number of states have enacted GST pick up taxes equal to the § 2604 credit amount. *See, e.g.*, Cal. Rev. & Tax Code §§ 16,700–16,950; N.Y. Tax Law §§ 1020–1033. How state legislatures will response to the repeal of § 2604 in unknown.

Problems

1. Decedent specifically devises $1.5 million to Grandnephew, with death taxes payable from the residue. The personal representative fails to allocate Decedent's GST exemption. What is the inclusion ratio?

2. In 1996, Grandparent made a gift to Grandchild of $500,000. Grandparent allocated $500,000 of GST exemption to this transfer. Grandparent died in 2002, having created a testamentary trust for the Grandchild of $1 million with all taxes payable from the residue. What is the lowest possible inclusion ratio?

3. In 1987, Grandparent created a lifetime trust of $1 million with income payable to Child for 15 years, the remainder passing to Grandchild. Grandparent allocated $700,000 of GST exemption to this trust. After 15 years the trust property is worth $2.1 million and trust termination expenses are $100,000. How much GST tax will be imposed on the taxable termination, assuming no state GST tax?

4. How would your answer change if the trust in Problem 3 was created in 2002 instead of 1987?

5. In 2002, Grandparent creates a trust with income payable to her child until the child reaches age 40 at which time the trust will terminate and the trust principal will be payable to the child, but if the child dies under age 40, to the children of the deceased child. Absent an election by the grandparent, what will be the inclusion ratio for the trust? Would your answer be different if the child would not get the principal before age 50?

6. Grandparent dies leaving $1 million to Grandchild 1 and another $1 million to a trust that benefits Child for life and remainder to Grandchild 2. Assume that Grandchild 1 and Grandchild 2 are both children of Child, why would the Grandparent's personal representative want to allocate part or all of the GST exemption to the trust that might later involve a generation-skipping transfer, rather than to the direct skip?

§ 5.03 Refinements Under the GST Tax System

[A] Exclusions

A variety of transactions are specifically excluded from application of the GST tax. First, some transfers to some skip persons are excluded if the parent of the skip person is dead. Second, the GST tax may be eliminated on amounts qualifying for the gift tax annual exclusion (and with respect to exclusions for transfers for educational and medical purposes) if certain conditions are satisfied. Third, the effective date provisions of the 1986 Act effectively exclude trusts that antedated the Act from application of the tax, notwithstanding later terminations or distributions. Fourth, the multiple-skip rule has the effect of an exclusion where a generation-skipping transfer has already occurred at a generation level. Fifth, the GST tax does not apply if the interest was previously subject to the GST tax at that generation. Finally, several special rules apply only to the spouse of the transferor.

[1] Predeceased Child Rule

Code: § 2651(e).

Regulations: None.

The Code alters the generation-skipping assignment in one significant way to provide an important exception to the GST tax.[22] Section 2651(e) defines a grandchild of the transferor as a nonskip person if the beneficiary's parent (who is a descendant of the transferor) is dead at the time the transfer is subject to either gift or estate tax. For example, when a transferor makes a gift to a grandchild and the transferor's child who is the parent of the grandchild is dead, the gift is not a direct skip because the grandchild is not a skip person under the statute. This provision also serves to bar the occurrence of a GST tax when the transferor's child is dead at the time the transfer is subject to either gift taxes or estate taxes. The move-up rule may prevent a taxable termination tax or a tax distribution tax from arising, but only when the circumstances of § 2651(e) apply. Generally, the rule will not prevent a taxable termination or a tax distribution from occurring. For example, assume that a trust is created for a child and the trust is scheduled to terminate before the child dies. If the child in fact dies before the trust terminates, however, and the child's children receive the trust assets, this is a taxable termination and the move-up rule does not prevent the application of the GST tax. The child was alive when the estate or gift tax was due on the initial creation of the trust.

Before 1998, § 2612(c)(2) excluded from the GST tax only direct skips to a grandchild of the transferor, if the grandchild's parent (the transferor's child) was dead. Under the rules of both § 2651(e) and repealed § 2612(c)(2), the grandchild is treated as being in his deceased parent's generation. Both sections apply to transfers to grandchildren of the transferor's spouse or former spouse. This moving-up rule may be reapplied if descendants in more than one generation are dead. As a result, great-grandchildren or younger lineal descendants could be moved-up several generations to become nonskip persons.

Section 2651(e) also permits GST-exempt transfers to grandchildren of the transferor's siblings if the transferor has no living lineal descendants and the related parent of the grandnephew or grandniece is dead.

---

[22] Section 511 of the Taxpayer Relief Act of 1997 amended § 2651 by renumbering existing subsection (e) as (f), and adding a new subsection (e), effective for GST taxable events occurring after December 31, 1997.

[2] GST Exclusions Based on Gift Tax Exclusions

[a] Exclusion for Transfers that Qualify Under the Gift Tax Annual Exclusion

Code: § 2642(c).

Regulations: None.

The effect of the gift tax annual exclusion for GST purposes depends on the type, form, and amount of generation-skipping transfer. Outright gifts that qualify for the annual exclusion under § 2503(b) are exempt from the GST tax. *See* § 2642(c)(1), (3). The Technical and Miscellaneous Revenue Act of 1988 made a major change concerning gifts qualifying for the $10,000 annual exclusion, effective March 31, 1988. Only nontaxable gifts that are direct skips are exempt from the GST tax. Moreover, for direct skips in trust, the trust must be solely for the benefit of a skip person. At the death of that skip person, the trust must be includable in the skip person's gross estate for estate tax purposes. *See* § 2642(c)(2).

Problem

If a direct skip exceeds the annual exclusion amount, will any effect be given to the exclusion under the GST tax system?

[b] Exclusion for Transfers that Would Have Qualified Under Section 2503(e)

Code: § 2611(b).

Regulations: None.

Section 2611(b)(1) provides that a generation-skipping transfer does not include "any transfer which, if made inter vivos by an individual, would not be treated as a taxable gift by reason of § 2503(e) (relating to exclusion of certain transfers for educational or medical expenses)."

Example: Grandparent creates a trust with income payable to Child for life, remainder to Grandchild. The trustee has the power to use corpus to pay for Grandchild's college education, and in fact pays the Grandchild's college tuition from trust corpus.

Because the payment would have qualified under § 2503(e) if made by an individual, the transfer will not constitute a taxable distribution. Absent this exclusion, the payment on behalf of Grandchild would constitute a taxable distribution.

[3] Effective Date Rules

Code: §§ 2611 and 2652.

Regulations: Treas. Reg. § 26.2601–1(a) and –1(b)(1)(i).

The GST tax system generally applies to any generation-skipping transfer that occurs after October 22, 1986, the date of enactment of the Tax Reform Act of 1986. Tax Reform Act of 1986 (Act), § 1433(a). Act § 1433, however, modifies the rules for some transfers occurring before and after October 22, 1986.[23] First, the GST tax system does not apply to transfers under wills (or revocable trusts) executed before October 22, 1986, if the testator died before January 1, 1987. *See* Act, § 1433(b)(2)(B). Second, in general, the system does not apply to trusts that were irrevocable on September 25, 1985. *See* Act, § 1433(b)(2)(A). Thus, lifetime transfers made between September 25, 1985 and October 22, 1986 are potentially subject to the tax. Third, the system generally does not apply to at-death transfers by individuals who were incompetent on October 22, 1986 and remained so until death. *See* Act § 1433(b)(2)(C).

The exemption for irrevocable trusts is not absolute. It does not apply, for example, to new transfers to corpus added after September 25, 1985, or from income therefrom. *See* Act, § 1433(b)(2)(A). Second, the regulations narrowly define the concept of "irrevocable." *See* Treas. Reg. § 26.2601–1(b). Third, grandfathering protection can be lost if powers are exercised in ways not sanctioned by regulation. In *Peterson Marital Trust v. Commissioner*, 78 F.3d 795 (2d. Cir. 1996), the Second Circuit upheld a then-temporary effective date regulation that treated a general power of appointment, held by a decedent who died after October 22, 1986, and created in an irrevocable trust established before September 26, 1985 as a constructive addition by the power holder, and thus, not grandfathered for GST tax purposes. The Eighth Circuit in *Simpson v. United States*, 183 F.3d 812 (1999), held that the GST tax applied only to the extent the general power in a grandfather trust was not exercised. The court distinguished *Peterson* on the basis that only assets remaining in the power of appointment trust after the exercise is a constructive addition and thus subject to the GST tax. In *Peterson*, the general power was not exercised. *Bachler v. United States*, 126 F. Supp. 2d 1279 (N.D. CA. 2000), followed *Peterson* although the facts were similar to *Simpson*.[24] The court found the reasoning of *Simpson* "unpersuasive."[25]

The exemption for transfers from incompetents is also defined carefully. It requires that the individual was incompetent on October 22, 1986, and did not regain competence before the date of his death. *See* Act, § 1433(b)(2)(C). The exemption applies to direct skips occurring by reason of the death of the incompetent (Act, § 1433(b)(2)(C)(ii)) and to generation-skipping transfers from trusts included in the gross estate of the incompetent. *See* Act, § 1433(b)(2)(C)(i). Thus, the exemption would not apply to taxable terminations or taxable distributions from trusts resulting from the incompetent's death, although those trusts would undoubtedly be grandfathered if created before the effective date.

The Service has fielded hundreds of private letter ruling requests regarding whether a particular modification of an otherwise grandfathered trust would cause the loss of grandfather status. In December of 2000, the Service published a taxpayer-friendly final regulation that generally allows trust

---

[23] Certain transfers that occurred before October 23, 1986 are deemed to have occurred on that date.

[24] A final regulation adopts the results in *Peterson* and *Bachler* and rejects *Simpson*. *See* Treas. Reg. § 26.2601-1(b)(1)(v)(A).

[25] *Bachler*, at 1283.

modifications provided the "modification does not shift a beneficial interest in the trust to any beneficiary who occupies a lower generation (as defined in section 2651) than the person or persons who held the beneficial interest prior to the modification, and the modification does not extend the time for vesting of any beneficial interest in the trust beyond the period provided for in the original trust." Treas. Reg. § 26.2601-1(b)(4)(i)(D). The regulation also provides other safe harbor rules for judicial construction, settlement agreement, or trustee action, together with numerous examples. *See* Treas. Reg. § 26.2601-1(b)(4).

[4] Multiple-Skip Rule

Code: § 2653.

Regulations: Treas. Reg. § 26.2653–1.

Not all generation-skipping trusts skip only a single generation. As a result, the Code addresses the application of the GST tax when property is held in trust for beneficiaries in successively lower generation levels. Section 2653(a) provides the general rule for multiple skips. In brief, that section treats a trust that has been taxed under the GST tax as having a new transferor; one generation above the generation of the oldest continuing beneficiary of the trust. The section further continues the inclusion ratio applied to the trust prior to the first generation-skipping transfer, adjusted for the GST tax applied to the transfer.

To illustrate the operation of § 2653, assume that Grandparent creates a trust with income to Child for life, income thereafter to Grandchild for life, remainder to Great-Grandchild. When Child dies, a generation-skipping transfer occurs in the form of a taxable termination, and a GST tax will be imposed. Because the property will continue to be held in trust, § 2653(a) applies. For the purposes of the next transfer, the transferor will be deemed to be in the same generation as Child. This result occurs because the Child's generation is the first generation above the generation assignment of the grandchild, and the grandchild is a member of the highest generation of any person who has an interest in the trust. Thus, when the grandchild dies, another taxable termination will occur because Great-Grandchild is a skip person relative to the transferor's generation assignment—the Child's generation level.

The multiple skip rule can also have the effect of preventing GST taxation from being imposed more than once at a generation level.

Example: Grandparent creates a trust for Grandchildren with income to Grandchild 1 for ten years, and corpus to Grandchild 2 after ten years.

In this example, a direct skip occurs upon the creation of the trust, because the trust is a skip person, having only skip persons as beneficiaries. Therefore, the GST tax is applied when the trust is created, and the trust is thereafter deemed to have been created by a transferor one generation above the grandchildren. Thus, when Grandchild 1 receives income and Grandchild 2 eventually receives the corpus, the trust is not a generation-skipping trust, having been "created" by a transferor only one generation above the beneficiary. In short, the § 2653 rule prevents the distributions from being taxable distributions or taxable terminations.

Note that although multiple skips in a trust are taxed, double skips are not at a rate higher than single skips. For example, a devise to a great-grandchild is not taxed differently than a devise to a grandchild.

[5] Exclusion for Prior Transfers

Section 2611(b)(2) provides an exclusion for transfers that were previously taxed by the GST tax at the same generation. Consider a disposition in trust for Grandchild 1 for ten years, with corpus then payable to Grandchild 2. A direct skip occurs on trust creation. Thereafter, distributions from the trust are protected by the prior transfer exclusion, to the extent of the initial direct skip amount. Thus, distributions of income or corpus would not be taxable, until the distributions (or terminations) exceeded the direct skip amount.

There is considerable overlap between this exclusion and the multiple skip rule. Although the multiple skip rule is on an "attributable to" basis, this exclusion is on a "to the extent of" basis. Therefore, the multiple-skip rule can be more advantageous.

Note the impact of the multiple-skip rule to the above facts. Unlike the prior transfer rule, which protected the trust only to the extent of the value of the prior transfer, the multiple-skip rule protects the entity. No taxable distribution or taxable termination occurs after creation of the trust because the transferor is deemed to be in the child's generation level. Thus, a grandchild is not a skip person, and the termination is not taxable.

[6] Spousal Issues

[a] Split Gifts

Code: § 2652(a)(2).

Regulations: Treas. Reg. § 26.2652–1(a)(4) and –(a)(5). Examples 1 and 2.

Section 2652(a)(2) provides that a split-gift election (a § 2513 gift tax election) will make a consenting spouse a GST transferor for one-half of the transferred property. The GST tax effect of the gift tax election is automatic.

[b] QTIPs[26]

Code: § 2652(a).

Regulations: Treas. Reg. § 26.2652–2(a) and –2(d). Examples 1 and 3.

Based on the general transferor rules of § 2652(a), the decedent or donee spouse who creates a QTIP disposition for which a marital deduction is allowed will not be the transferor. Instead the surviving or donee spouse will be the transferor. As a result, none of the decedent's or donor's GST exemption can be used in the QTIP disposition because that spouse is not the transferor. Pursuant to § 2652(a)(3), however, the decedent's personal representative or the donor may make an election (known as a reverse QTIP election) to

---

[26] For a discussion of QTIP trusts, see Chapters 3 and 4.

disregard the actuality that a QTIP election was made for gift or marital deduction purposes. Hence, for GST purposes the first spouse will be treated as the transferor of a QTIP disposition so that her GST exemption can be allocated to the QTIP disposition.

Although the *Peterson* court, *supra*, ruled that a general power of appointment will cause the loss of the grandfathering exemption for the GST tax, the same is not true of a QTIP trust, established before September 26, 1985. If the spouse-beneficiary dies before the general effective date of the GST tax, Treasury Regulation § 26.2601–1(b)(iii) provides that the QTIP trust will be treated as though the creator of the QTIP trust made the § 2652(a)(3) election. As a result, the QTIP is grandfathered from the GST tax.

Problems

1. Grandparent creates a trust with income to Child for life, remainder as that Child appoints by will, and in default of the appointment, to Grandchildren. Child appoints the property to Grandchild 1. Does a taxable termination occur on Child's death?

2. Decedent devises property to *X University* to be used to pay the college tuition of his Grandchild. Does a direct skip occur? Would the result change if Decedent directed that his personal representative pay the tuition directly to *XU*?

3. Grandparent devises $2 million in trust, with income payable to Child for life, then income payable to Grandchild for life, remainder to Great-Grandchild. Assuming no other generation-skipping transfers were made by Grandparent, what would be the GST tax consequences of the devise, Child's death, and Grandchild's death?

[B] Income Tax Changes Based on GST Tax System[27]

Code: § 2654.

Regulations: None.

The GST tax raises two significant income tax consequences: (1) basis is adjusted to reflect the tax, and (2) the tax is deductible from any income deemed distributed to the beneficiary as a result of the transaction. The basis adjustment is similar to that which occurs on the imposition of the estate or gift tax. If a taxable termination results from an individual's death, the basis of the subject property is stepped-up (or stepped-down) to fair market value as it is under § 1014, but not otherwise. *See* § 2654(a).

If the inclusion ratio for calculation of the GST tax is less than one, the basis step-up (or step-down) is proportional.

Example 1: In 2002, Grandparent transfers property to Grandchild with a value of $600,000 and an adjusted basis of $200,000. Disregard the gift tax annual exclusion and assume no part of the GST exemption is allocated

---

[27] *See* Act, § 1433(D)(1). Additional changes based on the GST system that are not discussed include: Code § 303(d) (relating to stock redemption); § 2032(c)(2) (relating to alternate valuation date election); and § 6166(i) (relating to extensions to pay taxes in installments).

to the property. The GST tax is $300,000. Further assume that there is no gift tax because of the unified credit.

On these facts, the portion of the GST tax attributable to the excess of the fair market value over the adjusted basis is $200,000. The excess is $400,000 ($600,000 value minus $200,000 basis), which divided by $600,000 and multiplied by the GST tax of $300,000 equals $200,000. Hence, the basis of the property is stepped-up by $200,000, raising the adjusted basis from $200,000 to $400,000.

In case of a gift, the basis of the subject property is adjusted in a manner analogous to § 1015. Therefore, the GST tax imposed on the net appreciation of the property may be added to the income tax basis of the property, provided the adjustment does not increase the basis above fair market value.

> **Example 2:** In 2002, Grandparent made a lifetime generation-skipping transfer of property worth $100,000 with a basis of $50,000. A $50,000 GST tax is imposed. Grandparent is in the 50% gift tax bracket.

Because 50% of the GST tax is on the net appreciation, $25,000 is added to the adjusted basis of the gift property, calculated as follows. The total value of the gift equals $150,000 (the $100,000 gift plus the $50,000 GST tax). *See* § 2515. Therefore, the gift tax due equals $75,000. One-third of $75,000 ($25,000) is the net appreciation of the gift property, and an additional $25,000 is added to the adjusted basis of the property. Therefore, the adjusted basis is $100,000.

Pursuant to § 164, when a GST tax is imposed on a distribution that will be included in the transferee's taxable income, an income tax deduction is permitted for the GST taxes paid. A comparable provision is made under § 691, discussed in Chapter 14, when GST taxes are imposed on income in respect of a decedent.

Problems

1. In 1992, Grandparent transfers property in trust to Child for life, remainder to Grandchild. The property has an adjusted basis of $100,000, which carries over to the trust. Assume Grandparent's GST tax exemption was allocated fully before the transfer. Thus, the inclusion ratio is one. In 2002, Child dies when the property is worth $500,000 and that value is used for generation-skipping tax purposes. What will be the Grandchild's tax basis for the property? *See* § 2654(a)(2).

§ 5.04 Procedural and Administrative Rules

Code: §§ 2661 and 2662.

Regulations: None.

As a general rule, the procedural and administrative rules that apply to gift and estate taxation also apply for GST tax purposes. *See* § 2661. Special rules, however, govern such matters as who is liable for paying the GST tax.

The taxpayer, the person liable for the GST tax, depends on the type of generation-skipping transfer. Section 2603(a) provides as follows:

(a) Personal Liability—

(1) Taxable Distributions—In the case of a taxable distribution, the tax imposed by § 2601 shall be paid by the transferee.

(2) Taxable Termination—In the case of a taxable termination or a direct skip from a trust, the tax shall be paid by the trustee.

(3) Direct Skip—In the case of a direct skip (other than a direct skip from a trust), the tax shall be paid by the transferor.

Consistently, the person liable for paying the GST tax under § 2603 must file the applicable return. *See* § 2662(a); Treas. Reg. § 26.2662–1.

Part III

APPLICATION OF PRINCIPLES

This Part investigates the tax impact of various lifetime transfers. Property owners often engage in transactions which have aspects warranting both estate and gift taxation, or in which it is difficult to determine whether either or both of the two taxes should apply. For example, a donor may retain property until just before death, giving it away on her deathbed to avoid probate. Such gifts are "gifts" in name only, and may be taxed as transfers at death. Similarly, a donor may create a future interest in the property while retaining its present use. Other donors may give property away conditionally, retaining the power to change their minds. In each case, the donor retains many of the attributes of ownership, and the Code may wish to treat this retention as the retention of ownership itself.

The following chapters investigate the transfer and income tax ramifications of such retentions. Chapter 6 discusses what happens when the transfer is near death. Chapter 7 considers the tax effects of retained interests in irrevocable transfers, including retained rights to income and reversions. Chapter 8 extends the discussion to the most extreme of the retained powers—the power to revoke. Chapter 9 turns to other retained powers, such as powers to change the beneficial interests of various parties, powers to change the time and manner of the enjoyment of the beneficial interests, administrative powers over the management and disposition of the trust property, and retained powers to remove trustees. Chapters 10 and 11 discuss contractual arrangements, including life insurance and survivor annuities. Chapter 12 considers the effect of creating powers in third parties. Chapter 13 addresses survivorship property interests, specifically joint tenancies and tenancies by the entireties.

Each chapter considers the impact of the particular transactions under the four applicable federal tax systems in the following order:

1. Gift Tax

2. Estate Tax

3. Generation-Skipping Transfer Tax

4. Income Tax

The income tax aspects generally involve the application of Subchapter J of the Code. Subchapter J's complex system for taxing the income of trusts (and decedents' estates) is studied in Chapter 14. In this Part, we are concerned primarily with one income tax issue: whether the trust creator, referred to as the grantor in the Code, has retained sufficient control over the transferred property to warrant taxing the income generated by the property to the grantor. If the grantor has relinquished sufficient control over all or part of the transferred property, then all or part of the income will be taxed under the regular rules of Subchapter J. In other words, the income will not be taxed to the grantor, but will be taxed to the trust or its beneficiaries.

In addition to considering the taxation of the grantor, Chapters 6 through 13 will look at the income tax basis issue, when it is an issue for the recipient of a lifetime transfer that may be included in a transferor-decedent's estate.[1]

---

[1] *See generally* John L. Peschel, *The Impact of Fiduciary Standards on Federal Taxation of Grantor Trusts: Illusion and Inconsistency,* 1979 DUKE L.J. 709.

Chapter 6

TRANSFERS NEAR DEATH

Transfers near death present unique transfer tax problems. Throughout history, they have been treated almost as wills for property law purposes because they are typically used as will substitutes. As seen in this Chapter, this treatment has impacted the tax treatment of transfers near death, especially for estate tax purposes.

§ 6.01 Gift Tax

The gift tax treatment of gifts near death depends on whether the gifts are treated under state law as gifts *causa mortis*. *Causa mortis* gifts are revocable until death as a matter of property law, and thus, are incomplete in the gift tax sense. *See* Treas. Reg. § 25.2511–2(c) and *Burnet v. Guggenheim*, reproduced at § 4.01[A][1], *supra*. If the gift is not *causa mortis* under local law, it is irrevocable, and the nearness to death does not matter—the gift is taxed in the normal manner as a completed gift. *See* Chapter 4.

§ 6.02 Estate Tax

Code: § 2035.

Regulations: None.

The very revocability that makes gifts *causa mortis* incomplete for gift tax purposes makes them taxable in the gross estate of the donor. Section 2038 specifically requires inclusion in the gross estate property previously transferred by the decedent that is subject to a power of revocation. The fact that the power exists because of local law, rather than affirmatively retained, does not make it any less a power in the tax sense.

Irrevocable gifts near death, however, can also have estate tax effects. The very nearness of death which led the common law courts to develop the concept of the *causa mortis* gift also led Congress to make certain transfers near death subject to the estate tax. These appear too testamentary to avoid treatment as transfers at death. The rules are contained in § 2035.

[A] Simple Gifts

Early History. From the inception of the gift tax until recently, transfers made near death were included in the gross estate of the donor. Because of the potential ease a dying person could use deathbed transfers to avoid the estate tax at death, the 1916 Act included provisions for the taxation of transfers *in contemplation of death* as a part of the decedent's estate. This provision was interpreted and refined over the years, both by the courts and Congress.

Court refinement centered on the definition of the statutory phrase: "contemplation of death." The term was finally interpreted by the Supreme Court to require less than a fear of death sufficient to support a finding that a gift was *causa mortis*, but more than the generalized appreciation that all persons must die. *See United States v. Wells*, 283 U.S. 102 (1931). It was further refined by a legion of cases which differentiated *death motives*, such as illness and old age, from *life motive* factors, such as income tax planning, a regular pattern of giving, holiday gifts, and the like. The Commissioner was never particularly successful in persuading District Court juries of the absence of *life motives*. The government's losses reached the sublime, however, with *Kniskern v. Commissioner*, 232 F. Supp. 7 (S.D. Fla. 1964), in which substantial transfers made by a 99 year old donor to his grandchildren slightly more than a year before dying were found not to have been made in contemplation of death.

Most congressional action has involved attempts to find a way to avoid the factual determinations inherent in the *contemplation of death* provision, while continuing to tax transfers near death. The Supreme Court concluded that an early attempt to create an irrebuttable presumption that transfers made within two years of death were made in contemplation of death was a denial of due process of law. *See Heiner v. Donnan*, 285 U.S. 312 (1932). A subsequent amendment to the Code provided that transfers more than three years before death irrebuttably were presumed not to be in contemplation of death, and transfers within three years of death rebuttably were presumed to be in contemplation of death. This amendment passed constitutional muster, but resulted in the type of fact questions illustrated by *Kniskern*.

Tax Reform Act of 1976. The willingness of judges and juries to find life motives for transfers meant that wealth holders could freely use gifts near death to take advantage of the pre-1977 difference in tax rates for gifts and estates. To reduce this technique, Congress in 1976 removed the *contemplation of death* requirement, and replaced it with an automatic gross estate inclusion rule. Subject to limited exceptions, gratuitous taxable transfers made within three years of death were includable in the decedent's gross estate without regard to whether the gifts were made in contemplation of death. This time the constitutionality of the automatic three-year rule was upheld. *See Estate of Ekins v. United States*, 797 F.2d 481 (7th Cir. 1986).

The 1976 Act continued to exclude nongratuitous transfers, *i.e.*, transfers made for full and adequate consideration in money or money's worth, no matter how close to death. The presence of consideration avoided the possibility that the transfer would deplete the decedent's estate by the transferred amount. Indeed, because the consideration received would be in the decedent's estate, the exception was (and still is under current § 2035(d)) required to avoid double taxation.

Congress further tightened § 2035 by requiring that any gift taxes paid by the decedent (or his estate) on any gifts within three years of death be added to the gross estate. *See* § 2035(b) [originally § 2035(c)]. Without this provision, a donor near death could diminish the gross estate not only by making gifts, but also by paying the gift tax with untaxed dollars. The effect of § 2035(b) is to levy an estate tax on gift taxes paid on transfers made within three years of death, thus equating the tax treatment of property owned at death, and removing from gifts made near death the tax advantage inherent in the gift tax.[2] Finally, to avoid double taxation, which would result if property was included in the gross estate and also treated as an *adjusted taxable gift*, the latter term was defined to exclude property included in the gross estate. *See* § 2001(b) (last sentence).

1981 and 1997 Acts. In large part, the unification of the estate and gift taxes under the 1976 Act made § 2035 unnecessary. Section 2001(b)(1)(B)'s addition of adjusted taxable gifts to the taxable estate for the purpose of calculating the tentative tax effectively includes gifts in the estate tax rate base, whether or not they were included in the gross estate.[3] Further, the requirement of § 2035 that gift taxes are included in the gross estate removes the largest remaining advantage of gifts near death. It is not surprising, therefore, that Congress acted in 1981, repealing its 1976 rule that most outright gratuitous transfers made within three years of death were subject to estate taxation. *But see* Jeffery G. Sherman, *Hairsplitting Under I.R.C. 2035(d): The Cause and the Cure,* 16 VA. TAX. REV. 111 (1996) (arguing for reinstatement of the 1976 rule of automatic inclusion).

Although the 1981 Act substantially reduced the application of § 2035, it remained applicable to certain transfers made within three years of death. The three year rule of § 2035 still applies to a transfer by the decedent of life insurance on the decedent's life, because § 2042 would have applied had the decedent continued to own the policy until death. Also, § 2035 applies to transfers that would have been included in the gross estate under §§ 2036 through 2038 had the decedent not relinquished control or enjoyment of the property within three years of death. These situations are better treated in the following chapters that consider §§ 2036 through 2038 and 2042. *See* Chapters 7 through 10.

The final change made by the 1981 Act was to require gifts made within three years of death to be considered when determining an estate's qualification for special treatment under §§ 303, 2032A, and 6166. *See* § 2035(c) (previously § 2035(d)).

The 1997 Act essentially clarified the scope of § 2035 and reworded the statute to reorganize awkward provisions and to remove obsolete provisions. The Act's one substantive change was the addition of § 2035(e). This section applies to revocable trusts and is discussed in Chapter 8.

Section 2035 is noteworthy for the transfers it does not reach:

Example: In 2002, *D* gave *C* stock worth $111,000, with an income tax basis of $11,000. *D*'s gift was reduced for one $11,000 annual exclusion and the

---

[2] As discussed in Chapter 4, gifts taxes are computed on a *tax exclusive* basis while estate taxes are computed on a *tax inclusive* basis. By including the gift tax in the gross estate, the gift becomes a tax inclusive transfer.

Note that federal gift taxation and the possible application of § 2035(b) will be confined to relatively large lifetime gifts because the unified credit increased to $345,800 in 2002. As a result, the exemption equivalent increases to $1 million in 2002.

[3] The only significant difference is valuation. Adjusted taxable gifts are included in the computation of estate taxes at their gift tax value, rather than fair market value at the time of the decedent's death.

gift tax liability on the $100,000 taxable gift was offset by the unified credit. When *D* died in 2004, the stock *C* received had a fair market value of $125,000.

In the example, the $125,000 value of the stock is not included in *D*'s gross estate. Because § 2035(a) only applies to transfers that would have been includable under §§ 2036 through 2038 and 2042, it does not apply to the transfer of stock in 2002 that would have been included under § 2033 if held until death. The $100,000 gift tax value of the stock, however, is included as an adjusted taxable gift in calculating the tentative tax on his estate. *See* § 2001(b)(1)(B). In short, the value of the gift is included, and post-transfer appreciation in the value of the transferred property escapes estate taxation. Under § 1015, *C* has a carryover income tax adjusted basis of $10,000. The $100,000 adjusted taxable gift does not result in *C* receiving a stepped-up adjusted basis under § 1014.

[B]　Application of Section 2035(b) (Formerly Section 2035(c))

Estate of Sachs v. Commissioner

88 T.C. 769 (1987), aff'd, 856 F.2d 1158 (8th Cir. 1988)

Cohen, Judge: Respondent determined a deficiency of $516,365.63 in petitioners' Federal estate tax. In an amendment to answer, respondent also asserted an additional deficiency of $58,678.62. The issues for decision are: (1) Whether gift tax paid by the donees of net gifts made within 3 years of decedent's death is includable in decedent's gross estate under section 2035(b); [other issues are omitted].

. . .

[Decedent died on June 27, 1980. On April 10, 1978, he gave 14,000 shares of Sachs Holding Co. to each of three irrevocable trusts established for the benefit of his grandchildren. The trust instruments provided that the gift was "made subject to and upon the conditions . . . that the Trustees shall promptly pay, or cause to be paid, any and all gift taxes which may be found to be due to the United States because of the making of such gifts." Decedent and his wife claimed split-gift treatment of the gifts, and reported a gift tax of $612,700, calculated on a gift of $1,786,340, [sic] which represented the $2,399,044 value of the stock less the amount of the gift tax. The trusts paid the tax using cash provided in a separate gift from the parents of the grandchildren.]

Pursuant to section 2035, the shares transferred to the trusts were included in decedent's gross estate at date of death value ($2,196,180) reduced by the amount of gift tax ($612,700) paid by the donee trusts. Although the gift tax paid by the trusts was not included in the gross estate, in the computation of estate tax it was deducted under section 2001(b)(2) from the tentative estate tax computed under section 2001(b)(1). In his notice of deficiency, respondent determined that the gift tax paid by the trusts is included in decedent's gross estate pursuant to section 2035(b).

. . .

Petitioners contend that section 2035(b) does not "gross up" decedent's estate to include gift tax paid by the donee on a net gift made within 3 years of decedent's death. Petitioners maintain that gift tax paid by the donee trust is not tax paid by "the decedent or his estate" and argue that the "concise and unambiguous" language of the statute thus dictates our decision. Respondent contends that section 2035(b) reaches gift tax paid by the donee of any gift included in decedent's gross estate pursuant to section 2035(a). Respondent argues that the legislative history of section 2035(b) supports this construction of the statute.

. . .

Application of the literal language of section 2035(b) would dictate a result inconsistent with the architecture of the transfer tax system. This case thus presents circumstances "plainly at variance with the policy of the legislation as a whole" that warrant our search for unequivocal evidence of the purposes of section 2035(b).

. . .

Insistence on the literal language of section 2035(b) would distort the framework erected by the Tax Reform Act of 1976. The act retained some of the prior law's preferences for lifetime gifts; however, these preferences were not made available to deathbed gifts. Petitioners' construction of section 2035(b) extends the benefit of one such preference to deathbed net gifts. Mechanical application of section 2035(b) would completely remove from the transfer tax base all funds used to pay gift tax on such gifts. This interpretation of the statute is wholly inconsistent with Congress' goal of sharply distinguishing deathbed gifts from other gifts and eliminating the disparity of treatment between deathbed gifts and transfers at death.

. . .

Section 2035(b) speaks of gift taxes "paid . . . by the decedent or his estate" rather than gift taxes "paid" without modification because payment of tax on gifts described in § 2035(a) does not always remove funds from the transfer tax base. The House Committee on Ways and Means explained as follows:

> [T]he amount of gift tax paid with respect to transfers made within 3 years of death are to be includable in a decedent's gross estate. The "gross-up" rule for gift taxes eliminates any incentive to make deathbed transfers to remove an amount equal to the gift taxes from the transfer tax base. The amount of gift tax subject to this rule would include tax paid by the decedent or his estate on any gift made by the decedent or his spouse after December 31, 1976. It would not, however, include any gift tax paid by the spouse on a gift made by the decedent within 3 years of death which is treated as made one-half by the spouse, since the spouse's payment of such tax would not reduce the decedent's estate at the time of death. [H. Rept. 94–1380, *supra*, 1976–3 (Vol. 3) C.B. at 748.]

The draftsmen of section 2035(b) thus tailored the statute to accommodate gifts split under section 2513. Although the language selected for this purpose does not, in isolation, describe net deathbed gifts, our analysis of section 2035(b), its legislative history, and the framework erected by the 1976 Act persuades us that Congress did not intend to distinguish net deathbed gifts from other deathbed gifts.[4]

. . .

[Concurring and dissenting opinions omitted.]

———

Application of § 2035(b) is illustrated by an example:

Example 1: Assume D made a large gift in 2002, which resulted in a gift tax liability (after exhausting the unified credit) of $41,000. D paid the $41,000 gift tax and later died in 2004.

In the example, § 2035(b) requires inclusion of $41,000 in D's gross estate, even though the value of the gift is not included in the gross estate (but is an adjusted taxable gift under § 2001(b)(1)(B)).

Section 2035(b) can also apply if the decedent paid gift taxes on a split-gift made by the decedent's spouse. If the decedent consents to the split-gift election under § 2513, each spouse is jointly and severally liable for the gift tax on the gift. If the decedent pays any or all of the tax, and dies within three years of the gift, § 2035(b) requires that the gift taxes paid be included in the gross estate, even if that includes the spouse's share of the tax liability.

Example 2: Assume W gave C $122,000 in 2002. W's spouse, H, consented to split the gift so that W and H were each deemed to have made a taxable gift of $50,000 ($61,000 from each as a result of the split gift election, less a $11,000 gift tax annual exclusion for each). Assume further that W and H had both exhausted their unified credits, so that a gift tax was due. H paid all of the gift taxes, and died within three years after the gift.

In the example, the entire amount of gift taxes H paid would be included in his gross estate under § 2035(b). Similarly, if W paid the taxes and died within three years, § 2035(b) would require that the taxes she paid be included in her gross estate.

The rule of § 2035(b) is an inclusion of gift taxes paid on transfers made within three years of death. However, it does not require the inclusion of all gift taxes paid within three years of death. An example demonstrates the difference:

---

[4] Affirming the Tax Court, the Eighth Circuit observed:

> If Mrs. Sachs had paid the gift tax on her half of the split gift from assets separate from her husband's estate, § 2035(b) would not include that payment in the gross estate. In this case, however, the payment of the gift tax was made entirely from the proceeds of the donated stock, all of which would have been included in the decedent's estate absent the gift. The assets which were used to pay the gift tax would have been part of the gross estate if the gift had never been made, and so the entire amount of the gift tax was properly included under § 2035(b).

856 F.2d 1158, 1165 (8th Cir. 1988).

Example 3: Assume *D* made a large gift in 2002 that resulted in a gift tax liability (after exhausting the unified credit) of $41,000. *D* paid the $41,000 gift tax on its due date—April 15, 2003. The decedent died on February 1, 2006.

In the example, § 2035(b) does not require the inclusion of the $41,000 of gift taxes paid in *D*'s gross estate, even though the gift taxes were paid less than three years before the decedent died. The taxable transfer occurred more than three years before the decedent died and § 2035(b) is applicable only to taxes paid on transfers made within three years of death.

[C] Impact of Tax Payment Provisions

To prevent decedents from manipulating the quantitative requirements of § 303 (corporate redemption is not a dividend), § 2032A (special use valuation) and § 6166 (deferred payment on taxes on business property), the automatic inclusion of gifts made within three years of death still applies for purposes of determining the qualification under these special provisions. *See* § 2035(c)(1).[5] This provision also retains the three-year rule for the purposes of collecting liens under Chapter 64 of the Code.

As discussed in Chapter 3, §§ 2032A and 6166 require that qualifying property be a minimum percentage of the total estate to qualify for the relief provisions. Under § 2032A, special use valuation is limited to cases in which qualifying real farm or business property constitutes 50% of the value of the decedent's gross estate, as adjusted. Section 6166 permits estate taxes to be paid in installments with respect to an interest in a closely held business if the decedent's interest exceeds 35% of the value of the gross estate, as adjusted. Retention of the three-year rule prevents manipulation of these percentage requirements. For example, a transfer of nonfarm assets within three years of death will not reduce the size of the gross estate for purposes of determining whether farm or business realty constitutes 50% of the value of the gross estate under § 2032A, or 35% under § 6166.

Example: *D* owns assets worth $10 million. The business is $3.4 million of that total. To ensure that the business property is worth more than 35% of the gross estate, *D* gives $400,000 worth of nonbusiness assets to *S*. *D* dies within three years with an estate valued at $9.6 million.

In the example, § 2035(c)(2) requires that the estate include the $400,000 gift in calculating the gross estate for purposes of calculating the minimum percentage requirements of § 6166. Thus, the $3.4 million business is only 34% of the gross estate as calculated for § 6166 purposes, and § 6166 does not apply. *See Estate of Slater v. Commissioner*, 93 T.C. 513 (1989) (involving an attempt to obtain special use valuation).

Finally, gifts within three years of death present special problems when the gift is split with a spouse under the provisions of § 2513. If the estate of the donor spouse is required to include the transferred property in the gross estate under § 2035, double taxation results if the nondonor spouse is also required

---

[5] Section 2035(c)(3) provides an exemption for transfers (other than of life insurance) for which a gift tax return was not required to be filed.

to treat the one-half split gift amount as an adjusted taxable gift for the estate tax calculation under § 2001(b). This problem is avoided by § 2001(e), which provides that in appropriate circumstances the term *adjusted taxable gifts* does not include the split-gift amount.[6]

> **Example:** W owned a $100,000 life insurance policy which insured her life. In 2002, when the policy was worth $32,000, she transferred the policy to her son. W's husband, H, agreed to split-gift treatment of the transfer under § 2513. After taking into account the gift tax annual exclusion, W and H each made a taxable gift of $5,000, but paid no gift tax because of the unified credit. W died in 2004.

In the example, W's gross estate would include the value of the policy proceeds under § 2035 because of the operation of § 2035(a), and the gift of the policy would be excluded from the decedent's adjusted taxable gifts because the policy was included in the gross estate. When H later dies, the policy will not be included in his gross estate because he did not transfer the policy for estate tax purposes. Notwithstanding this lack of inclusion in the gross estate, however, H's portion of the split gift of the policy also is not treated as an adjusted taxable gift by H because of § 2001(e). H's estate, however, would be barred from claiming a credit for any tax due on the gift. *See* § 2001(d); Rev. Rul. 82–198, C.B. 206; Rev. Rul. 81–85, C.B. 452. If W had survived for three years after the gift of the policy, of course, § 2035 would not have applied.

Problems

1. In 2002, H made a gift to his child, C, in the amount of $2,222,000. H's wife, W, consented to split-gift treatment of the gift, and H paid all of the taxes payable resulting from the gift.

   a. What would be the estate tax consequences if H died in Year 2006, assuming his taxable estate would otherwise be $1,750,000, which he left entirely to C?

   b. What would be the result if H died in 2004?

   c. Assume that W died in 2004 with a taxable estate of $1,250,000. She left her entire estate to C. What would be her estate tax, assuming that H paid all gift taxes on the split gift?

   d. What would be the tax result in (b) and (c) if at the time of the gift in 2002, W paid the $41,000 gift tax liability out of her own assets?

   e. What would be the tax result in (b) and (c) if at the time of the gift in 2002, W had paid both her gift tax liability and H's gift tax liability out of her own assets?

2. D, a farmer, sold 10,000 shares of publicly held corporate stock on the market for $1 million in Year 1. In Year 3, he died, owning farmland worth

---

[6] The relief provided by § 2001(e) does not correct all potential problems with split gifts, however. If one spouse transfers property in a gift taxable transaction, but retains an interest that causes an estate tax inclusion, § 2001(e) will not reduce the nondonor spouse's adjusted taxable gifts even though the gifted property is included in full in the donor spouse's estate. Section 2001(e) relief is available only if the estate tax inclusion results from the application of § 2035 and not if the inclusion results from other sections such as §§ 2036 through 2038.

$2 million and other farm property worth $1 million so that total farm assets totaled $3 million. His total estate is valued at $5.5 million, which includes the proceeds from the sale of the stock and the farm. At the time of his death, 10,000 shares of the stock he sold was worth $3 million. For the purposes of § 2032A, must the gross estate be increased by the $2 million—the amount the value of the stock at *D*'s death exceeds the value of the consideration *D* received for it?

§ 6.03　Generation-Skipping Transfer Tax

Code: § 2515.

Regulations: None.

The basic generation-skipping transfer tax system applies to transfers that fall within the category of simple gifts, *i.e.*, gifts made without strings. Because the gift is made within three years of death, the result does not change. Further, because simple gifts are no longer subject to gross estate inclusion under § 2035, only the lifetime generation-skipping transfer tax rules will apply.

The impact of the GST tax system on gifts with strings is more complex. If the gift is treated as a gift *causa mortis* under local property law, it is deemed revocable. As a general rule, the inclusion ratio cannot be established for an interest in property if one of the string provisions applies. *See* § 2642(f).

The delayed inclusion ratio rule does not apply if the property is includable in the decedent's gross estate only because of § 2035. The generation-skipping transfer tax may be avoided by allocating a sufficient amount of the transferor's GST exemption to the lifetime transfer. If this is done, the transferor can establish a zero inclusion ratio for the transferred asset, even if the transferred property is later included in the transferor's gross estate under § 2035. Section 2642(f) expressly excludes the application of § 2035 from barring an early determination of the inclusion ratio. Thus, it is not necessary for the decedent's personal representative to allocate any additional GST exemption to the transferred property. Further, if the transferred asset qualifies for the annual exclusion, the transfer may be exempt from the generation-skipping transfer tax without the allocation of GST exemption. *See* § 2642(c). In this event, a § 2035 inclusion will not require the decedent's estate to allocate GST exemption even though the decedent did not make an allocation either. This rule has its most important application when the asset transferred is a life insurance policy.

> **Example:** *D* transfers a $50,000 life insurance policy with a gift tax value of $8,000 to a grandchild. *D* does not file a gift tax return and no GST exemption is allocated to the direct skip transfer because both the gift and the GST transfer are exempt from tax. *See* §§ 2503(b), 2642(c). *D* dies within three years.

Section 2035(a)(2) includes the policy proceeds—$50,000—in *D*'s gross estate. No GST tax is due at *D*'s death, however, and it is not necessary for *D*'s estate to allocate GST exemption to the direct skip to exempt it from GST tax.

When direct skip gifts made during lifetime require the payment of GST taxes, an additional taxable gift may occur. Section 2515 provides that any

GST taxes paid on a direct skip represent an additional transfer that is subject to gift taxes. If the direct skip occurs within three years of the transferor's death, the gift tax on the GST tax will be includable in the gross estate under § 2035(b), and the additional taxable gift will be an adjusted taxable gift under § 2001(b). Although the gift tax on the generation-skipping transfer and the GST tax will reduce the estate tax liability under § 2001(b), no credit is allowed for the GST tax itself.

Section 2035 should have no application to taxable terminations or taxable distributions. The donor does not pay the GST tax when either of these taxable events occur.

§ 6.04   Income Tax

Code: §§ 1014(e), 1015(a), (d), and (e).

Regulations: Treas. Reg. §§ 1.1014–6(a) and 1.1015–1(a).

Transfers near death can also have income tax implications. A gift *causa mortis* is subject to the donor's power of revocation. Thus, the income from the asset is taxed to donor. *See* Chapter 8, *infra*. Further, if the transfer is incomplete for gift tax purposes, the provisions of § 1015, carrying over the donor's basis to the donee, will not apply because the estate tax inclusion in the donor's estate will provide a date of death basis for the donee under § 1014.

If the gift is complete, income is taxed to the donee, unless one of the grantor trust rules discussed in Chapters 7 through 13 applies. In addition, the donee has a carryover basis under § 1015. If, however, a completed gift is included in the decedent's estate under § 2035, the donee's basis in the asset is stepped-up (stepped-down) under § 1014.

When a donee dies shortly after receiving the gift, the donee's death can trigger the application of § 1014(e), which denies the donor or donor's spouse a stepped-up basis for the property. Congress added this section in 1981 to prevent an individual from receiving the benefit of stepped-up basis if the donor gave appreciated property to a donee shortly before the donee's death, and inherited the same property back from the donee on the donee's death. Before 1982, this "free" step-up in basis was not commonly attempted because the transfer to the donee would have been a taxable gift in all significant cases. Large gift-tax free transfers became possible, however, with the adoption of the unlimited marital deduction and the dramatic increase in the unified credit in 1981.

Section 1014(e) applies if: (1) appreciated property is transferred by a donor to a donee, (2) the donee dies within one year of receiving the property, and (3) the property returns to the donor or to the donor's spouse as a result of the donee's death. If § 1014(e) applies, the donor's basis in the property is the basis of the property in the hands of the donee immediately before his death.

Application of § 1014(e) may be illustrated as follows:

Example: *H* owns Blackacre, which is worth $100,000 and for which *H*'s basis is $60,000. *H* is married to *W*, who is suffering from terminal cancer.

In Year 1 *H* deeds Blackacre to *W*. Later in the year, *W* dies, devising Blackacre to *H*.

In the example, *H*'s basis in Blackacre under § 1014(a) is $100,000, which is the date of death value of the property. Because of § 1014(e), however, *H* keeps *W*'s basis in the property, which was $60,000, *H*'s basis before the gift from *H* to *W*. *See* § 1015(a).

The rule of § 1014(e) also prevents parents and children from transferring property to one or the other shortly before one of them dies when the estate is not sufficiently large to use all of the decedent's unified credit. For example, if a donor's elderly parent is about to die with a gross estate of $100,000, it was possible before the enactment of § 1014(e) for the child to give the parent low basis assets and then inherit them back with a new fair market basis.

When the estate tax is repealed for the year 2010, a carryover basis at death rule will generally apply. *See* § 1022 (effective for decedents dying after December 31, 2009) and the discussion at § 2.06[A], *supra*. Although the carryover-basis amount may be increased by up to $1.3 million and an additional $3 million dollars if the property is acquired by the decedent's surviving spouse in a qualifying manner, see § 1022(b) and (c), these exceptions may not be applicable for property acquired by the decedent by gift within 3 years of death. *See* § 1022 (d)(1)(C).

The repeal of § 2035 with respect to outright transfers is not always beneficial. Although its repeal allows post-transfer appreciation to be excluded from the decedent's gross estate, it also denies the donee the advantage of a stepped-up basis under § 1014. Because the transferred property is not in the estate, the donee takes the donor's carryover basis. *See* § 1015. In the case of a nontaxable estate, the result is a net tax loss. As a result, donors near death who own appreciated assets might well decide either not to give them during life, or to give them in a manner which triggers estate tax inclusion, thereby preserving the application of § 2035(a). For taxable estates, the transfer of property with a low income tax basis transferred shortly before the donor dies may produce a net "tax negative" depending on how much the fair market value exceeds the income tax basis, the amount of post-gift appreciation, and the applicable tax rates (income and estate tax).

Finally, § 2035 can have an impact on the estate's ability to use § 303, which allows a tax-favored redemption of shares in closely held companies for the purposes of paying the estate tax. Section 303 requires that the stock in the corporation exceed 35% of the value of the decedent's gross estate, with adjustments for §§ 2053 and 2054 items. Because § 2035(c) retains the automatic inclusion rule for the purposes of § 303, transfers cannot be made within three years of the decedent's death to increase the estate's percentage up to 35%.

Problems

1. Assume that on June 1 of Year 1, *H* gave his wife, *W*, property worth $100,000. *H*'s adjusted basis in the property was $60,000.

    a. What are the federal gift and income tax consequences of the transfer?

b. Assume that *W* dies on May 1 of Year 2, that the property is then worth $100,000, that *W*'s will bequeaths all of her property to *H*, and that on July 1 of Year 2, *H* sells the property for $125,000. What is *H*'s reportable gain?

c. Assume the same facts as in (b), but that *W* dies on June 30 of Year 2. What is *H*'s reportable gain?

d. Assume that *W* dies on May 1 of Year 2, that the property is then worth $100,000, that *W*'s will bequeaths the property to *B*, her only child, and that on July 1 of Year 2, *B* sells the property for $125,000. What is *B*'s reportable gain?

e. Finally, assume in (b) above *W*'s will leaves the property to a trust for the benefit of *H* instead of outright to him. Does that change your answer? *See* Priv. Ltr. Ruls. 9026036 (issue 6) and 9321050 (issue 6).

2. Assume that in a community property regime, *W* converts her separate property into community property. *H* dies within one year of *W*'s transfer and devises his one-half interest in the community property to *W*. How should *W*'s basis in the property be determined? Consider §§ 1014(b)(6) and 1014(e).

Chapter 7

RETAINED INTERESTS

Donors retain interests in transferred property for a number of reasons. For example, it is very common for individuals to establish an inter vivos trust as a substitute for a will. When the client dies, the property held in trust will not be subject to probate. The creator of such a trust (hereinafter referred to as the grantor) will retain the income from the trust for life, and the corpus will be distributed in the same way the grantor's will would have disposed of the decedent's estate. Similarly, a transfer may be made concomitant to remarriage, with the property owner establishing a trust. The income of the trust is payable to the new spouse for life and the corpus will revert to the grantor at the spouse's death, or, if the grantor is dead, to the objects of the grantor's bounty. These and other examples are discussed in this Chapter.

§ 7.01 Retention of an Income Interest

Transfers with retained income interests are common substitutes for wills. Retained income interests allow the grantor to enjoy the economic benefits of the transferred property until death while providing a valid disposition of the property outside of probate. Transfers of this type may also be used to protect the underlying assets from the grantor's creditors, or even to avoid the elective share claims of a surviving spouse.

[A] Gift Tax

[1] In General

Code: §§ 2501, 2511, 2512, 2503(b), and 2702.

Regulations: Treas. Reg. §§ 25.2512–5(f); 25.2702–1(a), –(b), –2(a)(1) through –2(a)(4).

A grantor who creates an irrevocable trust, retaining a life income interest with the remainder to another person at the grantor's death, has made a completed transfer of the remainder interest. *See* Treas. Reg. § 25.2511–1(e). Absent application of § 2702 or the *Robinette* doctrine, the gift of the remainder interest will equal its actuarially determined value based on the valuation rules of § 7520. Because a remainder interest in property is a future interest, the gift of the remainder does not qualify for the gift tax annual exclusion under § 2503(b). The gift tax liability exists even though the value of the transferred property will be included in the grantor's estate under § 2036, discussed below. Subjecting the same property to gift taxes and estate taxes does not result in double taxation, however. As discussed in Chapter 3, when the same property is subject to both taxes, the definition of adjusted taxable gifts removes the taxable gift from the amount that is added to the taxable estate to compute the estate taxes payable by the decedent's estate. *See* § 2001(b). Moreover, any gift taxes paid on the taxable gift will be a credit against the estate tax liability. *See* § 2001(b)(2). The net effect of the adjustment and the credit is to undo the gift tax consequences of the lifetime transfer at the time of the decedent's death, although the decedent lost the use of any money actually paid in gift taxes.

[2] Section 2702

If a grantor transfers a remainder interest in property, or any part of it, to a member of the grantor's family,[1] while retaining some interest in or control over the property, § 2702 applies to value the grantor's retained interest at zero.

> **Example:** *G* transfers property to a trust. *G* retains the income for life. The remainder is payable to his child, *C*. The zero value rule of § 2702 applies to the transfer. The value of the remainder interest will be the value of the transferred property rather than its actuarial value. Thus, the gift tax value of the remainder is the value of the property transferred even though the grantor has a retained interest. *See* Treas. Reg. § 25.2702–1(b). The result would be the same if the trust income were payable to *C*, and *G* retained a reversionary interest in the trust corpus.

Section 2702 is a gift tax valuation rule that determines the value of a grantor's retained interest. It does not determine if a gift has occurred, and it is not applicable to estate or GST taxes. For § 2702 to apply, the grantor must make a completed gift of an interest in property, but not the grantor's entire interest. Thus, if a donor makes a transfer that is not a complete gift of any portion of the transferred property, there is no taxable gift to be valued under the rules of § 2702. Moreover, if the transfer is a complete gift of the grantor's entire interest in property, there is no retained interest to be valued under § 2702. It is only when the transfer is an incomplete gift in part and completed gift in part of the donor's interest that § 2702 comes into play.

Section 2702 provides a few notable exceptions to the zero value rule that allow the actuarial value of the grantor's retained interest to be taken into account, resulting in a gift equal to the actuarial value of the remainder interest. These exceptions include qualified interests, such as grantor retained annuity trusts (GRATs), grantor retained unitrusts (GRUTs), personal residence trusts (PRTs), and qualified personal residence trusts (QPRTs). *See generally* Mitchell M. Gans, *Grits, GRATs and GRUTs: A Comparative Analysis*, 11 VA. TAX L. REV. 761 (1992).

It is difficult to overstate the impact of § 2702 on transfers with retained interests. In most situations, these transfers will involve family members. The effect of the statute is to discourage transfers with retained interests unless the transfer is structured to satisfy the parameters of one of the exceptions discussed in § 4.02[B][3], *supra* (regarding exceptions to § 2702). Throughout

---

[1] A member of the grantor's family includes the grantor's spouse, a sibling, or an ancestor or descendant of the grantor or the grantor's spouse, or the spouse of any such sibling, ancestor, or descendant. *See* § 2702(e), which incorporates the definition of family member used in § 2704(c)(2).

this Chapter and in Chapters 8 and 9, § 2702 will affect the gift taxation of many of the transactions examined.

[3]　Donors as Permissible Recipients of Trust Income

The following ruling considers the gift tax consequences when a grantor does not retain the right to receive trust income, but is only a permissible recipient of trust income.

Revenue Ruling 77–378

1977–2 C.B. 347

Advice has been requested as to the application of the federal gift tax to a transfer to a trust, in the circumstances described below.

On January 16, 1975, approximately one half of the grantor's income-producing property was conveyed to an irrevocable inter vivos trust created on that day. The terms of the trust require the trustee (a corporation) to accumulate income and add it to principal during the lifetime of the grantor. Upon the death of the grantor, the trust will terminate and its assets will be paid to the grantor's spouse and children.

Pursuant to the trust agreement the trustee was empowered to pay to the grantor such amounts of the trust's income and principal as it determines in its absolute and uncontrolled discretion. However, under the applicable state law the trustee's decision whether to distribute trust assets to the grantor is entirely voluntary. The grantor can not require that any of the trust's assets be distributed to the grantor nor can the creditors of the grantor reach any of the trust's assets.[2]

The question presented is whether the grantor has parted with dominion and control of the property transferred so that the Federal gift tax is applicable to the transfer, in view of the power of the trustee to return the property to the grantor.

. . .

The gift tax is an excise tax upon the donor's act of making the transfer and is measured by the value of the property passing from the donor. The tax is not imposed upon the receipt of the property by the donee, nor is it necessarily determined by the measure of enrichment resulting to the donee from the transfer. *See* Treas. Reg. § 25.2511–2(a).

Even though a trustee may have an unrestricted power to return all of the trust's assets to the grantor, if the grantor's interest in the trust is not enforceable either by the grantor or on the grantor's behalf, then the grantor has parted with dominion and control over the property transferred into trust. *See* Treas. Reg. § 25.2511–2(b). Furthermore, if the grantor retains such a mere expectancy that the trustee will distribute trust assets to the grantor

---

[2] Several states permit grantors to establish a trust for their own benefit without risk that creditors may reach the trust assets. *See, e.g.* 1997 Alaska Stat § 34.40.110; 12 Del. Code Ann. Title 12 §§ 3570–3575 (1997); and Mo. Rev. Stat. § 456.080.3. Eds.

rather than an enforceable interest in the trust, the mere expectancy does not prevent the completion or reduce the value of the gift. *Herzog v. Commissioner*, 41 B.T.A. 509 (1940), *aff'd*, 116 F.2d 591 (2d Cir. 1941).

In *Herzog*, the grantor transferred assets in trust with instructions to the trustee to pay the income to the grantor or the grantor's wife at such times and in such amounts as the trustee should deem proper with a remainder over to certain named beneficiaries. On the same day the trust was created the trustee directed that all of the trust income be paid to the grantor. The grantor argued that for gift tax purposes the value of property transferred in trust should be reduced by an amount representing the value of the income for life receivable by the grantor if the trustee in the trustee's uncontrolled discretion should so direct. The Board of Tax Appeals stated:

> There would be no doubt of his nonliability for gift tax upon the value of the income if he had reserved to himself the absolute right to the income for his life. But he made no such reservation. He transferred the entire property. Whether he would enjoy any of its income depended entirely on the trustee, who, in his uncontrolled discretion, could deprive him of it completely. It was only by virtue of the trustee's direction, which on this record must be regarded as entirely voluntary. [sic] that the donor received any of the income; and this direction might be terminated whenever the trustee deemed it proper that the wife should receive the income. Such a hope or passive expectancy is not a right. It is not enough to lessen the value of the property transferred. 41 B.T.A. at 510 (citations omitted).

Accordingly, the Board held that since the transfer by the grantor was complete the gift tax was, by its own terms, applicable to the value of the entire property transferred.

In the instant case, the grantor has parted with dominion and control over the property that the grantor transferred into trust. Although the trustee has an unrestricted power to pay trust assets to the grantor, the grantor cannot require that any of the trust's assets be distributed to the grantor nor can the grantor utilize the assets by going into debt and relegating the grantor's creditors to the trust. *See* Paolozzi v. Commissioner, 23 T.C. 182 (1954), *acq.*, 1962-2 C.B. 5. Whether the grantor would enjoy any of the trust's assets is dependent entirely on the uncontrolled discretion of the trustee. Such a hope or passive expectancy does not lessen the value of the property transferred. Accordingly, the Federal gift tax is applicable to the entire value of the property transferred to the trust by the grantor.

In Rev. Rul. 62-13, 1962-1 C.B. 181, the Service announced that it would follow the decisions in *Commissioner v. Vander Weele*, 254 F.2d 895 (6th Cir. 1958), and *Gramm v. Commissioner*, 17 T.C. 1063 (1951), *acq.*, 1962-1 C.B. 4. In the *Vander Weele* and *Gramm* cases the courts held that the grantors of irrevocable inter vivos trusts had not completely parted with dominion and control over the trust assets since they retained enforceable rights to some or all of the trusts' assets. For example, in *Vander Weele*, the court noted that under state law the grantor could in actuality retain the economic benefit and enjoyment of the entire trust income and corpus by borrowing money or by selling, assigning, or transferring the grantor's interest in the trust fund and relegating the grantor's creditors to the trust fund for payment. *See* 254 F.2d at 898. Thus, in view of the settlor's retained rights there was no assurance that anything of value would pass to the remaindermen and the gift was entirely incomplete. *See Holtz v. Commissioner*, 38 T.C. 37 (1962), *acq.*, 1962–2 C.B. 4. The court in *Gramm* made it clear that where the grantor reserves no interest, the gift is complete. It did this by distinguishing *Herzog* on the ground that there "the grantor did not reserve the income to himself, and whether he received it or not was in the uncontrolled discretion of the trustee." However, Rev. Rul. 62–13 may be read to imply that broad powers given to a trustee to invade trust income and corpus for the benefit of the grantor may be sufficient to render the gift incomplete even though the grantor's interest in the trust assets is unenforceable. Therefore, Rev. Rul. 62–13 is hereby clarified to remove any implication that an entirely voluntary power held by a trustee to distribute all of the trust's assets to the grantor is sufficient to render a gift incomplete either in whole or in part.

Accordingly, in the present case, the Federal gift tax is applicable to the entire value of the property transferred to the trust by the grantor.

Rev. Rul. 62–13 is clarified.

The result in Revenue Ruling 77–378 was applied in Private Letter Ruling 9837007. This ruling involved an asset protection trust created by the donor for herself and her descendants. The controlling state law permitted the donor to establish a spendthrift trust and retain a discretionary interest in income and principal.

In the 1990s asset protection trusts gained popularity and some states such as Delaware and Alaska enacted statutes that permit donors to create spendthrift trusts for their own benefit which are beyond the reach of creditors. *See* Footnote 2. Historically, donors could not create spendthrift trusts for their own benefit. *See* SCOTT ON TRUSTS §§ 156 and 156.2.

When the trustee's powers are subject to ascertainable standards such that it can be enforced to control the trustee's action, the standard defines fixed rights in the grantor and remaindermen. The value of the retained interest could be deducted from the value of the transferred property. *See Commissioner v. Irving Trust Co.*, 147 F.2d 946 (2d Cir. 1945); Treas. Reg. § 25.2511–2(b). *See also* Priv. Ltr. Rul. 8038163, in which a grantor who transferred property to a trust but retained a right to monthly income from the trust and a monthly payment from the trust principal, and who also provided that the trust principal could be used to pay the debts of his estate, made an incomplete gift to the remaindermen named in the trust. The Service held that "by retaining the power to subject the trust corpus to the payment of his debtors [sic] the donor has effectively retained the trust corpus for his own use."

It is unlikely, however, that a discretionary interest will be a qualified interest under § 2702, if the transfer is to a family member and the gift is complete in part, but incomplete in part. Thus, § 2702 will value the retained discretionary interest at zero for gift tax purposes, *i.e.*, the donor will report the entire value of the transferred property as a taxable gift and no portion will likely qualify for an annual exclusion.

Problems

1. In 2002, *G*, a 50-year-old widow, transfers $1 million of property to a trust. The income is payable to *G* for her life and, at *G*'s death, the corpus is to be distributed to *Y*, an unrelated person. *G* is the trustee. What are the federal gift consequences of this transfer, assuming *G* has made no previous taxable gifts, and that the applicable interest rate under § 7520 is 8%?

Alternatively, assume *Y* is *G*'s daughter. What is the impact of § 2702?

2. *G*, age 50, transfers $100,000 to a trust. She retains the right to a $6,000 annual annuity for life. The remainder is payable to *N*, a niece of *G*. What are the gift tax consequences? What would the gift tax consequences be if the remainder beneficiary was *G*'s brother, *B*?

3. *G* transfers $100,000 to a trust reserving the right to trust income for 5 years. At the end of the trust term, the trust is payable to *G*'s child. If *G* dies sooner than 5 years, the trust terminates and pays over to *G*'s estate. What is the gift tax consequence to *G*, assuming an 8% § 7520 rate. *See* Walton v. Commissioner, 115 T.C. 589 (2000) (*en banc*).

4. *G*, age 50, wants to live in her $200,000 house for the next ten years; thereafter she wants *C*, her child, to live in the house. What advice would you give *G*? *See* Treas. Reg. § 25.2702–5.

[B]   Estate Tax

[1]   In General

Code: § 2036(a)(1).

Regulations: Treas. Reg. § 20.2036–1.

Inter vivos transfers in which the decedent retained either lifetime possession or enjoyment, or the right to the income from the transferred property, have been includable in the decedent's gross estate since 1931. Before 1931, the Service argued that such transfers were "intended to take effect on or after death," under language in the Code (at that time). In 1931, language was added to specifically include such transfers. The 1931 language has since been transformed into § 2036(a)(1), which taxes the property whether the retained interest is (1) for the life of the decedent; (2) for a period not ascertainable without reference to his death; or (3) for a period which does not end before his death.

Section 2036 treats a transfer with retained enjoyment for life as a testamentary substitute because the decedent must die before someone else can enjoy the property. By retaining the right to the income from the trust property, the grantor retains the economic benefit of the trust property. The grantor has, in effect, made a testamentary disposition which justifies the imposition of the federal estate tax. A transfer in trust with a retained life estate is the practical equivalent of keeping the property, using only the income from it, and then leaving the property by devise.

The impact of applying § 2036 is that the entire estate tax value of the property producing the retained income is included in the gross estate, including any appreciation between the time of transfer and the date of death. If, of course, the decedent had only retained the right to income from a portion of the property, only that portion would be includable. *See* Treas. Reg. § 20.2036–1(a).

The most common example under § 2036(a)(1) involves a retained life interest in property:

> **Example 1:** *G*, age 55, transfers $100,000 of property to trust. She reserves the income for life and the remainder is distributable to *X*, an unrelated person. *G* later dies when the property in the trust has appreciated in value to $125,000. On the date of the gift, the applicable interest rate under § 7520 was 8%.

In Example 1, the value of the gift to *X* equals $21,166 ($100,000 times the actuarial factor for a remainder after a life interest in someone age 55), for which no present interest gift exclusion is available because *X*'s interest is a future interest. At *G*'s death, the $125,000 value of the trust property will be included in *G*'s gross estate under § 2036(a)(1), because *G* retained the income from the transferred property for her life.

Section 2036(a)(1) also applies if the transferor retains a legal life estate in transferred property:

> **Example 2:** *G* deeds real property to *X*, but *G* reserves a legal life estate in the property. *G* later dies.

At *G*'s death the value of the real property will be included in *G*'s gross estate because *G* retained the possession and enjoyment of the transferred property for life.

The retained interest need not, however, be phrased in terms of a life estate. Section 2036(a)(1) also applies to interests retained for periods not ascertainable without reference to the grantor's death, and to periods which do not end before the grantor dies. Thus, it would apply to the following examples:

> **Example 3:** *G* creates a lifetime trust. He reserves the income for ten years. The remainder is distributable to *X*, an unrelated person. *G* dies during the ten year period.

> **Example 4:** *G* creates a lifetime trust. He reserves the income for the life of his wife, *W*, and the remainder is distributable to *X*, an unrelated person. *G* dies before *W*.

> **Example 5:** *G* creates a lifetime trust, reserving the income for a period ending six months before his death, but payable six months after it is earned. The remainder is distributable to *X*, an unrelated person.

In Examples 3, 4, and 5, the value of the trust property will be includable in the grantor's gross estate at death. In Examples 3 and 4, *G* retained the income interest for a period which did not end before death. *See* Treas. Reg.

§ 20.2036–1(a). In Example 5, *G* retained the income interest for a period that could not be determined without reference to his death. *See* Treas. Reg. § 20.2036–1(b)(1)(i). In Examples 3 and 4, § 2033 would also apply because *G* owned the balance of the term at his death. Because this income interest is part of the entire value of the trust corpus, however, application of § 2033 would be redundant and the trust would be reported only under § 2036. Otherwise, double taxation of the interest would result.

Commissioner v. Nathan's Estate

159 F.2d 546 (7th Cir. 1947), cert. denied, 334 U.S. 843 (1948)

[Decedent transferred property to trust, making the income payable to his sister for life, and then to the decedent for life, then to a remainderman.]

Evans, C.J.:

. . .

The doubt, if any exists in this case, is over the question, was the property which was transferred and in which decedent retained a contingent life interest, terminable by his death or by that of his sister? Stated differently, was the period during which his contingent estate therein existed ascertainable without reference to his death or did the period of the contingent estate which decedent retained in the trust he created have a possible ending before his death?

Notwithstanding some doubt (in view of [*Estate of Curie v. Commissioner,* 4 T.C. 1175 (1945)]) we hold the language of the statute must be so construed as to impose an estate tax on the property covered by this trust less the value of the life estate of the sister . . . .

The Commissioner could not have found or held otherwise. The transfer in which the deceased retained a contingent estate was held by him for a period which did not in fact end before his death. It was his death, not his sister's death, which terminated his contingent interest . . . .

The factual difference between the instant case and the usual trust agreement which may be called testamentary has not been ignored. The decedent here retained only a contingent estate which became effective in case he survived his sister. Notwithstanding this rather important fact so far as enjoyment is concerned, it did not take the transfer out of the reach of the language of section [2036(a)(1)] which controls our decision. We cannot lessen the effect or the meaning of the words because the grantor's interest was less certain or the enjoyment of the estate reserved more remote. We feel we must give the words used their fair, rightful meaning and we can not make them depend on the size or nature of the grantor's reservation appearing in his transfer. The vital test of said reservation in grantor's favor necessitates an answer to the query—was the transfer one which was for a period not ascertainable without reference to his death?

———

The *Nathan* result is contained in Treasury Regulation § 20.2036–1(a), which provides, in the secondary life estate situation, that the gross estate includes the value of the entire trust property "less only the value of any outstanding income interest which is not subject to the decedent's interest or right and which is actually being enjoyed by another person at the time for the decedent's death."

The discussion in Chapter 4 considers the gift tax issues for donors of charitable remainder trusts. In addition, lifetime deferred giving transfers can also have estate tax consequences. For a donor who transfers property to a charitable remainder trust and retains a life interest, most or all of the value of the trust assets are included in the donor's gross estate. Revenue Ruling 82–105 illustrates the computation of the amount included by § 2036 of a charitable remainder trust where the donor retained a life interest. The decedent's estate will receive an estate tax charitable deduction for the value of the remainder interest that passes to the charitable beneficiary. If no other noncharitable beneficiaries have an interest in the trust property, the inclusion should be offset by the charitable deduction.

Revenue Ruling 82–105

1982–1 C.B. 133

For purposes of section 2036 of the Internal Revenue Code, what portion of the value of a charitable remainder annuity trust is includible in the grantor's gross estate when the grantor is the private annuitant for life?

FACTS

In 1974 *D* created a trust that qualified as a charitable remainder annuity trust under section 664 of the Code. The trust agreement provided for an annuity of 12x dollars to be paid each year to *D* for life and for the remainder upon *D*'s death to be distributed to *N*, a charitable organization described in section 2055(a). The trust was funded with 200x dollars. *D* died on March 1, 1980. The value of the trust assets on *D*'s date of death was 300x dollars. *D*'s executor did not elect to use the alternate valuation date.

LAW AND ANALYSIS

Section 2036(a)(1) of the Code provides, in part, that a decedent's gross estate shall include the value of any interest in property transferred by the decedent if the decedent retained for life the possession or enjoyment of, or the right to income from, the property.

Section 20.2036–1(a) of the Estate Tax Regulations provides generally that if the decedent retained or reserved an interest or right with respect to all of the property transferred by the decedent, the amount to be included in the gross estate under section 2036 of the Code is the value of the entire property on the date of death. If the decedent retained a right with respect to only part of the property transferred, the amount to be included in the decedent's gross estate under § 2036 is the proportionate amount of corpus.

Under the trust agreement D did not retain the right to the income from the cash transferred, but retained the right to receive the annuity amount. In effect, D has retained the right to income from a portion of the property transferred.

In order to determine the amount includible under section 2036 of the Code, it is necessary to ascertain the specific portion of corpus over which D, in effect, possessed an income interest.

In Northeastern Pennsylvania National Bank & Trust Company v. United States, 387 U.S. 213 (1967), Ct. D. 1916, 1967–2 C.B. 343, a bequest to the decedent's spouse of a fixed monthly stipend, payable from trust income or corpus, was held to satisfy the requirement of section 2056(b)(5) of the Code that the spouse receive all the income from a specific portion of trust corpus. The specific portion of corpus qualifying for the marital deduction was determined by computing the amount of corpus necessary to produce the guaranteed monthly payment, assuming a fixed rate of return.

This computation is discussed in Citizens National Bank of Evansville v. United States, 359 F.2d 817 (7th Cir. 1966), *cert. denied*, 387 U.S. 941 (1966), which involved an identical issue. The court computed the allowable marital deduction by capitalizing the annual annuity payment at an assumed rate of 3½ percent (rate specified under section 20.2031–7 of the regulations, applicable in the case of decedents dying prior to 1971).

In Estate of Marvin L. Pardee v. Commissioner, 49 T.C. 140 (1967), *acq.,* 1973–2 C.B. 3, the decedent created a trust and retained the right to use the income of the trust to satisfy a legal obligation of the decedent to pay, as child support, the sum of $500 per month. The court held that, under section 2036(a)(1) of the Code, the right retained by the decedent was the right to satisfy the legal obligation of $500 per month, and the amount includible in the decedent's estate was the amount that is required to yield monthly payments of $500 per month at 3½ percent (rate specified under section 20.2031–7 of the regulations, applicable in the case of decedents dying prior to 1971). *See also* United States National Bank of Portland v. United States, 188 F. Supp. 332 (D. Ore. 1960), which discusses a computation similar to the computation in *Pardee*.

For estate tax purposes, the annual rate of return of a charitable remainder annuity trust is presumed to be 6 percent in the case of decedents dying after December 31, 1970. *See* section 20.2031–10 of the Estate Tax Regulations. *See also* section 1.664–2(c) of the Income Tax Regulations, which refers to section 20.2031–10 of the Estate Tax Regulations, and Rev. Rul. 77–374, 1977–2 C.B. 329. Therefore, in accordance with *Northeastern*, the portion of corpus over which D has retained a right to income is that portion that will yield an annuity of 12x dollars a year, assuming a 6 percent annual rate of return. At a 6 percent rate of return on investment, the amount of corpus necessary to generate 12x dollars per year is 200x dollars:

$$12\text{x dollars}/.06 \ = \ 200\text{x dollars}$$

Accordingly, although the value of the corpus on *D*'s date of death was 300x dollars, only 200x dollars is includible in *D*'s gross estate under section 2036 of the Code. Alternatively, if the value of the trust assets was 200x dollars or less on *D*'s date of death, the entire corpus would be includible in *D*'s gross estate. Compare Rev. Rul. 76–273, 1976–2 C.B. 268, which demonstrates the application of section 2036 of the Code to a charitable remainder unitrust.

HOLDING

For purposes of section 2036 of the Code, the portion of the value of a charitable remainder annuity trust that is includible in *D*'s gross estate at death is the amount necessary, at the rate of 6 percent as specified under section 20.2031–10 of the regulations, to yield the guaranteed annual payment. In the instant case, the amount includible is 200x dollars:

$$(12\text{x dollars}/.06 \ = \ 200\text{x dollars})$$

However, because the 200x dollars constitutes part of the remainder interest passing to a charitable organization described in section 2055(a), the 200x dollars is deductible from *D*'s gross estate under section 2055. The amount of the charitable deduction cannot exceed the value of the transferred property required to be included in the gross estate. Section 2055(d).

The holding of this ruling applies only to the portion of the value of a charitable remainder annuity trust that is includible in the gross estate under section 2036. The ruling does not consider the amount, if any, that may be includible in the gross estate under any other provisions of the Code.

When the donor's spouse has a concurrent or successive interest in a charitable remainder trust that continues after the donor dies or arises upon the donor's death, but there are no other noncharitable beneficiaries of the trust, the combination of marital deduction permitted under § 2056(b)(8) and the charitable deduction should offset the inclusion of the trust in the donor's estate. Alternatively, if someone other than the donor's spouse has an interest in the charitable trust following the donor's interest or the spouse's interest, the inclusion in the donor's estate of the value of the charitable trust will have estate tax consequences. The charitable deduction will not offset the full amount of the inclusion. Moreover, the spouse's interest will not qualify for the estate tax marital deduction. None of the interests of any of the noncharitable beneficiaries will qualify for any deduction.

When a donor names someone other than himself or his spouse as the noncharitable beneficiary, but retains no interest in the property transferred, there is no estate tax inclusion in the donor's estate, regardless of when the donor dies. As noted in Chapter 4, however, the transfer will likely create a taxable gift, which reduces the ultimate estate and gift tax unified credit available to the decedent's estate.

As previously discussed, when § 2036 causes an estate tax inclusion of a transfer that was a taxable gift by the grantor, the amount of the gift is deducted when computing the decedent's adjusted taxable gifts. *See* § 2001(b). Moreover, any gift taxes paid on the taxable gift will be a credit against the estate tax liability. *See* § 2001(b)(2).

Problems

For purposes of the problems below, assume the § 7520 rate is 8%.

1. Five years ago, *G*, a 50-year-old widow, transferred $1 million of property to a trust. The income is payable to *G* for her life, and at her death, the corpus is to be distributed to *Y*, an unrelated person. *T* is the trustee. At *G*'s death, the property is valued at $1.2 million. What are the federal gift and estate tax consequences of this transfer? Does the transfer constitute an "adjusted taxable gift" for the purposes of § 2001 when *G* dies? Would your answers change if the trust was created by declaration of trust, so that *G* was the trustee? What if *Y* is *G*'s daughter?

2. *G* transfers $100,000 in property to an irrevocable trust. The income is payable to *G* for ten years and then the corpus is to be distributed to *C*. *G* pays a gift tax upon the value of the interest passing to *C*.

     a. What are the gift and estate tax consequences if *G* dies four years after creating the trust?

     b. What are the gift and estate tax consequences if *G* dies two years after creating the trust?

     c. What are the estate tax consequences if *G* dies three weeks after the end of the ten year term?

3. At age 53, *G* transfers $100,000 to a trust and reserves the right to an annual annuity of $6,000 for 12 years. On the termination of the trust, any accumulated income and principal is payable to *B*, her brother. *G* dies at age 64 when the trust assets are valued at $300,000. What are the gift and estate tax consequences? *See* Rev. Rul. 82–105, 1982–1 C.B. 133.

4. At age 53, *G* transfers $100,000 to a trust and reserves for life the annual right for life to receive 6% of the value of the corpus, with accumulated income and principal payable to *S*, her sister at death. *G* dies at age 64 when the trust assets are valued at $300,000. What are the gift and estate tax consequences? *See* Rev. Rul. 76–273, 1976–2 C.B. 268.

5. *D* transfers $100,000 to an irrevocable trust. The income is payable to *A* for life, then to *D* for life. The remainder is distributable to *B*. Assume that *D* is not related to *A* or *B*. At the time the trust is created, *A* is age 40. When *A* is age 55 and the trust assets are valued at $120,000, *D* dies.

     a. What are the gift tax consequences of creating the trust? Consider the impact of § 2702.

     b. What would be included in *D*'s gross estate? Consider the impact of § 2702.

     c. What are the estate tax consequences of the trust if *D* survives *A* and then dies?

d. What result in (a), (b), and (c) if D is related to A or B within the meaning of § 2702?

e. For D's estate, what is the amount of D's adjusted taxable gifts?

[2] Discretionary and Support Interests

Gokey v. Commissioner

72 T.C. 721 (1979)

Wiles, Judge . . .

[In 1961, the decedent, Joseph G. Gokey, created irrevocable trusts for the benefit of two of his children, Gretchen and Patrick. Mrs. Gokey was the trustee. The trust provided:

> Until each beneficiary becomes twenty-one (21) years of age, the Trustee shall use such part or all of the net income of his or her trust for the support, care, welfare, and education of the beneficiary thereof, payments from such net income to be made to such beneficiary or in such other manner as the Trustee deems to be in the best interest of the beneficiary, and any unused income shall be accumulated and added to the principal of such beneficiary's trust. After each beneficiary becomes twenty-one (21) years of age, the Trustee shall pay to him or her, in convenient installments, the entire net income of his or her trust. In the Trustee's discretion, said income payments may be supplemented at any time with payments of principal from a beneficiary's share whenever the Trustee deems any such payment necessary for the support, care, welfare, or education of the beneficiary thereof.

In 1969, Mrs. Gokey appointed First National bank as co-trustee. Thereafter, some of the trust income was regularly used to pay education expenses, professional fees, and Federal and state income taxes of each beneficiary. The rest of the income was transferred to Mrs. Gokey as guardian for the beneficiary. None of the income was ever accumulated and added to principal. Decedent died in October of 1969.]

Decedent's estate tax return did not include any portion of the value of assets in the irrevocable trusts created . . . for the benefit of Gretchen [and] Patrick . . . . Respondent determined under section 2036 that the entire value of the assets in Gretchen's and Patrick's trusts was includable in decedent's gross estate.

. . .

The . . . issue is whether decedent retained the possession or enjoyment of, or the right to the income from, property transferred by him to irrevocable trusts for the benefit of Gretchen and Patrick. If so, the value of the property in those trusts is properly includable in decedent's gross estate under section 2036. The resolution of this issue depends upon whether, within the meaning of section 20.2036–1(b)(2), Estate Tax Regs., the income or property of the trusts was to be applied toward the discharge of the decedent's legal obligation to support Gretchen and Patrick during his lifetime.

Respondent contends that under Illinois law decedent was under a legal duty to support his minor children, Gretchen and Patrick; that the terms of the children's trusts clearly require the trustees to use the trusts' income and property for their support; and that, therefore, the value of the trust property is includable in decedent's gross estate. Petitioners do not dispute decedent's obligation to support Gretchen and Patrick under Illinois law; however, they contend that the use of the property or income therefrom for the children's support was within the unrestricted discretion of the trustees; that even if the trusts did not give the trustees any discretion in this matter, the decedent nevertheless intended to grant them this discretion; that the use of the term "welfare" in the trusts creates an unascertainable standard which, even if ascertainable, is much broader than the standard for support; and that, therefore, the value of the trust property is not includable in decedent's gross estate. We agree with respondent on this issue.

Respondent relies upon sec. 20.2036–1(b)(2), Estate Tax Regs., which states that the use, possession, right to the income, or other enjoyment of the transferred property is considered as having been retained by or reserved to the decedent within the meaning of section 2036(a)(1) to the extent that the use, possession, right to the income, or other enjoyment is to be applied toward the discharge of a legal obligation of decedent which includes an obligation to support a dependent. "Is to be applied" is not to be read as "may be applied," which exists where an independent trustee is vested with discretion over distributions. *Estate of Mitchell v. Commissioner*, 55 T.C. 576, 580 (1970). This creates a factual question as to whether the income from the trust property must be restricted or confined to fulfilling the settlor's obligation to support his dependents. *Estate of Lee v. Commissioner*, 33 T.C. 1064, 1067 (1960).

We believe the language of the children's trusts found in section 2 of the 1961 trust agreement which relates "shall use such part or all of the net income . . . for the support, care, welfare, and education of the beneficiary" clearly manifests decedent's intent to require the trustees to apply the income for the stated purpose. In our view, it is impossible to construe the instrument as one which gives the trustees discretion as to whether or not income shall be used for "support, care, welfare and education." That standard completely controls the application of the trusts' funds. If those needs exceed the trusts' income, principal may be utilized. If those needs do not absorb all of the trusts' income, the remaining income is accumulated and added to principal. Moreover, the section 2 phrase "payments from such net income to be made to such beneficiary or in such other manner as the Trustee deems to be in the best interest of the beneficiary" does not alter our interpretation. Clearly, this phrase only grants the trustee discretion in the method of payment adopted. Since we find decedent's intent clearly expressed in the trust instrument, we need not look beyond the four corners of the instrument to determine intent.

Petitioners next argue that the use of the word "welfare" within the phrase "the Trustee shall use such part or all of the net income of his or her trust for the support, care, welfare, and education of the beneficiary thereof" in section 2 of the 1961 trust instrument, gives the trustee authority to make nonsupport expenditures which, in turn, violates the "is to be applied" language of section 20.2036–1(b)(2), Estate Tax Regs. They support this theory by arguing that the standard "support, care, welfare, and education" is not ascertainable under, among others, sections 2036(a)(2) and 2041; and even if ascertainable, "welfare" is broader than "support" under Illinois law.

In determining whether "support, care, welfare, and education" is subject to an ascertainable external standard, we must rely upon Illinois law. [Citations omitted.] In *Estate of Wood v. Commissioner*, 39 T.C. 919, 923–924 (1963), we held that the phrase "support, maintenance, welfare, and comfort" was subject to an ascertainable standard:

> We think that these four somewhat overlapping nouns were intended in the aggregate to describe the life beneficiary's standard of living in all its aspects . . . .
>
> Admittedly, the words "support," and "maintenance" are regarded as referable to a standard of living, and the addition of the naked words "comfort" and "welfare" in the context of the instrument before us merely rounds out the standard of living concept.

In *Estate of Bell v. Commissioner*, 66 T.C. 729, 734–735 (1976), we found that the phrase "well being and maintenance in health and comfort" was subject to an ascertainable standard in Illinois:

> Although providing a modicum of discretion to the trustees, this language created a standard enforceable in a court of equity. Under Illinois law, a court of equity would look to the beneficiary's accustomed living standard in compelling compliance by the trustees, either to require income distributions for the stated purposes or to restrain distributions for unauthorized purposes. *In re Whitman*, 22 Ill. 511 (1859) ("support, education, and maintenance"); *French v. Northern Trust Co.*, 197 Ill. 30, 64 N.E. 105, 106 (1902) ("properly maintained and comfortably provided for out of such property"); *Burke v. Burke*, 259 Ill. 262, 102 N.E. 293, 294 (1913) ("the comforts and necessities of life").

We similarly believe that under Illinois law, a court of equity would look to Gretchen's and Patrick's accustomed living standard in compelling compliance by the trustee to require income distributions for the stated purposes. As a result, we find that the terms "support, care, welfare, and education," when viewed in the aggregate, were intended to describe the children's standard of living and are, therefore, subject to an external ascertainable standard. *See Estate of Wood v. Commissioner, supra; Leopold v. United States*, 510 F.2d 617, 620 (9th Cir. 1975). Having found that the phrase in the aggregate created an ascertainable standard requiring the trustee to make expenditures for the children's accustomed living standard, we must reject petitioners' argument that the term "welfare" in the phrase allows the trustees to make nonsupport payments because "welfare" is broader than "support" under Illinois law.

Thus, it only remains for us to decide whether under Illinois law, support is synonymous, for this purpose, with accustomed standard of living. In *Rock*

Island Bank & Trust Co. v. Rhoads, 353 Ill. 131, 187 N.E. 139, 144 (1933), the Illinois Supreme Court stated:

> The word "comfort" must be construed as relating to her support and ease . . . . Had this clause provided only for her comfort, it cannot be doubted that such would be a limitation . . . to maintain her in the *station of life to which she was accustomed.* [Emphasis added.]

We view this language as indicative that, under Illinois law, support is equivalent to accustomed standard of living. We are satisfied that the instrument before us provides an ascertainable standard under Illinois law. Accordingly, we find that decedent's gross estate includes the value of Gretchen's and Patrick's trusts since we find them to be support trusts within the meaning of section 2036(a)(1) and section 20.2036–1(b)(2), Estate Tax Regs.

. . .

To reflect the foregoing,

Decisions will be entered under Rule 155.

———

In Private Letter Ruling 9122005, the Service ruled that the value of the trust is includable in the grantor's gross estate under § 2036(a)(1), because the grantor had the ability, as co-trustee, to use the trust principal to discharge his legal obligation to support his wife. The Service noted that under the applicable local law, as in most states, a husband has an obligation to support his wife. The Service reasoned that this obligation could be discharged under the trust provisions that authorized discretionary distributions for the spouse's "support, maintenance and health."

Inclusion under § 2036(a)(1) could also result if the decedent retains a discretionary power to make distributions to support his child. *See* Rev. Rul. 59–357, 1959–2 C.B. 212. If, however, an independent trustee has discretion whether to apply the trust income for the support of a dependent of the grantor, and the grantor cannot direct the use of the income from the trust for this purpose, the trust property will not be taxed to the grantor because he has not retained a right to the income. *See* Priv. Ltr. Rul. 8504011.

Whether income has been retained requires an interpretation of the governing instrument and local law. Section 2036(a)(1) applies if the decedent-transferor had the legal ability to enjoy the income after the transfer:

Example: *G* creates a trust. The income is payable to *A* for life and the remainder is distributable to *B. T,* the trustee, has the absolute discretion to distribute income to *G.*

If, under applicable state law, the trustee must use the income from the discretionary trust to discharge the grantor's debts, the grantor has retained the right to the income from the trust in the sense that he could anticipate the income by incurring debts. Given that *G*'s creditors could reach the trust income, *G* would be deemed to have retained the income. *Compare* Estate of Paxton v. Commissioner, 86 T.C. 785 (1986) (Washington law), *with* Estate of German v. United States, 7 Cl. Ct. 641 (1985) (holding that consent of an adverse party is necessary before discretionary payments are possible).

Problem

G creates a trust for the benefit of her minor children, *A* and *B*. A bank trustee, *T*, is granted unlimited discretion to make distributions of income or principal for the benefit of *A* and *B*. If *G* dies while *A* and *B* are minors, is the value of the trust included in *G*'s estate?

[3] Implied Retentions

Estate of McNichol v. Commissioner

265 F.2d 667 (3d Cir.), cert. denied, 361 U.S. 829 (1959)

Steel, District Judge.

More than nine years before his death, the decedent purported to convey certain income-producing real estate to his children. Thereafter, pursuant to an oral understanding with his children, the decedent continued to receive the rents from the properties until his death. The Tax Court held that the properties were includable in the decedent's gross estate under [§ 2036(a)(1)]. 29 T.C. 1179. That decision is before us for review.

. . .

Petitioners argue that [§ 2036(a)(1)] is inapplicable to a transfer with a retained income interest unless that interest is reserved in the instrument of transfer. This argument is based upon the statutory provision that the income must be retained "under" the transfer. This is too constricted an interpretation to place on the statute. The statute means only that the life interest must be retained in connection with or as an incident to the transfer . . . .

Next, petitioners point out that the statute speaks of the retention of "the right to the income." Emphasizing the word "right," petitioners argue that Congress has decreed that [§ 2036(a)(1)] is applicable only if a transferor reserves to himself an enforceable claim to the income. Since, according to petitioners, the statute of frauds of Pennsylvania would foreclose judicial enforcement of the oral understanding between the decedent and his children, petitioners conclude that the decedent had no "right" to the income from the property.[3]

It is not necessary for us to delve into Pennsylvania law, for the question is not one of local law. Rather, it is whether Congress intended that

---

[3] The law of Pennsylvania seems not to be as unqualified as petitioners state. If the decedent's children had refused to honor their oral agreement and had collected the rent themselves, the statute of frauds would not have barred the decedent from recovering the rents from the children if, as in the case at bar, they admitted the existence of the oral agreement. Under the circumstances hypothesized decedent would have had an enforceable claim against his children.

[§ 2036(a)(1)] should subject to an estate tax property conveyed under circumstances which here prevail. While state law creates legal interests and rights, it is the federal law which designates which of these interests and rights shall be taxed. *Morgan v. Commissioner*, 1940, 309 U.S. 78, 80–81.

In seeking to discover the type of transfers at which [§ 2036(a)(1)] is aimed, the words "right to the income" are not entitled to undue emphasis. Section [2036(a)(1)] states that property which has been transferred inter vivos is includable in the gross estate of a decedent when the decedent "has retained for his life . . . the possession or enjoyment of, or the right to the income from the property . . . ." Thus, the statute deals with two things: retention of "possession or enjoyment" and retention of "the right to the income."

The history of the statute discloses that "the right to the income" clause was not intended to limit the scope of the "possession and enjoyment" clause used in [§ 2036(a)(1)]. Section [2036(a)(1)] derives directly from section 302(c) of the Act of 1926, as amended in 1931 and 1932. The amendment of 1931 included for the first time express language taxing property which had been transferred inter vivos with a lifetime retention of "the possession or enjoyment of, or the income from" the property. This amendment said nothing about the "right to" income. The words "right to" were inserted for the first time by the 1932 amendment, and the language of the 1932 amendment was carried over into [§ 2036] of the I.R.C. of 1939. This insertion was to make clear that Congress intended that the statute should apply to cases where a decedent was entitled to income even though he did not actually receive it. H.R. Rep. No. 708, 72d Cong.; 1st Sess. pp. 46–7 (C.B. 1939–1, Part 2, pp. 490–1); Sen. Rep. No. 665, 72d Cong.; 1st Sess. pp. 49–50 (C.B. 1939–1, Part 2, p. 532).[4] Hence, the "right to income" clause, instead of circumscribing the "possession or enjoyment" clause in its application to retained income, broadened its sweep.

The conclusion is irresistible that the petitioners' decedent "enjoyed" the properties until he died. If, as was said in *Commissioner v. Estate of Church*, [335 U.S. 632 (1949)], the most valuable property attribute of stocks is their income, it is no less true that one of the most valuable incidents of income-producing real estate is the rent which it yields. He who receives the rent in fact enjoys the property. Enjoyment as used in the death tax statute is not a term of art, but is synonymous with substantial present economic benefit. *Commissioner v. Estate of Holmes*, 1945, 326 U.S. 480, 486. Under this realistic point of view the enjoyment of the properties which the decedent conveyed to his children was continued in decedent by prearrangement and ended only when he died. The transfers were clearly of a kind which Congress intended that [§ 2036(a)(1)] should reach.

This conclusion, petitioners insist, is irreconcilable with the decisions in *Nichols v. Coolidge*, 1927, 274 U.S. 531, and in *Burr's Estate*, 4 T.C. Memo 1289 (1945), *Scheide's Estate*, 6 T.C. Memo 1271 (1947), and *Richards' Estate*,

---

[4] In referring to the changes made by the 1932 Act to the Joint Resolution of March 3, 1931, H.R. Rep. No. 708 states: "(3) The insertion of the words 'the right to the income' in place of the words 'the income' is designed to reach a case where decedent had the right to the income, though he did not actually receive it. This is also a clarifying change." Sen. Rep. No. 665 says the same thing.

1953, 20 T.C. 904. The cited Tax Court decisions may be dispatched summarily. In none of them did it appear, as it does in the case at bar, that the transferor retained the income from the transferred property by virtue of an understanding between the transferor and transferee at the time of the transfer.[5]

Nichols v. Coolidge, supra, however, may not be so readily disposed of. There, the grantor without consideration had conveyed the fee of her residences to her children, with a contemporaneous lease back for a nominal consideration. It was understood that the lease would be renewed so long as the grantor desired. Four years later the grantor died. The Commissioner included the realty in the decedent's gross estate under section 402 of the Act of 1919, 40 Stat. 1097 on the ground that the transfer was "intended to take effect in possession or enjoyment at or after his death." The District Court held that the Commissioner's action was unauthorized. It reasoned that the grantor had no "valid agreement" for the renewal of the lease, that the conveyance gave the grantees full possession and enjoyment of the properties, and that the transaction vested in the grantees "complete title." The Supreme Court affirmed upon the basis of the District Court decision.

The present-day importance of *Nichols v. Coolidge* can be understood only when it is viewed in its historical setting. The statute under which it was decided provided that property transferred inter vivos should be included in the gross estate of a decedent when the transfer was [274 U.S. 531] "in contemplation of or intended to take effect in possession or enjoyment at or after his death."

Interpreting this same statutory language four years later, the Court held in *May v. Heiner*, 1930, 281 U.S. 238, that property which had been irrevocably transferred under a formal agreement of trust reserving to the settlor an interest in the income terminable at his death was not includable in the gross estate of the settlor since the title had vested in the transferee at the time of transfer. Although *May v. Heiner* made no reference to *Nichols v. Coolidge*, both decisions turned upon the fact that legal title had been technically transferred prior to death, and hence the transfer was not "intended to take effect in possession or enjoyment at or after his death". [281 U.S. 238] This dispositive principle was reaffirmed on March 2, 1931 in *Burnet v. Northern Trust Co.*, 1931, 283 U.S. 782; *Morsman v. Burnet*, 1931, 283 U.S. 783, and *McCormick v. Burnet*, 1931, 283 U.S. 784, by per curiam decisions based upon *May v. Heiner*. These decisions upset the long-standing Treasury interpretation of the "intended to take effect in possession or enjoyment" clause which had been in the Revenue Act since 1916, 39 Stat. 777.

The following day Congress, in order to close the obvious tax loophole which the decisions had opened, adopted the Joint Resolution of March 3, 1931. This resolution redefined the phrase "intended to take effect in possession and enjoyment at or after his death" so that it would include a transfer under which the transferor "retained for his life . . . the possession or enjoyment of, or the income from" the transferred property. This provision and its

---

[5] We intimate no opinion as to whether we would have followed these decisions if, in the case before us, the decedent had received the rents following the transfer without an agreement with his children that he might do so.

substantial embodiment in later amendments to the Revenue Act made taxable property which had been transferred inter vivos under a formal declaration of trust with a life estate reserved to the settlor. That was its purpose. By this resolution Congress rejected the view of *May v. Heiner* and its progeny that estate tax includability depended upon whether or not title had technically passed. The premise of *Nichols v. Coolidge* was precisely the same as that of *May v. Heiner*; hence, the effect of the Joint Resolution was to undo *Nichols v. Coolidge* as well. Since Congress barred resort to formal trust agreements with reserved life estates as a means of circumventing the payment of death taxes, it is unreasonable to conclude that it intended to permit the accomplishment of the same result by an oral agreement having an identical effect.

The saying that a man is as good as his bond is an expression born of experience which fortunately is not too uncommon. And when filial devotion and respect in fact justifies the faith which a parent reposes in his children in transferring property to them upon their oral assurance that the income is to be his for life, it is entirely artificial to hold that the parent did not retain the enjoyment of the property until his death simply because his receipt of its income accrued under an oral agreement rather than one more formal in nature. Nothing in the language of [§ 2036(a)(1)] suggests that such a tenuous distinction was intended.

   . . .

Section 7(b) of the Technical Changes Act of 1949, 63 Stat. 895, . . . did not impugn the basic soundness of the *Church* concept of "possession and enjoyment." While it nullified the prospective effect of the *Church* decision in its application to transfers antedating the Joint Resolution of 1931, this simply reflected Congressional solicitude for taxpayers who, in reliance upon *May v. Heiner*, refrained from divesting themselves of life estates reserved under trusts created prior to the Joint Resolution of 1931. *See* Sen. Rep. No. 831, 2 U.S.C. & Cong. Serv., 81st Cong., 1st Sess. 1949, pp. 2172, 2180. Since the transfers at bar were effected between 1939 and 1942 the rationale of the *Church* case is directly apposite.

The decision of the Tax Court will be affirmed.[6]

———

The determination of what constitutes the right to income, or the retention of either possession or enjoyment, has produced a significant amount of litigation. One of the most common situations was suggested in *Nichols v. Coolidge*, cited by the court in *McNichol*, in which one family member transfers a residence to another, but does not move out. Often, the transferee

———

[6] *Accord*, Estate of Whitt v. Commissioner, 751 F.2d 1548 (11th Cir.), *cert. denied*, 474 U.S. 1004 (1985); Estate of Paxton v. Commissioner, 86 T.C. 785 (1986); Treas. Reg. § 20.2036–1(a). *Cf.* Lee v. United States, 86–1 U.S.T.C. (CCH) ¶ 13,649 (W.D. Ky. 1985), *aff'd*, 59 A.F.T.R.2d 87–1251 (6th Cir. 1987) (section 2036(a)(1) applicable because of continued receipt of the income by the decedent, even though decedent had neither expressly retained the right to income nor entered into a prearrangement with the transferee to receive it).

and transferor both live in the house after the transfer. The Service attempts to include the house in the transferor's gross estate upon death. When the transferee is someone other than the spouse of the transferor, the courts have usually implied an agreement on the part of the transferee. The assumption is that the transferor can continue in possession. Therefore, the Service and courts have required that the house be taxed. *See, e.g.,* Guynn v. United States, 437 F.2d 1148 (4th Cir. 1971); Estate of Honigman v. Commissioner, 66 T.C. 1080 (1976) (mother to daughter); Estate of Linderme v. Commissioner, 52 T.C. 305 (1969); Rev. Rul. 70–155, 1970–1 C.B. 189. *But see,* Diehl v. United States, 68–1 U.S.T.C. ¶ 12,506, 21 A.F.T.R. 1607 (W. D. Tenn. 1968) (mother to son and his wife), *non acq.* Rev. Rul. 78–409, 1978–2 C.B. 234. In *Estate of Reichardt v. Commissioner,* 114 T.C. 144 (2000), the Tax Court held that § 2036(a)(1) applied because the decedent had an implied agreement to retain enjoyment over interests in a family limited partnership.

When, however, the transfer is to the transferor's spouse and both spouses continue to reside in the residence, the courts generally have refused to draw such an inference from the facts. *See, e.g.,* Union Planters Nat'l Bank v. United States, 361 F.2d 662 (6th Cir. 1966). This position was recognized by the Service in Rev. Rul. 70–155, 1970–1 C.B. 189, in which the Service stated that continued occupancy by the transferor spouse will not generally result in an inference that an agreement existed for such continued occupancy by the transferor spouse. Because of the unlimited marital deduction, this is likely a nonissue, unless the facts are unusual.

A variation of the same issue arises when the decedent sells her primary residence but continues to occupy it. In *Estate of Maxwell v. Commissioner,* 3 F.3d 591 (2nd Cir. 1993), *aff'g* 98 T.C. 594 (1992), the decedent sold her residence to her son on an installment basis and then leased the property from her son. The lease payments effectively negated the interest payments on the note. The son made no principal payments on the loan; the decedent forgave the debt at the rate of $20,000 per year with the unpaid balance forgiven in her will. The divided appellate court affirmed the Tax Court's ruling that the decedent retained a life estate in the transferred house.

A similar problem arises when state law recognizes income rights not expressly created by the instrument of transfer. For example, some community property laws treat the income from separate property as community property. Thus, if one spouse transfers separate property to the other, it could be argued that he retains a community income interest in the transferred property. When, however, the transferor has done all that he can to make a complete transfer, the courts typically refuse to treat the right as a retention of an income interest. *See, e.g., Estate of Wyly v. Commissioner,* 610 F.2d 1282 (5th Cir. 1980) (historically followed by the Service). See Rev. Rul. 81–221, 1981–2 C.B. 178.

Problems

1. Assume *S* transfers his personal residence in trust "for the use and possession of my spouse, *W*, for her life, remainder to our child, *C*." *S* is trustee. What are the gift tax consequences? Consider the impact of § 2702.

2. In Problem 1, S continues to live in the house with W and C. What are the estate tax consequences if:

a. S dies during W's life?

b. S dies after W?

3. By written instrument, D transfers title to his art collection to his son. At the time of D's death, one of the paintings he gave to his son was found hanging in D's home. *See Gruen v. Gruen*, 496 N.E.2d 869 (N.Y. 1986).

a. Will that painting, or all of the paintings, be included in D's gross estate?

b. Assume instead that the art collection was in the lobby of D's law firm and his son was a partner in the firm. What result?

[4]   Retention of Voting Rights: Section 2036(b)

Code: § 2036(b).

Regulations: None.

The problem of defining what constitutes retained possession or enjoyment can also raise perplexing problems if a shareholder transfers stock in a closely held corporation which the shareholder controls. This issue is discussed in Chapter 9.

[5]   Consideration: Section 2043

Code: § 2043.

Regulations: None.

Section 2036(a)(1) does not apply if the decedent receives full and adequate consideration in money or money's worth for the transferred interest. By receiving full consideration for the relinquished interest (the remainder interest), the transferor merely substitutes one item of property for another of equivalent value. Assuming that the consideration is invested, it should cumulate to the value of the corpus by the time of the decedent's death. Theoretically, the transferor's wealth (the total value of the retained interest plus the consideration) remains the same and will remain the same until death. Thus, the transaction is deemed to be merely a change in the form of the property, and not to be a testamentary substitute requiring gross estate inclusion. As *Wheeler* below explains, courts have not always agreed with this analysis.

If the transferor receives some consideration but not full consideration in money or money's worth, then the transferred property must be included in the decedent's gross estate under § 2036 or one of the other retained interest Code sections. Section 2043(a) allows a reduction for the actual consideration received at the time of the gift, however.

Example: G retains a legal life estate in property and sells the legal remainder to X. The actuarial value of the remainder is $25,000, but X only pays $15,000 to G. At G's death the property has a value of $200,000. By application of § 2043(a), G's gross estate will include $185,000 ($200,000 less the consideration received of $15,000). *See* Treas. Reg. § 20.2043–1(a).

Wheeler v. United States

116 F.3d 749 (5th Cir. 1997)

Garwood, Circuit Judge:

This case involves the determination of the federal estate tax due from the estate of Elmore K. Melton, Jr. (Melton). On July 13, 1984, Melton, then age sixty, sold to his two adopted sons, John Wheeler and David Wheeler, the remainder interest in his ranch located in Bexar County, Texas. Melton retained a life estate in the ranch and used the actuarial tables set forth in the Treasury Regulations to determine the price to be paid by the Wheelers for the remainder interest. On May 25, 1991, Melton, then age sixty-seven, died. Melton's federal estate tax return did not include any value for the ranch. The Internal Revenue Service (IRS) issued a notice of deficiency, claiming that the sale of the remainder interest in the ranch to the Wheelers for its actuarial value did not constitute adequate and full consideration, and that accordingly the fair market value of the full fee simple interest in the ranch, less the consideration paid by the sons, should have been included in Melton's gross estate. The court below agreed and, following a line of cases stating that the sale of a remainder interest for less than the value of the full fee simple interest in the property does not constitute adequate consideration for the purposes of section 2036(a) of the Internal Revenue Code determined that Melton's estate had been properly assessed an additional $320,831 in federal estate tax. We reverse.

Facts and Proceedings Below

I.

. . .

[O]n July 13, 1984, Melton executed a warranty deed conveying to John and David his 376-acre ranch, located in Bexar County, Texas. The deed reserved to Melton a life estate in the ranch. [Footnote omitted.] For many years prior to the sale, and until the time of his death, Melton used the ranch as his personal residence. John and David paid for the remainder interest with a personal liability real estate lien note in the amount of $337,790.18, secured by a vendor's lien expressly retained in the deed and additionally by a deed of trust on the ranch. The deed and deed of trust were promptly recorded. The purchase price for the remainder interest in the ranch was determined by multiplying the sum of the appraised fair market value of the ranch's fee simple interest, $1,314,200, plus $10,000, by 0.25509, the factor set forth in the appropriate actuarial table in the Treasury Regulations for valuing future interests in property where the measuring life was that of a person of Melton's age. *See* Treas. Reg. § 25.2512–5(A).

. . .

Melton died testate on May 25, 1991, at the age of sixty-seven, more than six years after the sale of the remainder interest to the Wheelers and more than three years after the note had been paid in full. The cause of death was heart failure. Melton had suffered from coronary artery disease and arterio-sclerosis for approximately ten years. The undisputed evidence, however, was that Melton's death was not (and was not thought to be) imminent in July 1984 when he sold the remainder interest to the Wheelers (nor is there any evidence that it was ever imminent before 1991).

. . .

[On audit of Melton's estate tax return, the Service determined a deficiency based on the inclusion of the farm's date of death value of $1,074,200 reduced by the consideration of $338,000 that decedent received from his sons when he sold the remainder interest six years earlier.

. . .

The district court affirmed the magistrate's report that upheld the Service's position.] Melton's estate appeals.

Discussion

I.

. . .

Central to this case is section 2036(a) of the Code [and the parenthetical exception for adequate and full consideration] . . . .

The estate concedes that the fee simple value of the ranch would have to have been brought back into the estate had the remainder been transferred to the Wheelers without consideration or for an inadequate consideration. However, the Wheelers paid Melton for the remainder interest transferred an amount which the government concedes is equal to (indeed slightly in excess of) the then fair market value of the fee simple interest in the ranch multiplied by the fraction listed in the Treasury Regulations for valuing a remainder following an estate for the life of a person of Melton's age. *See* 26 C.F.R. § 25.2512–5(A). The estate contends that accordingly under the parenthetical clause of section 2036(a) the ranch is not brought back into the estate, as Melton was paid full value for the transferred remainder. Indeed, there is no evidence to the contrary. The government, however, contends that because Melton was paid for the remainder interest an amount indisputably less than the value of the full fee interest, that therefore the parenthetical clause of section 2036(a) cannot apply, and hence the ranch must be brought back into the estate.

This case thus ultimately turns on whether the phrase "adequate and full consideration" as used in the italicized parenthetical clause of section 2036(a) is to be applied in reference to the value of the remainder interest transferred, as the estate contends, or in reference to the value of the full fee simple interest which the transferor had immediately before the transfer, as the government contends . . . .

That the proper construction of section 2036(a)'s "adequate and full consid-eration" has presented taxpayers, the IRS, and the courts with such persistent conceptual difficulty can be explained, in large part, by the absence of a statutory definition of the phrase combined with the consistently competing interests of all tax litigants—the government and the taxpayer. The crux of the problem has been stated as follows:

> "Because the actuarial value of a remainder interest is substantially less than the fair market value of the underlying property, the sale of a remainder interest for its actuarial value is viewed by many as allowing the taxpayer to transfer property to the remainderman for less consideration than is required in an outright sale. Consequently, the sale of a remainder interest for its actuarial value, although such value represents the fair market value of the remainder interest, raises the question of whether the seller has been adequately compensated for the transfer of the underlying property to the remainderman. If the actuarial value of the remainder interest does not represent adequate compensation for the transfer of the underlying property to the remainderman, the taxpayer may be subject to both the gift tax and the estate tax . . . . If the taxpayer holds the retained interest until death, section 2036(a) of the [Code] pulls the underlying property back into the taxpayer's gross estate, unless the transfer is a bona fide sale for adequate and full consideration." Martha W. Jordan, *Sales of Remainder Interests: Reconciling Gradow v. United States and Section 2702*, 14 Va. Tax Rev. 671, 673 (1995).

Both parties agree that, for the purposes of the gift tax (section 2512 of the Code), consideration equal to the actuarial value of the remainder interest constitutes adequate consideration. *See also* Treas. Reg. § 25.2512–5(a). For estate tax purposes, however, authorities are split. Commentators have generally urged the same construction should apply . . . and the Third Circuit has held that "adequate and full consideration" under section 2036(a) is determined in reference to the value of the remainder interest transferred, not the value of the full fee simple interest in the underlying property. *D'Ambrosio v. Commissioner*, 101 F.3d 309 (3d Cir. 1996), *cert. denied*, . . . On the other hand, *Gradow v. United States*, 11 Cl. Ct. 808 (1987), *aff'd*, 897 F.2d 516 (Fed. Cir. 1990), and its faithful progeny, . . . have stated that a remainder interest must be sold for an amount equal to the value of the full fee simple interest in the underlying property in order to come within the parenthetical exception clause of section 2036(a). This Court has yet to address the precise issue.

II.

A. *Gradow v. United States* **and the Widow's Election Cases**

As the government's position rests principally on an analogy offered by the Claims Court in *Gradow*, a preliminary summary of the widow's election mechanism in the community property context is appropriate.

In a community property state, a husband and wife generally each have an undivided, one-half interest in the property owned in common by virtue of their marital status, with each spouse having the power to dispose, by testamentary instrument, of his or her share of the community property.

Under a widow's election will, the decedent spouse purports to dispose of the entire community property, the surviving spouse being left with the choice of either taking under the scheme of the will or waiving any right under the will and taking his or her community share outright. One common widow's election plan provides for the surviving spouse to in effect exchange a remainder interest in his or her community property share for an equitable life estate in the decedent spouse's community property share.

In *Gradow*, Mrs. Gradow, the surviving spouse, was put to a similar election. If she rejected the will, she was to receive only her share of the community property. *Id.* 11 Cl. Ct. at 809. If she chose instead to take under her husband's will, she was required to transfer her share of the community property to a trust whose assets would consist of the community property of both spouses, with Mrs. Gradow receiving all the trust income for life and, upon her death, the trust corpus being distributed to the Gradows' son. *Id.* Mrs. Gradow chose to take under her husband's will and, upon her death, the executor of her estate did not include any of the trust assets within her gross estate. *Id.* The executor asserted that the life estate received by Mrs. Gradow was full and adequate consideration under section 2036(a) for the transfer of her community property share to the trust, but the IRS disagreed. *Id.* Before the Claims Court, the parties stipulated that the value of Mrs. Gradow's share of the community property exceeded the actuarial value of an estate for her life in her husband's share. *Id.* However, the estate contended that the value of the life estate in the husband's share equaled or exceeded the value of the *remainder* interest in Mrs. Gradow's share. The Claims Court did not clearly resolve that contention because it determined that the consideration flowing from Mrs. Gradow was "the entire value of the property she placed in the trust, *i.e.,* her half of the community property," and that thus the life estate was inadequate consideration, so the exception to section 2036(a) was unavailable. *Id.* at 810.

The court in *Gradow* concluded that the term "property" in section 2036(a) referred to the entirety of that part of the trust corpus attributable to Mrs. Gradow. *Id.* at 813. Therefore, according to the court, if the general rule of section 2036(a) were to apply, the date-of-death value of the property transferred to the trust corpus by Mrs. Gradow—rather than the zero date-of-death value of her life interest in that property—would be included in her gross estate. *Id.* Citing "[f]undamental principles of grammar," the court concluded that the bona fide sale exception must refer to adequate and full consideration for the property placed into the trust and not the remainder interest in that property. *Id.*

Fundamental principles of grammar aside, the *Gradow* court rested its conclusion equally on the underlying purpose of section 2036(a), observing that:

> "The only way to preserve the integrity of the section, then, is to view the consideration moving from the surviving spouse as that property which is taken out of the gross estate. In the context of intra-family transactions which are plainly testamentary, it is not unreasonable to require that, at a minimum, the sale accomplish an equilibrium for estate tax purposes." *Id.* at 813–14.

. . .

It is not our task to address the merits of *Gradow*'s analysis of how section 2036(a) operates in the widow's election context but rather to determine whether the *Gradow* decision supports the construction urged by the government in the sale of a remainder context. We conclude that the widow election cases present factually distinct circumstances that preclude the wholesale importation of *Gradow*'s rationale into the present case.

As noted, a widow's election mechanism generally involves an arrangement whereby the surviving spouse exchanges a remainder interest in her community property share for a life estate in that of her deceased spouse. Usually, as in *Gradow*, the interests are in trust. Necessarily, the receipt of an equitable life estate in the decedent-spouse's community property share does little to offset the reduction in the surviving spouse's gross estate caused by the transfer of her remainder interest. It is precisely this imbalance that the commentators cited in *Gradow*—and the "equilibrium rule" gleaned from *United States v. Allen*—recognized as the determinative factor in the widow's election context. Because a surviving spouse's transfer of a remainder interest depletes the gross estate, there can be no "bona fide sale for an adequate and full consideration" unless the gross estate is augmented commensurately. *See* Charles L. B. Lowndes, *Consideration and the Federal Estate and Gift taxes: Transfers for Partial Consideration, Relinquishment of Marital Rights, Family Annuities, the Widow's Election, and Reciprocal Trusts*, 35 Geo. Wash. L. Rev. 50, 66 (1966); Stanley M. Johanson, *Revocable Trusts, Widow's Election Wills, and Community Property: The Tax Problems*, 47 Tex. L. Rev. 1247, 1283–84 (1969) ("But in the widow's election situation, the interest the wife receives as a result of her election-transfer is a life estate in her husband's community share—an interest which, by its nature, will not be taxed in the wife's estate at her death. It appears that the wife's estate is given a consideration offset for the receipt of an interest that did not augment her estate."). Accordingly, we need not address the issue whether the value or income derived from a life estate in the decedent-spouse's community property share can ever constitute adequate and full consideration. For our purposes it is enough to observe that, in most cases, the equitable life estate received by the surviving spouse will not sufficiently augment her gross estate to offset the depletion caused by the transfer of her remainder interest. [Footnote omitted.] This depletion of the gross estate prevents the operation of the adequate and full consideration exception to section 2036(a). [Footnote omitted.] Had the court in *Gradow* limited its discussion of section 2036(a)'s adequate and full consideration exception to the widow's election context, the nettlesome task of distinguishing its blanket rule of including the value of the full fee interest on the underlying property when a remainder interest is transferred might be somewhat easier. In *dicta*, however, and apparently in response to a hypothetical posed by the taxpayer, the *Gradow* court let loose a response that, to say the least, has since acquired a life of its own. The entire passage—and the source of much consternation—is as follows:

> "Plaintiff argues that the defendant's construction would gut the utility of the 'bona fide sales' exception and uses a hypothetical to illustrate his point. In the example a 40-year-old man contracts to

put $100,000.00 into a trust, reserving the income for life but selling
the remainder. Plaintiff points out that based on the seller's life
expectancy, he might receive up to $30,000.00 for the remainder,
but certainly no more. He argues that this demonstrates the unfairness of defendant insisting on consideration equal to the $100,000.00
put into trust before it would exempt the sale from § 2036(a).

There are a number of defects in plaintiff's hypothetical. First,
the transaction is obviously not testamentary, unlike the actual
circumstances here. In addition, plaintiff assumes his conclusion by
focusing on the sale of the remainder interest as the only relevant
transaction. Assuming it was not treated as a sham, the practical
effect is a transfer of the entire $100,000.00, not just a remainder.
More importantly, however, if plaintiff is correct that one should be
able, under the 'bona fide sale' exception to remove property from
the gross estate by a sale of the remainder interest, the exception
would swallow the rule. A young person could sell a remainder
interest for a fraction of the property's worth, enjoy the property for
life, and then pass it along without estate or gift tax consequences."
Gradow, 11 Cl. Ct. at 815.

The Claims Court went on to conclude that "[t]he fond hope that a surviving
spouse would take pains to invest, compound, and preserve inviolate all the
life income from half of a trust, knowing that it would thereupon be taxed
without his or her having received any lifetime benefit, is a slim basis for
putting a different construction on § 2036(a) than the one heretofore consistently adopted." *Id.* at 816.

One can only imagine the enthusiasm with which the IRS received the news
that, at least in the view of one court, it would not have to consider the time
value of money when determining adequate and full consideration for a
remainder interest. [Footnote omitted.] Subsequent to the *Gradow* decision,
the government has successfully used the above quoted language to justify
inclusion in the gross estate of the value of the full fee interest in the
underlying property even where the transferor sold the remainder interest
for its undisputed actuarial value. *See Pittman v. United States*, 878 F. Supp.
833 (E.D.N.C. 1994). *See also D'Ambrosio v. Commissioner,* 105 T.C. 252, *rev'd,*
101 F.3d 309 (3d Cir. 1996), *cert. denied,* [citations omitted].

Pittman (and the Tax Court's decision in *D'Ambrosio*) presents a conscien-
tious estate planner with quite a conundrum. If the taxpayer sells a remainder
interest for its actuarial value as calculated under the Treasury Regulations,
but retains a life estate, the value of the full fee interest in the underlying
property will be included in his gross estate and the transferor will incur
substantial estate tax liability under section 2036(a). If the taxpayer chooses
instead to follow *Gradow*, and is somehow able to find a willing purchaser
of his remainder interest for the full fee-simple value of the underlying
property, he will in fact avoid estate tax liability; section 2036(a) would not
be triggered. The purchaser, however, having paid the fee-simple value for
the remainder interest in the estate, will have paid more for the interest than
it was worth. As the "adequate and full consideration" for a remainder interest
under section 2512(b) is its actuarial value, the purchaser will have made a

gift of the amount paid in excess of its actuarial value, thereby incurring gift tax liability. [Footnote omitted.] Surely, in the words of Professor Gilmore, this "carr[ies] a good joke too far." [Footnote omitted.]

. . .

C. In Pari Materia

As alluded to above, significant problems arise when "adequate and full consideration" is given one meaning under section 2512 and quite another for the purposes of section 2036(a). In a pair of companion cases in 1945, the Supreme Court set forth the general principle that, because the gift and estate taxes complement each other, the phrase "adequate and full consideration" must mean the same thing in both statutes. *See Merrill v. Fahs*, 324 U.S. 308, 309–11 (1945) (" 'The gift tax was supplementary to the estate tax. The two are in pari materia and must be construed together.' ") . . . ; *Estate of Friedman v. Commissioner*, 40 T.C. 714–19 ("The phrase 'an adequate and full consideration in money or money's worth,' common to both the estate and gift tax statutes here pertinent, is to be given an 'identical construction' in regard to each of them.") (citing *Fahs*, 324 U.S. at 309–11). In *Fahs*, the Court observed:

> "Correlation of the gift tax and the estate tax still requires legislative intervention. [citations omitted] But to interpret the same phrases in the two taxes concerning the same subject matter in different ways where obvious reasons do not compel divergent treatment is to introduce another and needless complexity into this already irksome situation." *Id.* at 313.

. . .

The sale of a remainder interest for its actuarial value does not deplete the seller's estate. "The actuarial value of the remainder interest equals the amount that will grow to a principal sum equal to the value of the property that passes to the remainderman at termination of the retained interest. To reach this conclusion, the tables assume that both the consideration received for the remainder interest and the underlying property are invested at the table rate of interest, compounded annually." Jordan, *Sales of Remainder Interests*, at 692–93 (citing Keith E. Morrison, *The Widow's Election: The Issue of Consideration*, 44 Tex. L. Rev. 223, 237–38 (1965)). In other words, the actuarial tables are premised on the recognition that, at the end of the actuarial period, there is no discernible difference between (1) an estate holder retaining the full fee interest in the estate and (2) an estate holder retaining income from the life estate and selling the remainder interest for its actuarial value—in either case, the estate is not depleted. This is so because both interests, the life estate and the remainder interest, are capable of valuation. Recognizing this truism, the accumulated value of a decedent's estate is precisely the same whether she retains the fee interest or receives the actuarial value of the remainder interest outright by a sale prior to her actual death. *Id.* at 691–92; Morrison, *The Issue of Consideration*, at 237–38.

Two possible objections—which are more properly directed at the wisdom of accepting actuarial factors than at the result just described—should be addressed. The first, to paraphrase the Claims Court in *Gradow*, is that the fee interest holder, in such a situation, might squander the proceeds from the sale of the remainder interest and, therefore, deplete the estate. *See Gradow*, 11 Cl. Ct. at 816 (noting that "[t]he fond hope that a surviving spouse would take pains to invest, compound, and preserve inviolate all [proceeds from a sale of the remainder interest], knowing that it would thereupon be taxed without his or her having received any lifetime benefit, is a slim basis" for holding the actuarial value of a remainder interest is adequate and full consideration under section 2036(a)). This objection amounts to a misapprehension of the estate tax. [Footnote omitted.] Whether an estate holder takes the "talents" received from the sale of the remainder interest and purchases blue chip securities, invests in highly volatile commodities futures, funds a gambling spree, or chooses instead to bury them in the ground, may speak to the wisdom of the estate holder, *see* Matthew 25:14–30, but it is of absolutely no significance to the proper determination of whether, at the time of the transfer, the estate holder received full and adequate consideration under section 2036(a). If further explanation is required, we point out that *Gradow* itself seems to have reached the same conclusion in an earlier portion of the opinion. *See Gradow*, 11 Cl. Ct. at 813 ("Even if the consideration is fungible and easily consumed, at least theoretically the rest of the estate is protected from encroachment for lifetime expenditures."). *See also* Jordan, *Sales of Remainder Interests*, at 695–96 & n.105; Morrison, *The Issue of Consideration*, at 236–44.

The second objection is no more availing. If a sale of a remainder interest for its actuarial value—an amount, it is worth noting, that is nothing more than the product of the undisputed "fair market value" of the underlying estate multiplied by an actuarial factor designed to adjust for the investment return over the actuarial period—constitutes adequate and full consideration under section 2036(a), then the estate holder successfully "freezes" the value of the transferred remainder at its date-of-transfer value. Accordingly, any post-transfer appreciation of the remainder interest over and above the appreciation percentage anticipated by the actuarial tables passes to the remainder-man free of the estate tax. But, of course, this is a problem only if the proceeds of the sale are not invested in assets which appreciate as much (or depreciate as little) as the remainder. Moreover, those who recall the Great Depression, as well as more recent times, [footnote omitted] know that assets frequently do not appreciate. Indeed, Melton's ranch did not appreciate, but rather at his death was worth less than eighty-two percent of its value when the remainder was sold . . . .

D. Section 2036(a)'s Bona Fide Sale Requirement

[Court rejected that bona fide had special application in the family transfers.]

. . .

E. Intrafamily Transactions

At oral argument the government pursued a line of reasoning not fully anticipated by their brief's *Gradow* no-bona-fide-transaction theory. Stated concisely, the government asserted that, because the purpose of section 2036(a) is to reach those split-interest transfers that amount to testamentary substitutes and include the underlying asset's value in the gross estate, the adequate and full consideration for *intrafamily transfers*—which are generally testamentary in nature because the interest passes "to the natural objects of one's bounty in the next generation"—must be measured against the entire value of the underlying asset in order to accomplish section 2036(a)'s purpose. [Footnote omitted.] This argument is necessarily at odds with *Gradow's* "fundamental principles of grammar" approach that rested on a construction of the bona fide sale exception that did not purport to distinguish between either the identity or the subjective intent of the parties. [Footnote omitted.] We reject the government's proffered construction as not supported by the statutory language.

. . .

F. Former Section 2036(c) and Chapter 14

. . .

Congress enacted former section 2036(c) in 1987 to address certain estate "freezing techniques" [Footnote omitted.] enabling taxpayers to take advantage of the assumptions underlying the valuation tables in the Treasury Regulations. Omnibus Budget Reconciliation Act of 1987, Pub. L. No. 100–203, 101 Stat. 1330–1431; *see also* Mitchell M. Gans, *GRIT's, GRAT's and GRUT's: Planning and Policy*, 11 Va. Tax Rev. 761, 791 & n.63 (1992). Under the terms of former section 2036(c), the "exception contained in subsection [2036](a) for a bona fide sale shall not apply to a transfer described in paragraph (1) if such transfer is to a member of the transferor's family." I.R.C. § 2036(c)(2) (West 1989), repealed by P.L. 101–508, sec. 11601, 104 Stat. 1388 (1990). *See also id.* at § 2036(c)(3)(B) (defining "family" to include a "relationship by legal adoption"). [Footnote omitted.] A paragraph (1) transfer involved a transfer by the holder of a "substantial interest in an enterprise" while retaining an interest in the income or rights of the transferred enterprise. Former § 2036(c)(1)(A)–(B). Although "enterprise" as used in the legislative history and the subsequent interpretation offered by the IRS was capable of a more restrictive application, the reach of former section 2036(c) could have "potentially embrace[d] almost any activity relating to property held for personal use as well as business or investment property." . . .

In response to severe criticism of former section 2036(c) passed in 1987, Congress enacted the Omnibus Budget Reconciliation Act of 1990, Pub. L. No. 101–508, 104 Stat. 1388, which repealed former section 2036(c) retroactively and replaced it with the valuation rules set forth in I.R.C. §§ 2701–2704. *See* 5 Bittker & Lokken, *supra,* 136–3 to 136–4. Under section 2702, transfers of interests in trust to a member of the transferor's family trigger special valuation rules. [Footnote omitted.] The general rule of section 2702 values the remainder interest transferred as having the value of the full fee interest by setting the value of the retained interest at zero. I.R.C. § 2702(a)(2). In other words, the general rule of section 2702 seems to accomplish, explicitly, precisely what the government argues that 2036(a) accomplishes by implication. [Footnote omitted.] Because there are overwhelming indications that the estate freeze provisions adopted by Congress in 1990 were designed to address the perceived shortcomings of section 2036(a), we find unconvincing the government's suggestion on brief that "there is nothing in [section] 2702 or its legislative history indicating that a transfer with a retained life estate, even if within [section] 2702, was not already subject to the provisions of [section] 2036(a)."

. . .

Accordingly, we hold that the sale of a remainder interest for its actuarial value as calculated by the appropriate factor set forth in the Treasury Regulations constitutes an adequate and full consideration under section 2036(a).

————

Whether *Wheeler* or *Gradow* is the correct interpretation of § 2043 is unsettled. The Service has not acquiesced in *Wheeler*, although the Ninth Circuit has followed *Wheeler*. *See* Estate of Magnin v. Commissioner, 184 F.3d 1074 (9th Cir. 1999). Moreover, § 2702 was enacted after the tax year involved in *Wheeler*. Under the Regulations, the sale of a remainder interest to a family member is subject to the valuation rules of § 2702. *See* Treas. Reg. § 25.2702–4(d), Example 2. The application of § 2702 to a sale of a remainder is significant if *Wheeler* is correct. Under the valuation rule of § 2702, the entire value of the transferred property, less the consideration actually received, is subject to gift taxes, but no estate tax consequence follows. If § 2702 is not applicable, then there is no gift tax consequence to the transfer and no subsequent estate tax inclusion either. This is the transfer tax result the taxpayer sought in *Wheeler*.

For sales of remainders to individuals that are outside of the statutory definition of a family member, such as a niece or nephew, § 2702 is not applicable. Moreover, students are reminded that § 2702 is a gift tax valuation provision and has no impact on the issue of whether § 2036 applies or not. Thus, even if a sale of a remainder is subject to the gift tax valuation rule of § 2702, the estate tax consequence is determined by *Wheeler* or *Gradow* and not § 2702.

If *Gradow*, rather than *Wheeler*, is the correct interpretation of the law, the estate tax inclusion of the transferred property will have an impact on the decedent's adjusted taxable gifts if § 2702 applied to the initial transfer. The amount of the prior gift will be deducted from taxable gifts to determine adjusted taxable gifts.

See generally Ronald H. Jensen, *Estate and Gift Tax Effects of Selling a Remainder: Have D'Ambrosio, Wheeler, and Magnin Changed the Rules?*, 8 FLORIDA TAX L. REV. 537 (2000); Wendy C. Gerzog, *Why Gradow is Correct*, 89 TAX NOTES 551 (2000).

Problems

1. In *Gradow* (discussed in *Wheeler*), the consideration received for the transfer of the remainder in the transferor-spouse's share of the community

property was a life estate in her deceased husband's share of community property. In *Wheeler*, the consideration was a cash equivalent. Could this difference explain the differing results in the two cases?

2. What are the gift tax consequences of a sale of the remainder interest like the one in *Wheeler* if § 2702 applies? *See* Treas. Reg. § 25.2702–1(a), –(b).

3. Can the harshness of § 2043(a) be avoided by dividing the property to be transferred into separate properties and then making separate transfers of the two properties where full consideration is received for one transfer and no consideration is received for the other?

[6]　Reciprocal Trusts

Faced with the broad reach of § 2036(a)(1), planners noted that the section applied only to interests retained in property transferred by the decedent. This suggests that its application could be avoided by having someone else transfer the property. The Service and courts have not always agreed.

United States v. Estate of Grace

395 U.S. 316 (1969)

Mr. Justice Marshall delivered the opinion of the Court.

. . .

Decedent was a very wealthy man at the time of his marriage to the late Janet Grace in 1908. Janet Grace had no wealth or property of her own, but, between 1908 and 1931, decedent transferred to her a large amount of personal and real property, including the family's Long Island estate. Decedent retained effective control over the family's business affairs, including the property transferred to his wife. She took no interest and no part in business affairs and relied upon her husband's judgment. Whenever some formal action was required regarding property in her name, decedent would have the appropriate instrument prepared and she would execute it.

On December 15, 1931, decedent executed a trust instrument, hereinafter called the Joseph Grace trust. Named as trustees were decedent, his nephew, and a third party. The trustees were directed to pay the income of the trust to Janet Grace during her lifetime, and to pay to her any part of the principal which a majority of the trustees might deem advisable. Janet was given the power to designate, by will or deed, the manner in which the trust estate remaining at her death was to be distributed among decedent and their children. The trust properties included securities and real estate interests.

On December 20, 1931, Janet Grace executed a trust instrument, hereinafter called the Janet Grace trust, which was virtually identical to the Joseph Grace trust. The trust properties included the family estate and corporate securities, all of which had been transferred to her by decedent in preceding years. The trust instruments were prepared by one of decedent's employees in accordance with a plan devised by decedent to create additional trusts before the advent of a new gift tax expected to be enacted the next year. Decedent selected the properties to be included in each trust. Janet Grace, acting in accordance with this plan, executed her trust instrument at decedent's request.

Janet Grace died in 1937. The Joseph Grace trust terminated at her death. Her estate's federal estate tax return disclosed the Janet Grace trust and reported it as a nontaxable transfer by Janet Grace. The Commissioner asserted that the Janet and Joseph Grace trusts were "reciprocal" and asserted a deficiency to the extent of mutual value. Compromises on unrelated issues resulted in 55% of the smaller of the two trusts, the Janet Grace trust, being included in her gross estate.

Joseph Grace died in 1950. The federal estate tax return disclosed both trusts. The Joseph Grace trust was reported as a nontaxable transfer and the Janet Grace was reported as a trust under which decedent held a limited power of appointment. Neither trust was included in decedent's gross estate.

The Commissioner determined that the Joseph and Janet Grace trusts were "reciprocal" and included the amount of the Janet Grace trust in decedent's gross estate. A deficiency in the amount of $363,500.97, plus interest, was assessed and paid.

. . .

The doctrine of reciprocal trusts was formulated in response to attempts to draft instruments which seemingly avoid the literal terms of [§ 2036(a)(1)], although still leaving the decedent the lifetime enjoyment of his property. The doctrine dates from *Lehman v. Commissioner*, 109 F. 2d 99 (2d Cir.), *cert. denied*, 310 U. S. 637 (1940). In *Lehman*, decedent and his brother owned equal shares in certain stocks and bonds. Each brother placed his interest in trust for the other's benefit for life, with remainder to the life tenant's issue. Each brother also gave the other the right to withdraw $150,000 of the principal. If the brothers had each reserved the right to withdraw $150,000 from the trust that each had created, the trusts would have been includible in their gross estates as interests of which each had made a transfer with a power to revoke. When one of the brothers died, his estate argued that neither trust was includible because the decedent did not have a power over a trust which he had created.

The Second Circuit disagreed. That court ruled that the effect of the transfers was the same as if the decedent had transferred his stock in trust for himself, remainder to his issue, and had reserved the right to withdraw $150,000. The court reasoned:

> "The fact that the trusts were reciprocated or 'crossed' is a trifle, quite lacking in practical or legal significance . . . . The law searches out the reality and is not concerned with the form." 109 F.2d, at 100.

The court ruled that the decisive point was that each brother caused the other to make a transfer by establishing his own trust.

The doctrine of reciprocal trusts has been applied numerous times since the *Lehman* decision. It received congressional approval in section 6 of the Technical Changes Act of 1949, 63 Stat. 893. The present case is, however, this Court's first examination of the doctrine.

The Court of Claims was divided over the requirements for application of the doctrine to the situation of this case. Relying on some language in *Lehman* and certain other courts of appeals' decisions, the majority held that the crucial factor was whether the decedent had established his trust as consideration for the establishment of the trust of which he was a beneficiary. The court ruled that decedent had not established his trust as a quid pro quo for the Janet Grace trust, and that Janet Grace had not established her trust in exchange for the Joseph Grace trust. Rather, the trusts were found to be part of an established pattern of family giving, with neither party desiring to obtain property from the other. Indeed, the court found that Janet Grace had created her trust because decedent requested that she do so. It therefore found the reciprocal trust doctrine inapplicable.

The court recognized that certain cases had established a slightly different test for reciprocity. Those cases inferred consideration from the establishment of two similar trusts at about the same time. The court held that any inference of consideration was rebutted by the evidence in the case, particularly the lack of any evidence of an estate tax avoidance motive on the part of the Graces. In contrast, the dissent felt that the majority's approach placed entirely too much weight on subjective intent. Once it was established that the trusts were interrelated, the dissent felt that the subjective intent of the parties in establishing the trusts should become irrelevant. The relevant factor was whether the trusts created by the settlors placed each other in approximately the same objective economic position as they would have been in if each had created his own trust with himself, rather than the other, as life beneficiary.

We agree with the dissent that the approach of the Court of Claims majority places too much emphasis on the subjective intent of the parties in creating the trusts and for that reason hinders proper application of the federal estate tax laws. It is true that there is language in *Lehman* and other cases that would seem to support the majority's approach. It is also true that the results in some of those cases arguably support the decision below. Nevertheless, we think that these cases are not in accord with this Court's prior decisions interpreting related provisions of the federal estate tax laws.

Emphasis on the subjective intent of the parties in creating the trusts, particularly when those parties are members of the same family unit, creates substantial obstacles to the proper application of the federal estate tax laws. As this Court said in *Estate of Spiegel v. Commissioner*, 335 U. S. 701, 705–706 (1949):

> "Any requirement . . . [of] a post-death attempt to probe the settlor's thoughts in regard to the transfer, would partially impair the effectiveness of . . . [§ 2036] as an instrument to frustrate estate tax evasions."

We agree that "the taxability of a trust corpus . . . does not hinge on a settlor's motives, but depends on the nature and operative effect of the trust transfer." *Id.*, at 705.

We think these observations have particular weight when applied to the reciprocal trust situation. First, inquiries into subjective intent, especially in intra family transfers, are particularly perilous. The present case illustrates that it is, practically speaking, impossible to determine after the death of the parties what they had in mind in creating trusts over 30 years earlier. Second, there is a high probability that such a trust arrangement was indeed created for tax-avoidance purposes. And, even if there was no estate tax-avoidance motive, the settlor in a very real and objective sense did retain an economic interest while purporting to give away his property.[7] Finally, it is unrealistic to assume that the settlors of the trusts, usually members of one family unit, will have created their trusts as a bargained-for exchange for the other trust. "Consideration," in the traditional legal sense, simply does not normally enter into such intra family transfers.

For these reasons, we hold that application of the reciprocal trust doctrine is not dependent upon a finding that each trust was created as a quid pro quo for the other. Such a "consideration" requirement necessarily involves a difficult inquiry into the subjective intent of the settlors. Nor do we think it necessary to prove the existence of a tax-avoidance motive. As we have said above, standards of this sort, which rely on subjective factors, are rarely workable under the federal estate tax laws. Rather, we hold that application of the reciprocal trust doctrine requires only that the trusts be interrelated, and that the arrangement, to the extent of mutual value, leaves the settlors in approximately the same economic position as they would have been in had they created trusts naming themselves as life beneficiaries.[8]

Applying this test to the present case, we think it clear that the value of the Janet Grace trust fund must be included in decedent's estate for federal estate tax purposes. It is undisputed that the two trusts are interrelated. They are substantially identical in terms and were created at approximately the same time. Indeed, they were part of a single transaction designed and carried out by decedent. It is also clear that the transfers in trust left each party, to the extent of mutual value, in the same objective economic position as before. Indeed, it appears, as would be expected in transfers between husband and wife, that the effective position of each party vis-a-vis the property did not change at all. It is no answer that the transferred properties were different in character. For purposes of the estate tax, we think that economic value is the only workable criterion. Joseph Grace's estate remained undiminished to the extent of the value of his wife's trust and the value of his estate must accordingly be increased by the value of that trust.

The judgment of the Court of Claims is reversed and the case is remanded for further proceedings consistent with this opinion.

It is so ordered.

---

[7] For example, in the present case decedent ostensibly devised the trust plan to avoid an imminent Federal gift tax. Instead of establishing trusts for the present benefit of his children, he chose an arrangement under which he and his wife retained present enjoyment of the property and under which the property would pass to their children without imposition of either estate or gift tax.

[8] We do not mean to say that the existence of "consideration," in the traditional legal sense of a bargained-for exchange, can never be relevant. In certain cases, inquiries into the settlor's reasons for creating the trusts may be helpful in establishing the requisite link between the two trusts. We only hold that a finding of a bargained-for consideration is not necessary to establish reciprocity.

Mr. Justice Douglas, dissenting [opinion omitted].

––––––

The Service issued Rev. Rul. 74–533, 1974–2 C.B. 293, to provide guidance on how to compute the amount to include in a decedent's estate if the reciprocal trust doctrine applies, but different amounts are transferred to each trust. In the ruling, *H* transfers $400,000 to a trust for the benefit of *W*. Simultaneously, *W* transfers $300,000 to a trust for *H*. When *H* dies, the value of the trust *W* created is then worth $500,000. When *W* dies, the trust that *H* created is valued at $600,000.

At the time of *H*'s death, the full value of the trust *W* created is included in his estate because *W*'s trust was the smaller of the two trusts when they were created; thus, reciprocity exists to the extent of mutual consideration ($300,000). The value of *W*'s trust for *H* is $500,000 at the time of *H*'s death, and that amount is includible in *H*'s estate.

When *W* dies, only three-fourths ($300,000/$400,000) of *H*'s trust is included in her estate because the trust *H* created for her was larger than the trust that *W* created for *H*. There was mutual consideration only to the extent of $300,000, or three-fourths of the trust that *H* created for *W*. Because *H*'s trust for *W* was valued at $600,000 at the time of *W*'s death, $450,000 (¾ × $600,000) is the amount includible in *W*'s estate.

The conclusions of the Rev. Rul. 74–533 are consistent with *Estate of Cole v. Commissioner*, 140 F.2d 636 (8th Cir. 1944).

Subsequent to *Grace*, the Tax Court in *Estate of Levy v. Commissioner*, T.C. Memo 1983–453, decided that the reciprocal trust doctrine does not apply when one trust provides a remainder to described persons, but the other trust provides that the remainder will be determined through the exercise of a special power of appointment.

––––––

The reciprocal trust doctrine has been applied to lifetime transfers to impose a gift tax liability. In *Sather v. Commissioner*, 251 F.3d 1168 (8th Cir. 2001), the donors were trying to increase the number of available annual exclusions. The court found:

> The Sather brothers, Larry, John, Duane, and Rodney (collectively the "brothers"), along with Larry's, John's, and Duane's wives, Kathy, Sandra, and Diane, respectively (collectively the "wives"), owned 100% of the stock in Sather, Inc., which they previously received from the brothers' parents. At the time of the transfers at issue, Rodney was unmarried and had no children. Larry, John, and Duane each had three children. In an effort to transfer the stock of Sather, Inc., to the next generation of Sathers, the brothers consulted their accountant for advice on structuring the transfer. Upon their accountant's advice, Larry, John, and Duane and each of their respective wives transferred $9,997 worth of stock to each of their children

and to each of their nieces and nephews on December 31, 1992. Larry, John, and Duane also transferred additional shares to their own children to effect the full transfer of Sather, Inc., stock to the next generation of Sathers. On January 5, 1993, Larry, John, and Duane each transferred $19,994 worth of stock to each of their nieces and nephews and approximately $15,000 worth of stock to each of their own children. The wives each transferred $3,283 worth of stock to each of their own children. [Footnote omitted] The transfers were made to irrevocable trusts for each set of children (Larry's, John's, and Duane's).

Each donor filed a separate gift tax return for 1992, claiming nine $10,000 gift tax exclusions, one for each donee (each individual's own three children and six nieces and nephews, or nine nieces and nephews in Rodney's case). Each donor likewise filed a gift tax return for 1993, again claiming nine $10,000 gift tax exclusions and electing to have each gift treated as made one-half by each spouse, as allowed under the Internal Revenue Code (I.R.C.) § 2513, 26 U.S.C. § 2513 (1994). . . .

Estate of Grace establishes a two-part test to apply the reciprocal trust doctrine to gifts. First, the gifts must be interrelated and second, the donors must be left in approximately the same economic position. As to the first test, the court concluded:

> Applying the reciprocal trust doctrine to this case, there can be no doubt that the gifts were interrelated. The Sather brothers together sought advice on how to transfer the stock to the next generation of Sathers. The transfers to all the children were made on the same days and were for the same amounts of stock. We cannot say that the tax court erred—clearly or otherwise—in determining that the transfers were interrelated.

As to the second test, the court determined:

> . . . Uncrossing the gifts in the present case, the tax court made the factual finding that each immediate family was in the same position as if each donor had made gifts only to the donor's own children. Thus, using the reciprocal trust doctrine to identify the actual transferor, each donor made transfers to each of his or her own children but no gifts to any of the nieces and nephews. *See Schultz*, 493 F.2d [1225 (4th Cir. 1974)] at 1226. We cannot say that the tax court clearly erred in making this factual finding. Under I.R.C. § 2503(b), each transferor—Larry, Kathy, John, Sandra, Duane, and Diane—was entitled to one $10,000 exclusion for gifts made to each uncrossed donee, their own children, for each year in which gifts were made. Because each transferor has only three children but claimed nine exclusions, the IRS correctly determined that the transferors understated their gift tax liabilities.

Problems

1. Must the Service establish that the reciprocal nature of the trusts was intended by the grantors of both trusts to apply the reciprocal trust doctrine?

2. Assume that *G*, age 60, transfers $400,000 to a trust. The income is payable to *C*, age 60, for life and then the remainder is distributable to *C*'s children. At nearly the same time, *C* transfers $300,000 of her own assets to a trust. The income from that trust is payable to *G* for life and the remainder is distributable to *G*'s children.

   a. What are the gift tax consequences to *C* and *G* on creating their respective trusts?

   b. Is either trust included in *G*'s gross estate upon his death?

   c. Assume further that at *G*'s death, the trust created by *C* is valued at $500,000, and at *C*'s death the trust created by *G* is valued at $700,000. How much should be included in each estate?

[C] Generation-Skipping Transfer Tax

Code: § 2642(f).

Regulations: Treas. Reg. § 26.2632–1(c).

The transferor's retention of an income interest does not trigger any immediate GST tax consequences. The retention will, however, have subsequent generation-skipping consequences.

> **Example 1:** Grandparent transfers $100,000 to a trust and retains the income for life, with remainder to Grandchild. When Grandparent dies, the trust property has a value of $200,000.

A direct skip does not occur on trust creation unless the trust is a *skip person* under § 2612(c)(1). Under the "look through to see who are the beneficiaries" rules, the trust in Example 1 is not a skip person because the transferor has an interest held in the trust. *See* § 2651(e). The transferor is, by definition, a nonskip person. *See* § 2613(b).

A generation-skipping transfer (GST) will occur on Grandparent's death. A direct skip occurs because the property is subject to estate tax under § 2036(a)(1) and the property interest passes to a skip person.[9] The GST tax imposed depends on the applicable rate (§ 2641) and the taxable amount (§ 2623). Ultimately, a GST tax will be imposed if the inclusion ratio is greater than zero.

Normally, a transferor may establish an inclusion ratio by allocating GST exemption to a transfer which might later be deemed a generation-skipping transfer. *See* § 2632. If a transferor could allocate GST exemption with a retained interest transfer, and if the inclusion ratio was zero as a result of the allocation, the ultimate transfer of possession to the skip person would be free from generation-skipping tax. Thus, in Example 1, if Grandparent allocated sufficient GST exemption to the trust to obtain an inclusion ratio of zero, when Grandparent died, Grandchild would receive the $200,000 free of the generation-skipping tax.

Congress determined that the advantages of allocation of GST exemption while retaining an interest were too good to be true. Section 2642(f) and

---

[9] A taxable termination does not occur because the gross estate inclusion is a superseding transfer. *See* Treas. Reg. § 26.2612-1(b)(1)(ii).

Treasury Regulation § 26.2632–1(c) do not permit a GST allocation to be effective in this situation, even if the donor attempts to make an allocation on a gift tax return. Instead, the allocation, although irrevocable, is given effect only when the property will not be included in the transferor's gross estate if the transferor had died immediately after the transfer (other than by reason of § 2035). The time between the date of the transfer and the time when an effective allocation can be made is known as an Estate Tax Inclusion Period (ETIP). If the allocation is made after the ETIP closes, the allocation is effective as of the time it is made.

As applied to Example 1, the ETIP will not close until the Grandparent dies because § 2036 would have applied any time before the Grandparent's death. On the Grandparent's death, the inclusion ratio will be determined based on the estate tax value of the property ($200,000) plus the amount of any GST exemption allocated by the decedent's personal representative or by operation of law. *See* § 2632(c).

Problem

Grandparent, *GP*, creates a trust. The income is payable to *GP* for ten years, and the remainder to Grandchild. Must *GP* allocate a GST exemption after ten years? What happens if *GP* never allocates a GST exemption to the trust? *See* § 2632(C)(4).

[D] Income Tax

Code: § 677(a).

Regulations: Treas. Reg. § 1.677(a)–1.

The grantor's retention of the right to income from a trust has significant income tax consequences.[10] Section 677(a)(1) provides that "[t]he grantor shall be treated as the owner of any portion of a trust, . . . whose income without the approval or consent of any adverse party . . . may be—(1) distributed to the grantor or the grantor's spouse." To the extent that the grantor has a right to the current distribution of income, § 677 merely duplicates the normal rule regarding taxation of the income of trusts. See the discussion of §§ 652 and 662, in Chapter 14, *infra*, which taxes trust income to the beneficiary currently entitled to receive it.

The scope of § 677(a)(1) is far more extensive, however, than §§ 652 and 662. First, unlike the estate and gift tax provisions, § 677 does not treat the grantor's spouse as a separate entity. Express statutory language treats income payable to the spouse as the equivalent of income payable to the grantor. Section 672(e) treats the grantor as holding any power or interest held by the spouse, whether they (1) were married at the time the power or interest was created or (2) married subsequent to the creation of the power or interest. For example, *H* creates a trust. The income is payable to his wife, *W*, and the remainder is distributable to *X*. For income tax purposes, the trust income is taxed to *H*. Contrast this income tax result with the consequences

---

[10] The right to income as used in this section comprehends current income.

of § 2036, which would not include the trust property in *H*'s estate, if he died while *W* was still living.

Second, § 677(a)(1) applies to income which *may be* distributed to the grantor or the grantor's spouse. Thus, if the grantor creates a discretionary trust for her own benefit, the trust income will be taxed to her under § 677(a), unless the discretionary power is held by an *adverse party*. The mere existence of a power to make a distribution to the grantor, and not the power's exercise, makes the income taxable to the grantor.

The term *adverse party* is defined by § 672(a) and requires that the party have a substantial beneficial interest which would be adversely affected by the exercise of the power. In this context, § 672(a) requires that the power holder have the right to the income distributed to the grantor. Operation of the section is illustrated in the following example:

> **Example 1:** *G* creates an irrevocable trust. The income is payable to *A* for life and the remainder is distributable to *B*. The trustee, who is not an adverse party, has the power to distribute the trust income to *G*.

In this example, the trust income is taxed to *G* because the income may be distributed to him. The same result would obtain if *G*'s spouse, rather than *G*, was the permissible recipient of trust income, but not if *A* were the trustee. As long as the income may be distributed to the spouse, it is taxable to the grantor.

The following decision of the Tax Court illustrates the application of § 677(a).

Krause v. Commissioner

56 T.C. 1242 (1971)

Featherston, Judge:

Respondent determined a deficiency in petitioners' Federal income tax for 1964 in the amount of $91,249.05. The issue for decision is whether funds derived by trusts from dividends and loans and used, pursuant to the trust instruments, to pay the gift taxes resulting from the creation of the trusts are income taxable to petitioners.

Victor W. Krause (hereinafter referred to as petitioner) and Gordon C. Krause, administrator of the Estate of Gertrude C. Krause, were legal residents of Rockford, Mich., at the time they filed their petition. Gordon C. Krause is a petitioner herein only because Gertrude C. Krause and petitioner filed a joint income tax return for 1964. They filed the return with the district director of internal revenue, Detroit, Mich.

The facts, all stipulated, show that during September of 1963, petitioner created three trusts: One for the benefit of the children of his son, Gordon C. Krause (hereinafter the Gordon trust), and one for the benefit of the children of each of his daughters, Elizabeth K. Sherwood and Ruth K. Sherwood (hereinafter the Elizabeth and Ruth trusts, respectively). To the Gordon trust, petitioner transferred 12,000 shares of common stock in Wolverine Shoe & Tanning Corp. To the Elizabeth and Ruth trusts, respectively, he transferred 8,000 shares of common stock in the same corporation. The total value of the stock was $807,000, and petitioner's basis in it was $21,700.

The Gordon trust agreement provides:

> 2. The Trustees shall promptly pay all Federal Gift Taxes and all other taxes which shall arise out of or be attributable to the transfer by this Trust Agreement of the above mentioned shares of corporate stock, and said corporate stock is transferred hereby subject to the duty and obligation of the Trustees to promptly pay all such taxes. In order to provide funds with which to pay said taxes the Trustees in their sole and absolute discretion may sell and convert to cash such portions of said corporate stock as they may deem necessary for that purpose or they may borrow sufficient funds for that purpose from such sources, including themselves or either of them, as they may deem proper, and pledge any part of the principal and income of this Trust as security for such loan, or they may obtain funds for the payment of all such taxes partly by sale of assets of said Trust and partly by loan secured by all or any part of the principal and income of this Trust, all in accordance with their sole and absolute discretion.

> 3. All income and earnings of this Trust shall be used and applied by the Trustees in such amounts and at such times as they in their sole and absolute discretion from time to time shall determine for the following purposes, namely:

> First—for the payment of all taxes and assessments and other governmental charges which may be lawfully imposed upon the principal and/or income of this Trust.

> Second—for the payment of all proper charges and expenses incurred by the Trustees and their agents and attorneys in and about the faithful administration of this Trust.

The Elizabeth and Ruth trust agreements contain basically similar provisions, differing only in that each further provides that the trustees—

> may obtain funds for the payment of all such (gift) taxes partly by sale of assets of the principal of said trust, partly from income thereof, and partly by loan secured by all or any part of the principal and/or income of this trust . . . .

In April of 1964, the trustees of the three trusts pledged the stock which they had received from petitioner to Old Kent Bank & Trust Co., one of the trustees, as security for loans in the total amount of $134,500. With these funds, the trustees, on April 14, 1964, paid the joint and several gift tax liabilities of petitioner and his wife, both of whom had consented pursuant to section 2513 to having the gifts treated as made one-half by each of them. The total amount of taxes so paid was $134,331.65.

During their fiscal years ending August 31, 1964, the trusts received the following amounts of dividend income:

	Sept. to Apr. 14	Apr. 15 to Aug. 31	Total
Gordon	$3,600	$4,050	$7,650
Elizabeth	2,400	2,700	5,100
Ruth	2,400	2,700	5,100
	8,400	9,450	17,850

Beginning in September of 1964 and continuing through August of 1970, the trusts made periodic payments to Old Kent Bank & Trust Co. to discharge the loans and the interest thereon. These payments were made with dividend income received by the trusts from the stock.

The Code provides generally that the gift tax "shall be paid by the donor." Sec. 2502. When a husband and wife have consented to have a gift made by one of them treated as if made one-half by each of them, they are jointly and severally liable for the full amount of the tax liability arising from the transfer. Sec. 2513(d). The donee, under section 6324(b), is personally liable for the tax only if it is not paid when due. *Fletcher Trust Co. v. Commissioner*, 141 F.2d 36, 39 (C.A. 7, 1944), *affirming* 1 T.C. 798 (1943), *certiorari denied* 323 U.S. 711 (1944). Thus, notwithstanding his agreements with the trustees and his wife, petitioner was liable under the Code for the payment of all the gift taxes arising from the transfers to the trusts.

Relying upon these Code provisions, respondent determined that petitioner transferred "stock in trust for several donees, reserving an income interest in the transfer for the payment of . . . (his) gift tax liability in the amount of $134,331.65; and that . . . (his) reservation of the income interest subjects . . . (him) to the provisions of section 677 of the Internal Revenue Code . . . . Accordingly, the net income of the trusts in 1964 is taxable to . . . (him) in the amount of $14,091.62." Respondent further determined that petitioner's "income interest in the trusts terminated in 1964 when the trusts paid . . . (his) gift tax liability in full; and that such payment, from funds other than trust income, constitutes a purchase in liquidation of . . . (his) income interest and results in ordinary income" in the additional amount of $120,240.03.

Section 677(a) provides in pertinent part:

> The grantor shall be treated as the owner of any portion of a trust . . . whose income without the approval or consent of any adverse party is, or, in the discretion of the grantor or a nonadverse party, or both, may be—
>
> (1) distributed to the grantor; . . .

Amplifying this provision, section 1.677(a)-1(d), Income Tax Regs., provides:

> (d) Under section 677 a grantor is, in general, treated as owner of a portion of a trust whose income is, or in the discretion of the grantor or a nonadverse party, or both, may be applied in discharge of a legal obligation of the grantor . . . .

When the grantor is treated as "the owner of any portion of a trust," section 671 provides that there shall be included in the computation of his taxable income 'those items of income, deductions, and credits against tax of the trust which are attributable to that portion of the trust to the extent that such items would be taken into account . . . in computing taxable income or credits against the tax of an individual.'

Sections 671 and 677 are part of subpart E, part I, subchapter J, of the 1954 Code. This subpart includes revised versions of 1939 Code sections 166 and 167 and certain regulations issued under 1939 Code section 22(a), the so-called Clifford and Mallinckrodt regulations. The subpart "provides rules to determine when a trust's income is to be taxed to the grantor because of the grantor's substantial dominion and control of the trust property or income." S. Rept. No. 1622, to accompany H.R. 8300 (Pub. L. No. 591), 83d Cong., 2d Sess., p. 86 (1954). Section 677 corresponds with section 167 of the 1939 Code, and it deals with the grantor's retention of dominion and control over the trust income.

To the extent of the amount of the income realized by the trusts prior to the payment of the gift taxes ($8,400), respondent's position is quite clearly correct. Where a person transfers property to a trust and, as a condition to the transfer, the trustee agrees to pay the resulting gift tax liability, the donor is taxable on any trust income which the trustee may use for that purpose. Within the meaning of section 677, he is treated as an owner of a portion of the trust because its income, in the discretion of the trustee, may be used to discharge his legal obligation. Under section 671, the donor is taxable on the income attributable to such portion of the trust—*i.e.,* the income which may be used to discharge his legal obligation to pay the gift tax. *Estate of Craig R. Sheaffer,* 37 T.C. 99 (1961), *affd.* 313 F.2d 738 (C.A. 8, 1963), *certiorari denied* 375 U.S. 818 (1963); *Estate of A. E. Staley, Sr.,* 47 B.T.A. 260 (1942), *affd.* 136 F.2d 368 (C.A. 5, 1943), *certiorari denied* 320 U.S. 786 (1943). It is of no avail to petitioner in the instant case that the proceeds of the loans rather than the trust income were used for this purpose. The controlling consideration under section 677 is the described "discretion," not the way in which that discretion is actually exercised.

Petitioner contends that the trustees of the Gordon trust were prohibited from using trust income for the payment of the gift taxes. In support of his contention, petitioner points out that paragraph 2 of the Gordon trust agreement does not specifically authorize the use of the income to pay such taxes, whereas the corresponding provisions in the Elizabeth and Ruth trust instruments do. We, however, do not attach the same significance to this difference in language as does petitioner.

Paragraph 2 of the Gordon trust agreement, quoted above, is permissive; it allows the trustee to sell part of the corpus or to borrow on the corpus to pay the gift taxes, but it does not prohibit the use of trust income for this purpose. Indeed, paragraph 3, dealing with trust income, gives the trustee wide discretion to use the trust income "for the payment of all taxes and assessments . . . which may be lawfully imposed upon the principal and/or income" of the trust and "for the payment of all proper charges and expenses incurred by the Trustees and their agents and attorneys." Since the trust agreements required the trustees to pay the gift tax liabilities arising from the transfers in trust, such liabilities became proper charges against the principal and income of the trusts. The trustees, therefore, had the discretionary power to use the trust income to meet this charge without violating the trust agreement. In these circumstances, sections 671 and 677 require all such income received prior to the payment of the taxes to be included in petitioner's taxable income.

The income received by the trusts after April 14, 1964, when the gift taxes were paid, however, is not taxable to petitioner. As a result of the payment of the taxes, all of his obligations with respect thereto were satisfied, and, within the meaning of section 1.677(a)-1(d), *supra*, he had no further obligations to which the trust income could be applied. Thus, the payment of the gift taxes denuded petitioner of every interest in the trusts, and section 1.667(a)-1(c), Income Tax Regs., provides:

> If the grantor strips himself permanently and definitively of every interest . . . he is not treated as an owner under section 677 after that divesting . . . .

Since petitioner, after April 14, 1964, no longer had any interest in the trusts within the meaning of section 677, none of the trust income received after that date is taxable to him. This is the rationale and holding of *Estate of Annette S. Morgan*, 37 T.C. 981 (1962), *affirmed per curiam* 316 F.2d 238 (C.A. 6, 1963), *certiorari denied* 375 U.S. 825 (1963); *David Keith*, 45 B.T.A. 644 (1941), *acq.* 1942-1 C.B. 10.

Although the income which the Commissioner sought to tax in *Estate of Annette S. Morgan* and *David Keith* was actually received by the trusts in years subsequent to the ones in which the gift taxes were paid, the reasoning which those cases employ does not permit a different rule for the trust income received during the portion of the taxable year remaining after the taxes are paid. Neither represents trust income received during a period when the donor is treated as the owner of a portion of the trusts under section 677. Quite obviously if a beneficiary dies during a trust's fiscal year and after his death the trust income is to be distributed to someone else, he is not taxable on the income received by the trust during the entire year. *See, e.g., D. G. McDonald Trust*, 19 T.C. 672 (1953), *acq.* 1953-2 C.B. 5, *affirmed sub nom. Chase National Bank v. Commissioner*, 225 F.2d 621 (C.A. 8, 1955). Similarly, where, as in the instant case, the grantor is divested of all interest in the trust during a taxable year, he is not taxable on the subsequently received income of the trust. We hold petitioner is not taxable on the income received by the trusts between April 14, 1964, the date of the gift tax payment, and August 31, 1964, the end of the trusts' fiscal years.

Contrary to respondent's contention, payment of the gift taxes with borrowed funds did not constitute a purchase or liquidation of income interests retained by petitioner. His retained interests were not limited to the right to have the trust income applied toward the payment of the gift taxes. He had the right to have the gift taxes paid out of any available funds, whether borrowed, obtained from corpus, or derived from dividends on the transferred stock. In a very real sense, his gifts in trust consisted of only the excess of the value of the stock over the amount of the gift taxes. *Richard H. Turner,* 49 T.C. 356, 363 (1968), *affirmed per curiam* 410 F.2d 752 (C.A. 6, 1969); *Sarah Helen Harrison,* 17 T.C. 1350, 1357 (1952), *acq.* 1952-2 C.B. 2. If petitioner had transferred to the trusts, along with the stock, sufficient cash to pay the gift taxes, the use of the cash for that purpose would not have generated any taxable income. Similarly, the use of cash derived from pledging the entrusted stock did not generate any taxable income. Significantly, the pre-April 14, 1964, trust income is taxable to petitioner not because of any requirement that the gift taxes be paid out of income but because the trust income, within the meaning of section 677, was subject to being used for that purpose at a time when petitioner was personally liable for the tax. When the gift taxes were paid through use, in part, of the reserved portions of the corpora, petitioner's interests in the trust terminated, but he realized no taxable income therefrom. . . .

We adhere to the authority of that case.

Reviewed by the Court.

Sterrett, J., dissents. . . .

The only significant limitation on this *"may be"* aspect of § 677 is that income which may be used for the support of someone that the grantor is obligated to support is not taxable to him unless it is actually used for support or the grantor holds the distribution power other than as a trustee. *See* § 677(b); Treas. Reg. § 1.677(b)–1(a).[11] Note, however, that this limitation does not apply to income that may be used to discharge the grantor's legal obligation to support his spouse or that is available to discharge legal obligations of the grantor or the grantor's spouse, other than their obligation to support or maintain a trust beneficiary.

Third, by requiring that the grantor is "treated as the owner of [the] portion," the grantor can also be liable for capital gains that might otherwise be taxed to the trust. This assumes that capital gains may be allocated to income or the trustee has the discretion to distribute principal to the grantor. If capital gains must be allocated to corpus and the trustee cannot invade the corpus for the grantor, that income would not be attributable to the *portion* owned by the grantor as income beneficiary of a trust. *See* Treas. Reg. § 1.677(a)–1(g), Example 1.

The following Revenue Ruling illustrates the rule.

Revenue Ruling 66-161

1966-1 C.B. 164

Where, under the terms of a trust indenture, corpus is to revert to the grantor after ten years, capital gains are to be added to corpus, and all such

---

[11] Section 674(a) *also* requires taxation of the grantor if he has a power to distribute income, to the extent that the power is not exempted by § 677(b). *See* § 674(b)(1).

gains as are taxable to the grantor are, subject to his demand, payable to him, then all capital gains plus income attributable to the portion of the trust, title to which the grantor may revest in himself, must be included in the computation of the grantor's taxable income for the taxable year in which the items of income are realized.

Advice has been requested as to the taxability to the grantor of capital gains and other income realized by the trust described below.

The trust indenture provides that trust income is to be currently distributed to a named beneficiary for ten years and that upon the termination of such period, the corpus of the trust is to revert to the grantor. The trust is irrevocable and may not be modified. The indenture further provides:

All gains derived from the sale or exchange of capital assets shall be deemed to be corpus and any such gains as are taxable to the grantor under any Federal income tax law shall be paid to the grantor at such time and to such extent as he may request.

Section 677(a) of the Internal Revenue Code of 1954 provides, in part, that the grantor shall be treated as the owner of any portion of a trust whose income without the approval or consent of any adverse party is, or, in the discretion of the grantor or a nonadverse party, or both, may be held or accumulated for future distribution to the grantor.

Section 1.677(a)-1(f) of the Income Tax Regulations provides, in part, that if income is accumulated in any taxable year for future distribution to the grantor, section 677(a)(2) of the Code treats the grantor as an owner for that taxable year. Thus, if income (including capital gains) of a trust is to be accumulated for ten years and then will be, or at the discretion of the grantor may be, distributed to the grantor, the grantor is treated as the owner of the trust from its inception.

Section 676 of the Code treats the grantor of a trust as the owner of that portion of the trust, title to which he can revest in himself at any time. Section 1.671-3(a) of the regulations provides in part, that when a grantor is treated under sections 671 through 678 of the Code as the owner of any portion of a trust, there are included in computing his tax liability those items of income attributable to or included in that portion.

Since the terms of the trust indenture provide that capital gains are to be added to corpus which is to revert to the grantor, the grantor is treated as the owner under section 677(a) of the Code of that portion of the trust to which the capital gains are attributable.

In addition, since the accumulated capital gains lose their identity as capital gains and become merged with corpus following the year of realization, the quoted provisions of the trust indenture, in effect, give the grantor the power to revest in himself title to a portion of the corpus. Therefore, the grantor is treated as owner of such portion of the trust under section 676 of the Code.

Accordingly, all capital gains plus income attributable to the portion of the trust corpus title to which the grantor may revest in himself must be included in the computation of the grantor's taxable income for the taxable year in which the income is realized.

————

Problems

1. Five years ago, a 50-year-old widow, *T*, declared herself trustee of an irrevocable trust for property valued at $1 million. Trust income was payable to *T* for her life. At *T*'s death, the corpus is to be distributed to *T*'s minor child, *C*. When *T* dies, the property is valued at $1.2 million.

a. What are the federal income, gift, estate, and GST tax consequences of this transfer if *T* made no previous taxable gifts and assuming 8% assumed rate under § 7520?

b. How would the results differ if *T* had transferred the property to a bank trustee, and given the bank the discretion to distribute income to *T*, or accumulate it?

c. How would the results in (b) differ if instead the bank was given the discretion during *T*'s life to pay income for the support of *C*?

d. How would the results differ in (a) if the remainderman was *T*'s spouse?

2. Assume the facts in Problem 1, except that *C* paid *T* the value of the remainder when *T* created the trust. What are the gift and estate tax consequences?

§ 7.02 Reversionary Interests

Reversionary interests can also have significant gift, estate, generation-skipping transfer, and income tax consequences to the grantor. The scope of these ramifications depends significantly upon the nature of the interest retained.

[A] Indefeasible Reversions

As used in this book, and as commonly understood, an indefeasible reversion is an interest that is retained by the transferor. The possession or enjoyment of the transferred property must, on the termination of a present interest, return to the transferor (or if dead, to the transferor's successors in interest). Consider the following trust disposition. *G* creates a trust. The income is payable to *A* for life. *G* has an indefeasible reversion. When *A* dies, *G* (or if *G* is then dead, *G*'s successors-in-interest) will have the right to possession of the trust property. Note that a reversion (whether or not indefeasible) does not have to be expressly retained. Rather, a reversion is created whenever a transferor does not transfer away her entire interest in the property.

[1] Gift Tax

Code: § 2511.

Regulations: Treas. Reg. § 25.2511–1(e).

If an irrevocable trust provides that income is distributable to a third party for a term of years or for life, and the grantor retains an indefeasible reversion, the transfer of the income interest is a completed gift. *See* Treas. Reg. § 25.2511–1(e). Absent application of § 2702 or the *Robinette* doctrine, the gift of the income interest will equal its actuarially determined value based on the valuation rules of § 7520. Because an income interest usually is not a future interest, the gift of the income interest should qualify for the gift tax annual exclusion under § 2503(b).

If the income interest, or any part of it, is transferred to a member of the grantor's family,[12] § 2702 applies, and the grantor's reversion will be valued at zero, unless the grantor retained a qualified interest. If this zero value rule applies to the transfer, the value of the income interest will be the value of the entire property transferred rather than its actuarial value. *See* Treas. Reg. § 25.2702–1(b).

Section 2702(b)(3) provides an exception to this zero-valuation rule for certain indefeasible reversions. Provided the reversion is preceded only by a § 2702 blessed annuity or unitrust interest, the actuarial value of the reversion will be taken into account. Only the actuarial value of the gifted annuity or unitrust interest will be considered for gift tax purposes.

[2] Estate Tax

Code: §§ 2033 and 2702.

Regulations: Treas. Reg. § 25.2702–6.

Reversions constitute an interest in property owned at death. Thus, they are included in the owner's estate under § 2033. The same is true of resulting trust interests (interests impliedly retained because not given away), even though the transfer of the intervening income interest is subject to the gift tax. In both cases the personal representative may elect to defer payment of estate taxes attributable to inclusion of the reversionary interest in the gross estate. *See* § 6163.

If the reversion was valued at zero for gift tax purposes because of § 2702, and the grantor owned the same reversion at death, a double tax problem arises. In this circumstance, the regulations prescribe an adjustment to ameliorate the effects of double taxation. *See* Treas. Reg. § 25.2702–6.

Problems

1. On January 1, 1997, *G* transfers $100,000 to a trust. The income is payable to *G*'s niece or her estate for ten years, and the corpus reverts to *G*. What are the gift tax consequences of the transfer assuming a § 7520 rate

---

[12] A "member of the grantor's family" includes the grantor's spouse or sibling, an ancestor or descendant of the grantor or the grantor's spouse, or the spouse of any such sibling, ancestor, or descendant. Section 2702(e) incorporates the definition of *family* provided by § 2704(c)(2).

of 8%? What are the estate tax consequences if *G* dies on January 1, 2003? What are the gift and estate tax consequences if the income beneficiary is *G*'s mother?

[3] Generation-Skipping Transfer Tax

The normal generation-skipping tax rules will likely apply when a transferor creates a trust, but retains the indefeasible right to the trust property after termination of the prior interests. Thus, if Grandparent creates a trust for Grandchild for ten years, reversion to Grandfather, a direct skip would occur on the trust's creation. Only skip persons have a present interest in the trust. *See* Treas. Reg. § 26.2612–1(d), (e). However, the amount of the direct skip should be limited by the value of the ten year term.

[4] Income Tax

Code: §§ 673(a) and 677(a)(2).

Regulations: Treas. Reg. § 1.677(a)–1(g).

Section 673(a) taxes trust income to the grantor if the grantor (or the grantor's spouse) has a reversionary interest in trust principal or income, provided that "as of the inception of that portion of the trust, the value of such interest exceeds 5% of the value of such portion." Actuarially, assuming an 8% rate, it is necessary for the grantor to dispose of 39 years of income to avoid being currently taxed on the trust's income. The only exception to this rule is § 673(b), which allows the income interest to be limited by the death of the income beneficiary before age 21, if that beneficiary is the minor dependent of the grantor. Section 673(c) provides that for the purposes of determining whether a reversionary interest has a value in excess of 5% of the trust, it will be assumed that any discretionary powers in favor of the grantor are exercised to maximize the value of the reversionary interest.

The current language of § 673(a) was added by the Tax Reform Act of 1986. Before then, the grantor could avoid income taxation by retaining a reversionary interest in the principal or income of a trust, unless it would or might reasonably be expected "to take effect in possession or enjoyment within ten years, commencing with the date of the transfer of that portion of the trust." Under the prior law, the income from a simple trust (known as a *Clifford* trust or a short-term trust) could be reported by the income beneficiary if the income interest lasted for at least ten years and a day, although the grantor had a reversion at the end of the trust term.

Reversionary interests can also result in the taxation of capital gains to the grantor, even if the 5% rule of § 673 is satisfied. Under § 677(a)(2), the grantor is taxed on trust income as the owner of any portion of a trust in which the income of which may be "held or accumulated for future distribution to the grantor or the grantor's spouse." To the extent that capital gains are allowable to principal—the usual pattern—this provision requires that capital gains are taxed to the grantor. *See* Treas. Reg. § 1.677(a)–1(g), Example 2.

The following Private Letter Ruling discusses the rule.

Private Letter Ruling 9402011

In August 1992, the grantor transferred all of her right, title, and interest in her personal residence to a trust. The residence is the grantor's personal residence... The trust instrument provides that the grantor shall have the right, rent free, to the use of the residence (or any replacement residence acquired by the trustee) as a personal residence for a term of 3 years beginning at the creation of the personal residence trust. The trustee shall pay over or apply any net income of the trust at the end of each calendar year to or for the benefit of the grantor. The trustee shall not pay over or apply any portion of the principal of the trust estate to or for the benefit of any person other than the grantor. The trustee may pay expenses properly chargeable to the trust estate.

The trust instrument provides that the trust shall terminate upon the first to occur of 1) the death of the grantor or 2) the expiration of the fixed term. If the grantor dies prior to the expiration of the fixed term, the trust estate shall be payable to the trustee of the grantor's revocable living trust, and if such trust is not then in existence, to the grantor's executor or administrator, to be disposed of as part of the grantor's probate estate. If the grantor survives the fixed term, then upon the expiration of the fixed term, the trust estate is to be distributed in trust to the children of the grantor.

You represent that the grantor was age 76 at her birthdate nearest the creation of the personal residence trust in August 1992. The applicable federal rate under section 7520 of the Code for the month of August 1992, was 7.8%.

You request that we rule as follows:

. . .

3. The grantor will be considered the owner of both the income and principal of the qualified personal residence trust for federal income tax purposes under section 673 of the Code.

. . .

ISSUE 3 (Income Taxation of Qualified Personal Residence Trust)

Section 671 of the Code provides that where it is specified in subpart E that the grantor or another person shall be treated as the owner of any portion of a trust, there shall then be included in computing the taxable income and credits of the grantor or the other person those items of income, deductions, and credits against tax of the trust that are attributable to that portion of the trust to the extent that such items would be taken into account under chapter 1 in computing taxable income or credits against the tax of an individual. Section 1.671-3(a) of the Income Tax Regulations provides that when under subpart E (section 671 and following) a grantor or another person is treated as the owner of any portion of a trust, there are included in computing his personal income tax liability those items of income, deduction, and credit against tax attributable to or included in that portion. For example, if a grantor or another person is treated as the owner of the entire trust (corpus as well as ordinary income), the grantor takes into account in computing the grantor's income tax liability all items of income, deduction, and credit (including capital gains and losses) to which the grantor would have been entitled had the trust not been in existence during the period that the grantor is treated as the owner.

Section 1.671-3(b)(3) of the regulations provides that both ordinary income and other income allocable to corpus are included where the grantor has an interest in or a power over both ordinary income and corpus, or an interest in or power over corpus alone that does not come within the provisions of section 1.671-3(b)(2). For example, if a grantor is treated under section 673 as the owner of a portion of a trust by reason of a reversionary interest in corpus (i.e., an interest in or power over corpus alone that does not come within the provisions of section 1.671-3(b)(2)), both ordinary income and other income allocable to corpus are included in the portion.

Section 673(a) of the Code provides that the grantor shall be treated as the owner of any portion of a trust in which he has a reversionary interest in either the corpus or the income therefrom, if, as of the inception of that portion of the trust, the value of the reversionary interest exceeds 5% of the value of such portion. Section 673(c) provides that for purposes of section 673(a), the value of the grantor's reversionary interest shall be determined by assuming the maximum exercise of discretion in favor of the grantor.

In the present case, the grantor retains a reversionary interest in the corpus of the entire trust because if the grantor dies prior to the expiration of the fixed term, the corpus of the entire trust will be distributed to the trustee of the grantor's revocable living trust, and if such trust is not then in existence, to the grantor's executor or administrator, to be disposed of as part of the grantor's probate estate. Based on the applicable federal rate of 7.8% for the month of August 1992, and the grantor's age of 76 at her nearest birthdate, the value of the reversionary interest is 13.4689% of the value of the trust at its creation. Accordingly, since this exceeds the 5% requirement in section 673(a), we conclude that the grantor will be considered the owner of the entire trust under section 673(a), and must include in computing her personal income tax liability all items of income, deduction, and credit against tax attributable to the trust under section 671 . . . .

Problems

1. In 2002, *G* creates a trust. The income is payable to *X* for 11 years and then the corpus is distributable to *G*'s spouse. Will trust income be taxable to *G*? Assume that after 11 years the trust property is payable to *Y*, but the trustee had the power to invade corpus for *G*. Would income be taxable to *G*? *See* § 673(a), (c).

2. *G* establishes a lifetime trust. The income is payable to *X* for five years, then the trust is to terminate and the corpus reverts to *G*. Is the transfer subject to the gift tax, given that the trust will be taxed to *G* for income tax purposes? *See Lockard v. Commissioner*, 166 F.2d 409 (1st Cir. 1948).

[B] Reversions Subject to a Condition

[1] Gift Tax

It is well settled that a gift occurs where one transfers a remainder interest, despite the possibility that it may not become possessory because the grantor may regain possession on the happening of a contingency. *See* Smith v. Shaughnessy, 318 U.S. 176 (1943). In *Smith*, G created a trust with income payable to his wife for life. The trust corpus was to revert to G if then living, and if not, to B. There was no dispute that a gift of the income interest occurred. The Court rejected the contention, however, that the remainder interest was not subject to gift taxation because it might later be included in G's gross estate under the predecessor to § 2037, discussed at § 7.02[B][2], *infra*. Double reporting is not equivalent to double taxation.

Apart from the double reporting issue, the Court in *Smith* explained:

> We cannot accept any suggestion that the complexity of a property interest created by a trust can serve to defeat a tax. The essence of a gift by trust is the abandonment of control over the property put in trust. In cases such as this, where the grantor has neither the form nor substance of control and never will have unless he outlives his wife, we must conclude that he has lost all "economic control" and that the gift is complete except for the value of his reversionary interest.

(318 U.S. 180–81)

As indicated in *Robinette v. Helvering* (reproduced in Chapter 4 at § 4.02[B][1], *supra*), certain contingencies upon the grantor's interest can result in the grantor being denied the right to subtract the value of the retained interest from the value of the transferred property. If those contingencies are not capable of actuarial valuation, the retained interest is valued at zero, and the entire transfer is taxed to the grantor. Similarly, if § 2702 applies, the value of the reversionary interest will be zero.

Problem

Would § 2702 apply if the trust in *Smith v. Shaughnessy* was created in 2002?

[2] Estate Tax

Code: § 2037.

Regulations: Treas. Reg. § 20.2037.1(a) through (e).

As noted in Chapter 3, and as illustrated in Example 1 below, a contingency which terminates the grantor's interest negates taxation under § 2033 because the interest becomes nontransmissible and has no value.

Example 1: S creates a lifetime trust. The income is payable to A for life and then the trust property reverts to S, if S survives A, or is distributable to B if S does not survive A. S dies before A.

In Example 1, *S* only regains the property if she survives *A*. Because *S* did not survive *A*, the reversionary interest fails and no part of the trust is included in her estate under § 2033. *See* Rev. Rul. 55–438, 1955–2 C.B. 601.

On the other hand, any contingencies on the grantor's interest that survive her death, can raise valuation problems similar to those in *Robinette v. Helvering* (reproduced in Chapter 4 at § 4.02[B][1], *supra*), but in the estate tax context.

> **Example 2:** *S* creates a lifetime trust. The income is payable to *A* for life and then the trust property is to revert to *S* if *A* dies childless or is distributable to the children of *A*, if *A* is survived by children. *S* dies before *A* while *A* is childless.

Robinette would suggest that the contingency cannot be actuarially determined. If *Robinette* is then read to require that the interest be valued at zero, no estate tax would result under § 2033, even though the right to the property passed to his heirs or legatees at his death. *See, e.g., Estate of Cardeza v. Commissioner*, 5 T.C. 202 (1945), *aff'd*, 173 F.2d 19 (3d Cir. 1949). This interpretation would leave the estate in the same position for estate tax purposes as for gift tax purposes. *Robinette* requires that the retention of the interest be ignored for gift tax purposes, resulting in the taxation of the entire trust as a gift. In a sense, the heirs' or legatees' rights were taxed with the gift tax.

It is easily argued, however, that *Robinette* flips over on the taxpayer in this context. *Robinette* put the burden on the taxpayer to justify why the transaction should not be taxed and the retained interest valued at zero. This result can be justified on the basis that a grantor should not to be able to take a tax advantage of self-created uncertainties. Therefore, in the gift tax context the grantor should be taxed on the full value of the transfer, other than the value of the portion that she can prove was retained. If a similar reasoning is applied to the estate tax (in which there is difficulty in valuing a contingency on a decedent's retained interest), the estate has the burden of establishing the value of the contingency, which is the value of the likelihood of the grantor not regaining the transferred property. Applied this way, *Robinette* requires that contingencies that are not capable of being actuarially valued, are included in the gross estate without regard to the contingency. Accordingly, in Example 2 it is assumed that *A* would die childless. Thus, the entire value of a remainder after *A*'s life interest would be included in the grantor's gross estate. Double taxation is avoided by the mechanism of § 2001(b)—adjusted taxable gifts—at the time of the decedent's death.

Section 2037 requires the taxation of all reversionary interests if possession or enjoyment requires surviving the decedent and the decedent's interest and that interest is worth at least 5% of the value of the property immediately before the decedent's death. The decedent's interest can arise under the express language of the instrument or by operation of law. *See* Treas. Reg. § 20.2037–1(c)(2).

Under § 2037(b)(2), the term *reversionary interest* has its own special statutory meaning. This can include the possibility that the transferred property will return to the grantor, or the grantor's estate, or may be subject to a power of disposition by the grantor.

The first requirement of § 2037 is that a beneficiary can obtain the possession or enjoyment of the property only by surviving the grantor. If the beneficiary is required to survive the grantor to obtain possession or enjoyment of the trust property, the transfer is deemed a substitute for a testamentary disposition. The Code looks to possession or enjoyment as the essence of ownership of the interest. If, on the other hand, the beneficiary can take possession without surviving the grantor, such as by surviving the life tenant or by surviving for a set period, § 2037 does not apply. This requirement may be restated a different way that is a bit more understandable: Does death terminate the grantor's reversion? Neither the Code nor Regulations phrase this requirement in this manner, but it has the same effect. No one can receive the property until the decedent dies without the contingency being satisfied.

The second requirement of § 2037 is that the grantor retain a reversionary interest. This requirement is imposed because the reversion suggests that the grantor did not want to dispose of the property until death. The reversion gives the transaction a testamentary aspect. The term *reversion* includes any interest not given away by the grantor when the transfer was made. *Reversion* does not, however, include the retention of a secondary life interest or estate. *See* Treas. Reg. § 20.2037–1(c)(2). Even though a secondary life interest is technically a reversionary interest for property law purposes, § 2037 specifically excludes income interests from the definition of *reversion* under § 2037. This confirms the history of §§ 2036 and 2037, both of which arose from early estate tax provisions taxing transfers "intended to take effect at . . . death." Section 2036 later specifically addressed income interests, including secondary income interests, so that § 2037 excluded them when it was adopted.

The final requirement is that the decedent's interest be worth in excess of 5% of the value of the property immediately before death. This requirement arose from a desire by Congress to limit the effect of *Spiegel* to cases in which the decedent retained an interest sufficient to make the transaction reasonably considered as testamentary in nature. The requirement was applied when § 2037 was adopted as a part of the 1954 Code, and mirrors a 5% limitation which Congress imposed in 1949, on the taxation of pre-*Spiegel* transfers, but which the 1949 Act had not applied to post-*Spiegel* transactions.

The 5% test makes valuation of the retained interest critical to the question whether the property subject to the test is included in the Code. If, after all, the retained interest is worth less than 5% of the value of the property, § 2037 does not apply. As *Allen* holds, applying the test requires comparing the value for the transferred property with the value of the reversionary interest, immediately before the decedent's death. *See* Treas. Reg. § 20.2037–1(a)(3); *Estate of Allen v. United States*, 558 F.2d 14 (Ct. Cl. 1977).

Estate of Allen v. United States

558 F.2d 14 (Ct. Cl. 1977)

Kashiwa, Judge:

*   *   *

On October 28, 1949, Henrietta Allen, the decedent, established an irrevocable trust designating the First National Bank of Belfast, Maine, as trustee. The trustee was directed to pay the net income of the trust fund to the decedent's sister, Rebecca Ross ("Rebecca"), for her life. Upon the death of Rebecca, the trust was to terminate and the corpus was to revert to the decedent if she still was living. The decedent died on January 1, 1971, survived by Rebecca. In valuing the decedent's reversionary interest, the plaintiffs, as co-executors of decedent's estate, took into account the actual health and physical condition of the decedent and Rebecca and determined that the value was less than 5 percent of the value of the trust corpus.[13] Consequently, plaintiffs did not include the value of the reversion in decedent's gross estate.

On audit of the estate tax return, the Commissioner of Internal Revenue ("Commissioner") valued decedent's reversionary interest in accordance with Treas. Regs. § 20.2037-1(c)(3)(1958) and § 20.2031-10(a)(2), (e), using the tables of mortality and actuarial principles therein provided, and determined the value of decedent's reversion to be 34.158 percent of the value of the trust corpus. Accordingly, the Commissioner included the value of the trust corpus, reduced by the value of Rebecca's life estate, in the gross estate of the decedent under section 2037. . . .

The plaintiffs and defendant have differing views on the meaning of one sentence under section 2037(b). That sentence is:

> . . . The value of a reversionary interest immediately before the death of the decedent shall be determined (without regard to the fact of the decedent's death) by usual methods of valuation, including the use of tables of mortality and actuarial principles, under regulations prescribed by the Secretary or his delegate.. . .

*   *   *

Plaintiffs' position is that section 2037(b) authorizes consideration of the actual facts relating to the health and physical condition of the parties to the

---

[13] The stipulated facts are that decedent was afflicted with a fatal and incurable disease and that when the actual health and physical condition of the decedent and her sister are considered, the value of the reversionary interest immediately prior to death was less than 5 percent of the value of the trust corpus.

It should be noted that the percentage value of the reversionary interest is independent of the monetary value of the property subject to the reverter. The reverter's value depends on the transferor's chance of recovering the property. Thus, the value of the reversionary interest contingent on survivorship is a function of the relation between the life expectancies of the transferor and transferee. The shorter the expected life of the transferor or the longer the expected life of the transferee, the less the reverter is worth.

transfer in valuing reversionary interests under section 2037. . . . Generally, plaintiffs contend that the Treasury's and Service's positions that mortality tables are the exclusive tool for the valuation of reversionary interests under § 2037 conflict with congressional intent which, to plaintiffs, permits consideration of the actual health of persons. . . .

The parties do not dispute the purpose of section 2037. As demonstrated in the legislative history, section 2037 was introduced into the estate tax laws to eliminate the harsh results of *Estate of Spiegel v. Commissioner*, 335 U.S. 701 . . . (1949), and to provide a dividing line between taxable and nontaxable reversions.[14] However, neither the parties nor we can find anything in the legislative history which specifically precludes consideration of the health of the decedent in valuing a reversionary interest, or anything which specifically says that mortality tables are the sole method of valuation. Since it appears that Congress did not actually consider the problem of which method of valuation should be utilized, we must focus on the general background and purpose of section 2037 and the cases cited by the parties.

* * *

As plaintiffs recognize, section 2037(b) requires that the value of reversionary interests be determined by "usual methods of valuation." Initially, this language makes it appear difficult to conclude that mortality tables alone may be used in valuation. . . . We, however, do not place any independent meaning on this requirement. We feel that the specific delegation to the Secretary of authority to issue regulations dealing with valuation suggests that "usual methods" should be those defined by Treasury decision and that the methods chosen should include tables of mortality and actuarial principles. The Secretary has followed this mandate and issued regulations dealing with valuation. The fact that those regulations provide for the exclusive and routine use of actuarial tables to measure the value of a reversionary interest when the particular interest is subject to actuarial valuation does not, in our opinion, exceed the scope of the delegated power. The regulations promulgated under this specifically delegated authority are commonly referred to as "legislative" regulations.[15] It may be broadly stated that legislative regulations are given force and effect of law unless the regulations exceed the scope of the delegated power, are contrary to the statute, or are unreasonable. . . . As we construe these regulations promulgated by the Secretary pursuant to his authority, we believe that they require an actuarial determination of life expectancy, without regard to extrinsic evidence such as the actual life expectancy of the decedent here involved. Those regulations neither exceed the scope of the delegated power nor are contrary to the statute; furthermore, we do not find them unreasonable since, in our opinion, they promote both ease of administration and even-handed relief of the tax laws without undermining the settled policy embodied in the basic plan of section 2037.

---

[14] [In Spiegel, the Court held that the estate tax reached a decedent's contingent reversionary interest even though it had a minuscule value immediately before death. In 1954, Congress modified the result in Spiegel to require the value of the reversionary interest to exceed 5% of the date of death value of the underlying property. Eds.]

[15] [Examples of the delegation of rule-making authority for legislative regulations include §§ 469(h), 274(o), 1274(d)(1)(B), and 168(h)(8). Eds.]

The background of section 2037 demonstrates that one of the purposes of the statute is to tax transfers with a reversionary interest contingent on survivorship when they are used as testamentary substitutes. To consider health in valuing this type reversionary interest seems to us to detract considerably from this purpose. To assume, as plaintiffs have done, that Congress intended estate tax consequences to turn on the decedent's state of health just before death would create discrimination between decedents who were in good health prior to death and decedents who died after a long illness. That is, if estate tax consequences turned on the decedent's state of health, the life expectancy of a decedent who was in good health prior to death would presumably be determined by mortality tables, while the life expectancy of a decedent who died after a long illness would be determined differently. This does not seem proper to us. . . .

If one thing is certain, it is that "* * * no single method of valuation of a reversion can be prescribed in view of the large variety of reversionary interests."[16] In other words, not all reversionary interests can be valued actuarially.[17] The more dependent a reversionary interest is on facts peculiar to a particular transfer, the less useful actuarial principles are in valuing that reversionary interest. As such, we believe that the provisions "usual methods of valuation" and "without regard to the fact of the decedent's death" only apply to interests which cannot be valued actuarially. When a reversionary interest can be valued actuarially, we interpret the Code to allow exclusive use of actuarial principles. . . .

[The court then found Regulations §§ 20.2031-1, -7 and -10 to be consistent with its holding.]

As the Tax Court noted:

> By adopting * * * [this] construction of section 2037 * * * we have stayed within the framework of the rule of statutory construction set down by the Supreme Court in *Sunshine Coal Co. v. Adkins*, 310 U.S. 381 . . . (1940), wherein it was said that an "alternative [which would seriously impair the effectiveness of a statute] will not be taken where a construction is possible which will preserve the vitality of the Act and the utility of the language in question."[18]

Nichols, Judge, concurring:

> . . . I found the case on its facts an easy one, as our cases go, because I reached the same result by a shorter and well trodden route-the rule that courts will not construe a statute literally to produce absurd results beyond the known or probable intention of the Congress. . . . If Congress intended the value of the possibility of reverter immediately before death to be appraised on the basis of the causes that produced the death, it intended to introduce a joker in the statute, for the five percent exception would all but obliterate the rule. The

---

[16] Estate of Roy v. Commissioner, 54 T.C. at 1322.

[17] For example, actuarial principles cannot value a reversionary interest contingent on death without issue. *See* Commissioner v. Estate of Sternberger, 348 U.S. 187 . . . (1955); Humes v. United States, 276 U.S. 487 . . . (1928).

[18] Estate of Roy v. United States, 54 T.C. at 1323.

only cases the rule would cover would be those of virtually instantaneous deaths, as, *e.g.*, in homicides and other accidental deaths, and even then, if the victim lingered an hour or two before expiring, presumably the life expectancy and therefore the application of the five percent rule would be evaluated as of that period. As to people dying of disease in bed, it is easy to picture the tax lawyer and accountant hovering about the premises to make sure the decedent still breathed when the magic five percent point was passed. In many cases, the inquiries for the tax man to make would be grisly and macabre. If a person died by drowning, do you determine his life expectancy as of when he was already in the water? Would it depend on how long he remained afloat? Or whether he knew how to swim? Congress may occasionally legislate with tongue in cheek, but it is not capable of the black humor our plaintiffs impute to it.

* * *

Problems

1. *G* creates a lifetime trust. The income is payable to *A* for life and then the trust property reverts to *G* if *G* survives *A* or is distributable to *B* if *G* does not survive *A*. *G* dies before *A*. What are the estate tax consequences? *See* §§ 2033, 2037.

2. *G* creates an irrevocable trust. The income is payable to his spouse, *W*, for her life and the remainder is distributable to *G*'s children if they are at least 21 years of age when *W* dies. If none of the children are at least 21, the trust assets revert to *G*. If *G* dies during the life of *W*, but before the children have reached age 21, is any part of the trust included in *G*'s gross estate? *See* Treas. Reg. § 20.2037–1(e), Example 1.

———

As is true in the case of §§ 2035 and 2036, the decedent's receipt of consideration for the interest which would have been included under § 2037 prevents the application of § 2037 to the extent of the consideration. On the other hand, if the decedent received partial consideration, the amount includable under § 2037 would be reduced by the application of § 2043.

Finally, § 2035(a) will not apply to transactions to which § 2037 applies, but § 2035(a) can apply if the transfer or a release occurs within three years of the transferor's death. *See* § 2035(a), *infra* at § 7.03.

[3] Generation-Skipping Transfer Tax

The generation-skipping transfer tax may apply to lifetime transfers that trigger § 2037 if the trust has skip persons as beneficiaries.

Example: *GM* creates a trust. The income is payable to her Daughter, *D*, for life. The corpus reverts to *GM* if she is living when *D* dies, but if not, the corpus is distributable to *GM*'s Granddaughter.

A direct skip does not occur on trust creation because *D*, a nonskip person, holds the only "interest" in trust. *See* §§ 2612(c), 2613(a)(2)(A), and 2652(c)(1). Although *GM* might like to establish a zero inclusion ratio when the trust is created, § 2642(f) provides that an allocation generally will not be effective until the ETIP ends. Treasury Regulation § 26.2632–1(c)(2)(ii)(A) provides an exception: if the actuarially determined value of the transferor's reversionary interest is less than 5%, then § 2642(f) does not apply.

In the example, a GST allocation is effective only at *GM*'s death if *GM*'s reversionary interest is 5% or greater. Note that a direct skip does not occur on *GM*'s death because *D*, a nonskip person, still has the intervening life interest. Accordingly, the generation-skipping transfer will not occur until *D* dies, although the inclusion ratio must be established at *GM*'s death.

Problem

Assume that in the example, *GM*'s Granddaughter was the income beneficiary rather than *D*. How might the results be different?

[4] Income Tax

Code: §§ 677 and 677(a)(2).

Regulations: None.

The income tax issues of reversionary interests subject to a contingency depend on the nature of the contingency. Section 673 applies if the value of the reversionary interest exceeds 5%, for example, a secondary life estate. More remote contingencies run afoul of § 677(a)(2), which is phrased in terms of income that "may be . . . held or accumulated for future distribution to the grantor . . . ." The issue, however, is unclear. *Compare* ARTHUR M. MICHAELSON & JONATHAN G. BLATTMACHR, INCOME TAXATION OF ESTATES AND TRUSTS 3–23 (14th ed., 1995) ("[a]pparently the rule is that the grantor will be taxable if an eventual distribution to him (personally, during his lifetime) depends upon a contingency, but not if the occurrence of the contingency is highly unlikely"), *with* BORIS I. BITTKER, FEDERAL TAXATION OF INCOME, ESTATES AND GIFTS ¶ 80.4.2 (2d ed., 1991) ("[r]eliance on the pre-1954 cases holding that the grantor is not taxable on income that can be distributed only if and when a remote contingency occurs is perilous").

Problems

Consider the impact of § 2702 in both problems below.

1. Stacy creates an irrevocable trust. The income is payable to her Father for life and then the trust property reverts to Stacy, if Stacy survives. If she does not survive, it is distributable to her Child.

   a. What are the gift tax consequences on the creation of the trust, assuming that the value of the corpus is $100,000, the value of Father's life estate is $70,000, and the value of Child's remainder is $24,000?

   b. What are the income tax consequences of the trust during its operation?

c. What are the estate tax consequences of the trust on Stacy's death during Father's life, assuming that the value of the trust corpus is $100,000, the value of Father's remaining life estate is $60,000, and the actuarial value of Stacy's reversion immediately before her death is $4,000?

2. *G* creates an irrevocable trust. The income is payable to her husband, *H*, for life and the remainder is distributable to her Child, *C*, if *C* survives *H*.

a. What are the gift and income tax consequences of the creation of the trust?

b. What are the estate tax consequences of the trust on *G*'s death, assuming that both *H* and *C* survive *G*?

c. What are the estate tax consequences on *H*'s death, assuming that *C* survives *H*? Does it matter whether *G* elected QTIP treatment of the trust when she created it?

§ 7.03   Transfer and Release of Retained Interests

After a transaction has occurred in which the grantor has retained an interest, she may decide for a number of reasons to transfer the retained interest. Typically, she would make the transfer by deed or other assignment. Such a relinquishment can have a variety of tax effects.

[A]   Gift Tax

Code: §§ 2511 and 2702.

Regulations: Treas. Reg. §§ 25.2511–1(f) and 25.2702–6.

Generally, the transfer of a retained interest is like the transfer of any interest in property. *See* Treas. Reg. § 25.2511–1(f). A gift occurs to the extent that the interest is transferred without full and adequate consideration. However, special treatment may be required if the transferred interest was valued initially at zero under § 2702. *See* Treas. Reg. § 25.2702–6.

The nature of the retained interest which is subsequently transferred may affect the availability of the annual exclusion and the marital deduction. The annual exclusion is available only if the donee receives a present interest. Similarly, because only non-terminable interests qualify for the gift tax marital deduction, transfers of many common contingent interests are disqualified. Consider the following.

Example: *H* creates an irrevocable trust. The income is payable to *H* for life and the remainder is distributable to *H*'s Nephew. Ten years later, *H* gives the retained life estate to his wife, *W*.

At the time of the first transfer, *H* made a taxable gift of the remainder interest, but did not receive the annual exclusion because Nephew's interest was a future interest. If he later gives *W* his retained life estate, that gift would qualify for the annual exclusion, but would not qualify for a marital deduction because the term would terminate at *H*'s death. *See* § 2523(f).

Problems

1. *G* creates a trust. The income is payable to *A* for life and *G* retains the reversion. The following year, *G* transfers her reversionary interest to *A*. Should this second transfer qualify for the gift tax annual exclusion? *See Clark v. Commissioner*, 65 T.C. 126 (1975). Would the result be different if the subsequent transfer were to *B*, rather than *A*? Answer the question both assuming that *G* and *A* are related within the meaning of § 2702 and assuming they are not related.

2. *G* creates a trust. The income is payable to *G*'s father, *F*, for life and then the corpus is distributable to *G*, if *G* survives, if not, to *C*. Later, *G* transfers his interest to his spouse. Would the subsequent transfer qualify for the marital deduction?

[B] Estate Tax

Code: §§ 2035(a) and 2038(a)(1).

Regulations: Treas. Reg. § 25.2702–6(c), Ex. 1.

United States v. Allen

293 F.2d 916 (10th Cir. 1961), cert. denied, 368 U.S. 944 (1961)

Murrah, Chief Judge.

This is an appeal from a judgment of the trial court awarding plaintiff-executors a refund for estate taxes previously paid.

The pertinent facts are that the decedent, Maria McKean Allen, created an irrevocable trust in which she reserved three fifths of the income for life, the remainder to pass to her two children, who are the beneficiaries of the other two fifths interest in the income. When she was approximately seventy-eight years old, the trustor-decedent was advised that her retention of the life estate would result in her attributable share of the corpus being included in her gross estate, for estate tax purposes. With her sanction, counsel began searching for a competent means of divestiture, and learned that decedent's son, Wharton Allen, would consider purchasing his mother's interest in the trust. At that time, the actuarial value of the retained life estate, based upon decedent's life expectancy, was approximately $135,000 and her attributable share of the corpus, *i.e.*, three fifths, was valued at some $900,000. Upon consultation with his business advisers, Allen agreed to pay $140,000 for the interest, believing that decedent's actual life span would be sufficient to return a profit to him on the investment. For all intents and purposes, he was a bona fide third party purchaser—not being in a position to benefit by any reduction in his mother's estate taxes. The sale was consummated and, upon paying the purchase price, Allen began receiving the income from the trust.

At the time of the transfer, decedent enjoyed relatively good health and was expected to live her normal life span. A short time thereafter, however, it was discovered that she had an incurable disease, which soon resulted in her untimely death. As a result of the death, Allen ceased receiving any trust income and suffered a considerable loss on his investment.

The Internal Revenue Commissioner determined that ⅗ths of the corpus, less the $140,000 purchase money, should be included in decedent's gross estate because (1) the transfer was invalid because made in contemplation of death, and (2) the sale was not for an adequate and full consideration.

Plaintiff-executors paid the taxes in accord with the Commissioner's valuation of the estate, and brought this action for refund, alleging that the sale of the life interest was for an adequate consideration; and that, therefore, no part of the trust corpus was properly includible in the gross estate.

The trial court held for plaintiffs, finding that the transfer was in contemplation of death, but regardless of that fact, the consideration paid for the life estate was adequate and full, thereby serving to divest decedent of any interest in the trust, with the result that no part of the corpus is subject to estate taxes.

Our narrow question is thus whether the corpus of a reserved life estate is removed, for federal estate tax purposes, from a decedent's gross estate by a transfer at the value of such reserved life estate. In other words, must the consideration be paid for the interest transferred, or for the interest which would otherwise be included in the gross estate?

In one sense, the answer comes quite simply—decedent owned no more than a life estate, could not transfer any part of the corpus, and Allen received no more than the interest transferred. And, a taxpayer is, of course, entitled to use all proper means to reduce his tax liability. *See Cravens v. C.I.R.*, 10 Cir., 272 F.2d 895, 898. It would thus seem to follow that the consideration was adequate, for it was in fact more than the value of the life estate. And, as a practical matter, it would have been virtually impossible to sell the life estate for an amount equal to her share in the corpus. *Cf. Sullivan's Estate v. C.I.R.*, 9 Cir., 175 F.2d 657.

It does not seem plausible, however, that Congress intended to allow such an easy avoidance of the taxable incidence befalling reserved life estates. This result would allow a taxpayer to reap the benefits of property for his lifetime and, in contemplation of death, sell only the interest entitling him to the income, thereby removing all of the property which he has enjoyed from his gross estate. Giving the statute a reasonable interpretation, we cannot believe this to be its intendment. It seems certain that in a situation like this, Congress meant the estate to include the corpus of the trust or, in its stead, an amount equal in value. *See Helvering v. Hallock*, 309 U.S. 106, *C.I.R. v. Wemyss*, 324 U.S. 303, *C.I.R. v. Estate of Church*, 335 U.S. 632.[19]

---

[19] In his treatise, *Cutting the "Strings" on Inter Vivos Transfers in Contemplation of Death*, 34 MINN. L. REV. 57, 70, 71, Professor Lowndes says:

> [T]he adequacy of the consideration which will prevent a tax when an incident of ownership in connection with a taxable inter vivos transfer is relinquished in contemplation of death, will be measured against the value of the interest which would be taxable apart from the transfer in contemplation of death, rather than the property interest which is transferred . . . . [T]he determination of what interest is transferred in contemplation of death and what is adequate consideration to prevent a transfer in contemplation of death from being taxable, should be made on

The judgment of the trial court is therefore reversed and the case is remanded for further proceedings in conformity with the opinion filed herein.

Breitenstein, Circuit Judge (concurring in result).

Section 811 of the 1939 Internal Revenue Code [now § 2036(a)(1)] provides for the determination of the value of the gross estate of a decedent for federal estate tax purposes. Among other things, it requires the inclusion of property "(1) to the extent of any interest therein of which the decedent has at any time made a transfer (except in case of a bona fide sale for an adequate and full consideration in money or money's worth), by trust . . . (B) under which he has retained for his life or for any period not ascertainable without reference to his death (I) . . . the right to income from, the property . . . ."

Trustor-decedent in 1932 created an irrevocable trust and received no consideration therefor. She retained for life the right to income from ⅗ths of the property which she placed in the trust. By the plain language of the statute that portion of the property held in the trust and devoted to the payment to her of income for life is includible within her gross estate. Such property is an "interest" of which she made a transfer with the retention of income for life.

The fact that the transfer of the life estate left her without any retained right to income from the trust property does not alter the result. As I read the statute the tax liability arises at the time of the inter vivos transfer under which there was a retention of the right to income for life. The disposition thereafter of that retained right does not eliminate the tax liability. The fact that full and adequate consideration was paid for the transfer of the retained life estate is immaterial. To remove the trust property from inclusion in decedent's estate there must be full and adequate consideration paid for the interest which would be taxed. That interest is not the right to income for life but the right to the property which was placed in the trust and from which the income is produced.

As the 1932 trust was irrevocable, trustor-decedent could thereafter make no unilateral transfer of the trust property. Granting that she could sell her life estate as that was a capital asset owned by her, such sale has no effect on the includibility in her gross estate of the interest which she transferred in 1932 with the retention of the right to income for life. For the reasons stated I would reverse the judgment with directions to dismiss the case.

———

The result in *Allen* has been codified in § 2035(a), which continues to apply § 2035 to a transfer of "property (or an interest therein) [that] would have been included in the decedent's gross estate under § 2036, 2037 . . . if such transferred interest . . . had been retained by the decedent on the date of his death."

the basis of the tax effect of the transfer and the effect of the consideration of the transferor's taxable estate, rather than by the comparatively irrelevant rules of property law.

Problems

Answer Problems 1–2, assuming, in the alternative, that § 2702 applies and does not apply.

1. In Year 1, D, age 65, transferred $100,000 to irrevocable trust. D reserved the income for his life and the remainder is payable to B. In Year 4, D, now age 69, makes a gift of his life income interest to B.

   a. Determine the amount of taxable gifts for the transfer in trust and the later gift of the life estate to B, assuming an 8% applicable interest rate under § 7520.

   b. What would be the estate tax consequences if D died in Year 8?

   c. What would be the estate tax consequences if D died in Year 5?

2. Assume the facts in Problem 1, but that in Year 4 D sold his life estate to B for its fair market value and in Year 5 died.

   a. What would be the gift tax consequences of the sale of the life estate?

   b. What would be the estate tax consequences upon D's death?

3. Assume that S created an irrevocable trust. The income is payable to A for life and the remainder reverts to S, if S survives A, if not, remainder to B. Within three years of his death, and while A was still alive, S transferred his reversionary interest to B. As of what date do you value that interest for the purposes of the 5% test under § 2037 (as of S's death, or as of the date of the transfer to B)? *See* Rev. Rul. 79–62, 1979–1 C.B. 295.

4. In year 1, H transferred $200,000 to a trust. The income is payable to W for life and the remainder is distributable to X. H made a QTIP election for gift tax purposes. In Year 4, when the trust assets were valued at $300,000 and W was age 65, W transferred 20% of her income interest to Z. At the time of W's transfer, she had made no previous taxable gifts. H died in Year 5 when the trust assets were valued at $400,000. W died in Year 6 when the trust assets were valued at $500,000.

   a. What were the gift and estate tax consequences to H?

   b. What were the gift and estate tax consequences to W?

5. Assume that H made a gift in Year 1 to a trust, reserving the income for his life and designating his son as the remainderman. His wife, W, consented to the split gift election for the gift of the remainder interest. Each spouse previously had exhausted his or her unified credit, and each gift generated $20,500 in tax, which each spouse paid out of his or her separate funds. H died in Year 4, and W died in Year 5. The trust corpus remained at $100,000 in value at all times.

   a. In Year 3, H made a gift of his retained income interest to his daughter. What would be the estate tax consequences of the trust with respect to the estates of H and W?

   b. How would the results differ if H had not transferred the retained income interest in Year 3?

[C] Generation-Skipping Transfer Tax

Code: § 2642(f).

Regulations: None.

The generation-skipping transfer tax consequences of assigning a retained interest depend on such factors as the type of trust, the kind of retained interest (current or reversionary), and the identity of the assignee (skip or nonskip person). Section 2642(f) generally bars the establishment of an inclusion ratio at the time of an initial transfer when the transferor retains an income interest.

[D] Income Tax

The transfer and release of a retained interest can result in the redirection of the income tax. In *Blair v. Commissioner*, 300 U.S. 5 (1937), the assignor-life tenant, who had only a right to income from the property, but no right to the property itself, gave his beneficial interest in the trust to his children. The Court held that the income had been redirected for income tax purposes. On the other hand, if a taxpayer who was the life income beneficiary under a trust assigned his interest for only a short period, the attempted redirection would fail, and the income would continue to be taxed to the taxpayer. *See Harrison v. Schaffner*, 312 U.S. 579 (1941). In the latter situation, the taxpayer-donor continues to be free to allocate subsequent payments as he chooses, and general assignment of income principles, as set forth in *Helvering v. Horst*, 311 U.S. 112 (1940), deny the temporary income tax deflection.

Chapter 8

REVOCABLE TRANSFERS

The revocable living trust is a common technique for avoiding probate. The grantor retains the income from the trust, total access to the corpus, and the power to revoke the trust during life. The grantor can change the management or terms of the trust in any way, including the provisions that apply after death. Powers of revocation are also used as a means of controlling the behavior of beneficiaries. For example, a parent might establish a trust for a child so that the child feels responsibility for money, but retain the power to revoke the trust if the child proved incapable of dealing responsibly with wealth. Contingent powers also have their place in the universe of asset planning. For example, a widow is contemplating remarrying. She wants to provide her second spouse financial security while ensuring that her property passes to her children by her first marriage. By establishing an irrevocable trust for the spouse for life, that goal may be satisfied. Nevertheless, she might want to reserve the right to revoke the interest of her children, but only if she survives her spouse. This Chapter investigates the tax ramifications of reserving these and similar powers.

§ 8.01   Absolute Powers

This section discusses the tax effects of outright powers to revoke all or part of a trust and other transfers. Typically, powers of revocation are over the entire property, although powers to revoke income interests and powers to revoke one or more future interests may also be retained.

[A]   Gift Tax

Code: § 2511.

Regulations: Treas. Reg. § 25.2511–2(e).

As was discussed in Chapter 4, the retention of the power to revoke a transfer or an interest makes the transfer incomplete for gift tax purposes. *See Burnet v. Guggenheim*, 288 U.S. 280 (1933) (reproduced at § 4.01[A][1], *supra*); Treas. Reg. § 25.2511–2.

Obviously, the incomplete transfer doctrine is not restricted to transfers in trust. Whenever the donor retains the power to revoke an interest in any transfer, the transfer is incomplete for gift tax purposes. This includes such commonplace transfers as designation of beneficiaries under life insurance policies (because the donor retains the right to cash in the policy or change the beneficiary), and transfers by a donor of a personal note to the donee in a jurisdiction which would hold the note unenforceable because it was gratuitous. *See* Rev. Rul. 67–396, 1967–2 C.B. 351.

The problem of incomplete transfers arises when a donor gives a personal check to a donee as an annual exclusion gift. Controversies have arisen when the check is not cashed until after the donor's death and when it is not cashed until the year after delivery. The first issue impacts the size of the decedent's gross estate and the second affects the annual exclusion.

The Tax Court held in *Estate of Belcher v. Commissioner*, 83 T.C. 227 (1984), that checks to charities were excludable from the gross estate even though the checks were cashed after the decedent's death. In the court's opinion, cashing the checks related back to the date the decedent delivered the checks to the charities. Thus, completed gifts were made during lifetime and were not part of the gross estate. With a check made out to a charity, failure to apply the doctrine usually means that the estate will receive a charitable deduction rather than the annual exclusion thereby creating a wash situation.

In similar cases in which the donee was not a charity, the Tax Court has refused to extend *Belcher* for estate tax inclusion purposes. *See Estate of Gagliardi v. Commissioner*, 89 T.C. 1207 (1987). The Tax Court rejected the relation-back theory, reasoning that the test for completeness of a gift is whether state law would permit the decedent to revoke the gifts with a stop payment order, and thus, render the gift incomplete for tax purposes.

The Second Circuit applied similar reasoning in *Rosano v. United States*, 245 F.3d 212 (2d Cir. 2001). The court held:

> The doctrine of relation-back is entirely judicially created. . . . Accordingly, in evaluating appellant's argument, we have no easy recourse to legislative authority. Rather, we must evaluate the policy goals that led the courts to create the doctrine, and determine whether the goals are met by applying the doctrine in the instant case. We conclude that they are not.
>
> Other courts have refused to apply the doctrine when the decedent died prior to payment of a non-charitable gift. *McCarthy v. United States*, 806 F.2d 129, 131–33 (7th Cir.1986); *Newman v. Commissioner*, 111 T.C. 81, 1998 WL 420689 (1998). In *McCarthy*, the court offered two reasons for its refusal to extend the doctrine of relation-back. First, a rationale for applying the doctrine in the charitable context was not present in the non-charitable context. Checks delivered by the decedent to a charity but not paid until after the decedent's death, if included in the estate, would generate a deduction for the estate. This deduction would result in a "wash" for estate tax purposes, meaning that the estate would obtain the benefit of the charitable deduction whether or not the doctrine of relation-back was applied. For practical purposes, it makes more sense to consider the checks as outside the estate. "No such practical consideration extends to noncharitable gifts. No offsetting deduction exists for gifts made to noncharitable donees." *McCarthy*, 806 F.2d at 132. Second, the court thought that extending the doctrine would allow for improper tax avoidance: "By issuing a check to a noncharitable donee with the understanding that it not be cashed until after his death, a decedent may effectively bequest up to $10,000 per donee,

thus avoiding the estate tax consequences normally attending such transactions." *Id. Accord Metzger,* 38 F.3d at 122.

We agree with the policy concerns expressed by the *McCarthy* and *Metzger* courts. Thus, we will not apply the doctrine where gifts are made to a non-charitable donee and the donor died prior to the date of payment. We express no opinion as to whether we would apply the doctrine where there is a non-charitable donee and the donor is alive on the date of payment.

In *Estate of Metzger v. Commissioner*, 100 T.C. 204 (1993), *aff'd* 38 F.3d 118 (4th Cir. 1994), the Tax Court applied the relation-back doctrine to a non-charitable donee *for annual exclusion purposes* when checks were timely presented in the year for which the gift tax annual exclusions were claimed, but were not charged against the account until later. The Fourth Circuit agreed with the Tax Court that the relation-back doctrine could be applied if: (1) the donor intended to make a gift; (2) the check was unconditionally delivered; and (3) the check was presented within a reasonable time after issuance for payment in the year for which the favorable tax treatment is sought. The Court also held that the doctrine would not apply to a check written to a noncharitable donee and cashed after the donor died. Subsequent to *Metzger*, the Service approved the Fourth Circuit's three-part test. *See* Rev. Rul. 96–56, 1996–2 C.B. 161. In *Estate of Dillingham v. Commissioner*, 903 F.2d 760 (10th Cir. 1990), *aff'g* 88 T.C. 1569 (1987), the Tenth Circuit refused to extend the relation-back doctrine when checks written in Year 1 and cashed in Year 2 were not unconditionally delivered.

Application of the incomplete transfer rule becomes more difficult when the gift appears to be complete, but a state court ruling permits the donor to "undo" the transfer. For example, in *Berger v. United States*, 487 F. Supp. 49 (1980), the taxpayer was on a short list for an appointment to a high level post at the Federal Aviation Administration. Based on various press reports, the taxpayer believed that he was required to transfer all of his assets to an irrevocable blind trust to comply with the Nixon administration's policy on conflicts of interest. As a consequence, the taxpayer sold all of his assets, including his residence, and transferred the proceeds to two irrevocable trusts for the benefit of his wife and children. At the time of the transfer, a trust officer with the bank serving as trustee asked whether revocable trusts would satisfy the requirements of the potential appointment, but the taxpayer insisted on making the trusts irrevocable. When the government job never materialized, the taxpayer sought state court relief to reform the trusts and make them revocable. The relief was granted by a Pennsylvania Orphan's Court after an attempt to reform the trust in another state court failed for lack of subject matter jurisdiction.

The Service rejected amended gift tax returns which reversed the prior filed returns that disclosed the irrevocable transfers. The taxpayer paid the assessed gift taxes under protest and filed suit for a refund in federal district court. Citing Pennsylvania state court decisions that permit a donor to revoke a gratuitous transfer resulting from a unilateral mistake of law or fact, the court ordered the refund based on several federal tax decisions that negated a gift tax when a mistake caused an unintended transfer of property. *See*

Dodge v. United States, 413 F.2d 1239 (5th Cir. 1969); *Commissioner v. Allen*, 108 F.2d 961 (3d. Cir. 1939), *cert. denied*, 309 U.S. 680 (1940); *Touche v. Commissioner*, 58 T.C. 565 (1972).

In *Neal v. United States*, 83 A.F.T.R. 2d 99-778 (3d Cir. 1999), an unreported decision, the Circuit Court affirmed a District Court ruling that refunded $420,000 in gift taxes previously paid. In 1988, Neal created a grantor retained income trust (GRIT) following the rules of § 2036(c). Thereafter in 1989, the Service issued Notice 89–99, 1989-2 C.B. 422, interpreting § 2036(c) to exclude a GRIT that included a reversionary interest worth more than 25% of the trust value. In response to the Notice, Neal released her contingent reversionary interests to satisfy the administrative interpretation of § 2036(c). Neal paid a gift tax as a result of the release of her reversionary interest.

In 1990, § 2036(c) was retroactively repealed. Thereafter, Neal executed a document rescinding the release and petitioned a state court to approve her rescission of the release because it was given as a result of a unilateral mistake of law. The Pennsylvania Orphan's Court "found that the release was rescindable because . . . of Neal's mistaken belief in the validity of section 2036(c) and the Notice."

The IRS refused to refund the gift tax paid and Neal sued. The Third Circuit held that "the retroactive repeal of § 2036(c) made the law at the time [the taxpayer] released her reversionary interests other than what she understood it to be." Neal understood the law when she made the release, but she mistook the effect that it would have on her tax liabilities.

Naturally, the corollary to the incomplete transfer doctrine is that a transfer becomes complete, and thus gift taxable, when the power terminates. *See Burnet v. Guggenheim*, reproduced at § 4.01[A][1], *supra*. Thus, the gift of the donor's personal check becomes complete when the check is cashed. Similarly, the receipt of income by a beneficiary of a revocable trust constitutes a completed gift by the grantor to the beneficiary at that time. *See* Treas. Reg. § 25.2511–2(f). Each distribution is a separate gift that can qualify for the annual exclusion because each income payment is outright.

Camp v. Commissioner

195 F.2d 999 (1st Cir. 1952)

Magruder, Chief Judge.

[Petition by Frederic E. Camp for review of a decision of the Tax Court holding that he was deficient in his gift tax for the years 1937 and 1943. On February 1, 1932, Camp established a trust with Bankers Trust Company as trustee. The income from the trust was payable to his wife during her life; upon her death the principal of the trust was to be paid to Camp's then living issue per stirpes; and in default of such issue the trustee was to continue to hold the principal in trust, paying the income to Camp's mother Johnanna R. Bullock for her life, with the principal to then pass, in the alternative, to Camp's half-brother H. Ridgely Bullock, to H. Ridgely Bullock's issue *per stirpes*, or to the trustees of Princeton University.

Under article ten of the trust, Camp retained the right to modify, alter or revoke the trust with the written consent of either his half-brother or his mother. He exercised this power three times: in 1934, he limited his wife's income interest to the period she was his wife and lived with him; in 1937, he clarified the term "issue" to include adopted children (he and his wife adopted four children between 1937 and 1942), and to substitute his wife as the person whose approval was necessary for amendment of the trust; in 1946 he made the trust irrevocable and not subject to amendment.]

. . .

Where a donor makes a transfer in trust for numerous beneficiaries, it is obvious that there may be several distinct gifts or potential gifts. For purposes of the gift tax, some of the interests created may be completed gifts, and others may not be, depending upon the facts of the particular case . . . .

(1) If the trust instrument gives a designated beneficiary any interest in the corpus of the trust property or of the income therefrom, which is capable of monetary valuation, and the donor reserves no power to withdraw that interest, in whole or in part, except with the consent of such designated beneficiary, then the gift of that particular interest will be deemed to be complete, for the purposes of the gift tax. *See accord*, our discussion in *Commissioner v. Prouty*, 1 Cir., 1940, 115 F.2d 331, 334, 131 A.L.R. 977 . . . . This is true, though at the time of the creation of the trust there might be extraneous considerations, whether of a pecuniary or sentimental nature, which would give the donor every confidence that such designated beneficiary would acquiesce in any future desire of the donor to withdraw the gift, in whole or in part . . . . In that respect the donor is taken at his word; he has legally given away something which he cannot take back except with the consent of the donee. The transfer fulfills the concept of a completed gift, quite as much as if a husband makes an outright gift of securities to his wife, being confident that his wife would reconvey the securities to him if he ever asked for them. If there were an advance agreement between the donor and the donee, prior to the transfer in trust, to the effect that the donee would acquiesce in any future exercise of the power of modification proposed by the donor, then the situation would be different. The trust instrument would not express the true intention of the parties. A real gift is not intended, where the purported donee has agreed ahead of time to hold the "gift" subject to the call and disposition of the purported donor.[1]

(2) If the only power reserved by the donor is a power to revoke the entire trust instrument (not a power to modify the trust in any particular), and this power may be exercised only in conjunction with a designated beneficiary who is given a substantial adverse interest in the disposition of the trust property or the income therefrom, then the transfer in trust will be deemed to be a present gift of the entire corpus of the trust, for purposes of the gift tax. In such cases, the gift of the entire corpus will be deemed to have been "put beyond recall" by the donor himself.

---

[1] In the present case, the Tax Court inferred from petitioner's deposition, which was read in evidence, that there was such an advance agreement here between petitioner and his half brother Ridgely. In the view we take, it is unnecessary for us to determine whether such an inference of fact was warranted.

(3) If the trust instrument reserves to the donor a general power to alter, amend or revoke, in whole or in part, and this power is to be exercised only in conjunction with a designated beneficiary who has received an interest in the corpus or income capable of monetary valuation, then the transfer in trust will be deemed to be a completed gift, for purposes of the gift tax, only as to the interest of such designated beneficiary having a veto over the exercise of the power. As to the interests of the other beneficiaries, the gifts will be deemed to be incomplete, for as to such interests the donor reserves the power to take them away in conjunction with a person who has no interest in the trust adverse to such withdrawal. The gifts to the other beneficiaries have not been "put beyond recall" by the donor . . . . when the donor has reserved the power to withdraw any of the donated interests with the concurrence of some third person who has no interest in the trust adverse to such withdrawal, it is in substance the same as if the donor had reserved such power in himself alone. In further support of this proposition, see the discussion in *Estate of Sanford v. Commissioner*, 1939, 308 U.S. 39, 46–47.

Coming back, then, to the terms of the trust which petitioner created in February, 1932: It is clear that there was not at that time a completed gift of the life income to petitioner's wife Alida. Under the original provisions of the trust indenture, this life estate was subject to revocation by the donor in conjunction either with the donor's half brother Ridgely or his mother Johnanna, neither of whose interests in the trust were adverse to the withdrawal of the life estate from Alida.

When the trust instrument was amended on December 11, 1937, so as to transfer to Alida alone the veto power over any further proposals by the donor for amendment of the trust, there was on that date a completed gift to Alida of the interest which she then held in the trust . . . . However, it is to be noted that Alida did not at this time hold an absolutely unqualified life interest in the income. By prior amendment, the indenture provided that the income of the trust was to be payable to Alida, wife of the donor, only "as long as she, during his lifetime, shall continue to be his wife and to reside with him." Whether, in the valuation of the gift to Alida on December 11, 1937, some allowance should be made for this qualification upon the life estate, we do not now undertake to say. *Cf. Robinette v. Helvering*, 1943, 318 U.S. 184, 188. The Tax Court was in error, we think, in ruling that upon the execution of the amendment of December 11, 1937, petitioner made a taxable gift of the whole corpus of the trust . . . . There were at that time no completed gifts to the succeeding income beneficiaries and beneficiaries in remainder, for Alida's interest in the trust was not adverse to the donor's revocation of those succeeding interests by an exercise of the reserved power.

By the amendment of June 6, 1946, whereby all power to revoke, alter or modify the trust was eliminated, there resulted a taxable gift of the then value of the corpus, minus the sum determined to be the value of the gift to Alida on December 11, 1937, and minus also the values of any completed gifts which may be deemed to have been made at the time of the creation of the trust on February 1, 1932. This latter point we do not have to determine in the present case, because petitioner's liability for the year 1946 is not before us. In passing, we simply allude to a possible difficulty, in that the donor originally reserved a power to revoke or modify the trust in conjunction with either Ridgely or Johnanna. Ridgely's contingent remainder interest might have been revoked by the donor, in conjunction with Johnanna, whose interest in the trust was not adverse to such revocation. Johnanna's contingent life estate could have been revoked by the donor in conjunction with Ridgely, whose interest in the trust was not adverse to such revocation. Where the veto power is thus lodged in the alternative, it may be that, for purposes of the gift tax, there is not a completed gift to either of such beneficiaries. *But cf. Estate of Leon N. Gillette*, 1946, 7 T.C. 219; *Commissioner v. Betts*, 7 Cir. 1941, 123 F.2d 534.

The decision of the Tax Court is vacated, and the case is remanded to that court for further proceedings not inconsistent with this opinion.

The substantial adverse interest concept discussed in *Camp* is reflected in Treasury Regulation § 25.2511–2(e). Camp's piecemeal release of his power of revocation resulted in two taxable events. The first was the 1937 modification that resulted in the gift tax issue that was before the court. The second gift occurred in 1946, when he completely released the power to alter the trust. The tax effect of the final modification was not before the court for review, but clearly Camp made a gift of the remainder interest in the trust, as the court noted in its opinion.

Problems

1. *D* transfers Blackacre to *B* in return for a series of secured notes equal to the value of the property less the annual exclusion. *D* intends each year to forgive a portion of the indebtedness equal to the annual exclusion. Has *D* made a completed gift at the time of the transfer of Blackacre? *See Haygood v. Commissioner*, 42 T.C. 936 (1964), *acq.*, 1965–2 C.B. 5; Rev. Rul. 77–299, 77–2 C.B. 343. Could it be argued that *D*'s power to enforce the note made the transfer incomplete until the portion of the note was forgiven?

2. *X* lends money to *Y* on a demand note, but fails to call the note. After a period of time, the applicable statute of limitations runs out.

a. Has a completed gift occurred on the running of the statutory period? *See Estate of Lang v. Commissioner*, 613 F.2d 770 (9th Cir. 1980).

b. Were the running of the statute to occur within three years of *X*'s death, would any portion of the note amount be included in *X*'s gross estate?

[B] Estate Tax

Code: §§ 2035(a), 2036(a)(2), and 2038.

Regulations: Treas. Reg. §§ 20.2036–1 and 20.2038–1(a).

The retention of a power of revocation can require inclusion of property in the gross estate under §§ 2038 and 2036(a)(2).

[1]   Section 2038

As noted in *Burnet v. Guggenheim*, § 4.01[A][1], *supra*, Congress, at an early date, included revocable interests in the decedent's estate. That provision is now § 2038, which includes in the gross estate property previously transferred by the decedent, if the decedent has, at death, a power to "alter, amend, revoke, or terminate" the transferred property interest.

The rationale behind § 2038 is that the nature of the transfer warrants estate taxation. The decedent has the power at death to control property he previously owned; he has not given up sufficient control to avoid estate taxation. The power to revoke is the equivalent of ownership of the transferred interest. The transaction is testamentary in the sense that it is the decedent's death which finally ensures enjoyment of the interests by others.

Section 2038 applies if several criteria are met: (1) the interest in property must previously have been transferred by the decedent; (2) the decedent must have a power to "alter, amend, revoke, or terminate;" and (3) the power must exist at the decedent's death. Those requirements, however, are expansively defined. The transfer can be by trust or otherwise. The section applies to any interest in property—present or future. The power can be exercisable in any capacity—fiduciary or individual. The power can be a sole power or held jointly, even with a person who has an adverse interest. Finally, the power need not be specifically retained if it arises by implication or operation of law.

[2]   Section 2036(a)(2)

In addition to taxing a decedent because of a retained income interest, § 2036 taxes the decedent if a power over the income is retained. Section 2036(a)(2) includes in a decedent's gross estate property interests previously transferred, if the decedent has retained for life (or a similar period) "the right . . . to designate the persons who shall possess or enjoy the property or the income therefrom." If the decedent's power of revocation applies to the possession or enjoyment of the property (typically the income from a trust), this section requires taxation of the entire trust in the decedent's estate.

Again, the Code treats the retention of a power to control an income interest the same as the retention of the interest itself by treating the retention of control as testamentary. All that is required is a transfer by the decedent and the retention of a power to revoke. Like § 2038, it applies to joint powers, and has been held to apply to powers held as a fiduciary, as well as to powers held individually. Unlike § 2038, however, a power which is not retained, but arises from a later transaction, does not trigger § 2036(a)(2). *See* Estate of Farrel v. United States (reproduced in § 8.02[B], *infra*).

> **Example:** *S* creates a trust with income to *A* for ten years, remainder to *B*. *S* retains the power to revoke the trust. Assume *S* dies without having revoked the trust.

In this example, both sections can be applied. The property was previously transferred by *S*, satisfying that requirement of each section. Under § 2038, *S* has a power at death to revoke each and every interest in the trust. Thus, the entire trust would be includable in his gross estate under that section. Under § 2036(a)(2), *S*'s power to revoke includes the power to revoke the income interest. This gives *S* the power to designate who possesses or enjoys the income, which, because it is a retained power, triggers § 2036(a)(2). This, in turn, requires inclusion of the property producing the income, *i.e.*, the entire trust corpus, in *S*'s gross estate.

[3] Joint Powers

Helvering v. Helmholz

296 U.S. 93 (1935)

Mr. Justice Roberts delivered the opinion of the Court.

This case . . . arises under [§ 2038]. The respondent is administrator and sole beneficiary of the estate of his wife, Irene C. Helmholz. In 1918 she, her father and mother and her brothers and sisters joined in an indenture conveying to a trustee all of the shares of stock in the Patrick Cudahy Family Company. Her contribution was 999 shares, the dividends from which the trustee was to receive, and pay, less expenses, to Mrs. Helmholz for life, remainder to her appointee by will and remainder to her issue; and in event she or any other subscriber should die without issue the net dividends on the stock delivered to the trustee by such decedent were to be paid "to the surviving subscribers or their issue living at the time of distribution proportionately by right of representation."

The paragraph of the indenture relative to the termination of the trust is:

> "Fifth: The term of the primary trust hereby created shall end (1) upon the death of the last surviving grandchild of Patrick and Anna M. Cudahy, they being then deceased, or (2) upon delivery to the said trustee of a written instrument signed by all of the then beneficiaries, other than testamentary appointees, declaring said trust term at an end, or (3) upon delivery to said trustee of a copy (certified by the president or secretary of the Patrick Cudahy Family Company and under its corporate seal) of a resolution adopted by a unanimous vote of the board of directors of said corporation declaring said trust term at an end, whereupon and in either of said events the said trustee shall distribute the capital stock of said the Patrick Cudahy Family Company to the beneficiaries then entitled to receive the net dividends thereof other than testamentary appointees . . . . ["]

. . .

Irene C. Helmholz left a will bequeathing all her property to respondent. The Supreme Court of Wisconsin held this a valid exercise of her power of appointment under the trust deed. [*See First Wisconsin Trust Co. v. Helmholz*, 225 N.W. 181.] The petitioner determined that the value of the 999 shares should be included in her gross estate. The Board of Tax Appeals reversed this determination. The United States Court of Appeals for the District of Columbia, to which an appeal was taken pursuant to stipulation for hearing by that court, affirmed the Board. We granted certiorari.

. . .

The words of [§ 2038] are, "where the enjoyment [of the transfer] was subject at the date of his death to any change through the exercise of a power, either by the decedent alone or in conjunction with any person, *to alter, amend or revoke* . . . ." The agreement under consideration contains no such power as that described. Like every well drawn instrument it embodies provisions for the termination of the trust. An examination of paragraph Fifth shows that these were, in the main, such as any far-sighted settlor would employ . . . .

The petitioner . . . pitches upon the only remaining event of termination, asserting it to be the equivalent of a power to revoke, or to amend, to be exercised by the settlor with others. This is found in the clause providing that the delivery to the trustee of a writing signed by all the then beneficiaries (other than testamentary appointees) declaring such purpose, shall be effective to end the trust. He points out that such a writing might have been executed by Mrs. Helmholz and her co-beneficiaries while she was alive, with the effect of revesting in her the shares which she had delivered into the trust. This argument overlooks the essential difference between a power to revoke, alter or amend, and a condition which the law imposes. The general rule is that all parties in interest may terminate the trust.[2] The clause in question added nothing to the rights which the law conferred. Congress cannot tax as a transfer intended to take effect in possession or enjoyment at the death of the settlor a trust created in a state whose law permits all the beneficiaries to terminate the trust.

. . .

The judgment is

Affirmed.[3]

———

The government did not assert estate tax inclusion under § 2036 in *Helvering v. Helmholz* because the transfer occurred before the effective date of that section.

Helvering v. Helmholz is an exception to the general rule that jointly held powers are subject to §§ 2036 and 2038 even if the joint power holder possesses an interest adverse to the exercise of the power. Both sections expressly tax powers held in conjunction "with any other person."

Besides the limited comfort of *Helvering v. Helmholz*, another technique is available for avoiding the strictures of §§ 2036(a)(2) and 2038. Because each section taxes the property in a decedent's estate to the extent of a power, each

---

[2] Restatement of the Law of Trusts, §§ 337, 338. We are referred to no authority to the contrary in Wisconsin, the place of the transaction.

[3] The conclusion of the court that a grantor, who has only a power to revoke in conjunction with all of the beneficiaries, does not have a § 2038 power is now reflected in Treasury Regulation § 20.2038–1(a)(2). The conclusion that a power to terminate does not constitute a power to "revoke, alter or amend" was reversed by an amendment of § 2038. [Eds.]

can be avoided by giving broad discretionary powers to one or more independent trustees. *See* Charles E. Early, *The Irrevocable Trust That Can Be Amended*, 18 U. MIAMI INST. ON EST. PLNG. ¶ 1700 (1984). When the decedent lacks the power, the transaction is not deemed testamentary. Similarly, although death terminates the decedent's power and may finally vest the beneficiary with the right of possession or enjoyment, vesting would not be the result of activity or inactivity of the decedent—the basis for taxation under string provisions. Although an independent trustee is normally willing to do what the grantor may suggest, the estate tax and gift tax do not assume that one who is a non-adverse party will abide by the wishes of the grantor. Thus, unlike the treatment of trustee powers under the income tax, powers given to a trustee are not treated as retained by the grantor under the gift tax and estate tax.

Furthermore, each string section is limited by the general proviso that the section does not apply if the transferred interest was for full and adequate consideration.

[4] Powers of Attorney

Because of the potential to save estate taxes with annual exclusion gifts, it is common for an attorney in fact to make gifts for incompetent principals using powers of attorney. When the action of an attorney-in-fact exceeds the authority granted in the power of attorney, the principal may void the transfer. As a result, the Service routinely examines transfers by attorneys-in-fact to determine if the gifts were revocable and thus, included in decedent's estates under § 2038.

Estate of Swanson v. United States

87 A.F.T.R.2d 2001–2345 (Fed. Cir. 2001)

BRYSON, Circuit Judge.

. . . .

Sylvia Swanson, an elderly widow, was the sole trustee of a survivor's trust; her nephew, Dean Stubblefield, was named as successor trustee. After Ms. Swanson was declared legally blind in 1985, Mr. Stubblefield took over responsibility for managing Ms. Swanson's finances.

In December 1990, after a 20-day period of hospitalization, Ms. Swanson entered a nursing home. On December 14, 1990, she executed a document entitled "durable power of attorney," which gave Mr. Stubblefield legal authority to manage and dispose of Ms. Swanson's property and accorded him "sole discretion" as to when and how to invoke those powers.

In February 1991, shortly before Ms. Swanson's death, Mr. Stubblefield wrote, signed, and delivered checks from the trust account to himself and 37 others in the amount of $10,000 each. Mr. Stubblefield testified that he proposed that Ms. Swanson make gifts of $10,000 each to 40 individuals for purposes of minimizing the impact of the estate tax on her estate, and that she approved 38 of the 40 proposed gifts by nodding her head when Mr. Stubblefield read each individual's name.

After making a federal estate tax payment, the appellant estate claimed a refund of $146,039 based on the 38 checks, which the estate contended should not have been treated as part of the estate at the time of Ms. Swanson's death. The Internal Revenue Service denied the claim on the ground that the purported gifts were not valid and that the $380,000 represented by the 38 checks signed by Mr. Stubblefield was therefore includible in the gross estate under 26 U.S.C. § 2038(a)(1).

The estate filed an action in the United States Court of Federal Claims seeking a refund of the claimed amount. On cross-motions for summary judgment, the court granted judgment for the government on the ground that the purported gifts were invalid under California law. Because the gifts were revocable, the court held that they were properly included in Ms. Swanson's estate and subject to tax on that basis. The estate then took this appeal.

II

This case turns on California law. The estate contends that under California law, Mr. Stubblefield was authorized to make gifts from the trust on Ms. Swanson's behalf. The government contends that under California law Mr. Stubblefield was not so authorized and that, as a consequence, the $380,000 represented by the 38 checks executed by Mr. Stubblefield was never validly removed from the trust and is therefore taxable in Ms. Swanson's estate. We agree with the trial court that under California law, Mr. Stubblefield was not authorized to make gifts from the trust funds and that the 38 purported gifts were therefore properly treated as part of Ms. Swanson's estate for tax purposes.

In challenging the ruling of the trial court, the estate makes two arguments. First, it argues that there was a factual question as to whether the durable power of attorney allegedly executed by Ms. Swanson on December 14, 1990, was validly executed. In particular, the estate suggests that the signature on the durable power of attorney may not have been Ms. Swanson's. The problem with that argument is that the estate did not challenge the validity of the power of attorney in the trial court. In fact, in the trial court one of the estate's arguments was that the power of attorney was valid and that it expressly authorized Mr. Stubblefield to make the gifts at issue in the case. The estate cannot now reverse field, contend that the power of attorney was invalid, and argue that the trial court erred by granting summary judgment without addressing the validity of the power of attorney.

The estate's second argument is more substantial. The estate contends that Mr. Stubblefield was not required to invoke the durable power of attorney to write the 38 checks at issue in this case. Instead, the estate argues, Mr. Stubblefield was authorized by common law agency principles to make the gifts, since Ms. Swanson directed him to make the gifts, and that he was authorized to act in the capacity of a common law agent without regard to the scope or limitation of the powers granted under the durable power of attorney he held from Ms. Swanson. Although this argument has some appeal, we agree with the trial court and the government that it is contrary to California law, and we therefore reject it.

Under California law, a durable power of attorney is not construed to confer the power to make gifts unless the document expressly provides that power in writing. That rule, which is now codified in statute, *see* Cal. Prob.Code § 4264, has been part of California's common law for many years, *see, e.g., Shields v. Shields,* 200 Cal.App.2d 99, 101 (1962); *Bertelsen v. Bertelson,* 122 P.2d 130, 133 (Cal. Dist. Ct. App.1942). Moreover, the California rule appears to be that when an agent has a power of attorney from the principal, the agent cannot exercise the authority to make gifts on behalf of the principal even if the principal purports to give the agent direct oral authority to do so. *See Estate of Huston v. Greene,* 51 Cal.App. 4th 1721, 1726–27 (1997).

The reason underlying that rule, which is followed in many jurisdictions, *see, e.g., Estate of Casey v. Commissioner,* 948 F.2d 895 (4th Cir.1991); *Townsend v. United States,* 889 F.Supp. 369 (D. Neb.1995); *Wade v. Northrup,* 70 Ore. 569 (1900); *Fender v. Fender,* 285 S.C. 260 (1985), is that to permit a person with a power of attorney to invoke ordinary agency principles to claim powers additional to those given by the power of attorney would make it too easy to bypass restrictions imposed by the parties or by law on the scope of a power of attorney. Thus, as in this case, a power of attorney that does not contain authorization to make gifts is treated under California law as reflecting the intention of the parties to deny the agent the power to make gifts. Yet if the agent could make gifts simply by invoking general agency principles as an alternative source of power, the legal limitation on the agent's authority under the power of attorney would be worth little. The policy against permitting subversion of the limits on the power of attorney counsels against permitting persons with a power of attorney to invoke other legal principles to exercise powers that are not available under the power of attorney. It is for that reason that the Restatement of Agency explains that "it is assumed that [a document conveying a power of attorney] represents the entire understanding of the parties." *Restatement (Second) of Agency* § 34, cmt. h (1958). Thus, if Mr. Stubblefield was not authorized to make gifts of Ms. Swanson's property under the power of attorney—and we think it clear that under California law he was not—he was likewise not authorized to make gifts under the general principles of agency law.

In the *Huston* case, the California case closest to this one, the court refused to sustain a gift to the agent purportedly made in accordance with the principal's oral instructions, because the gift was contrary to limitations in the power of attorney. The court refused to recognize the gift in that case, even though the principal stated to a neutral third party her intention to make the gift to the agent. The estate seeks to distinguish *Huston* on the ground that in that case the power of attorney expressly forbade the agent from making gifts to himself. In light of the California rule that a power of attorney is construed to forbid the agent from making gifts unless the power is expressly granted, that distinction is unavailing. While it is also true that the gift in *Huston* was solely to the agent and not in part to third parties, that distinction also has no legal force. The point of *Huston* was that the court declined to uphold a gift that was outside the authority granted to the agent by the power of attorney, notwithstanding the evidence that the principal wished to make the gift. Applying the same principle here, the 38 checks signed by Mr. Stubblefield purporting to make gifts to himself and others must be deemed to be revocable transfers.

In sum, we agree with the trial court that, absent authorization in the durable power of attorney or a written modification of the power of attorney, Mr. Stubblefield was not authorized to make the gifts as agent for Ms. Swanson, and that the funds represented by the 38 disputed checks were therefore properly included in Ms. Swanson's estate.

————

The Service's position is consistent with its long-held view that gifts made by an attorney-in-fact are revocable unless the instrument specifically authorizes such gifts or unless state law specifically implies such a power in the instrument. *See* Tech. Adv. Mem. 9231003; Tech. Adv. Mem. 9342003; Priv. Ltr. Rul. 9410028; Priv. Ltr. Rul. 9509034 Priv. Ltr. Rul. 9634004.

Swanson illustrates that whether an attorney-in-fact can make gifts with a power of attorney is a question of state law. In some jurisdictions, it is not necessary for the power of attorney to specifically include the power to make gifts. *See Estate of Pruitt v. Commissioner*, T.C. Memo 2000–287. In other jurisdictions, the state legislature has responded to decisions like *Swanson* to statutorily remove the requirement that the power to gift must be specifically granted. For example, the Virginia legislature responded to the Fourth Circuit's decision in *Estate of Casey v. Commissioner*, 948 F.2d 895 (4th Cir. 1991) with VA. CODE ANN. Sec. 11-9.5. In *Estate of Ridenour v. Commissioner*, 36 F.3d 332 (4th Cir. 1994), the court sanctioned the retroactive effect given the state statute by the Virginia Legislature to make the decedent's gifts with a power of attorney irrevocable.

Problems

1. Why didn't the Service contend in *Swanson* that § 2033 required inclusion because the transfer without authority was void?

2. Are Totten trust accounts taxable to the trustee at her death under (a) § 2036(a)(2), (b) § 2038, or (c) § 2033? *See Estate of Sulovich v. Commissioner*, 587 F.2d 845 (6th Cir. 1978).

3. *H* is a domiciliary of a community property state. *H* creates a revocable trust using community property, naming *X* to take at *H*'s death. What portion of the trust is included in *H*'s gross estate? *See Katz v. United States*, 382 F.2d 723 (9th Cir. 1967).

[C] Generation-Skipping Transfer Tax

Code: § 2642(f).

Regulations: Treas. Reg. § 26.2632–1(c).

Retention of a power of revocation can delay imposition of the generation-skipping transfer tax, just as it does the imposition of the gift tax. If the transaction is a direct skip without regard to the power, the fact that the power negates the gift tax also negates the generation-skipping transfer tax. *See* § 2612(c)(1). On the other hand, the Code does not define the retention of a power as retention of an interest, so that a retained power would not keep the trust from being a skip person if it had only skip persons as beneficiaries. *See* § 2613(a)(2). Still, the inclusion ratio cannot be established until the transferor's power terminates. *See* § 2642(f).

The generation-skipping transfer tax mirrors the gift tax and estate tax rule that the termination of a power to revoke completes the transfer for generation-skipping tax purposes. At that time, the transfer may constitute a direct skip. The release of the power is not, however, a taxable termination because the power holder is not defined as having an interest. Of course, if a distribution resulted from the termination of the power to revoke, such as a payment of income to a skip person, the distribution is a direct skip. Subsequent transfers from the trust may be taxable distributions or taxable terminations.

[D] Income Tax

Code: § 676(a).

Regulations: Treas. Reg. § 1.676(a)–1.

Retention of the power to revoke has long required the income of the revocable trust be taxed to the grantor. In *Corliss v. Bowers*, 281 U.S. 376 (1930), the grantor-taxpayer created a trust to pay income to his wife for life, with remainder to their children. In the trust instrument, the taxpayer reserved the power "to modify or alter in any manner, or revoke in whole or in part, this indenture and the trusts then existing, and the estates and interests in property hereby created." In taxing the income of a revocable trust to the grantor, the Supreme Court stated (281 U.S. at 378):

> [I]f a man disposes of a fund in such a way that another is allowed to enjoy the income which it is in the power of the first to appropriate, it does not matter whether the permission is given by assent or by failure to express dissent. The income that is subject to a man's unfettered command and that he is free to enjoy at his own option may be taxed to him as his income, whether he sees fit to enjoy it or not.

The result in *Corliss v. Bowers* is now codified. Section 676(a) taxes the income of a trust to the grantor if a power to revoke the trust and receive all or any part of the trust principal is exercisable by the grantor alone, by a nonadverse party (as defined in § 672(a) and (b)) alone, or by the grantor and a nonadverse party acting together. If a power to revoke exists, even if the power is not exercised, the grantor remains in substance the owner of the trust property, and is taxed on its income unless the power is remote. *See* § 676(b).

An *adverse party* is defined by § 672(a) as "any person having a substantial beneficial interest in the trust which would be adversely affected by the exercise or non-exercise of the power which he possesses respecting the trust." The requirement that an adverse party have a beneficial interest in the trust prevents most trustees from being characterized as adverse. Further, the "substantial" limitation on the beneficial interest requires more than mere monetary value. *See Paxton v. Commissioner*, 520 F.2d 923 (9th Cir. 1975), *cert. denied*, 423 U.S. 1016 (1975) (3.84% interest *insubstantial*). The regulations define a substantial interest as one whose "value in relation to the total value of the property subject to the power is not insignificant." *See* Treas. Reg. § 1.672(a)–1(a).

The fact that the wording of § 676 is limited to trusts is not significant. Even without express statutory language, the same result can be obtained (at least with respect to a pure power of revocation in the grantor) in nontrust transactions, under the reasoning of the Court in *Helvering v. Clifford*, reproduced in § 2.05[C][3], *supra*.

Problems

Consider § 2702 when answering the following problems and assume the § 7520 rate is 8%.

1. *S* transfers $1 million in trust. The income is payable to *A* for life and the remainder is distributable to *C. S* retains a power to revoke the trust.

a. What are the federal gift tax consequences of (1) transferring property to the trust and (2) paying income to *A*? Consider *Burnet v. Guggenheim* (reproduced in § 4.01[A][1], *supra*).

b. What are the federal gift tax consequences if *A* predeceases *S* and *S*'s power of revocation terminates upon *C*'s possession of the remainder?

c. What are the federal income tax consequences of the trust? Consider § 676(a).

d. What are the federal estate tax consequences of the trust if *S* predeceases *A*?

e. What are the federal GST tax consequences of the trust if *C* is a skip person?

2. *S* creates a trust. The income was payable to *A* for life and the remainder is distributable to *B. S* retains the right to revoke the trust with her husband's, *H*'s, consent.

a. What are the gift and income tax consequences of establishing the trust?

b. Would the answer in (a) change if *H* had a legal obligation to support *A* or *B*?

c. If *S* dies during the life of *A*, will any part of the trust be includable in her gross estate?

3. *S* transfers $1 million to a trust. The income is payable to *A*, age 65, for life and the remainder is distributable to *C. S* retains a power to revoke *A*'s life estate and designate himself income beneficiary for *A*'s life.

a. What are the federal gift tax consequences of (1) transferring the property to the trust and (2) paying trust income to *A*?

b. What are the federal estate tax consequences of the trust, assuming that S dies during the life of A?

4. S transfers $1 million to a trust. The income is payable to A, age 65, for life and the remainder is distributable to C. S retains a power to revoke C's remainder and designate himself remainderman.

    a. What are the federal gift tax consequences of (1) transferring property to the trust and (2) paying income to A?

    b. What are the federal gift tax consequences if A predeceases S and the trustee distributes the corpus to C?

    c. What are the federal income tax consequences of the trust? Consider §§ 673, 676(a) and 677(a).

    d. What are the federal estate tax consequences of the trust if S predeceases A?

5. How would the answers in problems 3 and 4 change if A were S's spouse?

§ 8.02   Contingent Powers

If the grantor attaches a condition on the power to revoke, the tax picture becomes more complicated. If the condition has not occurred at the time for the taxing decision, does the holder have a power for tax purposes? This question puts at issue the reasons for the various provisions of the Code dealing with retained powers.

[A]   Gift Tax

Code: None.

Regulations: Treas. Reg. § 25.2511–2(b).

With a contingent power, unlike an outright power, the grantor is not certain of being able to shift the interest from the donee. Rather, it is like a contingent interest, worth only the interest which might be shifted, times the likelihood of the power arising. Thus, retention of a contingent power should make the transfer incomplete only to the extent of the actuarial value of the contingency. The remaining interests have been given away. This impact of the gift tax can be illustrated by the following example:

> **Example:** D creates a trust. The income is payable to A for life and the remainder is distributable to B, provided, however, that D retains the right to revoke the remainder if D survives for five years.

In the example, the life estate in A is a completed gift, because D does not have, nor will he ever have, the power to change its ownership. The remainder, however, is only complete to the extent that D is not likely to survive for five years.[4] The likelihood of this occurring can be calculated using actuarial tables, which would reduce the value of the gift to B or, more accurately, would define the extent to which D has retained an interest or power which can be subtracted from the value of the transferred property.

---

[4] *See* RICHARD B. STEPHENS ET AL., FEDERAL ESTATE AND GIFT TAXATION ¶ 10.01[5][b] (7th ed. 1997).

[B] Estate Tax

Code: §§ 2036(a)(2), 2037, and 2038.

Regulations: Treas. Reg. §§ 20.2036–1(b)(3) and 20.2038–1(b).

The impact of applying a contingency to a power to revoke is more complex under the estate tax, and depends on which section is being applied to the transaction. The results under §§ 2036(a)(2) and 2038 are discussed in *Farrel*. In addition, § 2037 might also apply.

Estate of Farrel v. United States

553 F.2d 637 (Ct. Cl. 1977)

Davis, Judge.

The stipulated facts in this tax refund suit thrust upon us a narrow but knotty issue of estate tax law under section 2036(a)(2) . . . . In 1961 Marian B. Farrel established an irrevocable trust with a corpus of various securities and her grandchildren as beneficiaries. Two individuals were named as trustees. They were given discretionary power [which if held by Marian Farrel would have required taxation under §§ 2036(a)(2) and 2038. Although these powers would not constitute powers of revocation if held by Mrs. Farrel, Judge Davis' opinion applies equally to powers of revocation.]

The trust called for two trustees at all times, and provided for Mrs. Farrel to appoint a successor trustee if a vacancy occurred in that position through death, resignation or removal by a proper court for cause. However, neither the instrument nor Connecticut law (which governed the trust) permitted Mrs. Farrel to remove a trustee and thereby create a vacancy. The trust was silent as to whether Mrs. Farrel could appoint herself as a successor trustee in the event of a vacancy, but neither the trust instrument nor Connecticut law would have prevented her from doing so.

Two vacancies occurred in the office of trustee during Mrs. Farrel's life. In 1964 a named trustee died and Mrs. Farrel appointed a third person as successor trustee. In 1965 that successor trustee resigned and Mrs. Farrel, as settlor, appointed another individual to succeed him.

Mrs. Farrel died in October 1969. Her estate, plaintiff here, filed in 1971 a federal estate tax return which did not include the trust property in the gross estate, and paid the tax shown on the return. In 1973 the Internal Revenue Service assessed a deficiency on the ground that the trust property should have been included in the gross estate under section 2036(a)(2) . . . . Plaintiff paid the deficiency, filed a timely refund claim, and after the appropriate waiting period instituted the present refund suit.

Both parties agree that (a) the trustees had "the right, either alone or in conjunction with any person, to designate the persons who shall possess or enjoy the property or the income therefrom" within the meaning of section 2036(a)(2); (b) Mrs. Farrel, the decedent-settlor, could lawfully designate herself (under the trust and Connecticut law) as successor trustee if a vacancy occurred during her life; (c) the occurrence of a vacancy in the office of trustee was a condition which Mrs. Farrel could not create and which was beyond her control; and (d) Mrs. Farrel had the opportunity, before her 1969 death, to appoint a successor trustee only during the two periods in 1964 and 1965 mentioned above. The legal conflict is whether the right of the trustees (as to who should enjoy or possess the property or income) should in these circumstances be attributed to the decedent under section 2036(a) for any of the three periods designated in that statutory provision—her life; any period not ascertainable without reference to her death; any period which does not in fact end before her death. The Government's answer is yes and the plaintiff of course says no.

. . .

Plaintiff's primary point is that (i) it is now and has long been settled that section 2038 does not cover a power or right subject to a conditional event which has not occurred prior to and does not exist at the decedent's death, such as a discretionary power to distribute income or principal under specified conditions which have not occurred before the death, and (ii) the same rule has been and is applicable to section 2036(a).

There is no question that taxpayer is correct as to the construction of section 2038. That slant was given by the courts to the provision's predecessor under the 1939 Code . . . , and the Treasury has itself adopted the same interpretation for the 1954 Code as well . . . .

The initial and fundamental question we have to face is whether this settled understanding of section 2038 necessarily governs section 2036(a), as it now stands. We think not for two reasons which we shall consider in turn: first, that the critical points-of-view of the two provisions differ, and, second, that the regulations governing the two sections take diametrically opposed positions on the narrow issue of contingent rights and powers of the kind involved here.

The two separate provisions appear to diverge sharply in their perspective—the point from which the pertinent powers and rights are to be seen. Section 2038(a) looks at the problem from the decedent's death—what he can and cannot do at that specific moment. Excluded are contingent rights and powers (beyond the decedent's control) which are not exercisable at that moment because the designated contingency does not exist at that time. Section 2036(a), on the other hand, looks forward from the time the decedent made the transfer to see whether he has retained any of the specified rights "for his life or for any period not ascertainable without reference to his death or for any period which does not in fact end before his death." This language makes the transferor's death one pole of the specified time-span but the whole of the time-span is also significant. Because of the statute's reference to the time-span, differences of interpretation are quite conceivable. It is possible for instance, to hold the words to mean that the retained right has to exist at all times throughout one of the periods, but it is also possible to see the language as covering contingencies which could realistically occur at some separate point or points during the designated periods—always including the moment of decedent's death. We take it (from the argument's insistence on the parallel to 2038) that the taxpayer would not stand on the former ("at all times") interpretation if a vacancy in the trusteeship existed and had not been filled at [the settlor's] death. But under the language of 2036(a) there is no compelling reason why the moment of death has to be exclusively important. Unlike section 2038, this provision seems to look forward from the time of transfer to the date of the transferor's death, and can be said to concentrate on the significant rights with respect to the transferred property the transferor retains, not at every moment during that period, but whenever the specified contingency happens to arise during that period (so long as the contingency can still occur at the end of the period).

There is nothing unreasonable about this latter construction, which accords with Congress' over-all purpose to gather into the estate tax all transfers which remain significantly incomplete—on which the transferor still holds a string—during his lifetime. It is hard to believe, for instance that, whatever may be true of section 2038, 2036(a) would have to be seen as failing to cover a trust where the trustee, with discretionary powers, could be removed by the settlor, and the settlor substituted as trustee, whenever economic conditions fell below a stated level (*e.g.,* a designated level on a certain stock exchange index or a level of earnings of the trust) even though fortuitously that condition did not happen to exist at the time of death. In a case like that, the lifetime link between the decedent and the trust property (and income) would be so strong as plainly to measure up to both the letter and the spirit of section 2036(a) if the Treasury chose to see it that way. This case, though perhaps less clear, falls into the same class of a continuing substantial tie.

The other element which leads us to reject plaintiff's attempt to equate section 2036(a) with section 2038, for this case, is that the Treasury has affirmatively chosen to separate the two sections—there is a Treasury regulation under the former section 20.2036–1 which, to our mind, clearly covers this decedent's situation (in contrast to the regulation under section 2038 which excludes it). Taxpayer urges us to read the regulation otherwise, and if we cannot to hold it invalid.

The regulation [Treasury Regulation § 20.2036–1(b)(3)] says flatly that it is immaterial "(iii) whether the exercise of the power was subject to a contingency beyond the decedent's control which did not occur before his death (*e.g.,* the death of another person during the decedent's lifetime)." This would seem on its surface to blanket this decedent's position under her trust, but plaintiff would read it very literally and narrowly to apply only where the contingency relates to the "exercise" of an already existing power, and conversely, to be inapplicable where the power only springs into existence when a trustee vacancy occurs. Similarly, taxpayer sees in the broad sweep of the last sentence of section 20.2036–1(b)(3) the implied negative that a restricted power in the decedent to appoint herself a substitute trustee only in the event of a vacancy lies outside 2036(a). We cannot accept these strained (if not casuistic) analyses of the regulation because they go directly counter to its apparent purpose to cover just such contingencies as we have here. If proof of that objective is needed it is fully supplied by the companion regulation under section 2038 . . . section 20.2038–1(b) which declares in coordinate terms that "section 2038 is not applicable to a power the exercise of which was subject to a contingency beyond the decedent's control which did not occur before his death (*e.g.,* the death of another person during the decedent's life). *See, however, section 2036(a)(2) for the inclusion of property in the decedent's gross estate on account of such a power*" (emphasis added).

We are required, then, to consider whether section 20.2036–1(b)(3) should be overturned as invalid. Recognizing the deference due Treasury Regulations . . . , we cannot take that step. We have pointed out that 2036 is not the same as 2038 in its wording or in the viewpoint from which it appraises the decedent's link to the transferred property. We have also said that it is not unreasonable to regard 2036(a), in the way the Treasury does, as a blanket overall sweeping-in of property over which the decedent still has at death some significant, though contingent, power to choose those who shall have possession or enjoyment.

    . . .

We end by noting that the contingent right of Mrs. Farrel to make herself a trustee in the event of a vacancy—unlike the de facto "powers" involved in *United States v. Byrum*, 408 U.S. 125 (1972) and in *Estate of Tully v. United States*, 528 F.2d 1401, 208 Ct. Cl. 596 (1976)—was a legally enforceable right, in effect imbedded in the trust instrument, which bore directly on the designation of the persons to possess or enjoy the trust property or income. That the exercise of this right was foreseeable when the trust was created— that it was a real right, neither insignificant nor illusory—is shown by the fact that Mrs. Farrel had two opportunities to exercise it in eight years and, if she had lived, may well have had more.

CONCLUSION

For these reasons we hold that plaintiff is not entitled to recover and the petition is dismissed.

Kunzig, Judge, concurring [opinion omitted].

———

As suggested in the comment before *Farrel*, § 2037 specifically provides that the term "reversionary interest" includes "a possibility that property transferred by the decedent—(1) may return to him or his estate, or (2) may be subject to a power of disposition by him . . . ." If the decedent created a trust that provides that the income is payable to A for life and the remainder distributable to B, but the decedent retained the power to revoke the trust if he survived A, the transfer would leave him with the possibility of getting it back. That possibility triggers the application of § 2037, which continues the general premise of the "string provisions," *i.e.*, that a retained power over assets is to be treated the same as retaining the interest itself. The retention suggests that the decedent is treating the transfer as testamentary in nature.

On the other hand, § 2037 does not require inclusion in the case of every contingent power because remote powers would not satisfy the 5% value limitation on the operation of that section.

Problem

A gift is incomplete to the extent of a contingent power, and thus the gift tax is not applied to the entire value of the trust. Moreover, § 2038 does not apply to contingent powers. Does this produce a loophole in the transfer tax?

[C]   Generation-Skipping Transfer Tax

There are no special generation-skipping consequences to retaining contingent powers to revoke, other than the inability to allocate the GST exemption on the creation of the trust if the contingent power will cause the property subject to the power to be included in the transferor's estate. *See* § 2642(f).

[D]   Income Tax

Code: § 676(b).

Regulations: Treas. Reg. § 1.676(b)–1.

In general, contingencies on a power to revoke will not limit taxation of the income to the grantor. Section 676(b) states that "Subsection (a) [the section taxing income to the grantor because of a power to revoke] shall not apply to a power the exercise of which can only affect the beneficial enjoyment of the income for a period commencing after the occurrence of an event such that a grantor would not be treated as the owner under § 673 if the power were a reversionary interest." Section 673 requires taxation of income to the grantor if he retains a reversion valued at more than 5% of the value of the property at the time of the transfer. Thus, any contingency that gives the grantor more than a 5% chance of having the power to revoke would violate § 676, whether or not the contingency had occurred.

§ 8.03   Release of Retained Powers

[A]   Gift Tax

Code: § 2511.

Regulations: Treas. Reg. § 25.2511–2.

As noted in Chapter 4, the release or lapse of a power of revocation completes the gift of the property that was subject to the power. *See Burnet v. Guggenheim*, 288 U.S. 280 (1933) (reproduced at § 4.01[A][1], *supra*); Treas. Reg. § 25.2511–2. Thus, if income from a revocable trust is paid to the income beneficiary, a gift occurs to that extent, but qualifies for the annual exclusion under § 2503(b). Similarly, release of a power to revoke a remainder will complete the gift of the remainder (albeit without an exclusion, because it is a future interest).

There is one significant limitation on this principle: if the termination of the power is caused by the death of the grantor, no gift tax applies. The Regulations provide that transactions which are completed by death are not subject to the gift tax (although they are subject to the estate tax). *See* Treas. Reg. § 25.2511–2(f) (first sentence).

[B]   Estate Tax

Code: §§ 2035(a) and 2038.

Regulations: None.

The release of a power to revoke may produce estate taxation under either of two sections of the Code. First, § 2038 specifically requires gross estate inclusion when the decedent holds the power at death, and "where any such power is relinquished during the three-year period ending on the date of the decedent's death." Second, § 2035(a) applies when property "would have been included in the decedent's gross estate under §§ 2036, 2037, 2038, or 2042 if such interest or relinquished power had been retained by the decedent on the date of his death."

Before the Taxpayer Relief Act of 1997, the Service took a litigating position that gifts made from a taxpayer's revocable trust were subject to the three-year pullback rule. Taxpayers contested the Service's view on the basis that the inclusion was easily avoided by removing the assets to be gifted from the revocable trust before making the transfer to the donee. *See Estate of Jalkut v. Commissioner,* 96 T.C. 675 (1991), *acq.* 1992–002 (transfers from revocable trust includible in gross estate); *McNeely v. Commissioner,* 16 F.3d 303 (8th Cir. 1994) (transfers from revocable trust not includible in gross estate); *Kisling v. Commissioner,* 32 F.3d 1222 (8th Cir. 1994), *acq.* 1995–2 C.B. 1 (transfers from revocable trust not includible in gross estate). Such a two-step process took form over substance to the extreme.

In response to the issue, Congress adopted § 2035(e). The legislative history states: "[t]he House bill codifies the rule set forth in the *McNeely* and *Kisling* cases to provide that a transfer from a revocable trust (*i.e.,* a trust described under § 676) is treated as if made directly by the grantor. Thus, an annual exclusion gift from such a trust is not included in the gross estate." Conference Report, Taxpayer Relief Act of 1997 at 76–77.

Attention should also be given to the impact of the *Allen* case, reproduced in § 7.03[B], *supra,* on the release of powers. Because § 2035 applies to the relinquishment of powers, it could require substantial consideration to avoid taxation to the estate. Under the analysis of *Allen,* to avoid estate taxation under § 2035(a), the grantor would have to receive the full value of the property which would have been taxed to the estate in return for the release of the power. In the case of a § 2038 power, that is not particularly severe because that is the actual value received by the recipient of the property free from the power. If the power is a § 2036(a)(2) or § 2037 power, however, much greater consideration could be required. Assume, for example, a retained power to revoke a remainder, conditioned on the decedent surviving all of his living siblings. The decedent might have only a small chance of surviving, but if the chance were greater than 5%, the remainder would be taxed to his estate under § 2037. Thus, if he relinquished his power, he would have to receive the present value of the full remainder to avoid operation of § 2035.

[C]   Generation-Skipping Transfer Tax

The generation-skipping transfer tax consequences of relinquishing a retained power to revoke are based on the extent to which interests are thereby deemed transferred. Thus, the power is based on such factors as the type of trust, the identity of the trust beneficiaries, and the application of the ETIP rule.

[D]   Income Tax

Code: § 676.

Regulations: None.

Release of retained powers stops the taxation of trust income to the grantor. Section 676(a) (taxing property because of the power to revoke) applies only if "at any time the power to revest in the grantor title to such portion is exercisable by the grantor . . . ." Relinquishment of the power prevents the exercise, and thus income taxation based on the power. Indeed, § 676(b) expressly states that § 676(a) does not apply to remote powers which are relinquished, even if the powers would otherwise become currently exercisable.

Problems

1. S creates a trust. The income is payable to A, age 65, for life and the remainder is distributable to B. S retains the right to revoke the trust with the consent of her husband, H. What would be the gift and estate tax consequences if S released the power to revoke: (1) four years before her death; (2) two years before her death?

2. S transfers $1 million to a trust. The income is payable to A, age 65, for life and the remainder is distributable to C. S retains a power to revoke A's life estate and designate himself income beneficiary for A's life. What would be the gift and estate tax consequences if S released the power to revoke: (1) four years before his death; (2) two years before his death?

3. If a grantor releases his power to revoke a trust within three years of death, § 2038 will apply. In addition, the release will be a taxable event for gift tax purposes. What would be the result if four years after creating the trust the grantor revokes the trust, gives the property to the trust beneficiary, and dies the next year? *See* § 2035(e).

Chapter 9

RETENTION OF POWERS OTHER THAN THE POWER TO REVOKE

Although a grantor may be willing to irrevocably transfer all beneficial interests in assets, the grantor may wish to retain one or more powers to determine what happens to the assets after the transfer. This Chapter investigates the tax ramifications of retained powers other than the power to revoke.

Retained powers may be administrative in nature, as when the grantor serves as the trustee of an irrevocable trust. In that case, the grantor has inherently retained the powers of the legal title holder subject to the equitable duties of a trustee to the trust's beneficiaries. Another grantor might want a third party to act as trustee, while retaining the right to control trust investments or the allocation of receipts and expenses to income or principal. This enables the grantor to control the financial health of the trust.

A grantor may retain discretionary powers, such as the power to change beneficiaries of a trust or to determine whether payments should be made from a trust to one or more beneficiaries. If the grantor has two children, for example, she may want to retain a power to *sprinkle* income between them as they need it from time to time. Another grantor might want to retain the power to accumulate income and add it to corpus if he perceives that the income beneficiary does not need or merit it.

Retention of powers other than the power to revoke can have marked tax consequences. These powers may be divided into either dispositive or administrative powers. The term *dispositive power* means the right to alter or amend beneficial enjoyment of the income or corpus subject to the power, either by determining who will enjoy it or when it will be enjoyed. Common dispositive powers include powers to: (1) change beneficiaries; (2) alter the respective interests of the beneficiaries; (3) accumulate or distribute income; and (4) invade corpus or otherwise terminate a trust. Necessarily, the term also includes a general power to modify a trust, which is not limited to administrative modifications.[1]

Dispositive powers may be retained by a grantor over an otherwise irrevocable trust. Indeed, retaining dispositive powers is not necessary if the trust is revocable because the power to revoke usually includes the power to modify. This makes retaining the right to modify other dispositive powers superfluous. Whether a right to modify a dispositive power exists is determined under the general rules for the interpretation of trusts, which require that the power be reserved expressly or by implication from the terms of the trust agreement.

---

[1] Although a broad power of modification may be deemed to include the power to revoke, SCOTT & FRATCHER, 4 THE LAW OF TRUSTS § 331.2 (4th ed. 1989), the discussion here assumes that the power to modify would be limited.

Powers may also be indirectly retained, but exercisable only upon the occurrence of a contingency. *See Estate of Farrel v. United States* (reproduced in § 8.02[B], *supra*).

The complexity of the rules governing the taxation of grantor powers, coupled with the variety of powers which may be retained, necessitate some delineation for discussion purposes. This text divides dispositive powers into powers which: (1) may be exercised to change either the beneficiaries or their respective interests; (2) can change only the time or manner of enjoyment of interests previously determined; and (3) may be indirectly exercised by a retained power to remove the trustee. Administrative powers are discussed separately at the end of this Chapter.

§ 9.01 Powers to Change Beneficial Interests

The most significant tax effects accompany powers which can be used to change beneficial interests. These powers include, for example, the power to change beneficiaries and the power to accumulate income and add it to the corpus when different beneficiaries are entitled to income and corpus.

[A] Gift Tax

Code: §§ 2511 and 2702.

Regulations: Treas. Reg. §§ 25.2511–2, 25.2702–6(c), and Examples 6 and 7.

Estate of Sanford v. Commissioner

308 U.S. 39 (1939)

[Reproduced in Chapter 4, § 4.01[A][1].]

———

Whether a retained power to shift beneficial interests prevents a gift from being complete for gift tax purposes will depend on whether the power is deemed to be a power in the tax sense. Thus, powers subject to approval by an adverse party would be excluded under the reasoning of *Camp*, § 8.01[A], *supra*. Similarly, if the power "is a fiduciary power limited by a fixed or ascertainable standard" it will not make the transaction incomplete. *See* Treas. Reg. § 25.2511–2(c), –1(g)(2). The transfer is complete to the extent that the standard limits the grantor's power to deny a beneficiary the income or principal because the beneficiary has a legal right to the interest that may not be withheld by the grantor's exercise of the power.

The exercise of a retained power may be limited by acts of independent significance. For example, the ability to expand a class of beneficiaries by having or adopting children should not constitute a power to change the beneficial interests for gift tax purposes. *See.* Rev. Rul. 80–255, 1980–2 C.B. 272 (stating that "although [the settlor's] act of bearing or adopting children will automatically result in adding the child as beneficiary to the trust, such result is merely a collateral consequence of the bearing or adopting of children"). Similar results are obtained if, for example, exercising a power required the grantor to quit his job.

Remember also that termination of the retained power over an interest completes a previously incomplete gift of that interest. Thus, a gift of an income interest which is subject to a power to accumulate income is complete for any income paid to the income beneficiary. Alternatively, the gift is complete for the value of any income that is accumulated. It is not until the power is exercised (or not exercised) that the gift tax effects of the income can be determined. At that time, the income passes out of the grantor's control. *See* Treas. Reg. § 25.2511–2(f).

In *Smith v. Shaughnessy*, 318 U.S. 176, 179 (1943), the Court refused to extend *Sanford*'s logic to excuse gift taxation of a transfer of property subject to a reversionary interest, notwithstanding the estate taxation of the transfer under the predecessor to § 2037:

> As we said [in *Sanford*], the gift and estate tax laws are closely related and the gift tax serves to supplement the estate tax.[2] . . . The scope of that provision we need not now determine. It is sufficient to note here that Congress plainly pointed out that "some" of the "total gifts subject to gift taxes . . . may be included for estate tax purposes and some not." House Report No. 708, 72d Cong., 1st Sess., p. 45. Under the statute the gift tax amounts in some instances to a security, a form of down-payment on the estate tax which secures the eventual payment of the latter; it is in no sense double taxation as the taxpayer suggests.

Problems

1. *S* transfers $1 million to *T* in an irrevocable trust. The income is payable to *A* for ten years and the remainder is payable to *B* or *B*'s estate. *S* reserves the power to substitute or add income beneficiaries. Assuming in the alternative that *S* is related to *A*, *B*, both of them, or neither of them, what are the gift tax consequences of this transfer, if *S* has made no prior taxable gifts, and the applicable interest rate under § 7520 is 8%? (Consider § 2702 and its discussion in Chapter 7 when answering this question).

2. Assume in Problem 1 that in its first year the trust receives $80,000 of income and *T* distributes all of the income to *A*. What are the gift tax consequences to *S*, if any?

[B]   Estate Tax

Code: §§ 2036(a)(2) and 2038.

Regulations: Treas. Reg. §§ 20.2036–1 and 20.2038–1(a).

As you read the following cases and materials, note that there are four basic questions to consider in the application of §§ 2036(a)(2) and 2038: (1) what

---

[2] The gift tax was passed not only to prevent estate tax avoidance, but also to prevent income tax avoidance through reducing yearly income and thereby escaping the effect of progressive rates.

is the nature of a power implicating either or both of the sections; (2) when must the power exist; (3) who must hold the power; and (4) assuming the existence of the power, what interests must be included in the decedent's gross estate?

[1]　Discretionary Powers

United States v. O'Malley

383 U.S. 627 (1966)

Mr. Justice White delivered the opinion of the Court.

. . .

Edward H. Fabrice, who died in 1949, created five irrevocable trusts in 1936 and 1937, two for each of two daughters and one for his wife. He was one of three trustees of the trusts, each of which provided that the trustees, in their sole discretion, could pay trust income to the beneficiary or accumulate the income, in which event it became part of the principal of the trust. Basing his action on [§ 2036] . . . the Commissioner included in Fabrice's gross estate both the original principal of the trusts and the accumulated income added thereto. He accordingly assessed a deficiency, the payment of which prompted this refund action by the respondents, the executors of the estate. The District Court found the original corpus of the trusts includable in the estate, a holding not challenged in the Court of Appeals or here. It felt obliged, however, by *Commissioner v. McDermott's Estate*, 222 F.2d 665, to exclude from the taxable estate the portion of the trust principal representing accumulated income and to order an appropriate refund. 220 F. Supp. 30. The Court of Appeals affirmed . . . . We now reverse the decision below.

The applicability of [§ 2036(a)(2)] . . . depends upon the answer to two inquiries relevant to the facts of this case: first, whether Fabrice retained a power "to designate the persons who shall possess or enjoy the property or the income therefrom;" and second, whether the property sought to be included, namely, the portions of trust principal representing accumulated income, was the subject of a previous transfer by Fabrice.

Section [2036(a)(2)], which originated in 1931, was an important part of the congressional response to *May v. Heiner*, 281 U.S. 238 . . . and of the legislative policy of subjecting to tax all property which has been the subject of an incomplete inter vivos transfer. *Cf. Commissioner v. Estate of Church*, 335 U.S. 632, 644–645; *Helvering v. Hallock*, 309 U.S. 106, 114. The section requires the property to be included not only when the grantor himself has the right to its income but also when he has the right to designate those who may possess and enjoy it. Here Fabrice was empowered, with the other trustees, to distribute the trust income to the income beneficiaries or to accumulate it and add it to the principal, thereby denying to the beneficiaries the privilege of immediate enjoyment and conditioning their eventual enjoyment upon surviving the termination of the trust. This is a significant power, *see Commissioner v. Estate of Holmes*, 326 U.S. 480, 487, and of sufficient substance to be deemed the power to "designate" within the meaning of

[§ 2036(a)(2)]. This was the holding of the Tax Court and the Court of Appeals almost 20 years ago. *Industrial Trust Co. v. Commissioner*, 165 F.2d 142, affirming in this respect *Estate of Budlong v. Commissioner*, 7 T.C. 756. The District Court here followed *Industrial Trust* and affirmed the includability of the original principal of each of the Fabrice trusts. That ruling is not now disputed. By the same token, the first condition to taxing accumulated income added to the principal is satisfied, for the income from these increments to principal was subject to the identical power in Fabrice to distribute or accumulate until the very moment of his death.

The dispute in this case relates to the second condition to the applicability of [§ 2036(a)(2)]—whether Fabrice had ever "transferred" the income additions to the trust principal. Contrary to the judgment of the Court of Appeals, we are sure that he had. At the time Fabrice established these trusts, he owned all of the rights to the property transferred, a major aspect of which was his right to the present and future income produced by that property. *Commissioner v. Estate of Church*, 335 U.S. 632, 644. With the creation of the trusts, he relinquished all of his rights to income except the power to distribute that income to the income beneficiaries or to accumulate it and hold it for the remaindermen of the trusts. He no longer had, for example, the right to income for his own benefit or to have it distributed to any other than the trust beneficiaries. Moreover, with respect to the very additions to principal now at issue, he exercised his retained power to distribute or accumulate income, choosing to do the latter and thereby adding to the principal of the trusts. All income increments to trust principal are therefore traceable to Fabrice himself, by virtue of the original transfer and the exercise of the power to accumulate. Before the creation of the trusts, Fabrice owned all rights to the property and to its income. By the time of his death he had divested himself of all power and control over accumulated income which had been added to the principal, except the power to deal with the income from such additions. With respect to each addition to trust principal from accumulated income, Fabrice had clearly made a "transfer" as required by [§ 2036(a)(2)]. Under that section, the power over income retained by Fabrice is sufficient to require the inclusion of the original corpus of the trust in his gross estate. The accumulated income added to principal is subject to the same power and is likewise includable. *Round v. Commissioner*, 332 F.2d 590; *Estate of Yawkey v. Commissioner*, 12 T.C. 1164.

Respondents rely upon two cases in which the Tax Court and two circuit courts of appeals have concluded that where an irrevocable inter vivos transfer in trust, not incomplete in any respect, is subjected to tax as a gift in contemplation of death under [an earlier version of § 2035], the income of the trust accumulated prior to the grantor's death is not includable in the gross estate. *Commissioner v. Gidwitz' Estate*, 196 F.2d 813, *affirming* 14 T.C. 1263; *Burns v. Commissioner*, 177 F.2d 739, *affirming* 9 T.C. 979. The courts in those cases considered the taxable event to be a completed inter vivos transfer, not a transfer at death, and the property includable to be only the property subject to that transfer. The value of that property, whatever the valuation date, was apparently deemed an adequate reflection of any income rights included in the transfer since the grantor retained no interest in the property and no power over income which might justify the addition of subsequently accumulated income to his own gross estate. *Cf. Maass v. Higgins*, 312 U.S. 443.

This reasoning, however, does not solve those cases arising under other provisions of [§ 2036]. The courts in both *Burns*, 9 T.C. 979, 988–989 and *Gidwitz*, 196 F.2d 813, 817–818, expressly distinguished those situations where the grantor retains an interest in a property or its income, or a power over either, and his death is a significant step in effecting a transfer which began inter vivos but which becomes final and complete only with his demise. *McDermott's Estate* failed to note this distinction and represents an erroneous extension of *Gidwitz*.[3] In both *McDermott* and the case before us now, the grantor reserved the power to accumulate or distribute income. This power he exercised by accumulating and adding income to principal and this same power he held until the moment of his death with respect to both the original principal and the accumulated income. In these circumstances, [§ 2036(a)(2)] requires inclusion in Fabrice's gross estate of all of the trust principal, including those portions representing accumulated income.

Reversed.

Mr. Justice Stewart, with whom Mr. Justice Harlan joins, dissenting.

. . .

By its terms the statutory provision applies only to property "of which the decedent has at any time made a transfer." Fabrice "made a transfer" only of the original trust corpus. He never "made a transfer" of the income which the corpus thereafter produced, whether accumulated or not. I can put the matter no more clearly than did the Court of Appeals for the Seventh Circuit in *Commissioner v. McDermott's Estate*, 222 F.2d 665, 668:

> Irrespective of all other considerations, property to be includible must have been transferred. Obviously, the accumulations here involved were not transferred by the decedent to the trustee. It is true, of course, that the accumulations represented the fruit derived from the property which was transferred but, even so, Congress did not make provision for including the fruit, it provided only for the property transferred. If it desired and intended to include the accumulations, it would have been a simple matter for it to have so stated.

See also Michigan Trust Co. v. Kavanagh, 284 F.2d 502, 506–507 (6th Cir. 1960).

---

[3] The Court of Appeals in *McDermott's Estate* was clearly wrong in saying that the transfer there involved was as complete as was the transfer in *Gidwitz*. In *Gidwitz* the transfer was in trust and the grantor was one of the trustees but there was a specific direction to accumulate with no discretionary powers in the trustees over either income or principal. In *McDermott*, as in this case, the grantor retained the power, with other trustees, to accumulate or distribute trust income.

Nothing in the legislative history persuades me that the statute should not be applied as it was written, and I would therefore affirm the judgment.

———

Sections 2038 and 2036(a)(2) impose estate taxes upon retained powers to change beneficial interests, although the amount each section will include in a decedent's estate may be different.

Section 2038 applies to the power to "alter, amend, . . . or terminate" a trust, as well as the power to revoke a trust. The term *alter* has long been interpreted to apply to a retained power to name a new beneficiary or change the beneficial interests of the designated beneficiaries. *See, e.g., Porter v. Commissioner*, 288 U.S. 436 (1933). Thus, a power to invade corpus causes gross estate inclusion for the value of the corpus. The power to accumulate income causes inclusion for the value of the income interest. Similarly, if a grantor has a power to add new remainder beneficiaries, the value of the remainder is includable, as it would be if the grantor possessed the power to remove and replace remaindermen.

As illustrated by *O'Malley*, § 2036(a)(2) also expressly applies to retained powers "to designate the persons who shall possess or enjoy the [trust] property or the income therefrom." Nothing in that section requires that the grantor be able to personally benefit by the exercise of the power. For example, if the grantor retains the right to add or substitute an income beneficiary, § 2036 is triggered. Similarly, § 2036(a)(2) applies if the grantor retains the right to change the shares of the income beneficiaries designated in the trust instrument. The typical *sprinkle power*, *i.e.* a trust that permits the income be paid to X, Y, or both of them as the grantor may determine, is a taxable retained power.

Under § 2036(a)(2), the entire value of the trust property is included in the grantor's gross estate. *See* Treas. Reg. § 20.2036–1(a). Usually, all that is required is for the grantor to have the power to *designate* who may enjoy the income from the property. The retention of this power by the grantor amounts to sufficient dominion and control over the trust property to equal, for tax purposes, the retention of the enjoyment and ownership of the property. In a tax sense, the retained power is the equivalent of a testamentary transfer by the grantor. Therefore, the entire trust property is includable in the gross estate.

The separate effect of §§ 2036(a)(2) and 2038 can be shown by two examples:

Example 1: S creates a trust with income to A for ten years, remainder to B. S retains the power to change the remainderman. S dies during the trust term.

Example 2: S creates a trust with income to A for ten years, remainder to B. S retains the power to accumulate income and add it to corpus. S dies during the trust term.

In Example 1, § 2038 requires gross estate inclusion of the value of the remainder interest, the only interest which was subject to change by the decedent. *See* Treas. Reg. § 20.2038–1(a), last sentence. Similarly, in Example 2,

§ 2038 requires inclusion of the value of only the income interest. § 2036(a)(2) applies to Example 2 as well, because S could affect the enjoyment of the income which requires the inclusion of the entire value of the trust in S's gross estate. Section 2036(a)(2) would not apply in Example 1, however. *See* Treas. Reg. § 20.2036–1(b)(3). Consequently, in terms of its inclusionary impact, § 2038 is broader in scope than § 2036(a)(2), but § 2036(a)(2) when applicable may include more value in the decedent's estate.

In addition, § 2035(b) requires the inclusion in a decedent's estate any gift tax paid on transfers made within three years of death. *See also* § 9.05, *infra* (discussing the application of § 2035(a) to released powers).

Problems

1. S, age 60, transferred $100,000 to a trust. The income is payable to A, age 60, during the life of S. The corpus is payable to B on S's death. S retained the power to name a new remainderman. When S dies ten years later, what are the estate tax consequences of this trust?

2. D created an irrevocable trust for the benefit of his children. Under the terms of the trust, afterborn or adopted children, if any, are to share as beneficiaries. Does D's power to procreate or adopt require inclusion of the trust in his gross estate under either §§ 2036(a)(2) or 2038? *See* Rev. Rul. 80–255, 1980–2 C.B. 272.

[2]   Powers Subject to a Standard

Jennings v. Smith

161 F.2d 74 (2d Cir. 1947)

Swan, Circuit Judge.

This is an action by the executors of the will of Oliver Gould Jennings, a resident of Connecticut whose death occurred on October 13, 1936, to recover such part of the estate tax paid by them to the defendant collector as had been illegally collected. Their right to a refund of the amount claimed is clear under *Maass v. Higgins*, 312 U.S. 443, and was not disputed; but the defendant set up in defense an additional estate tax liability (greater than the alleged overpayment) based on the failure to include in the decedent's gross estate the value of certain property which he had transferred in trust in 1934 and 1935. Although assessment of an additional estate tax was barred by the statute of limitations, the plaintiffs do not contend that they are entitled to a refund unless the tax legally due was overpaid. *See Lewis v. Reynolds*, 284 U.S. 281. Hence the question presented at the trial and renewed here, is whether the value of the trust property should have been included in the gross estate. The district court held it includible under [§ 2038]. Accordingly judgment was given for the defendant, and the plaintiffs have appealed.

In December 1934 the decedent set up two trusts: one for the family of his elder son, B. Brewster Jennings, the other for the family of his younger son, Lawrence K. Jennings. The trust instruments were identical, except for the names of the beneficiaries and the property transferred. In discussing the terms of the trusts, it will suffice to refer to the one set up for the elder son's family. The trust was irrevocable and in so far as legally permissible its provisions were to be interpreted and enforced according to Connecticut law. It reserved no beneficial interest to the settlor. He and his two sons were named as the trustees; in case a vacancy should occur provision was made for the appointment of a successor trustee having like powers; there was always to be three trustees and they were authorized to act by majority vote. At the end of each year during the life of the son, the trustees were to accumulate the net income by adding it to the capital of the trust but they were given power, "in their absolute discretion" at any time during the year and prior to the amalgamation of that year's net income into capital, to use all or any part of it for the benefit of the son or his issue provided "the trustees shall determine that such disbursement is reasonably necessary to enable the beneficiary in question to maintain himself and his family, if any, in comfort and in accordance with the station in life to which he belongs." Upon the death of the son the capital of the trust was to be divided into separate equal trust funds, one for each of his surviving children and one for each deceased child who left issue surviving at the death of the son. The trustees also had power to invade the capital . . . . In the Lawrence K. Jennings trust all current net income for the years 1935 and 1936 was paid to him, the trustees, of whom the decedent was one, having unanimously determined that such payments were necessary to enable Lawrence to maintain himself and his family in comfort and in accordance with his station in life. No payment or application of income of the B. Brewster Jennings trust, and none of capital of either trust, was made or requested during the life of the decedent.

. . .

[The court held that a power exercisable in a fiduciary capacity is includible under § 2038(a)(2), as a similar power is under § 2038(a)(1) because the addition of the parenthetical clause "in whatever capacity exercisable" in § 2038(a)(1) was declaratory of existing law. *See Commissioner v. Newbold's Estate*, 158 F.2d 694 (2d Cir. 1946).]

The next question is whether the powers conferred upon the trustees in the case at bar are powers of the character described in [§ 2038(a)(2)], which requires that enjoyment of the trust property must be subject at the date of the decedent's death to change through the exercise of a power. The trustees' power to invade the capital of the trust property was exercisable only if the son or his issue "should suffer prolonged illness or be overtaken by financial misfortune which the trustees deem extraordinary." Neither of these contingencies had occurred before the decedent's death; hence enjoyment of the capital was not "subject at the date of his death to any change through the exercise of a power." In *Commissioner v. Flanders*, 2d Cir., 111 F.2d 117, although decision was rested on another ground, this court expressed the opinion that a power conditioned upon an event which had not occurred before the settlor's death was not within the section . . . . The question has recently been explored by the Tax Court in *Estate of Budlong v. Commissioner*, 7 T.C. 758. There it was held in a convincing opinion that the power of trustees to invade corpus in case of "sickness or other emergency" which had not occurred before the decedent's death, was not a power to "alter, amend or revoke" within the meaning of the statute. The court reasoned that the trustees had not unlimited discretion to act or withhold action under the power, since the trust instrument provided an external standard which a court of equity would apply to compel compliance by the trustees on the happening of the specified contingency or to restrain threatened action if the condition were not fulfilled. In the case at bar the district judge was of opinion that even if the trustees found that the stated conditions had been fulfilled, "their finding created no enforcible [sic] rights in any of the beneficiaries." 63 F. Supp. at 837. In this view we are unable to concur. The condition upon which the power to invade capital might arise is sufficiently definite to be capable of determination by a court of equity. As Judge L. Hand said in *Stix v. Commissioner*, 2d Cir., 152 F.2d 562, 563, "no language, however strong, will entirely remove any power held in trust from the reach of a court of equity." . . . Since the trustees were not free to exercise untrammeled discretion but were to be governed by determinable standards, their power to invade capital, conditioned on contingencies which had not happened, did not in our opinion bring the trust property within the reach of [§ 2038(a)(2)].

Similar reasoning leads to the same conclusion with respect to the trustees' power over net income. At the end of each calendar year they were to accumulate the net income of that year unless prior to its amalgamation into capital they exercised their power to disburse it to, or for the benefit of, the son or his issue. The power the trustees had with respect to disbursing income was exercisable year by year; and at the date of the decedent's death the only income of which the enjoyment was subject to change through exercise of a power was the income of the B. Brewster Jennings trust for the year 1936. But the exercise of this power was conditioned on the trustees' determination that disbursement of the income was necessary to enable the beneficiary to whom it might be allotted to maintain himself and his family "in comfort and in accordance with the station in life to which he belongs." The contingency which would justify exercise of the power had not happened before the decedent's death; consequently the 1936 net income of the B. Brewster Jennings trust was not subject at the date of the decedent's death "to any change through the exercise of a power." Hence it was not includible in the gross estate of the decedent under [§ 2038(a)(2)]. This conclusion is not inconsistent with *Commissioner v. Newbold's Estate*, 2d Cir., 158 F.2d 694, for there the trustees had unlimited discretion, the trust instrument expressly providing that no beneficiary should have any vested right to receive any payment from income.

> . . .

There remains for consideration the question whether the value of the trust property is includible in the decedent's estate under Sec. [2036(a)(2)] upon which the appellee also relies.

> . . .

The 'right' referred to in clause (2), to designate the persons who shall possess or enjoy the property or the income therefrom, . . . apparently overlaps the powers mentioned in Sec. 302(d), as amended, Sec. [2038] of the Code. *See* Art. 19, Treas. Reg. 80. At first glance it might seem that clause

(2) covers the present case, because the decedent, for a period that did not in fact end before his death, 'retained the right,' in conjunction with another of the trustees, to designate the persons who should enjoy the trust property or the income therefrom. But for the reasons that moved us when considering the applicability of Sec. [2038] we think the decedent effectively put that 'right' beyond his own control or retention by imposing conditions upon the exercise of it. A 'right' so qualified that it becomes a duty enforcible in a court of equity on petition by the beneficiaries does not circumvent the obvious purpose of Sec. [2036(a)(2)] to prevent transfers akin to testamentary dispositions from escaping taxation. In this respect the case at bar differs from the trust involved in *Budlong's Estate*, 7 T.C. 758, where the court held that [2036(a)(2)] was applicable to the unlimited power of the decedent, as sole trustee, to distribute the trust income or to accumulate and add it to the principal. In the Jennings trusts the rights of the beneficiaries were no more affected by the settlor's death in October 1936 than they would have been had he resigned as a trustee in January 1936. In either event the contingent power of the trustees to invade corpus or to disburse the net income of 1936 or any subsequent year would remain the same as before his death or resignation. Only when the interest of some beneficiary is enlarged or matured by the decedent's death, is Sec. [2036(a)(2)] applicable, in our opinion. In the case at bar the decedent's death had no such effect.

The judgment is reversed and the cause remanded with directions to enter judgment for the plaintiffs.

———

The *ascertainable standard* concept applies to §§ 2036(a)(2) and 2038. If a grantor's exercise of the power is subject to an ascertainable standard, the retained power is regarded as part of the terms of the trust instrument, rather than as a power to exercise any independent discretion. This assumes that the ascertainable standard provides sufficient guidance for a state court to enforce the rights of the trust beneficiary. The presence of ascertainable standards prevents trust assets from being taxed in the grantor's estate under § 2036(a)(2). The standard negates the concept of a *power*. Furthermore, because an ascertainable standard inherently puts conditions on the exercise of powers, it also protects the grantor's estate from the operation of § 2038. In developing a rationale for the ascertainable standard exception, one commentator stated that where the grantor's powers

> [t]o designate the enjoyment of the property interests or to [alter, amend, revoke, or terminate] such interests are . . . controlled by an external standard, and thus the duties are enforceable in a court of equity, the property so transferred is not includable in the [settlor-trustee's] gross estate when he dies. The reasoning supporting the doctrine is entirely consistent with the policy underlying Sections 2036(a)(2) and 2038. The rationale previously stated for Sections 2036(a)(2) and 2038 is that since retention of powers over the interest transferred is equivalent to retention of the interest itself, they should be taxed as such. If, however, such powers over the

interest are not freely exercisable by the transferor but are in effect limited ministerial duties enforceable in an equity court, such powers are not equivalent to holding the interest itself and should not require inclusion of the property in the transferor's estate at death.

Note, *The Doctrine of External Standards Under Sections 2036(a)(2) and 2038,* 52 MINN. L. REV. 1071, 1078–79 (1968).

Considerable litigation surrounds the ascertainable standard gloss used by federal courts. Although a federal court will decide the issue of the sufficiency of the ascertainable standard, the standard must be enforceable in a state court which would "compel compliance by the trustee on the happening of the specified contingency or to restrain the threatened action if the condition were not fulfilled." *Jennings v. Smith*, 161 F.2d 74, 77 (2d Cir. 1947) (reproduced *supra*). The power to invade the trust property for the life income beneficiary to the extent "necessary to suitably maintain her in as much comfort as she now enjoys" was held to create a standard for invasion that is "fixed in fact and capable of being stated in definite terms of money." *Ithaca Trust Co. v. United States*, 279 U.S. 151, 154 (1929). An ascertainable standard exists if words such as *comfort, support, maintenance, welfare, care, well-being, need, necessity, education,* or *living expenses* are used. *See also Estate of Budd v. Commissioner*, 49 T.C. 468 (1968) (stating that the grantor-trustee had the power to invade the trust principal for the beneficiary in the event of "sickness, accident, misfortune or other emergency"). *See, e.g., Leopold v. United States*, 510 F.2d 617 (9th Cir. 1975) ("support, education, maintenance and general welfare"); *Estate of Wier v. Commissioner*, 17 T.C. 409 (1951), *acq.* 1952–1 C.B. 4, *partially withdrawn on other point*, 1966–2 C.B. 8) ("education, maintenance and support"). These words may be modified by adjectives, such as *proper, reasonable, necessary, comfortable,* or *appropriate*. Furthermore, the trust instrument need not expressly refer to the beneficiary's customary standard of living.

A power to change beneficial interests for a beneficiary's *happiness, pleasure,* or *enjoyment* introduces elements of speculation too large to be overcome. Such a power is probably not subject to an ascertainable standard. *See also Estate of Yawkey v. Commissioner*, 12 T.C. 1164 (1949), *acq.*, 1949–2 C.B. 3 (stating that the power to use income or invade principal for the "best interests" of the beneficiary was insufficiently limited). *See, e.g., Merchants Nat'l Bank v. Commissioner*, 320 U.S. 256 (1943).

Consider, however, *United States v. Powell*, 307 F.2d 821 (10th Cir. 1962), in which the court, in construing a power held by the grantor-cotrustee to invade trust principal "for the maintenance, welfare, comfort or happiness of the Grantor's wife, . . . or Grantor's daughter," concluded (307 F.2d at 828):

> We are of the opinion that the word "happiness," in the sense it is used in the trust instrument, is synonymous with "welfare" and "comfort."

> It is well settled that the words "welfare" and "comfort" provide an ascertainable and judicially enforceable external standard.

We conclude that the provisions in the trust instrument giving the trustees power to use the corpus "for the maintenance, welfare, comfort or happiness" of the beneficiaries and for the "education" of the daughters, the remaindermen, "provided . . . the purpose for which the payments are to be made, justifies the reduction in" the corpus, established an ascertainable, external and judicially enforceable standard and that the trustees, in exercising such power, were limited by such standard and the supervision and control of the courts of Kansas in the exercise of their equity powers.

Hence, the authority given the trustees to invade the corpus did not give to the settlor power to alter or amend the trust, within the meaning of [§ 2038(a)(2)].

[3] Joint Powers

As was true with joint powers of revocation, retained dispositive powers that are exercisable only with the consent of an adverse party are not clearly excused from the operation of §§ 2036 and 2038. Both sections expressly apply to powers exercisable in conjunction "with any other person," although this broad language undoubtedly should be limited in the case of a power exercisable only with the consent of all beneficiaries. *See Helvering v. Helmholz*, 296 U.S. 93 (1935) (discussed in § 8.01[B][4], *supra*).

[C] Generation-Skipping Transfer Tax

The GST tax consequences of retained powers vary depending on the type of power retained. For example, an immediate direct skip of an income interest cannot occur if the transferor retains a power to modify that interest because a completed gift has not occurred. Presumably, a direct skip will occur on the distribution of income to a skip person.

Section 2642(f) may also apply when a transferor retains a dispositive power. For example, if grandparent creates a trust for grandchild for ten years, remainder to great-grandchild, and grandparent retains a power to change the income beneficiary, an inclusion ratio cannot be immediately established for the transfer. The trust would be includable in the grandparent's gross estate if he died immediately after creation and § 2642(f) does not permit an effective allocation of GST exemption until the estate tax inclusion period (ETIP) has ended. The establishment of an inclusion ratio should be possible for actual distribution of trust income.

Problem

Grandmother creates a trust. The income is payable to her grandson for ten years and the remainder is payable to her granddaughter. Grandmother retains the power to change the remainder beneficiary. What are the GST tax ramifications of the trust?

[D]   Income Tax

Code: § 674.

Regulations: Treas. Reg. § 1.674.

Section 674(a) expressly provides that a grantor is treated as the owner of any portion of a trust to the extent that he can make any change in the beneficial enjoyment of the corpus or the income by exercise of a power of disposition. Section 674 focuses on trusts that cannot directly benefit the grantor. The section addresses the grantor's ability to alter a beneficiary's enjoyment. Thus, if the grantor reserves the right to name new beneficiaries, either as to income or corpus, the income of the trust is taxed to the grantor. The section also covers powers to shift economic benefits between beneficiaries. Thus, the section applies if the grantor reserves the power to distribute corpus to the income beneficiary, accumulate and add it to corpus, or sprinkle it among a class of beneficiaries. This is assuming that different recipients could benefit from the exercise or nonexercise of the power.

Carson v. Commissioner

92 T.C. 1134

Nims, Chief Judge:

FINDINGS OF FACT

. . .

On June 30, 1981, petitioners, as co-owners, transferred the real property, furnishings and equipment used in Dr. Carson's dental practice to the trustee. On June 30, 1981, Jean Carson as trustee and Dr. Carson as President of John M. Carson, D.D.S., Inc., executed a lease agreement whereby John M. Carson, D.D.S., Inc., leased the real property from the trust.

. . .

The trustee received the lease payments and deposited them in the trust's checking account. After depositing the lease payments, the trustee disbursed the trust's net income under the terms of the trust agreement, which stated in part:

Net Income of Trust

1. During the term of this Trust, the Trustee shall pay to or apply for the benefit of . . . [the] children of the Trustor, all of the net income of the Trust Estate, in monthly or other convenient installments, in no event less than annually, until they die or this Trust shall terminate, as hereinafter set forth, whichever shall first occur . . . .

Termination of Trust

2. On the death of both of the beneficiaries, if there are no issue of the beneficiaries, or on the expiration of ten (10) years and one (1) month after

the date of this declaration, whichever first occurs, this Trust shall terminate and all the Trust Estate . . . shall [be] . . . transferred, conveyed, and delivered in fee to the Trustor.

[For the tax years in question, the Trustee made unequal distributions to the Trustor's children.]

Jean Carson, as trustee, filed the trust's fiduciary income tax returns (Form 1041) for the trust's fiscal years ending in 1982, 1983 and 1984. Petitioners did not report any of the trust income as taxable income on their joint returns for the taxable years at issue. In the statutory notice of deficiency respondent determined that all of the trust income was taxable to petitioners.

OPINION

. . .

Section 674(a) codifies a line of cases arising out of the Supreme Court's decision in *Helvering v. Clifford*, 309 U.S. 331 (1940). H. Rept. 1337, 83d Cong., 2d Sess., 63–64 (1954); S. Rept. 1622, 83d Cong., 2d Sess., 86–87 (1954). These cases establish, among other things, that if a grantor retains the power to "spray" or "sprinkle" income unevenly between members of a class of beneficiaries he then has the power to dispose of the beneficial enjoyment of the trust income. *Stockstrom v. Commissioner*, 148 F.2d 491, 493–495 (8th Cir. 1945), *revg.* and *affg. in part* 3 T.C. 255 (1944). *Commissioner v. Buck*, 120 F.2d 775 (2d Cir. 1941), *revg.* and *affg. in part* 41 B.T.A. 99 (1940); *Corning v. Commissioner*, 24 T.C. 907 (1955), *affd. per curiam* 239 F.2d 646 (6th Cir. 1956). The power to sprinkle income allows the grantor to control the beneficial enjoyment of trust income so that under section 674(a) he then is treated as owning that portion of trust income over which he retained the sprinkling power. Such income thereby becomes taxable to the grantor. *Commissioner v. Buck*, *supra* at 777–778; *Corning v. Commissioner*, *supra* at 913; *see also* section 1.674(a)–1(b)(3), Income Tax Regs.

The issue here is whether Jean Carson, as grantor, retained the power to sprinkle trust income between the beneficiaries. (If we find that she retained a sprinkling power, then her co-grantor and spouse, Dr. Carson, will also be deemed to have retained such a power under section 672(e).)

Petitioners do not argue that any of the statutory exceptions to the general rule of section 674(a) apply here. *See* sections 674(b), (c) and (d); *see also* sections 1.674(b)-1, 1.674(c)-1 and 1.674(d)-1, Income Tax Regs. Instead, petitioners assert that Jean Carson did not retain a sprinkling power because petitioners as grantors did not intend for her, as trustee, necessarily to equalize income distributions annually, but did so intend for her to do so cumulatively over the entire term of the trust. Alternatively, petitioners assert that the trustee was legally obligated to equalize distributions so any unequal distributions merely constituted misadministration of the trust. *See Bennett v. Commissioner*, 79 T.C. 470 (1982).

In his brief respondent contends that the unequal distributions in the trust's fiscal years 1983 and 1984 indicate "that Mrs. Carson as grantor and a nonadverse party with respect to Carson, retained the power to sprinkle income among the beneficiaries of [the] trust and that the retention of such power is violative of section 674(a)." We agree with respondent.

Jean Carson testified that "the boys [*i.e.,* her sons] would always tell [her] what amount they needed," and she would then distribute income on the basis of need. The record supports her testimony . . . .

While she made roughly equal distributions to or on behalf of her sons in 1982, she distributed income unequally in 1983 and 1984. The unequal distributions indicate that as a grantor she believed that she had retained the power to sprinkle income in those fiscal years.

Petitioners testified that although distributions were unequal in 1983 and 1984, it was their intent as grantors to equalize distributions over the 10-year and one-month term of the trust. We find their intent, which we note was not expressed in the trust agreement, to be irrelevant here. Section 674(a) requires the taxation of trust income to grantors when they retain the power to sprinkle income—regardless of whether they choose to exercise such power. *Stockstrom v. Commissioner, supra* at 493–495. To determine the proper period for analyzing whether a grantor retained a sprinkling power, we look to the terms of the trust agreement. These specifically require that all net trust income would be distributed "in no event less than annually."

Petitioners argue in the alternative that although one of the grantors may have exercised a sprinkling power as trustee, she did not legally possess such a power under the trust agreement and therefore she misadministered the trust by making unequal distributions in 1983 and 1984. *See Bennett v. Commissioner, supra* at 486–488. To determine whether the trustee breached her fiduciary duty, we look to the relevant trust provision (paragraph 1, Net Income of Trust, *supra*). Petitioners assert that the language "in the same proportion . . . as would have been done for the benefit of the beneficiary" creates an implied duty to equalize distributions. We do not agree. The trust agreement does not specify the beneficiaries' income proportions.

We note that in the critical dispositive language of section 1 of the trust agreement, there is conspicuously absent the word "equal" as a modifier of the "monthly or other convenient installments" of income distribution requirement. Thus, the language in the trust agreement does not limit the trustee's discretion in dividing distributions between the two beneficiaries. Although not expressly granting the trustee full discretionary powers, the only restriction imposed on her by the trust provision is that all net trust income has to be paid to or applied for the benefit of both beneficiaries at least annually.

In *Bennett v. Commissioner, supra* at 487, we held that "The grantor-trustees' misadministration of the trust is not the equivalent of the authority to dispose of the beneficial enjoyment of the trust income [under section 674(a)]." But here, as we have held, the administration of the trust (as regards unequal income distributions) by a grantor-trustee was consistent with the terms of the trust, so there could have been no misadministration on that score.

Next, we must decide over what "portion" the sprinkling power was retained. Petitioners assert that, if Jean Carson did retain a sprinkling power, she did not retain a sprinkling power over all of the trust income but only over the excess portion of trust income which was actually sprinkled. Petitioners note that the beneficiaries both received $6,640 during 1983, with an excess of $2,425 being paid to Jon. Petitioners further note that during 1984 both beneficiaries received $4,564 with an excess of $4,806 being paid to Derrick. Thus, petitioners contend that because the trustee exceeded making equal distributions by $2,425 and $4,806 in 1983 and 1984, respectively, the trustee retained the power to sprinkle only the $2,425 and $4,806 portions of trust income. Respondent asserts that the trustee retained a sprinkling power over all of the trust income and as such all of the trust income should be taxable to petitioners as grantors under section 674(a). We agree with respondent. As we have held, petitioners retained the power to sprinkle all of the trust income, not just the $2,425 and $4,806 excess portions.

. . .

————

Section 674(c) permits broader discretionary powers to be held by the trustee(s) without invoking grantor trust treatment, but the grantor has less freedom in choosing the trustee(s). Specifically, powers may be given to: distribute, apportion, or accumulate income, or pay principal to or for an existing beneficiary, beneficiaries, or within a class of beneficiaries. The trustee may not only accumulate income or distribute trust principal, but may also decide which individual or individuals from among a group of beneficiaries will receive the income or principal, in what proportions, and when. For example, the trustees may be given discretion to sprinkle income and corpus among all beneficiaries. The powers need not be subject to any standards, but the addition of beneficiaries is not permitted, except as to after-born or after-adopted children.

Section 674(c) excludes the grantor or the grantor's spouse as possible trustees, and requires that at least one-half of the trustees be independent trustees. Independent trustees are trustees who are not related, or subordinate, to the grantor and who are not subservient to the grantor's wishes or the wishes of the grantor's spouse. Related and subordinate parties are defined in § 672(c). Section 674(c) is based on the premise that an independent trustee is subject to a fiduciary duty to act in the best interests of the beneficiaries.

Under § 674(d), a grantor's close relative (excluding the grantor's spouse who is living with the grantor) or employee can serve as trustee and be given discretionary power to distribute, apportion, allocate, or accumulate income (but not principal) to or for an existing beneficiary, beneficiaries, or within a class of beneficiaries, including the remainderman, if the power is limited by a reasonably definite standard set forth in the trust instrument. Thus, a grantor can create a *sprinkle* trust in which the income can be shifted from one beneficiary to another as long as the power is limited by an approved standard. A reasonably definite standard is addressed in Treasury Regulation § 1.674(b)–1(b)(5). The trustee may be a related or subordinate party, but no one, including the grantor, can have a power to veto the trustee's exercise of discretion. Again, the trustee cannot add new beneficiaries.

Estate of Goodwyn v. Commissioner

T.C. Memo 1976-238

Quealy, Judge:

. . .

OPINION

Trusts created by Hilton W. Goodwyn

By deed dated January 9, 1943, the decedent caused to be transferred certain real properties to himself and N. B. Goodwyn, his brother, as trustees, to be held for the use and benefit of his three sons. By deed dated January 4, 1944, certain additional properties were transferred to the decedent and his brother, as trustees, for the same purposes. Subsequently, the decedent resigned as trustee, causing Lloyd M. Richards and Charles C. Russell, attorneys at law, to be appointed as trustees. Notwithstanding any lapses in their original appointments, it is admitted that as of the date of death of the decedent Richards and Russell were, and for some years prior thereto, had been trustees in name, if not in fact, of these trusts.

Similarly, by deed dated June 8, 1943, the decedent caused to be transferred to Hallie M. Goodwyn, his wife, and N. B. Goodwyn, his brother, certain real properties to be held in trust for the use and benefit of other members of the family. By deed dated January 4, 1944, additional real properties were transferred to said trustees for the same purposes. Upon the death of N. B. Goodwyn, and the resignation of Hallie M. Goodwyn, as trustee, Richards and Russell likewise became trustees in name, if not in fact, of these trusts and were so acting upon the death of the decedent.

Under the terms of the deeds creating these trusts, the trustees were granted broad discretionary powers with respect to both the distribution of income to the beneficiaries and the investment and management of the corpus of the trusts. Notwithstanding the designation of Richards and Russell as trustees, it further appears that at all times from the establishment of the trusts until his last illness, with the acquiescence of the trustees, the decedent made all decisions with respect to the purchase and sale of trust assets and the investment of any proceeds and determined the amounts, if any, to be distributed to the respective beneficiaries.

There is no question that Goodwyn created legally valid trusts under state law. The provisions of these trust instruments, including those regarding the rights, duties and obligations of the trustees demonstrate the grantor's intent to relinquish the ownership of the involved assets. Although many of the beneficiaries were unaware of the existence of these trusts, such notice is not a requirement for a valid trust.

Regarding the effect of the Federal income tax laws on these trusts, it is not contended here that the decedent reserved any right or power in any of the trusts whereby the income of these trusts could be attributed to the grantor. Additionally, it is clear that during the years in issue the trustees were not related or subordinate parties within the definition of 672(c) whose discretionary power to distribute or accumulate income to beneficiaries would attribute the income to the grantor. Rather, these trustees were independent trustees within the meaning of section 674(c), who may have such a discretionary power over income.

While the record indicates that the legal formalities have been complied with, it also indicates that the designated "independent" trustees whether by agreement or otherwise, entrusted the management of the trusts' assets and the distribution of income therefrom to the sole discretion of the decedent. The decedent kept all the records, made all of the investments and decided the amount to be distributed to beneficiaries. The trustees merely acquiesced in these actions.

On the basis of these facts, the judicial decisions following the Supreme Court's decision in *Helvering v. Clifford*, 309 U.S. 331 (1940), and the later so-called *Clifford* regulations might well warrant the attribution of the income from these trusts to the decedent. However, to the extent these previous principles are not embodied in the present statutory provisions of the Code, they must be considered no longer applicable. Section 671 provides that subpart E represents the sole criterion of dominion and control under section 61 (relating to the definition of gross income) and thereby also under the *Clifford* doctrine.

The Report of the Committee on Ways and Means on the Internal Revenue Code of 1954 explains clearly that this exclusivity was the intent of Congress:

> It is also provided in this section (671) that no items of a trust shall be included in computing the income or credits of the grantor (or another person solely on the grounds of his dominion and control over the trust under the provisions of section 61 (corresponding to sec. 22(a) of existing law). The effect of this provision is to insure that taxability of *Clifford* type trusts shall be governed solely by this subpart. However, this provision does not affect the principles governing the taxability of income to a grantor or assignor other than by reason of his dominion and control over the trust. Thus, this subpart has no application in situations involving assignments of future income to the assignor, as in *Lucas v. Earl* (281 U.S. 111), *Harrison v. Schaffner* (312 U.S. 579), and *Helvering v. Horst* (311 U.S. 112), whether or not the assignment is to a trust; nor are the rules as to family partnerships affected by this subpart.

Consequently, in order for a grantor to be held taxable pursuant to subpart E on the income of a trust which he has established, he must have one of the powers or retained interests proscribed by subpart E.

The grantor's power to control beneficial enjoyment of either the principal or the income, within the limits defined in section 674, would result in attribution of the income to the grantor.

. . .

Although the trustees here would not be adverse parties, section 674(c) excepts the application of the general rule in certain circumstances which are applicable here.

Respondent would concede that none of the provisions of the trusts in issue would give the decedent the power proscribed by this section. It is respondent's argument, however, that although grantor does not specifically have such a power, his relationship to the trust res through its management and to the administration of these trusts generally is such that he should be deemed to be a trustee, in fact, during his life. Being considered a trustee, the trustee's power under the trust agreement to distribute or accumulate the income from these trusts would then make such income attributable to him under subpart E.

Respondent's contention in this respect is similar to that respondent raised in the *Estate of Hilton W. Goodwyn, supra.* As relevant here, respondent argued in that case that the decedent should be treated as trustee, in fact, possessing such rights and powers as to cause the inclusion of the assets thereof in his gross estate under section 2036(a)(2). That section requires the inclusion in decedent's gross estate any property for which the decedent has retained the right, either alone or in conjunction with any person, to designate the persons who shall possess or enjoy the property or the income therefrom.

We found in that case there was no basis for such inclusion. The Supreme Court has held in *United States v. Byrum*, 408 U.S. 125, 136–7 (1972), that the right, upon which the inclusion under section 2036(a)(2) is predicated, is "an ascertainable and legally enforceable power," reserved in the trust instrument or by some other means. *See also Estate of Charles Gilman*, 65 T.C. 296, 316 (1975), on appeal (2d Cir., February 6, 1976). We found that Goodwyn had not retained such a right in the case of the Richards and Russell Trusts of which he was grantor.

In this case, while a different test is applicable, the tests are similar in character. Where section 2036(a) uses the term "right," section 674 uses the term "power." The House Ways and Means Committee Report, cited *supra*, in its explanation of this section uses the term power in the legal sense of having an enforceable authority or right to perform some action. The use of this term in this legal sense suggests that the power of a grantor upon which he will be taxed is a power reserved by instrument or contract creating an ascertainable and legally enforceable right, not merely the persuasive control which he might exercise over an independent trustee who is receptive to his wishes. Such interpretation is also, we believe, indicated by the holding in the *Byrum* case.

In this case, the trustees in question accepted the rights, duties and obligations granted them in the trust instruments. Regardless of the fact they had entrusted to the decedent the complete management and control of these trusts, this informal delegation did not discharge them from the legal responsibility they had as the trustees. As a matter of law, the trustees were liable and answerable for the decedent's acts on their behalf. See 2 Scott, TRUSTS 1388, 1391 (3rd ed., 1967); 3 Scott, TRUSTS 1794 (3rd ed., 1967). There is nothing in the record to show that the trustees could not have undertaken exclusive control of the trust res if they had elected to do so. Whatever power Goodwyn exercised over the trust assets, administration or distribution, he did so on the trustee's behalf and not in his own right. Because of Goodwyn's failure to have a legally enforceable right, we have already held, following

Byrum, that the assets of these trusts were not includable in the decedent's estate under 2036(a)(2). Since a similar legal right or power is a prerequisite under section 674(a), consistency appears to require the same decision with respect to the applicability of this section. We see no other possible decision.

Section 671 precludes attributing the income to Goodwyn on any other theory of dominion and control under the definition of gross income, including the *Clifford* doctrine. We interpret this limitation to mean that if Goodwyn cannot be considered as a trustee, in fact, under the statutory provisions of subpart E, he cannot be considered as such by virtue of the judicial doctrines arising from the *Clifford* case which Congress intended to limit through the enactment of subpart E. But the protection of section 671, as explained in the House Ways and Means Committee Report, cited *supra*, does not extend to situations involving the assignments of future income.

––––––

In summary, § 674(d) permits dispositive powers, limited by a standard to be held by a wide range of trustees. Section 674(c) allows even broader powers to be held by independent trustees.

Furthermore, under § 674(b), § 674(a) does not apply to a variety of situations in which a grantor wants to retain a discretionary power. A retained power to use income for the support of dependents is not taxed, unless it is, in fact, exercised to provide support. *See* § 674(b)(1). Remote contingent powers (powers over less than 5 percent future interests) are immune. *See* § 674(b)(2). These exceptions are intended to correlate § 674(a) with §§ 677 and 673 so that § 674 does not result in tax consequences to the grantor if the grantor would not be taxed under the latter two sections. The remaining exceptions in § 674(b) raise true exceptions. A retained testamentary power to name additional corpus beneficiaries is excepted by § 674(b)(3), and a power to distribute income to a minor under 21 (or a legally disabled person) or accumulate it for a corpus beneficiary is excepted under § 674(b)(7). Powers to choose between charitable beneficiaries are exempt under § 674(b)(4). Powers to invade corpus for any existing beneficiary which are limited by an ascertainable standard are acceptable under § 674(b)(5)(A). The scope of the standards is described in Treasury Regulation § 1.674(b)–1(b)(5)(i). Accumulation powers may be retained if the accumulated income must be paid to the income beneficiary, his estate, or his appointees (§ 674(b)(6)(A)), or to previously defined income beneficiaries on termination of the trust. However, the power cannot be used to shift accumulated income to a remainderman. Finally, the power to allocate receipts and disbursements between income and corpus pursuant to state law is exempt under § 674(b)(8). The powers a grantor may retain under § 674(b) over the beneficial enjoyment of a trust, without triggering trust status, is analyzed in Frank R. Fink, *Grantor May Have Powers Over Trust, Yet Not Be Subject to Tax*, 19 Est. Plan. 232 (1992).

According to Treasury Regulation § 1.674(a)–1(a), § 674 reaches "every case in which [the grantor] or a nonadverse party can affect the beneficial enjoyment of a portion of a trust." Thus, it does not apply to powers that require the consent of an adverse party.

Problems

1. *S* transfers $1 million to an irrevocable trust. The income is payable to *A* for ten years. At the end of ten years, the corpus is to be distributed to *B*. *S*, as the sole trustee, reserves the power to substitute *C* as income beneficiary. Assume that *S* is not related to either *A* or *B*; alternatively, assume that *S* is the father of both.

   a. What are the gift tax consequences of this transfer on:

   i. the creation of the trust if the applicable interest rate under § 7520 is 8%, and

   ii. the distribution in the current year of $80,000 to *A*? Consider §§ 2501, 2512, 2503, 2505, and Treas. Reg. §§ 25.2511–2 and 25.2512–5(f).

Alternatively, assume that *S* is *A*'s father, then *B*'s father and then *C*'s father. Consider § 2702.

   b. What are the estate tax consequences assuming *S* dies (i) two years, or (ii) four years after creating the trust, and that, at his death, the value of the trust property is $2 million? Assume that all income from the trust is currently distributed. Consider §§ 2036(a)(2), 2038, and 2035(b), and Treasury Regulations §§ 20.2036–1(a) and (b) and 20.2038–1(a).

   c. What are the income tax consequences of the trust? Consider §§ 674 and 676(a)?

   d. In creating the trust would you have recommended that *S*, as grantor-trustee, retain the power to substitute *C* as beneficiary if limited by an ascertainable standard? Consider Treasury Regulation § 25.2511–1(c), –1(g)(2) and (3), and *Jennings v. Smith*. What are the income tax consequences of such an approach? Consider § 674(b) and (d).

   e. Should another trustee, not *S*, have been given the power to substitute *C* as beneficiary? Consider Treasury Regulations §§ 20.2036–1(b)(3), 20.2038–1(a), 25.2511–2(c), –2(f). What are the income tax consequences of such an approach? Consider § 674(c).

2. *S*, age 60, transfers $1 million to a trust. The income is payable to *W*, his wife, for life and the remainder is distributable to *C*, his child. *S* retains the power to accumulate the trust income and add it to corpus.

   a. What are the gift tax consequences on the creation of the trust and the payment of income to *W* if the § 7520 rate is 8%?

   b. What are the income tax consequences?

   c. What are the estate tax consequences if *S* predeceases *W*?

3. Assume in Problem 2 that *S* exercises the power to accumulate income, and accumulates $100,000 of income.

   a. What are the gift tax consequences if the § 7520 rate is 8%?

   b. What are the estate tax consequences if the § 7520 rate is 8%? Would it make a difference if *S* holds the power to accumulate as trustee?

4. *D* declares himself trustee of a $1 million irrevocable trust. The income is payable to *A* and *C* in equal shares for 20 years and the remainder is

distributable to *E*. *A* and *C* are *D*'s children. *D* dies during the 20-year term. What would be the gift, income, and estate tax consequences of the trust, assuming that the § 7520 rate is 8% and:

    a. The facts as given?

    b. That the trustee has the power to sprinkle income between *A* and *C*, if their health and educational needs mandate?

    c. That the trustee has the power to invade the trust corpus for the health or educational needs of *A* or *C*?

    d. That the trustee has the power to add additional income beneficiaries?

  5. Assume the facts in Problem 4. What would be the results if:

    a. There is an independent trustee, rather than *D*?

    b. The trustees were *D*'s ex-spouse and current spouse?

    c. The trustees were *D*'s spouse and father?

    d. The trustees were a bank, *D*'s attorney, and *D*?

  6. Should the reciprocal trust doctrine apply if the grantors have no interests in the trusts, but have powers that would invoke §§ 2036 or 2038 if the powers had been retained by the grantor? *See Estate of Grace, Swanson,* and the discussion of reciprocal trusts in Chapter 7, § 7.01[B][6], *supra. Compare Estate of Green v. United States,* 68 F.3d 151 (6th Cir. 1995) (no), *with Estate of Bischoff v. Commissioner,* 69 T.C. 32 (1977) (yes).

§ 9.02   Powers to Change Time or Manner of Enjoyment of Beneficial Interests

  Not all retained dispositive powers allow the grantor to control who enjoys the interest or the extent of the interest. Some are limited to determining when the holder of the interest may possess and enjoy it. This section investigates the tax ramifications of retaining these dispositive powers.

[A] Gift Tax

Code: § 2511.

Regulations: Treas. Reg. § 25.2511–2(d).

  The retention of a power merely to affect time or manner of enjoyment of property does not make a transfer incomplete for gift tax purposes. *See* Treas. Reg. § 25.2511–2(d). Thus, in an irrevocable trust created for a single beneficiary, the retention of the power to terminate the trust, or to accumulate income for future distribution to the sole beneficiary, would not delay gift taxation of the transfer to the trust. Furthermore, termination of that power would not constitute a gift, so that the income or corpus from the trust could be paid to the beneficiary without further gift tax exposure. In effect, a completed gift of the income interest occurs when the trust is established, even though the grantor retains the power to accumulate the income.

  If, of course, the power is apparently one that alters the time or manner of enjoyment, but in reality can change beneficial interests, its retention causes the transfer of those interests that are subject to the power to be incomplete for gift tax purposes.[4] Thus, if a grantor places property in trust for 20 years, directing that the income be paid to A, with corpus payable to A if he is alive when the trust terminates, and if not, to A's heirs, and retains the power to accumulate income, the gift of the income interest is incomplete to the extent that A might not live 20 years. The power could be used to deny A the ultimate right to the income.

[B]   Estate Tax

Code: §§ 2036(a)(2) and 2038.

Regulations: Treas. Reg. §§ 20.2036–1 and 20.2038–1(a).

Lober v. United States

346 U.S. 335 (1953)

Mr. Justice Black delivered the opinion of the Court.

This is an action for an estate tax refund brought by the executors of the estate of Morris Lober. In 1924 he signed an instrument conveying to himself as trustee money and stocks for the benefit of his young son. In 1929 he executed two other instruments, one for the benefit of a daughter, the other for a second son. The terms of these three instruments were the same. Lober was to handle the funds, invest and reinvest them as he deemed proper. He could accumulate and reinvest the income with the same freedom until his children reached twenty-one years of age. When twenty-one they were to be paid the accumulated income. Lober could hold the principal of each trust until the beneficiary reached twenty-five. In case he died his wife was to be trustee with the same broad powers Lober had conveyed to himself. The trusts were declared to be irrevocable, and as the case reaches us we may assume that the trust instruments gave Lober's children a "vested interest" under state law, so that if they had died after creation of the trusts their interests would have passed to their estates. A crucial term of the trust instruments was that Lober could at any time he saw fit turn all or any part of the principal of the trusts over to his children. Thus he could at will reduce the principal or pay it all to the beneficiaries, thereby terminating any trusteeship over it.

Lober died in 1942. By that time the trust property was valued at more than $125,000. The Internal Revenue Commissioner treated this as Lober's property and included it in his gross estate. That inclusion brought this lawsuit. The Commissioner relied on [§ 2038] of the Internal Revenue Code . . . . That section, so far as material here, required inclusion in a decedent's gross estate of the value of all property that the decedent had previously transferred by trust "where the enjoyment thereof was subject at the date of his death to any change through the exercise of a power . . . to alter, amend, or revoke . . . ." In *Commissioner v. Holmes*, 326 U.S. 480, we held that power to terminate was the equivalent of power to "alter, amend, or revoke" it, and we approved taxation of the Holmes estate on that basis. Relying on the

---

[4] *See* Treas. Reg. § 25.2511–2(c).

Holmes case, the Court of Claims upheld inclusion of these trust properties in Lober's estate. 124 Ct. Cl. 44, 108 F. Supp. 731. This was done despite the assumption that the trust conveyances gave the Lober children an indefeasible "vested interest" in the properties conveyed. The Fifth Circuit Court of Appeals had reached a contrary result where the circumstances were substantially the same, in *Hays' Estate v. Commissioner*, 181 F.2d 169, 172–174. Because of this conflict, we granted certiorari. 345 U.S. 969.

Petitioners stress a factual difference between this and the *Holmes* case. The Holmes trust instrument provided that if a beneficiary died before expiration of the trust his children succeeded to his interest, but if he died without children, his interest would pass to his brothers or their children. Thus the trustee had power to eliminate a contingency that might have prevented passage of a beneficiary's interest to his heirs. Here we assume that upon death of the Lober beneficiaries their part in the trust estate would, under New York law, pass to their heirs. But we cannot agree that this difference should change the *Holmes* result.

We pointed out in the *Holmes* case that [§ 2038] was more concerned with "present economic benefit" than with "technical vesting of title or estates." And the Lober beneficiaries, like the Holmes beneficiaries, were granted no "present right to immediate enjoyment of either income or principal." The trust instrument here gave none of Lober's children full "enjoyment" of the trust property, whether it "vested" in them or not. To get this full enjoyment they had to wait until they reached the age of twenty-five unless their father sooner gave them the money and stocks by terminating the trust under the power of change he kept to the very date of his death. This father could have given property to his children without reserving in himself any power to change the terms as to the date his gift would be wholly effective, but he did not. What we said in the *Holmes* case fits this situation too: "A donor who keeps so strong a hold over the actual and immediate enjoyment of what he puts beyond his own power to retake has not divested himself of that degree of control which [§ 2038] requires in order to avoid the tax." *Commissioner v. Holmes, supra,* at 487.

Affirmed.

Mr. Justice Douglas and Mr. Justice Jackson dissent.

———

The transfer in *Lober* occurred before the forerunner of § 2036(a)(2) was enacted and thus, it was not considered by the Court.

A retained power to determine the time or manner of enjoyment can result in property being taxed to the grantor's estate under both §§ 2036(a)(2) and 2038. As indicated in *Lober*, § 2038 clearly applies to powers that affect time or manner of enjoyment. Moreover, § 2038 is not limited to powers over corpus. A power to accumulate income would also be a § 2038 power, as would virtually any power which could determine when the beneficiary would receive corpus or income of a trust and which was not limited by an ascertainable standard.

The language of § 2038, including powers to alter, amend, revoke, or terminate, is broadly inclusive. First, note that reference to powers to *terminate* trusts was added to § 2038 in 1936, and thus applies only to transfers made after June 22, 1936. *See* § 2038(a)(1). Given the result in *Lober*, however, this distinction may be practically meaningless. The power to invade corpus in *Lober* was equivalent to the power to partially terminate the trust to the extent of the invasion. If such a power constitutes a power to "alter or amend" the trust, as the Court held, then it is difficult to see why a power to terminate the trust would not be equal to a power to "alter or amend" it.

Second, § 2036(a)(2) applies to powers that affect the time or manner of enjoyment of income interests. Most § 2036(a)(2) powers which result in the inclusion of lifetime transfers in the estate of the grantor allow the grantor to shift income to a remainderman, or other individual. Courts have held that § 2036(a)(2) applies even if the income beneficiary is also the remainderman. *See Struthers v. Kelm*, 218 F.2d 810 (8th Cir. 1955); *Estate of Alexander v. Commissioner*, 81 T.C. 757 (1983). In *Alexander*, the decedent created a trust, naming himself as trustee and his nine months old daughter, Louise, as the sole beneficiary. The decedent retained the right, as trustee, to accumulate the trust income as he might *desire*. When Louise reached age 21, she would receive distributions from the trust in $5,000 installments every five years until she reached age 66. At 66, all remaining accumulated income and principal would be paid to Louise. In the event of Louise's prior death, the funds were to be paid to her estate or as she might designate by will. Because the decedent's right as trustee to accumulate income restricted Louise's present enjoyment of income, this constituted "the right . . . to designate the persons who shall possess or enjoy the property or the income therefrom" under § 2036(a)(2).

Struthers was a similar case which relied on *Lober* by implicitly treating the income beneficiary and that beneficiary's successors in interest as separate persons for the purposes of the *who* language in § 2036(a)(2). *Struthers* also requires that the "possession or enjoyment" language of § 2036(a)(2) be interpreted to require actual possession, rather than vesting of a legal right. Such a reading of § 2036(a)(2) seems to downplay the importance of the *who* language of the section. Is that interpretation totally unreasonable?[5] If nothing else, the reading gives a consistent interpretation to the "possession or enjoyment" language of §§ 2036(a)(2) and 2037, which clearly refers to actual possession. Yet, if the court is right, then the likelihood of the income beneficiary surviving to possess or enjoy should be taken into account in determining the value of the interest included in the grantor's estate.

Section 2036(a)(2) is inapplicable to powers which can affect only corpus interests, because those interests are unrelated to the possession or enjoyment of, or the income from, property. *See* Treas. Reg. § 20.2036–1(b)(3).

Application of the two sections to powers that can effect time or manner of enjoyment can be illustrated by assuming that the decedent established a trust in which income was payable to X for 20 years with the corpus then distributable to X. Assume further that the grantor retained the right to

---

[5] *See* RICHARD B. STEPHENS ET AL., FEDERAL ESTATE AND GIFT TAXATION § 4.08[5][c] (7th ed. 1997) (arguing that *Struthers* and *Alexander* were wrongly decided).

invade the trust property, in whole or in part, in favor of X, which would accelerate X's enjoyment of the principal. If the decedent died during the 20-year term, the value of the remainder interest, but not the income interest, is includable under § 2038. X has the right to the income whether or not the grantor exercises the retained right. The grantor lacks the ability to shift income from X, and thus, the right to determine who gets the income. *See* Treas. Reg. § 20.2036–1(b)(3).

Contrast this situation with a trust in which the income is payable to X for 20 years and the principal is then payable to Y. Assume further the grantor retains the right to invade the trust property, in whole or in part, for Y, which would accelerate Y's enjoyment of the principal. In this situation, both §§ 2038 and 2036(a)(2) can apply. Section 2038 applies to the right to invade the whole trust property, because the grantor can modify all interests, either by anticipating Y's enjoyment of the remainder or shifting X's income interest to Y. Furthermore, the latter shifting calls into play § 2036(a)(2). By giving all or part of the trust property to the remainderman, the grantor can divert income from the income beneficiary to the remainderman, thus "designating" who possesses or enjoys it.

Problems

1. D declares himself trustee of an irrevocable trust. Under the trust, income is payable to D's child, C, until C reaches age 30 at which time the trust is distributable to C. The trustee is given the power to invade corpus for C. Answer alternatively assuming that D and X are related, and are not related.

   a. What are the gift and estate tax consequences of the trust, assuming that D dies before C reaches age 30?

   b. How would the results in (a) differ if the trustee was instead given the power to accumulate income?

   c. How would the results in (a) and (b) differ if the respective powers were exercisable only for the health or education of C?

   d. How would the results in (a) and (b) differ if the powers were held by D and a bank as co-trustees?

   e. What would be the tax results if D retained the power to invade the corpus for X?

2. S transfers $1 million in an irrevocable trust, income to Child for 20 years, remainder to grandchild. What are the gift and estate tax consequences if S retains the power to accumulate the income and pay it to Child after 20 years?

[C]   Generation-Skipping Transfer Tax

When the transferor merely retains the power to alter the time or manner of enjoyment, a completed gift occurs and possibly may trigger a direct skip. Nonetheless, § 2642(f)(1) defers a direct skip which occurs on trust creation if the gift would be subject to estate tax, assuming the transferor immediately dies. A taxable distribution will occur if a distribution of income is made to a skip person. In that circumstance, an effective GST exemption may be allocated to exempt taxable termination distribution from tax. *See* Treas. Reg. § 26.2632–1(c)(5), Example 2.

Problem

Grandparent creates a trust, income to grandchild for ten years, remainder to grandchild. Grandparent retains the power to terminate the trust in favor of grandchild. What are the GST tax ramifications of the trust?

[D]   Income Tax

Code: § 674.

Because a power to affect time or manner of enjoyment cannot normally be used to shift income or corpus between beneficiaries, retention of this power will not normally produce adverse income tax consequences to the grantor. A variety of exceptions to § 674(a) lead to this result. First, § 674(b)(6) expressly excepts from the operation of § 674(a) powers to distribute or accumulate income for a beneficiary as long as the income accumulated must pass to the beneficiary, his estate or appointees, or to other irrevocably designated, current income beneficiaries. *See* § 674(b)(6)(A), (b)(6)(B).

Second, under § 674(b)(7), common powers to withhold income during the legal disability of the income beneficiary, or during the period before the income beneficiary reaches age 21, are excepted from § 674(a). Indeed, the effect of such a power may even be to transfer the income accumulated to the corpus beneficiary, as long as no one has the power to add income or corpus beneficiaries to the trust.

Third, under § 674(b)(5), the widely used power to invade corpus for the present enjoyment of the income beneficiary is excepted, as long as a proportionate share of corpus is chargeable against the portion of the trust held for that beneficiary. This is true even if the power can be used to divert corpus from the remainderman to the income beneficiary. *See* Treas. Reg. § 1.674(b)–1(b)(5)(iii), Example 3.

Remember also that joint powers are subject to the adverse interest rules under §§ 674(a) and 672.

Problems

1. *D* creates an irrevocable trust. The income is payable to *A* for 20 years. After 20 years, the corpus is payable to *A*. *D* retains the power to invade the corpus for *A*.

   a. What will be the income tax consequences of this trust? Consider § 674(a) and (b)(5)(B).

   b. Can you suggest a better way of handling the transaction? What if *D* wants to reserve the right to distribute the trust principal to *A* if in *D*'s opinion it will make *A* happy? Consider § 674(b)(5).

§ 9.03 Power to Remove or Appoint a Trustee

Because of the tax costs involved in retaining various powers, it is not uncommon for the grantor to appoint a third party trustee to whom he gives the desired powers. In that case, the grantor may want to retain the power to remove the trustee. This protects the grantor from unjustified reliance on the discretion of the trustee, and allows him to find a new trustee who will act in a manner more consistent with what the grantor considers as the proper operation of the trust. Retention of a removal and replacement power, however, had been under attack until publication of the following ruling.

Revenue Ruling 95–58

1995–2 C.B. 191

The Internal Revenue Service has reconsidered whether a grantor's reservation of an unqualified power to remove a trustee and appoint a new trustee (other than the grantor) is tantamount to a reservation by the grantor of the trustee's discretionary powers of distribution. This issue is presented in Rev. Rul. 79–353, 1979–2 C.B. 325, *as modified by* Rev. Rul. 81–51, 1981–1 C.B. 458. An analogous issue is presented in Rev. Rul. 77–182, 1977–1 C.B. 273. The reconsideration is caused by the recent court decisions in *Estate of Wall v. Commissioner*, 101 T.C. 300 (1993), and *Estate of Vak v. Commissioner*, 973 F.2d 1409 (8th Cir. 1992), *rev'g* T.C. Memo 1991–503.

Section 2036(a) of the Internal Revenue Code, in general, provides that the value of the gross estate includes the value of all property to the extent of any interest in the property that was transferred by the decedent (for less than adequate consideration) if the decedent has retained for life the right, alone or in conjunction with any person, to designate the person who shall possess or enjoy the property or the income therefrom.

Section 2038(a)(1), in general, provides that the value of the gross estate includes the value of all property to the extent of any interest in the property that was transferred by the decedent (for less than adequate consideration) if the decedent held a power, exercisable alone or in conjunction with any person, to change the enjoyment of the property through the exercise of a power to alter, amend, revoke, or terminate.

Section 25.2511–2(c) of the Gift Tax Regulations provides that a gift of property is incomplete to the extent that the donor reserves the power to revest the beneficial title to the property in himself or herself or the power (other than a fiduciary power limited by a fixed or ascertainable standard) to name new beneficiaries or to change the interest of the beneficiaries among themselves. *See also* § 25.2511–2(f).

For purposes of §§ 2036 and 2038, it is immaterial in what capacity the power was exercisable by the decedent. Thus, if a decedent transferred property in trust while retaining, as trustee, the discretionary power to distribute the principal and income, the trust property will be includible in the decedent's gross estate under §§ 2036 and 2038. The regulations under §§ 2036 and 2038 explain that a decedent is regarded as having possessed the powers of a trustee if the decedent possessed an unrestricted power to remove the trustee and appoint anyone (including the decedent) as trustee. Sections 20.2036–1(b)(3) and 20.2038–1(a) of the Estate Tax Regulations.

Rev. Rul. 79–353 concludes that, for purposes of §§ 2036(a)(2) and 2038(a)(1), the reservation by a decedent-settlor of the unrestricted power to remove a corporate trustee and appoint a successor corporate trustee is equivalent to the decedent-settlor's reservation of the trustee's discretionary powers.

Rev. Rul. 81–51 *modifies* Rev. Rul. 79–353 so that it does not apply to a transfer or addition to a trust made before October 29, 1979, the publication date of Rev. Rul. 79–353, if the trust was irrevocable on October 28, 1979.

Rev. Rul. 77–182 concludes that a decedent's power to appoint a successor corporate trustee only in the event of the resignation or removal by judicial process of the original trustee did not amount to a power to remove the original trustee that would have endowed the decedent with the trustee's discretionary control over trust income.

In *Estate of Wall*, the decedent had created a trust for the benefit of others and designated an independent corporate fiduciary as trustee. The trustee possessed broad discretionary powers of distribution. The decedent reserved the right to remove and replace the corporate trustee with another independent corporate trustee. The court concluded that the decedent's retained power was not equivalent to a power to affect the beneficial enjoyment of the trust property as contemplated by §§ 2036 and 2038. *See also Estate of Headrick v. Commissioner*, 93 T.C. 171 (1989), *aff'd* 918 F.2d 1263 (6th Cir. 1990).

In *Estate of Vak*, the decedent had created a trust and appointed family members as the trustees with discretionary powers of distribution. The decedent reserved the right to remove and replace the trustees with successor trustees who were not related or subordinate to the decedent. The decedent was also a discretionary distributee. Three years later, the trust was amended to eliminate both the decedent's power to remove and replace the trustees and the decedent's eligibility to receive discretionary distributions.

The issue considered in *Estate of Vak* was whether the decedent's gift in trust was complete when the decedent created the trust and transferred the property to it or, instead, when the decedent relinquished the removal and replacement power and his eligibility to receive discretionary distributions. The Eighth Circuit concluded that the decedent had not retained dominion and control over the transferred assets by reason of his removal and replacement power. Accordingly, the court held that under § 25.2511–2(c) the gift was complete when the decedent created the trust and transferred the assets to it.

In view of the decisions in the above cases, Rev. Rul. 79–353 and Rev. Rul. 81–51 are revoked. Rev. Rul. 77–182 is modified to hold that even if the decedent had possessed the power to remove the trustee and appoint an individual or corporate successor trustee that was not related or subordinate to the decedent (within the meaning of § 672(c)), the decedent would not have retained a trustee's discretionary control over trust income.

EFFECT ON OTHER DOCUMENTS

Rev. Rul. 79–353 and Rev. Rul. 81–51 are revoked. Rev. Rul. 77–182 is modified.

———

Of course, if the grantor's retained power to remove a trustee includes the power to name the grantor as the successor trustee, § 2036 will apply even if a condition precedent to the exercise of the power exists. *See* Treas. Reg. § 20.2036–1(b)(3). Section 2038 will also apply if no condition precedent exists on the exercise of the power or the condition precedent has been satisfied at the time of the grantor's death. *See* Treas. Reg. § 20.2038–1(b).

Problems

1. *S* created an irrevocable trust. The income is payable to her spouse *H* for his life and the remainder is distributable to *S*'s children. The Lost Trust Company was named as trustee and given the power to terminate the trust by immediate distribution of the corpus to the children. In the trust agreement, *S* retained the power to remove the trustee at any time, and to appoint a successor.

    a. If *S* dies while the trust is in existence without replacing the trustee, will any part of the trust be included in her gross estate? *See* Treas. Reg. § 20.2038–1(a)(3); *Mathey v. United States*, 491 F.2d 481 (3d Cir. 1974).

    b. Would the result be any different if *S*'s power were limited to appointing successors in the event of resignation or disqualification of the trustee? *See Estate of Farrel v. United States*, 553 F.2d 637 (Ct. Cl. 1977) (discussed in § 8.02[B], *supra*).

    c. Would it matter if *S*'s power were limited to replacing the corporate trustee with another corporate trustee?

§ 9.04   Administrative Powers

Powers that are not strictly dispositive are often retained, and may have tax effects. The power to control investments, or the power to allocate receipts between income and principal accounts are typical examples. These powers could be used to minimize current income and inflate the growth of corpus or vice-versa. This section describes the effects of such powers. *See generally* Martin D. Begleiter, *Administrative and Dispositive Powers in Trust and Tax Law: Toward a Realistic Approach*, 36 U. Fla. L. Rev. 957 (1984).

[A] Gift Tax

In general, the retention of administrative powers does not have gift tax consequences because the power holder does not truly have the power to shift beneficial interests, nor the power to affect the value of the interests outside of fiduciary controls. *See, e.g., Chambers v. Commissioner*, 87 T.C. 225 (1986).

If, of course, the powers are so broad as to belie the existence of a fiduciary duty, then they might well negate the existence of any duty at all, and thus, be treated as dispositive powers by the court. That, in turn, would require an analysis of the tax treatment in accord with the principles applicable to dispositive powers.

[B]   Estate Tax

Code: §§ 2036(a)(2), (b), and 2038.

Regulations: None.

Old Colony Trust Co. v. United States

423 F.2d 601 (1st Cir. 1970)

[Decedent established an inter vivos trust, the income of which was payable to his son, with the remainder payable to the son's widow and children. Decedent was a trustee with broad powers to distribute or accumulate income and corpus for the son's *best interests* and with broad administrative powers as described in the opinion. What follows is that portion of the opinion dealing with the administrative powers.]

Aldrich, Chief Judge.

. . .

Article 7 gave broad administrative or management powers to the trustees, with discretion to acquire investments not normally held by trustees, and the right to determine, what was to be charged or credited to income or principal, including stock dividends or deductions for amortization. It further provided that all divisions and decisions made by the trustees in good faith should be conclusive on all parties, and in summary, stated that the trustees were empowered, "generally to do all things in relation to the Trust Fund which the Donor could do if living and this Trust had not been executed."

. . .

If *State Street Trust Co. v. United States*, 1 Cir., 1959, 263 F.2d 635, was correctly decided in this aspect, the government must prevail because of the Article 7 powers. There this court, Chief Judge Magruder dissenting, held against the taxpayer because broad powers similar to those in Article 7 meant that the trustees "could very substantially shift the economic benefits of the trusts between the life tenants and the remaindermen," so that the settlor "as long as he lived, in substance and effect and in a very real sense . . . 'retained for his life . . . the right . . . to designate the persons who shall possess or enjoy the property or the income therefrom; . . .'" 263 F.2d at 639–640, *quoting* 26 U.S.C. § 2036(a)(2). We accept the taxpayer's invitation to reconsider this ruling.

It is common ground that a settlor will not find the corpus of the trust included in his estate merely because he named himself a trustee. *Jennings v. Smith*, 2 Cir., 1947, 161 F.2d 74. He must have reserved a power to himself that is inconsistent with the full termination of ownership. The government's brief defines this as "sufficient dominion and control until his death." Trustee powers given for the administration or management of the trust must be equitably exercised, however, for the benefit of the trust as a whole. *Blodget v. Delaney*, 1 Cir., 1953, 201 F.2d 589; *United States v. Powell*, 10 Cir., 1962, 307 F.2d 821; Scott, Trusts §§ 183, 232 (3d ed. 1967); *Restatement (Second) Trusts* §§ 183, 232. The court in *State Street* conceded that the powers at issue were all such powers, but reached the conclusion that, cumulatively, they gave the settlor dominion sufficiently unfettered to be in the nature of ownership. With all respect to the majority of the then court, we find it difficult to see how a power can be subject to control by the probate court, and exercisable only in what the trustee fairly concludes is in the interests of the trust and its beneficiaries as a whole, and at the same time be an ownership power.

The government's position, to be sound, must be that the trustee's powers are beyond the court's control. Under Massachusetts law, however, no amount of administrative discretion prevents judicial supervision of the trustee. Thus in *Appeal of Davis*, 1903, 183 Mass. 499, 67 N.E. 604, a trustee was given "full power to make purchases, investments and exchanges . . . in such manner as to them shall seem expedient; it being my intention to give my trustees . . . the same dominion and control over said trust property as I now have." In spite of this language, and in spite of their good faith, the court charged the trustees for failing sufficiently to diversify their investment portfolio.

The Massachusetts court has never varied from this broad rule of accountability, and has twice criticized *State Street* for its seeming departure. *Boston Safe Deposit & Trust Co. v. Stone*, 1965, 348 Mass. 345, 351, n. 8, 203 N.E.2d 547; *Old Colony Trust Co. v. Silliman*, 1967, 352 Mass. 6, 8–9, 223 N.E.2d 504. *See also, Estate of McGillicuddy*, 54 T.C. No. 27, 2/17/70, CCH Tax Ct. Rep. Dec. 29, 1965. We make a further observation, which the court in *State Street* failed to note, that the provision in that trust (as in the case at bar) that the trustees could "do all things in relation to the Trust Fund which I, the Donor, could do if . . . the Trust had not been executed," is almost precisely the provision which did not protect the trustees from accountability in *Appeal of Davis, supra*.

We do not believe that trustee powers are to be more broadly construed for tax purposes than the probate court would construe them for administrative purposes. More basically, we agree with Judge Magruder's observation that nothing is "gained by lumping them together." *State Street Trust Co. v. United States, supra*, 263 F.2d at 642. We hold that no aggregation of purely administrative powers can meet the government's amorphous test of "sufficient dominion and control" so as to be equated with ownership.

———

The possession by a grantor-trustee of administrative and investment powers, such as the power to allocate trust receipts between principal, income, and the composition of trust investments, generally does not bring § 2038 into play. The exercise of such powers is subject to fiduciary restrictions and strict judicial scrutiny. *See, e.g., Estate of Graham,* 46 T.C. 415, 429 (1969) ("a trustee must act in good faith in accordance with his fiduciary responsibility").

Problem

Would the result in *Old Colony* be different if the grantor reserved the administrative powers in his individual, rather than trustee, capacity?

———

There are many types of powers that a grantor might retain over a trust. In addition, a grantor might retain a power over only certain assets held in a trust. In *Byrum, infra,* the decedent transferred stock in three closely held corporations to a trust, but retained the right to vote the shares, to veto their sale or transfer, to veto any investment or reinvestment, and to remove the trustee and appoint another corporation as successor trustee. The Court considered whether the retained powers were sufficient to invoke § 2036(a)(2).

United States v. Byrum

408 U.S. 125 (1972)

Mr. Justice Powell delivered the opinion of the Court.

Decedent, Milliken C. Byrum, created in 1958 an irrevocable trust to which he transferred shares of stock in three closely held corporations. Prior to transfer, he owned at least 71% of the outstanding stock of each corporation. The beneficiaries were his children or, in the event of their death before the termination of the trust, their surviving children. The trust instrument specified that there be a corporate trustee. Byrum designated as sole trustee an independent corporation, Huntington National Bank. The trust agreement vested in the trustee broad and detailed powers with respect to the control and management of the trust property. These powers were exercisable in the trustee's sole discretion, subject to certain rights retained by Byrum: (i) to vote the shares of unlisted stock held in the trust estate; (ii) to disapprove the sale or transfer of any trust assets, including the shares transferred to the trust; (iii) to approve investments and reinvestments; and (iv) to remove the trustee and 'designate another corporate Trustee to serve as successor.' Until the youngest living child reached age 21, the trustee was authorized in its 'absolute and sole discretion' to pay the income and principal of the trust to or for the benefit of the beneficiaries, 'with due regard to their individual needs for education, care, maintenance and support.' After the youngest child reached 21, the trust was to be divided into a separate trust for each child, to terminate when the beneficiaries reached 35. The trustee was authorized in its discretion to pay income and principal from these trusts to the beneficiaries for emergency or other 'worthy need,' including education.

When he died in 1964, Byrum owned less than 50% of the common stock in two of the corporations and 59% in the third. The trust had retained the shares transferred to it, with the result that Byrum had continued to have the right to vote not less than 71% of the common stock in each of the three corporations. There was minority stockholders, unrelated to Byrum, in each corporation.

Following Byrum's death, the Commissioner of Internal Revenue determined that the transferred stock was properly included within Byrum's gross estate under § 2036(a). That section provides for the inclusion in a decedent's gross estate of all property which the decedent has transferred by inter vivos transaction, if he has retained for his lifetime '(1) the possession or enjoyment of, or the right to the income from, the property' transferred, or '(2) the right, either alone or in conjunction with any person, to designate the persons who shall possess or enjoy the property or the income therefrom.' The Commissioner determined that the stock transferred into the trust should be included in Byrum's gross estate because of the rights reserved by him in the trust agreement. It was asserted that his right to vote the transferred shares and to veto any sale thereof by the trustee, together with the ownership of other shares, enabled Byrum to retain the 'enjoyment of . . . the property,' and also allowed him to determine the flow of income to the trust and thereby 'designate the persons who shall . . . enjoy . . . the income.

The executrix of Byrum's estate paid an additional tax of $13,202.45, and thereafter brought this refund action in District Court. The facts not being in dispute, the court ruled for the executrix on cross motions for summary judgment. 311 F. Supp. 892 (S.D. Ohio 1970). The Court of Appeals affirmed, one judge dissenting. 440 F.2d 949 (C.A.6, 1971). We granted the Government's petition for certiorari. 404 U.S. 937 (1971).

I

The Government relies primarily on its claim, made under § 2036(a)(2), that Byrum retained the right to designate the persons who shall enjoy the income from the transferred property. The argument is a complicated one. By retaining voting control over the corporations whose stock was transferred, Byrum was in a position to select the corporate directors. He could retain this position by not selling the shares he owned and by vetoing any sale by the trustee of the transferred shares. These rights, it is said, gave him control over corporate dividend policy. By increasing, decreasing, or stopping dividends completely, it is argued that Byrum could 'regulate the flow of income to the trust' and thereby shift or defer the beneficial enjoyment of trust income between the present beneficiaries and the remaindermen. The sum of this retained power is said to be tantamount to a grantor-trustee's power to accumulate income in the trust, which this Court has recognized constitutes the power to designate the persons who shall enjoy the income from transferred property.

At the outset we observe that this Court has never held that trust property must be included in a settlor's gross estate solely because the settlor retained the power to manage trust assets. On the contrary, since our decision in *Reinecke v. Northern Trust Co.*, 278 U.S. 339 (1929), it has been recognized that a settlor's retention of broad powers of management does not necessarily subject an inter vivos trust to the federal estate tax. Although there was no statutory analogue to § 2036(a)(2) when *Northern Trust* was decided, several lower court decisions decided after the enactment of the predecessor of § 2036(a)(2) have upheld the settlor's right to exercise managerial powers without incurring estate-tax liability. In *Estate of King v. Commissioner*, 37 T.C. 973 (1962), a settlor reserved the power to direct the trustee in the management and investment of trust assets. The Government argued that the settlor was thereby empowered to cause investments to be made in such a manner as to control significantly the flow of income into the trust. The Tax Court rejected this argument, and held for the taxpayer. Although the court recognized that the settlor had reserved 'wide latitude in the exercise of his discretion as to the types of investments to be made,' *id.*, at 980, it did not find this control over the flow of income to be equivalent to the power to designate who shall enjoy the income from the transferred property.

Essentially the power retained by Byrum is the same managerial power retained by the settlors in *Northern Trust* and in *King*. Although neither case controls this one—*Northern Trust*, because it was not decided under § 2036(a)(2) or a predecessor; and *King*, because it is a lower court opinion—the existence of such precedents carries weight. The holding of *Northern Trust*, that the settlor of a trust may retain broad powers of management without adverse estate-tax consequences, may have been relied upon in the drafting of hundreds of inter vivos trusts. The modification of this principle now sought by the Government could have a seriously adverse impact, especially upon settlors (and their estates) who happen to have been 'controlling' stockholders of a closely held corporation. Courts properly have been reluctant to depart from an interpretation of tax law which has been generally accepted when the departure could have potentially far-reaching consequences. When a principle of taxation requires reexamination, Congress is better equipped than a court to define precisely the type of conduct which results in tax consequences. When courts readily undertake such tasks, taxpayers may not rely with assurance on what appear to be established rules lest they be subsequently overturned. Legislative enactments, on the other hand, although not always free from ambiguity, at least afford the taxpayers advance warning.

The Government argues, however, that our opinion in *United States v. O'Malley*, 383 U.S. 627 (1966), compels the inclusion in Byrum's estate of the stock owned by the trust. In *O'Malley*, the settlor of an inter vivos trust named himself as one of the three trustees. The trust agreement authorized the trustees to pay income to the life beneficiary or to accumulate it as a part of the principal of the trust in their 'sole discretion.' The agreement further provided that net income retained by the trustees, and not distributed in any calendar year, "shall become a part of the principal of the Trust Estate." *Id.*, at 629 n. 2. The Court characterized the effect of the trust as follows:

> 'Here Fabrice (the settlor) was empowered, with the other trustees, to distribute the trust income to the income beneficiaries or to accumulate it and add it to the principal, thereby denying to the beneficiaries the privilege of immediate enjoyment and conditioning their eventual enjoyment upon surviving the termination of the trust.' *Id.*, at 631. As the retention of this legal right by the settlor, acting as a trustee 'in conjunction' with the other trustees, came squarely

within the language and intent of the predecessor of § 2036(a)(2), the taxpayer conceded that the original assets transferred into the trust were includable in the decedent's gross estate. *Id.*, at 632. The issue before the Court was whether the accumulated income, which had been added to the principal pursuant to the reservation of right in that respect, was also includable in decedent's estate for tax purposes. The Court held that it was.

In our view, and for the purposes of this case, *O'Malley* adds nothing to the statute itself. The facts in that case were clearly within the ambit of what is now § 2036(a). That section requires that the settlor must have 'retained for his life . . . the right . . . to designate the persons who shall possess or enjoy the property or the income therefrom.' *O'Malley* was covered precisely by the statute for two reasons: (1) there the settlor had reserved a legal right, set forth in the trust instrument; and (2) this right expressly authorized the settlor, 'in conjunction' with others, to accumulate income and thereby 'to designate' the persons to enjoy it.

It must be conceded that Byrum reserved no such 'right' in the trust instrument or otherwise. The term 'right,' certainly when used in a tax statute, must be given its normal and customary meaning. It connotes an ascertainable and legally enforceable power, such as that involved in *O'Malley*. Here, the right ascribed to Byrum was the power to use his majority position and influence over the corporate directors to 'regulate the flow of dividends' to the trust. That 'right' was neither ascertainable nor legally enforceable and hence was not a right in any normal sense of that term.

Byrum did retain the legal right to vote shares held by the trust and to veto investments and reinvestments. But the corporate trustee alone, not Byrum, had the right to pay out or withhold income and thereby to designate who among the beneficiaries enjoyed such income. Whatever power Byrum may have possessed with respect to the flow of income into the trust was derived not from an enforceable legal right specified in the trust instrument, but from the fact that he could elect a majority of the directors of the three corporations. The power to elect the directors conferred no legal right to command them to pay or not to pay dividends. A majority shareholder has a fiduciary duty not to misuse his power by promoting his personal interests at the expense of corporate interests. Moreover, the directors also have a fiduciary duty to promote the interests of the corporation. However great Byrum's influence may have been with the corporate directors, their responsibilities were to all stockholders and were enforceable according to legal standards entirely unrelated to the needs of the trust or to Byrum's desires with respect thereto.

The Government seeks to equate the de facto position of a controlling stockholder with the legally enforceable 'right' specified by the statute. Retention of corporate control (through the right to vote the shares) is said to be 'tantamount to the power to accumulate income' in the trust which resulted in estate-tax consequences in *O'Malley*. The Government goes on to assert that '(t)hrough exercise of that retained power, (Byrum) could increase or decrease corporate dividends . . . and thereby shift or defer the beneficial enjoyment of trust income.' This approach seems to us not only to depart from the specific statutory language, but also to misconceive the realities of corporate life.

There is no reason to suppose that the three corporations controlled by Byrum were other than typical small businesses. The customary vicissitudes of such enterprises—bad years; product obsolescence; new competition; disastrous litigation; new, inhibiting Government regulations; even bankruptcy— prevent any certainty or predictability as to earnings or dividends. There is no assurance that a small corporation will have a flow of net earnings or that income earned will in fact be available for dividends. Thus, Byrum's alleged de facto 'power to control the flow of dividends' to the trust was subject to business and economic variables over which he had little or no control.

Even where there are corporate earnings, the legal power to declare dividends is vested solely in the corporate board. In making decisions with respect to dividends, the board must consider a number of factors. It must balance the expectation of stockholders to reasonable dividends when earned against corporate needs for retention of earnings. The first responsibility of the board is to safeguard corporate financial viability for the long term. This means, among other things, the retention of sufficient earnings to assure adequate working capital as well as resources for retirement of debt, for re- placement and modernization of plant and equipment, and for growth and expansion. The nature of a corporation's business, as well as the policies and long-range plans of management, are also relevant to dividend payment decisions. Directors of a closely held, small corporation must bear in mind the relatively limited access of such an enterprise to capital markets. This may require a more conservative policy with respect to dividends than would expected of an established corporation with securities listed on national exchanges.

Nor do small corporations have the flexibility or the opportunity available to national concerns in the utilization of retained earnings. When earnings are substantial, a decision not to pay dividends may result only in the accumu- lation of surplus rather than growth through internal or external expansion. The accumulated earnings may result in the imposition of a penalty tax.

These various economic considerations are ignored at the directors' peril. Although vested with broad discretion in determining whether, when, and what amount of dividends shall be paid, that discretion is subject to legal restraints. If, in obedience to the will of the majority stockholder, corporate directors disregard the interests of shareholders by accumulating earnings to an unreasonable extent, they are vulnerable to a derivative suit. They are similarly vulnerable if they make an unlawful payment of dividends in the absence of net earnings or available surplus, or if they fail to exercise the requisite degree of care in discharging their duty to act only in the best interest of the corporation and its stockholders.

Byrum was similarly inhibited by a fiduciary duty from abusing his position as majority shareholder for personal or family advantage to the detriment of the corporation or other stockholders. There were a substantial number of minority stockholders in these corporations who were unrelated to Byrum. Had Byrum and the directors violated their duties, the minority shareholders would have had a cause of action under Ohio law. The Huntington National

Bank, as trustee, was one of the minority stockholders, and it had both the right and the duty to hold Byrum responsible for any wrongful or negligent action as a controlling stockholder or as a director of the corporations. Although Byrum had reserved the right to remove the trustee, he would have been imprudent to do this when confronted by the trustee's complaint against his conduct. A successor trustee would succeed to the rights of the one removed.

We conclude that Byrum did not have an unconstrained de facto power to regulate the flow of dividends to the trust, much less the 'right' to designate who was to enjoy the income from trust property. His ability to affect, but not control, trust income, was a qualitatively different power from that of the settlor in *O'Malley*, who had a specific and enforceable right to control the income paid to the beneficiaries. Even had Byrum managed to flood the trust with income, he had no way of compelling the trustee to pay it out rather than accumulate it. Nor could he prevent the trustee from making payments from other trust assets, although admittedly there were few of these at the time of Byrum's death. We cannot assume, however, that no other assets would come into the trust from reinvestments or other gifts.

We find no merit to the Government's contention that Byrum's de facto 'control,' subject as it was to the economic and legal constraints set forth above, was tantamount to the right to designate the persons who shall enjoy trust income, specified by § 2036(a)(2).

II

The Government asserts an alternative ground for including the shares transferred to the trust within Byrum's gross estate. It argues that by retaining control, Byrum guaranteed himself continued employment and remuneration, as well as the right to determine whether and when the corporations would be liquidated or merged. Byrum is thus said to have retained 'the . . . enjoyment of . . . the property' making it includable within his gross estate under § 2036(a)(1). The Government concedes that the retention of the voting rights of an 'unimportant minority interest' would not require inclusion of the transferred shares under § 2036(a)(1). It argues, however, 'where the cumulative effect of the retained powers and the rights flowing from the shares not placed in trust leaves the grantor in control of a close corporation, and assures that control for his lifetime, he has retained the 'enjoyment' of the transferred stock.' Brief for United States 23.

It is well settled that the terms 'enjoy' and 'enjoyment,' as used in various estate tax statutes, 'are not terms of art, but connote substantial present economic benefit rather than technical vesting of title or estates.' *Commissioner of Internal Revenue v. Estate of Holmes*, 326 U.S. 480, 486 (1946). For example, in *Reinecke v. Northern Trust Co.*, 278 U.S. 339 (1929), in which the critical inquiry was whether the decedent had created a trust "intended . . . 'to take effect in possession or enjoyment at or after his death," *id.*, at 348, the Court held that reserved powers of management of trust assets, similar to Byrum's power over the three corporations, did not subject an inter vivos trust to the federal estate tax. In determining whether the settlor had retained the enjoyment of the transferred property, the Court said:

"Nor did the reserved powers of management of the trusts save to decedent any control over the economic benefits or the enjoyment of the property. He would equally have reserved all these powers and others had he made himself the trustee, but the transfer would not for that reason have been incomplete. The shifting of the economic interest in the trust property which was the subject of the tax was thus complete as soon as the trust was made. His power to recall the property and of control over it for his own benefit then ceased and as the trusts were not made in contemplation of death, the reserved powers do not serve to distinguish them from any other gift inter vivos not subject to the tax." 278 U.S., at 346–347.

The cases cited by the Government reveal that the terms 'possession' and 'enjoyment,' used in § 2036(a)(1), were used to deal with situations in which the owner of property divested himself of title but retained an income interest or, in the case of real property, the lifetime use of the property. Mr. Justice Black's opinion for the Court in *Commissioner of Internal Revenue v. Estate of Church*, 335 U.S. 632 (1949), traces the history of the concept. In none of the cases cited by the Government has a court held that a person has retained possession or enjoyment of the property if he has transferred title irrevocably, made complete delivery of the property and relinquished the right to income where the property is income producing.

The Government cites only one case, *Estate of Holland v. Commissioner*, 1 T.C. 564 (1943), in which a decedent had retained the right to vote transferred shares of stock and in which the stock was included within the decedent's gross estate. In that case, it was not the mere power to vote the stock, giving the decedent control of the corporation, which caused the Tax Court to include the shares. The court held that "on an inclusive view of the whole arrangement, this withholding of the income until decedent's death, coupled with the retention of the certificates under the pledge and the reservation of the right to vote the stock and to designate the company officers" subjects the stock to inclusion within the gross estate. *Id.*, at 565. The settlor in *Holland* retained a considerably greater interest than Byrum retained, including an income interest.

As the Government concedes, the mere retention of the right-to-vote shares does not constitute the type of 'enjoyment' in the property itself contemplated by § 2036(a)(1). In addition to being against the weight of precedent, the Government's argument that Byrum retained 'enjoyment' within the meaning of § 2036(a)(1) is conceptually unsound. This argument implies, as it must under the express language of § 2036(a), that Byrum 'retained for his life . . . (1) the possession or enjoyment' of the 'property' transferred to the trust or the 'income' therefrom. The only property he transferred was corporate stock. He did not transfer 'control' (in the sense used by the Government) as the trust never owned as much as 50% of the stock of any corporation. Byrum never divested himself of control, as he was able to vote a majority of the shares by virtue of what he owned and the right to vote those placed in the trust. Indeed, at the time of his death he still owned a majority of the shares in the largest of the corporations and probably would have exercised control of the other two by virtue of being a large stockholder in each. The statutory language plainly contemplates retention of an attribute of the property transferred—such as a right to income, use of the property itself, or a power of appointment with respect either to income or principal.

Even if Byrum had transferred a majority of the stock, but had retained voting control, he would not have retained 'substantial present economic benefit,' 326 U.S., at 486. The Government points to the retention of two 'benefits.' The first of these, the power to liquidate or merge, is not a present benefit; rather, it is a speculative and contingent benefit which may or may not be realized. Nor is the probability of continued employment and compensation the substantial 'enjoyment of . . . (the transferred) property' within the meaning of the statute. The dominant stockholder in a closely held corporation, if he is active and productive, is likely to hold a senior position and to enjoy the advantage of a significant voice in his own compensation. These are inevitable facts of the free-enterprise system, but the influence and capability of a controlling stockholder to favor himself are not without constraints. Where there are minority stockholders, as in this case, directors may be held accountable if their employment, compensation, and retention of officers violate their duty to act reasonably in the best interest of the corporation and all of its stockholders. Moreover, this duty is policed, albeit indirectly, by the Internal Revenue Service, which disallows the deduction of unreasonable compensation paid to a corporate executive as a business expense. We conclude that Byrum's retention of voting control was not the retention of the enjoyment of the transferred property within the meaning of the statute.

For the reasons set forth above, we hold that this case was correctly decided by the Court of Appeals and accordingly the judgment is affirmed. Judgment affirmed.

Mr. Justice White, with whom Mr. Justice Brennan and Mr. Justice Blackmun join, dissenting. [Dissenting opinions omitted.]

———

In response to *Byrum*, Congress enacted § 2036(b), which requires that transferred stock in a controlled corporation be included in the gross estate if voting stock is transferred, but the voting rights are retained by the transferor. A controlled corporation is defined as a corporation in which the decedent retains at least 20% of the voting power of all classes of stock. Section 2036(b) defines the retention of voting rights as a retained interest under § 2036(a)(1). Because § 2036(b) equates the retention of voting rights to the retention of an interest in the stock under § 2036(a)(1), the Court's conclusion that some indirect retention of the power to control the income flow from transferred assets may be excepted from § 2036(a)(2) may continue to be viable. *See* John T. Gaubatz, *The Nontaxation of Nontestamentary Acts: Will Byrum Survive the Tax Reform Act of 1976?*, 27 CASE W. RES. L. REV. 623 (1977); Willard H. Pedrick, *Grantor Powers and the Tax Reform Act; End of an Era?*, 71 N. W. L. REV. 704 (1977).

Problem

D owns all of the stock of XYZ. An insurance agent has suggested that *D* recapitalize XYZ into voting and nonvoting common stock. Thereafter, *D* will give all of the nonvoting stock to his children. Should § 2036(b) apply to this transaction? Does it?

[C] Generation-Skipping Transfer Tax

Absent the retention of a *Byrum* type power, which could result in estate taxation of transferred interests and trigger a delay in the effective allocation of GST tax exemption as a result of § 2642(f), retained administrative powers should have no independent effect for GST tax purposes.

[D] Income Tax

Code: § 675.

Regulations: § 1.675.

The impact of retained administrative powers on income taxation can be more severe. Administrative powers which can be used to control the flow of income, including the power to vote controlling stock and the power to control investment in a situation similar to *Byrum*, will result in taxation of the income to the grantor if the powers are exercisable by anyone not in a fiduciary capacity. *See* § 675(4). Other powers which can cause taxation of income to the grantor include powers to allow the grantor to deal with the corpus or income of the trust for less than full and adequate consideration or to allow the grantor to borrow trust corpus or income without adequate interest or security. *See* § 675(1), (2).[6] Furthermore, these powers should be carefully distinguished from fiduciary powers to allocate receipts between corpus and income, which are specifically excepted from the list of discretionary powers that cause the grantor to be taxed. *See* § 674(b)(8).

Courts have also been clear that reality, not form, determines the existence of rights and powers in the grantor. Indeed, even some transactions which may not, in themselves, be sufficient to indicate retention of control can, in fact, result in taxation of the trust income to the grantor. For example, § 675(3) taxes income from the trust to the grantor if he actually borrows trust assets without adequate security or interest, even if there was no express authority for the loan in the trust instrument. *See Benson v. Commissioner*, 76 T.C. 1040 (1981).

---

[6] Section 675(3) also taxes income to the grantor if the grantor or the grantor's spouse, borrows trust funds at less than adequate interest or security, or if the loan was made by a related or subordinate trustee subservient to the grantor or to the grantor's spouse, who lives with the grantor.

Revenue Ruling 86–82

1986-1 C.B. 253

ISSUE

If the grantor of a trust borrows the entire trust corpus and makes complete repayment of principal and interest within the same year is that grantor treated as owner of the trust under section 675(3) of the Internal Revenue Code?

FACTS

On May 11, 1985, *A* created an irrevocable trust for the benefit of *A*'s children. The trust instrument names *A* trustee and gives *A* power to borrow trust corpus or income at the market rate of interest with adequate security. On June 11, 1985, *A* borrowed 100x dollars from the trust in compliance with these requirements. The borrowed funds comprised the entire trust corpus. On November 3, 1985, *A* repaid the loan plus interest. Both *A* and the trust are calendar year taxpayers.

LAW AND ANALYSIS

Section 671 of the Code provides that if any section of subpart E of subchapter J treats the grantor as the owner of any portion of the trust, then the grantor must include in computing taxable income those items of income, deductions, and credits which are attributable to that portion of the trust.

Section 675(3) of the Code provides that, generally, the grantor of a trust will be treated as the owner of any portion of a trust in respect to which the grantor has borrowed the corpus or income and has not completely repaid the loan, including any interest, before the beginning of the taxable year.

In *Mau v. United States*, 355 F. Supp. 909 (D. Hawaii 1973), the taxpayer established five separate trusts, with the taxpayer designated trustee of each. In 1965, the taxpayer borrowed money from each of the trusts. These amounts were not repaid until 1969. The taxpayer argued that section 675(3) of the Code did not cause the taxpayer-grantor to be liable for federal income tax on the trusts' 1965 income because the loans were not outstanding at the beginning of the year. The court rejected this interpretation of the statute, reasoning that section 675(3) was enacted to prevent the shifting of taxable income in situations where a grantor retained control and use of trust properties through borrowing. Therefore, the court held that the borrowing of trust corpus or income by a grantor at any time during a taxable year would result in the grantor being taxed on trust income for that entire year under section 675(3). The court concluded that the taxpayer was taxable on income of the trusts in 1965, the year the borrowing occurred, even though the loans were made after the beginning of the year. If section 675(3) otherwise applies for a given year, its effect is not avoided by making repayment before the year closes. *Mau* therefore stands for the principle that section 675(3) applies for any year during any part of which a loan by a trust to the grantor-trustee is outstanding.

In the present case, *A* borrowed the entire trust corpus during calendar 1985. Accordingly, *A* is treated as the owner of the entire trust under section

675(3) of the Code in spite of the fact that A made full payment of principal and interest before the close of 1985. See section 1.671-3(b)(3) of the regulations. Hence, under section 671, A must include in gross income all income earned by the trust in 1985.

HOLDING

Under section 675(3) of the Code, a grantor-trustee who has both borrowed the entire trust corpus and repaid the borrowed funds plus interest in the same year will be treated for federal income tax purposes as the owner of the entire trust for that year.

———

Problems

1. S wants to transfer property to a trust and to name himself as the sole trustee. His child will be the income beneficiary for life and remainder will be payable to his grandchild. S also wants to retain substantial administrative rights over the trust.

a. What income, gift, and estate tax problems are raised by the following language?

> The Trustee shall have power . . . to exchange property for other property; . . . to exchange and invest and reinvest in securities or properties although of a kind or in an amount which ordinarily would not be considered suitable for a trust investment, including, but without restriction, investments that yield a high rate of income or no income at all and wasting investments, intending hereby to authorize the Trustee to act in such manner as it is believed by him to be for the best interests of the Trust Fund, regarding it as a whole, even though particular investments might not otherwise be proper; . . . to determine what shall be charged or credited to income and what to principal notwithstanding any determination by the courts and specifically, but without limitation, to make such determination in regard to stock and cash dividends, rights, and all other receipts in respect of the ownership of stock and to decide whether or not to make deductions from income for depreciation amortization or waste and in what amount; . . . and generally to do all things in relation to the Trust Fund which I, the Donor, could do if living and the Trust had not been executed.
>
> . . .
>
> All such acts and decisions made by the Trustees in good faith shall be conclusive on all parties at interest and my Trustees shall be liable only for their own willful acts or defaults, but in no case for acts in error of judgment.

b. Would the answer change if the grantor appointed an independent trustee and retained the above administrative powers in the grantor's individual capacity?

2. *D* transfers undeveloped land that currently produces no income to a corporate trustee. The trust provides that the income is payable to *W* for life and the remainder is distributable to whomever she appoints by will. In default of appointment, the property is to be divided among *D*'s children. *D* retains the power to veto any sale or other disposition of trust assets (other than at termination).

    a. What are the gift tax consequences? Is all or any part of the transfer a taxable gift? Will any part qualify for the gift tax annual exclusion or gift tax marital deduction? Consider Treasury Regulation § 25.2523(e)–1(f)(4) and *Maryland National Bank*, reproduced in Chapter 4, § 4.01[B][1][a], *supra*.

    b. Is the income taxable to *D*?

    c. Will any part of the trust be includable in *D*'s gross estate if he dies before the trust terminates?

§ 9.05 Termination of Retained Powers

Code: §§ 2035(a)(2), 2038(a)(1) last clause, and 2038(a)(2) end of first sentence.

Regulations: None.

Sanford, reproduced in Chapter 4, § 4.01[A][4] *supra*, provides that the termination of a dispositive power acts to complete the gift of the interests subject to the power. *See, e.g., Robinson v. Commissioner*, 675 F.2d 774 (5th Cir. 1982), *cert. denied*, 459 U.S. 970 (1982) (release of a retained power to appoint remainder among children). For example, if the donor retains the power to accumulate income of a trust so that income may ultimately be paid to the remainderman, rather than to the income beneficiary, actual payment of income constitutes a completed gift to the income beneficiary. Conversely, accumulation may be a completed gift to the remainderman, depending on whether income, once accumulated, must be held for the remainderman. Payment or accumulation constitutes a termination of the power to determine who enjoyed the income.

Termination of retained powers can also have estate tax ramifications. The express language of § 2038 includes property subject to powers released within three years of the death of the grantor in the grantor-power holder's estate. *See* § 2038(a)(1), (a)(2). Furthermore, the release of powers within three years of death are transfers for purposes of § 2035. Section 2035(a) includes property in the gross estate if a "decedent relinquished a power with respect to any property, during the 3-year period ending on the date of the decedent's death, and . . . the value of such property (or an interest therein) would have been included in the decedent's gross estate under section 2036. . . [or] 2038 . . . if such . . . relinquished power had been retained by the decedent on the date of his death." Thus, the release of any *hot* power within three years of death will not prohibit estate taxation of the interest which would have been subject to the power. Whether a power has terminated is a question of state law. *See* Rev. Rul. 79–177, 1979–1 C.B. 298 (concerning joint powers).

Problem

What GST tax consequences might occur on releasing a dispositive power?

Chapter 10

LIFE INSURANCE

This Chapter investigates the tax ramifications of life insurance. Insurance is one common form of third party contractual arrangement used to pass wealth in our society. Other common forms include retirement plans and "joint and survivor" accounts with banks and other financial institutions. Retirement plans are discussed in Chapter 11. Joint interests are discussed in Chapter 13.

§ 10.01 In General

A life insurance policy is a contract between an insurance company (*the insurer*) and the policy owner (*policyholder*). Under the contract, the insurer promises to pay a specified sum (*the face amount*) to a designated person (*the beneficiary*) on the death of a named person (*the insured*) in consideration for premium payments. Typically, the insured and the owner are the same person, but this is not a legal necessity. The insured-owner of a policy may assign the rights to another individual or an entity. Similarly, a person who is not the insured but who has an interest in the life of the insured, may purchase a policy and be the owner from the inception.

Many different types of life insurance policies are available. *See generally* Lawrence Brody, *Life Insurance is Like a Box of Chocolates—You Never Know What You Are Going to Get Until You Open It Up: A Perspective on Contemporary Life Insurance Products and Their Uses*, 30 U. Miami Inst. on Est. Plan., Ch. 7 (1996). Three types of insurance policies are considered below: *term*, *ordinary*, and *universal* life insurance policies.

Under a term policy, the insurer must pay the death benefit if the insured dies during a defined period of time, usually one year. If the insured does not die during the policy term, the insurer's promise ends. However, the insurance contract may provide that the policy may be renewed for additional periods of time if additional premiums are paid. If the insured dies during the policy term, the insurer pays the beneficiary the face amount of the policy. Because term insurance premiums are based on mortality rates, the amount of the annual premium increases with the age of the insured. Term insurance is *pure insurance* in the sense that it has no value to the owner other than the insurer's promise to pay if the insured dies before a specified date.

Compared to term insurance, ordinary (or *whole*) life insurance consists of three elements: pure insurance, savings, and mortality gain (or loss). Ordinary life insurance is usually characterized by constant annual premiums over a substantial number of years; typically the life of the insured. A portion of ordinary life premiums are used to provide pure (term) insurance. The remainder of the policy premiums represent the savings element, which the insurer invests, usually guaranteeing a minimal rate of return. The investment of the savings element produces earnings which build the cash value of the policy. The cash value is the amount for which the policy can be redeemed, borrowed against,[1] or used to purchase fully paid-up insurance before the insured's death or the maturity of the policy.[2] The mortality gain (or loss) is the degree that mortality expectations change during the life of the policy. Because ordinary life policies last for substantial periods of time, changes in mortality figures can change the risk factors on the insurance portion from the risk factors used when the policy was issued.

Universal life insurance, like whole life, has a savings element. In a typical universal life insurance policy, the amounts and frequency of the premium payments are determined by the policyholder, and may be increased or decreased at any time. The policyholder may switch back and forth between ordinary life and term coverage, and may decrease (or in some instances, increase) the amount of coverage. To permit a variation in potential insurance plans, the policy permits the policyholder flexibility in determining the amount and frequency of premium payments, as well as the ability to specify and change the policy's maturity date. The cash value of the policy equals the sum of the net premium for the period in question (gross premium paid less expense charges), plus the cash value for the preceding period. This amount is increased by one period's interest for this combined sum and is reduced by the cost of insurance for the period. The insurance company guarantees a minimum rate of interest for the life of the policy. The company may increase this rate in advance of each policy year to provide extra interest. The company may also reduce the cost of term insurance in advance of each policy year.

A universal life insurance policy permits a policyholder to invest a substantial amount of cash without increasing the amount of pure insurance protection offered by the contract. This can have marked income tax advantages to the policyholder. The increased cash fund, represented by the policyholder's account with the insurance company, earns interest for the policyholder, without subjecting the owner to tax consequences on any interest credited to the policy. The interest may be used to fund future insurance costs on the policy, or the policyholder may cash in the policy before maturity and withdraw the entire cash value at that time. Furthermore, the interest is not taxable when the policyholder borrows against the cash value. However, the accumulated interest is taxed if the policy is surrendered for an amount in excess of the taxpayer's basis in the policy (typically, total premiums paid). In short, a universal life policy may be an attractive vehicle for tax deferred savings.

As compared to a tax deferred savings vehicle, universal life insurance permits a policyholder to pay less in premiums than is typically required for a whole life policy. The owner may choose to deposit less money in the savings element of the contract to reduce the annual cost. If the policy investments perform better than projected performance, the growth in value of the policy can partially offset the insurance cost portion of the policy.

---

[1] If the insured dies while a loan against the policy is outstanding, the beneficiary receives the face amount of the policy less the unpaid loan balance.

[2] The savings element also offsets the increasing cost of insurance as the insured gets older by allowing a level premium.

Because of abuses, Congress enacted § 7702 in 1984, to define a *life insurance contract* for federal tax purposes. The thrust of the section is to distinguish life insurance from income tax deferred investments being marketed under the life insurance label.

[A] Gift Tax

Code: §§ 2503, 2511, and 2512.

Regulations: Treas. Reg. §§ 25.2503–3; 25.2511–1(h)(8), –1(h)(9); and 25.2512–6.

Because life insurance constitutes a type of property, transfers of policies can have federal gift tax consequences.

[1] Taxable Transfers

[a] In General

A gift may occur when a policyholder transfers ownership by assigning the policy to someone, including a trustee. Mere designation of a policy beneficiary, however, usually does not constitute a completed gift. In the typical case, the third party contract rights of the beneficiary are subject to being revoked by the owner's reserved contractual right to change the policy's beneficiary. *See* Treas. Reg. § 25.2511–1(h)(8). Indeed, even if the owner assigns the policy to another, but retains the right to change the beneficiary, the gift is incomplete. *See* Treas. Reg. § 25.2511–1(h)(8).

When a policy is assigned irrevocably to a trustee, the gift tax consequences depend on whether the trust is revocable or irrevocable. If the trust is revocable by the policyholder, the gift is incomplete for gift tax purposes. If the trust is irrevocable, a completed gift has been made, unless the owner retained an interest or power over the trust that makes the gift incomplete to some extent. For example, if the trustee is directed to pay the debts of the transferor, the gift may be considered incomplete because of the donor's power to create debts that must be paid with policy proceeds. *See Paolozzi v. Commissioner*, 23 T.C. 182 (1954), *acq.*, 1962–1 C.B. 4.

A gift may also occur when someone other than the owner pays a premium on the policy. The payment improves the owner's financial position. Thus, for example, a gift occurs if the insured continues to pay the premiums after irrevocably assigning ownership of the policy. *See* Treas. Reg. § 25.2511–1(h)(8).

Finally, the death of the insured may cause a gift if the policy is owned by someone other than the insured and the policy proceeds are payable to a third person. The death of the insured completes the gift of the proceeds from the owner of the policy to the designated beneficiary. *See Goodman v. Commissioner*, 156 F.2d 218 (2d Cir. 1946); Rev. Rul. 77–48, 1977–1 C.B. 292. The owner has made a gift to the beneficiary who receives the policy proceeds. *See* Treas. Reg. § 25.2511–2(f).

[b] Community Property

The death of the insured may also produce gift tax consequences if the life insurance policy was held as community property at the death of the insured. *See* Treasury Regulation § 25.2511–1(h), Example 9, which treats the surviving spouse as making a gift of one-half the insurance proceeds in the following circumstances: the deceased spouse is the insured, a third party is a beneficiary of the proceeds, all premiums were paid with community property, and the policy was owned as community property. *But cf. Estate of Street v. Commissioner*, 152 F.3d 482 (5th Cir. 1997) (rejecting gift theory based on Texas law). However, even if community property funds were used to pay the premiums, under applicable state law the policy may be treated as the separate property of the noninsured spouse who is the policy owner. As a result, when the insured dies the noninsured owner-spouse will be treated as making a gift of the entire proceeds to the third party beneficiary under the insurance contract. *See* Rev. Rul. 94–69, 1994–2 C.B. 241 (applying Louisiana law).

[2] Valuation

When the transfer of a policy constitutes a gift, the value of the gift depends on the type of policy assigned and when the assignment takes place. Valuation of life insurance for gift tax purposes is governed by Treasury Regulation § 25.2512–6. First, if the purchase and assignment of the policy occur at substantially the same time, the value of the policy equals its cost. The cost is the initial premium paid. *See Guggenheim v. Rasquin*, 312 U.S. 254 (1941) (single premium policy); *Phipps v. Commissioner*, 43 B.T.A. 790 (1941) (annual premium policy). Second, the value of a paid-up policy[3] which has been in force for some time is established through the sale of comparable contracts by the insurer. These contracts are valued based on the amount the insurance company would charge for the same insurance on a person of the insured's health and age at the date of the gift. *See* Treas. Reg. § 25.2512–6(a), Example 3. Third, if a policy has been in force for some time and additional premiums are to be paid, the value equals the *interpolated terminal reserve*. This is the reserve the insurer maintains to cover its liability under the policy and the unused portion of the last premium paid before the date of the gift which covers the time period after the date of the gift. *See* Treas. Reg. § 25.2512–6(a).

A group term policy[4] transferred to a donee has been held to have no ascertainable value for gift tax purposes when given on a premium due date. *See* Rev. Rul. 76–490, 1976–2 C.B. 300. If given at any other time, the gift tax value is presumably the unearned premium.

Because the value of a policy is often low as compared to its face amount, the transfer of a policy or the payment of a premium may produce no gift tax. As discussed below, the annual exclusion covers the gift. A gift of a term policy, in particular, usually passes tax free because the fair market value of the policy at the date of the transfer is likely to be minimal. For example, the

---

[3] A paid-up policy is one that requires no further premium payments before maturity.

[4] Group term insurance is an employer provided fringe benefit that may be exempt from income taxation in whole or part under § 79.

annual premium for a term policy of $500,000, based on the insured's age and assuming excellent health, may be under $1,000 a year.

[3] Annual Exclusion

Whether the transfer of a policy or the payment of premiums qualifies for the annual exclusion depends on the nature of the rights created or assigned. The exclusion is available only for transfers of present interests. *See* § 4.02[B][1], *supra*. An outright transfer of the incidents of ownership to one donee, as absolute owner, constitutes the gift of a present interest. In this situation, the annual exclusion is available. *See* Treas. Reg. § 25.2503–3(a); Rev. Rul. 55–408, 1955–1 C.B. 113.

The presence of restrictions on the transferee's control over a policy can easily void the present interest qualification. The impact of restrictions on ownership is evident when a single policy is given to more than one donee. Because a single owner cannot exercise all the ownership rights without the consent of the co-owners, the gift to several donees does not qualify as a gift of a present interest for gift tax exclusion purposes. *See Skouras v. Commissioner*, 14 T.C. 523 (1950), *aff'd*, 188 F.2d 831 (2d Cir. 1951).

Whether post transfer premium payments made by the insured qualify for the annual exclusion turns on whether the beneficial owner of the policy has a present or future interest in the policy. If the owner has an unrestricted right to the policy, then premiums paid on the policy by another should constitute a gift of a present interest and qualify for the annual exclusion. *See* Treas. Reg. § 25.2503–3(c), Example 6.

Obtaining the annual exclusion for a gift of life insurance to a trust is more difficult than obtaining it for an outright gift to an individual. For a variety of reasons, unless an identifiable trust beneficiary has a present interest transfer to a trust, a gift of a policy to an insurance trust or the gift of cash to the trustee to allow the trustee to pay premiums on the policy will be a gift of a future interest for which the annual exclusion will not be available. *See* Treas. Reg. § 25.2503–3(c), Example 2; *Jessie S. Phillips v. Commissioner*, 12 T.C. 216 (1949); *Dora Roberts v. Commissioner*, 2 T.C. 679 (1943); Rev. Rul. 79–47, 1979–1 C.B. 312.

As the following Private Letter Ruling illustrates, the use of a *Crummey* demand power, discussed in § 4.02[B][1][b], *supra*, may facilitate the allowance of a gift tax annual exclusion for a gift in trust.

Private Letter Ruling 8134135

This is in response to the letter . . . concerning an irrevocable life insurance trust which you propose to create.

According to the letter, you would like to know whether the annual exclusion provided by section 2503(b) of the Internal Revenue Code is available to you under the following circumstances:

(1) at the time you initially fund the trust with whole life and group term life insurance policies,

(2) at the time you make subsequent contributions to the trust, and

(3)   at the time your employer pays the premiums on certain group term life insurance policies placed into trust.

The letter provides the following facts. You propose to establish an irrevocable inter vivos life insurance trust that will be funded with an initial contribution of $500 and four whole life policies, two term policies, and two group term policies the premiums for which will be provided by your employer. All policies name you as the insured. Article II, paragraph 2 of the trust instrument directs the trustee to apply all available funds toward the payment of premiums. Article III, paragraph 1, provides that before your death, any income of the trust in excess of the amount paid toward premiums or other charges due and payable under the insurance policies will be accumulated and added to principal. You have named your wife as trustee and beneficiary, and your children as the other beneficiaries. Article I, paragraph 1 permits additional contributions to the trust. With respect to any contributions to corpus, and premiums paid by your employer, Article I, paragraph 2 provides that the beneficiaries (or the guardian of a minor beneficiary) may demand $3,000 or their proportionate noncumulative shares within 30 days after written notification. The trustee is required to maintain sufficient liquid assets during each such period of withdrawal to enable immediate payment to any beneficiary exercising his or her right of withdrawal.

Upon your death, the trustee will pay to your wife or for her benefit the entire income of the trust estate and such principal as the trustee deems necessary for her support, care, and maintenance. If she survives you, then at her death, the trustee will distribute the trust estate in equal shares to your children if surviving, if not surviving, then to their issue then living.

Section 2503(b) of the Internal Revenue Code provides an annual . . . exclusion from gifts in computing taxable gifts for the calendar [year]. In order to qualify, however, the transfer must be of a present rather than a future interest in property (see section 25.2503–3(a) of the Gift Tax Regulations). Section 25.2503–3(a) of the regulations defines "future interests" as a legal term that includes reversions, remainders, and other interests or estates, whether vested or contingent, and whether or not supported by a particular interest or estate, which are limited to commence in use, possession or enjoyment at some future date or time. The term has no reference to such contractual rights as exist in a bond, note (though bearing no interest until maturity), or in a policy of life insurance, the obligations of which are to be discharged by payments in the future. But a future interest or interests in such contractual obligations may be created by the limitations contained in a trust or other instrument of transfer used in effecting a gift. Subsection (b) of that regulation defines a present interest in property as an unrestricted right to the immediate use, possession, or enjoyment of property or the income from property (such as a life estate or term certain).

    . . .

The United States Supreme Court stated in *Fondren v. Commissioner*, 324 U.S. 18 (1945), Ct. D 1627, 1945 C. B. 421, that "the crucial thing" in determining whether a gift is one of a future interest in property "is postponement of enjoyment." Rev. Rul. 73–405, 1973–2 C. B. 321 states that it is not the actual use, possession, or enjoyment by the donee which marks the dividing line between a present and a future interest, but rather the right conferred upon the donee, in the case of a trust, by the trust instrument to such use, possession, or enjoyment. A gift in trust to a minor is not a "future interest" if the donee has a present right to the use, possession, or enjoyment, although such use, possession, or enjoyment may require the appointment of a legal guardian. *See also Crummey v. Commissioner*, 397 F.2d 82 (9th Cir. 1968).

In this case, Article I, paragraph 2 of the trust instrument provides the beneficiaries (and guardian of any minor or disabled beneficiary) the right to receive notification of contributions and premium payments, and the right within 30 days of notification to withdraw $3,000 or the beneficiary's fractional share of the market value of the property contributed, whichever is less, provided that the annual amounts withdrawn do not exceed $5,000 per beneficiary (paragraph 7). These rights terminate upon your death. Thus, we conclude that, during your life, the beneficiaries of the proposed trust have the present right to use, possess, or enjoy the property contributed to it:

(1) at the time you initially fund the trust with whole life and group term life insurance policies,

(2) at the time you make subsequent contributions to the trust, and

(3) at the time your employer pays the premiums on certain group term life insurance policies placed into trust.

Consequently, the annual gift tax exclusion of $3,000 [now $11,000, as adjusted for inflation] per donee under section 2503(b) of the Code is available to you under those circumstances. *Fondren v. Commissioner*, 324 U.S. 18 (1945), Ct. D 1627, 1945 C. B. 421; *Crummey v. Commissioner*, 397 F.2d 82 (9th Cir. 1968); Rev. Rul. 73–405, 1973–2 C. B. 321; Rev. Rul. 76–490, 1976–2 C. B. 300.

. . .

———

Students should note that Private Letter Rulings have no precedential value and are binding on the Service only for the taxpayer who requested the letter ruling.

Problems

1. *O* owns a life insurance policy on her own life. She assigns ownership of the policy to *A*, who later names *X* as beneficiary of the policy.

a. What are the gift tax consequences when *O* assigns the policy to *A*?

b. What would be the gift tax consequences on the assignment if *O* and *A* were married?

c. What are the gift tax consequences of *A* naming *X* as beneficiary?

d. What are the gift tax consequences if *O* continues to pay annual premiums? If *A* pays the premiums? If *X* pays the premiums?

e. What are the gift tax consequences if, after the assignment, *O* predeceases *A*?

[B] Estate Tax

Code: § 2042.

Regulations: Treas. Reg. §§ 20.2031–8(a); 20.2042–1, and –2.

The treatment of life insurance policies and proceeds has been a particularly difficult area of estate taxation. Because of its inherent risk shifting characteristics, life insurance does not easily fit into the regular patterns of transfer taxation. It is similar to other assets only for its investment value: roughly the sum of the cash surrender value and the unearned premium of the particular policy. In the case of a paid-up policy, that total may approach the face value of the policy.

The difficulty with taxation of insurance is deciding to whom to tax the risk value of the policy, *i.e.,* the difference between the investment value of the policy and the value of the face amount at the death of the insured. *See Guggenheim v. Rasquin*, 312 U.S. 254 (1941) (determining the value of single premium policies for gift tax purposes); Treas. Reg. § 25.2512–6. Because the value of the risk portion of the policy inflates markedly near (and at) the death of the insured, legislating a scheme which will treat equitably all varieties of policies, beneficiary designations, and assignments is difficult.

[1] Taxation Based on Current Ownership

The response of Congress to these issues has been to divide life insurance policies into three groups: (1) those policies which the decedent owns on the life of another; (2) those policies payable to the estate of the decedent-insured; and (3) those policies insuring the decedent's life which are payable to others. The first category is subject to § 2033 as property owned at death. The other two categories are dealt with in § 2042.

[a] Policies Not Insuring the Decedent

Insurance policies that the decedent owns, but which insure the life of someone else, are like any other contractual right, and are taxed as property owned by the decedent at death under § 2033. On the other hand, if the decedent does not own the policy, but has a power to surrender the policy for cash, borrow against the policy without adequate security, or a similar power, these powers may constitute a general power of appointment requiring the policy to be included under § 2041. Policies insuring the life of another are valued at their fair market (not face) value using the same valuation techniques that apply to gift taxation of life insurance policies. *See* Treas. Reg. §§ 20.2042–8(a)(2), 20.2031–8(a)(3), Example 3.

[b] Policies Payable to the Insured's Estate

Policies insuring the life of a decedent that are payable to the decedent's estate present few tax difficulties. This category of policies have been taxed in the decedents' estates since 1919. Section 2042(1) requires that the face value of a life insurance policy insuring the decedent's life be included in the gross estate whenever the proceeds of the policy are payable to the decedent's personal representative.

Example: The decedent's sister owned a life insurance policy which insured the decedent's life, and the decedent's estate was the named beneficiary. The decedent died while the policy was in force.

Section 2042(1) includes the proceeds of the policy in the decedent's gross estate. Although the decedent did not own the policy—his sister did—it was payable to his personal representative. Therefore, the Code requires gross estate inclusion.

If the decedent purchases and pays the premiums for the policy, inclusion in the decedent's gross estate is explainable on the grounds that the economic situation is similar to the purchase and ownership at death of an asset by the decedent. If, on the other hand, someone else purchased the policy, the result may be explainable on the ground that the decedent, through the ability to direct the distribution of the proceeds, has the equivalent of a general power of appointment over the policy.

Whether the proceeds are "receivable by the executor" is a question of fact. The term clearly includes policies payable to the decedent's administrator or to the decedent's estate. *See* Treas. Reg. § 20.2042–1(b). Further, normal substance over form analysis is used in deciding whether the proceeds are, in fact, payable to the estate of the insured. Thus, if the policy is payable to someone other than the estate, but the beneficiary is under a legal obligation to use all or a portion of the insurance proceeds to pay taxes or other obligations of the estate, then the proceeds are taxed under § 2042(1) to the extent of the beneficiary's obligation. *See* Treas. Reg. § 20.2042–1(b)(1). For example, life insurance payable to the decedent's creditor, such as *credit life,*[5] are included in the decedent's gross estate.

Problem

The decedent's spouse owned a policy on the decedent's life which was payable to the spouse. The spouse, however, murdered the decedent. Under applicable state law, the spouse could not collect the proceeds. The proceeds were payable to decedent's heirs, unless otherwise directed in decedent's will. Are the proceeds taxable under § 2042(1)? *See First Kentucky Trust Co. v. United States,* 737 F.2d 557 (6th Cir. 1984).

[c] Policies Payable to Others

Policies insuring the decedent's life, but payable to beneficiaries other than the decedent's estate, are taxed to the estate if the decedent possessed any "incidents of ownership" at death. *See* § 2042(2). Under the 1918 Act, this category of policies was includable in the insured decedent's estate only if "taken out by" him. By Regulation, this was interpreted to require that the decedent paid the premiums and possessed the incidents of ownership over the policy. Later, the Act was interpreted to require that the decedent *either* paid the premiums *or* possessed the incidents of ownership.

---

[5] Common examples of credit life are insurance payable to the decedent's mortgage company in the event of death or to the decedent's credit card company. In each of these examples, the insurance pays off the balance due on the debt.

When the Regulations were changed to only require premium payments by the decedent, Congress responded with the codification of this interpretation in 1942. Policies on the life of the decedent, but not payable to the estate, were taxed to the estate only if the decedent had either paid the premiums or, at death, possessed incidents of ownership over the policy. Finally, in 1954, the law was set into its present form by leaving only the "incidents of ownership" test.

Incidents of ownership include such rights as the ability to borrow against the policy, the right to cash in the policy, and the power to change beneficiaries. *See* Treas. Reg. § 20.2042–1(c)(2), –1(c)(3).

Example: The decedent died owning a life insurance policy insuring her life. Her children were named as beneficiaries.

As owner of the policy, the decedent has all incidents of ownership at death, even though her ownership interest ceased at death and the policy became payable to the beneficiaries. Accordingly, the proceeds payable under the policy are includable in the decedent's gross estate pursuant to § 2042(2), although they are not included under § 2033.

Commissioner v. Estate of Noel

380 U.S. 678 (1965)

Mr. Justice Black delivered the opinion of the Court.

This is a federal estate tax case, raising questions under section 2042(2) of the Internal Revenue Code . . . , which requires inclusion in the gross estate of a decedent of amounts received by beneficiaries other than the executor from "insurance under policies on the life of the decedent" if the decedent "possessed at his death any of the incidents of ownership, exercisable either alone or in conjunction with any other person . . . ." The questions presented in this case are whether certain flight insurance policies payable upon the accidental death of the insured were policies "on the life of the decedent" and whether at his death he had reserved any of the "incidents of ownership" in the policies.

These issues emerge from the following facts. Respondent Ruth M. Noel drove her husband from their home to New York International Airport where he was to take an airplane to Venezuela. Just before taking off, Mr. Noel signed applications for two round-trip flight insurance policies, aggregating $125,000 and naming his wife as beneficiary. Mrs. Noel testified that she paid the premiums of $2.50 each on the policies and that her husband then instructed the sales clerk to "give them to my wife. They are hers now, I no longer have anything to do with them." The clerk gave her the policies, which she kept. Less than three hours later Mr. Noel's plane crashed into the Atlantic Ocean and he and all others aboard were killed. Thereafter the companies paid Mrs. Noel the $125,000 face value of the policies, which was not included in the estate tax return filed by his executors. The Commissioner of Internal Revenue determined that the proceeds of the policies should have been included and the Tax Court sustained that determination, holding that the flight accident policies were insurance "on the life of the decedent"; that

Mr. Noel had possessed exercisable "incidents of ownership" in the policies at his death; and that the $125,000 paid to Mrs. Noel as beneficiary was therefore includable in the gross estate. 39 T. C. 466. Although agreeing that decedent's reserved right to assign the policies and to change the beneficiary amounted to "exercisable incidents of ownership within the meaning of the statute," the Court of Appeals nevertheless reversed, holding that given "its ordinary, plain and generally accepted meaning," the statutory phrase "policies on the life of the decedent" does not apply to insurance paid on account of accidental death under policies like those here. 332 F.2d 950. The court's reason for drawing the distinction was that under a life insurance contract an insurer "agrees to pay a specified sum upon the occurrence of an *inevitable* event," whereas accident insurance covers a risk "which is *evitable* and not likely to occur." (Emphasis supplied.) 332 F.2d at 952. Because of the importance of an authoritative answer to these questions in the administration of the estate tax laws, we granted certiorari to decide them. 379 U.S. 927.

I.

In 1929, 36 years ago, the Board of Tax Appeals, predecessor to the Tax Court, held in *Ackerman v. Commissioner*, 15 B.T.A. 635, that "amounts received as accident insurance" because of the death of the insured were includable in the estate of the deceased. The Board of Tax Appeals recognized that "there is a distinction between life insurance and accident insurance, the former insuring against death in any event and the latter . . . against death under certain contingencies . . . ." The Court of Appeals in the case now before us considered this distinction between an "inevitable" and an "evitable" event to be of crucial significance under the statute. The Board of Tax Appeals in *Ackerman* did not, stating "we fail to see why one is not taken out upon the life of the policy-holder as much as the other. In each case the risk assumed by the insurer is the loss of the insured's life, and the payment of the insurance money is contingent upon the loss of life." This view of the Board of Tax Appeals is wholly consistent with the language of the statute itself which makes no distinction between "policies on the life of the decedent" which are payable in all events and those payable only if death comes in a certain way or within a certain time. Even were the statutory language less clear, since the Board of Tax Appeals' *Ackerman* case it has been the settled and consistent administrative practice to include insurance proceeds for accidental death under policies like these in the estates of decedents. The Treasury Regulations remain unchanged from the time of the *Ackerman* decision and from that day to this Congress has never attempted to limit the scope of that decision or the established administrative construction of section 2042(2), although it has re-enacted that section and amended it in other respects a number of times. We have held in many cases that such a long-standing administrative interpretation, applying to a substantially re-enacted statute, is deemed to have received congressional approval and has the effect of law. *See, e.g., National Lead Co. v. United States*, 252 U.S. 140, 146; *United States v. Dakota-Montana Oil Co.*, 288 U.S. 459, 466. We hold here that these insurance policies, whether called "flight accident insurance" or "life insurance," were in effect insurance taken out on the "life of the decedent" within the meaning of section 2042(2).

II.

The executors' second contention is that even if these were policies "on the life of the decedent," Mrs. Noel owned them completely, and the decedent therefore possessed no exercisable incident of ownership in them at the time of his death so as to make the proceeds includable in his estate. While not clearly spelled out, the contention that the decedent reserved no incident of ownership in the policies rests on three alternative claims: (a) that Mrs. Noel purchased the policies and therefore owned them; (b) that even if her husband owned the policies, he gave them to her, thereby depriving himself of power to assign the policies or to change the beneficiary; and (c) even assuming he had contractual power to assign the policies or make a beneficiary change, this power was illusory as he could not possibly have exercised it in the interval between take-off and the fatal crash in the Atlantic.

(a) The contention that Mrs. Noel bought the policies and therefore owned them rests solely on her testimony that she furnished the money for their purchase, intending thereby to preserve her right to continue as beneficiary. Accepting her claim that she supplied the money to buy the policies for her own benefit (which the Tax Court did not decide), what she bought nonetheless were policy contracts containing agreements between her husband and the companies. The contracts themselves granted to Mr. Noel the right either to assign the policies or to change the beneficiary without her consent. Therefore the contracts she bought by their very terms rebut her claim that she became the complete, unconditional owner of the policies with an irrevocable right to remain the beneficiary.

(b) The contention that Mr. Noel gave or assigned the policies to her and therefore was without power thereafter to assign them or to change the beneficiary stands no better under these facts. The contract terms provided that these policies could not be assigned nor could the beneficiary be changed without a written endorsement on the policies. No such assignment or change of beneficiary was endorsed on these policies, and consequently the power to assign the policies or change the beneficiary remained in the decedent at the time of his death.

(c) Obviously, there was no practical opportunity for the decedent to assign the policies or change the beneficiary between the time he boarded the plane and the time he died. That time was too short and his wife had the policies in her possession at home. These circumstances disabled him for the moment from exercising those "incidents of ownership" over the policies which were undoubtedly his. Death intervened before this temporary disability was removed. But the same could be said about a man owning an ordinary life insurance policy who boarded the plane at the same time or for that matter about any man's exercise of ownership over his property while aboard an airplane in the three hours before a fatal crash. It would stretch the imagination to think that Congress intended to measure estate tax liability by an individual's fluctuating, day-by-day, hour-by-hour capacity to dispose of property which he owns. We hold that estate tax liability for policies "with respect to which the decedent possessed at his death any of the incidents of ownership" depends on a general, legal power to exercise ownership, without regard to the owner's ability to exercise it at a particular moment. Nothing we have said is to be taken as meaning that a policyholder is without power to divest himself of all incidents of ownership over his insurance policies by a proper gift or assignment, so as to bar its inclusion in his gross estate under section 2042(2). What we do hold is that no such transfer was made of the policies here involved. The judgment of the Court of Appeals is reversed and the judgment of the Tax Court is affirmed.

———

Estate of Lumpkin v. Commissioner

474 F.2d 1092 (5th Cir. 1973)

[Decedent-employee was covered by an employer provided group term life insurance policy whose beneficiaries (spouse, minor children, and parents, in that order) were set by the employer. Proceeds were to be paid to the beneficiaries in monthly increments for a period determined by the length of the employee's service. The only rights the employee had over this policy, purchased by the employer, was the power to delay payment of one-half of the monthly payments due the surviving spouse, or to negotiate other forms of payment with the employer and the insurer. The employee had no right to modify the order of beneficiary designation.]

Gewin, Circuit Judge:

This federal estate tax case squarely presents the question of whether an employee who under the provisions of a group term life insurance policy is given nothing more than the right to alter the time and manner of enjoyment of the proceeds possesses an "incident of ownership" with respect to that policy so that at his death the value of the proceeds must be included in his gross estate under section 2042 of the Internal Revenue Code . . . . Decedent, James H. Lumpkin, Jr., died on March 15, 1964. After his estate's tax return was received, the Commissioner of Internal Revenue assessed a deficiency because the value of the proceeds from a group term life insurance policy covering Lumpkin's life were [sic] not included in his gross estate. Lumpkin's estate brought this action in the United States Tax Court to contest the Commissioner's deficiency determination. The Tax Court decided that section 2042 does not require the value of the proceeds to be included in decedent's gross estate, and the Commissioner has appealed. We reverse.

. . .

Section 2042 is the statute in the federal estate tax scheme under which the value of life insurance proceeds is taxed to the estate of the insured. With respect to proceeds receivable by beneficiaries other than the insured, it is triggered only if at death the insured possessed any "incidents of ownership" in the insurance. When the "incidents of ownership" term first appeared as part of an amendment to section 2042's predecessor, no definition accompanied it; however, Congress, in its committee reports, did include an illustrative list of the kinds of rights comprehended by the phrase. Among these were the right of the insured to the economic benefits of the insurance, the right to change beneficiaries, the right [sic] to surrender or cancel the policy, the right to assign the policy, the right to pledge the policy for a loan, and others.

From this list it can be inferred that by using the "incidents of ownership" term Congress was attempting to tax the value of life insurance proceeds over which the insured at death still possessed a *substantial degree* of control. This inference is strengthened if we recognize that by enacting section 2042 Congress intended to give life insurance policies estate tax treatment roughly equivalent to that accorded other types of property under related sections of the Code. Under sections 2036 (transfers with retained life estate), 2037 (transfers taking effect at death), 2038 (revocable transfers), and 2041 (powers of appointment) substantial control is often the touchstone by which the determination is made that inclusion is necessary . . . .

The question before this court is whether the right to alter the time and manner of enjoyment, a fractional right to be sure, affords its holder the kind of control over the proceeds that will make it an "incident of ownership" within the meaning of section 2042(2). The Tax Court thought not. In reaching this decision it relied on an earlier Board of Tax Appeals case which to our knowledge is the only one in which the question has been considered. In *Billings v. Commissioner*[6] the decedent had a right to elect optional modes of settlement similar to that conferred upon Lumpkin by the group term policy in this case; the Tax Court's predecessor held that the right to determine when the proceeds should be paid to the beneficiary was too limited and insignificant to amount to control over the proceeds.

To offset the impact of this 1937 decision, the Commissioner relies upon two relatively more recent Supreme Court decisions. In *Lober v. United States*[7] the decedent had created three separate irrevocable trusts . . . . Thus Lober had forsaken the right to determine who the beneficiaries of the trust would be but had retained the right to determine when the trust property would be enjoyed. The court held that retention of this right rendered the value of the trust property includible in Lober's gross estate under the forerunner to section 2038 . . . . In reference to Lober's right to alter the time of enjoyment, the court said: " '[A] donor who keeps so strong a hold over the actual and immediate enjoyment of what he puts beyond his own power to retake has not divested himself of that degree of control which § [2038] requires in order to avoid the tax.' "[8]

In essence *United States v. O'Malley*,[9] the second case relied upon by the Commissioner, is not substantially different from *Lober* . . . . [There the power] extended to the trust income only and not the principal which was

---

[6] B.T.A. 1147 (1937), *acq.* 1937–2 Cum. Bull. 3. Although it has since been withdrawn, the Commissioner's acquiescence in the *Billings* case remained outstanding at the time taxpayer filed its return and at the time the litigation commenced, and at oral argument the taxpayer argued that its justifiable reliance upon this acquiescence estopped the Commissioner from reversing his position retroactively. But it is well-established law that the Commissioner has plenary power to modify, amend or revoke his acquiescences and to make suit changes retroactively as to all taxpayers or, in the exercise of his discretion, certain classes of taxpayers. *Dixon v. United States*, 381 U.S. 68 (1965).

[7] 346 U.S. 335 (1953).

[8] *Lober v. United States*, 346 U.S. 335, 337 (1953).

[9] 383 U.S. 627 (1966).

inalterably committed to pass to the beneficiary (or his estate) when the trust terminated.[10] Nevertheless the Supreme Court held that O'Malley's power over the time and manner of enjoyment was significant and of sufficient substance to activate the predecessor to section 2036 which required inclusion whenever the transferor of property in trust had retained the right to "designate" who was to enjoy it.

. . .

The only significant distinction between sections 2036 and 2038 on the one hand and section 2042 on the other is that under the former there must be an incomplete transfer by the decedent whereas under the latter a transfer is unnecessary. Thus under sections 2036 and 2038 the decedent must have *retained* some control over property he initially transferred while under section 2042 it is enough if at death the decedent merely *possessed* an incident of ownership, the means by which he came into possession being irrelevant. This distinction does not, however, suggest that there is a further difference among these sections of the estate tax as to the degree of power a decedent must hold over the property in question—whether it be life insurance or some other form of wealth—in order to render its value includible in his gross estate.

These sections are all part of a Congressional scheme to tax the value of property transferred at death, whether the decedent accomplishes the transfer by will, by intestacy, or by allowing his substantial control over the property to remain unexercised until death so that the shifting of its economic benefits to the beneficiary only then becomes complete. It is the lapse of substantial control at death that triggers their application. *Lober* and *O'Malley* teach that one endowed with power over the time of enjoyment has the kind of substantial control Congress intended to reach by enacting these sections. Because the control it affords is substantial, we conclude that a right to alter the time of enjoyment such as that conferred upon Lumpkin by the optional modes of settlement provision in this case is an "incident of ownership" under section 2042(2). Lumpkin could easily have assigned the right to elect optional settlements, thereby completely divesting himself of control over the insurance proceeds and avoiding inclusion of their value within his gross estate. Since he did not, his estate must suffer the consequences.

. . .

Vacated and remanded.

———

In contrast with *Lumpkin*, the Third Circuit has held that settlement options do not constitute incidents of ownership, provided that the decedent cannot enjoy any economic benefits by exercising the power. *See Estate of Connelly v. Commissioner*, 551 F.2d 545, 552 (3d Cir. 1977) (right to select a settlement option with the mutual agreement of the insured's employer and the insurer did not give the insured a substantial degree of control sufficient

---

[10] The district court held that the original corpus of the trusts was includible in the estate, and that holding was not challenged on appeal.

to constitute an incident of ownership).[11] In *Estate of Rockwell v. Commissioner*, 779 F.2d 931 (3d Cir. 1985), the court extended the economic benefit rationale. In *Rockwell*, the court held that the decedent's right to veto third party ownership of a policy did not constitute an incident of ownership because the decedent could not enjoy any economic benefit by exercising the veto power over a policy held in trust. The court distinguished Rev. Rul. 75–70, 1975–1 C.B. 301, in which the decedent had the ability to enjoy economic benefits by exercising veto power. *See also Billings v. Commissioner*, 35 B.T.A. 1147 (1937), *nonacq.* 1972–1 C.B. 3.

In *Schwager v. Commissioner*, 64 T.C. 781, 791–92 (1975), the court noted:

> [I]t is not the number of powers possessed that is the determining factor. Rather it is the existence of even a "fractional" power not the "probability" of its exercise that controls . . . .

> The distinction between the power to make changes and the power to bar change by the expedient of denying permission was found insufficient to alter the result in *Karagheusian's Estate* [233 F.2d 197 (2d Cir. 1956)] where the Court of Appeals stated that it made "no difference whether under the trust instrument the decedent may initiate changes or whether he must merely consent to them . . . ."

> Although certain powers may be retained which will not constitute incidents of ownership [such as the right to receive policy dividends], the ability to bar the change of beneficiary to a part of the policy does, in our judgment, constitute a substantial incident of ownership.

The Service concedes that § 2042(2) will not apply if the decedent was listed mistakenly as the owner. *See* Priv. Ltr. Rul. 8610068. Nor will § 2042(2) apply if a valid contract or other binding arrangement overrides powers granted by the terms of the policy. *See Estate of Beauregard v. Commissioner*, 74 T.C. 603 (1980), *acq.* 1981–1 C.B. 1 (California court order prevented decedent from changing beneficiary designation). At the other extreme, a contract may operate to give the decedent rights that constitute taxable incidents of ownership even though those rights are not accorded under the policy. *See Estate of Tomerlin v. Commissioner*, T.C. Memo. 1986–147.

Treasury Regulation § 20.2042–1(c)(2) and –1(c)(3) provides guidance on what constitutes an incident of ownership for purposes of § 2042(2). The test is satisfied by many powers which do not rise to the level of interests, such as the power to change beneficiaries, borrow against the policy, assign the policy, pledge the policy as collateral for a loan, or select a settlement option. Thus, the operation of § 2042 is difficult to analogize to the *string* sections of the Code (such as §§ 2036, 2037, and 2038), which require gross estate inclusion of property not owned by the decedent at death. The *incidents of ownership* test is far broader in operation than §§ 2036, 2037, or 2038 because it does not require the decedent to initially purchase or pay for the policy. Likewise, to the extent that the *incidents of ownership* test does not allow the decedent to exchange the policy for cash or make the policy payable to his

---

[11] The Service has announced that it will not follow *Connelly*. *See* Rev. Rul. 81–128, 1981–1 C.B. 469.

estate, creditors, or to the creditors of his estate, it is more far reaching in operation than § 2041. Section 2041 analogizes the holder of a general power of appointment to the owner of the property for estate tax purposes.

Section 2042(2) specifically adopts a § 2037 test for determining whether a contingent right over a policy will constitute an incident of ownership. Thus, a reversionary interest constitutes an incident of ownership if the right is valued at more than 5% of the value of the policy immediately before the insured's death. A reversionary interest is the possibility that the policy or its proceeds may return to the insured or become subject to a power of disposition by the decedent. The possibility, however, that the insured might receive the policy or its proceeds by inheritance through the estate of another is not considered to be a reversionary interest. *See* Treas. Reg. § 20.2042–1(c)(3). Furthermore, Treasury Regulation § 20.2042–1(c)(3) provides that if the assignee has an unqualified right to cash in the policy immediately before the insured's death, this right prevents the reversionary interest from having a value in excess of 5% of the value of the policy.

If the decedent owns a controlling interest in a corporation, the substance-over-form analysis dictates that the policy is taxed as though it is owned by the decedent. *See* Treas. Reg. §§ 20.2042–1(c)(6), 20.2031–2(f). A controlling interest is defined as more than 50% of the total combined voting power of a corporation which owns a policy on the decedent's life. If, however, the policy is payable to the corporation, which is typical when the policy is *key person* insurance, inclusion of the policy in the decedent's estate results in double taxation, because the policy also should be taken into account in determining the value of the decedent's interest in the corporation. Therefore, the Regulations specifically negate attribution of the corporate ownership to the decedent when the corporation receives the policy proceeds. *See id.* Comparable rules apply in the partnership area. *See* Rev. Rul. 83–147, 1983–2 C.B. 158; Rev. Rul. 83–148, 1983–2 C.B. 157.

Problems

1. *H* purchased an ordinary life insurance policy on *W*'s life and named himself as the policy beneficiary. *H* retains full ownership of the policy and pays all premiums.

    a. What would be the estate tax consequences if *H* predeceases *W*?

    b. How would the results differ if *H* had purchased a paid-up policy? What effect does the *Cartwright* decision, reproduced in § 3.03[A][2], *supra*, have on the valuation of the policy in *H*'s estate?

2. *H* created a revocable trust that benefits his children. A bank is the trustee. His wife, *W*, owns a policy of insurance on his life and makes the trust the beneficiary. She retains the incidents of ownership. When *H* dies, with the policy in force, is any part of it includable in his gross estate under §§ 2042 or 2041? *See Margrave v. Commissioner*, 618 F.2d 34 (8th Cir. 1980). Would a gift tax be due? *See* Rev. Rul. 81–166, 1981–1 C.B. 477.

3. Donna purchased a life insurance policy on her life and named Anna as beneficiary. What would be the estate tax consequences if, more than four years before her death, Donna irrevocably assigns the policy to Anna, but:

a. Donna retains the power to change the policy beneficiary with the permission of Anna?

b. the assignment provides that Anna cannot change the beneficiary without Donna's consent?

4. Dave is an employee of Smith & Associates, but not a shareholder. His company provides group term insurance coverage for each employee in an amount equal to two times an employee's annual salary. The plan contains a conversion feature allowing, but not requiring, each employee to convert the policy to an ordinary life policy after voluntary termination of employment. The policy may be canceled if the employee is fired. Each employee may designate a beneficiary and may change that designation at any time.

a. Will there be any estate tax inclusion when Dave dies four years after designating his wife as the policy beneficiary if he gave her the power to change the beneficiary and to exercise the conversion feature?

b. What would be the estate tax consequences if Dave retained the conversion feature? *See Estate of Smead v. Commissioner*, 78 T.C. 43 (1982), *acq.*, Rev. Rul. 84–130, 1984–2 C.B. 194.

c. How would the estate tax consequences differ if Dave owned 40% of the company stock and his wife owned 15%, so that together they could cause the corporation to cancel the group policy?

5. Don is the sole shareholder of Production Corporation. The corporation owns a life insurance policy on Don's life and the proceeds are payable to the corporation.

a. What are the estate tax consequences of the policy when Don dies?

b. Would the estate tax consequences be different if Don's wife were the beneficiary under the policy?

6. Four years ago, *H* assigned his interest in a group life insurance policy to *W*. Two years later, a new policy was issued to *H*, but *W* had to agree to surrender the first policy. Will the second policy be includable in *H*'s gross estate? *See American Nat'l Bank & Trust Co. v. United States*, 832 F.2d 1032 (7th Cir. 1987).

Revenue Ruling 84–179

1984–2 C.B. 195

ISSUE

For purposes of section 2042(2) of the Internal Revenue Code, does an insured decedent possess incidents of ownership in an insurance policy if the decedent transferred all incidents of ownership to another person who, in an unrelated transaction, transferred the policy in trust and, at death, the decedent was a trustee with discretionary powers which, although broad, could not be exercised for *D*'s personal benefit?

FACTS

In 1960, *D*, the decedent, purchased an insurance policy on *D*'s life and transferred all incidents of ownership to *D*'s spouse. The spouse designated their adult child as the policy beneficiary.

The spouse died in 1978 and, by will, established a residuary trust for the benefit of the child. *D* was designated as trustee. The insurance policy on *D*'s life was included in the spouse's residuary estate and was transferred to the testamentary trust. The drafting of the spouse's will to provide for the residuary trust and the appointment of *D* as trustee were unrelated to *D*'s transfer of the policy to the spouse.

As trustee, *D* had broad discretionary powers in the management of the trust property and the power to distribute or accumulate income. Under the terms of the policy, the owner could elect to have the proceeds made payable according to various plans, use the loan value to pay the premiums, borrow on the policy, assign or pledge the policy, and elect to receive annual dividends. The terms of the will did not preclude *D* from exercising these rights, although *D* could not do so for *D*'s own benefit. *D* paid the premiums on the policy out of other trust property.

D was still serving as trustee when *D* died in 1984.

LAW AND ANALYSIS

Section 2042(2) of the Code provides that the value of the gross estate includes the value of all property to the extent of the amount receivable as insurance under policies on the life of the decedent by beneficiaries (other than the executor), with respect to which the decedent possessed at date of death any of the incidents of ownership in the policies, exercisable either alone or in conjunction with any other person.

Section 20.2042–1(c)(2) of the Estate Tax Regulations provides that the meaning of the term "incidents of ownership" is not confined to ownership of the policy in the technical legal sense. The term includes the power to change the beneficiary, to surrender or cancel the policy for a loan, or to obtain from the insurer a loan against the surrender value of the policy, etc.

Section 20.2042–1(c)(4) of the regulations provides that a decedent is considered to have an incident of ownership in a policy held in trust if under the terms of the policy the decedent (either alone or in conjunction with another person) has the power (as trustee or otherwise) to change the beneficial ownership in the policy or its proceeds, or the time or manner of enjoyment thereof, even though the decedent has no beneficial interest in the trust.

The legislative history of section 2042 indicates that Congress intended section 2042 to parallel the statutory scheme governing those powers that would cause other types of property to be included in a decedent's gross estate under other Code sections, particularly sections 2036 and 2038. S. Rep. No. 1622, 83rd Cong., 2d Sess. 124 (1954). *See Estate of Skifter v. Commissioner*, 468 F.2d 699 (2d Cir. 1972).

Sections 2036(a)(2) and 2038(a)(1) concern lifetime transfers made by the decedent. Under these sections, it is the decedent's power to affect the beneficial interests in, or enjoyment of, the transferred property that required [sic] inclusion of the property in the gross estate. Section 2036 is directed at those powers retained by the decedent in connection with the transfer. *See, for example, United States v. O'Malley*, 383 U.S. 627 (1966), 1966–2 C.B. 526. Section 2038(a)(1) is directed at situations where the transferor-decedent sets the machinery in motion that purposefully allows fiduciary powers over the property interest to subsequently return to the transferor-decedent, such as by an incomplete transfer. *See Estate of Reed v. United States*, Civil No. 74–543 (M.D. Fla., May 7, 1975); *Estate of Skifter v. Commissioner*, above cited, at 703–05.

In accordance with the legislative history of section 2042(2), a decedent will not be deemed to have incidents of ownership over an insurance policy on decedent's life where decedent's powers are held in a fiduciary capacity, and are not exercisable for decedent's personal benefit, where the decedent did not transfer the policy or any of the consideration for purchasing or maintaining the policy to the trust from personal assets, and the devolution of the powers on decedent was not part of a prearranged plan involving the participation of the decedent. This position is consistent with decisions by several courts of appeal. *See Estate of Skifter; Estate of Fruehauf v. Commissioner*, 427 F.2d 80 (6th Cir. 1970); *Hunter v. United States*, 624 F.2d 833 (8th Cir. 1980). *But see Terriberry v. United States*, 517 F.2d 286 (5th Cir. 1975), *cert. denied*, 424 U.S. 977 (1976); *Rose v. United States*, 511 F.2d 259 (5th Cir. 1975), which are to the contrary. Section 20.2042–1(c)(4) will be read in accordance with the position adopted herein.

The decedent will be deemed to have incidents of ownership over an insurance policy on the decedent's life where decedent's powers are held in a fiduciary capacity and the decedent has transferred the policy or any of the consideration for purchasing and maintaining the policy to the trust. Also, where the decedent's powers could have been exercised for decedent's benefit, they will constitute incidents of ownership in the policy, without regard to how those powers were acquired and without consideration of whether the decedent transferred the property to the trust. *Estate of Fruehauf; Estate of Skifter*, above cited at 703. Thus, if the decedent reacquires powers over insurance policies in an individual capacity, the powers will constitute incidents of ownership even though the decedent is a transferee.

In the present situation, *D* completely relinquished all interest in the insurance policy on *D*'s life. The powers over the policy devolved on *D* as a fiduciary, through an independent transaction, and were not exercisable for *D*'s own benefit. Also, *D* did not transfer property to the trust. Thus, *D* did not possess incidents of ownership over the policy for purposes of section 2042(2) of the Code.

HOLDING

An insured decedent who transferred all incidents of ownership in a policy to another person, who in an unrelated transaction transferred powers over the policy in trust to the decedent, will not be considered to possess incidents of ownership in the policy for purposes of section 2042(2) of the Code, provided that the decedent did not furnish consideration for maintaining the policy and could not exercise the powers for personal benefit. The result is the same where the decedent, as trustee, purchased the policy with trust assets, did not contribute assets to the trust or maintain the policy with personal assets, and could not exercise the powers for personal benefit.

EFFECTS ON OTHER REVENUE RULINGS

Rev. Rul. 76–261, 1976–2 C.B. 276, is revoked.

———

[d]   Community Property

Revenue Ruling 80–242

1980–2 C.B. 276

ISSUE

What amount is includible in *D*'s gross estate with respect to insurance on *D*'s life, under the circumstances described below?

FACTS

D, a resident of Texas, obtained, when unmarried, a whole life policy of insurance on *D*'s life, in face amount of $100,000. *D* paid $3,000 in premiums before marriage. After marriage, $12,000 in premiums were paid with funds that were, under the law of Texas, community property. *D* held the incidents of ownership in the policy until death. The surviving spouse, *S*, was the designated beneficiary of the policy.

LAW AND ANALYSIS

Section 2033 of the Internal Revenue Code provides that a decedent's gross estate shall include the value of all property to the extent of the decedent's interest therein at the time of death.

Section 2042(2) includes in the gross estate the proceeds of insurance on the decedent's life if the decedent possessed incidents of ownership in the policy.

Under Texas law the proceeds of an insurance policy belong to the insured's separate estate, if the policy was initially separate property of the insured when acquired. However, if after the policy is acquired premiums are paid with community funds, then the proceeds are subject to the community estate's right of reimbursement for the return of community funds used to pay the premiums.

In the present case, the policy was the separate property of *D* when acquired and therefore the proceeds belong to *D*'s separate estate. However, since $12,000 in insurance premiums was paid with community funds, the insurance proceeds are subject to the community claim for reimbursement of premiums paid. Therefore, the amount includible in *D*'s gross estate under section 2042(2) of the Code is the face amount of policy proceeds less the amount of premiums paid with community funds, or $88,000. In addition, one-half of the reimbursed premiums ($6,000) is separately includible in *D*'s gross estate under section 2033 of the Code as the value of *D*'s interest, at death, in community property.

The above conclusions regarding the amount includible with respect to the decedent's insurance policy proceeds are in direct conflict with *Rev. Rul. 54–272*, 1954–2 C.B. 298, which applies a discussion of Louisiana law contained in Paragraph (E) of *Rev. Rul. 232*, 1953–2 C.B. 268, to similar situations arising under Texas law. Applying *Rev. Rul. 54–272*, to the facts in the present situation, $100,000 would be includible under section 2042 of the Code. The Service will no longer follow the position stated in *Rev. Rul. 54–272* that in cases when the surviving spouse is the beneficiary the full value of the insurance proceeds, purchased in part with community funds, is includible in the gross estate under section 2042. However, in such cases the Service will continue to disallow a deduction under section 2053 for the community's claim for reimbursement, since under Texas law the community's claim for reimbursement of the insurance premiums paid for community funds is a claim on the insurance proceeds rather than a claim on the decedent's estate. *See* sections 20.2053–4 and 20.2053–7 of the Estate Tax Regulations. For the same reason, when the decedent's estate, or someone other than the surviving spouse is the beneficiary, the Service will not allow a deduction under section 2053 with regard to the community's reimbursement claim. However, the community's reimbursement claim will be reflected as a reduction in the amount includible in the gross estate under section 2042.

. . .

———————

Estate taxation of life insurance in community property regimes depends on the applicable state law. *See Lang v. Commissioner*, 304 U.S. 264 (1938); Treas. Reg. § 20.2042–1(c)(5). For example, Revenue Ruling 80–242 relied on Texas' inception of title approach where the surviving spouse is only entitled to the return of one-half of the premiums paid for a policy that was acquired by the insured spouse as separate property. As a result, the entire proceeds of the policy, less those reimbursable premium payments, were includible in the decedent's estate. On the other hand, under California's apportionment approach the surviving spouse is entitled to a ratable share of the proceeds that were purchased by one half of the community property funds. Accordingly, a lesser amount should be includible in the deceased spouse's estate. *See Scott v. Commissioner*, 374 F.2d 154 (9th Cir. 1967).

In *Estate of Burris v. Commissioner*, T.C. Memo. 2001-210, the Tax Court held that only one-half of the proceeds were includable in the deceased spouse's estate when a life insurance was purchased with community property funds. The linchpin for the decision was the court's construction of Louisiana law to the effect that the noninsured spouse has a community property interest in a policy purchased with community property, resulting in the conclusion that the deceased spouse had incidents of ownership in only one-half of the policy.

If under applicable law the noninsured spouse can be shown to be the owner of the entire policy, the proceeds can be entirely excluded from the insured's estate on the theory that he possessed no incidents of ownership over it. *See, e.g.*, Rev. Rul. 94–69, 1994–2 C.B. 241 (Louisiana); *Parson v. United States*, 460 F.2d 228 (5th Cir. 1972) (Texas). But, as in Rev. Rul. 94–69, the surviving spouse will be treated as then making a completed gift of the proceeds if a third party is the beneficiary.

Estate taxation under § 2041(1) also depends on community property rights in insurance that is payable to the estate of the insured. Based on the theory that the surviving spouse will be entitled to one-half of the proceeds, the general rule is that only one-half of the proceeds is includible in the insured's gross estate if the insurance is owned as community property. *See* Treas. Reg. § 20.2042–1(b)(2). If, however, the deceased spouse's estate was designated beneficiary and under applicable state law the surviving spouse does not have a valid claim to one-half of the proceeds receivable by the estate, then the full amount receivable by the decedent's estate will be included in its gross estate under section 2041(1). *See Estate of Steet v. Commissioner*, 152 F.3d 482 (5th Cir. 1997) (Texas law). On the other hand, only one-half of the face value may be included in the insured's gross, estate even if the noninsured spouse predeceases the insured and all proceeds are payable to the insured's estate if the predeceased spouse's estate or successor has a claim to one-half of the proceeds. *See Estate of Cervin v. Commissioner*, 111 F.3d 1252 (5th Cir. 1997); *following Estate of Cavenuaugh v. Commissioner*, 51 F.3d 597 (5th Cir. 1995) (Texas Law).

[e] Life Insurance Proceeds and the Marital Deduction

Proceeds of life insurance included in the gross estate which pass to the decedent's surviving spouse generally qualify for the marital deduction. *See* § 2056(c)(7). Care must be taken to avoid the terminable interest rule under some settlement options. An arrangement that is equivalent to the life estate—general power of appointment trust,[12] however, is deductible under § 2056(b)(6). That section provides that the marital deduction is allowed for a life insurance settlement in which the proceeds of a life insurance policy are held by an insurance company under a contract in which the surviving spouse is to receive the proceeds in installments or the interest on the proceeds, and the spouse has a power to appoint all interests. The rationale is that the surviving spouse has rights under the installment or interest options analogous to those required for an interest qualifying for the marital deduction under § 2056(b)(5). When insurance proceeds are payable to a trust, the arrangement may qualify for the marital deduction if the rules governing

---

[12] *See* discussion of § 3.04[C][4][b], *supra*.

marital deduction and power of appointment or QTIP trusts are met, as discussed in Chapter 3.

[f] Interaction with Section 2206

Although the determination of who bears the burden of death taxes is generally a matter of state law, § 2206 apportions the estate tax attributable to life insurance to the beneficiaries, unless the decedent's will provides otherwise. *See McAleer v. Jewell*, 804 F.2d 1231 (11th Cir. 1986). That section does not, however, apply to insurance proceeds which qualify for the estate tax marital deduction because the proceeds generate no tax. *See also Estate of Boyd v. Commissioner*, 819 F.2d 170 (7th Cir. 1987), *rev'g* 85 T.C. 1056 (1985) (qualified disclaimer of right to have decedent's estate pay taxes attributable to life insurance proceeds triggered § 2206 and enlarged the marital deduction).

[2] Transfers Within Three Years of Death

Code: § 2035(a).

Regulations: None.

[a] In General

Revenue Ruling 82–13

1982–1 C.B. 132

ISSUE

Is the value of a renewable group term life insurance policy includable in the decedent's gross estate under section 2035 of the Internal Revenue Code when the decedent has assigned the policy more than three years before death, but is considered to make premium payments until death?

FACTS

D, the decedent, was an employee of *X* company, which covered its employees with a renewable group term life insurance policy. All premiums were paid by the *X* company. The policy was renewable upon payment of the annual premium at standard rates. No evidence of insurability was necessary for renewal.

On February 1, 1975, *D*, gratuitously assigned all rights under the policy (including any conversion privilege) to *A* and each subsequent yearly premium was paid by *D*'s employer, the *X* company. *D* died on May 1, 1980, possessing no incidents of ownership in the policy.

LAW AND ANALYSIS

Section 2035(a) of the Code generally provides that the gross estate shall include the value of all property interests transferred by a decedent within three years before death.

The initial purchase of a life insurance policy by a decedent who designates a third party as owner of the policy is a transfer of the policy for purposes of section 2035 of the Code and the entire proceeds will be includable in the decedent's gross estate if such purchase is within three years of death. *Detroit Bank & Trust Co. v. United States*, 467 F.2d 964 (6th Cir. 1972), *cert. denied*, 410 U.S. 929 (1973); *First National Bank of Oregon v. United States*, 352 F. Supp. 1157 (D.C. Ore. 1972), *aff'd*, 488 F.2d 575 (9th Cir. 1973). The result is the same if the policy is initially purchased by the decedent as owner more than three years before death but is subsequently transferred by the decedent to a third party owner within three years of the decedent's death. The result is also the same where the decedent annually repurchases a policy that expires in its entirety each year and upon each repurchase designates a third party as owner. In such a case, each repurchase constitutes a new transfer for purposes of section 2035 of the Code, and the proceeds will be includable in the decedent's gross estate at death. *See Bel v. United States*, 452 F.2d 683 (5th Cir. 1971), *cert. denied*, 406 U.S. 919 (1972).

A term life insurance policy furnishes life insurance protection for a specified term, the face value of which is payable only if death occurs during stipulated term. At the end of the policy term all premiums are fully earned, and all rights of the policy owner terminate. S. HUEBNER AND K. BLACK, LIFE INSURANCE 73 (8th ed. 1972). If, however, the policy contains a provision granting a right of renewal, the contract must be renewed upon demand (and payment of the premium) by the policy owner, without regard to the insurable status of the insured at the time. D. GREGG AND V. LUCAS, LIFE AND HEALTH INSURANCE HANDBOOK 57 (3d ed. 1973).

In the instant case, the premiums paid by *X* company are attributable to *D*, for estate tax and gift tax purposes. *See* Rev. Rul. 76–490, 1976–2 C.B. 300. Thus, if the premium payment was deemed to purchase a new insurance contract each year, then the policy proceeds would be subject to inclusion under section 2035.

Under the group term policy considered here, there was an option for automatic renewal upon payment of the premium. This renewal was accomplished without providing evidence of insurability. The rights and obligations of the parties continued without interruption from the policy's inception, as long as the policy was renewed on each anniversary date. Thus, the payment of the premium at the time for the policy's renewal did not create new rights, nor was such payment a repurchase of insurance. The payment merely effectuated the continuation of an existing agreement. Therefore, when *D*, through *X* company, paid each renewal premium, it was not a new transfer of insurance coverage under section 2035 of the Code and the proceeds from the insurance policy are not includable in *D*'s gross estate.

Compare *Bel v. United States*, where payments of annual premiums after creation of the policy were each considered purchases of a new policy. In *Bel*, an accidental death policy was involved that did not provide a renewal privilege.

HOLDING

The value of the renewable group term life insurance policy is not includable in the decedent's gross estate under section 2035 of the Code when the decedent assigned the policy more than three years before death, but is considered to have made premium payments until death.

———

The tax consequences of transfers of, and premium payments on, life insurance policies near death have produced considerable controversy between the Service and taxpayers. This occurs, in large part, because the premiums or *replacement cost* policies are minuscule relative to the face amount of such policies. To avoid § 2042(2), owners have gifted policies on their lives to third persons. However, if the owner transferred the policy after 1976, and died within three years of the transfer, the policy proceeds would automatically be included in the insured's gross estate pursuant to § 2035. The only limitation has been that, to the extent that the transferee makes premium payments after the transfer of the policy and within three years of the transferor's death. The Tax Court has held that the amount includable in the decedent's gross estate is that portion of the policy proceeds which equals the ratio of the premiums paid by the decedent before the transfer to the total premiums paid before and after the transfer. *See Estate of Silverman v. Commissioner*, 61 T.C. 338 (1973), *aff'd on the grounds raised in the appeal*, 521 F.2d 574 (2d Cir. 1975).

The *Silverman* holding may be illustrated by the following example: Assume insurance proceeds were $1,000,000. If the decedent had paid $8,000 in premiums and the assignee had paid $2,000 in premiums, the assignee would be deemed to have contributed 20% of the value or $200,000. As a result, gross estate inclusion under section 2035 would be only $800,000. *See* Douglas Kahn and Laurence Waggoner, *Tax Consequences of Assigning Life Insurance-Time for Another Look*, 4 FLA. TAX REV. 381 (1999) (criticizing the *Silverman*-loophole).

[b] Pre-1982 Applications

Before the Economic Recovery Tax Act of 1981 (ERTA), taxpayers attempted to avoid the reach of § 2035 by furnishing the funds to acquire policies on their lives but with actual ownership of the policy initially acquired and held in a third person. Nonetheless, § 2035 was held applicable if the insured died within three years of the policy's acquisition based on a theory that the insured had constructively transferred the policy for purposes of § 2035.[13] *See Bel v.*

---

[13] Taxpayers attempted to avoid the constructive transfer doctrine by having a trust purchase the policy. In operation, the insured transferred sufficient funds to a trust to allow the trust to purchase a policy on the insured's life. If the transfer was within three years of death, however, § 2035 was applied willingly by the courts even though the trust was technically the purchaser; thus, recognizing that the trustee was nothing more than an agent of the insured for the purposes of purchasing the policy. *See First Nat'l Bank v. United States*, 488 F.2d 575 (9th Cir. 1973); *Detroit Bank and Trust Co. v. United States*, 467 F.2d 964 (6th Cir. 1972), *cert. denied*, 410 U.S. 929 (1972); *Estate of Kurihara v. Commissioner*, 82 T.C. 51 (1984) (summarizing cases). To apply the agency theory, however, it was necessary to establish more than just that the decedent furnished funds to the trustee who then acquired the policy; rather, it "require[d] a factual determination that the trustee . . . [had] no discretion to invest the trust assets, but was in fact controlled by the decedent, acting as the decedent's agent when he paid the premiums." *Hope v. United States*, 691 F.2d 786, 789 (5th Cir. 1982).

United States, 452 F.2d 683 (5th Cir. 1971), *cert. denied*, 406 U.S. 919 (1972) (the leading case in the area).

[c] Post-1981 Law

Changes made to § 2035 by ERTA altered the inclusion rule for policies acquired within three years of the decedent's death if the decedent never had any incidents of ownership.

Estate of Leder v. Commissioner

893 F.2d 237 (10th Cir. 1989), aff'g 87 T.C. 235 (1987)

Tachia, Circuit Judge.

The Commissioner of Internal Revenue ("Commissioner") appeals the decision of the United States Tax Court ("Tax Court") that the proceeds from an insurance policy are not includable in the insured's gross estate under section 2035(a)[14] of the Internal Revenue Code, 26 U.S.C. § 2035(d), where the decedent never possessed any of the incidents of ownership in the policy under section 2042. We affirm.

I.

The parties stipulated to the facts of this case. The decedent, Joseph Leder, died on May 31, 1983. At the time of his death, Joseph Leder was insured under a $1,000,000 policy issued by TransAmerica Occidental Life Insurance Company on January 28, 1981 ("the policy"). Jeanne Leder, the decedent's wife, signed the policy application as the owner and the decedent signed as the insured. The policy initially reflected that Jeanne Leder was the policy owner and sole beneficiary.

The premiums for the policy, $3,879.08 per month, were paid by preauthorized withdrawals from the account of Leader Enterprises, the decedent's wholly owned corporation. All of the policy premiums were paid less than three years before the decedent's death. Leader Enterprises treated the premium payments as loans made to the decedent. Neither Leader Enterprises nor the decedent received any consideration from Jeanne Leder in exchange for these premium payments.

On February 15, 1983, Jeanne Leder, as the owner of the policy, transferred the policy to herself as trustee of an inter vivos trust. The trust agreement provided that upon receipt of the trust corpus, the trustee would divide the trust into four equal shares for the benefit of Jeanne Leder and the Leders' three children. No further assignments of the policy proceeds or changes in the beneficiaries of the policy were made.

Upon the decedent's death the proceeds of the policy, $971,526.49, were distributed as provided for in the trust agreement. The proceeds were not

---

[14] In 1997, Congress amended section 2035. Subsection (d) was modified somewhat, reworded, and renumbered as subsection (a).

included in the decedent's gross estate on the federal estate tax returned filed for the decedent's estate.

The Commissioner determined that the proceeds of the policy were properly includable in the decedent's gross estate under section 2035 and sent Jeanne Leder, the executrix of Joseph Leder's estate, a notice of deficiency. The estate challenged the Commissioner's determination in the Tax Court.

The Tax Court held that the policy proceeds were not includable in the decedent's gross estate under section 2035. Section 2035 provides in relevant part:

> SEC. 2035. Adjustments for Gifts Made Within 3 Years of Decedent's Death . . . .
>
> (a) *Inclusion of Gifts Made by Decedent.* — [T]he value of the gross estate shall include the value of all property to the extent of any interest therein of which the decedent has at any time made a transfer, by trust or otherwise, during the 3-year period ending on the date of the decedent's death.
>
> (d) *Decedents Dying After 1981.*
>
> (1) *In general.* — Except as otherwise provided in this subsection, subsection (a) shall not apply to the estate of a decedent dying after December 31, 1981.
>
> (2) *Exceptions for certain transfers.* — Paragraph (1) of this subsection . . . shall not apply to a transfer of an interest in property which is included in the value of the gross estate under section 2036, 2037, 2038, or 2042 or would have been included under any of such sections if such interest had been retained by the decedent. 26 U.S.C. § 2035.[15]

Section 2035(a) generally requires that the value of any property or interest transferred by the decedent within three years of death for less than full and adequate consideration be included in the decedent's gross estate (the "three year inclusionary rule"). The Economic Recovery Tax Act of 1981, Pub. L. No. 97–34, section 424, 95 Stat. 172, 317 [hereinafter ERTA], added section 2035(d), which applies to the estates of decedents dying after 1981. Construing section 2035 as a whole, the Tax Court found that for decedents dying after 1981, subsection (d)(1) nullifies the three year inclusionary rule of subsection (a), except for those transfers described in subsection (d)(2). Section 2035(d)(2) specifically references transfers under section 2042 . . . .

Critically, under section 2042 the decedent's *payment of premiums is irrelevant* in determining whether the decedent retained any "incidents of ownership" in the policy proceeds. *See First Nat'l Bank v. United States*, 488 F.2d 575, 578 (9th Cir. 1973); *Bel v. United States*, 452 F.2d 683, 689 (5th Cir. 1971), *cert. denied*, 406 U.S. 919 (1972); *Estate of Headrick v. Commissioner*, 93 T.C. 171, 178–79 (1989). Congress intended to eliminate the premium payment test used in the 1939 Code when it adopted section 2042. *See First Nat'l Bank*, 488 F.2d at 578. Both the House and Senate committee

---

15 [Section 2035(d)(2) is now found in revised § 2035(a). Eds.]

reports stated that section 2042 "revises existing law so that payment of premiums is no longer a factor in determining the taxability *under this section* of insurance proceeds." *Id.* (emphasis in *First Nat'l Bank*) (quoting H.R. Rep. No.1337, 83d Cong., 2d Sess. A316, *reprinted in* 1954 U.S. Code Cong. & Admin. News 4017, 4459; citing S. Rep. No. 1622, 83d Cong., 2d Sess. 472 (1954)).

The Tax Court examined section 2042 and determined that the decedent never possessed any rights to the insurance policy that would constitute "incidents of ownership." Because the policy proceeds were not includable under section 2042, the Tax Court concluded that the section 2035(d)(2) exception did not apply, and thus under the general rule of section 2035(d)(1) the proceeds from the insurance policy were not includable in the decedent's gross estate. In so holding the Tax Court emphasized that it did not reach the issue of the includability of the policy proceeds under the "constructive transfer" caselaw doctrine developed under section 2035(a) because section 2035(d)(1) overrides section 2035(a).[16]

II.

The proper application of section 2035 to the estate of a decedent dying after December 31, 1981, is a statutory construction question of first impression. The principal issue on appeal is whether the term "transfer" in section 2035(d)(2) includes so called "constructive transfers" as described in *Bel*, 452 F.2d at 691–92, or if section 2035(d)(2)'s cross reference to section 2042 implicitly limits the term's scope. The Tax Court held that the subsection (d)(2) cross reference did limit "transfer." The Commissioner contends on appeal, however, that Congress did not intend subsections (d)(1) and (d)(2) to exclude "constructive transfers" from the decedent's gross estate for estate tax purposes.

The constructive transfer doctrine developed under section 2035(a) prior to the passage of the ERTA and the addition of subsection (d) to section 2035. Under section 2035(a), a "transfer" is not limited to the passing of property directly from the donor to the transferee, but encompasses a donation 'procured through expenditures by the decedent with the purpose, effected at his death, of having it pass to another,'" *Bel*, 452 F.2d at 691. The typical example of a constructive transfer is where the decedent purchases a life insurance policy on himself or herself, pays all the premiums, and designates his or her children or spouse as the owners and beneficiaries. In these situations courts construing section 2035(a) view the decedent's actions as acts of transfer, because the decedent "beamed" the policy proceeds to the children or spouse by paying the policy premiums and creating in the children or spouse all of the contractual rights to the insurance benefits. *Bel*, 452 F.2d at 691; *see also First Nat'l Bank*, 488 F.2d at 576–77; *Detroit Bank & Trust Co. v. United States*, 467 F.2d 964, 967–68 (6th Cir. 1972), *cert. denied*, 410 U.S. 929 (1973); *Estate of Kurihara v. Commissioner*, 82 T.C. 51, 60–61 (1984).

---

[16] The Tax Court in two subsequent cases has continued to adhere to its interpretation that I.R.C. § 2035(d)(1) nullifies § 2035(a) except for the transfers referenced in § 2035(d)(2). *See Estate of Headrick v. Commissioner*, 93 T.C. 171 (1989), *aff'd*, 918 F.2d 1263; *Estate of Chapman v. Commissioner*, 56 T.C.M. (CCH) 1451 (1989).

We decline the Commissioner's invitation to create a judicial gloss on the express language of section 2035(d) by incorporating into section 2035(d)(2) the *Bel* constructive transfer doctrine. Section 2035(d)(2) *expressly refers to section 2042*, a fact which, viewed in light of the *Bel* opinion, compels us to reject application of the constructive transfer doctrine to section 2035(d)(2).

In *Bel*, 452 F.2d 683, upon which the Commissioner relies heavily, the decedent purchased a life insurance policy on himself and paid the premiums out of community funds. The decedent designated his three children as owners and beneficiaries of the policy proceeds. The executors of the decedent's estate did not include on the estate tax return the policy proceeds in the decedent's gross estate, and the Commissioner assessed a deficiency. The estate argued that because Congress specifically rejected a premium payment test for determining whether insurance policy proceeds are included in the decedent's gross estate under section 2042, a premium payment test should not be used to determine a "transfer" includable in the decedent's gross estate under section 2035(a). *See Bel*, 452 F.2d at 688–690. The *Bel* court disagreed, finding that the scope of transfers includable in the decedent's gross estate under sections 2042 and 2035(a) were not equivalent:

> In arguing that this court should affirm the lower court's ruling that no part of the insurance proceeds is includable in the decedent's gross estate, the taxpayers would have us apply a section of the Code dealing with lemons (section 2042), to one pertaining to oranges (section 2035[a]). Section 2042, which deals strictly with life insurance, provides, *inter alia*, that a decedent's gross estate shall include the value of the proceeds of life insurance policies on which the decedent possessed at his death any of the incidents of ownership. However, section 2035[a] provides that *all property* which is transferred in contemplation of death is includable in a decedent's gross estate. We do not think that [sections 2042 and 2035(a)] were designed or conceived to be read in *pari materia*. They came into being at different times, their respective targets were diverse, and we perceive no philosophical confluence to twin them.

452 F.2d at 690 (emphasis in original).

Like the taxpayer's argument in *Bel*, the Commissioner's interpretation of section 2035—that the constructive transfer doctrine of section 2035(a) applies to 2035(d), and specifically section 2035(d)(2)—would have us mixing lemons and oranges. Section 2035(d)(2) *specifically cross references* section 2042. The only inference we can draw from this express cross reference is that Congress, in enacting subsection (d), meant to construe sections 2035(d)(2) and 2042 in *pari materia*. "It is a well established law of statutory construction that, absent ambiguity or irrational result, the literal language of a statute controls." *Edwards v. Valdez*, 789 F.2d 1477, 1481 (10th Cir. 1986) (citations omitted). In *Bel* terms, section 2035(d)(2), like section 2042, is a lemon; section 2035(a) remains an orange. The fundamental rationale behind the *Bel* court's invocation of the constructive transfer doctrine—that section 2042 and its rejection of a premium payments test are not limitations on section 2035(a)—thus becomes inapplicable to section 2035(d)(2), which, as applied to the disputed insurance proceeds in this case, is by its very terms expressly limited to transfers under section 2042. To apply the constructive transfer doctrine in the manner requested by the Commissioner would be to resurrect under section 2042 the premium payment test "phoenix-like from the language of section 2035," *First Nat'l Bank*, 488 F.2d at 578, in contravention of the express language of section 2035(d)(2) and the undisputed intent of section 2042, *see* discussion of sections 2035(d) and 2042, *supra*, Part I at 4–6.

Having concluded that section 2035(d)(2) transfers are defined through the cross referenced sections, we turn to section 2042 to determine its application to the facts of this case. Section 2042 includes in the decedent's estate the proceeds of life insurance policies on the life of the decedent where the decedent at the time of his death possessed any of the incidents of ownership in the policies. Treas. Reg. § 20.2042–1(c)[(2)] . . . .

Under the section 2042 definition of "incidents of ownership" the decedent Joseph Leder never held any ownership, economic, or other contractual rights in the policy. Jeanne Leder was the owner of the policy from the time of application for the policy until the policy was transferred to the trust for the benefit of herself and the Leder's [three] children. The policy states that "the owner will be entitled to the rights granted by this policy," and that only "[t]he owner may change the beneficiary. Jeanne Leder, first in her own right and later as trustee, enjoyed the legal and shared the equitable rights granted under the policy with her three children. Nor did the decedent hold a reversionary interest in the policy proceeds. The policy states that "[i]f the owner . . . dies before the Insured, the rights of the owner belong to the executor or administrator of the owner." Finally, the payment of the policy premiums by the decedent's wholly owned corporation does not render the policy proceeds includable in the decedent's gross estate, because payment of premiums is not an incident of ownership under section 2042. *See* discussion of section 2042, *supra*, Part I at 5–6.

On these facts we find that the policy proceeds are not includable in the decedent's estate under section 2042. Because the decedent did not transfer an interest in the policy proceeds under section 2042, and none of the other exceptions listed in section 2035(d)(2) apply, we hold that the general rule of section 2035(d)(1) governs. Section 2035(d)(1) excludes the policy proceeds from the decedent's gross estate.

III.

We hold that the constructive transfer doctrine is inapplicable to section 2035(d)(2) because of Congress's cross reference to section 2042. In addition, we determine that applying the constructive transfer doctrine to a transaction governed by section 2042 would contravene Congress's intent in enacting section 2042 by effectively resurrecting the premium payment test.

The judgment of the Tax Court is affirmed.

In *Estate of Perry v. Commissioner*, 927 F.2d 209 (5th Cir. 1991), the court held that proceeds from life insurance policies purchased by the decedent within three years of his death were not includible in his gross estate because he never possessed any incidents of ownership in the policies. In *Perry*, the decedent, who paid the premiums, was named as the insured, and his sons were named as policy owners and beneficiaries from the inception of the policy. The Circuit that had earlier embraced the constructive transfer directive (*Bel v. U.S., supra*), rejected its application and held that an actual transfer of ownership was a prerequisite for inclusion of life insurance proceeds under § 2035(a). Subsequently, the court awarded attorneys' fees under § 7430, because the Service's position was not substantially justified. *See Perry v. Commissioner*, 931 F.2d 1044 (5th Cir. 1991).

The Service threw in the towel (*AOD 1991–012*) and will no longer litigate the includability of life insurance in the gross estate of a nonowner insured who dies within three years of the policy's inception. In *AOD 1991–012*, the Chief Counsel's Office recommended acquiescing in *Estate of Headrick v. Commissioner*, 918 F.2d 1263 (6th Cir. 1990). The *AOD* also encompasses the *Estate of Leder* and *Estate of Perry* cases. Despite the fact that it will no longer litigate the issue, the Service maintains that "substance should prevail over form" and the proceeds should be includable in the gross estate.

Section 2035, as it applies to most transactions, was repealed in 1981. It was retained for transfers of life insurance policies which, but for the transfer, would have been includable under § 2042. *See* § 2035(a). Thus, if a decedent-insured actually transfers ownership of a life insurance policy within three years of death, it will be taxed to the decedent's estate because it would have been includable in the gross estate under § 2042 if the decedent had retained the policy until death. As did its predecessor, the current version of § 2035 will apply even though the annual per donee exclusion made the filing of a gift tax return on the transfer of the policy unnecessary.

The current application of § 2035 to transfers of life insurance is limited in two circumstances. First, as indicated in *Estate of Leder*, § 2035 only applies if the policy would have been includable in the gross estate but for the transfer. *See* § 2035(a). Second, if the transfer was for full consideration, the policy is not includible in the gross estate. *See* § 2035(d). If, however, the transferor received only partial consideration, then the value of the policy less the consideration will be includible in the gross estate under § 2043(a). Further, if the transferee pays premiums after the policy is transferred, the amount includable in the gross estate under § 2035 will be affected. *See Estate of Silverman v. Commissioner*, 61 T.C.338 (1973), *aff'd on the limited grounds raised in the appeal*, 521 F.2d 574 (2d Cir. 1975), discussed in § 10.02[B][2][a], *supra*.

Problems

1. What would the result have been in *Estate of Leder* if the corporation had been the policy owner? Consider Treasury Regulation § 20.2042–1(c)(6).

2. If a policy is includible in the insured's gross estate under § 2035, and the decedent paid premiums after assigning the policy, must the premiums paid within three years of death also be included as a separate item? If not, are the premium payments adjusted taxable gifts under § 2001(b)?

3. *D* owns a life insurance policy on the life of *A* which *D* transfers to another within three years of *D*'s death. If the transfer was a present interest so that no gift tax return was required to be filed, should the policy value be included in *D*'s estate under § 2035(a)?

[C]　Generation-Skipping Transfer Tax

Because life insurance is property, generation-skipping transfer tax consequences may arise. However, there are few unique issues. The generation-skipping transfer tax can be avoided by allocating a sufficient amount of the transferor's GST exemption to the transfer. If an allocation is made, the transferor may establish a zero inclusion ratio for the policy proceeds, even if the proceeds are or would have been includible in the transferor's gross estate under § 2035. Section 2642(f) expressly excludes the application of § 2035 in barring early determination of the inclusion ratio. Further, if the policy has a value of $11,000 or less, and the transfer qualifies for the gift tax annual exclusion, the transfer may be exempt from the GST tax. *See* § 2642(c).

For most lifetime allocations of GST exemption made after the due date of the gift return, the property is valued as of the first day of the month that the late allocation occurs. *See* Treas. Reg. § 26.2642–2(a)(2). For life insurance or a trust owning life insurance, however, this special valuation rule is not applicable if the insured dies during the month.

Use of an irrevocable life insurance trust to leverage the sheltering effect of the GST exemption is discussed in Pam Schneider, *GST Planning With Irrevocable Trusts: Putting It All Together After the Final GST Regulations*, 31 U. MIAMI INST. ON EST. PLAN. 300 (1997).

[D]　Income Tax

Code: §§ 101 and 677(a)(3).

Regulations: None.

Life insurance raises three significant issues for income tax purposes. The first reflects that life insurance is an asset that can produce income or be disposed of for gain or loss. Income may result if the policy owner receives dividends before the death of the insured, based on the investment success of the company (although dividends which do not exceed premiums paid do not constitute taxable income). A dividend received in excess of the policy's cost constitutes dividend income to the policy owner. *See* § 72(e). Similarly, if the policy owner sells the policy for more or less than the amount invested in it, *i.e.* the adjusted basis, the difference is a gain or a loss. *See* §§ 101(a)(2), 1001(a).

The second income issue involves the receipt of policy proceeds and distributions on or after the death of the insured. Generally, life insurance proceeds are exempt from income taxation. *See* § 101(a)(1). The proceeds are treated in the same manner as a bequest or devise, which § 102 exempts from income taxation. A major exception exists, however, if the policy was ever transferred for value. *See* § 101(a)(2). Under the *transfer for value* rule, the beneficiary of life insurance proceeds has income to the extent the proceeds exceed that taxpayer's basis, *i.e.*, the amount paid for the policy, including premiums paid after the transfer.

Treasury Regulation § 1.101–1(b) broadly defines a transfer for value to include any transfer or assignment for *valuable consideration*. The definition does not apply, however, if the purchaser has a basis in the policy determined by reference to the transferor. A buyer with a carryover adjusted basis under § 1015 rather than a cost basis under § 1012, is not subject to the transfer for value rule. Thus, a policy can be transferred for some consideration without application of the rule, so long as the transfer is in part a gift and the amount paid is less than the transferor's basis (the total premiums paid before the transfer). Similarly, a policy may be transferred as a part of a tax-free reorganization of a corporation without the transfer for value rule applying.

Also excepted from the rule are transfers "to the insured, to a partner of the insured, to a partnership in which the insured is a partner, or to a corporation in which the insured is a shareholder or an officer." *See* Treas. Reg. § 1.101–1(b)(2). This exception is not applicable to a transfer to another shareholder of a corporation in which the insured is a shareholder or an officer, however. Thus a sale or transfer of a policy by a corporation to a shareholder other than the insured will invoke the rule.

The transfer for value rule can be a real problem when the owners of a corporation use life insurance as a part of a buy-sell agreement, but subsequently attempt to restructure the ownership of the policies. Care must be taken to avoid the loss of the income tax exemption.

The § 101(a) exclusion of gross income does not shield income produced by the proceeds. At death, the distribution of the proceeds of a life insurance policy may take the form of a policy settlement option: the proceeds may be left with the insurance company, as money manager, and paid out in the way established by the agreement. The settlement options may include the following.

 (1) An interest option whereby the insurance company retains the proceeds and the beneficiary receives only the interest on the proceeds until the time agreed on for the payment of the fund in a lump sum; or

 (2) a variety of installment options including:

  (a) a fixed amount to be paid periodically until the proceeds, with interest, are exhausted;

  (b) a fixed amount to be paid periodically for a specified number of years with the amount of each installment to include interest and to liquidate the amount of the insurance proceeds that are to be liquidated at the end of the stated period; or

(c)   an annuity to be purchased with the policy proceeds for the lifetime of the primary beneficiary, perhaps with a guaranteed minimum number of payments.

Amounts of interest paid on proceeds held by the insurer under a settlement option are taxable as income. *See* § 101(c), (d).

The third income issue arises when a trust owns an insurance policy on the life of the grantor or the grantor's spouse. If income from the trust *may* be used to pay insurance premiums, the grantor is treated as the owner of the trust for income tax purposes under § 677(a)(3). Thus, taxable income generated by insurance trusts is taxed to the grantor.

Because universal life insurance has a very substantial investment component—although the appreciation in value of life insurance has traditionally been shielded from tax—Congress became concerned that the new products were merely investment vehicles masquerading as life insurance to obtain the tax benefits. In response, in 1984 Congress enacted guidelines that universal life insurance contracts must meet if the policy is to be treated as life insurance for federal income tax purposes. Those guidelines apply to *flexible premium contracts* issued before January 1, 1985, payable by reason of death (§ 101(f)), and to *life insurance contracts* issued after December 31, 1984. *See* § 7702. The guidelines are designed to ensure that a universal life insurance policy provides a minimum amount of insurance protection at all times.

To discourage the purchase of life insurance as a tax shelter investment vehicle, the 1988 Tax Act modified the income tax treatment of loans and other amounts received under life insurance policies, statutorily defined as *modified endowments*. A modified endowment policy is a life insurance policy under which the cumulative amount of premiums paid in the first seven years exceeds the sum that would have been paid by aggregating seven level annual premium payments. *See* § 7702A(b). If a policy is deemed a modified endowment, there are two major income tax effects. First, amounts received under the policy, such as withdrawals from the cash surrender value or cash dividends, constitute taxable income to the extent of any gain (excess of total cash value of the policy over the basis) in the policy at the time of the distribution. For this purpose, policy loans are treated as distributions under the contract. On the other hand, distributions made before gain exists, or in excess of any gains, constitutes a tax free return of basis. Policy dividends used internally to pay premiums are not treated as distributions.

The second major impact of a policy being deemed a modified endowment is that distributions from the policy before the owner attains age 59½, or is disabled, are subject to a 10% additional income tax. *See* § 72(v). The taxation of policy gain on distributions from modified endowment contracts after age 59½ is essentially similar to the taxation of income received from an annuity.

The inside cash value buildup for all life insurance policies, including modified endowments, is tax free. The compounding effects of this growth may still make a modified endowment, such as a single premium policy, an attractive investment if the policy owner does not need the distributions for a number of years. Furthermore, the full death benefit is generally free from income taxation. *See* Ronald D. Aucutt and Catherine Veihmeyer Hughes, *Irrevocable Life Insurance Trusts Still Have Planning Possibilities After TAMRA*, 71 J. TAX'N 258 (Oct. 1989).

In recent years, some insurance companies have allowed terminally ill insureds to receive the policy's proceeds to meet medical and other expenses of the illness. In 1996, Congress codified rules that permit tax-free receipt of viatical settlements. *See* § 101(g). A policy may be sold or surrendered for an amount in excess of the premiums paid without an income tax consequence if the insured is *terminally ill* or *chronically ill*. The statute defines the applicable terms such as *terminally ill, chronically ill,* and *viatical settlement provider*. Notwithstanding the complexity of § 101(g), it is possible to cash in a policy before the insured dies without an income tax consequence if the conditions are met. *See generally*, Julia Brazelton and Rebecca Kaenzig, *Accelerated Death Benefits Finally Afforded Exclusion*, 75 TAXES, January 1997, pp. 57–63.

Problems

1. *G* names *S* beneficiary of a $100,000 ordinary life insurance policy. *G* executed a settlement option permitting the insurer to retain the policy proceeds, pay annual interest to *S*, and pay over the $100,000 principal to *S* (or *S*'s estate) in ten years. Can *S* exclude the interest and the policy proceeds from gross income?

2. *G* creates a trust for the benefit of his grandchildren and transfer cash, stocks, and bonds to the trust. *G*'s son, *S* is the trustee. As trustee, *S* uses the cash transferred to the trust to buy a life insurance policy on *G*'s life. Each year thereafter, *S* uses half of the trust income to pay annual life insurance premiums and he accumulates the other half of the annual income. Is *G* taxed on any of the income? If so how much? *See* Weil v. Commissioner, 3 T.C. 579 (1944), *acq.* 1944 C.B. 29.

[E] Review Problems

1. Your client believes he can assign his insurance to his wife, still pay the premiums, and avoid taxation of the proceeds to his estate. His insurance agent, who is advising him, says that the cost of doing this will be minimal, because the premiums on his term insurance policy of $1 million are minor compared to the face value. Would you advise him to do this?

    a. Would such an assignment be a taxable gift? *See* Treasury Regulation § 25.2511–1(h)(8). Would it qualify for the gift tax exclusion under § 2503(b)? For the gift tax marital deduction under § 2523? Would the transfer have any federal estate tax consequences to the insured?

    b. What would be the federal estate tax implications of the wife's ownership of the policy, if she died before he did? Consider Treasury Regulation § 20.2031–8(a).

    c. What alternative approach would you recommend to achieve the advantages he seeks without the concomitant disadvantages?

2. Five years ago, *A* purchased a $1 million ordinary life insurance policy on his life. The beneficiary of the policy is *S*, *A*'s son. Would you recommend that:

    a. *A* make an outright transfer of the incidents of ownership to *S*? What if *W*, *A*'s wife, were the assignee? *A* will continue to pay the policy premiums.

    b. *A* assign the policy to an irrevocable trust, with *S* as trustee and life income beneficiary, and with the remainder payable to *S*'s two children in equal shares? *A* will continue to pay the policy premiums.

    c. *A* do nothing?

In making your recommendation consider the following.

    (1)   The nontax advantages and disadvantages of an outright gift or a transfer in trust.

    (2)   The income tax consequences of a transfer under §§ 101(a)(1) and 677(a)(3).

    (3)   The gift tax consequences (including the availability of the annual exclusion) of an outright transfer or a transfer in trust of the incidents of ownership and *A*'s continued payment of the policy premiums. Especially consider Treasury Regulation §§ 25.2511–1(h)(8) and 25.2512–6(a).

    (4)   The estate tax consequences under §§ 2042 and 2035.

3. *A* transferred the policy to a trust. What would be the tax consequences if:

    a. *A* continues to pay the premiums on the policy and dies more than three years after the transfer?

    b. Each year *A* transfers an amount sufficient to pay the premiums to the trust, and dies within three years of transferring the policy?

    c. More than three years before his death, *A* transferred the policy and enough assets to the trust to pay all future premiums?

4. *A* assigned the policy outright to *W*, designated *S* as policy beneficiary, and predeceased *W*. What are the gift and estate tax consequences for *A* and *W*?

5. *A* irrevocably assigned the policy to an irrevocable trust and designated *S* as the trustee.

    a. What are the gift and estate tax consequences to *S* if he is given the power, during his lifetime or at death, or both, to appoint the remainder interest between his children or their issue? Consider §§ 2514(b), (c); 2041(a)(2), (b)(1).

    b. Could *A* safely be designated the co-trustee of the trust? *See* Treas. Reg. § 20.2042–1(c)(4); Rev. Rul. 84–179.

6. *D*, the insured, assigned a whole life insurance policy to an irrevocable trust for his wife and children. Immediately before the transfer, he exercised his option to borrow against the policy, and borrowed the entire cash value. What would be the federal gift tax consequences of the transfer of the policy to the trust? Assuming that he never repaid the loan, would the policy be

included in his gross estate? Would it be important to your answer to know the interest rate on the loan as compared to the market interest rate for secured loans to individuals charged by commercial banks?

Chapter 11

ANNUITIES AND OTHER RETIREMENT ARRANGEMENTS

Commercial annuity contracts may pass wealth from one individual to another. It is not uncommon for an individual, approaching retirement and desiring a steady source of income for the retirement years, to buy an annuity contract from an insurance company. The purchaser pays a lump-sum premium or a series of premiums. The insurer agrees to pay a set amount periodically (usually monthly) to the purchaser for as long as the purchaser (the annuitant) lives. If the purchaser is married, the contract may provide for the payments to continue, perhaps at a lesser amount, for the remainder of the spouse's life. This right to continued payments constitutes a valuable right in the spouse and raises gift and estate tax questions. Furthermore, the periodic payments to the annuitant raise income tax questions, because, to some extent, the payments result from the insurer's investment of the premium. Thus, the payments substitute for income the annuitant could have if he had not purchased the annuity.

Employment related annuities and other retirement benefits are discussed later in this Chapter, including important changes made by the 2001 Tax Act.

§ 11.01 Taxation of Annuities

[A] Gift Tax

Code: §§ 2512 and 2523(f).

Regulations: None.

Commercial annuities present no special gift tax problems. If survivorship rights are not vested, no gift tax issue exists. Vested survivorship rights are taxable. Valuation is computed using the § 7520 tables based on when the term begins and how long it will last. Furthermore, if the survivorship feature is payable to the annuitant's spouse, the gift tax marital deduction applies even though the annuity will terminate on the surviving spouse's death, provided no interest passes to another after the surviving spouse's death. *See* § 2523(f)(6).

[B] Estate Tax

Code: § 2039.

Regulations: None.

Survivorship interests under commercial annuity contracts are included in the gross estate under § 2039.

Example: The decedent purchases an annuity contract from an insurance company. Pursuant to the contract, the decedent receives annual payments for life. On death, a designated person receives either a payout for life or a lump-sum payment.

At the decedent's death, the value of the beneficiary's right to receive the survivorship payments will be includable in the gross estate under § 2039. That section only requires that at the decedent's death an annuity or other amount is *payable* to the decedent, and that after the decedent's death, a payment is receivable by a beneficiary. In the example, the decedent's annuity is *payable* to the decedent, and the survivorship annuity is receivable by another beneficiary.

Section 2039 applies whether the decedent's right is in the form of an annuity payout during life, or for a term certain, or in the form of a lump-sum payment. It also applies even if the decedent was not receiving annuity payments at death because of a deferred annuity arrangement, provided the decedent possessed the right to receive one or more payments from the annuity in the future. Thus, for example, a survivorship annuity to begin at age 65 is included in the decedent's estate, even if the purchaser did not live to age 65.

Section 2056(b)(7)(C) contains a special marital deduction rule under the QTIP provision. If the surviving spouse is the only person who is entitled to receive annuity payments before the surviving spouse's death and the value of the annuity is included in the decedent's gross estate under § 2039, the personal representative is treated as having made a QTIP election. In effect, a marital deduction is automatic for such annuity arrangements so that the personal representative must elect not to have the annuity qualify as a marital deduction if it is not wanted.

Estate of Montgomery v. Commissioner

458 F.2d 616 (5th Cir.), cert. denied, 409 U.S. 849 (1972)

Per Curiam:

. . .

The decedent, Lafayette Montgomery, on May 4, 1964 was approaching his seventy-fifth birthday and suffered from advanced pulmonary emphysema, chronic bronchitis, arteriosclerosis, labile hypertension, and hepatitis, his major health problem being severe pulmonary insufficiency due to emphysema and chronic bronchitis. On that date he executed instruments creating two irrevocable trusts for the benefit of his grandchildren. The co-Trustees of each trust were his two sons and the Trust Company of Georgia. The following day he made application to the National Life Insurance Company (National) for a life annuity on his life at a purchase price of $2,200,000, and the trustees of each of the two trusts made written application (executed by the decedent as the proposed insured) for life insurance in the amount of $1,000,000 on the decedent's life. The decedent presented no evidence of insurability and was of course not insurable at standard rates.

One day later, May 6, National issued its nonrefundable annuity contract to the decedent providing for monthly payments during his life of $22,682 with no survivor benefits. The same day National issued the two life insurance policies applied for to the trustees of the respective trusts in the face amount of $1,000,000 each. The annuity required payment of a single premium of $2,200,000, its face amount plus 10 percent, and the amount of the first annual premiums on each of the two life insurance policies was $132,938. The decedent procured a bank loan on May 8 in the amount of $2,500,000 and deposited the net proceeds of $2,465,876 in his personal bank account. From this account he paid the single premium on the annuity and issued to each of the two trusts his check in the amount of $132,938. The latter amounts were immediately used by the trusts to pay the premiums on the insurance policies.

National regularly offers a combination nonrefundable annuity and life insurance policy plan whereunder life insurance policies are issued, as here, without proof of insurability. As to annual premium life insurance National permits the purchase of a life insurance policy provided the consideration paid for the annuity is equal to 110 percent of the face amount of the policy. Thus National incurs no insurance risk or risks of economic loss in such transactions since the annuity premium offsets the insurance policy proceeds and the annual premiums on the insurance policy offset the monthly payments under the annuity contract. Insurance policies would not have been issued without the purchase of the annuity contract since no evidence of the decedent's insurability was submitted. Neither would the policies have been issued by National without the decedent's consent, which was required by Georgia law. The decedent's consent was evidenced by his witnessing the applications, though National had no concern with the identity of the named beneficiaries under the insurance policies so long as they were on the same life as the annuity contract.

The decedent died October 31, 1964, less than six months after the transactions above described. National paid the sum of $1,066,469 due under each of the policies to each of the trusts. The excess amount of $66,469 represented a refund of one-half of the annual premium paid on each policy.

A gift tax return for the year 1964 was filed by the taxpayer on behalf of the decedent on April 15, 1965, reporting as gifts the $132,938 given to each trust to pay the first annual premium on each policy. The estate tax return, filed January 31, 1966, also reported these amounts as transfers inter vivos subject to the estate tax and claimed a credit for the federal gift taxes paid with respect to the transfers. The sum of $2,465,876 representing the net proceeds of the bank loan obtained by the decedent to pay the premiums on the annuity and life insurance contracts was deducted as a debt of the estate. The amounts received by the trustees from the policies issued by National on the decedent's life were not included in the decedent's reported gross estate, but were specifically excluded on the asserted ground that the decedent had no interest in them.

The Commissioner of Internal Revenue did not question the claimed deduction pertaining to the estate's indebtedness to the bank. But the Commissioner determined that the proceeds ($2,132,938) of the two life insurance policies were includible in the decedent's gross estate under the provisions of . . . section 2039 of the Internal Revenue Code . . . . The Tax Court held the proceeds includible under section 2039 . . . .

On this appeal the taxpayer argues that the Tax Court was in error when it found as factual matters that:

1. Prior to the purchases of the annuity-insurance combination plan in this case, National, decedent, and the trustees of the trusts entered into an understanding and agreement with respect to the above transactions relating to the issuance of both the annuity and the life insurance policies.

2. That the decedent gave his consent to the issuance of the two policies of insurance on his life by paying the first annual premium on each through the trusts as conduits.

3. That there was a single investment contract between the decedent and National Life Insurance Company.

Regarding the Tax Court's legal conclusion, the taxpayer disputes the includibility of the proceeds of the two life insurance policies under section 2039.

Our scope of review of the decisions of the Tax Court under Title 26, U.S.C., Section 7482(a), is "in the same manner and to the same extent as decisions of the district courts in civil actions tried without a jury." Applying the "clearly erroneous" test of Rule 52(a), F.R. Civ. P., to the facts found by the Tax Court, we perceive no reason to disturb those findings of fact. Given these factual findings, no error is demonstrated in the Tax Court's holding that the proceeds of the insurance policies were includible in the decedent's gross estate under section 2039 of the Internal Revenue Code . . . .

The decision of the Tax Court is

Affirmed.

––––––

Montgomery illustrates that § 2039(a) includes the value of a survivor annuity in the decedent's gross estate if, under the contract, the decedent was entitled to a payout from the annuity or other payment during life. This language requires the inclusion of all common forms of survivor annuities under which the decedent received, or was entitled to receive, payments with unpaid amounts passing under the contract to a surviving beneficiary.

Under the provisions of § 2039(b), only the annuity payments attributable to contributions by the decedent are includable in the gross estate. The portion attributable to contributions by the survivor is excludable.

Because § 2039 applies only to contracts or other forms of agreement, it does not apply to current and future payments made from trusts established by the decedent. Those payments are covered by §§ 2036, 2037, and 2038. *See* Chapters 7 and 8. When a decedent establishes an annuity under her will, the annuity property is included in her gross estate under § 2033.

Problem

Decedent won the state lottery but died before receiving all installment payments. Pursuant to state law, the installment payments were not assignable by the decedent during life. Do you think the value of the unpaid lottery installments are includable in the gross estate? If includable, should the payments be valued as an annuity based on the annuity tables prescribed by § 7520? *Compare Estate of Shackleford v. United States*, 88 AFTR2d ¶ 2001-5250 (9th Cir. 2001) *with Estate of Gribauskas v. Commissioner*, 116 T.C. 142 (2001).

[C] Generation-Skipping Transfer Tax

Generation-skipping transfer tax consequences can also arise in conjunction with annuities if the annuitant is a skip person. An annuity arrangement has the effect of a trust and will be taxed accordingly. *See* § 2652(b). If the annuity is a survivor annuity that will be taxable under § 2039, § 2642(f) bars the immediate allocation of the GST exemption during the decedent's lifetime.

[D] Income Tax

Code: § 72.

Regulations: Treas. Reg. § 1.72–4(a), –5(a), –6(a), and –9.

The challenge for the income tax system is to determine the extent that annuity payments are taxed as income to the annuitant, and to what extent they are to be treated as a return of the purchase price of the annuity. Section 72 defers taxation of the interest on the capital invested until the payments are received. This means that any interest income earned on the money on deposit with the insurance company is not included in gross income before the annuity starting date. Unlike a savings account, an annuity defers the tax consequences on the interest income. Presumably, this deferral feature is based on the policy of encouraging people to save for old age and retirement. *See* S. Rep. No. 1622, 83d Cong., 2d Sess. 11 (1954). The deferral aspect usually allows the retired person to report the interest element at a lower tax rate than the rate during the individual's peak earning years.

If the annuitant withdraws funds from the contract before the annuity starting date, the tax ramifications depend on when the contract was purchased. Before 1982, early withdrawals were treated first as a withdrawal of capital and, therefore, taxable only after the entire investment in the contract had been recovered. Insurance companies began marketing annuities that provided investment yields competitive with other investments that did not enjoy the same deferral advantage. The benefits of tax deferral until the annuity starting date and the return of capital treatment for partial withdrawals allowed insurance companies to market annuities as tax shelters. In 1982, § 72(e) was amended to provide that amounts received under annuity contracts before the annuity starting date are treated as withdrawals of income already earned on the investment. Withdrawals constitute a return of capital only after all the accumulated income has been reported. *See* § 72(e)(2), (e)(3).[1]

> **Example 1:** *X* purchased a single premium annuity contract for $50,000. Ten years later, but before the annuity starting date, when the policy had a cash value of $125,000, *X* withdrew $100,000.

Under prior law, *X* could treat $50,000 as a return of capital. Since 1982, *X* must include $75,000 in gross income, which is the portion of the withdrawal allocated to income already earned. The remaining $25,000 withdrawn is a return of capital. Afterwards, *X* has an investment in the contract of only $25,000. Further, § 72(q) imposes a 10% penalty tax on early distributions not resulting from such events as disability or death of the annuitant.

After the annuity starting date, payments received are allocated between income and the return of capital—allowing the annuitant to recover the investment in an annuity contract over the recipient's projected life expectancy. Operation of the annuity rule can be illustrated by a simple example.

> **Example 2:** Assume that the taxpayer purchases an annuity contract for $9,000 which provides for annual payments of $1,000 for the rest of her life, beginning in one year.

If the annuitant's life expectancy is 27 years, the annuity will provide the annuitant with $27,000 of payments during her life. The cost of the annuity, *investment contract*, divided by the expected payments, *return*, yields the ratio of payments which may be excluded from income, *exclusion ratio*. *See* § 72(b), (c); Treas. Reg. § 1.72–4(a), –5(a), –6(a). In this case, the exclusion ratio would be 33.3%. Therefore, 33.3% of the first annual payment of $1,000 would be excluded from the annuitant's gross income. Thereafter, a similar amount is excluded annually until the annuitant has recovered her investment in the contract, *i.e.*, for 27 years. *See* § 72(b)(2). Subsequently, the full value of annuity payments would be fully taxable for income tax purposes because no part of the payments would represent a return of the purchase price. *i.e.*, starting in the 28th year. In short, if the annuitant lives for her 27-year life expectancy, $9,000 of the total annuity payments, but no more, would be excluded from her gross income.

Of course, the annuitant may die before the projected life expectancy. If so, not all basis will be recovered. In that case, § 72(b)(3) allows a deduction for the unrecovered investment in the contract (as defined in § 72(b)(4)) in the decedent's last taxable year. Section 72(b)(3) does not apply, however, if the annuitant dies before the annuity starting date. In such a case, no loss is deductible because this is a mortality loss.

[E] Private Annuities

Because life annuities depend on actuarial assumptions, only life insurance companies and other commercial entities regularly market annuities. In contrast, a private annuity—usually involving family members—is quite risky as an economic transaction. Consider a mother who transfers funds to a child

---

[1] Investments in annuity contracts purchased prior to August 14, 1982, are exempt from the new provisions of § 72(e).

in return for the child's promise to pay his mother an annuity for life. From the mother's perspective, she takes the risk that her child may dissipate the transferred property, or that creditors may attach the property, so that child would lose the resources to pay the annuity—leaving the mother as annuitant without the anticipated income for the duration of her life. On the other hand, the mother may outlive her life expectancy so that the total payments made by the child to mother exceed the value of funds initially transferred in exchange for the private annuity.

Despite the risks, a private annuity arrangement is a successful and recognized estate planning technique designed to avoid § 2036(a)(1).[2] Also, § 2039 will not apply if the only annuitant is the decedent.

Example: The decedent transferred property to her son in consideration for the son's promise to pay decedent an annuity of $10,000 per year for life.

Section 2036 should not apply because the decedent did not retain a right to the income from the property transferred to her son, unless $10,000 was less than the expected income from the property. *See* Rev. Rul. 79–94, 1979–1 C.B. 296 (applying § 2036(a)(1)). This type of transfer in return for a promised annuity undercuts the technical requirement that there be retained enjoyment of the transferred property. Under a private annuity, the transferor receives only a personal obligation of the promisor-buyer, rather than a retained right in the property itself. *See, e.g., Estate of Fabric v. Commissioner*, 83 T.C. 932 (1984).

Whether § 2036(a)(1) applies to a private annuity arrangement is determined by the substance of the transaction, rather than its form. *See Ray v. United States*, 762 F.2d 1361 (9th Cir 1985). *See generally* Robert O. Loftis, Jr., *When Can a Trust be Used to Fund a Private Annuity Without Creating a Retained Interest?*, 14 EST. PLAN. 218 (1987). If the transferor effectively retained the enjoyment of the property, it will be included in her gross estate. This would be true for example when the annuity payment is less than the anticipated income generated by the property. *See* Rev. Rul. 79–94, 1979–1 C.B. 296. This is also true if the grantor retained a security interest in the transferred property. *See, e.g., Updike v. Commissioner*, 88 F.2d 807 (8th Cir. 1937), *cert. denied*, 301 U.S. 708 (1937).

Problems

1. For $5,000, *D* purchased a straight life annuity and gave it to his wife, *W*. What would be the gift and estate tax consequences of the annuity if:

a. *D* died two years after purchasing the annuity?

b. *D* died more than three years after purchasing the annuity, and *D* reserved the right to add additional annuitants during *W*'s life, but *D* died without exercising the right?

c. The annuity provided that if *W* died before receiving 120 payments, the remaining payments would be made to *D* if living, or to *X*, if *D* were then dead, but *D* died while *W* was alive?

---

[2] *See* § 7.01[B], *supra* (discussing § 2036(a)(1)).

2. *A* purchased a joint and survivor annuity under which she would receive fixed monthly payments for her life and upon her death the payments would continue to her sister, *B*, for *B*'s life. The annuity starts when *A* retires at age 62. What would be the gift and estate tax consequences if:

    a. *A* supplies all of the funds for the purchase of the annuity and dies at age 70 while *B* is still alive?

    b. *A* supplies all of the funds, but *B* predeceases *A*?

    c. *A* and *B* each supply half of the consideration and *A* predeceases *B*?

    d. *A* supplies all of the funds and dies at age 60 while *B* is still alive? The contract provides that if *A* dies before age 62, the company will start paying the annuity payments to *B*.

3. Decedent, during her life, purchased a nonrefundable life annuity from an insurance company. At the same time she transferred a significant portion of her remaining assets to an irrevocable trust under which the income was to accumulate. The trust is to terminate at her death and the corpus and accumulated income are to be distributed in equal shares to her surviving children. What are the gift tax consequences of the transactions? Is any part of the trust includable in her gross estate under either § 2036 or § 2039?

4. Mother, *M*, wants to transfer Blackacre to her daughter, *D*. Your senior partner has suggested that *M* transfer Blackacre to *D* in exchange for a private annuity. If *M* is age 67, Blackacre is valued at $500,000, and the § 7520 rate is 8%, what is the amount of the annual annuity payment? What is the amount of the monthly annuity payment? What facts do you think are relevant for *M* and *D* to consider before consummating the transaction?

§ 11.02 Employment Related Retirement Benefits

A variety of annuity and death benefit programs are related to a decedent's employment.

The employee's retirement plan benefits often constitute a major asset in the estate.

The taxation of employment related benefits is exceedingly complex.[3] In general terms, employment related retirement benefits may be divided into two categories for tax purposes: qualified and nonqualified plans. Qualified plans, including employer plans and individual retirement arrangements (IRAs), are those plans that receive special income tax treatment under §§ 401 through 417. The text treats any plan that is not a qualified plan as a nonqualified plan.

This section, in summary form, provides a brief overview of the different types of qualified plans and the tax ramifications of qualified employment-related retirement and death benefit plans, as well as spousal rights in retirement assets. The section concludes with the tax treatment of nonqualified plans.

---

[3] This discussion focuses on the taxation of private sector retirement benefits. Social security death benefits are not subject to federal estate taxation. *See* Rev. Rul. 67-277, 1967-2 C.B. 322; Rev Rul 55-87, 1955-1 C.B. 112.

[A] Description of Qualified Employment Related Retirement Plans

[1] Employer Plans

Many of the common qualified retirement and death benefit plans are maintained by employers.[4] Most include provisions for death benefits if the employee dies during employment, as well as retirement income for the employee and her spouse.

Noncontributory plans are funded entirely by the employer, while contributory plans require or permit contributions by the employee. If funded, a plan may be in the form of a contract with an insurance or other company external to the employer, or in the form of a trust maintained by the employer or another.

In general, qualified employer plans are of three types: pension plans, profit sharing plans, and stock bonus plans. These three types of plans are discussed below.

> *Pension plan.* A pension plan . . . is a plan established and maintained by an employer primarily to provide systematically for the payment of definitely determinable benefits to his employees over a period of years, usually for life, after retirement. Retirement benefits generally are measured by, and based on, such factors as years of service and compensation received by the employees. The determination of the amount of retirement benefits and the contributions to provide such benefits are not dependent upon profits. . . . A pension plan may provide for the payment of a pension due to disability and may also provide for the payment of incidental death benefits through insurance or otherwise. However, a plan is not a pension plan if it provides for a payment of benefits not customarily included in a pension plan such as layoff benefits or benefits for sickness, accident, hospitalization, or medical expenses . . . .

Treas. Reg. § 1.401–1(b)(1)(i).

> *Profit sharing plan.* A profit-sharing plan is a plan established and maintained by an employer to provide for the participation in his profits by his employees or their beneficiaries. The plan must provide a definite predetermined formula for allocating the contributions made to the plan among the participants and for distributing the funds accumulated under the plan after a fixed number of years, the attainment of a stated age, or upon the prior occurrence of some event such as layoff, illness, disability, retirement, death, or severance of employment. A formula for allocating the contributions among the participants is definite if, for example, it provides for an allocation in proportion to the basic compensation of each participant . . . . A profit-sharing plan . . . is primarily a plan of deferred compensation, but the amounts allocated to the account of a

---

[4] Individual retirement arrangements (IRAs) are discussed in § 11.02[A][2][b], *infra.*

participant may be used to provide for him or his family incidental life or accident or health insurance.

Treas. Reg. § 1.401–1(b)(1)(ii).

> *Stock Bonus Plan.* A stock bonus plan is a plan established and maintained by an employer to provide benefits similar to those of a profit-sharing plan, except that the contributions by the employer are not necessarily dependent upon profits and the benefits are distributable in stock of the employer company. For the purpose of allocating and distributing the stock of the employer which is to be shared among his employees or their beneficiaries, such a plan is subject to the same requirements as a profit-sharing plan.

Treas. Reg. § 1.401–1(b)(1)(iii).

The two basic types of qualified retirement plans are "defined benefit plans" and "defined contribution plans." Defined contribution plans are plans with benefits based on contributions (§ 414(i)); defined benefit plan benefits are determined by a predetermined formula applied as of retirement. Pension plans usually are defined benefit plans, however, money purchase pension plans are defined contribution plans. Profit sharing and stock bonus plans are defined contribution plans.

401(k) plans are part of a profit sharing or stock bonus plan. *See* § 401(k)(2). The employee participant elects to have the employer deduct a certain percentage of salary from the employee's paycheck and contribute the money to the plan. How much money can be contributed depends on the employer, but it may not exceed a dollar limitation. Based on the changes made by the 2001 Act under § 402(g)(1)(B), the limitations on exclusion for elective deferrals under 401(k) plans are as follows:

For 2001	$10,500
For 2002	$11,000
For 2003	$12,000
For 2004	$13,000
For 2005	$14,000
For 2006	$15,000[5]

Many employers will match employee contributions for example by $.25 or $.50 for each dollar the employee contributes but there is no tax law requirement that an employer match any portion of the employee's contributions.

[a] ERISA Limitations

Congress passed The Employee Retirement Income Security Act of 1974 (ERISA) to prevent a variety of retirement plans abuse. ERISA imposes minimum standards on participation, vesting and funding of employee retirement plans, requires termination insurance for defined benefit plans, imposes annual reporting of plan performance to the Labor Department, and annual

---

[5] After 2006, there will be indexing for inflation based on $500 increments. *See* § 402(g)(2). Pursuant to § 414(v)(2)(B)(i) and effective January 1, 2002, employees age 50 or older may be allowed to make additional annual catch-up contributions if the employer establishes catch-up contributions as a plan feature.

disclosure to plan participants. It further imposes fiduciary responsibilities on plan trustees and other fiduciaries and creates civil and criminal sanctions for violation of those responsibilities. ERISA compliance is a complex matter.

[b]   Income Tax Limitations

ERISA also prescribes stringent income tax rules for qualified employer plans. These rules are designed to inhibit the use of creative fringe benefits. A most significant rule imposes anti-discrimination rules so that highly compensated employees cannot be singled out to receive retirement benefits to the exclusion of nonhighly compensated employees. *See* §§ 401(a)(4) and 410(b).

[c]   Tax Advantages

Assuming an employer plan satisfies all tax requirements, the plan will be qualified, resulting in several income tax advantages. First, the employer's contributions to the plan are not taxed as income to the employee when made. *See* Treas. Reg. §§ 1.402(a)–1(a), 1.403(a)–1(a). [6] Second, income generated by a qualified plan is exempt from income taxation until distributed. *See* § 501(a).

In addition, the employer generally is permitted a current deduction subject to complex limitations, for contributions permanently set aside to fund the plan. *See* § 404.

Lastly, distributions from the qualified plan may be taxed favorably, as discussed in § 11.02[B][3], *infra*.

[2]   Individual Plans

The Code allows deferral of income for two types of individually established plans, known as H.R. 10 (or Keogh) plans and individual retirement accounts (IRAs). This is in an attempt to allow self employed individuals, and those for whom an employer has not provided a retirement plan, some of the tax deferral advantages available under qualified plans of employers.

[a]   H.R. 10 (or Keogh) Plans

H.R. 10 plans were approved in 1962, for use by self employed individuals, including partners in partnerships. A self employed person is allowed an income tax deduction for allowable contributions to an H.R. 10 plan based on the rules under § 404.

---

[6] Based on 2001 Tax Act changes, in 2002 deductible contributions to defined contribution plans may not exceed the lesser of the following: 100% of the employee's compensation or $ 40,000. *See* §§ 415(d)(1)(C), (d)(4)(B). For years after 2002, the dollar limitation will be the lesser of 100% of the employee's compensation or $40,000 as indexed for inflation in $1,000 increments. *See id.*

For defined benefit plans, and taking into account the changes under the 2001 Tax Act, contributions in 2002 may not exceed amounts that will produce benefits no greater than the lesser of 100% of the participant's average compensation for his or her three highest years or $160,000. *See* § 415(b). For years after 2002, the dollar limitation will be indexed for inflation in $5,000 increments. *See* I.R.C. § 415(d)(1)(A), (D)(4)(A).

[b] Individual Retirement Arrangements (IRAs)

Individual retirement arrangements (IRAs) are either accounts, annuities, or trusts established under § 408 for the exclusive benefit of a single individual or her beneficiaries. *See* § 408(a) through (c).

IRAs may be established by an individual, or by an employer, or association of employers, for employees, with separate accounting of individual employee interests. Two popular employer-sponsored plans use IRAs as the vehicle for the contribution: Simplified Employee Pension Plans (SEPs) and SIMPLE IRAs. Both plans permit an employee to elect to make voluntary employee contributions to IRAs.

The most common IRA is created by an employee. Depending on an individual's income level and whether the individual or the individual's spouse is covered by a qualified employer plan, a taxpayer may make deductible contributions to an IRA. Based on the changes made by the 2001 Tax Act, § 219(b)(1), (b)(5)(A) provides that the maximum annual amounts that may be contributed to an IRA is the lesser of the individual's compensation or the following amounts:

For 2002-2004	$3,000
For 2005-2007	$4,000
For 2008	$5,000[7]

IRAs are available to all individuals who have compensation income and are not active participants in pension plans. If, however, the individual (or his or her spouse) is an active participant in an employer sponsored retirement plan, then the deduction may be reduced or even disallowed. *See* I.R.C. § 219(g)(5). For the years 2002 and thereafter, the deduction will be disallowed entirely if an unmarried, active participant's adjusted gross income exceeds the following amounts. *See* I.R.C. § 219(g)(3)(B)(ii):

For 2002	$44,000
For 2003	$50,000
For 2004	$55,000
For 2005 and thereafter	$60,000

For the years 2001-2006, the deduction will be disallowed entirely if a joint return is filed and the adjusted gross income exceeds the following amounts. *See* I.R.C. § 219(g)(3)(B)(i):

For 2002	$64,000
For 2003	$70,000
For 2004	$75,000
For 2005	$80,000
For 2006	$85,000[8]

---

[7] For years after 2008, the limit would be adjusted for inflation based on $500 increments. *See* I.R.C. § 219(b)(5)(C). Pursuant to the 2001 Tax Act, employees 50 years of age and older can make additional annual catch-up contributions of $500 for the years 2002-2005 and $1,000 thereafter. *See* I.R.C. § 219(b)(5)(B).

[8] For 2007 and thereafter, the safe harbor amount jumps by $15,000 to $100,000. *See* I.R.C. § 219(g)(2)(A)(ii), (g)(3)(B)(i). If, however, the individual is not an active participant, but his or her spouse is an active participant, then the IRA deduction will be disallowed if the couple's adjusted gross income exceeds $160,000, or $170,000 after 2006. *See* I.R.C. § 219(g)(2) and (g)(7).

Although deductible IRA contributions are disallowed for an individual whose adjusted gross income exceeds threshold levels, such individual is allowed to make nondeductible IRA contributions. *See* I.R.C. § 408(o). The amount that may be contributed may not exceed the deduction limits under § 219, as reduced by any deductible IRA contributions. *See* § 408(o)(2).

No contributions to a traditional IRA (other than rollover contributions) are allowed once the individual reaches age 70½. *See.* § 219(d)(1). IRAs cannot invest in collectibles, *see* § 408(m)(2), because their acquisition will be deemed a taxable distribution. Nor may an IRA owner pledge an IRA as security because a deemed distribution will result. *See* § 408(k)(4).

Traditional IRAs, whether funded by deductible or nondeductible contributions, and whether funded by the employee or his employer, receive favorable tax treatment to the extent of income earned by the account. *See* § 408(e). Income is allowed to accumulate, without current income taxation, until withdrawn.

In 1997, Congress created another type of IRA, known as a *Roth* IRA. *See* § 408A. This type of IRA has different tax incentives than a traditional IRA. *See* Martin Silfin, *Roth IRA or Regular IRA: How To Decide Which One is Preferable*, 25 EST. PLAN. 108 (1998). In summary, a Roth IRA permits nondeductible contributions, but the distributions are generally exempt from income tax. Unlike a traditional IRA, contributions can be made to a Roth IRA after an individual reaches age 70½. Like traditional IRAs, however, Roth IRAs have restrictions on contributions related to the amount of the contributor's income. The effect of these income limitations is to exclude higher income taxpayers from making tax-advantaged contributions.

[B] Taxation of Employment Related Retirement Plans

Death benefit and retirement plans have a variety of tax ramifications under the gift, estate, and income tax laws. There should be no special generation-skipping transfer tax consequences beyond those discussed earlier in this Chapter.

[1] Gift Tax

There are no gift tax effects that are specific to qualified retirement plans. To the extent that the employee-owner of the plan benefit irrevocably designates someone to receive a survivor annuity or lump-sum payment, there is a taxable gift. This gift is typically a future interest that does not qualify for the annual exclusion, but which can qualify for the gift tax marital deduction. *See* § 2523(f)(6). Generally, the designation of a beneficiary is revocable and thus, no gift tax issue exists.

[2] Estate Tax

Code: § 2039.

Regulations: None.

Qualified employer provided retirement plans are subject to § 2039 to the same extent as privately purchased annuities. Survivorship interests are, therefore, taxable to the employee's gross estate. Before 1982, there was an unlimited exemption from estate taxes for survivor interests in employer financed plans and IRAs. This was reduced to $100,000 by the Tax Equity and Fiscal Responsibility Act of 1982, and Congress then repealed the exemption in the Deficit Reduction Act of 1984.

Notwithstanding the 1982 repeal of the unlimited exemption and the 1984 repeal of the $100,000 exemption, both continue to be available for some grandfathered benefits.[9]

Operation of § 2039 with respect to qualified retirement plans is illustrated by the following example.

Example 1: In 2001, the decedent created a rollover IRA[10] to receive a $500,000 distribution from a qualified retirement plan. Pursuant to the IRA agreement, X, a named beneficiary, would receive the remaining balance in the account on the decedent's death as an annuity for life. The decedent dies in 2003, when the account has a remaining balance of $540,000.

Under § 2039, the entire $540,000 is includable in the decedent's gross estate.

Section 2039 also applies to employer created benefit plans. Employer contributions are deemed to be made by the employee pursuant to § 2039(b):

Example 2: D, as a participant in a qualified plan established and funded by his employer, had the right to receive retirement benefits. If D died before retirement, a lump sum would be payable to his designated beneficiary. D died in 2001, before retirement. The death benefit is payable to his designee, X.

The payments to X are includable in D's gross estate under § 2039, because D "possessed the right to receive" payments for a period which did not, in fact, end before death, even though he did not receive any payments because he had not yet retired. *See* Treas. Reg. § 20.2039–1(b)(2), Example 3. Federal estate taxes attributable to qualified plan benefits being included in an employee's gross estate qualify as an income tax deduction for the recipient of the distribution. *See* § 691(c). This qualification mitigates, but does not eliminate, the double tax burden.[11]

If the surviving spouse is named as the sole beneficiary, then a martial deduction should be allowed in full. It may also be possible to obtain a marital

---

[9] Plan benefits are grandfathered if: (1) the decedent was still employed (*in pay status*) and had irrevocably chosen the form of benefit on the grandfathering date; or (2) the decedent was no longer employed (*i.e., separated from service*) on the grandfathering date and does not change the form of benefit before he dies.

[10] An IRA rollover is the transfer of a plan distribution to an IRA. The plan distribution may be made directly to the IRA or it may be distributed to the participant. When the distribution is to the participant, the rollover to the IRA must occur within 60 days of the distribution for the participant to avoid current taxation on the distribution. The students should note that if the distribution is not made directly to an IRA and the distribution is not a "retirement type" distribution, the plan sponsor is required to make a 20% tax withholding. The effect of the rollover is to provide the participant with a deferral of income until distributions are received from the IRA.

[11] To the extent the participant has basis in this account balance, typically from nondeductible contributions, the distribution is not income and no deduction is available under § 691(c). For a discussion of § 691(c), see § 14.02[C], *infra.*.

deduction if a QTIP trust is named as beneficiary. *See* Rev. Rul. 2000-2, 2000-1 C.B. 305. Because the use of a QTIP trust interfaces with the minimum required distribution rules, discussed at § 11.02[B][3], *infra*, we defer consideration of Rev. Rul. 2000-2 to later in this Chapter. *See* § 11.02[C][2], *infra*.

By naming a qualified charity as the beneficiary of retirement benefits, a charitable contribution deduction will be allowed under § 2055. Designating a charitable remainder trust or charitable remainder unitrust as beneficiary of a qualified plan or IRA benefits should result in a charitable contribution for the remainder value.

[3] Income Tax

This discussion concentrates on the income tax consequences of distributions from qualified employer plans (including Keogh plans) and IRAs.[12] As will be seen, these rules are basically the same for qualified employer plans and IRAs, with some variations for nondeductible and Roth IRAs. Other income tax consequences were discussed in § 11.02[A][1][a] and [2], *supra*.

[a] General Rules for Distributions

Generally, distributions whenever made are subject to being taxed as annuities under Internal Revenue Code § 72, discussed in § 11.01[D], *supra*. *See* § 402(a). The constructive receipt rules do not apply to plan distributions; § 402(a)(1) provides that only amounts *actually distributed* are taxed.

In the usual case, the entire amount distributed will be includible in the participant's gross income in the year of distribution. For example, when a participant under a traditional, deductible IRA makes a withdrawal, the amount distributed will be included in the participant's gross income. Similarly, when a retired employee receives a distribution under a qualified employer plan, the amount distributed will be included in the employee's gross income.

On the other hand, if the participant had a traditional IRA that was nondeductible, she would only be required to include a portion of the distribution, because the other portion would be treated under the annuity rules as a return of capital. *See* § 72(b). Also, if the participant had a Roth IRA, then the entire amount would be excluded from gross income provided there was a qualified distribution as defined by § 408A(d)(2).

[b] Lump Sum Distributions

If the plan allows the participant the option to elect a lump sum distribution, immediate federal income tax recognition on the amount received will be triggered unless the participant elects to rollover the lump sum distribution into an eligible qualified plan including an IRA. *See* § 18.02[B][3][b], *supra*. Unfortunately, the favorable five year forward averaging method for lump sum distributions is no longer in effect. *See* § 1401(a) of The Small Business Job Protection Act of 1996. However, certain transitional rules are still in

---

[12] Portions of this section have been adapted from Harold D. Klipstein & Ira Mark Bloom, DRAFTING NEW YORK WILLS, Ch. 18 (Matthew Bender 2001).

effect. First, if the employee reached age 50 before 1986, 10-year averaging may be elected. Second, if plan participation started before 1974, there may be special capital gains treatment for a portion of the lump sum distribution. *See id.*

These transitional rules for lump sum distributions do not apply to IRAs. *See* I.R.C. § 408(d)(1). As a result, a lump sum distribution from an IRA will be included in the participant's gross income. Pursuant to the Roth IRA rules, the participant will not have to include anything in gross income from a qualified distribution.

[c] Rollover Distributions

Eligible rollover distributions provide a significant exception to the general rule that retirement benefits are taxable in the year of distribution based on the annuity rules of § 72. Eligible rollovers are not taxed at all in the year of distribution if an eligible rollover occurs. *See* § 402(c)(1). As a general matter, eligible rollovers involve the transfer from one eligible retirement plan to another eligible retirement plan.

Assuming the distribution is eligible for rollover treatment, then the amount distributed to the individual must be rolled over within 60 days of its receipt to another eligible retirement plan, which include IRAs, qualified employer plans under § 401, and annuity plans under § 403(b). *See* I.R.C. § 402(c)(8)(B). Alternatively, the result of a rollover may be accomplished without a rollover distribution to the individual. Under this direct transfer method, the amount of an eligible rollover distribution from one retirement plan is transferred directly by the trustee to the trustee of the eligible retirement plan. *See* I.R.C. § 401(a)(31).

Most rollovers are made into IRAs because they generally are more flexible than qualified employee plans. The rules for IRA rollovers are comparable to those for qualified employer plans. *See* I.R.C. § 408(d)(3); Prop. Treas. Reg. § 1.408-8.

[d] Premature Distributions

The underlying basis for the favorable income tax treatment of retirement benefits is to encourage provision for a participant's retirement. Accordingly, distributions to a participant from a retirement plan made before normally scheduled payments may be prohibited outright under the plan or if allowed, subject to a 10% penalty tax under § 72(t) for distributions before the participant reaches age 59½. However, the penalty will not apply in certain circumstances, including the death or disability of the participant.

[e] Minimum Required Distribution Rules

As previously discussed, *see* § 11.02[A][1][b] and [b], *supra*, qualified employer plan and IRA retirement benefits accumulate free of income taxation during the life of the participant. In recognition of the tax deferral advantages, federal law limits both the length of the period over which payments can be made from a qualified employer plan or IRA and the amount of the distribution. Specifically, § 401(a)(9) imposes minimum required distribution (MRDs) rules for qualified employer plans. These MRD rules also apply under IRAs.[13] Failure to distribute the MRD results in a 50% penalty tax on the deficient amount. *See* § 4947.

The MRD rules are exceedingly complex, as evidenced by the lengthy final regulations that were published in April 2000. *See generally*, Louis A. Mezzullo, *Did They Get it Right? The Final Minimum Distribution Rules*, 37 HECKERLING INST. EST. PLNG Ch. 7 (2003).

Only the briefest overview of the MRDs is possible here. The MRD rules depend on whether the participant is alive or dead. If alive, the MRD rules generally require that the participant begin receiving MRDs by the required beginning date (RBD), which is no later than April 1st of the calendar year following the later year of—(1) the calendar year in which the participant reaches age 70½ years of age; or (2) the calendar year in which the employee retires. *See* § 401(a)(9)(c). *See also* Treas. Reg. § 1.401(a)(9)-2, Q&A 2.

The process for determining a MRD involves three steps: (1) determine the value of the account on December 31st of the year before the distribution; (2) determine the life expectancy factor from the newly-published Lifetime Distribution Table;[14] and (3) divide the value of the account by the life expectancy factor. If the participant is a 5% owner, or the qualified benefit is an IRA, the RBD is strictly age-driven and distributions must begin regardless of the 5% owner's work status.

Example: Alice, who owned an IRA, turned 70½ during 1995. As a result, her first MRD was required no later than April 1, 1996. In 2003, she will mark her 78th birthday. The MRD for 2003 will be the value in the account on December 31, 2002, divided by 20.3 which is the life expectancy factor for a person aged 78 under the Uniform Distribution Table. Assuming the account balance on December 31, 2002 was $203,000, Alice must receive a MRD of $10,000($203,000/20.3) in 2003.

If the participant dies before her entire account has been distributed, then complex MRD rules apply, depending on whether the participant died before or after his RBD, to ensure that the participant's designated beneficiary receives MRDs. Under the new regulations, the designated beneficiary is not determined until September 30th of the year following the participant's death. If there is no designated beneficiary, then less favorable payout rules will apply.

If the participant's spouse is the sole beneficiary, very favorable treatment is provided under the MRDs. In addition, the surviving spouse, but only the surviving spouse, has the option to rollover the account so that the spouse becomes the new participant. *See* § 402(c)(9) and 408(d). However, this option will not be suggested if the surviving spouse has reached her RBD, but the deceased spouse had not.

---

[13] Roth IRAs are not subject to the minimum required distribution rules during the participant's lifetime. *See* § 408A(c)(5)(A). However, the MRD rules will apply if the participant dies before the account balance has been distributed completely to the participant. *See* I.R.C. §§ 408(g)(6) and 408A(c)(5).

[14] *See* Treas. Reg. § 1.401(a)(9)-9, Q&A-2. This table is based on the participant's age in the year of distribution. *See* Treas. Reg. § 1.401(a)(9)-5, Q&A-4(a).

[4] Income in Respect of a Decedent (IRD)

All taxable amounts received by a beneficiary of a deceased participant are taxed to the beneficiary as IRD.[15] As a consequence, the participant's interest does not receive a step-up in adjusted basis under § 1014, but federal estate taxes attributable to the qualified retirement benefits are deductible for purposes of computing income tax under § 691(c). *See* § 14.02, *infra,* for a detailed discussion of IRD.

A taxable disposition of a qualified plan benefit by an estate or trust will cause an immediate income tax liability. *See* § 691(a)(2), (3). Unless some basis exists from nondeductible employee contributions or the inclusion of pure insurance (PS-58) costs in income, the value of the entire account balance is income. For example, a taxable disposition of a qualified retirement benefit occurs when the qualified retirement benefit is distributed in satisfaction of a pecuniary marital bequest. *See* Rev. Rul. 60–87, 1960–1 C.B. 286 (reproduced in § 14.05[E][1], *infra*). The disposition can also occur if distributed in satisfaction of any other pecuniary devise. On the other hand, income taxes are not triggered immediately if the qualified retirement benefit is distributed as part of the decedent's residuary estate or trust. Similarly, if the qualified retirement benefit is given in a specific bequest, no income is triggered by the distribution.

[C] Spousal Interests and Issues in Retirement Assets

A participant's spouse may have an interest in a plan participant's retirement plan, either because of the terms of the plan (with or without an election by the participant), the specific requirements of federal law, or a court order. Of particular importance is the impact of the Employee Retirement Income Security Act (ERISA), as amended. Title II of ERISA forms the substance of the rules governing qualified plans under Internal Revenue Code §§ 401 through 417.

[1] ERISA Plans

Most retirement plans maintained by employers other than governmental and church entities are subject to ERISA. *See* ERISA § 4(b). Further, most retirement plans that are subject to ERISA (whether they are qualified employer plans for tax purposes or not) are required to contain certain provisions protecting the participant's spouse.[16] Most importantly, since 1984, defined benefit plans must give the surviving spouse of a participant an annuity for life of at least 50%, but not greater than 100%, of the amount payable during the couple's joint lives. *See* ERISA § 205(d). Defined contribution plans must provide that a surviving spouse is the automatic beneficiary of the participant's account. In either circumstance, a participant's spouse can waive the right to these required protective provisions.

---

[15] To the extent the participant has basis in the account balance, typically from nondeductible contributions or under Roth IRAs, the distribution is not income and thus no § 691(c) deduction is available.

[16] ERISA only applies to employee benefit plans. *See* ERISA § 4(a). Because individual IRAs are not employee benefit plans, ERISA rules do not apply to such accounts.

In addition, a family court may order that a portion of the participant's benefits be paid to the nonparticipant spouse and/or dependent children in the case of divorce. *See* ERISA § 206(d)(3).

[a] Joint and Survivor Annuities

The 1984 Retirement Equity Act amended ERISA § 205 to require ERISA plans to provide the participant's surviving spouse with a *Qualified Joint and Survivor Annuity* (QJSA). The requirement applies if:

(1)   the plan provides for distributions in annuity form;[17]

(2)   the participant has been married for one year as of the annuity starting date;[18] and

(3)   the participant's spouse does not consent to a different form of payout.

Further, to protect the spouse in case of the death of the participant before retirement, such plans are required to provide the participant's surviving spouse with a qualified pre-retirement survivor annuity (QPSA), which is roughly equivalent to the survivor annuity that the spouse would have received if the participant had retired before his death. *See* ERISA § 205(e).

As noted above, the QJSA and the QPSA may be waived by the spouse. In the case of the QJSA, however, the waiver is valid only if it occurs within 90 days of the participant's annuity starting date. *See* ERISA § 205(c). In the case of the QPSA, the waiver may occur at any time during the period beginning in the plan year in which the participant is 35 years of age and ending at the participant's death.

Because the survivor annuities have value, the Service has taken the position that creation of such rights is the transfer of an item of value to the spouse, and therefore, a taxable gift. *See* § 2511; Treas. Reg. § 25.2511–1(h)(10). Under § 2523(f), however, the spouse's interest is treated as qualified terminable interest property for marital deduction purposes (unless the donor irrevocably elects out of QTIP treatment). Further, wavier of the survivor annuity, or consent to the waiver, is excluded from the definition of a taxable gift. *See* § 2503(f).

If the participant-spouse dies first, the value of the survivor's annuity should be included in the decedent's gross estate under § 2039. The interest, however, would qualify for the marital deduction as QTIP property. *See* § 2056(b)(7)(C).

---

[17] Most defined contribution plans, including profit sharing and § 401(k) plans, are exempt from the annuity rules provided that the participant's entire vested account balance is payable to the surviving spouse on the participant's death absent the spouse consenting to the designation of another beneficiary. *See* ERISA § 205(b).

[18] A participant's annuity starting date is (1) the first day of the first period for which an amount is payable as an annuity, or (2) if benefits are not payable as an annuity, the first day on which all events have occurred which entitle a participant to the benefit. *See* ERISA § 205(h)(2).

[b] Qualified Domestic Relations Orders (QDROs)

ERISA also requires most pension or profit-sharing plans that are subject to ERISA to provide that the benefits under the plan cannot be assigned or alienated. *See* ERISA § 206(d)(1) and § 401(a)(13). This limitation, however, does not protect against division of the benefit in the case of divorce. The Retirement Equity Act of 1984 recognized the power of domestic relations courts to enter what are known as qualified domestic relations orders (QDROs) with respect to plan benefits. *See* ERISA § 206(d)(3).

A QDRO is an order made pursuant to state domestic relations law (including approval of a property settlement agreement) relating to child support, alimony, or the marital property rights. *See* ERISA § 206(d)(3)(B)(ii). Among other rules domestic relations order is qualified if it creates or recognizes the existence or rights of an alternate payee, or assigns to an alternate payee the right to receive all or a portion of the benefits payable to a participant under a plan. *See* ERISA § 206(d)(3)(B)(i). An alternate payee includes a spouse, former spouse, child or other dependent of a participant who is recognized by a QDRO as having a right to receive some or all of the benefit payable under a qualified plan with respect to a participant. *See* ERISA § 206(d)(3)(K).

Division of pension rights under a QDRO would avoid transfer taxation either under § 2516 or by application of the principle of the *Harris* decision, discussed in § 4.01[B][2], *supra*.

Although IRAs are not subject to ERISA's anti-alienation rules and to the QDRO, exception, IRAs transfers incident to divorce or separation will generally not be treated as a distribution to the IRA participant. *See* § 408(d)(6). A division of IRA benefits pursuant to a separation agreement or divorce decree should not result in adverse gift tax consequences.

[c] Community Property

ERISA also limits the application of community property rights with respect to pension and profit-sharing benefits. Although general principles of community property law would treat deferred compensation as community property, ERISA preempts the application of such laws with respect to ERISA plan benefits. *See Boggs v. Boggs*, 117 S. Ct. 1754 (1997). As a result, the nonparticipant spouse who predeceases the participant lacks a disposable interest in the participant's ERISA plan benefits. *Id. See generally* Philip H. Wile, Boggs v. Boggs: *Good News and Bad News*, 76 TAX NOTES 679 (1997).

To the extent that plans are not subject to ERISA, state laws regulating their ownership are not preempted by ERISA. Because IRAs other than employer-sponsored IRAs are not subject to ERISA, a nonparticipant spouse should have cognizable community property rights in a participant's IRA. *See, e.g., Estate of Mundell v. Mundell*, 857 P.2d 631 (Id. 1993) (holding that § 408(g) does not preempt application of Idaho's community property law to IRAs); *Estate of McDonald v. McDonald*, 794 P.2d 911 (Ca. 1990).[19]

---

19 In *Estate of McDonald v. McDonald*, the California Supreme court held that the predeceasing spouse had not, by consenting to a third party beneficiary designation, transmuted the community property IRA into the separate property of her husband. As a result, her beneficiaries were entitled

Of course, to the extent that community property rights are recognized in the nonparticipant spouse, ownership for transfer tax purposes is affected. Thus, if the nonparticipant spouse dies with a transmissible interest, the gross estate will include the interest under § 2033. If the surviving spouse is then entitled to an annuity in the plan, it would be treated as QTIP property unless the personal representative elects out. *See* § 2056(b)(7)(C), as amended by the Taxpayer Relief Act of 1997.

Problem

What would the federal tax consequences be if the nonowner spouse consented to a third party designation in an IRA held as community property, and then died without revoking the consent. What would be the tax consequences if the owner-spouse died first?

[2] QTIP Trusts for Qualified Plan Benefits

Revenue Ruling 2000-2

2000-1 C.B. 305

. . . .

ISSUE

May an executor elect under § 2056(b)(7) of the Internal Revenue Code to treat an individual retirement account (IRA) and a trust as qualified terminable interest property (QTIP) if the trustee of the trust is the named beneficiary of decedent's IRA and the surviving spouse can compel the trustee to withdraw from the IRA an amount equal to all the income earned on the IRA assets at least annually and to distribute that amount to the spouse?

FACTS

A died in 1999 at the age of 55, survived by spouse, *B*, who was 50 years old. Prior to death, *A* established an IRA described in § 408(a). The IRA is invested only in productive assets. *A* named the trustee of a testamentary trust established under *A*'s will as the beneficiary of all amounts payable from the IRA after *A*'s death. A copy of the testamentary trust and a list of the trust beneficiaries were provided to the custodian of *A*'s IRA within nine months after *A*'s death. As of the date of *A*'s death, the testamentary trust was irrevocable and was a valid trust under the laws of the state of *A*'s domicile. The IRA was includible in *A*'s gross estate under § 2039.

Under the terms of the testatmentary trust, all trust income is payable annually to *B*, and no one has the power to appoint trust principal to any

---

to her one-half interest in the community property IRA. In 1992, California legislatively overruled *McDonald*. *See* Cal. Prob. Code §§ 5010–5030. Although a spouse's consent to a provision for a nonprobate transfer of community property is revocable until the death of the first spouse, if the consenting spouse's consent is not revoked by the death of the first spouse, the consent becomes irrevocable.

person other than B. A's children, who are all younger than B, are the sole remainder beneficiaries of the trust. No other person has a beneficial interest in the trust. Under the terms of the trust, B has the power, exercisable annually, to compel the trustee to withdraw from the IRA an amount equal to the income earned on the assets held by the IRA during the year and to distribute that amount through the trust to B. The IRA document contains no prohibition on withdrawal from the IRA of amounts in excess of the annual minimum required distributions under § 408(a)(6).

In accordance with the terms of the IRA instrument, the trustee of the testamentary trust elects, in order to satisfy § 408(a)(6), to receive annual minimum required distributions using the exception to the five year rule in § 401(a)(9)(B)(iii) for distributions over a distribution period equal to a designated beneficiary's life expectancy. Because B's life expectancy is the shortest of all the potential beneficiaries of the testamentary trust's interest in the IRA (including remainder beneficiaries), the distribution period for purposes of § 401(a)(9)(B)(iii) is B's life expectancy. Because B is not the sole beneficiary of the testamentary trust's interest in the IRA, the trustee elected to have the annual minimum required distributions from the IRA to the testamentary trust begin no later than December 31 of the year immediately following the year of A's death. The amount of the annual minimum required distribution for each year is calculated by dividing the account balance of the IRA as of the December 31 immediately preceding the year by the remaining distribution period. On B's death, any undistributed balance of the IRA will be distributed to the testamentary trust over the remaining distribution period.

LAW AND ANALYSIS

Section 2056(a) provides that the value of the taxable estate is, except as limited by § 2056(b), determined by deducting from the value of the gross estate an amount equal to the value of any interest in property that passes from the decedent to the surviving spouse.

Under § 2056(b)(1), if an interest passing to the surviving spouse will terminate, no deduction is allowed with respect to the interest if, after termination of the spouse's interest, an interest in the property passes or has passed from the decedent to any person other than the surviving spouse (or the estate of the spouse).

Section 2056(b)(7) provides that QTIP, for purposes of § 2056(a), is treated as passing to the surviving spouse and no part of the property shall be treated as passing to any person other than the surviving spouse. Section 2056(b)(7)(B)(i) defines QTIP as property that passes from the decedent, in which the surviving spouse has a qualifying income interest for life, and to which an election applies. Under § 2056(b)(7)(B)(ii), the surviving spouse has a qualifying income interest for life if (I) the surviving spouse is entitled to all the income from the property, payable annually or at more frequent intervals, or has a usufruct interest for life in the property, and (II) no person has a power to appoint any part of the property to any person other than the surviving spouse.

Section 20.2056(b)-7(d)(2) of the Estate Tax Regulations provides that the principles of § 20.2056(b)-5(f), relating to whether the spouse is entitled for life to all of the income from the entire interest, apply in determining whether the surviving spouse is entitled for life to all of the income from the property for QTIP purposes.

Section 20.2056(b)-5(f)(1) provides that, if an interest is transferred in trust, the surviving spouse is entitled for life to all of the income from the entire interest, if the effect of the trust is to give the surviving spouse substantially that degree of beneficial enjoyment of the trust property during the surviving spouse's life which the principles of the law of trusts accord to a person who is unqualifiedly designated as the life beneficiary of a trust.

Section 20.2056(b)-5(f)(8) provides that the terms "entitled for life" and "payable annually or at more frequent intervals" require that under the terms of the trust the income referred to must be currently (at least annually) distributable to the spouse or that the spouse must have such command over the income so that it is virtually the spouse's. Thus, the surviving spouse will be entitled for life to all of the income from the interest, payable annually, if, under the terms of the trust instrument, the spouse has the right exercisable annually (or more frequently) to require distribution to the spouse of the trust income, and otherwise the trust income is to be accumulated and added to corpus.

In the present situation, the IRA is payable to a trust the terms of which entitle B to receive all trust income, payable annually. In addition, no one has a power to appoint any part of the property in the trust or the IRA to any person other than B. Therefore, whether A's executor can elect to treat the trust and the IRA as QTIP depends on whether B is entitled to all the income for life from the IRA, payable annually.

Under the terms of the testamentary trust, B is given the power, exercisable annually, to compel the trustee to withdraw from the IRA an amount equal to all the income earned on the assets held in the IRA and pay that amount to B. If B exercises this power, the trustee must withdraw from the IRA the greater of the amount of income earned on the IRA assets during the year or the annual minimum required distribution. Nothing in the IRA instrument prohibits the trustee from withdrawing such amount from the IRA. If B does not exercise this power, the trustee must withdraw from the IRA only the annual minimum required distribution.

B's power to compel the trustee's action meets the standard set forth in § 20.2056(b)-5(f)(8) for the surviving spouse to be entitled to all the income for life payable annually. Thus, B has a qualifying income interest for life within the meaning of § 2056(b)(7) in both the IRA and the testamentary trust. Furthermore, B has a qualifying income interest for life in the IRA and the testamentary trust for purposes of §§ 2519 and 2044. Because the trust is a conduit for payments equal to income from the IRA to B, A's executor needs to make the QTIP election under § 2056(b)(7) for both the IRA and the testamentary trust.

The result would be the same if the terms of the testamentary trust require the trustee to withdraw from the IRA annually an amount equal to all the income earned on the IRA assets and pay that amount to the surviving spouse.

HOLDING

An executor may elect under § 2056(b)(7) to treat an IRA and a trust as QTIP when the trustee of the trust is the named beneficiary of the decedent's IRA, the surviving spouse can compel the trustee to withdraw from the IRA an amount equal to all the income earned on the IRA assets at least annually and to distribute that amount to the spouse, and no person has a power to appoint any part of the trust property to any person other than the spouse.

EFFECT ON OTHER REVENUE RULING(S)

Rev. Rul. 89-89, 1989-2 C.B. 231, is obsoleted.

———

Until Revenue Ruling 2000-2, the Internal Revenue Service required that the IRA or qualified employer plan and the conduit QTIP trust be drafted in a way that prevented maximizing the use of tax-free build-ups in plan benefits. Specifically, Revenue Ruling 89-89, 1989-1 C.B. 231, effectively required that all IRA or plan benefit income be distributed to the QTIP trust and that the trust distribute out all of the IRA or plan benefit income annually to the surviving spouse.

By insisting that all plan benefit income be distributed annually to comply with the QTIP rules, the Service forced QTIP trusts to receive income from the retirement benefits that may have exceeded the MRD for the year. For example, if the MRD was 3% of the value in the IRA account, but the IRA actually earned 5% for the year, Revenue Ruling 89-89 effectively amounted to a minimum distribution of 5%, when only 3% was required under the income tax rules. Rev. Rul. 89-89 was obsoleted by Rev. Rul. 2000-2. *See generally* Marcia Chadwick Holt, *Revenue Ruling 2000-2—What Does It Mean for You?*, 139 TR. & EST. 16 (2000); Robert S. Keebler, *Minding Your P's and Q's: QTIPping an IRA*, 78 TAXES 8 (Apr. 2000).

[D] Nonqualified Plans

[1] Gift Tax

The transfer tax consequences of nonqualified plans depend on the rights and powers of the participant and beneficiaries of the plan. If the plan is discretionary with the employer, the participant may lack any interest that could trigger a transfer tax. Even if the plan is not discretionary, it may give the participant the right to change plan beneficiaries, so that the designation of a beneficiary would be an incomplete gift, while an irrevocable designation would constitute a gift. *See* Treas. Reg. § 25.2511–1(h)(10). Depending on the form or benefit, a gift to the participant's spouse may qualify for the gift tax marital deduction. Section 2523(f), for example, allows a gift tax marital deduction for joint and survivor annuities where only the two spouses have the right to receive payments. In this situation, the donee spouse's interest is treated as qualified terminable interest property, unless the donor irrevocably elects out of QTIP treatment.

Revenue Ruling 81–31, below, and the judicial response in *DiMarco*, discussed in Chapter 4, illustrate the difficulty in resolving this issue in particular situations.

Revenue Ruling 81–31

1981–1 C.B. 475

. . .

D, the donor, and *X* corporation entered into an employment contract whereby, in consideration of future services to be rendered by *D* to the corporation, the corporation agreed to pay a death benefit to *D*'s surviving spouse if *D* was employed by the corporation at the date of death. Under the terms of the agreement, the death benefit was to be equal in amount to twice the annual salary of *D* at the date of *D*'s death. *D* had no right to change the beneficiary, nor was any amount payable to *D*'s estate in the event *D*'s spouse predeceased *D*. The benefit was not funded in any manner.

At *D*'s death in 1978, *D* was still employed by *X*, and the death benefit was paid to *D*'s surviving spouse.

. . .

Holding

D made a gift of the value of the death benefit passing to *D*'s surviving spouse. For federal gift tax purposes, the transfer became a completed gift in the calendar quarter in which *D* died, at which time the amount of the gift first became susceptible of valuation. . . .

––––––

In *Estate of DiMarco v. Commissioner*, 87 T.C. 653 (1986), *acq. in result* 1990-2 C.B. 1 (reproduced in § 4.01[A][2], *supra*), the Tax Court expressly rejected Revenue Ruling 81–31, stating:

> [T]o the extent that [Rev. Rul. 81–31] can be read as holding either that a transfer of property can become complete for gift tax purposes by reason of the death of the donor, or that it is permissible to treat a completed transfer of property as an open transaction and to value the transferred property and impose the gift tax at some time other than when the completed transfer occurs, we regard the ruling as being inconsistent with the gift tax statute and the regulations.

87 T.C. at 661, n.8.

In 1992, the Service revoked Revenue Ruling 81–31. *See* Rev. Rul. 92–68, 1992–2 C.B. 257.

[2] Estate Tax

A survivor benefit under most plans would be included in the participant's gross estate under § 2039 because it would constitute amounts receivable by "any beneficiary by reason of surviving the decedent under any form of contract or agreement." Again, however, the marital deduction should be available if the survivor is the participant's spouse. Section 2056(b)(7)(B) provides, as the default rule, that the personal representative is deemed to have made a valid QTIP election over the annuity. Thus, absent a personal representative's election out, an estate tax marital deduction will be allowed for the value of the annuity included in the participant's gross estate.

In some situations, the Service has difficulty in applying the estate tax to employee death benefits which are payable to the surviving spouse or others. *See generally* Howard M. Esterces, *Analysis of Gift and Estate Tax Consequences of Death Benefits under Nonqualified Plans*, 56 J. TAX'N 100 (1982). It must first show that the payments were contractual obligations of the employer rather than discretionary payments. *See Estate of Bogley v. United States*, 514 F.2d 1027 (Ct. Cl. 1975). Then it must be shown that the contractual obligation falls under one of the inclusionary provisions of the Code. On the latter question, inclusion under § 2036(a)(2) or § 2038 has been rejected, in the absence of the power to change beneficiaries with respect to the benefit. *See Estate of Tully v. United States*, 528 F.2d 1401 (Ct. Cl. 1976) (§§ 2036 and 2038 inapplicable even though the decedent, his employer, and other shareholders might have amended their agreements, or the decedent might have terminated his employment, altered his compensation, or divorced his wife (the beneficiary)); Rev. Rul. 76–304, 1976–2 C.B. 269. *But cf. Estate of Levin*, 90 T.C. 723 (1988) (§ 2038 applied because the decedent as corporate director could amend plan). Coverage under § 2037 also has been an elusive target, because that section requires that payment be made to the employee's estate if the beneficiary predeceases the employee. *See Estate of Bogley v. United States*, 514 F.2d 1027 (Ct. Cl. 1975).

Inclusion under § 2033 turns on whether the decedent was deemed to have a transmissible interest at death. The court in *Estate of Tulley* concluded that if the decedent's possible controls did not rise to a § 2038(a) power then they did not create a § 2033 interest. Note, however, that §§ 2033 or 2041 should apply if the proceeds were payable to the decedent's estate. *See Goodman v. Granger*, 243 F.2d 264 (3d Cir. 1957), *cert. denied,* 335 U.S. 835 (1957) (reproduced in § 3.03[A], *supra*).

The congressional solution to these questions was § 2039, but questions have arisen regarding the meaning of the phrase *contract or agreement* as used in § 2039(a). The regulations define the term to include "any arrangement, understanding or plan . . . arising by reason of the decedent's employment." Treas. Reg.§ 20.2039–1(b)(1). In *Estate of Courtney v. United States*, 84–2 U.S.T.C. (CCH) ¶ 13,580 (N.D. Ohio 1984), the court explained that the payments must arise out of an enforceable obligation. Thus, no contract or agreement was found where payments to an employee's spouse were made pursuant to a nonbinding resolution of a corporation's board of directors. *Id.* On the other hand, an unenforceable corporate resolution will constitute a contract or agreement if the beneficiary by controlling the corporation could obtain payment. *See Neely v. United States*, 613 F.2d 802 (Ct. Cl. 1980).

Another issue concerns what constitutes *an annuity or other payment* receivable by the decedent. *Hetson*, below, illustrates the problem.

Hetson v. United States

209 Ct. Cl. 291 (1976)
(adopting report of Court of Claims Trial Div.,
75–2 USTC ¶ 13,098 (1975),
36 A.F.T.R.2d 75–6505 (Ct. Cl. Trial Div. 1975))

Bernhardt, Trial Judge:

[Beginning in late 1955, Purity Paint Products Corporation (hereafter *Purity*) was wholly owned by Isidor Hetson and his two adult sons, Leonard and Harold. By virtue of his ownership of all voting stock, Isidor had effective control over Purity.]

Opinion

. . .

Leonard and Harold [were] dissatisfied over their lack of control over corporate affairs, and threatened to quit unless firm assurances were given them of their future security. Consequently, on April 20, 1960, Isidor entered into a written agreement with his sons and wife, Fannie, and with Purity, wherein the sons were guaranteed employment for 10 years at minimum yearly salaries of $20,000; voting control of Purity was to remain in Isidor during his life; and he was assured a salary no greater than his sons which was to be paid to him "regardless of the amount of time devoted by him to the Corporation's business and regardless of his being disabled, incapacitated or otherwise unable to perform services for the Corporation." The agreement also assured that the corporation would pay Fannie a life-time pension of $13,000 per year after Isidor's death, which pension was . . . guaranteed by the sons individually in a separate agreement with Fannie.

[Isidor died on September 18, 1963. His estate included the value of Fannie's lifetime annuity in the decedent's gross estate. Thereafter, a claim for refund was filed and denied by the Service. This suit in the US Court of Claims (now US Claims Court) was then commenced.]

Annuity Contract

. . .

Section 2039 provides "[t]he gross estate shall include the value of an annuity or other payment receivable by any beneficiary under any form of contract or agreement . . . , if, under such contract or agreement, an annuity or other payment was payable to the decedent, or the decedent possessed the right to receive such annuity or payment, . . . for his life . . . or for any period which does not in fact end before his death." There is no question but that the April 1960 agreement was a "contract or agreement" within the statutory terms. Nor is it subject to doubt that the payments receivable by Isidor did "not in fact end before his death." The facts show clearly that Isidor was receiving payments from Purity at the time of his death . . . .

Serious questions have been raised as to whether the payments contracted for by Isidor were "an annuity or other payment" and as to whether the payments were "payable to the decedent, or the decedent possessed the right to receive [them]." Both of these issues are decided adversely to the plaintiffs, and consequently the payments to Isidor fall within the ambit of Section 2039.

Plaintiffs argue, as was similarly and successfully argued in *Kramer v. United States*, 186 Ct. Cl. 684, 406 F.2d 1363 (1969), that the payments contracted for represent salary or compensation for services rendered and do not constitute "an annuity or other payment."[20] In *Kramer* the decedent contracted to receive $12,000 per year as general manager of a company, a job which he was actively discharging at the time of his unexpected demise. The same contract further provided "[i]n the event of illness and/or in the event that due to any circumstances which may make it impossible for Mr. Kramer to continue to act as General Manager, the Company agrees that he shall remain with it as an Advisor and Counselor and to assist the officers and Employees in formulating plans and programs for the continuation of the business, for the remainder of his life."[21] *Id.*, at 687. Kramer's salary as advisor was to continue at $12,000 per year and upon his death while working in either capacity his wife would receive $150 per week for life. The court found that payment for services as an advisory counselor was not a "post-employment period" payment and that "the parties contemplated that Mr. Kramer would render services worth $12,000." *Id.*, at 694.

The Hetson agreement of April 1960 is distinguishable from the Kramer agreement. Isidor was to receive his stipend *regardless* of the amount of time devoted by him to the Corporation's business and *regardless* of his being disabled, incapacitated or otherwise unable to perform services for the Corporation" [emphasis added]. The April 1960 agreement did not by its terms contemplate a reduced form of active employment in lieu of disability payments as did the Kramer contract. Kramer was to be employed as general manager or, if disabled, as an active advisor/counselor. Isidor could participate to any degree of activity he wished or, if disabled, not at all; yet he would

---

[20] The *Kramer* decision relied upon *Bahen v. United States*, 158 Ct. Cl. 141 (1962), where this court held that an individual's regular salary was not comprehended within the statutory phrase "annuity or other payment." This view of the Court of Claims has since been adopted by the Tax Court in *Fusz' Estate*, 46 T. C. 214 (1966), and acquiesced in by the Internal Revenue Service, 1967–2 Cum. Bull. 2.

[21] The court cautioned with respect to its factual determination on this point that "[t]he result in this case turns entirely on the stipulation and under different stipulated or proven background facts, an identical contract might have different tax consequences." *Kramer v. United States, supra*, at 691. "Any court, construing a similar contract, will not regard this case as a precedent if it appears that the services to be rendered were nominal or pro forma or that the prescribed payments were really a retirement annuity." *Id.*, at 694. *See, e.g., Silberman v. United States*, 333 F. Supp. 1120 (W. D. Pa. 1971) ("the obligations on the part of the retiring or incapacitated President . . . is [sic] at the very most an ephemeral obligation in consideration of the 50% payment which would be made to him for the rest of his life").

still receive his stipend. Kramer apparently could not receive payments if he performed no services. For this reason, the Kramer case is inapplicable to the present situation insofar as establishing Isidor's disability payments as salary or wages.

Other decisions clarify that Isidor's payments were "an annuity or other payment." In *Silberman v. United States*, 333 F. Supp. 1120 (W. D. Pa. 1971), the district court found that a contract, similar to Isidor's, which paid the decedent wages while he was performing services and which continued the payments as non-wages if he became disabled, constituted an annuity or other payment. "The purpose of the plan here was to provide an income for Silberman throughout the course of his life, no matter what the condition of his physical health and upon his decease to provide certain benefits for his widow, conditioned only upon her surviving him . . . . Thus, the plaintiff's characterization of the agreement as one anticipating continuing active employ is ill founded." *Id.*, at 1125–26. And this court in *Gaffney v. United States*, 200 Ct. Cl. 744 (1972), considered "a written contract of employment . . . between decedent and his employer, . . . which . . . employed decedent as Office Manager for ten years at $35,000 a year fixed salary, and provided that in the case of decedent's disability, to the extent he was unable to perform his duties as Office Manager, . . . he should be paid 50% of his fixed salary . . . ." The court ruled that "the provision for Mr. Gaffney's disability satisfies the requirements of § 2039(a)", because, inter alia, "the decedent possessed the right to receive an 'annuity or other payment.'" *Id.*, at 745. These precedents, and the lack of applicability of *Kramer*, establish that the April 1960 agreement provided Isidor with "an annuity or other payment" within the purview of Section 2039(a) and not with wages or compensation for services as plaintiffs have contended. Indeed, this court has expressly said that "[t]he statute covers—as an 'other payment,' at least—disability compensation benefits of the type here involved." Bahen v. United States, *supra*, at 147.

It is unnecessary to decide for purposes of Section 2039 whether the money Isidor actually accepted from Purity at the time of his death was a disability payment or compensation for services. Plaintiffs have contended that he was actively employed until the moment of his death. Under Section 2039(a), the annuity receivable by the beneficiary is includable in the decedent's estate as long as the decedent's annuity or other payment was "payable to the decedent, *or the decedent possessed the right to receive such annuity or payment*" [emphasis added]. Thus Fannie's annuity is includable in Isidor's estate if he simply had the right to receive disability payments regardless of whether he was in fact earning them at the time of death.

In *Bahen* it was held the decedent "possessed the right to receive payments" where his right to disability payments was contingent on fulfilling conditions of the plan. Relying on the treasury regulations,[22] this court said "in

---

[22] The treasury regulations, then as now, provided "[t]he decedent 'possessed the right to receive' an annuity or other payment if, immediately before his death, the decedent had an enforceable right to receive payments at some time in the future, whether or not, at the time of his death, he had a present right to receive payments. In connection with the preceding sentence the decedent will be regarded as having had 'an enforceable right to receive payments at some time in the future' so long as he had complied with his obligations under the contract or agreement up to the time of his death." Reg. § 20.2039–1(b)(1)(ii).

circumstances like these, the decedent's interest in future benefits, even if contingent, is sufficient" [footnote omitted]. 158 Ct. Cl. at 148. The "circumstances" to which the court referred was the fact that decedent had died before becoming disabled and therefore had never actually received any disability payments. Likewise in *Silberman v. United States, supra*, the court found the value of a spouse's annuity includable in the decedent's estate where the annuity was payable pursuant to a retirement-disability plan. Silberman died before retiring or becoming disabled, but the court observed that "Silberman could have received the retirement benefit upon become disabled." 333 F. Supp. at 1127. The court decided that "[t]he rights which the decedent possessed immediately prior to his death, were rights which were solely dependent upon him, and in no way dependent upon his employer. The employer's obligations were fixed by the terms of the contract, and nothing the employer could do would alter its obligation. Effectuation of the provisions of the agreement was solely dependent upon conditions which would befall the employee, *i.e.*, he would reach the age of 70 or suffer some prior incapacity which would then have created immediately enforceable obligations on the employer." *Id.* The court then concluded "[s]ince at the time of his death Mr. Silberman possessed the right to receive retirement payments, any benefits which would inure to his wife as a consequence of this employment agreement considered as a whole, are includable in Mr. Silberman's gross estate." *Id. See also In re Wadewitz' Estate v. Comm'r*, 339 F. 2d 980 (7th Cir. 1964) (decedent "possessed the right to receive" retirement benefits even though contingent on his refraining from competition with his employer).

As in these cases, it is similarly found that Isidor "possessed the right to receive . . . [an] annuity or other payment" even though he may not have been receiving any such income at his death. The facts disclose that Isidor upon his disability or retirement had an enforceable right to receive payments from Purity. This right was "solely dependent upon him, and in no way dependent upon his employer." *Silberman v. United States, supra*, at 1127.

The requisites for inclusion of Fannie's annuity in Isidor's gross estate are therefore met, and her annuity must be included in Isidor's gross estate at its commuted value.[23] Plaintiffs have argued that the Commissioner's determination of the commuted value is erroneous, because it relies on standardized tables contained in the treasury regulations and designed for the purposes of commuting the values of private annuities. The standard assumptions, plaintiffs allege, which underlie these tables do not comport with the realities of Purity's financial stability, and thus the tables should not be used as the sole determinant of commuted value. No evidence has been presented as to the "proper" calculation of commuted value. There is, of course, a presumption in favor of the Commissioner not only that he is correct, but that his tables are correct. Unless plaintiffs adduce persuasive evidence showing not only that the Commissioner's tables are inapplicable but also what the correct

---

[23] The fact that Fannie received an annuity smaller than the payments which Isidor had the right to receive does not affect the includability of her annuity under Section 2039. *See Gray v. United States*, 410 F. 2d 1094 (3d Cir. 1969), quoting with approval Estate of Beal, 47 T. C. 269, 272 (1966): "[W]e can perceive no reason to limit the section only to those payments to a beneficiary which are a continuation of the payments to the decedent or to those payments to a beneficiary which are a substitution for amounts otherwise payable to the decedent."

amount is, then the issue will be decided in favor of the Government. *Missouri Pacific R. R. Co. v. United States*, 168 Ct. Cl. 86 (1964).

[Other estate tax issues have been omitted.]

---

[3] Income Tax

Nonqualified plans may be eligible for treatment under special rules, such as qualified stock options under §§ 421 through 424, or they may be subject to the Byzantine rules of § 83 concerning restrictive property. A comprehensive consideration of the tax treatment of nonqualified plans is beyond the scope of this book.

Chapter 12

THIRD-PARTY POWERS

Previous chapters have explored the tax ramifications of interests and powers that are directly or indirectly retained by the transferor (creator of the power). Any of the powers that can be retained by the transferor, however, may also be granted to a third party. For example, a settlor may give a trusted friend the power to control or approve trustee actions. Further, as illustrated in Chapter 8 in the discussion of joint powers, third parties may be given the power to veto the revocation or modification of a trust. Similarly, third parties can be given the power to direct a modification or termination of a trust.

This Chapter focuses on those powers that are commonly held by third parties, but which are not attributed to the creator of the power. Third-party powers are defined and classified in a number of ways. The most significant distinction is between fiduciary powers, the exercise of which is made subject to a duty, and therefore controllable by the equity courts, and nonfiduciary powers, which are not so limited.[1] Further, fiduciary powers may be discretionary or nondiscretionary. Lastly, discretionary powers may be called powers of appointment or invasion powers, and nondiscretionary powers may be described using terms such as *mandatory special powers of appointment*, *investment powers*, or *administrative powers*.

The rights of a power holder depend on the type of the power. If the power is defined as an agency power, it ceases upon the death or incompetence of the principal[2] unless it is coupled with an interest in the power holder. Powers of appointment, on the other hand, are similar to interests in property and may survive the incompetence or death of the creator. Indeed, a common source of powers of appointment is a donor's will, which requires the death of the donor if the power is to be effective. The type of power will also determine the tax ramifications. This Chapter first considers dispositive powers (including powers of appointment), and then administrative powers.

§ 12.01 Dispositive Powers

A variety of powers can be held by persons other than the grantor. The classic is the power of appointment, which gives the holder the power to pass title to himself or others. Property law has denominated these powers as *general*—if the holder may appoint to anyone, including himself—or *special*—if the class of possible appointees is limited.[3] Further, some powers

---

[1] Trust law defines and controls the power if the holder is a trustee or is exercising trustee functions. The law of agency defines the limits of powers held by the third party as the agent or attorney of the grantor.

[2] In many jurisdictions, durable powers of attorney can be created that will survive the incompetence of the principal,

[3] Section 2041(b)(1) defines general powers of appointment. Any power that is not *general* is *special*.

commonly given to trustees, such as the power to invade trust corpus for one or more trust beneficiaries, have an effect equal to a power of appointment, whether given to the trustee, beneficiary, or other nontrustee.

In this Chapter, these powers will be categorized by the way in which the transfer tax systems respond to their existence. For transfer tax purposes, any dispositive power that can be exercised, directly or indirectly, in favor of the power holder is referred to as *general*. All other powers are referred to as *special*.

[A]   General Powers of Appointment

Section 2041 includes in a decedent's gross estate property over which the decedent possessed a general power of appointment exercisable at death. This Chapter investigates whether a power is a general power for estate tax purposes. It also analyzes the basic concept of taxing an individual because a power is exercised in favor of someone else (or because the individual failed to exercise the power at all), when the decedent could have exercised it in her own favor. A power that can be exercised in favor of the power holder is the economic equivalent of ownership of the interest subject to the power. Therefore, the power holder is deemed the owner of the interest for tax purposes, and normal transfer tax principles are applied to this deemed ownership.

[1]   Gift Tax

Code: § 2514.

Regulations: Treas. Reg. § 25.2514–1, –3.

Section 2514 treats the lifetime exercise or release of a general power in favor of someone other than the power holder as a transfer for gift tax purposes. *See* § 2514(b).[4] By exercising the power in favor of the other person, the power holder has diminished his worth: he could have obtained control over the assets for his own benefit.

> **Example:** *X* transfers $100,000 to *T* in an irrevocable trust, income to *A* for life, remainder to *B*. *T* has the power to invade corpus for anyone, including himself. *T* invades $40,000 of corpus for *C*.

In the example, § 2514 treats *T* as making a gift to *C* of $40,000, which also qualifies as a present interest under § 2503(b). *T* As a result, only $60,000 from the trust remains to be taxed under § 2041. Had T not invaded the corpus for *C*, the entire $100,000 would have been taxed in his estate under § 2041.

Section 2514 also applies if the power holder *releases* the power, so that she will not thereafter have the power. The release diminishes her estate by preventing operation of § 2041, which requires that the power be held at death. Not surprisingly, the definition of general power is the same for both gift and estate tax purposes. Compare §§ 2041(b)(1) and 2514(c).

---

[4] Section 2514(a) taxes the power holder on the exercise, but not the release, of powers created before October 22, 1942.

Furthermore, the lapse of a general power constitutes a release for gift tax purposes, but only to the extent that the property subject to the power exceeds $5,000 or 5% of the property that could be used to satisfy the exercise. *See* § 2514(e). The power holder is taxed for not exercising the power in favor of herself. By not exercising the power, and allowing it to lapse, the power holder has diminished her potential estate.

Obviously, the exercise of a general power in favor of the power holder is not a gift for tax purposes because the gift tax applies only to transfers that diminish the wealth of the donor. In this setting the power holder is not poorer as a result of the exercise. The same logic applies if after a release or lapse the power holder still has the beneficial enjoyment of the property or has some limited control. In both circumstances, the estate tax will apply when the power holder dies, even though the power holder no longer has an inter vivos general power of appointment.

[2]   Estate Tax

Code: § 2041.

Regulations: Treas. Reg. §§ 20.2041–1(a), –(b)(1), –(c); 20.2041–3(a), (b), (c).

For a discussion of the general estate tax aspects of general powers of appointment, see *Estate of Alperstein v. Commissioner* and the related discussion in § 3.02[A] *supra*.

[3]   Limitations on the Taxation of Powers

For a discussion of the ascertainable standard limitation on general powers of appointment, see *Estate of Vissering v. Commissioner* and the related discussion in § 3.02[B] *supra*.

[4]   Release of a General Power

Code: §§ 2041(b) and 2514(e).

Regulations: Treas. Reg. §§ 20.2041–3(c) and 25.2514–3(c).

de Oliveira v. United States

767 F.2d 1344 (9th Cir. 1985)

Sneed, Circuit Judge:

Jose de Oliveira, Jr., executor of the estate of Serafina de Oliveira, appeals from a judgment entered in proceedings for the determination of entitlement to an estate tax refund. The district court held that estate taxes were properly assessed against Serafina's estate and granted the Internal Revenue Service's (IRS) motion for summary judgment . . . .

I.

FACTS AND PROCEEDINGS BELOW

Jose de Oliveira, Sr. (the testator) died testate in 1956. His last will and testament created a testamentary trust to hold his half of the community property and named his wife, Serafina, as lifetime beneficiary and trustee. The will also gave the trustee certain powers. The nature and scope of those powers are the principal matters of dispute between the parties in this action.

In 1972, Serafina executed a document entitled "Power of Attorney." Under that document Serafina agreed to confer with the family members and to abide by a majority vote on any proposed sale, lease, loan or transaction regarding any of the family property.

Serafina died testate in 1978. Her son, Jose Jr., was appointed executor of her estate. A timely federal estate tax return was filed for the estate. This return did not include as assets of the estate the property in the testamentary trust established by the testator, Jose Sr.

On audit, the IRS determined that the provisions of the testator's will creating the trust gave Serafina the power, exercisable in favor of herself, to consume, appropriate, or dispose of the corpus of the trust. Based on this determination the IRS concluded that Serafina possessed a general power of appointment and that the trust assets were required to be included in her gross estate for estate tax purposes under the provisions of 26 U.S.C. section 2041.

. . .

The provisions of the testator's will that gave rise to this dispute are the sixth, seventh, and ninth paragraphs. Paragraph six reads in part:

> Said estate to be held and administered thereafter by said Trustee in trust. . .
>
> a) *for the benefit of my said wife* so long as she lives,
>
> b) with all the powers and subject to the conditions specifically designated hereinafter in paragraph Ninth for my said Trustee and/or Executrix,
>
> c) and shall continue until the death of my said wife. Upon the death of my said wife, this trust to cease and terminate and all the rest, residue and remainder of my trust estate I hereby give, devise and bequeath to my ten children . . . .

(emphasis added).

Paragraph nine gives the trustee various powers "[i]n addition to any inherent or implied or statutory powers" and places no limitations on the use of the trust assets.[5]

---

[5] Paragraph nine provides in part:

In addition to any inherent or implied or statutory powers my Executrix and/or Trustee may have in either capacity, I grant the following powers to such Executrix and Trustee and her successor:

. . .

Paragraph seven contains the following language: "I hereby direct that *all provisions for support herein* are intended to take effect as of the date of my death." (emphasis added).

II.

DISCUSSION

To determine whether the trust assets were properly included in Serafina's gross estate, we must determine whether the testator's will created a general power of appointment in the trustee (Serafina), and, if so, whether this power was terminated by Serafina's execution of the "Power of Attorney" document in a manner that removed the trust assets from Serafina's gross estate.

. . .

B. The Existence of a General Power of Appointment

The executor argues that the language in the testator's will creating the trust did not expressly grant to Serafina a general power of appointment. If such a power might be implied, he argues, the will is latently ambiguous since this was not the testator's intent. The executor maintains that certain extrinsic evidence offered below proves that the testator intended that the trust could be invaded only for Serafina's support.

Our analysis begins by recognizing that state law determines the property rights and interests created by a will, but federal law determines the tax consequences of those rights and interests . . . .

The district court concluded that the will created a power of appointment under California law. The executor does not contest that conclusion on appeal. Rather, the issue on appeal is whether the power of appointment created by the will was a general power of appointment within the meaning of the federal estate tax law.

Section 2041 of the Internal Revenue Code includes within the gross estate of a decedent the value of property over which the decedent possessed a general power of appointment. Such a general power is defined by section 2041(b)(1) . . . . Serafina's power of appointment is derived from paragraphs six and nine of the testator's will. Paragraph six provides that the trust was "for the benefit" of Serafina. In addition, paragraph nine grants extensive powers to Serafina as trustee to own, control, possess and use the trust assets, to collect and receive rents, issues and profits for the benefit of the trust, and to sell, convey, lease or mortgage property of the trust as deemed necessary

---

(b) During the continuance of the administration of my estate, and for the trust herein created, my Trustee shall own, control, possess and use the said trust estate and all property therein; shall collect and receive the rents, issues and profits thereof and shall apply them to the uses and purposes of said trust; said Trustee is hereby empowered to sell, convey, lease, mortgage, hypothecate, encumber by deed or trust and/or convert the property of said trust as from time to time shall be deemed necessary or convenient; to invest and reinvest the trust estate in any property or securities . . . hereby giving to my said Trustee every power and discretion in the management of the trust estate that she would have if she were the absolute, unqualified and unlimited owner thereof . . . .

or convenient. Serafina's power to consume, invade, or appropriate property is limited only by the requirement that it be exercised for her "benefit."

The executor does not deny that "benefit" is not an "ascertainable standard" sufficient to bring the power within the exception stated in subsection 2041(b)(1)(A). *See, e.g., Lehman v. United States*, 448 F.2d 1318 (5th Cir. 1971) (holding that the words "comfort" and "welfare" rendered a power of appointment general); Treas. Reg. section 20.2041–1(c)(2) (1954). Accordingly, Serafina [sic] power remains one exercisable in her favor, her estate, or the creditors of her estate.

Paragraph seven of the will states that "all provisions for support herein" shall take effect on the day of the testator's death and directs the executrix "to make the same provisions for the beneficiary [Serafina] as provided in said trust" during the probate administration of the estate. This does not alter the conclusion that Serafina's power was a general power. The purpose of paragraph seven was to free Serafina from the need to seek court-ordered maintenance pursuant to Cal. Prob. Code sections [6540–6545 (West 1998)].

Nonetheless, the executor argues that the use of the "provisions for support" creates an ambiguity which requires the extrinsic evidence be examined to determine the testator's intent. The extrinsic evidence offered below, the executor insists, shows that the testator intended that the trust could be invaded only for Serafina's support. Thus, her power was not general because limited by an "ascertainable standard."

. . .

The essence of the executor's argument is that the testator intended to create an arrangement that would allow the trust assets to pass to the children without being taxed as part of Serafina's estate. In an affidavit, the attorney who drafted the testator's will stated that both he and the testator intended to limit Serafina's use of the trust assets to the funds necessary for her "support." In effect, the executor is urging this court to rewrite the will to effectuate the testator's intent . . . . While it is possible the testator intended to limit Serafina's power over the trust assets by an ascertainable standard, he did not do so. Accordingly, the will should not be construed to limit Serafina's power to invade the trust assets to "support." The federal estate tax consequences must be determined on the basis of the testator's will as it is written, not on the basis of how it might have been written.

C. "Power of Attorney" Document

The executor also argues that the power of attorney document eliminated the general power of appointment by requiring that Serafina exercise the power only upon the authorization by a majority of her children. While it is true that the power of appointment would not have been general if that requirement had been in the testator's will, the subsequent creation of the requirement does not achieve the legal effect that the executor desires. Section 2041(a)(2) of the Code states that the decedent's gross estate includes the value of all property "with respect to which the decedent has at any time . . . released [a general] power of appointment by a disposition which is of such nature that if it were a transfer of property owned by the decedent, such property would be includible in the decedent's gross estate under sections 2035 to 2038, inclusive." The document constituted a release of Serafina's general power of appointment. *See* Treas. Reg. section 20.2041–3(d) (1954) . . . . If the power of attorney document had been a transfer of property owned by Serafina, it is obvious that property would have been includible in Serafina's estate under section 2036(a). Her retained powers fit snugly within that section. Accordingly, the value of the trust assets is includible in Serafina's estate pursuant to section 2041(a)(2). The fact that Serafina perhaps was not aware that she had a general power of appointment when she executed the power of attorney document is irrelevant. Serafina had a general power of appointment regardless of whether she was aware of that fact. It follows that the property subject to the general power of appointment was includible in Serafina's gross estate both before and after the execution of the power of attorney document.

AFFIRMED.

――――――

De Oliveira raises two questions. The first—what constitutes a general power—was considered in *Vissering v. Commissioner*, discussed in § 3.02[B], *supra*. The second question—whether the release of the widow's power prevented taxation under § 2041—and its answer explains when a general power of appointment is analogized to ownership of the property that is subject to the power. The court's response, addressing the interaction of § 2041(b)(2) with §§ 2036, 2037, and 2038, establishes that the analogy is complete.

Thus, if a decedent transferred property to a trust, retaining an interest or power over the property, §§ 2036, 2037 and 2038 include the property or interest in property in the decedent's gross estate. If, on the other hand, a power holder *transfers* property to a trust by exercising or releasing a general power of appointment, the result is the same under the cross-reference in § 2041 to §§ 2036 through 2038.

The possible estate tax on inter vivos releases of general powers raises the question of what constitutes a release for purposes of §§ 2514 and 2041. The term obviously applies to actions that are deemed a release under local law, such as when the power holder gives up the power in a document delivered to the takers in default. This was the nature of the release in *de Oliveira*. The concept is more inclusive, however. First, the term *release* can also apply to any other transaction that has the impact of terminating the power, even if the transaction is not categorized as a release under local law. Thus, for example, the renunciation of a power could constitute a release, if the renunciation did not satisfy the qualified disclaimer rules of §§ 2046 and 2518. *See* Treas. Reg. § 20.2041–3(d)(6)(i). *See also Goudy v. United States*, 86–2 U.S.T.C. (CCH) ¶ 13,690, *rev'd and remanded*, 851 F.2d 360 (9th Cir. 1988). A qualified disclaimer of a general power, on the other hand, would not constitute a release for the purposes of § 2041. *See* Treas. Reg. § 20.2041–3(d)(6)(i).

Second, § 2041(b)(2) provides that the lapse of a power, *i.e.*, the termination of the power by its own terms, constitutes a release to the extent that the value of the property subject to the power exceeds 5% of the property in the trust or $5,000, whichever is greater. As a general proposition, therefore, it is not possible to avoid the full effect of § 2041 by providing for the automatic termination of the power, rather than its release.

The "five or five rule." The *lapse equals release* rule in § 2041(b)(2) is limited to the extent that the property subject to the power exceeds the greater of $5,000 or 5% of the "aggregate value, at the time of such lapse, of the assets out of which, or the proceeds of which, the exercise of the lapsed powers could have been satisfied." Thus, powers of a limited nature may lapse without estate tax effects. *See generally Estate of Noland v. Commissioner*, T.C. Memo 1984–209; Treas. Reg. § 20.2041–3(d). As a result of this exception, trust instruments typically will limit invasion powers to the greater of $5,000 or 5% of the trust corpus. Indeed, such powers are sufficiently common in estate planning as to have earned the name *five or five powers.*

Finally, the existence or exercise of third-party powers usually does not have estate tax consequences to the grantor of the power. In the absence of facts that imply a retention of the power by the grantor, third-party powers do not trigger §§ 2036, 2037 or 2038, even if the power could be exercised in favor of the grantor. *See* Treas. Reg. §§ 20.2036–1(b)(3) (second from last sentence), 20.2038–1(a). Of course, the grantor's initial transfer establishing the power of appointment was likely a transaction that subjected the grantor to gift tax.

[5] Joint Powers and Contingent Powers

More complex issues arise when a power of appointment is contingent or is exercisable only with the concurrence or consent of another person. Treasury Regulation § 20.2041–3(b) provides that a power of appointment is a general power even if:

> . . .
>
> the exercise of the power is subject to the precedent giving of notice, or even though the exercise of the power takes effect only on the expiration of a stated period after its exercise, whether or not on or before the decedent's death notice has been given or the power has been exercised.

The regulations provide examples of conditions that prevent a power from being a general power of appointment:

> . . .
>
> a power which by its terms is exercisable only upon the occurrence during the decedent's lifetime of an event or a contingency which did not in fact take place or occur during such time is not a power in existence on the date of the decedent's death. For example, if a decedent was given a general power of appointment exercisable only after he reached a certain age, only if he survived another person, or only if he died without descendants, the power would not be in existence on the date of the decedent's death if the condition precedent to its exercise had not occurred.

In *Estate of Kurz v. Commissioner*, 68 F.3d 1027 (7th Cir. 1995), *aff'g* 101 T.C. 44 (1993), the decedent was the beneficiary of two trusts. One trust was a marital deduction trust and the other was a nonmarital or by-pass trust. (For a discussion of marital trusts and by-pass trusts, see § 3.04[C][5], *supra*.) The decedent had a power to withdraw all of the marital trust at any time by notice to the trustee. The decedent had a power to appoint to herself up to 5% of the nonmarital trust, if the principal of the marital trust had been depleted. The Service included 5% of the nonmarital trust in the decedent's gross estate, although the marital trust had not been depleted. The Tax Court agreed with the government. The condition on exercise had no substantial nontax purpose and the decedent had the right to withdraw the marital trust funds at will. The Seventh Circuit affirmed the Tax Court's ruling, but refused to hold that a condition precedent to the exercise of a power of appointment may be disregarded as too subjective solely because it lacks a significant nontax consequence. The court instead focused on whether the condition was one that could have been satisfied by the decedent on the date of death. The Seventh Circuit determined that requiring the decedent to exhaust the marital trust was a notice requirement only. She could have exhausted the marital trust at any time.

The rule concerning jointly exercisable powers is addressed similarly in the Regulation. *See* Treas. Reg. § 20.2041–3(c). A joint power by definition is one that requires a second person to either consent to the exercise or join affirmatively in the exercise. Two rules covered the alternative scenarios for joint powers.

(1) A joint power exercisable only with the joinder or consent of the grantor of the power is not a general power of appointment.

(2) A joint power exercisable only with the joinder or consent of someone who has an adverse interest in the exercise is not a general power of appointment.

The more problematic aspect of the Regulations is the determination of who has an adverse interest. The Regulations provide that an interest is adverse if it is substantial in value "in relation to the total value of the property subject to the power." *See* Treas. Reg. § 20.2041–3(c)(2). A taker in default of the exercise of the power is an example of an adverse interest, but merely being one of several permissive appointees is not.

When several individuals hold a power of appointment, the determination of the existence of a power of appointment is difficult. The following Revenue Ruling illustrates the types of situation that may arise.

Revenue Ruling 76–503

1976–2 C.B. 275

. . .

In 1973, three siblings named *A*, *B*, and *C* owned equal interests in their family business. They decided to place the business in trust for the benefit of their descendants and with a view toward keeping the family enterprise intact. Each sibling-grantor designated one of the sibling's adult children as one of the three trustees of the trust. Under the terms of the trust, income is to be accumulated and added to principal until the trust terminates. The trust shall terminate exactly twenty years after the death of the last surviving descendant of A, B, and C who is living at the date of creation of the trust.

The trustees are empowered to manage the trust assets in their complete discretion. They are also empowered to distribute trust property to whomever they select, including themselves, in such proportions, at such times, and for such purposes as they see fit. Each trustee is privileged to designate one of the trustee's relatives to serve as a successor trustee in the event of the trustee's death or resignation. In the absence of such a designation, the oldest adult living descendant of the deceased or resigned trustee who is willing to serve as the new trustee shall occupy the vacant trustee position. The decedent, D, was selected by A to be one of the three trustees and D continued in that position until D's death in 1975.

The question presented is whether any amount is includible, with respect to the trust described above, in D's gross estate under section 2041 of the Code as the value of property subject to a general power of appointment, in view of the fact that the power was held jointly by D and two cotrustees. Section 2041(a)(2) of the Code requires inclusion in the gross estate of the value of all property with respect to which the decedent has, at the time of death, a 'general power of appointment' created after October 21, 1942. Section 2041(b) of the Code provides, in relevant part, the definition of the term 'general power of appointment' . . . .

Section 20.2041–3(c) of the Estate Tax Regulations provides the following with respect to jointly held powers of appointment created after October 21, 1942:

> (2) Such power is not considered a general power of appointment if it is not exercisable by the decedent except with the consent or joinder of a person having a substantial interest in the property subject to the power which is adverse to the exercise of the power in favor of the decedent, his estate, his creditors, or the creditors of his estate. An interest adverse to the exercise of a power is considered as substantial if its value in relation to the total value of the property subject to the power is not insignificant. For this purpose, the interest is to be valued in accordance with the actuarial principles set forth in § 20.2031–7 or, if it is not susceptible to valuation under those provisions, in accordance with the general principles set forth in § 20.2031–1. A taker in default of appointment under a power has an interest which is adverse to an exercise of the power. A coholder of the power has no adverse interest merely because of his joint possession of the power nor merely because he is a permissible appointee under a power. However, a coholder of a power is considered as having an adverse interest where he may possess the power after the decedent's death and may exercise it at that time in favor of himself, his estate, his creditors, or the creditors of his estate. Thus, for example, if X, Y, and Z held a power

jointly to appoint among a group of persons which includes themselves and if on the death of X the power will pass to Y and Z jointly, then Y and Z are considered to have interests adverse to the exercise of the power in favor of X. Similarly, if on Y's death the power will pass to Z, Z is considered to have an interest adverse to the exercise of the power in favor of Y . . . .

(3) A power which is exercisable only in conjunction with another person, and which after application of the rules set forth in subparagraphs (1) and (2) of this paragraph constitutes a general power of appointment, will be treated as though the holders of the power who are permissible appointees of the property were joint owners of property subject to the power. The decedent, under this rule, will be treated as possessed of a general power of appointment over an aliquot share of the property to be determined with reference to the number of joint holders, including the decedent, who (or whose estates or creditors) are permissible appointees. Thus, for example, if X, Y, and Z hold an unlimited power jointly to appoint among a group of persons, including themselves, but on the death of X the power does not pass to Y and Z jointly, then Y and Z are not considered to have interests adverse to the exercise of the power in favor of X. In this case X is considered to possess a general power of appointment as to one-third of the property subject to the power.

In the above-quoted portion of section 20.2041–3(c)(2) of the regulations, the example provided describes Y and Z as having substantial interests, in the property subject to the jointly held power of appointment, that are adverse to exercise of the power in favor of the decedent X because the power will pass to Y and Z upon the death of X. In such a situation, Y and Z will be able to exercise, by themselves, the power in their own favor after the death of X, so it is in their economic interest to refuse to agree to exercise the power in favor of X during X's lifetime. Their ability to benefit themselves is thus enlarged by the death of X. In such circumstances, the Code and regulations (quoted above) provide that the potential survivors of the decedent hold an interest and that it is adverse to the exercise of the power in favor of the decedent.

Where, however, as in the example in section 20.2041–3(c)(3) of the regulations, the surviving coholders of the power do not receive, at the death of the decedent, the entire power of appointment between themselves but must continue to share the power with the decedent's replacement, they would not necessarily be in a better economic position after the decedent's death than they are before the death. In such a situation, the fact that the coholders may survive the decedent does not mean that they stand to profit by refusing to exercise the power in favor of the decedent during the decedent's lifetime. Therefore, the coholders of the power do not have an interest that is adverse to exercise of the power in favor of the decedent for purposes of section 2041(b)(1)(c)(ii) of the Code.

If the coholders of the power, who must share their power with the decedent's replacement upon the death or resignation of the decedent, have no interest in the subject property other than as coholders of, and permissible appointees under, the power, those facts alone cannot support the conclusion that they hold adverse interests. As a result, the decedent's power meets the definition of a 'general power of appointment' because the coholders of the power in actuality have no substantial interest in the subject property, which is adverse to the exercise of the power in favor of the decedent. If the coholders of the decedent's general power of appointment are, along with the decedent, permissible appointees of the subject property, the amount includible in the decedent's gross estate is the value of the subject property divided by the total number of holders of the power who are also permissible appointees, pursuant to section 2041(b)(1)(C)(iii) of the Code and section 20.2041–3(c)(3) of the regulations, quoted above. Accordingly, in the instant case, one third of the value of the trust (as of the date of death of D or appropriate alternate valuation date) is includible in the gross estate of D under section 2041 of the Code as property subject to a general power of appointment.

Problems

1. What is the difference between a lapse and a release, and why is it important to distinguish between the two concepts?

2. Z transfers property to an irrevocable trust. The income is payable to D for life and the remainder is payable to B. D has the power to invade the corpus for his own benefit at any time after his thirty-fifth birthday. D dies at age 26.

    a. What are the estate tax consequences of the power?

    b. How would the results differ if the power were exercisable only after D married, and D died unmarried?

3. S transfers property to an irrevocable trust. The income is payable to D for life and the remainder is distributable to whomever D should appoint with the consent of S. The remainder in default of appointment goes to X. D dies without exercising the power.

    a. What are the gift and estate tax consequences of the trust and power?

    b. How would the results differ if D needed the consent of X to exercise the power? Consider § 2041(b)(1)(C) and Treasury Regulation § 20.2041–3(c)(2).

4. X transfers property to an irrevocable trust. The income is payable to D for life and remainder is payable to A. D is given the power to change the remainderman by deed or will. D releases the power four years before his death.

    a. What are the estate and gift tax consequences of the release of the power?

    b. What would be the results if D renounced the power six months after learning of its existence? Consider § 2518.

5. On January 1 of Year 1, X transfers $200,000 to an irrevocable trust. The income is payable to D for life and the remainder is payable to B. D has

the noncumulative power to withdraw $22,000 from corpus each year (if *D* has not exercised the power by the end of the year, the power for that year terminates, but a new power exists for the succeeding year). *D* never exercised the power during his life, and died in Year 2. What are the gift and estate tax consequences if:

a. The value of the trust corpus at all times was $200,000?

b. The value of the trust on January 1 of Year 2 was $200,000 and on the date of *D's* death the value was $300,000?

c. The value of the trust on January 1 of Year 2 was $200,000 and on the date of *D's* death the value was $100,000?

6. Consider the impact of § 2702 when answering Questions 4 and 5.

[6] Generation-Skipping Transfer Tax

Code: § 2652(a).

Regulations: None.

The possession, exercise, release, or lapse of a general power of appointment may also have generation-skipping transfer tax consequences. Because the GST tax uses the normal transfer tax definitions, the exercise, release, or lapse of a general power is a transfer for GST tax purposes. Thus, for example, a direct skip will occur on the lifetime exercise of a general power of appointment in favor of a skip person. Similarly, a direct skip will occur if the donee of a power fails to exercise a testamentary power that in default passes to a skip person.

Furthermore, care must be taken in the exercise of any power of appointment under a trust or will that is grandfathered under the effective date rules. *See* § 1433, Tax Reform Act of 1986; Treas. Reg. § 26.2601–1. The Regulations provide that a gift or estate taxable release, exercise, or lapse of a power of appointment constitutes a constructive addition to the trust of the value of the entire trust principal involved (not merely the taxable portion) and will cause the trust to lose its exempt status. *See* Treas. Reg. § 26.2601–1(b)(1)(v). In general, however, those powers that cause the loss of the GST grandfathered status must be general powers under §§ 2041 and 2514; the exercise or release of special powers should not affect the grandfathering of otherwise exempt trusts. *See id.*

[7] Income Tax

Code: § 678.

Regulations: None.

General powers of appointment may also have income tax consequences. Property subject to a power that can be exercised in favor of the power holder is taxed to the holder. Subject to exceptions not relevant here, § 678(a) specifically requires that a person other than the grantor of a trust "shall be treated as the owner of any portion of a trust with respect to which: (1) such person has a power exercisable solely by himself to vest the corpus or the income therefrom in himself, . . ." *See Mallinckrodt v. Nunan*, 146 F.2d 1 (8th

Cir. 1945). Thus any general power of appointment over corpus or income interests effectively results in the taxation of trust income to the power holder. *See, e.g.*, Rev. Rul. 67–241, 1967–2 C.B. 225.

Section 678 may also treat a person as the owner of the trust (or a portion of the trust) after exercise or release of a general power. If, after the exercise or release of the power, the power holder retains the kind of interest or control over the property that would have required taxation of the income to her under §§ 671 through 677 if she had transferred the property to the trust, then she continues to be taxed consistent with the latter sections. *See* § 678(a)(2). The exercise or release of the power is treated the same as is a transfer of property, paralleling the treatment of exercises and releases of powers for transfer tax purposes under § 2041. Curiously, however, § 678 does mention lapses of powers of appointment. Nevertheless, the Service consistently has held that lapsed powers such as "five or five" powers, which are generally exempt from gift tax and estate tax consequences, have significant income tax consequences.

Private Letter Ruling 200022035

On D[ate]1 *G* created a revocable trust, Trust 1. Following *G*'s death on D[ate]2, a marital trust and residual trust, Trust 2, were created pursuant to the provisions of Trust 1. Under the provisions of Trust 2, *B*, as the income beneficiary, has a lifetime power to appoint all or any part of the Trust 2 income. In addition, *B* has the noncumulative power to withdraw annually from the corpus of Trust 2 an amount not exceeding five thousand dollars or five percent of the market value of the net principal of Trust 2. This type of power in a trust is commonly referred to as a "five or five" power. With the exception of a partial withdrawal in Year 1, *B* has not exercised this five or five power.

Section 678(a) provides that a person other than the grantor shall be treated as the owner of any portion of a trust with respect to which (1) such person has a power exercisable solely by himself to vest corpus or the income therefrom in himself, or (2) such person has previously partially released or otherwise modified such a power and after the release or modification retains such control as would, within the principles of §§ 671 to 677 of the Code inclusive, subject a grantor of a trust to treatment as the owner thereof.

Section 677 provides that the grantor of a trust shall be treated as the owner of any portion of the trust whose income without the approval or consent of any adverse party is distributed to the grantor.

In Rev. Rul. 67–241, 1967–2 C.B. 225, the beneficiary of a trust held a noncumulative power, exercisable solely by the beneficiary, to withdraw certain amounts of corpus annually from the trust. Rev. Rul. 67–241 concludes that, for each year that this demand power is held, under § 678(a)(1)of the Code the beneficiary is the owner of that portion of the trust which is subject to this demand power, whether or not it is exercised.

We conclude that *B*'s five or five power is a power to vest in *B* part of the corpus of Trust 2. Therefore, until the power is exercised, released or allowed to lapse, B will be treated as the owner for each year of that portion of Trust 2 that is subject to the power to withdraw under § 678(a)(1).

For each year that B fails to exercise the five or five power, B will be deemed to have partially released a power to withdraw a portion of the trust corpus. B has also retained a power over the income of Trust 2 that would subject a grantor of a trust to treatment as the owner under § 677. Therefore, B will also be treated as an owner of a portion of Trust 2 corpus under § 678(a)(2).

After each succeeding year in which B fails to exercise the five or five power, B will be treated as the owner of an increasing portion of the corpus of Trust 2. The annual increase of the portion of the corpus of Trust 2 of which B is treated as the owner is the product of the amount which B could withdraw multiplied by a fraction the numerator of which is the portion of trust corpus which B is not already treated as owning and the denominator of which is the total of trust corpus from which the withdrawal could be made.

We further conclude that to the extent that B exercises the five or five power during a calendar year, such distribution shall be deemed to have been made from B's pro rata share of each asset of Trust 2 corpus that B is treated as owning.

Section 671 provides that where a grantor or other person is treated as the owner of any portion of a trust, the income, deductions, and credits against tax of the trust attributable to such portion of the trust shall be included by the grantor or other person in computing his taxable income and credits.

Section 1.671–3(a) of the Income Tax Regulations provides that a deemed owner of corpus must include his or her share of the capital gains realized by the trust if allocable to the portion of corpus which that person is deemed to own.

Section 1.671–3(a)(3) provides that if a person is treated as owning an undivided fractional share of trust corpus or an interest represented by a dollar amount, then a pro rata share of each such item of capital gain shall be allocated to that person.

We conclude that B must include, in computing B's tax liability, items of income, deductions, and credits that are attributable to that portion of the corpus of Trust 2 which B is treated as owning. Also, as the owner of an undivided fractional share of the corpus of Trust 2, B shall be allocated a pro rata share of each item of any capital gain realized by Trust 2.

The impact of the Service's position on Crummey Trusts is discussed below in § 12.01[C][4].

[B] Other Dispositive Powers

Although powers that are not general powers in the tax sense usually do not trigger transfer or income taxation, particular exercises of nongeneral powers may.

[1] Gift Tax

Code: § 2514.

Regulations: None.

When third-party powers cannot be exercised in favor of the power holder, usually no gift tax ramifications flow from the existence or exercise of the power. Although the power may adjust interests among beneficiaries, no transfer is made by the power holder at the time of exercise; the only transfer is by the donor, and that usually is taxed at the time the power is created. The application of § 2514 to only general powers means that the exercise of a nongeneral power does not trigger gift taxation, unless the exercise creates a new power valid without reference to the time of the creation of the first power. *See* § 2514(d).

Notwithstanding the general rule that the exercise of special powers does not result in gift taxation, in some circumstances a taxable gift can indirectly result from the exercise.

Estate of Regester v. Commissioner

83 T.C. 1 (1984)

. . .

George L. Bignell, a resident of Michigan, died on September 29, 1973 . . . .

The provisions of the Bignell will with which we are concerned created a trust (the Bignell trust) as follows:

> I give, devise and bequeath to my Trustee hereinafter named, IN TRUST, with the powers and duties hereinafter set forth, and to dispose of the income and principal thereof as follows:
>
> A. He shall pay the net income thereof, at least as often as quarter-annually, to my daughter Ruth B. Regester, as long as she lives.
>
> B. If the net income payable to my said daughter from this trust, together with her income from other sources, is insufficient in the opinion of my Trustee to maintain her in the comfort and manner to which she has been accustomed in my lifetime; or if there is need to supplement said income to meet extraordinary needs of her and/or her family arising from accident, physical or mental illness, or the like; I authorize my Trustee in such case to make such payments to her out of the principal thereof as from time to time may be required for the purpose.
>
> C. During the lifetime of my said daughter, my Trustee shall distribute the principal thereof, in whole or in part and from time to time, either in trust or otherwise, but free of this trust, to or for her son Charles Regester and/or his issue, and in such proportions to or for each, as my said daughter shall appoint by instruments signed, sealed and acknowledged by her and delivered to my Trustee.

D. Upon the death of my said daughter, the remaining principal thereof and all increase and income then on hand, if any, shall be distributed as my said daughter shall by her last will and testament appoint among any one or more of the following: her son, and the issue of her son; but not the estate of my said daughter, her creditors, or the creditors of her estate.

By a trust agreement dated May 24, 1974, Charles L. Regester created a trust (the Regester trust) for the benefit of his three children. By an instrument dated June 6, 1974, decedent exercised her special power of appointment over the corpus of the Bignell trust and transferred the entire amount to the trustee of the Regester trust. Assets from the estate of George L. Bignell were transferred to the trustee of the Bignell trust in October 1974. On or about November 20, 1974, the corpus of the Bignell trust, consisting solely of 26,811 shares of stock of Rospatch Corporation and a check for $2,412.99 attributable to dividends paid on the stock on November 15, 1974, were delivered to Charles L. Regester as the trustee of the Regester trust. No distributions of income or principal were ever made from the Bignell trust to decedent.

Prior to her death on December 30, 1977, at age 75, decedent filed a gift tax return for the calendar quarter ended December 31, 1974. On September 28, 1978, petitioner filed a United States Estate Tax Return. Neither tax return included an amount attributable to the life income interest of decedent in the Bignell trust or her exercise of the special power of appointment with respect thereto.

By notice of deficiency dated October 8, 1981, respondent determined that the inter vivos exercise of the special power of appointment over the corpus of the Bignell trust by decedent concomitantly effected a gift of her life income interest in the Bignell trust during the calendar quarter ended December 31, 1974; that the value of the gift was $100,474, the then present value of the life income interest of a 72-year-old female in property having a value of $227,894; and that the tax due on such gift was $18,362. Petitioner has agreed that if a taxable gift occurred, the value and tax are as computed by respondent. Petitioner contends, however, that no taxable gift occurred and that section 25.2514–1(b)(2), Gift Tax Regs., which respondent seeks to apply here, is an unreasonable and invalid attempt by respondent to circumvent prior case law.

The federal gift tax is imposed on property transferred by gift, whether the transfer is in trust or otherwise and whether the gift is direct or indirect. *See* sections 2501(a) and 2511(a). The gift tax statutes are intended to include "every species of right or interest protected by law and having an exchangeable value." S. Rept. No. 665, 72d Cong., 1st Sess. (1932), 1939–1 (Part 2) C.B. 496, 524.

Powers of appointment, *i.e.*, a power of disposition given a person over property not his own, were not taxable until 1942 when the predecessor to section 2514 was enacted. *Walston v. Commissioner*, 8 T.C. 72 (1947), *affd* 168 F.2d 211 (4th Cir. 1948); section 452(a) of the Revenue Act of 1942, ch. 619, 56 Stat. 798. Section 2514 provides that, in certain circumstances, the exercise or release of a power of appointment is a taxable transfer of property by the individual possessing the power. Section 2514 applies only to general powers of appointment, *i.e.*, those exercisable by the donee of the power in favor of himself, or in favor of his estate, his creditors, or the creditors of his estate.

Section 25.2514–1(b)(2), Gift Tax Regs., provides as follows:

. . .

Petitioner acknowledges that the life income interest of decedent in the Bignell trust was property for federal gift tax purposes and does not argue that any consideration passed to decedent in connection with her surrender of that interest upon the exercise of the special power of appointment. Further, petitioner concedes that a donee of a life estate may make a gift of an income interest in trust property. *See Hrobon v. Commissioner*, 41 T.C. 476 (1964).

Petitioner argues, however, that the interest of decedent in the income of the Bignell trust should be treated as extinguished, and not as transferred, upon exercise of the special power of appointment. Petitioner cites *Walston v. Commissioner, supra*, and *Self v. United States*, 135 Ct. Cl. 371, 142 F. Supp. 939 (1956), in support of the contention that no taxable gift occurs when the beneficiary of a life estate in income from a trust transfers the underlying trust property by exercising a special power of appointment.

In *Walston v. Commissioner, supra*, which was a Court reviewed opinion, the petitioner received a power to appoint to her brother the corpus of a trust established under her father's will. The will also contained conflicting language with respect to the income of the trust, and after considering extrinsic evidence, the majority held that the will directed the petitioner to transfer the income interest to her brother; thus the income interest was not petitioner's to give away but belonged to her father's estate.

Six judges dissented in the *Walston* case. The disagreement between the majority opinion and the dissenting opinion was that the dissent construed the will to make an outright disposition to the daughter of the income interest, unrestricted by the additional language empowering her to transfer the income interest to her brother. In affirming our decision in the *Walston* case, the Court of Appeals for the Fourth Circuit agreed that the daughter held only a special power of appointment over the trust corpus and income and noted that she did not at any time consider the income or principal of the trust to be her property. 168 F.2d at 217–218. Nothing in any of the opinions is inconsistent with a conclusion that the transfer of a life estate over which the transferor had an absolute interest is a taxable gift.

Respondent maintains the position, consistent with that taken by him in the *Walston* case, that the life income interest transferred was separate from the corpus, and, because only the corpus was the subject of the special power, the transfer of the income interest should be treated and taxed separately. Respondent argues persuasively that neither court in *Walston* ruled contrary to that position because each court concluded that the petitioner held only a special power of appointment over the income interest. We agree with respondent that *Walston* is thus distinguishable, and neither opinion compels the result sought by petitioner here.

Petitioner also cites *Self v. United States, supra*, in support of his argument that decedent's income interest was extinguished upon the exercise of the special power of appointment. In *Self*, the Court of Claims summarized the government's argument:

> that a gift tax should be imposed on the donee of a limited power of appointment upon the exercise of the power when the donee has a beneficial interest in the property transferred pursuant to the power. This argument is based on the theory that such a donee is giving up an economic interest when he exercises the power. This same argument and precise question were presented to the court in *Commissioner v. Walston*, 4 Cir., 168 F.2d 211 . . . . The Tax Court and the Court of Appeals held that the right to the income was transferred under the power of appointment and not by the taxpayer in her independent capacity and therefore the transfer was not taxable. Each court pointed out that where the income beneficiary had a life estate subject to a power of appointment, the income beneficiary had a temporary interest which might last for life, but which was subject to termination if and when the power of appointment was exercised. Consequently, to the extent the power is exercised, the income beneficiary's estate is terminated by reason of the power and not by a desire on the part of the income beneficiary to give up the life estate irrespective of the power.

> The donor of the power of appointment is considered the transferor of the gift and the donee merely acts as his agent and gives direction to the gift pursuant to the donor's wishes. [142 F. Supp. 941–942.]

The Court of Claims in the *Self* case ignored the factual basis for the holding in the *Walston* case, viz, that the taxpayer there, unlike here, did not have the unrestricted right to enjoy the income from the trust for life or the unlimited ability to make an inter vivos transfer of her income interest. Both the Tax Court and the Court of Appeals in *Walston* found that the taxpayer's income interest was to be transferred only to the taxpayer's brother, either separately or along with the corpus. Neither court deciding *Walston* addressed the distinction between the situation where the inter vivos control over the life estate is absolute, as it is here, and the case where the inter vivos control over the life estate is such as to make the donee of that life estate the mere agent of the donor, as he was in *Walston*. That distinction is substantial and must be addressed; to the extent that the Court of Claims relied upon *Walston* to support its holding that an unrestricted life interest is extinguished and not transferred when the underlying corpus is transferred pursuant to a special power of appointment, we conclude that such reliance is misplaced.

In responding to the government's citation of the predecessor of section 25.2514–1(b)(2), Gift Tax Regs., the Court of Claims in the *Self* case stated (at page 942):

> The defendant refers us to Treasury Regulations 108, sec. 86.2(b)(2) (as amended by T.D. 6077, 1954–2 C.B. 308) as authority for its position . . . . We do not deem this portion of the regulation necessarily inconsistent with our decision because the plaintiff in the instant case did not have, in addition to his special power, a

general power to appoint by will, as is the case in the example given in the regulation. However, to the extent that the example given in the regulation implies that a donee, who has only the right to the income from the corpus subject to a special or limited power of appointment, is subject to a gift tax on the exercise of the special or limited power of appointment, we disagree with it.[6]

The Court of Claims suggests that respondent, by adopting the predecessor section 25.2514–1(b)(2), Gift Tax Regs., is trying to tax the exercise of a special power of appointment. The regulation, however, distinguishes between property a taxpayer owns outright, transfer of which may result in a taxable gift, and property of another over which the taxpayer has merely the power to convey to a third party. When a person has the right to income for life and the ability to transfer that right to anyone or to retain it as long as she lives, transfer of that property without consideration gives rise to a taxable gift. Had decedent chosen to transfer her life interest to a third party prior to her exercise of the special power of appointment, she would have made a taxable gift of her life interest. *Cf., Monroe v. United States*, 301 F. Supp. 762 (E.D. Wash. 1969), *affd.* 454 F.2d 1169 (9th Cir. 1972). The fact that she chose to convey that interest to the ultimate owner of the corpus does not disguise the fact that she chose to give her income from the trust property to another without compensation. The transfer of the property should, therefore, be treated as a gift by the life tenant, *i.e.*, decedent, who had an absolute interest in the income. *See* sections 2501(a) and 2511(a). Such a transfer is taxable irrespective of section 2514. A discussion of section 2514 is relevant only because the taxable transfer here was accomplished by decedent's exercise of the special power of appointment over the corpus. Because the income from the corpus follows the corpus, the method used to transfer the income interest was to "piggyback" it onto the property that was transferred under the power of appointment.

The conceptual response to petitioner's argument that decedent's interest was terminated and not transferred is that although decedent's interest in the trust terminated after the underlying trust property was transferred, the property, *i.e.*, the income interest, was not extinguished. When the trust corpus was transferred, the income generated by the corpus was also transferred. There was nothing left in the trust to generate income for petitioner and no reason for the trust to continue. Under the doctrine of merger, the trust would then be terminated; but the enjoyment of the income continued in the hands of the transferee of the corpus. *See* Bogart, Trusts and Trustees, sec. 1003, pp. 363–364 (Rev. 2d Ed. 1983); IV Scott on Trusts, sec. 337.1, pp. 2658–2659 (1967).

Petitioner contends that section 25.2514–1(b)(2), Gift Tax Regs., is invalid because it is "directly contrary to well-established case law which pre-dates the regulation." It is apparent from the discussion above that the regulation

---

[6] In 1979, respondent issued Rev. Rul. 79–327, 1979–2 C.B. 342, in which he announced that the Internal Revenue Service would not follow the *Self* case to the extent that it is contrary to the regulations. The revenue ruling takes the position that an individual's exercise of a special power of appointment results in a taxable gift if the individual also possesses an income interest for life in the property subject to the power of appointment.

is only contrary to the *Self* case, with which we disagree, and that the substantially identical predecessor regulation pre-dated the opinion of the Court of Claims in the *Self* case. There is no basis here for holding the regulation invalid.

Finally, petitioner argues that a decision for respondent in this case would violate the principle that taxpayers should be afforded a degree of certainty. We give that argument little weight where respondent's position was consistent in the cases and in the regulations, and petitioner's claimed reliance was on a single case in point.

We have considered the other arguments made and authorities cited by each party and find them inapplicable in this case.

———

The creation of third-party dispositive powers can occasionally inhibit gift taxation of the transfer. If the third party can distribute all of the trust assets to the grantor, and it does not appear that the intent was for anyone other than the grantor to benefit from the transaction, then the transfer may be deemed incomplete. *See Commissioner v. Vander Weele*, 254 F.2d 895 (6th Cir. 1958); *see also Outwin v. Commissioner*, 76 T.C. 153 (1981), *acq.*, 1981–2 C.B. 2 (creditors' right to attach trust for benefit of grantor). *Cf.* Rev. Rul. 77–378, 1977–2 C.B. 347. For a discussion of incomplete transfers see § 7.01[A], *supra.*

[2]   Estate Tax

Code: § 2041(a)(3).

Regulations: None.

For estate tax purposes, § 2041 applies if a decedent exercises a special power by creating another power that is valid under local law without regard to the date of the first power. *See* § 2041(a)(3). This section was adopted to estate tax the exercise of special powers that create new special powers, which in Delaware may be exercised without regard to the Rule Against Perpetuities. *But see Estate of Murphy v. Commissioner*, 71 T.C. 671 (1979) (inapplicability of § 2041(a)(3) by applying Wisconsin law). *See generally* Ira Mark Bloom, *Transfer Tax Avoidance: The Impact of Perpetuities Restrictions Before and After Generation-Skipping Taxation*, 45 ALB. L. REV. 261 (1981).

Although § 2041(a)(3) was passed to address the problem of successive special powers, the section is not so limited; it may be triggered by the exercise of a special power to create a life estate coupled with a general power of appointment exercisable by the appointee. The new power, being general, is valid without reference to the date of the creation of the first power in many jurisdictions because it may be exercised to vest the property in the power holder. As a result, there is the danger that § 2041 will cause gross estate inclusion on careless exercise of a special power. On the other hand, a planner may want to intentionally incur estate taxation by exercising a special power to cause estate tax inclusion. For example, estate taxation may be desirable to avoid imposition of the generation-skipping transfer tax. *See* Jonathan G.

Blattmachr & Jeffery N. Pennell, *Using "Delaware Tax Trap" To Avoid Generation-Skipping Taxes*, 68 J. TAX'N 242 (1988).

A second exception to the nontaxation of special powers under the estate tax occurs when the asset is insurance on the power holder's life. *See Estate of Lumpkin v. Commissioner*, 474 F.2d 1092 (5th Cir. 1973) (reproduced in § 10.01[B][1][c], *supra*). Section 2042 taxes insurance to the estate of the insured if at death the decedent possesses "incidents of ownership" over the policy. The section does not expressly require that the incidents of ownership be retained. The incidents may be obtained from someone else. *See* Chapter 10.

[3] Generation-Skipping Transfer Tax

Generation-skipping transfer taxation can also be triggered by the exercise of special powers of appointment. The exercise can operate to cause a taxable termination or distribution. For example, assume that *G* creates an irrevocable trust with the income payable to his son for the son's life, remainder as the son appoints by will to his spouse or issue. Assume further that the son appoints the remainder to his daughter (*G'* s granddaughter). On the son's death, a taxable termination occurs because after the son's death, only skip persons have interests in the trust. If, of course, the appointment was to the son's widow, a taxable termination would not occur, because the widow would not be a skip person. She is only a single generation below *G*'s generation.

[4] Income Tax

Code: §§ 674 and 677(b).

Regulations: None.

Although the creation of a special power, *i.e.*, a power not exercisable in favor of the power holder, generally does not require that the income from the property that is subject to the power be taxed to the power holder, the existence of the power can have significant income tax consequences. Under § 674(a), the grantor is treated as the owner of any part of a trust in which the beneficial enjoyment of income or corpus is subject to a power of disposition exercisable by a *nonadverse party*, even if not by the grantor. Thus, normal trustee-held dispositive powers may result in taxation of the trust income to the grantor as most trustees are not holders of beneficial interests adverse to the exercise of the power.[7] *See, e.g., Holt v. United States*, 669 F. Supp. 751 (W. D. Va. 1987), *aff'd*, 842 F.2d 1291 (4th Cir. 1988). The major limitation on the operation of this provision is § 674(c), which excepts powers from grantor taxation unless more than half of the trustees are subordinate or related to the grantor or the grantor's spouse. *See* David Westfall, *Trust Grantors and Section 674: Adventures In Income Tax Avoidance*, 60 COLUM. L. REV. 326 (1960).

Importantly, the existence of powers in third parties can limit application of exceptions to the operation of § 674(a). For example, if the trustee has the

---

[7] The same analysis applies to powers of revocation held by nonadverse parties. *See* § 676(a). It may also apply to powers held by nonadverse parties to determine whether income is distributed to or held for the benefit of the grantor or the grantor's spouse. *See* § 677(a).

power to add to a class of beneficiaries to whom corpus may be distributed, the exception in § 674(b)(5) does not apply. *See* § 674(b)(5) (last sentence). Similarly, a power to add to a class of beneficiaries for whom income may be accumulated prevents the operation of § 674(b)(6), which excepts accumulation powers from the operation of § 674(a). *See* § 674(b)(6) (last sentence). As to other exceptions limited by the existence of special powers, see § 674(c) and (d) (last sentence), excepting powers to add afterborn or adopted children to an existing class.

Nonetheless, the existence of some powers in the hands of third parties is acceptable from the income tax point of view, but the exercise of those powers can generate tax consequences. For example, the mere existence of a power to distribute income from a trust to a person (other than the grantor's spouse) whom the grantor is legally obligated to support does not constitute a power to distribute income to the grantor. Section 677(b) specifically excludes a dependent-benefit power from the operation of § 677(a), with the result that the grantor is not considered the owner for income tax purposes. If, however, the power is exercised to apply or distribute income in payment of that support obligation, the exception does not apply and the grantor is taxed. *See* § 677(b). Similarly, the exercise of a trustee-held power to distribute income for the support or maintenance of a person the trustee is obligated to support will result in the income distributed being taxed to the trustee under § 678(c), even though the mere existence of the power would not produce this result.

Stone v. Commissioner

T.C. Memo. 1987-454

MEMORANDUM OPINION

Raum, Judge:

[Husband and wife, petitioners, created trusts for minor children with their attorney as trustee. Income was to be used to pay for the private school and college education of petitioners' children. The primary issue was whether trust income paid to educational institutions was taxable to the petitioners under section 677(b). Although the trusts were not § 2503(c) trusts, the same issue can arise when trust income is used to pay for educational expenses. The tax years involved were 1980–1982.]

. . .

Section 677(b), IRC 1954, provides in relevant part that:

> *Income of a trust shall not be considered taxable to the grantor under subsection (a)* or any other provision of this chapter *merely because such income* in the discretion of another person, the trustee, or the grantor acting as trustee or co-trustee, *may be applied or distributed for the support or maintenance of a beneficiary (other than grantor's spouse) whom the grantor is legally obligated to support or maintain, except to the extent that such income is so applied or distributed.* [Emphasis Supplied]

. . .

The subsection was added to the Code in 1943 as an exception to the more general provisions of the predecessor to section 677(a).

Under section 677(a) the grantor of a trust is treated as "the owner of any portion of a trust . . . whose income without the approval or consent of any adverse party is, or, in the discretion of the grantor or a nonadverse party, or both, *may be* — (1) distributed to the grantor or the grantor's spouse; . . ." (Emphasis supplied.) It is clear under section 677(a) that the grantor may be treated as the owner of a portion of a trust if trust income merely *may be* distributed to him or for his benefit, even if it is not actually so distributed. Section 677(b) provides an exception to section 677(a) to the extent trust income may be, but is not, "applied or distributed for the support or maintenance of a beneficiary (other than grantor's spouse) whom the grantor is legally obligated to support or maintain." Only "to the extent that such income is so applied or distributed" is it taxable to the grantor "under subsection (a)."[8]

There is no question that the beneficiaries involved here, petitioners' minor children, are beneficiaries that petitioners are "legally obligated to support." The California Civil Code provides that "The father and mother of a child have an equal responsibility to support and educate their child in the manner suitable to the child's circumstances, taking into consideration the respective earnings or earning capacities of the parents." Cal. Civ. Code sec. 196 (West 1982). It is significant that both support and education are recognized in section 196 of the Civil Code as a part of the responsibility owed by parents to their minor children. Moreover, children in California are "subject to compulsory full-time education." Cal. Educ. Code sec. 48200 (West 1978). The required education can be attained through attendance at "public full-time day school." Attendance at public school is excused for those children "instructed in a private full-time day school" that complies with the state requirements. Cal. Educ. Code sec. 48222 (West 1978).

---

[8] . . .

Petitioners misconceive the manner in which they would be taxed under section 677(b) . . . . It is petitioners' understanding (and the basis of their argument) that if they are to be taxed on trust income under sec. 677(b), such income will "be taxed to them as if distributed to them as beneficiaries." They depend on sec. 1.662(a)–4, Income Tax Regs., for this proposition. However, sec. 1.662(a)–4, which petitioners read as requiring treatment as a beneficiary in the situation before us, in no way governs whether a *grantor* is to be treated as a beneficiary. Instead, it interprets sec. 662 so that when a trust makes a payment which discharges a *beneficiary's* (as opposed to a *grantor's*) legal obligation, that payment is treated "as though directly distributed to him as a beneficiary." Sec. 662 does not determine whether a taxpayer will be treated as a grantor or as a beneficiary, but merely sets forth the consequences of the treatment prescribed by other sections. It is sec. 667(b) that directs how the grantor will be treated if trust payments are used to discharge the grantor's support obligations. Under sec. 667(b) a grantor is taxed under sec. 662, as a beneficiary, only when the support obligation discharged by the trust is "paid out of corpus or out of other than income for the taxable year." Sec. 677(b), IRC 1954. *See* Scheft v. Commissioner, 59 T.C. 428, 434 (1972); sec. 1.677(b)–1(a) and (b), Income Tax Regs. Otherwise, the grantor is taxed under subsection (a), as the owner of a portion of a trust. To the extent the grantor is so treated as the owner of a portion of a trust, the income from it is taxed to him and the trust is disregarded. Scheft v. Commissioner, 59 T.C. at 432. There is no evidence that the payments made here for the educational expenses of petitioners' children were "paid out of corpus or out of other than income," and thus petitioners are not properly taxable as beneficiaries.

Petitioners do not challenge that they are legally obligated to support their minor children or that education is a basic part of their obligation. Instead, they contend only that "under California law . . . they do not have a legal obligation to send their children to private school." The Commissioner agrees that the issue before us is "whether under California law private schooling constitutes a support obligation," but maintains that under the circumstances presented private schooling does constitute a support obligation of petitioners.[9]

The issue must be decided with reference to California state law. Consequently, the holdings of other courts with respect to similar obligations under the laws of other states are of only limited aid here.[10] It is, instead, the conclusion drawn from a close examination of California law that will be determinative. It has long been stated by the state courts of California that "the minor is entitled to be maintained in a style and condition consonant with his parent's financial ability and position in society." The concept has been codified in section 196 of the Civil Code which in relevant part provides that parents have a "responsibility to support and educate their child in the manner suitable to the child's circumstances, taking into consideration the respective earnings or earning capacities of the parents."

While the issue of a parent's obligation to support his child generally occurs in the divorce context, the child's right to support is not limited to that context. The right under section 196 is the child's right and the child can maintain an action against his parent for support.

This Court has previously treated, in a case involving the same type of determination under section 677(b) as is required here, state court decisions relating to child support in the divorce context as having some import on the section 677(b) issue. *See Braun v. Commissioner*, T.C. Memo. 1984-285. In *Braun*, the Court considered New Jersey cases arising in the divorce context, but recognized that some of the factors relevant therein "would have no bearing except in a controversy between divorced parents or between a child and a noncustodial parent." We do the same here.

---

[9] The parties' framing of the issue to focus on whether private education is a legal obligation under California law appears to be at least to some extent inconsistent with the language of sec. 677(b). That section governs the treatment of amounts "applied or distributed for the support or maintenance of a beneficiary . . . whom the grantor is legally obligated to support." The legal obligation required by the language seems to be a general one towards the beneficiary, not a specific obligation to expend particular amounts on particular expenses connected with the person to whom the obligation is owed. However, to the extent an expenditure is found to be a legal obligation, it will surely also be an expenditure for the "support or maintenance of a beneficiary . . . whom the grantor is legally obligated to support." Consequently, we deal with the issue as narrowly formulated by the parties in their presentation of the case to us here.

[10] For instance, petitioners rely heavily on Brooke v. Commissioner, 468 F.2d 1155 (9th Cir. 1972). In that case, the 9th Circuit upheld the District Court of Montana's conclusion that "the expenditures made were not the legal obligations of the taxpayer under Montana law." Brooke v. Commissioner, 468 F.2d at 1158. While that case too involved expenditures made for private school tuition, few facts were reported therein and of those that were reported many appeared to be markedly different from those here. In addition, the determinative Montana statute, though similar, was not identical to the California statute before us. Moreover, the Government was evidently able to find only one Montana case interpreting the Montana support statute that awarded child support to cover a child's education, and that case was decided in 1936.

The California cases which deal with the issue of the proper level of educational support to be granted a child are few and far between. Even less available are cases dealing specifically with the obligation to provide a private high school education. As to the expenses of a college education, the California district courts of appeal have generally allowed stand the trial court decisions awarding support to a child that would finance that child's attendance at college, so long as "it is for the best interests of the child to be sent to college and the father is financially able to pay the expense."

The parents' legal obligation under section 196 of the California Civil Code to provide their child with support for education was in 1985 limited by statute to continue to apply only to "any unmarried child who has attained the age of 18, is a full-time high school student, and resides with a parent, until such time as he or she completes the 12th grade or attains the age of 19, whichever first occurs." Cal. Civ. Code sec. 196.5 (West 1987 Supp.). While this amendment substantially limits the obligation under California law of parents to send their children to college, it in no way reduces the obligation of support owed under section 196 for the high school education of a minor child.

The obligation to educate a minor child was dealt with in *In re Marriage of Aylesworth*, 106 Cal. App. 3d 869, 165 Cal. Rptr. 389 (Ct. App. 1980). In that case, private school tuition was requested for two children, but was awarded to only one of the two. The tuition was awarded to a child who had been enrolled in private school for at least 23 months and who had "educational difficulties" apparently connected with epileptic seizures. The private school education was found to be of "personal benefit to him in helping to alleviate his past anxieties related to school." *In re Marriage of Aylesworth*, 106 Cal. App. 3d at 879. The tuition was not awarded to a child who had never attended private school and who showed no evidence that she would derive any special benefit from private school.

Here, it is stipulated that Matthew attended Harvard School during the years 1978 through 1982 and that Samantha attended Marlborough School during the years 1979 through 1982. There is no evidence that the children did not attend private schools in the years before they entered Harvard and Marlborough Schools. Additionally, there is no evidence that would indicate whether either of the children had any special need for or derived any special benefit from their private school education. These lapses in the evidence with respect to the benefit to the children of private education weigh against petitioners' case. Moreover, the limited evidence of petitioners' financial ability to pay for the education involved here, which we have obtained from petitioners' returns, indicates that they could well afford to finance their children's private school education.

What is even more indicative of both the benefit to petitioners' children of private school education and petitioners' ability to pay for that education is the action of petitioners during the years involved here. Petitioners sent their children to private school for at least two or three years before the trust was created. They apparently believed that such an education was of benefit to their children. We can only assume that, as in *Braun v. Commissioner*, T.C. Memo. 1984-285, the education that petitioners chose for their children was "imminently reasonable in the light of the background, values and goals of the parents as well as the children." The benefits of the private education were apparently perceived as such that petitioners were willing to pay the costs of tuition in the years before the trust was created. They were clearly both willing and able to finance the private high school education of their children. Under these circumstances, we conclude that the expenses paid by the trust in 1981 and 1982 for the private high school education of petitioners' children are amounts "distributed for the support or maintenance of a beneficiary . . . whom the grantor is legally obligated to support or maintain" under section 677(b), IRC 1954. Consequently, under section 677(a), IRC 1954, petitioners are treated as "the owner of [the] portion of [the] trust whose income" has been so distributed.

Decision will be entered under Rule 155.

———

Finally, nearly all distributions from trusts have the potential to "carryout" income to the recipient to the extent the trust has income for the taxable year. This occurs under the normal DNI rules discussed briefly in Chapter 2 and discussed in detail in Chapter 14.

Problems

1. S transfers property to an irrevocable trust. The income is payable to A for life and remainder is payable to B. D has an inter vivos power to appoint the remainder (effective after his death) to someone other than A or B. D dies survived by A and B. What are the estate and gift tax consequences if:

a. D dies having failed to exercise the power? Consider Treasury Regulation § 20.2041–1(b)(3).

b. Four years before his death, D appoints irrevocably the remainder to C?

c. One year before his death, D releases the power? Consider § 2035(a)(2).

d. What is the estate tax consequence of D paying gift taxes on the exercise of the power in (b) and (c)?

2. X transfers property to an irrevocable trust. The income is payable to Y and the remainder is payable to Z. Y has the power to invade corpus for either of the trust beneficiaries. Y exercises the power to distribute $50,000 each to Y and Z.

a. How many gifts are subject to the tax?

b. What would be the estate tax consequences if Y dies without having exercised the power?

3. If a parent had contracted with a college to pay her child's tuition, would trust distributions to the college be taxable to the parent? *See Morrill v. United States*, 228 F. Supp. 734 (D. Me. 1964), applying § 677(a), but not § 677(b).

[C] Additional Tax Problems Raised by *Crummey* Trusts[11]

Crummey trusts were discussed earlier in the context of the annual exclusion. *See* § 4.01[B][1][b], *supra*. Besides the issues discussed there, the beneficiaries' right to withdraw the property added to the trust is a general power of appointment. Under the provisions of virtually all *Crummey* trusts, the right to demand a distribution of recent transfers to the trust will expire shortly after the gift is made. Thus, the lapse of the withdrawal right is a lapse of a general power of appointment. Moreover, if the beneficiary dies before the power lapses, the withdrawal right is a § 2041 general power of appointment. In addition, income and generation-skipping transfer tax consequences potentially exist.

[1] Gift Tax

Code: § 2514(b) and (e).

Regulations: None.

The donee of the *Crummey* power may have gift tax issues, depending on the amount the donor transfers to the trust for the beneficiary each year and the terms of the *Crummey* trust.

[a] Gifts of Less than $5,000 or 5% of the Trust

If the annual amount the donor transfers to a *Crummey* trust for the donee is less than $5,000, there are no gift tax implications for the donee on the lapse of the withdrawal power. *See* § 2514(e). Alternatively, if the total amount a donee may withdraw in a year exceeds $5,000, no gift tax consequences arise upon the lapse of the power unless the amount donated exceeds 5% of the value of the trust. *See* § 2514(e). Of course, if the donee exercises the withdrawal power in his own favor, no gift tax issues arise for the donee no matter the size of the donor's gift because no lapse occurs and no transfer to a third person has occurred.

When the donee is the beneficiary of several *Crummey* powers, Rev. Rul. 85–88, 1985–2 C.B. 201, aggregates all powers held by the beneficiary that annually lapse, under all instruments, for purposes of calculating the tax consequences of the lapsing of powers. This rule clearly is intended to prevent one donor from creating several *Crummey* trusts for the same beneficiary and qualifying each for the five or five exception of § 2514(e). If the Service's position were incorrect, a single donor could create two *Crummey* trusts for a single beneficiary, or a married donor whose spouse consented to a split gift under § 2513 could create four *Crummey* trusts, without exceeding the annual exclusion and at the same time avoid any gift tax consequences to the donee. Stacking of *Crummey* trusts in this manner would certainly be contrary to the congressional intent of § 2514(e). Whether the Service's position in Rev.

---

[11] The discussion below is adapted from F. Ladson Boyle, *Present Interest Gifts in Trust: Donor and Donee Problems*, 29 GONZ. L. REV. 453 (1994). *See also* John R. Price, Crummey v. Commissioner *Revisited: Opportunities and Pitfalls of Trust Withdrawal Powers*, 33 HECKERLING INSTITUTE ON ESTATE PLANNING, Ch. 8 (1999)

Rul. 85–88 applies to different trusts created by different donors, with different terms, all for the same beneficiary, is unknown. Neither the Service nor a court has addressed the issue since the Revenue Ruling was issued.

[b]   Gifts in Excess of $5,000 or 5% of the Trust

If the amount that may be withdrawn by a *Crummey* power holder in a year exceeds the greater of $5,000 or 5% of the value of the trust, the beneficiary may make a gift of a future interest to the trust beneficiaries upon the lapse of the *Crummey* power. The general rule of § 2514 provides that the exercise or release of a general power of appointment is considered a transfer of property by the power holder. Section 2514(e) provides that a lapse of a power of appointment is not considered a release of the power unless it exceeds the greater of $5,000 or 5% of the value of the property subject to the power. As a result of § 2514, when a lapsed *Crummey* power exceeds the five or five exception, the power holder is deemed to be making a transfer to the trust. This results in applying to the donee all of the rules applicable to donors of *Crummey* trusts, and unless the donee is the only beneficiary of the *Crummey* trust, a gift of a future interest occurs.[12]

The potential gift tax consequences for the power holder may be eliminated in one of several ways. First, if the donee is the sole beneficiary of the trust or of a separate share of the trust and upon the donee's death the trust or separate share of the trust is distributed to the power holder's estate, the lapsing power will not cause the power holder a gift tax problem. *See* Treas. Reg. § 25.2511–2(c). In the alternative, if the donee has a special or general testamentary power of appointment over the property that is subject to his withdrawal power, the power of appointment will prevent a gift tax problem for the donee because the gift resulting from the unprotected lapse would be incomplete for gift tax purposes. *See* Treas. Reg. § 25.2511–2(b); *see also Priv. Ltr. Ruls. 8229097, 8517052.*

Some commentators have suggested that the potential gift tax problem for the donee may be eliminated by a provision in the trust that provides that the amount that may be withdrawn will not lapse until and unless it will lapse within the five or five protection of § 2514(e). *See* Henry Gissel, Jr. and Robert J. Rosepink, *Irrevocable Trusts and Crummey Powers*, 15 PROB. NOTES 128 (Fall 1989); HOWARD M. ZARITSKY, TAX PLANNING FOR FAMILY WEALTH TRANSFERS: ANALYSIS WITH FORMS, 4–34 to 4–38 (2d ed. 1991); RICHARD B. COVEY, PRACTICAL DRAFTING, Jan. 1983 at 77. These specially drafted *Crummey* powers are sometimes called *hanging powers*. If any portion of the transfers has not lapsed at the time of the donor's death, the unlapsed portion will be included in the power holder's estate under § 2041.

Hanging powers are not the panacea to all problems that may arise when a *Crummey* power lapses. First, if the donor plans to continue making

---

[12] The valuation of this gift may be difficult. Under the principles of Robinette v. Helvering, 318 U.S. 184 (1943), discussed in Chapter 4, unless the taxpayer can prove the value of the retained interest in transferred property, the gift tax value of the transferred property may not be reduced by the value of the retained interest. Moreover, § 2702 may apply. Whether a taxpayer can actuarially determine the value of a retained interest will vary with the terms of each *Crummey* trust.

maximum gifts to the *Crummey* trust each year into the indefinite future, the unlapsed portions of early contributions will not have the opportunity to lapse. Second, and more importantly, donors who create *Crummey* trusts do so to give donees limited access to the transferred property. If a hanging power is used, the unlapsed portion of the transferred property is subject to the donee's demand at any time until the power lapses, and that is not what the donor wants.

Finally, whether hanging powers are effective as proposed is not settled. In Technical Advice Memorandum 8901004, the Service opined that a hanging power was not effective as proposed. It reasoned that the hanging power was a condition subsequent and thus ineffective under the rationale of *Commissioner v. Procter*, 142 F.2d 824 (4th Cir. 1944), *cert. denied*, 323 U.S. 756 (1944). *See also* Rev. Rul. 85–41, 1986–1 C.B. 300; Rev. Rul. 65–144, 1965–1 C.B. 442. The reasoning of this Technical Advice Memorandum has been criticized, however. *See* Richard B. Covey, *Recent Developments Concerning Estate, Gift and Income Taxation—1989*, 24 U. MIAMI INST. ON EST. PLAN. 1–87 (1990); Gissel and Rosepink, *Irrevocable Trusts and Crummey Powers*, *supra*.

[c] A Related Issue: Two Lapses per Year

When the gift to a *Crummey* trust is made late in a calendar year, the lapse of the power will not occur until the following year if a reasonable period for withdrawal is permitted. Rev. Rul. 83–108, 1983–2 C.B. 167, provides that the donor's gift for annual exclusion purposes occurs in the year of the transfer. For the donee, the lapse occurs in the second year. If the donor makes a new transfer to the trust in the second year and the right to withdraw that amount expires in the second year as well, the donee may have a gift tax problem if the value of the two lapsed amounts exceeds the limitations of § 2514(e). For example, this can happen if the donor makes a transfer on December 15 of the first year and a second transfer on March 15 of the second year. For the donor, the gifts have occurred in separate years and both qualify as annual exclusion gifts in the separate years. If the *Crummey* power expires thirty days after the transfer to the trust, the donee has two lapses in a single calendar year—year two—and if the total amount of both transfers exceeds the five or five limitation of § 2514(e), a taxable gift may occur for the donee upon the second lapse. Treasury Regulation § 25.2503–2(a) excludes the first gifts made to a donee in a calendar year from the definition of a taxable gift.

Some practitioners have suggested that donees of *Crummey* powers should notify the trustee that they do not wish to exercise the right to withdraw a specific gift to the trust, or in the alternative that they do not wish to receive future notices because they do not intend to exercise the power. The suggestion is made to accomplish two objectives. When a *Crummey* trust is created late in the calendar year, the objective is to make the lapse occur in the first year so that an additional gift can be made to the *Crummey* trust in the next year without exceeding the five or five limitation. The second objective is to relieve the trustee of the obligation to give actual notice each year.

The proposal raises unanswered questions. Whether such affirmative action by the donee is a release of the power or a lapse is not clear, but the classification makes a tax difference.[13] If the beneficiary's notice to the trustee not to exercise the right of withdrawal is a release and not a lapse, the five or five limitation is not applicable because § 2514(e) applies only to lapses. On the other hand, if the notice to the trustee is not a release, the two lapses in one year problem may not be resolved, because the first power will not lapse, under its own terms, in the first year.

In addition, relieving the trustee of the duty to give notice of future gifts may provide the Service with ammunition to attack future gifts as future interests and not present interests because the donee has given up the right to withdraw before the transfer is made. Alternatively, the beneficiary's action may be viewed as a disclaimer, in which event the Service might argue that no right to withdraw existed because the disclaimer is effective retroactive to the date of creation.[14]

[2] Estate Tax

Code: § 2041(a)(2).

Regulations: None.

The estate tax picture for donees of *Crummey* trusts is complex. The donee may have full inclusion, partial inclusion, or no inclusion. The terms of the trust, that is, how the donor chose to solve, or not solve, some of the gift tax issues when the trust was drafted, will determine the outcome.

A donee with a tax vested interest in the trust will have an estate tax inclusion. The estate tax inclusion will depend on whether the beneficiary has a general power of appointment that will cause an inclusion under § 2041 or whether the trust is payable to her estate with an inclusion under § 2033. For non-tax vested beneficiaries of *Crummey* trusts, the issue is more complex and depends on the size of the contributions to the trust for the beneficiary and how the donor chose to deal with the lapsing power problem under the terms of the trust. If the amount a beneficiary may withdraw in a year does not exceed $5,000 or 5% of the value of the trust and the document was drafted with that limitation in mind, the assets of the *Crummey* trust should not be included in the beneficiary's estate unless some provision of the trust, unrelated to the lapsing power issue, causes an inclusion or the beneficiary dies while the power is still exercisable.

When annual gifts to a *Crummey* trust for a beneficiary exceed the five or five limitation, the donee's estate tax situation will depend on how and whether the donor dealt with the lapsing power, gift tax issue. If the potential lapse problem was solved by tax vesting the beneficiary there is obviously an estate tax inclusion. If the problem was solved by giving the beneficiary a hanging power, § 2041 will cause an estate tax inclusion to the extent the

---

[13] Under § 2514(b) the release, as well as the exercise of a power of appointment is a taxable event. Subsection (e) provides the limited exception that a lapse is not the equivalent of a release up to $5,000 or 5% of the value of the trust.

[14] Such a disclaimer might not be effective under § 2518 because the donee has a continuing interest in the property after the disclaimer, and thus, § 2518(b)(4) is not satisfied. In addition, if the disclaimer is effective under state law, the adverse effect on the *Crummey* power still might occur because the right has effectively been released.

power has not lapsed. If the problem was solved by giving the donee a special power of appointment so that the potential gift to the donee on the lapse of the *Crummey* was an incomplete gift, an estate tax inclusion still occurs, even though it is not a tax vested interest in the usual meaning of the word. Under § 2041(a)(2) an estate tax inclusion occurs if a decedent holds a power of appointment that is exercised or released, and after the exercise or release there would be an estate inclusion under §§ 2035 through 2038 if the decedent had been the transferor. When the beneficiary is given a special power of appointment to avoid the gift tax issue, that power is an interest that would be included in the beneficiary's estate under § 2036(a)(2) if the beneficiary had been the donor of the transferred property.

Alternatively, if the donor did not deal with the lapsing power problem at all, such as in *Estate of Cristofani*, (reproduced in § 4.01[B][1][b], *supra*), the donee still will have at least a partial inclusion under § 2041(a)(2). In the typical *Crummey* trust, the beneficiary has an interest in the trust that would be included in the beneficiary's estate under § 2036(a)(1) if the beneficiary had been the donor of the transferred property. The amount that is included is limited, however, by § 2041(b)(2), which provides that a lapse of a power of appointment is not deemed a release except to the extent that it exceeds the greater of $5,000 or 5% of the value of the trust.

Finally, if a donee dies before any *Crummey* power expires, the amount of property subject to the power is included in the donee's estate under § 2041, because the power is a general power of appointment to the extent of the property subject to the power.

[3] Generation-Skipping Transfer Tax

Code: None.

Regulations: Treas. Reg. § 26.2652–1(a)(5), Example 5.

The GST implications for donees of *Crummey* powers are relatively straight forward. If the amount contributed to the trust did not exceed the five or five limitation of § 2514(e), the donee should not have any GST issues with which to contend. The GST regulations have adopted the five or five benchmark of § 2514(e) to exempt transfers that fit within the gift tax exclusion. *See* Treas. Reg. § 26.2652–1(a)(5), Example 5. However, if the donee of the power is making a gift for gift tax purposes because of the lapsing power, the donee becomes the transferor of the property for generation-skipping tax purposes as well. *See* Treas. Reg. § 26.2652–1(a)(5), Example 5. The net result of the regulation is to require the donee of a *Crummey* power to allocate exemption to a GST trust if the trust is to be exempted from the generation-skipping tax and the contribution exceeded $5,000 or 5%.[15] The GST exemption

---

[15] Whether it is really necessary for the donee of the power to allocate requires an examination of the terms of the trust to determine whether any trust assets may be distributed to skip persons when the donee is the new transferor. For example, if the donee is the donor's grandchild, then distributions to the donee, other grandchildren of the donor, or great-grandchildren of the donor would not be subject to the generation-skipping tax. Only distributions to the donor's great-great-grandchildren would involve a generation-skipping transfer for the portion of the trust where the donee is the transferor. When the donee is related to the donor within the meaning of § 2651(b), the generation assignment is based on the number of years the donee is younger than the donor. *See* § 5.02, *supra* (discussing § 2651).

assumes the original donor allocated exemption to the trust as well, to keep it fully exempt.

Problem

GP creates a trust and gives his child a *Crummey* demand power up to $5,000. Child is the principal beneficiary of the trust. Is *GP* the transferor for GST tax purposes although the transfer is not subject to gift taxes? *See* § 2652.

[4] Income Tax

Code: § 678.

Regulations: None.

The existence of a right to demand distribution of trust corpus, even for a limited period of time, will cause the holder of such power to be deemed the owner of a portion of the trust. *See* § 678(a)(1); Rev. Rul. 81–6, 1981–1 C.B. 385. In a *Crummey* trust, each item of income, credit, and deduction is attributed pro rata to the beneficiary according to the amount of his demand right and the period of time during which the power may be exercised. *See* Treas. Reg. § 1.671–3(a)(3).

Private Letter Ruling 8545076

You propose to create the Trust for the exclusive benefit of the Beneficiary. The Trust Agreement provides that the Trust will terminate when the Beneficiary reaches age 30 or upon the death of the Beneficiary, whichever occurs first. When the Trust terminates, the Trustee will distribute its assets to the Beneficiary or to such persons as the Beneficiary designates by will.

You propose to fund the Trust initially with up to $10,000 in cash. You anticipate making additional contributions in future years of cash or property of varying amounts or values, probably not in excess of $10,000 each year.

You have represented that the Trust corpus will not consist substantially of insurance policies. According to the Trust Agreement, the Trustee is prohibited from: satisfying your or her legal obligation to support the Beneficiary; paying the life insurance premium on your life or the life of your spouse; and exercising any power other than in a fiduciary capacity. You have released any right to be named a substitute or successor trustee.

The Trust Agreement gives the Beneficiary the right to withdraw from the Trust any property you add to the Trust in an amount equal to the total value of property contributed to the trust during the year. The maximum amount that may be withdrawn each year is $10,000. The Trust Agreement requires that the Trustee give the Beneficiary written notice of his right of withdrawal when property is received from you. As the Beneficiary's natural guardian, the Trustee will receive this notice of the right to withdraw. The power to withdraw may be exercised by the Beneficiary's guardian, except that you are expressly prohibited from exercising the power on the Beneficiary's behalf. If not exercised within 30 days of written notice, the right to withdraw expires.

You have asked, first, who will be taxed on the income of the proposed Trust.

Under section 671 of the Internal Revenue Code, if a grantor or another person is treated as the owner of any portion of a trust, then there shall be included in computing the taxable income and credits of the grantor or the other person those items of income, deductions and credits against the tax of the trust that are attributable to that portion of the trust to the extent that those items would be taken into account under subtitle A, chapter 1, in computing taxable income or credits against the tax of an individual.

The Agreement discloses no provision that would cause you, the grantor, to be considered the owner of any portion of the Trust under §§ 673, 674, or 676 of the Code.

None of the circumstances which cause administrative controls to be considered exercisable primarily for the benefit of the grantor under section 675 of the Code are authorized under the Agreement. Thus, whether you will be treated as the owner under section 675 will depend upon the circumstances attendant upon the operation of the Trust. This is a question of fact, the determination of which must be deferred until the federal income tax returns of the parties involved have been examined by the office of the District Director that has jurisdiction over the returns.

Section 677(b) of the Code provides that income of a trust shall not be taxable to the grantor under section 677(a) merely because such income may be applied or distributed for the support or maintenance of a beneficiary (other than the grantor's spouse) whom a grantor is legally obligated to support or maintain, except to the extent that such income is so applied or distributed.

Accordingly, the Grantor shall not be treated as the owner of a portion of the Trust under section 677 of the Code, except to the extent the current income of the Trust is applied or distributed in satisfaction of the Grantor's legal obligation to support or maintain the Beneficiary.

Section 678(a) of the Code provides, in relevant part, that a person other than the grantor shall be treated as the owner of any portion of a trust to which such person has the power exercisable solely by himself to vest the corpus or the income therefrom in himself.

Any new property transferred to the Trust by you will be an addition to the trust corpus. Since the Beneficiary has the power to vest in herself any new property, she has the power to vest in herself part of the trust corpus. Therefore, until her power is exercised, released or allowed to lapse, the Beneficiary will be treated as the owner of each item of income, deduction and credit that is attributable to any new property transferred by gift to the Trust (subject to the $10,000 per Grantor limitation contained in the Agreement). *See* section 1.678(a)–1 of the Income Tax Regulations. Accordingly, the Beneficiary will include in computing her taxable income a pro rata share of each item of income, deduction and credit of the entire Trust. *See* section 1.671–3 of the regulations for rules used in computing the pro rata share of those items.

If the Beneficiary fails to exercise the power to vest in herself any new property that is transferred by gift to the Trust, it will become a permanent part of the trust corpus. Because the income from that portion, in the discretion of a nonadverse party without the approval or consent of any adverse party, may be distributed to the Beneficiary or accumulated for future distribution to her, the Beneficiary will be treated as the owner of that portion of the Trust under sections 671 and 677(a) of the Code.

Section 678(b) of the Code provides that section 678(a) shall not apply if the grantor of the trust is otherwise treated as the owner under provisions of subpart E of subchapter J, other than section 678. Therefore, this ruling under section 678(a) of the Code is based on the condition that the Grantor is not treated as the owner of the Trust under section 677(b) or section 675 as a result of the manner in which the Trust is operated.

. . .

Trust ownership is also attributed to anyone who has "partially relesed or otherwise modified" a power of appointment over the trust property, and who, after such release or modification, retains control sufficient to treat the grantor of the trust as the owner. *See* § 678(a)(2). In Private Letter Ruling 8521060, the Service stated that a lapsed power "will be treated as if [the beneficiary] released the power to withdraw the amount under section 678 (a)(2)." *Compare* Charles E. Early, *Income Taxation of Lapsed Powers of Withdrawal: Analyzing Their Current Status,* 62 J. Tax'n 198 (1985) (disagreeing with this position), *with* David Westfall, *Lapsed Powers of Withdrawal and the Income Tax,* 39 Tax L. Rev. 63 (1983) (agreeing with Service's position).

The applicablility of this rule to beneficiaries of *Crummey* trusts may be questioned, as the provision contains no reference to the lapse of a power, only to a "release or other modification." In addition a five or five limitation is absent. Nevertheless, if the lapse of a *Crummey* demand power is treated as a release or other modification without the five or five safe harbor, as the Service ruled in *Private Letter Ruling* 9034003, the beneficiary could be deemed the owner of the portion of the trustover which he could demand distribution. This ownership could increase over time.

Consider a beneficiary who fails to exercise the *Crummey* demand power over trust contributions. When the power lapses, the contributions become part of the trust principal. If the income from that portion may be distributed to the beneficiary (or accumulated for future distribution to the beneficiary), the beneficiary becomes the owner of that portion of the trust if the grantor would be treated as the owner of the trust under §§ 671 through 677.

Problems

1. *S* wants to place property in an irrevocable trust for his 14-year-old granddaughter. The trust instrument provides for the accumulation of the trust income until the granddaughter reaches age 21, at which time the accumulated interest and principal will be paid to the granddaughter, if she is then living. The trust instrument will further provide that the granddaughter—in December of any year in which the settlor transfers property to the

trust—can demand the immediate distribution to her of a sum equal to the property put into the trust during that year, up to a maximum of $5,000 per year. *S* places $5,000 in trust.

    a. Is the annual exclusion available under § 2503(b)?

    b. Who is taxed on the income generated by the trust corpus?

    c. What would be the gift, estate and income tax consequences of the trust if *S* put $6,000 into the trust in one year?

    d. Do your answers change if *S* makes the transfer in June rather than December?

2. Why is the demand right in the above problem limited to $5,000 per year in light of the $10,000 annual exclusion (as adjusted for inflation)?

§ 12.02 Administrative Powers

By definition, a trust requires that a trustee have active duties. In turn, the trustee must have administrative powers to carry out those duties. The settlor of a trust may generally have administrative powers without significant adverse tax consequences. *See* Chapter 9. It follows that there are few adverse tax consequences when a third party serves as trustee. This section discusses those consequences.

The granting of administrative powers to a trustee invokes no special gift, estate, or generation-skipping transfer tax consequences. A transfer in trust that otherwise is complete is not made incomplete by granting administrative powers to the trustee. Quite simply, these powers do not give rise to any claim that the settlor has not relinquished dominion and control in either the gift, estate, or GST tax sense.

Granting a third party normal administrative powers may also be done without requiring trust income to be taxed to the grantor. As long as the power cannot be used to control the flow of income, there should not be income tax consequences. Even powers to allocate receipts between corpus and income are specifically excepted from the list of discretionary powers that require taxation of trust income to the grantor. *See* § 674(b)(8). On the other hand, certain administrative powers can result in the taxation of trust income to the grantor under § 675. If, for example, a nonadverse party has the power to allow the grantor to deal with the corpus or income of the trust for less than full and adequate consideration, or to allow him to borrow the trust corpus or income without adequate security, the grantor will be taxed on the income. *See* §§ 675(1) and 675(2). Similarly, a power to vote controlling stock and the power to control investments in a *Byrum*-type situation (*see* § 9.04[B], *supra*) will result in taxation of the income to the grantor if the powers are exercisable by anyone not in a fiduciary capacity. *See* § 675(4). Finally, the power to loan trust funds to the grantor or the grantor's spouse, even for an adequate interest rate and security, if held by someone subservient to the grantor or the grantor's spouse, will produce taxation of trust income to the grantor if the grantor (or spouse) in fact borrows trust funds. *See* § 675(3).

Chapter 13

CONCURRENT PROPERTY INTERESTS

The creation of concurrent interests (*e.g.,* tenancies in common, joint tenancies, and tenancies by the entireties) can have federal gift, estate, generation-skipping transfer, and income tax consequences. This Chapter discusses these tax effects. It begins with a discussion of concurrent interests between persons other than spouses, and then investigates spousal joint property, both in noncommunity property and in community property situations. The Chapter also considers severing joint tenancies and the effects of disclaiming joint interests.

§ 13.01 Non-Spousal Concurrent Property Interests

[A] Gift Tax

Code: § 2511.

Regulations: Treas. Reg. § 25.2511.

Because the creation of concurrent interests in property inherently requires a transfer of property from one person to another, it is not a surprise that such transfers can have federal gift tax ramifications. Such ramifications are, however, not simple to outline. First, the result depends upon whether the transfer is for adequate consideration. Second, if the donor is not one of the concurrent owners after the transfer, the transfer is a normal gift and is subject to the general gift tax rules discussed in Chapter 4. Third, if under the terms of the concurrent ownership, the donor cannot take the property back, the gift is complete for gift tax purposes. *See* Treas. Reg. § 25.2511–1(h)(5). On the other hand, a transfer creating a concurrent interest (such as a joint bank account) in which the donor-tenant can recover full ownership, is nontaxable. *See* Treas. Reg. §§ 25.2511–1(h)(4), –2.

The following is a brief outline of these basic distinctions in the various forms of nonspousal concurrent ownership: tenancies in common and joint tenants with right of survivorship.

[1] Tenancies in Common

The gratuitous creation of a tenancy in common interest is a taxable gift, whether or not the donor is a co-tenant after the interest is created. If *A* buys land for $100,000 with his own funds, and title is taken in the names of *A* and *B* as tenants in common, *A* has made a gift to *B* because *B* has received an interest in property without paying for it. A tenancy in common gives each owner the absolute right to an aliquot portion of the underlying assets, without obligation to the other tenant. The transfer is a complete gift. Because the donee-tenant can, in the normal course, dispose of his share at will, without the control or permission of the donor, the interest is *severable* as that term is used in the Regulations, and subject to tax. *See* Treas. Reg. § 25.2511–1(h)(5). Due to the restrictive nature of a tenant's interest, a discount should apply for valuation purposes. Further, the transfer should qualify for the gift tax annual exclusion.

Not all interests denominated as *tenancies in common* necessarily produce the normal gift tax results, however. In contractual tenancies, the terms of the contract define the property interests of the parties to the contract. Contractual *tenancies* may lack the irrevocability necessary for completed gift treatment. If, for example, the depositor may withdraw the account balance at will, classification of the interests of the signatories to the account as tenants in common will not cause taxation as the interest of the donee-tenant are not beyond the recall of the donor-tenant. *See* Treas. Reg. § 25.2511–1(h)(4), –2(c). Further, even if the interests created are *severable*, the special terms of the contract may affect the value of a particular interest relative to the interests of the co-tenants. If this is true, this value will be reflected in valuation of the gift for tax purposes under § 2512. Nevertheless, to the extent that particular terms of contractual tenancies prevent valuation of the donee-tenant's interests, they may also prevent qualification for the annual exclusion. *See* Treas. Reg. § 25.2503–4(c).

[2] Joint Tenancies

The creation of a joint tenancy in property owned by one of the joint tenants will normally result in a taxable gift being made from the donor-tenant to the donee-tenant. Similarly, a joint tenancy created by a donor who is not one of the joint tenants constitutes a taxable gift to the joint tenants. This is true for the creation of joint tenancies in real property and with severable tenancies in personalty. *See* Treas. Reg. § 25.2511–1(h)(5). Again, however, it is important to determine exactly the rights of the donee-tenant under local law. The donor's power to reverse or modify the rights of the donee will prevent taxation. Thus, creation of joint tenancy bank accounts is usually not a completed gift for tax purposes because the donor-tenant retains the right to withdraw the entire balance. *See* Uniform Probate Code § 6–103(a); Treas. Reg. § 25.2511–1(h)(4). For example, assume that *A* deposits funds into a joint and survivor bank account in the name of *A* and *B*, payable on death to the survivor. *A* may revoke the entire arrangement by withdrawing all the funds on deposit and, therefore, the transfer is incomplete for gift tax purposes. The gift is completed when *B*, the nondepositing joint tenant, withdraws any funds from the account without any obligation to account to *A* for the sums withdrawn. *See* Treas. Reg. § 25.2511–1(h)(4). This result is dependent upon state law. For example, New York banking law gives the joint tenant an interest protected from the donor-tenant. *See* N.Y. Banking Law § 675.

Valuation of joint tenancy gifts for tax purposes is normally not difficult, notwithstanding the survivorship nature of the interests involved. Even if the likelihood of the younger tenant taking through the survivorship provision is high, that does not determine the value of the interest for gift tax purposes. Because either tenant may destroy the tenancy by alienation, each has a present one-half interest in the property. The joint tenancy is worth what the tenant could convert it into—a tenancy in common interest. Thus, if *A* pays for 100 shares of common stock (or buys a parcel of land) and takes title in the name of *A* and *B* as joint tenants with right of survivorship, *A* makes a completed gift of one-half of the property to *B*, the noncontributing co-owner, at the time of the acquisition. *B* has the unilateral right, at any time, to partition or sever the joint tenancy and take one-half of the property. The Regulations take the position that the value of *B*'s interest in the joint tenancy arrangement equals one-half of the value of the property at the time of the transfer. *See* §§ 2501(a)(1), 2511(a); Treas. Reg. § 25.2511–1(h)(5). Both the annual per donee exclusion (§ 2503(b)) and the unified credit against the gift tax (§ 2505) may be used to eliminate or minimize the amount of the gift tax due. If both *A* and *B* make a contribution to the purchase of the shares, a taxable gift results if one of the joint tenants contributes more than her proportionate share of the purchase price. Thus, if *A* and *B* buy land for $100,000 and take title jointly, but respectively provide $70,000 and $30,000 of the purchase price, *A* has made a gift to *B* for the amount that the value of *B*'s half of the property exceeds *B*'s consideration paid.

Revenue Ruling 78–362

1978–2 C.B. 248

ISSUE:

Are a co-tenant's monthly payments of a mortgage debt on property held jointly regarded as gifts to the other joint tenants?

FACTS:

On January 15, 1974, *D*, the donor, paid 30x dollars as a down payment for the purchase of real property. *D* had title to the property conveyed to the joint ownership, with rights of survivorship, of *D*, *A*, and *B*. *A* and *B* were the children of *D*. The fair market value of the property was 150x dollars.

The property was subject to a mortgage of 120x dollars that was to be paid in monthly installments of 3x dollars. The payment included principal and interest on the mortgage plus escrow payments of local real property taxes and casualty insurance premiums. As each monthly payment to the mortgage became due, *A* and *B* lacked funds to contribute to the payment. Therefore, *D* made all of the monthly payments and at the time of each payment advised *A* and *B* that *D* did not expect any reimbursement from them.

Under local law, a joint tenant may unilaterally sever the joint tenant's interest in the jointly held property at any time. Interests of joint tenants are presumed to be owned in equal shares.

Local law provides that co-tenants are equally responsible for the payment of the expenses of jointly held property. A co-tenant who has paid all of the expenses of the property is entitled to reimbursement from the other joint tenants for their aliquot shares of the indebtedness.

LAW AND ANALYSIS

Section 2511(a) of the Internal Revenue Code . . . provides that the gift tax applies whether the transfer is in trust or otherwise, whether the gift is direct or indirect, and whether the property is real or personal, tangible or intangible.

A transfer is taxable as a gift to the extent that the value of the property transferred exceeds the consideration in money or money's worth received by the transferor. *See* section 25.2512–8 of the regulations. If an individual with the individual's own funds purchases property and has title conveyed to the individual and others as joint tenants with rights of survivorship, and any joint tenant acting alone may sever the joint tenant's interest, the individual is deemed to have made a gift to the other joint tenants of equal shares of the property. *See* section 25.2511–1(h)(5) of the regulations.

In addition, the payment of money or property on behalf of an individual can result in a taxable gift. For example, the gratuitous payment of the debt of another person is a transfer subject to the gift tax. *See Estate of Woody v. Commissioner*, 36 T.C. 900 (1961).

A mortgage debt on property that is subject to the mortgage is regarded as the obligation of the owner of the property in that the payment of the mortgage debt by someone else is equivalent to a cash payment directly to the owner of the property. Further, the value of the owner's interest in the property is increased as the mortgage debt on the property is reduced.

In the present situation, *D*, *A*, and *B* owned equal interests in the jointly owned property that could be unilaterally severed. Since *D* provided the funds for the down payment and received no consideration from *A* and *B*, *D* made taxable gifts of one-third interests to *A* and *B* when the property was purchased and placed in joint ownership. Inasmuch as the expenses of the property were the obligations of *D*, *A*, and *B* in equal shares, *D*'s monthly payments to the mortgage were gifts to *A* and *B* when *D* paid their respective one-third shares of the obligations without the expectation of reimbursement from *A* and *B*.

HOLDING:

On January 15, 1974, *D* made gifts to *A* and *B*, valued at 10x dollars for each gift, of one-third interests in the net value of the property placed in joint ownership. Thereafter, *D* made monthly gifts to *A* and *B* of 1x dollars each, which is one-third of the total monthly payment to the mortgage lender.

————

Note that if the contractual terms of the tenancy prevent alienation, the gift would still be complete, but valuation would depend on the relative likelihood of the various tenants surviving. This would in turn depend on their relative ages. With such a restriction, the value of the younger tenant's interest would inherently be greater, reflecting the increased likelihood of surviving the older tenant. This value is calculated under § 2512, using supplemental two-life tables provided by the Commissioner.

[B] Estate Tax

Code: § 2040(a).

Regulations: Treas. Reg. § 20.2040–1.

The estate tax consequences of nonspousal concurrent property interests turn on whether the concurrent property interests have survivorship rights. Tenancies in common are included in the gross estate as property owned at death under § 2033. Only the value of the decedent's aliquot portion of tenancy in common property is included: what he or she owned. If there are two co-tenants, the value on one-half of the property is included in the deceased co-tenant's gross estate. If there are three, the value of one-third of the property is included. *See Estate of Bonner v. United States* (reproduced at § 3.04[C][4][f], *supra*) for a discussion of the valuation of undivided interest in property.

Because the values of the interests of the other tenants do not depend on surviving the decedent, their interests are not taxed to the decedent. Rather, only the decedent's interest is taxed, whether the decedent or a third party created the interests.

Taxation of joint tenancy property is more complex. Unlike tenancies in common, joint tenancies cannot be taxed as property owned at death under § 2033, because the survivorship right of the tenancy terminates the decedent's interest. On the other hand, the decedent's power during life to convert the tenancy to a tenancy in common suggests that economic value passes at death. Further, joint tenancies are commonly used as will substitutes, suggesting that all interests in the property ought to be taxed to the decedent.

Section 2040 controls the taxation of joint interests. Taxation of nonspousal joint tenancies depends on who created the joint tenancy. The aliquot share of the joint tenancy gratuitously created by someone other than a co-tenant is included in the gross estate although death terminated the decedent's interest in the property. *See* § 2040(a). The fact that the decedent could have converted the joint interest into a tenancy in common is sufficient reason to include the terminated interest in the gross estate. The decedent is taxed as though the joint tenancy had been converted, or the decedent had a general power over a portion of the property.

Example: The decedent's father devised real property to the decedent and her two brothers as joint tenants with the right of survivorship. The value of the property was $30,000 on the date of the father's death. The decedent died survived by her two brothers and the realty is worth $60,000.

Under § 2040(a), the decedent's gross estate includes $20,000, determined by dividing the property's value ($60,000) by the number of joint tenants (three). This valuation is potentially different than the value of a one-third interest of tenants in common. The regulations for § 2040(a) specifically provide that the inclusion is based on the decedent's proportionate interest in the value of the entire property. *See* Treas. Reg. § 20.2040–1(b)(7).

In *Estate of Young v. Commissioner*, 110 T.C. 297 (1998), the decedent and his spouse owned real property as joint tenants. The decedent's estate return asserted a fractional interest discount for the decedent's one-half interest. The estate argued that § 2040 requires inclusion of the joint interest in the decedent's estate, but that valuation is similar to valuation under § 2033. The court was not persuaded, however. It concluded that (110 T.C. at 316):

> The fractional interest discount, as applied in section 2033, is based on the notion that the interest is worth less than its proportionate share, due in part to the problems of concurrent ownership. These problems are created by the unity of interest and unity of possession. However, at the moment of death, the co-ownership in joint tenancy is severed, thus alleviating the problems associated with co-ownership.

For valuation of undivided interests in property, see § 3.03[A][4], *supra*.

If, on the other hand, the joint tenancy was created by one of the joint tenants, the extent to which the entire property (not just the decedent's aliquot portion) is taxed is determined by how much of the consideration for the acquisition was supplied by the decedent. Section 2040(a) requires that the entire property is taxed to the estate of the first tenant to die, except to the extent that the survivor (or survivors) can show that he (or they) contributed to the acquisition. This treats the tenancy as a testamentary substitute, and rebuttably presumes that the decedent is using the tenancy to pass the entire property at death.

Taxing joint tenancies has existed in the Code since the beginnings of the federal estate tax in 1916. It was required to prevent massive avoidance of the estate tax by means of survivorship interests. Without the joint tenancy rule, the estate tax could easily be avoided by transferring property into joint tenancy at the time it is heavily mortgaged. The minimal value of the equity would have prevented gift taxation; later principal payments would also have been excludable under the annual exclusion; and the recipient would have received an item of significant value on the donor's death without significant transfer taxation. Section 2040(a) prevents this result.

[1] Interests to which Section 2040 Applies

Section 2040 applies both to traditional survivorship interests, as well as to contractual joint arrangements such as joint bank accounts and jointly-owned U.S. Savings Bonds, which are payable to either owner or the survivor. *See* Treas. Reg. § 20.2040–1(b). Applicable state or federal property rules determine the rights of both the survivor and the decedent in the property, and thus, whether the property is subject to § 2040. For example, although an account is in both names, as joint tenants, it may be shown under state law that it was merely an account for the convenience of the survivor. If it was, then the interest was not joint for estate tax purposes. Similarly, controlling substantive law may invalidate pre-death changes from joint ownership. For example, in *United States v. Chandler*, 410 U.S. 257 (1973), the Supreme Court held that ownership of U.S. Savings Bonds can be changed only by complying with federal regulations, that the decedent's manual delivery of bonds to the joint owner with the intent to divest the decedent of ownership was ineffective without re-registering the bonds, and that therefore, the bonds were taxable under § 2040.

[2] Consideration Furnished Test

Under § 2040(a), the survivorship property is included to the extent that it cannot be shown that the survivor contributed to its acquisition. This is the *consideration furnished* test.

Example 1: The decedent used $80,000 of his own funds to acquire stock and named himself and his daughter as joint tenants with right of survivorship. When the father died, the stock was worth $100,000 for estate tax purposes. He was survived by his daughter.

Because the daughter in Example 1 contributed nothing to the acquisition of the stock, § 2040(a) includes the entire value of the stock in the decedent's gross estate. Thus, the estate reports $100,000, the full value of the jointly-owned stock. On the other hand, if the daughter died first, none of the stock would be included in her gross estate, because the father provided all of the consideration for the acquisition.

If each of the joint tenants contributes separate funds to the creation of the tenancy, the first tenant to die includes only the proportionate share of the value of the property in the gross estate.

Example 2: Assume in Example 1 that the daughter furnished $20,000 of her own funds and the decedent furnished $60,000 to acquire the stock costing $80,000. Further assume the father predeceased the daughter and the stock had a date of death value of $100,000.

On these facts, § 2040(a) would require the father's gross estate to include $75,000 (three-fourths) of the value of the jointly owned stock, because the daughter provided one-fourth of the consideration for the acquisition. *See* Treas. Reg. § 20.2040–1(a)(1).

To determine what consideration was furnished by the survivor, the personal representative must submit "facts sufficient to show that the property was not acquired entirely with consideration furnished by the decedent, or was acquired by the decedent and the other joint owner or owners by gift, bequest, devise or inheritance." *See* Treas. Reg. § 20.2040–1(a).

Example 3: In Example 2, assume that the $20,000 provided by the daughter was from funds previously given to her by her father.

In Example 3, the daughter may not claim that she furnished any consideration because the original source of the daughter's contribution was funds provided by the decedent. Therefore, the entire value of the property will be taxed to the decedent's gross estate. Section 2040(a) disregards the daughter's contribution because it came from a prior gift from her father, the other joint tenant. Contrast this result with the result if the contribution was from funds provided by someone other than a co-tenant.

Example 4: In Example 2, assume that the $20,000 provided by the daughter was from funds previously given to her by her aunt.

In Example 4, the daughter is treated as supplying consideration for the purposes of § 2040(a). Income from gifts is also treated as consideration provided by the donee.

Example 5: In Example 2, assume that the $20,000 provided by the daughter was interest income earned from property she originally received as a gift from her father.

In Example 5, the daughter is treated as supplying consideration for the purposes of § 2040(a), notwithstanding the fact that the property generating the income was acquired by gift from the co-tenant. *See* Treas. Reg. § 20.2040–1(c)(5). The income, which the daughter had to report as interest income for income tax purposes, is also correctly treated as her property for § 2040 contribution purposes.

Estate of Goldsborough v. Commissioner

70 T.C. 1077 (1978), aff'd without opinion
673 F.2d 1310 (4th Cir. 1982)

Featherston, Judge:

. . .

Section 2040 provides in general that the decedent's gross estate includes the entire value of jointly held property but that section "except[s] such part thereof as may be shown to have originally belonged to . . . [the surviving joint tenant(s)] and never to have been received or acquired by the latter from the decedent for less than an adequate and full consideration in money or money's worth." Section 2040 further provides that if the decedent owned property jointly with another, the amount to be excluded from the decedent's gross estate is "only such part of the value of such property as is proportionate to the consideration furnished by . . . [the surviving joint tenant(s)]."[1] Mathematically this "consideration furnished" exclusion can be expressed as follows:

$$\text{Amount excluded} = \text{Entire value of property (on the date of death or alternate valuation date)} \times \frac{\text{Survivor's consideration}}{\text{Entire consideration paid}}$$

In the instant case, the decedent (Goldsborough) acquired on May 12, 1937, real property (St. Dunstans) in her individual name. On April 4, 1946, decedent transferred St. Dunstans, valued at $25,000 on that date, to her two daughters (Eppler and O'Donoghue) as a gift. On July 17, 1949, the daughters sold St. Dunstans to H. W. Ford and his wife for $32,500. Sometime in that same year, each daughter invested her share of the proceeds from the sale of St. Dunstans in various stocks and securities; each daughter took title to her respective stocks and securities in joint tenancy with decedent. These stocks and securities remained in joint tenancy until December 21, 1972, the date of decedent's death, and during the period of joint tenancy the stocks and securities appreciated in value to $160,383.19, the value on the alternate valuation date.

---

[1] Brackets in original. Eds.

Thus, the section 2040 exclusion depends on the amount, if any, of the consideration Eppler and O'Donoghue, the surviving joint tenants, furnished toward the $32,500 purchase price of the jointly held stocks and securities.

Respondent contends that all the funds used to purchase the stocks and securities in question were derived from decedent and thus the entire value of the jointly held property ($160,383.19) is includable in her gross estate.

Petitioners Buppert and Eppler argue that only the value of St. Dunstans at the time the gift was made to decedent's two daughters (*i.e.,* $25,000) is includable in decedent's gross estate. In the alternative, petitioner Eppler contends that the gain of $7,500, measured by the appreciation in value from the time St. Dunstans was given to the two daughters in 1946 until that property was sold by them in 1949, constitutes consideration furnished by the daughters toward the $32,500 purchase price of the jointly held stocks and securities. Thus Eppler argues that $37,011.50 ($7,500/$32,500 of $160,383.19), the value of the jointly held property on the alternate valuation date, should be excluded from decedent's gross estate. We agree with this alternative argument.

To be sure, section 2040 is not a paragon of clarity, and the courts and Internal Revenue Service have wrestled with the question of whether a contribution made out of gain representing appreciation in value of property received gratuitously from decedent is attributable to the decedent or, instead, is to be treated as income from the property and thus separate funds of the surviving tenant.[2] [T]he law, as we perceive it, recognizes two distinct situations and treats the two differently. In one situation, the surviving joint tenant receives property gratuitously from the decedent; the property thereafter appreciates, and the property itself is contributed in an exchange for jointly held property. In this circumstance section 20.2040–1(c)(4), Estate Tax Regs., treats all the property as having been paid for by the decedent, and the entire value of the property is included in the decedent's gross estate. *See Estate of Kelley v. Commissioner,* 22 B.T.A. 421, 425 (1931).

In the second situation, the surviving joint tenant receives property gratuitously from the decedent; the property thereafter appreciates or produces income and is sold, and the income or the sales proceeds are used as consideration for the acquisition of the jointly held property. In this situation, the income or the gain, measured by the appreciation from the time of receipt of the gift to the time of sale, has been held to be the surviving joint tenant's income and a part of that joint tenant's contribution to the purchase price. *Harvey v. United States,* 185 F.2d 463, 467 (7th Cir. 1950). Thus, in the words of the statute, "such part of the value of such property as is proportionate to the consideration furnished by [the surviving joint tenant]" is excluded.

The facts of the instant case fall precisely within this second situation. In *Harvey v. United States, supra* at 465, the court characterized the facts and framed the issue as follows:

> "The jointly held property is not the gift property itself, in either
> its original or transmuted form, but property traceable to (1) the

---

[2] It is clear that income from property acquired gratuitously from the decedent constitutes a contribution from a surviving joint tenant's separate funds. Sec. 20.2040–1(c)(5), Estate Tax Regs.

profits made through sales of the original gift property and successive reinvestments of the proceeds of such sales or (2) the rents, interest and dividends produced by such property in its original or converted form, while title thereto was in the wife. The question presented by this appeal, then, is whether such profits and income, realized from property originally received by the wife as a gift from her husband and traceable into property which was held by them as joint tenants at the time of the husband's death, came within the exception to the requirement of [§ 2040] that the entire value of property held in joint tenancy shall be included in the decedent's gross estate."

The Government in *Harvey* argued that the full value of the jointly held property should be included in the decedent's gross estate, and the court dealt with that argument in the following manner (185 F.2d at 467):

"It seems clear that none of the cases cited contains any support for the novel proposition that income produced by gift property, after the gift has been completed, belongs to the donor and is property received or acquired from him by the donee; nor is there, in these cases, anything to impeach the conclusion of the trial court, or that of the Tax Court in the *Howard* case,[3] that the income produced by property of any kind belongs to the person who owns the property at the time it produces such income and does not originate with a donor who has made a completed gift of that property prior to its production of the income . . . .

. . .

Moreover, no reason is suggested for holding that one form of income, *i.e.,* "profit gained through a sale or conversion of capital assets," . . . is outside the exception, whereas other forms of income, such as dividends, rentals and interest, fall within its terms. It follows that the government's contention that the full value of the property held in joint tenancy by decedent and his wife at the time of his death should have been included in decedent's gross estate must be rejected."

Thus we conclude that Eppler and O'Donoghue furnished $7,500 toward the $32,500 purchase price paid for the stocks and securities they held in joint tenancy with decedent until her death on December 21, 1972. Under the terms of the statute, such part of the value of the property, *i.e.,* $160,383.19 on the alternate valuation date, as is proportionate to the $7,500 of consideration Eppler and O'Donoghue furnished is excluded from decedent's gross estate. Under the mathematical formula, set out above, the amount of the exclusion is $37,011.50.

. . .

To reflect the foregoing,

---

[3] Estate of Howard v. Commissioner, 9 T.C. 1192, 1202–1203 (1947).

Decisions will be under Rule 155.

Problem

In *Estate of Goldsborough*, what would be included in the decedent's gross estate if the daughters had transferred the realty itself in exchange for the stocks?

The consideration-furnished test imposes a substantial burden on the estate. Besides the difficult questions raised in *Estate of Goldsborough*, practical problems of proving the source of contributed funds exist. It is usually very difficult to trace the contributions of the co-owners to establish that the surviving co-owner originally owned all or a portion of the property, or furnished all or a portion of the consideration used for the acquisition of the property. The consideration furnished test obviously places a premium on meticulous record keeping.

Contribution questions often arise in the context of mortgaged property:

Example 1: In 1995, the decedent and a sibling purchased a vacation home for $100,000. They made a $20,000 down payment, paid with funds provided by decedent, and borrowed $80,000, secured by a mortgage on the property. They were jointly and severally liable on the mortgage. Between 1995 and the decedent's death in 2002, the decedent paid $60,000 on the mortgage, of which $10,000 represented repayment of principal and $50,000 represented payment of interest. The decedent dies when the property is worth $200,000.

Rev. Rul. 79–302, 1979–2 C.B. 328, deems the survivor to have contributed one-half of the remaining mortgage liability, or $35,000, because the survivor was personally liable on the mortgage and that liability constituted a separate contribution. On the other hand, the decedent's earlier payments were traceable to him, and thus, cannot be deemed a contribution by the survivor, even if they reduced the survivor's liability on the mortgage. Because $100,000 was originally paid for the property (in the form of a down payment plus the mortgage), 35/100ths of $200,000 would be excludable. *See* Rev. Rul. 81–183, 1981–2 C.B. 180; Rev. Rul. 81–184, 1981–2 C.B. 181 (second mortgages and refinancing).

Two situations illustrate the difficulties that the contribution requirement can present:

Example 2: Father and Daughter each contribute $10,000 to jointly purchase realty for $20,000. When the property is worth $100,000, Father makes a capital improvement costing $10,000. Father dies when the property is worth $200,000.

Example 2 raises the question whether appreciation should be taken into account when contributions are made subsequent to the original purchase.

If only actual dollar outlays are considered, the father's estate would report two-thirds ($20,000/$30,000) of the $200,000. The daughter would be deemed to have furnished only one-third ($10,000/$30,000) of the consideration. This approach, however, fails to take into account the value of her interest when the father made his second contribution. A more realistic approach would account for the appreciation, so that each would be considered as having contributed one-half of the value of the property at the time of the improvement ($100,000/2 equals $50,000). Father would then add the new contribution of $10,000. On this analysis, Father would report 6/11ths ($60,000/$110,000) of the $200,000. The only case on this issue, *Peters v. Commissioner*, 46 T.C. 407 (1966), *aff'd*, 386 F.2d 404 (4th Cir. 1967), did not clearly resolve the problem.

> **Example 3:** Two unmarried individuals agreed to live together. In the early years they rented an apartment. One worked outside the home, and provided the money for rent, food, etc.; the other maintained the home and did the shopping, etc. They opened and maintained joint savings and checking accounts. Later they bought a condominium, using funds from joint savings, put the title in their joint names, and paid the mortgage from the joint checking account, replenished by the outside worker. The outside worker dies.

Example 3 raises the issue whether homemaking and other services may constitute consideration for the purposes of § 2040. Litigation involving married couples suggests that services may not. *See Estate of Otte v. Commissioner*, T.C. Memo 1972–76. On the other hand, a different result is possible if the unmarried persons acquired property through business arrangements, such as partnership agreements. *See Estate of Neel v. United States*, 235 F.2d 395 (10th Cir. 1956). In *Estate of Anderson v. Commissioner*, T.C. Memo 1989–643, the decedent and her son were joint tenants of property acquired solely with her funds. The Tax Court held that only one-half of the joint property is includable in the decedent's gross estate because the son's management services constituted adequate consideration for his half interest.

[3] Simultaneous Death Situations

Finally, what is the result if joint tenants die simultaneously and one tenant has furnished all the consideration for the jointly owned property? The following ruling involves simultaneous death of tenants by the entirety, which now falls under the rules of § 2040(b). However, its reasoning is applicable to nonspousal joint tenancies.

Revenue Ruling 76–303

1976–2 C.B. 266

The Internal Revenue Service has reconsidered the holdings of Rev. Rul. 66–60, 1966–1 C.B. 221, with regard to the includability of the value of the property held in tenancy by the entirety in the gross estate of the husband and wife.

In Rev. Rul. 66–60, a husband and wife were killed in an automobile accident under circumstances wherein there was not sufficient evidence as to which spouse may have died first. The husband furnished the entire consideration for the purchase of certain realty which was held by them as tenants by the entirety. The husband's will contained no statement as to which should be considered to have survived the other in case they died in a common disaster. The decedents resided and perished in a state which has adopted the Uniform Simultaneous Death Act, and the property in question was located in that state. Section 3 of the Act provides that "[w]here there is no sufficient evidence that two joint tenants or tenants by the entirety have died otherwise than simultaneously the property so held shall be distributed one-half as if one had survived and one-half as if the other had survived."

Under section 2040 of the Internal Revenue Code . . . and section 20.2040–1(a)(2) of the Estate Tax Regulations, the decedent's gross estate includes the entire value of all jointly owned property including property held as tenants by the entirety (not acquired by the decedent and the other joint owner(s) by gift, devise, bequest, or inheritance), except the part, if any, attributable to the consideration in money or money's worth furnished by the other joint owner(s).

Section 2033 of the Code provides that the value of the gross estate shall include the value of all property to the extent of the interest therein of the decedent at the time of death.

Rev. Rul. 66–60 holds that inasmuch as the estate of the wife is entitled to a half interest in the property, one-half of the value of the property is includable in the wife's gross estate under section 2033 of the Code.

Rev. Rul. 66–60 also holds that inasmuch as the property in question was held in tenancy by the entirety at the time of the husband's death and since there is no evidence to indicate that the wife furnished any consideration for the property, the full value of the property is includable in the husband's gross estate under section 2040 of the Code.

However, in order for any of the value of jointly held property or property held in tenancy by the entirety to be includable in a decedent's gross estate under section 2040 of the Code, the decedent must be survived by a joint tenant or a tenant by the entirety. Under the Uniform Simultaneous Death Act, the husband and wife are each considered to have survived with respect to one-half of the property. Thus, section 2040 will be applicable for determining the includability of the value of one-half of the property in each of their gross estates. Since there is no evidence to indicate the wife furnished any consideration for the property, the value of one-half of the property with respect to which the wife is considered to have survived is includable in the husband's gross estate under section 2040. Since the husband furnished all the consideration for the property, none of the value of the one-half of the property with respect to which the husband is considered to have survived is includable in the wife's gross estate under section 2040.

In addition, since each is considered to have survived as to one-half of the property, each is considered to have acquired an absolute, sole ownership interest in one-half of the property before death. Thus, the value of one-half of the property is includable in each of their gross estates under section 2033 of the Code.

Rev. Rul. 66–60 stated that the value of one-half of the property was includable in the wife's gross estate under section 2033 of the Code because her estate was entitled to a half interest in the property. However, the mere fact that property becomes part of a decedent's estate does not make the property includable in a decedent's gross estate under section 2033. *See* Rev. Rul. 75–126, 1975–1 C.B. 296; Rev. Rul. 75–127, 1975–1 C.B. 297; and Rev. Rul. 75–145, 1975–1 C.B. 298, where the decedent had no interest in the property at death. In the instant case, the requirement of section 2033 is satisfied with respect to the one-half of the property as to which the wife is deemed to have survived and which she therefore is considered to have owned at death.

Thus, the result here is the same as in Rev. Rul. 66–60, that is, inclusion of the full value of the property in the husband's gross estate and inclusion of the value of one-half of the property in the wife's gross estate. However, the basis for inclusion in each of the gross estates is different.

Rev. Rul. 66–60 is hereby modified.

———

If joint tenants do not die simultaneously, Revenue Ruling 76–303 obviously does not apply. *See Vaughan v. United States,* 536 F. Supp. 498 (W.D. Va. 1982), requiring full inclusion in daughter's gross estate because the death certificate showed that the father predeceased the daughter. In *Estate of Racca v. Commissioner,* 76 T.C. 416 (1981), *acq.* 1982–1 C.B. 1, the court held that the decedent could not unilaterally dispose of or make survivorship presumptions with respect to jointly owned property. It also declared inapplicable to jointly owned property a provision in his will to the effect that if he and his wife died simultaneously, his wife would be presumed to predecease him.[4] Thus, where the husband and wife died simultaneously in an auto accident, one-half of the joint property was distributed as if the wife survived.

[C] Generation-Skipping Transfer Tax

Generation-skipping transfer tax consequences depend on the interest created. Thus, if the donor-tenant furnishes some or all of the consideration, then § 2642(f) bars the establishment of an inclusion ratio greater than zero if the other tenant(s) are skip persons. On the other hand, if the donor was not a co-tenant, an immediate direct skip may occur with a mandatory allocation of the GST exemption, unless the donor elects otherwise. *See* § 2632(b). Of course, if the joint interest was created at the donor's death, an allocation of the GST exemption may then be made.

---

[4] *Estate of Racca v. Commissioner* involves spousal joint tenants, but for a tax year when the inclusion rules for spouses was the same as for nonspouses.

[D] Income Tax

The federal income tax effects of irrevocable transfers into concurrent ownership depend upon state law. The state law determination as to who is entitled to the income produced from the property largely determines who must report the income for income tax purposes. Thus, when a tenant in common is entitled to an aliquot portion of the income from the property, that portion of the income will be included in the transferor's gross income. The same will normally be true for joint tenants. Thus, if under local law each joint tenant is entitled to one-half of the income, each should report one-half for income tax purposes. If, on the other hand, each tenant is entitled only to a proportion of income reflecting contribution to the purchase of the property, that proportion is taxable as income to the tenant. For example, a special rule exists for U.S. Savings Bonds. Interest is reportable based upon contribution. *See* Rev. Rul. 54–143, 1954–1 C.B. 12.

The major income tax effect of concurrent interests is the basis of the property. If the tenancy is created by gift, the donee's basis is a portion of the donor's basis, with a possible adjustment for gift taxes. *See* § 1015(a). Later, if the donee succeeds to the remainder of the property, basis is determined by the portion that is included in the gross estate at its estate tax value, *i.e.,* the fair market value at the date of death for the portion included in the estate (or the alternate valuation date). *See* § 1014(a), (b)(9). If the tenancy is created by will or intestacy, the estate tax value will also control.

Problems

1. *A* transferred to *B* a one-half tenancy in common interest in Blackacre. Thereafter, *B* died still owning that interest. Would any part of the interest be included in *B*'s gross estate? If *A* predeceased *B*, what would be included in *A*'s gross estate?

2. Decedent was a joint tenant with right of survivorship with his sister. The property was purchased with funds supplied by the sister. Assuming that decedent could have severed the tenancy during his life, is any portion of the property included in his estate under § 2040(a)? *See* Treas. Reg. § 20.2040–1(c)(3). Would the result be different under § 2041?

3. *A* and *B* are unmarried individuals who live together. They are considering the purchase of a house for $60,000. *B* would provide the down payment of $10,000. The balance will be financed by a note and mortgage payable monthly over thirty years for which both *A* and *B* are liable. *B* will make all subsequent monthly payments for mortgage principal and interest, real estate taxes, and insurance on the property.

   a. Consider the gift tax consequences of the joint tenancy arrangement. Specifically:

      (i) What are the gift tax consequences on a creation of the joint tenancy? Assume *B* has made no previous taxable gifts.

      (ii) What are the gift tax consequences when *B* makes the monthly payments, which include the mortgage principal and interest, insurance, and real estate taxes?

b. Consider the estate tax consequences of the joint tenancy arrangement. Specifically:

(i) What are the estate tax consequences on *B*'s death and on *A*'s subsequent death?

(ii) Assume that *A* and *B* died simultaneously. What would be included in the estate of each?

(iii) Assume *A* and *B*, both of whom are employed, made the monthly payments, which include the mortgage principal and interest, insurance, and real estate taxes, from their joint checking account. What are the estate tax consequences on *B*'s death. What if *A* dies first?

c. Assume *A* predeceases *B* and the fair market value of the house on *A*'s death equals $120,000 and the balance due on the mortgage is $40,000. For income tax purposes, what is *B*'s basis in the house? Consider § 1014(a) and (b)(9).

4. *R* gives her sister, *S*, stock with a fair market value of $38,000 at the time of the gift. *R*'s basis in the stock equals $30,000. *S* sells the stock for $40,000, reporting a gain of $10,000 for income tax purposes. *S* uses the $40,000 proceeds as her contribution towards the acquisition of $100,000 in stock, which was acquired in joint ownership by *R* and *S*. What portion of the jointly owned stock is included in *R*'s gross estate, assuming that *R* predeceases *S* and the stock is still valued at $100,000?

5. *A* and *B*, unmarried cohabitants, pool their cash and other property, contribute labor and services to a variety of joint and several undertakings, and exercise authority, control, and management over the business endeavors which they operate jointly. What part of their property—the title of which was held at *A*'s death in joint tenancy—or of their joint bank accounts, must be included in *A*'s gross estate? Would the result differ if all outside income was earned by *A*, but *B* provided efforts in running the farm owned in joint tenancy? In running the home similarly owned?

§ 13.02   Spousal Concurrent Property Interests: Noncommunity Property

When the concurrent interest is between spouses, sometimes the tax consequences are the same as between nonspousal tenants. In particular, tenancies in common are taxed the same way whether between spouses or between nonspouses, except that interests passing to the spouse qualify for the marital deduction. When the concurrent interest is of a survivorship nature, whether joint tenancy or tenancy by the entireties, however, there are significant differences in how spousal interests are taxed. In either type of tenancy, there will be no generation-skipping transfer tax consequences if one spouse creates the joint tenancy because a spouse is assigned to the same generation level as the grantor. *See* § 2651(c) (assigning spouses to the same GST generation).

[A]   Gift Tax

Code: § 2523(d).

Regulations: Treas. Reg. § 25.2523(d)–1.

The gift tax ramifications on creating spousal joint tenancies are virtually identical to those flowing from creation of nonspousal joint tenancies. Although special provisions existed before 1982 governing the taxation of spousal joint tenancy interests, the adoption of the unlimited marital deduction made those provisions unnecessary, and as a result were repealed.

Concurrent interests created in the donor's spouse generally qualify for the gift tax marital deduction. Even if, as a result of the tenancy, the donor spouse retains a survivorship interest in the property, the donee spouse's interest is not deemed to be a terminable interest. *See* § 2523(d). It is, after all, convertible into a tenancy in common interest. The same analysis explains why the interest qualifies for the gift tax annual exclusion. Thus, even if one spouse furnishes all of the consideration for the purchase of the property, no gift tax will result on completed gifts of joint interests in personalty or realty. Indeed, because § 6019(a) exempts most interspousal transfers from the gift tax filing requirement, no return would be required in the typical case.

Problems

1. In 2002, *H* created a spousal joint tenancy in a noncommunity property state with property valued at $50,000. What are the gift tax consequences? *See* §§ 2503(b), 2523, 2524.

[B]   Estate Tax

Code: § 2040(b).

Regulations: None.

[1]   In General

Unlike the gift tax, major differences exist between the estate taxation of spousal joint tenancies and tenancies by the entireties, and similar survivorship interests between nonspouses. For estate tax purposes, property held as spousal joint tenancies and tenancies by the entireties are deemed to be owned one-half by each spouse, irrespective of contributions. Section 2040(b) recognizes the partnership nature of the marital enterprise, and in effect treats both spouses as having contributed equally to the property's acquisition.

Section 2040(b) was added to the Code in 1981. It was the final step in a transition which began with treating spousal joint tenancies on a monetary contribution basis. Before 1977, spousal joint interests were taxed using the contribution-furnished rules of § 2040(a). The Tax Reform Act of 1976 changed this result to allow spouses to treat the property as contributed one-half by each, if the creation of the tenancy was taxable for gift tax purposes. The condition was necessary because § 2515, as then in effect, did not tax the creation of spousal joint tenancies in realty unless an election was made to make them taxable. The 1981 amendments completed the transition.

Section 2040(b) is not applicable, however, when the decedent's surviving spouse is not a U.S. citizen. Section 2056(d)(1)(B) overrides § 2040(b). In *Estate of Young v. Commissioner*, 110 T.C. 297 (1994), the court acknowledged this exception, but did not apply it because the Commissioner did not raise the issue until its final post-trial reply brief and conceded inclusion of only half to avoid prejudicing the Estate.

Section 2040(b) avoids the tracing problems and ends the confusion and litigation over the extent to which a nonworking spouse was deemed to have furnished consideration for the acquisition and improvement of jointly held property. As the legislative history indicates, "[t]he effect of including only one-half the value of the property in the gross estate in these situations is to implicitly recognize the services furnished by a spouse toward the accumulation of the jointly owned property even though a monetary value of the services can not be accurately determined." Estate and Gift Tax Reform Act of 1976, Report of the Committee on Ways and Means, United States House of Representatives, H.R. Rep. No. 94–1380, 94th Cong., 2d Sess. 20 (1976).

Section 2040(b) applies to *qualified joint interest* property. See § 2040(b)(1). The latter term is defined to include tenancies by the entirety and joint interests with a right of survivorship if the decedent and her spouse are the only joint tenants. See § 2040(b)(2).

> **Example:** Husband purchases stock for $80,000 with his own funds. Title is taken in the name of Husband and Wife as joint tenants. Local law recognizes a right of survivorship in joint tenancies. Assume Husband dies survived by his spouse when the stock is worth $100,000. Alternatively, assume that Wife dies first.

Pursuant to § 2040(b), when Husband dies first, his gross estate will include $50,000, which equals one-half of the value of the qualified joint interest. When Wife later dies, the entire then value of the stock would be includable in her gross estate as property owned at death under § 2033. If Wife dies first, one-half would be included in the Wife's estate under § 2040(b), and then the entire value would be included in the estate of Husband under § 2033.

Any interest that passes to the surviving spouse as a result of the death of the co-tenant qualifies for the estate tax marital deduction. Joint and entireties interests are specifically deemed to have passed from the decedent spouse. See § 2056(c)(5). The marital deduction is limited to the half included as a part of the decedent's gross estate. The other half is deemed already to have been owned by the surviving spouse. In *Estate of Reno v. Commissioner*, 945 F.2d 733 (4th Cir. 1991) (en banc), a will provision directing the payment of taxes from tenancy by the entirety property was ineffective under applicable state law. As a result, the marital deduction was not reduced by the taxes which were charged ineffectively to the tenancy by the entirety property.

In the case of other spousal survivorship interests (such as a joint tenancy in which at least one tenant is a nonspouse), any interest deemed contributed by the decedent and passing to the spouse would qualify, even though § 2040(a) continues to apply, because there also is a nonspouse tenant. *See* § 2040(b)(2)(B). Thus, for example, if the decedent, his spouse and one other person were joint tenants with respect to property contributed 80% by the decedent and 20% by the other person, 80% would be included in the decedent's gross estate under § 2040(a). For purposes of the decedent's estate, his interest would be deemed to pass 50% to the surviving spouse, and 30% to the other person. It is unclear whether the amount passing to the spouse would qualify for the estate tax marital deduction, even if the spouse had the usual right to sever the interest. *Cf. Jeschke v. United States*, 814 F.2d 568 (10th Cir. 1987) (joint bank account).

[2] Pre-1977 Joint Tenancies

Before 1977, a decedent's interest in joint property with a spouse was determined under the contribution rule of § 2040(a). This rule was changed in 1976, and again in 1981. Since 1982, a disagreement has developed between taxpayers and the government over the inclusion rule for pre-1977 spousal joint tenancies.

In *Gallenstein v. United States*, 975 F.2d 286 (6th Cir. 1992), the Circuit Court held that § 2040(b) did not apply to real property acquired in joint tenancy by a husband and wife before January 1, 1977. The portion each spouse contributed to the purchase of such property determined the amount includable in the gross estate of the first joint tenant. The Fourth Circuit in *Patten v. United States*, 116 F.3d 1029 (4th Cir. 1997), agreed with the Sixth Circuit. In *Patten*, property was inherited by the husband in 1952, and conveyed to the couple as tenants by the entirety in 1955. When the husband died first, the property was worth $500,000; a year later, the surviving spouse sold the property for $625,000. The surviving spouse reported her gain using an adjusted basis in the property that assumed that half of the property was inherited from her spouse, *i.e.,* $250,000, and the remainder of her basis came from original basis that was established when her husband inherited the property in 1952. After the surviving spouse died, the personal representative of her estate asserted that all of the property should have been included in the first decedent's estate. Thus, the basis should have been $500,000: the value when the first decedent died. The Service rejected a claim for refund of income taxes, and the personal representative sued. The District Court agreed with the taxpayer and the Fourth Circuit affirmed.

Both Circuit courts considered the effective date rule of the Economic Recovery Tax Act of 1981 (ERTA) and the effective date rule of the Tax Reform Act of 1976 (TRA 1976). TRA 1976, which added § 2040(b), applies to "all joint interests created after December 31, 1976." ERTA, which amended § 2040(b) to add the 50% inclusion rule for qualified joint interests, applies to "estates of decedents dying after December 31, 1981." The issue was whether the 1976 date was superseded by the 1981 Act or created a new rule for post-1981 estates. Both Circuit Courts held that the 1981 Act amended, rather than superseded, the 1976 Act. *Accord Anderson v. United States*, 96–2 U.S.T.C. ¶ 60,235 (D. Md. 1996). In 2001, the Service acquiesced in *Hahn v. Commissioner*, 110 T.C. 140 (1998), a decision that followed *Gallenstein*. *See* I.R.B. 2001–42 (Oct. 15, 2001).

The *Gallenstein* rule may result in a greater portion of a property's value being included in the estate of the first spouse to die, but no estate tax cost results because the increased inclusion qualifies for the unlimited estate tax marital deduction. A larger inclusion provided the surviving spouse a new adjusted basis in a larger portion of the property for income tax purposes, if the first spouse to die contributed more than one-half the consideration for jointly owned property. This rule can work against that taxpayer when the first spouse to die contributes less than one-half the consideration or the property has declined in value and the first spouse to die has contributed more than one-half the consideration.

Problem

In 1952, H purchased real property for $300,000. In 1975, when the property was valued at $400,000 in 1955, H transferred the property to H and W as joint tenants. H died in 2001, when the value of the property was $500,000. In 2002, W sold the property for $650,000. How much gain does W realize?

[C] Income Tax

Because most married couples file jointly, no significant income tax advantages to concurrent ownership of property by spouses exist. Whatever may be the proportion of income taxed to each, the total of their incomes will be the same. This lack of income tax advantage to marital joint ownership is not, however, mirrored by the absence of tax disadvantages. For example, because only one-half of spousal joint property is in the decedent's gross estate, only the one-half is entitled to a stepped-up basis at death. *See* § 1014(a). Second, because survivorship property passes directly to the surviving tenant, income from it cannot be deflected to the estate during the period of estate administration. Thus, that income will be taxed at the surviving spouse's marginal income tax rate during administration, rather than at the estate's rate (which might be lower).

Problems

1. Assume that H and W are considering the purchase of a vacation home for $200,000. H will provide the down payment of $40,000 by selling securities he owns in his own name. The balance will be financed by a mortgage payable monthly over a period of thirty years. H will make all subsequent monthly payments for the mortgage principal and interest, real estate taxes, and insurance on the property from his salary.

   a. From a nontax standpoint, should title be taken in the name of H and W as joint tenants with right of survivorship?

   b. What would be the gift consequences of the joint tenancy arrangement:

      (i) On the creation of the joint tenancy?

      (ii) When H makes the monthly payments, which include payment of the mortgage principal and interest, insurance on the property, and real estate taxes?

      (iii) If W pays for these items?

   c. What would be the estate tax consequences of the joint tenancy on the deaths of H and W:

(i) Assuming *H* predeceases *W*? Is the marital deduction available? *See* Tech. Adv. Memo. 200104008.

(ii) Assuming *W* predeceases *H*? Is the marital deduction available? *See* Tech. Adv. Memo. 200104008.

(iii) Assuming *H* and *W* die together, for example, in an automobile accident, and it is impossible to establish the order of their deaths? Under §§ 3 and 6 of the Uniform Simultaneous Death Act, each is deemed to die last with respect to joint tenancy property. *See* Rev. Rul. 76–303. Does § 2040(b) change the result?

d. What would be the income tax consequences of the joint tenancy if on *H*'s death the value of the home equals $300,000? Consider § 1014(a), (b)(9).

§ 13.03   Spousal Concurrent Property Interests: Community Property

This text has considered community property issues in the context of specific transfer and income tax provisions. *See e.g.*, §3.01[B][2][b], *supra*. The community property discussion in this Chapter continues the integrated approach by exploring the comparable tax issues for spousal concurrent interests in community property.

[A]   Gift Tax

The gift tax ramifications for a third person who transfers property to be held as community property should be the same as if the third person created a tenancy in common in the spouses. In effect, the transferor will make a completed gift of the property and because each spouse has a present interest in the community property, two gift tax annual exclusions should be available.

When one spouse makes a gift to the other spouse of community property, no gift tax issues arise. The transfer should qualify for the gift tax marital deduction. In Nevada, Texas, and Wisconsin, a right of survivorship may be attached to community property. Nonetheless, the possibility of the donor spouse recovering the property if the donee spouse dies first should not bar the allowance of the gift tax marital deduction. *See* § 2523(d). When the transfer qualifies for a gift tax marital deduction, a gift tax return need not be filed.

The taxation of gifts of community property by one or both spouses to a third party depends on the applicable state community property law. In all community property states, a gift of community property can be made if joined in by both spouses. Each spouse will be deemed to have made a gift of one-half of the property. Indeed, the § 2513 split-gift election was enacted in 1948, to allow spouses with separate property to accomplish the gift-splitting that automatically exists for community property.

Depending on the type of property, the value of each spouse's gift may involve a discount to reflect the minority interest being transferred. The discount theory adopted in *Estate of Bright v. United States* (reproduced at § 3.05[A][3][b], *supra*) for the estate tax valuation of community property should apply to each spouse's gift of her one-half interest in community property.

State specific rules determine the gift tax consequences if only one spouse purports to transfer community property to a third person. Absent constructive fraud on the donee spouse, a donor spouse under Texas law may make a valid gift of community property. *See Land v. Marshall*, 426 S.W.2d 841 (Tex. 1968). As a result, each spouse should be taxed as if both had joined in the making of the gift. *See Commissioner v. Chase Manhattan Bank*, 259 F.2d 231 (5th Cir. 1958). New Mexico allows one spouse to make reasonable gifts, but the non-joinder of one spouse makes an unreasonable gift void so that no immediate gift tax consequences should occur for either spouse.

Under California law one spouse is not allowed to make a gift of any community property and the gift is voidable by the donee spouse. *See* Cal. Fam. Code § 1100(b). Because the donor has relinquished control over his interest in the gift property, the donor spouse should be treated as making a gift of his interest. On the other hand, because the nonconsenting spouse has the power to void the transfer, she has not relinquished control for gift tax purposes. *See Estate of Kelly v. Commissioner*, 31 T.C. 493 (1958).

[B] Estate Tax

As discussed in § 3.01[B][2][b], *supra*, the death of one spouse subjects that spouse's one-half community property interest to estate taxation under § 2033. The other half is not subject to estate taxation. It was not owned by the surviving spouse.

In 1948, Congress enacted the marital deduction provisions to level out the tax treatment of community property and separate property. Before the change, only one-half of community property was subject to estate (and gift) taxation, but all property titled in a decedent's name was subject to estate (and gift) taxation if separately owned by one spouse. In 1981, Congress modified the marital deduction to remove the quantitative limits. *See* § 3.04[C][1], *supra*. Accordingly, the deceased spouse's estate may obtain an estate tax marital deduction if that spouse's interest (either in the entire property if separate property or the value of the deceased spouse's one-half in community property) passes to the surviving spouse in qualifying form.

In some community property states, spouses may agree to modify the traditional community property rule that each spouse owns a vested one-half interest in the property. For example, in Nevada and Texas the survivor may take the entire property by right of survivorship. In contrast, in California survivorship rights are limited to bank accounts and similar arrangements. In Washington, spouses may have a lifetime agreement for the disposition of community property at the death of the first spouse. An estate tax marital deduction should be allowable for these arrangements if property passes to the surviving spouse in qualifying form, *i.e.*, not in violation of the nondeductible terminable interest rules of § 2056(b).

[C] Income Tax

Code: §§ 1014(a)(6), (a)(9), and 1041.

Regulations: None.

Section 1041 applies to transfers between spouses with two primary results: (1) there is no taxable event and (2) the basis of property in the hands of the donor spouse carries over to the donee spouse. As a result, there is no immediate income tax consequence when spouses create or transmute interests in property.

Section 1014(b)(6) provides that on the death of the first spouse the basis in both halves of the community property is the estate tax value of the assets. The surviving spouse's basis in one-half of the property is stepped up (or stepped down) on the death of the decedent spouse. Moreover, the step-up (or step-down) of the survivor's one-half interest does not depend on the survivor receiving the decedent spouse's one-half interest.

In comparison, if property is held by a couple in a community property state as joint tenancy property with right of survivorship (or as tenants by the entirety), the surviving spouse receives a new basis in only the one-half interest that she succeeds to as the surviving co-tenant. *See* § 1014(b)(9).

When property has appreciated in value, it will be important for spouses to hold property as community property rather than as joint tenancy property. In fact, there is considerable litigation in community property jurisdictions to determine whether property was held as joint tenants or as community property. *See, e.g., Estate of Peterson*, 28 Cal. App. 4th 1742, 34 Cal. Rptr. 449 (1994).

Problems

1. What is the justification for § 1014(b)(6)?

2. Could the benefits of § 1014(b)(6) be obtained over separate property if the surviving spouse created a revocable trust pursuant to which the deceased spouse had the lifetime power to appoint the assets in the trust to the creditor's of the deceased spouse's estate? Consider Tech. Adv. Memo. 9308002 (denying basis step-up based on application of § 1014(e)), criticized in Paul M. Fletcher, *Drafting Revocable Trusts to Facilitate A Stepped-Up Basis*, 22 EST. PLAN. 100 (Mar./Apr. 1995).

3. Community property rules in some states may have a survivorship feature so that the survivor automatically becomes the owner. What will be the basis of community property with a right of survivorship feature in the hands of the survivor?

§ 13.04   Severing Joint Tenancies

If clients own property as joint tenants or as tenants by the entireties, severing the tenancy may be necessary as part of their estate planning. This is particularly likely when the clients jointly own most or all of their property. This is often the case with married clients who have not done any estate planning. Under either tenancy, the property passes to the survivor upon the death of one tenant. This prevents control of its devolution by will or trust, and, in the marital setting, will ultimately over-fund the survivor's estate, *i.e.,* there will be no transfer of assets to a by-pass trust because all of the decedent's estate passed directly to the surviving spouse by right of survivorship. Severing the tenancy is, therefore, necessary to minimize taxes on the survivor's death.

To understand the need to sever joint tenancies, assume that spouses H and W own property worth $2 million, all of which is owned jointly. If W dies, one-half will be included in her estate under § 2040(b), but because it passes to H, W's taxable estate is reduced to zero. Later, when H dies, all of the property will be in his estate, because he owns all of the property as a result of the survivorship provision. This is exactly the result good tax planning seeks to avoid.

To appreciate the reason for severing tenancies in the nonmarital setting, assume that nonspouses A and B own property worth $100,000 in joint tenancy, and that A had paid the entire $40,000 purchase price. If A dies, the entire $100,000 value at his death will be included in his estate, even though he owns only half of the property, and even though creation of the tenancy was a taxable gift. Yet, if B dies first, none of the property will be included in her estate, because she furnished no consideration. If they convert their ownership to tenancy in common, however, then only one-half of the property will be included in the estate of either, because § 2040 does not apply to tenancies in common. This permits the first to die of A or B to fund a by-pass trust, if desired.

The manner of severing joint tenancies or tenancies by the entireties is governed by state law.[5] Joint tenancies may be severed by one tenant conveying his interest to a third party, and in some states, to himself, thereby creating tenancy in common interests in the two tenants. They also may be severed by joint deed to the co-tenants, which changes the tenancy. The conversion of tenancies by the entireties generally requires the joint action of both spouses.

If a tenancy is to be severed, the gift and estate tax effects of the severance must be considered. Each nonspousal tenant should receive an interest in the property equal to the value of his interest before the transaction; if not, a gift to the co-tenant occurs in the amount of any excess value over that tenant's interest. Thus, if A and B hold securities as joint tenants with right of survivorship, each has a one-half interest in the property. If the securities are sold for $100,000 and A receives $60,000 and B $40,000, B has made a gift of $10,000 to A that should qualify for the annual exclusion. The termination of a joint tenancy while the nonspousal co-tenants are alive will not constitute a gift for federal gift tax purposes if the co-owners become tenants in common or each co-owner receives his or her share of the proceeds.

If the tenancy is between spouses, it may be severed without gift tax liability, even if consideration for its purchase came from only one spouse no matter which spouse receives the proceeds. The unlimited gift tax marital deduction applies to any amounts that the donee spouse receives in excess of his contribution to the purchase price.

---

[5] Federal regulation controls transfers of federal obligations. *See* United States v. Chandler, 410 U.S. 257 (1973).

Black v. Commissioner

765 F.2d 862 (9th Cir. 1985)

Canby, C.J.

Petitioner Phyllis Black, personal representative of the estate of Richard Black, appeals from a judgment of the United States Tax Court finding an estate tax deficiency of $39,666.00. The issue is whether the entire value of the assets formerly held in joint tenancy by the decedent and his spouse, less the contribution of the surviving spouse, should be included in the gross estate under I.R.C. section 2040, even though the assets were transferred shortly before the decedent's death into a revocable trust that modified the surviving spouse's right of survivorship.[6] We hold that the creation of the trust severed the joint tenancy and placed the surviving spouse's share of the trust assets beyond the reach of section 2040 . . . .

On June 10, 1977, Mr. and Mrs. Black created the Black Revocable Trust [containing, *inter alia*, a number of securities held as joint tenants]. During their joint lives, the Blacks retained unrestricted rights to all trust principal and income. The also reserved a joint power to amend or revoke the trust.

The trust agreement provided that, upon the death of the first spouse to die, the trust assets would be divided into two separate trusts, the "Survivor's Trust" and the "Decedent's Trust." The agreement allocated to the Survivor's Trust the "Surviving Trustor's separate property and the Surviving Trustor's interest in community property," plus the amount necessary to obtain the maximum marital deduction. The remainder of the assets was allocated to the Decedent's Trust.

With respect to the Survivor's Trust, the surviving spouse was given the unfettered right to all principal and income, and a general power of appointment. She also could amend or revoke the trust. With respect to the Decedent's Trust, however, the surviving spouse had fewer rights. The surviving spouse and Black's daughter, Dorothy Gayle Standish, were co-beneficiaries entitled to discretionary distributions of principal and income. The trust agreement provided that the trustee "shall consider the respective needs of the beneficiaries" in determining whether to make distributions from the Decedent's trust, and limited the power to invade principal to those amounts necessary for the health, education, and reasonable support of the beneficiaries. Although the agreement designated the surviving spouse as trustee, it prohibited her from "participat(ing) in any decision to invade principal for . . . her benefit." The decision to invade principal was vested in a co-trustee or successor trustee other than the surviving trustor. The surviving spouse had a special power of appointment over the remaining principal and accumulated income.

Mr. Black died on August 2, 1977. On that date, the trust contained the [jointly held securities. The estate reported only one-half of the securities in

---

[6] Neither party suggests that section 2040(b) applies in this case. Section 2040 was adopted in 1976 to provide that one-half of the value of a "qualified joint interest" held by a husband and wife is includable in the gross estate of the first spouse to die. Tax Reform Act of 1976, Pub. L. No. 94–455, § 2002(c)(3), 90 Stat. 1520, 1855 (1976). Section 2040(b) does not apply, however, to joint interests created before 1977. Section 2002(d)(3), *id.* at 1856.

the gross estate.] In his notice of deficiency, the Commissioner determined that the Blacks held [the securities] as joint tenants on the date of Mr. Black's death. Accordingly, he included the entire value of the trust assets, less the contribution of the surviving spouse, in the gross estate pursuant to I.R.C. section 2040.

. . .

The tax court affirmed the Commissioner's decision . . . . Nowhere did the court refer to general common-law joint tenancy principles or the Arizona law of joint tenancy. Instead, the court relied on a line of tax cases which holds that section 2040 includes in the gross estate the entire value of joint tenancy property placed in a revocable trust.

. . .

The common law governing severance of joint tenancies is relatively simple. Joint tenants can end a joint tenancy by express agreement. They can also sever the estate by implication if they enter into a contract the terms of which are inconsistent with the continued existence of the joint tenancy. Since the distinguishing feature of a joint tenancy is the right of survivorship, a contract which modifies the right of survivorship severs the joint tenancy relationship. *In re Estate of Estelle*, 122 Ariz. 109, 111–113, 593 P.2d 663, 665–667 (1979).

. . .

According to these rules, the creation of the Black Revocable Trust severed the joint tenancy in the trust assets. Arguably the express terms of the trust agreement were sufficient to destroy the joint tenancy, since the Blacks listed the securities that they contributed to the trust as their respective separate property. But even if the Blacks did not sever their joint tenancy holdings merely by dividing them and labeling them "separate," they clearly did so by mutually agreeing to alter the right of survivorship. Under the trust agreement, the surviving spouse shares with her daughter the income interest in the one-half of the securities allocated to the Decedent's Trust. She may not invade the principal of the Decedent's Trust except at the discretion of an independent trustee. Upon her death, she may exercise only a special power of appointment over the remaining trust principal and accumulated income. These provisions substantially diminish the undisputed right of ownership that the surviving spouse would otherwise have acquired at the death of her husband. By including them in the trust agreement, the Blacks created a property interest that common law would not characterize as a joint tenancy.

The Commissioner suggests that the decedent's interest in the trust assets so closely resembled a joint tenancy that Congress must have intended to tax it as if it were in fact a joint tenancy. But we have previously rejected the notion that Congress intended section 2040 to apply where joint tenants have severed a joint tenancy under state law and taken the property in another form of joint ownership. In *Sullivan's Estate v. Commissioner*, 175 F.2d 657 (9th Cir. 1949), two joint tenants had agreed to terminate their joint tenancy ownership and to hold their property as tenants in common. Even though each co-owner retained substantial rights in the property, including unlimited lifetime rights of management and control and the undisputed right to direct the disposition of half of the property at death, we summarily rejected the idea that the predecessor of section 2040 justified the inclusion of the entire value of the property in a co-owner's gross estate. We reasoned that "the joint tenancy was terminated (by the agreement to sever) before the husband's death. Hence, as to the joint tenancy, the deceased had no 'interest therein . . . at the time of his death.'" *Id.* at 660.

Sullivan applied the established rules of joint tenancy severance even though Congress had specifically provided that an analogous transfer of an outright ownership interest would not have removed the transferred property from the decedent's gross estate. The decedent in *Sullivan* terminated the joint tenancy in contemplation of his death. *Id.* At that time, the gross estate included property "to the extent of any interest therein of which the decedent has at any time made a transfer" in contemplation of death. But we refused to hold that the severance of the joint tenancy constituted a taxable "transfer," even though the effect of the severance was to reduce the decedent's estate at his death by one-half of the value of the property. We stated that "(t)here was no compulsion on the co-tenants to continue the joint tenancy so that (a) taxable event would occur." *Id.* at 659.

. . .

The Commissioner argues that the *Sullivan* line of cases should be distinguished on the ground that none of them involved a revocable trust like the one that the decedent here established. The Commissioner contends, and the tax court held, that the revocation clause in the trust agreement makes the trust assets includable under section 2040.

. . .

Neither the logic of the Commissioner's position nor the above authority on which he relies is persuasive. In the first place, if "revocability" distinguished taxable transfers of joint tenancy property from nontaxable ones, section 2040 would apply whenever joint tenants sever their joint tenancy and take a tenancy in common or some other form of joint ownership.[7] Owners of jointly held property can always change the form of ownership of the property by agreement among themselves. Thus former joint tenants who hold as tenants in common can "revoke" the severance at any time and resume the joint tenancy. In light of *Sullivan*, we cannot read the statute so broadly that it would tax this kind of "revocable" tenancy in common.

. . .

---

[7] We speak here only of transfers which are "revocable" by the transferors jointly during their joint lives. We do not decide a case in which the trust agreement provides that the surviving spouse may revoke the trust after her husband's death, or that the surviving spouse may receive unlimited distributions of principal and interest without regard to the interests of the remaindermen. In such cases, the surviving spouse arguable retains a right of survivorship even though her interest may not be labeled as such. *See* Estate of May v. Commissioner, 37 T.C. Memo 137 (1978).

REVERSED.

————

Black and *Sullivan's Estate* illustrate the Commissioner's lack of success in attempts to compel gross estate inclusion when joint tenants transfer property to a revocable trust and retain income interests for life. Similar results were reached in *United States v. Heasty*, 370 F.2d 525 (10th Cir. 1966), in which a husband and wife transferred property owned as tenants by the entirety to an irrevocable trust reserving the right to income for life. The court held that § 2036(a)(1) required inclusion of only 50% of the property despite the fact that the decedent furnished all the consideration for the transfer. The Service will no longer contest this issue. *See* Rev. Rul. 76–348, 1976–2 C.B. 267.

Problems

1. Do you think the result in *Black* would have been the same if the power of revocation had not been joint, but had been the decedent's alone?

2. *A* and *B*, unmarried cohabitants, purchase shares of stock for $100,000. *A* supplies $60,000, and *B* contributes $40,000, of the consideration. They take title as tenants in common.

    a. What are the gift tax consequences of the creation of the tenancy in common?

    b. More than a year after the purchase, *A* and *B* sell the stock for $200,000. What are the gift tax consequences if:

      (i) they divide the proceeds equally?

      (ii) *A* receives all of the proceeds?

3. Assume the same facts as in Problem 2, except that *A* and *B* take title as joint tenants with right of survivorship.

    a. What are the gift tax consequences of the creation of the joint tenancy?

    b. More than a year after the purchase, *A* and *B* sell the stock for $200,000. What are the gift tax consequences if:

      (i) they divide the proceeds equally?

      (ii) *A* receives all of the proceeds?

      (iii) *B* receives $80,000 and *A* receives $120,000 of the proceeds?

§ 13.05   Disclaimers of Concurrent Property Interests

Code: § 2518.

Regulations: Treas. Reg. § 25.2518–2(c)(4) and (5).

McDonald v. Commissioner

853 F.2d 1494 (8th Cir. 1988), cert. denied sub. nom
Corelius v. Commissioner, 490 U.S. 1005 (1989).

Wollman, Circuit Judge

. . .

Gladys L. McDonald (Gladys) appeals from a tax court order upholding a determination by the Commissioner that her disclaimer of the survivorship interest in jointly-held property was a taxable transfer because such disclaimer was not made within the time period prescribed by [Treasury Regulation] section 25.2511–1(c). *McDonald v. Comm'r*, 89 T.C. 293 (1987). We reverse and remand for further proceedings consistent with this opinion. [Another issue involving § 2032A is omitted.]

John McDonald (Decedent), a resident of North Dakota, died testate on January 16, 1981, survived by his widow, Gladys, four children and three grandchildren. Except for some small specific bequests, the will provided that Gladys was to inherit all of Decedent's property. In addition, Decedent and Gladys had owned certain property, including several parcels of farmland, as joint tenants with right of survivorship.

On September 23, 1981, Gladys disclaimed her interest in the farmland she stood to inherit under the terms of Decedent's will, as well as the survivorship interest in most of the farmland the couple had owned in joint tenancy. As a result of the disclaimer, this property passed to three of Decedent's children, Virlyn McDonald, Dorothy Spicer, and Gladys Jean Cox, in equal shares.

. . .

Federal gift tax is imposed "on the transfer of property by gift." *See* section 2501(a)(1). The scope of this tax is broad, applying "whether the transfer is in trust or otherwise, whether the gift is direct or indirect, and whether the property is real or personal, tangible or intangible." *See* section 2511(a). Moreover, in construing the gift tax provisions, " '[t]he terms "property," "transfer," "gift," and "indirectly" are used in the broadest and most comprehensive sense; the term "property" reaching every species of right or interest protected by law and having an exchangeable value.' " *Jewett v. Comm'r.*, 455 U.S. 305, 309 (1982) (quoting S.R. No. 665, 72nd Cong., 1st Sess. 39 (1932); H.R. No. 708, 72nd Cong., 1st Sess. 27 (1932)). Thus, absent an applicable exception, a disclaimer, which is an indirect transfer, would fall within the encompassing language of the gift tax statute.

Such an exception exists, however, for certain disclaimers made within a specified period after the disclaimed property is transferred to the disclaimant. *See* section 2518 (applicable for transfers creating an interest in the disclaimant after December 31, 1976); Treas. Reg. § 25.2511–1(c)(2) (applicable for transfers creating an interest in the disclaimant before January 1, 1977).[8] The effect of these disclaimer provisions is to collapse the entire transaction into a single transfer from the original owner to the ultimate recipient, *Kennedy v. Comm'r*, 804 F.2d 1332, 1334 (7th Cir. 1986), thereby ignoring the gift tax consequences of the intermediate disclaimer.

Gladys disclaimed the survivorship interest in the property she had formerly held with decedent as joint tenants on September 23, 1981, less than nine months following decedent's death. The question before us is whether the transfer relative to which the timeliness of the disclaimer is measured refers to the transfer creating the joint tenancy or the transfer of the survivorship interest at the joint tenant's death.

The tax court, relying primarily on *Jewett v. Comm'r*, 455 U.S. 305 (1982), adopted the Commissioner's position that "transfer" as used in the disclaimer provisions refers to the transfer creating the joint tenancy. Because the joint tenancies in question were created prior to 1977, the court concluded that Gladys' September 23, 1981, disclaimer was not "made within a reasonable time" as required by section 25.2511–1(c)(2).

In *Jewett*, Jewett's grandmother established a testamentary trust providing that the trust income should be paid to Jewett's grandfather for life, and thereafter to Jewett's parents. Upon the death of the surviving parent, the trust principal was to be divided " 'into equal shares . . . so that there shall be one share for each child of my said son [petitioner's father] then living and one share for the issue then living representing each child of my said son then dead.' " 455 U.S. at 306 (quoting trust instrument). While Jewett's mother was still living, and therefore before his interest vested, Jewett disclaimed his interest in the trust. At the time, Jewett was forty-five years old, and the trust had been in existence for thirty-three years. The Supreme Court held that the transfer referred to in [Treasury Regulation] section 25.2511–1(c) occurred when the contingent interest was created and not when it vested, and that a disclaimer made thirty-three years after the transfer was not made "within a reasonable time" under section 2501(a)(1) and 2511(a). *Id.* at 312, 318–19.

Gladys, on the other hand, urges this court to adopt the Seventh Circuit's position in *Kennedy v. Comm'r*, 804 F.2d 1332 (7th Cir. 1986). Kennedy had received a gift of a joint tenancy in 1953 when she and her husband acquired the farm. Her husband died in 1978, and in 1979 she disclaimed the survivorship interest under Illinois law. The Seventh Circuit concluded that the relevant transfer occurred when Kennedy acquired the survivorship interest on her husband's death in 1978, making section 2518 the applicable disclaimer provision.

Kennedy distinguished *Jewett* on the basis of the power of partition that is associated with joint tenancy. *Kennedy* found the deceased joint tenant's

---

[8] 26 C.F.R. section 25.2511–1(c)(2) provides in relevant part:

[W]hen the law governing the administration of the decedent's estate gives a beneficiary, heir, or next-of-kin a right completely and unqualifiedly to refuse to accept ownership of property transferred from a decedent . . . , a refusal to accept ownership does not constitute the making of a gift if the refusal is made within a reasonable time after knowledge of the existence of the transfer. The refusal must be unequivocal and effective under the local law. There can be no refusal of ownership of property after its acceptance.

power of partition to be equivalent to a general power of appointment over the survivorship interest, because by partitioning the property a joint tenant could direct his half to his creditors and legatees of his choice.[9] Kennedy, 804 F.2d at 1335. Under the gift tax regulations, "[a] person to whom any interest in property passes by reason of the . . . lapse of a general power [of appointment] may disclaim such interest within a 9-month period after the . . . lapse." [Treas. Reg.] section 25.2518–2(c)(3). Applying this concept to the transfer of the survivorship interest, *Kennedy* concluded that the surviving joint tenant should have nine months after the lapse of the decedent's power of partition in which to disclaim a survivorship interest.

The Commissioner contends that the tax court correctly concluded that the deceased joint tenant's right to partition or sever is merely another contingency and does not distinguish *Kennedy* from *Jewett*. The Commissioner notes that under North Dakota law, "[a] joint tenancy may be described as a life estate with each joint tenant having a contingent remainder in fee—the contingency being based upon survival of the other joint tenant." *Jamestown Terminal Elevator, Inc. v. Knopp*, 246 N.W.2d 612, 613 (N.D. 1976). In this respect, the Commissioner oversimplifies the nature of the deceased joint tenant's interest. In *Jamestown*, the North Dakota Supreme Court further clarified the nature of this interest: "The deceased joint tenant had, essentially, a life estate which no longer exists, a power in himself and his judgment creditor to sever which was never exercised and lapsed upon death, and a contingent remainder which never vested." 246 N.W.2d at 614. This power to sever, which the Seventh Circuit analogized to a general power of appointment over the survivorship interest, distinguishes the right to partition or sever from the survival contingency addressed in *Jewett*.

Accordingly, we conclude that the relevant transfer for the purpose of the disclaimer provisions occurs at the death of the joint tenant and not at the creation of the joint tenancy. Thus, the time period in which Gladys could disclaim the survivorship interest began to run in 1981 and therefore is governed by the provisions of section 2518. Although there is no question that Gladys' disclaimer was timely under this statute, the parties disagree as to whether the disclaimer otherwise qualified under section 2518. Accordingly, we remand the case to the tax court for the purpose of that determination. Kennedy, 804 F.2d at 1336 (the tax court should have the initial opportunity to apply the terms of section 2518 and its implementing regulations).

. . .

On remand in *McDonald v. Commissioner*, T.C. Memo 1989–1401 (1989), the Tax Court held that a surviving spouse's disclaimer of her survivorship interest in certain real property previously owned in joint tenancy with her deceased husband, made within nine months of the husband's death, constituted a qualified disclaimer for gift tax purposes. The court viewed a gift of

---

[9] In the gift tax context, a general power of appointment generally means "any power of appointment exercisable in favor of the person possessing the power . . . , his estate, his creditors, or the creditors of his estate." [Treas. Reg.] section 25.2514–1(c)(1).

a joint tenancy with right of survivorship as more than one transfer, with the first being an undivided right given on the date the joint tenancy was created, and an additional transfer occurring at the death of the other joint tenant. The court concluded that the disclaimer was qualified because it referred to the survivorship interest that was deemed to have been transferred at the time of the husband's death.

The controversy over disclaimers of survivorship interests in joint tenancies and tenancies by the entirety was apparently resolved by an amendment to the disclaimer regulations. Treasury Regulation § 25.2518–2(c)(4)(i) permits a

> qualified disclaimer of the survivorship interest to which the survivor succeeds by operation of law upon the death of the first joint tenant to die . . . [if] made no later than 9 months after the death of the first joint tenant to die regardless of whether such interest can be unilaterally severed under local law.

For disclaimers of joint ownership where the transferor has a unilateral right to withdraw her contribution to the account, such as joint bank, brokerage, mutual fund and other investment accounts, without the consent of the noncontributing owner, the surviving tenant may disclaim "funds contributed by a deceased cotenant, . . . [if] made within 9 months of the cotenant's death." *See* Treas. Reg. § 25.2518–2(c)(4)(iii). The contributing tenant "may not disclaim any portion of the joint account attributable to consideration furnished by that surviving joint tenant." *Id.*

Two examples in the Regulations illustrate the rules.

> **Example (7).** On February 1, 1990, *A* purchased real property with *A*'s funds. Title to the property was conveyed to "*A* and *B*, as joint tenants with right of survivorship." Under applicable state law, the joint interest is unilaterally severable by either tenant. *B* dies on May 1, 1998, and is survived by *A*. On January 1, 1999, *A* disclaims the one-half survivorship interest in the property to which *A* succeeds as a result of *B*'s death. Assuming that the other requirements of section 2518(b) are satisfied, *A* has made a qualified disclaimer of the one-half survivorship interest (but not the interest retained by *A* upon the creation of the tenancy, which may not be disclaimed by *A*). The result is the same whether or not *A* and *B* are married and regardless of the proportion of consideration furnished by *A* and *B* in purchasing the property.

> **Example (8).** Assume the same facts as in Example (7) except that *A* and *B* are married and title to the property was conveyed to "*A* and *B*, as tenants by the entirety." Under applicable state law, the tenancy cannot be unilaterally severed by either tenant. Assuming that the other requirements of section 2518(b) are satisfied, *A* has made a qualified disclaimer of the one-half survivorship interest (but not the interest retained by *A* upon the creation of the tenancy, which may not be disclaimed by *A*). The result is the same regardless of the proportion of consideration furnished by *A* and *B* in purchasing the property.

Chapter 14

INCOME TAXATION OF ESTATES, TRUSTS AND BENEFICIARIES

This Chapter focuses on subchapter J of the Code—the taxation of decedents' estates and trusts, and the beneficiaries of estates and trusts. Understanding the income tax consequences of subchapter J assumes a working knowledge of the basic income tax system for individuals. *See generally* Jeffrey G. Sherman, *All You Really Need to Know About Subchapter J You Learned from This Article*, 63 Mo. L. Rev. 1 (1998).

§ 14.01   The Decedent's Final Income Tax Return

Code: §§ 6012(b)(1) and 6013(a)(2).

Regulations: None.

Income earned before a decedent's death, and not reported on a previously filed return, is reported on a return that is filed after death. The Code requires the personal representative to file a decedent's final return for a tax reporting period ending with the decedent's death. *See* § 6012(b)(1). The personal representative of a married decedent may file a joint return with the surviving spouse. *See* § 6013(a)(2).

A decedent's last taxable year starts on January 1 of the year of death and ends with the date of death.[1] The final year is always less than a full taxable year, unless the decedent died on December 31st. The short period can produce tax savings. For example, § 443(c) does not require proration of the personal exemption deductions under § 151. The decedent is, therefore, entitled to full use of the exemptions, even if on an accrual basis.

One problem faced by the personal representative when filing the final return is determining what constitutes income during the final taxable year. This question raises the timing issues normally covered in a separate course on federal income taxation. Cash basis taxpayers usually report only actual or constructive receipts as income, while those who report on the accrual basis report income for which the right to receive has accrued, whether or not the income was actually received in the taxable year. The only major exception to this rule is that amounts that accrue to the decedent solely because of death are excluded from taxable income on the decedent's final return even if the income was otherwise reported on the accrual basis. *See* § 451(b).

Income received on the date of death for a cash basis taxpayer or accrued for an accrual basis taxpayer is reported on the decedent's final return regardless of the time of day the decedent dies.

---

[1] If the decedent had been filing an income return on a fiscal year, the first day of the final year would be the first day of the fiscal year instead of January 1. Fiscal year individuals are most rare.

Questions often arise over whether an exclusion, deduction, or credit normally available to an individual is available on a decedent's final return. For a cash basis taxpayer, many of these questions are resolved by determining whether the deductible item was in fact paid before the decedent's death. For example, a debt paid by the decedent with a check prior to death is deductible if the bank pays the check; the amount is not deductible, however, if the bank does not pay the check. *See Estate of Hubbell v. Commissioner*, 10 T.C. 1207 (1948). *Cf. Flint v. United States*, 237 F. Supp. 551 (D. Idaho 1964). For an accrual basis taxpayer, deductions are normally available if liability can be ascertained in *all events* during the last taxable year, and economic performance has generally occurred. *See* § 461(h).

An exclusion or deduction may also be available on the final return of a cash basis taxpayer, even if not paid during the last taxable year. For example, § 213(c)(1) expressly treats as paid, at the time incurred, medical expenses paid by the decedent's estate within the year after death.[2] Further, § 1033 allows gains from condemnation awards to be deferred if the reinvestment occurs after the decedent's death. *See Goodman v. Commissioner*, 199 F.2d 895 (2d Cir. 1952). Provisions that permit accruals by a cash basis taxpayer may also be available. Thus, for example, a personal representative can claim prorated § 167 depreciation deductions for property the decedent used in trade or business or held for the production of income.

The personal representative of an estate that includes U.S. Savings bonds, whether series E, EE, H, or HH, may elect to include any interest accrued up to the date of the decedent's death, but unpaid, as income on the decedent's final return.[3] *See* § 454(a). Alternatively, the personal representative may elect to report all accrued interest up to the year of the election on the estate's fiduciary income tax return. Finally, the recipient of the bonds may elect to defer reporting the income until the savings bonds are redeemed or mature. *See* Rev. Rul. 68–145, 1968–1 C.B. 203; Rev. Rul. 64–104, 1964–1 C.B. 223; Rev. Rul. 58–435, 1958–2 C.B. 370.

Problems

1. Under what circumstances would a personal representative choose to report savings bond interest on a decedent's final income tax return?

2. The decedent suffers a property loss during her final taxable year. A reimbursement claim against the person causing the loss exists, but has not been collected by the time of death. Is the loss deductible? Would the result be any different if there was an insurance claim for the loss of the item? *See* Treas. Reg. § 1.165–1(d)(2), –1(d)(3) (limiting deductibility of losses to those situations in which there is no *reasonable certainty* that reimbursement will be obtained).

---

[2] Alternatively, the decedent's personal representative may elect to deduct medical bills as a debt of the decedent under § 2053. *See* § 213(c)(2).

[3] It is possible that the decedent had elected under § 454 to annually report the income accruing on the bonds as income.

§ 14.02   Income in Respect of a Decedent

Code: §§ 691 and 1014(c).

Regulations: Treas. Reg. §§ 1.691(a)–1, 1.691(a)–2, 1.691(a)–4, and 1.691(a)–5.

[A]   In General

When a taxpayer has a right to income but it has not been received (or accrued for an accrual basis taxpayer), the income is not reported on the decedent's final return. Nevertheless, because of the decedent's entitlement to the income at death, special rules apply. Under § 691(a), income in respect of a decedent (IRD) is taxable to the recipient as income, rather than as return of capital. As income, IRD items are denied stepped-up basis treatment. *See* § 1014(c). As suggested by *Estate of Peterson, infra*, this is true whether the decedent's estate (§ 691(a)(1)(A)), or some other person (§ 691(a)(1)(B) and (C)), inherits or takes the income item from the decedent before its been taxed as income.

Although the definition of "income in respect of a decedent" can be difficult to apply, many types of IRD are easily recognized. The most common types are salaries and wages unpaid at death. *See* Treas. Reg. § 1.691(a)–(1). *Cf. Halliday v. United States*, 655 F.2d 68 (5th Cir. 1981). IRD also includes bonuses not yet declared, but earned by the decedent. *See O'Daniel's Estate v. Commissioner*, 173 F.2d 966 (2d Cir. 1949). If the bonus has not accrued at death, however, it will not be includable in the decedent's gross estate. *See* Rev. Rul. 65–217, 1965–2 C.B. 214. Qualified retirement benefits, including IRAs, are also classic examples of IRD.

Normal investment proceeds such as accrued interest,[4] unpaid dividends on stock (if the decedent was alive on the record date),[5] and accrued rents[6] are also items easily identified as IRD income.

Over the years, the identification of IRD has been problematic in many instances, however. The government and taxpayers have disputed the classification of certain items of income as IRD. The cases and material below provide a sampling of how courts, the Service, and taxpayers have struggled with the concept of income in respect of a decedent.

[1]   Contracts to Sell Property

Defining income in respect of a decedent is most difficult in cases such as *Estate of Peterson, infra*, in which there has been a sale of assets. If the sale is complete but the purchase price is yet to be paid in full or in part, the presence of IRD is apparent. Further, the Code contains specific provisions for determining the IRD of installment sales (§ 691(a)(4)) and annuity proceeds (§ 691(a)(5)). However, when the sale is in any stage prior to completion, the categorization of the transaction for IRD purposes is difficult

---

[4] *See* Rev. Rul. 58–435, 1958–2 C.B. 370; Rev. Rul. 79–340, 1979–2 C.B. 320.

[5] *See Estate of Putnam v. Commissioner*, 324 U.S. 393 (1945).

[6] *See* Rev. Rul. 64–289, 1964–2 C.B. 173, 175.

and important. Courts have tended to use either an *economic activities* test or a *right to income* test to determine whether the transaction has produced IRD. The former looks to whether the economic activities of the decedent produced the gain. *See Commissioner v. Linde*, 213 F.2d 1 (9th Cir. 1954), *cert. denied*, 348 U.S. 871 (1955) (holding that sale proceeds of crops delivered to co-op prior to death constituted IRD). *Compare Keck v. Commissioner*, 415 F.2d 531, 533 (6th Cir. 1969) (discussed in *Peterson* and *Claiborne, infra*), *with Claiborne v. United States*, 648 F.2d 448 (6th Cir. 1981), *infra*. The latter test considers the time the sale contract became effective.

Sales of IRD items by an estate can also affect the taxation of these items. Because the right to income is an asset, the estate or other recipient may sell or otherwise dispose of the right. To prevent a sale of IRD (or other disposition not pursuant to inheritance, devise, or bequest from the decedent) from transferring income taxation of the IRD to the purchaser, the proceeds of the sale are considered to be an anticipation of IRD and taxed as income to the seller of the IRD item. *See* § 691(a)(2).

Claiborne v. United States

648 F.2d 448 (6th Cir. 1981)

Edwards, Chief Judge.

The United States (Internal Revenue Service) appeals from a judgment entered in favor of plaintiff taxpayer allowing recovery of a refund of federal taxes which plaintiff had paid under protest. The United States contended before the District Court, and contends before us, that the refund should be denied because the funds at issue were income in respect of a decedent, and hence taxable to the estate of the deceased Simcoe under § 691(a) of the Internal Revenue Code of 1954.

The facts in the case were stipulated before the District Judge who decided in favor of the administratrix. Our question is whether or not the stipulated facts showed that at the time of Simcoe's death she was entitled to the income from the sale of a piece of property.

Decedent Simcoe in 1967 was an elderly widow living on her farm in Jefferson County, Kentucky. The preceding year the Ford Motor Company had decided to purchase real estate for the site of a Ford heavy duty truck assembly plant in the vicinity of Louisville, and for that purpose had signed a contract with the Louisville and Nashville Railroad (L & N). A wholly-owned subsidiary of L & N (Houston-McCord Realty Company) began negotiations with landowners, including Simcoe, and entered into an option contract with Simcoe for the purchase of her property at $4,000 per acre. With the signing of the option contract, Simcoe received $6,000, which was described in the contract as being the total of liquidated damages the purchaser would be subject to pay in the event the option was not picked up or the contract for sale was not consummated.

Four events happened thereafter: Simcoe appointed her son, Newton Simcoe, as her personal representative and gave him power of attorney to act on her behalf. Thereafter on August 12, 1967, Houston-McCord exercised its option rights on the Simcoe property. On August 15, Newton Simcoe entered into an agreement with Houston-McCord giving them immediate possession of the property at issue. In early September, Ford actually entered upon the Simcoe farm and began clearing and site preparation work for the construction of an access road.

Maude Simcoe died October 1, 1967, before the closing of the sale and before anything had been paid except the $6,000 previously referred to.

The applicable statute [§ 691(a)(1)(A)] does not in its specific language appear to shed much light upon the issue which is currently before us:

. . .

The history of this particular provision has been previously considered by this court in *Keck v. Commissioner*, 415 F.2d 531, 533 (6th Cir. 1969), as follows:

> Under the prior law, only the items which were accruable to a taxpayer at the time of his death were required to be included in the last return. This discriminated against accrual-basis taxpayers and allowed much income of cash-basis taxpayers to escape income tax. To correct this situation, Congress provided that in the case of both cash and accrual taxpayers, the last return must include all items accruable at death. The Supreme Court, in *Helvering v. Enright*, 312 U.S. 636, held that the term "accrual" in the statute was not to be construed narrowly in its accounting sense, but broadly to effectuate the purpose of the statute. However, such broad construction resulted in the bunching of income in the last return and its resultant taxation in higher surtax brackets.
>
> It was to remedy this situation that Congress enacted the forerunner of Section 691, above quoted, which provides that such income as was formerly required to be included in the last return, because it was accrued though not actually received, is taxable to the recipient and has the same character in his hands that it would have had in the hands of the decedent.

The Treasury Regulation adopted to elucidate § 691 adds at least something to the construction of the statute in applicable part as follows:

> (b) *General definition.* In general, the term "income in respect of a decedent" refers to those amounts *to which a decedent was entitled as gross income* but which were not properly includible in computing his taxable income for the taxable year ending with the date of his death or for a previous taxable year under the method of accounting employed by the decedent. See the regulations under section 451. Thus, the term includes—
>
> (1) All accrued income of a decedent who reported his income by use of the cash receipts and disbursements method;
>
> (2) Income accrued solely by reason of the decedent's death in case of a decedent who reports his income by use of an accrual method of accounting; and

(3) Income to which the decedent had a contingent claim at the time of his death.

Treas. Reg. § 1.691(a)–1(b) (1965) (emphasis in original).

The legal arguments which have followed the enactment of this statute and the regulation just quoted have divided approximately as follows: The taxpayers have contended that entitlement meant an immediate and legally enforceable right to payment as of the date of death. The IRS, on the contrary, has taken the point of view that where the income was produced by the activities of the decedent prior to death, it was income "in respect of a decedent" within the meaning of the statute, regardless of whether or not the decedent could on the date of death have enforced payment through legal process. The District Judge who heard this case reasoned as follows:

> The terms of the contract concerning liquidated damages are plain and unambiguous. They are such that they can only reasonably be construed to be a limitation of the rights of the parties, and not security for the performance of the contract. The terms specifically refer to the consideration as liquidated damages. True it is that the Court must look at the entire agreement. If it is clear that the intention of the parties was to limit their rights, the Court must give that interpretation to the contract. The Court must also look at the surrounding circumstances.

> Here, Houston-McCord was not negotiating for itself but for Ford. Had Ford, for whatever reason, changed its plans, Houston-McCord cannot be found to have intended to purchase the property for itself. Thus, the liquidated damages provision must be interpreted as just that . . . .

> Defendant further urges that Ford, by taking possession of Mrs. Simcoe's property in August, indicated that the contract would be performed by Houston-McCord and that both Ford and Houston-McCord treated the transaction as having been consummated except for the formal signing of the deed. Whether or not this position has merit, it is agreed that Ford entered the property pursuant to authority granted by Newton Simcoe under the power of attorney referred to above. The reading of that power of attorney raises serious doubt as to the validity of Newton Simcoe's acts. The Court finds no special significance in Houston-McCord's and Ford's activities.

> In sum, the Court finds that, at the date of her death, Mrs. Simcoe was not entitled to the amounts yet unpaid by Houston-McCord and that, therefore, the amounts ultimately paid were not income in respect of a decedent as that term is used in Section 691. Since there was no right, there was no taxable income. *Keck v. Commissioner of Internal Revenue*, 415 F.2d 531 (6th Cir. 1969).

We observe that our examination of the power of attorney Mrs. Simcoe gave her son does not raise in this court's mind such serious doubts as to the validity of Newton Simcoe's actions as the District Judge found therein. We recognize, of course, that the broad power granted in the first sentence was limited by

Mrs. Simcoe by the phrase "under such terms or conditions as I may deem proper." Nothing in this record, however, suggests that Mrs. Simcoe disagreed with her son's grant of authority to the Ford Motor Company to enter upon her land and begin site preparation, and the second paragraph of the power of attorney seems to us to resolve any question of Newton Simcoe's authority.

At that point where the Ford Motor Company began the work of site preparation, Houston-McCord had already exercised its option to purchase this property. In addition, the purchasing parties (Ford, L & N and Houston-McCord) had had Mrs. Simcoe's property rezoned to industrial use and had secured a building permit for it.

Furthermore, Houston-McCord had agreed with Mrs. Simcoe to purchase a farm and some income-producing property which would be accepted by her as part of the purchase price. These negotiations were far advanced at the time of Mrs. Simcoe's death and were completed shortly thereafter. The closing of the purchase of Mrs. Simcoe's farm (with the exchange of properties referred to above and payment of $690,258.86 in cash) took place just 16 days after Mrs. Simcoe's death.

Assuming that the test for taxability of the current disputed income is the enforceability of Mrs. Simcoe's right to the full purchase price as of the date of her death, we find it impossible to agree that no such enforcement rights existed. While as a strict matter of law Mrs. Simcoe would not be "entitled" to the purchase price until after the closing, we believe that Ford's entry upon the land after Houston-McCord had exercised its option would have occasioned the success of a suit by Mrs. Simcoe for specific performance if at that advanced point in the transaction the Ford Motor Company had for some reason refused to complete the purchase. As we construe the term "entitlement," it includes both legal and equitable rights.

Kentucky, of course, recognizes an action for specific performance . . . .

Under the factual posture of this case, at the moment of decedent's death, we believe that there was entitlement in Mrs. Simcoe to the specific performance of the purchase agreement on tender of a deed. We also believe where, by agreement, Ford Motor Company had taken possession of Mrs. Simcoe's land and had begun reshaping it, Ford's agent would be regarded by the Kentucky courts as having so exercised its contract rights as to be liable for full payment of the contract price . . . .

In leading, if now somewhat elderly, cases, the optionor's right to specific performance of a land purchase agreement at full purchase price, rather than liquidated damages, has been recognized where (as here) the optionee has taken full possession of the realty which is the subject of the contract. *Milby v. Martin*, 280 S.W.2d 196 (Ky. 1955); *Brown v. Norcross*, 59 N. J. Eq. 427, 45 A. 605 (Ch. 1900). In this last case the court said:

> If the contract should be held to tender a choice to accept performance, or to refuse and pay the liquidated sum, the defendant long ago has exercised his election, and has chosen to accept performance. He has paid a part of the purchase money, accepted delivery of possession, which he yet retains, and has declared his willingness fully to perform if his construction of the amount yet due be made

the basis of settlement. Under these circumstances, having already elected, and still retaining the benefits of his choice, he cannot, without even offering to restore those benefits, now choose again, and take the other alternative.

Brown v. Norcross, supra, 45 A. at 607.

The leading case in this Circuit upon interpretation of § 691 of the Revenue Act of 1954 is *Keck v. Commissioner*, 415 F.2d 531 (6th Cir. 1969). *Keck* relied in part on *Trust Co. of Georgia v. Ross*, 392 F.2d 694 (5th Cir. 1967), *cert. denied*, 393 U.S. 830 (1968). In *Keck* we said:

> We agree with the United States Court of Appeals for the Fifth Circuit in holding that the right to income, under the provision of the statute here pertinent, is to be distinguished from the economic activities that create that right and that, absent such a right, no matter how great the activities, there is no taxable income under Section 691.

> It is our conclusion that, at the date of his death, decedent Arthur D. Shaw possessed neither the right nor the power to require the corporations to liquidate and did not, prior to his death, possess the right to receive any proceeds from the contemplated liquidation. It follows that the amounts herein involved are not taxable under Section 691.

Keck v. Commissioner, supra at 534–35.

In *Keck* the transaction involved required the approval of the Interstate Commerce Commission before there could be any consummation of the sales of the shares concerned. Such approval was not received until a year and a half after the death of the owner of the shares concerned. Neither in law nor in equity could the owner of the shares have enforced the purchase agreement there involved.

We recognize that the United States in this appeal argues for an "economic activities" test which would exclude any consideration of enforceability as an aspect of entitlement. To this degree the government appears to be asking for an overruling of the *Keck* opinion. Since we believe that for the reasons outlined above the factual situation in this case is sufficiently distinguishable from the facts in *Keck* to warrant a different result, we decline the suggestion which we believe is strongly implied in the government's brief that we now overrule the legal conclusion in *Keck*.

For the reasons set forth above, we hold that decedent was entitled to the completion of this transaction and the payment of the funds as of the time of her death. The basic thrust of the Congressional purpose appears to us to be to include in income accounted for under § 691 all income where economic activities had progressed to the point of either legal or equitable entitlement.

The judgment of the District Court is therefore vacated and this case is remanded to the District Court for further proceedings in accordance with this opinion.

————

Estate of Peterson v. Commissioner

667 F.2d 675 (8th Cir. 1981)

McMillian, Circuit Judge.

This is an appeal from the decision of the Tax Court holding that the sale proceeds received by the estate of Charley W. Peterson from the sale of 2,398 calves did not constitute "income in respect of a decedent" under § 691(a)(1) of the Internal Revenue Code . . . .

The facts are not disputed . . . . The decedent, Charley W. Peterson, was in the business of raising and selling cattle. On July 11, 1972, he entered into a "livestock sales contract" with the Max Rosenstock Co., through its agent R. E. Brickley. Under the terms of this contract, the decedent was to raise and sell to the Max Rosenstock Co. "approximately 3,300 calves" at $ 0.49 per pound, with the date of delivery to be designated by the decedent upon five days notice. One group of calves (the Brown County calves) was to be delivered no later than November 1, 1972; the other group (the Holt County calves) was to be delivered no later than December 15, 1972. The calves were to be from three to eleven months old and in "merchantable condition" when delivered. As provided in the contract, the Max Rosenstock Co. paid $ 46,500 in "earnest money" to the decedent on July 13, 1972. The risk of loss was on the decedent until delivery.

The decedent did not designate a delivery date or deliver any calves by the November 1 delivery date. The record contains no reason why the decedent did not designate a delivery date or deliver the Brown County calves on or before the November 1, 1972, delivery date specified in the contract. The decedent died on November 9, 1972. The estate (the taxpayer) assumed responsibility for the calves, designated several December delivery dates, and delivered a total of 2,929 calves, 2,398 owned by the estate and 531 owned by the decedent's sons, Willis Peterson and Charles R. Peterson. The calves were accepted by the Max Rosenstock Co. As found by the Tax Court, approximately two-thirds of the calves were in a "deliverable" condition as of the date of the decedent's death. The remaining calves were not "deliverable" on that date because they were too young.

The estate reported the sale of the calves on its fiduciary income tax return and computed the gain from the sale by subtracting the fair market value of the calves on the date of the decedent's death from the sale proceeds. The Commissioner, however, determined that the gain from the sale constituted "income in respect of a decedent" under § 691(a)(1) and recomputed the estate's gain on the sale by subtracting the decedent's adjusted basis in the calves from the sale proceeds. *See* §§ 691(a)(1), 1014(a) (basis of property acquired from decedent is the fair market value at date of decedent's death), 1014(c) (§ 1014(a) does not apply to property which constitutes a right to receive an item of income in respect of a decedent under § 691). The characterization of the sales transaction thus determines whether the estate uses the decedent's adjusted basis or a stepped-up basis (fair market value on date of death) in calculating the gain from the sale. The amount of income tax deficiency at issue is $185,384.10.

The Tax Court decided that the sale proceeds did not constitute "income in respect of a decedent" under § 691(a)(1) . . . . After noting that § 691 does not itself define "income in respect of a decedent," the Tax Court reviewed the history of the section,[7] referred to the applicable regulations, . . . § 1.691(a)(1)–(3) (1981), examined the case law, and distilled a four-factor test for determining whether sale proceeds constitute "income in respect of a decedent": (1) whether the decedent entered into a legally significant arrangement regarding the subject matter of the sale,[8] (2) whether the decedent performed the substantive (nonministerial) acts required as preconditions to the sale, (3) whether there existed at the time of the decedent's death any economically material contingencies which might have disrupted the sale, and (4) whether the decedent would have eventually received the sale proceeds if he or she had lived.

Stated in misleadingly simple terms, whether income is considered income in respect of a decedent under § 691 depends upon whether the decedent had a right to receive income at the time of his or her death. The focus is upon the decedent's right or entitlement to income at the time of death.

> Although it is pertinent to inquire whether the income received after death was attributable to activities and economic efforts of the decedent in his lifetime, these activities and efforts must give rise to a right to that income. And the right is to be distinguished from the activity which creates the right. Absent such a right, no matter how great the activities or efforts, there would be no taxable income under § 691.

Trust Co. v. Ross, 392 F.2d 694, 695 (5th Cir. 1967) (per curiam), *cert. denied*, 393 U.S. 830 (1968).

---

[7] As summarized in *Keck v. Commissioner*, 415 F.2d 531, 533 (6th Cir. 1969):

> Under the prior law, only the items which were accruable to a taxpayer at the time of his death were required to be included in the last return. This discriminated against accrual-basis taxpayers and allowed much income of cash-basis taxpayers to escape income tax. To correct this situation, Congress provided that in the case of both cash and accrual taxpayers, the last return must include all items accruable at death. The Supreme Court in *Helvering v. Enright*, 312 U.S. 636, . . . (1941), held that the term "accrual" in the statute was not to be construed narrowly in its accounting sense, but broadly to effectuate the purpose of the statute. However, such broad construction resulted in the bunching of income in the last return and its resultant taxation in higher surtax brackets.
>
> It was to remedy this situation that Congress enacted the forerunner of Section 691, . . . which provides that such income as was formerly required to be included in the last return, because it was accrued though not actually received, is taxable to the recipient and has the same character in his hands that it would have had in the hands of the decedent.

[8] As noted by the Tax Court, "[t]his arrangement may take a variety of forms: an express executory contract of sale [as in *Trust Co. v. Ross*, . . . 392 F.2d 694]; an implied contract for sale A delivers apples to Y, Y accepts the apples, A dies before Y can pay for them]; or a contractual arrangement with a cooperative marketing association [as in *Commissioner v. Linde*, . . . 213 F.2d 1 (no contract or sale, just delivery of grapes to marketing cooperative; proceeds held income in respect of a decedent when received)]." Estate of Peterson v. Commissioner, 74 T.C. 630, 639 (1980) (parentheticals substituted and expanded). *See also* Halliday v. United States, 655 F.2d 68, 72 (5th Cir. 1981) (the right to income need not be legally enforceable).

The leading commentators have proposed the following as a "tentative working definition" of income in respect of a decedent:

> Items of income in respect of a decedent . . . are payments received toward satisfaction of a right or expectancy created almost entirely through the efforts or status of the decedent and which, except for his death and without further action on his part, the decedent would have realized as gross income. Two observations should be made. First, the concept is manifestly broader than the mere accrued earnings of a cash basis decedent. Second, despite the breadth of this tentative definition, § 691 does not reach the income potential in a decedent's appreciated property, even if that appreciation is due to the decedent's own efforts. Further action on the decedent's part (*e.g.*, a sale) would have been required for such appreciation to be realized as income. Within this definition farm produce inventories grown, harvested, and processed for market, but not delivered by the decedent before his death, even though they come very close to representing ordinary income actually realized, are "property" rather than a bare right to income until they are sold. Not being income in respect of a decedent, they qualify for a new basis at death under the fair market value provision of § 1014(a).

M. Ferguson, J. Freeland & R. Stephens, Federal Income Taxation of Estates and Beneficiaries 146 (1970).

"The impact of § 691 may vary according to the nature or origin of the income. Such variation extends to questions of timing and characterization and even to the question whether a particular receipt must be treated as income in respect of a decedent at all." *Id.* at 162. For example, items of income attributable to the decedent's services are generally income in respect of a decedent.[9] Characterization of items of income attributable to sales proceeds, as in the present case, however, is less clear, particularly because of the operation of the basis rules of § 1014. *Id.* at 177–78.

. . .

As noted by Ferguson, Freeland and Stephens, "the definitional problem under § 691(a) is complicated by the general rule of § 1014(a) according a basis equal to estate tax value to the decedent's "property" other than such § 691(a) "rights." *Id.* at 180. As illustrated by the present case, the tax consequences of characterizing a particular item of income may be substantial. Ferguson, Freeland and Stephens apparently do not favor characterizing sales

---

[9] "The decedent's personal services are the most common source of IRD [income in respect of a decedent], including payment for the decedent's final pay period, compensation paid in installments continuing after his death, billed but uncollected fees and commissions, and accrued vacation and leave pay. Items attributable to the decedent's services but dependent on future events can also constitute IRD, such as an insurance agent's right to receive renewal commissions on life insurance policies sold by him, a lawyer's right to share in contingent fees received by his firm in cases that are uncompleted at the time of his death, and a bonus paid after an employee's death by an employer under a plan that did not vest enforceable rights in the employees. More controversial are cases holding that allowances paid by employers to the surviving spouse or other dependents of a faithful employee, if not excludable from gross income as 'gifts' or employee death benefits under IRC § 102 or § 101(b)(1), constitute IRD . . . ." 3 B. Bittker, Federal Taxation of Income, Estates and Gifts, *supra*, ¶ 83.1.2, at 83–5 to –6.

proceeds from sales transactions substantially "incomplete" at the time of the decedent's death as income in respect of a decedent:

> [W]here there is a contract of sale which would have been completed during the decedent's life but for his death, the proceeds received upon culmination of the sale by the decedent's transferee will be taxed as income in respect of a decedent if no substantial conditions remained to be performed by the decedent at his death. Thus, if the executor had only a passive or ministerial role to play in completing the sale, the proceeds should be taxed as income in respect of a decedent.
>
> Whenever the decedent negotiates a contract enforceable by his executor after death, the profit may properly be attributed to the decedent's bargaining and other efforts, which would seem to suggest income treatment for a part of the post-death receipts. On the other hand, the basis rules of § 1014(a) suggest that, wherever the risks inherent in ownership remain with the decedent until death, adjustments to the property's basis (and hence variations in the amount of gain or loss under the contract) remain possible until actual disposition by the decedent's successor.

Id. at 183–84.

Here, the task remaining to be performed by the estate was performance of the contract. We agree with the conclusion of the Tax Court that performance of the contract, which, under the circumstances, involved care and feeding of livestock and delivery, cannot be characterized as a ministerial or minor act. However, we think that characterization of the tasks which remain after the death of the decedent should not necessarily depend upon the nature of the subject matter of the sales transaction. For example, the subject matter of the sales transaction in the present case was livestock, which obviously required care and feeding. What if the subject matter was not livestock but logs or refrigerators? It would still be the task of the decedent's transferee to deliver or otherwise dispose of the logs or refrigerators, even though that type of property does not require the care that livestock does.

We recognize that the analysis followed by the Tax Court emphasizes delivery or disposal of the subject matter of the sales transaction and, to a certain degree, discounts the significance of the sales contract. Compare Gordon, *Income in Respect of a Decedent and Sales Transactions*, 1961 WASH. U. L. Q. 30, 37–38 (proposing that § 691 should apply to sales proceeds if the contract of sale is incomplete at death "only as to delivery of the res and receipt of the purchase price"). Nonetheless, this analysis is not inconsistent with *Trust Co. v. Ross, supra*, 392 F.2d at 697, where the contract of sale was executed and the stock was placed in escrow before the death of the decedent and the tasks remaining for the estate were "minor," and *Commissioner v. Linde, supra*, 213 F.2d at 4–8, where the decedent had delivered the property before death to the marketing cooperative, thus "converting" the property into a right to receive income. Moreover, "while the death of a decedent can be a fortuitous event tax-wise, it is certainly hard to visualize death as a tax avoidance scheme." Note, *Sales Transactions and Income in Respect of a*

Decedent, supra, 3 GA. L. REV. at 615. After all, the decedent in a sales case does not prearrange his death in order to shift the responsibility for delivering the subject matter of the sale transaction to his executor or to take advantage of the fair market value basis rule of § 1014(a) and thus avoid the reach of § 691.

Accordingly, the decision of the Tax Court is affirmed.

————

In *Estate of Napolitano v. Commissioner*, T.C. Memo. 1992–316, the court held that proceeds of a real estate sales contract, which closed after the decedent's death, were not IRD because the decedent, as of the date of his death, had not corrected certain housing authority violations as required by the contract of sale. According to the court, two conditions must be satisfied for the decedent to have a right to the proceeds from a contract of sale on the date of death. The decedent must have: (1) entered into a contract regarding the subject matter of his claim, and (2) performed the substantive (non-ministerial) acts required of him as a precondition to closing the sale. Citing *Estate of Peterson*, the court explained that the second requirement, which was not met, requires that the subject matter of the sale be in a deliverable state at the date of the decedent's death.

[2] Other IRD Items

The IRD classification arises with types of right to income other than contracts to sell property.

Estate of Riegelman v. Commissioner

253 F.2d 315 (2d Cir. 1958)

Waterman, Circuit Judge.

Petitioners, executors of the estate of Charles A. Riegelman, seek reversal of a decision of the Tax Court sustaining a deficiency assessed by the Commissioner in the estate tax reported by the executors. The sole issue is whether the gross estate of the deceased includes the value of the right of his estate to receive from a law partnership of which he had been a member certain payments which represented a share of post-death partnership income.

The relevant facts are not in dispute. Charles A. Riegelman on the date of his death, July 20, 1950, was the senior partner of the law firm of Riegelman, Strasser, Schwarz and Spiegelberg. The partnership owned no significant tangible property, though it did own nominal assets such as office furniture, fixtures, and a library. Decedent had not made any capital contributions to the partnership. The partnership agreement in effect at Riegelman's death provided that upon the death of a partner the partnership should not thereby be dissolved, but that the estate of the deceased partner should be entitled to receive specified payments. Specifically, these payments (as found by the Tax Court) consisted of

(i) The deceased partner's share of the undistributed profits realized and collected by the partnership prior to his death, plus his share of the profits realized and collected after his death which were attributable to work completed prior to his death, and

(ii) A share, for a specified period of time, of the post-death partnership fees and profits which were attributable to work completed after the deceased partner's death on matters in process at the date of his death and matters upon which work was commenced and completed after the date of his death.

The petitioners timely filed an estate tax return and included therein, as part of the gross estate, the value of the payments to which they were entitled under (i) above, and, in addition, the value of any further payments which they were entitled to receive for the work done during the lifetime of the decedent. They did not include as part of the gross estate the value of payments to be received by the estate for work done subsequent to Riegelman's death . . . .

The rationale underlying inclusion in the gross estate of the value of an estate's right to receive a portion of the income earned by a partnership subsequent to the death of a deceased partner has been adequately considered elsewhere and does not require an extended discussion here. *See McClennen v. Commissioner, 1 Cir., 1942*, 131 F.2d 165, . . . The right of Riegelman's estate to share in the profits of the partnership for the stipulated period after his death was a chose in action, in lieu of that to which it would have succeeded in the absence of an agreement, which passed from Riegelman to his estate as a part of his wealth and hence was properly includable in his gross estate for the purpose of computing an estate tax. *McClennen v. Commissioner, supra.*

The petitioners, however, rely upon *Bull v. United States, 1935*, 295 U.S. 247 as controlling authority for the proposition that the value of such payments is not subject to an estate tax unless capital was a material income-producing factor in the business conducted by the partnership or the deceased partner had made capital contributions to the partnership. The decedent there was a partner in a firm of shipbrokers, the business of which did not require the use of a significant amount of capital. The articles of partnership provided that upon the death of a partner his estate should have "the option of withdrawing his interest from the firm within thirty days after the probate of will" and that if it did not so elect "the survivors should continue the business for one year subsequent to his death, and his estate should 'receive the same interests, or participate in the losses to the same extent,' as the deceased partner would, if living," 295 U.S. 247, 251. Bull's executors did not exercise the option of withdrawing, and the business continued as contemplated by the agreement. The estate tax return filed by the executors included only the partnership profits earned prior to Bull's death; but, upon the assessment of a deficiency by the Commissioner, they paid an estate tax on the entire amount paid to Bull's estate by the partnership. Subsequently, the estate filed its income tax return and did not include therein the amounts received after Bull's death as post-death partnership income. The Commissioner determined that an income tax was payable on the amounts so received. The Court of

Claims sustained him, and rejected the estate's demand for refund of the estate tax on the ground that a refund was barred by the statute of limitations. On certiorari the Supreme Court sustained the Court of Claims as to the imposition of income tax, holding that since the firm had no capital assets the payments made to the estate could not constitute the purchase price of decedent's interest in the partnership—therefore the payments were income to the estate. In addition, the Court held the Commissioner erred by including in the decedent's gross estate the exact amount of the payments so received.

. . .

We think, however, that there is a . . . fundamental reason for holding *Bull* inapplicable to the case at bar. That decision was handed down in 1935 and involved estate tax liability accruing during the year 1920. During the intervening years Congress has enacted substantial changes in the Internal Revenue Code. We deem of particular importance § 134(e) of the Act of October 21, 1942, 56 Stat. 831, incorporated as [§ 691] of the Internal Revenue Code . . . Subsection (c) of . . . section [691] provides for a deduction of the portion of the estate tax attributable to inclusion in the estate of the right to receive such income. A reading of subsection (c) indicates that it contemplates that an estate tax is payable on the value for estate tax purposes of all the items described in subsection (a)(1). The question here, therefore, is whether the post-death partnership income received by Riegelman's estate constitutes "income in respect of a decedent," for it is clear that the right to receive these amounts was acquired by the estate from the decedent.

. . .

The payments were not gifts, nor were they attributable to anything done by Riegelman's estate. They were the fruits of the man's professional activity during his lifetime; and this is so whether the payments are considered to be in the nature of additional compensation for services performed by him during his lifetime or are considered to be in lieu of the chose in action to which his estate would have succeeded in the absence of a specific agreement. *See* Note, 65 HARV. L. REV. 1024 (1952).

Insofar as *Bull v. United States* is contrary to this conclusion, we think that it no longer states the applicable law. The decision of the Tax Court sustaining the deficiency assessed by the Commissioner is affirmed.

Estate of Cartwright v. Commissioner

183 F.3d 1034 (9th Cir. 1999)

SILVERMAN, Circuit Judge:

. . . .

FACTUAL AND PROCEDURAL BACKGROUND

In 1969 Cartwright and others incorporated CSB. Only CSB attorneys were shareholders. The firm distributed no dividends, but paid to each associate and shareholder a salary and distributed its profits as bonuses. CSB's shareholders determined the amounts of the yearly bonuses based on each attorney's contribution to the firm.

In a 1973 shareholders' agreement, CSB addressed what would happen to the interest of a shareholder upon his death. The agreement provided that CSB would purchase the deceased shareholder's interest in the firm and, in return, pay to the shareholder's surviving spouse or estate the following amounts: (1) the shareholder's actual purchase price for his CSB stock; (2) any earned but unpaid profits prior to death; (3) any earned but unpaid salary prior to death; (4) incurred but unreimbursed expenses or loans; (5) 25 percent of the net amount received after death for cases that the shareholder brought to CSB; (6) ten percent of the net amount received for cases pending at the date of death that came to the firm due to the firm name or the efforts of an associate; (7) 25 percent of the net amount received during the three years following the shareholder's death from cases for clients that the shareholder brought to the firm who provide continuing legal business; and (8) one-half of any life insurance proceeds from policies on the shareholder's life, to be applied toward the previous obligations.

In 1988 CSB amended the shareholders' agreement only as it related to the disposition of Cartwright's interest in the firm upon his death. The amendment recited that CSB had purchased two life insurance policies on Cartwright's life totaling $5,000,000. Pursuant to the amendment, CSB, the beneficiary under the polices, would use the proceeds upon Cartwright's death exclusively to purchase his interest in the firm. The precise language of the 1988 amendment, which is crucial to our decision, is as follows:

> In the event of the death of Robert E. Cartwright, the proceeds of said policies payable to the Corporation *will be exclusively used to purchase and acquire from the estate and heirs of Robert E. Cartwright all of Mr. Cartwright's stock in the Corporation together with any claim to any cases or work in process that may otherwise be made on behalf of Robert E. Cartwright.* In this regard, the Corporation agrees to buy all of said stock and Robert E. Cartwright agrees to sell it. The value of said stock and claim in said cases and work in process is hereby fixed as the amount of proceeds of said life insurance policies. Any amounts owed to Mr. Cartwright for unpaid salary or expenses will be additionally paid or reimbursed to his Estate . . . . [emphasis added]

Cartwright died on June 30, 1988, the owner of 71.43 percent of the outstanding shares of CSB. As the shareholders had agreed, CSB paid the proceeds that it received from the two policies to Cartwright's estate. The total amount was $5,062,029, which included $62,029 in premium adjustments and interest. CSB issued a Form 1099-MISC, stating that it had paid $4,080,256 to the estate as non-employee compensation. The estate, however, did not report the proceeds it received from CSB as taxable income in its fiduciary income tax return. Instead, it took the position that the full amount of the proceeds were paid to redeem Cartwright's stock. The IRS disagreed, finding that $4,080,256 of the $5,062,029 was compensation and that the estate owed $1,142,472 for its tax deficiency.

Cartwright's estate appealed to the tax court. The court held that the plain language of the 1988 amendment made clear that CSB's payment of the insurance proceeds to Cartwright's estate was for both Cartwright's stock and for his claim to the firm's cases or work in process. It found that the amendment valued the total of these items at $5,000,000.

The tax court also concluded that neither CSB's work in process nor the insurance proceeds, which CSB paid directly to the estate, should have been considered an asset of CSB for purposes of valuing Cartwright's stock. Similarly, the court determined that the IRS's exclusion of advanced client costs in appraising CSB's assets was proper. Finding that the value of Cartwright's stock was $1,105,762, the court concluded that the other $3,956,267 of the payment to the estate was taxable as income in respect of a decedent.

DISCUSSION

We review decisions of the United States Tax Court on the same basis as decisions of a district court in a civil bench trial. *Delk v. Commissioner of Internal Revenue,* 113 F.3d 984, 986 (9th Cir.1997). Thus, we review the tax court's interpretation of contract provisions de novo. *Confederated Tribes of Siletz Indians v. Oregon,* 143 F.3d 481, 484 (9th Cir.1998). We review its determination of the value of stock for clear error. *Trust Servs. of Am., Inc. v. United States,* 885 F.2d 561, 568 (9th Cir.1989).

I.

The first issue for decision is whether the payment to Cartwright's estate was made solely to redeem Cartwright's stock or whether it was for *both* Cartwright's stock *and* his claim to the firm's cases or work in process. The estate contends that extrinsic evidence established an intent merely to buy out Cartwright's shares in the firm and that the 1988 amendment set the stock redemption value at $5,000,000. It argues that because the corporation, and not any individual shareholder, owns CSB's cases and work in process, Cartwright could have no interest in these items other than in his capacity as a shareholder. The tax court held that both the language of the amendment and the surrounding circumstances evidenced an intent to purchase more than Cartwright's shares.

We agree with the tax court. As the plain language of the 1988 amendment explicitly provides, CSB's distribution of the insurance proceeds to Cartwright's estate constituted payment for both "Mr. Cartwright's stock together with any claim to any cases or work in process." This unambiguous language reflects what Cartwright and his colleagues understood when drafting it—that Cartwright, at the time of his death, would have or might have an interest in the firm's "cases or work in process" that the firm agreed to buy out. The uncontradicted evidence of the firm's practices supports this conclusion as well. The primary component of Cartwright's compensation was not his salary. It was his bonus, paid at the end of each year based on his contribution to the firm. As the firm's majority shareholder, chairman of the board, and chief rainmaker, Cartwright, at the time of his death, had a reasonable expectation that he again would be voted a bonus for the cases that he had brought into the firm or had worked on himself.

The tax court correctly distinguished other cases in which payments made to a shareholder or his estate were held to redeem only the shareholder's stock. In *Smith v. Commissioner of Internal Revenue,* 82 T.C. 705, 1984 WL 15567 (1984), the evidence demonstrated an intent to enter into a stock purchase agreement and that the $25,000 payment was equivalent to the fair market value of the stock. Similarly, in *Steffen v. Commissioner of Internal Revenue,* 69 T.C. 1049, 1978 WL 3394 (1978), the language of a corporate redemption agreement conclusively established that the $40,000 paid to a shareholder was solely for his stock and was not compensation. In *Estate of Bette v. Commissioner of Internal Revenue,* 36 T.C.M. (CCH) 1636 (1977), the tax court relied on the clear terms of a stock redemption agreement. Finally, *Erickson v. Commissioner of Internal Revenue,* 56 T.C. 1112, 1971 WL 2470 (1971), also involved an unambiguous agreement providing only for the purchase of stock. In the instant case, both the clear language of the 1988 amendment and the underlying facts compel the conclusion that the parties intended that CSB buy out more than just Cartwright's shares of CSB stock. Any claims to work in process were included in the purchase price. [Footnote omitted]

II.

Having determined that the insurance proceeds constituted payment for both Cartwright's stock and his claim to cases or work in process, we must now decide whether the tax court correctly apportioned the payment between these two components. After hearing conflicting expert testimony from witnesses called by both parties, the court adopted the findings of the IRS's expert, who relied upon the 1973 agreement and its 1988 amendment in ascertaining the intent of the parties.

The estate argues that, even if the proceeds redeemed Cartwright's stock plus his claim to cases or work in process, the court made three errors in its valuation of his stock: (1) it failed to consider the effect of CSB's advanced client costs, (2) it ignored CSB's work in process on its contingent fee cases, and (3) it should have included the insurance proceeds as a nonoperating asset of CSB.

The estate is correct that the tax court should have included advanced client costs, which CSB maintained as a negative asset account, among the firm's assets, because they properly are treated as loans. *See Canelo v. Commissioner of Internal Revenue,* 447 F.2d 484, 485 (9th Cir. 1971). The tax court also should have included the firm's work in process on contingent fee cases as an asset, since it would have influenced what a willing buyer would have paid for CSB stock. *See Estate of James E. Curry v. Commissioner of Internal Revenue,* 74 T.C. 540, 546–47, 1980 WL 4454 (1980).

The tax court did not err, however, by not including the life insurance proceeds as an asset of the firm for stock valuation purposes. It is true that in valuing stock, "consideration shall also be given to nonoperating assets, including proceeds of life insurance policies payable to or for the benefit of the company, to the extent such nonoperating assets have not been taken into account in the determination of net worth, prospective earning power and dividend-earning capacity." 26 C.F.R. § 20.2031-2(f)(2). The court, however, properly determined that CSB's insurance policy would not necessarily affect what a willing buyer would pay for the firm's stock because it was offset dollar-for-dollar by CSB's obligation to pay out the entirety of the policy benefits to Cartwright's estate. *See Estate of John L. Huntsman v. Commissioner of Internal Revenue,* 66 T.C. 861, 875, 1976 WL 3635 (1976).

CONCLUSION

The tax court correctly determined that CSB's payment of life insurance proceeds to Cartwright's estate redeemed both Cartwright's stock and his claim to the firm's cases or work in process. The unambiguous language of the 1988 amendment and an understanding of CSB's practices compel this conclusion. The court erred, however, in calculating what portion of the proceeds was for Cartwright's stock and what portion was for his claim to cases or work in process. We remand to the tax court for a redetermination of the value of the stock to take into account advanced client costs and work in process. We affirm in all other respects.

AFFIRMED IN PART AND REMANDED.

THOMAS, Circuit Judge, concurring in part and dissenting in part:

[dissenting opinion omitted]

———

Section 706(c)(2) closes a partnership's tax year with respect to a partner who dies during the year. The result of this rule is to include on the partner's final income return the deceased partner's portion of the partnership income earned before the partner died. Section 1366(a)(1) provides a similar rule for shareholders of S corporations. The effect of these rules is to eliminate an estate from having IRD as a result of the decedent being a partner or S corporation shareholder.

———

Problems

1. *Estate of Riegelman* suggests that payments which constitute income in respect of a decedent are necessarily subject to estate tax. Do you agree?

2. The decedent died owning the following assets. Which are IRD items and why?

a. IRA valued at $100,000 and payable to the decedent's surviving spouse.

b. Stock in a closely held business subject to a mandatory buy-sell agreement.

c. A $50,000 payment to the decedent's surviving spouse under a death benefit only plan similar to the one described in *Estate of DiMarco v. Commissioner,* 87 T.C. 653 (1986), reproduced in § 4.01[A][2], *supra*.

d. The decedent was the beneficiary of a QTIP trust established by the decedent's spouse.[10] The trust made distributions at the end of each calendar quarter. The decedent died on May 15th. The trust earned $30,000 in the second quarter and thus, distributed one-half of the quarterly income ($15,000) to the decedent's estate.

e. What if the *stub* income in (d) were payable to the remainder beneficiaries of the QTIP trusts? What if the trust instrument was silent about the distribution of income earned during the quarter in which the decedent died?

3. The decedent owned Series EE US Savings bonds, but had not elected to accrue interest in income. *See* § 454. What will be the effect if the personal representative elects to *cash in* the bonds? *See* Rev. Rul. 64–104, 1964–1 C.B. (Part 1) 223.

4. At the end of each month, *D* is paid wages earned during the month. He is a cash basis taxpayer using calendar year accounting. *D* works two weeks in February before he dies. On the last day of February, his employer pays his estate for the February work. How is the February payment reportable for income and estate tax purposes?

5. Decedent owns Blackacre, which he purchased for $125,000, and which is worth $150,000 when he dies.

a. What are the income tax consequences of the sale if the personal representative sells the land for $200,000 eight months after decedent's death?

b. Assume that four months before his death the decedent contracted to sell Blackacre to *X* for $150,000, with the closing to be one year after the contract date. Assume further that the contract was binding on the decedent's personal representative. What would be the estate and income tax consequences of the contract and sale?

c. Assume that in (b), the personal representative distributed Blackacre to the residuary legatee before the closing and the legatee closed on the contract. What would be the income tax consequence?

d. In (c), could the estate avoid the adverse income tax consequences by selling the property to a third party subject to the outstanding contract? Consider § 691(a)(2).

6. Alice was a partner in the *ABCD* law firm, a service partnership in which capital is not a factor in the production of income. Alice died on March 1. At the time of her death, she was entitled to $24,000 of profits earned during the two months before her death. The $24,000 had not been distributed to Alice. Her estate received the payment on March 15th. How is the $24,000 treated for estate and income tax purposes?

7. In Problem 6, assume that the partners in the law firm had entered into a partnership agreement. The agreement provided that, upon the death of any partner, the remaining partners would be entitled to continue the practice of law under the firm name and would be entitled to the assets of the firm. However, the remaining partners would be obligated to pay to the estate of

---

[10] *See* § 3.04[C][4][c] (discussing QTIP trusts).

the deceased partner one-quarter of the firm's net profits for one year after the partner's death. Under this agreement, Alice's estate received an additional $200,000, which represented one-quarter of the firm's profits for the one year period after her death. How is this sum treated for estate and income tax purposes?

[B]   Deductions in Respect of Decedents

Code: § 691(b).

Regulations: Treas. Reg. § 1.691(b)–1.

Paralleling the taxation of income in respect of a decedent, § 691(b) also allows an estate and beneficiaries to claim some deductions which the decedent could have claimed had he lived. These deductions are commonly called *deductions in respect of a decedent* (DRD).

The deductions subject to § 691(b) are limited to trade or business expenses deductible under § 162, interest deductible under § 163, taxes deductible under § 164, investment and other expenses deductible under § 212, and depletion deductions allowable under § 611.[11] Moreover, the deductions must exist at the time of the decedent's death. For example, interest on a decedent's loan that has accrued as of the date of death is subject to § 691(b), but the interest on the same loan accruing after death is not. Property taxes due at the time of death are § 691(b) deductions, but taxes arising after the date of death are not.

The depletion deduction is available to the person receiving the depletion income in respect of a decedent. *See* § 691(b)(2). Other expenses, interest, and taxes are deemed to be deductible by the estate, or the person who is liable for their payment. *See* § 691(b)(1).

A positive consequence of being classified as a § 691(b) deduction is that the double deduction disallowance rule of § 642(g) is not applicable. *See* § 642(g) (last sentence).

[C]   Section 691(c) Deduction

Code: § 691(c).

Regulations: Treas. Reg. § 1.691(c)–1.

As *Riegelman, supra*, illustrates, if IRD items are assets in the gross estate of the decedent for tax purposes, they generate estate tax consequences as well as income tax. To reduce the impact of applying two taxes to the IRD item, the recipient of items of income in respect of a decedent is entitled to deduct from IRD income the portion of the decedent's federal estate tax attributable to the IRD's inclusion in the decedent's gross estate. *See* § 691(c).

Treasury Regulation § 1.691(c)-1(a) provides guidance on how the deduction is computed:

> (1) Ascertain the net value in the decedent's estate of the items which are included under section 691 in computing gross income.

---

[11] The foreign tax credit permitted under § 27 is also subject to § 691(b).

This is the excess of the value included in the gross estate on account of the items of gross income in respect of the decedent (see § 1.691(a)-1 and paragraph (c) of this section) over the deductions from the gross estate for claims which represent the deductions and credit in respect of the decedent (see § 1.691(b)-1). . .

(2) Ascertain the portion of the estate tax attributable to the inclusion in the gross estate of such net value. This is the excess of the estate tax over the estate tax computed without including such net value in the gross estate. In computing the estate tax without including such net value in the gross estate, any estate tax deduction (such as the marital deduction) which may be based upon the gross estate shall be recomputed so as to take into account the exclusion of such net value from the gross estate.

The net effect of the Regulation computation is to compute the estate taxes attributable to the net IRD items at the marginal estate tax rate. Determining the estate tax on the reduced hypothetical estate can be complex when the estate is entitled to a marital or charitable deduction based on a formula or residuary devise. Taxpayers and the Service have argued over the amount of § 691(c) deduction for the reduced estate. *See Estate of Kincaid v. Commissioner*, 85 T.C. 25 (1985); *Chastain v. Commissioner*, 59 T.C. 461 (1972).

In *Estate of Cherry v. United States*, 133 F.Supp. 2d 949 (W.D. Ky. 2001), the court concluded:

[T]he purpose of Section 691 deduction is to diminish the tendency toward double taxation by allowing a deduction from income tax for the portion of the estate tax fairly attributable to the presence of the IRD in the estate. The logical way to accomplish this goal is first to calculate the estate tax on the entire amount (including therein the ordinary consideration of marital share), and then to begin the recomputation by removing the IRD before proceeding in the customary fashion (including therein a *recomputation* of the marital share). [emphasis in original]

An example (applying *Cherry*) illustrates the computation.

Example 1: In 2002, *D* died with a gross estate of $4.2 million and a net estate (before deducting the marital devise) of $4 million. The estate included $1.2 million specific devise to *D*'s child, that was not charged with the payment of estate taxes. The balance of the estate, after the payment of estate taxes, was devised to the decedent's surviving spouse. Among the estate assets was an IRA valued for estate tax purposes at $1.2 million that was payable to the surviving spouse. All of the estate's $200,000 in debts were § 691(b) deductions in respect of a decedent. Thus, the § 691(c) net value amount was $1 million.[12]

The total estate taxes for D's estate are $142,105 ($101,384 federal tax and $40,721 of state estate tax based on the maximum credit permitted by § 2011 in 2002). The amount of the residue, *i.e.*, the marital devise is $2,657,895 ($2.8

---

[12] Section 691(c)(B) provides that the net amount for § 691(c) purposes is the value of the § 691(a) items less the § 691(b) deductions.

million less $142,105). The reduced estate is $3 million ($4 million less $1 million net § 691(c) amount). Because the residue marital devise is still charged with taxes, the marital is reduced to $1,657,895. This result occurs because the pre-residuary devises are still entitled to $1.2 million which leaves only $1.8 million to pay taxes and fund the marital devise. Thus, in this hypothetical there is no § 691(c) deduction because the reduced estate does not pay a smaller tax. All of the IRD items are being attributed to the marital devise.

The § 691(c) computation changes dramatically if the IRA designates someone other than the estate or the surviving spouse as beneficiary.

Example 2: Assume the same facts as Example 1 except *D*'s will leaves the entire estate to the surviving spouse and the estate is still chargeable with the payment of estate taxes. The only non-marital deduction gift is the IRA is now payable to *D*'s child.

The total estate taxes for *D*'s estate is still $142,105. The reduced estate is $3 million ($4 million less $1 million of net § 691(c) amount). Because the estate no longer includes any devises to someone other than the surviving spouse, the hypothetical estate is now -0-. Thus, the § 691(c) deduction is $101,384 (the amount paid in state death taxes does not qualify for the § 691(c) deduction). *See* § 691(c)(2)(A). When *D*'s child reports the IRA in income, the child will be entitled to an income tax deduction of $101,384.

The § 691(c) deduction is not subject to the 2% rule of § 67. *See* § 67(b)(8).

Problem

The decedent died in 2002, with a gross estate of $1.2 million and a taxable estate of $1,150,000. Included in the estate was an installment note valued for estate tax purposes at $100,000. The income tax basis in the decedent's hands equaled zero. The decedent's final paycheck (undelivered at death) was valued at $10,000. One of the deductible estate expenses was $10,000 of accrued interest on a loan that was outstanding at the time of the decedent's death. Assume that the $100,000 installment note is specially devised to the decedent's daughter, *D*, and she collects the note in 2003. What is the amount of gross income the daughter must report? What is the amount of the § 691(c) deduction?

§ 14.03 Fiduciary Accounting

Code: § 643(b)

Regulations: Proposed Treas. Reg. § 1.643(b)-1

State Law: Applicable Principal and Income Act assigned by instructor.

An integral part of taxing the income of estates and trusts is a determination of fiduciary accounting income and principal. Indeed, the Code's scheme for taxing trusts, estates, and beneficiaries specifically relies on the definition of income as prescribed under applicable state fiduciary accounting rules. The following provides a brief overview. [13]

[A] The Relationship Between Subchapter J Taxation and Traditional State Income and Principal Fiduciary Accounting Rules

Section 643(b) generally adopts state fiduciary accounting rules as the benchmark for determining what is "income" for Subchapter J purposes. In turn, Treasury Regulation § 1.643-1(b) requires that trust provisions defining income which fundamentally depart from the applicable state law concepts of principal and income be disregarded. Thus, a general understanding of fiduciary accounting principles is essential. The following provides a brief overview of the traditional state rules for determining principal and income.

Uniform Laws

The National Conference of Commissioners on Uniform State Laws (NCC-USL) has promulgated three pertinent acts. In 1931, NCCUSL adopted the original Uniform Principal and Income Act and it is the law of fiduciary accounting in only two states. The Commissioners revised the original Act and adopted the Revised Uniform Principal and Income Act in 1962 (hereinafter the "1962 Act"). The 1962 Act is the law in approximately 20 states. A third version of the Uniform Principal and Income Act—Uniform Principal and Income Act (hereinafter the "1997 Act")—was approved in 1997, and is the law in at least 25 states. *See generally* E. James Gamble, *If It's the 1990s, It Must Be Time For Another Principal and Income Act*, 32 INST. ON EST. PLAN. 8.1-.80 (1998). The remaining states either do not have statutory rules for fiduciary accounting or have statutory rules that are not based on any of the Uniform Acts. Many of the rules of the 1962 Act are applicable only to estates. The 1997 Act extends many of the estate rules to revocable trusts. The change reflects the growing popularity of revocable trusts: many testators are choosing to avoid probate and estate administration by creating and funding revocable trusts before dying. Because of the predominance of the 1962 Act and the 1997 Act, this discussion will focus on the provisions of these two Acts (hereinafter the "Acts").

The Acts define principal and income. *See* 1962 Act § 3, 1997 Act § 102. For example, they provide that receipts which are due at a decedent's death are classified as principal. *See* 1962 Act § 4(b)(1), 1997 Act § 302(a). The 1962 Act provides that unpaid items from periodic payments of income, such as rent or interest, are prorated on a daily basis. *See* 1962 Act § 4(b)(2). All other receipts from income producing property are income if received after a decedent's death. *See* 1962 Act § 4(c). The 1997 Act § 302(b) changes this rule to provide that income that periodically accrues is not income if the income interest terminates between payments. Only payments that do not have either a due date or periodic due date accrue ratably. The Comments to 1997 Act

---

[13] Discussion of 1962 Act is adapted from F. Ladson Boyle, *Fiduciary Accounting Basics*, 1 PROB. PRAC. REP. 8 (Aug. 1989). For additional discussion of 1962 Act, see Dave L. Cornfeld, *It's the Principal of the Thing: Fiduciary Accounting Problems*, 22 U. MIAMI INST. ON EST. PLAN. 16–1 (1988).

§ 302 provide examples of each exception. Interest on a tax refund does not have a due date and zero coupon bonds do not have periodic due dates.

Both the 1962 Act and the 1997 Act provide that an income beneficiary of a trust is entitled to income as soon as the trust receives an asset. *See* 1962 Act § 4(a), 1997 Act § 301. If assets are to pass to a trust from an estate, the trust income beneficiary is entitled to the income as of the death of the testator. *See* 1962 Act § 4(a), 1997 Act § 301. Income in respect of a decedent is generally fiduciary accounting principal as are capital gains realized on the disposition of trust principal. *See* 1962 Act § 4, 1997 Act § 302.

Unproductive and Underproductive Property

Section 12 of the 1962 Act (as well as § 11 of the original Act) provides an unproductive and underproductive property rule. If an asset does not produce at least an average of 1% net income for more than a year, then upon the sale of the asset, a portion of the proceeds are classified as income and not principal. The 1962 Act provides for 4% imputed income if the section applies (the original Act imputes 5%). The 1997 Act deletes the unproductive property rule by incorporating the Uniform Prudent Investor Act and its rule that a trustee's management of investments should consider collectively all assets and not any one asset in isolation. *See* 1997 Act § 413. In the alternative, 1997 Act § 104(a) grants a trustee the power to make adjustments between principal and income.

Income from a Business

Section 8 of the 1962 Act provides that income from a sole proprietorship or partnership of a decedent is estate income. Nevertheless, losses from either of these enterprises are charged to principal and are not carried forward to determine net income in a future year. On the other hand, generally accepted accounting principles are used to determine income and principal allocations from a farm operation. Finally, timber sales are classified as either income or principal using the reasonable and equitable standard that persons of ordinary prudence, discretion, and judgment would determine, as provided in § 2(a)(3). (*See* Rev. Rul. 85–116, at § 14.05[D][1], *infra*, for an example of when § 8 applies.) The 1997 Act provides that cash receipts from a business are generally income, unless one of the exceptions apply. *See* 1997 Act § 401(b). Partnership distributions are categorized in a manner similar to corporate distributions. For timber receipts, § 412 of the 1997 Act provides more specific instructions to a trustee on how to account for sales of timber and related products.

Wasting Assets

The 1962 Act contains special provisions for wasting assets. Section 9 provides that a reserve of 27½% of gross receipts, not to exceed 50% of net income, is maintained out of royalties from natural resources; the balance is income. The 1997 Act abandons the 27½/50% rule and provides instead that 10% of receipts from natural resources are income and the balance are principal. *See* 1997 Act § 411. For other wasting assets such as patents, copyrights, and leaseholds, the income beneficiary is entitled to a payment equal to 5% of the *inventory value* of the asset, as defined in 1962 Act. *See* 1962 Act § 11. The balance is principal. The 1997 Act abandons the 5% of inventory rule and provides instead that 10% of receipts from a wasting asset is income and the balance is principal. *See* 1997 Act § 410(b).

Other Issues

Section 6 of the 1962 Act contains extensive rules governing distributions by corporations. Generally, corporate distributions are income, but stock dividends and distributions that are a result of mergers or partial or complete liquidations are principal. The 1997 Act provides similar rules. *See* 1997 Act § 401.

Section 505 of the 1997 Act addresses the income tax issues that arise when a trust or estate owns an interest in a partnership or S corporation. The 1962 Act contained no guidance. The 1997 Act also provides guidance for modern investments such as derivatives, options, asset-backed securities, annuities, deferred compensation agreements, and other nontraditional investments. *See* 1997 Act §§ 414, 415.

Expenses

Section 5 of the 1962 Act provides that all estate administration expenses, including taxes, funeral expenses, debts, and attorneys' fees are paid out of principal. Similarly, compensation for the personal representative is paid out of the principal of the estate. Trustee commissions, however, are paid one-half from principal and one-half from income. *See* § 13. Of course, all of these rules may be modified by the governing document. The 1997 Act grants a personal representative discretion to pay estate expenses from either income or principal. *See* 1997 Act § 201(2)(B). Debts of the decedent, funeral expenses, taxes and penalties are still charged to principal, however. *See* 1997 Act § 201(2)(C). Trustees of revocable trusts that are probate estate substitutes are granted the same discretion.

Although ordinary expenses of an estate are charged to principal under the 1962 Act, ordinary expenses of administering a trust are charged against income. This does not include all trust expenses, however. For example, trustee fees, legal fees, and court costs are charged one-half to income and one-half to principal. Charges to invest the principal of a trust are charged to principal, not income. Under both Acts, taxes on ordinary income are charged to income, but capital gains taxes are charged to principal. *See* 1962 Act § 13 and 1997 Act § 505. And to the surprise of many, the 1962 Act requires a trustee to maintain, out of income, a depreciation reserve for property subject to depreciation under generally accepted accounting principles, unless the governing instrument provides otherwise. *See* 1962 Act § 13(a)(2). 1997 Act § 501 provides that trustee fees, investment advisory fees, costs of accountings, and judicial costs are charged half to income and half to principal. All other ordinary expenses, including insurance premiums, are charged fully to income. In addition, the 1997 Act makes a depreciation reserve optional in the trustee's discretion. *See* 1997 Act § 503(b).

[B] The Relationship Between Subchapter J Taxation and New Trust Paradigms

[1] In General

As explained in the following excerpt from Proposed Treasury Regulation § 1.643(b)(1), the Service has responded favorably to new state law developments based on the trustee's power to adjust and the unitrust paradigm:

Background

Section 643(b) provides a definition of the term income for purposes of subparts A through D of part I of subchapter J of the Internal Revenue Code (Code). The term income, when not modified by any other term, means the amount of income of the trust or estate determined under the terms of the governing instrument and applicable local law. Section 1.643(b)-1 further provides that trust provisions that depart fundamentally from the concepts of local law in determining what constitutes income will not be recognized.

These statutory and regulatory provisions date back to a time when, under state statutes, dividends and interest were considered income and were allocated to the income beneficiary while capital gains were allocated to the principal of the trust. Changes in the types of available investments and in investment philosophies have caused states to revise, or to consider revising, these traditional concepts of income and principal.

The prudent investor standard for managing trust assets has been enacted by many states and encourages fiduciaries to adopt an investment strategy designed to maximize the total return on trust assets. Under this investment strategy, trust assets should be invested for total positive return, that is, ordinary income plus appreciation, in order to maximize the value of the trust. Thus, under certain economic circumstances, equities, rather than bonds, would constitute a greater portion of the trust assets than they would under traditional investment standards.

One of the concerns with shifting trust investments toward equities and away from bonds is the potential adverse impact on the income beneficiary. Based on the traditional concepts of income and principal, the income beneficiary is entitled only to the dividends and interest earned by the trust assets. The dividend return on equities as a percentage of their value traditionally has been substantially less than the interest return on bonds.

To ensure that the income beneficiary is not penalized if a trustee adopts a total return investment strategy, many states have made, or are considering making, revisions to the definitions of income and principal. Some state statutes permit the trustee to make an equitable adjustment between income and principal if necessary to ensure that both the income beneficiary and the remainder beneficiary are treated impartially, based on what is fair and reasonable to all of the beneficiaries. Thus, a receipt of capital gains that previously would have been allocated to principal may be allocated by the trustee to income if necessary to treat both parties impartially. Conversely, a receipt of dividends or interest that previously would have been allocated to income may be allocated by the trustee to principal if necessary to treat both parties impartially.

Other states are proposing legislation that would allow the trustee to pay a unitrust amount to the income beneficiary in satisfaction of that beneficiary's right to the income from the trust. This unitrust amount will be a fixed percentage, sometimes required to be within a range set by state statute, of the fair market value of the trust assets determined annually.

Questions have arisen concerning how these state statutory changes affect the definition of income provided in section 643(b) and the other Code provisions that rely on the section 643(b) definition of income.

Explanation of provisions

Definition of Income

The proposed regulations will amend the definition of income under section 1.643(b)-1 to take into account certain state statutory changes to the concepts of income and principal. Under the proposed regulations, trust provisions that depart fundamentally from traditional concepts of income and principal (that is, allocating ordinary income to income and capital gains to principal) will generally continue to be disregarded, as they are under the current regulations. However, amounts allocated between income and principal pursuant to applicable state law will be respected if state law provides for a reasonable apportionment between the income and remainder beneficiaries of the total return of the trust for the year, taking into account ordinary income, capital gains, and, in some situations, unrealized appreciation. For example, a state law that provides for the income beneficiary to receive each year a unitrust amount of between 3% and 5% of the annual fair market value of the trust assets is a reasonable apportionment of the total return of the trust. Similarly, a state law that permits the trustee to make equitable adjustments between income and principal to fulfill the trustee's duty of impartiality between the income and remainder beneficiaries is a reasonable apportionment of the total return of the trust.

In addition, an allocation of capital gains to income will be respected under certain circumstances. Such an allocation will be respected if directed by the terms of the governing instrument and applicable local law. Similarly, if a trustee, pursuant to a discretionary power granted to the trustee by local law or by the governing instrument (if not inconsistent with local law), allocates capital gains to income, the allocation will be respected, provided the power is exercised in a reasonable and consistent manner.

The proposed changes to the regulations will permit trustees to implement a total return investment strategy and to follow the applicable state statutes designed to treat the income and remainder beneficiaries impartially. At the same time, the limitations imposed by the proposed regulations ensure that the Code provisions relying on the definition of income under section 643(b) are not undermined by an unlimited ability of the trustee to allocate between income and principal.

Supplementary Information for Proposed Treasury Regulations redefining income, 66 F.R. 10396, 10396–10397 (Feb. 15, 2001).

[C] Tax Accounting vs. Fiduciary Accounting

Although Subchapter J generally relies on fiduciary accounting principles under state law to determine what constitutes "income," defined income is not the ultimate determinant for taxation under Subchapter J. In other words, what constitutes state law "income" does not necessarily determine what is taxable. The most significant difference involves the treatment of capital gains. As seen in the above discussion, capital gains are generally allocable to principal for traditional fiduciary accounting purposes. On the other hand, capital gains are treated as gross income for fiduciary income tax purposes. As will be seen in the next section, this difference can dramatically affect to whom capital gains are taxable, especially in the context of trusts.

Another difference involves the treatment of estate expenses. Under the 1962 Act estate expenses are a fiduciary charge to principal for fiduciary accounting purposes and the 1997 Act grants the fiduciary discretion to charge estate expenses to income or principal (but debts and taxes remain a charge to principal). *See* 1962 Act § 5, 1997 Act § 201(2). However, for federal tax purposes estate expenses may be deducted on the estate tax return or the income tax return, but not both (unless permitted by § 691(b)). To claim the income tax deduction, the personal representative, pursuant to § 642(g), must elect to forgo the estate tax deduction in favor of the income tax deduction. This election is discussed in § 14.04[B] [4], *infra*.

Estate Income

Although the Code permits the personal representative to deduct the administration expenses against the estate's income, the 1962 Act does not (the 1997 Act grants discretion to charge to either income or principal). The right to estate income is determined by state law (the applicable principal and income law). Specific devisees are entitled to the net income generated by the devised property. *See* 1962 Act § 5(b); 1997 Act § 201-202. Except for pecuniary bequests *not in trust*, the remaining net estate income is distributable among all other beneficiaries in proportion to their undistributed interests in the estate. According to the 1962 Act, pecuniary devises not in trust provided for under a will are not entitled to any estate income. Section 201(3) of the 1997 Act provides that an outright pecuniary amount provided for in a decedent's will is entitled to interest or such other amount provided by state law, but like the 1962 Act, not a share of estate income. Section 201(3) of the 1997 Act, unlike the 1962 Act, makes a similar provision for pecuniary amounts due from trusts, *i.e.*, a pecuniary amount provided for in a revocable trust is treated the same as an outright devise in a will. Both Acts permit pecuniary devises to share in income. *See* 1962 Act § 5(b); 1997 Act § 201(4).

The Uniform Probate Code (UPC) remedies the failure to give any portion of estate income to pecuniary bequests *not in trust.* UPC § 3–904 provides that all pecuniary bequests, including bequests in trust, earn interest beginning one year after the appointment of the personal representative, unless the will provides otherwise. Thus, the pecuniary bequest not in trust receives interest at the legal rate under applicable state law.[14]

Statutory Inconsistency

Close examination of the UPC provision for pecuniary bequests and the provisions of both the 1962 Act and the 1997 Act reveal an overlap. The UPC provision applies to all pecuniary bequests, even those in trust. Both Principal and Income Acts except from the share of income rule only pecuniary bequests not in trust. Thus, a pecuniary bequest in trust seems to be entitled to interest and a share of income. This duplication appears to be an error. The editor's comment to the UPC provision indicates that the UPC provision is consistent with the 1962 Act, although it is not. For states that have adopted the UPC and 1962 Act or 1997 Act provisions, it is not clear whether a pecuniary bequest in trust is entitled to interest, a share of estate income, or both. In his book, MARITAL DEDUCTION PLANNING AND CREDIT SHELTER DISPOSITIONS AND THE USE OF FORMULA PROVISIONS, at 68 (4th Edition 1997), Richard Covey suggests that if both statutes are applicable, only pecuniary bequests not in trust should receive interest.

Finally, rather than relying on state law, a document may specify that a pecuniary bequest is entitled to either interest or a share of income. In his book, Covey suggests that documents provide that all pecuniary marital bequests receive interest at 5%. Although this is permissible, a drafter should not provide that a marital bequest receives no interest. This may affect the marital deduction. *See* Treas. Reg. §§ 20.2056(b)–5(f)(9), 20.2056(b)–4(a).

Problems

1. The testator's will provided that the residue of the estate is to be held in a marital deduction trust. The surviving spouse was to receive all trust income at least annually. The testator died in 2002. The trust was not funded until 2004. The testator's surviving spouse demanded distribution of the net trust income retroactive to the date of the testator's death. As of what date is the spouse entitled to the trust income? Why?

2. The decedent's will created a QTIP trust for the benefit of the decedent's second spouse. After the second spouse dies, all of the trust assets are distributable to the decedent's children from the decedent's first marriage. At the time of the decedent's death, his estate included the following assets which were eventually distributed to the marital trust:

---

[14] Treas. Reg. § 1.663(c)-5, Example 7 declares that interest on a pecuniary devise is not deductible for federal income tax purposes. Section 163 permits an interest deduction only for business interest, investment interest, and qualified home mortgage interest. The interest on the pecuniary devise is none of these.

a. A patent valid for 15 more years valued at $50,000. After the decedent's death, Microsoft bought a license for the patent. Annual royalties payable to the trust are $100,000. What portion of the $100,000 is principal and what is income and why?

b. Stock in closely held business X valued at $4 million on the estate tax return filed for the decedent's estate. The corporation had a Subchapter S election in place when the decedent died and it has been retained by the estate and marital trust. X was in two equally valuable lines of business, but recently sold one line for $5 million. Because of corporate tax rules, X must distribute the net sales proceeds to its shareholder, the trust. Is the receipt income or principal?

c. A one-year certificate of deposit due December 31 of the year of death. (Assume decedent died on June 30.) When the certificate matured, it paid $6,000 interest and returned the decedent's $100,000. How much of the $106,000 is principal and how much is income?

3. G created a trust many years ago for the benefit of B. All income is distributable to B at least annually. The trust assets are valued at $1 million and consist solely of cash and certificates of deposit. For this year, the trustee charged an annual fee of $8,000 for serving as trustee. In addition, the trustee charged a special fee of $1,000 to prepare the trust's income tax return. If the trust earned $50,000 of interest income this year, what amount of cash flow can the beneficiary expect to receive and what is the fair market value of the trust at year's end?

§ 14.04   Taxable Income of Estates and Trusts

Code: §§ 1(e), 63(a), 167(d), 641(b), 642(e) and (g), 691(b), and 2053.

Regulations: None.

Section 1(e) imposes a tax on the taxable income of estates and trusts. With certain important modifications, the taxable income of estates and trusts is computed in the same manner as for individuals. *See* § 641(b); Treas. Reg. § 1.641(a)–2. For example, if an estate or trust receives dividends or interest, these items are included in gross income. Similarly, capital gains are includable in an entity's gross income. Because trusts and estates are not entitled to a standard deduction, however, their taxable income is computed by reducing the amount of gross income by allowable deductions only. *See* § 63(a).

This part considers gross income and deduction issues that arise in applying the income tax system for individuals to estates and trusts. The income and deduction issues for income in respect of a decedent was considered previously. *See* § 14.02, *supra*. The all-important distribution deductions under §§ 651 or 661 are considered separately in § 14.05[D], *infra*.

[A]   Gross Income: Identifying the Taxpayer

Revenue Ruling 75–61

1975–1 C.B. 180

. . .

The questions presented involve the manner in which the income generated by the corpus of an estate should be reported under the circumstances described below.

A died testate in 1963. His will provided that after the payment of his just debts and funeral expenses one-third of the estate be "allotted and assigned" to his wife, *B*, as satisfaction of her dower interest. Real property was transferred by the executor of *A*'s estate to *B* in 1964 to carry out this provision in the will. Under local law, real property and income therefrom is subject to administration.

A's will further provided that the income from certain property, comprising one-third of the estate, was to be paid to his son, *C*, for life and at *C*'s death, such property was to be distributed to those of *C*'s children living at the time of his death. In the event any portion of such property should vest in any person before such person attained his or her majority, then such portion would be retained by a trustee under a power in trust to invest and reinvest the principal, to collect the income and apply the net income, or as much thereof as the trustee should in his sole discretion determine, to the support and maintenance of such person during his or her minority.

C died in the year 1971 leaving only a minor child, *D*. Under the laws of the appropriate jurisdiction legal title to property held under a power in trust is in the beneficiaries, in this case *D*.

The final third of the estate consisted of real estate and under the will was to be held by *A*'s daughter, *E*, in fee simple, with the limitation that she would have no right to sell, convey, mortgage, incumber or dispose of, in any way, the real estate or rights therein before January 1, 1971, or to control, receive, or collect income from such real estate before January 1, 1967, unless permitted to do so at an earlier date by the action of the trustee. On and after January 1, 1967, however, she could lease the real property and receive the income from it.

The specific issues are whether the income derived from the property held by the executor and ultimately distributed to *B* is income to *B* or to the executor; whether the income derived from the property held subject to the power in trust is income of a trust or of *C*'s child; and whether income derived from the property conveyed to *A*'s daughter is her income or income of a trust.

Section 641 of the Internal Revenue Code of 1954 provides, in part, that the taxes imposed on individuals shall apply to the taxable income of any kind of property held in trust, including income accumulated in trust for the benefit of persons with contingent interests, income accumulated or held for future distribution under the terms of a will or trust and income which, in the discretion of the fiduciary, may be either distributed to the beneficiaries or accumulated. The tax on such taxable income shall be paid by the fiduciary. *See* section 1.641(a)–2 of the Income Tax Regulations.

Section 1.641(a)–2 of the regulations provides, in part, that the gross income of an estate or trust is determined in the same manner as that of an individual. Thus, the gross income of an estate or trust consists of all items of gross income received during the taxable year, including:

(a)   Income accumulated in trust for the benefit of unborn or unascertained persons or persons with contingent interests;

(b)   Income accumulated or held for future distribution under the terms of the will or trust;

(c)   Income which is to be distributed currently by the fiduciary to the beneficiaries, and income collected by a guardian of an infant which is to be held or distributed as the court may direct;

(d)   Income received by estates of deceased persons during the period of administration or settlement of the estate; and

(e)   Income which, in the discretion of the fiduciary, may be either distributed to the beneficiaries or accumulated.

The several classes of income enumerated above do not exclude others that also may come within the general purposes of section 641 of the Code.

Section 301.7701–4 of the regulations provides, in part, that generally, an arrangement will be treated as a trust under the Code if it can be shown that the purpose of the arrangement is to vest in trustees responsibility for the protection and conservation of property for beneficiaries who cannot share in the discharge of this responsibility and, therefore, are not associates in a joint enterprise for the conduct of business for profit.

Section 301.7701–6 of the regulations provides, in part, a definition of the term "fiduciary." Fiduciary is a term which applies to persons who occupy positions of peculiar confidence toward others, such as trustees, executors, and administrators. A fiduciary is a person who holds in trust an estate to which another has the beneficial title or in which another has beneficial interest or receives and controls income of another, as in the case of receivers.

Section 301.7701–7 of the regulations provides, in part, that there may be a fiduciary relationship between an agent and a principal, but the word "agent" does not denote a fiduciary. An agent having entire charge of property, with authority to effect and execute leases with tenants entirely on his own responsibility and without consulting his principal, merely turning over the net profits from the property periodically to his principal by virtue of authority conferred upon him by a power of attorney, is not a fiduciary within the meaning of the Code. In cases where no legal trust has been created in the estate controlled by the agent and attorney, the liability to make a return rests with the principal.

A "power in trust" involves a form of express fiduciary obligation similar to that of an express trust, and it therein differs from a mere agency, revocable at pleasure, which imposes no duty, but merely grants authority to act. A power in trust places on the grantee a duty to execute a trust in favor of a person or persons other than himself and involves the idea of a trust as much as does a trust estate. *See Brooklyn Trust Company*, 295 N.Y.S. 1007.

The will, in the instant case, passed legal title to one-third of the estate to *B*, one-third to *D*, and one-third to *E*. However, it is manifest that complete control over the realty conveyed to *D* and *E* was given to the trustee. *D* and *E* could not collect the rental income themselves regardless of where the bare legal title to the real estate might vest. It was *A*'s intent that the income from the real estate held by *D* should be received by *C*, until *C*'s death, then controlled by the trustee for the benefit of *D* until such time as *D* reached his majority, then to *D*. Furthermore, it was *A*'s intent that the income from the real estate held by *E* should be controlled by the trustee until January 1, 1967, and the power to convey the real estate was to be withheld until January 1, 1971.

Thus, the trustee of the properties of *D* and *E* is vested with the responsibility for the protection and conservation of property for beneficiaries who cannot share in the discharge of the responsibility.

Accordingly, it is held that the trustee must file U.S. Fiduciary Income Tax Returns (Form 1041) reporting therein the income from the property held under the power in trust for the benefit of *D*, for the taxable years in which he, as trustee, received such income. It is further held that the trustee must also report the income received from the real property left by *A* for the benefit of *E* for the taxable years in which such income was received by the trustee. Furthermore, it is noted that the dower interest of *B* has been satisfied by the transfer to her of real property of the estate by the executor, since under local law the property and income therefrom was subject to administration during that period. *Rev. Rul. 57–133*, 1957–1 C.B. 200. The income from such property that was received prior to the transfer to *B* is held to be income to the estate and reportable by the executor. After the transfer of the real estate to *B*, the income is held to be the personal income of *B*.

———

Uniform Probate Code § 3–101 provides that a decedent's property passes at death to the decedent's devisees or heirs. This rule is sometimes called *title popping*, as the effect of the statute is to pass title at the moment of the decedent's death to the beneficiaries of the decedent's estate. Nevertheless, § 3–101 provides that the title popping rule is "subject to homestead allowance, exempt property and family allowance, to rights of creditors, elective share of the surviving spouse, *and to administration*." [Emphasis added.]

Uniform Probate Code § 3–711 provides that a decedent's "personal representative has the same power over the title to property of the estate that an absolute owner would have, in trust however, for the benefit of the creditors and others interested in the estate." Also, Uniform Probate Code § 3–907 requires a personal representative to execute a deed or other document "assigning, transferring or releasing the assets to the distributee as evidence of the distributees title to the property."

The net result of these Uniform Probate Code sections is to vest title in the devisees at the decedent's death, but the decedent's property remains subject to the personal representative's control and the property is subject to probate administration. When the personal representative determines that the decedent's property is no longer needed for administration, a deed of distribution provides objective proof that the personal representative has released the property from administration.

The effect on title to property of the three Uniform Probate Code sections easily satisfies the guidelines of Revenue Ruling 75–61, and the income generated by assets of a decedent's estate, including real property, is property reportable by the personal representative until a deed of distribution is executed and delivered.[15] Gross income inclusion for an estate is limited only to the extent that the income was taxed on the decedent's final return because the decedent was on the accrual basis.

[B] Deductions

[1] In General

Estates and trusts may generally claim deductions that are allowed for individuals. *See* Treas. Reg. § 1.641(b)–1. For individuals there are three classes of deductions: (1) those described by § 62 (deductions used to calculate adjusted gross income), (2) those allowed for personal exemptions, and (3) the balance of allowable deductions, known as itemized deductions. Estates and trusts do not have adjusted gross income per se, but for purposes of § 67, an adjusted gross income amount is determined. Section 67(e) provides that the adjusted gross income for the estate or trust is determined in the same manner as it is for an individual, except "the deductions for costs which are paid or incurred in connection with the administration of the estate or trust and which would not have been incurred if the property were not held in such trust or estate" are allowable in arriving at adjusted gross income. *See* § 67(e)(1). In addition, the estate or trust is permitted a personal exemption, § 642(b), and the distribution deduction (§§ 651 and 661) to calculate adjusted gross income. *See* § 67(e)(2).

In contrast with individuals who are entitled to a $2,000 personal exemption (as indexed for inflation) under § 151, an estate is limited to a $600 personal exemption deduction. *See* § 642(b). A trust's personal exemption will be $300 or $100 depending on whether it is required to distribute all of its income. *See* § 642(b).

Estates and trusts also are generally subject to the same rules that are applicable to individuals in calculating itemized deductions (*i.e.,* deductions other than those described by § 62 and the personal exemption deduction). *Lamkin*, reproduced in § 14.02[B][2], *infra*, illustrates the special rules for allocating the depreciation deduction. Estates and trusts are also subject to the 2% floor on miscellaneous itemized deductions under § 67, but may fully deduct expenses unique to the existence of the trust or estate, without regard to the 2% limit for individuals in § 67. In *O'Neill v. Commissioner*, 98 T.C. 227 (1992), the Tax Court held that investment advice expenses incurred by

---

[15] In states that have not adopted the Uniform Probate Code, applicable state law determines whether Revenue Ruling 75–61 is applicable.

a trust were subject to the 2% floor under § 67. On appeal, the Sixth Circuit reversed (994 F.2d 302 (6th Cir. 1993)), and held that a trust's payments for investment advice were fully deductible to determine adjusted gross income because they stemmed from a fiduciary obligation and would not have been incurred if the assets had not been held in a trust.

In *Mellon Bank v. U.S.*, 265 F.3d 1275 (Fed. Cir. 2001) the Court of Appeals for the Federal Circuit, affirmed a ruling of the Court of Federal Claims that investment advice expenses are subject to the 2% rule of § 67. The trustee paid for investment-strategy advice provided by private investment advisors and for private accounting, tax preparation and management services. The Trustee relied on the Sixth Circuit's opinion in *O'Neill* "for the proposition that the taxpayer may satisfy section 67(e)(1) by proving that the expenses incurred were necessary to fulfill his fiduciary obligations under state law." The *Mellon* court agreed that the statute requires that expenses " 'are paid or incurred in connection with the administration of the estate or trust,' " but concluded that the statute imposes a second requirement (265 F.3d at 1280–1281):

> The second clause of section 67(e)(1) serves as a filter, allowing a full deduction only if such fees are costs that "would not have been incurred if the property were not held in such trust or estate." The requirement focuses not on the relationship between the trust and costs, but the type of costs, and whether those costs would have been incurred even if the assets were not held in a trust. Therefore, the second requirement treats as fully deductible only those trust-related administrative expenses that are unique to the administration of a trust and not customarily incurred outside of trusts.

> Investment advice and management fees are commonly incurred outside of trusts. An individual taxpayer, not bound by a fiduciary duty, is likely to incur these expenses when managing a large sum of money. Therefore, these costs are *not* exempt under section 67(e)(1) and are required to meet the two percent floor of section 67(a).

[2] Depreciation

Code: § 167(d).

Regulations: Treas. Reg. § 1.167(h)–1.

Lamkin v. United States

533 F.2d 303 (5th Cir. 1976)

Roney, Circuit Judge:

This appeal involves an issue of tax law which has, apparently, reached the courts on only one previous occasion. We are called upon to decide whether 26 U.S.C.A. § 167[(d)] permits an estate in administration to take a depreciation deduction on real property when the estate distributed the income generated by that property to income beneficiaries of the trust that will eventually hold the property. The Government allocated a pro rata share of the depreciation deduction to the distributees of the income and assessed a deficiency against the estate. The taxpayer estate paid the deficiency and brought this suit for refund, in which the district court granted the Government's motion for summary judgment. We affirm.

Under the second sentence of § 167[(d)], the depreciation deduction may be taken by the trust only when the trustee is "directed" by local law or by the trust instrument to retain income in a depreciation reserve for the purpose of preserving corpus. Treas. Reg. § 1.167(h)–1(b)(2) (1960). *See Sue Carol*, 30 BTA 433 (1943). Had the distributees received the real property income from the incipient trust rather than from the estate, the depreciation deduction would be allocated pro rata to the income distributees, there being no indication in the record of a required depreciation reserve.

The present dispute arises in the interpretation of the third sentence of § 167[(d)], which controls the disposition of this case. That portion of the statute provides:

> In the case of an estate, the allowable deduction shall be apportioned between the estate and the heirs, legatees, and devisees on the basis of the income of the estate allocable to each.

This provision does not in specific terms cover distributions, made during the administration of an estate, to the income beneficiaries of a testamentary trust which is not yet operative. The question before this Court, therefore, is whether the income beneficiary of the yet-to-be-established trust may be considered either an heir, legatee or devisee of the estate for purposes of § 167[(d)]. The taxpayer contends that the income beneficiary does not fall within any of these three categories, and therefore, a pro rata portion of the depreciation deduction is not to be allocated to the beneficiary, but may be taken by the estate.

The estate relies, in support of its position, on a Fourth Circuit case which is similar to ours, yet distinguishable in one critical respect. *In re Nissen*, 345 F.2d 230 (4th Cir. 1965). That action was brought to determine whether an estate could properly take a property depreciation deduction during its administration, the court ruling that the deduction was available to the estate. The property giving rise to the deduction would, upon closing of the estate, be distributed to testamentary trusts which would distribute all income to life beneficiaries. Acting under authorization in the will, the executor made discretionary income distributions to the future life beneficiaries, but the estate took the depreciation deduction. The executor acted in accordance with the following provision in the will:

> I authorize my Executor pay to or apply from the net income of my estate such sums and at such intervals and in such manner as my Executor in its sole discretion shall from time to time deem requisite or desirable in providing for the reasonable support, maintenance and education of my granddaughter . . . [and] my son . . . .

See Estate of Nissen, 41 T.C. 522, 525 (1964). Because these discretionary distributees, the son and granddaughter of the testatrix, were also the future life income beneficiaries, it is easy to misunderstand the holding of *In re*

Nissen, supra, 345 F.2d 230. Since the son and granddaughter received income distributions from the estate in accordance with their status under the will as income distributees at the discretion of the executor, and not in accordance with their status as future trust beneficiaries, we understand the Fourth Circuit's holding to be that those who so receive income under the will during estate administration are not heirs, devisees or legatees of specific real property, entitled to the depreciation deduction accruing to that property. Indeed, it is entirely possible that the Nissen distributees received income generated by assets other than the real property.

By contrast, in the case before us the will did not provide for the distribution of income during the period of administration. Therefore we can only conclude that the distribution to the future life income beneficiary was based on her status vis-a-vis the trust. Our case is in this critical respect distinct from *Nissen*.

As a generally accepted matter, an executor can legally distribute income only to a legatee, or heir if the will is silent. *See, e.g.*, Vernon's Tex. Civ. Stat. Ann., Probate Code, § 239. To be legal the income distributions here in question must be viewed in either of two ways. First, treating the real property as constructively being in the trust, the distribution could have constructively been made from the trust to the estate and then from the estate to the income beneficiaries. By this view the depreciation deduction would be allocated under the second sentence of § 167[(d)], there being no local law or trust instrument provision directing a depreciation reserve. Alternatively, the will might be construed to permit direct distribution to the trust beneficiaries as if they were, during administration, legatees of the real property. Under this concept, depreciation allocation is mandated by the third sentence of § 167[(d)]. According to either view, the distributee clearly takes according to her status vis-a-vis the real property under the trust. It is equally clear that the income she receives is income generated by the real property which gives rise to the depreciation deduction.

The statute appears to follow a general policy that the depreciation deduction travels with the income from the property. Thus, the first sentence of § 167[(d)] directs that in every instance life tenants will receive the depreciation deduction, and the third sentence mandates allocation of the deduction pro rata, on the basis of the receipt of income. The second sentence is consistent, even though it allows the settlor of a trust to preserve corpus by setting aside a depreciation reserve, because under the statute and longstanding regulations, the trust may take the depreciation deduction, but only to the extent that it withholds income in its reserve. In view of the policy of this statute, it would be anomalous to permit an estate to distribute income which can be identified as coming from the real property, but retain the depreciation deduction as an offset against income from unrelated sources.

Affirmed.

The taxpayer in *Dusek v. Commissioner*, 376 F.2d 410 (10th Cir. 1967), created a short-term trust for the benefit of his wife, and named himself trustee.[16] The trust provided that the income of the trust could be distributed to the beneficiary in the trustee's discretion. The trust corpus initially consisted of cash, but that was invested in rental real estate.

The trust document required the trustee to maintain a depreciation reserve "out of income," although another provision of the trust instrument authorized the trustee to apportion the depreciation deduction "in such manner as he may see fit." For tax years 1959 through 1961, the trust had net income, but only $100 per year of it was distributed to the taxpayer's wife. The trustee allocated all of the depreciation deduction to the beneficiary.

The *Dusek* court interpreted § 167(d) as requiring the depreciation deduction to be apportioned, to the extent the trust's income is allocated, to the beneficiary. Income set aside in a depreciation reserve is not allocable to the beneficiary because it is retained by the trust. Because the trust's income was retained by the trustee, the trust, not the beneficiary, incurred the depreciation.

The 1962 Revised Principal and Income Act § 13(a)(2) provides that income of a trust is charged with "a reasonable allowance for depreciation . . . under generally accepted accounting principles." Section 2(a)(1) and (a)(2) provide that the governing instrument may override the requirement for a depreciation reserve. In contrast, § 503 of the 1997 Act gives the trustee the discretion to decide whether to transfer net cash receipts from income to principal for depreciation.

Treasury Regulation § 1.167(h)–1(b) and Revenue Ruling 74–530, 1974–2 C.B. 188, explain how the depreciation deduction is apportioned between a trust and its beneficiary when a reserve is being maintained. First, the depreciation deduction is allocated to the trust to the extent of the reserve. The remainder of the deduction, if any, is then apportioned between the trust and beneficiary "on the basis of the trust income [in excess of the income set aside for the reserve] allocable to each." *See* Rev. Rul. 74–530, 1974–2 C.B. 188. If the amount of the deduction exceeds the income of the trust, the depreciation deduction is still allocated on the basis of the income retained by the trust compared with the income distributed to the beneficiary, and the deduction is not limited by the amount of the net income of the trust. In other words, the beneficiary may have a net deduction if the amount of the depreciation deduction is larger than the income earned.

The amount of depreciation deduction allowable by §§ 167 and 168 is unlikely to be the same as the reasonable allowance determined under generally accepted accounting principals (GAAP). Various political policies have determined the useful life of property for tax purposes. Moreover, the practical useful life of an asset is not the same as the economic life that GAAP attempts to establish.

---

[16] Before the Tax Reform Act of 1969, it was possible to create a trust for the benefit of a taxpayer's spouse and have the income taxed under normal trust rules as long as the trust had a term of more than ten years.

Problem

A trust receives net rental income of $100,000. The depreciation deduction under §§ 167 and 168 for the property owned by the trust is $50,000, but under GAAP, the amount of a reasonable allowance for wear and tear is $40,000. Although the trust instrument generally grants the trustee discretion to determine the allocation of receipts between principal and income, the trust instrument is silent concerning whether a depreciation reserve is required or excused. If the trust is required to distribute all of its income at least annually to *B*, what amount of fiduciary accounting income (*i.e.*, cash flow) should *B* expect under your state law? How is the depreciation deduction divided between *B* and the trust?

[3] Charitable Deduction

The income tax charitable deduction permitted for an estate or trust is unlimited. The percentage limitations of § 170 do not apply. Besides permitting a deduction for amounts paid to a charity, an estate is permitted a deduction for any amount permanently set aside for charity. Generally, trusts, except a pooled income fund, are not permitted a similar deduction for a set aside. Nevertheless, under § 645, discussed in § 14.05[D][4], *infra*, some trusts may elect to be treated as an estate for tax purposes. The legislative history indicates that when that election is made, a deduction for amounts permanently set aside for charity will be available.

[4] Double Deducting Administrative Expenses on the Estate's Income Return and Estate Tax Return

[a] In General

Although §§ 212 and 2053 allow the deduction of administration expenses, § 642(g) expressly bars deducting these items from both the estate tax and fiduciary income tax returns. It also prohibits an estate from claiming sales expenses as an "offset against the sales price," effectively barring the double use of the expense to obtain tax advantages.[17]

Notwithstanding a bar on deducting the same amount on both the estate and income tax returns, § 642(g) does not prevent a personal representative from splitting the amount between the returns. Amounts not claimed as a deduction against income may be claimed on the decedent's estate tax return. Treasury Regulation § 1.642(g)–1 provides that the fiduciary income tax return should be accompanied by a statement that the amount claimed on the income tax return neither has been, nor will be, claimed as a deduction on the estate tax return. If the statement is not included with the return, the estate must eventually file the statement before the statute of limitations expires on the return. Until the statement is filed, it is permissible to claim the deduction on both returns, but eventually one of them must be amended. Once the statement is filed, the deduction may not be claimed on the estate tax return. *See* Priv. Ltr. Rul. 8022023.

---

[17] Section 642(g) similarly bars a double deduction for income and GST tax purposes.

The one major exception to the double deduction bar is deductions in respect of a decedent (DRD). *See* § 691(b), which is discussed in § 14.02 [B], *supra*. The last sentence of § 642(g) excludes such deductions. Thus, the DRD deductions continue to be allowable on both returns to the extent that they qualify for normal deductibility. For example, if the decedent had borrowed money before his death, but he died before repaying the loan, the payment of interest which accrued before death would be deductible both as to the income tax and as a claim against the estate under § 2053. *See Estate of Hornor v. Commissioner*, 44 B.T.A. 1136 (1941), *aff'd on other grounds*, 130 F.2d 649 (3d Cir. 1942). In effect, § 691(b) permits a double deduction for certain expenses that have accrued before the decedent died, but which are not deductible on the decedent's final return.

[b]   Marital and Charitable Deduction Regulations

In 1999, the Treasury issued final Regulations detailing the tax treatment of estate administration expenses that are charged against marital or charitable shares. Estate administration expenses that can be paid from the share of an estate passing to a surviving spouse or charity and deducted for income tax purposes without reducing the estate tax marital or charitable deduction produce a substantial tax savings. The Supreme Court allowed such deductions for estate administration expenses that were not, on the date of death, expected to be material. *Commissioner v. Estate of Hubert*, 500 U.S. 93 (1997).

The Regulations make a distinction between "estate transmission expenses" and "estate management expenses." Estate management expenses are those expenses that could have been incurred by the decedent during life or by the beneficiaries, had they received the property on the date of death without any intervening period of administration. Estate management expenses include, for example, costs of maintaining and preserving estate assets during the estate administration, investment advisory fees, stock brokerage commissions, custodial fees, and interest. Treas. Reg. §§ 20.2055-3(b)(1)(i), 20.2056(b)-4(d)(1)(i). Estate management expenses may be paid from the income of a marital or charitable share and deducted for income tax purposes without a corresponding reduction in the estate tax marital or charitable deduction. The final Regulations clarify that such estate management expenses deducted on the estate tax return as administration expenses, rather than on the fiduciary income tax return, reduce the marital or charitable deduction. *See* Treas. Reg. §§ 20.2055-3(b)(3), 20.2056(b)-4(d)(3), 20.2056(b)-4(d)(5) (Example 4). Estate management expenses paid from a marital or charitable share also reduce the estate tax marital or charitable deduction, if the expense is attributable to another share of the estate. *See* Treas. Reg. §§ 20.2055-3(b)(4), 20.2056(b)-4(d)(4), 20.2056(b)-4(d)(5) (Example 3).

Estate transmission expenses are expenses that would not have been incurred but for the decedent's death and the resultant need to collect the decedent's assets, pay debts and wealth transfer taxes, and distribute the decedent's property to the beneficiaries. Estate transmission expenses include, for example, executor commissions and attorney fees (except to the extent they are specifically related to investment, preservation, and maintenance of the assets), probate fees, expenses incurred in construction proceedings and defending against will contests, and appraisal fees. Any expense that is not an estate management expense is an estate transmission expense. *See* Treas. Reg. §§ 20.2055-3(b)(1)(ii), 20.2055-3(b)(2), 20.2056(b)-4(d)(1)(ii), 20.2056(b)-4(d)(2).

Estate transmission expenses paid from a marital or charitable share will reduce the estate tax marital or charitable deduction, regardless of whether they are deducted on the estate tax return or the fiduciary income tax return. The final Regulations illustrate the application of these new rules to an estate with a marital share large enough to reduce the estate tax liability to zero. The Regulations show that when the fiduciary has discretion to charge expenses to either income or principal: (i) estate transmission expenses that are claimed as estate tax deductions should be paid from the marital share, to maximize the nonmarital share and minimize the estate tax at the surviving spouse's death; (ii) estate transmission expenses deducted on the fiduciary income tax return should be paid from the nonmarital share, to avoid reducing the marital deduction and generating an estate tax liability; and (iii) estate management expenses should be paid from the income of the marital share, to minimize the surviving spouse's taxable estate, while maximizing the nonmarital share. *See* Treas. Reg. §§ 20.2056(b)-4(d)(5) (Examples 5 and 6).

The final Regulations also explain how these rules apply to pecuniary bequests to a charity or surviving spouse. No estate tax deduction is allowed for the income earned on a pecuniary charitable or marital bequest that is not, under the governing instrument or applicable local law, entitled to a share of income earned prior to distribution. Therefore, the charitable or marital deduction is not reduced by estate transmission or estate management expenses paid from the income of such a share. *See* Treas. Reg. § 20.2056(b)-4(d)(5) (Example 7).

[C] Timing Issues

Code: None.

Regulations: Treas. Reg. §§ 1.652(c)–1, –2, and 1.662(c)–1, –2.

Schimberg v. United States

365 F.2d 70 (7th Cir. 1966)

Swiggert, Circuit Judge.

The facts were stipulated. Anna H. Collins died on November 29, 1957. The plaintiff, as the executor of the estate, filed an income tax return for the decedent covering the period from January 1, 1957 to the date of death. The decedent was the sole income beneficiary of the Philip Henrici trust, which kept its books and filed its income tax returns for fiscal years beginning February 1 and ending January 31, and a forty per cent income beneficiary of the William M. Collins trust, which kept its books and filed tax returns for fiscal years beginning April 1 and ending March 31. The decedent kept her books and filed tax returns on the cash basis for calendar years.

In the decedent's final income tax return, the plaintiff included the following: (1) the decedent's distributive share of the income of the Henrici and Collins trusts for their fiscal years ending January 31, 1957 and March 31, 1957, respectively; (2) $27,621.69, that portion of the income from the Henrici trust for its fiscal year ending January 31, 1958 which was actually distributed to the decedent prior to her death; (3) $7,041.57, that portion of the income from the Collins trust for its fiscal year ending March 31, 1958 which was actually distributed to the decedent before her death. The plaintiff subsequently sought a refund of the taxes attributable to the inclusion in the return of the amounts distributed to the decedent prior to her death which related to the fiscal years of the trusts ending after her death. The district court held that these amounts were properly included in the decedent's final return and dismissed that part of the claim. *Schimberg v. United States*, 245 F. Supp. 616 (N.D. Ill. 1965).

The general rule that an individual taxpayer must report his income in the year that it is received is different as to income received by the beneficiary of a trust. Section 652(c) of the Internal Revenue Code provides that "if the taxable year of a beneficiary is different from that of the trust, the amount which the beneficiary is required to include in gross income . . . shall be based upon the amount of income of the trust for any taxable year or years of the trust ending within or with his taxable year." The literal language of this "different taxable years" provision has been modified by the regulations in an attempt to resolve the anomaly arising when the death of the trust beneficiary presents a situation in which the taxable year of the trust will not end "within or with" the final taxable year of the beneficiary. In such cases Treasury Regulation section 1.652(c)–2 provides that the "gross income for the last taxable year of a beneficiary on the cash basis includes only income actually distributed to the beneficiary before his death" and that trust income distributed to the beneficiary's estate is to be included in the gross income of the estate as "income in respect of a decedent" under section 691 of the Internal Revenue Code.

The plaintiff concedes the applicability of the regulations but contends, drawing support from commentators, that they are invalid because the Commissioner is without power to depart from a literal reading of section 652(c). He argues that the statute permits a beneficiary to be taxed on trust income only when the taxable year of the trust ends within or with the beneficiary's taxable year, that the statute does not authorize a different rule in the event of the death of the beneficiary, and that therefore all trust income attributable to the taxable year of a trust not ending within or with the beneficiary's last taxable year must be reported as income by the beneficiary's estate. We do not agree. The problem resolved by the regulations in question, the treatment of trust income actually received by a cash basis beneficiary prior to his death, is either one not contemplated by the statute or one as to which the application of the statute is unclear, given the general Congressional policy with respect to the time and incidence of income taxation. In such a case the regulations must be sustained unless they are unreasonable. *Commissioner of Internal Revenue v. South Texas Lumber Co.*, 333 U.S. 496, 501 (1948). As the district judge commented, "It is difficult to find oppressive a regulation which attempts only to impose tax liability on income the taxpayer has actually received and enjoyed prior to the taxing date."

The plaintiff maintains that the regulations are unreasonable because they permit "bunching" of more than twelve months' trust income in the decedent's final return. He also notes that the regulations do not afford deceased trust beneficiaries the same tax treatment extended to a deceased partner's share of partnership income in the year of the partner's death, in that the rule applicable to partnerships avoids "bunching" in the final return of a deceased partner. Insofar as a "bunching" hardship may be permitted by the regulations, however, it should be noted that "bunching" generally occurs as a result of the trust having adopted a fiscal tax year, which may well have given the beneficiary the advantage of postponing the reporting of trust income of several months over a period of years. And again, the restriction of "bunching" to trust income actually received prior to the beneficiary's death militates against the alleged hardship. As to the objection regarding partners, if, as is doubtful, it is necessary to justify the difference in treatment, the treatment afforded a deceased partner's share of partnership income is the product of a conceptually different legal relationship with respect to the time at which "income" is received by a partner and also of specific Congressional action. The district judge's opinion adequately traces the unique problems of reporting partnership income and the series of decisions that prompted Congress "to finally alleviate the burdens of bunched income, as it affected partnerships" by adding section 706(c) to the Internal Revenue Code.

The decision of the district court is affirmed.

Major, Senior Circuit Judge (dissenting).

In my judgment, under the plain, unambiguous language of the statutory provisions involved, the taxpayer should prevail. The Treasury Regulations relied upon should not be sustained on the pretext that they are no more than a permissible interpretation or construction of such provisions. The government in its brief states, "Certainly, Congress did not intend any income from a trust should escape taxation unless definitely exempted." The point is that the income in the instant case was by statute "definitely exempted," and it is only by reason of the Treasury Regulations that it was "definitely" required to be reported. The government continues, "Obviously, the trust income herein is not definitely exempted and therefore will have to be reported some place in order that it be subjected to tax." So, based on the premise that it should be reported someplace and being unable to find any place provided by Congress, the Commissioner promulgates the regulations contrary to the statutory provisions. This must be a novel approach in seeking to justify the regulations. In June 1956, at the time the regulations were proposed, the Section of Taxation of the American Bar Association, through its committee on the Taxation of Estates and Trusts, transmitted to the Commissioner its comments on the proposed regulations. Inasmuch as I thoroughly agree with the views therein expressed, I take the liberty of quoting in part as follows:

> Sections 652(c) and 662(c) unequivocally provide that, if the taxable year of the beneficiary is different from that of the trust, the amount which the beneficiary includes in gross income "shall be based upon the amount of income of the trust for any taxable

year or years of the trust ending within or with his taxable year." There are no exceptions in the statute. Thus, since the taxable year of the beneficiary will end with his death, he should include nothing under the statute with respect to any year of the trust which ends after his death. The regulations contain the statement that Sections 652(c) and 662(c) of the Code do not apply to amounts paid to the beneficiary during the taxable year of the trust in which he dies. There is absolutely no statutory justification for this statement.

The same committee included in its comments the further pertinent observation: "Furthermore, the rule which the regulations purport to set forth with no statutory justification can result in the bunching of income in the final taxable year of the beneficiary. For example, let us assume that the beneficiary is on a calendar year and that the trust is on a January 31 fiscal year. The beneficiary dies on December 1, 1956. The regulations would require that the beneficiary's last tax return include all of the income from the trust for its fiscal year 1956, plus the income of the trust payable to the beneficiary for the period from February 1, 1956 to December 1, 1956. This result is most unjust and is completely contrary to the statute."

I would reverse the judgment.

—————

The taxable income of an estate is computed on an annual basis. An estate's first taxable year, however, need not end on the first anniversary of the decedent's death, nor on the date the decedent's taxable year would have ended had he survived. Instead, the personal representative may elect to end the estate's first taxable year on the last day of any month that falls within one year of the decedent's death. *See* § 441. For example, if the decedent died on April 13, 2002, the estate's first taxable year could end on April 30, 2002, on March 31, 2003, or on any last day of the month between those two dates. Assuming the first year does not end exactly one year after the decedent dies, a short-period return must be filed under § 443. Very likely, the decedent's last taxable year will be a short-period. Shortperiods allow the estate to spread income over more tax years. Moreover, the fact that the first year is short does not require adjustments to deduction and exemptions. *See* § 443(a)(2).

The first day of the estate's tax year is the day of the decedent's death.[18] This is true although the decedent's final return includes the day of death and any income received on the day of death is reported on the decedent's final return. This rule can be a trap for decedents who die the last day of a month. When the tax year beginning on the 31st, the longest tax year the estate may elect ends approximately 11 months later. For example, the estate of a decedent who dies on January 31 may elect any tax year so long as that year ends no later than December 31 of the year of the decedent's death. For a trust, the first day of its first tax year is the day of creation.

Before 1987, trusts also had the right to report income on a fiscal year basis. This right was removed by the Tax Reform Act of 1986. Section 644 mandates

---

[18] *See* Rev. Rul. 69–563, 1969–2 C.B. 104.

that trusts (other than tax exempt and wholly charitable trusts) determine taxable income on a calendar year basis.[19] This requirement was explained as follows:

> In the case where the trust has a taxable year different than the taxable year of its beneficiaries, the present and prior law rules governing the taxation of trusts permit the deferral of taxation by one month for each month that the taxable year of the trust ends sooner than the taxable year of its beneficiaries. Thus, in the case of a taxable year of a trust ending on January 31 and the trust beneficiary on a calendar year, the taxation of trust income which is distributed to the beneficiary is deferred eleven months.
>
> The Congress believed that the ability to defer taxation on income through the selection of taxable years of trusts should be limited.[20] Accordingly, the Act requires all trusts to have a calendar year as its taxable year. Where the beneficiaries of the trust use a calendar year for their taxable year (which is typically the case), this rule will eliminate any deferral of taxation of income.

Report, Joint Committee on Taxation, General Explanation of the Tax Reform Act of 1986, 99th Cong., 2d Sess. 1250 (1987).

As in the case of individuals, estates and trusts must have an accounting method. The method can include the cash receipts and disbursement method, the accrual method, or some other allowable method.

When a trust provides that the trust terminates upon the happening of an event such as the death of the trust's income beneficiary, the trust's tax year does not end on the day the beneficiary dies. Rather, Treasury Regulation § 1.641(b)-3(b) provides that the trustee is allowed a reasonable period of time after the terminating event to complete the administration of the trust. Once all assets have been distributed, except for a reserve to pay unascertained expenses and contingent liabilities, a trust is terminated for tax purposes. The winding up affairs of a trust or estate cannot be unduly prolonged. When this occurs, the Treasury Regulations deem the trust or estate to be terminated. *See* Treas. Reg. § 1.641(b)–3(a) and (b).

Problems

1. The decedent died on December 1, 2002. At the time of his death, he owned publicly traded stock that paid a quarterly dividend (on March 31, June 30, September 30, and December 31) of $5,000. The decedent's two children

---

[19] As discussed later in the chapter, an election may be made under § 645 to treat certain revocable trusts as estates; in such a case, a fiscal year close may be allowed for the revocable trust.

[20] Under both present and prior law, a decedent's estate is treated as a separate taxable entity beginning as of the date of death. The estate may elect a taxable year different than the decedent's taxable year. Congress recognized that the same possibilities of deferral are also present in the case of estates. Nonetheless, the duration of estates is generally much shorter than the duration of trusts. There is often a greater need for executors of estates to select an accounting period that coincides with the administration of the estate. The Act does not, therefore, affect the present law treatment of the taxable years of estates.

are the sole beneficiaries of the estate. If they are interested in the maximum tax savings, what tax year do you recommend the estate elect? Based on your election, when is the income tax return due for the dividend income?

2. If an estate seeks the maximum deferral for the payment of income taxes on estate income, what tax year should the estate elect? How long will the deferral last?

3. If a decedent dies on December 31, when is the latest date a tax year may be elected?

§ 14.05 Trust and Estate as Conduits

[A] In General

Code: §§ 67(e)(1), 102, 167(d), 273, 1001(e), 2622 and 2654(a)(2).

Regulations: Treas. Reg. §§ 1.641(b)–1, 1.1014–5, and 25.2512–5(d).

Irwin v. Gavit

268 U.S. 161 (1925)

Mr. Justice Holmes delivered the opinion of the Court.

This is a suit to recover taxes and penalties exacted by the Collector under the Income Tax Act of October 3, 1913 . . . .

The question is whether the sums received by the plaintiff under the will of Anthony N. Brady in 1913, 1914 and 1915, were income and taxed. The will, admitted to probate August 12, 1913, left the residue of the estate in trust [in which the plaintiff was entitled to receive income therefrom, and did receive trust income, during the years in controversy]. The Courts below held that the payments received were property acquired by bequest, were not income and were not subject to tax.

The [applicable] statute provides that there shall be levied a tax "upon the entire net income arising or accruing from all sources in the preceding calendar year to every citizen of the United States." If these payments properly may be called income by the common understanding of that word and the statute has failed to hit them it has missed so much of the general purpose that it expresses at the start. Congress intended to use its power to the full extent. *Eisner v. Macomber*, 252 U.S. 189, 203. [The statute further provides that] the net income is to include "gains or profits and income derived from any source whatever, including the income from but not the value of property acquired by gift, bequest, devise or descent." . . . The language quoted leaves no doubt in our minds that if a fund were given to trustees for A for life with remainder over, the income received by the trustees and paid over to A would be income of A under the statute. It seems to us hardly less clear that even if there were a specific provision that A should have no interest in the corpus, the payments would be income none the less, within the meaning of the statute and the Constitution, and by popular speech. In the first case it is true that the bequest might be said to be of the corpus for life, in the second it might be said to be of the income. But we think that the provision of the act that exempts bequests assumes the gift of a corpus and contrasts it with the income arising from it, but was not intended to exempt income properly so-called simply because of a severance between it and the principal fund. No such conclusion can be drawn from *Eisner v. Macomber*, 252 U.S. 189, 206, 207. The money was income in the hands of the trustees and we know of nothing in the law that prevented its being paid and received as income by the donee.

The Courts below went on the ground that the gift to the plaintiff was a bequest and carried no interest in the corpus of the fund. We do not regard those considerations as conclusive, as we have said, but if it were material a gift of the income of a fund ordinarily is treated by equity as creating an interest in the fund. Apart from technicalities we can perceive no distinction relevant to the question before us between a gift of the fund for life and a gift of the income from it. The fund is appropriated to the production of the same result whichever form the gift takes. Neither are we troubled by the question where to draw the line. That is the question in pretty much everything worth arguing in the law. *Hudson County Water Co. v. McCarter*, 209 U.S. 349, 355. Day and night, youth and age are only types. But the distinction between the cases put of a gift from the corpus of the estate payable in installments and the present seems to us not hard to draw, assuming that the gift supposed would not be income. This is a gift from the income of a very large fund, as income. It seems to us immaterial that the same amounts might receive a different color from their source. We are of opinion that quarterly payments, which it was hoped would last for fifteen years, from the income of an estate intended for the plaintiff's child, must be regarded as income within the meaning of the Constitution and the law. It is said that the tax laws should be construed favorably for the taxpayers. But that is not a reason for creating a doubt or for exaggerating one when it is no greater than we can bring ourselves to feel in this case.

Judgment reversed.

Mr. Justice Sutherland, dissenting.

By the plain terms of the Revenue Act of 1913, the value of property acquired by gift, bequest, devise, or descent is not to be included in net income. Only the income derived from such property is subject to the tax. The question, as it seems to me, is really a very simple one. Money, of course, is property. The money here sought to be taxed as income was paid to respondent under the express provisions of a will. It was a gift by will,—a bequest. *United States v. Merriam*, 263 U.S. 179, 184. It, therefore, fell within the precise letter of the statute; and, under well settled principles, judicial inquiry may go no further. The taxpayer is entitled to the rigor of the law. There is no latitude in a taxing statute,—you must adhere to the very words. *United States v. Merriam, supra*, pp. 187–188.

The property which respondent acquired being a bequest, there is no occasion to ask whether, before being handed over to him, it had been carved from the original corpus of, or from subsequent additions to, the estate. The corpus of the estate was not the legacy which respondent received, but merely the source which gave rise to it. The money here sought to be taxed was not the fruits of a legacy; it was the legacy itself. *Matter of Stanfield*, 135 N.Y. 292, 294.

With the utmost respect for the judgment of my brethren to the contrary, the opinion just rendered, I think without warrant, searches the field of argument and inference for a meaning which should be found only in the strict letter of the statute.

Mr. Justice Butler concurs in this dissent.

———

Irwin v. Gavit is the seminal case resolving the inherent conflict between the concept of the trust as a conduit of trust income, and the concept that gifts and bequests do not enter into the computation of taxable income because of the gift exemption under § 102(a). The *Irwin* Court held that receipts which constitute income to the trust and are distributed, are considered income to the recipient. Without this holding, income tax avoidance through the medium of trusts would have proved a simple affair. The result in *Irwin* is now codified as § 102(b)(2).

In addition to the cases in this section, the following explanation for trusts that distribute their income provides the underpinnings for taxing estates, trusts, and their beneficiaries:

> The trust is a taxable entity, whose net income is to be initially determined by the application of the rules governing the net income of individuals. At the same time, a beneficiary currently receiving the income of a trust is also treated as a person in receipt of taxable income. The Supreme Court early decided in *Irwin v. Gavit* that the policy decision to exempt gifts from taxable income did not extend to a gift of annual income from property. The Court thus made the receipt of trust income by the beneficiary a taxable event even though the income was in effect the current manifestation of the gift that had been made to the beneficiary when the property was placed in trust.[21] This conclusion is essentially premised on the sound view that a progressive income tax applied to an individual's annual income could not sensibly exclude from that base funds received annually from a trust. But if nothing more were done the combination of *Irwin v. Gavit* and treatment of the trust as a taxable entity would produce a double tax on trust income. Whatever might be the merits of the double tax in the corporate relationship, they clearly do not extend to situations where present and future interests in property are created and the property itself placed in the hands of a caretaker. Yet ceasing to recognize the trust as a taxable entity was not an acceptable solution for this double tax problem

---

[21] The Court, in effect, rejected the view that the discounted value of the future distributions constituted the gift to the current beneficiary, and hence did not amortize that discounted value over the annual distributions. The gift exemption was thus reserved for the corpus rather than divided between corpus and income.

since it would not meet a case where the income was being accumulated, especially for unascertained beneficiaries. So the solution adopted was that of preserving the taxable status of both trust and current beneficiary, but eliminating the double tax through the allowance to the trust of a special deduction for the income taxable to the beneficiary. This solution has been characterized as the conduit principle of trust taxation.

H. Brian Holland et al., *A Proposed Revision of the Federal Income Tax Treatment of Trusts and Estates—American Law Institute Draft*, 53 COLUM. L. REV. 316, 317–318 (1954).

Section 273 provides basis rules when a life or term interest in property is acquired by gift or inheritance. A life or term holder is denied any amortization for the declining value of the life or term interest. For example, if a decedent devises a life estate in Blackacre to her daughter, remainder to her granddaughter, no amortization deduction is allowed even though the actuarial value of the daughter's life interest at the time of the decedent's death was, for example, $150,000, and will eventually decline to zero, when she dies.

If a term or life interest (including an income interest in a trust) is sold, § 1001(e) permits the life tenant a basis in the term or life interest only if the sale is of the entire property and not just the term or life interest. For example, if a decedent devises a life estate in Blackacre to her daughter, remainder to her granddaughter, the daughter is allowed no basis for purposes of determining gain if she sells the life interest for $100,000, unless the granddaughter simultaneously sells her remainder interest. Thus, the daughter will have a $100,000 gain even though Blackacre was valued at $200,000 in the decedent's estate, the life interest was actuarially valued at $150,000 at the time of the decedent's death, and $90,000 at the time of the sale.

Treasury Regulation § 1.1014-4(a) provides rules to determine gain realized on the sale of a remainder. The basis of the property is actuarially divided between the life estate and the remainder, based on the age of the life tenant at the time of the sale. *See* Treas. Reg. § 1.1014-5(c), Examples 1 and 2. Any amount realized in excess of the proportional part of the adjusted basis is gain (or loss if the amount realized is less than the remainderman's share of the adjusted basis). The division of basis for the remainderman occurs whether or not the life interest is simultaneously sold. Thus, if the life estate and remainder are sold at different times, there is no full recover of basis. Nevertheless, once the life tenant's interest has expired, the remainderman will have a basis equal to the entire original basis if the remainder is not disposed of before the life tenant dies. *See* Treas. Reg. § 1.1014-4(a)(2).

Section 2702, discussed in § 4.02[C][3], *supra*, provides the gift tax rules when an income or remainder interest in property is gifted or sold to a family member.

Problems

1. Parent transfers $100,000 in cash to a trust with the direction that the income from the trust corpus is to be paid annually to his 58-year-old Child

for life. On Child's death, the corpus of the trust is to be distributed to Child's only child, Grandchild, who is 15 years old at the time the trust is created. The trustee invests the money in a corporate bond paying 8% interest each year.

a. Assuming the income distributed by the trust is not otherwise excluded from income, when and why is all of the income taxed to the life tenant?

b. What will be the remainderman's basis for the trust property on the death of the life tenant? Will a GST tax at Child's death change the result?

2. *D* created a testamentary trust for her Child, *C*. Upon *C*'s death, the trust is to be distributed to the daughter's only child, *GC*. At the time of *D*'s death, the trust was funded with $500,000 of stock. Five years later, *C* sells her interest in the trust to *GC* for $300,000. For purposes of answering this problem, assume the applicable rate under § 7520 is 8%.

a. What is the tax consequence to *C*, if she was 64 when the decedent died and the value of the trust is still $500,000?

b. What is GC's income tax basis? *See* Rev. Rul. 62–132, 1962–2 C.B. 73.

c. Would your answer change if *C* and *GC* joined in a sale of all the trust assets and the proceeds were divided between *C* and *GC*, based on the actuarial value of their interests as determined under § 7520?

[B] Distributable Net Income: The Conduit Mechanism

Code: § 643(a), (b).

Regulations: Treas. Reg. §§ 1.643(a)–0 through–5, 1.643(b), and 1.643(d)–2.

Trusts and estates are treated in part as conduits of income to their beneficiaries because the income and deductions may pass through the trust or estate to the beneficiary. By adopting the conduit approach, Congress created a need for a standard that identifies income taxable to beneficiaries and for income which an estate or trust receives a distribution deduction. Before 1954, Congress relied on state law fiduciary accounting principles to define income. However, as the following legislative history explains, the 1954 Congress adopted the standard of *distributable net income*.

> Your committee's bill contains the basic principles of existing law under which estates and trusts are treated as separate taxable entities, but are generally regarded as conduits through which income passes to the beneficiary. The estate or trust is taxed in general in the same manner as an individual, but is allowed an additional deduction for income distributions to its beneficiaries.
>
> . . .
>
> The bill adopts the general principle that to the extent of the trust's current income all distributions are deductible by the estate or trust and taxable to the beneficiaries. This approach represents a basic departure from the general rule of the existing law that taxable distributions must be traced to the income of the estate or trust for the current year.

This approach, however, requires the use of a measure to impose an outside limit on the total distributions deductible by the estate or trust and taxable to the beneficiary. In general, the measure adopted by the bill for this purpose is taxable income, [with several modifications].

The bill adheres to the conduit theory of the existing law. This means that an estate or trust is in general treated as a conduit through which income passes to the beneficiary. In order to implement this theory in a satisfactory manner, it is necessary to include in the measure items of income and deductions which are not reflected in taxable income. The bill adopts the concept of "distributable net income" as the measure and adjusts the amount of the distributions deductible by the estate or trust and taxable to the beneficiaries by eliminating not only capital gains and losses but items of income and expenses which do not enter into the computation of taxable income. Thus, the distributable net income of an estate or trust is defined as its taxable income for the current year, excluding capital gains and losses not distributed by the estate or trust, the portion of extraordinary cash dividends and taxable stock dividends allocated to principal (in the case of simple trusts described below), and the dividends received exclusion, but including tax exempt interest and foreign income of foreign trusts.

The approach adopted by the bill eliminates the necessity, in determining the taxability of distributions, of tracing such distributions to the income of the estate or trust for the current taxable year.

S. Rep. No. 1622, H.R. 8300, 83rd Cong., 2d Sess. 82–83 (1954).

The statutory term of art *distributable net income* (DNI) is the cornerstone of determining the income tax liability of estates, trusts, and beneficiaries of estates and trusts. By the mechanics of § 643, taxable income is allocated among the entity and its beneficiaries. DNI quantifies the amount of the deduction an estate or trust is allowed for distributions to beneficiaries (§§ 651(a) and 661(a)) and the amount beneficiaries must report as income (§§ 652(a) and 662(a)). Moreover as will be discussed later, DNI determines the character of income that beneficiaries must report (*i.e.*, interest, dividends, and tax exempt income). *See* Treas. Reg. §§ 1.652(b), 1.662(b).

The computation of DNI begins with the taxable income of the entity. *See* § 643(a). Thus, it is necessary to determine the gross income and deductions of the entity and compute taxable income before determining DNI. Taxable income is then adjusted by:

(1)   adding back the amount of the distribution deduction permitted by §§ 651 or 661, if any (§ 643(a)(1));

(2)   adding back the personal exemption permitted by § 642(b) (§ 643(a)(2));

(3)   subtracting capital gains and adding back deductible capital losses,

if any (§ 643(a)(3));[22]

(4)　for a simple trust, subtracting extraordinary dividends and taxable stock dividends that are not included in fiduciary accounting income, if any (§ 643(a)(4));[23] and

(5)　adding any tax exempt income earned by the entity, reduced by any related expenses (§ 643(a)(5)).

The computation of DNI involves a catch-22. The taxable income of the entity cannot be determined until the amount of the distribution deduction is computed. Sections 651 and 652 permit estate and trust income deductions for distributions to beneficiaries. Nevertheless, the amount of the distribution deduction cannot be computed until the amount of DNI is calculated. Sections 651(b) and 661(a) limit the distribution deduction to the taxable portions of DNI. To resolve the dilemma, it is necessary to compute the taxable income of a trust or estate without a distribution deduction. Then DNI is computed without adding back the distribution deduction as required by § 643(a)(1) because the deduction was not claimed in computing taxable income.

Before a trustee can determine DNI and taxable income, receipts and disbursements must be allocated between principal and income under the terms of the governing instrument or applicable state law. Fiduciary accounting income plays an important role in determining the tax liability of beneficiaries. It is the measuring stick to determine if a trust is a simple or complex trust.

The following example illustrates how fiduciary accounting income (FAI) and DNI are computed:

Example 1: A trust is required to distribute all of its income to its sole beneficiary and makes no other distributions. It has the following income and deductions:

Gross income from real estate rentals	$15,000
Interest on corporate bonds	$25,000
Extraordinary cash dividend allocated to principal	$10,000
Long term capital gain	$25,000
Long term capital loss	-$15,000
Trustee fees chargeable ½	-$12,000
Real estate rental expenses	-$5,000

FAI of the trust is computed as follows:

Rental income	$15,000
Corporate bond interest	$25,000

---

[22] The adjustment for capital gains is dependent on the capital gains being allocated to corpus for fiduciary accounting purposes, not being required to be "paid, credited, or required to be distributed to any beneficiary" or not being required to be "paid, permanently set aside, or to be used" for a qualified charity. *See* § 643(a)(3). The adjustment for capital losses is dependent on the loss not affecting the amount to be "paid, credited, or required to be distributed to any beneficiary."

[23] As will be discussed later in this Chapter, a simple trust is a trust that is required to distribute all of its income, makes no distributions of principal, and makes no distributions to charity.

Less rental expenses	-$5,000
Less one-half of the trustee fee	-$6,000
FAI	$29,000

The computation of tentative taxable income needed to determine DNI is calculated as follows:

Gross income from real estate rentals	$15,000
Interest on corporate bonds	$25,000
Extraordinary cash dividend allocated to principal	$10,000
Long term capital gain	$25,000
Trustee fees[24]	-$12,000
Long term capital loss (§ 1211)	-$15,000
Real estate rental expenses	-$5,000
Personal exemption	-$300
Tentative Taxable Income	$42,700

DNI is computed as follows:

Tentative Taxable Income[25]	$42,700
Plus personal exemption	$300
Less capital gains	-$25,000
Plus capital loss	$15,000
Less extraordinary cash dividend allocated to principal	-$10,000
DNI[26]	$23,000

Example 2: Assume the same facts as in Example 1, except that the trust receives $10,000 in tax exempt income and $15,000 in taxable interest. The trust is required to distribute all of its income to its sole beneficiary and the trust makes no other distributions. The computations of FAI and DNI are made as follows:

Gross income from real estate rentals	$15,000
Interest on corporate bonds	$15,000
Interest on (tax exempt) municipal bonds	$10,000
Extraordinary cash dividend allocated to principal	$10,000
Long term capital gain	$25,000
Long term capital loss	-$15,000
Trustee fees chargeable ½ to income and ½ to principal	-$12,000

---

[24] The entire fiduciary fee is deductible in determining taxable income and tentative taxable income, although one-half is charged to FAI and one-half is charged to fiduciary accounting principal.

[25] This text refers to taxable income without a distribution deduction as *tentative taxable income*.

[26] The distribution deduction is not added back to compute DNI because it was not deducted in determining tentative taxable income.

Real estate rental expenses	-$5,000

FAI of the trust is computed as follows:

Rental income	$15,000
Corporate bond interest	$15,000
Tax exempt income	$10,000
Less rental expenses	-$5,000
Less one-half of the trustee fee	-$6,000
FAI	$29,000

The computation of tentative taxable income needed to determine DNI is calculated as follows:

Gross income from real estate rentals	$15,000
Interest on corporate bonds	$15,000
Extraordinary cash dividend allocated to principal	$10,000
Long term capital gain	$25,000
Trustee fees allocable to taxable income[27]	-$9,000
Long term capital loss (§ 1211)	-$15,000
Real estate rental expenses	-$5,000
Personal exemption	-$300
Tentative Taxable Income	$35,700

DNI is computed as follows:

Tentative Taxable Income	$35,700
Plus personal exemption	$300
Less capital gains	-$25,000
Plus capital loss	$15,000
Less extraordinary cash dividend allocated to principal	-$10,000
Plus tax exempt interest (less related expenses)[28]	$7,000
DNI[29]	$23,000

---

[27] Because of § 265, a portion of the trustee's fee must be apportioned to the tax exempt income of the tax. As a result, that portion is not allowable as a deduction used in computing taxable income. The fiduciary is allowed a deduction for the entire amount of the trustee fee not disallowed by § 265, although one-half of the fee is charged to income and one-half is charged to principal for fiduciary accounting purposes. *See* Treas. Reg. § 1.643(d)–2(a).

The deduction is disallowed under § 265 on the proportion of exempt income included in FAI (before reduction for expenses). Thus, the rents are not reduced by the directly related rental expenses. *See* Treas. Reg. §§ 1.652(c)–4, Example, 1.661(c)–2, 1.662(c)–4, 1.643(d)–2(a). *But see* Treas. Reg. § 1.652(b)–3(b). The ratio in the example is $10,000/$40,000 times $12,000 equals $3,000. It is *not* $10,000/$35,000 times $12,000 equals $3,429.

[28] $10,000 minus $3,000.

[29] The distribution deduction is not added back to compute DNI because it was not deducted in determining tentative taxable income.

Treasury Regulation § 1.643(d)–2 provides another detailed example of how to compute DNI when a trust has received tax exempt income.

If the trust is a complex trust because it is not required to distribute all of its income, the computation of DNI is different because of the reduction of taxable income required by § 643(a)(4) does not apply.

Example 3: Assume the same facts as in Example 1, except that the trustee is not required to distribute all of its income, but chooses to distribute $29,000 to the beneficiary. The computation is as follows:

Gross income from real estate rentals	$15,000
Interest on corporate bonds	$25,000
Extraordinary cash dividend allocated to principal	$10,000
Long term capital gain	$25,000
Long term capital loss	-$15,000
Trustee fees chargeable ½ to income and ½ to principal	-$12,000
Real estate rental expenses	-$5,000

FAI of the trust is computed as follows:

Rental income	$15,000
Corporate bond interest	$25,000
Less one-half of the trustee fee	-$6,000
Less rental expenses	-$5,000
FAI	$29,000

The tentative taxable income needed to compute DNI is computed as follows:

Gross income from real estate rentals	$15,000
Interest on corporate bonds	$25,000
Extraordinary cash dividend allocated to principal	$10,000
Long term capital gain	$25,000
Trustee fees[30]	-$12,000
Long term capital loss	-$15,000
Real estate rental expenses	-$5,000
Personal exemption	-$100
Tentative Taxable Income	$42,900

DNI is computed as follows:

Tentative Taxable Income	$42,900
Plus personal exemption	$100
Less capital gains	-$25,000

---

[30] The entire fiduciary fee is deductible in determining taxable income and tentative taxable income, although one-half is charged to FAI and one-half is charged to fiduciary accounting principal.

Plus capital loss	$15,000
DNI [31]	$33,000

Example 4: Assume the same facts as in Example 3, except that the trust has $10,000 of exempt income and $15,000 of taxable interest income. The computation of FAI and DNI is as follows:

Gross income from real estate rentals	$15,000
Interest on corporate bonds	$15,000
Interest on (tax exempt) municipal bonds	$10,000
Extraordinary cash dividend allocated to principal	$10,000
Long term capital gain	$25,000
Long term capital loss	-$15,000
Trustee fees chargeable ½ to income and ½ to principal	-$12,000
Real estate rental expenses	-$5,000

FAI of the trust is computed as follows:

Rental income	$15,000
Corporate bond interest	$15,000
Tax exempt income	$10,000
Less rental expenses	-$5,000
Less one-half of the trustee fee	-$6,000
FAI	$29,000

The tentative taxable income needed to compute DNI is computed as follows:

Gross income from real estate rentals	$15,000
Interest on corporate bonds	$15,000
Extraordinary cash dividend allocated to principal	$10,000
Long term capital gain	$25,000
Trustee fees allocable to taxable income [32]	-$9,000
Long term capital loss	-$15,000
Real estate rental expenses	-$5,000

---

[31] The distribution deduction is not added back to compute DNI because it was not deducted in determining tentative taxable income.

[32] Because of § 265, a portion of the trustee's fee must be apportioned to the tax exempt income of the tax. As a result, that portion is not allowable as a deduction used in computing taxable income. The fiduciary is allowed a deduction for the entire amount of the trustee fee not disallowed by § 265, although one-half of the fee is charged to income and one-half is charged to principal for fiduciary accounting purposes. *See* Treas. Reg. § 1.643(d)–2(a).

The deduction is disallowed under § 265 on the proportion of exempt income included in FAI (before reduction for expenses). Thus, the rents are not reduced by the directly related rental expenses. *See* Treas. Reg. §§ 1.652(c)–4, Example, 1.661(c)–2, 1.662(c)–4, 1.643(d)–2(a). *But see* Treas. Reg. § 1.652(b)–3(b). The ratio in the example is $10,000/$40,000 times $12,000 equals $3,000. It is *not* $10,000/$35,000 times $12,000 equals $3,429.

Personal exemption	$100
Tentative Taxable Income	$35,900

DNI is computed as follows:

Tentative Taxable Income	$35,900
Plus personal exemption	$100
Less capital gains	-$25,000
Plus capital loss	$15,000
Plus tax exempt interest (less related expenses)	$7,000
DNI	$33,000

Problem

A trust that provides income to *A* for life, remainder to *B*, has the following items of gross income: dividends of $30,000 and taxable interest of $20,000. The trust also has allowable deductions for trustee's commissions allocable to income in the amount of $5,000. What is the amount of DNI?

a. Would your answer change if the commissions were allocable to principal instead of income?

b. Would your answer change if the trust also had $10,000 of tax exempt income?

[C] Capital Gains in DNI

Code: § 643(a)(3).

Regulations: Treas. Reg. § 1.643(a)–3.

Although the general rule of § 643(a)(3) excludes capital gains from the computation of DNI, three exceptions exist. The following Revenue Ruling explains the exceptions provided in Treasury Regulation § 1.643(a)–3.

Revenue Ruling 68–392

1968–2 C.B. 284

Advice has been requested whether capital gains are excludable from distributable net income of a trust under the circumstances described below.

Under the will of *A*, assets with a fair market value of 268x dollars were transferred to a trust for the benefit of his daughter, *B*. The testator directed that 24x dollars be paid annually to *B* for her lifetime, first out of income of the trust and if necessary, out of corpus.

For its first taxable year, the trust had income of 10x dollars all of which was distributed by the trustee to *B*. In satisfaction of her right to receive an additional 14x dollars, *B* agreed to accept securities that were part of trust corpus. The securities had a fair market value of 14x dollars at the time of distribution and a basis of 12x dollars in the hands of the trust.

The governing instrument is silent on the treatment of capital gains. However, in the absence of a provision in the trust instrument, local law requires that such gains be allocated to corpus.

The transaction whereby the trustee distributed securities to *B* in partial satisfaction of the annuity payments, to the extent of their fair market value, is treated as though the trustee sold the securities to *B* for cash, and immediately thereafter the trustee distributed the entire proceeds from the sale to her. Since the securities distributed had a fair market value in excess of their basis at the time of distribution, this excess must be included in the gross income of the trust as capital gain.

Under the provisions of section 1014 of the Internal Revenue Code of 1954 as implemented by section 1.1014–4(a)(3) of the Income Tax Regulations, when property is transferred by a trustee to a beneficiary under such circumstances that the transfer is considered a sale or exchange, the beneficiary acquires a basis equal to the fair market value of the property on the date of the transfer.

Section 643(a)(3) of the Code provides, in part, that gains from the sale or exchange of capital assets shall be excluded from distributable net income to the extent that such gains are allocated to corpus and are not (A) paid, credited, or required to be distributed to any beneficiary during the taxable year, or (B) paid, permanently set aside, or to be used for the purposes specified in section 642(c) of the Code.

Section 1.643(a)–3(a) of the regulations provides that gains from sale or exchange of capital assets are ordinarily excluded from distributable net income, and are not ordinarily considered as paid, credited, or required to be distributed to any beneficiary unless they are:

(1) Allocated to income under the terms of the governing instrument or local law by the fiduciary on its books or by notice to the beneficiary,

(2) Allocated to corpus and actually distributed to beneficiaries during the taxable year, or

(3) Utilized (pursuant to the terms of the governing instrument or the practice followed by the fiduciary) in determining the amount which is distributed or required to be distributed.

The first instance under the regulations for inclusion in distributable net income requires that capital gains be allocated to income under the terms of the governing instrument or local law by the fiduciary on its books or by notice to the beneficiary. This requisite is not met in the instant case since the governing instrument is silent as to allocation of capital gains and, in the absence of a provision therein, local law requires that capital gains be allocated to corpus.

The second instance under the regulations for inclusion in distributable net income requires that capital gains be allocated to corpus and actually distributed to beneficiaries during the taxable year. As illustrated by Examples (3), (4) and (5) of section 1.643(a)–3(d) of the regulations, this provision regarding the inclusion of capital gains in distributable net income applies only where there is a distribution required by the terms of the governing instrument upon the happening of a specified event. In the instant case, such a condition for inclusion of capital gains in distributable net income is not present.

The third instance under the regulations for inclusion in distributable net income requires that capital gains be utilized (pursuant to the terms of the governing instrument or the practice followed by the fiduciary) in determining the amount that is distributed or required to be distributed. In the instant case, capital gains are not being utilized pursuant to the terms of the governing instrument in determining the amount that is distributed or required to be distributed. Furthermore, since this is the first taxable year of the trust, capital gains are not utilized pursuant to the practice followed by the fiduciary in determining the amount that is distributed or required to be distributed.

Accordingly, under the facts set forth above, where income of the trust for its first taxable year is insufficient to make the annuity payment to *B* and in accordance with the agreement with her, the trustee distributes securities to her in partial satisfaction of the annuity payment, capital gain of 2x dollars resulting from the transaction is includible in gross income of the trust but is excludable from its distributable net income.

B is required to include 10x dollars (the trust's distributable net income as determined under section 643 of the Code) in gross income as ordinary income.

Also *B* is treated as having received 14x dollars (such amount being in excess of the trust's distributable net income) as a distribution of corpus.

The basis of the securities in the hands of *B* is 14x dollars representing fair market value on the date of transfer.

———

The examples in Revenue Ruling 68–392 describe three exceptions to the general rule that capital gains are not included in DNI. First, the underproductive property rule of 1962 Revised Uniform Principal and Income Act § 12 requires gain, in some instances, to be categorized as fiduciary accounting income; the 1997 Principal and Income Act does not. *See* 1997 Act § 413. The 1962 Act requirement is an example of when local law may allocate capital gains to fiduciary accounting income. Second, when a trust terminates, capital gains realized in the final year are actually distributed. This is an example of the second exception to the general rule of § 643(a)(3).

Finally, a fiduciary may establish a practice of considering capital gains when determining the amount to be distributed to a beneficiary. This exception is the most problematic. In Revenue Ruling 68–392, the Service asserted that no practice existed on the part of the fiduciary in the first year a fiduciary considers capital gains in determining distributable income. This implies that in the second year a practice may exist, but the fiduciary's conduct is the same in both instances.

In 2001, the Treasury issued Proposed Treas. Reg. § 1.643(a)-3(b) which alters the third example of the *Rev. Rul 68-393, supra*. The Proposed Regulations permit the practice to exist the first year the fiduciary allocates capital gains to DNI on its books, records, and tax returns. In Prop. Treas. Reg. § 1.643(a)-3(e), Example 2, the Trustee treats discretionary distributions of principal "as being first paid from any net capital gains." The inclusion of capital gains in DNI "is a reasonable exercise of the Trustee's discretion," but thereafter, all distributions must include capital gains.

The proposed regulation goes well beyond modifying the above result. As explained by the Service:

> The proposed regulations will amend section 1.643(a)-3(a) to clarify the circumstances in which capital gains are includible in distributable net income for the year. In general, capital gains are included in distributable net income to the extent they are, pursuant to the terms of the governing instrument or local law, or pursuant to a reasonable and consistent exercise of discretion by the fiduciary (in accordance with a power granted to the fiduciary by the governing instrument or local law): allocated to income; allocated to corpus but treated by the fiduciary on the trust's books, records, and tax returns as part of a distribution to a beneficiary; or allocated to corpus but utilized by the fiduciary in determining the amount which is distributed or required to be distributed to a beneficiary. . . .

> Under the proposed regulations, capital gains will be included in distributable net income under certain circumstances that are directed by the terms of the governing instrument and applicable local law. Thus, any capital gain that is included in the section 643(b) definition of income is included in distributable net income. Similarly, any capital gain that is used to determine the amount or the timing of a distribution to a beneficiary is included in distributable net income.

> Capital gains are also included in distributable net income if the fiduciary, pursuant to a discretionary power granted by local law or by the governing instrument (if not inconsistent with local law), treats the capital gains as distributed to a beneficiary, provided the power is exercised in a reasonable and consistent manner. Thus, if a trustee exercises a discretionary power by consistently treating any distribution in excess of ordinary income as being made from realized capital gains, any capital gain so distributed is included in distributable net income. The provisions of sections 643(b) and 643(a)(3) are further intertwined when consideration is given to the new state statutory provisions defining income. If, under the terms of the governing instrument or applicable local law, realized capital gains are treated as income to the extent the unitrust amount or the equitable adjustment amount exceeds ordinary income, capital gains so treated are included in distributable net income. A similar result is achieved for capital gains consistently allocated to income by the fiduciary pursuant to a discretionary power. In any other situation, capital gains will be excluded from distributable net income and will be taxed to the trust.

Explanation of Proposed Treas. Reg. § 1.643(a)-3, 66 Fed. Reg. 10396, 10398 (Feb. 15, 2001)

Revenue Ruling 85–116

1985–2 C.B. 174

ISSUE

Under the circumstances below, is any portion of a capital gain realized by a trust that is allocated to trust income under state law deductible by the trust and includible by the income beneficiary of the trust in the taxable year the gain is realized?

FACTS

T is a trust established in 1977 under A's will for the benefit of A's family. The terms of the trust instrument require that all trust income be paid out currently to A's child B for life. A's grandchildren are the remaindermen. T was funded exclusively with all the shares of X, a closely held corporation that A founded. In 1979, X adopted a plan of liquidation and sold all of its assets. In 1980, the proceeds of the sale in the amount of 390x dollars were distributed to T in complete liquidation of X.

Under the law of state V which is applicable to T, a portion of the proceeds of any transaction with respect to underproductive property, that is, trust property that has not produced for more than a year an average net annual income of one percent of its cost or value when acquired by the trust, is treated as "delayed income" which, in the absence of trust provisions to the contrary, is allocated to trust income rather than principal. The portion of the proceeds that is treated as delayed income is the difference between the proceeds and the amount which, had it been invested at five percent annually during the time the property was underproductive, would have produced the proceeds, less any income received by the beneficiary during that time. The balance is treated as principal. The trust instrument is silent concerning the allocation of the sale proceeds to trust income or principal.

The trustee of T allocated the liquidating distribution from X to principal and petitioned the state surrogate's court for approval of that action. T made no distribution to any beneficiary in 1980. In 1981, the court ordered that a portion of the liquidating distribution should be allocated to T's income account as delayed income because the X stock was underproductive property. In that year, after appropriately adjusting the books of T to reflect the allocation, the trustee made a distribution to B in the amount of 91x dollars, which was the amount of delayed income ordered by the court to be allocated to T's income account.

Both T and B file income tax returns on the calendar year basis. On its 1980 fiduciary income tax return, T reported a capital gain of 30x dollars as a result of the liquidation of X. B did not include any of the capital gain on B's individual income tax return for 1980 or for 1981.

LAW AND ANALYSIS

Section 651 of the Internal Revenue Code provides that, in the case of any trust the terms of which (1) provide that all of its income is required to be distributed currently, and (2) do not provide that any amounts are to be paid, permanently set aside, or used for the purposes specified in section 642(c) (relating to the deduction for charitable, etc., purposes), there shall be allowed as a deduction in computing the taxable income of the trust the amount of the income for the taxable year which is required to be distributed currently. If the amount of the income required to be distributed currently exceeds the distributable net income of the trust for the taxable year, the deduction shall be limited to the amount of the distributable net income.

Section 652 of the Code provides that the amount of income for the taxable year required to be distributed currently by a trust described in section 651 shall be included in the gross income of the beneficiaries to whom the income is required to be distributed, whether or not distributed. If that amount exceeds the distributable net income of the trust, there shall be included in the gross income of each beneficiary an amount which bears the same ratio to distributable net income as the amount of income required to be distributed to that beneficiary bears to the amount of income required to be distributed to all beneficiaries. The amount which the beneficiary is required to include in gross income is based upon the amount of income of the trust for any taxable year or years of the trust ending within or with the beneficiary's taxable year.

Income received by a trust that is required to be distributed currently to a beneficiary is taxable to the beneficiary in the taxable year of the beneficiary ending within or with the taxable year of the trust in which the income is received, even though the beneficiary receives the income at a later time due to the trustee's erroneous belief that the receipt constituted corpus and not income. *DeBrabant v. Commissioner*, 90 F.2d 433 (2d Cir. 1937). *See Polt v. Commissioner*, 233 F.2d 893 (2d Cir. 1956); *United States v. Higginson*, 238 F.2d 439 (1st Cir. 1956); Rev. Rul. 62–147, 1962–2 C.B. 151.

Section 643(a) of the Code defines distributable net income to mean the taxable income of the trust computed with the modifications set forth in section 643(a)(1) through (7). Section 643(a)(3) provides that gains from the sale or exchange of capital assets are excluded to the extent that such gains are allocated to corpus and are not (A) paid, credited, or required to be distributed to any beneficiary during the taxable year, or (B) paid, permanently set aside, or to be used for the purposes specified in section 642(c).

Section 1.643(a)–3(a)(1) of the Income Tax Regulations provides that gains from the sale or exchange of capital assets are not ordinarily considered as paid, credited or required to be distributed to a beneficiary unless they are (1) allocated to income under the terms of the governing instrument or local law by the fiduciary on its books or by notice to the beneficiary, (2) allocated to corpus and actually distributed to beneficiaries during the taxable year, or (3) utilized (pursuant to the terms of the governing instrument or the practice followed by the fiduciary) in determining the amount which is distributed or required to be distributed.

Section 643(b) of the Code provides that for purposes of subparts A through D of subchapter J of the Code (sections 641 through 668 of the Code), the term "income," when not preceded by the words "taxable," "distributable net," "undistributed net," or "gross," means the amount of income of the trust for the taxable year determined under the terms of the governing instrument and applicable local law.

In the present case, the trust realized a capital gain in 1980 on the liquidation of X corporation. Under applicable local law, the law of state V, 91x dollars of the amount received by T in 1980 was treated as income and, therefore, was "income" within the meaning of section 643(b) of the Code. Under the terms of the trust instrument, all trust income was required to be distributed currently to B. Accordingly, under section 651, T is allowed a deduction in computing its taxable income for 1980 for the amount of income required to be distributed currently to B, limited to the distributable net income of T. Under section 652, B is required to include in gross income for 1980 an amount equal to the amount deductible by the trust under section 651. This is so despite the fact that the 91x dollars was not distributed to B until 1981. *DeBrabant v. Commissioner.*

To the extent that capital gains are allocated to income, they are included in computing distributable net income for purposes of section 651 of the Code. Section 1.643(a)–3(a)(1) of the regulations. In this case, 91/390 of the proceeds received by T is allocated to income under the law of state V. Therefore, a proportionate part of the capital gain realized by T, 7x dollars (91/390 × 30x dollars), is considered allocated to income and hence includible in the computation of distributable net income. See Example 5 of section 1.643(a)–3(d), showing that where half the proceeds of the sale of stock by a trustee was distributed to a beneficiary, half the capital gain is considered allocable to the beneficiary.

HOLDING

The 91x dollars of delayed income constitutes trust income required to be distributed to B in 1980. The total amount of trust income required to be distributed to B in 1980 is included in B's gross income for that year, and is allowed as a deduction to T, to the extent this amount does not exceed T's distributable net income for 1980. T's distributable net income for that year includes 7x dollars of the capital gain T realized on the liquidation of X.

Problem

A trust that provides income to A for life, remainder to B, has the following items of gross income: dividends of $30,000, taxable interest of $20,000, and a long term capital gain of $10,000 (but no tax exempt income). The trust also has allowable deductions for trustee's commissions allocable to income in the amount of $5,000. What is the amount of DNI? Would your answer change if the trustee distributed the gain to A pursuant to a mandatory direction in the trust instrument or a regular practice?

[D]   Operation of the Conduit System

[1]   Taxation of Simple Trusts and Their Beneficiaries

Code: §§ 641, 642(b) through (g), 643, 651, and 652.

Regulations: Treas. Reg. §§ 1.651(a) and (b), 1.652(a), 1.652(b), and 1.652(c)–4.

The concept of the trust as a conduit is illustrated in its most basic form by the taxation of simple trusts and their beneficiaries. *See* §§ 641, 643, 651 and 652. A *simple trust* is one which requires that all income be distributed currently, and which makes no charitable distributions and no distributions out of principal. *See* § 651. The term, *simple trust*, is not used in the statute, but is used in the Senate Finance Committee Report to the 1954 Act. *See* Sen. Rep. No. 1622, 83rd Cong. 2d Sess., 82–87 (1954). *Income* for these purposes is *accounting income*, as determined by the trust instrument and local law. *See* § 643(b).

As suggested by Revenue Ruling 85–116, *supra*, and *Tucker*, *infra*, the property law designation of an item as income or principal will not affect the initial determination of whether the item is taxable to someone as income; that is a matter of federal tax law. For example, most income in respect of a decedent (§ 691) received by an estate is treated as principal for trust accounting purposes because the right to it was an asset owned by the decedent at his death. *See* 1962 Act § 4; 1997 Act § 302. It is, however, an item of gross income for income tax purposes.

Although state law does not determine whether a receipt is taxable, it usually determines to whom the income is taxable. The decision regarding allocation of a receipt normally dictates to whom the income is payable and taxable. Thus, if an item is considered to be income for accounting purposes, it is normally taxed to the income beneficiary of a simple trust, because it is required to be distributed currently or because it is actually distributed. On the other hand, if the receipt is considered to be principal for accounting purposes, it is normally taxed to the trust.

Revenue Ruling 85–116 and *Tucker* also illustrate the second half of the conduit aspect of simple trusts—the taxation of trust income to the income beneficiary. Section 652 requires that the income of simple trusts (income required to be distributed currently) be included in the gross income of the beneficiary to whom it is supposed to be distributed. Even if such income is not distributed, but is retained in the trust, it constitutes gross income to the beneficiary entitled to it, and income must be reported. Paralleling the limitation that *distributable net income* places on the distribution deduction available to the trust, the amount of income includable in the beneficiary's gross income is limited by § 652(a) to the amount of distributable net income, as adjusted by net tax exempt items.

Under § 652(b), income has the same character in the hands of the beneficiary as it had in the hands of the trustee. Thus, as illustrated by *Tucker*, tax exempt income (less allocable deductions) remains tax exempt in calculating the taxable income of the beneficiary.

Simple trusts with more than one income beneficiary present an additional problem that is addressed by the Code: how is the taxable income divided among beneficiaries? No such problem exists if the income distributed equals the distributable net income, and if it all comprises ordinary income. When, however, the distributable net income is less than the distributed fiduciary accounting income, or when the distributed fiduciary accounting income contains items such as tax exempt income, then allocation of income among beneficiaries becomes more difficult.

If a trust's DNI is less than the distributed fiduciary accounting income, each income beneficiary must report as income a proportion of the DNI. Section 652(a) requires that each income beneficiary report as income a portion of the DNI equal to a proportional share of the fiduciary accounting income. *See* Treas. Reg. § 1.652(b)–2. Thus, the tax burden of the income is spread among all of the income beneficiaries.

When it comes to the allocation of types of income and deductions the Code takes a different approach. The settlor may provide for the allocation of such items to particular beneficiaries. If the trust instrument so specifies, the tax costs and benefits of that allocation pass as directed. *See* § 652(b). For example, if one beneficiary is to receive all tax exempt income, another is to receive a capital gains item, and yet another an item of ordinary income, the allocation results in the three beneficiaries receiving the specified type for tax purposes. *See* Treas. Reg. § 1.652(b)–2(b). If the trust instrument does not provide for the allocation of items, § 652(b) requires proportionate allocation of these items among beneficiaries.

Tucker v. Commissioner

322 F.2d 86 (2d Cir. 1963)

Leonard P. Moore, Circuit Judge.

This is a petition for review of a decision of the Tax Court.

. . .

[The Court determined] a deficiency of $28,703.71 in the income tax of the petitioner, Marcia Brady Tucker, and her deceased husband for the calendar year 1955. Marcia Brady Tucker is the income beneficiary of a trust created under the will of her father. The entire net income from the trust, other than capital gains, is payable to her for life. The income of the trust for 1955 consisted of $380,122.21 of tax exempt municipal bond interest, $607,497.84 of taxable dividends and interest, and $1,408,887.31 of net long term capital gains.

The trust expenditures not directly attributable to any specific class of income amounted to $148,817.36. These expenses were all chargeable to and paid out of the corpus of the trust.[33] The sole controversy between the parties

---

[33] Under the 1954 Code, the income beneficiary receives the benefit of all the deductions of the trust not attributable to tax exempt interest, including those deductions, if any, properly allocable to capital gains. This change from the practice under the Internal Revenue Code of 1939 was made to avoid the wasting of deductions that was possible under that Code. *See generally* H. Rep. No. 1337, 83rd Cong., 2d Sess., A196–198 (1954); S. Rep. No. 1622, 83rd Cong., 2d Sess., 345–47 (1954), U.S. Code Congressional and Administrative News, p. 4025 *et seq.*

is over the method of allocation of these administrative expenses between the tax exempt and taxable income of the trust. The trustee allocated these expenses pro rata among all items of tax exempt and taxable income, including capital gains, thereby arriving at an allocation of $23,464.09 to tax exempt income and $125,353.27 to taxable income. The Commissioner made the allocation only among the items of tax exempt and taxable income distributable to the income beneficiary. By excluding capital gains, he arrived at an allocation of $56,456.84 of the expenses to tax exempt income and $92,360.52 to taxable income, thus increasing the amount of the expenses allocated to tax exempt income by $32,992.77. The Commissioner's allocation has no effect on the amount of income which is taxable to the trust,[34] but it does increase by $32,992.77 the amount of the distribution which must be included in the gross income of the taxpayer. This increase produced the deficiency of $28,703.71. The Tax Court upheld the Commissioner's determination on the ground that Section 652(b) of the Internal Revenue Code of 1954 mandated the allocation as made by the Commissioner. We affirm.

[The court set forth § 652(b) of the 1954 Code.]

. . .

Section 643 defines the term "distributable net income" to mean the taxable income of the estate or trust computed with certain modifications. One of the modifications enumerated is the exclusion of capital gains to the extent that these gains are allocated to corpus and are not paid, credited, or required to be distributed to any beneficiary during the taxable year. Section 643(a)(3). As noted earlier, the capital gains of the trust in question are not distributed to the beneficiary but are required to be retained in the trust corpus. Thus, the capital gains of the trust are not part of the distributable net income of the trust as defined in section 643 and are, therefore, not an "item of distributable net income" for purposes of allocation under section 652(b). According to the terms of the statute itself, then, the allocation of the Commissioner is the proper one.[35]

Taxpayer seeks to avoid the mandate of section 652(b) and the regulations promulgated thereunder by arguing that section 265, and not section 652(b), controls the allocation in question. She argues that trust disbursements (expenses) are to be allocated to tax exempt interest according to the principles of section 265,[36] and that the amount of the expenses held to be nondeductible, because allocated to tax exempt interest under section 265, is not an item of deduction entering into the computation of distributable net income for purposes of section 652(b). According to the taxpayer, section 652 is concerned only with the allocation of deductions, for the purpose of determining the income character in the hands of the beneficiary, after the amount of the deduction has been determined under section 265.

---

[34] This method of allocation does not change the total amount of the deductions available to the trust. When the trust's deductible expenses are decreased, the deduction allowed for the amount of the income required to be distributed to beneficiaries is increased by an equal amount. *See* § 651 of the Internal Revenue Code of 1954.

[35] The Regulations to § 652(b) also call for the allocation made by the Commissioner. *See* Treas. Reg. § 1.652(b)–3(b).

[36] Treas. Reg. § 1.265–1(c) provides that if an expense is allocable to both exempt and nonexempt income, a "reasonable proportion thereof . . . shall be allocated to each."

Taxpayer argues that the trustee's allocation of the expenses among all classes of income is the only reasonable one under this section. The Court of Claims, however, has held that the Commissioner's allocation is reasonable under section 265. *Manufacturers Hanover Trust Co. v. United States*, 312 F. 2d 785 (Ct. Cl. 1963).

Taxpayer's analysis would leave no operative significance for section 652(b). Carrying the analysis to its logical conclusion and still giving effect to section 652(b) would produce strange results. For example, section 652(b) requires that deductions entering into the computation of distributable net income be allocated among the items of distributable net income. One of the items of distributable net income is tax exempt income. Section 643(a)(5). Allocating a portion of the deduction (defined by taxpayer to exclude the amount allocated to tax exempt income under section 265) to tax exempt income would mean that expenses clearly attributable to taxable income would be lost to the taxpayer. The only way to avoid that result would be to exclude tax exempt interest from the base for the purpose of the section 652(b) allocation. This would do violence to the clear requirement of that section.

The basic fallacy in taxpayer's argument is that it contemplates two allocations, one to determine the trust's deductions and the other to allocate those deductions among the items of distributable net income. The statutory pattern calls for one allocation and that allocation is governed by section 652. To hold otherwise would be to deny any effect to the language of that section.

Affirmed.

The result in *Tucker* is confirmed and expanded in Revenue Ruling 77–355, 1977–2 C.B. 82, Revenue Ruling 77–466, 1977–2 C.B. 83, and *Fabens v. Commissioner*, 519 F.2d 1310 (1st Cir. 1975).

Revenue Ruling 85–116 and *Tucker* illustrate the interplay of tax law and state property law designations. Both also highlight the default rule: if the testator does not specify the interests of the beneficiaries, the Code will.

The following example illustrates how taxable income and the income of the beneficiary are computed.

Example 5: Assume the same facts as in Example 1, § 14.05[B]. The trust is required to distribute all of its income to its sole income beneficiary. The trust makes no other distributions. It has the following income and deductions:

Gross income from real estate rentals	$15,000
Interest on corporate bonds	$25,000
Extraordinary cash dividend allocated to principal	$10,000
Long term capital gain	$25,000
Long term capital loss	-$15,000
Trustee fees chargeable ½ to income and ½ to principal	-$12,000

Real estate rental expenses	-$5,000

FAI of the trust is computed as follows:

Rental income	$15,000
Corporate bond interest	$25,000
Less rental expenses	-$5,000
Less one-half of the trustee fee	-$6,000
FAI	$29,000

The computation of tentative taxable income needed to determine DNI is calculated as follows:

Gross income from real estate rentals	$15,000
Interest on corporate bonds	$25,000
Extraordinary cash dividend allocated to principal	$10,000
Long term capital gain	$25,000
Trustee fees [37]	-$12,000
Long term capital loss (§ 1211)	-$15,000
Real estate rental expenses	-$5,000
Personal exemption	-$300
Tentative Taxable Income	$42,700

DNI is computed as follows:

Tentative Taxable Income	$42,700
Plus personal exemption	$300
Less capital gains	-$25,000
Plus capital loss	$15,000
Less extraordinary cash dividend allocated to principal	-$10,000
DNI [38]	$23,000

Computation of taxable income for the trust picks up with tentative taxable income and is reduced by the distribution deduction.

Tentative Taxable Income	$42,700
Less distribution deduction [39]	$23,000
Taxable Income	$19,700

The beneficiary of the trust must report as gross income the amount that is required to be distributed, whether or not it is distributed. *See* § 652(a). If the amount required to be distributed exceeds DNI, the amount of income

---

[37] The entire fiduciary fee is deductible in determining taxable income and tentative taxable income, although one-half is charged to FAI and one-half is charged to fiduciary accounting principal.

[38] The distribution deduction is not added back to compute DNI because it was not deducted in determining tentative taxable income.

[39] The distribution deduction is the lesser of DNI or FAI. *See* § 651(b)

the beneficiary must report is limited by the amount of DNI. For a simple trust with several beneficiaries, the DNI is shared proportionately. *See* § 652(a), last sentence.

The following example illustrates how taxable income and the income of the beneficiary are computed when the trust receives tax exempt income:

Example 6: Assume the same facts as in Example 5, except the simple trust has $10,000 of tax exempt income and $15,000 of taxable interest. The computation of taxable income for the trust and the amount of income the beneficiary must report is computed as follows:

Gross income from real estate rentals	$15,000
Interest on corporate bonds	$15,000
Interest on municipal bonds	$10,000
Extraordinary cash dividend allocated to principal	$10,000
Long term capital gain	$25,000
Long term capital loss	-$15,000
Trustee fees chargeable ½ to income and ½ to principal	-$12,000
Real estate rental expenses	-$5,000

FAI of the trust is computed as follows:

Rental income	$15,000
Corporate bond interest	$15,000
Tax exempt income	$10,000
Less rental expenses	-$5,000
Less one-half of the trustee fee	-$6,000
FAI	$29,000

The computation of tentative taxable income needed to determine DNI is calculated as follows:

Gross income from real estate rentals	$15,000
Interest on corporate bonds	$15,000
Extraordinary cash dividend allocated to principal	$10,000
Long term capital gain	$25,000
Trustee fees allocable to taxable income[40]	-$9,000

---

[40] Because of § 265, a portion of the trustee's fee must be apportioned to the tax exempt income of the tax and, as a result, that portion is not allowable as a deduction used in computing taxable income. The fiduciary is allowed a deduction for the entire amount of the trustee fee not disallowed by § 265 although one-half of the fee is charge to income and one-half is charged to principal for fiduciary accounting purposes. *See* Treas. Reg. § 1.643(d)–2(a).

The deduction is disallowed under § 265 on the proportion of exempt income included in FAI (before reduction for expenses). Thus, the rents are not reduced by the directly related rental expenses. *See* Treas. Reg. §§ 1.652(c)–4 Example, 1.661(c)–2, 1.662(c)–4, 1.643(d)–2(a). *But see* Treas. Reg. §§ 1.652(b)–3(b). The ratio in the example is $10,000/$40,000 times $12,000 equals $3,000. It is *not* $10,000/$35,000 times $12,000 equals $3,429.

Long term capital loss (§ 1211)	-$15,000
Real estate rental expenses	-$5,000
Personal exemption	-$300
Tentative Taxable Income	$35,700

DNI is computed as follows:

Tentative Taxable Income	$35,700
Plus personal exemption	$300
Less capital gains	-$25,000
Plus capital loss	$15,000
Less extraordinary cash dividend allocated to principal	-$10,000
Plus tax exempt interest (less related expenses)[41]	$7,000
DNI[42]	$23,000

Computation of taxable income for the trust picks up with tentative taxable income and is reduced by the distribution deduction.

Tentative Taxable Income	$35,700
Less distribution deduction[43]	$16,000
Taxable Income	$19,700

The beneficiary of the trust must report as income the amount that is required to be distributed whether or not it is distributed. *See* § 652(a). If the amount required to be distributed exceeds DNI, however, the amount of income the beneficiary must report is limited by DNI. For a simple trust with several beneficiaries, the DNI is shared proportionately. *See* § 652(a), last sentence.

Under § 652(b), the character of the income earned by the trust retains its character when it passes out to the beneficiary. Unless the trust agreement provides otherwise, the character of the income passes out proportionately based on the character of the income that entered into the computation of DNI. For trusts with multiple beneficiaries, the DNI is shared proportionally. *See* Treas. Reg. § 1.652(b)–2.

In Example 6, FAI equals $29,000 and DNI equals $23,000. Thus, the amount of income the beneficiary must report is limited by DNI. Moreover, $7,000 of

---

[41] $10,000 minus $3,000.

[42] The distribution deduction is not added back to compute DNI because it was not deducted in determining tentative taxable income.

[43] The distribution deduction is the lesser of DNI or FAI. *See* § 651(b). In addition, the distribution deduction is limited to the portion of DNI attributable to taxable income. In the example, DNI is computed without adding back the net exempt income, resulting in a "special § 651(b) DNI" of $16,000 ($23,000 less $7,000). The amount required to be distributed is similarly adjusted to reflect the portion that is not taxable income. Thus, FAI of $29,000 is reduced for the net tax exempt income ($10,000 minus $3,000 of related expenses) for a net amount of $22,000. Thus, the distribution deduction is limited to the lesser of the special § 651(b) DNI ($16,000 in the example) or the taxable amount distributed to the beneficiary ($22,000). *See* Treas. Reg. § 1.651(b)–1.

the DNI is attributable to exempt income which leaves the beneficiary with $16,000 of taxable income.

In Examples 5 and 6, *supra*, the amount of income that the beneficiary must report has been computed without regard to the nature of that income. Under Treasury Regulation § 1.652(b)–2, the beneficiary receives a portion of each class of income received by the trust, unless the governing instrument has a specific provision or local law provides for a different apportionment of the income. For multiple beneficiaries, the classes of income are shared proportionately. Treasury Regulation § 1.652(b)–2(a) provides a simple example:

> Assume that under the terms of the governing instrument, beneficiary *A* is to receive currently one-half of the trust income and beneficiaries *B* and *C* are each to receive currently one-quarter, and the distributable net income of the trust (after allocation of expenses) consists of dividends of $10,000, taxable interest of $10,000, and tax exempt interest of $4,000. *A* will be deemed to have received $5,000 of dividends, $5,000 of taxable interest, and $2,000 of tax exempt interest; *B* and *C* will each be deemed to have received $2,500 of dividends, $2,500 of taxable interest, and $1,000 of tax exempt interest. However, if the terms of the trust specifically allocate different classes of income to different beneficiaries, entirely or in part, or if local law requires such an allocation, each beneficiary will be deemed to have received those items of income specifically allocated to him.

When the trust has deductions, Treasury Regulation § 1.652(b)–3 provides rules to determine which class of income is reduced by the deduction. First, the expenses directly attributable to one class of income must offset that income when determining the class of income received by the beneficiary. *See* Treas. Reg. § 1.652(b)–3(a). Second, if DNI includes any tax exempt income, a portion of the expenses must be allocated to the exempt income. *See* Treas. Reg. § 1.652(b)–3(b). For purposes of making the § 265 allocation, any item of income with directly attributable expenses is not reduced by those expenses for purposes of determining the disallowance fraction. *See* Treas. Reg. § 1.652(c)–4, Example. This was illustrated in Example 6 when the deduction for trustee's fee was disallowed in part. *See* footnote 45, *supra*.

The remainder of the expenses may be allocated against any class of income. *See* Treas. Reg. § 1.652(b)–3(b). The trustee may make this allocation irrespective of local law or provisions of the governing document. Finally, if expenses directly attributable to a class of income exceed that class of income, the excess deductions may be allocated against any other class of income, except that excess expenses attributable to exempt income may not be allocated to taxable income. *See* Treas. Reg. § 1.652(b)–3(d).

Using the facts presented in Example 6, the class of income received by the beneficiary and the allocation of deductions is determined as follows:

> The Trustee fees not allocated to tax exempt income may be allocated to either the rental income or apportioned among them. Thus, the $9,000 may be allocated all to the rental income to produce a net rental income of $1,000 and bond interest of $15,000.

	Tax exempt income	Rental Income	Corporate Bond Interest
Gross Income	$10,000	$15,000	$15,000
Related Expense	$ 3,000	$ 5,000	0
Discretionary Expense Allocation	0	$ 9,000	0
NET	$ 7,000	$ 1,000	$15,000

Alternatively it may be apportioned all to the bond interest to produce a net of $6,000 and rents of $10,000.

	Tax exempt income	Rental Income	Corporate Bond Interest
Gross Income	$10,000	$15,000	$15,000
Related Expense	$ 3,000	$ 5,000	0
Discretionary Expense Allocation	0	0	$ 9,000
NET	$ 7,000	$10,000	$ 6,000

Finally it may be apportioned between the two classes of income as the trustee elects. For example, an allocation of 50/50 results in $5,500 of rental income and $10,500 of bond interest.

	Tax exempt income	Rental Income	Corporate Bond Interest
Gross Income	$10,000	$15,000	$15,000
Related Expense	$ 3,000	$ 5,000	0
Discretionary Expense Allocation	0	$ 4,500	$ 4,500
NET	$ 7,000	$ 5,500	$10,500

In all of the alternatives, the total amount received by the beneficiary is $23,000 of DNI, of which $16,000 is subject to income taxes.

For another example of the allocation of deductions see Treasury Regulation § 1.652(c)–4(f).

A trustee's discretion to allocate deductions to or away from various classes of income can be important to the beneficiary. For example, if the beneficiary is subject to the passive activity rules of § 469, the allocation of deductions to dividends or interest rather than to rental income of the trust might permit the beneficiary to increase the amount of the passive activity loss deduction permitted by § 469.

Problems

1. *D*'s will establishes a testamentary trust. Net income is payable to *D*'s spouse, *S*, for life, with the corpus to be distributed upon *S*'s death to *D*'s child, *C*. The corpus consists of corporate bonds which, during the current tax year,

produce $30,000 in taxable interest income. During the year, the trust expends $1,000 on investment advice, which is deductible as a § 212 expense, but is not subject to the 2% floor on miscellaneous itemized deductions under § 67(a). *See O'Neill v. Commissioner*, 994 F.2d 302 (6th Cir. 1993) *rev'g* 98 T.C. 227 (1992). *But see Mellon Bank v. United States*, 265 F.3d 1275 (Fed. Cir. 2001), *supra*, § 14.04[B][1]. The trust instrument provides that, for fiduciary accounting purposes, the expense is to be charged to corpus. The trustee, therefore, distributes $30,000 to *S* as fiduciary accounting income.

a. First, calculate the trust's taxable income and then calculate the amount of gross income that *S* must report.

b. How would your answers change if $10,000 of the $30,000 trust income was tax exempt interest income?

c. How would your answers to (a) and (b) change if the trust had two income beneficiaries, *X*, who is entitled to 60% of the trust income, and *Y*, who is entitled to 40% of the trust income?

d. How would your answers to (a) through (c) change if the trust also had a capital gain of $10,000?

e. Would the answer in (a) change if the investment advice expense is subject to § 67? *See Mellon Bank v. United States*, 265 F.3d 1275 (Fed. Cir. 2001)

2. The income beneficiary of a trust successfully objected to the trustee's accounting and obtained for the trust a surcharge of $500,000 against the trustee. The state court determined that $70,000 of this amount represented lost income to the trust and ordered its payment to the income beneficiary. Should this receipt by the beneficiary constitute the distribution of taxable income? *See Plunkett v. Commissioner*, 118 F.2d 644 (1st Cir. 1941). What would be the tax treatment of the remaining amount of the surcharge?

3. On the death of the primary life tenant a simple trust continues in existence. The income is to be split among secondary beneficiaries. The instrument is unclear about which of several possible takers are entitled to the income. As a result, the trustee impounded the income and petitioned for instructions. Four years later a state court decided to pay the impounded income to *A*. To whom should the income be taxable, and when? *See Estate of Bruchmann v. Commissioner*, 53 T.C. 403 (1969).

4. A simple trust receives an item of income in respect of a decedent which is includable in its gross income despite its characterization as principal under state law. The trust also generates taxable interest income, as well as tax exempt income. In addition, the trust incurs expenses which are allocable to principal, but deductible for fiduciary income tax purposes. When the trust distributes its income for the year, should the income in respect of a decedent be taken into account in allocating trust expenses to tax exempt income? *See VanBuren v. Commissioner*, 89 T.C. 1101 (1987); *Steingold v. Commissioner*, T. C. Memo 2000-225.

5. *A* was entitled to receive income from a trust for life. On August 1 of Year 1, *A* died having previously received $20,000 from the trust in Year 1.

a. Will the $20,000 be taxable to *A* or to *A*'s estate because the trust's taxable year will end on December 31 of Year 1, assuming DNI exceeds $20,000?

b. Assuming *A* was on the cash basis, who will be taxable on the income that was due *A* from the trust, but distributed after *A*'s death by the trust to *A*'s estate? *See Estate of Schimberg v. United States*, 365 F.2d 70 (7th Cir. 1966); § 14.01[C], *supra*; Treas. Reg. § 1.652(c)–2.

6. In Problem 1, assume the trust received $15,000 of rents and $15,000 of corporate bond interest. What is the amount of each class of income that *S* must report, assuming the investment advice is directly attributable to the interest income? What if the investment advice is not directly attributable to the interest income?

[2] Taxation of Complex Trusts and Their Beneficiaries

Code: §§ 641, 642, 643, 661, 662, and 663.

Regulations: Treas. Reg. §§ 1.661(a)–2(e), 1.661(b) and (c), and 1.662(a) and (b).

Complex trusts are trusts that need not distribute all income currently, or have charitable beneficiaries, or make corpus distributions during the taxable year. In some ways, the taxation of complex trusts is similar to the taxation of simple trusts. For example:

(1) FAI is computed identically for both;

(2) taxable income is calculated in the same way. *See* §§ 641(b), 67(e)(2);

(3) distributable net income is generally calculated in the same way, except for § 643(a)(4) (*i.e.,* extraordinary dividends and taxable stock dividends are included in DNI); *see* § 643(a);

(4) both types of trusts are entitled to a *personal exemption* deduction. The exemption for simple trusts is $300, but for complex trusts it is only $100, unless all income is required to be distributed currently; *see* § 642(b); and

(5) a complex trust, as with a simple trust, is allowed a deduction for income required to be distributed currently, limited only by the amount of distributable net income; *see* § 661(a)(1).

In other ways, however, the taxation of complex trusts is completely different. Although simple trusts are generally conduits for tax purposes,[44] complex trusts are treated, in part, like corporations because they can be taxed on income which is not distributed.[45] Furthermore, limited only by the extent that distributable net income exists (§ 661(a)), a complex trust may claim:

(1) a distribution deduction for amounts paid to the beneficiaries out of income in satisfaction of trustee obligations to make distributions which may be out of income or corpus (§ 661(a)(1)); and

---

[44] A simple trust that has taxable income that is excluded from DNI is taxable on that income.

[45] Simple trusts are taxed only as to items that constitute income for tax purposes, but that are not income for fiduciary accounting purposes. *See* Rev. Rul. 85–116 (reproduced in § 14.05[D][1], *supra*).

(2)   a distribution deduction for any other amounts of income or corpus "properly paid or credited or required to be distributed for such taxable year." *See* § 661(a)(2); § 1.661(a)–2(c).

Income actually accumulated and not required to be distributed currently is taxed to the trust, unless there are corpus distributions requiring income tax treatment under § 661(a)(2).

The taxation of the beneficiary of a complex trust reflects this corporate tax-like treatment. Just as the trust is allowed to take a distribution deduction for amounts distributed or required to be distributed, a beneficiary is required to report as gross income similar amounts, but limited by the amount of distributable net income of the estate or trust (§ 662) for the taxable year(s) ending within the beneficiary's taxable year. *See* § 662(c).

The following example illustrates how taxable income of a complex trust and the income of the beneficiary are computed.

Example 7: Assume the same facts as in Example 3, § 14.05[B]. A complex trust is not required to distribute all of its income. The modification of taxable income required by § 643(a)(4) to compute DNI does not apply. The trustee distributes $29,000 to the beneficiary in its discretion. The computation of taxable income for the trust and its beneficiary are as follows:

Gross income from real estate rentals	$15,000
Interest on corporate bonds	$25,000
Extraordinary cash dividend allocated to principal	$10,000
Long term capital gain	$25,000
Long term capital loss	-$15,000
Trustee fees chargeable ½ to income and ½ to principal	-$12,000
Real estate rental expenses	-$5,000

FAI of the trust is computed as follows:

Rental income	$15,000
Corporate bond interest	$25,000
Less one-half of the trustee fee	-$6,000
Less rental expenses	-$5,000
FAI	$29,000

The tentative taxable income needed to compute DNI is computed as follows:

Gross income from real estate rentals	$15,000
Interest on corporate bonds	$25,000
Extraordinary cash dividend allocated to principal	$10,000
Long term capital gain	$25,000
Trustee fees[46]	-$12,000

---

[46] The entire fiduciary fee is deductible in determining taxable income and tentative taxable income, although one-half is charged to FAI and one-half is charged to fiduciary accounting principal.

Long term capital loss	-$15,000
Real estate rental expenses	-$5,000
Personal exemption	-$100
Tentative Taxable Income	$42,900

DNI is computed as follows:

Tentative Taxable Income	$42,900
Plus personal exemption	$100
Less capital gains	-$25,000
Plus capital loss	$15,000
DNI[47]	$33,000

Taxable income for the trust picks up with tentative taxable income and completes the computation as follows:

Tentative Taxable Income	$42,900
Less distribution deduction[48]	$29,000
Taxable Income	$13,900

The beneficiary of the trust must report as income the amount of income that is required to be distributed whether or not it is distributed, and must report any other amounts paid, credited, or required to be distributed. *See* § 662(a). If the amount required to be distributed exceeds DNI, the amount of income the beneficiary must report is limited by DNI. *See* § 661(a)(1). Trusts with several beneficiaries share the DNI proportionately. *See* § 662(a)(1).

In Example 7, FAI equals $29,000 and DNI equals $33,000. Thus, the amount of income the beneficiary must report is limited by the amount of the distribution.

The following example illustrates how taxable income and the income of the beneficiary are computed when a complex trust has received tax exempt income:

Example 8: Assume the same facts as in Example 7, except that the complex trust has $10,000 of exempt income and only $15,000 of taxable interest. The computation of taxable income for the trust and the amount of income the beneficiaries must report is computed as follows:

Gross income from real estate rentals	$15,000
Interest on corporate bonds	$15,000
Interest on municipal bonds	$10,000
Extraordinary cash dividend allocated to principal	$10,000
Long term capital gain	$25,000
Long term capital loss	-$15,000

---

[47] The distribution deduction is not added back to compute DNI because it was not deducted in determining tentative taxable income.

[48] The distribution deduction is the lesser of DNI ($33,000) or the amount required to be distributed to beneficiaries and other amounts actually distributed ($29,000).

Trustee fees chargeable ½ to income and ½ to principal	-$12,000
Real estate rental expenses	-$5,000

FAI of the trust is computed as follows:

Rental income	$15,000
Corporate bond interest	$15,000
Tax exempt income	$10,000
Less rental expenses	-$5,000
Less one-half of the trustee fee	-$6,000
FAI	$29,000

The tentative taxable income needed to compute DNI is computed as follows:

Gross income from real estate rentals	$15,000
Interest on corporate bonds	$15,000
Extraordinary cash dividend allocated to principal	$10,000
Long term capital gain	$25,000
Trustee fees allocable to taxable income[49]	-$9,000
Long term capital loss	-$15,000
Real estate rental expenses	-$5,000
Personal exemption	-$100
Tentative Taxable Income	$35,900

DNI is computed as follows:

Tentative Taxable Income	$35,900
Plus personal exemption	$100
Less capital gains	-$25,000
Plus capital loss	$15,000
Plus tax exempt interest (less related expenses)	$7,000
DNI	$33,000

Taxable income for the trust picks up with tentative taxable income and completes the computation as follows:

Tentative Taxable Income	$35,900

---

[49] Because of § 265, a portion of the trustee's fee must be apportioned to the tax exempt income and, as a result, that portion is not allowable as a deduction used in computing taxable income. The fiduciary is allowed a deduction for the entire amount of the trustee fee not disallowed by § 265 although one-half of the fee is charged to income and one-half is charged to principal for fiduciary accounting purposes. *See* Treas. Reg. § 1.643(d)–2(a).

The deduction is disallowed under § 265 on the proportion of exempt income included in FAI (before reduction for expenses). Thus, the rents are not reduced by the directly related rental expenses. *See* Treas. Reg. §§ 1.652(c)–4 Example, 1.661(c)–2, 1.662(c)–4, 1.643 (d)–2(a). *But see* Treas. Reg. §§ 1.652(b)–3(b). The ratio in the example is $10,000/$40,000 times $12,000 equals $3,000. It is *not* $10,000/$35,000 times $12,000 equals $3,429.

Less distribution deduction[50] $22,848

Taxable Income $13,052

The beneficiary of the trust must report as income the amount of fiduciary accounting income that is required to be distributed, whether or not it is distributed and must report any other amounts that are paid, credited, or required to be distributed. *See* § 662(a). If the amount required to be distributed exceeds DNI, the amount of income the beneficiary must report is limited by DNI. *See* § 661(a)(1). Trusts with several beneficiaries share the DNI proportionately. *See* § 662(a)(1).

Under § 662(b), the character of the income earned by the trust retains its character when it passes out to the beneficiaries. Unless the trust agreement provides otherwise, the character of the income passes out proportionately based on the character of the income that entered into the computation of DNI. For trusts with multiple beneficiaries, characterization is shared proportionally. *See* Treas. Reg. § 1.662(b)–1.

In Example 8, the amount distributed equals $29,000 and DNI equals $33,000. Thus, the amount of income the beneficiary must report is limited by the amount of the distribution. Moreover, a portion[51] of the amount distributed is attributable to exempt income which leaves the beneficiary with $22,848 of taxable income. If the DNI had not exceeded the amount required to be distributed, then only the taxable portion of DNI would have been income to the beneficiary.

Treasury Regulation § 1.662(b)–1 provides that deductions that are used in the calculation of DNI are allocated in accordance with Treasury Regulation § 1.652(b)–1. Deductions that are directly attributable to an item of income offset that income. Other deductions are allocated to all items of income that are included in DNI. Thus, a portion of the deductions must be allocated to exempt income, if any, that is included in DNI. The portion of the deductions not disallowed by § 265 may be allocated to any class of taxable income. For purposes of making the § 265 allocation, any item of income with directly attributable expenses is not reduced by those expenses for purposes of determining the disallowance fraction. *See* Treas. Reg. § 1.662(c)–4, Example.

---

[50] The distribution deduction is the lesser of DNI or the amount required to be distributed to beneficiaries and other amounts actually distributed. *See* Treas. Reg. § 1.661(a)–2(a). In addition, the distribution deduction is limited to the portion of DNI or the amount distributed that is attributable to taxable income. *See* §§ 661(b) (last sentence), 661(c); Treas. Reg. § 1.661(c)–1. In the example, DNI is computed without adding back the net exempt income, resulting in a "special § 661(c) DNI" of $26,000. The amount distributed is similarly adjusted to reflect the portion of a distribution that represents tax exempt income. *See* Treas. Reg. § 1.661(c)–1. The DNI of the trust ($33,000) is composed of $7,000 of exempt income and $26,000 of taxable income. Consequently, $7,000/$33,000 of amount distributed is not deductible. Thus, $26,000/$33,000 times $29,000 or $22,848 is the taxable portion of the amount distributed. Thus, the distribution deduction is limited to the lesser of the special section 661(c) DNI ($26,000 in Example 8) or the taxable amount distributed to the beneficiary ($22,848). *See* Treas. Reg. § 1.661(a)–2. Compare with note 43.

[51] The DNI of the trust ($33,000) is composed of $7,000 of exempt income and $26,000 of taxable income. Conversely, $7,000/$33,000 of the amount distributed is not deductible. Thus $26,000/$33,000 times $29,000 or $22,848 is the taxable portion of the amount distributed. Thus, the distribution deduction is limited to the lesser of the special § 661(c) DNI ($26,000 in the example) or the taxable amount distributed to the beneficiary ($22,848). *See* Treas. Reg. § 1.661(a)–2.

In § 14.05[D][1], *supra*, the determination of the character of income received by a beneficiary of a simple trust is discussed. Treasury Regulation § 1.662(b)–1 provides a similar rule for complex trusts. Classes of income are shared proportionally, unless the governing instrument has a specific provision or local law provides for a different apportionment of the income. Additional rules are necessary to complete the allocation of deductions because complex trusts may have a charitable deduction. Under Treasury Regulation § 1.662(b)–2, when a trust is entitled to a charitable deduction, the charity is deemed to receive a ratable share of each class of income, unless the governing instrument has a specific provision or local law provides for a different apportionment of the income.

The trustees of complex trusts are free to allocate deductions to various classes of income, subject to the same limitations that apply to simple trusts. *See* Treas. Reg. § 1.652(b)–3(b). Treasury Regulation § 1.662(c)–4(e) provides a complex example that illustrates the trustee's discretion to allocate deductions.

A trustee's discretion to allocate deductions to or away from various classes of income can be important to the beneficiary. For example, if the beneficiary is subject to the passive activity rules of § 469, the allocation of deductions to dividends or interest rather than to rental income of the trust might permit the beneficiary to increase the amount of the passive activity loss deduction permitted by § 469. Moreover, if DNI includes capital gains, the allocation of deductions away from capital gain income might permit a beneficiary to deduct capital losses generated outside of the trust or qualify more income for the special capital gains rates provided in § 1(h).

When a trust has more than one beneficiary to whom income is required to be currently distributed or to whom income or corpus may be distributed, rules are necessary to determine who reports receipts, and what amounts, as gross income. To treat the recipient of corpus as having received income would be inconsistent with the basic thrust of § 102 that gifts are not taxed as income. It would also seem inherently unfair to require a beneficiary who properly receives corpus to report gross income, or to allow an income beneficiary to receive tax free distributions of trust income. On the other hand, the complex trust rules were designed to avoid the possibility of trust accounting varying the income tax result merely by designating an item as *income* or *corpus*. The solution devised by Congress is a tier system under which beneficiaries who are entitled to receive the income that is required to be currently distributed are forced to report income, before any beneficiary is forced to report as income other payments, credits, or amounts required to be distributed by the trust. In the case of multiple beneficiaries, the tier system operates as follows:

Tier 1

(1)   When the trust's income is required to be currently distributed, each beneficiary reports either:

    (a)   the amount of income required to be currently distributed, or

(b)   if the *distributable net income* is less than the total of all income required to be currently distributed, the proportion of the distributable net income equal to the beneficiary's proportion of income required to be currently distributed. *See* § 662(a)(1).

Tier 2

(2)   When the trust properly pays, credits, or is required to distribute other cash or property to beneficiaries, each beneficiary reports either:

(a)   the *other amount* properly paid, credited, or required to be distributed; or

(b)   if the *distributable net income* of the trust or estate is less than the sum of such *other amounts* plus amounts of income required to be currently distributed, then:

(i)   if income required to be distributed currently equals or exceeds distributable net income, none of the distribution is income in the hands of the Tier 2 beneficiary; but

(ii)   if the income required to be distributed does not exceed DNI, an amount equal to the proportion of such *other amounts* multiplied by the difference between the distributable net income and such income required to be distributed currently. *See* § 662(a)(2).

The basic operation of the tier system can best be illustrated with an example.

Example 9: A trust has $100,000 in DNI. Under the terms of the trust, the trustee is required to pay $50,000 of trust income to *A*. The trustee may, in addition, distribute corpus or income to either *A* or *B*. In the taxable year, the trustee distributes the required $50,000 in income and $50,000 in corpus to *A* and $50,000 in corpus to *B*.

On the trust return for the year, the trustee deducts $100,000 as distributions to *A* and *B* because actual distributions exceeded DNI. *A* reports the $50,000 required income payment, plus one-half ($50,000 of *other amounts* divided by the $100,000 total of those Tier 2 amounts) of the remaining $50,000 in distributable net income. Thus, *A* reports $75,000 of income. *B* reports the other $25,000, which is treated as income even though paid out of corpus for accounting purposes.

Tier 1½.[52] When a trust makes a distribution of income to a qualified charity it is entitled to a charitable income tax deduction under § 642(c). The charity is not treated as a beneficiary, however, for purposes of §§ 661 and 662.[53] This rule has no effect on the computations that are made under § 661, but it has an impact on the noncharitable beneficiaries tax liability determined under § 662.

---

[52] Tier 1½ is not an official name, but reasonably describes the position of charities between Tier 1 and Tier 2.

[53] Any trust with a charitable beneficiary is a complex trust. Thus, §§ 651 and 652 are not applicable.

Section 662(a)(1) provides that DNI is computed without the charitable income tax deduction. Thus, a special § 661(c) DNI must be determined for purposes of computing the income that must be reported by a Tier 1 beneficiary. However, when the income reportable by a Tier 2 beneficiary is computed, regular, statutory DNI is used to limit the amount that is deemed income that the Tier 2 beneficiary must report.

The net effect of the difference between DNI computed under § 662(a)(1) and (2), is to allocate the DNI first to the Tier 1 beneficiaries, next reduce DNI by the charitable deduction, and finally allocate the remaining DNI to the Tier 2 beneficiaries.

The conduit system treats distributions as income, regardless of the source and type of property, to the extent the trust has distributable net income for the taxable year. The Code contains special provisions to avoid the possibility of inherently unfair results caused by the conduit system's potential treatment of all distributions as income. First, under a pure form of this statutory scheme, a beneficiary could be required to report a particular item of income in each of two years. If the terms of the trust required the trustee to distribute some income currently, the beneficiary would have to report that income in the year the trust earned it. If, however, the trustee did not in fact distribute that income until a succeeding taxable year, the beneficiary would be required to report it again as property actually distributed. To avoid this result, § 663(a)(3) makes §§ 661(a) and 662(a) inapplicable to amounts required by §§ 651 or 661 to be treated as distributed in a prior taxable year.

A second inherent unfairness is the taxation of a specific gift or devise of a sum of money or of property, when it is made during a year in which the trust has distributable net income. As *other payments* these specific items would ordinarily be treated as income to the beneficiary if the trust had undistributed DNI. To avoid this result, § 663(a)(1) specifically makes §§ 661(a) and 662(a) inapplicable to such gifts or devises, unless these payments can be credited only from income of the trust.

A third unfairness is raised by trusts in which two or more beneficiaries have substantially separate shares. The classic example is a trust in which the trustee is directed to divide the corpus into separate shares (but not separate trusts) for children of the grantor. Application of the normal subchapter J rules would produce an unfair result if the trustee did not make equal distributions to all beneficiaries in any taxable year. For example, if income and corpus were distributed to beneficiary *B* from his share, but nothing was distributed to the beneficiaries of the other shares, the normal rules would require *B* to report as income even the corpus distributions, up to the amount of distributable net income of the entire trust for the tax year. *B* would thus bear the tax costs of income properly chargeable to the other beneficiaries. To avoid this result, § 663(c) allows distributable net income for *shares* of trusts and estates to be calculated on a *share* basis. Thus, *B* would be taxed only on the distributable net income of his share of the trust, and the corpus distribution would pass out tax free. The separate share rule is considered in more detail later, including its application to estates. *See* § 14.05 [D] [4], *infra.*

Finally, the simple tax structure described above does not reflect the possibility that one beneficiary may be entitled to tax exempt income, another to capital gains and losses, and yet another to ordinary income. To tax each, as though the beneficiary received some of each type of income, would allocate tax burdens in a manner inconsistent with the provisions of the trust terms. Thus, § 662(b) provides that, as with simple trusts, income of complex trusts retains its character in the hands of the beneficiary. If the will or trust instrument requires a particular allocation of specific classes of income to certain beneficiaries, that allocation may be respected for tax purposes. It is only where the instrument does not effectively allocate classes of income that all classes are deemed to have been distributed proportionately to all beneficiaries.

To ease the possible problems inherent in calculating income before it can be distributed, § 663(b) allows the trustee of a trust to elect to have distributions made within 65 days of the close of the taxable year treated as though they were made during the prior taxable year.

Problems

1. A trust has annual interest income of $45,000 and fully deductible expenses of $5,000 which are chargeable to income. On the following trust terms, what amount will the trustee deduct under § 661 given the described distributions, and what amount will the beneficiary include in gross income under § 662? What will be the trust's taxable income in each situation?

a. The trust provides income must be paid to A and B for life, remainder to C. Trustee, T, has power to invade the corpus for C. T distributes $20,000 each to A and B, and invades corpus for C in the amount of $20,000.

b. The trust provides that T has the discretion to distribute income to D, or accumulate it and add it to corpus. On D's death, the trust will terminate and the accumulated corpus will pass to E. T has the power to invade corpus for E. T distributes $40,000 of income to D, and invades corpus for E in the amount of $25,000.

c. The trust provides income to X for life, remainder to Y, and gives Z the annual right to receive $25,000, to be paid out of corpus. T pays $40,000 to X, and $25,000 to Z. Would your answer change if T could accumulate or distribute income to X, and T distributes $40,000 from income to X, as well as $25,000 to Z.

d. The trust provides income equally to A and C for the life of A, remainder to B. C is a qualified charity. Trustee T has power to invade corpus for B. T distributes $20,000 each to A and C, and invades corpus for B in the amount of $20,000.

e. The trust provides income equally to A and B for the life of A, remainder to D. Also, the trustee is required to distribute $20,000 a year to charity, C. Trustee, T, has power to invade corpus for D. T distributes $20,000 each to A, B, and C, and invades corpus for D in the amount of $20,000. *See Mott v. U.S.*, 462 F.2d 512 (Ct. Cl. 1972).

f. The trust requires the trustee to distribute $10,000 per year from income to a charity, C, and permits the trust to distribute income and principal to A and B. Trustee, T, has power to invade corpus for D. T distributes $10,000 to the charity, $20,000 each to A and B, and invades corpus for D in the amount of $20,000.

g. Assume the expense is $15,000 instead of $5,000 and assume that the expense is charged to principal. The terms of the trust require the trustee to distribute $5,000 of income per year to a charity, C, directs that $30,000 of income must be distributed to A, and permits the trust to distribute income and principal to B. T distributes $5,000 to C, $30,000 to A, and $10,000 to B.

2. D establishes a testamentary trust, the net income of which must be paid to his wife, W, for her life, with the corpus to be distributed to his child, C, on W's death. The corpus consists of corporate bonds which, during the current tax year, produce $30,000 in taxable interest income. During the year, the trust expends $1,000 on investment advice, which is charged to principal and which is deductible as a § 212 expense and is not subject to § 67. Assume further that the trustee has the power to distribute corpus to the single income beneficiary, W. How would the income of the trust be taxed to the trust and its beneficiaries?

3. In Problem 2, assume that the trustee has the power to withhold income from W, but that the trustee does not exercise the power. How would this fact change the analysis of the problem?

4. In Problem 3, would the results differ depending on whether the trustee charged the $30,000 distribution to the income account, the principal account, or part to each?

5. In Problem 2, assume that the trustee is required to pay W $10,000 in income each year, and has the power to pay W or C additional income or corpus. During the taxable year, the trustee pays W $20,000, allocating $15,000 to income and $5,000 to corpus, and pays C $20,000, allocating $5,000 to income and $15,000 to corpus. What would be the income tax consequences to the trust and its beneficiaries?

6. Assume the facts in Problem 5, except that the trust instrument directs the trust to be divided into separate equal shares for W and C, so that the trust's accounting income is allocated one-half to each. What would be the income tax consequences of this change?

7. Assume the facts in Problem 6, except that the trustee distributes the required $10,000 in income to W, and specifically bequeaths an automobile worth $10,000 to W. The trustee also distributes $10,000 in discretionary income and $10,000 in corpus to C. What are the income tax consequences of the distributions to the trust and its beneficiaries?

8. A trust has annual interest income of $25,000 and rental income of $20,000. It also pays $5000 for investment advice that is chargeable to income. The trust provides income to A and B for life, remainder to C. Trustee, T, has power to invade the corpus for C. T distributes $20,000 each to A and B, and invades corpus for C in the amount of $20,000. What is the amount of each class of income that A, B, and C must report, assuming the investment advice is directly attributable to the interest income? What if the investment advice is not directly attributable to the interest income?

[3]   Taxation of Estates and Their Beneficiaries

Code: §§ 642(b), 661, and 662.

Regulations: Review regulations previously assigned.

The distribution deduction for estates and the gross income inclusion rules for beneficiaries are determined in the same manner as for complex trusts. *See* §§ 661–663. Thus, the statutory exception under § 663(a)(1) also applies to bequests of a specific sum of money and of specific property; however, it does not apply to residuary bequests. *See* Treas. Reg. § 1.663(a). Also, the 65-day rule of § 663(b) applies to decedents' estates. Decedents' estates are, however, entitled to a personal exemption deduction of $600 rather than $100 for complex trusts. *See* § 642(b).

Notwithstanding the fact that §§ 661 through 663 apply to estates and complex trusts, there are some differences due to the unique nature of decedents' estates. Thus, an estate will usually have only Tier 2 distributions because an estate will rarely be required to distribute income. *See* Priv. Ltr. Rul. 8306003. Because amounts paid under a widow's allowance and similar provisions are governed by §§ 661 and 662, a judicially imposed widow's allowance or other support allowance may constitute a Tier 1 distribution if the estate has income. *See* Treas. Reg. § 1.662(a)–2. Also, not all estate assets and income will automatically form part of the subchapter J estate. For example, if real property is deemed to pass to heirs or devisees by operation of law at the decedent's death and the property is not subject to estate administration, the income from this property will not be treated as an amount paid by the estate under § 661. *See* Treas. Reg. § 1.661(a)–2(e). The property is deemed to be received by the heir or legatee as a gift under § 102(a). However, if the property is subject to administration, the income from it may be taxable to the estate and the beneficiaries. *See* Rev. Rul. 75–61, 1975–1 C.B. 180 (reproduced in § 14.04[A], *supra*); Rev. Rul. 69–49, 1968–1 C.B. 304.

[4]   Taxation of Certain Trusts as Estates

Code: § 645.

Regulations: § 1.645.

For many years prior to 1998, the income tax treatment of trusts and estates varied. Rules applicable to estates were not always applicable to trusts and vice versa. Each had tax advantages and disadvantages. The Taxpayer Relief Act of 1997 amended subchapter J rules to generally equalize the treatment of estates and trusts. Among the provisions are the 65-day election for estates and the mandatory application of the separate share rule as discussed in § 14.05[D][5]. In addition, the § 267 disallowance of losses between related taxpayers was made applicable to estates as discussed in § 14.05[E][1], *infra*.

The Taxpayer Relief Act of 1997 added § 645 which allows the personal representative of a decedent's estate and the trustee of a revocable trust, together, to elect to treat a revocable trust created by the decedent as if it were part of the decedent's estate for income tax purposes. In 2001, the IRS proposed Regulations providing guidance on how the 645 election should be made and how it affects the taxation of the trust and estate. *See* Prop. Treas. Reg. §§ 1.645-1(d)(1)(i), 1.645-1(d)(1)(ii)(A).

Section 645 applies only to a "qualified revocable trust" (QRT), which the Regulation defines as a domestic trust or portion of a domestic trust that, on the date of the decedent's death, was deemed owned by the decedent under § 676 because the decedent held a power to revoke the trust and revest its assets in the decedent. *See* § 8.01[D], *supra*, discussing § 676. For this purpose, a trust is not a qualified revocable trust merely because the decedent's spouse or other nonadverse party holds a power to revoke the trust and revest the assets in the decedent, nor because of a power to revoke held by the decedent if that power is exercisable solely with the consent of a nonadverse party. *See* Prop. Treas. Reg. § 1.645-1(b)(1).

The trustee of the QRT and the personal representative of the decedent's estate together make the election under § 645 by attaching a statement to the estate's fiduciary income tax return (Form 1041) for the estate's first taxable year.[54] The trustee makes the election alone, when there is no personal representative for the estate. *See* Prop. Treas. Reg. § 1.645-1(c).

The trustee and personal representative may choose not to obtain a TIN for the trust or file a fiduciary income tax return for the trust's short taxable year between the date of death and December 31 of that year if the § 645 election is made on the filing of the Form 1041 with the required statement attached.

An election under § 645 causes the trust to be treated as part of the estate for fiduciary income tax purposes. The separate share rules cause the trust to be treated as a separate share of the estate for purposes of computing distributable net income (DNI) and applying the distribution rules of §§ 661 and 662. The Regulation explains how to adjust the DNI of a QRT where distributions are made from the trust to the estate.

An election under § 645 will:

- permit the trust to elect a fiscal tax year;

- eliminate the need for separate income tax returns for the trust and the estate;

- allow the trust an income tax charitable deduction for amounts permanently set aside for charitable purposes, as well as amounts paid to charities;

---

[54] The election must include a written statement that:

- states that the election is made under § 645;

- states the decedent's name, address, date of death, and taxpayer identification number (TIN);

- states the trust's name, address, and TIN (if one has been obtained);

- states the estate's name, address, and TIN;

- represents that the electing trust is a QRT under § 645 and the Regulation;

- states, under penalties of perjury and with the dated signature of the personal representative, that the personal representative elects to treat the QRT as part of the related estate under § 645; and

- states, under penalties of perjury and with the dated signature of the trustee, that the trustee elects to treat the QRT as part of the related estate under § 645.

See Prop. Treas. Reg. § 1.645-1(c)(1)(ii).

- eliminate the active participation requirement for the use of passive loss under § 469, for two years after the owner's death; and

- enable qualification for amortization of reforestation expenditures in the same manner as estates, under § 194.

The trust may own S stock for potentially longer periods of time. A trust that does not make the election may own S stock for only 2 years after the grantor's death.

If made, the election is effective as of the decedent's death and it expires:

(i) the day preceding the date two years after the decedent's death, if a federal estate tax return (Form 706) is not required to be filed, or

(ii) If an estate tax return is filed, the day that is six months after the "final determination of liability for estate tax."

Upon termination of the election, there is a deemed distribution of all the assets of the electing trust to a new trust.

[5]　Separate Share Rules

Code: §§ 663.

Regulations: § 1.663(c).

The statutory exception under § 663(a)(1) also applies to bequests of a specific sum of money and of specific property, but not to residuary bequests. *See* Treas. Reg. § 1.663(a). In addition, the Taxpayer Relief Act of 1997 expanded the coverage of the separate share rule for trusts to estates. Subsequently, the Treasury Department issued regulations that provide guidance on when and how the separate share rules are applicable to estates. *See* Treas. Reg § 1.663(c)–4.

Having separate shares mean that an estate or a complex trust must separately compute distributable net income (DNI) for each separate share to determine the limitation on the §661 distribution deduction and to compute the amount of income §662 requires each beneficiary to report separately for each share. The separate share rules are mandatory—if applicable, the fiduciary must compute DNI under these rules. *See* Treas. Reg. § 1.663(c)-1(d). A separate share does not mean separate tax ID numbers, separate tax returns, separate tax payments (including separate estimated payments), or multiple personal exemptions. *See* Treas. Reg. 1.663(c)-1(b). However, the separate share rules are not applicable to "sprinkle" trusts, *i.e.*, trusts in which the fiduciary has discretion to distribute principal or income, however.

What is a separate share of an estate? Generally, Treasury Regulation § 1.663(c)-4 treats each share of an estate that has multiple beneficiaries with substantively separate and independent shares as a separate taxable entity solely for purposes of computing DNI. Treasury Regulation § 1.663(c)-4 provides that:

> Ordinarily, a separate share exists if the economic interests of the beneficiary or class of beneficiaries neither affect nor are affected by the economic interests accruing to another beneficiary or class of beneficiaries.

Separate shares include, for example, the income on bequeathed property if the recipient of the specific bequest is entitled to such income and a surviving spouse's elective share that under local law is entitled to income and appreciation or depreciation.

Furthermore, a qualified revocable trust for which an election is made under § 645 is always a separate share of the estate and may itself contain two or more separate shares.

See § 14.05[D][4], *infra* (discussing § 645).

Treasury Regulation § 1.663(c)(5) provides a number of examples that clarify the application of the separate share rule to estates. Treas Reg § 1.663(c)(2).

For example, when a personal representative makes proportionate distributions to residuary beneficiaries of an estate, the DNI is shared proportionately. *See* Treas. Reg. § 1.663(c)-5, Example 2. In this circumstance, having separate shares makes no difference because the distributions are proportionate. Under § 662 (without the separate share rule), the residuary beneficiaries of an estate divide the DNI (*i.e.*, report income) in the same proportions as the distributions were made.

When, however, the personal representative makes distributions to some residuary beneficiaries, but not all, the fiduciary must use a reasonable and equitable method to allocate income and expenses to the estate's or trust's shares. *See* Treas. Reg. § 1.663(c)-5, Example 3. Depending on when during the tax year the distribution is made, it may no longer be reasonable or equitable to determine the distributable net income by allocating a proportionate share of the estate's income and expenses for the year to the beneficiaries who receive a distribution. The computation of the DNI received by the beneficiaries should take into consideration the relative size of the after-the-partial-distribution size of their smaller separate shares of the estate and the relative size of the other beneficiaries' larger separate shares.

Example 3 does not mandate any automatic allocation formula. Rather, it is requiring the fiduciary to determine what is a fair allocation. For example, if the distribution is made the first day of the tax year, *i.e.*, before the estate has earned any income, and is for the full amount due beneficiaries who receive distributions, fairness might dictate that no DNI be attributed to them.

Before the separate share rule was applicable to estates, it was possible to shift the income tax liability between groups of beneficiaries. For example, if the distribution in Example 3 of the Regulation had been solely to one beneficiary, it was possible to have that beneficiary report as income the entire net income the estate received for the entire tax year. In a subsequent year, the other beneficiaries receive their share of the fiduciary accounting income free of income taxes if the estate has no DNI. This would happen if the second distribution occurred at the beginning of the final tax year and no assets remained in the estate after the distribution to generate any income or DNI.

When the estate beneficiary is not entitled to a share of estate income, distributions to that beneficiary do not carryout DNI. *See* Treas. Reg. § 1.663(c)-5, Example 4.

Example 7 illustrates how the separate share rule applies to elective share claims. *See* Treas. Reg. § 1.663(c)–5, Example 7. In the example, the testator is survived by a spouse and three adult children. The testator's will divides the residue of the estate equally among the three children. The surviving spouse files an elective share claim. Under state law, a surviving spouse is entitled to one-third of the decedent's estate after the payment of debts and expenses. The surviving spouse is not entitled to any estate income and does not participate in appreciation or depreciation of the estate's assets. However, under the elective share statute, the surviving spouse is entitled to interest on the elective share. During the taxable year, the estate makes a distribution in partial satisfaction of the elective share and pays $200,000 of interest on the delayed payment of the elective share. The estate has four separate shares—the surviving spouse's elective share and each of the three children's residuary bequests. Because the surviving spouse is not entitled to any estate income under state law, none of the estate's gross income is allocated to the spouse's separate share. The $200,000 of interest paid to the spouse must be included in the spouse's gross income under § 61. The estate's $200,000 interest payment is a nondeductible personal interest expense described in § 163(h).

The courts had split over the proper treatment of a distribution made in satisfaction of a surviving spouse's statutory share of a decedent's estate. In *Deutsch v. Commissioner*, T.C. Memo. 1997-470, the Tax Court held that a distribution in satisfaction of a surviving spouse's share of a decedent's estate did not carry out DNI to the surviving spouse. Thus, the surviving spouse did not include in gross income the payment in satisfaction of her elective share.

In *Brigham v. United States*, 983 F. Supp. 46 (D. Mass. 1997), *aff'd*, 160 F.3d 759 (1st Cir. 1998), however, the court held that the elective share distribution fully carried out DNI to the surviving spouse. Treasury Regulation § 1.663(c)–4(b) supersedes these decisions by providing that a surviving spouse's statutory elective share is a separate share of the estate for purposes of determining DNI, whether or not state law allows the surviving spouse to share in estate income or in appreciation and depreciation in estate assets. When the elective share is entitled to a share of estate income, a distribution of a surviving spouse's elective share will carry out only a proportionate share of the estate's DNI.

When an estate reports income from an S corporation or a partnership, Treasury Regulation § 1.663(c)-2(b)(4) provides a special rule for gross income not attributable to cash.

> This paragraph (b)(4) governs the allocation of the portion of gross income includible in distributable net income that is not attributable to cash received by the estate or trust (for example, original issue discount, a distributive share of partnership tax items, and the pro rata share of an S corporation's tax items). Such gross income is allocated among the separate shares in the same proportion as § 643(b) income from the same source would be allocated under the terms of the governing instrument or applicable local law.

For IRA distributions that are fiduciary accounting principal, several special rules to allocate DNI are provided. *See* Treas. Reg. § 1.663(c)-5, Examples 6, 9, and 10.

Although § 663 exempts specific devises from DNI rules and thus is not a separate share, the income on specifically devised property is a separate share. Distribution of the specifically devised property will not give rise to a distribution deduction or cause the beneficiary to receive taxable income, but when the income generated by the property is received by the estate and distributable to beneficiary, that distribution will carry out DNI. *See* Treas. Reg. § 1.663(c)-5, Example 8.

Problems

1. This year an estate has interest income of $45,000 and fully deductible expenses of $5,000 which are chargeable to principal. *D* and *E* are equal residuary beneficiaries. The personal representative distributes $40,000 of estate income to *D* and $25,000 of estate principal to *E*. What amount can the personal representative deduct under § 661? What amounts will *D* and *E* include in gross income under § 662? What will be the estate's taxable income and other income tax imposed?

2. A will provides as follows:

> I give assets, in cash or in kind or partly in each, the selection of which shall be in the absolute discretion of my personal representative with a fair market value at the date of distribution equal to $2,000, to the trustee hereinafter named, to be held, administered, and distributed as hereinafter provided.

If the personal representative distributes $2,000 to the testamentary trustee, will § 663(a)(1) apply? *See* Rev. Rul. 86–105, 1986–2 C.B. 82.

3. A will leaves $10,000, plus interest at 10%, to *X*. How should the interest payment be treated? *Compare United States v. Folckemer*, 307 F.2d 171 (5th Cir. 1962), *with Davidson v. United States*, 149 F. Supp. 208 (Ct. Cl. 1957). *See Tech. Adv. Mem. 9604002*; Uniform Probate Code § 3–904. *See* Treas. Reg. 1.663(c)-5, Example 7.

4. An estate is on a fiscal year ending on January 31st. The estate distributes $10,000 to *A* on June 1 of both Year 1 and Year 2. The estate's distributable net income for each year is greater than the distribution to *A*. How much, and in what years, will the distributions be includable in *A*'s gross income? *See* § 662(c). Would your answer change if *A* died on August 1 of Year 2? *See Schimberg v. United States* (reproduced at § 14.04[C], *supra*).

[E]   The Impact of Property Distributions

Code: §§ 267(b)(13), 643(d) and (e), 661, 663, 691, 1001, and 1014.

Regulations: Treas. Reg. § 1.691(a)–4; Prop. Treas. Reg. §§1.651(a)-2(d) and 1.661(a)-2(f).

When a trust or estate distributes property (other than cash), the distribution may result in a gain to the entity. In addition, the basis of the property in the hands of the beneficiary must be determined. This section explores these and other consequences of property distributions. *See generally* James J.

Freeland, *Estate and Trust Distributions of Property in Kind After The Tax Reform Act of 1984*, 40 Tax. L. Rev. 449 (1985).

[1] Mandatory Recognition of Gain or Loss

As suggested by *Kenan v. Commissioner, infra,* satisfaction of a pecuniary obligation of an estate or trust by means of distributions in kind can result in immediate recognition by the estate or trust of gain or loss on assets that have appreciated or depreciated in value. *See* Rev. Rul. 67–74, 1974–1 C.B. 194. However, § 267 permits neither an estate nor a trust to recognize a loss on a sale or exchange to a beneficiary. Excepted from the disallowance rule is a distribution by an estate in satisfaction of a pecuniary bequest. *See* § 267(b)(13).

Kenan v. Commissioner

114 F.2d 217 (2d Cir. 1940)

Augustus N. Hand, Circuit Judge.

The testatrix, Mrs. Bingham, died on July 27, 1917, leaving a will under which she placed her residuary estate in trust and provided in item "Seventh" that her trustees should pay a certain amount annually to her niece, Louise Clisby Wise, until the latter reached the age of forty, "at which time or as soon thereafter as compatible with the interests of my estate they shall pay to her the sum of Five Million ($5,000,000.00) Dollars." The will provided in item "Eleventh" that the trustees, in the case of certain payments including that of the $5,000,000 under item "Seventh," should have the right "to substitute for the payment in money, payment in marketable securities of a value equal to the sum to be paid, the selection of the securities to be substituted in any instance, and the valuation of such securities to be done by the Trustees and their selection and valuation to be final."

Louise Clisby Wise became forty years of age on July 28, 1935. The trustees decided to pay her the $5,000,000 partly in cash and partly in securities. The greater part of the securities had been owned by the testator and transferred as part of her estate to the trustees; others had been purchased by the trustees. All had appreciated in value during the period for which they were held by the trustees, and the Commissioner determined that the distribution of the securities to the niece resulted in capital gains which were taxable to the trustees . . . . On this basis, the Commissioner determined a deficiency of $367,687.12 in the income tax for the year 1935.

The Board overruled the objections of the trustees to the imposition of any tax . . . and confirmed the original deficiency determination. The taxpayers contend that the decision of the Board was erroneous because they realized neither gain from the sale or exchange of capital assets nor income of any character by delivering the securities to the legatee pursuant to the permissive terms of the will . . . .

The amount of gain is to be determined under Section [1001] which provides:

"(a) *Computation of gain or loss.* The gain from the sale or other disposition of property shall be the excess of the amount realized therefrom over the adjusted basis . . . .

"(b) *Amount realized.* The amount realized from the sale or other disposition of property shall be the sum of any money received plus the fair market value of the property (other than money received)."

Section [1014(a)(1)] is claimed by the taxpayers to be relevant and provides:

(a) the basis or property of a person acquiring the property from a decedent or to whom the property passed from a decedent shall . . . be—

(1) the fair market value of the property at the date of the decedent's death . . . .

In support of their petition the taxpayers contend that the delivery of the securities of the trust estate to the legatee was a donative disposition of property pursuant to the terms of the will, and that no gain was thereby realized. They argue that when they determined that the legacy should be one of securities, it became for all purposes a bequest of property, just as if the cash alternative had not been provided, and not taxable for the reason that no gain is realized on the transfer by a testamentary trustee of specific securities or other property bequeathed by will to a legatee.

We do not think that the situation here is the same as that of a legacy of specific property. The legatee was never in the position occupied by the recipient of specific securities under a will. She had a claim against the estate for $5,000,000, payable either in cash or securities of that value, but had no title or right to the securities, legal or equitable, until they were delivered to her by the trustees after the exercise of their option. She took none of the chances of a legatee of specific securities or of a share of a residue that the securities might appreciate or decline in value between the time of the death of the testator and the transfer to her by the trustees, but instead had at all times a claim for an unvarying amount in money or its equivalent.

If there had merely been a bequest to the legatee of $5,000,000 and she had agreed with the trustees to take securities of that value, the transaction would have been a "sale or other disposition" of the securities under *Suisman v. Eaton*, 15 F. Supp. 113, *affirmed*, 2 Cir., 83 F.2d 1019, *cert. denied*, 299 U.S. 573. There, a will creating a trust provided that each of the testator's children was to receive $50,000 on attaining the age of twenty-five. The trustee transferred stock of the value of $50,000 to one of the children, Minerva, in satisfaction of her legacy. Judge Hincks said in the district court (15 F. Supp. at page 115), that the "property which the trust estate received from the 'sale or other disposition' of said stocks was the discharge of the corpus from Minerva's equitable right to receive $50,000 therefrom; the amount realized, *i.e.*, the 'fair market value of the property (other than money) received,' . . . was $50,000; and the excess of the amount realized over the basis was properly computed by the Commissioner, legally assessed as part of the taxable income of the trust estate, and the tax thereon was legally collected."

In the present case, the legatee had a claim which was a charge against the trust estate for $5,000,000 in cash or securities and the trustees had the power to determine whether the claim should be satisfied in one form or the other. The claim, though enforceable only in the alternative, was like the claim in *Suisman v. Eaton, supra*, a charge against the entire trust estate. If it were satisfied by a cash payment securities might have to be sold on which (if those actually delivered in specie were selected) a taxable gain would necessarily have been realized. Instead of making such a sale the trustees delivered the securities and exchanged them pro tanto for the general claim of the legatee, which was thereby satisfied.

It is said that this transaction was not such a "sale or other disposition" as is intended by Section [1001(a)] or was dealt with in *Suisman v. Eaton*, because it was effectuated only by the will of the trustees and not, as in *Suisman v. Eaton*, through a mutual agreement between the trustee and legatee. The Board made no such distinction, and we are not inclined to limit thus the meaning of the words "other disposition" used in Section [1001(a)], or of "exchange" used in Section [1222]. The word "exchange" does not necessarily have the connotation of a bilateral agreement which may be said to attach to the word "sale." Thus, should a person set up a trust and reserve to himself the power to substitute for the securities placed in trust other securities of equal value, there would seem no doubt that the exercise of this reserved power would be an "exchange" within the common meaning of the word, even though the settlor consulted no will other than his own, although, of course, we do not here advert to the problems of taxability in such a situation.

The board alluded to the fact that both here and in *Suisman v. Eaton* the bequest was fixed at a definite amount in money, that in both cases there was no bequest of specific securities (nor of a share in the residue which might vary in value), that the rights of the legatee, like those in the *Suisman* case, were a charge upon the corpus of the trust, and that the trustees had to part either with $5,000,000 in cash or with securities worth that amount at the time of the transfer. It added that the increase in value of the securities was realized by the trust and benefited it to the full extent, since, except for the increase, it would have had to part with other property, and it cited in further support of its position *United States v. Kirby Lumber Co.*, 284 U.S. 1. Under circumstances like those here, where the legatee did not take securities designated by the will or an interest in the corpus which might be more or less at the time of the transfer than at the time of decedent's death, it seems to us that the trustees realized a gain by using these securities to settle a claim worth $5,000,000 just as the trustee in *Suisman v. Eaton* realized one.

It seems reasonably clear that the property was not "transmitted at death" or "acquired by bequest . . . from the decedent." Section [1014(b)(1)]. It follows that the fears of the taxpayers that double taxation of this appreciation will result because the legatee will take the basis of the decedent . . . are groundless. . . . The legatee's basis would seem to be the value of the claim surrendered in exchange for the securities; and the Board of Tax Appeals has so held. *Sherman Ewing v. Commissioner of Internal Revenue*, 40 B.T.A. 911.

. . .

Orders affirmed.

———

Revenue Ruling 74–178

1974–1 C.B. 1996

Advice has been requested whether, under the circumstances described below, a decedent's estate realizes gain upon the transfer of appreciated property to satisfy a claim against the estate.

At the time of his death on February 1, 1973, the decedent owned 150 shares of common stock in a domestic corporation. These shares were acquired from the decedent by his estate and valued for Federal estate tax purposes at $70 per share, which was the fair market value of a share at the date of his death. On the Federal estate tax return filed on behalf of the decedent's estate, the executor did not elect the alternate valuation date prescribed by section 2032 of the Internal Revenue Code of 1954. An unrelated creditor of the decedent subsequently filed a claim against the estate for $8,000. The claim was based upon an indebtedness of $8,000 that the decedent owed the creditor at the date of his death. In an arm's-length transaction the executor of the estate transferred 100 shares of the stock to the creditor in satisfaction of the claim. The fair market value of a share at the time of the transfer was $80.

Section 1001(a) of the Code provides, in part, that the gain from the disposition of property shall be the excess of the amount realized therefrom over the adjusted basis provided in section 1011 for determining gain.

Section 1011(a) of the Code provides, in part, that the adjusted basis for determining the gain from the disposition of property shall be the basis determined under the applicable provisions of the Code.

Section 1014(a) of the Code provides, generally, that the basis of property in the hands of a person acquiring the property from a decedent shall be the fair market value of the property at the date of the decedent's death or, where there is an appropriate election, at the alternate valuation dates as provided in section 2032.

Section 1.1014–2(a)(1) of the Income Tax Regulations provides, in part, that property acquired by the decedent's estate from the decedent is considered to have been acquired from a decedent.

Rev. Rul. 66–207, 1966–2 C.B. 243, holds, in part, that where an executor distributes appreciated property in partial satisfaction of a pecuniary legacy, the estate realizes gain to the extent of the difference between the amount of the bequest satisfied and the estate's basis in the property. That Revenue Ruling states that the effect of the distribution will be the same as if the executor sold the assets of the estate and distributed the proceeds.

In the instant case the fair market value of the shares of stock at the time such stock was transferred to the creditor is equal to the amount of the claim satisfied ($8,000). However, since the executor did not elect the alternate valuation date, the estate's basis in the shares transferred is the fair market value of the shares at the date of the decedent's death ($7,000).

Accordingly, it is held that upon such transfer the estate realized a gain of $1,000, which is the excess of the amount of the claim satisfied by the transfer over the estate's basis in the shares. Had the estate's basis in the shares of stock transferred exceeded the amount of the claim satisfied, the estate would have sustained a loss deductible to the extent allowed in sections 1211 and 1212 of the Code.

————

Revenue Ruling 60–87

1960–1 C.B. 286

Advice has been requested whether gain or loss is recognized upon the distribution of securities by the executor of an estate to a marital deduction testamentary trust under the circumstances described below.

The decedent was a resident of a community property state. The estate consisted almost entirely of community property. The decedent's will provided that, after certain distributions of his personal property, a part of the residue and remainder of the estate be placed in trust for the benefit of his wife. The trust was to include the wife's share of certain community property, plus an amount of the decedent's separate property which, when added to the value of certain other property included in the decedent's gross estate, would equal one-half of his adjusted gross estate as finally determined for Federal estate tax purposes. On the date the will was executed, the decedent's wife executed a statement to the effect that her election to accept its provisions would be effective upon demise of her husband upon condition that his will be admitted to probate. The will has been admitted to probate and she elected to take under it. The testamentary trust is to continue during the lifetime of the decedent's wife and during such period of time she is to receive the income therefrom, with a general testamentary power of appointment, but in default of appointment with remainder over to named persons.

After the final determination of the value of the decedent's adjusted gross estate for Federal estate tax purposes, the executor of the estate transferred to the testamentary marital deduction trust securities sufficient in value, together with the other items to be included therein, to bring the value of the trust to the required one-half of the adjusted gross estate. In determining the value of the property to be transferred to the trust, the executor of the estate used the fair market value of the property at the date of the distribution. However, since the fair market value of the property transferred, at the date of the transfer to the trust, was greater than the value used for Federal estate tax purposes, the specific question arises whether gain is realized by the estate because of such transfer. A corollary question is whether such marital deduction trust may be considered as being provided for in a fixed and definite 'dollar amount.'

Revenue Ruling 56–270, C.B. 1956–1, 325, stands for the proposition that, if a marital deduction trust comprises a fraction or percentage of the 'adjusted gross estate' of a decedent, the marital trust fund is considered to have been provided for in a fixed and definite 'dollar amount.' Therefore, capital gain or loss is recognized upon the distribution of property to a trust.

Insofar as is here pertinent, section 663(a) of the Internal Revenue Code of 1954 provides, in general, that a gift or bequest of a specific sum of money shall neither be allowed as a deduction to an estate or trust under section 661 of the Code nor included in the gross income of the beneficiary under section 662(a) of the Code. To qualify for this exclusion, the amount of money bequeathed must be ascertainable as of the date of death. The effect of the regulations is that a bequest under a marital deduction trust formula clause does not qualify for exclusion since the amount of the trust fund is not ascertainable at the date of the decedent's death.

[The Revenue Ruling quotes Treasury Regulation § 1.663(a)–1(b)(1).]

. . .

Unlike section 1.663(a)–1(b)(1) of the regulations, *Revenue Ruling 56–270*, *supra*, is not concerned with the ascertainability of a specific amount at the date of death, but rather whether the marital trust fund is provided for in a fixed and definite amount at the time of the distribution. Thus, to qualify for the exclusion in section 663(a) of the Code, the above-quoted regulation prescribes an entirely different test from that prescribed in *Revenue Ruling 56–270*. The ruling only has application for capital gain purposes.

Further, the last sentence of the above-quoted regulations recognizes the fact that a different rule applies for capital gain purposes and clearly implies that the regulations are not to be considered inconsistent with that rule.

In the instant case, the marital deduction trust comprises a portion of the residue of the decedent's estate. However, instead of using a residuary formula clause, which leaves a percentage or fraction of the value of the residuary estate to the surviving spouse or trust, the will uses a pecuniary formula clause similar to *Revenue Ruling* 56–270, *supra*. The pecuniary formula clause leaves a percentage of the 'adjusted gross estate' to the surviving spouse or trust. There is a significant distinction between a marital deduction trust of the pecuniary formula type and one of the residuary formula type.

The rationale of *Revenue Ruling* 56–270, *supra*, is that a marital deduction trust of the pecuniary formula type provides for a trust fund in a fixed and definite amount once the value of the adjusted gross estate is finally determined. The amount is unaffected by any appreciation or depreciation in the value of the assets comprising the estate.

Under a pecuniary formula clause, the trust will receive assets of a fixed and definite amount at the time of distribution. On the other hand, under the residuary formula clause, the percentage or fraction will be applied for the purpose of making distribution of the residuary estate as constituted at the time of distribution. Therefore, under a residuary formula clause, the trust will share in appreciation and depreciation of the value of the estate, which is not the case under a pecuniary formula clause. Thus, *Revenue Ruling* 56–270, *supra*, is not inconsistent with section 1.663(a)–1(b)(1) of the regulations.

The facts in the instant case show that the marital deduction trust comprising a portion of the residue of the estate is measured by a percentage of the value of the adjusted gross estate. Under such circumstances, the marital trust fund is provided in a fixed and definite 'dollar amount.' Accordingly, gain or loss is realized by the estate; measured by the difference between the fair market value of the property at the date of distribution and the value of the property determined for Federal estate tax purposes.

Revenue Ruling 56–270, C.B. 1956–1, 325, is clarified.

––––––––

Because of the potential for gain on funding pecuniary, estate planners drafted estate planning documents to provide that pecuniary marital devises were to be funded using date of death values for assets. The Service responded with Rev. Proc. 64–19, 1964–1 C.B. 682, discussed in Chapter 3. The Revenue Procedure disallows the marital deduction if date of death values are used to determine the funding of the marital trust unless the requirements of the Revenue Procedure are satisfied.

––––––––

Revenue Ruling 69–486

1969–2 C.B. 159

Advice has been requested as to the Federal income tax treatment of a final distribution of property in kind by a trustee to the two beneficiaries of a trust under the circumstances described below.

Under terms of the trust instrument, the trustee is required to distribute currently all trust income to B for her life and upon her death distribute one-half of the trust corpus to C, an individual, and one-half to X, a charitable organization exempt from tax under section 501(c)(3) of the Internal Revenue Code of 1954.

B died on July 1, 1967. At the time of her death, the trust had ordinary income of 20x dollars to be reported in its current calendar year period. Subsequent to B's death the trust received no income up to its termination on August 1, 1967. The distributable net income of the trust for 1967 as defined by section 643(a) of the Code was 20x dollars. The trustee properly distributed currently 20x dollars to B's successor in interest. At the time of B's death, the trust corpus to be distributed to C and X consisted in part of notes that had been purchased by the trust and that had a total adjusted basis of 300x dollars and a total fair market value of an equal amount. The balance of the trust corpus consisted of common stock acquired by purchase with a total adjusted basis of 100x dollars and a total fair market value of 300x dollars.

The trust instrument as well as local law was silent as to the authority of the trustee to make a non-pro rata distribution of property in kind. By mutual agreement, the two beneficiaries requested that the trustee distribute all of the notes to C and all of the common stock to X. The trustee complied with this request on August 1, 1967.

The first issue to be decided is how the non-pro rata distribution by the trustee to C and X will be treated for Federal income tax purposes. Since the trustee was not authorized to make a non-pro rata distribution of property in kind but did so as a result of the mutual agreement between C and X, the non-pro rata distribution by the trustee to C and X is equivalent to a distribution to C and X of the notes and common stock pro rata by the trustee, followed by an exchange between C and X of C's pro rata share of common stock for X's pro rata share of notes.

The second issue to be decided is the basis of the pro rata share of notes and common stock in the hands of C and X.

Section 661 of the Code as implemented by section 1.661(a)–2(f)(3) of the Income Tax Regulations provides, in pertinent part, that the basis of property in the hands of the beneficiary is its fair market value at the time it was paid, credited, or required to be distributed, to the extent such value is included in the gross income of the beneficiary. To the extent that the value of property distributed in kind is not included in the gross income of the beneficiary, its basis in the hands of the beneficiary is governed by the rules in sections 1014 and 1015 of the Code and the regulations thereunder. Section 661 of the Code provides for a deduction (limited to the distributable net income of the trust) to the trust for distributions properly made and section 662 of the Code provides for the inclusion of a corresponding amount in gross income of a beneficiary.

Inasmuch as the 20x dollars of income required to be distributed currently to the estate of B is equal to the distributable net income of the trust, no amount is includible in the gross income of C and X as a result of the pro rata distribution of notes and common stock by the trustee. See section 662(a) of the Code as implemented by section 1.662(a)–2 of the regulations. The basis of the pro rata shares of notes and common stock in the hands of C and X is the same as the adjusted basis in the hands of the trust. *See* section 1.1015–2(b).

Furthermore, C in substance exchanged his pro rata share of common stock with X for X's pro rata share of notes. The amount of recognized gain to C is determined under sections 1001 and 1002 of the Code. Since X is a charitable organization exempt from tax under section 501(c)(3) of the Code, it has no tax consequence as a result of the exchange.

Estate of Dean v. Commissioner

T.C. Memo 1983–276

Fay, Judge:

Respondent determined the following deficiencies in petitioners' 1974 Federal income tax:

Docket No.	Amount
7003–79	$ 4,814.00
14281–81	21,275.00

14354–81   20,035.00
14355–81   25,584.79

After concessions, the only issue is whether an estate is entitled to a deduction under section 661(a)(2) when it makes a distribution to its beneficiaries of a promissory note representing a right to receive income in respect of a decedent under section 691.

Jack Dean (decedent) died on July 26, 1972. Prior to his death, he sold cattle to Paul C. Dean (Buyer). Buyer executed a $221,252.69 promissory note (the Note) payable in 8 equal annual installments with interest of 7% on the unpaid balance. Decedent elected to report gain on the sale on the installment basis under section 453.

Pursuant to his Last Will and Testament, the Estate succeeded to the right to receive payments on the Note. The residue of the Estate was bequeathed in equal shares to three beneficiaries, petitioners Jack L. Dean, Bonnie D. Evans, and Deborah K. Dean.

As of January 1, 1974, the balance due the Estate on the Note was $221,252.69. On March 18, 1974, the Estate received a principal payment of $22,344.00 and an interest payment of $15,480.00 from Buyer in partial satisfaction of the Note. On November 18, 1974, with a balance owing of $198,908.69 (its fair market value), the Estate distributed the Note in equal shares to its three beneficiaries. This was the only distribution out of the Estate during its 1974 taxable year. The Estate had distributable net income of $61,418.00 in 1974. On December 16, 1974, the beneficiaries received $189,477.10 in further payment on the Note.

In its petition, the Estate claimed an overpayment of tax based in part on its claim for a deduction for distribution of the Note. In his answer, respondent disallowed this deduction.

The parties agree the Note is income in respect of a decedent under section 691. At issue is whether an estate is entitled to a section 661(a)(2) deduction when it distributes a note representing a right to receive income in respect of a decedent. The Estate claims it is entitled to the deduction since such distribution comes within the literal language of section 661(a)(2) as "amounts properly paid." Respondent acknowledges a literal reading of that section might include a distribution of a right to receive income. Respondent contends, however, that section 691 overrides section 661(a)(2) and, therefore, governs the tax treatment of both the Estate and its beneficiaries upon distribution of the Note.

This very issue was decided in respondent's favor in a recent opinion of this Court wherein we held section 691 must take precedence over section 661. *Rollert Residuary Trust v. Commissioner*, 80 T.C. [619 (1983), *aff'd* 752 F.2d 1128 (6th Cir. 1985)].

Briefly, the basis of our decision is as follows. The taxation of trusts, estates, and their beneficiaries is governed by Subchapter J, sections 641 through 692. Congress has adopted the "conduit principle" of taxation whereby income is taxed only once between an estate and its beneficiaries. Allocation of this income is accomplished through the combined operation of the concept of distributable net income (DNI—defined as the estate's taxable income with certain modifications) and the distribution rules of sections 661–663.

Generally, section 661 allows an estate, to the extent of its DNI, a deduction for distributions to its beneficiaries. Under section 662, the beneficiaries must include this amount in their gross income. When property is distributed, it is taken into account at its fair market value for purposes of these distribution rules and, accordingly, takes a basis equal to its fair market value in the hands of the beneficiaries. Sec. 1.661(a)–2(f)(2) & (3), Income Tax Regs.

Section 691, on the other hand, provides special rules for income which a decedent had a right to or an entitlement to at or prior to his death, but which was never includible in his gross income. Generally, section 691(a) requires such income to be reported by and when the person actually receives the income, whether it be the estate or a beneficiary.

When the right to receive income in respect of a decedent is distributed by an estate, the distribution rules of sections 661 and 662 conflict with the provisions of section 691.

Although most property acquired from a decedent receives a stepped-up basis equal to its date of death value, section 691 property receives no such step-up in basis. Sec. 1014(c). By allowing the estate a deduction for a distribution of the section 691 property (in the same manner as a distribution of any other property) the estate and its beneficiaries escape income taxation by the amount of such deduction.[55] This effectively subverts sections 691 and 1014(c) which contemplate that the entire amount of income in respect of a decedent be subject to income tax.

Moreover, the timing and characterization rules of sections 661 and 662, and section 691, are inconsistent. Sections 661 and 662 require income to be included at the time of distribution whereas section 691 requires income to be reported at the time of its actual receipt. Additionally, section 691(a)(3) requires the character of section 691 property to be the same as it would have been in the hands of the decedent had he lived to receive such income. Under the distribution rules, the character of the income is determined by reference to the character of the estate's distributable net income.

Given these inconsistencies, and given the well-settled principle that a specific statute controls over a general one, we held that section 691 overrides

---

[55] The following example taken from respondent's brief illustrates this point. An estate has distributable net income (DNI) of $100,000 in 1974 representing interest paid on a certificate of deposit held by the estate. The estate also holds sec. 691 property in the form of a note with a value of $120,000 and with zero basis. In 1974 the estate distributes the sec. 691 property and retains the interest income. In 1974, soon after the distribution, the beneficiary received the $120,000 payment on the note.

Applying sec. 661(a)(2), the estate receives a $100,000 deduction in 1974 based on its distribution of the note. The deduction carries out all distributable net income totally eliminating any tax liability of the estate. Under sec. 662, the beneficiary is required to include $100,000 in his gross income at the date of distribution. He also takes a $100,000 basis in the note. Sec. 1661(a)–2(f)(3), Income Tax Regs. Because of this increased basis, the beneficiary need only include $20,000 in his gross income when he receives actual payments of $120,000 on the note. Thus, although $220,000 in income has been realized, only $120,000 has been taxed. Moreover, no income will result upon the later distribution by the estate of the $100,000 of interest income. Therefore, $100,000, the amount of the distribution deduction, escapes income taxation altogether.

sections 661 and 662. *Rollert Residuary Trust v. Commissioner*, 80 T.C. 619 (1983).[56] Property representing a right to receive income in respect of a decedent is subject to its own statutory provisions. Thus, the transfer by an estate of section 691 property is treated as a neutral event, and is not subject to the distribution rules of sections 661 and 662.

Accordingly, we hold for respondent on this issue. To reflect concessions, decisions will be entered under Rule 155.

The result in *Dean* is confirmed by § 643(e)(2).

A taxable event does not ordinarily occur when an estate distributes the legal right to receive payments which constitute income in respect of a decedent (IRD). *See* Treas. Reg. § 1.691(a)–4(b)(2). However, a recognizable gain or loss may take place if the estate distributes IRD property in satisfaction of a pecuniary bequest. *See* § 691(a)(2).

In a *Kenan*-type distribution, the recipient's basis in the property equals the property's fair market value at the time of the distribution. This result is obtained because the entity is deemed to have constructively distributed cash equal to the property's fair market value, and the beneficiary is then deemed to have purchased the property from the trust with the cash.

The distribution deduction for the entity depends on whether the pecuniary bequest is described by § 663(a)(1). If so, there is no deduction under § 661. *See* Rev. Rul. 86–105, 1986–2 C.B. 82. If, however, § 663(a)(1) does not apply, the entity, which is constructively deemed to have distributed cash, is entitled to a deduction under § 661.

[2] Elective Recognition of Gain or Loss

Code: §§ 643(e) and 662(a)(2).

Regulations: Treas. Reg. § 1.661(a)–2(f).

The following legislative history explains the enactment of § 643(e) by the Tax Reform Act of 1984. The section was amended by the Tax Reform Act of 1986 to require that the election apply to all distributions made in a tax year.

---

[56] This result is consistent with *Mott v. United States*, 462 F.2d 512 (Ct. Cl. 1972), which disallowed an estate a deduction under sec. 661(a)(2) for a distribution to a qualified charitable beneficiary. The court held that to the extent the distribution did not comply with sec. 642, which deals specifically with the deductibility of charitable distributions, the deduction was not allowable.

Trust [and Estate] Distributions

Prior Law

Under prior law, beneficiaries were taxed on amounts distributed from a trust or estate to the extent of the trust's or estate's distributable net income. The trust or estate was allowed a deduction for amounts taxed to its beneficiaries. Prior Treasury Department regulations provided that distributions of property were deemed to carry out distributable net income to the extent of the property's value at the time of distribution. In such a case, no gain or loss was realized on the distribution by the trust or estate and the basis of the property in the hands of the beneficiary was its value to the extent it carried out distributable net income. *See* Treas. Reg. § 1.661(a)–2(f).

Reasons for Change

Where a trust or estate had distributable net income and distributed property, the effect of the prior Treasury Department regulations was to exempt the gain or loss entirely from tax. Congress believed that the gain or loss should be taxed to either the beneficiary or the trust (or estate).

Explanation of Provisions

The Act provides that distributions of property from a trust or estate are treated as carrying out distributable net income only to the extent of the lesser of the property's basis or its fair market value at the time of distribution. Under this rule, the basis of the property in the hands of the beneficiary will be the same as the trust's or estate's basis in the property. Alternatively, the Act permits the trustee or executor to elect to treat distributions of property as taxable events resulting in recognition of gain or loss on the distribution as if the property had been sold to the beneficiary.

The Act does not change prior law in those cases where a distribution of property to a beneficiary results in the recognition of gain or loss to the trust or estate (*e.g.*, the rule providing a basis adjustment for property received in satisfaction of a pecuniary bequest continues to apply).[57] Additionally, Congress did not intend that this provision change the prior-law tax effects of charitable contributions. For example, if a trust beneficiary makes a gift to a charitable organization of property received in an in-kind distribution from a trust or estate, that transfer is not to be considered a taxable disposition within the meaning of the Code. The prior-law rules governing gifts of appreciated property to charitable organizations (as modified by the Act) also will continue to apply to such gifts.

---

[57] In the case of a distribution by a trust or estate of property whose value is less than its basis, § 267 would deny a loss deduction to the trust or estate. Excepted from the disallowance rule is a distribution by an estate in satisfaction of a pecuniary bequest. *See* § 267(b)(13).

General Explanation of the Tax Reform Act of 1984, at 253–54.

The primary purpose of § 643(e) is to limit the amount of DNI carried out by a distribution of property to the adjusted basis of the property. This rule reverses a Regulation that permitted, in some circumstances, the trust to have a distribution deduction equal to the fair market value of the distributed asset. *See* Treas. Reg. § 1.661(a)–2(f)(2). Moreover, the recipient will take a carryover basis, rather than a fair market value basis. Again, this rule reverses a Regulation that permitted, in some circumstances, the recipient to have a new fair market basis in the distributed asset. *See* Treas. Reg. § 1.661(a)–2(f)(3).

For example, under the now obsolete Regulation, if an estate with DNI of $100 distributed stock with a fair market value of $100 and income tax basis of $60 to the residuary beneficiary of the estate (and makes no other distributions during the year), the stock distribution would have carried out DNI of $100 and the beneficiary would have a basis of $100. The $40 potential gain inherent in the appreciated asset was not taxed. Under § 643(e), the distribution will carry out only $60 of DNI and the beneficiary will have an income tax basis of $60.

Section 643(e)(3) permits a fiduciary to elect to recognize gain on the distribution of appreciated or depreciated assets. The election is made on a yearly basis. Once it is made, the election applies to all distributions of the estate or trust for the year. The Treasury has not issued regulations to explain the full ramifications of an election. Nevertheless, it appears that losses will not likely be allowed because of § 267. Under the provisions of § 267 the loss is disallowed, but the recipient is permitted, under some circumstances, to realize the loss on a disposition of the asset to an unrelated party. As an alternative to making a distribution of loss asset, the fiduciary may realize the loss by selling the loss asset to a third party instead of distributing it to a beneficiary of the estate or trust.

Notwithstanding the non-recognition of loss issue, an election under § 643(e)(3) likely increases taxable income for the entity. Whether that additional income will increase DNI will probably depend on the nature of the asset. When the deemed sale generates capital gains, those items are in DNI only if the provisions of § 643(a)(3) do not exclude the capital gains and losses from DNI. However, the election will likely effect the amount of DNI being carried out by the distribution. With the recognition of gain, the distribution will carry out DNI to the extent of the new adjusted basis of the distributed asset, *i.e.,* the fair market value. There is no effect on adjusted basis from the recognition of losses. Under the old rules of Treasury Regulation § 1.661(a)–2(f)(2), the distribution of an asset with a fair market value less than basis carried out DNI only to the extent of fair market value.

Problems

1. Under § 691(a)(2), the transfer of an item of income in respect of a decedent (IRD) by way of "sale, exchange, or other disposition" results in immediate recognition of IRD to the extent of the sales price or fair market value of the right in excess of adjusted basis. "Transmission at death to the

estate of the decedent or a transfer to a person pursuant to the right of such person to receive such amount by reason of the death of the decedent or by bequest, devise, or inheritance from the decedent" is specifically excluded from the definition of *transfer*. Assume the decedent's will provides that a testamentary trust is to be funded with a specified pecuniary amount.

a. In light of § 691(a)(2), can a personal representative fund the trust with IRD items without immediate recognition of the income?

b. If § 663(a)(1) did not apply, would the estate be entitled to a distribution deduction under § 661?

2. An estate distributes stock having a basis of $20,000, but with a fair market value of $30,000 to the sole residuary beneficiary. Assuming that the estate makes no other distributions, and that apart from this distribution the estate's distributable net income is $25,000, what would be the tax consequences of the distribution if:

a. The personal representative does not make an election under § 643(e)(3)?

b. The personal representative makes the § 643(e) election?

See generally Alan S. Acker, *The Impact of TRA '84 on Trust and Estate Distributions of Property*, 124 Tr. & Est. 54 (1985).

3. The decedent's will authorizes the personal representative to make non-pro rata distributions to two residuary beneficiaries. For this tax year, distributions occur as follows:

A receives:

	Fair Market Value	Adjusted Basis
Land	$100,000	$25,000
Stock	$100,000	$25,000
Cash	$ 0	n/a

B receives:

	Fair Market Value	Adjusted Basis
Land	$ 50,000	$ 50,000
Stock	$ 50,000	$ 50,000
Cash	$100,000	n/a

How much income must *A* and *B* report if the trust has DNI of $200,000 this year?

4. Would your answer to Problem 3 change if A only received the stock with a fair market value of $100,000 and an adjusted basis of $25,000?

5. Would your answer to Problem 3 change if B only received $100,000 in cash?

[F] Termination of a Trust or Estate

Code: §§ 67, 443, 641, 642(h), 662, 663, and 643.

Regulations: Treas. Reg. §§ 1.641(b)–3, 1.642(h), 1.663(c)–3(e), and 1.643(a)–3.

The conduit principle also applies in the year a trust or estate terminates. The Regulations provide guidance on when an estate or trust is considered terminated. This usually occurs when all assets have been distributed, not when amounts are allocated to the distributees' accounts. *See Estate of Johnson v. Commissioner*, 88 T.C. 225 (1987). However, an estate or trust will be deemed terminated if the administration period is unduly prolonged, with the tax consequences attributable to the beneficiaries. *See Chick v. Commissioner*, 166 F.2d 337 (1st Cir. 1948), *cert. denied* 334 U.S. 845; Treas. Reg. § 1.641(b)–3. *Cf. Estate of Johnson v. Commissioner*, 88 T.C. 225 (1987) (holding that where personal representative had not collected all estate assets, administration was not unduly prolonged).

Note that trusts do not terminate at the time specified for termination in the instrument. Rather, trusts terminate after the trustee has completed trust administration; a trust is deemed to continue for a reasonable period of time for tax purposes. *See* Treas. Reg. § 1.641(b)–3(b). During this interim period, income and capital gains (in excess of losses) may be considered as amounts required to be distributed currently to the ultimate beneficiaries. *See* Treas. Reg. §§ 1.641(b)–3(c)(1). For example, if the trust is to terminate at the death of the income beneficiary with the corpus then paid to the remainderman, the trust does not terminate until the corpus is in fact paid, or at such earlier time after the death of the life income beneficiary as distribution would have been appropriate.

A trust's termination produces some tax results that differ from those during normal trust operation. For example, capital gains, which are normally excluded from DNI, are included in the entity's final year because they are required to be distributed during the year. *See* Treas. Reg. § 1.643(a)–3. In turn, beneficiaries have to include in gross income capital gains realized and recognized by the trust during the year of termination because the gain will be deemed properly paid for purposes of § 662. *See id.* Another difference is that the trust's or estate's last taxable year will invariably be less than a full year, requiring the filing of a short period return. *See* § 443. In the case of estates (but not trusts) that report on a fiscal year basis, estate beneficiaries' may have to include gross income amounts from two taxable years of the estate. *See* Rev. Rul. 71–180, 1971–1 C.B. 204.

Section 642(h)(1) provides special rules which entitle the beneficiaries who succeed to the property of terminating estates or trusts to deduct the estate or trust's capital loss and net operating loss carryovers. In addition, § 642(h)(2) entitles these beneficiaries to deduct *excess deductions*. Excess deductions arise in the year of termination when an entity's deductions (other than the personal exemption and charitable deductions) exceed gross income. Section 642(h)(2) prevents the wasting of these deductions. Note, however, that the deductions in the hands of the beneficiary may be *wasted* in part or in whole because the deductions are subject to the 2% floor of § 67.

Revenue Ruling 57–31

1957–1 C.B. 201

Advice has been requested whether excess deductions allowable to a residuary testamentary trust on the termination of an estate, which trust distributes all of its current income, will be available to the income beneficiary of the trust should such deductions exceed the gross income of the trust for its taxable year.

Section 642(h)(2). . . provides that any deductions (other than deductions for personal exemption and charitable contributions) in excess of the gross income of an estate or trust for its year of termination may be allowed as a deduction to the beneficiaries succeeding to the property of the estate or trust. A testamentary trust may be a legatee or beneficiary of an estate for purposes of section 642(h). *See* G.C.M. 24749, C.B. 1945, 237.

In the instant case, the decedent provided in his will that the rest and residue of his estate be placed in trust and that the income therefrom be distributed currently to his surviving spouse. Deductions of the estate for the year in which it was terminated exceeded gross income and resulted in the allowance of the excess thereof to the residuary trust. The excess deductions exceeded the gross income of the trust for its taxable year.

Since the amount of trust income taxable to a beneficiary of a trust is limited to that beneficiary's proportionate share of the distributable net income of the trust, excess deductions from an estate which become available through operation of section 642(h)(2) to a testamentary trust having the status of a beneficiary under section 642(h) would in turn reduce the amount of income taxable to the beneficiary of the trust.

If a testamentary trust has deductions in excess of its gross income after the allowance of deductions from an estate made available to it through section 642(h)(2), the amount in excess of the gross income would not be deductible by the income beneficiary of the trust. However, if the trust also terminates during the taxable year in which it is allowed the section 642(h)(2) deductions, the deductions in excess of its gross income will be available under section 642(h)(2) to the remaindermen succeeding to the property.

In view of the foregoing, it is held that where a residuary testamentary trust, which has the status of a beneficiary succeeding to the property of the estate within the meaning of section 642(h) of the Internal Revenue Code of 1954, has deductions in excess of its gross income after the allowance of excess deductions from an estate as authorized by section 642(h)(2), the amount in excess of the gross income of the trust would not be deductible by the income beneficiaries of the trust; but, if the trust terminated in the year in which it was allowed the section 642(h)(2) deductions, they would be available to the remaindermen.

———

O'Bryan v. Commissioner

75 T.C. 304 (1980)

Nims, Judge:

. . .

After concessions by Petitioner, the sole issue remaining for the Court's determination is the proper method of calculating under section 642(h)(2) an estate's "excess deductions" when the estate has made charitable contributions in its year of termination which are deductible under section 642(c).

I

The facts in this case were fully stipulated and are so found. Faye Marie O'Bryan (the petitioner) resided in Chicago, Ill., at the time she filed her petition.

The estate in question is that of petitioner's husband, Leslie L. O'Bryan, who died on November 21, 1970. Mr. O'Bryan's will contained various specific bequests to petitioner, and it also left property to a marital trust sufficient for the estate to obtain the maximum marital deduction. The residue of the estate was left to a residuary trust, which required that all the trust income be distributed currently to the petitioner.

The final return for the estate, representing the period from August 1, 1973, to June 30, 1974, inclusive, reflected a gross income of $879,446.55 and the following deductions:

Interest	$ 10,599.71
Taxes	1,176.79
Charitable deduction	776,500.00
Miscellaneous expense	593.46
Personal Representative's commissions	65,000.00
Attorney's fee	85,000.00
Accounting fees	2,980.00
	941,849.96

The charitable deduction was claimed pursuant to section 642(c)(2)(B). Claimed deductions exceeded reported income by $62,403.41.

The residuary trust established pursuant to the terms of the will, the Leslie L. O'Bryan Trust, received gross income during 1974 of $72,739.59. Relying on section 642(h)(2), the trust claimed an excess deduction from the estate in the amount of $62,403.41. The parties stipulated that under the rules of subchapter J the excess deduction claimed by the trust had no effect on the trust's taxable income. The deduction did, however, reduce the income beneficiary's (*i.e.*, the petitioner's) taxable income by the aforesaid $62,403.41.

In the notice of deficiency the Commissioner determined that the estate's excess deductions under section 642(h)(2) had been calculated incorrectly and that petitioner's taxable income for 1974 was to be increased by $62,403.41.

II

This is a case of first impression. At issue is the interpretation and construction of section 642(h)(2), which provides as follows: . . .

The focal point of the dispute before us is the application of the parenthetical clause "(other than the deductions allowed under subsections (b) or (c))." Section 642(b) permits a $600 personal exemption deduction and section 642(c) permits a deduction for amounts paid or permanently set aside for a charitable purpose.

Like many simple rules, the rule contained in section 642(h)(2), when applied to a concrete set of facts, creates an enigma. We are told that no part of the charitable deduction may be included in "excess deductions," but we are not told how to determine whether, on facts such as ours, the excess of deductions over income actually includes any charitable deduction.

Respondent contends that section 642(h)(2) invokes a simple one-step procedure in which all deductions are totaled, except for the personal exemption and charitable contribution, and that figure is given first priority in reducing gross income to determine whether there are any excess deductions.[58]

Petitioner reads the section 642(h)(2) parenthetical clause as excluding the section 642(c) deduction, not from total deductions calculated under section 642(h)(2), but only from the amount determined to be the excess. Arithmetically, this translates into a two-step calculation: the first step is to determine the amount by which total deductions exceeds gross income, and the second step is to determine what amount of this excess consists of deductions other than the section 642(b) and (c) deductions. In essence, says petitioner, the amount by which total estate deductions exceed gross income is an excess deduction under section 642(h)(2) to the extent that the estate has deductions other than a section 642(c) deduction.[59]

---

[58] Respondent's computation is as follows:

a. Gross income of estate	$879,446.55
Less deductions:	
b. Interest, taxes, fees and miscellaneous expenses	($165,349.96)
c. Sec. 642(c) charitable deductions	
d. Total deductions	(165,349.96)
e. Excess of deductions over gross income (0 if line a exceeds line d)	0

[59] The following computation results from petitioner's approach:

a. Gross income of estate	$879,446.55
Less deductions:	
b. Interest, taxes, fees, and miscellaneous expenses	($165,349.96)
c. Sec. 642(c) deduction	(776,500.00)
d. Total deductions	(941,849.96)
e. Excess of deductions over income	(62,403.41)
f. Amount attributable to deductions other than Sec. 642(c) deductions	(165,349.96)
g. Deduction allowable to beneficiary (lower of e or f)	(62,403.41)

From the above it is apparent that, regardless of the arguments made to support the respective positions, each party is simply asking us to afford priority to a preferred type of deduction in reducing estate gross income. If, under petitioner's theory, gross income is first to be reduced (but not below zero) by the charitable deduction, the excess deductions allowable to the trust, and ultimately in fact to petitioner, must perforce consist of allowable deductions. Under respondent's theory, the reverse would be true.

There can be little argument that respondent's construction follows more comfortably the literal dictates of the statute. Petitioner asks the Court to look beyond a literal construction of the statute and to read section 642(h) in the context of the entire statutory scheme of subchapter J. Petitioner argues that her interpretation preserves the integrity of the section 642(c) charitable deduction and also balances the goal of section 642(h) to ameliorate wastage of deductions with what she perceives as the purpose of the parenthetical in section 642(h)(2) to prevent any charitable deduction from being passed from an estate or trust to a noncharitable beneficiary.

Section 642(h) is only one part of a tightly woven and intricate statutory scheme. Before turning to the specifics of this case, we need to review the basic provisions and underlying principles of subchapter J of the Code, which deals with the taxation of estates, trusts, beneficiaries, and decedents, generally. We have couched this overview in terms of the tax treatment of estates; but the rules of subchapter J apply with equal force, with appropriate modifications, to trusts as well.

Subchapter J sets forth the rules for determining the proper amount of estate income subject to tax as well as the rules for determining whether the beneficiary or estate should bear the burden of this tax. Simply stated, subchapter J is built on the "conduit principle" of taxation; i.e., estate income is taxed only once, either to the estate or to the beneficiaries, or partly to each. The estate is treated as a taxable entity and is taxed, in general, on income which it realizes but does not distribute to its beneficiaries. Income distributed to a beneficiary is not taxable to the estate but instead is taxable to the beneficiary. This result is accomplished by permitting the estate a deduction for the amount of the distribution.

The device that serves as the linchpin for this statutory scheme is the concept of distributable net income (D.N.I.). D.N.I., which is defined in section 643 and is essentially the estate's taxable income (with some modifications), serves generally as a ceiling on the combined tax liability of the estate and beneficiary. D.N.I. is allocated between the estate and beneficiaries in accord with the distribution rules of sections 661–663.

When distributions to beneficiaries exceed D.N.I., the tier structure of section 662 determines who among the beneficiaries are deemed to have received taxable distributions out of income and who have received nontaxable distributions out of corpus. D.N.I. is allocated under section 662(a)(1) first to beneficiaries who have a right to income that is "required to be distributed currently to such beneficiary," and the distribution to those beneficiaries is taxable to that extent. Sec. 1.662(a)–2(a), Income Tax Regs. All distributions within that tier are treated ratably should D.N.I. be less than total first-tier distributions. Any remaining D.N.I. is allocated pursuant to section 662(a)(2) among all other taxable beneficiaries, so called second-tier beneficiaries, and distributions to those beneficiaries are taxable to that extent. Sec. 1.662(a)–3(a), Income Tax Regs.

Section 661 complements section 662 by providing the estate a deduction up to the estate's D.N.I. for amounts distributed to its beneficiaries.

The rules of subchapter J become more complex when charitable beneficiaries are involved. In lieu of the charitable deduction allowed under section 170, section 642(c) in general allows an estate an unlimited charitable deduction for amounts of "gross income" which, pursuant to the governing instrument, are paid, permanently set aside, or to be used for charitable purposes.

On the estate side of the equation, the charitable contribution authorized by section 642(c) is simply one of numerous deductions that may be claimed in computing the estate's taxable income. To avoid duplicating deductions, section 663(a)(2) provides that distributions qualifying for the charitable deduction under section 642(c) are not included for purposes of calculating the estate's section 661 distribution deduction.

On the beneficiary side, however, the effect of the section 642(c) charitable distribution depends upon whether the beneficiary is a first- or second-tier beneficiary. Section 662(a) is structured so that first-tier beneficiaries do not benefit from the charitable deduction. Conceptually, section 662 accomplishes this by factoring charitable distributions into the tier system of priorities in such a way that the pool of income that can potentially be taxed to the beneficiaries (potentially taxable income) is deemed to flow first to first-tier beneficiaries. It is only if the pool of potentially taxable income exceeds first-tier distributions that the distribution to charitable beneficiaries is deemed to come out of that pool. In effect, the section 642(c) charitable distribution is an "intermediate tier" between tier-one and tier-two beneficiaries. We say intermediate tier because section 662(a)(2) is designed so that tier-two beneficiaries benefit from the section 642(c) charitable distribution deduction: the pool of potentially taxable income for determining the amount of a distribution that is taxable to tier-two beneficiaries is reduced by the section 642(c) charitable distributions (as well as the tier-one distributions). Section 662 (a) and (b).

Finally, we reach section 642(h)(2), which allows estate beneficiaries to take a deduction on their individual return for certain excess deductions of the estate in the year of termination. Section 642(h) had no counterpart in the 1939 Internal Revenue Code. Prior to 1954 excess deductions of an estate could not be passed onto beneficiaries. The problem was particularly acute in the estate's final year when the windup expenses of estate administration are generally heaviest and the deductions for those expenses often are greater than income. Congress, as part of a general effort to prevent wastage of deductions, ameliorated this problem through the enactment of section 642(h)(2).

III

Petitioner has drawn on two themes present in subchapter J in an attempt to show her construction of section 642(h)(2) best implements policy considerations underlying subchapter J. One is the familiar axiom that Congress seeks to encourage charitable contributions and foster charitable organizations and that this policy is manifested in section 642(c). The second is that unused deductions for expenses incurred in the year of termination should be passed on to beneficiaries.

While these themes are present in subchapter J, countervailing considerations surface in section 642(h)(2). Charitable deductions are allowed "without limitation" on the estate side only for purposes of calculating the estate's taxable income. On the beneficiary side, the section 662(a) tier system imposes a substantial limitation by barring first-tier beneficiaries from gaining any tax benefit from the presence of a section 642(c) charitable distribution deduction. The structure of section 662 reflects a distinct lack of concern on the part of Congress for "wastage" of charitable deductions insofar as determining the tax liability of income beneficiaries.

In the instant case all the deductions, other than the section 642(b) personal exemption and the section 642(c) charitable deduction, have already been taken into account in determining the pool of income potentially taxable to beneficiaries. The only deduction that has been wasted here, *i.e.*, that does not operate to reduce the income beneficiary's tax liability, is the section 642(c) deduction for charitable distributions. Given the lack of concern evinced by Congress in section 662 for wasted charitable deductions, we are not troubled by a reading of section 642(h)(2) which allows these deductions to go unused. Mathematically, this result is accomplished by excluding altogether the section 642(c) charitable deduction from the section 642(h)(2) computation, which is the construction of the statute called for by respondent.

Under the circumstances, we reject petitioner's argument that the policy considerations underlying subchapter J are best implemented by her reading of section 642(h)(2). In summary, we hold that to determine whether there are excess deductions available to beneficiaries under section 642(h)(2), deductions exclusive of the personal exemption under section 642(b) and the charitable deduction under section 642(c) are to be totaled and matched against the gross income of the terminating estate or trust. If the deductions so computed in fact exceed such gross income, then, and only then, will there be excess deductions as contemplated by section 642(h)(2).

To reflect concessions made by the parties on other issues, Decision will be entered for the respondent.

Problem

D's will leaves $100,000 to *A*, and the residue of the estate equally to *B* and *C*. The estate is sufficient to pay only $90,000 to *A*, and nothing to *B* and *C*. There is an excess of deductions over gross income for the last taxable year of the estate of $5,000, and a capital loss carryover of $15,000. Section 642(h) applies to both. How is the excess deduction and capital loss carryover allocated among *A*, *B*, and *C*?

[G] Trapping Distributions

An anomaly occurs when a trust or estate makes a distribution to a trust of fiduciary accounting principal that nevertheless results in a distribution of DNI. In this situation, the second trust may be required to treat the principal distribution as gross income, although the receipt by the second trust is retained because it is fiduciary accounting principal and not income that is normally distributable to the income beneficiary. This scenario is sometimes called a *trapping distribution*. An example illustrates the situation:

Example 1: The decedent's estate makes a $100,000 distribution to the $1 million credit-shelter, residuary trust.[60] Because the estate has $100,000 of DNI that is attributed to the residue under the separate share rules, the trust receives $100,000 of gross income. Nevertheless, the fiduciaries of both the estate and trust account for the distribution as fiduciary accounting principal. Assuming the residuary trust is a simple trust, *i.e.*, it is required to distribute all of its income to its sole beneficiary, no amount is distributable to the beneficiary because the trust has no fiduciary accounting income. Thus, the DNI is *trapped* in the trust and taxed to the trust at its applicable tax rates.

Alternatively, if in Example 1 the fiduciaries had both accounted for the distribution as fiduciary accounting income and not as principal, the $100,000 distribution by the estate to the residuary trust would be income required to be distributed by the trust. Thus, the second trust would receive $100,000 of DNI, but would be entitled to a $100,000 distribution deduction and the beneficiary of the trust would be required to report $100,000 of gross income under § 652.

Trapping distributions offer fiduciaries the opportunity to move income from one trust to another without having the income flow out to the beneficiary. Depending on all of the facts, this type of planned distribution may result in overall tax savings. For example, the receiving trust may have a tax loss, but trapping income will allow the trust to use the loss deductions to offset the income.

[H] Equitable Adjustments

[1] Ordered Adjustment

The following provides an overview of the circumstances under which courts and fiduciaries might make an equitable adjustment.[61]

The personal representative of an estate is a fiduciary and must act in the best interests of the estate beneficiaries. To do otherwise is a breach of his duty for which he can be surcharged. While a personal representative has many specific fiduciary duties, it is possible to identify at least four that can interact to create the need for equitable adjustments. These four are the

---

[60] *See* § 3.04[C][5][c], *supra* (discussing *credit-shelter* trusts).

[61] The discussion of equitable adjustments is an adaptation of F. Ladson Boyle, *Tax Consequences of Equitable Adjustments*, 37 S.C. L. Rev. 583 (1986). The discussion has been revised to reflect changes in the law and tax rates that have occurred since 1986.

duties: (1) to be impartial, (2) to conserve the estate, (3) to account for estate principal and income in accordance with state law, and (4) to report income of the estate in the manner required by subchapter J. In the context of equitable adjustments, the duty to conserve the estate can be described as the duty to minimize the total taxes of the estate, both income and estate taxes.

Potential for conflict is inherent among the personal representative's duties. For example, the duty to conserve the estate and save taxes may require the personal representative to violate the duty to be impartial. Similarly, the duty to conserve estate or trust assets may conflict with the duty to account for estate income and principal according to local fiduciary accounting principles. Under established precedent, the need for equitable adjustments arises when two duties conflict in such a way that the personal representative cannot avoid breaching one of them.

Equitable adjustments first arose as a judicial reaction to the unfair consequences that arise from the breach of a fiduciary duty. An equitable adjustment allocates estate income to the disadvantaged beneficiaries to compensate for the inequity, even though the allocation is often contrary to state fiduciary accounting principles.

Two types of equitable adjustments, both derived from New York surrogate court cases, are well established in some states—the *Warms* adjustment and the *Holloway* adjustment. *See In re Estate of Warms*, 140 N.Y.S.2d 169 (Sur. Ct. 1955); *In re Estate of Holloway*, 323 N.Y.S.2d 534 (Sur. Ct. 1971), *rev'd*, 327 N.Y.S.2d 865 (Sur. Ct. 1972).

The Warms Adjustment

The *Warms* adjustment, which is the best known equitable adjustment, derives its name from *In re Estate of Warms, supra*, the first reported decision to recognize the fiduciary obligation to adjust the shares of beneficiaries for the adverse impact of a tax election. In *Warms*, the decedent bequeathed two-fifths of his estate to his nieces and the remaining three-fifths in trust with his spouse as life income beneficiary. The bequest in trust apparently did not qualify for the estate tax marital deduction. The personal representative of Mr. Warms' estate elected to deduct the estate administration expenses as income tax deductions rather than as estate tax deductions. The failure to claim the expenses as estate tax deductions increased the estate taxes payable out of the principal of the residuary. Deducting the administration expenses on the income tax returns, on the other hand, reduced the estate income tax liability. Because the residuary beneficiaries did not receive all the tax savings of the income tax deduction, a New York surrogate's court required the estate's income account to reimburse the estate's principal account for the extra estate taxes.

The following example illustrates the need for a *Warms* adjustment:

Example 1: *D* dies in 2002, with a $2 million gross estate. He leaves everything to a trust that is to pay all the income to *A* for life and the remainder to *B* at *A*'s death. The will directs that all estate taxes and expenses of administration be paid out of the residuary estate. Deductible administration expenses total $200,000.

If the personal representative elects to deduct the administration expenses on the estate tax return, the principal passing to the trust, after taxes and expenses, totals $1,455,000. In 2002, estate taxes payable on a $1.8 million taxable estate (gross estate of $2 million less $200,000 of expenses) equal $345,000.[62] The net estate passing to the trust is thus $1,455,000 ($2 million less $200,000 of expenses and less $345,000 of estate taxes).

On the other hand, if the personal representative of the estate elects to deduct the administration expenses on the estate's income tax returns,[63] the net estate passing to the trust totals $1,365,000. Estate taxes payable on a $2 million taxable estate in 2002, equal $435,000.[64] The net estate passing to the trust is thus $1,365,000 ($2 million, less $200,000 of expenses, still chargeable to principal, and less $435,000 of estate taxes).

If it is assumed that the estate can deduct the expenses in a 47½% income tax bracket (combined state and federal tax rates), the $200,000 of administration expenses saves the estate $95,000 in income taxes, but estate taxes increase by $90,000.

Thus, the personal representative's decision to deduct the administration expenses on the income tax returns reduces the principal of the residuary estate by $90,000. Because fiduciary accounting income is normally computed without reduction for estate administration expenses, net income increases by $95,000, which produces a dramatic shift of assets from the trust to A. Nevertheless, if the estate's income tax bracket is higher than the estate tax bracket, the personal representative has a clear duty to make the election to reduce the total tax liability.

Although the tax law permits the personal representative to elect between the estate tax deduction, the 1962 Revised Uniform Principal and Income Act does not. See 1962 Act § 5(a). Estate administration expenses are a charge against principal, not income. See id.[65] Because the election provides a benefit for the estate's income account at a substantial cost to the principal account, the election violates the fiduciary duty to be impartial and is contrary to fiduciary accounting rules. At the same time, however, the election discharges the personal representative's duty to conserve the estate.

When the duty to conserve conflicts with the duty to be impartial and violates fiduciary accounting rules, equity intercedes. A *Warms* adjustment reallocates estate income to offset the adverse consequences of the tax election. The mechanics of effecting this adjustment in Example 1 are easy to illustrate. Under accounting rules, A would receive all the income generated in the estate. See § 5(b). The *Warms* adjustment, however, directs $90,000 of the

---

[62] This example assumes that state death taxes equal the state death tax credit.

[63] Section 642(g) permits a personal representative to elect between an income tax deduction or an estate tax deduction for most estate expenses unless § 691(b) is applicable. If § 691(b) is applicable, these expenses are deductible on both returns.

[64] This example assumes that state death taxes equal the state death tax credit.

[65] The 1997 Uniform Principal and Income Act grants discretion to charge estate expenses to either principal or income. See § 201(2). If the fiduciary elects to charge estate expenses to principal, the same situation occurs under the 1997 Act.

estate income to the principal account. *A* then receives the remaining income.[66]

The personal representative who makes the *Warms* adjustment accomplishes the entire transaction on the books of account with no money actually changing hands. The personal representative simply makes a charge to the income account and a credit to the principal account. It is as though the personal representative takes money out of one pocket and puts it into another. Thus, the adjustment restores the amount of the estate principal to the size it would have been if the personal representative had not made the income tax election.

Other Adjustments

A number of other situations also create *inequities* that might justify equitable adjustments. Nearly every election or decision by a personal representative has the potential to cause a shift of assets from one group of beneficiaries to another. Disproportionate distributions to equal beneficiaries of an estate can create the need for an adjustment. *See In re Estate of Cooper v. Parkinson*, 186 So. 2d 844 (Fla. Dist. Ct. App. 1966); *Salesky Estate*, 15 Pa. Fiduc. 213 (Orphans' Ct. 1965). The potential differences between tax accounting and fiduciary accounting cause a net after tax difference probably not intended by the testator. Electing a tax year for the estate or the timing of the final distributions to close an estate can also create inequities among beneficiaries.

Before the Treasury issued the separate share regulations, the potential for an equitable adjustment existed when an estate made a distribution of principal to a beneficiary, and a portion of the distribution was treated as taxable income. Under the distributable net income (DNI) rules, funds designated as principal for fiduciary accounting purposes may be taxable income for federal income tax. An estate's distribution of principal carried out taxable income to the recipient unless § 663(a)(1) provided an exception, even if the distribution was fiduciary accounting principal.[67]

---

[66] The *Warms* opinion did not discuss the mechanics of the *Warms* adjustment. It is arguable that there is more than one way to divide the tax savings if the potential recipient of an equitable adjustment receives a portion of the income tax savings under the local principal and income act.

An example better illustrates the issue.

D dies in 2002, with a $2 million gross estate. He leaves $727,500 to a trust for the benefit of *A* and the residuary outright to *B*. If estate administration expenses are $200,000, the value of the residuary estate is also $727,500. An election by the personal representative to deduct the estate administration expenses on the estate's income tax returns, however, increases the estate taxes by $90,000 and reduces the residuary estate by the same amount. If it is assumed that the income tax deductions save $95,000 in income taxes, a *Warms* adjustment can restore the residuary to its former size with $5,000 left over.

Based on these facts, without considering the tax election and a possible equitable adjustment, the trust and the residuary bequest evenly divide estate income under the RUPIA. If the tax election is made and an equitable adjustment is considered, the question becomes whether the estate income is divided before or after the *Warms* adjustment. If the income is divided first, each beneficiary receives $50,000. The *Warms* adjustment then takes $40,000 of income from the trust, but leaves the trust with the $5,000 of overall tax savings. In the alternative, if the residuary receives the income after the *Warms* adjustment, the residuary receives the $90,000 it needs to be made whole, and then receives $5,000, or one-half of the remaining estate income, that results from the tax election.

[67] *See* Harkness v. United States, 469 F.2d 310 (Ct. Cl. 1972).

Because the principal distributions carried out DNI, a recipient reported income to the extent of DNI received. *See* § 662. As a consequence, the estate's fiduciary accounting income was not taxed in full because the estate received an income tax deduction equal to the distribution. Subsequent distribution of the accumulated estate income in a later year had no income tax consequence if the distribution of the accumulated income occurred at a time when the estate had no DNI. In summary, the recipient of the principal paid income taxes on fiduciary accounting principal, while the estate's accumulated income is subsequently distributed free of any income tax.

Here, as in the *Warms* scenario, the disparity between fiduciary accounting rules and income tax reporting created a conflict for the fiduciary. In *In re Estate of Holloway*, *supra*, a New York surrogate's court ordered an equitable adjustment when a distribution of principal was treated as income for federal income tax purposes.

A potential adjustment exists because of § 643(e), which provides that a distribution of assets in kind by an estate carries out DNI only to the lesser of the asset's adjusted basis or fair market value. The beneficiary's adjusted basis in the asset received equals the estate's adjusted basis. In the alternative, the personal representative can elect to recognize gain or loss on the distribution. If the election is made, the distribution carries out DNI to the extent of fair market value, and the beneficiary's adjusted basis equals fair market value.

The § 643(e) election, as other tax elections, has the potential to cause an equitable adjustment. For example, the recipient of the assets reports more income if the election is made. The estate has less income tax, but a gain is incurred. Fiduciary accounting rules are unlikely to place the benefit of the election where the taxes fall, and the basis for an equitable adjustment exists.

The qualified terminal interest property (QTIP) election presents an additional equitable adjustment problem that is unresolved.[68] A personal representative with the discretion to make a QTIP election has the power to defer estate taxes by making the election or to forgo any election and cause a current estate tax. The following example illustrates the problem.

Example 3: *D* died in 2002, with an estate of $2 million. *D*'s will leaves the maximum marital deduction (less the unified credit equivalent) in a QTIP trust for the surviving spouse. When the spouse dies, the QTIP trust assets will go to their children. The residuary estate goes outright to *D*'s children by an earlier marriage.

Putting aside the administration expenses issue, each set of children will eventually receive $1 million, free of Federal estate taxes. If, however, the surviving spouse is wealthy and has $1 million of assets, the spouse might decide, if named personal representative, to forgo the QTIP election in *D*'s estate. This causes *D*'s estate to pay $435,000 in estate taxes out of the residuary (*i.e.,* out of the assets passing to *D*'s first set of children after taxes, assuming the decedent's will directs that estate taxes are paid from the residue).

---

[68] QTIP trusts are discussed in Chapter 3.

If the surviving spouse also dies in 2002, the second set of children receives $2 million ($1 million from each estate), and the first set of children receives $565,000 ($1 million residue less taxes of $435,000). Alternatively, if *D*'s estate elects the QTIP marital deduction and the surviving spouse dies in 2002, either the QTIP marital trust or the spouse's separate assets pay $435,000 of estate taxes. The second set of children receives $1,565,000 ($1 million from each estate less $435,000 of estate taxes), and the first set of children receives $1 million (the residue from the first estate). The surviving spouse with the discretion to make a QTIP election, has the power to take $435,000 away from *D*'s other children and give it to their children.

It is not clear that the surviving spouse can make such a selfish election without violating the fiduciary duty to be impartial. At least one court has determined that when a conflict of interest arises, the fiduciary owes a higher duty to the other beneficiaries and must exercise elections to her own detriment. *See In re Estate of Colp, N.Y.L.J.*, Jan. 20, 1976, at 8, col. 2 (Sur. Ct. 1976). If this case is representative of the law generally, the surviving spouse may be surcharged if she forgoes the QTIP election. For more discussion of QTIP election issues, *see* Mark L. Ascher, *The Quandary of Executors Who Are Asked to Plan the Estates of the Dead: The Qualified Terminable Interest Property Election*, 63 N.C. L. Rev. 1 (1984).

[2] Equitable Adjustments Under the 1997 Uniform Principal and Income Act

Section 506(a) of the 1997 Principal and Income Act grants a fiduciary discretion to make equitable adjustments when tax elections create inequities. The Reporter's Comment to the Uniform Act provides several examples of when an adjustment might be appropriate. For example, if a trust owns S corporation stock, the trust beneficiary must report the S corporation income whether or not the S corporation makes an appropriate cash distribution to the trust. In this situation, it might be prudent for the trustee to reallocate a portion of principal to income and distribute it to the income beneficiary. *See* UNIFORM PRINCIPAL AND INCOME ACT, 7B U.L.A., 189 (1997).

When a fiduciary tax election potentially endangers either the estate tax marital or charitable deductions, 1997 Act § 506(b) requires an equitable adjustment to preserve the deduction. The Reporter's Comment notes that the result of the mandatory adjustment is intended to provide the same result that the Tax Court reached in *Estate of Brittenstool v. Commissioner*, 46 T.C. 711 (1966), in which the court determined that a mandatory adjustment required by New York probate law saved the estate's charitable deduction. *See id.*

Problems

1. The decedent died with a net estate of $2 million. Her will leaves one-half of the net estate to the surviving spouse and one-half of the net estate to her children by a prior marriage. The deductible expenses of administration are $100,000 this year. On which return (estate tax or income tax) should the personal representative claim the deductions? Should an equitable adjustment

be made? If so, why or if not, why not? Does it matter who is serving as personal representative? How does your answer change if the estate expenses are classified as management expenses or transmission expenses under the *Hubert* Regulations? *See* § 14.04[B][4][b], *supra*.

§ 14.06   Controlling Abuses of Trusts

Code: §§ 643(f), 661, and 665 through 667.

Regulations: Treas. Reg. § 1.665(a)–0(A)(d).

The basic structure of subchapter J allows income tax manipulation. For example in 2002 and 2003, by creating multiple trusts for the same beneficiary, a certain amount of undistributed income in each trust could be taxed at the 15% rate. If instead, one trust were created, taxable income in excess of the amount taxable at the 15% bracket would be taxed at a 27%, 30%, 35%, 36% or 38.6% rate. In 1984, Congress enacted the *multiple trust rule* to curb this abuse. *See* § 643(f).

Other structural aspects of subchapter J allow both estates and trusts to be used for income tax manipulation. However, Congress has only responded by curbing the abuses in trusts. It has left estates alone because estates exist for only a short period of time and they are not voluntary entities.

This section considers how Congress has minimized income tax abuses. The most complex provision involved the *throwback rules*, which were severely limited in application by the Taxpayer Relief Act of 1997.

[A]   Taxation of Multiple Trusts

As explained below, Congress enacted § 643(f) in the Tax Reform Act of 1984:

Prior Law

Trusts are treated as separate taxable entities with respect to certain accumulated and undistributed income (Code sec. 641). Trusts are taxed under a separate progressive rate schedule (sec. 1(e)).

Treasury Department regulations adopted following the Tax Reform Act of 1969 provided that multiple trusts were treated as one trust if the trusts had (1) the same grantor and substantially the same beneficiary, (2) no substantially independent purposes (such as independent dispositive purposes), and (3) as their principal purpose the avoidance or mitigation of progressive rates of tax (including mitigation as a result of deferral of tax) or avoidance or mitigation of the alternative minimum tax.[69]

In Edward L. Stephenson Trust v. Commissioner, 81 T.C. 283 (1983), the Tax Court held that the Treasury Department regulations regarding multiple trusts were invalid because the Internal Revenue Code did not support a subjective test of tax avoidance motive as a basis

---

[69] Treas. Reg. § 1.641(a)–0(c).

for determining the existence of multiple trusts. The court further held
that Congress, by enacting a series of more limited rules relating to
multiple trusts in the Tax Reform Acts of 1969 and 1976, had implicitly accepted an earlier Tax Court decision which held that the motive
for establishing and maintaining multiple trusts was irrelevant for tax
purposes.[70]

Reasons for Change

Because of the progressive tax structure, it would be possible to
reduce income taxes significantly by establishing multiple trusts
having the same grantor and the same or similar beneficiaries unless
there were rules providing for aggregation of trusts in certain cases.
For example, if, instead of establishing one $1 million trust, a taxpayer
established ten essentially identical $100,000 trusts, the taxpayer
would be able to secure a significantly lower marginal tax rate for the
undistributed income of the trusts.

Congress was concerned that, without the restrictions of the Treasury Department regulations, persons would be able to reduce significantly the taxation of investment income through the creation of
multiple trusts. Accordingly, Congress believed that rules similar to
the rules contained in the prior Treasury regulations should be
legislated.

Explanation of Provision

The Act provides that, under Treasury regulations, two or more
trusts will be treated as one trust if (1) the trusts have substantially
the same grantor or grantors and substantially the same primary
beneficiary or beneficiaries, and (2) a principal purpose for the existence of the trusts is the avoidance of Federal income tax . . . .

For purposes of these rules, a husband and wife are treated as one
beneficiary or grantor. Also, trusts will not be treated as having
different primary beneficiaries merely because the trusts have different contingent beneficiaries. Similarly, trusts will not be treated as
having different grantors by having different persons making nominal
transfers to the trusts. For example, Congress expects that the
Treasury regulations will treat the trusts in the following example as
one trust:

> *A* establishes, with the principal purpose of avoidance of Federal
> income tax, Trust 1 for the benefit of his sister *S1*, his brother
> *B1*, and his brother *B2*; Trust 2 for the benefit of his sister *S2*,
> his brother *B1*, and his brother *B2*; Trust 3 for the benefit of his
> sister *S1*, his sister *S2*, and his brother B1; and Trust 4 for the
> benefit of his sister *S1*, his sister *S2*, and his brother *B2*. Under
> each trust instrument, the trustee is given discretion to pay any

---

[70] Estelle Morris Trusts v. Commissioner, 51 T.C. 20 (1968), *aff'd per curiam*, 427 F.2d 1361
(9th Cir. 1970).

current or accumulated income to any one or more of the beneficiaries.

Where there are substantial independent purposes, and tax avoidance is not a principal purpose for the existence of separate trusts, the trusts will not be aggregated. The following is an example of where separate trusts will not be aggregated under the Act:

> X establishes two irrevocable trusts for the benefit of X's son and daughter. Son is the income beneficiary of the first trust and the trustee (Bank of P) is required to pay all income currently to son for life. Daughter is the remainder beneficiary. X's daughter is an income beneficiary of the second trust and the trust instrument permits the trustee (Bank of D) to accumulate or to pay income, in its discretion, to daughter for her education, support, and maintenance. The trustee also may pay income or corpus to son for his medical expenses. Daughter is the remainder beneficiary and will receive the trust corpus upon son's death.

Report, Joint Committee on Taxation, General Explanation of Revenue Provisions of Deficit Reduction Act of 1984, 98th Cong., 2d Sess. 255–257 (1985).

Problems

1. Given that the income of simple trusts is taxed to the beneficiary in the year earned, can you see any tax advantages to multiple simple trusts?

[B]   Calendar Year Requirement for Trusts

Nearly all trusts are now required to file tax returns using a calendar year. *See* § 644. Only trusts that are totally exempt from income, *i.e.*, charitable trusts, may still use a fiscal year. For this purpose, a § 664 split interest charitable trust is not exempt from the calendar year rule.

[C]   Throwback Rules

Sections 665 through 667 govern the taxation of accumulated trust income when it is distributed to the beneficiaries.[71] *See generally* Alan S. Acker, *The Throwback Rule: Its Historical Development and How It Works*, 10 REV. OF TAX. OF INDIV. 107 (1986). These provisions, known as the throwback rules, were enacted to discourage use of accumulation trusts as devices for obtaining significant tax savings. The rules contained in §§ 665 through 667 apply only to trusts and do not apply to estates. *See* § 666(a). The short term nature of the normal estate was enough to permit its exclusion from the rules.

Under the throwback rules, distributions of accumulated income are treated as if the distributions were made in the year in which the income was earned. These rules reflect a belief that income will most often be accumulated by a trust when the tax on that trust income will be less than the income tax in the hands of the beneficiaries.

---

[71] For taxation of distributions from foreign trusts, see § 668.

The Taxpayer Relief Act of 1997 generally repealed the application of the throwback rules to all trusts, but excepted from repeal foreign trusts and trusts created before March 1, 1984, which would be considered multiple under the provisions of § 643(f).

§ 14.07 Income Taxation of a Charitable Trust Beneficiary

Code: §§ 664(a) through (c), and 642(c)(3).

Regulations: Treas. Reg. § 1.664–1(d).

The estate and gift taxation of charitable remainder trusts was discussed briefly in Chapters 3 and 4. Once the trust is created and funded, additional income tax issues must be considered.

Qualified charitable remainder trusts are exempt from income tax, except to the extent they have unrelated business income (which is rare). *See* § 664(c). This exemption permits the trustee of a charitable remainder trust to sell assets contributed to the trust without incurring gain. So long as the trustee was not obligated to sell the gifted property at the time contributed to the trust, assignment of income principles should not be applicable. *See* Rev. Rul. 60–370, 1960–2 C.B. 203. The income tax exempt nature of the charitable trust is one of the highly touted features of charitable remainder trusts: capital gain associated with the disposition of appreciated property is not recognized.

When the income from a qualified charitable remainder trust is distributed to the noncharitable beneficiary, however, those distributions may be, and are generally, income. The exact income tax consequences to the beneficiary depend upon the character of the payment under a four tier distribution system. Distributions are taxed according to the following tiered system:

(1) ordinary income to the extent that the trust currently has ordinary income or has undistributed ordinary income from a prior year;

(2) capital gains to the extent that the trust currently has capital gains or has undistributed capital gains from a prior year (short term first);

(3) any other income (for example, tax exempt income), to the extent that the trust has other income currently or has undistributed other income from a prior year;

(4) distribution from trust principal.

Section 664(b) and Treasury Regulation § 1.664–1(d).

The tiered system requires the income beneficiary to defer receipt of any tax exempt income earned by the trust until all taxable income has been distributed. Ordinary losses are not distributable to the income beneficiary, but instead offset any ordinary income in the trust. If a trust has both short term and long term capital gains, the short term capital gains are deemed distributed before the long term capital gains. The beneficiary is deemed to receive the income distribution in a year that the trust is required to distribute property as well.

Pooled income funds, unlike charitable remainder trusts, are not exempt from income tax.[72] *See* § 642(c)(3). Rather, pooled income funds are considered *complex trusts* under subchapter J. *See* Treas. Reg. § 1.642(c)–5. Although subject to tax, a pooled income fund usually does not pay income tax for two reasons: (1) the fund is required to distribute its income every year to its beneficiaries and receives a concomitant deduction and (2) the fund is allowed a charitable contribution deduction for long term capital gains. Distributions to the income beneficiaries are not determined under the tiered distribution applicable to charitable remainder trusts. Instead, the distributions are taxed under normal trust distribution rules. The beneficiaries are taxed pro rata according to the character of the income earned by the fund. The beneficiaries must report that income during the tax year of the fund.

Charitable lead trusts are taxed as complex trusts, unless the grantor trust rules of §§ 671 through 677 apply. Amounts distributed to the charity are deductible in determining taxable income of the trust or the grantor.

---

[72] Pooled income funds are defined and discussed in § 3.04[D][8], *supra*.

Part IV
_____

POLICY CONSIDERATIONS

This part contains Chapter 15, which includes excerpts from a number of articles that discuss reforms of, and alternatives to, the transfer tax system. As policy articles, they challenge the assumptions and solutions of the current transfer tax system, and spotlight the weaknesses of current law.

Chapter 15

PERSPECTIVES ON THE CURRENT WEALTH TRANSFER TAX SYSTEM

This chapter contains excerpts from a number of articles that discuss reforms of, and alternatives to, the transfer tax system. As policy articles, they challenge the assumptions and solutions of the current transfer tax system, and spotlight the weaknesses of current law. We begin the chapter with a discussion of issues raised by the Tax Act of 2001.

§ 15.01 Issues Raised by the Tax Act of 2001[1]

William G. Gale and Joel Slemrod, The Estate Tax: Not Dead Yet

93 Tax Notes 807 (2001)

I. INTRODUCTION

After decades of relative neglect, the estate tax became a red-hot political issue over the last few years. Supporters believe it to be an important part of the federal tax system, on the grounds that it imposes progressive burdens, plugs income tax loopholes, and encourages charitable contributions. Opponents believe that as a complex, unfair, and inefficient levy, the so-called "death tax" violates every norm of good tax policy.

Faced with these divergent views, politicians examined three choices: live with the estate tax, reform it, or throw it out. In the spirit of Yogi Berra's[2] admonition, "If you come to a fork in the road, take it!" in the recent tax legislation, Congress and the president chose all three options! Under the new tax law, the estate tax will be slightly reformed and reduced between 2002 and 2009. In 2010, the estate tax and the generation-skipping transfer tax will be repealed, but the gift tax will be retained. These changes are coupled with changes in the taxation of inherited assets with capital gains. In 2011, all of these changes are removed, and the tax reverts to its current form. Overall, the changes introduced in the new law make taxes more complex and more uncertain and generate an end-point outcome — the currently existing tax — that many people find less than optimal. For all of these reasons, policymakers will likely revisit the estate tax in the near future.

A remarkable feature of the recent estate tax debate was the almost complete lack of hard evidence about any of the alleged effects of the estate

---

[1] *See generally Symposium: The Death of the Death Tax*, 48 CLEVE. ST. L. REV. 653-791 (2000).

[2] YOGI BERRA AND DAVID KAPLAN, WHEN YOU COME TO A FORK IN THE ROAD, TAKE IT!: INSPIRATION AND WISDOM FROM ONE OF BASEBALL'S GREATEST HEROES (Hyperion Books 2001).

tax or its alternatives. For example, despite seemingly never-ending discussion of how the estate tax destroyed family farms, The New York Times[3] reported that the American Farm Bureau Federation — an ardent supporter of estate tax abolition — could not identify a single family farm that had been put under by the estate tax. Likewise, the impact on small businesses, saving, and capital formation was the subject of much rhetoric but virtually no evidence. Thus, the next time the estate tax emerges as a live policy issue, it would be useful to have a coherent framework, plus facts and analysis, to guide the debate and help frame the choices.

Providing this framework is exactly the purpose of *Rethinking Estate and Gift Taxation*[4] . . . The book stems from a conference convened in May 2000 at the Brookings Institution and sponsored jointly by the Office of Tax Policy Research at the University of Michigan Business School and Brookings. The conference centered around 10 research papers, covering the history and features of the estate tax; the optimal taxation of estates and gifts; methods of estate tax avoidance; the extent and determinants of estate tax evasion; theoretical, simulation, and empirical work on how estate taxes affect capital accumulation and the distribution of income; the impact of estate taxes on charitable contributions; the distributional impacts of taxing capital gains at death; and the role of health in wealth management decisions by elderly households. The book contains those papers, discussant comments, and an overview chapter. The goal of the papers is to apply rigorous research methods to better understand the economics of estate taxes, not to advocate particular policy changes.

In this report, we provide an overview of the estate tax debate with special reference to the contributions made by the papers in the new volume. [Parts II and III, which summarize the transfer tax system before and after the 2001 Tax Act, are not included since a more comprehensive discussion is found in Chapter 1, § 1.01, *supra*.]

IV. ANALYZING ESTATE AND GIFT TAXES

Transfer taxes raise a number of difficult issues within and beyond the bounds of economics. The issues range from considerations as private as the nature of relationships between parents and their children, and as socially encompassing as the definition and implementation of equal opportunity.

A. Why Do People Give Transfers?

An important theme to emerge from the conference is the simple but fundamental point that the effects of transfer taxes will depend on why people give transfers in the first place. Some bequests may be "accidents," in the sense that people accumulate assets to save for retirement, but face uncertain lifespans. Even if they do not plan or desire to give bequests, they may end up bequeathing their accumulated assets to descendants. Other bequests may

---

[3] David Cay Johnston, *Talk of Lost Farms Reflects Muddle of Estate Tax Debate*, New York Times April 8, 2001, P.1.

[4] WILLIAM G. GALE, JAMES R. HINES JR., AND JOEL SLEMROD, EDS., RETHINKING ESTATE AND GIFT TAXATION (Brookings Inst. Press 2001).

be motivated by parental altruism toward their children. Some people may be motivated by the sheer joy of giving resources away. Finally, some bequests or transfers may represent a sort of payment by parents to their children in exchange for help and attention.

Each possibility above draws support from at least some research, but none is the sole explanation of all wealth transfers. Many households are influenced by several motives, and the importance of each motive may vary across households. It is also worth emphasizing that analysis of the estate tax requires evidence on the motives for giving among the very wealthiest households. But there is even less known about the very wealthy than about the moderately wealthy or middle-class households that are the mainstay of most research, and the richest households may well have different motives for, and patterns of, giving and saving.

B. Equity

Transfer taxes are highly progressive if they are ultimately borne by either the donors or recipients of bequests. A simulation study by John Laitner in the conference volume suggests that the estate tax is for the most part not indirectly passed on to other — nonwealthy — people by gradually reducing saving and the economy's capital intensity. Laitner finds that removing the estate tax would increase the concentration of wealth, especially among the top 1 percent of wealth-holders. This implies the tax is progressive, even allowing for its economywide effects. The estate tax also serves as a backstop to the income tax, taxing components of income — such as unrealized capital gains — that otherwise go untaxed.

Transfer taxes raise difficult issues of horizontal equity. Among families with the same lifetime resources, the taxes discriminate on the basis of how resources are spent, violating the notion that those with equal means should pay equal taxes. Those that spend down their wealth avoid these taxes, while others do not. But among recipients with the same (noninheritance) wealth, transfer taxes reduce the inequality of inheritances and thus ameliorate unequal opportunity. These two perspectives appear to create irreconcilable differences in views about whether taxes on transfers are fair in principle.

Another issue is whether taxing at death is appropriate. Death, however, is neither necessary nor sufficient to trigger transfer taxes. It is unnecessary because transfers between living persons can trigger gift taxes. It is insufficient because 98 percent of people who die pay no estate tax. While death may be unpleasant to contemplate, the costs of taxing at death do not appear to be significant, relative to taxation during life. Thus, to the extent that it really is a problem, taxation at death could be avoided by replacing the estate tax with equally progressive taxes imposed during life.

C. Efficiency

In his conference paper, Louis Kaplow shows that whether an estate tax is part of an efficient tax system — one that minimizes the economic cost per dollar raised — depends crucially on several factors, most notably on why people give transfers. For example, to the extent that bequests are "accidental," as described above, the estate tax is a highly efficient tax — it places a burden on something the donor does not care about. On the other hand, if parents are altruistic toward their children, Kaplow shows that there may even be a case for subsidizing transfers, rather than taxing them.

However, if society desires an equitable tax system as well as an efficient one, the case for an estate tax is improved, because the tax is highly progressive, and hence can "buy" a lot of equity. This suggests that simple descriptions of optimal tax policy toward transfers are difficult to establish.

D. Tax Complexity, Avoidance, and Evasion

Critics argue that the tax spawns a host of avoidance schemes and call the estate tax "voluntary." But it is hard to believe that financially sophisticated, wealthy households voluntarily part with upwards of $ 30 billion per year. It is also sometimes claimed that transfer taxes are both easy to avoid and a serious deterrent to wealth accumulation. But if they were so easy to avoid, why would the taxes hurt wealth accumulation? In his conference paper, Richard Schmalbeck suggests that the typical estate tax shelter (for example, a trust) features a fixed fee that reduces the effective tax rate on an unlimited amount of wealth that is passed through the device. Schmalbeck's findings imply that shelters do reduce the effective marginal tax rate at high wealth levels, and therefore reduce the deterrence to wealth accumulation below what the statutory rate structure suggests.

Estimates of the costs of complying with and administering the estate tax vary enormously — from 7 percent of revenues to 100 percent — partly because the data and methodologies are imperfect; the more reliable estimates are at the lower end of the range. In their contribution to the conference, Martha Britton Eller, Brian Erard, and Chin-Chin Ho estimate an estate tax evasion rate of about 13 percent, and suggest that this is a lower bound for the true value. This figure is about the same as estimates for income tax noncompliance.

E. Saving, Labor Supply, and Entrepreneurship

Critics argue that the estate tax significantly reduces the saving, labor supply, and entrepreneurship that are essential to economic prosperity, but little evidence has been available to evaluate these claims. A distinctive feature of the volume is the presence of the three papers on wealth accumulation and the taxation of estates.

Laitner provides the most sophisticated simulation model of the economic impact of estate taxes to date, embedding them in an overlapping generations model which features individuals with altruistic bequest motives. He finds that removing estate taxes would have a small positive effect on the long-term ratio of capital to labor. William Gale and Maria Perozek show that the impact of transfer taxes on saving, like the efficiency effects, will depend critically on why people give transfers. If bequests are unintentional, for example, estate taxes will not affect saving by the donor, but they will reduce the net-of-tax inheritance received by the recipient and thereby raise the recipient's saving.

If bequests are motivated by altruism, the effects are ambiguous, but simulations suggest that the estate tax could actually raise private saving under many circumstances.

Wojciech Kopczuk and Joel Slemrod analyzed estate tax return data from 1916 to 1996 and found that the size of aggregate reported estates is generally negatively associated with the estate tax rate, holding constant other influences. Using data on specific decedents, they found that the tax rate that prevailed at age 45, or 10 years before death, is more clearly (negatively) associated with reported estates than the tax rate prevailing in the year of death. These results could reflect the impact of estate taxes on the donor's saving, or avoidance, or both.

Other empirical work has shown that recipients of large inheritances increase their consumption spending and reduce their labor supply. By extension, if estate taxes reduce net-of-tax inheritances, they should raise saving and labor supply by the recipient.

The impact of the estate tax on family-held businesses and farms has taken on a hugely disproportionate role in public policy debates. This issue is reviewed extensively in the introductory survey by Gale and Slemrod, but the basic points are straightforward. There is virtually no reliable evidence suggesting that the impact of estate taxes on the viability of businesses and farms is very significant. Businesses and farms already receive substantial subsidies under the existing estate tax, not to mention subsidies under the income tax. The vast majority of estates have no business or farm assets, and only about 3 percent of estates have more than half of their wealth in businesses and farms. Most of the value of small businesses in estates consists of unrealized capital gains and would never be taxed if not for the estate tax. These findings suggest that the case for existing business subsidies in the estate tax is weak, the case for expanding those subsidies is weaker still, and the notion that the estate tax should be abolished because of its effect on businesses and farms is misguided.

F. Effects on Gift-Giving and Charity

Although estate and gift taxes are said to be "unified," a number of features of the tax code favor gifts over bequests, and evidence suggests that changes in the tax treatment of gifts and bequests affect the composition and timing of transfers. In their paper at the conference, Jonathan Feinstein and Chin-Chin Ho (2001) extend this work by showing that an individual's health status (and by extension, the likelihood of dying and facing estate taxes), has important effects on giving behavior. They document a series of patterns among saving, gift giving, and health that suggest that a significant amount of giving is tax-motivated.

A number of analyses find that the estate tax deduction for charitable donations generates a significant increase in contributions at death. The estate tax may encourage charitable giving during life, too, since this would reduce both income and estate taxes. David Joulfaian's (2001) contribution to the volume matches estate tax returns filed between 1996 and 1998 with income tax returns for the same people filed between 1987 and 1996. He finds that the magnitude of giving during life relative to giving at death changes markedly with wealth, with the extremely wealthy giving a much greater share of their contributions at death. His estimates also document that giving at death is sensitive to the marginal tax rates applied in the estate tax, and so indicate that abolishing the tax would lead to a significant decline in charitable bequests.

V. REFORM OPTIONS

Given the changes made in EGTRRA, the first question for reform has to be "why do anything?" Why not let the tax act run its course? The answer is that the new tax law, even though it repeals the estate tax at one point, creates numerous complexities and uncertainties. First, although few people believe the tax cut will simply be allowed to sunset as of 2011, the existence of the sunsetting provisions creates unnecessary uncertainty about how, whether, and when the tax change will be extended. Second, the long transition period before the estate tax is abolished implies that different estate planning techniques, allocations, or investments may be most appropriate depending on when a person is likely to die. This will undoubtedly complicate optimal estate planning. The third problem stems from the repeal of basis step-up at death. Under pre-EGTRRA law, when an heir receives an asset from an estate, the basis price is "stepped up." The new bill features "basis carryover" as of 2010[5] : in general, heirs inherit an asset's original basis price, but each estate would be allowed to increase the basis of assets by up to $ 1.3 million on transfers to any person, and by an additional $ 3 million on transfers to a spouse. Exemptions would apply to transfers of some assets below $ 1.3 million and to interspousal transfers of $ 3 million.

Carryover basis not only would raise virtually no revenue, it also raises vexing administrative issues.[6] For example, some families would have to keep records for generations to keep track of asset purchase prices and improvements unless a safe harbor rule were created. A carryover basis provision was enacted in the late 1970s, but was repealed before it took effect because taxpayers complained about the new complexities and problems in implementation. There is little reason to think these issues would be any easier to deal with now.

If the estate tax is abolished, and basis carryover proves inadministrable or undesirable, some other tax treatment of capital gains at death must be applied.[7] Coupling the current tax treatment of gains — basis step-up — with estate tax repeal would create a gaping loophole in the income tax that would drain revenues, provide huge tax cuts to the wealthiest households, and exacerbate the "lock-in" effect of capital gains taxation.

---

[5] [Carryover basis, effective for the year 2010, is discussed in Chapter 2, § 2.06[A], *supra*. Eds.]

[6] [*See generally* Joseph M. Dodge, *What's Wrong With Carryover Basis Under H.R. 8*, 91 TAX NOTES 961 (2001) (discussing technical and policy faults). Eds.]

[7] [*See generally* Stephen Vasek, *Death Tax Repeal: Alternative Reform Proposals*, 92 TAX NOTES 955 (2001). Eds.]

Abolition could be coupled with the extension of the capital gains tax to the gains accrued but unrealized at death.[8] This proposal, however, would raise only about a quarter of the revenue of the estate tax, and would be much less progressive, as James Poterba and Scott Weisbenner show in their conference paper. In addition, this would have many of the complexities of the estate tax, so it is neither an attractive or likely option by itself.

Moreover, it is not evident that repeal of the estate tax is the best policy.[9] Repeal would eliminate what is by far the most progressive tax instrument in the federal tax arsenal, just after an extended period over which the distributions of pre-tax income and wealth have become far more skewed and after which highest-income households received a substantial tax cut. It could hurt nonprofit organizations. It may not even raise saving, labor supply, or growth, as its advocates hope, and would probably reduce state tax revenues as well.

Perhaps the most plausible reform would be to follow the strategy invoked for income taxes in the Tax Reform Act of 1986: keep the exemption level high, close loopholes, and keep rates low, relative to the current status. Raising the exemption would reduce the number of people paying the tax while still taxing the "truly wealthy," and chipping away at the concentration of wealth. It would also help smaller family-owned businesses, but without the horizontal equity problems that are involved in giving preferential treatment to business assets. Closing loopholes by treating different assets in a more similar fashion would reduce sheltering opportunities, and thus make the tax simpler and fairer. Modestly reducing rates would reduce the incentive to shelter or change behavior in the first place. In addition to these changes, indexing the effective exemption and the tax brackets for inflation would automatically keep the tax burden at any particular real wealth level constant over time. To some extent, these changes — at least regarding tax rates and the effective exemption — are consistent with the estate and gift tax as of 2009 in the current legislation, before the off-and on-again treatment now planned for 2010 and 2011.

VI. CONCLUSION

The appropriate role and effects of transfer taxes are still open questions. Any conclusion about the appropriate taxation of intergenerational transfers must take into account transfer motives, the political and technical limitations on other tax instruments, the limited knowledge about these taxes that is currently available, and other factors.

In a real world filled with practical difficulties, political compromises, and economic uncertainties, it may take a variety of taxes to meet social goals, and the estate tax may well play a small but important role in the government's portfolio of tax instruments. It adds to progressivity in a way that the

---

[8] [Professor Dodge advocates this approach. *See* Joseph M. Dodge, *A Deemed Realization Approach Is Superior to Carryover Basis (And Avoids Most of the Problems of Estate and Gift Tax)*, 54 TAX L. REV. 421 (2001). Eds.]

[9] [*See id.* at 424–429 (summarizing debate on transfer tax repeal, with useful citation to references). Eds.]

income tax cannot easily do because of capital gains issues, and that society may choose not to do via income taxes, because taxing at death may have smaller costs than taxing during life. The supposed negatives of the estate tax — its effects on saving, compliance costs, and small businesses — lack definitive supporting evidence and in some cases appear to be grossly overstated. And there are some presumed benefits from increased charitable contributions and improved equality of opportunity.

Nevertheless, it is equally clear that there is a problem. A tax with high rates and numerous avoidance opportunities is ripe for change. Even given the goals and constraints noted above, many people feel that transfer taxes could be better structured. Many others feel that having no transfer taxes would be preferred to the existing situation.

Economic analysis cannot fully resolve these issues. What it can do is clarify the various trade-offs involved in tax policy decisions, illuminate which value judgments — about which economics has no say — are involved, and identify the crucial conceptual and empirical issues. Compared to many tax questions, the tradeoffs that affect estate taxes are more difficult to analyze, because they involve more than one generation. The value judgments are more difficult, because they involve life-and-death issues about which people feel strongly. And empirical analysis is more difficult, because the data are more elusive and the relevant behaviors span at least a lifetime.

The studies in *Rethinking Estate and Gift Taxation* address all of these issues — they rethink the estate and gift tax in a rigorous way. It is our hope and expectation that the papers will provide a solid base of knowledge to inform future policy discussions and a springboard to encourage continuing analysis of transfer tax issues.

§ 15.02 Reform of the Current Wealth Transfer Tax System

Tax Reform for Fairness, Simplicity, and Economic Growth

*2 Treasury Department Report to the President
378–80, 382, 384, 385, 393, 400–01, 402 (1984)*[10]

. . .

Simplification of Rules Pertaining to
Completed Gifts and Testamentary Strings

Application of the gift tax on a tax-inclusive basis would eliminate the major disparity between the transfer tax treatment of lifetime gifts and transfers at death. Therefore, it would be possible to eliminate the rule requiring inclusion in the gross estate of gift taxes paid on transfers made within three

---

[10] *See* David H. Brockway, *Comprehensive Estate and Gift Tax Reform,* 67 TAX NOTES 1089 (1995) (including proposal to correlate the transfer tax rates with the income tax rates); *see also* Joseph M. Dodge, *Redoing the Estate and Gift Taxes Along Easy-to-Value Lines,* 43 TAX L. REV. 241 (1988).

years of death. The complex retained interest rules would be replaced with a simpler set of rules determining when a transfer of less than an entire interest constitutes a completed gift for Federal transfer tax purposes. These new rules would ensure that a transfer is subject to gift or estate tax, but not to both taxes. In addition, the rules would assure a more accurate valuation and provide greater consistency between the transfer tax rules and the rules governing when trust income is taxed at the grantor's rate.

Retained beneficial enjoyment. The proposal would simplify present law by providing that a transfer tax would be imposed only once, when the beneficial enjoyment retained by the donor terminates. Thus, if a donor makes a gift of a remainder interest in property, but retains the intervening income interest, no gift would occur until the termination of the donor's income interest. At that time, the property would be subject to gift or estate tax at its full fair market value. Because the transferor would be treated as the owner of the property during the interim, any distributions made to beneficiaries other than the transferor would be treated as transfers when made.

The transferor would continue to be treated as owner of the property for all transfer tax purposes. Such treatment would foreclose any opportunity for tax avoidance through the transferor's repurchase of the remainder interest free of gift tax.

The proposal would also apply to the creation of inter vivos charitable lead trusts. The creator of such a trust would be treated as owning the property for transfer tax purposes until the vesting of the non-charitable interest or his or her death, if sooner. (Testamentary charitable lead trusts would be taxed as under present law.)

Revocable transfers. The rules of present law would continue with respect to any transfer where the transferor retains the right to regain possession or enjoyment of the property. Such a transfer would be treated as incomplete for gift and estate tax purposes, and would be treated as complete only when the transferor's retained right or power to revoke terminates. Distributions from the property to beneficiaries other than the donor would be treated as gifts when made, thereby providing consistency with the rules governing the income taxation of trusts as well as the rules governing the income and gift tax treatment of demand loans.

Retained powers. In determining whether a gift is complete for transfer tax purposes, the proposal would treat a retained power to control the beneficial enjoyment of the transferred property as irrelevant where the power could not be used to distribute income or principal to the donor. Thus, the fact that the transferor as trustee or custodian can exercise control over the identity of the distributee of the property or over the amount or timing of a distribution would be irrelevant in determining whether a gift is complete (although such factors may be relevant in determining whether the transfer qualifies for the annual gift tax exclusion). Under this rule, a transfer would be complete for gift tax purposes where the grantor creates an irrevocable trust but retains the absolute right to determine who (other than himself) will receive the trust income or principal.

Reversionary interests. Current rules regarding retained reversionary interests would be replaced by a rule that disregards reversionary interests retained by the grantor in valuing transferred property for Federal gift tax purposes. The existence of the reversionary interest would be relevant only for purposes of determining the timing of the transfer for estate and gift tax purposes.

If the donor makes a gift of property for a term of years or for the life of one or more beneficiaries, and if the donor retains a reversionary interest that is more likely than not to return the property to the donor or his or her estate, the transfer would be treated as incomplete. Interim distributions of income or principal (or the value of the use of the property) would be treated as gifts by the donor on an annual basis. On the other hand, if it is more likely than not that the reversionary interest will not return the property to the donor or his or her estate, the transfer will be treated as complete and the full fair market value of the property will be subject to gift tax, without reduction for the actuarial value of the reversionary interest. If the donor dies with the reversion outstanding, the value of the reversionary interest will be excluded from the donor's estate, whether or not the reversion terminates at that time. If the property reverts to the donor prior to his or her death, the donor would have the right to retransfer the property at any time free from additional gift tax liability. If not retransferred during the donor's lifetime, the property would be excluded from the donor's estate. In order to prevent disputes arising from the reversion and subsequent retransfer of fungible assets, however, the proposal would require the donor to place the reverted property in a segregated account in order to benefit from the exclusion.

The determination of whether a reversionary interest is more likely than not to return property to the donor during his lifetime generally would depend on the life expectancy of the donor and the anticipated duration of the intervening interest. For example, a reversion following a term of years less than the donor's life expectancy or following the life of a beneficiary older than the donor would be more likely than not to return the property to the donor.

. . .

Analysis

Application of the gift tax on a tax-inclusive basis would remove the primary tax incentive for lifetime gifts and therefore would make tax considerations a relatively neutral factor in the decision whether to dispose of property during one's lifetime or to retain it until death. Moreover, the proposal would provide greater fairness in the application of the transfer tax system because all persons paying the transfer tax would do so on the same tax-inclusive basis. Finally, by removing the major incentive for disguising testamentary transfers as lifetime gifts, the proposal would permit the simplification of the rules governing when a transfer is complete for estate and gift tax purposes.

The proposed rules for determining when a transfer is complete would ensure that each transfer is subject to estate or gift tax, but not to both taxes. By delaying the imposition of transfer tax liability until the donor's interest terminates, the proposed rules would reduce the number of instances in which it is necessary to consult an actuarial table to value the transfer of a partial interest in property and would provide greater accuracy in the valuation of the transferred interest.

Finally, the proposal would provide greater consistency between the gift tax rules governing when a transfer is complete and the rules governing when trust income is taxed at the grantor's rate.

. . .

REVISE POWER OF APPOINTMENT RULES

. . .

Reasons for Change

The present rules governing general powers of appointment are largely ineffective. They can be circumvented easily by creation of a power that is purportedly limited by an ascertainable standard but that, in reality, gives the holder substantial discretion and control over the trust property.

In addition, present law can often trap the unwary taxpayer. For example, the general power of appointment rule may be invoked where neither the creator of the power nor the donee of the power is aware that a particular power is likely to be construed as a general power of appointment. To a great extent, this uncertainty exists because State law determines whether a limitation placed on the exercise of the power constitutes an "ascertainable standard."

. . .

Proposal

The current power of appointment rules would be replaced by a rule treating an individual as the owner of property for transfer tax purposes where the individual possesses a nonlapsing right or power to vest the property or trust corpus in himself or herself. For purposes of this rule, a power or right would be treated as nonlapsing if it did not, by its terms, expire prior to the death of the powerholder.

The release of such a power (or the extinguishment of such a power at death) would be treated in the same manner as a transfer by the outright owner of the underlying property. . . .

. . .

EXPAND CREDIT FOR TAX ON PRIOR TRANSFERS

. . .

Reasons for Change

In certain situations, the current credit for tax on prior transfers is inconsistent with the rationale underlying the proposed tax on generation-skipping transfers, i.e., that the transfer tax ought to be imposed once per generation. For example, if A leaves property to his brother B, and if B dies more than two years after A, the property will be subject to more than one full estate tax in the generation of *A* and *B*. If *B* dies more than ten years after *A*, the property will be subject to two full estate taxes in that generation.

In many cases, *A* can avoid the necessity of a second estate tax payable at *B*'s death by leaving the property in trust for *B*'s benefit during his lifetime or by giving *B* a life estate in the property. Both these alternatives, however, require advance planning and entail administrative costs. More significantly, they place restrictions on *B*'s use of the property that *A* may not wish to impose.

Proposal

In a case where a decedent's estate includes property inherited from a member of the same generation or a lower generation, a full estate tax credit would be given to the estate for any estate tax paid by the original transferor of the property. The credit would not phase out over time.

. . .

REVISE INCOME IN RESPECT OF A DECEDENT RULES

. . .

Reasons for Change

The double deduction generated by DRD [Deductions in Respect of a Decedent] items grants an undue benefit to estates that can take advantage of it and should be eliminated. The section 691(c) deduction is available only to taxpayers who itemize their deductions.

Proposal

The deduction allowed by section 691(c) would be replaced by a rule providing for a basis increase in each item of IRD [Income in Respect of a Decedent] equal to the estate tax liability attributable to such item.

Upon payment of an item of DRD, the income tax deduction otherwise allowable would be reduced by an amount equal to the estate tax savings attributable to the deduction of the liability for Federal estate tax purposes. The amount of estate tax savings would be computed in a manner similar to that utilized to compute the estate tax attributable to an item of IRD. Thus, the estate tax liability (including liability for State death taxes) would be computed with and without the deductions attributable to the items of DRD, with the difference allocated among each DRD item according to their relative amounts.

. . .

LIMIT STATE DEATH TAX CREDIT

. . .

Reasons for Change

The original purpose of the State death tax credit was to prevent States from competing with each other for high-income residents by having low (or no) State death taxes. Today, however, almost all States have enacted estate or inheritance taxes that provide significant revenue; arguably, therefore, the State death tax credit is no longer needed to prevent competition among the States for wealthy residents.

In its present form, the State death tax credit functions largely as a device for sharing Federal estate tax revenues with the States. This purpose can be served without the use of a highly detailed, graduated credit schedule.

Proposal

The present schedule setting forth the maximum state death tax credit would be replaced by a flat rate maximum credit equal to five percent of the decedent's Federal taxable estate.[11]

. . .

———

Report on Transfer Tax Restructuring

*Task Force on Transfer Tax Restructuring, Section of Taxation,
American Bar Association (1987),
reprinted in 41 TAX LAW. 395 (1988)*[12]

1. *Introduction*

. . .

A. Some view, as the worst feature of the present transfer tax system, the complexity it generates for estate planning and will and trust drafting. They state that revision efforts should focus on a simpler and more neutral transfer tax system.

B. Others observe that change itself is complex. They find even more need for repose in the transfer taxes than in the income tax. At a minimum, if transfer tax revision must be attempted, it should be done carefully and with adequate opportunity for outside study and comment before enactment.

C. Most agree that transfer tax reform would be more acceptable if it were revenue neutral. Broadening of the transfer tax base . . . should be offset by

---

[11] The 2001 Tax Act repeals the credit for state death taxes by 2004 and replaces it with a deduction under § 2058.

[12] *See also* Harry L. Gutman, *A Comment on the ABA Tax Section Task Force Report on Transfer Tax Restructuring*, 41 TAX LAW. 653 (1988).

lower rates, a larger exemption (or equivalent credit) or both. The issue of the optimum transfer tax revenue yield should, if addressed, be addressed independently.

. . .

3. *The Issue of Complexity*

. . .

B. *Proposed flat rate tax*

Tax rate levels are primarily a political and economic issue. Nevertheless, the choice between the scheduled post-1987 rate structure and a flat rate presents also an issue of simplification.

The purpose of a progressive rate structure is to implement the concept of taxation in accordance with ability to pay. However, that purpose could also be served by utilization of a substantial exemption and a flat rate. The table below compares, for estates of stated sizes, the progressivity of (a) a low-exemption progressive-rate estate tax (we have used the pre-1977 estate tax, with a $60,000 exemption and 25 rate brackets ranging from 3% to 77%) and (b) a high-exemption flat-rate tax (we have assumed a $600,000 exemption and a flat 50% rate). The two right-hand columns show that the effective rate of the latter tax is approximately as progressive as that of the former.

Taxable estate before exemption	Tax under clause (a) above	Tax under clause (b) above	Effective tax rate under (a)	Effective tax rate under (b)
$ 500,000	$ 126,500	$ -0-	25.30%	-0-
1,000,000	303,500	200,000	30.35%	20%
2,000,000	726,200	700,000	36.31%	35%
3,000,000	1,231,400	1,200,000	41.05%	40%
4,000,000	1,802,000	1,700,000	45.07%	42.5%

The scheduled post-1977 seven-bracket rate table (37% to 50%) is a truncation of the more progressive rate table enacted in 1976. For a taxable estate that reaches the top 50% bracket, the post-1987 rate table will produce a tax of only $117,000 less than a flat 50% rate and a $600,000 exemption would produce. The complexity in estate planning required to duplicate that tax saving for a married couple is, as we have shown, substantial. Some testators and their lawyers sacrifice that tax saving, in part to avoid the complexity.

Substitution of a flat rate for the present rate table would simplify estate planning and still preserve progressivity.

. . .

D. *Proposed exemption rather than credit*

If the proposal outlined . . . above for a flat tax rate is adopted, a unified exemption should be substituted for the unified credit.

An exemption is preferable to a credit because an exemption is easier to understand and use. With a flat rate, the argument in favor of a credit, namely, that an exemption is worth more to the wealthier who are in higher brackets, disappears.

E. *Proposed portability of exemption between spouses*

Any exemption unused by a married individual or his estate should be made available for use after his death by his surviving spouse during her life or by her estate at her death.

If that change were made, married testators would no longer need to utilize . . . the complex credit shelter trust clauses . . . . They would also no longer be required to consider lifetime transfers to the nonpropertied spouse to permit consumption of her exemption if she dies first.

This proposal for portability of the exemption is consistent with the existing gift-splitting and marital deduction provisions in treating husband and wife as, in effect, a single taxable unit.

The considerations that support portability of the exemption between spouses apply also to the generation-skipping transfer tax exemption. Techniques similar to those described above may be used today to duplicate that exemption where one spouse is unpropertied or insufficiently propertied. Portability would simplify.

In proposing portability of the exemption, we have not overlooked two problems that we now address. On balance, we submit, our proposal is simplifying despite the presence of those problems.

(i) *Situation where nonpropertied spouse dies first*

Assume that the first spouse to die is *W,* who has either no monetary assets or insufficient such assets to utilize fully the exemption.

We recommend that, as a condition to the proposed portability, *W*'s executor be required to file a timely estate tax return. A simplified return form (say, Form 706EZ) might be promulgated for that purpose.

Because that return would show no estate tax liability, the Internal Revenue Service would not be expected to audit the return. For that reason, the Service should be permitted to adjust values on *W*'s return when it audits *H*'s subsequent return, but, if three years have expired after the filing of *W*'s return, only for the purpose of determining *H*'s estate tax liability.

Any human tendency to understate the value of *W*'s assets would, at least to some extent, be offset by the human tendency not to lose some income tax basis by understating their value.

. . .

The above procedure would be simplified where, as would frequently occur, *W* left everything to *H.* In that case, *W*'s executor could, by checking the appropriate box on the return, avoid having to list on the return *W*'s properties and their values.

(ii) *Successive marriages*

The other problem is whether the prospect of successive marriages makes portability unworkable.

. . .

Today, *W1*'s exemption is utilized if *H* makes a sufficient lifetime transfer to her or for her benefit and she does not return the property to *H.* By making part of his estate ineligible for the marital deduction, *H* utilizes his exemption and enables *W2* to utilize her exemption. Three exemptions are, with careful planning, thus utilized today. Allowance of three exemptions under portability would, therefore, not exceed the number available today.

. . .

The prospect of successive marriages did not prevent enactment of the marital deduction or the subsequent lifting of the 50% limitation thereon. We are aware of no evidence of significant abuse. The same should be true, we suggest, of the proposed portability.

. . .

6. *Gross-up of Gift Tax*

Under the present law, the estate tax base is tax-inclusive and the gift tax base tax-exclusive.

A. *The Treasury proposal*

The Treasury Department, in its 1984 report to the President on tax reform, proposed that the gift tax base be made tax inclusive. The Treasury advanced two arguments in support of that proposal. First, its adoption would, by eliminating one of the preferences accorded lifetime gifts, make the transfer tax system more neutral. Second, its adoption would facilitate adoption of a uniform and simpler set of gift and estate tax rules for determining when a transfer is complete.

B. *Introductory comment*

If this feature of the transfer taxes is viewed in isolation, there are arguments for and against the Treasury proposal. The argument for the proposal is, simply stated, a vote for tax rate neutrality. The arguments against the proposal are two:

(1) Many believe that a transfer tax system that encourages lifetime giving is socially and economically beneficial because such a system causes business and investment capital to be moved into the hands of younger, more vigorous owners.

(2) If the gift tax is regarded as an advance payment of estate tax, the Treasury has the earlier use of the tax money. The gift tax advantage, therefore, may be analogized to a discount for early payment. To obtain that discount, the payment must be substantially (more than three years) early, because of the gross-up of gift tax required by Code section 2035(c) for gifts made within three years of death.

On the narrowly-focused debate outlined above, views (including those of members of the task force) might be expected to diverge. However, when other features of the existing transfer tax system are taken into account, the case for the Treasury proposal becomes more tenuous, as we shall now show.

C. *Income tax basis*

Property that has appreciated in value, if transferred at death, is given a new income tax basis equal to its fair market value on the estate tax valuation date. If transferred by gift, the basis of such property is augmented only by the gift tax allocable, under a proportional formula, to the element of the gift consisting of unrealized appreciation in value.

In his letter to Mr. Calkins . . . Mr. Pearlman observed that, for gifts in the top 50% rate bracket, the Treasury proposal would cause basis to be stepped up to fair market value. We have several problems with that observation.

First, the result is merely fortuitous. If rates are reduced, disparity will be reintroduced.

Second, relatively few gifts are taxed in the top bracket. For all gifts below that bracket, i.e., for almost all gifts, the gift tax basis adjustment does not fully eliminate gain.

Third, the adjustment described by Mr. Pearlman does not aid the donor who must sell other appreciated property to pay the gift tax. Assume . . . that the donor must sell other property, which is also worth $800,000 but has a basis of $300,000, to make the gift tax payment. The donor thus incurs income tax on the $500,000 of gain. No similar problem arises for transfers at death, because the basis of all property so transferred (including the portion that has to be sold to pay estate tax) is adjusted to fair market value.

D. *Other differences*

Other Code provisions that provide relief or benefits in connection with the estate tax, but not the gift tax, are section 303 (redemption of stock to pay estate taxes), section 2032 (alternate valuation), section 2032A (special use valuation), and sections 6161(a)(2), 6163, and 6166 (deferment of payment of estate tax).

. . .

8. *Transfers for Partial Consideration*

The application of the estate tax to lifetime transfers for partial consideration should be revised and clarified. Code section 2043(a) should be replaced . . . . The peculiar results of valuing the consideration at the date of transfer and the property at the date of death would thus be eliminated. Proportional inclusion is more logical than the holdings in cases such as *Estate of Davis v. Commissioner* [440 F.2d 896 (3d Cir. 1971)].

9. *Survivor Benefits (Section 2039)*

Code section 2039 should be amended to eliminate as a test for inclusion of an annuity or other payment in the gross estate thereunder, the possession by the decedent of a right to receive an annuity or payment. All contractual or statutory survivor benefits economically attributable to the decedent would thus be includible in the gross estate. Examples are Social Security death benefits and copyright renewal or termination rights. These rules would cover all payments to a survivor because of the decedent's services, whether as employee or independent contractor.

. . .

All survivor benefits would be taxable at death only, and would in no case constitute lifetime gifts. If the nonemployee spouse were to die first, no property right in the benefit would be included in that spouse's gross estate, but there would be full taxation on the subsequent death of the employee spouse. These rules would apply to community property, to awards on divorce or separation, and to rights created by the Retirement Equity Act of 1984.

. . .

12. *Marital Deduction (Sections 2044, 2056, 2519, and 2523)*

The marital deduction provisions should be modified in the following respects:

A. Code sections 2056(b)(5) and 2523(e) should be repealed, thus eliminating the power-of-appointment trust as a separate category of interest qualifying for the marital deduction. Power-of-appointment trusts should instead be qualified for the marital deduction as QTIP trusts under Code section 2056(b)(7) or 2523(f) if the QTIP election is made. To accommodate this proposal, the definition of a QTIP trust should be changed to permit the donee spouse or surviving spouse to be given a lifetime power (either general or limited) to appoint out of the trust to third parties. Enactment of this and related proposals would promote simplification and eliminate unneeded rules.

. . .

G. The harsh rule of section 2519 should be repealed, so that a QTIP trust would not become wholly taxable upon any disposition of part of a qualifying income interest. A substitute set of rules should be enacted that would properly treat (1) donations out of the income interest of the surviving spouse or donee spouse and (2) exercise by such spouse of a lifetime power of appointment in favor of another person. The problem in each situation is when the gift made by the donee spouse or surviving spouse should be measured (1) by the property given or appointed or (2) by an amount determined because such gift is of an income interest, which appropriately should be capitalized (*i.e.,* treated as a gift of a corresponding portion of principal). The following suggestions, which may not be comprehensive, are made:

(i) Assignment by the spouse of a fractional share of her income interest for life would result in a gift of the assigned portion of the income interest under section 2511 and of a corresponding fraction of principal under section 2519 as proposed to be revised.

(ii) If the trust has a charitable remainderman and the spouse assigns one-third of her income interest to, say, her child, there would be no charitable deduction for the one-third of the principal taxed under section 2519 as proposed to be amended, because the trust is not a unitrust or annuity trust.

(iii) Any assignment of income by the spouse for a period shorter than her life should leave her taxable on the assigned income and, therefore, the trust would remain taxable under section 2044 at her death. Section 2519 would have no application.

(iv) Assume that the spouse remarries and assigns (say) one-third of her income interest to her new husband. Under present law, neither the income interest transferred to the new husband nor the remainder interest deemed under Code section 2519 to be transferred to the trust remainderman qualifies for the marital deduction. That should, we believe, remain the rule.

. . .

I. The rule that possession by W of a nongeneral power of appointment prevents a so-called "estate trust" from qualifying for the marital deduction should be overruled by statute. Although the concept that such a power causes such a trust to fall afoul of the terminable interest principle is technically correct, no valid tax policy is served by the rule, and it operates as a trap for the unwary.

. . .

———

§ 15.03   Wealth Tax

George Cooper, A Voluntary Tax?

New Perspectives on Sophisticated Estate Tax Avoidance 107–10 (1979)

. . .

What purpose is served by having major tax burdens turn on when and how property is transferred?

If we define the purpose of the estate and gift tax as imposing a levy on the value of all property at the time the property is transferred, the question is of course circular, and it answers itself. However, that seems an odd way to state the purpose of the tax. The purpose of the transfer tax is no more to tax transfers than the purpose of the income tax is to tax income. This is rather only a description of the tax base. Its purpose must be found in its economic or social goals. In the case of the estate tax, it is difficult to find a consensus on these goals. The historical record indicates that the estate and gift tax was originally intended to serve as a revenue producer. This most likely is at least a part of its purpose today, although some would disagree. In addition, a variety of social goals are stated for the tax: supplementing the income tax, breaking up large fortunes, and preventing the creation of a coupon-clipper class. All of these purposes or goals might better be served by an annual or a periodic wealth tax than by the estate and gift taxes.

From a revenue viewpoint, a wealth tax is clearly superior to an estate and gift tax. The wealth tax base is not eroded by post-gift appreciation, since wealth in the hands of transferees would continue to be subject to taxation when the next tax period rolled around, rather than shifted out of the clutches of the tax for a generation. This simple fact means that the significance of estate freezing as an avoidance technique would be sharply diminished. (This is not to say that tax revenues might not continue to be affected by intergenerational transfers. Assuming that the wealth tax had progressive rates and was imposed on individuals, rather than family groupings, a transfer of some wealth to a poorer taxpayer would reduce tax collections by reducing the tax bracket, but it could not completely remove property from the tax base.

Moreover, the value of intergenerational transfers as a tax avoidance technique would be inherently self-limiting because the more that was given to a person the closer his tax bracket would move to that of the donor. Assuming that a flat top rate would come into effect at some level, the super rich would soon hit that level and thereby have exhausted the tax avoidance opportunities in bracket-lowering transfers.)

As a supplement to the income tax, the wealth tax seems preferable to transfer taxation. The primary goal in this respect is to take account of the fact that the existing income tax underrates accumulated wealth as a source of ability to pay because it reaches only the net realized returns on capital; all the indirect benefits of wealth—power, security, appreciation—must be reached by some other tax, if at all. Another asserted income tax supplementary goal is adding to the progressivity of the overall tax system. While the estate and gift tax serves both these goals, it does so only erratically; the wealth tax would do it more consistently and more evenhandedly. The wealth tax is also far superior in attacking large fortunes because it does so regularly and promptly and cannot be evaded through generational shifting of ownership.

The choice of taxes is not quite so easy when we turn to the goal of preventing coupon clippers, because the wealth tax strikes all wealth holders equally, whether they created their fortunes or were given them. However, a major point of this book is that much of the growth of property in the hands of a wealthy person is attributable to his or her parents or the result of his or her having been given capital. To the extent that property growth is derived from such sources, the wealth tax is a superior means of taxing the idle rich. (In other words, the wealth tax addresses the problem we have referred to as intra-family fringe benefits.) On the other hand, to the extent that the wealth tax sweeps in self-produced wealth, it can be viewed as inferior.

One other major advantage of the periodic wealth tax should also be mentioned. It has always been difficult for people to accept the idea of having a large chunk of property seized by the government in one fell swoop; particularly when the property is in an illiquid form and payment of the tax may require disposition of some or all of it. This in large part explains why Congress has consistently been sympathetic to mitigating the estate tax payment of farmers and small businessmen and why the courts have been so sympathetic to valuation discounts for closely held stock. The result of this understandable sympathy has been a substantial complication of the estate tax and an erosion of its base.

This problem could be eliminated under a periodic wealth tax. Because such a tax would be imposed much more frequently than an estate tax, it could carry correspondingly lower rates than the existing scale for estate and gift taxes. For example, an annual net wealth tax with a flat rate of 1 percent imposed only on net wealth in excess of $200,000 (thus limiting the tax to only the richest 1 percent to 2 percent of the population and even for them exempting the first $200,000) would have produced approximately the same revenue in 1972 as did the estate and gift tax in that year. Given the greatly increased exemption levels and consequent lowered revenue estimates for the post-1976 estate and gift tax, it is probable that this hypothetical 1 percent net wealth tax on top wealth holders would be a better revenue producer than the new estate and gift tax, as well as being superior for the other reasons discussed above. Such a 1 percent tax would of course be far easier on holders of nonliquid assets than the existing high rate estate and gift tax.

This is, of course, only a brief look at the periodic wealth tax. A fuller evaluation requires a more careful articulation of the goals of taxation in this area and a careful choice among those goals. Unfortunately, and perhaps surprisingly, that evaluation cannot be undertaken easily because these goals have never been thought through in any coherent way. The goals discussed above have grown up more as slogans than rationally developed policies. Until the quality of this underlying analysis is improved and the role of estate and gift taxation in our overall tax structure is clarified, no solid conclusion can be reached regarding the ultimate merits of different approaches to taxation in this area.

Moreover, even apart from this lack of clarity as to underlying goals, there is not space here to undertake an extended discussion of the periodic net wealth tax which, of course, has a number of special practical and legal problems of its own. This is simply the place to observe that such a tax or some variation on the theme has much to be said for it, and that a large part of the dissatisfaction with the treatment of estate freezing under the estate and gift tax is the result of a tendency to want it to do what a net wealth tax can do and to be disturbed because the sow's ear is not better at tapping silk purses.

Gerald R. Jantscher, The Aims of Death Taxation

Death, Taxes and Family Property 46–49
(E. Halbach, Jr., ed. 1977)

. . .

TAXING CAPITAL PERIODICALLY

Death taxes are sometimes said to serve the purpose of imposing a periodic tax on capital—of imposing a once-a-generation tax on family wealth, as the aim is often expressed. According to this view a death tax substitutes for a regular tax on the wealth of the living, a new wealth tax of the kind imposed annually in a growing number of foreign countries . . . .

I leave aside the question of whether wealth is a suitable object of taxation and therefore whether a net wealth tax would be an appropriate addition to a nation's tax system. These questions have elsewhere been answered affirmatively, both by scholars and by governments, generally on the ground that wealth often provides a better measure of taxpaying ability than income. Nicholas Kaldor's vivid example of the beggar and the gold hoarder, both of whom may have zero income but whose capacities to bear a tax are very different, is often cited to illustrate this point. The questions we have to consider are, granting the desirability of a tax on wealth, is a death tax an acceptable substitute for a net wealth tax, and if so, what characteristics must it have?

Death taxes easier to administer

Why bother imposing a death tax, one might ask, as a substitute for a net wealth tax if the latter is feasible? Apart from the constitutional question that the tax raises in this country, its attraction is considerably diminished by the formidable difficulty of administering it well. Death taxes are much easier to impose. They are an established part of the American tax structure and the problems they raise are familiar to tax administrators and taxpayers. Administrative costs are kept low both by the infrequency with which the taxes are imposed and by the fact that they are levied at a time when a person's property must be inventoried anyway.

Differences between a death tax and net wealth tax

The essential difference between death tax and a net wealth tax is that a death tax only reaches savings that have not been consumed during the owner's lifetime. The consequences of omitting savings that were consumed are considerable. On the assumption that much saving is undertaken to even out variations in lifetime income flows—to finance consumption after one's working life has ended—a large amount of property is sure to be missed.

The incidence of a death tax is also apt to differ appreciably from that of a net wealth tax. The equity argument for net wealth taxation supposes that a wealth tax would be borne primarily by the owner of the property and would force him to curtail his consumption, his saving, or his leisure, or a combination of these. Death taxes normally have either no effect or only a small effect on the owners of wealth and are borne instead by the heirs of the owners.

Furthermore, a tax on wealth that is imposed only once and is intended to substitute for an annual wealth tax should bear some relation to the average wealth of the person over his lifetime. A death tax does not—witness a person who accumulates much wealth during his life, dissaves in retirement, and dies owning nothing, or a person who dies suddenly in late middle age when his savings are greatest, before he has begun a program of dissaving. The two taxes also strike certain forms of property quite differently: annuities and term life insurance, for example.

Death tax as a substitute for a net wealth tax on heirs

Perhaps a death tax would be a more attractive substitute for a periodic tax on net wealth if it were viewed as an impost on the wealth of heirs instead of an impost on the wealth of decedents. That is, rather than tax the inherited wealth of heirs annually at low rates, the government might tax it just once—at high rates when they receive it. There is then some justification for taxing transfers outright to remote descendants more heavily than transfers to near descendants, on the basis that the former are on average younger than the latter and that the stream of annual taxes that the former avoid is greater in value and must be replaced by a larger death tax.

This formulation invites the objection that it is hardly feasible to imagine substituting a single tax for a stream of annual taxes without knowing how long an heir will retain his property. Some heirs will cling to their property all of their lives; others will consume their inheritances within a few years. Obviously death taxes of different sizes are called for if they are intended to replace annual taxes that would have been imposed during the duration of the heirs' ownership.

Rate discrimination

If death taxes are intended to tax wealth once a generation, there is a clear case for either exempting transfers between spouses, but taxing all transfers from parents to children, or taxing transfers between spouses, but subsequently exempting the transfer of the same property to children (because the property had already been taxed once in that generation). Transfers to one's parents should be tax free, or even occasion a refund of tax, but transfers to grandchildren should be charged at double the rate that applies to transfers to children.

It may be significant that no death tax to my knowledge has ever incorporated this kind of discrimination, a fact that suggests that the aim of taxing property once a generation has not figured prominently in the minds of tax authorities. But the partial abatement of tax on property in a decedent's estate that was recently taxed upon its transfer from another estate—a feature found in many tax statutes—may reflect a feeling that death taxes should not be imposed too frequently on one bundle of property.

Conclusion

The differences of result between a death tax and a periodic tax on net wealth are so substantial that I do not believe a death tax can be supported as a substitute for the other. If my view is correct, rate discrimination according to age or generational differences between the transferor and transferee is uncalled for. There may still be good reasons for exempting transfers between spouses from tax, but not on the ground that death taxes should not be imposed more than once a generation. There is also less reason to be troubled by transfers that skip a generation. I have in mind here outright bequests to decedents' grandchildren, not transfers in trust that provide life tenancies to members of successive generations. The case for placing a surtax on the latter is based on equity considerations: the unfairness of imposing a heavy tax on one decedent's property because he owned it outright, while exempting another's because it was only held in trust for him.

George Cooper, Taking Wealth Taxation Seriously

34 Rec. A. B. City N.Y. 24, 34–43, 46–48 (1979)

. . .

THE PRACTICAL PROBLEMS OF THE TAX

The valuation procedure under a wealth tax would of course commence with a self-assessment return as under our existing income and transfer taxes. The concern about valuation problems under the wealth tax stems from the assumption that this tax will then require us each year, and for every taxpayer, to go through the same process we now go through in assessing the estate tax for the much smaller group of decedents. If true, this would create an impossible administrative burden and would be ample grounds for rejecting the wealth tax.

However, what seems to be ignored in making this assumption is that the agony of estate tax evaluation is a product of two things—the high rates involved and the fact that it is a once-in-a-generation controversy—both of which change dramatically with the wealth tax. When every dollar of valuation means 70 cents of tax, you are going to get a lot of resources thrown into the fray, especially when there is no second chance. But only a lunatic would devote the same effort year in and year out to valuations for a wealth tax of a few percent. Possibly, a taxpayer might fight hard in one year to establish a precedent for how his assets ought to be valued and what factors ought to be emphasized, but that precedent, once established, would likely be followed in ensuing years. The Service has more important things to do than refight the same battle every year. Indeed, the initial controversy would possibly cover several years at once, since the likelihood of recurrent issues under a wealth tax makes multiple-year audits a sensible policy. This fact of wealth-tax life is actually institutionalized in the wealth-tax law of Germany. In Germany valuations are made only once every three years. The triennial valuation provides the basis of tax for the full period unless there are defined percentage changes in circumstances, in which case either the taxpayer or the government can request a revaluation. Thus, the worst horror stories about the need for a replay of the estate tax every year clearly are hyperbolic.

Moreover, the fact that a wealth tax deals with repeated small-impact valuations in lieu of a single high-impact valuation, has an even more profound significance than merely reducing the level of controversy from year to year. It means that, in place of subjective attempts at perfection in valuation, we can comfortably shift to more objective, formula-based techniques that can be applied almost automatically. In Germany, among other countries, it is conventional to value real estate, farms and closely-held securities by use of standard formulae. The taxpayer and the government both have some right to insist on subjective, fair market valuation, but, at least in the case of closely-held stock, the courts have ruled that the formula can be overridden only where the result is "unbearable." Even without such judicial chariness, we could expect that very few persons would bother to contest a reasonable formula. Unless the formula was drastically wrong, the stakes would not be high enough to challenge it, and there would always be the comfort that what is a little off in one direction in one year might be a little off in the other direction the next year. We could also reinforce the tendency to use the formula by barring subjective values unless shown to vary from the formula by more than a fixed percent, say 20%.

If this casual attitude toward valuation shocks you, you might reflect a moment on how accurate are the valuations we get today with our subjective adversarial process. Competing experts commonly come up with valuations for such things as untraded securities that are so different you might well ask if they looked at the same company. The latest case I just saw in the advance sheets is a typical example. Two experts for a taxpayer valued the same stock at $150 per share and $867 per share. The government expert put it at $2,325. The court after several pages of musing over the divergent analyses, seized on $1,250 as a compromise. As always the valuation result was ultimately reached by arbitrary compromise, after the expenditure of ridiculous time and money by lawyers and experts. For taxpayers who can afford to match the government, the result is usually pretty good, too good for my taste. But for taxpayers with less at stake, the result may well turn out unfairly to them. A compromise could well be built into a formula, especially a formula using new computerized techniques which I will discuss in a moment, which would be fairer to all.

Moreover, and I think the importance of this point needs to be stressed, even if the estate tax valuations reached in the current way were perfect, which they surely are not, they would be inherently arbitrary because they represent the value in a single fortuitously selected year. The company might have been worth double or half in the next or preceding year because of general changes in the market or specific events relating to the company. The decedent probably held the stock for years and the beneficiaries will also likely hold it for a while. What conceivable sense is there in making massive tax burdens turn on the value in one particular year selected by the fickle hand of death? It is difficult to imagine any wealth tax valuation process that could help but be more fair than this.

To put these valuation issues in better perspective, let's look for a moment at specific classes of assets.

The largest single category in terms of aggregate value is real estate. As of 1972, almost a third of privately-held wealth was in the form of real estate ($1.4 trillion out of a total of $4.3 trillion). Realty poses difficult valuation problems, as we all know, but in a sense it is the easiest of all from the viewpoint of practical administrative burdens. Every single piece of real estate in the country is already being valued and, in most cases, is already being taxed at rates higher than those likely to be imposed by a national wealth tax. There is no new administrative burden, only an administrative opportunity to improve and modernize the existing systems which are often admirable but more often wretched. The time is especially ripe for doing this because modern computer techniques for real estate valuation have been developed over the past decade which are fast and simple to use and capable of giving results as or more accurate and reliable than traditional techniques.

These new techniques use a statistical procedure known as multiple regression analysis [MRA] to determine the relationship between various factors which contribute to property value—such as house size, location, existence of a garage or swimming pool, lot size—and the actual sale price of property. The MRA formula does this in a mathematical way which determines the most accurate possible weights for each factor. Of course, in doing this the computer is merely replicating what a human appraiser tries to do by intuition and subjective examination of comparable sales but the computer does it more scientifically. Well conducted MRA studies have produced estimates of property values which consistently average within 10% of actual sale prices or better. It is now generally accepted that MRA-based assessment is the wave of the future; 11% of all jurisdictions and 31% of large jurisdictions now use it. Some states, including New York, have developed modified systems for use by smaller governmental units which do not have the wherewithal to go it on their own. New York reports that its system "has gone far beyond the theoretical and testing stages, it is up and operating," and it has successfully withstood judicial scrutiny. The adoption of a wealth tax would give impetus to this trend.

The next most important category of property is corporate stock, which constitutes 20% of all privately held assets and almost half (47%) of the holdings of the richest 1% of the population. Much of this is traded stock, as to which valuation is simple. For the untraded securities, I suggest that standard formulae be used, subject to the right of either side to demand subjective valuation. A number of formulae have been developed in Europe and are a conventional means of valuing untraded securities there. I think we could do even better with a modern use of MRA techniques, using factor weights derived from traded stocks, and I have been encouraged in this regard by discussions with real estate MRA experts and with securities analysts who have done related work. The literature of securities evaluation already includes many reports of MRA models which have had reasonable success in estimating current stock values. In the words of one experienced Wall Street analyst, the formulation of a reliable MRA system for closely-held stock valuation is "practical, doable, and not expensive with presently available software." This formula procedure should also be adaptable, as it is in Europe, to valuation of business in noncorporate form.

Most of the remaining major classes of assets are relatively easy to value and do not raise any particular administrative problems: bonds (4% of all holdings), category is non-business, non-investment, personal property, including household furnishings, jewelry and art.

There is, admittedly, no entirely satisfactory manner of dealing with this property. In terms of pure theory, all assets ought to be in the tax base, just as all income including fringe benefits and the imputed rental value of a washing machine ought theoretically to be in the income tax base. But we are talking practically, and that means there must be some manner of avoiding the need to account for and value every last dishtowel. A basic general tax exemption—the wealth tax's zero bracket amount, if you will—would be a significant contributor to mitigating this problem because it would drastically cut down the number of families subject to the tax. With a zero bracket of $60,000 (like the pre-'76 estate tax) only about 7% of the population would be covered by a wealth tax; and with a zero bracket of $175,000 . . . , less than 1% would be covered. Even a low zero bracket of $25,000 would exclude all but 15% of the population.

Still, it does not seem worthwhile to worry about the dishtowels of even the super rich, and we would undoubtedly have additional exemptions for much non-business personal property using dollar floors and exempt categories.

The formulation of the precise exemptions is troublesome. A broad exemption eases administration and reduces equity, a narrow exemption does the opposite. But we should not exaggerate the significance of the equitable problems raised by a broad exemption. The opportunities for tax avoidance through investment in art or jewelry, even if it is totally exempt, would be essentially self-limiting because of the non-income producing nature of these assets and because the simple pressures of supply and demand would naturally tend to make such investments less and less attractive. Nor are the economic implications of diverting funds to art all that serious, since the purchase of art does not consume resources but merely shifts cash from one person to another. For these reasons, and on the assumption that a new tax should start as simply as possible, I think it makes sense to err on the side of administrative ease in this marginal area and grant a broad exemption for most non-business, non-investment property, or at least for all such items below a very high floor. This is the general pattern in Europe and no overwhelming abuses seem to occur. If, after a time, abuses are perceived the exemption could be tightened, and the reforms would be effective immediately, not a generation later.

. . .

There are a number of other serious questions which must be answered in drafting wealth tax legislation, but for the most part these are simple variations on income tax or estate tax themes and give no particular cause for new concern under the wealth tax. For example, there is the issue of pension expectations under qualified plans. These expectations are wealth of a sort, but not realizable or controllable currently and possibly subject to forfeiture through voluntary or involuntary job change. You can easily see arguments both ways for how such plans should be treated, and I would expect some compromise, possibly paralleling the income tax compromise on the treatment of pension arrangements.

There is not time to run through all these issues, but there is one that provokes such controversy among lawyers that I cannot in good faith shirk it—this is the treatment of trusts. Trusts were originally developed as tax avoidance devices and they survive in large part as tax avoidance devices. As a consequence they create endless problems for most broad-based taxes, notably the income tax and the estate tax, and the wealth tax will be no different. There are a variety of ways to deal with the trust question.

. . .

Here are some specific suggestions, which are not intended as a definitive answer but to indicate some possibilities. The straight-forward solution, to treat trusts as separate taxable entities, is too generous if there is any substantial zero bracket amount or progressivity in the wealth tax rates. However, if a workable multiple trust consolidation rule could be formulated it might be feasible to treat consolidated groups of trusts as taxable entities. One approach to consolidation is suggested by regulations recently adopted under the income tax, where the same problem of artificial multiple trusts arises. The British Board of Inland Revenue suggested a different plan which seems promising—consolidate all trusts created by a single settlor. This gives one extra zero bracket per settlor, but only one, and the trust zero bracket should be set rather lower than that for individuals.

An alternative to consolidation for trusts, also proposed by the Inland Revenue, is to levy a tax on each trust, but to deem the trust assets to be owned by specific persons and calculate the tax according to the wealth status of the deemed person. For simple trusts, the deemed person would be the income beneficiary. For an accumulating discretionary trust with several beneficiaries, there are a number of options for deeming. The Inland Revenue proposed to use the settlor's wealth as the reference point; the Law Society favored using the wealth of the wealthiest potential beneficiary. In each case, of course, the outside person would be only a deem [sic] in the trustee's eye; the trust itself would always pay the tax. To the extent this deeming caused harsh results, the British proposal left it open for the trustee to change the deemed person by making actual distributions of income. Still another alternative is to tax trusts at an arbitrary rate when they accumulate and then to recompute the tax when distributions occur. This approach, proposed by the British Institute of Chartered Accountants, is similar to our existing income tax treatment.

In other words, there are answers to the trust problem.

So far we have been talking about the practical problems of tax design and administration—largely the problems of the government. However, there is a very important practical problem for taxpayers that cannot be ignored. Where does a taxpayer whose assets are not generating current income get the money to pay his tax—the liquidity problem. But here again, as in the case of valuation, I think the wealth tax is not the creator of liquidity problems but the solution to them.

Liquidity is not a problem unique to the wealth tax. In addition to being a hot issue in local property taxation, it received much attention with respect to the estate tax in the 1976 Tax Reform Act. Liquidity problems are particularly severe under the estate tax because of its very high rates. The severity would be much less under a wealth tax because of its inherently lower rates. Moreover, a capital-directed wealth tax should be accompanied by an elimination or substantial reduction of the estate tax. The wealth tax would thus become a built-in mechanism for paying a portion of present low estate tax obligations in a series of small installments spread out over many years rather than in one large installment. It might even enable us to do away with the existing awkward deferral provisions.

On the other hand, if repeal or reduction of the estate tax does not accompany adoption of the wealth tax, then the wealth tax should be limited to the income-directed class. Its rate would have to be very low, around 1% if the European tradition prevails, and it should be accompanied by reduction in top bracket income tax rates. In these circumstances, while there would surely be sympathetic cases, it is difficult to believe that the low-rate wealth tax would cause intolerable liquidity burdens on very many taxpayers. Of course, persons with large holdings in Krugerrands, gold bullion, or other nonexempt unproductive property would be under some pressure to sell off a portion or shift to more productive investments. If so, I assume this would be a beneficial and desired result of the tax.

The only liquidity problem area of real concern under an income-directed tax is the situation of farmers and owners of closely-held business who can't easily sell small portions of their assets and, justifiably, do not want to liquidate their entire operation. Indeed such cases are so sympathetic that we may tend to exaggerate how much of a problem they are. As a practical matter, any business has to be generating some income—you can't stay in business if you are losing money indefinitely. If this income year in and year out is only enough to cover the value of the owner's services, the capital value of the business is not likely to be very great and the wealth tax should be minimal or nonexistent. Only a business producing a fair return over and above the value of the owner's services is going to have high capital value and be subject to a significant wealth tax. Moreover, even for such a business, there might well be aspects of the valuation formula which would tend to hold down capital value for wealth tax purposes. Personal goodwill, that is, the value of the owner's own name and reputation which will disappear with him, arguably should be excluded. It is not bequeathable and it is an aspect of "human capital" which is generally excluded from the base of the proposed tax. Another mitigating feature of the formula would likely be a reasonable allowance for the difficult marketability and consequent reduced sale value of a closely-held business. Altogether, there is no need to expect generally intolerable liquidity burdens on closely-held business from an income-directed wealth tax.

If there are a few special problem situations, such as the farmer whose return on his land is reasonable in light of farming value but not in light of developmental value, or the business that is temporarily experiencing losses, limited ameliorative provisions, such as the special valuation and deferral rules in present law, could be considered. I repeat, however, such problems are less likely under the wealth tax than the estate tax because of the built-in installment payment nature of the wealth tax.

In sum, I believe this analysis indicates that the wealth tax is practical. It is inherently no more difficult to administer nor harsher than an estate tax except for the issue of more frequent assessment. On closer examination it seems to me that frequent assessment may well make the tax easier to administer rather than more difficult, and less harsh on taxpayers. In any event, the practicality issue is not all one-sided. There are tradeoffs and the balance is at least not clear. Moreover, it is not really fair to look at the wealth tax alone and ask if it imposes unreasonable burdens. The tax should be viewed as an alternative to other reform measures since it is a substitute for more complex provisions attacking income and estate tax loopholes. Compared to steps such as increased capital gains taxes (with by-product lock-in), the minimum income tax, the carryover basis rules and the generation skipping tax—some of which may become unnecessary with a wealth tax—the wealth tax may not seem so troublesome.

THE ECONOMIC IMPLICATIONS

The wealth tax is unlikely to be a major revenue generating tax. For example a 1% flat rate wealth tax, imposed on approximately the same wealth that is now subject to the estate tax (individual wealth holdings in excess of $200,000) would have produced, as of 1972, approximately $5 billion, assuming no deductions, credits or loopholes other than a basic $200,000 exemption. Some, unavoidable, erosions of the tax base would undoubtedly cut into that revenue potential. On the other hand, if the tax base were expanded by reducing the basic exemption, or the rate were increased, the revenue potential might double or triple, but that is the most we could reasonably expect unless the wealth tax became a broad-based substitute for the income tax. Compared to the income tax revenues (individual and corporate) in the same year of $121 billion, or total federal budget receipts of $209 billion, the wealth tax revenue is modest, particularly when it is realized that much of the revenue from the tax will likely be offset by reductions in estate and gift taxes and high bracket income taxes.

This limited revenue potential also means that the wealth tax is unlikely to have any dramatic effect on our overall national economic life. The wealth tax will affect equity and it may seriously affect some people's capital, but it is not going to have major macroeconomic repercussions unless its rates are set higher than any of us find imaginable. Nonetheless, some modest effects may be foreseen, and I will briefly comment on those.

One economic argument for the wealth tax is that it is more economically efficient than an income tax. Under the income tax, in the name of promoting risk-taking we have provided avoidance avenues which seem more to promote absurd tax shelter deals than risk-taking. The wealth tax, on the other hand, directly rewards and encourages seeking high returns. The wealth tax rate effectively goes down as the rate of return increases because the wealth tax on a given amount of capital is fixed without regard to return. This simple and neutral manner of encouraging risk-taking seems much preferable to the complex pattern of incentives evolved under our income tax law, and it is presumably a desirable aspect of wealth taxation.

However, the wealth tax is also accused of a rather sinister effect, the erosion of the national stock of capital. At the present time, when national concern about "capital formation" runs high, this is tantamount to accusing the wealth tax of being contrary to apple pie. However, despite its superficial logic, there is not really much to this accusation.

Much of any wealth tax will be income-directed and paid out of income, including that newly gained by persons who shift to more productive investments in response to the tax. To the extent it is capital-directed, the burden of the tax will be offset, in part, by the reductions in high bracket income and estate and gift tax rates. The only serious erosion of capital that is plausible will occur in the case of heirs who may for the first time find themselves paying a substantial tax. If desired, the very limited anticapital effects of this aspect of the tax could be offset by a requirement that a portion of revenue be earmarked for government capital purposes, for example the social security trust fund. Such earmarking is unlikely to be necessary, however, because, as I said, any macroeconomic concern is probably a tempest in a teapot if we are talking about a fairly modest wealth tax.

———

Barry L. Isaacs, Do We Want a Wealth Tax in America?

32 U. Miami L. Rev. 23, 33, 35–37, 46–49 (1977)

. . .

V. GENERAL PRINCIPLES: THE CONTROVERSY

. . .

B. Arguments Against a Wealth Tax

While it is suggested by some that the general arguments against a wealth tax are reducible to concerns about practical difficulties in administering the tax and the possible adverse economic consequences, particularly on saving, the arguments are in fact more numerous. In a subjective sense, it is impossible to be sure if individuals are equally wealthy since personal satisfaction cannot be measured directly. Materialistic wealth has always been an extremely incomplete index of taxable capacity, since it does not consider the human resources of individuals who depend on earnings from personal services. A wealth tax concerns itself only with the status quo and not how the situation arose in the first place, suggesting that if all wealth were taxed as it was transferred into new ownership, the claim that wealth represented additional taxable capacity would no longer stand. Indeed, this argument points in the direction of an integrated estate, gift, and income tax system, rather than the introduction of a wealth tax as a check on concentrations of wealth.

There is no definition of what constitutes an unacceptable wealth distribution. Wherever there is a relatively high exemption limiting the application of a wealth tax, it is indicative only to the point at which wealth accumulation may be considered unacceptable. But to tax wealth only when it reaches a certain level proves that it is not aimed at ownership of wealth per se, but only at excessive inequalities of wealth. This would tend to weaken the equity argument of additional taxable capacity unless it too was intended to apply only to excessive concentrations of wealth.

Redistribution of wealth can take two forms: it can flow from one individual to other individuals or from an individual to the state. The static nature of a wealth tax demonstrates that it can achieve only the latter since it operates only when the unacceptable level of wealth has been reached. Thus, it merely serves to confiscate accumulations above that level. For there to be a significant redistribution to the state, a confiscating marginal rate approaching one hundred percent is required, a rate which clearly would be unacceptable. The argument that great concentrations of wealth bring power to those who possess them might suggest that the power be controlled, not necessarily that the wealth itself should be confiscated or broken up.

It has been said that those who decry inequalities in wealth distribution often advance such criticism only to hide their basic envy and political discontent. Discrimination of this sort against a wealthy minority of a population without any criteria for limiting the extent of such discrimination is incompatible with the governing principles of democracy and the rule of law. A majority of persons should not be able to decide the appropriate limit on another citizen's wealth. The consumption of the wealthy, however extravagant or wasteful, is always conspicuous, but even conspicuous waste must be countenanced as the price of freedom. A world in which a majority could prevent all that it did not like would probably be a stagnant and a declining world.

Those who seek to justify wealth tax on equitable grounds fail to consider the significance of the fact that income from different kinds of property of the same value can still differ greatly. Taxes levied on the basis of property values discriminate against those whose income yield on investments is negligible. The lead time for enterprises to become productive can be lengthy, causing an individual who holds shares in such an investment to pay a tax based on the market value of his shares, notwithstanding that no dividends may be payable for years. He is thus forced to consume his capital to meet his tax liability.

. . .

VII. ECONOMIC ASPECTS OF A WEALTH TAX

The practical effects of a wealth tax on economic behavior are unpredictable because they generally encompass but a small part of the economy as a whole and because economic behavior is influenced by many more considerations than a particular form of taxation. Numerous economic benefits are claimed for the net wealth tax relative to its effects upon investment and economic development generally. An important asserted benefit is that since the tax will not impinge upon the incremental gain from investment or expansion but rather upon the total accumulation of an individual, there should be a disincentive to avoid earning income; that is, past and future effort will be taxed regardless of yield, so the assets might as well be directed towards meeting the tax payments. In addition, as mentioned earlier, there may be a tendency to push investments out of cash, gold, and low income securities and into higher-yield investments, presumably contributing to economic growth and efficiency. No economic benefits, however, are seriously asserted for a wealth tax when the combination of wealth and income tax levies approaches or exceeds 100% of net income. . . . [A] tax on 3% of net worth . . . would be the equivalent of a 60% tax on income derived from net wealth on which the yield is 5%. Depending on an individual's tax bracket, the yield on his assets, and the source of that yield, the prospect of certain individuals being unable to meet reasonable consumption requirements from disposable net income becomes very real. This would not be as serious if the tax were designed to reduce higher marginal rates of taxation on both income and investments. Advocates of such an additive wealth tax, however, are usually contemptuous of any tax provision aimed at reducing high marginal rates and would rather see them made more effective. There is scant empirical evidence to support the proposition that any particular combined rate of income and wealth tax will have any adverse effect on work effort, incentives to produce, and savings. It is expected, nevertheless, that rates above a 70% level will seriously diminish the foregoing endeavors. A study in India was made to analyze the impact of a similar wealth tax which, when combined with the income tax, took between 90% and 120% of net income on savings and investment. The study was done by comparing aggregate savings and investments seven years before and seven years after the tax was introduced. The conclusion was that capital formation in the national aggregate had not been affected in any appreciable degree nor had it substantially reduced private savings in the community. It was conceded, however, that the wealth tax had had a considerable effect on capital formation—there existed unaccounted for money, income and wealth which had escaped assessment. Tax evasion in India was found to be widespread and growing rapidly, concentrated mainly in the higher income groups comprising the wealth tax assessees. The data collected about the amounts that had been concealed tended to suggest that overall tax evasion had a considerable effect on reducing otherwise productive utilizations of capital. The efficiency of the wealth tax in this instance was severely criticized, even to the point of encouraging its abolition.

Whether or not there are investment incentives caused by the introduction of a wealth tax, even when it is substituted for a higher rate of income tax of equal yield, is highly complex and debatable question. A wealth tax would allow losses to be offset against taxable wealth up to the full extent of the investor's net worth. Such a set-off would seem to encourage investment enterprise. On the other hand, the ultimate effect of a capital levy depends so heavily on such matters as the use to which the levy is put, the unexpectedness of the levy, the likelihood of repetition, and inflation, that prediction is difficult. It is safe to say only that any reward resulting from risk-taking will increase wealth tax liability only in the event that it is added to net worth.

The effect of a wealth tax on savings appears to be much easier to assess because the tax falls directly on all accumulations as such. The opportunity to add to future consumption through saving would seem to be restricted among the affected taxpayers, with no likelihood that the incidence of the tax can be shifted. On the other hand, it has been found that large wealth tends to be associated with individuals whose marginal propensity to save is very high and who would be likely to save any increment in income or assets if they were able to do so. Additionally, the psychological effect of a wealth tax spread over the entire amount rather than an income tax concentrated on the fruits of additional savings may not prove negative after all. Whether or not a potential decline in aggregate saving would condemn a wealth tax depends to a great extent on government savings and prevailing employment conditions. Thus, this question too remains unanswered.

§ 15.04 An Accessions Tax

W. Andrews, The Accessions Tax Proposal

22 Tax L. Rev. 589, 591–95 (1967)[13]

Summary Description

Accessions

Accessions are defined generally as including all property received by way of gift or inheritance. More specifically, accessions include the receipt of life insurance proceeds if the insured retained incidents of ownership; the receipt of employee benefits by an employee's survivors after his death; the amount of property acquired by the survivor in a joint tenancy in excess of the portion contributed by him or on which he was taxed when the joint tenancy was created. With several minor exceptions and one major exception, the events that represent included transfers by the transferor under the unified transfer tax represent accessions to the transferee under the accessions tax proposal.

The major exception is a transfer in trust. In the accessions tax proposal no accession is ordinarily deemed to occur on account of the creation of a trust or the transfer of property to a trustee. On the other hand, a distribution from a trust, whether of income or corpus, is treated as an accession to the distributee from the settlor. This rule applies even after the settlor's death, and it applies to testamentary as well as inter vivos trusts. There are various exceptions and qualifications, described below, but the accessions tax proposal is built around the concept that ordinarily the distribution of trust property, rather than contribution to the trust, is the taxable event.

Exclusions and Deductions

There is a complete exclusion of interspousal accessions. There is an exclusion of money or property received (and expended) for current consumption, and on top of that an annual per donor exclusion for outright inter vivos gifts of up to $1,500 (which will cover $3,000 from a married donor if nothing is received from his spouse). The annual exclusion is inapplicable to transfers at death and to trust distributions. There is a lifetime exemption of $24,000 (described as a zero percent bracket in the rate schedule) applicable to taxable accessions from all sources.

No exclusion is necessary for charitable contributions; charitable organizations are simply exempt from the tax. On the other hand, there is need to provide an exclusion for charitable distributions if it is thought desirable to exempt them from the tax.

A deduction is also provided of 40 per cent of the amount of any accession from a parent, parent-in-law, sibling, child, or parent of a deceased parent ("immediate relations"). The effect of this deduction, like that of the 50 per

---

[13] *See also* Edward C. Halbach, Jr., *An Accessions Tax*, 23 Real Prop. Prob. & Tr. J. 211 (1988).

cent marital deduction under the present gift tax, is to make the effective rate of tax on accessions from these people lower than that on accessions from other sources ("remote accessions"). The reasons for this rate differential are described below in the discussion of the rate structure.

Computation of Tax

The tax is computed and paid annually. Each year's tax is based on the year's taxable accessions, but the rate, which is graduated, depends on a taxpayer's cumulative total taxable accessions during his whole lifetime. The mechanics of computation are exactly the same as under the present gift tax: read the tax in the table for the taxpayer's taxable accessions for the taxable year and all prior years; then read the tax in the table for the taxpayer's taxable accessions in prior years only; the tax for the current year is the excess of the former over the latter.

There is a special elective provision for income beneficiaries of a trust under which a fixed rate can be established to apply to income distributions. The beneficiary computes hypothetically the tax that would result from an accession equal to the actuarial value of this interest; then he uses the ratio between that hypothetical tax and the actuarial value on which it is predicated as a rate to be applied to all subsequent accessions on account of the income interest in question. The effect of this provision is to enable an income beneficiary to avoid the decline in after tax income that would result if distributions were taxed separately at successively higher rates.

This provision also permits an income beneficiary to go further, if he wishes, and pay the hypothetical tax computed on the actuarial value of his interest. If he does that subsequent distributions are free of tax.

Another provision undertakes to give relief from the effects of successive taxation when a person dies within ten years after receipt of a taxable accession. The device proposed is a reduction or refund of tax on the basis of a recomputation in which accessions received during a decedent's last years are wholly or partially excluded, on condition that the executor identify and segregate an amount of property equal to that being excluded, and that the property so segregated be treated by the next taker as an accession from the decedent's transferor. The effect of this provision is to enable the executor to reconstruct the situation for tax purposes as if the property had been left in trust for the decedent during his lifetime, and then to the decedent's appointees. This recomputation is permitted with respect to all or any part of any accession received within six years before death, and with respect to decreasing percentages of the amount of any accession received during the seventh to tenth years before death.

The Special Estate Tax on Property Left in Trust

Part of the accession tax proposal is that there be, in some cases, a separate tax on property left in trust. This tax is imposed only in the case of decedents who leave moderately large estates ($500,000, excluding property left to or for a spouse or charity); and only if a significant amount ($100,000) is left in trust. The tax is imposed only on property left in trust (including property still held in any inter vivos trusts created by the decedent during his lifetime), but at a rate determined by reference to the decedent's whole probate estate. The special estate tax is designed to approximate, very roughly and rather conservatively, the accessions taxes that would be due on a distribution of the trust property. The special estate tax paid on any trust is made the basis for a credit against accessions taxes on subsequent distributions from the trust. The effect of the credit is to make the special estate tax operate principally as a device for prepayment of accessions taxes on trust distributions, not as an instrument for imposing any substantial additional tax burden. The purpose is simply to curb the otherwise unlimited opportunity for tax deferral that would exist under the general rule that trust property is taxed on the way out of the trusts, not on the way in.

Trust Beneficiaries

The treatment of trust beneficiaries—the fact that generally a tax is imposed only on the distribution of trust property, not on the creation of the trust or the vesting of a beneficiary's interest—is perhaps the central structural feature of the accessions tax proposal. This rule and the reasons for it will now be examined in greater detail.

Exceptions and Qualifications

There are several exceptions and qualifications to the rule that trust beneficiaries are taxed only on distributions of the trust property:

1. Any person interested in a trust is permitted to elect, as of the end of any taxable year, to be treated as having received a distribution of the property in the trust. The consequences of such an election are (i) that the amount of the property in the trust is deemed to be an accession to the person making the election; (ii) that the person making the election will not be taxed on subsequent distributions from the trust, and any other person subsequently receiving a distribution from the trust may treat it as an accession from the person who made the election; and (iii) that any property in the trust on the death of the person making the election will be part of his taxable estate for purposes of the special estate tax on property left in trust. An election may be made with respect to less than all the property in a trust only if the trustees identify and segregate the property to which the election relates. Any action that will enable the trustees to account separately for the identified property, and income from it, constitutes a satisfactory segregation. A person may elect under this rule even if no tax results, as when the person making the election is the spouse of the creator of the trust.

2. If a person sells an interest in a trust, the sales proceeds are to be treated like a distribution from the trust on account of such interest. The purchaser will not be subject to accessions tax on subsequent distributions to him; and if he causes distributions to be made to someone else the distributions will be accessions from the purchaser, not from the creator of the trust.

3. If a trust beneficiary is permitted to enjoy his interest by occupation or direct use of trust assets rather than by the distribution of income, then the

value of such use shall be treated as a distribution from the trust for accessions tax purposes.

4. If a trust beneficiary at any time has a general power of appointment over the trust property, then he shall be treated as having received a distribution of the property subject to the power, and subsequent distributees of the property and the income therefrom, may treat it as if the powerholder were the creator of the trust. A general power of appointment is defined in much the same way as under the unified transfer tax, except that it does not include a power that can only be exercised on death.

5. As indicated before, a trust income beneficiary may elect to establish a fixed rate of tax or to pay up his accessions tax in advance on the actuarial value of his interest.

6. The special estate tax on property left in trust may be viewed as a qualification of the general rule regarding trust beneficiaries.

The Tax Deferral Problem

The general rule for taxing trust beneficiaries gives rise to the problem of tax deferral. Thus if property is left by A on his death to a trustee to pay income to B for his life and then to distribute the corpus to B's issue, no accessions tax is payable by any beneficiary with respect to the trust corpus until B's death. A tax would have been payable on A's death if the property had been left outright to B; and under a transfer tax, the tax would have been payable on A's death whether the property were left outright to B or in trust. Under the accessions tax proposal therefore, the trust disposition can be said to defer the tax on the trust corpus for the period of B's lifetime.

This result has been considered to be unacceptable in the case of large estates. That is the reason for imposing the special estate tax on substantial trust dispositions. Insofar as the special estate tax operates as a prepayment of accessions taxes all that is deferred is the final reckoning by which trust property is accounted for as an accession to a particular beneficiary.

Tax deferral is not considered to be a serious problem in small or middle-sized estates, however, because the corollary of deferral is inclusion in the tax base of all income (including capital appreciation) during the period of deferral. In the case given above, for example, income distributions to B during his life will be subject to tax as accessions to B from A. If the trust assets are invested to produce capital appreciation rather than (or addition to) current income, the government will share in that too by virtue of valuing the corpus on B's death, not A's, for purposes of taxing the transfer to B's issue. Neither the income nor the capital appreciation would be taxed under a transfer tax imposed at the time of A's death . . . .

Gerald R. Jantscher, The Aims of Death Taxation

Death, Taxes and Family Property 40, 54–55
(E. Halbach, Jr., ed. 1977)

Inheritance tax, estate tax or other form?

The anti-concentration aim calls for a death tax tailored to the circumstances of the recipient rather than to those of the decedent: a levy of the inheritance tax form rather than of the estate tax form. Moreover, the tax should take account of the heir's separate wealth, including wealth that he had saved from his own earnings. Bequests received by wealthy persons should be taxed more heavily than bequests received by less wealthy ones.

In practice, discrimination of this kind would be denounced as inequitable. One man's inheritance would be taxed differently depending on whether he received it early in life, when his savings were small, or later in life, when his savings were large. Probably the most highly developed form of inheritance tax that is a practical possibility is the "accessions tax," a cumulative, progressive tax on all the gifts and bequests that one person receives throughout his life. Each gift or bequest would be taxed at a rate that depended not only on its size but also on the size of all previous gifts and bequests that the person received, much as gifts and bequests are now taxed to donors under the new donor-based, unified federal gift and estate taxes.

Like an estate tax, an accessions tax would reduce inequality by taxing away portions of all large estates and depriving the heirs of a part of their inheritance. Unlike an estate tax, an accessions tax would also encourage testators to distribute their property widely by providing a reduction in tax in exchange for their doing so. Although proponents of the tax like to emphasize this feature, I am skeptical whether at current levels of taxation many persons would react to it. Many wealthy persons already distribute their property widely—typically half of the estate to the surviving spouse, the balance divided among the children—and may not be able to distribute it more widely without passing it outside their families. This I presume they will not do except in response to far higher rates of tax than have hitherto been proposed.

If my guess is correct, the principal effect of substituting an equal-yield accessions tax for an estate tax would be to alter the distribution of tax burdens among relatively few persons, such as the estate of a person with only one heir, or that are divided very unequally among a larger number would attract a heavier tax than they do now. Estates that are divided evenly among several heirs would pay a smaller tax. These changes would tend to reduce inequalities of inheritance and would therefore promote a more equal distribution of wealth.

———

§ 15.05   Taxing Gifts and Bequests as Income

Joseph M. Dodge, Beyond Estate and Gift Tax Reform: Including Gifts and Bequests in Income

91 Harv. L. Rev. 1177 (1978)

. . .

Suggestions for change have included not only the refinement of the existing structure, which taxes wealth transfers to the decedent or donor, but also the taxation of such transfers to the recipient. Such alternatives to the present system have included an inheritance tax, an accessions tax, and the inclusion of gifts and bequests in the recipient's income tax base. This Article will focus on the last of these alternatives, the "income tax proposal," . . .

I. Legislative Enactment of the Proposal

The enactment of the income tax proposal for gifts and bequests would be accomplished by amending the Internal Revenue Code to repeal the gift, estate, and generation-skipping taxes, and section 102 of the Code, which excludes gifts and bequests from the gross income of the recipient.

. . .

It has . . . been argued that gifts and bequests are not income since they do not represent additions to the existing stock of capital in the economy but rather are mere transfers of capital. This argument, while perhaps partially explaining the historical basis for the exclusion of gifts and bequests, confuses income in the economic sense with income in the tax sense. . . . "[I]ncome" in the tax sense is the term that has been used to describe the measurement of the taxable unit's capacity to contribute to the public sector relative to other taxable units. It is true that the income tax proposal involves "double taxation" in the economic sense in that the grantor is giving after-tax dollars on which the recipient is again taxed, but whatever hindrance to capital formation may arise from this double taxation can easily be offset in other ways. The area of gifts and bequests is not one where economic considerations should predominate over principles of tax equity.

. . .

Those concerned with double taxation (in the economic sense) under the income tax proposal must acknowledge that double taxation of amounts transferred by gift or bequest has existed since 1916 in the form of the estate tax and its subsequent complements, the gift tax and the generation-skipping tax.

. . .

Under the existing transfer tax system, double taxation is proper because the aim of such taxes is to place a levy on the transfer of wealth. The income tax proposal, on the other hand, has the objective of measuring relative ability to pay, and it therefore considers only the economic position of the individual tax unit when imposing taxes. The method of accession to wealth is irrelevant.

Double taxation, that is, taxing the recipient on wealth previously taxed to someone else, is consistent with an attempt to measure each person's ability to pay. While the present system subjects unrealized appreciation both to the transfer taxes and, through the carryover basis mechanism of sections 1015 and 1023, to the income tax of the transferee upon realization, the income proposal taxes it only once because carryover basis would be dropped. The income tax proposal, however, would not preclude additionally taxing the transferor on previously unrealized appreciation, resulting in full double taxation on transfers of appreciated property.

. . .

It might seem that these recipient-oriented taxes would be less effective in raising revenue since the number of transferees is usually greater than the number of transferors. But the effectiveness of any transfer tax scheme in raising revenue—as well as in breaking up accumulations of wealth—depends upon its rates and exemptions. Although the present transfer taxes have considerable potential for accomplishing these goals, recent experience indicates that the political system is unwilling to tap this potential. The income tax proposal, while still subject to some manipulation through exemptions, at least precludes independent tampering with the rate structure. Finally, if any important objective of a transfer tax cannot be accomplished by the income tax proposal, transfer taxes, reduced in scope to bear only on the extremely wealthy, could be retained to supplement the income tax plan.

. . .

Of the recipient-oriented taxes, only the income tax proposal does not contemplate a separate rate schedule for gifts and bequests. Such a separate schedule would contradict a basic premise of the proposal: that the source of receipts should not affect tax liability.

. . .

A separate rate schedule for gifts and bequests would also have the undesirable consequence of resurrecting the troublesome distinction between income and corpus. It is true that the accessions tax has been formulated to eliminate the income-corpus distinction, but this elimination is more a matter of convenience than principle. If a justification of the accessions tax is curbing the accumulation of wealth, then income (as opposed to corpus) distributions from trusts should not be counted as accessions.

. . .

Adoption of the income tax proposal for gifts and bequests would contribute greatly to the simplification of the tax code. This simplicity of the proposal is both a consequence of its theoretical foundations and an additional justification for its enactment. The existing estate, gift, and generation-skipping taxes would be removed. The portions of subchapter J dealing with the taxation of trusts and beneficiaries would likewise be excised, although those provisions concerned with "grantor trusts" should probably be retained. In addition, the calculation of the basis of in kind property received as a gift or bequest would be vastly simplified for individuals and eliminated for trusts and estates.

The question of what constitutes a gift, now a question of fact which results in much litigation, would be eliminated. Under the income tax proposal, gratuitous transfer exclusions should be allowed only under a de minimis rule to protect the integrity of the tax system in the public eye. Only gifts that are administratively difficult to discover or which are generally not considered transfers of wealth by the public, such as occasional holiday and anniversary gifts, should be excluded from income. Transfers in trust and payments of life insurance premiums, which often qualify—perhaps unjustifiably—for the gift tax present interest exclusion, would not be taxed currently at all under the income inclusion approach. Small distributions from trusts, however, do not fall within the administrative exclusion rationale for small gifts and would therefore be taxed in full.

. . .

Any transfer tax system will have some predictable effects on the pattern and techniques of distribution of wealth. Since the income tax proposal would not tax trust gains or income, an incentive would exist to use trusts as vehicles for postponing and spreading out the taxation of distributees. This incentive to use trusts to minimize tax exposure of recipients will affect the role of the trustee. The burden of timing transfers will in many cases be shifted from the transferor to the trustee in order to permit distribution when the marginal tax rates of the distributees are lowest. Trustees may also receive increased control over choosing the recipients of distributions within an expansively defined group. The trustee would be permitted to dispense wealth among many—and particularly low bracket—donees in order to avoid high marginal rates. The end result of these tendencies will be that the trustee will transfer wealth more often on the basis of need than at present. While trustees and executors would be quite tax conscious under the income tax proposal, there would no longer be the emphasis on extreme sophistication as under present law, since the trust or estate itself would not be taxed and the income to the beneficiary would all be taxed as ordinary income.

The income proposal would also probably discourage inter vivos gifts to persons outside the tax unit since they would have to include them in full as income, and present interest exclusions might be diminished, and the unified transfer credit would not be available. In addition, donors would have no particular reason to create complex irrevocable trusts with retained powers and potential economic benefits designed to avoid transfer tax. In general, the donor's own situation would not affect his decision to made gifts, except for any desire to eliminate future income and appreciation from his tax base.

. . .

The present system of taxing transferors of wealth, combined with the uncertainty of which spouse will die first, encourages spouses to equalize their estates before the death of either, so that neither estate will be subject to high marginal tax rates. Even with sophisticated tax planning, this task of equalization is difficult to accomplish with precision. Since the income tax proposal eliminates taxation of interspousal gifts and removes the incentive to split estates to minimize aggregate taxes, the proposal neither encourages nor discourages transfers to spouses. Moreover, there would be no tax differences between common law and community property jurisdictions.

§ 15.06 Consumption Tax

In 1994, Professor McCaffery published an article that argued, from a liberal's perspective, for the repeal of the income and wealth transfer tax systems and adoption of a progressive consumption-without-estate tax.[14] *See* Edward J. McCaffery, *The Uneasy Case for Wealth Transfer Taxation*, 104 YALE L.J. 283 (1994). As explained by Professor Schenk, Editor-in-Chief, Tax Law Review:

> Not surprisingly, many scholars, particularly those who consider themselves liberal egalitarians, take exception to Professor McCaffery's arguments and to the interpretive method he uses to ascertain liberal values. In May, 1996, the Tax Law Review brought together some of those scholars to debate the role of wealth transfer taxation, especially from a liberal egalitarian perspective. The articles and commentary from that Colloquium appear in this issue of the Tax Law Review.

Deborah Schenk, *Colloquium of Wealth Transfer Taxation,* 51 TAX L. REV. No. 3 (1996 Foreword).

An excerpt from Professor McCaffery's Yale Law Journal article follows. Thereafter, two excerpts from the Colloquium are provided. The attempt here is merely to show the flavor of the debate. Consult the Colloquium issue for the full nine responses and commentaries to Professor McCaffery's proposal, as well as to Professor McCaffery's reply to his critics.

E. McCaffery, The Uneasy Case for Wealth Transfer Taxation

104 Yale L.J. 283, 288, 348–49 (1994)

My argument follows three basic steps: (1) The current gift and estate tax does not work, is in deep tension with liberal egalitarian ideals, and lacks strong popular or political support. (2) While the failure of the status quo may suggest a stronger wealth transfer tax as an alternative, such an answer suffers from two distinct problems: (a) a stronger tax is neither practical nor popular, and (b) given the many imperfections of the real world and the likely consequences of a strengthened transfer tax, such as reduced work, reduced savings, and increased inequality in consumption, a stronger wealth transfer tax may not be preferable even on ideal liberal grounds. (3) Motivated by the first two points to think through matters more deeply, we can arrive at alternative tax systems that both comport better with liberal first principles and fit well with the implicit spirit of our actual practices and beliefs, without any form of estate tax at all.

This argument leads naturally to a proposal for comprehensive tax reform, specifically a progressive consumption-without-estate tax. By responding to our objective preferences for work and savings while giving institutional form

---

[14] Professor McCaffery's reference to only estate tax is merely his way of shorthanding his proposal to not impose any wealth transfer taxes.

to our suspicions over the large-scale private use of wealth, such a tax system indeed fits best with liberal principles and with the often-inchoate spirit of our actual practices. To those who would immediately object that the private possession of wealth alone is a distinct liberal concern, not reached by a progressive consumption-without-estate tax, I hasten to add that the altered tax regime changes the very meaning, and hence the risks and dangers, of the "private possession" of wealth. The meaning of this phrase is not a constant, but rather depends on the legal rules in place. A liberal society's reasonable concerns over possession alone reduce largely to dual concerns over possession *qua* potential or actual use; the ability to use one's wealth, the threat of doing so, or the actual ongoing use of wealth as consumptive investment is what ought to concern the liberal. But a progressive consumption-without-estate tax, designed under a political theory of tax, changes matters by redefining property rights. In the end, it appears that our practices may be moving toward a better place, on strictly liberal grounds, than any answers that our most rarefied political theory alone could produce.

. . .

To be sure, two rather large sets of problems remain. First, there appear to be equitable and political issues involving the concentration of power accompanying private wealth and investment decisions, and some benefits flow from possession alone. Second, as the liberal egalitarian case reminds us, the use of wealth by those deemed to have "earned" it may not be as offensive as any use of such wealth made by subsequent generations, although skepticism over the relevance or meaning of "earnings" weakens this point, perhaps fatally. These objections are common and well founded; the key response is that we do not need an estate tax to deal with either issue.

As to the first point, a combination of progressive rates and investment regulation under a nominal "consumption" tax can check the liberal dangers of possession alone. A progressive consumption tax changes the very meaning and hence the risks and dangers of private "possession." Many, and maybe all, of the normative problems with the private possession of . . . wealth turn out to relate to possession *qua* actual or potential use. . . . On the other hand, one might consume or exercise power directly through investment; this is possession *qua* use. Think, for example, of William Randolph Hearst buying up newspapers. But we can readily enough deal with that problem by compelling the private saver to save in certain forms—a blind trust is a limiting example, but any qualified form of savings accounts will do—in order to get the benefits of the nontaxation of savings. Such vehicles can preserve the efficiency of decentralized decisions while checking abuse, much as the loose form of government oversight of the current pension and charitable activity sectors now does. In both of these responses, the progressive consumption-without-estate tax plan aims to make literal the common pool metaphor of Hobbes and Rawls. Possession is no longer narrowly "private."

As to the second problem, of inheritance and inequality, we can deal with the issue of use by later generations through modifications in the consumption tax's rate structure. Society may actually have a greater concern with the inequities of inherited wealth. I have not denied that there might be such a concern; I have simply emphasized that a crude attempt to choke off intergenerational transfers may: (1) interfere with important intra-generational norms, in part by its dependence on a naive division between intra- and intergenerational spheres of activity; and (2) clash with settled and normatively appropriate practices and beliefs evincing more of a concern with the use than with the mere possession of wealth. Indeed, we can see that the use-possession distinction extends down through the generations. While society no doubt has some concerns over the possession of unearned wealth by later generations, and such concerns may be greater than those over possession alone at the earlier generation, the concern vis-a-vis the later generation may once again be even greater when it comes to use. Society may have some worry over imprudent investment decisions by heirs, say, but we can again deal with this point by regulating the favorable consumption tax treatment. Moreover, it is not clear that the alternative uses of that capital—now understood to be either investment decisions by the government or increased consumption by the prior generation—are any better. In contrast, society may have a much heightened concern with the decadent use of wealth by the later generation, and here may decisively prefer the alternatives of any other use. Yet under current law, society places no burden on the act of consumption by an heir; we exert no control whatsoever over how or when heirs spend their wealth. Under a progressive consumption-without-estate tax, this hands-off attitude would change, and we can change it even more fundamentally with a separate rate schedule on spending out of inherited wealth.

Details as to the precise rate schedule will of course need to be worked out, and they may require difficult and ultimately somewhat arbitrary decisions. For now, I seek mainly to illustrate where a consistent liberal egalitarian focus on use, implicit in consumption tax theory, might naturally lead: to a progressive consumption-without-estate tax. Such a structure responds to concerns over possession alone by changing our conception of what "possession" means. This tax plan is also what our practices seem to be suggesting; we can go a long way toward resolving many problems by making the inchoate themes more conscious and deliberate.

Anne L. Alstott, The Uneasy Liberal Case Against Income and Wealth Transfer Taxation: Response to Professor McCaffery

51 Tax L. Rev. 363, 363–367 (1996)

Professor McCaffery's novel claim is that his proposal is grounded in liberal egalitarian political theory, particularly that of John Rawls.

. . .

To understand the nature of Professor McCaffery's surprising claim, one must understand both the traditional liberal justification for the estate and income taxes and the nature of consumption taxation. Traditionally, Rawls and other liberal egalitarians have considered an estate tax and, under some conditions, a progressive income tax, to be central to a liberal regime. In Rawls' theory, the estate tax is an important means of correcting disparities in the distribution of wealth and power that tend to undermine important principles of justice—the fair value of political liberty and fair equality of opportunity. Rawls also argues that progressive income taxation may be appropriate under conditions of extreme and continuing economic inequality, a condition that arguably is met in the United States today. Professor McCaffery, in contrast, argues that neither an estate tax nor an income tax is a prerequisite for distributive justice in a liberal egalitarian regime. Instead, he contends, a progressive consumption tax would best promote liberal objectives.

The defining characteristic of a consumption tax is that it removes from the tax base income that is saved or invested (for example, in financial investments like stocks or bonds or in real investments like plant and equipment). A consumption tax, by definition, taxes only income spent on current, personal consumption (for example, on cars, food and travel). By deferring tax on saved income until the money is spent, a proportional consumption tax essentially exempts the earnings on the investment from taxation. A progressive consumption tax of the kind Professor McCaffery advocates would offer significant tax benefits to savers while penalizing those with high levels of consumption spending. In contrast, an income tax encompasses both consumed and saved income, and an estate tax taxes all inherited wealth, whether saved or consumed.

Professor McCaffery's argument differs significantly from prior scholarship advocating a consumption tax. Many previous proposals for consumption taxation have been framed in explicitly utilitarian terms: Economists, in particular, have long argued that a consumption tax, relative to an income tax, would promote aggregate well-being by increasing economic efficiency. Other advocates have argued that the consumption tax would avoid the considerable administrative challenge of measuring income from capital. Some prominent proponents of consumption taxation have recommended an additional tax on wealth, for instance, an estate tax, in order to preclude an undue advantage for the rich, who own a disproportionate share of capital and income from capital. In contrast, Professor McCaffery's case for a progressive consumption tax does not rely on utilitarian norms, but instead on the principles of liberal egalitarian political theory, and his argument rejects not only the income tax but also the estate tax.

In this Article, I argue that Professor McCaffery's argument is untenable at three key points. First, Professor McCaffery contends that traditional liberal theory has ignored an important distinction between the possession and the use of wealth, and that it is primarily the use, or consumption, of wealth that is objectionable on grounds of equality of opportunity or political liberty. Thus, he concludes, a tax on consumed income is ideally suited to a liberal tax regime. A closer examination shows that Professor McCaffery's argument discounts the significant political, economic and social power that possession of wealth confers. His claim ultimately turns on an ethically unconvincing characterization of private savings and investment as liberal values. In attempting to reconcile private power with public benefit, Professor McCaffery advances institutional innovations that are both unworkable and in tension with the premises of his argument.

Professor McCaffery's second argument concerns the economic effects of the estate and income taxes. He argues that liberal society appropriately values work and savings, which a consumption tax would encourage but which income and estate taxation discourage. In addition, he claims, the economic gains created by repeal of the income and estate taxes would tend to increase, rather than reduce, economic equality. Professor McCaffery's economic case rests on an overly optimistic account of the relevant empirical evidence and relies on comparisons of an idealized consumption tax with the flawed, real-world income and estate taxes.

Finally, Professor McCaffery defends his interpretation of liberal egalitarian principles by reference to current social practices. He argues that liberal political theory has inappropriately ignored public opposition to the estate tax and contends that, in this case, public opinion is an appropriate guide to liberal egalitarian ideals. Social interpretation is, however, a tricky business, and Professor McCaffery's overly simple reading of public opinion and political rhetoric comes dangerously close to equating illiberal sentiments with liberal principles.

Joseph M. Dodge, Taxing Gratuitous Transfers Under a Consumption Tax

51 Tax L. Rev. 529, 593–95 (1996)

C. Taxation of Gratuitous Transfers Outside of the Income or Consumption Tax

If transferred endowment is not taxed at least once per generation, the various consumption taxes would fail to reach accumulated invested wealth until such time as such wealth is reduced to consumption in the indefinite future. (In the case of a wage tax, wealth would be taxed up front, but all returns on such wealth to the end of time would escape tax, even if spent on consumption.) This point, however, is only descriptive, not argumentative. The argument based on this point would be that the untaxed growth of dynastic wealth is harmful to society by expanding the gap between the rich and the poor and allowing undue concentrations of power in the hands of a few. The final step in the argument is that the federal government can and should do something about this prospect by taxing wealth as it passes from generation to generation.

There are debatable normative and empirical points along the path of this argument, which I call the wealth-redistribution argument. To take one, would undue dynastic accumulations occur in the absence of government policy to the contrary? At what point would such accumulations become socially harmful? Would a wealth transfer tax be the most effective government tool to remedy the problem? These and other questions are beyond the scope of this Article.

It is true that the case for a Table 3 CIT[15] would be reinforced by the wealth-redistribution argument. But the crucial point is that such case does not depend on the argument and its various components. The case for the Table 3 CIT is based on arguments relating to fairness, economic efficiency and net incentives for investment. The wealth-redistribution argument clearly falls within the realm of policy. Although government policy can intervene in tax design to achieve certain goals, the tax system will exist regardless of its use to carry out policy. For that reason, it is essential to design a tax system initially along lines relating to fairness and economic efficiency; deviations from such system in the name of policy are, in a sense, afterthoughts. (I am not arguing that policy interventions in tax systems are per se illegitimate in any sense.)

Thus, stating that the issue is whether transfers of wealth should be taxed either within the CIT (or income tax) or without it by a separate wealth transfer (or wealth) tax is to misstate the issue. If taxing transfers within the annual personal tax is proper on various grounds that are independent of the wealth-redistribution argument, and if wealth maldistribution is perceived to be a serious problem, then the issue would be whether transfers should be taxed *both* within the CIT (or income tax) and under a separate tax. Of course, in the context of either designing the CIT or repealing § 102, this question is only hypothetical: If taxation *within* the basic tax structure should turn out to be effective to curb undue accumulations of wealth, the separate tax would not be needed as a policy instrument.

This last point leads to the conclusion that the short-term strategy should be to tax transfers within the basic income or consumption tax and to repeal the existing wealth transfer taxes, which, at best, are clumsy and inefficient policy tools. If such a move is insufficient to curb undue accumulations of wealth, or raises other policy concerns, then it would be necessary to consider the desirability and design of a separate tax on wealth or wealth transfers.

An argument can be made that gratuitous transfers should be taxed within the basic income or *consumption tax* and that wealth (or, by way of proxy, wealth transfers) should be taxed separately without regard to conventional distributional policy. This position is based on a utility rationale: To the extent wealth is *"consumption power,"* the tax base should include actual consumption plus gratuitous transfers; to the extent wealth entails utility (power and control over things and people) over and above consumption power (including freedom of testation), it should be taxed again. This argument, of course, is the basic argument for preferring an income tax to a consumption tax or for preferring an income tax either without § 102 or with a wealth transfer tax to a bare income tax with § 102. My point is that the argument would justify a Table 3 CIT (or other consumption-tax equivalent) combined with a separate wealth (or wealth transfer tax) containing "small estate" exemptions and a

---

[15] Earlier in his article, Professor Dodge explained the meaning of the Consumed Income Tax (CIT) as follows: The consumption tax that has received the most attention in the literature of the legal academy is the cash-flow consumption tax . . . . The cash-flow consumption tax is referred to herein as the "CIT," meaning "consumed income tax." 51 Tax L. Rev. at 537. Thereafter, Professor Dodge constructed three different CIT models based on whether gratuitous transfers were taxed as consumption. Table 3 CIT refers to a CIT where "all assets would be taxed to each person acquiring the same by purchase or by accession." *Id.* at 542.

separate rate schedule. Stated differently, my preference for a Table 3 CIT (as opposed to a CIT that ignores gratuitous transfers and receipts) is not dependent upon acceptance of the wealth-is-more-than-consumption-power argument, which seems to be the main focus of debate in the original McCaffery article and elsewhere in this Colloquium issue.

———

Problems

1. You have joined the staff of the Joint Committee on Taxation of the United States Congress. You are asked to prepare a memorandum analyzing federal wealth transfer taxes and alternative tax arrangements. Specifically, you should consider whether and why you favor or oppose:

  a. The revision of federal wealth transfer taxes.

  b. The adoption of a federal wealth tax.

  c. The adoption of a federal accessions tax.

  d. The inclusion of gifts and bequests in income.

2. Do you favor the outright repeal (without replacement) of all federal wealth transfer taxes? *Compare* Joel C. Dobris, *A Brief for the Abolition of All Transfer Taxes,* 35 SYRACUSE L. REV. 1215 (1984), *with* Michael J. Graetz, *To Praise the Estate Tax, Not To Bury It,* 93 YALE L.J. 259 (1983). Reconsider the excerpted articles in § 15.01 and in this section, § 15.06. *See generally* Henry J. Aaron & Alicia H. Munnell, *Reassessing the Role for Wealth Transfer Taxes,* 45 NAT'L TAX J. 119 (1992).

TABLE OF CASES

[References are to page numbers; principal cases are in capital letters.]

[References are to page numbers; principal cases are in capital letters.]

[References are to page numbers; principal cases are in capital letters.]

[References are to page numbers; principal cases are in capital letters.]

H

[References are to page numbers; principal cases are in capital letters.]

[References are to page numbers; principal cases are in capital letters.]

[References are to page numbers; principal cases are in capital letters.]

TABLE OF STATUTES

[References are to page numbers.]

[References are to page numbers.]

Internal Revenue Code—Cont.

Internal Revenue Code—Cont.

[References are to page numbers.]

[References are to page numbers.]

[References are to page numbers.]

[References are to page numbers.]

[References are to page numbers.]

[References are to page numbers.]

[References are to page numbers.]

Treasury Regulations—Cont.

Treasury Regulations—Cont.

[References are to page numbers.]

[References are to page numbers.]

INDEX

A

ABUSE OF TRUSTS, CONTROL OF
Calendar year requirement for trusts 710
Multiple trusts, taxation of . . . 708
Throwback rules . . . 710

ANNUITIES
Estate tax . . . 168, 491
Generation-skipping transfer tax . . . 495
Gift tax . . . 491
Income tax . . . 495
Private annuities . . . 496
Retirement benefits (See RETIREMENT BENEFITS)

C

COMMUNITY PROPERTY
Concurrent property interests of spouse (See CONCURRENT PROPERTY INTERESTS, subhead: Spousal concurrent property interests)
Estate tax
    Expenses and debts . . . 117
    Interests of the surviving spouse . . 65
    Marital deduction . . . 154
Life insurance (See LIFE INSURANCE)
Retirement assets, spousal interests . . 510

CONCURRENT PROPERTY INTERESTS
Disclaimers . . . 587
Joint tenancies . . . 559, 581
Non-spousal concurrent property interests
    Estate tax . . . 563
    Generation-skipping transfer tax 572
    Gift tax . . . 559
    Income tax . . . 573
    Joint tenancies . . . 559
Spousal concurrent property interests
    Community property
        Estate tax . . . 580
        Gift tax . . . 579
        Income tax . . . 581
    Non-community property
        Estate tax . . . 575
        Gift tax . . . 575
        Income tax . . . 578

CRUMMEY TRUSTS
Minors, gifts to . . . 221
Third party powers (See THIRD-PARTY POWERS)

E

ERISA (See RETIREMENT BENEFITS)

ESTATE TAX
Annuities . . . 168, 491
Charitable deduction
    Comparison between CRATS and CRUTS . . . 170
    Deferred charitable devises . . . 166
    General rules for charitable remainder trusts . . . 167
    Lead trusts . . . 172
    Marital deduction and charitable remainder trusts . . . 170
    Partial interest contributions (not in trust) . . . 171
    Pooled income fund . . . 171
    Remainder annuity trust . . . 168
    Remainder unitrust . . . 169
    Restrictions on charitable remainder trusts . . . 166
Community property (See COMMUNITY PROPERTY)
Concurrent property interests (See CONCURRENT PROPERTY INTERESTS)
Credits against the estate tax imposed
    Foreign death taxes . . . 182
    Gift taxes paid credit . . . 178
    Prior transfers, tax on . . . 179
    State death taxes . . . 176
    Unified credit . . . 175
Deduction provisions
    Casualties . . . 118
    Charitable deduction (See subhead: Charitable deduction)
    Expenses and debts (See subhead: Expenses and debts as deduction)
    Family-owned business deduction 173
    Marital deduction (See subhead: Marital deduction)
    State death tax deduction . . . 174
Determining the gross estate
    Assets owned at death
        Generally . . . 61
        Surviving spouse, interests of . . . 65
    Generally . . . 59
Expenses and debts as deduction
    Administration expenses . . . 104
    Claims and mortgages . . . 108
    Community property . . . 117
    Consideration requirement . . . 116
    Funeral expenses . . . 108
    Generally . . . 103
    Settlement of claims . . . 117
Family-owned business (See FAMILY-OWNED BUSINESSES)
Generally . . . 174
History . . . 3

I–1

W